Claire L'Heureux-Dubé

PATRONS OF THE OSGOODE SOCIETY

Blake, Cassels & Graydon LLP
Chernos, Flaherty, Svorkin LLP
The Law Foundation of Ontario
McCarthy Tétrault LLP
Osler, Hoskin & Harcourt LLP
Paliare Roland Rosenberg Rothstein LLP
Torys LLP
WeirFoulds LLP

The Osgoode Society is supported by a grant from
The Law Foundation of Ontario

The Society also thanks The Law Society of Upper Canada
for its continued support.

LAW AND SOCIETY SERIES
W. Wesley Pue, General Editor

The Law and Society Series explores law as a socially embedded phenomenon. It is premised on the understanding that the conventional division of law from society creates false dichotomies in thinking, scholarship, educational practice, and social life. Books in the series treat law and society as mutually constitutive and seek to bridge scholarship emerging from interdisciplinary engagement of law with disciplines such as politics, social theory, history, political economy, and gender studies.

For a list of the titles in this series, see the UBC Press website, www.ubcpress.ca.

Claire L'Heureux-Dubé
A Life

CONSTANCE BACKHOUSE

PUBLISHED BY UBC PRESS FOR
THE OSGOODE SOCIETY
FOR CANADIAN LEGAL HISTORY

UBC Press • Vancouver • Toronto

© UBC Press 2017

All rights reserved. No part of this publication may be reproduced, stored in a retrieval system, or transmitted, in any form or by any means, without prior written permission of the publisher, or, in Canada, in the case of photocopying or other reprographic copying, a licence from Access Copyright, www.accesscopyright.ca.

26 25 24 23 22 21 20 19 18 17   5 4 3 2 1

Printed in Canada on paper that is processed chlorine- and acid-free, with vegetable-based inks.

Library and Archives Canada Cataloguing in Publication

Backhouse, Constance, author
    Claire L'Heureux-Dubé: a life / Constance Backhouse.

(Law and society series)
Includes index.
Issued in print and electronic formats.
ISBN 978-0-7748-3632-6 (hardcover). – ISBN 978-0-7748-3634-0 (PDF). – ISBN 978-0-7748-3635-7 (EPUB). – ISBN 978-0-7748-3636-4 (Kindle)

    1. L'Heureux-Dubé, Claire. 2. Canada. Supreme Court – Biography. 3. Judges – Canada – Biography. 4. Women judges – Canada – Biography. I. Osgoode Society for Canadian Legal History, issuing body II. Title. III. Series: Law and society series (Vancouver, B.C.)

KE8248.L44B33 2017   347.71'03534   C2017-903771-4
KF345.Z9L44B33 2017   C2017-903772-2

Canadä

UBC Press gratefully acknowledges the financial support for our publishing program of the Government of Canada (through the Canada Book Fund), the Canada Council for the Arts, and the British Columbia Arts Council.

This book has been published with the help of a grant from the Canadian Federation for the Humanities and Social Sciences, through the Awards to Scholarly Publications Program, using funds provided by the Social Sciences and Humanities Research Council of Canada.

Printed and bound in Canada by Friesens
Set in Garamond by Artegraphica Design Co. Ltd.
Copy editor: Francis Chow
Proofreader: Sarah Wight
Indexer: Margaret de Boer
Cover designer: Jessica Sullivan

UBC Press
The University of British Columbia
2029 West Mall
Vancouver, BC V6T 1Z2
www.ubcpress.ca

Contents

Foreword / ix

Acknowledgments / xi

Chronology / xv

Introduction / 3

1 *Ewanchuk* / 8

Family Heritage and Childhood

2 Lineage: Of Elephants, Literary Salons, the Military, and Mozart / 23

3 Early Years: Quebec City and Rimouski / 33

4 Growing Up in Rimouski / 51

Early Education

5 Life as a *Pensionnaire* with the Ursulines, 1937–43 / 63

6 Collège Notre-Dame-de-Bellevue: Classical Studies for a *Baccalauréat*, 1943–46 / 76

A Legal Education

7 The Decision to Go to Law School, 1946–48 / 93

8 Laval Law School Student Body, 1948–52 / 103

9 Laval Law School Faculty and Curriculum, 1948–52 / 111

10 Life Outside of Law School, 1949–52 / 123

Law Practice

11 Entry: A Law Firm Job, 1952 / 135

12 Sam Bard: The Man behind the Employment Offer / 141

13 Business Law Practice / 150

14 Marriage and Children / 162

15 Family Law: The Later Years of Practice / 176

16 Practising as a Woman / 193

Quebec Superior Court

17 New Career Directions: "No" to Electoral Politics, "Yes" to the Bench, 1972–73 / 211

18 First Months on the Bench, February to October 1973 / 230

19 Immigration Commission of Inquiry, October 1973 to January 1976 / 238

20 Quebec Superior Court, 1976–79 / 253

21 Family Tragedy: Arthur's Death, 11 July 1978 / 269

Quebec Court of Appeal

22 Appointment to the Quebec Court of Appeal, 1979 / 283

23 Appellate Judging, 1979–87 / 293

24 More Family Traumas / 307

Contents

Supreme Court of Canada

25 Appointment to the Supreme Court of Canada, 1987 / 319

26 Early Days on the Supreme Court of Canada / 330

27 Continuing Isolation on the Supreme Court / 347

28 Fifteen Years of Jurisprudence, 1987–2002: "The Great Dissenter" / 359

Selected Cases

29 Sexual Assault: *Seaboyer*, 1991 / 379

30 Family Law and Spousal Support: *Moge*, 1992 / 395

31 Human Rights for Same-Sex Couples: *Mossop*, 1993 / 412

32 Tax Law and Sex Discrimination: *Symes*, 1993 / 428

33 More Deaths, 1987–94 / 442

34 The Quebec Secession Reference: "The Most Important Case," 1998 / 454

35 Fairness in Immigration Law: *Baker*, 1999 / 470

36 Epilogue on *Ewanchuk* / 486

A Wider Stage

37 Judicial Education and International Influence / 505

38 Retirement: A Much-Heralded Exit / 520

Conclusion / 540

Notes / 547

Illustration Credits / 707

Index / 713

Foreword

The Osgoode Society for Canadian Legal History

Claire L'Heureux-Dubé was the second woman appointed to the Supreme Court of Canada, and the first from Quebec. This deeply researched biography takes us from the judge's origins and life in the Quebec of the 1920s to the present. The portrait of Quebec society in the 1920s through the 1950s wonderfully enriches the book's comprehensive, intimate, and insightful examination of Justice L'Heureux-Dubé herself. We learn a great deal about the role of women and women lawyers in Quebec society, the Quebec legal profession, legal education, and the judiciary as we trace L'Heureux-Dubé's rise in the province's legal hierarchy to the Court of Appeal and then to the Supreme Court of Canada in 1987. Our understanding of the Supreme Court of Canada during the early *Charter* era is also considerably augmented by this account, which deals with the gender and cultural dynamics, the relations between Anglophone and Francophone judges, and the jurisprudential debates and controversies of the period. The book also takes us beyond Justice L'Heureux-Dubé's retirement and into the various high-profile interventions she made in public life, including her contribution to the Quebec Charter of Values debate. This book is essential reading for anyone interested in Canada's and Quebec's modern legal history, in the role of women in law, and in what made this judge such a compelling personality.

The purpose of the Osgoode Society for Canadian Legal History is to encourage research and writing in the history of Canadian law. The Society, which was incorporated in 1979 and is registered as a charity, was founded at the initiative of the Honourable R. Roy McMurtry and officials of the

Law Society of Upper Canada. The Society seeks to stimulate the study of legal history in Canada by supporting researchers, collecting oral histories, and publishing volumes that contribute to legal-historical scholarship in Canada. This year's books bring the total published since 1981 to 103, in all fields of legal history – the courts, the judiciary, and the legal profession, as well as on the history of crime and punishment, women and law, law and economy, the legal treatment of ethnic minorities, and famous cases and significant trials in all areas of the law.

Current directors of the Osgoode Society for Canadian Legal History are Susan Binnie, Bevin Brooksbank, Shantona Chaudhury, David Chernos, Linda Silver Dranoff, Michael Fenrick, Timothy Hill, Ian Hull, Trisha Jackson, Mahmud Jamal, C. Ian Kyer, Virginia MacLean, Rachel McMillan, Roy McMurtry, Yasir Naqvi, Dana Peebles, Paul Reinhardt, William Ross, Paul Schabas, Robert Sharpe, Jon Silver, Alex Smith, Lorne Sossin, Mary Stokes, and Michael Tulloch.

Robert J. Sharpe
President

Jim Phillips
Editor-in-Chief

Acknowledgments

I have George Thomson to thank for suggesting that I write a biography of Claire L'Heureux-Dubé. A former judge, senior civil servant, and executive director of the National Judicial Institute, George Thomson had been a long-time friend to Justice L'Heureux-Dubé when, in 2006, he spotted me in a plane. He approached me as we disembarked to stress that this was an important biography and that I was the person to write it. It seemed a substantial departure from the legal history I had pursued before, profiling previously unacknowledged women who sought to use the law to redress discrimination in the face of overwhelming odds, typically in losing battles. A biography of the second woman to ascend to the Supreme Court of Canada was hardly in the same vein. However, on the spur of the moment, I agreed that I would consider it if Justice L'Heureux-Dubé consented. It took George Thomson another year to secure that consent, and in late 2007 she and I began a project we thought might take three years. It turned out to take three times as long.

I had known of Claire L'Heureux-Dubé long before that, because her colourful personality and remarkable record as a judge had made her a household name in legal circles and beyond. As a law professor, I had followed her career with interest because of the many groundbreaking decisions she had delivered regarding equality rights. In the wake of the explosive *Ewanchuk* case in 1999, I felt strongly that the public abuse she withstood reflected broader pent-up hostility toward feminism. It seemed unfair that she had been individually targeted. It was one of the reasons I became interested in commencing the research for her biography. When

I undertook the task, I think neither of us fully anticipated what this entailed, or how deeply immersed I was to become in the project.

It often felt as if I was traversing completely foreign territory. I grew up on the prairies in Winnipeg, where the definition of a river was the Assiniboine tributary that flowed into the muddy Red and drained north to Hudson Bay. I attended secular public schools. I went to law school in an era when the women students were no longer an anomaly. Then a unilingual Anglophone, I pursued my law career entirely in Ontario. Claire L'Heureux-Dubé grew up in Rimouski, on the banks of the Lower St. Lawrence, a massive river that looked more like the sea, salty and swelling with tides from the Atlantic Ocean. She received her education as a boarder in a Catholic convent. She went to law school when it was virtually unthinkable for women to do so. A bilingual Francophone, she lived and practised in Quebec during some of its most formative decades: through the Duplessis era, the Quiet Revolution, and Lévesque's separatist vision. As the years passed, I began to joke that I came to know more about Quebec than Manitoba, more about Claire L'Heureux-Dubé's life than my own family, and occasionally more than she knew about herself.

The biography introduced me in a deeply personal way to the politics, culture, economy, and lives of the people of Quebec. Multiple French-language immersion courses were necessary, despite Justice L'Heureux-Dubé's request that the biography be in English because that was the language spoken by her grandsons, who were growing up in the United States. Some of the original sources were in English, some in French. I have chosen to retain some of the original French phrases in this book, because it may help to underscore Claire L'Heureux-Dubé's lifelong attachment to her mother tongue, a language she speaks and writes with eloquence. It may also remind readers about the challenges of functioning in two languages. To ensure that unilingual Anglophone readers do not miss the essence of the material, however, translations are inserted at the bottom of the relevant pages.

This is not an "authorized" biography. Justice L'Heureux-Dubé has neither requested nor received any control over the final manuscript. However, it has been researched and written with her cooperation, and she has helped me identify and connect with individuals who can shed light on her life and career. With her generous assistance, I have completed over two hundred oral history interviews with her, her siblings and daughter, childhood friends, school and university classmates, law school classmates, law partners, law clerks, journalists, politicians, litigants, law professors, lawyers, and judges across Canada and beyond.[1] She also arranged for me to have access to the closed records that contain her papers at Library and Archives Canada.[2] Some of my interpretations may differ from the ones she would have drawn, and it is a tribute to her trademark openness and strength of character that she did not attempt to shape either the research or my conclusions.

This research has been complicated by my commitment to feminism as a way of being in the world. Feminism as a philosophical, political, social, and cultural perspective has given rise to a multitude of interpretations across diverse communities, as the different opinions evident in this book illustrate so well. Although feminism has sometimes been criticized for impeding objectivity, feminists have been quite adept at unmasking concepts such as "objectivity," "balance," "common sense," and "point-of-view-lessness" to demonstrate that all perspectives are partial. Feminists try to admit theirs. I have attempted to conduct this research through a lens that calls upon the core of feminist principles: a recognition that gender matters, that discrimination exists, that resistance and backlash follow, that our society would be a better place if there were greater inclusion and equality, and that biographical research should take account of all of this. It is, then, a feminist legal biography. It must also be noted that Justice L'Heureux-Dubé's relationship to feminist ideology and practice is an uneasy one, that we often do not view law and society the same way, and that the exercise of completing this biography has caused both of us to reflect upon our distinct ways of viewing the world.

I wish to thank many friends, colleagues, and archivists who contributed expertise and ideas during this research: Beth Atcheson, Barbara Babcock, Nancy Backhouse, Olga Backhouse, Natasha Bakht, Felice Batlan, Edwige Beaudin, Sylvie Bédard, Marie-Claire Belleau, Suzanne Bouclin, Bettina Bradbury, Jacqueline Briggs, Kim Brooks, Tomiko Brown-Nagin, Rosemary Cairns Way, Yvan Carette, Soeur Claire Chénard, Sharon Cook, Elaine Craig, Colombe Dallaire, Florian Daveau, Jane De Hart, Nathalie Des Rosiers, Adam Dodek, Davison Douglas, Jocelyn Downie, Donald Fyson, Chloe Georas, Philip Girard, Marie Gordon, Deborah Gorham, Lorraine Greaves, Michael Grossberg, Richard J. Harkin, Rosemary Hunter, Rebecca Johnson, Bill Kaplan, Sally Kenney, Linda Kerber, Diane Kirkby, Craig Klafter, Evelyn Kolish, Pnina Lahav, James Harold Lambert, Véronique Larose, Annie Leclerc, Andrée Lévesque, Jennifer Llewellyn, Constance MacIntosh, Diana Majury, Bruce Mann, Lorna McLean, Philippe Michaud, Renate Mohr, James Muir, Sylvio Normand, Lorraine O'Donnell, Peter Oliver, Maureen O'Neil, Lucie Paquet, Yasmeen Peer, Jim Phillips, Mae Quinn, Ed Ratushny, Teresa Scassa, Mitra Sharafi, Elizabeth Sheehy, Peter

Showler, Crystal Sissons, Veronica Strong-Boag, Beth Symes, Sophie Tellier, Marlene Trestman, Geneviève Vezeau, Barbara Welke, David Wexler, Brian Young, Leandra Zarnow, and Ellen Zweibel.

I have been aided by remarkably talented research assistants: Mark Bourrie, Yasmine Butlin, Fouz Abdel Hadi, Emelie Kozak, Jessica Kozak, Mayoori Malankov, Falon Milligan, Jessica Reid, Devon Robertson, and Carly Stringer. My research has also benefited from engaging, provocative discussions with the gifted law students who have participated in the legal history seminars over the past few years at the University of Ottawa.

I am grateful to the team at UBC Press, Randy Schmidt, Ann Macklem, and Melissa Pitts, who went far beyond what any author has a right to expect in assisting with the editing and publication of this book. Their exquisite professional guidance was superbly supported by copy editor Francis Chow, cover designer Jessica Sullivan, copywriter Camilla Blakeley, proofreader Sarah Wight, indexer Margaret de Boer, and intern Carmen Tiampo. Martin Dufresne provided expert translations for the French texts.

Where references are not specified by way of an endnote, the source of all other information is my interviews with Claire L'Heureux-Dubé in Quebec City, Ottawa, Rimouski, and Clearwater, Florida, on 17 September, 30 October, 1 November, and 2 December 2007; 29–30 April, 1–2 May, and 23–25 July 2008; 5 March, 7 March, 27–28 April, 10–14 May, and 21 September 2009; 10 March, 30 June, and 13 September 2010; 3 May and 30 August 2012; 4–5 July 2013; and 30 June and 25–27 November 2014.

Chronology

1885	Napoléon L'Heureux is born in St. Paul, Minnesota
1890	Antoinette Fortin marries Victor Dion
1903	Marguerite Dion is born in Quebec City
1904	Napoléon L'Heureux marries Bruna Lavoie
1905	Paul L'Heureux is born in Quebec City
1910	Victor Dion dies
1924	Paul L'Heureux becomes a commissioned officer in the Régiment de Montmagny
1926	Paul L'Heureux marries Marguerite Dion in Quebec City
1927	Claire L'Heureux is born in Quebec City on 7 September
1929	Louise L'Heureux is born in Quebec City
1932	Lucie L'Heureux is born in Quebec City
1933	Claire L'Heureux starts school at Saint-Joseph de Saint-Vallier, Quebec City, at age 6
1934	Nicole L'Heureux is born in Quebec City
	Bruna Lavoie L'Heureux dies
1935	Paul L'Heureux is promoted to collector of customs and excise in Rimouski
	L'Heureux family moves from Quebec City to Rimouski
	Claire L'Heureux starts school at L'École Saint-Germain, run by les Sœurs de la Charité

1936	Marguerite L'Heureux is sent for medical treatment to the Sanatorium Prévost
	The L'Heureux girls are sent to the orphanage, Orphelinat du Couvent des Sœurs de la Charité
1937	Claire begins boarding at the Monastère des Ursulines de L'Immaculée Conception de Rimouski at age 10
1939	Paul L'Heureux enlists in the Canadian Armed Forces
1940	Napoléon L'Heureux marries Aurore Lavoie
	Antoinette Fortin Dion dies
1941	Claire moves to Quebec City for one year to attend the Collège Notre-Dame-de-Bellevue
1942	Claire returns to finish her studies at the Monastère des Ursulines in Rimouski
1943	Claire graduates from the Monastère des Ursulines in Rimouski, completing the matriculation course at age 15
	Claire returns to board at the Collège Notre-Dame-de-Bellevue in Quebec City
1946	Claire graduates from the Collège Notre-Dame-de-Bellevue, obtaining a *baccalauréat-ès-arts magna cum laude* at age 18
	Paul L'Heureux returns to Rimouski from overseas military service
1948	Claire begins studying law at Laval University at age 21
1949	Paul L'Heureux is promoted to collector of customs and excise in Quebec City
	Paul and Marguerite L'Heureux move from Rimouski to Quebec City
1950	Fire destroys Rimouski and the old L'Heureux home
1951	Claire graduates with an LL.L. *cum laude* from Laval University at age 23
	Claire begins working as a secretary for Sam Schwarz Bard in Quebec City
	Claire meets Arthur Dubé
1952	Claire L'Heureux is admitted to the Quebec bar at age 25
	Lucie L'Heureux dies at age 20
	Claire L'Heureux begins practising law with Sam Schwarz Bard

Chronology

1955	Napoléon L'Heureux dies at age 71
1957	Paul L'Heureux is appointed collector of customs and excise in Montreal
	Claire L'Heureux, age 30, marries Arthur Dubé, age 38, on 30 November
1960	Daughter Louise Dubé is born in Quebec City on 13 May; Claire L'Heureux-Dubé is 32
1963	The Dubé family moves to 940 Adolphe-Routhier, Quebec City, in October
1964	Son Pierre Dubé is born in Quebec City on 29 January; Claire L'Heureux-Dubé is 36
1969	Sam Schwarz Bard is appointed to the Superior Court of Quebec
	The L'Heureux-Dubé family moves to 1014 Mont-Saint-Denis, Sillery
1972	Claire L'Heureux-Dubé refuses Prime Minister Pierre Trudeau's request that she run for the Liberals in the federal election of 30 October
1973	Claire L'Heureux-Dubé is appointed to the Superior Court of Quebec on 9 February, at age 45
	Claire L'Heureux-Dubé takes leave of absence from Superior Court on 13 August, to serve with the Commission of Inquiry Relating to the Department of Manpower and Immigration in Montreal
	Claire L'Heureux-Dubé is appointed to chair the Montreal immigration inquiry on 30 October
1974–75	Hearings of the Montreal immigration inquiry run from 23 April 1974 to 19 August 1975
1976	Claire L'Heureux-Dubé files final report of Montreal immigration inquiry on 19 January
	Claire L'Heureux-Dubé returns to the Superior Court and begins sitting in January
1978	Arthur Dubé commits suicide on 11 July; Louise is 18, Pierre 14
1979	Claire L'Heureux-Dubé is appointed to the Quebec Court of Appeal on 16 October, age 52

1982	*Canadian Charter of Rights and Freedoms* comes into force
1983	Marguerite Dion L'Heureux dies on 16 December
1985	Section 15 of the *Charter* comes into force on 17 April
1987	Claire L'Heureux-Dubé is appointed to the Supreme Court of Canada on 15 April, age 59
	Claire L'Heureux-Dubé moves to 174 Dufferin, Ottawa, in September
1989	Paul L'Heureux dies, age 84
1994	Pierre Dubé dies on 17 March, age 30
2002	Claire L'Heureux-Dubé retires from Supreme Court of Canada on 1 July; she is allowed six months, until 31 December, to finish writing any outstanding decisions
2003	Claire L'Heureux-Dubé moves to Grande Allée Ouest, Quebec City

Claire L'Heureux-Dubé

Introduction

Claire L'Heureux-Dubé is a judge who shaped our notions and legal doctrines of equality, and whose influence upon constitutional, family, criminal, and administrative law was transformative. In an era of groundbreaking *Charter* interpretation, she stands out as one of the most dynamic, forceful, and controversial judges on a controversial court in a controversial time. The second woman appointed to the Supreme Court of Canada and the first from Quebec, she has been characterized as "the Great Dissenter," her unique judgments both applauded and roundly criticized during her term.

Her innovative legal approach was anchored in context, giving explicit recognition to the social, economic, and political realities that impacted her cases. This is a socio-legal biography that borrows from that approach, examining how context can also shape a life. It steps beyond the traditional format for legal biographies, which often focus upon high-profile cases and jurisprudential legacies. This biography explores the rich social, political, economic, and cultural setting in which L'Heureux-Dubé's career unfolded. It can contribute to our understanding of legal education, the profession, the judiciary, the distinctive socio-legal experience of Quebec, the complex concepts of class and race, the position of Francophone women within the male legal world of Quebec and beyond, the inner workings of the top court, changing norms of gender roles, and women's experience in law. This biography also trains a more concentrated focus on Claire L'Heureux-Dubé's personal life. Women often have their personal lives placed under the microscope, and there is a risk that a more personalized judicial biography may play into that gendered dynamic. However, the hope here is that fuller analysis of important personal details may ultimately become more regular inclusions in biographies of male and female judges alike.

We tend to have settled notions about the careers of famous lawyers and judges. In the typical narrative, they get their start in a comfortable middle-class family, where they are encouraged to pursue their education. Their private lives are uncomplicated: intact birth families, happy lifelong marriages with supportive partners, children who grow up to be self-supporting adults, tidy personal lives that enable them to succeed. They develop flourishing practices and are elevated to the bench with the support of the wider legal community. They sit with wise judicial colleagues and make collegial efforts to discern the fairest responses to complex legal problems.

Claire L'Heureux-Dubé's life rarely conforms.

She was born in Quebec City in 1927, the eldest of four sisters in an intensely "female" family. Her childhood was spent in Rimouski, a town on the Lower St. Lawrence with a landscape and climate that imprinted itself vividly upon her personality. She had a complicated relationship with her father, Paul L'Heureux, a customs inspector, military officer, and strict disciplinarian, who tried to prevent her from going into law. Her mother, Marguerite L'Heureux, an intellectually gifted woman paralyzed by multiple sclerosis, urged Claire to aim for a professional career. Her influence upon Claire was so great that an alternative subtitle for this biography might have been "Marguerite's daughter."

Claire was educated as a convent *pensionnaire* at the cloistered Monastère des Ursulines in Rimouski, where she excelled as one of the most academically gifted (and unruly) pupils. After leaving the Ursuline convent, she studied at the Collège Notre-Dame-de-Bellevue, where she received her *baccalauréat* in 1946. Her youthful immersion in Roman Catholicism touched her deeply, and at one point she aspired to become a nun. The inclination disappeared with adulthood, and in her later years she became strongly opposed to religion.

The only one from her convent class to enrol in law school, Claire thrived in the novel setting. She was the ninth woman to graduate from Laval University in law, the only woman to enter private practice in Quebec City in 1952, and the first to establish a successful law practice there. Her entry was premised upon a job offer from Jewish lawyer Samuel Schwarz Bard at a time when no French Canadian lawyer would hire her. She did not let her marriage derail her career, partnering at age thirty-one with

Arthur Dubé, a brilliant Laval engineering professor who supported her decision to continue practice even after the birth of their two children. She had few role models as she struggled to negotiate the challenges of work/life balance. The anguish of witnessing her husband's battle with depression, alcoholism, and suicide, and of dealing with her son's juvenile delinquencies and premature death in a hospital lock-up, took an enormous toll. Yet her resilience and optimism, self-consciously patterned upon her mother's formidable strength of character, carried her through. Her trailblazing business law practice at Bard's firm (much of it conducted for Jewish clients in English) and her switch to divorce practice after the 1968 *Divorce Act* reshaped family law in Quebec, brought her to prominence as the capital city's most illustrious female lawyer.

She received judicial appointments from three different governments, becoming the first woman appointed to sit in Quebec City on the Quebec Superior Court in 1973, the first to the Quebec Court of Appeal in 1979, and the second to the Supreme Court of Canada in 1987. In none of these elevations does she seem to have been the candidate of choice from the bench or bar. She had entered the legal profession prior to the Quiet Revolution that transfigured *La belle province,* but by the time she was appointed to the Superior Court, feminism was growing in influence, especially in Quebec. She did not self-identify as a feminist, and does not recall being introduced to the term during her formative years. Yet she was on the cusp of change. When the forces of political, social, and cultural reform pressed in upon the world of law, and pressure mounted to put a woman on the bench, she was the obvious candidate. She became a standard-bearer for a movement to which she had never belonged, a situation of some complexity.

L'Heureux-Dubé negotiated her path through a masculinist terrain surrounded by men in power, marked irrefutably as an outsider by gender, captured in group portraits as the lone female in the crowd. Masculinity was a culture she had to master, and there were lessons she had to absorb from the men around her. Yet her options were limited. The early female professionals who pushed beyond the bounds of contemporary femininity had to present themselves in high heels, hair carefully coiffed, good wives, mothers, cooks, and proud of it. How did Claire L'Heureux-Dubé frame herself within this contradictory setting? How did stereotypical gender norms hijack perceptions of her? How did a woman with a reputation as a *femme fatale,* short in stature with a high-pitched voice, come to be perceived as a judge whose charisma dominated the rooms she entered? How did she relate to the men in power around her, to the few women who joined her within the halls of power – and they to her? How did her French Canadian heritage, her coming of age in an increasingly nationalistic Quebec, complicate the "outsider" picture?

She joined the Supreme Court as an appellate judge with a reputation for painstaking research, formidable powers of organization, an elegant mastery of written French, and a traditionally formalistic approach to law. She left it fifteen years later as a judge who was revered and reviled for her innovative use of social science evidence, her insistence on examining the real-world implications of rulings, and her outspoken embrace of novel equality claims. Analysts tripped over themselves in confusion – uncertain whether to categorize her as "conservative" or "progressive," a proponent of "law and order" or of "victim's rights." Did she change during her time on the bench? Or was it the real core that she revealed in her last decade, aspects that had been muted until she reached the pinnacle of the top court?

How did her personal and professional life and the context of the times transport her to a place of articulated pride in being an egalitarian, a renegade, a risk taker without fear of standing alone? How did her isolation at the Supreme Court affect her? Was she influenced by fellow judges, law clerks, public audiences, or the press? Why did she champion gender and LGBT issues, while showing less leadership on racial, ethnic, and religious discrimination? Did her philosophy and method of judging differ from accepted norms? Why did her judicial career elicit such contradictory public responses? In addition to a vilification that was truly singular in content and vehemence, L'Heureux-Dubé experienced a virtual canonization as a "heroine," as the tributes during the fêtes that attended her retirement in 2002 so clearly demonstrated. Throughout this trajectory, she also became a towering presence on the international stage.

Who was the woman behind the success? Was she talented, ambitious, flamboyant, driven, hard-working, and fundamentally insecure? Did she self-consciously position herself to aim for spectacular success in a discriminatory milieu, or was she oblivious to elevation and power? Claire L'Heureux-Dubé is direct in her observations but not particularly self-reflective. Her daughter, Louise, observed: "She's a very complicated person. What you see is not what you get. She says things and really means the exact opposite."[1] Other family members, friends, colleagues in law, and fellow judges maintain disparate views.

What is undeniable is that L'Heureux-Dubé lived through years of unprecedented change. In the early twentieth century, the Quebec legal profession and judiciary were unrelievedly male. L'Heureux-Dubé witnessed heated debates over the entry of women to law schools, to practice, and to the bench; the burning question was whether women would "make a difference." By the time she retired, the question of why women should be included, so central to the earlier discussion, was passé. Whether they had made or will make a significant difference remains unclear. What is clear is that Claire L'Heureux-Dubé's story offers a curious and remarkable tale of a truly singular woman and an extraordinary judge.

1
Ewanchuk

Claire L'Heureux-Dubé became both an icon and a lightning rod during her years on the Supreme Court. Within vulnerable communities, she was iconized for courageous decisions that forged deeper understandings about discrimination. Her judgments were all the more celebrated because they often took her out on a limb, isolated on the courtroom bench. The same decisions also turned her into a pariah within some sectors of the legal profession and the public, excoriated for her perspectives on equality. The apex of this icon/lightning rod polarity was reached in *Ewanchuk,* a sexual assault case that catapulted her onto the front pages of the newspapers, made her the subject of nightly telecasts and radio talk shows, and plunged her into the centre of public debates across the land. The case would eventually become so well known that it acquired two memorable tag lines of its own: "the bonnet and crinolines case" and "No means No."[1]

The *Ewanchuk* Case

On 2 June 1994, forty-four-year-old Steve Ewanchuk approached a young woman in an Edmonton mall parking lot and asked whether she had any interest in a part-time job staffing a display booth at the mall. The seventeen-year-old woman, described only as the "complainant" to preserve her privacy, needed a job. When she arrived for the interview the next day, Ewanchuk lured her to his private trailer in the parking lot. He closed the trailer door, explained that he was an "open" and "affectionate" employer, hugged her, and asked her to give him a massage. The complainant was half Ewanchuk's age and size. She testified that she complied because she thought the door was locked and she was "very scared."[2]

Ewanchuk's advances escalated. Each time the complainant said "no" or "just stop," often with tears in her eyes, he paused. Then he would begin afresh, massaging her inner thigh and pelvic area, reaching inside her shorts. The complainant told the court she believed that if Ewanchuk knew how afraid she was, it would increase the risk of a violent sexual assault. She explained that she lay "bone straight" when he pushed her backward so he could lie on top of her, "grinding his pelvis into hers." He took his penis out of his shorts and stuck it between her legs rubbing against her vaginal area, on top of her underwear. When she objected once more, Ewanchuk ceased, saying: "See, I'm a nice guy, I stopped." He let her leave the trailer, handed her $100, and asked her not to tell anyone.[3]

She reported all this to the police, who were well acquainted with her assailant, a man with four previous sexual assault convictions. One of the convictions involved forced intercourse with a teenage girl whom Ewanchuk had also approached regarding possible employment. He had twice violated a court order not to attempt to employ any female under eighteen, but by law none of this information was available to the judge at trial.[4] Ewanchuk would later be quoted in the press as saying that women were "one of [my] weaknesses," that it was "like placing a drink in front of an alcoholic."[5] The judge concluded that the complainant had not actually consented, but acquitted Ewanchuk upon the defence of "implied consent," because she had not communicated her fear by words, gestures, or facial expressions.[6]

The Alberta Court of Appeal upheld the acquittal in a two-to-one decision.[7] Justice John Wesley McClung's majority decision dismissed the complainant's no's as irrelevant. He emphasized that she had had a child out of wedlock and was living common-law. He critiqued feminist slogans such as "No means No." He stated that "in a less litigious age, going too far in the boyfriend's car was better dealt with on site – a well-chosen expletive, a slap in the face, or, if necessary, a well-directed knee." He depicted Ewanchuk's advances as "clumsy passes" in aid of "romantic intentions" that were more "hormonal" than "criminal." He rebuked the complainant for dressing in shorts, adding that she "did not present herself to Ewanchuk or enter his trailer in a bonnet and crinolines." The press described him as a "staunch conservative" with a "crusading desire ... to refute the twentieth century."[8]

Steve Ewanchuk as photographed by the *Edmonton Journal*, 1999.

The Supreme Court of Canada Intervenes

The Supreme Court of Canada heard the case in 1998. After the lawyers completed their arguments, the nine judges retired to their conference room. L'Heureux-Dubé recalled all of them speaking around the table about the misconceptions that ran through McClung's decision, agreeing that a guilty verdict should be substituted for the acquittal. It was "not one of those cases where people argued at length," she stressed. "The case was so clear ... She didn't consent, period ... We had all the elements to convict ... It was a very short meeting."[9]

There are several versions as to who was designated to write the decision for the unanimous court. The practice at the time was for the chief justice to choose the author, customarily the volunteer with the most seniority.[10] After Chief Justice Antonio Lamer, who did not wish to write this decision, L'Heureux-Dubé was then the most senior. She recalled that she offered to write for the court, as she wanted to develop a clear refutation of what she saw as a decision filled with erroneous assumptions. Instead, the chief justice assigned the task to Justice John (Jack) Major. When she objected that she was more senior, Lamer justified his decision by saying that Major came from Alberta, where the case had originated.

L'Heureux-Dubé remembered being upset at this departure from the seniority protocol, and wondering whether Major was really chosen because he was a friend of McClung, his former colleague from the Alberta Court of Appeal.[11] She also wondered whether Lamer, known to be a hunting pal of McClung's, was trying to shield McClung from criticism.[12]

Major's recollection was that the chief justice asked him to write because he was from Alberta. "I don't think it was any kind of a plot," he added.[13] Justice Ian Binnie recalled that L'Heureux-Dubé had been "very hard" on McClung during the judges' discussion in their conference room, and "generally the court tries not to whack away at judges in the court of appeal. Being an Alberta appeal, a controversial one, if the Court of Appeal of Alberta was going to get straightened out, it was good to have an Alberta judge do it." Binnie also thought Lamer probably went to Major because he would be less likely to take "personal shots" at a former colleague.[14] Justice Michel Bastarache recalled it still differently. He thought L'Heureux-Dubé was initially asked to write, but when her draft came in, the others thought it too strongly worded to sign. According to Bastarache, Major then decided that he would write a separate decision, most of the others signed onto Major's, and L'Heureux-Dubé's draft was relegated to a concurring opinion.[15]

Whatever the truth, the end result was that Major circulated his draft clarifying that there was no legal basis for implied consent to sexual assault, but offering no other critique of McClung's ruling. "It was just as if they were approving what he said," complained L'Heureux-Dubé. "I found it so offensive."[16] When it became clear that most of her colleagues would sign Major's decision, she observed that *"le courage ne court pas les corridors de notre cour!"*[†, 17] She believed that McClung's intemperate language cried out for comment, and decided to draft her own opinion, concurring in the result with separate reasons.[18] "I wrote it all myself one evening," she remembered. "I wrote with rage."[19] She was able to convince just one colleague, Charles Doherty Gonthier, to sign on. Beverley McLachlin, the only other woman on the Supreme Court at the time, wrote a brief but separate concurring judgment denouncing the "specious defence of implied consent" and rejecting "stereotypical assumptions."[20]

---

† "Courage does not abound in the corridors of our court!"

Justice John (Jack) C. Major.

L'Heureux-Dubé's decision refuted McClung's reasoning more thoroughly. She identified the case as rooted in women's and children's equality rights, citing statistics about the pervasiveness of sexual violence in Canada, with 99 percent of the offenders male and 90 percent of the victims female. She referred to international human rights instruments that urged signatory countries, including Canada, to implement effective legal measures against sexual assault, along with "gender-sensitive training of judicial and law enforcement officers." She cited the research of feminist legal scholars Catharine MacKinnon, Christine Boyle, and Elizabeth Sheehy.[21]

She critiqued the sexism inherent in the lower court decisions, derived from "mythical assumptions" that portrayed women who said no as "really saying 'yes,' 'try again,' or 'persuade me.'" She took issue with McClung's comment that the victim was an unwed mother who was living with her boyfriend. "Why [was it] necessary to point out these aspects of the trial record? Could it be to express that [the complainant] is a person of questionable moral character?" She objected to McClung's use of phrases such as "romantic intentions" and "clumsy passes" and his characterization of the assault as "far less criminal than hormonal." She critiqued McClung's suggestion that a woman should have to "fight her way out" of sexual assault, using physical force like "a well-directed knee":

> Complainants should be able to rely on a system free from myths and stereotypes, and on a judiciary whose impartiality is not compromised by these biased assumptions ... It is part of the role of this Court to denounce this kind of language, unfortunately still used today, which not only perpetuates archaic myths and stereotypes about the nature of sexual assaults but also ignores the law.[22]

As national legal affairs reporter Stephen Bindman observed, "she wasn't one to mince words."[23]

McClung's "Open Letter"

The public furor began the next day with an "open letter" from McClung in the *National Post*. Many judges take umbrage when overruled by a higher court, and some grumble to themselves or privately to trusted colleagues. But it was unprecedented for a sitting judge to critique a Supreme Court decision in a public forum.[24] McClung attacked L'Heureux-Dubé for "feminist bias" and a "graceless slide into personal invective," asserting that "personal convictions" delivered "again from her judicial chair" could be responsible for the "disparate (and growing) number of male suicides being reported in the Province of Quebec."[25] The reference to suicide struck many as inexplicable until it was disclosed that L'Heureux-Dubé's husband had committed suicide. McClung later apologized and claimed that he did not know.[26] His explanation was unconvincing given the otherwise illogical nature of the reference. It was also widely known within legal and judicial circles that L'Heureux-Dubé's husband had died by suicide. It was something she often spoke about openly.[27]

Whatever had occurred to bring this to pass? Some thought that McClung represented a group of male judges who had become increasingly uneasy over the entry of women into the judiciary. Jack Major described the Alberta Court of Appeal as "an old boys' club," where "after a session [the judges] retired to somebody's office and mulled over the case [with] a drink of scotch. When women started to invade that world ... they just [didn't] feel comfortable."[28] Some speculated that McClung had never got over being bypassed for the position of Alberta chief justice by a younger female judge.[29] Kirk Makin, a *Globe and Mail* reporter, wondered whether McClung had been thinking, "Somebody has to bell the cat. I'm the guy. The day has come."[30] Makin described McClung as a man "waiting to explode," adding that it was like observing a "poison sac bursting."[31] Sean Fine, another *Globe* reporter, suggested that McClung would not have cast such aspersions upon a male judge.[32] As if to prove his point, the name of Charles Gonthier, who had signed L'Heureux-Dubé's opinion, never came up.

As the story unfolded, observers were also startled to discover that McClung's grandmother was none other than the famous Canadian suffragist Nellie McClung. Moreover, McClung's father, a prominent Crown prosecutor with a drinking problem, had committed suicide himself after disclosure of his misappropriation of public funds.[33] Some wondered whether McClung's unusual family history had taken a toll, turning him into a man with a reputation as a bit of an eccentric who loved to use "colourful words and phrases" often "shocking" in their import.[34]

The *Ewanchuk* explosion was also explained as a "casualty of the newspaper wars."[35] The decision was released on 25 February 1999. McClung's open letter appeared the morning after. It left L'Heureux-Dubé wondering whether he had been tipped off with an advance copy of her judgment.[36] In fact, the letter was the result of a direct intervention by the *National Post*, which was hoping to beat the *Globe and Mail* to a high-profile news story.[37] Janice Tibbetts, who had covered McClung's earlier decision for the *Post*, thought the Alberta judge's reference to "bonnets and crinolines" was "ridiculous." Knowing that the Supreme Court was due to deliver its ruling on 25 February, she had written a piece speculating that McClung might be in for a bit of a "dressing down" by the top court.[38] It was her guess that the reporter on the night desk grabbed the newly released ruling and, unaware that it was a breach of protocol for a judge to comment on the appeal of his own decision, phoned McClung for a quote.[39] McClung took the bait, but replied he would rather send a letter to the editor. The

Justice John Wesley "Buzz" McClung.

Post undertook to publish it the next day.[40] And although McClung's colleagues apparently tried valiantly to talk him out of it, he would not be deterred.[41]

The *National Post* had launched one year earlier, after corporate investor Conrad Black gained control of the Southam newspaper chain. Under Black's ownership, the chain fired many of its feminist columnists and "declared war" on feminism.[42] The paper also began to wage a fierce campaign against what it called the efforts of unelected "activist" judges to refashion the law in Canada based on *Charter* principles. Tibbetts explained that the Supreme Court of Canada became one of the chain's "pet projects" and L'Heureux-Dubé emerged as "the embodiment of the *National Post* attack on judicial activism."[43]

McClung's letter was the first bolt of lightning but not the last, and the media swelled with invective against L'Heureux-Dubé. Voices of support for her judgment then surfaced to counter the critique.[44] The *National Post* and *Globe and Mail* both published twenty articles about the *Ewanchuk* decision within fourteen days of its release.

Flashpoints of Reaction

The *Toronto Star* published the comments of Alan Gold, a high-profile criminal defence lawyer, who characterized L'Heureux-Dubé's decision as a "radical feminist judgment." He complained that the sex act was governed by "ambiguity and nuance and all kinds of things that aren't susceptible to this kind of subsequent verbalization," adding that this "protocol for human sexuality is ridiculous."[45] The *Calgary Herald* reported that Gold had labelled her opinion "totalitarian."[46] University of Calgary political science professor Ted Morton took issue with the research L'Heureux-Dubé had cited, complaining that she and others who shared her views were allowed "to quote whatever they like from radical feminists."[47] The *National Post* quoted Gwen Landolt, founder of the socially conservative REAL Women of Canada, who complained that Canadians "shouldn't have to pay the salary of a radical feminist who sits on the bench and uses her position to promote her own personal agenda."[48] REAL Women then lodged a formal complaint against L'Heureux-Dubé to the Canadian Judicial Council, the organization charged with reviewing judicial misconduct.[49]

Labelling L'Heureux-Dubé as "a friend of the feminists," a *Toronto Star* columnist criticized her "slagging of Mr. Justice John McClung."[50] The editors at the *National Post* described her decision as a "sanctimonious attack."[51] A *Globe and Mail* columnist claimed that the "unfortunate decision" was now turning the "war of the sexes" into a "unilateral declaration of war against all men and their very sexuality."[52] The *Ottawa Citizen* editors depicted L'Heureux-Dubé as "the Supreme Court's resident zealot" and her decision as "feminist cant" that read "less like a Supreme Court judgment on a specific case than a manifesto on feminist legal theory."[53] Dave Rutherford, the host of an Alberta radio talk show, estimated that 90 percent of his callers defended McClung.[54]

Even stronger critique came from Edward Greenspan, another famous Toronto defence lawyer. His letter to the editor in the *National Post* began: "When the Supreme Court judges swore their oath ... [t]hey were not given the right to pull a lower court judge's pants down in public and paddle him." It continued:

> By labelling Judge McClung, in effect, the male chauvinist pig of the century, the chief yahoo from Alberta, the stupid, ignorant, ultimate sexist male jerk, Judge L'Heureux-Dubé did an unnecessary and mean-spirited thing ... Judge L'Heureux-Dubé drew first blood and whatever he said will not be recorded in Canadian judicial history like her vicious comments about him will ...

Toronto criminal lawyer Edward Greenspan.

It is clear that the feminist influence has amounted to intimidation, posing a potential danger to the independence of the judiciary ... Feminists have entrenched their ideology in the Supreme Court of Canada and have put all contrary views beyond the pale.

The feminist perspective has hijacked the Supreme Court of Canada and now feminists want to throw off the bench anyone who disagrees with them. Judge L'Heureux-Dubé was hell-bent on re-educating Judge McClung, bullying and coercing him into looking at everything from her point of view. She raked him over the coals for making remarks that may, in fact, be accurate in the given case. I don't know. But just as he had no empirical evidence to support his view (if you discount all of human history), she has no empirical evidence to say what she says (if you discount Catharine MacKinnon's collected works) ... Madam Justice L'Heureux-Dubé has ... disgraced the Supreme Court.[55]

Even Steve Ewanchuk got into it. He was quoted in the *Toronto Star* as saying: "Mrs. Dubé, she never should've said what she said about him being an archaic and ignorant man, because he's not. She started it. What came back to her, personally, is something she started. Not him."[56]

Those who defended Justice L'Heureux-Dubé insisted that she was being unfairly "demonized" for exposing the sexism of a senior male judge.⁵⁷ Montreal's *La Presse* characterized McClung's letter as *"une sortie publique sans précédent dans l'histoire juridique canadienne."*†, ⁵⁸ Francophone Laval University law professor Ann Robinson explained that the Québécois viewed McClung's shocking response as doubly insulting: "an attack on women" and also "an attack from an Anglophone on a Francophone," emphasizing that in Quebec, linguistic issues were understood to be inextricably intertwined with sexism.⁵⁹ Francophone University of Ottawa law professor Nathalie Des Rosiers extolled L'Heureux-Dubé as the *"miroir de son époque"*‡ and her decision for recognizing that *"les femmes ne sont pas des objets sexuels mais des agents de leur sexualité."*§, ⁶⁰ University of Toronto political scientist Peter Russell described McClung's comments as "appalling" and suggested that he had behaved more like a politician than a judge.⁶¹ University of Calgary law professor Kathleen Mahoney characterized McClung's comments as "completely unprecedented," adding: "I've seen judges make some fairly intemperate comments, but ... I've never seen anything like this in my lifetime."⁶²

Bouquets of flowers began to arrive, sent in solidarity to L'Heureux-Dubé's judicial chambers.⁶³ At a Canadian Bar Association meeting shortly after the fracas, conference attendees gave L'Heureux-Dubé a "standing ovation," and CBA president Barry Gorlick observed that sentiments ranged "from a minimum of disappointment to a maximum of utter outrage and disgust."⁶⁴ Alberta law professors Bruce Elman and Barbara Billingsley compared L'Heureux-Dubé's critique of McClung with other Supreme Court decisions, and concluded that her judgment was neither "unique" nor "aberrant."⁶⁵ *Globe and Mail* columnist Rick Salutin registered his astonishment that anyone could find venom in L'Heureux-Dubé's concurring decision, when all he could find was "dry legalistic language."⁶⁶ Twenty-four individuals and organizations filed complaints of judicial misconduct against McClung with the Canadian Judicial Council.⁶⁷

Queen's University law professor Sheila McIntyre equated the attacks on L'Heureux-Dubé with "nightmarish caricatures" and "distortions of fact," which had unfairly converted McClung into the "injured innocent." The act of "naming sexism" had been turned on its head and transformed

---

† "a public outburst unprecedented in Canadian judicial history"
‡ "the mirror of her time"
§ "Women are not sexual objects but agents of their own sexuality."

into the "violence in the story," while the "far worse injury" was "a rape victim demeaned, discredited, and denied justice because of sexism from the bench."[68] Toronto rape crisis centre counsellor Anna Willats expressed strong support for L'Heureux-Dubé: "Finally someone is saying, 'Judges, join the real world.' Women don't wear bonnets and crinolines anymore."[69] A *Law Times* editorial added: "Male judges have been driven by their own assumptions and ideologies – most of us call them biases – for eons. Only now that we've had a few women sit on the Supreme Court of Canada have gender biases become politically unacceptable."[70]

The conflagration began to consume international judicial conversations. California Federal Court of Appeals Justice Alex Kozinski wrote to the *National Post* defending L'Heureux-Dubé's judgment as "neither particularly strident nor particularly ideological," but mere "common sense shared, I am confident, by most Canadians." He added: "The only dismaying thing about the Supreme Court's decision is that most of the other justices did not see fit to condemn Judge McClung's unfortunate language. But there is a very significant difference between disagreeing with someone's words and ideas, and descending into personal invective. It is a line Justice L'Heureux-Dubé respected scrupulously. Unfortunately, Mr. Greenspan and Judge McClung did not."[71]

L'Heureux-Dubé's *Ewanchuk* decision was lambasted as dead wrong by some and as the gold standard in sexual assault jurisprudence by others. No Supreme Court judge had ever been so publicly vilified and positively extolled at the same time. Her Supreme Court colleague Michel Bastarache, remarking on L'Heureux-Dubé's "colourfulness" and "flair," summed it up well: "She leaves no one indifferent."[72]

Who was the woman behind the *Ewanchuk* decision? How did she attain such legendary stature, ground zero for the pitched battles over sexual consent, reviled and revered at the same time, icon and lightning rod to Canadians across the country?

Family Heritage and Childhood

2

Lineage

Of Elephants, Literary Salons, the Military, and Mozart

Claire L'Heureux was born in Quebec City on 7 September 1927, into a family whose Quebec records stretched back ten generations.[1] She was the first-born child of Paul Henri L'Heureux and Marguerite (Dion) L'Heureux. The lineage of stature came primarily from her mother's side. It was adventure that characterized her father's family history.

Paternal Family History

The paternal ancestor who loomed largest in Claire's life was her colourful grandfather, Napoléon L'Heureux. Napoléon was born in 1885 in St. Paul, Minnesota, where his family had moved in search of work opportunities, part of the great nineteenth-century Quebec diaspora.[2] Napoléon's father's life ended tragically when he drowned on a bridge-building job. Napoléon's destitute mother took her ten children back to a Quebec City Catholic orphanage. It was a harsh upbringing for Napoléon, who lost touch with his siblings and obtained little education.[3]

When the British army began to recruit colonial soldiers for the Boer War, Napoléon resisted the anti-imperialist critique of Quebec nationalists and took up the only career that presented itself to him. He saw active cavalry service and brought back stories that would entrance his first granddaughter, of travelling to war in South Africa on the back of an elephant. "I've never verified that," Claire confided. "He was such a raconteur that you could never believe him."[4]

On 9 May 1904, Napoléon married Bruna Lavoie, a wealthy, beautiful woman from the Lac Saint-Jean region. On 28 May 1905, in Quebec City, the couple produced one son, Paul Henri, who would become Claire's father. Napoléon's devil-may-care attitude coupled with an indifferent education kept his work history chronically unstable. His jobs as a longshoreman and travelling salesman had promise that never seemed to materialize, and he was constantly in debt. Bruna's family tried to protect the family money by appointing her uncle as *tuteur*† to exert some control over the estate. But it took Napoléon, a man of generosity, extravagance, and zest for life, little time to run through his wife's inheritance.[5]

With the outbreak of the Great War in 1914, Napoléon enlisted to fight with the French Canadian Royal 22e Régiment in Europe, leaving his wife and young son behind. He had a penchant for stories, but one that was verified involved heroism during battle, when he saved the life of a comrade, Charles (Chubby) Gavan Power. Power would later rise to fame as a federal minister in the Liberal cabinet of Mackenzie King. The friendship forged on the battlefield lasted for decades and made of Napoléon a lifelong Liberal "with connections."[6] His military distinction also won him promotion to the post of major. He sent none of his salary home to his family and the government forwarded no family stipends, but Bruna managed somehow despite the birth of a second child, Marie.[7]

Claire remembered her grandfather as "brilliant, "extremely handsome," "outgoing," and "optimistic," someone who was completely "outside of the ordinary."[8] During her childhood, he would take her for summer sojourns on Lac Sergent and Lac Saint-Jean, where he had constructed cottages. Everything about him was larger than life, including the time he took six-year-old Claire across the lake by boat during a terrifying thunder and lightning storm, heedless of the risk. He impressed his granddaughter with his purchase of a panelled Ford, one of the first cars Claire saw up close. She recalled Napoléon as someone who liked to drink, to joke, and to talk. In politics, he was "so Liberal that people would say *'Il est teindu'* – slang for saying 'he's so red it's as if he were put in a vat to tint him.'"[9] His generosity generated a flood of acquaintances seeking his help to find jobs. He was particularly known for going to bat for widows who needed government pensions, and occasionally he was able to deliver. He was a "populist" at heart.[10]

But Napoléon was a controversial figure, and Claire's parents had a troubled relationship with him. Paul L'Heureux, who had had aspirations

---

† guardian

for higher education as a young man, resented his father's roller-coaster life. After Paul was accepted at the Séminaire de Québec, the spendthrift Napoléon paid for his son's first year and furnished him with a car too. Paul had not gone beyond classes in rhetoric when the money ran out, and he was forced to leave school and abandon his dreams of becoming an architect.[11] He would harbour a lifelong resentment over the abrupt termination of his education. In recompense, Napoléon arranged for his son to sit the federal civil service examinations, and Paul began work as a customs and immigration officer in Quebec City.[12]

Claire's mother, Marguerite, disapproved of her father-in-law, whom she regarded as highly irresponsible. In later years, she refused even to have him in the house.[13] She used many choice phrases to describe Napoléon: *"menteur, comme un arracheur de dents"*[†] was one; *"bon cœur et tête folle"*[‡] was another. Claire, who took after her grandfather in looks, remembered her mother often scolding her: *"Lorsque je te dis que tu ressembles à ton grand-père, ce n'est pas un compliment."*[§, 14]

Napoléon and Bruna's marriage deteriorated over the years. Mental illness diagnosed at the time as *mélancolie chronique*[||] eventually rendered Bruna unable to communicate. Claire's childhood memory of her grandmother is of a woman seated in front of a window, staring out endlessly, never spoken to and never speaking. Bruna died in 1934.

In 1940, fifty-five-year-old Napoléon remarried. His new wife was twenty-six-year-old Aurore Lavoie. Some critiqued Napoléon's promiscuous ways, but Claire was gentler in her assessment. *"Il aimait les femmes,"*[#] was how she explained it. Aurore was working in a munitions factory at Valcartier and would later set up shop as a hairdresser. She was pregnant at the time of the marriage, and by all accounts she adored Napoléon. The newlyweds sent a picture of their newborn son to Claire's family. The photograph of the nude baby lying on his stomach on a bear rug left Marguerite beside herself with dismay. "A man of that age!" was her horrified reaction.[15]

Napoléon died of a heart attack in 1955, leaving behind the only property he had accumulated in his seventy-one years: a car, a small Lac Saint-Jean chalet, and, in what seemed something of a miracle to his family, no debt.[16]

---

† "an arrant liar [or he lies through his teeth]"
‡ "a good heart but a hothead"
§ "When I tell you that you look like your grandfather, I am not paying you a compliment."
|| chronic melancholy
"He loved women."

Maternal Ancestors

Among Claire's markedly more respectable maternal ancestors, her strongest memories were of her grandmother, Antoinette (Fortin) Dion.[17] Deeply religious, Antoinette was an adherent of Jansenism, an austere, prohibition-laced, heretical theological movement.[18] Her passionate affiliation with the Conservative party would lead to heated exchanges with Napoléon, sparking family shouting matches around the radio as the adults dissected the political disputes of the day. Claire described Antoinette as "an intellectual" and a "very powerful woman," who was "very decisive" and "interested in everything."[19]

She was born in a grand ancestral home in L'Islet, Quebec, in 1862, and was raised in a socially elite milieu. Her father was a land surveyor and her mother was from the prominent seigneurial Lepage family in Rimouski. The Lepage line had been studded with doctors, lawyers, and priests, people "of the world" who travelled widely and read voraciously.[20] When it came time for Antoinette to marry, she set her heart on Victor Dion from L'Islet. When Victor married her best friend instead, Antoinette announced that she would wait, and she married Victor after all, after her friend died giving birth to a third child. Antoinette and Victor had four more children, among them Marguerite, Claire's mother, who was born in 1903.[21]

Also from a wealthy family, Victor Dion began his career as the Canadian National Railway stationmaster in L'Islet and then moved to Quebec City to enter the hotel business with his brother. Victor eventually took over the management of the Hôtel Saint-Louis, at the corner of rues Saint-Louis and Haldimand in Vieux Québec. The growing Dion family resided in the stylish hotel, which was said to rival the Château Frontenac for grandeur and beauty. The environment was intellectually invigorating, with lawyers and politicians coming and going through the hotel salons and dining room to discuss important matters of the day. Antoinette organized some of the most impressive of the literary events. Claire remembered hearing about the polished silver, the delicately patterned china, and the grand cuisine of the Hôtel Saint-Louis.

Family finances took a dramatic turn for the worse when Victor lent $60,000 to an individual who invested it in a western Canadian mine. With the demise of the mine, the loan became worthless. A heart attack apparently triggered by the financial disaster killed Victor in 1910. What was left of the family fortune was placed in the hands of a notary for safekeeping, but between Antoinette's profligate spending and the notary's bad investments, the money soon disappeared. Antoinette hoped to continue living in the hotel with her children, but her debts overwhelmed her. Her furniture was seized, she could no longer afford to pay for heat, and her daughter Marguerite was forced to give music lessons to help earn her way.[22]

Antoinette's unexpected poverty was probably what brought young Marguerite Dion and Paul L'Heureux into contact. By the ages of fifteen and thirteen, respectively, they found themselves living one street over from each other in Quebec City and became childhood sweethearts. Although their current situation erased the disparity between their original class positions, Marguerite never quite forgot that Paul's was the sort of family that was raised on "jello and ice-cream," while hers had been used to fine cuisine and gracious dining.[23]

Marguerite Dion L'Heureux: *"Talents de toutes sortes"*[†]

Marguerite L'Heureux, Claire's mother, was the person Claire would later single out as the individual who most influenced her life.[24] Steeped in the culture of Quebec City's social elite, Marguerite grew up as a vivacious person with an active mind, sure of her own judgment. Never one to hide her opinions, she blended strong will with great charm. A talented individual of wide-ranging interests, she had an extraordinary sense of humour and was quick at mocking repartee. Known for her elegance of speech, she treasured her ancestral French culture, persistently identifying as "French" rather than "Canadian." Enthusiastic and playful, she could also exhibit driving perfectionism. Above all, she was deeply optimistic, a woman with a marked sense of *joie de vivre* who savoured life. Slim, of slender waist and medium build, Marguerite had dark-brown hair and green eyes with just a touch of brown. Her scrutinizing family pronounced her nose too long for classical beauty, but buoyed Marguerite's self-esteem by repeating that *"un grand nez ne défigure pas un joli visage."*[‡]

In her youth, Marguerite had worn dresses designed by the best couturiers in Quebec, and her refined sense of fashion never left her despite her diminished means. She loved beautiful furnishings, elaborate table settings, and haute cuisine, but she could also stretch a little money a long way, a skill honed during the financially strained years after her father's death. The organist at the cathedral gave the musically talented Marguerite

---

† "a multi-talented person"
‡ "a long nose does not spoil a beautiful face"

Marguerite Dion.

private lessons, and she often played the organ in the church. She was proficient in composition, and under the watchful eye of her mother sometimes practised piano for eight hours a day. She adored opera and Mozart.

As a young woman with a thirst for learning, Marguerite deeply regretted her limited options. Convent schools were then the only route for Francophone Catholic women wishing to obtain schooling beyond the few years offered in the public elementary system. Those wishing admission to university had to complete five additional years of private "classical" education. Although classical courses were first opened to female students in 1908, very few enrolled and Marguerite was not among them.[25] Instead, she studied at the Académie Saint-Louis, a traditional Quebec City convent for the daughters of the elite, where young women obtained the equivalent of a finishing-school education. She then enrolled at the Ursuline Collège in Stanstead in the Eastern Townships, where she pursued musical studies and improved her English. Although the Ursuline Collège interlude lasted less than a year, she would remember it with pleasure all her life.[26]

Prematurely cut off from higher education, Marguerite buried herself in books and literary magazines. She had a superb memory and could absorb and retain every detail from her reading. On her own, she studied Latin, Greek, Spanish, poetry, and mythology. She sought out people of ideas, with whom she loved to discuss politics as well as play poker and bridge. She obtained her *diplôme de professeur avec grande distinction*[†] from the Dominium College of Music, which enabled her to teach music at the convent boarding school of the Sœurs du Bon Pasteur in Chicoutimi.[27] She toyed briefly with the idea of becoming a nun, but by this time Paul L'Heureux was writing to her, urging her to return to Quebec City. Captivated by his entreaties, Marguerite returned home and took a position as a secretary until her marriage in 1926.[28]

Claire's childhood memories of her mother were glowing: *"Somme toute, ma mère avait de la classe, elle était instruite et elle avait des talents de toutes sortes. Elle était toujours gaie et disait qu'elle aimait tout ce qu'elle faisait. C'est ainsi que je voyais ma mère lorsque j'étais encore dans ma tendre enfance."*[‡, 29]

Paul L'Heureux: *"Il se perfectionnait sans cesse"*[§]

Paul L'Heureux was a man of sharp contrasts.[30] His daughters described him as having two sides to his personality: public and private. They explained that outside of the home, he was regarded as a man who respected others and thought well of people. He was open, smiling, friendly, and generous. Others confirmed this, characterizing Paul L'Heureux as "well-liked," "kind," "charismatic," "easy to talk to," and "a hell of a nice guy."[31]

[†] a professor's diploma with great distinction
[‡] "All in all, my mother had class, she was educated and she had talents of every kind. She was always cheerful and said she loved everything she did. This is how I saw my mother when I was still in my early infancy."
[§] "He was constantly striving to improve himself."

Charming and fun, he was the life of the party, who "loved to dance." Claire described her father in these moods as *"éblouissant,"* or dazzling in personality.[32]

But this was a side of Paul L'Heureux that his children rarely saw. Underneath the exterior lustre, at home he was stern, taciturn, and severe – a man of few words and fewer compliments. Within his own family, he was the undisputed boss, a stern disciplinarian who rarely smiled, a man who was "preoccupied," closed in on himself and unable to express his feelings. In retrospect, his children suspected that his mood shifts might have masked anxiety, lack of self-confidence, and possibly even depression. Claire admitted that she had never had the courage to "invade his personal universe," that her father frightened her, and that she suspected he was "not a happy man."[33]

Paul L'Heureux seems to have spent much of his life defining himself in relation to his father. Occupationally, he rebelled against Napoléon's legacy. The son of a man who couldn't hold a steady job, Paul himself never strayed from the stability of the civil service. Napoléon may have helped set him up in his first post, but it was shrewd perseverance and laborious hard work that brought Paul advancement in his career. Competent and dedicated, he did not shirk responsibility or cut corners. He was an individual of enormous energy, who seized opportunities, willingly shouldered extra tasks, eagerly took on overtime, never procrastinated, was never late, and took charge of a growing workload with capability and pride. His reward would be a series of prestigious promotions over the next decades.[34]

In politics, Paul refused to follow his father's lead into the Liberal party, in part because he was a civil servant but also because he was not anxious to engage in tumultuous party politics. With razor-sharp intelligence, a dry sense of humour, and definite opinions, he was more of a "thinking liberal" with a zealous desire for self-improvement. Committed to rising above his father's and his own lack of education, Paul immersed himself in literature, read everything he could find on military history and biography, and accumulated an impressive private library with a plethora of French books. At a time when elite Quebecers prided themselves on their proficiency in English, Paul built upon the rudimentary English he had learned in school to become fluently bilingual.[35]

On the other hand, Paul wrapped himself in his father's military mantle and followed that path with pride. Serving with the reserves from a young age, he began with the navy and switched to the armed forces. By 1924, he was a commissioned officer in the Régiment de Montmagny, rising in

Paul Henri L'Heureux, officer of the Régiment de Montmagny, ca. 1924.

rank from lieutenant to captain, major, and finally *officier d'état-major-général*† by 1937.³⁶ He was one of the first to enlist at the outbreak of the Second World War. While others in Quebec resisted military service and opposed conscription, Paul was committed to raising the profile of French

---

† general staff officer

Canadian troops. His immersion in martial life also left a significant imprint on his personality. His children described him as obsessed with military precision, a man who prized order, efficiency, and organization in every aspect of life, down to the last minute detail of the placement of socks and personal toiletries in his bedroom drawers.[37]

Physically, Paul was a "handsome" man with pale blue eyes and blondish hair, of medium height and a trim figure. He sported a tidy moustache that set off his chiselled facial features. He smoked cigarettes but never a pipe. A close childhood friend of Claire's described him as emanating a "quiet elegance" with "a smile that was a bit laconic" – a definite "ladies' man."[38]

Trying to reflect the positive aspects of the complex and difficult man who was her father, Claire wrote: *"Il était dévoué et rendait service facilement. Il était généreux, avait beaucoup d'esprit, aimait la vie (et les femmes) et en profitait. Je le trouvais beau. Dans mon enfance, je crois que je l'aimais. À l'adolescence, j'étais fière de lui."*[†, 39]

It was a lineage filled with contradictions, an astonishing assortment of characters with forceful personalities and larger-than-life dimensions. It was also a foreshadowing of L'Heureux-Dubé's own complex personality, moulded in the reflection of her colourful antecedents.

---

† "He was devoted and naturally helpful. He was generous, had a lot of wit, loved life (and women), and took advantage of it. I thought he was handsome. In my childhood, I think I loved him. As a teenager, I was proud of him."

3
Early Years
Quebec City and Rimouski

Quebec City, the four-hundred-year-old site of North America's first hospital, Canada's first university, and Canada's first symphony orchestra, prides itself as the cradle of French civilization in North America.¹ After its capture by the British in 1759, the French populace took care to secure the right to their French language, Roman Catholic religion, and civil law traditions. Architect Eugène-Étienne Taché sculpted *"Je me souviens,"*† a motto that would become ubiquitous, on the facade of the Quebec Parliament Building in 1883.² By 1927, the year of Claire L'Heureux-Dubé's birth, Quebec's growing population made it the seventh-largest city in Canada.³

During the interwar years of the 1920s and '30s, the city's economy suffered restless ups and downs. In good times, there was unprecedented growth, although the spread of industrial capitalism led to a troubling concentration of power in the hands of Anglophone financiers and entrepreneurs from Montreal, Toronto, and the United States. The depression of the 1930s brought the whole economy tumbling down. Provincial unemployment, 15 percent by the end of 1929, had doubled to 30 percent by 1933.⁴ Premier Louis-Alexandre Taschereau's Liberal party, which had reigned for forty years, fought back against growing charges of corruption, tired leadership, and complicity with monopolistic hydroelectric trusts. In 1936, opposition leader Maurice Duplessis, waiting in the wings with

---

† "I remember."

his newly formed Union Nationale, toppled the Liberals. He would usher in an even more conservative regime that would be dubbed *La Grande Noirceur,* the Great Darkness.⁵

The Quebec of Claire's youth was marked by hierarchical ideology and clerical power. The patriarchal family was proclaimed the foundation of religious morality, social order, and civilization. Even the nascent feminist movement accepted the husband as "minister of external affairs" and the wife as "minister of the interior."⁶ Defined as *les gardiennes de la race,*† women experienced smothering paternalism in the family, church, state, and workplace. Denied access to higher education, they were notably absent from universities, corporate life, and traditionally male professions. In 1935, the Quebec Legislative Assembly debated a bill that would deny employment to any woman who could not demonstrate financial need, as vouched for by a responsible male such as the curé, the mayor, or an alderman. Upon marriage, women suffered *la mort civile,* legal death. Between 1919 and 1940, of thirteen women's suffrage bills brought before the legislature, only the last achieved success. The year Claire turned thirteen, Quebec became the final province in Canada to extend the vote to women.⁷

This was the Quebec City of Claire's early years, the city to which she would return as a Quebec judge and finally again in retirement.

Claire's Early Childhood

On 17 August 1926, when Marguerite Dion was twenty-three years old and Paul L'Heureux twenty-one, they wed in the Notre-Dame-du-Chemin church in Quebec City.⁸ Marguerite's mother, Antoinette, was gravely concerned that her daughter was marrying a man who was her inferior in social class. Insistent that it was a mistake to marry for love rather than security and status, she never renounced her position. She disparaged Paul's pale blue eyes as colourless, calling her son-in-law *"ce grand corps mou et ses yeux blancs."*‡,⁹ Claire's sister Louise recalled: "She was opposed to the marriage. She came from a family that had doctors, intellectuals. She didn't think the L'Heureux family was on the same level."¹⁰

The young couple's intimate correspondence from their first decade of marriage, saved for years and later treasured by Claire, was effusively

---

† the guardians of the race
‡ "this lanky man with a limp body and blank eyes"

romantic. Paul's letters in flowing handwriting and poetic phrases, and Marguerite's peppered with philosophy and household details, are filled with declarations of love.[11] Claire's birth, on 7 September 1927, was followed by the arrival of three more girls: Louise in 1929, Lucie in 1932, and Nicole in 1934. The timing matched the traditional Quebec pattern. In the absence of birth control, most wives gave birth about every second year throughout their childbearing years.[12] All the L'Heureux girls were born at home.

Claire's parents moved several times before settling into 695 avenue Désy, a modest rented row house almost at the city limits.[13] Claire described the house as filled with light, warmth, and happiness. Perhaps the positive memories relate to the privilege of being the first-born, because Louise, her younger sister, recalled the house as small, crowded, and uncomfortable. Both remembered the bed bugs, *"des punaises à profusion,"*† which, despite all efforts at eradication, plagued the household until the family moved to Rimouski in 1935.[14] The diverse middle-class neighbourhood contained accountants, lawyers, insurance agents, bank employees, journalists, carpenters, salesmen, and civil servants. To Claire, it seemed that all the neighbouring families were wealthier than her own.[15]

Paul's salary may have been modest, but his secure job as an immigration officer left the family better economically insulated than many. It was Napoléon L'Heureux whose fiscal irresponsibility posed problems for his son and daughter-in-law. One family story, often repeated, involved a gift he gave the young couple: a new Frigidaire. Napoléon had taken up selling refrigerators. Marguerite suspected he had insufficient funds to pay for the one he brought them and urged her husband not to accept it. Paul reassured her that it was a gift, but sure enough, Napoléon lost the job and Claire's parents had to pay for a refrigerator they would not have chosen to buy. Marguerite's fury over the strain on the tight family finances also became etched in family lore.[16]

Scarlet fever, whooping cough, measles, mumps, and chickenpox – the typical childhood diseases of the time – descended on 695 Désy, forcing the girls into bed and quarantine. In the era before vaccines, "when one got it, we all got it," remembered Claire. In retrospect, she saw benefit in the contagion: "We had all these sicknesses, and we battled them. It made us stronger. We had immunities."[17] Claire's overriding memory of her early years was the freedom to play and roam without danger, secure within a

---

† "a multitude of bed bugs"

Claire at age three with carriage, Quebec City.

loving family. Trying to convey the sense of openness in the neighbourhood, she explained that her mother taught the girls to say a few phrases in English, including, "Would you come and play with us," a query that they put to anyone who passed by on the sidewalk. Laughing, she added, "Can you imagine that today?"[18]

Claire began school on 7 September 1933, her sixth birthday, and spent her first two years at the convent of the Sœurs de Saint-Joseph de Saint-Vallier on Chemin Sainte-Foy, close enough to walk. Her mother had already begun to teach her to read and write, and she recalled her early lessons from the nuns as effortless, *"une fête."*[†, 19] She topped the class in religious instruction.[20] Some of the credit for that must have been due to Marguerite, who would tuck the girls into bed at night telling them they were only "loaned" to her by God, that it was her responsibility to take them to heaven, where the family would be reunited after death.[21]

---

† "a holiday"

The leisure activities of the growing young family revolved around church, religious festivities, and family celebrations for special occasions, mostly spent with Antoinette and with Marguerite's sister Marie-Marthe and her husband, Wilfrid, who lived nearby. Memorable summer days were spent at Anse au Foulon, on the beach of the small cove about one and a half miles outside the city, where General Wolfe had landed with his British soldiers before scaling the cliffs to fight Montcalm's troops on the Plains of Abraham. Occasionally, the family also strolled the legendary Plains, where Claire and Louise posed for a photograph on the historic cannons.[22]

Louise and Claire on cannon, ca. 1935, Plains of Abraham.

Louise and Claire with Paul L'Heureux at Anse au Foulon.

Promotion to Rimouski

In 1935, Paul L'Heureux was promoted to the position of collector of customs and excise in Rimouski. It was a wrench for Paul and Marguerite to leave behind the city of their birth for a provincial town three hundred kilometres east on the south shore of the St. Lawrence, but the prospect of a more responsible post with a significantly higher salary beckoned. Marguerite's initial anxiety over the move evaporated as her characteristic sunny world-view resurfaced. She stayed behind with one-year-old Nicole for several months to pack up furniture and enable her husband to find a new home in Rimouski. Louise went to live temporarily with her aunt Marie-Marthe and uncle Wilfrid, who had no children of their own and doted on the little girl. Seven-year-old Claire was taken out of school to make the move to Rimouski with her father and sister Lucie.[23]

It was the two girls' first trip by train along the south shore of the St. Lawrence, and they were fascinated to pass through L'Islet, about which they had heard so much from their grandmother Antoinette.[24] By the time they reached Rimouski, at the mouth of the river that bore the same name, the St. Lawrence had turned salty and had swollen to forty miles wide. Directly across, the north shore was not visible to the eye. It was like looking out on the ocean. With mounting excitement, the girls disembarked with their father at the Canadian National Railway station.[25]

Their destination was the Hôtel Saint-Louis, where they would reside for the next five months. One of four hotels in Rimouski, the Saint-Louis was a short walk from the imposing red brick and stone edifice that housed the customs office. Originally a four-room guesthouse opened by a Rimouski widow renowned for her cooking, it had expanded to forty rooms in 1929. The tariff was $1.50 per room with meals, and one could feast on *fruits de mer:*[†] crab, lobster, clams, and salmon fresh from the wharf.[26] For Claire, the months at Hôtel Saint-Louis seemed like a delightful adventure. She and Lucie were warmly greeted by the effusive family that ran the hotel, and they spent their days playing in the lobby or at the home of Marguerite's uncle in Rimouski. Their father joined them for dinner at noon most days.[27]

The Cathédrale Saint-Germain, of medieval design with a vaulting Gothic steeple, dominated the Rimouski skyline with one of the best vantage

---

† seafood

Cathédrale Saint-Germain, Rimouski.

points on the shore. It served 99 percent of the populace with four or five Masses full to bursting every Sunday. The city's wealthiest citizens had constructed homes with decorative towers, grand balconies, and beautiful stone facades, still known by the names of their original owners: *la maison Caron, le château Rouleau, la maison Gauvreau.* Rimouski was also known for its wide wooden boardwalk that followed the course of the river. On summer evenings, crowds would come out to stroll along the boardwalk in the moonlight at high tide.[28]

If people asked Claire about Rimouski, she would exclaim that it was the "most beautiful place in the world."[29] Others might have emphasized different things. Poor soil and miserable weather. Fog, mist, and haze. Rain, snow, and wind. In the fall, the ice ascended and descended the river at the whim of the currents. Bitterly cold, humid winds blew continuously from the north. During the winter, temperatures could dip to −35°C. Spring came late, "three weeks behind Quebec City in the growing season," as Marguerite would gauge it. The L'Heureux family used to joke that "the summer in Rimouski came on the 8th and 9th of July – *c'est tout*."[†, 30] Summer days could be beautiful, with median temperatures of 17°C, but many were eclipsed by rain and thunderstorms. Mornings and rainy days brought *bancs de brume,* dense fog banks that rolled along the river, enveloping everything. Even under full sun, an almost imperceptible light fog floated on the river, giving a grey-blue tint to the landscape. Children would swim in the river, but the water was so cold that it would turn their skin blue.[31] What was there about this harsh environment that inspired Claire's lifelong passion for Rimouski?

"La mer, l'horizon, les vagues"[‡]

Rimouski inhabitants were in thrall to the dominion of the sea. Years after her retirement, Claire's joy at returning regularly to visit old friends remained unmistakable. There was a buoyancy in her step, a relaxation of tension, and pure happiness on her face: "We had to fight nature. Maybe that gave us the spirit of fighting. We built up confidence living in that small place."[32] She found the climate and landscape life-affirming:

> *L'air de la mer, cet air frais, iodé, à senteur de varech qu'on respirait à plein nez, malgré le vent et le rude climat, je lui attribue ma bonne santé physique et mentale. Le grand vent m'a fait des poumons, le grand air et les grands espaces m'ont donné le goût de la liberté. La mer, l'horizon, les vagues, tout nous inspire.*[§, 33]

---

† "that's all"
‡ "The sea, the horizon, the waves"
§ "The air of the sea, that fresh, iodized air, with a smell of kelp, that we breathed in deeply, despite the wind and harsh climate, I credit my good physical and mental health to it. Strong winds built my lungs, while the outdoors and wide open spaces gave me a taste for freedom. The sea, the horizon, the waves, all inspire us."

Settled in the nineteenth century, Rimouski traced its unusual name to the language of the original inhabitants, the Mi'kmaq.[34] By mid-century, the village had positioned itself as the "door to the east country," a judicial, religious, and educational metropolis for the Gaspésie and Matapédia.[35] Claire L'Heureux-Dubé, whose judicial career would lead her to grapple with complex debates about equality, diversity, and difference, acknowledged that she grew up in a town of "total homogeneity." From its founding to the 1960s, Rimouski's population held steady at 98 percent French Canadian. "We could say that Rimouski was a very closed society," she added. "Nobody from the outside, really, would come in to work or live."[36]

The few newcomers who did were segregated. The largest group of *étrangers* were Anglophones, many of whom managed the Price Brothers lumber company and lived in large houses in an enclave on the side of the river near the ski hill. There was one Chinese man who ran a laundry and lived in the basement on the premises. There was one French-speaking Syrian family who managed a clothing store in the west end of town.[37] Claire's sister Louise recalled that their mother used to say: "Don't go near that store. Cross the street!" She explained: "For some reason, people thought they were Jewish. They had never seen any foreigners. There were all kinds of stories about them."[38] Years later, she discovered that the Syrians were Catholic. There were no Jews in Rimouski, but that did not deter the bishop from spouting anti-Semitism. "The Catholic church called them Christ-killers," recalled Louise. "The Jews were at fault for everything. They put everything on the back of the Jews." Then she added that it was not something discussed at home: "We never talked about Jews in our house. It was more that foreigners were not to be trusted."[39]

It took two weeks before the sleepy town's daily press picked up the story of the October 1929 stock market crash, and even then it printed the brief article on page 4.[40] But by the depths of winter in 1930, the local curé confirmed that the Depression had plunged nine-tenths of Rimouski's inhabitants into poverty. Malnourished children showed up in school with bowed legs. Fortunately, 1935, when the L'Heureux family arrived, proved to be the bottom of the economic trough.[41] Forestry dominated Rimouski's industrial base, and despite disastrous fires that destroyed the flammable Price Brothers sawmill three times over, the company added a second mill in 1938 and was employing over five hundred factory workers by 1940. The bustling port of Rimouski was open from April to November, and ships of all tonnage dropped anchor. A total of 516 ships docked in 1935, discharging coal, oil and gas, and fish, and picking up lumber, pulp, and other forest products for export to the United States, Holland, and Germany.[42]

Quai de Rimouski, 1913.

As one of the few inhabitants of Rimouski with a steady income, Paul L'Heureux weathered the Depression better than most. A few months after his arrival, he purchased 188 rue Saint-Germain, the dwelling that would become Claire's favourite home, her childhood castle in Rimouski.[43] The thirteen-room house was on the market because the previous owner had defaulted on the mortgage, and the selling price of $3,750 was substantially below its real worth. To help meet the payments, Paul rented the front room to a physician for his office. The house had separate servants' quarters, and due to the low cost of domestic help, the family was able to hire one or two live-in maids, impoverished young women from Gaspésie to help with cooking, laundry, housekeeping, and childcare. Claire recalled that although it was common for families to refer to all their maids as "Marie," her mother always used the proper name for their servants, and although the maids were fed separately, they ate the same food as the family, unlike in many other homes.[44]

Rue Saint-Germain was one of the town's most prestigious residential and commercial thoroughfares.[45] The neighbourhood did not boast Rimouski's wealthiest families, but it was slightly above middle class in status.[46] Nearby lived Henri Labrie, military commander of the Fusiliers du St-Laurent Régiment, and Sir Eugène Fiset, the former deputy minister of defence, Rimouski's Liberal member of Parliament from 1924 to 1939 and later lieutenant-governor.[47] Of more interest to the L'Heureux girls

Saint-Germain children's birthday party in park, ca. 1936. *Kneeling, left to right,* Lucie L'Heureux, [unidentified], Nicole L'Heureux; *top row, left to right,* Andrée Ouellet, [unidentified], Jacques Ouellet, Huguette Cloutier, Lucie Lavoie, Raymonde Ouellet, Claire L'Heureux, Michèle Cloutier, Anita Lachance, Louise L'Heureux *(cut off)*.

was the abundance of new playmates. Raymonde and Andrée Ouellet lived next door, above the grocer. Huguette and Michèle Cloutier, daughters of the electrical inspector, lived across the street. The Masson family, which kept a shoe store down the street, had eight children and a badminton court in the backyard. Jean and Marguerite Drapeau, the children of neighbours Dr. Octave Drapeau and his wife, Cécile Paradis, became lifelong friends. It made for a whirlwind of birthday parties, neighbourhood affairs that served as occasions for party dresses and birthday cakes with candles.

The new L'Heureux home backed onto the river, buttressed by a retaining wall and small wharf to keep the blustery sea at bay. Several times a year, ferocious storms washed over the retaining wall, rendering the wharf repeatedly in need of repair, to the continuing despair of Claire's parents. Watching the storms roll in over the water, Marguerite would utter one of her favourite expressions: *"Le temps se graisse."*[†, 48] But on the rare warm summer days, the family could arrange chaise lounges on the reinforced terrace and stretch out in the sun. The girls could dangle their toes in the sea and watch the whales swim past. With windows that opened onto the St. Lawrence, "the house was almost *in* the water. It was like we were on top of it," recalled Louise. "The river was so deep that the sea was always there. It almost felt like we were in a boat all the time ... right on the water."[49] For young Claire, who watched her father search for ships on the horizon through his binoculars, it seemed to be a window on the world. She dreamed of becoming "a captain on a ship, a sea-pilot, free to roam beyond the horizon."[50]

The house itself was a two-storey wooden dwelling with the traditional J-shaped slope to the roof, characteristic of the Quebec countryside. In the winter, the snow would be piled so high that the girls could climb to the roof and jump off into the snow banks. The struggling old coal-burning furnace in the basement forced Paul L'Heureux to get up to add fuel in

188 rue Saint-Germain, late 1940s. The original balcony that extended around the front of the house had been removed.

---

† "The weather is greasing up."

the middle of every winter night. When the weather permitted, the girls loved to sit on the balcony, sheltered from the rain, and watch passers-by. On cool August evenings, the whole family would stay out there, tucked warmly into chairs with blankets and cushions, to watch the aurora borealis. Marguerite would sometimes wake the girls at 5 a.m. to see the sunrise from a large window in the upstairs hall.[51]

In later years, after the physician moved his office elsewhere, the spacious front room became Paul's private study, where he could listen to the news on the radio, smoke cigarettes, and read in peace. The private retreat housed a growing library of books, including church-banned literature that both Paul and Marguerite read voraciously. The girls were forbidden to enter but nothing was under lock and key, and as they grew older, they read through the collection as well.[52]

Marguerite's influence was evident in the living room, where the centrepiece was a grand player piano on which she would play in the evening, often Mozart or Liszt. On Saturday afternoons, the family would gather around the radio to listen to opera: "Texaco Sky Chief Direct from the Met." When grandmother Antoinette visited, she was annoyed to see Paul regularly interrupt his wife's evening piano recitals with the gramophone or the radio, and complained that Paul was unappreciative of Marguerite's beautiful piano playing. Antoinette would also criticize him for being too severe with her grandchildren, accusing him of acting like a "tyrant" and "martyring" Marguerite and the children, giving orders as if he were "the commanding general in his army."[53] For his part, Paul made fun of Antoinette and tried to stay away from the house during her visits. Eventually the two stopped speaking to each other, and the impasse ended only with Antoinette's death in 1940.[54]

The grand dining room with built-in mirrored buffet was where the family took all their meals. Claire's father walked home at noon to have dinner, the main meal of the day. Marguerite was formal about these, with heirloom linens, perfect table settings, and a full menu of soup, main course, and dessert. Louise described how her father dominated the room: "My father expected things to be orderly. No talking at the table. Mealtimes were not very happy. You couldn't really do much ... sit there straight, and don't put your arms and elbows on the table. You were just there, worried that something bad was going to happen."[55] Claire's memory was similar:

> Les repas en général n'étaient pas toujours sereins. D'une part, nous devions rester à table, maman, elle, se levait et papa dépeçait la viande. Souvent (peut-être moins souvent que je ne l'imagine) lorsque nous parlions, papa nous faisait taire

en disant que tout ce qu'on disait était stupide. Il n'y avait pas de dialogue avec papa: il avait toujours raison et on avait tort. Il vivait en militaire: il commandait et on devait obéir.[†, 56]

All agreed that Paul L'Heureux was the disciplinarian in the family. He ruled with an iron fist, delivering painfully severe corporal punishment whenever Marguerite reported wrongdoing on the part of the children. There were the ordinary childhood indiscretions such as sibling spats and pillow fights, but the scrapes occasionally escalated. Claire climbed through the main floor guest-room window, sneaking outside more than once when her parents had forbidden her to leave. Once the girls went into their father's bedroom dresser and took out his gun. And the sisters all described a disastrous incident with the player piano. Fascinated by the rollers and mechanical parts, Claire destroyed it when she cut the wires.[57]

Claire was the main culprit, and was physically punished more severely and frequently than the others. Her sister Nicole explained: "He would forbid her to do something, and she'd do it just the same. Or she would say in front of him that she was going to do it. He got very mad at her sometimes."[58] Jean Drapeau, a family friend, tried to capture Claire's personality as a young girl: "She was determined, and sometimes she loved to make a scene. A little *maligne.* We have an old French term we use in Quebec: *un air de grippette,* an affectionate way of saying 'mischievous.'"[59] Louise added: "Claire wasn't afraid. She said what she thought. She was a rebel from the time she was born. I think the reason that Claire and he clashed was because they were too much alike. She has more of my father's qualities than she thinks."[60]

The girls' recollections of their mother's cooking were more positive. Marguerite's talents were inherited from Antoinette, who had learned at the feet of the fancy chefs at her father's hotel. She guarded her favourite recipes, *cochon de lait*[‡] and *l'agneau au chou,*[§] like state secrets. Marguerite's specialties were desserts: charlotte russe, bavaroises, petit fours, galettes des rois, gâteau des anges, sponge cake, strawberry shortcake, custards, meringues. Louise described her mother as a "perfectionist in the kitchen,"

---

† "Meals in general were not always serene. First, we had to remain seated at the table, while Mom served us and Dad carved the meat. Often (perhaps less often than I imagine) when we spoke, Dad silenced us by stating that everything we said was stupid. There was no dialogue with Dad: he was always right and we were always wrong. He lived as a soldier: he commanded and we had to obey."
‡ suckling pig
§ lamb and cabbage

who would show off her talents by serving tiny sandwiches, vol au vents with oysters and mushrooms, cookie-sized meringues, and "perfect chocolate éclairs" for afternoon tea parties and bridge club.[61]

Claire's favourite room in the house was a windowed solarium behind the kitchen, which overlooked the river. During the summer, this was where the family ate dinner. In the evenings, the girls would gather to watch the extraordinary sunsets, which Claire remembered vividly:

> *Le ciel devenait pourpre et l'astre du jour se cachait finalement en splendeur derrière l'île St-Barnabé, en face de Rimouski, au milieu du fleuve St-Laurent. Élevée sur le bord du fleuve, j'adore l'eau et j'ai de la difficulté à vivre un autre paysage. La mer, c'est l'évasion, l'infini. Ce solarium vitré du côté de la mer m'a peut-être marquée pour la vie.*[†, 62]

This was often the setting where Marguerite would read aloud to the girls after all the dishes were done. Television had not yet arrived, and the evening readings were enticing. The other little girls from the neighbourhood would clamour to join the group. Michèle Cloutier was among the rapt audiences that sat perfectly quietly on the floor beside Marguerite L'Heureux's chair during these memorable sessions. "I can still hear her voice," she recalled. "There was such expression. She had a high-pitched voice, very strong, and it was almost crystal-like."[63] It was a vocal register that Claire herself would inherit, and something that her sister Louise remembered vividly from her mother's evening readings: "My mother had a distinctive voice – very high voice – and very dramatic. She would read just one chapter a night. When she read the Comtesse de Ségur books, we used to cry and cry. She made it come to life, and we were all eyes and ears."[64]

The fourteen-volume Comtesse de Ségur series that transfixed the young listeners had been written in the nineteenth century by a Russian-born countess from Paris. Her novels transported generations of Québécoises into the fictional world of nineteenth-century French children, whose adventures were designed to instil lessons of deportment and character. *Les petites filles modèles* offered young readers clear lessons in gender. The adorable good girls, who gave joy to their dear mothers, were the ones

---

† "The sky turned purple and the sun finally hid in splendour behind St. Barnabé Island, opposite Rimouski, in the middle of the St. Lawrence River. Brought up on the riverside, I love water and have difficulty inhabiting another landscape. The sea is escape, the sea is infinity. That glass-windowed seaside solarium may have marked me for life."

Doll with melted legs, from *Les malheurs de Sophie*.

who epitomized love, obedience, modesty, charity, forgiveness, absence of temper, and no hint of gluttony. Good boys were honest, hardworking, and brave, defenders of family and friends even to the point of regular fisticuffs.[65]

But proscriptive literature often contains the seeds of its own opposition. Claire's undisputed favourite in the series was *Les malheurs de Sophie*. Good behaviour eluded young Sophie. Headstrong and disobedient, the best that could be said, as her mother would often exclaim, was that Sophie was not *vilaine*† but *malchanceuse*.‡ Sophie defied feminine norms of docility and was not above indulging in physical scraps, even with boys if they teased her.[66]

In one episode, Sophie's father sent her a beautiful wax doll from Paris. She thought it looked pale, and despite her mother's warning, she left it in the sun "to warm it." Its eyes melted away. Then, using the curling iron, she burned the doll's hair. Next she washed its feet in boiling water, and

---

† naughty
‡ unlucky

melted the doll's legs right off. Finally, she orchestrated an elaborate burial ceremony for the battered amputee, to the astonished delight of her friends. Sophie's antics were legendary. She ate so much heavy cream, wild berries, and warm bread that she took sick. She fell in the sea, got lost in the woods, and tumbled into the hollow of a tree. Ashamed and contrite after every adventure, Sophie never seemed to learn.

The escapade that most delighted Claire involved the pet fish that Sophie's mother kept in a fishbowl. Sophie caught the fish, lined them up on a plate, sprinkled them with salt, and then cut them into tiny pieces with a knife. Confronted by her furious mother, Sophie retorted that she didn't think the fish were hurt because they didn't cry. Claire was captivated by Sophie's boundless capacity for trouble. "We loved the stories," she exclaimed. The endless havoc wreaked by the indomitable Sophie became one of her favourite memories.[67]

Claire's early years were filled with contrasts. She took away happy memories of a carefree childhood, a doting mother, a beautiful family home in Rimouski, a beloved seascape, and a bracing climate. She also witnessed acrimonious discord between her strong-willed grandparents and her father and mother. She was controlled by and rebelled against her father's strict disciplinary regimen. In retrospect, she would insist that the happy memories took precedence. But the disruptive experiences must also have taken a toll, planting seeds of rebellion that would emerge in years to come.

4
Growing Up in Rimouski

A Female-Dominant World

The L'Heureux girls grew up in pairs, the two eldest, Claire and Louise, and the two youngest, Lucie and Nicole, developing special bonds.[1] Claire was the most assertive and outgoing one. Louise was quieter, shy and conciliatory, a bit in the shadow of her elder sister.[2] Lucie was thought to be the beauty in the family. Blonde, dark-eyed, pale in complexion, and delicate in health, she was her father's favourite because she reminded him of his mother.[3] Nicole was the baby of the family, widely recognized as intelligent, self-sufficient, creative, and self-sacrificing.[4]

Claire sometimes resented being tied down by her younger sisters, and Louise had strong memories of Claire's emphatic orders not to tag along after her. Most of the time, however, the four girls played together, providing each other's best entertainment.[5] Between the L'Heureux home and the cathedral was a vacant field with tall trees, bushes, and wild grass for playing hide-and-seek. There were so few cars that the girls held tea parties in the middle of the road in front of the house. There was a swing in the back, where the girls would mimic the popular singers of the day: Tino Rossi, the French cabaret tenor, and Madame Bolduc, the revered Gaspésie singer-songwriter who combined the traditional folk music of Quebec and Ireland.[6]

In the winter, the girls skated to Strauss waltzes in the town arena, and skied – without a ski lift – on the hills near the Price Brothers mills. Claire became proficient at badminton, tennis, and swimming. The girls bicycled

Four L'Heureux sisters relaxing by the water at Le Bic, mid-1940s. *Left to right,* Lucie, Claire, Louise, Nicole.

to the nearest beach, Rocher Blanc, a few kilometres away, and still further, to Pointe-au-Père. Claire and Michèle Cloutier, her closest friend, would often plan the night before to take off for a morning cycle to the beach at 5:00 before anyone else was up. "It seemed so far. It was maybe two miles, but it was not built up, and we'd go in the quiet of the morning," mused Michèle. "Those bicycle rides were so lovely." Occasionally, Michèle's father, who used a car in his business, would drive the neighbourhood children about ten miles downriver and leave them at the beach for the day. Describing her friend Claire, Michèle laughed: "She was just a well-fed, happy, outgoing, good-looking young girl. And always, like her mother, her face had a big smile. She had so much energy!"[7]

The L'Heureux family had no automobile, and the children used the garage as a playhouse for impromptu plays. Marguerite composed the musical scores and wrote the scripts and lyrics. Rehearsals would last two or three days, and then the group would present *"une véritable explosion théâtrale"*[†] before audiences of neighbours.[8] The setting, with the St. Lawrence as the backdrop, was breathtaking. The girls' costumes included long dresses, sashes, shawls, turbans, cloche hats, and old shoes. Louise

---

† "a truly theatrical explosion"

Growing Up in Rimouski

Claire as a teenager with bicycle.

Children at the beach at Rocher Blanc. *Front row, sitting, left to right,* Nicole L'Heureux, Lucie L'Heureux, Louis Cloutier, Pierre Cloutier, [unidentified]; *middle group, sitting, left to right,* Huguette Cloutier, Denis Cloutier; *top row, standing, left to right,* Monique Jacob *(floating device around waist),* Louise L'Heureux, Andrée Ouellet, Raymonde Ouellet, Claire L'Heureux *(top middle, hands on hips),* Michèle Cloutier, Jacques Cloutier *(in front of Michèle),* Marthe Jacob.

described Claire as the natural leader, always in charge: "'You do this, and you do that,' she would command. She picked everything in the plays and the costumes."⁹

Michèle Cloutier was reluctant to characterize Claire as dominant or bossy, but she did think her friend knowledgeable beyond her years:

> When Claire was just twelve years old, my mother was expecting her sixth child. She was about two weeks from the end. I can still picture my mother standing outside. It must have been an early day of spring. Claire came to see me, and there was my mother in her *robe de chambre*.† Claire looked at my mother with a grown-up look, and asked, "When is it going to be?" My mother said, "Oh, it's very soon."
>
> Then I looked at my mother, and at Claire, and I suddenly saw the way they looked. I hadn't seen that my mother was pregnant! I remember thinking, how does Claire know? I just never put it together. She was clearly more advanced than I was.¹⁰

For summer vacations, Claire's mother would rent a cabin on the beach at Le Bic or Saint-Fabien for a week or two. The small cabins were rustic, with wood stoves upon which Marguerite cooked French crêpes for breakfast. The children swam in the ice-cold water, picked wild blueberries, and dug clams out of the mud, especially at Saint-Fabien, where they were plentiful at low tide.¹¹ The girls washed them, threw them in a big kettle, and then feasted on boiled clams dipped in melted butter. The holidays were always without Paul L'Heureux, who "never took vacations."¹²

A highlight of the L'Heureux children's lives was watching the ships pull into the Rimouski harbour. It was one of the few links they had to their father's more worldly affairs. Claire was thrilled on the rare occasions when her father took the girls by tugboat to inspect the incoming vessels. The girls climbed the ladder onto the big ships and sat quietly while their father examined the customs papers. Occasionally, Paul would bring ship captains home for special dinners. Once in a while, the captains would invite Paul and Marguerite (and more rarely the whole family) to dine on board.¹³

The Complicated Question of Class

Class status is a slippery matter. It shifts over time and place, and is affected

---

† dressing gown

by diverse factors such as ancestry, occupation, the economy, age, religion, family status, gender, race, ethnicity, linguistic environment, and cultural tradition. In the early years in Quebec City, the L'Heureux family was perceived as lower middle-class, a fact that rankled deeply with Antoinette, who had hoped her daughter might attain her family's stature of years gone by. Paul's promotion offered some potential for upward mobility. In smaller Rimouski, he rubbed shoulders with the town's most powerful citizens and social luminaries. As the customs officer, he was accorded privileges such as an invitation to join the Club Rimouski, a private facility with rooms for dining, reading, billiards, and cards. This apparently placed him on the fringe of the Rimouski elite.[14]

Yet both Claire's father and mother were bilingual, something that marked them out as unusual and elevated their status in Rimouski. Paul had learned English in the military, where all operations were still conducted in English.[15] It was a skill he honed on the job and through daily exposure to the *Montreal Star* and BBC radio. Bilingualism was something he aspired to for the whole family, so Marguerite and the children read the English newspapers as well. Perhaps as a result of their bilingualism, Paul and Marguerite were among the few French Canadians who socialized with the Price Brothers managers and their wives. Louise remembered her mother getting dressed for receptions at the private curling and golf club, putting on a long gown with a turquoise belt and brooch and dabbing on Shalimar perfume from her dresser.[16]

Marguerite took afternoon tea with a circle of female friends that included the wives of the doctor, judge, lawyer, notary, mayor, and engineer, and of the town's most successful businessman. Her social life with Paul revolved around *soirées mixtes*,† and cocktail, bridge, roulette, and poker parties. She seemed not to have succumbed to her mother's unwavering insistence upon class demarcations. Her children recall that Marguerite was in search of friends who were interested in culture, reading, and intellectual debate. Always hoping to learn something from the people she socialized with, she was quite intolerant of people she did not find interesting, whatever their social status.[17]

Attitudes toward money are often rooted in family background, and Claire pointed to her mother as a primary influence. Although Marguerite often worried about bills, she was critical of people whose lives revolved around the accumulation of wealth. "My mother was very economical,

---

† mixed parties

Marguerite and Paul L'Heureux beside their home in Rimouski.

and we knew not to ask for things when money was tight," explained Claire. "But in our house, money was not a goal in life. We never had a sense that money was important." Claire added, laughing: "Perhaps it's why I am not careful with money. There is a phrase: 'Build a nest egg but make an omelette once in a while.' And I make omelettes."[18] Perhaps her grandfather Napoléon's influence had crept in too.

Claire would eventually come to reject rigid class distinctions herself. Years later, it surprised and bothered her when others often perceived her as coming from an elite background. Although her family was clearly not underprivileged, elite status was something she felt she had escaped growing up in Rimouski. As an adult, she came to consider elitism destructive and unfair, and was dismissive of people she perceived to be "snobs" and "socialites." André Legault, who would work as a court attendant for Claire at the Supreme Court of Canada, explained: "She was the type of person who didn't differentiate. If she liked you, it didn't matter whether you washed floors, or were the prime minister of a country. She could like one and hate the other or vice versa."[19]

Medical Complications: Marguerite Falls Ill

The years in Rimouski witnessed a slow but significant deterioration in Marguerite's health. In retrospect, she realized that the signs of illness had shown up during her first pregnancy, when for several months she could not feel the floor with her feet. After Claire was born, everything returned to normal. During her second pregnancy, the problem recurred for a longer period, but it disappeared again after the birth of Louise. By the time she had settled into the new house in Rimouski, Marguerite often needed to lean on walls to steady her balance. By 1936, both of Marguerite's legs were beginning to fail her; soon she could no longer walk the thousand feet from home to church without a cane.[20]

The family sought help from a Quebec City clinic, where the doctors took fluid from her spine and a neurologist diagnosed multiple sclerosis. To Marguerite's horror, a nursing sister at the clinic explained that this was equivalent to a death sentence: "When you'll be older, you'll ask God to kill you. You'll be so crippled you will want to die."[21] Marguerite's family doctor referred her to a specialist named Dr. Gustave Gingras at the Sanatorium Prévost in Montreal, and she travelled to his clinic in the spring of 1936. Her stay from March to September cost $198.70, placing a heavy burden on the family budget.[22] The doctors experimented with keeping Marguerite's body temperature at 107°F, but it did not help.

Frantic with worry, Marguerite wrote scores of love letters to her husband in Rimouski. She despaired over what her illness would do to her marriage, lamenting that Paul would not love her any more and that there would be no place for her in the life of a man who loved to socialize and dance. She wrote with anguish about the plight of her children, who she was certain would never understand her situation. Decades later, the letters were handed down to Claire, who confessed that she could not read them, that they made her weep.[23]

Back in Rimouski, alone with the girls that summer, Paul L'Heureux felt unable to cope. He left the children to the care of the maids but discovered that they had locked the girls outside and invited their boyfriends to visit. He sent Nicole to live with her aunt Marie-Marthe, and dispatched the three older girls to the Rimouski orphanage, the Orphelinat du Couvent des Sœurs de la Charité, across the street from their home.[24] He must have been aware of the orphanage's dubious reputation. Former Rimouski residents recalled that it was widely known that the nuns "called the orphans names, were insulting, and did other things too awful to talk about."[25]

Entering the orphanage bereft of both her parents for the first time in her life was a shock for Claire. The nuns were cruel and the atmosphere was terrifying. As the eldest L'Heureux sister, Claire feared not only for her own safety but also that of her siblings. Still horrified decades later, Claire described watching the nuns administer corporal punishment to two little orphan twins: "They put a blanket over them and hit them on the head."[26] Her first brush with the vulnerability of the impoverished was seared indelibly into her consciousness. Louise was equally devastated. She described small children forced to stand in a corner wearing "a dunce hat" and covered with a "white sheet," along with other "very severe punishments."[27]

Claire denounced the orphanage food as *"infecte"* – foul – and complained that it was like eating *"des os dans du sirop."*[†, 28] She was often sent to the dormitory for disciplinary infractions, and it seemed to her that she was always in trouble. One day, enraged over what she felt was unjust punishment, she spotted a large tray in the dining room stacked with sliced bread, each piece thickly spread with molasses. She "redecorated the room" with the slices of bread and molasses, throwing them one by one, sticky-side down, at the walls around the dorm.[29] Years later, she managed to laugh over her effrontery. She tried to escape several times, and once gained entry to her locked house by sliding through the window of the coal chute, emerging black from head to foot but relieved to be home. When her father discovered her, he was furious at her disobedience and hustled her right back to the nuns.[30]

Marguerite returned home in the fall of 1936, and the children were repatriated from the disastrous orphanage. Marguerite's health continued to worsen, however. The loss of sensitivity extended slowly upward to her midsection. As she had anxiously predicted, it took a huge toll on her relationship with Paul, who resented the fact that his wife could no longer keep up the socializing, could no longer dance at parties. Marguerite tried to continue the outings but would lose her balance, causing people to wonder if she was drunk. She and Paul began arguing over the cards played at the

---

† "bones in syrup"

bridge parties after they got home late at night, shouting loudly enough to wake the children. Finally, the parties stopped for good.[31] Paul's growing estrangement from their mother must have been obvious to his children, exacerbating their already strong sense of distance from their father.

Paul's flirtatiousness with women began to rouse Marguerite's jealousy. Her fears grew as it became obvious that her husband was attracted to a host of other women. His severity with the children also troubled her, and she began scolding him for "treating the children like they were members of his army."[32] Paul's freedom with money worried Marguerite as well. He had a bit of his father in him, and liked to purchase new gadgets. He brought home an electric Mixmaster. He bought Marguerite one of the first automatic washers and dryers in the neighbourhood. While these were thoughtful gifts for a woman whose disability made household chores difficult, such expensive appliances strained the household budget.[33]

Every seven years or so, another attack would exacerbate Marguerite's multiple sclerosis. By 1946, she was using a wheelchair. The paralysis slowly worked its way up to her arms and hands, until the woman whose piano concerts her children still remember, with her "beautiful fingers gliding over the keyboard," lost the use of her fingers.[34]

Despite her disability – or perhaps because of it – she forged even stronger bonds with her children. She revelled in her eldest daughter's success at the coeducational public school run by the Sœurs de la Charité, L'École Saint-Germain, which Claire attended from age eight to ten. *"Je te félicite d'être première en classe. C'est une grande joie d'apprendre cela,"*† she wrote in March 1936.[35] Despite her physical incapacity, Marguerite followed each of her daughters' activities with intense interest, insisting on knowing everything about their lives. At the end of each day, she would ask them to give a full report. They were expected to tell her every single thing they had done, confessing even small indiscretions like "not being very nice to someone."[36] And throughout her long ordeal, she never lost her sense of optimism. Michèle Cloutier remembered that Marguerite "never complained," adding: "She was really a strong personality in the home. She would laugh and talk, and be very outgoing."[37] Claire agreed: "[My mother] was always making jokes, always uplifting us if we were down about something. She wouldn't let anybody be pessimistic in our house."[38] It was a trait that Claire, deeply moved by her mother's mental strength, determined to adopt for herself.

---

† "I congratulate you on placing at the top of your class. I was overjoyed to learn that."

One of the most significant repercussions of her mother's illness was the decision by Claire's parents to place all four girls into the full-time care of convent schools. The goal was to relieve Marguerite of the physically challenging day-to-day responsibilities of looking after an energetic brood of children. The additional hope was that the nuns might be able to inculcate a sense of discipline into the tempestuous Claire.[39] After careful research into the educational program and residential situation of the Monastère des Ursulines de L'Immaculée Conception in Rimouski, Marguerite and Paul registered their daughters. With the exception of one year, Claire would live there as a student boarder until her graduation in 1943. She must have faced the prospect with some consternation, given her experience at the hands of the nuns at the orphanage. Whatever her misgivings, in the fall of 1937, ten-year-old Claire entered the convent. What would befall her under the Ursulines?

Early Education

5
Life as a *Pensionnaire* with the Ursulines, 1937–43

"*Une étoile qui n'a pas été éclipsée.*"[1] She was "a star that has never been eclipsed," according to observers who described Claire's startling success within the world of a cloistered convent. She was irrepressible: bursting with energy, filled with *joie de vivre,* and thirsting for knowledge. Her strong-willed personality and her penchant for getting into trouble were clear from the outset. The question, as one of the nuns put it, was how to harness that energy, how to respond to her young pupil's need for a certain "framing."[2] What is indisputable is that Claire would leave an indelible mark on the Ursuline convent, as it would likewise leave one on her.

Le Monastère des Ursulines:
"*Une sorte d'abbaye avec des grilles*"[†]

The imposing Rimouski convent had two wings on each side of the main edifice, a curved mansard roof crowned with a bell tower, and symmetrical rows of windows in the Second Empire architectural fashion. A religious community with deep roots, the Ursuline nuns had marked the four-hundredth anniversary of the founding of their order in 1935. One year later, they celebrated the golden jubilee of Mère Marie-de-la-Présentation,

---
† "A sort of abbey with grilles"

Monastère des Ursulines, Rimouski.

the founding mother superior of the convent. The building housed more than fifty nuns, a novitiate, a *pensionnat* for boarding pupils, and an *école normale* for the instruction of primary school teachers.[3] Between 1906 and 1970, the first and last years of operation, the Ursulines would educate more than twenty thousand young girls in Rimouski.[4]

Claire entered on 14 September 1937, one of ninety-eight new student boarders that fall. To gain admission to the convent she rang the bell at the front entrance, pressed her face to a small grilled window, and awaited the arrival of *la Mère,* who alone could open the heavy double locks on the door. External excursions were limited to the mothers superior, and only for pressing travel to sister congregations or religious events. The cloistered nuns, who never left the convent, received visitors behind grilled bars.[5] Apart from two months of summer holidays, a few days in November, a week at Christmas, and a few days at Easter, the boarding pupils – the *pensionnaires* – were also forbidden to leave the convent.[6] Parents could visit their children only on Thursdays in the student parlour, a room that housed a glass-enclosed menagerie of stuffed dead birds, from the smallest titmouse to intimidating eagles, owls, falcons, and vultures. For Claire, whose mother was increasingly disabled and whose father chose not to come, there would be few visits. Marguerite wrote often, but the nuns vetted all correspondence and books before delivery to the students.[7] Except for one year away, Claire would be sequestered in the Ursuline convent from age ten until she completed her matriculation in 1943 at age fifteen.[8]

The nuns' "starched wimples, headdresses and veils, dazzling white on black robes," created an intimidating image. They walked in silence, their tread noiseless except for the ubiquitous "rattling of rosary beads hanging from [their] belts."[9] The students' uniforms eschewed all signs of vanity or feminine fashion. Long-sleeved black serge dresses featured white braided collars and cuffs. Skirts were originally hemmed three fingers from the ground. In the 1920s, when shorter skirts came into vogue, some emboldened students arrived with hems as much as sixteen fingers from the ground. The scandal took years to resolve, but eventually all dresses were hemmed at mid-calf. Long black stockings and regulation black shoes filled out the picture. For graduation, the girls were dressed all in white.[10]

Despite the strict regimen, convent life presented quite a contrast to Claire's terrifying months in the orphanage. First, she had family members within the Ursuline community, two first cousins to Marguerite who were delighted to find the L'Heureux girls entrusted to their care. Second, unlike the abandoned waifs of the orphanage, the convent boarders came from families that paid for their education. They stood out in a province where the majority of female students did not go beyond their ninth year of schooling until the 1950s.[11] The nuns looked at us like "precious little gems," explained Claire.[12] The *pensionnaires* were meant to serve as role models, to become perfect wives and devoted mothers whose piety would guarantee the religious security of their families.[13]

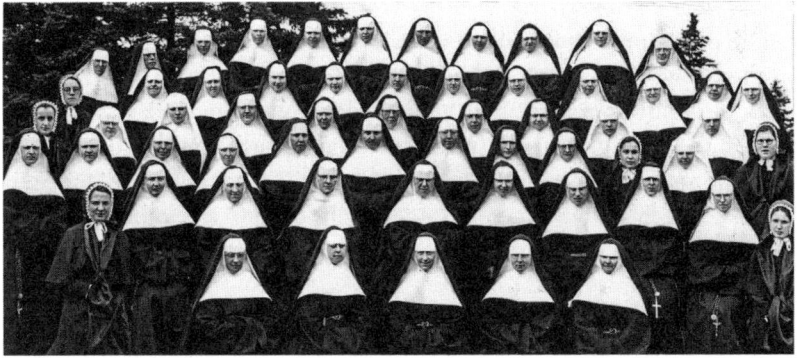

Community of Ursulines, 1931.

Certain convents deliberately recruited their students from the privileged classes. At the Ursuline convent, the *maîtresse générale* discreetly reviewed each boarder prior to admission to ensure that her family was *recommendable*.[†, 14] Les Sœurs des Saints-Noms de Jésus et de Marie, the Congrégation de Notre-Dame, and the Ursulines drew clients principally from the daughters of doctors, notaries, lawyers, and others at the top of the social hierarchy.[15] Even among the elite *pensionnaires,* however, distinctions of class could persist. Those whose parents could afford to pay for extra glasses of milk and treats of candy were visibly privileged over their peers. The occasional impoverished student who was admitted free worked in the garden or the laundry, or serving other students in the dining room.[16]

Claire's first-year tuition cost over $130, an amount higher than her family's quarterly mortgage payment and a substantial investment at the time.[17] Some families incurred the cost to ensure that their daughters would possess the elite imprimatur of a convent education, *"la mode pour la classe professionnelle du milieu."*[‡, 18] The L'Heureux family may have been less concerned than others about badges of elite status, and Paul's decision to make the financial sacrifice was driven primarily by Marguerite's growing infirmity rather than any deep commitment to female higher education.[19]

STUDENT LIFE: *"UN CONTEXTE RÉGLÉ COMME UNE HORLOGERIE"*[§]

Convent routines were rigidly modelled upon religious life in the Ancien Régime, iron-clad rules that would hold sway until the Quiet Revolution of the 1960s: *"Aucun geste ne semble désordonné ou impulsif. Toute action s'insère dans un contexte rigoureusement réglé comme une horlogerie."*[‖, 20] Up before dawn, present for Mass every day, required to observe total silence in the hallways and dining room, forbidden to bathe more than once a week, and put to bed at 7 p.m., the students' every minute was circumscribed.[21] There were no excursions or class outings, no gym or physical education classes. When the girls moved through the building, they did so in silence in straight lines. They ate their breakfast of oatmeal porridge

---

† respectable
‡ "a 'must' for the local professional set"
§ "A context set like clockwork"
‖ "No gesture seems out of order or impulsive. Every action takes place in a context that is rigorously set like clockwork."

Dramatic production at the Monastère des Ursulines. Claire is far left, top row.

and toast, their midday dinner, and their evening supper in silence while a nun read the Bible aloud from a pedestal. Claire shrugged off the enforced silence with the observation that the children cheated by playing secret games under the table, even cards sometimes. As for the Bible reading at every meal, she laughed, "I don't remember listening."[22]

Visits from church dignitaries and principal citizens offered the only relief from the regimented routine. The *fêtes patronales* honouring the bishop and Marie de l'Incarnation were occasions for pageantry, art, theatre, and music. During the *fête de Mère Sainte-Ursule,* celebrating the new mother superior, the students staged *Judith,* a Biblical drama in five acts with multiple actors and exotic backdrops. Claire, an enthusiastic participant, would get her father to lend her military uniforms as costumes.[23]

There was little to no physical contact allowed between the nuns and the students: no hugging, no physical affection of any kind.[24] The nuns were also vigilant in preventing particular friendships – *amitiés particulières* – between the girls, fearing that they might become too attached. Where friendships blossomed too strongly anyway, the girls were separated.[25] At 7 p.m., the lights went out and the nuns enforced *le grand silence, "pour offrir son âme à Dieu."*[†, 26] The rules required the girls to sleep with their hands on top of their blankets.[27]

---

† total silence, "to better offer one's soul to God"

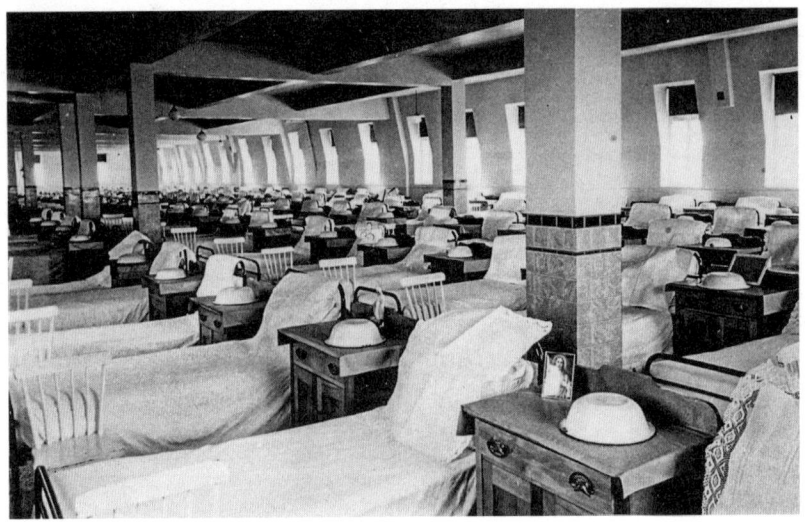

Dormitory of the *pensionnaires* at the Monastère des Ursulines.

Claire's Performance under Ursuline Rules

Sister Caroline Tanguay, one of Claire's most inspirational teachers, was among the first to take the measure of her new student.²⁸ She thought Claire had *"le tempérament de chef"* that would mark her out for *"une destinée extraordinaire,"* but found her equally *"espiègle, dissipée, impossible même."*†,²⁹ She agreed with Claire's parents that someone needed to help the young girl channel her energies positively. And she recognized what most others did not – that Claire's bravado masked a lack of self-confidence.³⁰

Right from the start, Claire showed academic promise. In her first year, she received first prize in catechism, writing, grammatical analysis and logic, composition, and vocabulary; second prize in religious history and French grammar; first honourable mention in geography, English, and piano; and second honourable mention in Canadian history. She also received prizes for "good conduct, correct language, devotion and foresight, studious effort, and musical scales."³¹ The stellar grades continued for years.³²

Those who knew Claire then described her as a sociable young student who was very popular with the other girls.³³ Yet her study habits rankled with her classmates, who were bitter that the top student "didn't study

---

† "a leader's character"; "a fate out of the ordinary"; "mischievous, dissipated, impossible at times"

very much" but "got A's anyway." Claire's retort, that she "didn't *have* to study," did little to console them.³⁴ Yves Dubé, later Claire's brother-in-law and himself an exceptional student at the nearby Rimouski seminary, characterized Claire as the brightest student at the convent: "She was a very able writer" and had "tremendous imagination."³⁵ Jean Drapeau, one of Claire's childhood friends, recalled her performance as "brilliant." Her mother "always pushed her" to study, he explained. "She was ambitious and she could work very quickly. She was always first."³⁶

Claire's troublemaking continued to focus attention on her. In contrast to the orphanage, the Ursulines never resorted to cruel disciplinary practices or corporal punishment, but every Sunday students had to line up to confess their sins. Those caught disobeying the rules were made to stand or kneel in the corner or assigned demerit points. A certain number of points meant loss of privileges, including access to parental visits. Claire knew that her mother was too sick to come and her father rarely showed. Her sensitivity about the absence of visitors sometimes caused her to forfeit points deliberately. She developed a reputation as someone who courted disaster. She put glue on the chairs. She stole and hid the bell the nuns used to wake up the children. Disrupting the dormitory at night was the worst offence, and when the rounds were made, Claire would hide under the bed. She inflated a brown paper bag and smashed it in the dark. *"Elle a bien des tours dans son sac,"*† was the verdict of the nuns.³⁷

One night, she plotted to be the last girl in line to turn off the light, and then she jumped on one of the nuns and hugged and kissed her. "It was such a scandal. It was like I had committed a crime. I liked her very much, and I just kissed her. I guess I missed my mother and needed some affection. They paraded me to the Mother Superior for that." On another occasion, Claire slipped away from the convent. She remembered her outraged father bringing her directly back with a curt retort: "You keep her." "I was doing all kinds of things to bring attention to myself. Maybe it was out of a desire to be loved or cared for. I was known as strong-minded, *tête forte, mauvais esprit*,‡ a trouble-maker."³⁸ Expulsion was the most serious penalty, summed up in the oft-repeated threat, *"Vous prendriez la porte, mademoiselle."*§ But Claire knew her mother was too sick to take her and, equally important, that the nuns were reluctant to expel their star pupil. Her sister Louise believed that "the teachers were nice" to Claire "because

---

† "She has plenty of tricks up her sleeve."
‡ hotheaded, bad attitude
§ "You would be expelled, Miss."

she was very bright. She was always the one who stood first. She made a big impression on them. They kind of catered to her."[39] Yves Dubé agreed, adding that Claire's sterling grades so impressed the nuns that they "spoiled" her.[40]

Claire's acting out, reminiscent of the impish Sophie in her beloved Comtesse de Ségur books, belied what were for her generally happy years at the convent. Not all of the students felt the same. Some of the homesick young ones cried themselves to sleep at night.[41] Louise L'Heureux tearfully begged her parents each year not to be forced to go. She found it particularly difficult to be the sister following Claire, whose reputation for brilliance and misbehaving preceded her siblings: "I would arrive in class and the first thing teachers would say is 'You're Claire's sister!'" Louise's memories of the convent were not positive: "I don't remember any of the nuns fondly. They were not mean, but the regimen of boarding school was very strict. You had to line up, all lined up in a row marching. You had to lay down all the time. We had a lot of religion. And it was all study, study, study. No extras."[42]

Claire's memories, by contrast, were of a challenging, nurturing, positive experience. Years later, her daughter would observe that her mother tended to use "rose-coloured glasses," selectively remembering "only the bits that were positive" and "avoid[ing]" or "sublimat[ing]" the rest.[43] Yet Claire was insistent that the nuns understood her, that she was well cared for, secure, and even loved during her years with the Ursulines. Looking back, she concluded: "[The nuns] were maternal and loving. Discipline was important to them, but they had their way about it. They were dedicated educators and extraordinary women. I loved being there."[44] And it was their understanding that she took away with her, a lifelong lesson to sympathize with rebellious youngsters. Decades later, friends who spoke with her about their own wayward teenagers remembered her advice: "Don't worry. The most intelligent ones are the ones you have the most trouble with."[45]

The Second World War Intrudes

On 9 September 1939, Prime Minister Mackenzie King declared war on Germany, and Canada entered the Second World War. As customs officer, Paul L'Heureux's first responsibility was to impound the ships of enemy countries and take their personnel as prisoners. Already a reserve officer and second-in-command of the Fusiliers du St-Laurent, he entered active service within days. On 14 October, naval authorities spotted two enemy submarines moving up the St. Lawrence. The all-night search for German U-boats was futile, but it brought the peril close to home.[46] The Fusiliers set up a regional training camp to recruit 1,500 soldiers and train 500 men for military service. In September 1940, Major Paul L'Heureux was promoted to the rank of lieutenant-colonel and named commander of the camp.[47]

Although Rimouski would witness serious public demonstrations against conscription, it also became a military city, flooded with soldiers in training along with air force trainees who were posted at Mont-Joli, twenty miles downriver.[48] Recruits came from all regions of the Lower St. Lawrence: Rivière-du-Loup, Témiscouata, Matapédia, Gaspé, Côte-Nord, and Îles-de-la-Madeleine. Most of the men, eighteen to twenty years old, had never been away from home and parish or seen a military uniform. They underwent medical examinations, documentation, and registration. They were transformed from civilians into soldiers, and were taught to handle arms and to work as vehicle mechanics, plumbers, electricians, carpenters, and welders.[49]

In 1941, Lieutenant-Colonel Paul L'Heureux was named commander of Camp Valcartier and was posted outside of Quebec City.[50] According to Major Jean R. Brillant, the officer who succeeded him as commanding officer of the Fusiliers, Paul's army files were filled with written testimonials from military authorities and civilians confirming his distinguished service.[51] Paul felt strongly that French Canadian soldiers should train and serve in their own language, under the command of French Canadian officers. It was a position he advocated forcefully but unsuccessfully in Ottawa. To his disappointment, the French Canadian recruits were integrated with other regiments and dispersed across the country.

Paul was also dispatched to military bases across eastern and western Canada to supervise training. He wrote home from Nanaimo, Prince Rupert, Vancouver, Prince Albert, Gagetown, and Halifax. One dramatic incident lives in the family lore. Claire described a confrontation in a training camp out west: French Canadian soldiers mounted a near-revolt, and her father bravely defused the incendiary moment, standing in front of his troops, saying, "If you want to shoot, shoot."[52]

The Gaspésie suffered direct German assault during the war. A torpedo exploded in Saint-Yvon, a small village on the north of the St. Lawrence, and twelve merchant ships were torpedoed between Métis Beach and Cap-des-Rosiers. By May 1942, there were estimates of twenty-three German submarines in the Gulf. Soldiers kept watch from bunkers on the beach and sirens wailed out submarine alerts. Householders blacked out their

Lieutenant-Colonel Paul L'Heureux, centre, with military colleagues.

windows every evening to allow no hint of light to escape, a precaution particularly critical for those, like the L'Heureux family, whose homes backed onto the St. Lawrence. Distribution of gas masks and rationing of tea, coffee, sugar, butter, and meat followed.[53]

Although safe inside the convent walls, Claire feared for her father's safety and was anxious about how her disabled mother was coping alone at home. She wrote her mother often, telling her not to worry about the housecleaning, because "with dust ... there was always more."[54] But there was an upside to the military upheaval. As a commanding officer, Paul's salary almost doubled, bringing the family an affluence they had never experienced before and never would again. Tuition payments to the convent no longer strained the family budget. "World War Two was the best thing that ever happened to us, I'm sorry to say," confided Claire. "We would not have been able to pursue these studies without the war. And we were alone with my mother, which was great. She was such a good mother. Five women together – it was more intimate."[55] At home and in the convent, Claire's world was truly a female one.

The First Classical Courses

It was an auspicious time to be a female student in Quebec. When Claire began her studies at the Rimouski convent, the nuns did not offer the prerequisite classical courses for admission to university, but Claire had the good fortune to be in the thick of changing times. Although many, including her father, still saw little use in higher education for girls, her mother was anxious to see her girls receive what she herself had been denied. Marguerite watched with interest in 1928 when Monseigneur Georges Courchesne granted the Ursulines permission to add one year of supplementary courses and to seek affiliation with Laval University. She was pleased to see the convent introduce its first classical course, *Éléments Latins,* in 1934 and gain formal affiliation with Laval in 1939.[56] While the Ursulines were gearing up for an expanded curriculum, Claire's mother arranged for her two eldest daughters to be sent for one academic year, 1941–42, to study at the Collège Notre-Dame-de-Bellevue in Quebec City, which had expanded its courses more quickly than the Rimouski convent.[57] It turned out to be a scholarly boost for Claire and Louise both.

In 1942, Claire returned to the Rimouski convent to join its second class of students studying classical courses, *le cours d'immatriculation.*[†, 58] The curriculum included French literature, Canadian history, English composition, mathematics, geography, natural sciences, and religion. Latin and Greek, never taught to girls in the past, had also been added. Several additional courses, not prescribed for male students in the seminaries, were explicitly gendered: domestic studies and family studies.[59] Most students and their parents were skeptical about the value of higher education for girls, and the numbers showed it. The year Claire was away, nine students had registered for the Rimouski convent's first year of classical studies. In Claire's cohort, just eight did.[60] Claire was not among the skeptics, however, and she put aside her shenanigans to concentrate wholly on her studies. She was hungry for education, always asking questions of the nuns. "They were building up those courses just for us," she explained. "Sister Caroline Tanguay wanted so much for us to succeed. I never remember being bored – never."[61]

Claire's favourite subject was French. She was fascinated by the nuances of the language and excelled in French composition. She prized the rigorous training in grammatical analysis. "We were taught to dissect sentences, piece by piece, studying each part. I adored it. French grammar is

---

† the entry course

very complicated. We would learn the rules and all the exceptions with little verses and jingles. It permitted us to learn how languages were built." She would later attribute her facility for learning languages to the discipline of being taught to "understand the parts of a sentence so clearly." Mathematics was her second favourite, because she could reason out the answers rather than having to memorize material.⁶²

The course she most disliked was Quebec history. "I had no interest whatsoever in learning French Canadian history," she recalled. "It was all sanitized. We learned about the savages – *'sauvages'* was the word used at the time!"⁶³ The austere 545-page text by Pères Gustave Lamarche and Paul Émile Farley did little to commend itself to students who hated memorization. Even learning about Lord Durham's infamously nasty 1839 quip, that *"les Français sont demeurés un peuple inéduqué, inactif et stationnaire,"*† did not rouse her as it did many of her classmates.⁶⁴

Although Claire always placed first, Mère Sainte-Thérèse de l'Enfant Jésus, who taught Latin, insisted she could do better. "You are lazy, you rely on your intelligence, you'll go nowhere with that," was her repeated complaint. "She was angry that I never went to the full length, exploring my full possibilities," explained Claire. Decades later, with some ruefulness, Claire conceded: "That's true. She saw that. I'm lazy by temperament. It doesn't look like that, it doesn't show, because I succeeded based on my intelligence." Jokingly, she added, "If I had given my potential, I might have become prime minister."⁶⁵

Claire's teachers did indeed extol her intellectual capacity:

Élève intéressée et intéressante! Elle ne quittait pas le texte des yeux quand on l'analysait au tableau. Ses questions pertinentes aidaient à l'approfondissement du sens. En latin, le thème ou la version accrochait toute son attention. Elle s'était fait une méthode pour décortiquer le plus rapidement et exactement possible un texte de César, de Tite-Live, ou de quelque autre auteur latin. En mathématiques, elle était une étoile qui n'a pas été éclipsée jusqu'à la fin de l'année.‡, ⁶⁶

---

† "the French have remained an uneducated, inactive and stagnant people"
‡ "Interested and interesting student! Her eyes never strayed from the text being analyzed on the blackboard. Her pertinent questions helped deepen its meaning. In Latin, every Latin or French translation exercise commanded all of her attention. She had created a method to dissect as quickly and exactly as possible a text by Caesar, Livy, or any other Latin author. In mathematics, she was a star whom no one eclipsed throughout the school year."

Graduation at the Monastère des Ursulines, June 1943. *Left to right*, Fernande Poirier from Matapédia, Cécile Dubé from Mont-Joli, Jeanne Marion from Rimouski, Claire L'Heureux, Françoise Dumont from Campbellton, New Brunswick, Gisèle Bélanger from Mont-Joli, Rachel Pelletier from Rimouski.

Claire L'Heureux graduated on 18 June 1943, carrying off the Lieutenant-Governor's Medal along with nearly every other prize. At the formal ceremony, she stood in the centre of her row of classmates. The girls were gowned in long white dresses, with jewelled tiaras and white gloves, rolled diplomas in hand. Reunited with her mother in the parlour, her arms filled with the books she had won as prizes, she was, her teachers recalled, *"rayonnante de joie."*[†, 67]

Claire would become one of the Ursulines' most famous alumnae. The photograph of her graduation was the only such photo printed in the official history of the Monastère des Ursulines, *À Rimouski, il était un monastère,* published in 1995.[68] Many years later, her Supreme Court colleague, Justice Charles Gonthier, concluded that Claire's convent education had been formative for her. "Right from the start, back in her school days, she asserted herself," he noted. "Perhaps she did not remain attached to the religion, but she remained attached to the nuns."[69] Claire had surmounted uprooting from home and family, sadness over her mother's increasing disability and absence, growing estrangement from her father, and rebellion against the strictness of convent life. She had emerged a sociable and popular young woman, an intellectual leader with greater self-confidence. The charisma that would become her trademark characteristic had begun to take shape.[70]

---

† "beaming with joy"

6
Collège Notre-Dame-de-Bellevue
Classical Studies for a *Baccalauréat*, 1943–46

The day her father left for overseas military service was a turning point for Claire's family.¹ In September 1943, Paul L'Heureux was dispatched to Great Britain to train officers at Balliol College in Oxford.² He had been away from home almost continuously since the war began, but this move foreshadowed a deepening rupture. The girls watched their father kiss their mother goodbye at home, and stood on the staircase, hugging and kissing each other to mimic their parents. "We were trying so hard not to cry," Claire remembered. "We were mocking them, trying to take the pain away."³

Marguerite closed up the Rimouski house for the winter months and moved back to Quebec City, bringing the four girls with her. She enrolled them all as *pensionnaires* in the Collège Notre-Dame-de-Bellevue. Deeply committed to her daughters' higher education, she easily financed the tuition with Paul's inflated wartime salary.⁴ Her letters to Claire convey unmistakably her high hopes for her eldest daughter:

> *Je voudrais que tu ... sois toujours un peu mieux que les autres; ça donne un peu plus de distinction et tu es le genre pour inspirer cet air de distinction qui élève au-dessus des autres. Tout ceci pour te dire que l'on doit tenir haut notre idéal, le voir mieux que la moyenne, lorsque l'on n'est pas faite pour les diminutions de la vie commune, et que nous valons mieux que cela. Il faut tendre au sommet de nos aspirations et avoir la maîtrise de soi-même.*†,⁵

---

† "I would like for you ... to be always a little better than others; it accords you a little more distinction, and you are the kind to inspire this air of distinction that elevates

Claire in front of Hôtel Clarendon.

Her insistence that Claire excel was uncompromising. Marguerite herself took up residence at the Hôtel Clarendon. It may have reminded her of her youth, and for decades after, she would ask her girls to make her a brunch "like the one at the Hôtel Clarendon."[6]

Collège Notre-Dame-de-Bellevue: *"Un gros privilège"*[†]

Higher education for women remained a matter of controversy. Professor Jean Flahaut of Montreal's École Polytechnique had a few choice phrases for female students: *"Des cervelles d'oiseaux. Des intelligences mutilées. On empêchait autrefois les pieds des chinoises de grandir."*[‡,7] It was not a pretty picture. Some fretted that educated women would find it difficult to get husbands, while others thought they would marry and have no use for

---

    one above the others. All this to say that we should hold high our ideal, to see it as better than the average when we are not made for the vagaries of common life, and that we are worthier of a better fate. We must strive to reach our highest aspirations and to achieve mastery of ourselves."
† "A great privilege"
‡ "Bird brains. Mutilated intelligence. One used to bind the feet of Chinese women to stunt their growth."

higher degrees. "It was the mentality of that time," recalled Jeanne D'Arc LeMay, who graduated five years before Claire.[8] The anxieties intensified in the crucible of early-twentieth-century Quebec, where traditional Catholic education and prolific maternity were stoutly defended as the antidote to industrialization, urbanization, emigration, British imperialism, American encroachment, and Anglo-Canadian confederation.[9]

Not surprisingly, the number of women taking classical courses grew slowly, and Claire was among the very first Québécoises to climb such rarefied heights.[10] The first class to graduate from Bellevue in 1940 consisted of six students. Three graduated in 1941, and only one in 1942, the year before Claire began.[11] But for the few who were given the opportunity to study, it was cause for jubilation. "I was proud [to be] learning Latin and the old Greek. I said – 'Oh, a girl can learn that!' I loved to study. I felt superior," recalled LeMay.[12] *"C'était vraiment un gros privilège,"*[†] exclaimed another student from the 1940s.[13]

Claire and Louise were also pleased to find Bellevue less rigid than the Ursuline convent. The uniforms were equally severe – black jackets with a medallion of the holy Virgin at mid-neck, black skirts eight inches from the ground, black shoes and stockings, and black gloves – but the teaching was not as strict and the nuns, who were not cloistered, seemed more worldly than the Ursulines. They would put on white gloves and take the girls to concerts and symphony rehearsals on Saturday mornings. They let the students listen to the Saturday opera radio broadcast in study hall. Small groups were permitted unsupervised outings to a nearby restaurant for a Coke and a sandwich, or for ice cream cones at the pharmacy, provided they were back by 8 p.m.[14]

The girls' aunt Marie-Marthe would appear at the convent parlour for monthly visits, bringing fruit, a great treat since none was served otherwise. Their grandfather Napoléon also came to visit, and took them home for dinner once in a while. The girls remembered their astonishment at his poorly furnished apartment and the lax decorum that characterized the household. Napoléon and his new wife allowed the baby, Gaston, to stand on top of the table wearing only a diaper.[15] Napoléon never came empty-handed and was always laden with candies and trinkets. Claire marvelled when he brought her a watch; she knew his income was too small for such extravagance and wondered, both aghast and in some admiration, whether the watch might have been stolen.[16]

---

† "It was really a great privilege."

Students from Collège Notre-Dame-de-Bellevue, 1941–42. Claire is third from right.

Perhaps she had inherited some of Napoléon's insouciance, for Claire continued to have trouble even at the more relaxed Bellevue convent. She often returned from outings after 8 p.m. She once helped a fellow student run away. Her sister Louise thought it was their father's sternness, not their grandfather's freewheeling approach to life, that was the source of Claire's refusal to follow rules: "She got in trouble. She didn't like rules and regulations. It goes back to my father's rules and regulations at home. She'd break every rule."[17] Whether her rebellion stemmed from her grandfather's devil-may-care attitude or from a stubborn refusal to submit to her father's militaristic orders, it was an impetus to mutiny that Claire would carry through life.

The Bellevue academic program was far richer than that at the Ursulines. There were physics classes, which Claire liked, and chemistry, which she did not. Speaking French perfectly became a competition, with students trading tokens that were paid by those who made mistakes to those who corrected them. The nun Claire most admired was Sister Sainte-Héléna, who taught mathematics and philosophy. Claire described her as a "good psychologist" and an "amazing" and "formidable" woman who pushed her students hard and impressed upon the young girls that they must become strong, independent role models for others. The talented nun would go on to become Mère Sainte-Héléna, the head of the congregation and chief administrator of the order.[18]

For the first time in Claire's studies, there was also a male teacher, a charismatic priest named Abbé Potvin. To the consternation of all concerned, Potvin contributed to the downfall of one of the young students, Gisèle Blondeau, who became enamoured of the handsome priest. When the nuns reported this to Gisèle's father, he transferred her immediately to a convent in Kamouraska. Gisèle was devastated at being uprooted from her friends, particularly because she believed herself misjudged over something quite innocent. She never forgot how Claire wrote to her every day after her transfer. "When I speak of friendly loyalty, it is Claire I speak of," she reflected years later.[19]

Claire's classmates remembered her as a lively student who was "always asking questions."[20] Gisèle Blondeau, in the class just behind Claire's, recalled her as brilliant, funny, and warm, as well as someone who "would make friends easily with those that were very capable." Blondeau added laughingly: "She would say 'life is too short to be with imbeciles.'"[21]

The academic competition was more intense than at the Ursuline convent, and the best students were a little miffed to find a new contender from Rimouski catapulted into their midst. "We realized we had serious competition," explained Marcèle Dorion, who would become Claire's closest friend in the class. "Claire was more aggressive. I remember she usually won."[22] There were seven girls in Claire's class. Three entered medicine,[23] a fourth did further studies in sociology and worked in a penitentiary,[24] and a fifth studied agriculture.[25] Only one, Cécile Dubé, who would become Claire's sister-in-law, chose not to pursue further professional studies.[26] Claire was the loner who would go into law.

The Place of Religion in Claire's Life: From Fervent Belief to the Seeds of Doubt

Religion dominated Claire's convent years. Besides formal instruction in religion, daily Mass, and confessions, the Ursulines held closed retreats at the beginning and end of each school year, during which the entire community observed total silence for three days of spiritual meditation. At Bellevue, the rules were more relaxed, but the devotion of the nuns continued to influence Claire. She treasured her first communion cards and kept them all her life. She joined the Société des enfants de Marie, with its special songs, pink ribbons, and rose sash. She participated in the Jeunesse Étudiante Catholique (JEC), a religious movement for Francophone Catholics between the ages of twelve and twenty.[27] She attended the JEC national congress in Montreal in 1945, an event that brought thirty thousand male and female students from Canada and the United States together for a grand parade, a Pontifical Mass, and *un jeu scénique*[†] under the stars. Seventeen-year-old Claire was excited to travel with her classmates to Montreal, "the big city."[28] She met youth organizers Jeanne Sauvé and Gérard Pelletier, and came away deeply inspired.[29]

"That was during my period of Jesus, Jesus, Jesus. I came back saying, 'There is only one reality and it is Jesus,'" was how Claire described it.[30] Her childhood friend Jean Drapeau, who later became a Catholic priest, agreed: "When Claire was young, she was very devout, like many of the girls who were under the tutelage of the nuns."[31] Gisèle Blondeau, who observed Claire keenly at Bellevue, described it as "true religious fervour."[32] Claire even briefly considered becoming a nun. It was a spiritual perspective that did not last.

The seeds of disbelief were sown within Claire's own family. Her mother practised Catholicism diligently, kneeling to say the rosary every night. The L'Heureux family had its name on one of the front pews in the church, and the whole family, like most everyone else in Rimouski, went to church every Sunday.[33] But Claire's father often refused to sit in the family pew. Along with some of the other men, he stayed outside to smoke and talk during the sermon. Claire suspected that neither Napoléon nor her father believed in religion. She wondered whether her mother privately shared some of Paul's skepticism, but noted that after the onset of Marguerite's illness, the church became "a crutch."[34] For Claire, it was the trappings of religion that appealed the most. Sunday Mass was an occasion to meet friends. "You put on your best dress and it was just like going to a *fête*."[‡,][35] She loved the religious music, the sense of community, and the Catholic values, but confessed that she paid little attention to the sermons, sleeping or using the time to reflect on her own thoughts.

There was also the matter of Georges Courchesne, the first archbishop of Rimouski, a tall, imposing, and magnificent orator, and an ultramontane conservative.[36] "He was very narrow-minded and he had a hold on the town," recalled Philippe Casgrain, a Rimouski resident who

---

† a theatrical play
‡ party

later became a law classmate of Claire's. "In the summer, priests had to ride their bicycles with full cassocks and square hats. It was very Catholic, very rigid."[37] Jean-Marie Joly, who grew up on the same street as Claire, recalled one of Archbishop Courchesne's Christmas Masses that opened with this statement: *"Les hommes sont des salauds, les femmes sont des salopes, et nous allons tous mourir dans les crottes."*[†] Pointedly, he added, "And that was the Christmas sermon."[38] Nicole L'Heureux explained: "We could say he was more Catholic than the pope."[39]

Archbishop Courchesne's religious edicts kindled growing doubts in Claire. "I'm sure he was very bright, but as far as his contribution to the progress of civil society, it was back there. He forbade dancing, and would refuse communion to the young people who went dancing on Saturday. We had to wear long sleeves. We couldn't wear shorts. He didn't like the Kiwanis. He didn't like the Rotary. They were not Catholic, and he didn't like that. He also had the idea that the cities were sinful, and so he put the people on the soil where nothing could grow. People were dying of poverty!"[40] Ultimately, Claire retreated from the religious saturation of the convents. The church's treatment of women was a major factor. "They separated women from men, then they taught the young men in the seminaries that women were sinful. Women could not become priests. Priests could not marry. When I was young, I just followed along. But eventually, I could not accept it."[41] Jokingly, she added: "And I met a boyfriend right after the JEC congress. That was the end of any thoughts of becoming a nun."[42]

Full religious disengagement would take quite a number of years. "I was aged nineteen or twenty by the time I washed my hands of religion," she mused. "We lived in a house where there was make-believe about these things. We felt our parents didn't really believe. We came to see the irrationalities, the stupidities of the teaching. We inherited the values but not the stupidities."[43]

First Taste of Romance:
"Boys Would Turn Their Heads and She Would Turn Too"

The woman who would grow into a notorious *femme fatale* began early. Initially, it was men her father's age who were the subject of the young girl's interest. Claire used to ask to sit beside Michèle Cloutier's father

---

[†] "Men are scoundrels, women are sluts, and we will all die in excrement."

when he drove the neighbourhood girls to the beach. Michèle added with laughter: "She was admiring him! That just came back to me!"[44] Thérèse Dionne, another childhood friend, offered a further illustration. Her father, Yves, held prominent administrative positions in Rimouski's local courts, and was a man who read widely about philosophy and politics. Thérèse remembered that when Claire came over, she seemed mesmerized by Yves and he by her, and that the two talked on and on. "He thought she was the brightest girl in Rimouski. My mother said, 'Don't bring her too often, because your father gets excited.'"[45]

Claire's first romantic flame, at age sixteen, was Paul Masson, who lived down the street in Rimouski. The Masson family hosted neighbourhood badminton competitions on their night-lit court, where the attraction first began. Then one day young Paul rescued Claire when she fell off a wharf and twisted her ankle. Under the strict chaperonage of the Masson parents, hand holding was the limit of the relationship, which ended tragically after Paul enlisted and was drowned at a military training camp. Claire and her mother attended the funeral. As with so many young women who lost admirers and lovers in the war, life moved on.[46]

Claire's social activities were simple pleasures. On holidays at home in Rimouski, young boys and girls skated, skied, swam, and bicycled together. They rented horses for sleigh rides, and came back for a big pot of beans, which they ate in the basement of one of their friends' houses. Teenagers would host small parties at their homes with sandwiches, cakes, and soft drinks. They sang together and listened to 78 rpm records – French music as well as Nat King Cole, Bing Crosby, Frank Sinatra, Dinah Shore, and Tommy Dorsey. Despite the disapproval of the religious authorities, sometimes they even pushed back the rugs and danced.[47]

Romance was strictly contained. Parents "attended and watched the whole thing," explained Claire. She was permitted to bring male friends home occasionally, but her mother set the rules first: she would not tolerate kissing. Claire described bringing a young pilot from the aviation camp in Mont-Joli to her home. At ten o'clock, her mother came into the room, wound the clock, and told the young man to go. "That was the end of it," laughed Claire.[48] Another time, she wrote a "love letter" to a young officer in her father's military camp. Word reached Claire's father, and when he confronted his young daughter with the evidence, Claire's "crush" on the attractive young soldier quickly disintegrated. "It was not a glorious day for me," she admitted.[49]

Quebec cinemas were not open to persons under sixteen, so it was 1943 before Claire had her first outing to the movies.[50] She and her Bellevue

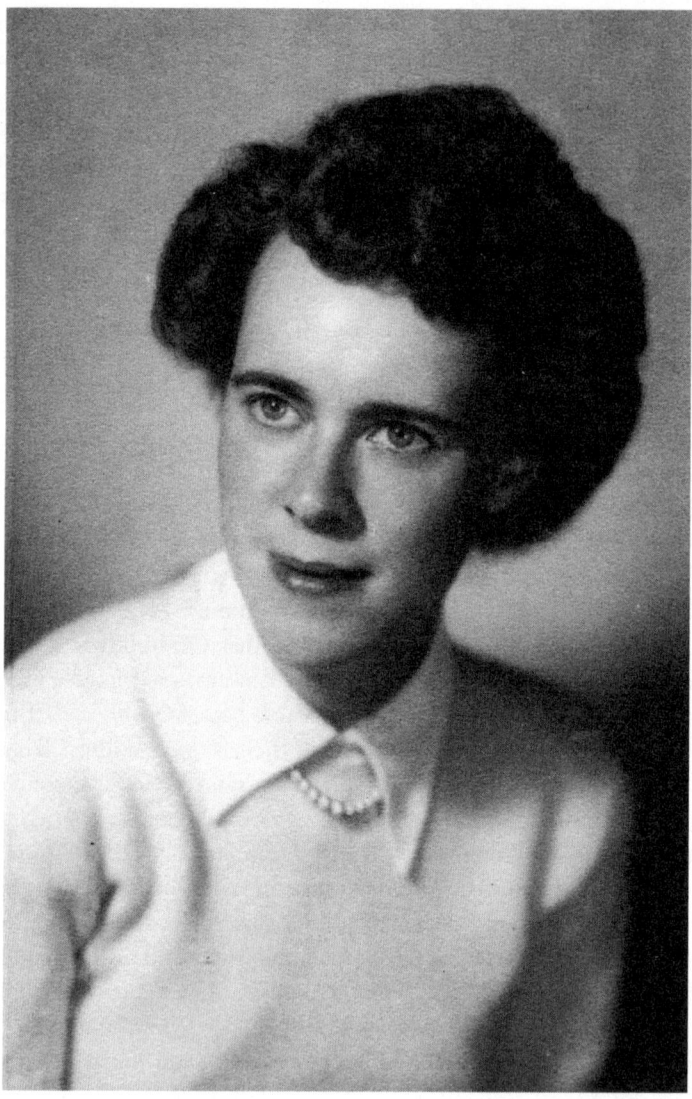

Claire L'Heureux, age sixteen.

classmates revelled in their first cinematic romance, *Le paradis perdu,* an interwar tearjerker about steadfast love. Philippe Casgrain recalled taking Claire to another French movie, *Les bateliers de la Volga,* in Rimouski. The plot involved the capture of the film's hero by Russians, who were trying to burn his eyes out with a hot iron. Claire became so emotionally wrapped up in the plot that she could not stop sobbing. "I had to say, don't cry, it's just a movie," Philippe remembered. He described Claire as a "hell of a nice girl," "well brought up," who "giggled" a lot. Indeed, he added, she was "good looking and had sex appeal." Did she have lots of boyfriends? "I think so," he replied, "but then I would not have noticed that. I would have thought I was the only one."[51]

From her earliest years, Claire's friends remarked on her interest in boys, and the corresponding attraction she inspired in males. Michèle Cloutier explained: "Claire liked boys. We were always talking about boys. Boys would turn their heads, and she would turn too."[52] Thérèse Dionne recalled that she was "popular" with boys: "Although she never said bad things about the other girls, every girl was afraid to leave their boyfriend with Claire. She had a way to talk to boys. She was friendly, joking easily, talking about everything. She was never with any boy for long."[53] Jean Drapeau added: "She was quite good looking and attractive to men, even when she was a girl. I think she has always had a sensual attraction along with an intellectual attraction."[54]

Philippe Michaud, who met Claire in Rimouski when he was about fifteen and home for holidays from the seminary, agreed that Claire had "a lot of boyfriends." "She has not changed for as many years as I've known her," he added. "[It's] the same in a small or a big group. [She is always] speaking loud, laughing. Every person, when we are talking about her, they smile. It's because she is so special."[55] One of Claire's Bellevue classmates, Monique Perron, recalled that her brother, who had met Claire previously and hoped to renew the acquaintance, dropped by to visit Claire at the convent. The more relaxed rules at Bellevue allowed familial visitors, and the plot was to have the young man identify himself as Claire's cousin. But the nuns quickly suspected something was up, and the subterfuge was completely exposed when young Claire became positively exuberant over her new visitor.[56]

The young women relished the relative freedom they were given at the Collège Notre-Dame-de-Bellevue to go out in groups. One of their favourite haunts was the Pharmacie Boissinot, a local drugstore about five minutes away, where they walked to buy ice cream cones or chocolate. That was where, at the age of seventeen, Claire met her first serious boyfriend, André Boissinot, the son of the pharmacist, who was in first-year medicine.[57] The innocent but enjoyable relationship lasted for some years of letter writing and occasional visits in the summer when Claire was back in Rimouski. André would take Claire dancing to the Hôtel du Rocher Blanc, and they swam and played badminton together. And, as Jean

Drapeau added, "I saw them kissing very often."[58] Claire's last school year at Bellevue ended with a formal ball. A photograph taken at the time captured the girls and their dates, Claire and André Boissinot among them, in long gowns, corsages, and finery.

Claire and André Boissinot on the beach at Rocher Blanc, ca. 1946.

FACING PAGE: Formal ball at the Collège Notre-Dame-de-Bellevue, 1946. *Front row, left to right,* Thérèse Martel, Lili (Éliane) Depeyre, Claire L'Heureux, Marcèle Dorion, Cécile Dubé. Other individuals in middle row: André Boissinot *(extreme left)*, Fabienne Tousignant *(girl at extreme left)*, Thérèse Drouin *(third girl from left)*, Marthe Godbout *(second girl from right)*, Marguerite Drapeau *(girl at extreme right)*, Pascal Lévesque *(extreme right)*.

Quebec City restaurant. *Left to right,* Claire, André Boissinot, Pascal Lévèsque, Cécile Dubé.

The Reluctant Return of Paul L'Heureux

Paul returned from overseas in 1944 and Marguerite moved home to Rimouski, but her husband was immediately reposted to British Columbia. His continuous absences did not end with the war. In May 1945, he was named commander of the second depot in Aldershot and sent back to England to supervise the repatriation of the Canadian soldiers.[59] Despite the tensions that had beset their marriage for some years, Marguerite tried to remain optimistic about the future. *"L'absence est à l'amour, ce qu'au feu le vent est; il éteint le petit et ranime le grand,"*† was her constant refrain to her daughters.

Her faith may have been misplaced. Paul's letters became less and less frequent, and his correspondence with the children dwindled to nothing. Louise remembered receiving only one postcard from him from England, with the curt message: "Learn English."[60] Marguerite began to suspect, accurately, that Paul was having an affair overseas.[61] As the months stretched on, she worried that he might not come back, and took the unusual step of approaching military officials in Rimouski to have her husband recalled. It was January 1946 by the time Paul L'Heureux returned.[62]

Marguerite's hopefulness pervaded the homecoming. "The day he came home," explained Louise, "my mother laid out a special dinner and opened a bottle of champagne at the table." Nothing could paper over the rift. Even before the end of the dinner, Paul's temper exploded. Louise described the blow-up: "My father had been used to tea in England, and it was a great tragedy that we forgot to put the tea on the table. I remember running to the kitchen, 'the tea, the tea ...' He had been the commanding officer in the army. He was used to ordering people around."[63] Nicole also perceived that whatever bond her father had with his family had disintegrated. "My father loved my mother very much. But because she was sick, it was not easy. When he lived in Europe for two to three years, he met a lot of people. He was like a bachelor. When he came back from Europe, he said he regretted being married with children."[64]

There were also difficulties from Marguerite's perspective. She had been used to having her own money, to being independent and in charge of the household, but after Paul's return, she had to ask for money for everything. It only increased the tension. Louise emphasized: "I think at

---

† "Absence is to love what wind is to fire; it extinguishes the small, it inflames the great."

the beginning my mother was very much in love with my father. But one thing she used to repeat was that it was a mistake to love somebody more than he loves you. I think that was her case. It ended up to be a bad match."[65]

Marcèle Dorion, a Bellevue classmate of Claire's, first met Marguerite at the Hôtel Clarendon and later became her lifelong friend. She offered her own assessment of the breakdown of the marriage: Madame L'Heureux became "crippled" when Lieutenant-Colonel L'Heureux was "still active," "young," and "charismatic." "They loved each other, but it was difficult to live together in those circumstances."[66] Jean Drapeau felt it had more to do with Paul. He conceded that Marguerite's "terrible disease" wore her husband down, but believed that the relationship unravelled because Paul was someone who "loved women," a proclivity he indulged during his absence in the war.[67] Many times before her death, Antoinette Dion had repeated the aphorism that "it was a great mistake to marry for love," and Marguerite seems to have eventually come around to believing her own mother. It was a lesson she would press home to her own daughters repeatedly, although the girls showed little interest in her romantic advice.[68]

Although it was many more years before Marguerite and Paul began to live separately, the rupture was irreparable by 1946. Claire's own views were crystal-clear: "If my mother had not got sick, I believe she would have made him happy, that they would have stayed together. My father was very good to my mother, but he couldn't accept that she was a cripple. My father came back from war in 1946 and found her in a wheelchair and that was the end of a great romance."[69] It was also another nail into the heart of the troubled relationship between Paul and his eldest daughter.

Claire let none of this interfere with her *baccalauréat* studies. She threw herself into preparations for her final provincial examinations that spring. When she came out of the philosophy examination, Sister Sainte-Héléna was waiting anxiously to find out how it had gone, and was aghast when she learned that Claire had chosen to answer the most difficult question. There was great jubilation when the results confirmed Claire as the recipient of multiple academic awards, including the philosophy prize. She was elated at having overachieved in Sister Sainte-Héléna's eyes. Her mother must have been equally thrilled by the results. Her sister Louise recalled that their mother "always encouraged everything Claire did. She was always pushing her to do more."[70]

In the spring of 1946, eighteen-year-old Claire received her *baccalauréat-ès-arts magna cum laude,* as well as the Lieutenant-Governor's Medal.[71] The girls retired for a celebratory party to the home of Lili Depeyre, whose mother cooked them a grand and memorable meal. Claire's classmates, merry fortunetellers all, gave her a miniature version of the Civil Code as a graduation present.

Collège Notre-Dame-de-Bellevue graduation, 1946. *Left to right,* Cécile Dubé, Gisèle Blouin, Thérèse Martel, Marcèle Dorion, Marthe Godbout, Lili (Éliane) Depeyre *(hidden behind Claire),* Claire L'Heureux.

A Legal Education

7
The Decision to Go to Law School, 1946–48

Law was an unusual career for women. Clara Brett Martin, the first female lawyer in Canada, had waged a six-year battle to secure her call to the Ontario bar in 1897. It provoked huge controversy. Opponents predicted catastrophe: nurseries attached to courtrooms, shrill demands to change laws perceived as discriminatory, women litigators who would use their gender to unfair advantage with judges and juries, abandoned families in unkempt homes.[1] Only a handful of women followed Martin, and the law societies in other jurisdictions dragged their heels. New Brunswick opened its doors in 1906, British Columbia in 1912, Nova Scotia and the remaining western provinces between 1915 and 1918, Prince Edward Island in 1926, and Newfoundland in 1933.[2] Quebec was the last holdout, barring the gate to women lawyers until 1941.[3]

The Battle for Entry in Quebec: Not for Lack of Trying

It was not for lack of trying. Quebec's first female law graduate, Annie MacDonald Langstaff, obtained first-class honours from McGill in 1914.[4] When the Barreau du Québec denied her application to write the entrance exams, she took her case to court in 1915. Her Montreal lawyer, Samuel William Jacobs, KC, a champion of minority rights, was no stranger to discrimination himself. He was conspicuously passed over for elevation to the post of *bâtonnier* of the Quebec bar, appointment to the federal cabinet, and appointment to the Senate because of his Jewish religion.[5]

The pairing of a Quebec woman and a Jewish lawyer was significant, foreshadowing Claire's own experience decades later.

Seventy-two-year-old Superior Court judge Henri-Césaire Saint-Pierre rejected Langstaff's claim. "Nature never intended her to take part along with the stronger sex in the bloody affrays of the battle field," he concluded, warning Langstaff that her "ambition in life" should be directed to something "more suitable to the sex."[6] The ruling found favour in the press. Montreal's *Le Pays* reminded its readers that although judges liked to present fronts of granite, they were men of flesh like others, and could be unfairly felled by "seductive" advocates whose "velvet tones" would flow from "satin throats."[7] The reporters agreed with Judge Saint-Pierre's assessment that female advocates would never be able to handle the rape cases, sexual repartee, shameful insinuations, and perfidious double entendres that pervaded the courtroom. What honourable woman would choose to immerse herself in such a milieu?[8]

Encouraged by members of the Montreal Local Council of Women who protested the "narrow-minded ruling," Langstaff appealed to the Court of King's Bench, but her claim failed there as well.[9] Provincial legislator Lucien Cannon then introduced two bills in 1916 to open the profession to women. *L'Action Catholique* charged that the measure was *"une invention yankee,"*[†] put forward at the instigation of *"cette Israélite montréalaise qu'est madame Langstaff, protégée aussi de Maître S.W. Jacobs, un avocat juif de la métropole."*[‡, 10] Jacobs wrote back to reassure readers that Annie Langstaff was a practising member of the Roman Catholic Church, but both bills went down to defeat.[11] Quebec City's *Le Soleil* expressed sarcastic regret that women would have to wait to add *"la toge noire de l'avocat"*[§] to their wardrobes.[12]

Further efforts at legislative reform in the 1920s and '30s, supported by Quebec women's organizations, fared no better. Some legislators asserted that legal careers might be acceptable for Anglo-Saxon women but did not accord with the values of French Canadian women or Quebec, a "province of tradition."[13] A 1925 parish bulletin suggested that only *"la Vierge Marie peut se prévaloir du titre d'avocate suprême de l'humanité devant le Dieu souverain juge."*[‖, 14] Laval law student Gérard Lacourcière insisted

---

† "a Yankee invention"
‡ "this Montreal Israelite who is Madam Langstaff, also a protégée of Maître S.W. Jacobs, a Jewish lawyer of the metropolis"
§ "the lawyer's black robe"
‖ "the Virgin Mary can take for herself the title of Mankind's supreme lawyer before the Divine Sovereign Judge"

The Decision to Go to Law School

First four women called to Quebec bar, 1942: Elizabeth C. Monk, Constance Garner Short, Suzanne Raymond-Filion, Marcelle Hémond.

that marriage and maternity were the true destiny for women, *"les gardiennes vigilantes du foyer, les éducatrices soigneuses des enfants et [ainsi] les conservatrices ... de l'intégrité de notre foi."*†,15 University of Montreal law student Joseph Noonan urged would-be female lawyers to turn their energies toward works of charity instead.16

It took the election of Liberal premier Adélard Godbout, who had ushered in female suffrage in 1940 and whose daughter would study with Claire at Bellevue, to turn the tide. On 1 April 1941, in spite of an angry protest petition signed by two hundred Montreal lawyers, the Godbout government passed *La loi concernant le barreau*, admitting women to law.17 When the doors opened in 1942, the first four women granted admission were Elizabeth Carmichael Monk, Suzanne Raymond-Filion, Marcelle Hémond, and Constance Garner Short.18 They attended the opening of the Superior Court that fall, where Chief Justice Robert-Alfred-Ernest

---

† "the vigilant caretakers of the hearth, the careful educators of children, and thus the keepers ... of the integrity of our faith"

Greenshields welcomed them as "members of the gentler sex" and expressed hope that their presence would "soften and even sweeten the atmosphere of the courts."[19]

A Peer Group of One

The chief justice's remarks capped a battle for admission that had been anything but easy, but times were about to get worse. With the end of the Second World War, women were buffeted by cultural headwinds that kept many from seeking careers of any kind. They were pressured to free up jobs for soldiers returning from the front, and the Quebec government turned its energy to pulling women out of the paid labour force and dismantling nurseries. Quebec women's magazines glorified "the joys of domestic life and femininity."[20] Decades later, at a University of Montreal lecture celebrating fifty years of women in law, Claire L'Heureux-Dubé would state:

> [C]'était l'époque où la société, la société québécoise en particulier, ne permettait aux femmes ni le choix de leur destinée ni la possibilité de faire un choix libre. Leur vie était tracée à l'encre indélébile: mariage, maternité, compagne effacée, d'une part, célibataire, enseignante ou secrétaire, d'autre part.[†, 21]

Claire's interest in law made her even more anomalous. She was "the only girl from Rimouski who took lawyers' lessons," said her childhood friend Thérèse Dionne.[22] "Women got married and stopped," explained another Rimouski friend, Michèle Cloutier. "Women weren't in the professions."[23] By Claire's graduation from Bellevue, only eleven women had been called to the bar in Quebec.[24] A mere 1.6 percent of Canadian lawyers were female.[25] Claire was the only Bellevue graduate in her class to set her sights on law. It worried her classmate Marcèle Dorion, one of three Bellevue graduates to enrol in medical school: "We were not that many women newcomers, so we were bunching together. We were happy to have the other girls with us. 'You're going [to medical school], I'm going there with you.' Not for Claire, though. She chose law alone."[26]

---

† "This was the time when society, especially Quebec society, allowed women neither the choice of their destiny nor the possibility of making a free choice. Their life was traced in indelible ink: on the one hand, marriage, maternity, and the role of a faceless partner, and on the other hand, the life of a spinster, teacher, or secretary."

The Decision to Go to Law School 97

Justice Jeanne D'Arc Lemay-Warren at time of appointment to the bench.

What led Claire L'Heureux to choose law?[27] It was a decision that she recalled making at Bellevue, influenced at least in part by the one Bellevue student who had preceded her into law. Jeanne D'Arc Lemay, five years older than Claire, had graduated from Bellevue in 1941 and enrolled in law school in 1942. She was the first woman to graduate with an LL.L. degree from Laval University, in 1946, and was called to the bar the same year.[28] While Lemay was still studying at Laval, Sister Sainte-Héléna, who was bucking social norms by pressing her students to think about professional careers, invited Lemay back to speak to the girls at Bellevue.[29] Claire described the presentation as a powerful moment:

> She spoke about what she was doing. I remember clearly, after that, I thought – hey, if she can do it, I can do it. You had to be motivated by someone, otherwise why would you go into a man's field? I liked writing. I liked

arguing. And I liked to win. It was good to know that some other people had done it. When she came to talk to us about law, I think it crystallized a latent desire.[30]

Claire's family background also played a role. She cited her family's four daughters as an important influence, explaining that with no one but sisters, she was never forced to share the limelight with boys and never developed a "feeling of inferiority toward men."[31] Her parents were equally influential, with her mother topping the list of those whom Claire considered the major motivations for her choice of career. Marguerite L'Heureux longed to have been a lawyer herself, Claire recalled. "She always said, 'I would have loved to continue my studies.' She would have loved to go on, to be independent, and to become a lawyer. Justice was very important to her."[32] Marguerite had come from a family whose milieu was professional and elite, and she was familiar with lawyers and judges from Quebec City and Rimouski. "She had talent galore, but she couldn't get to her full potential," explained Claire. "She couldn't do it, but her children would."[33] Living out their mothers' dreams was a theme that would echo for many women who formed part of the next generation of Quebec and Canadian lawyers.[34]

Marguerite's influence was underscored by Claire's appreciation of her mother's powerful inner strength and positive outlook on life. "My mother would say, 'The sky is the limit, nothing is impossible,'" recalled Claire.[35] It was a sentiment that she embraced and to which she attributed much of her later success. Years later, Charles Gonthier, the Supreme Court justice who would co-sign the *Ewanchuk* decision with Claire, mused: "What drove her? [Claire] had what seemed to be boundless energy. Claire was a person of authority. She asserted herself. She had to overcome many things, and always stood up to adversity. I never knew her mother, but Claire spoke of her often. She may have inherited this from her mother. They both had very marked personalities, remarkable in their own ways."[36]

Claire's father was equally influential, although in reverse. "He didn't want her to be a lawyer. He was against it," recalled Claire's sister Louise.[37] Their sister Nicole agreed: "He would have liked us just to go to high school and be a clerk at the Kresge store. My mother said, 'They have the potential to do better than that.' For him, that was enough. It's amazing, because he himself would have liked to go to university. But for us, he didn't think women needed an education."[38] Paul L'Heureux's views were well known among Claire's convent friends. Marcèle Dorion summed

Four L'Heureux sisters in front of Rimouski home.

up his position: "He was saying, 'What's good for this one is just to get married.' Why should he pay for higher education? [It] didn't enter his brain to think like that."³⁹

His strong views toppled the dreams of at least one of Paul's daughters. Louise yearned to continue university studies, but her father insisted she become a nurse. She complied but regretted the decision and quickly abandoned nursing for marriage.⁴⁰ Claire, the rebel, refused to knuckle under. "My father thought it was silly that I went into law. He thought I would marry, [that it was] not worth it. Marriage was the profession for women. But it was not for me. I never thought in terms of marriage. [It was] not my goal. I wanted to learn."⁴¹ It was a sentiment shared by Jeanne D'Arc Lemay: "My father wanted us to be debutantes, and [we] said, 'No way, we are not for sale.'"⁴² Claire's choice of law was as much a challenge to her father's sexism as it was a desire to fulfill her mother's ambitions.⁴³ It was an early illustration of the dogged, inspired resistance that she would exhibit on the top court. And it set her on a path that her youngest sister, Nicole, would follow after her.

Two-Year Hiatus

Paul L'Heureux's lower postwar salary at customs and immigration intensified his disapproval. The family's shifting economic fortunes tipped it into the lower middle class again. After her graduation from Bellevue, Paul declared law financially out of the question and insisted that Claire learn to support herself. He bought her a typewriter and instruction books, and ordered her to teach herself typing and stenography.

Putting a positive spin on the wrench in her plans, Claire decided that being able to earn her living as a secretary might prove a useful skill. "I never believed I could succeed in getting a job as a lawyer," she reflected. "[I] always thought I would earn my living as a secretary, relying on my second skill."[44] Few women with law degrees imagined that they could earn a living as a lawyer.[45] Louise Weibel Britton, one of the early McGill graduates, thought her law degree would be "very good training for a high-class secretary."[46] Secretarial employment was the early fate of Margaret Hyndman, called to the Ontario bar in 1926. She prefaced her legal studies by working as a secretary for a Toronto real estate lawyer.[47] Florence Margulis Rosenfeld, who graduated from law in Manitoba in 1945, recalled: "I probably would have had more difficulty had I not been able to type and do stenographic work."[48] In 1952, future United States Supreme Court justice Sandra Day O'Connor, who graduated from Stanford law school with high honours, was also offered a job in a law firm as a stenographer.[49]

Beginning in the fall of 1946, Claire struggled to make a living as a secretary in Rimouski. She worked initially at the Wartime Prices and Trade Board until it closed, then at the small federal veterans' office. Secretarial positions were typically obtained through patronage, and Claire owed her first jobs to her father's influence.[50] Her friend Thérèse Dionne, who was typing alongside Claire, helped her learn the ropes: "She was ambitious. She was funny. When [Claire] didn't know how to do something, she tried, she tried, and she did it. She never said she couldn't do it. She was typing with two fingers and then she got the whole method."[51] When a young woman with more connections bumped her from the job, her father helped her land another position at the Canadian Cod Liver Oil Research Institute.[52] It involved communicating primarily in English with American chemists visiting the Gaspésie region to test cod tongues. Claire's bilingualism improved.

The atmosphere at home remained volatile, with Paul L'Heureux's stormy temperament disrupting the household all too often. Claire's increasingly unhappy father ventured briefly into local politics, and was

Thérèse Dionne Lecomte, late 1940s.

elected to the Rimouski municipal council in 1946. From 1947 to 1949, he held the position of assistant mayor,[53] but his restlessness continued to alarm his family. At one point, he threatened to sell the house and throw everything out. Claire's drive to embark upon an independent legal career only strengthened.

She filled every spare hour with social activities. She joined the Rimouski Lecture Club, whose members read books and gave short presentations. She met with girlfriends to knit and chat in the evenings. She set up spontaneous mixed parties for long-time friends and new acquaintances. Her youngest sister, Nicole, recalled that Claire would arrive home around 5 p.m., rush around to vacuum the rug, set out sandwiches, cake, and soft drinks, put on the music, and then whirl around greeting the guests. Her energy amazed her siblings, as did her level of flirtatiousness. The earlier romance with André Boissinot came to an end, and a dizzying array of suitors followed. The complications that ensued when she would break off romances became legendary. Once Claire claimed to have fallen ill with tuberculosis, writing to the young pilot of a small ship that she could no longer see him because she had to seek treatment at a sanatorium. Her mother surreptitiously read the letter and suffered great maternal anguish before the ruse was unmasked to great sibling hilarity.[54]

The two-year hiatus came to a precipitate end in 1948, hastened by Claire's resentment at having to take orders from a man at the Canadian Cod Liver Oil Research Institute who had less education than she did. He dictated a letter, and Claire tried to correct his mistakes. Her recollection was that he angrily called her into the office complaining, "I didn't say that," and threw her revised letter into the basket. Claire announced that she had had enough of the job, because he "should be on her side of the desk and she should be on his."[55] On the heels of this explosion, her mother insisted that Claire go on to law school without delay.

Together they devised a plan. Claire would move to Quebec City and enrol at Laval University's Faculty of Law. There was no debate over which school to select. McGill drew primarily Anglophone students, and the University of Montreal primarily Francophones from Montreal, whereas Claire's family connections were all to Quebec City. The greatest challenge was financial. When they discovered that classes at Laval ran from 8 to 10 a.m. and from 4 to 6 p.m., they realized that much could be done with the six hours in between. The schedule was designed to accommodate the professors, who were practising lawyers with busy offices to run. If Claire could continue working as a secretary in the capital city between 10 and 4, she could pay for her legal education.

Marguerite L'Heureux enlisted the support of Jules-A. Brillant, Rimouski's most prominent businessman, who controlled the region's banking, electricity, and communications industries.[56] She was a close friend of Brillant's wife, Agnès, and the two women interceded with Jules. He was persuaded to assist the bright young girl from Rimouski who needed a helping hand.[57] Brillant sat on the board of Sun Trust, and he found a secretarial opening for Claire with the notary in the company's stately Quebec office, conveniently located on rue Saint-Pierre, right next to the law school. Arrangements were made for Claire to board with her aunt Marie-Marthe and uncle Wilfrid. The $150 registration fee was paid with Marguerite's housekeeping savings. The aged and yellowed receipt still remains in the family papers.

8
Laval Law School Student Body, 1948–52

Claire moved to Quebec in August 1948, ready to take her first steps toward becoming a lawyer.[1] The first order of business was to pay a visit to the home of Professor Marie-Louis Beaulieu. Claire's grandmother Antoinette had known him socially, and her mother, Marguerite, sent Claire with a letter of introduction begging the Laval law professor to assist a young woman who wished to study law. As an effort to trade on social capital, it fizzled. Claire recalled the meeting as short: "He said, 'This is a man's world. Don't go there. You'll never succeed. There's no future in it for you. Go into social work.'"[2] Marguerite found the news sobering, but Claire was undeterred: "[It] didn't impress me very much, to be frank."[3]

The next day, she walked to the Laval campus in the heart of the old city. The law school was on the third floor of an imposing five-storey stone building, just above the medical school.[4] All law registrants had to report to the university secretary, Alphonse-Marie Parent, an influential Catholic monseigneur. His reception was no warmer. When Claire asked to register, he said, "No, it's only for men."[5]

How many women before and after her were told the same? How many turned on their heels and ran? Claire saw it as reflecting the era: "They were not wrong in many ways. It was a world of men. We were the first trying to get there. It was a difficult undertaking. Jeanne D'Arc [Lemay] didn't get a job as a lawyer, but as a civil servant. But they might have been a little more encouraging."[6] Claire demanded to know whether there was any law against her registration. The two argued while Parent tried to persuade her to study social work instead.[7] When she stood her ground, he filed the registration. Apart from her gender, there was no barrier. "They didn't reject anybody because they didn't have enough people," she recalled.[8]

Next Claire met with the faculty academic director, Professor Guy Hudon, with whom she had corresponded earlier about financial assistance. Hudon had written that scholarships varied from $100 to $200, but that there was no guarantee of subsidy.[9] In person, he was blunter. He said the scholarships were only for men. When the awards were later posted, not only were all the recipients male, many from wealthy families, but most had known affiliations with the Duplessis party.[10] Claire was chagrined but held her peace. "Who am I to fight the system alone? We accepted what they told us, and that was it. Although I was a rebel who fought to get into the law school ... I had enough. I was not destitute. I was working. And my uncle gave me a dollar every week that he won playing cards."[11]

Laval law students were overwhelmingly from the privileged class. Half came from affluent families of lawyers, doctors, professionals, or senior managers; another third represented office workers and salespeople. Only 20 percent came from families of farmers, transportation or communication workers, labourers, or service personnel, sectors that represented over 70 percent of the Quebec workforce at the time.[12] One former student explained that there was a real difference between those who were "bourgeoisie" and born in Quebec City and those who were not.[13] Another recalled that the few students from the farms were quiet and "kept their heads down, hands folded."[14] The law school reflected the rigid social structure of Quebec City, where family origins mattered intensely.[15]

But class is never straightforward, and is often a matter of perception as well as means. It was obvious that Claire did not come from one of the old-line legal families boasting endless generations of lawyers and judges, as many of her classmates did. She grew up in Rimouski, she did not live in a mansion on the Grande Allée, and she had to work through law school. Yet she was born in Quebec City of a maternal line of ancestors that was comfortable mixing with the social elite. She had spent years in a Quebec City convent among daughters of the well-to-do. Some of her Laval classmates from the smaller villages perceived her as elite; others saw her as significantly below that.[16] It remained to be seen how gender would factor in.

Laval Classmates: Outnumbered in a Man's World

When she first stepped into the classroom in September 1948, Claire would have seen more than fifty chairs jammed together in narrow rows, filled

Jean Bienvenue, Claire's Laval classmate.

with male law students neatly attired in dress pants, jackets, and neckties.[17] It was an extraordinary group, many of whom would go on to distinction and notoriety. Some of their success was the result of raw talent and hard work. The rest was attributable to the insular, interlinked world of the Quebec legal system.

The flamboyant Philippe Casgrain, whom Claire knew from Rimouski, had already taken his seat in the centre of the front row. His lawyer father, Perreault Casgrain, would later serve as president of the Canadian Bar Association. Although Philippe would fight an uphill battle just to pass his bar exams, he would become a successful Montreal commercial lawyer, *bâtonnier* of the bar, and founder of the Quebec arm of the national firm of Fraser Milner Casgrain.[18] Jean Bienvenue, who always sat up front with Casgrain, impressed his classmates with tales of his father, Valmore Bienvenue, a powerful lawyer and provincial cabinet minister, who would soon be appointed to the Superior Court. Jean followed in his father's footsteps, and was appointed to the Superior Court in 1977 after a successful legal career and a stint as a Liberal politician. In 1995, his sexist and anti-Semitic comments from the bench would ignite a spectacular cause célèbre leading to a judicial inquiry that resulted in his resignation.[19]

Julien Chouinard, a young man who commanded attention because of his "ramrod-stiff" military bearing, athleticism, and focused intelligence, would be elected class president. He would become "the most powerful civil servant in Quebec" and be appointed to a seat on the Supreme Court of Canada eight years before Claire.[20] Martial Asselin showed political promise right from the start, and was elected president of the Laval student association in 1949. After graduation, he practised law in Charlevoix, serving as mayor of La Malbaie, Conservative member of Parliament, Canadian parliamentary representative to NATO, and senator, before being named lieutenant-governor of Quebec in 1990.[21]

Roch Bolduc would forge a brilliant career in the Quebec public service, transforming Duplessis-era patronage practices into a modernized civil service. He was named to the Senate of Canada in 1988.[22] The charismatic Gabriel Lapointe would become a renowned Montreal criminal lawyer and *bâtonnier* of the bar. His colourful career got a spirited start when his "school-boy prank" to kidnap the Laval carnival queen the evening she was due to be crowned almost got him and his co-conspirators expelled.[23]

Gérard Bertrand and Jacques Dupuis-Couillard achieved success in the diplomatic corps.[24] Robert Auclair-Hallé became a pillar of the labour movement during its most militant years, organizing alongside Jean Marchand and helping to lead the most divisive strikes in the country. He would later sit as a judge of the provincial labour court.[25] Pierre Marseille became a high-profile corporate and commercial lawyer in Quebec City with Louis St. Laurent's law firm.[26]

William Tetley, the only Anglophone student, had moved from Montreal to study at Laval in order to improve his French. He served as a Liberal Quebec cabinet minister and then became a McGill law professor renowned for his expertise in maritime law.[27] Jacques Alleyn would head up legal affairs for the CBC.[28] André Desgagné obtained a doctorate in law in Paris, returned to spearhead academic reform at the Laval law faculty, and became the president of the Université du Québec à Chicoutimi.[29] No fewer than ten of the fifty-one graduates would be appointed to the bench.[30]

Some of these students may have taken their future success for granted. Yet for most of them, on that first day at law school, such stellar achievements would have constituted nothing more than a gleam in their eye.

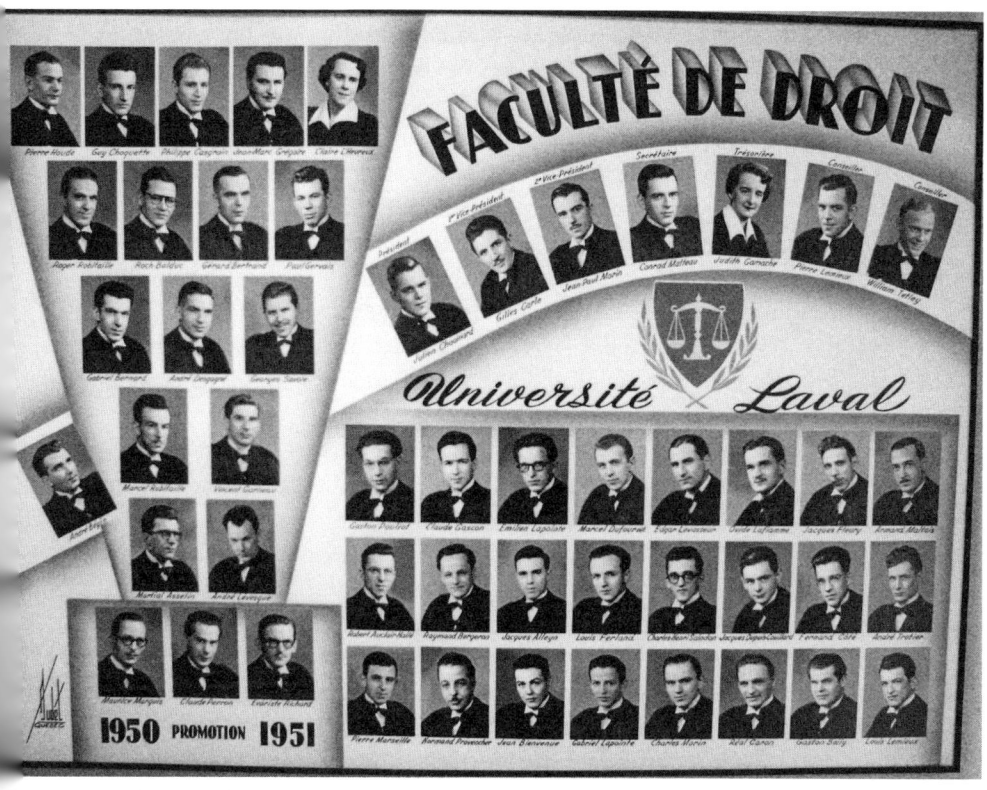

Laval Law graduating class, 1951. Claire L'Heureux is fifth from the left at the top row; Judith Gamache is third from right at the top curved row.

And none of them, even in their wildest dreams, would have guessed that a female student would stand a chance at glory.

A close inspection of the class that first day would reveal one other woman in the room, Judith Gamache.[31] Although she and Claire had not met before, Judith had also studied with the Ursulines in Rimouski. She lived with her widowed mother across the river in Lévis. She was extremely intelligent, with a practical bent and a wicked sense of humour. The two young women became inseparable. They studied together, socialized as a duo, and slept over at each other's homes. Equally pressed for money, Judith also worked, peddling newspaper ads and doing other odd jobs on the side.[32]

A handful of women had passed through Laval Law since Jeanne D'Arc Lemay's first admission in 1942. Eight preceded Judith and Claire's arrival, and nine more would enrol before their graduation in 1951. In 1954, Nicole

Women law students relaxing at Lac Sept-Îles, Quebec. *Left to right,* Calin Morin, Claire L'Heureux, Judith Gamache.

L'Heureux, Claire's youngest sister, would join the group, and Monique Perron, who became a lifelong friend, would follow in 1955.[33] The women chose not to set up a women's student association, as had occurred at Toronto's Osgoode Hall Law School a few years earlier.[34] But they spent some of their leisure time together, and Margot Choquette hosted a reception for them at her parents' lavish home on the Grande Allée. At least some of the male students thought that their female classmates deliberately maintained some distance. André Desgagné recalled that Claire and Judith "stayed always together in the classroom," and that they did not mix too much, especially at the start.[35] Jacques Alleyn described the two girls as existing "in a unit by themselves, probably for joint support."[36]

Canada's first female lawyer, Clara Brett Martin, had endured complete ostracism and loud hissing when she joined the class at Osgoode Hall in 1892.[37] The reaction was less voluble by the mid-twentieth century, but some male law students continued to display discomfort around female colleagues. Female law students at McGill, the University of Montreal, the University of Ottawa, Osgoode Hall, and the University of Manitoba described "gentle lechery present in the halls of learning," as well as "baiting" from colleagues who accused them of "husband-hunting," "status-seeking," and "over-ambition." The early women found their male classmates condescending and given to "making sexist remarks."[38] Jeanne D'Arc Lemay felt compelled to defend her presence in the Laval student newspaper, arguing that the obligations of being a spouse and mother did not require women to renounce other occupations.[39]

Claire and Judith too experienced some male displeasure. "We would come to the school, and they would close the door in our face," remembered Claire. "It was kind of an expression of 'you don't belong here.'"[40] Calin Morin, who began law studies at Laval a year after Claire, remembered one surprise incident when a male student brushed by her in the corridor and shoved a candle into her hand. "It was in the shape of a penis," she explained. "It was so stupid. He thought maybe I would make a commotion." Instead, a male student who witnessed the prank rescued her, quietly placing the candle in his pocket.[41] Yet most of the male classmates of these early women seem to have been largely oblivious to any discrimination. They took the view that Claire and Judith received no differential treatment and that it was easy for the two women to adapt to the environment.[42] Reflecting on this decades later, Robert Auclair-Hallé wondered: "Today, I think what if we had been two boys among a gang of women? How would we react?"[43]

Cross-gender friendships eventually blossomed. The strongest connections that Claire and Judith made were with Roch Bolduc from Saint-Raphaël-de-Bellechasse and Gilles Carle from Grand-Mère. Claire described Roch Bolduc as extremely intelligent and very friendly, someone who was always laughing, and a born communicator. Gilles Carle was elected vice president of the class and was generally acknowledged as the cleverest of the group. It may have been ill health that kept him from rivalling the career achievements of some of his classmates. He struggled for many years with tuberculosis, worked as a Crown prosecutor in Mont-Joli, and finished his career as a judge of the Provincial Court.[44] His conservative Duplessis politics ran contrary to the liberal philosophy of Roch Bolduc, and Claire remembered many fascinating hours with the foursome ensconced in the rooming house that the two young men shared, passionately debating local and national politics. Occasionally, the four also went out walking, skating, to dances, and to the cinema.[45]

Years later, Bolduc reflected on how much he had enjoyed the time at law school with Claire and Judith. Although he admitted that it was "new" for the male students to have female colleagues, since they had all come

Roch Bolduc, Laval graduation photo, 1951.

from gender-segregated colleges, he believed that they brought an important addition to the law school. He was one of the few male students who recognized that the young women had "to fight a lot" to be accepted. He described Judith as the "romantic type" who "used to fight with her charm," and Claire as "competitive," a young woman who "fought with her wit." Claire went "against the trend," noted Bolduc. "She wanted to be first. She was involved in everything. She was very intense. She has a steel will, I would say."[46]

9
Laval Law School Faculty and Curriculum, 1948–52

For the students who had come from studies in philosophy, literature, and the new discipline of social science, law was a distinct shock.¹ The professors were lawyers, "practical people" who saw themselves as "technicians of law."² They held forth in front of the class, seated upon a chair raised up on a platform. Claire's classmate Robert Auclair-Hallé recalled: "It was *une école technique de droit*.† Our professors would open up *le Code civil*. They would begin to read: *Ar-ti-cle un. Ar-ti-cle deux ... Ar-ti-cle mille neuf.* They would lecture with such long sentences and complicated terms that by the time you finished writing the sentence, you couldn't know where you were." It was all rules and "no reflection."³ Classmate André Desgagné agreed, adding that there was "very little for the mind in law."⁴

The professors never called on pupils to answer questions, and they did not take kindly to the odd student who asked one. When someone asked Professor Hudon about the labour implications of the law, he was dismissive: "That is not my business. I plead the case. It is a matter of what the law is."⁵ Hudon looked askance at students involved in social issues of the day, and chastised Robert Auclair-Hallé and Roch Bolduc for fundraising on campus on behalf of the workers in the 1949 Asbestos strike.⁶

The law school, almost a century old, remained under clerical direction. It was dedicated to the formation of a professional and social elite, rather

---

† a technical law school

Library of the Laval Faculty of Law, 1933.

than meant as a centre for intellectual and critical inquiry.[7] The faculty was "a veritable Family Compact," with professors drawn from the most illustrious members of the bar, a quarter of them sitting judges, intricately linked by professional and familial ties. The training inculcated a static vision of law and a conservative perspective on the role of law in society.[8] All courses were compulsory. The *Civil Code* and civil procedure swallowed up half the timetable.[9] Roman law was not just taught as an introductory framework but "treated as though it were a living law actually in force," even down to the inclusion of "the institution of slavery."[10]

Teaching materials were limited: the *Civil Code* and the *Criminal Code of Canada*, with a few stray references to French and Quebec treatises.[11] The mentality was that everything students needed to know was in the codes, which the students toted in their pockets everywhere they went.[12] Students read only a few cases: some from Quebec and the odd one from the Supreme Court of Canada that dealt with Quebec matters. The faculty used an "expository and didactic" style of pedagogy. In the hands of a master, these lectures could be an aesthetic experience, but in the hands of someone less skilled, this risked descent to an "arid exercise."[13] At least one of the professors simply reread the lectures his father had composed when he taught on the faculty a generation earlier.[14]

Laval was not anomalous in this. Pierre Elliott Trudeau was so bored in law school at the University of Montreal in the early 1940s that he studied only what was "barely necessary."[15] Across the border in Ontario, it was much the same. Ian Scott, who would go on to become a brilliant barrister and Ontario attorney-general, described Osgoode Hall as having "very large classes, very small permanent faculty, an imported dean of uncertain distinction, black letter law, printed notes, few questions asked, fewer answered."[16] It was a far cry from the elite American law schools, where proponents of the new "legal realism" were discrediting the view that disputes could be resolved by reference to certain, fixed, immutable principles, disentangled from politics and ideology.[17]

Laval students took notes in class, but wrote no papers and did no outside research. They annotated their codes, enumerated "constitutive elements," defined "juridical notions," and prepared tables that were "veritable catechisms" of structured questions and answers in preparation for regurgitation on examinations.[18] For many, this did not amount to a full forty-hour week. The majority spent their midday hours playing cards or ping-pong, smoking, drinking coffee, or drinking beer at the tavern.[19] The more impoverished students, such as Claire L'Heureux and Judith Gamache, took on paid employment. Some of the male students worked at jobs in nearby law offices secured through family connections or simply by knocking on doors. William Tetley, the Anglophone Protestant classmate who knew no one when he arrived, managed to obtain two offers from prestigious Francophone law firms. Tetley's bilingualism may have eased his path, since much business law was transacted in English at the time.[20] But such positions were never open to the women.

THE LAVAL FACULTY: TECHNICIANS OF LAW

Guy Hudon, the man who had refused Claire a scholarship, joined Laval's faculty as one of its first full-time professors two years before Claire arrived. He would later become its first full-time dean.[21] A conservative adviser to Maurice Duplessis and deeply versed in civil law doctrine, Hudon would put his hand on his forehead and "recite in a deep voice for one and a half hours ... with not a word out of place." His students described him as mixing law, poetry, and history "like Charles De Gaulle," intoning sentences that could stretch upwards of ten minutes without grammatical errors. Frowning and severe in manner, he rarely looked at his audience, and lectured as if there were no one in the room. Although many found his teaching "brilliant," Hudon's drinking was also legendary, with students astonished to smell liquor on his breath at eight in the morning. Some speculated that he rested his head in his hands when he lectured because he was too drunk to hold it up without a prop.[22]

Although there would be no substantial transformation of legal education for decades, the arrival of Marie-Louis Beaulieu signalled winds of change.[23] The professor who had earlier tried to shift Claire into social work, Beaulieu taught the first course in industrial legislation in 1942. He advocated new ways of teaching that examined the connections between social science and law. He and Hudon might have shared views about the unsuitability of women to law, but they clashed over the mission of a law school and the role of law in society.[24] Claire much preferred Beaulieu's perspectives: "For the first time, he made me understand what law was all about. He was the only professor who did that. But he was the best prof I ever had, who illuminated the whole thing."[25] Her classmate Roch Bolduc reminisced admiringly that Beaulieu could have been a real university professor, even at Oxford, but was a bit out of place in Quebec at the time. He also came in for a fair bit of student ribbing. A short man with an unusually large, bald head and a reputation as a gambler, Beaulieu was tagged with the unfortunate nickname *la tête à deux jaunes*.[†, 26]

Louis-Philippe Pigeon, who would be appointed to the Supreme Court of Canada in 1967, taught constitutional law. An erudite technician whose probing oral exams terrified generations of students, he depicted law as composed of "concision" and "good sense" without "any doubts or concessions," and ran his classrooms in a strict old-school manner.[27] William Tetley recalled a hot spring day, when the students sat "packed together in rows in a small room, with the windows closed." He could not recall whether it was Jean Bienvenue, Philippe Casgrain, or Gaby Lapointe, but one of the trio raised his hand to ask a question:

> We all drew in our collective breath at such audacity and Pigeon was also very surprised. Finally Pigeon said *"oui"* in his very high-pitched voice and the student said *"Puis-je poser une question?"* Pigeon reflected and said *"oui"* and the student said *"Puis-je ouvrir la fenêtre?"*[‡] Pigeon reflected again and said *"non"* and that was the end of Professor Pigeon's version of the Socratic

---

† the two-yolked head (or egghead)
‡ May I ask a question? May I open the window?

method for the day. The next day the same student raised his hand, we students were doubly astounded and Pigeon delayed, being himself quite suspicious. Eventually he said *"oui"* and the student asked *"Puis-je réitérer ma question de hier?"*† Pigeon replied *"non"* in his high-pitched voice and that was the beginning and end of Pigeon's Socratic method for the year and no doubt thereafter.[28]

William Tetley added that Pigeon had been indirectly responsible for the fate of Parti Québécois premier René Lévesque, who dropped out of third-year law a few years before Claire arrived. Pigeon threw Lévesque out of class for smoking. Lévesque refused to apologize, and left for good.[29]

Jacques Alleyn remembered well the "little black book" from which Pigeon lectured, "maybe forty pages long," adding, "It's as if his whole mind was contained there. He would go on and on." Robert Auclair-Hallé added that Pigeon would rhyme off citations by heart. The effect was magnified by Pigeon's odd mannerisms: twisting his face, rubbing his nose, and speaking in a falsetto sing-song voice. But Auclair-Hallé emphasized that "when Pigeon was speaking, you could hear a moth flying."[30] Claire was of a different view, admitting bluntly that she "didn't particularly understand it at that time" and was not "interested in constitutional law one bit."[31]

She was more enthusiastic about Professor Jean Turgeon,[32] who offered a few lectures in family law although there was no such practice at the time, since, as Claire explained, "There was no divorce, women had no rights, and there was no money in it."[33] Claire shared the sentiment, then widespread in the bar, of not wanting to "touch" family law, but she found Turgeon mesmerizing. Indeed, she admitted to developing a bit of a schoolgirl crush on the dark, handsome professor. It made the early-morning class bearable.

Jean-Charles Bonenfant, an intellectual described as *"une bibliothèque vivante,"*‡ taught Roman law.[34] Bonenfant was a sarcastic individual, and loved to quiz Claire and Judith about the "perpetual tutelage of women in old Rome."[35] Although she found Roman law interesting, Claire found it difficult to keep the complex details straight. Her mother, Marguerite, who became fascinated with the course, helped Claire study, and Roman law eventually became Claire's favourite subject.

---

† May I reiterate my question of yesterday?
‡ "a living library"

She was less enamoured of criminal law, which furnished a fault line for the early female law students. Opponents of women's admission to law had flagged sexual assault as improper for respectable women to study, and once they arrived, the young women faced continuing resistance. At some schools, professors spiced up their lectures with off-colour humour in order to embarrass female students.[36] At Laval, criminal law professor Gérard Lacroix asked both Claire and Judith to excuse themselves from class during his lectures on sexual offences, telling them that his wife, who was a friend of Claire's mother, would receive them for tea instead.[37] For years to come, female students at Laval would be asked to excuse themselves when the law of rape was taught in criminal class.[38] Was Professor Lacroix's invitation one they were free to refuse? Claire said it never entered their minds to refuse. "They would have locked the door! Anyway, we loved the break. We were not interested in criminal law."[39] Ironically, Claire, who was completely shut out of law school instruction on sexual assault, would make this area one of her signature legacies in her later decades on the Supreme Court.

Although it was less talked about, there were also incidents of sexual harassment. Both Claire and Judith had to contend with this in one of the professors' offices. Reluctant to name the offender even decades later, Claire explained: "He would invite us on one pretext or another. He would get up and put his hands on our behinds. I would push away. He would try again, often enough. We had names for him – *le cochon*.† But we never thought of reporting it. We were shy about it. Judith and I would exchange [stories] but we wouldn't mention it to anybody else. We felt it was something we shouldn't talk about."[40]

The students often wandered down to the Quebec Legislative Assembly to watch the political debates, sitting spellbound while Premier Maurice Duplessis of the Union Nationale party jousted nimbly with his Liberal adversaries. The cast of characters was familiar, since many of the politicians were Laval faculty members and the fathers and uncles of fellow law students. During question period, Professor Hudon would stand behind the green curtain to the left of the Speaker's chair, providing advice to Duplessis. Professor Pigeon would stand behind the same curtain on the other side, feeding questions and advice to opposition leader Adélard Godbout. When question period was over, Hudon and Pigeon would "walk out arm-in-arm, complaining audibly about the state of politics

---

† the swine

and politicians."⁴¹ "It was better than going to the movies," laughed Claire.⁴²

She also marvelled at Duplessis's talent for remembering everyone he met. She would cross his path walking to school in the morning as he was strolling from his residence in the Château Frontenac to the Legislative Assembly. He would stop, greet her with *"La petite L'Heureux!"*† and continue on his way. His formidable charisma enabled Duplessis to control a powerful electoral machine that imposed his anti-labour, anti-communist, church-based ideology, extolling Quebec nationalism while opposing increased government intervention in the social sector.⁴³ "I was very naive, and didn't know much about Duplessis's political ideology. I had great admiration for him as a human being, as our fierce leader, protecting the interest of Quebec," admitted Claire.

Occasionally, the students also followed their professors into court, to watch the proceedings at the Palais de Justice.⁴⁴ Although family law was not an actual field of practice yet, some of the rare cases that did arise made an indelible mark. In a petition for marital separation, Claire remembered graphic testimony about wife beating, involving a man who forced his wife to wash the floor naked. Yet it remained a matter of heated debate whether the husband's behaviour was sufficiently abusive to warrant separation from bed and board.⁴⁵ Another cause célèbre involved a civil claim for $35,000 for alienation of affection. Claire was horrified over the essence of the action. "She was his wife. They were talking of her like she was furniture or property, saying 'you took her from me.'"⁴⁶

One case involved a young couple who had been making love behind a cord of wood when the young woman's father surprised them. In the ensuing fight, the young man struck the older man on the head with a log, killing him. In Claire's mind, there was "no intention to murder, it was evident it was manslaughter," but the verdict was murder and the sentence was death. The scene still upset Claire years later: "I saw [the accused] on the stand with the lump in his throat. The judge was telling him solemnly he would be hanged by the neck until dead. It was barbarous, a terrible injustice. He was too young. I was terrified." Although the capital sentence appears not to have been carried out, Claire "never forgot it."⁴⁷

Sitting as observers in court, the young women were anomalies, their presence occasionally the subject of rebuke. Two Laval students from the class a year after Claire's, Calin Morin and Édith Lemay, happened to

---

† "The L'Heureux kid!"

be in court when a homosexual prosecution was in process. "The judge called us, the two girls, into his office," recalled Calin Morin. "He said, 'Do you think girls should come to trials like this?' We had to convince him that such topics were no longer completely taboo. Every day was not a fight exactly, but we had to make our place."[48]

Academic Results:
"I Studied Hard, but Not Harder than the Male Students"

Claire did not work particularly hard in the first two years. Judith admired her friend's ability to negotiate her way through law school so effortlessly: "Claire was not panicky ever. She laughed all the time."[49] It was a repeat of Claire's years at Bellevue, where her intellectual prowess enabled her to coast initially, and she waited until the end to bear down on her studies. At Laval, Claire stepped up the pace in her third year, as she came to realize that there was coherence in the materials. "I studied hard [but] not harder than the male students," she insisted.[50] Her classmates, however, were only too aware of Claire's competitive side. André Desgagné recalled: "She did not pass unnoticed."[51]

All the students found their anxieties heightened during exam time. They heaved sighs of relief when they learned that the written exams did not call for long-winded answers. "Those guys were practitioners. They didn't have much time to amuse themselves reading those things," joked Roch Bolduc.[52] In contrast, the oral exams were hair-raising. Students were taken one by one into a large room, where they sat across the table from three professors who took turns peppering them with questions.[53] Much depended on their ability to express themselves well at fever pitch. The mood of the examiners was also a factor, and their ill-humour could doom the chances of the best-prepared candidate. It was something of a "cat-and-mouse game," even according to the professors of the time.[54]

Three students led the class. Pierre Marseille had a talent for impersonating professors and students to the delight of his classmates, and scored some of the highest grades.[55] Ranking above him, Claire and Julien Chouinard jostled over the top spot every year. The two leading students, both eventually named Supreme Court judges, were complete opposites in philosophy and personality. Chouinard was an incisive leader, vigorous in pursuit of his objectives but strait-laced, conservative, quiet, and studious.[56] As their classmate Martial Asselin put it, he was "somebody who liked only to study, study, study. He was alone all the time. He will not accept to

Martial Asselin, retired in Quebec City, 2008.

come and have a glass of beer with the group."⁵⁷ In contrast, her classmates regarded Claire as a young woman who excelled academically but was socially convivial as well. She was "obviously bright as a light," but she was also all for "going out" and "having fun."⁵⁸

In the end, it was Julien Chouinard who obtained first prize in civil law. Claire carried off the labour law prize and finished second in civil law. Pierre Marseille obtained the Tessier medal.⁵⁹ Despite her achievement, her graduation, when she received her LL.L. *cum laude* in 1951, was not a celebrated rite of passage at all. Claire remembered nothing of the day or the speakers. "I think there was a ceremony. They gave us our diploma. My mother couldn't come, and my father didn't."⁶⁰

Admission to the Bar

Then an announcement from the Barreau du Québec stopped the graduates in their tracks. Previous students sat the bar exams directly after their third year, but in 1951 the Barreau imposed a fourth year of professional and practical training. Eventually this would turn into a one-year articling *stage*† at a law firm, but initially, the fourth year was assigned to the law schools, and Claire's class was forced to continue courses at Laval.[61] Speculation ran rampant about the motivation for the change. Some suggested that the profession distrusted the new social science influence that Professor Beaulieu was bringing to the law school, and others suggested that the Barreau was trying to stem the tide of returning veterans seeking to enter the bar.[62]

Several of Claire's classmates hoped to defer the fourth year by competing for the Rhodes Scholarship, which would fund a year of legal training at Oxford University in England. Claire was told that women were not eligible, but she was somewhat mollified when the faculty advised the entire class that because of the fourth year requirement, none of them was eligible to apply. To everyone's surprise, however, Julien Chouinard ignored the advice, submitted an application, and carried off the Rhodes. Roch Bolduc never got over his chagrin. "Julien didn't say a damn word, but he applied anyway. [He] got it because he was the only one who applied. We didn't like it. It was not fair play. In a proper competition, I'm not sure who would have won. Maybe Claire."[63] Upon his return, Chouinard also managed to evade the fourth year. He secured his call to the bar with a private member's bill in the legislature.[64]

For those left behind, the fourth year was something of a "charade," according to Jacques Alleyn, who perceived that the law school had to scramble to meet the new requirement.[65] The practitioners and judges who had taught the first three years soldiered on for a fourth, and tried to refashion their lectures to reflect a more practical focus. "We had to learn procedure, go to court, and learn how to make a will," explained Claire. "The bar was not organized enough to set up true articling positions, so our professors just tried to switch their classroom lectures from theory to practice."[66] At the end of the year, the Laval students travelled to Montreal to write the province-wide bar exams in a huge university hall. The last exam was scheduled for the full day of 24 June 1952. It was Saint-Jean-Baptiste Day, and a grand holiday parade tied up traffic, delaying the students who were trying to get back after lunch. The anxious Laval group arrived sweaty and dishevelled just in the nick of time, before the examiners closed the doors. That evening, Claire celebrated with fellow students at the Montmartre Cabaret.

---

† clerkship

Claire L'Heureux, call to the bar, 1952.

The bar examination results were released at the end of the summer. Claire did well, graduating *cum laude* once again. The call to the bar took place in the fall of 1952, although Claire has no more memory of it than of her law school graduation. Across the province, only twenty-six women had preceded her to the bar.[67] At least two other young women were called the same day. Marie-Claire Kirkland (later Kirkland-Casgrain) from McGill would become the first woman elected to the Quebec Legislative Assembly, the first female cabinet minister, and the first female judge of the Provincial Court.[68] Réjane Laberge-Colas from the University of Montreal, who had top marks in the bar exam, would become the first woman appointed to the Quebec Superior Court, and the first such appointee in Canada.[69]

Despite the challenges faced by the early female law students, Claire had triumphed academically, excelling at the doctrinal recitations demanded by her professors. She had also used her considerable social skills to overcome some of the disadvantages posed by her gender. Her Laval years were peopled with memorable and eccentric professors, many of whom she admired greatly. But the formalistic legal education they offered did little to prepare future practitioners and judges for a complex legal world. With the exception of Marie-Louis Beaulieu, the Laval professors were more interested in burying the real-world consequences of legal rules than exploring them. Although the *Canadian Charter of Rights and Freedoms* may have been unforeseeable in the 1940s and '50s, its enactment in 1982 would underscore even further the limitations of a traditional legal education.

10
Life Outside of Law School, 1949–52

During Claire's studies, life continued to unfold beyond the grey stone walls of Laval.[1] In 1949, Claire's father was promoted to the post of collector of customs and excise in Quebec City. Paul L'Heureux sold the Rimouski house for more than twice what he had paid for it, and moved his family back to the capital.[2] It was fortuitous because in 1950, a terrible fire broke out at the North Shore Paper Company, jumped the river, and razed a third of Rimouski, destroying 230 buildings and leaving two thousand people homeless. The former L'Heureux home was burnt to the ground.[3] The family was sad but relieved to have escaped the disaster. Paul purchased a newly constructed two-storey house at 1690 Parc de la Chesnaye, and in 1951 Claire joined her family in its new Quebec City home.[4]

Secretarial Woes

Trouble was brewing at Sun Trust, where Claire was the target of sexual harassment. One of the senior managers often came to work drunk and insisted that Claire take dictation in his office, where he made sexual overtures. The problem worsened in her third year of law. "I would try to avoid going to his office but I had no choice," recalled Claire. "At one point, I remember he was physically pushing me. It was too much pressure. I felt so bad ... so dirty. I couldn't stand it."[5] Finally, she mustered the courage to complain to her boss, and was shocked to learn that the older manager's proclivities were common knowledge. They told her it was just part of life. She quit.

Worried that without employment income Claire would not be able to complete her fourth year, her mother, Marguerite, intervened. She arranged for Claire to return to Rimouski for the summer of 1951, to work temporarily as Jules Brillant's secretary. A more permanent solution materialized when Claire returned to Laval that fall: "My mother said, 'If I were you, I would write a little [advertisement] for your secretarial services in the English newspaper, the *Quebec Chronicle-Telegraph*. You will see. Either the English or the Jews will hire you. They are looking for cheap labour.'" Somewhat ruefully, Claire added: "She was racist in that sense."[6]

Almost immediately, there was a reply from M. Pollack Ltd., a department store founded by Jewish businessman Maurice Pollack, who, contrary to Marguerite's negative stereotype, would go on to become one of Quebec's most generous philanthropists. His company offered to employ Claire in the credit department and she accepted. On the heels of the first offer came a second, by way of a letter from Sam Schwarz Bard, a Jewish lawyer who needed a secretary. Claire was inclined to ignore the letter since she already had a job, but Marguerite insisted it would be impolite not to reply. Claire phoned Bard to explain, and he prevailed upon her to

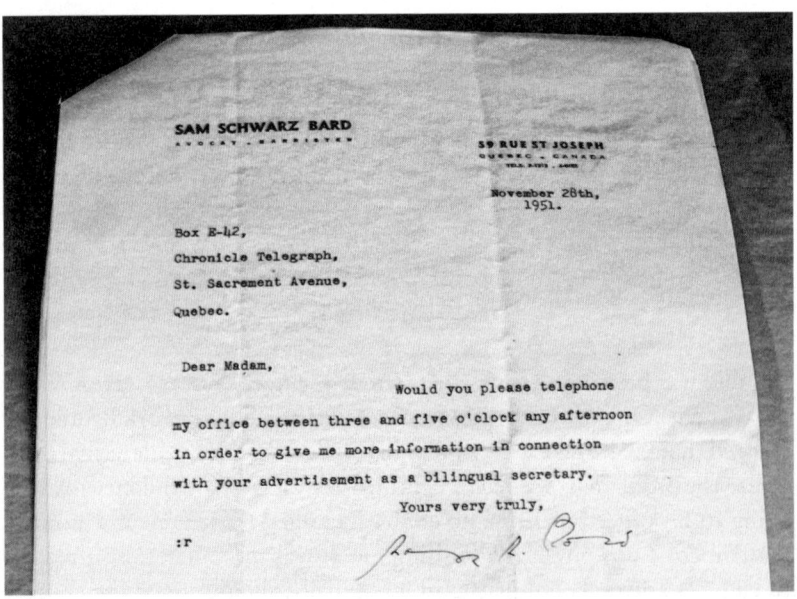

Letter from Sam Schwarz Bard regarding employment interview, 1951.

come to his office. Impressed by Claire's legal background and bilingualism, he offered her a job at higher pay than she had earned at Sun Trust, allaying any suspicions Marguerite had harboured about "cheap labour." "Don't worry," Bard said when she told him that she had accepted another job. "He's my client. I'll settle that."[7] Claire's grateful acceptance of Bard's offer would become pivotal to her career.

Romance: From a Broken Engagement to True Love

Early marriage and pregnancy felled many female law students in Claire's era, with temporary or permanent departure from the profession all too common.[8] Claire did not succumb. Had she done so, her entire career might have taken a different trajectory. This is not to suggest that Claire avoided romantic liaisons throughout her studies. Her female classmates regarded her as more modern than most, an "audacious" young woman who "liked men" and was not afraid to "show it."[9]

One of Claire's more serious relationships involved a man almost ten years older, Gabriel Gagnon, an engineer who worked for Jules Brillant's hydro company. Gaby was much wealthier than the other young men Claire had dated, and invited her to the theatre and out for scenic drives. He was bright and ambitious, and when he proposed with a beautiful diamond ring, she initially accepted. The family was dubious. Although Marguerite believed that Gaby's career offered welcome financial stability, she worried that he was not her daughter's type. Claire's sister Nicole agreed: "He was too plain. He didn't have a large perspective. [He] would count how many lights on the pole ... [He was] very bright [but] not fancy enough for Claire."[10] Claire eventually broke off the engagement, and Marguerite consoled Gaby, telling him that he was a lucky man to be out of what would have been a most unhappy relationship. Claire's classmates agreed.[11]

The breakup was accelerated by the presence of Arthur Dubé, whom Claire met the evening before her job interview with Sam Bard. She and Judith Gamache had agreed to have a drink with two brothers of a convent classmate at the Château Frontenac bar. It was Claire's first introduction to Arthur. The evening was so magical that Claire never forgot what she was wearing: "a little wine-red coat, very simple, and a little black hat."[12] Arthur and Claire became engrossed in conversation and the spirited discussion turned to religion. They began to debate the existence of God, Arthur against and Claire for. Arthur's reply was one often repeated in the

Formal ball with Gabriel Gagnon, Claire's first fiancé.

years ahead: "In the world of the unknown, theories abound."[13] Claire was enchanted by the brilliant debater and Arthur was intrigued by his fiery adversary. Although he could not afford it, he took her to a dance at the Auberge de la Colline and dinner at one of the city's finest restaurants. Looking back, Claire described it as love at first sight.[14]

Thirty-two-year-old Arthur Dubé was born in 1919 in Mont-Joli, east of Rimouski. His father, Joseph Dubé, was a notary and secretary of the municipality. His mother, Josephine Bérubé Dubé, raised seven children. Arthur's sister Cécile had been a classmate of Claire's at the Rimouski and Bellevue convents. His brother Georges-Henri knew Claire because he was studying at Laval to become a notary. Arthur had been the star pupil at the Rimouski Seminary, where his intellectual prowess gained great notoriety. The three brothers who followed him recalled with chagrin that after Arthur won all the scholastic prizes, the younger ones were nicknamed *Arthur deux, Arthur trois,* and *Arthur quatre.*† It was like "inheriting a dynasty," reflected Yves Dubé, who would go on to earn a doctorate in economics at the University of Chicago and become dean of social sciences at Laval.[15]

Yves described his older brother as the most intellectual member of the family, something of a "rebel" as well as a "jovial," "enterprising," and "popular" fellow who loved to debate the philosophy of Thomas Aquinas.[16] At the seminary, Arthur excelled in physics, chemistry, and math. A skillful athlete who trounced his competitors in tennis, he was also a gifted musician who soloed on the saxophone with the college orchestra. Generous to a fault, he lent money to friends any time they asked, even when he had none. He had no interest in material possessions but loved to gamble at the races and at cards. The priests hoped he would follow their path into the priesthood, but Arthur surprised everyone when he became the first in the history of the seminary to pursue graduate studies in science. He earned a bachelor of science degree at Laval, worked briefly for the Department of Mines in Ottawa, and then enrolled at the Carnegie Institute of Technology in Pittsburgh, reputed to be the best in the world for metallurgy. After completing his doctorate in engineering, he returned to Quebec to become a professor in Laval's department of mines and metallurgy at the impoverished salary of $3,000 a year.[17]

Arthur Dubé's courtship of Claire was neither swift nor smooth. The couple had many disagreements, but Claire was always drawn back to Arthur's magnetic conversational ability. "We could talk until four or five in the morning about all kinds of subjects," she explained. "He was the brightest man I ever met."[18] Arthur's brothers worried that Claire was too intelligent to get along with him, and Claire's sisters were equally wary of Arthur as a life mate for Claire.[19] Marguerite L'Heureux was no more enamoured of Arthur than she had been of Gaby. She fretted that marriage would derail Claire's career, although her second daughter, Louise, begged

---

† Arthur the Second, Arthur the Third, Arthur the Fourth

Arthur Dubé graduating from Carnegie Institute of Technology, Pittsburgh.

her to recognize that modern married women no longer automatically left the paid workforce.[20] Marguerite also disapproved of Arthur's heavy drinking, and was alarmed to discover that he had been so disruptive one night at the Château Frontenac bar that Claire was forced to bail him out of jail.[21] Over the next eight years, Claire and Arthur would break up and reconcile repeatedly.

Illness and Death Transform the L'Heureux Family

The L'Heureux family was weighed down by illness, with Marguerite's multiple sclerosis taking a heavy toll on her physical capacity to look after herself or her home. Lucie, the third-born L'Heureux sister, who disliked studying at the convent, was designated as caregiver, and in 1950 arrangements were made for her to return home to assist her mother full-time.[22] But Lucie herself became desperately ill and died of heart failure at the age of twenty, on 1 July 1952, one week after Claire's final bar exam.

Lucie had been diagnosed with rheumatic fever as a child, which some cited as the possible cause of her terminal illness. Some also speculated that the rheumatic fever might have been the result of a childhood operation to remove her tonsils. Dr. Victor Lepage, Marguerite's cousin, brought his instruments to the house, attached anesthetic masks to his four patients, performed the operations on the dining room table, and then left. "It was *à la mode*† at the time," explained Claire. "I always wondered whether that was the source of Lucie's rheumatic fever, whether he transmitted a virus or some bacterial infection that destroyed her heart."[23] Others wondered whether Lucie had been born with a malfunctioning heart valve, or whether she might have had scarlet fever as a child. "We really didn't go to the doctor at all," explained her sister Louise. "Nobody picked it up, [although] she was never well."[24] Pericarditis caused by viral, bacterial, or fungal infection was most likely the actual cause.[25] Claire always regretted that no proper diagnosis was made in Lucie's lifetime and that penicillin was discovered too late to cure her sister.

Lucie's illness was initially misdiagnosed as depression, and her wheezing and gasping for breath as psychosomatic. The exercise prescribed as a cure only made her more fatigued. Her illness may have affected her studies, for she consistently stood at the bottom of her class.[26] No one realized how ill she was until the spring of 1952. Then, after she had spent a month in the hospital, the doctors said that nothing could be done and Lucie went home to die. Marguerite was too ill to nurse her sick daughter, so Paul called Louise, who was practising as a nurse in New Rochelle, New York. Louise had been married two months earlier, and her young husband had just left for service in Korea. Summoned home in May, Louise took the first plane back.[27]

At home, she shouldered much of the physical and emotional round-the-clock care, ministering to both Marguerite and Lucie, administering

---

† in fashion

morphine injections, cooking all the meals, and taking care of the house. The other sisters were of little assistance. Claire, studying day and night for the bar exams and working midday at Sam Bard's law office, was home only for meals. Nicole was out much of the time, studying at the Bellevue convent. Louise searched all of her medical books for answers, but no one seemed able to diagnose what was wrong. She watched horrified as her sister's hair turned grey overnight. She spent hours at her sister's bedside, listening as the young girl expressed her sadness about failing several grades and never completing her *baccalauréat*.[28] Lucie's death was extremely traumatic for the whole family. Marguerite was overcome with grief when the open casket was set up in the living room and neighbours and friends came to pay their respects.[29]

Lucie's death coincided with Claire's decision to cut her ties with the Catholic Church. She was angered by the behaviour of the priest who was present at the time. "The priest came and told her she was going to die. Why was he so cruel? [There was] no reason to tell her this. We were devastated." It was the last sharp blow to Claire's waning religious zeal: "I resented that so much ... I revolted against the church."[30] This view strengthened with time: "I'm against religion, all religions, not only the Catholic one. I think they cause wars and other conflicts. I think religion is destructive. I'm totally agnostic. I don't believe in anything. The one thing that remained with me, as it did for most French-Canadians [who left the church], is the portrait of the community coming together."[31] It was that sense of community, she said, that ultimately shaped her belief that "collective rights" could be "more important than individual rights."[32]

Lucie's tragically premature death never lost its capacity to move Claire to tears: "I think of her very often. Our deaths don't leave us, especially as we grow older. You have a tendency to regret things more. That was probably the greatest pain that I ever had."[33]

Nicole, the youngest daughter, now took on the role of long-term caregiver to her invalid mother. Apparently, the family never discussed assigning this responsibility to her; it was just assumed. Nicole's sisters characterized their youngest sibling as an individual with a keen intellect and marvellous sense of humour, one who had inherited her mother's many creative talents, as well as a strikingly optimistic personality. In 1954, she followed Claire into law school, although she insisted that she was not simply following her sister's lead but had independently chosen this career because the class schedule made it possible for her to continue caring for her mother full-time. Except for two hours at class early in the morning and two hours later in the afternoon, she could monitor her mother's needs at home for most of the day.[34]

Called to the bar in 1958, Nicole continued to care for her mother while grading papers for professors who taught the bar admission course and helping faculty members conduct research and prepare lectures. When Laval began offering a master of law degree, Nicole was one of the first graduates, in 1964. In 1969, she joined the faculty of law at Laval, one of the first two female faculty members the law school appointed that year.[35] It was a route that Claire herself might have taken had she been the one required to care for her mother, and had Sam Bard's intercession not come at a critical juncture.

Law Practice

11
Entry
A Law Firm Job, 1952

"*Mlle Claire L'Heureux est reçue avocate*"† read the bold announcement that appeared in the Quebec newspaper *L'Événement Journal* in the fall of 1952. The paper spelled the traditional *"avocat"* with a feminine *"e,"* and congratulated the daughter of Lieutenant-Colonel and Madame Paul-H. L'Heureux for being one of fifty-one candidates who had passed the bar exams.[1] The job she took next would lay the foundation for all that followed. Experience in private practice was the key to professional influence and judicial appointment; without it, L'Heureux could never have made the mark she did on Canadian legal history. But it was an era of brutal gender discrimination. In 1952, out of 239 lawyers practising in Quebec City, 238 were male. L'Heureux would become the *only woman* from her class to embark upon private law practice in the city that year, and the second woman ever.[2]

The Elusiveness of Jobs: "No Place for Us"

Getting started in law was a difficult proposition for anyone, male or female, who did not have an elite family background or legal connections.[3]

Explanatory note: I have referred to Justice L'Heureux-Dubé previously as "Claire" when describing her youth and her student years. After her call to the bar in 1952, I switch to "L'Heureux" in recognition of her independent adulthood. After 1957, I use her married name, "L'Heureux-Dubé."
† "Miss Claire L'Heureux is admitted as a lawyer"

One of L'Heureux's Laval classmates described it as a "closed society, like the mafia."[4] Male law grads with coveted connections used familial social capital to secure entry. Their female counterparts noted cynically that some male classmates also courted and married women whose fathers were lawyers and judges, in hopes of obtaining that first job offer.[5] Securing that all-important first job was even tougher for women.[6]

Laval classmate William Tetley explained: "It was pretty hard being a girl. The law was made in those days by men for men. Women stayed home and had babies."[7] Raymond Lessard, who began legal practice in 1962, recognized that women "were received as foreigners" who had "invaded a male profession."[8] Louis LeBel, who was admitted to the bar ten years after L'Heureux and practised in Quebec City until he embarked on a judicial career that took him to the Supreme Court, recalled that male lawyers "were uncomfortable with the idea of women lawyers. The senior partners had been raised and lived and practised law at a time when women were not even allowed to join the Quebec bar. So they had this understanding that the place of women was essentially at home."[9]

L'Heureux sent out three job applications. She wrote to inquire about a position as a junior lawyer with the federal Department of Justice. The joint secretary of the Civil Service Commission responded that the minister wished her to know that there were no vacancies for women.[10] Her request to work as an agent or secretary with the Foreign Service was similarly rejected. Her application to the United Nations International Labour Organization in Geneva was also unsuccessful. The ILO replied that it did not employ women.[11] With three rejections in hand, L'Heureux had no idea what to do next.

Her self-confidence was so bruised by the realities of the gendered job market that she chose not to apply to law firms. Many of her contemporaries felt the same way. The first female Laval law graduate, Jeanne D'Arc Lemay, called to the bar in 1946, had thought her chances for a job in a law firm were so slim that she never bothered to apply: "There was no other woman out there. Maybe I didn't have the courage."[12] Calin Morin, called to the bar in 1953, recalled that when one of her Laval professors inquired what she planned to do after graduation, she told him she had no job. Although his law firm hired male graduates, he "certainly didn't propose a position for me," she explained. "None of the professors were interested in what we did after. They had such closed minds. It was so new to have women in the law school. I should have told him, 'Well, do you want to hire me?' But we lacked self-confidence. Nobody thought they had the right to go and ask."[13]

In an ironic twist of fate, L'Heureux's great break, the one that would set her successful career in motion, occurred because of the secretarial detour that she had taken to finance her legal studies. The dictating, typing, and filing services she rendered at Sam Schwarz Bard's law office to finance her last year of studies provided the opening. Had Bard been a different sort of employer, he might have kept her on in a secretarial capacity, benefiting from her legal knowledge while compensating her at the lower wages of a clerical worker. Instead, he made her a full-time lawyer immediately. It was something she had not thought to request. It was not a matter they discussed. Bard simply converted her position to that of a lawyer, joining the long line of Jewish lawyers who made room for female and racialized candidates across the country.[14]

L'Heureux's classmate Calin Morin was impressed: "Claire was lucky to go to the [Sam Bard] firm. Jewish people were open-minded. I don't think French Canadian lawyers would have given her the same chance."[15] Reflecting upon the significance of Bard's generosity, L'Heureux said: "He hired me at a time when women lawyers couldn't get a job. I accepted his offer and it made my life."[16]

The First Laval Cohort: Twenty Women-at-Law, 1945–54

Claire L'Heureux's unusual good fortune was shared by few of the first twenty female law students from Laval.[17] Some dropped out before qualifying, others left their careers for marriage, and still others were diverted to positions understood to be of lower status, such as jobs in government or corporations. The few who were intrepid enough to make cold calls on law firms, seeking coveted positions in private practice, were told flat-out that law firms would never hire women, and that clients would never agree to retain female professionals. There were no laws prohibiting discrimination in employment, and the early women were too few in number, and their entry into the profession too fresh, to challenge the discriminatory professional environment. The Quiet Revolution would not usher in significant change until the 1960s and '70s, too late to make a difference for the first Laval grads.[18]

Of these first twenty women, only five others managed to join Claire L'Heureux in securing those all-important first jobs in private practice.[19] Ginette Fournier, the first, opened a solo practice on boulevard Langelier, in the same building where her brother François practised law. That proved to be no ticket to entry, since François's firm never hired his sister. Her

Marguerite (Margot) Choquette, one of Laval's first female law graduates, photo taken in 1950.

practice struggled, and by 1957 she gave it up for social work. An unsung hero whose name has been forgotten by history, the first woman to practise in Quebec City, who took the courageous step of opening her own law firm, never crossed professional paths with Claire L'Heureux. Her imprint on the profession was so tenuous that L'Heureux was unaware she had even practised law in the city.[20]

Marguerite (Margot) Choquette followed Ginette Fournier and Claire L'Heureux into practice in 1953. The Choquette family name was legendary in legal circles. Margot's grandfather and father were judges, and four of her brothers became lawyers. She was the only one of the twenty to land a position with a well-established law firm.[21] Thérèse Lemay-Lavoie was the first to practise outside the capital. After the hiatus in her legal studies due to marriage, she moved with her surgeon husband to Saint-Georges-de-Beauce, where, in 1955, she became the first woman to set up a solo practice there.²²

Gabrielle Vallée entered private practice in 1956. Although some anticipated that she would practise within government, since her father had served as Quebec's deputy minister of public works, she joined a law firm that three of her male classmates had opened a year earlier. The firm added her as an equal partner at once. Her fellow Laval graduates remembered Gaby Vallée as bright, gregarious, and ambitious. She was someone who stood apart from the other women: "one of the boys," and very much at home in the "boys' club."²³ Louise Galipeault, admitted to the bar in 1955,

Louise Galipeault, another of Laval's first female law graduates, on her admission to the Quebec Bar, 1955.

also entered practice in 1956. Her way was smoothed by family connections. Her grandfather was chief justice of Quebec, and she joined the law office of her father, Langis Galipeault.[24]

Claire L'Heureux may have been one of the favoured six who landed a position in private practice, but it was Sam Bard's initiative that took her there. Her first job with him was "like gold." She had had no capital to set up a practice on her own, as Ginette Fournier had, and reflecting back, she added: "I would never have done that. I didn't have the self-confidence."[25] Unlike Margot Choquette and Louise Galipeault, she had no connections to pave the way into established family firms. Nor did she have a professional husband to take her away to a smaller town and support her while she hung out her shingle, as Thérèse Lemay-Lavoie did. And the prospect of hitching her star to a group of male classmates, as Gaby Vallée did, never occurred to her. "I was not in the gang," she explained, laughing about it years later.[26]

Decades later, in 1974, L'Heureux chaired a panel at a conference in Windsor, Ontario. The implications of career choice must have been starkly on display before the burgeoning group of female law students who had travelled from across the country to meet together at the first Canadian Women and the Law event. At one end of the table sat Sydney Robins, then head of the Ontario bar. He spoke about a new equality resolution that the Law Society had just passed. At the other end sat Joan Sullivan, a legal secretary who had left the picket line in front of her Windsor law firm to speak about her efforts to unionize her fellow secretaries. After the presentations, L'Heureux stood to thank the panellists. Robins remembered the peals of laughter that greeted her quip that Joan Sullivan would have made a great lawyer and that Syd Robins would have made a great legal secretary.[27] The gender implications that convulsed the audience that day were only just becoming visible. In 1952, when Claire L'Heureux took her first steps into the practice of law, she was a woman on the front line of career transformation.

12
Sam Bard
The Man behind the Employment Offer

Claire L'Heureux may have been the second woman to enter private practice in Quebec City, but Sam Bard was one of only two Jews.[1] Belying once again her mother Marguerite's depiction of Jews as miserly, he raised L'Heureux's salary to $100 a month and urged her to develop her own client base.[2] She could keep 75 percent of any income she brought in, paying Bard 25 percent for overhead. "It was very fair. He was not making a lot of money and I was assured of a living wage," recalled L'Heureux.[3] In an era when men and women were rarely paid equally, it was the same arrangement that Bard made with the male lawyers who worked with him.[4] Years later, he quietly downplayed his role. "I wasn't the kind of person to make a distinction," he said. "I just wanted someone capable and she turned out to be very capable indeed."[5] In retrospect, he might also have conceded that he was just a little mesmerized by the vivacious young girl in the wine-red coat and little black hat who had answered his ad for a secretary a year earlier.

What kind of person was Sam Bard, whose outsider status was on a par with that of the woman he hired? How had he come to establish a law practice in the city? And how did the position of the Jewish community in Quebec influence the legal practice that L'Heureux joined?

Sam S. Bard, founder of L'Heureux's first law firm.

Anti-Semitism in Quebec: *"À bas les juifs!"*†

In the late-nineteenth century, Bard's parents, Rose Ortenberg and Jacob Schwarzbard, fled from pogroms, persecution, and war in Romania and Russia and settled in Quebec City along with seventy-five other Jewish families from Eastern Europe.[6] The first families started as impoverished peddlers but soon opened small shops selling groceries, millinery, and dry goods, as well as tailored and ready-to-wear clothing.[7] Bard's parents did not flourish. His father's businesses often failed; his mother suffered long-term illness.[8] The Jewish presence in the city was a contested one. Bard's elderly grandfather, David Ortenberg, was swarmed and beaten by an unruly mob in 1910. The incident was one of the disruptive events that sparked the famous *Affaire Plamondon,* when a Quebec City notary initiated a campaign against Jewish individuals and property and the Jewish community filed a lawsuit for group defamation. There were no Jewish lawyers in Quebec City then, so Montreal lawyer Sam Jacobs, the same man who would later take the bar to court over its refusal to admit women, acted as counsel. The lawsuit, ultimately successful, may have helped the Jewish community recognize the role that law could play in stemming discrimination.[9]

Samuel Schwarzbard was born in Quebec City on 13 August 1913, one year before the legal victory.[10] He attended the Protestant English-speaking Quebec High School along with the other Jewish children.[11] He showed intellectual promise early, skipping two grades and taking the Governor-General's Medal in mathematics. The Jewish community made every effort to assist its second-generation children to obtain university and professional degrees, recognizing that self-employment was one way of evading pervasive employment discrimination.[12] Despite his family's impoverishment, Bard obtained a BA from McGill University in 1933, freelancing with the *Montreal Gazette* to help pay the bills. His horizons expanded significantly when he lodged with a working-class French Canadian family and socialized with international students of diverse racial backgrounds.[13] Next, he enrolled at Laval law school,[14] hoping to improve his fluency in French and to secure a position in a profession that would allow independent self-employment.[15] He completed his LL.L. degree in 1936, the only Jewish member of his class, and was admitted to the bar that same year.[16]

For Sam Bard, getting started in law after his admission to the bar posed almost as many challenges as it did for the first women. Discrimination

---

† "Down with Jews!"

barred Jews from all jobs with French Canadian or Anglo-Canadian law firms in Quebec. The public service and private corporations were no more welcoming. The 1930s economic doldrums were soul destroying for lawyers of any linguistic and religious background, but especially for Jewish lawyers in Quebec.[17] Sydney Lazarovitz, who opened a law practice in Quebec City in 1932, had to close his office for five years during the heart of the Depression.[18] Bard sat out the bad years until 1938, when he set up as a sole practitioner on rue Saint-Joseph.[19] He used the name Sam Schwarz Bard, derived from his family name of Schwarzbard. He would later shorten it further to Sam S. Bard.[20]

In 1942, Sam Bard married McGill arts graduate Brauna Lax, whose family owned one of the larger manufacturing businesses in Quebec City.[21] Her aunt, Clara Goodman, appears to have been the first Jewish woman to graduate from McGill law school. Although Goodman was never admitted to the bar, she and Bard became very close friends, and he admired her greatly.[22] To augment his minimal legal earnings, Bard went to work for his wife's father in the family business. It was a "brief and unhappy" time, for his personality did not mesh well with the trade.[23] In 1943, he closed his law office and joined the Canadian Forces, first as an artillery officer and then as a military judge advocate in Ottawa.[24]

He was thus away from Quebec City during the incendiary explosion of May 1944, when arsonists torched the new synagogue on the eve of its opening. The culprits were never caught.[25] The province was still reeling from the vilification of Jews that had peaked in the 1930s under the fanatical direction of journalist Adrien Arcand, who was sometimes labelled "the Canadian Führer."[26] Discrimination against Jews was so pervasive that when Pierre Elliott Trudeau wrote an anti-Semitic play as a student in 1938, its production at his Montreal Jesuit college was deemed a "great triumph" by priests, parents, and students.[27]

Many Jewish residents had hoped for more protection in Quebec City, where their numbers were so few that they were often viewed as a curiosity rather than a threat.[28] But Sam Bard's daughter Perry sensed that her parents were "walking on eggshells" in Quebec. "In small Jewish communities, we were on display. People knew who we were. If we made one false move, there would be trouble."[29] The Quebec City Jewish cemetery was regularly vandalized, with tombstones broken and defaced. Gentile parents disciplined unruly children by threatening to *"les donner au juif."*†

---

† "give them to the Jew"

The parish priest preached *"l'achat chez nous,"*† urging Catholics not to shop in Jewish stores. Jewish schoolchildren were taunted with chants of *"Maudit juif"*‡ and *"À bas les juifs!"* and were occasionally forced to run the gauntlet of Gentile bullies on their way home.³⁰

The Optimism of Sam Bard

Anti-Semitism was something that Sam Bard refused to dwell upon. "The world was divided into English and French, with a little Jewish subset," recalled his son Joel, "[but my father] didn't like to talk about our status there as minorities. He believed in integration."³¹ Perry Bard noted that her father would admit that he had been stoned as a Jew on the way to school, but, in the same breath, deny that there was any anti-Semitism in Quebec City. "If it was pouring out, my father would say the sun will be out tomorrow," she added.³²

Bard's optimism was strengthened when, with the close of the Second World War and the wider disclosure of the tragedy of the Holocaust, public anti-Semitism became less respectable.³³ He reopened his Quebec City office in 1948, at 771 rue Saint-Joseph est, in the back office of the Pollack Department Store. He was just getting on his feet when he hired L'Heureux, but his path was already set. He would work continuously from the rue Saint-Joseph premises, steadily building up a general practice with two or three other lawyers over the next twenty years.³⁴

When L'Heureux joined his law office, Bard was thirty-eight years old, with pale blue eyes and a neatly trimmed moustache, of short but lithe athletic build. As a male authority figure, he was markedly different from L'Heureux's father. In contrast to Paul L'Heureux's domineering, militaristic demeanour, contemporaries described Bard as "a gentleman," who was "kind," "gentle," "humane," "refined," "well-mannered," "steady," "charming," "courteous," and "dignified."³⁵ He may have been the first Quebec City lawyer to hire a woman, and he was familiar with feminist authors such as Mary Wollstonecraft and Simone de Beauvoir, but he was also socially conservative, a man who preferred that his wife stay at home rather than establish her own career.³⁶ And he was not above warning young women that it was difficult to mix legal careers with motherhood.³⁷

---

† "buy at home"
‡ "Damn Jew"

Sam Bard skiing on the Plains of Abraham, 1930s.

He was fluent in French, English, Hebrew, and Yiddish. He was an avid skier, artistic, musical, widely read, and always impeccably dressed. He valued clarity and meticulous precision. He wrote poetry, could recite Racine and Molière by heart, and became a skilled calligrapher. Although he was understated and quiet, someone who never raised his voice, he was also an accomplished public speaker. More spiritual than religious, he was fascinated all his life with the scholarly commentaries on the Talmud. A freethinker who was open-minded in his views, he helped found the Amitiés Judéo-Chrétiennes, one of the only inter-faith activities undertaken with Jewish, Protestant, and Roman Catholic leaders.[38]

Observers sometimes described Quebec as comprising "three solitudes": French, English, and Jewish.[39] But within the small Jewish and Anglo communities in Quebec City, Bard stood out for his Francophile perspectives.[40] He embraced French culture and the French Canadian community so fully that L'Heureux described him as speaking better French and having more knowledge about French literature than she did. His relatives said that he was completely comfortable in both French and English cultures, but identified first and foremost as French.[41]

Perhaps because of his fluency, Bard was one of the first to gain acceptance within the wider community. He was among the first Jews to be admitted to the Quebec Winter Club and the Club de la Garnison.[42] In 1956, he became the first Jew appointed as a part-time faculty member at Laval law school. There he impressed a generation of law students with his well-organized courses on bills of exchange. One of his students who went on to become a professor at McGill recalled that Bard never wasted class time boasting about his professional victories, and used innovative pedagogical techniques to focus on practical matters instead.[43] Bard's nephew Steven Katkin, who later studied law at Laval, recalled that his uncle never rolled his "r's" properly, causing some students to mimic his accent, but emphasized that Bard was an excellent instructor, whose passion for law was obvious.[44] In 1961, Sam Bard would be named Queen's Counsel. This honorary designation was traditionally reserved for the most eminent jurists, but it is worth noting that it came only after the death of Duplessis.[45]

Mentorship: "We Were the Perfect Match"

Claire L'Heureux described Bard as an exceptional supervisor. In an era when the transfer of most professional skills occurred outside the classroom, ambitious young lawyers were completely dependent upon their seniors for mentoring. With trademark wit, Ian Binnie, a Toronto barrister who would later join L'Heureux on the Supreme Court, explained:

> The junior lawyers followed the senior lawyers around, and eventually we grew into mutant copies. So Walter Williston's juniors learned how to mumble, some of Barry Pepper's juniors acquired fake English accents, and George Finlayson's juniors developed what today would be called an "attitude problem" … I had the privilege of articling for Bert MacKinnon, who was a perfect gentleman.[46]

With so much riding on this role modelling, mentoring across boundaries of gender, religion, and ethnicity came to pose special challenges.[47] Yet one-on-one support was the *sine qua non* that distinguished the early women who succeeded in private practice from many who did not.[48] Some relationships blossomed magnificently; others were characterized by discriminatory treatment and sexual harassment.

L'Heureux's assessment of Sam Bard was that he navigated the barriers of gender with unfailing sensitivity. "He trusted me, he supported me, he pushed me, he protected me [and he] sheltered me," she recalled.[49] Bard bolstered her self-esteem, insisting that she had a great future. He taught her to write with acuity, borrowing skills honed during his journalism days: "He was always telling me to be more succinct, more direct. He could shorten anything and write so every word mattered. And he never left anything unchecked."[50] Most importantly, she added, "We discussed everything. He would say, 'We win the war with details.' I said, 'Yes, but that's not my line.' He was a small comma guy. I was big picture. We were the perfect match."[51] It was the opposite of what many young women lawyers complain of today, being forced to take on the "handmaiden" role, consigned to tedious detail work while senior men meet with important clients and handle the big files.[52] Claire L'Heureux found in Sam Bard the perfect supervisor. The two became professionally and personally intertwined. They functioned seamlessly as a unit.

And what of the fact that her employer and mentor was a Jew? Some of L'Heureux's classmates marvelled that she had accepted such a position. Philippe Casgrain emphasized that Quebec was "full of prejudice. It was damn tough for her. She was a woman, and then she chose to practise with a Jewish firm!"[53] Anti-Semitism was rampant, according to William Tetley: "That Claire L'Heureux-Dubé was obliged to indenture herself in a Jewish law office" indicated "the general attitude at the time in Quebec towards women *and* Jews."[54] Roch Bolduc added that L'Heureux's decision was not *"la mode"*† in Quebec.[55] L'Heureux was also clearly aware of the anti-Semitism pervading the wider community. She recognized that joining a Jewish firm would pose challenges, but she downplayed the problem.

Years later, she asserted that her family did not share the level of anti-Semitism that affected some of their neighbours. "I knew that Jews were not very much accepted at the time, but no one in my family had ever said I shouldn't work for a Jew," she added. "Although we didn't talk about

---

† "in fashion"

it at home, I think they were just happy I had a job."[56] Her sister Louise confirmed that the matter was not a topic of discussion at home, that none of the family questioned Claire L'Heureux about the fact that her employer and clients were Jewish.[57] While everyone was undoubtedly happy that she had any legal job at all, the characterization of the family as less anti-Semitic than others seems to be something of an optimistic gloss. This was a family where the girls were warned not to enter or shop in a Rimouski store that their mother, Marguerite, mistakenly thought was owned by Jews. The fact that there were no Jews in Rimouski had not stopped their Catholic bishop from preaching against "Christ-killers." Sam Bard was the first Jewish person Claire L'Heureux had ever met. Their relationship would inspire in her a deep respect for Jewish culture, but overcoming the pervasive anti-Semitic environment that surrounded them would be a more complicated matter.[58]

13
Business Law Practice

The Quebec City bar that Claire L'Heureux joined in 1952 was a conservative and close-knit group of 239 lawyers, representing 15 percent of the province's total.[1] At the top end was Prime Minister Louis St. Laurent's firm, the largest in the city at nine lawyers, which managed the corporate needs of international pulp and paper companies and English financial interests, and drew lots of work through well-honed political connections.[2] Gagnon et de Billy was the next largest, a veritable family dynasty with three Gagnons and three de Billys.[3] At the bottom were eighty-five sole practitioners who scrambled for clients injured in automobile accidents and handled petty collections. Some recalled pleading cases for debts of $10 a month.[4] Sam Bard had been among the solo practitioners until one year earlier, when he expanded to a two-man firm.[5] With L'Heureux's name added to the masthead, his became one of the mid-sized offices in the city.[6]

L'Heureux purchased space in the newspaper *Le Soleil* to announce the opening of her law practice. On 29 September 1952, a front-page photograph showed her in barrister's gown, with an article describing her educational background, academic honours, and affiliation with the Bard law firm.[7] The editor sent her a copy of the announcement, along with his wishes for *"succès dans votre carrière."*[†,8] A short piece in *L'Événement Journal*

---

† "success in your career"

Business Law Practice 151

titled *"Charmant précédent à la cour du Recorder"*† credited L'Heureux with adding *"un élément féminin"*‡ to the court proceeding.⁹

Despite its growing size, Sam Bard's firm was neither top-end nor specialized, and no one pretended otherwise.¹⁰ For the duration of his practice, he rented the same space on the third floor of the Édifice Florence, a building attached to the back of the Pollack Department Store. The front door opened into a simple waiting room lined with a row of grey metal filing cabinets, behind which sat two or three secretaries hard at work. There was no receptionist. The dockets consisted of pink file cards, with jotted handwritten notes summarizing the work performed. The rent was cheap and the no-frills decor matched: no carpet, no art, no fancy furniture. It was modest, tidy, and clean. The bottom line reflected as much. The firm's accountant marvelled that Bard kept the operating costs to 42 percent of revenue, significantly below the typical 60 percent of the city's other legal offices.¹¹

The relationship between Sam Bard and Sydney Lazarovitz, the other Jewish lawyer in Quebec City, was amicable but distant. Born in 1908, Lazarovitz had graduated from Quebec High School, Bishop's College, and Laval law school, and had been admitted to the bar in 1931.¹² He practised one floor below Bard, on the second floor of the Édifice Florence. Lazarovitz's gregarious and flamboyant demeanour contrasted with Bard's reserved manner, and he took on clients whom Bard refused because he was suspicious of their integrity. "People used to say, if you want an honest lawyer, go to the third floor," laughed L'Heureux. "If you want a trickster, go to the second."¹³ Some of the gossip directed at Lazarovitz may have been tinged with anti-Semitism, because he was more publicly linked with the Jewish community.¹⁴ But both lawyers took their share of both impoverished and paying clients, and both prospered.¹⁵

THE CLIENTS OF A BILINGUAL JEWISH FIRM

In its early years, the Bard firm had few opportunities to build a French Canadian clientele. "It was a Jewish firm," emphasized L'Heureux, "so there would be a number of French Canadians who would never deal with them."¹⁶ The anti-Semitism of the English did not seem to constrain their

---

† "Charming precedent at the Recorder's Court"
‡ "a woman's touch"

Sydney Lazarovitz, Quebec City lawyer.

business in equal measure, probably because there were so few Anglophone lawyers in the city. The fluently bilingual Sam Bard serviced many clients from the small British and Irish populations, as well as people referred by the American and British consulates. By 1960, Bard had secured the Bank of Montreal branch nearest the office as a client as well.[17]

The majority of Bard's clients were drawn from the Jewish business sector, including grocers, tailors, butchers, jewellery store owners, real estate operators, pharmacists, physicians – and even a bordello proprietor. The mainstay of the firm, however, was Maurice Pollack, a brilliant entrepreneur who was often referred to as *"le doyen de la communauté juive de Québec."*[†, 18] Born in Konela, Ukraine, in 1885, Maurice arrived in Quebec City in 1902 *sans le sou*.[‡] He started as an itinerant salesman, purchasing

---

† "the dean of Quebec City's Jewish community"
‡ penniless

goods in Montreal and peddling them throughout the countryside. His satisfied customers reported that he never exaggerated and his wares were exceptional. Pollack plowed his slim profits into a men's clothing store that he opened on rue Saint-Joseph four years later. With the help of his wife, Rivka Tarantour Pollack, who set up women's and children's departments, the store grew to occupy almost all of the space between rue Saint-Joseph, rue du Pont, and boulevard Charest.[19]

In 1931, the architect for one of Pollack's new buildings inscribed the Star of David on the grillwork above the front door. The Catholic clergy asked Pollack to remove the Jewish religious symbol. When he refused, they prophesied that the building would topple in divine retribution. A church-sponsored boycott that lasted for nine months almost destroyed Pollack's business. He survived by taking his name signs off the delivery trucks and paper bags, and convincing loyal customers to send in orders by telephone or mail. When the priests discovered that Pollack had also discontinued his regular contributions to church funds, they called off the boycott and the store survived.[20]

Pollack was a driven man whose success came from innovation, risk taking, and overwork. In 1940, the federal government put out a call for bids for battledress uniforms. None of the other merchants would bid because machines and labour were in short supply. Pollack bought up second-hand machinery in New York, and convinced more than a thousand workers to move to Quebec City to work in his three new Mastercraft uniform factories. At one point, he became financially overextended and his creditors offered to settle on lower terms. Pollack refused, insisting he would pay off the loans at 100 percent, and he did. The wartime venture eventually brought him his greatest business success.[21] By 1950, he was running his retail store from a six-floor international-style emporium, one of the largest companies in Quebec City.[22]

By the time he brought his legal work to the Bard firm, Pollack's needs were multifaceted: he was "into everything," according to L'Heureux.[23] A demanding client, he would telephone repeatedly, insisting that he speak with Sam Bard personally. L'Heureux remembered his larger-than-life presence when a union was attempting to get certified to represent the workers at the Mastercraft premises. "The union agent would come [to our office] and they would meet. Pollack would be shouting. The guy from the union lost consciousness – he fainted. I had to get the water. Sam would say to me, 'Don't worry, it's only fake.' I was frightened. Pollack frightened the poor man who was in charge of the union. When they started to win, he closed the factory."[24] Pollack may have been ruthless in his business

Maurice Pollack, client of the Bard firm.

dealings, but he was also renowned as a philanthropist whose generosity stemmed from his religious principles.[25] The Bard law firm incorporated the Pollock Foundation in 1955, and under Sam Bard's supervision it became one of the largest charitable organizations in the province.[26]

Occasionally the Bard firm ventured into entirely new areas. Its most notorious clients were the Jehovah's Witnesses, members of a religious sect that abhorred organized religion and claimed that Roman Catholicism represented Satan on earth and that the Pope was the devil's main instrument of seduction. At the request of the Quebec wing of the Catholic Church, Premier Maurice Duplessis launched 1,665 prosecutions against the Witnesses between 1946 and 1953, in a battle he described as a "War without Mercy." The religious proselytizers were charged with blasphemous libel, sedition, disturbing the peace, and breaching municipal ordinances. They fought back in court.[27] Leading the defence was W. Glen How, a Jehovah's Witness who had been called to the Ontario bar in 1944.[28] He solicited help from counsel across Canada, but the pool of lawyers willing to champion the unpopular defendants was small.[29] In Quebec City, Sam Bard volunteered his office as command central.

Bard recognized that it was a dangerous position for a Jewish lawyer to take, but he was incensed that Duplessis would send his thugs out to disrupt religious meetings.[30] His son, Joel, remembered that it was a bold move "to step out of line that way, to take on the city and Duplessis."[31] Bard's nephew Steven Katkin recalled that other lawyers publicly admitted that to represent Jehovah's Witnesses meant to risk losing their law practice completely.[32] Bard warned L'Heureux that she should be concerned for her own position. "He said that I was free to leave his office if I could not work on such issues because I was Roman Catholic, and that he was worried I would suffer harassment."[33] She was adamant that she wanted not only to stay but also to help. She had watched Glen How argue a Jehovah's Witness case when she was still at Laval, and was fascinated by the man. She participated in lengthy discussions about legal strategy, and watched mesmerized as How cross-examined Duplessis. "Glen How was a very handsome man [and] a superb lawyer. A master of interrogation. For Duplessis, it was personal animosity towards Jehovah's Witnesses. To have Duplessis in the box took some guts. I don't think any lawyer from Quebec would have done that."[34] But there were personal consequences for the Quebec lawyers who assisted. "There were death threats and letters," L'Heureux explained, but neither she nor Bard backed down.[35]

The firm's most important contribution to the Jehovah's Witnesses cause was the *Saumur* case, which began as a challenge to a municipal ordinance banning the distribution of literature without a permit from the chief of police. A Witness named Laurier Saumur had been arrested numerous times for violating the flyer by-law. With Glen How and Sam Bard as co-counsel, Saumur claimed that the prohibition interfered with his freedom of religion and speech. The Quebec government argued that the sect did not constitute a religion, that its acts were incompatible with peace and order, and that the by-law simply prohibited distribution of literature in the streets. In October 1953, a slim majority of the Supreme Court of Canada found in favour of Saumur. Although only a minority of the judges endorsed How's and Bard's arguments, *Saumur* has been credited with advancing civil liberties and paving the way for the *Canadian Bill of Rights* and the *Canadian Charter of Rights and Freedoms*.[36]

L'Heureux's interaction with her law firm's clients was minimal at first, because she was at a distinct gender disadvantage. One of her colleagues bluntly explained that "some people hesitated to consult with a woman."[37]

L'Heureux described the problem: "They would come to the office, see me, and say, 'I want to see the lawyer.' At the beginning I would say, 'I'm a lawyer.' They would say, 'I want to see a man.' It didn't bother me. I would say, 'They will learn.'"[38] The impetus for the change of heart was often Sam Bard. "He would say to his clients, 'Go see Claire. She'll settle that. She's better than me. She will be faster. I've too much to do here.' He integrated me into the Jewish community."[39] The integration did not include inviting L'Heureux to bar mitzvahs and other social gatherings, but the Jewish clients came to accept her as their lawyer.

One of her first files was an unqualified disaster. The client was defending a civil claim for damages that the plaintiff had commenced in Sherbrooke. The client wanted the action transferred to Quebec City. It should have been an open-and-shut case, since the law was clear that Quebec City was the proper venue. L'Heureux retained a Sherbrooke lawyer to act as her agent, and asked him to file a jurisdictional objection with the Sherbrooke court. The lawyer failed to file the motion in time. "I remember it so clearly," she exclaimed. "This lawyer that we had chosen as correspondent – he was even the bar president – he was sloppy and let it drag, so we lost it. I was responsible for the file, so I felt it was my fault. It was expensive for the client. I lost the case, my first one!"[40] To her great embarrassment, when she learned of the fiasco, she started to cry and had to leave the office.

Crying was then, and still remains, a gendered experience. Our culture teaches males to restrain their tears while women are typically permitted a wider range of emotional expression. Many female lawyers have stories about tears betraying them at desolate moments in their early careers. And nothing underscores more the uneasy position of a female lawyer within a masculine profession than crying on the job. It can be humiliating, it can be soul destroying, and it can sometimes be career ending. Whatever happens, it is not quickly forgotten. L'Heureux's response in the wake of the tears reflected the determined optimism that marked her personality. She did not slink away and she did not torture herself with recriminations for crying. She spent the rest of the afternoon at the cinema to shore up her spirits. Recomposed, she returned to the office and confessed the disaster to Sam Bard. Decades later, she still remembered his response: "He said, 'Claire, it happens!' Not one word of criticism. I was crying and he would say, 'Count your blessings. Roll with the punches.'"[41] Such bolstering of her self-confidence was exactly what she needed.

Slowly L'Heureux built a small cluster of her own personal clients. The first were referred to her by Judith Gamache, who came across many impoverished people at the Juvenile Court, where she had taken a position as court clerk after her graduation from Laval.[42] L'Heureux represented them without fee. She also gave speeches to the Club Richelieu, Rotary Club, Kiwanis-Quebec, the Ligue catholique féminine, and other women's clubs, on topics such as inheritance laws, insolvency, and family law. Some were picked up by the press.[43] She spoke at a round-table on *"l'engagement de la femme"*† organized by the Association des femmes diplômées des universités, where she urged women to take positions on social, political, and economic questions of the day, while carefully stressing that her message was addressed to all citizens, male and female.[44] She drafted by-laws for the University Women's Club and the constitution for the Association des femmes de carrière du Québec métropolitain, later affiliated with the Business and Professional Women's (BPW) Club.[45] She served as legal adviser for the BPW, wrote reports on the law of succession, translated their reports into French, and sat at their luncheon head tables.[46] "I guess [women's organizations] felt more comfortable with a woman lawyer, and I was one of the only ones in practice," she explained. This helped her establish connections with young female entrepreneurs – a chiropractor, a pharmacist, and others – who were interested in hiring female lawyers. "It was five years or so before I attracted my own business clients. It built up very slowly, mostly through women's networks."[47]

L'Heureux acted for the YWCA when it appeared that the organization might lose its tax-exempt status under new government regulations. She carried the campaign directly to the legislative assembly, where she made a stirring speech about the history of the Y and its important role in the protection of women. She took the precaution of filling the spectators' seats with rows of YWCA members. "Premier Duplessis could see all the ladies sitting there, and realized it was a political matter. He said to the lawyer for the city, 'Go down the corridor and settle this with Mme L'Heureux.' So we did."[48]

Occasionally, her principles came into conflict with the firm's clients. Part of the practice involved drafting leases for one businessman who owned rental properties in Quebec City. When his tenants complained that the premises were rat-infested, "I told him these were slums. I threatened to tell the other poor people who were about to sign up as tenants that it was full of rats."[49] To her surprise, despite the chastisement, the client continued to do business with her. To her even greater pleasure, Sam Bard later suggested to the client that he set up a philanthropic foundation.

---

† "the promise (and responsibility) of women"

The Practice:
"We Were Honest and We Didn't Charge Very Much"

The firm's clients sought legal services to incorporate, to create partnership agreements, to set up leases for apartments, and to do the background legal work for the new shopping centres that were sprouting up in the 1950s. Some of this work was traditionally done in Quebec by notaries, a profession parallel to law peopled with legally trained professionals who handled real estate, wills, contracts, and other matters that were resolved out of court. But many Jewish clients came first to Bard's firm and transferred the files to the notaries only after the titles had been searched and the deals completed. The firm also drafted contracts, promissory notes, corporate by-laws, minutes, and demand letters for unpaid bills. Small collections of routine accounts and chasing after bad debts took up a large portion of the day. The firm launched personal injury and negligence claims and defended others for car accidents, workplace injuries, flooding, and landlord and tenant problems. Labour and employment law occupied a niche of the practice. Some clients, whose dreams outstripped their grasp, also required bankruptcy services.

There were many referrals from Montreal and Toronto lawyers, who retained Bard to incorporate companies in Quebec. There were very few criminal clients, and in the first fifteen years family law was virtually nonexistent in a province without divorce. Much of what is now understood as family law was then handled by notaries: marriage contracts, gifts *inter vivos*, estate planning. Although many lawyers deliberately cultivated political affiliations as a way to build business, Sam Bard chose to stay apolitical. He preferred philosophical independence to toeing "the party line."[50] It was a position that L'Heureux happily followed in turn. Consequently, there was no government-referred business.[51]

The Bard firm built an impressive reputation for servicing its clientele. Melvin Rothman, who practised with the Montreal firm of Phillips and Vineberg, recalled that every time his firm incorporated a Quebec company, it turned to Bard. "Sam and his partners, of whom Claire was the senior at the time, had a very efficient way of processing these things. It was a pretty active and successful firm for Quebec City standards."[52] L'Heureux smiled at this assessment: "We were honest and we didn't charge very much. Lawyers were not making money then."[53]

Some lawyers found this type of work repetitive, with one describing it bluntly as "dull, dull, dull."[54] In contrast, L'Heureux was enthusiastic about every facet. "I liked drafting. I had a client who was a pharmacist.

How well I remember drafting that contract. There was no model at that time. You had to invent every clause. You had to know your law, and you had to be sure that if the contract was breached, your client would be protected. It was very creative."[55] Even the incorporation referrals did not daunt her. The Quebec government had neglected to open an office in Montreal for incorporations, and so the Montreal lawyers were required to retain agents in Quebec City. The work was simple: locate an available corporate name, attend the appropriate government office, get the documents stamped and filed. Some days L'Heureux would do up to twenty. "It was a foundation from which to run the office [and] to pay for the basics. Sam was smart to have made all these Montreal contacts [who referred that business to us]. We charged $10 per incorporation. It didn't involve a lot of brains. But I did it for fifteen years."[56]

A great deal of the practice was conducted in English.[57] It was something that grated upon the French-speaking bar and would provoke concerted resistance when the Quiet Revolution ushered in new norms. Years later, L'Heureux-Dubé would roundly chastise the wider profession for its monolingual Anglophone linguistic assumptions.[58] But at the time, she made the decision to become proficient in English. "I worked in English most of the time I was with Sam. I learned the legal terminology first in English, so it became easier for me to write in English. And I think it's a simpler language, with fewer nuances, so the work goes faster."[59] It was a spirit of generosity that rarely characterized English-speakers.

Sam Bard's work may have been more English than others, given his client base. Although the Jewish residents of Quebec City did a great deal to integrate themselves into French Canadian life, many also opted for acculturation in English Canada, lived in Anglophone neighbourhoods, and conducted their business in English.[60] Even Francophone lawyers worked between 20 and 40 percent of their time in English.[61] The language of the legal work also influenced income, with Quebec lawyers who worked predominantly in English earning substantially more. It was something that the Royal Commission on Bilingualism and Biculturalism would document in the 1960s, unveiling explosive statistical evidence that French-speaking people in Quebec were unjustifiably positioned below the Anglophones who controlled the economy.[62]

There were no personal secretaries in the firm, and everyone, including Bard, made use of the "secretarial pool." Once hired, the staff tended to stay, many for twenty-five to thirty years. There were no dictaphones, photocopiers, or computers, and all the drafting was done longhand and then typed. Secretaries typed correspondence on multiple onionskin sheets separated by carbon paper. Every typographical error meant erasing the error on the original and on each of the carbon copies, and then retyping. Nevertheless, L'Heureux continued to do a lot of her own typing, because she insisted that she could think while she typed, and it was more efficient that way.

Nicole L'Heureux, her younger sister, took a summer position with the firm during her legal studies at Laval. She recalled the bustle of the working day: "The telephone was ringing all the time. People were coming and going, settling their debts. It was a very, very busy office."[63] It was an observation shared by Steven Katkin, Sam Bard's nephew, who also worked "for the experience – a euphemism for without remuneration" – while he studied law at Laval. "I well remember turning out copy after copy on the mimeograph machine [a low-cost printing machine that forced ink through a stencil onto paper]. Sam was tops in commercial law, so people came to learn. It was a busy office."[64]

The workday began promptly at 8 a.m., when Bard drove up to L'Heureux's home to offer her a lift to work. His daughter, Perry, who used to catch a ride to school with them, had a vivid image of Claire L'Heureux jumping into the car. "She was so full of energy, she *filled* the car. She would start talking the second she got in, and when I left the conversation hadn't stopped."[65] The short drive was devoted to detailed planning for the day's work. The early morning in the office was spent preparing cases for court, which commenced at ten o'clock. In the 1950s, the office would still close at noon so everyone could go home for lunch. It was a traditional French custom that had already died out in the Montreal law firms and would disappear in Quebec City in the 1960s.[66]

The afternoon was filled with appointments to see clients, meetings with other lawyers, case conferences, and drafting of documents. There were no law clerks or court runners, and the lawyers walked to court and personally filed documents "the old-fashioned, artisan way."[67] The office generally shut down around five o'clock, but both Bard and L'Heureux often worked at home after dinner or went back to the office. The scheduled week consisted of five and a half workdays, Monday morning to Saturday noon.

Lawyers in the province reported working between forty-one and forty-six hours a week, with some putting in up to forty-nine hours.[68] L'Heureux's working hours were longer than average. Joel Bard recalled that no matter how hard his father worked, Claire L'Heureux worked harder. The janitor of the building even expressed concern to Bard. "He was very worried about Mme. L'Heureux. She was always there."[69] Steven

Business Law Practice 161

Justice Louis LeBel, Supreme Court of Canada judge's chambers, June 2010.

Katkin said the same: "Claire would work late, and the night watchman in the building would tell Sam that she was working too long."[70] L'Heureux stressed that there was no external pressure to work long hours. She wanted to do so.

Montreal lawyer Melvin Rothman was effusive about L'Heureux's practice: "She was highly intelligent, very professional. She had the personality to maintain relationships with clients and other lawyers. She certainly had a substantial role in the firm."[71] Quebec lawyer Raymond Lessard described her as "a very smart woman" and "a natural organizer," adding: "The way she asks things, the way ... her mind is built ... [it] seems to others kind of easy."[72] But it was the image of the relentless worker that more accurately epitomized the female lawyers who made a go of practice. Louis LeBel, who practised at the same time as L'Heureux and went on to sit with her at the Supreme Court of Canada, noted that "women were slow to enter the practice of law in Quebec City," and those who did mostly stayed "for a few years and then left." He characterized those who made a career in the law, such as Claire L'Heureux and Gaby Vallée, as women who "had to be tough." He recalled that L'Heureux had "a very good reputation" as a "lawyer who really knew her law." His verdict on the plight of the early women: "It was not always easy."[73]

14
Marriage and Children

Although she never lacked for male attention, Claire L'Heureux was not quick to enter into matrimony.[1] "I never waited for a man to support me," was how she described it.[2] It had been career enhancing to practise as a single woman for the first five years at the Bard firm. "If I had married earlier, I don't think I would have had time ... to make my name. I was free to work twenty-four hours a day, free to do everything I wanted to do."[3]

The ground shifted in 1957, when L'Heureux's father, Paul, was promoted to the position of collector of customs and excise in Montreal.[4] He put the family home up for sale and warned his daughter that she would have to move with them. He was not prepared to have the family face the scandal of an unmarried daughter living alone in Quebec City, even one who was thirty-one years old and well established in her professional career. L'Heureux now had to make a final decision about her on-again, off-again relationship with Arthur Dubé. Musing about the mores of the times, she regretted that she was forced to choose. "If it had been today, I would never have considered marriage."[5] That she was prepared to knuckle under to her father's dictates reveals how much of a grip he still retained.

But first there was a delightful hiatus, a last-ditch attempt to forestall the finality of conjugality. It came courtesy of one of her clients, the Swiss Arosa Line, whose cruise ships docked in Quebec City. L'Heureux had settled the company's lost baggage claims with characteristic efficiency, and the owner offered her free passage on a European cruise in April 1957. The woman whose childhood dreams had been filled with visions of sailing

Claire L'Heureux on the deck of the cruise ship *Arosa Star*, 1957.

the world did not have to be asked twice. She convinced Sam Bard to give her several months' leave, found him a lawyer to fill her spot, and was en route without delay. The cruise would be a test of her attachment to Arthur. Could their relationship withstand the separation?

The cruise was a fantasy come true. L'Heureux was assigned a luxurious first-class cabin on the *Arosa Star*, and she marvelled over her fellow passengers (one an Italian contessa with her lover in tow), the fine restaurants, the live music, the flowers, the night-long dancing. She was mesmerized by her first sight of Paris, the Côte d'Azur, Monaco, Stockholm, Helsinki, the fiords of Norway, the Hermitage in St. Petersburg, the moon over the North Sea.

Fascinated by this cosmopolitan world so removed from the rigid domestic mores of the 1950s, L'Heureux experimented with the Bohemian lifestyle of her cruisemates years before a generation of young people popularized it in the late 1960s and 1970s.[6] She flirted, she toyed with marriage proposals, and she danced till dawn in seaside cafés. She may have been a woman who worked in an exclusively masculine world, but she was eager to display a feminine persona with a decidedly modern veneer. It was a deliberate casting off of the sexual mores of the convent years, a freethinking, attractive woman who wanted to stretch her wings. She also spent every cent of the $3,000 in savings she had brought along.

Claire L'Heureux at cocktail hour on the cruise ship *Arosa Star*, 1957.

Despite the exhilaration, her feelings for Arthur did not diminish. She could not shake the magnetic physical and intellectual attraction that had captivated her from the first evening they met. It was a shared ardency. For months, Arthur had been sending her love letters in care of American Express, letters she would keep all her life. When she arrived home, Arthur was at the dock to meet her with $60 in hand because he knew she was penniless and needed help to tip the crew. It was only a matter of days before the two were engaged.

A Proposal in the Woods and a Wedding at the Château

It was Claire L'Heureux who put the proposal forward during a walk through the woods in La Malbaie, Charlevoix. She explained that her parents were moving to Montreal and were insisting that she go with them. She saw no possibility of living together at the time, and because she loved him and wanted to be with him, the only alternative seemed to be marriage. Arthur's immediate affirmative response did not surprise his brother Yves. "Claire was probably the only woman that Arthur would ever have married and vice versa."[7] She agreed, adding: "To marry was a hard decision, but I think it was still the best."[8]

The choice of a mate can be life changing. This is particularly true for individuals whose paths are unusual, controversial, or groundbreaking.

Biographers of famous women are often curious about whom they select as spouses. Are they attracted to men in positions of power who can help them? Do they prefer men they perceive as equals who will be allies? Do they seek sensitive, gentle men who will nurture them? Does the right choice of husband seal their success? Does the wrong choice derail them?[9] Decades afterward, Claire L'Heureux-Dubé's daughter, Louise, offered her own insight. She did not think her mother chose to get married because she ever bought into the notion "that a man would take care of you, as was prevalent at the time, or that you could find fulfillment in marriage." Louise pointed to Claire's father, who had never presented the storybook image of a husband. "Traditional marriage wasn't something [my mother had] experienced" or "was looking for," she added. According to Louise, Claire L'Heureux married Arthur Dubé because he was "the smartest guy she ever met."[10]

The wedding of thirty-year-old Claire L'Heureux and thirty-eight-year-old Arthur Dubé took place during a big snowstorm on 30 November 1957 in the chapel of the Cathedral-Basilica of Notre-Dame de Québec before fifty family members and friends. The priest who officiated was the Abbé Larue, a Laval professor and close friend of Arthur's. In an era when white wedding dresses were not yet the norm, the bride wore a dark, tailored V-neck suit with a floral corsage and a string of pearls. At the reception in the Royal Suite of the Château Frontenac, the guests drank Mumm's champagne, admired the ice sculptures, and dined on salmon.

Arthur's brother Yves marvelled over what a "liberated woman" Claire L'Heureux was, observing that this was a bond that could serve the couple well, that they both loved their freedom.[11] Arthur's mother was pleased with the match, admiring the bride's professional status but also slightly aghast over her modern ways. Arthur's emotionally distant father gave the couple $1,000 to pay for the reception. A notary by profession, he also crafted their marriage contract, an agreement approved by the lawyer-bride with separation as to property and a will that left all worldly goods to the surviving spouse.[12] Marguerite L'Heureux was resistant to the end. "Marrying a man you know is an alcoholic will bring you a lot of tears. It's good that he has a great mind, but in a marriage you live with your heart and your emotions. He's very bright, but you will suffer," was her tight-lipped refrain.[13]

In the meantime, Paul and Marguerite's own marriage unravelled further. Although Marguerite and their youngest daughter, Nicole, accompanied Paul to Montreal, he rented a second-floor apartment that kept his

Claire L'Heureux and Arthur Dubé's wedding, 30 November 1957.

wife imprisoned in her wheelchair. His amorous escapades continued, and he often stayed out all night. In despair, Marguerite moved back with Nicole to the Quebec City house, which was still unsold. Paul began a new life in Montreal with Francine Teasdale, a woman just ten years older than his eldest daughter, with whom he lived for the next twenty-five years.[14] He never formally separated from Marguerite, visiting monthly, helping to support her financially, and keeping up the pretence that he was just away working in Montreal.[15]

Reflecting on the demise of her parents' marriage, L'Heureux-Dubé explained: "My parents lived apart for a long time. My father loved my mother, but he couldn't accept the fact that she was a cripple. She couldn't dance, and she couldn't go out with him. My father took the easy way out."[16] It was an indictment that she would occasionally voice in the future about other men, observing that they too often just took the "easy way out." She was distraught by what she saw as her father's insensitive abandonment of her beloved mother. It would take her years to forgive him.

A Modern Marriage between Spouses Committed to "Freedom"

After her marriage, Claire chose to use a hyphenated last name, L'Heureux-Dubé. "I wanted to keep my name because I had practised law as 'L'Heureux,'" she explained. "I didn't even ask Arthur, I just did it, and he didn't mind a bit."[17] There was no question of her becoming a stay-at-home wife. She knew from the outset that she would maintain her law practice because her desire to succeed as a lawyer had never wavered. Arthur supported her decision because it accorded with his own commitment to individual independence. He knew his new wife was ambitious and intelligent, someone who would flourish in a career setting. Given his reputed inability to manage money, he must also have been pleased that the family would have two incomes.

L'Heureux-Dubé was quick to credit Arthur for his support: *"Tout cela fut possible grâce à la collaboration et à la compréhension de mon mari."*[†, 18] Like her all-important first job with a law firm, this was pivotal to her future success. It was something she would stress again when she was elevated to the judiciary: *"Mon mariage a été un défi ... pour mon mari. Ce n'était pas facile d'épouser une femme tout en sachant qu'elle ne remplirait pas les rôles traditionnels qu'on lui a dévolus. Mon mari m'a apporté la liberté, liberté sans laquelle je n'aurais sûrement pas pu poursuivre cette carrière."*[‡, 19]

---

† "All this was made possible by my husband's cooperation and understanding."
‡ "My marriage was a challenge ... for my husband. It was not easy to marry a woman while knowing that she would not fulfill the traditional roles that befell her. My husband brought me freedom, freedom without which I certainly would not have been able to pursue this career."

Arthur and Claire.

The couple postponed their honeymoon until the spring of 1959, when Arthur could take a sabbatical from his Laval University post. Sam Bard gave her another leave, and the couple travelled through Europe from April to August. In England, she became pregnant, an unplanned conception that came as quite a shock to both of them.[20] Financial worries were uppermost, since Arthur had accumulated large debts from uncontrolled gambling and a lifelong habit of putting generosity well beyond his means.[21] The prospect of children was problematic on other levels as well. Arthur was struggling with bouts of severe depression and trying to cope with more alcohol, which led to further downward spirals. Both depression and alcoholism had a long lineage within the Dubé family. Yet the young couple remained deeply in love. "I loved his brilliance and that never stopped," explained L'Heureux-Dubé.[22]

A daughter, Louise, was born in the spring of 1960.[23] Her birth transformed both parents, who, overcoming their initial reluctance, decided to have another baby. When L'Heureux-Dubé became pregnant a second time in 1963, it was clear that new quarters were required. With careful household budgets and a five-year mortgage, the family purchased its

Marriage and Children

Mother and children at Christmas, ca. 1964.

first home: 940 Adolphe-Routhier. All the financial planning fell to L'Heureux-Dubé, since Arthur had no interest in money matters. She paid the bills, mortgage, and taxes on each of the homes the family would live in, all of which were registered in her name. Pierre was born shortly after the move, in the winter of 1964. The physicians insisted that he remain in the hospital for two months because of intestinal problems that were eventually diagnosed as coeliac disease.[24] His baptism was cause for great celebration when it finally took place.

Claire L'Heureux-Dubé described Arthur as a "good father," but admitted that most of the parenting was left to her. [25] He liked to garden and took out the garbage, but never shouldered an equal share of the family chores. Her sister Nicole explained that Arthur was "an old bachelor" when he got married, and the fact that he had a family "didn't change his life. He was a professor. He was interested in his students, in his research. He continued to do what he had done before. I would say he wasn't a 'family man.'"[26] It was left to L'Heureux-Dubé to organize a schedule that would enable her to combine parenting with a full-time career. She did it at a time when many, including other trailblazing women lawyers and judges, were insistent that women could never successfully combine a career and a family.²⁷

The stark realities were evident from the very first day, when L'Heureux-Dubé chose not to ask for maternity leave. "It was not in the mores of the time. In the maternity room before the birth, I had my files with me. I was calling clients, talking on the phone, and conducting business. I took fifteen days at home, not more than that, after each birth. Maternity leaves were unknown." She explained her reasoning: "First, I had pressing business, and I liked to be in the office. And I wasn't paid when I wasn't there. I really am a businesswoman by temperament. I'm not an at-home mother. Second, I had help – a specialized paediatric nurse, so I was confident that everything was ok. And I recuperated fast."²⁸

L'Heureux-Dubé hired full-time help, caregivers who lived in as well as those who did not. She emphasized that Sam Bard was helpful at his end, insisting that she stay at home if there was an emergency or the children were sick. She micro-planned the family's schedule, the household chores, and the meals. She cooked eggs over a hot stove for breakfast every morning. She drove the children to school. She rushed home around 4 or 5 p.m. to spend evenings with the children, and returned to the office after they had gone to sleep. If the floors needed cleaning, it was she who got up early in the morning to wash them. She started what would become a lifelong regimen of short sleep: four hours a night on average.²⁹ She seemed driven by the gendered expectations placed on women, who were traditionally assessed entirely upon their prowess as good wives, mothers, cooks, and housekeepers. It was a recipe for exhaustion, but L'Heureux-Dubé insisted that the enjoyment of her work kept her from noticing the fatigue.

The number of married women who worked outside the home in Quebec had more than doubled since 1941, but it was still under 18 percent.³⁰ L'Heureux-Dubé's path-breaking lawyer-mother status attracted much media interest, with reporters asking her to account for her two-track lifestyle. *"Je serais la dernière à recommander la même vie à toutes les femmes,"* she told *La Presse*. *"Ce qui est important, c'est d'avoir le choix de pouvoir suivre ses inclinations."*†,³¹ And she was quick to defend her choices, insisting that the children never suffered because she worked. Crediting her success with *"une santé de fer"* and *"une bonne organisation familiale,"*‡ L'Heureux-Dubé emphasized:

---

† "I would be the last person to recommend the same life to all women ... What is important is having the choice to be able to follow one's inclinations."
‡ "an iron constitution"; "a well-organized household"

Je ne les délaisse pas pour autant: je les vois autant que si j'étais à la maison et eux, à l'école. J'ai une personne fiable qui en prend soin quand je ne suis pas là et pour eux, c'est très normal de me voir partir tous les matins pour le bureau. Je travaille par goût et par besoin d'activité. Si je le faisais pour m'éloigner de la maison, les enfants le sentiraient et en seraient peut-être malheureux. Ils le sentent bien quand on les aime.[†, 32]

Yet L'Heureux-Dubé did not escape the feelings of guilt that have plagued working mothers over the generations. She tried to choose excellent childcare workers, but at times their very skills exacerbated her anxiety over her absence. Brutally honest, she admitted to worrying that they were displacing her, bonding more closely with her own children than she was able to do while working so feverishly. Occasionally she also agonized over her perception that they were mismanaging her children's upbringing. If she fired them, she blamed herself for disrupting the nurturing relationships her children had formed with the childcare workers. The woman who characterized her otherwise preoccupied husband as a "good father" was mercilessly self-critical: "At the time, I was a bad mother – Louise will tell you that, and I will agree. I was not often there. I'm a much better grandmother than I was a mother."[33]

The social expectations placed upon working mothers made other female professionals chafe under the obvious gender bias. Mary Gaudron, the first woman to be appointed to the Australian High Court, voiced her dismay over the situation: "[If the mother] does not say 'I will subordinate my interests,' the values of this society will immediately judge her to be a bad mother. We are dealing with notions, male notions, that are going to be imposed on any woman in this situation which are essentially, in my view, unfair and it puts the mother in an absolutely impossible position."[34]

L'Heureux-Dubé's friends were less critical than she of her performance as a mother. Childhood friend Gisèle Blondeau, a mother of five, commented: "Before having her children, [Claire] had no sense of motherhood. But the minute her children were born, that bloomed in her. She had cases in court when the children were sick, [and] she wouldn't leave their side."[35]

---

† "But I do not forsake them: I see them as much as if I were at home and they, at school. I have a reliable person who takes care of them when I am not home, and for them it is very normal to see me leave every morning for the office. I work out of personal inclination and to remain active. If I did so to get away from the house, the children would feel it and perhaps be unhappy. They are well aware of being loved."

Gisèle Blondeau, former convent student and lifelong friend of Claire L'Heureux-Dubé, ca. 2008.

Another lifelong friend from Rimouski, Jean Drapeau, agreed: "She was a good mother. She was very attentive to her children, and she loved them, but in the same time she was a woman of career. I think she has always been a woman who could manage many things. She could be a good mother and a great worker. I saw her with her children ... she [took] care of them. I don't know how she can find the time to do that, but she found time for her kids. She has always been a woman that was extraordinarily efficient."[36] Simone Tardif, a long-time friend, added: "I told her one hundred times you have no guilt. I don't know of anybody who has done so much for [her children] as you have."[37]

Working mothers struggle at the best of times, but L'Heureux-Dubé faced additional challenges. Two-year-old Louise came down with severe asthma when Arthur was in Europe doing research. When her daughter stopped breathing, the terrified mother rushed her to the emergency ward. Louise was hospitalized for ten days, and was released only when injections of expensive medication finally brought the asthma under control. Repeat attacks, often requiring hospital treatment, would plague the young girl into adulthood. By the age of two, Pierre also began exhibiting signs of asthma.

L'Heureux-Dubé described waking up between 11 p.m. and 5 a.m. as often as once a month with both children unable to breathe. "My husband would have Pierre in his arms, and I would hold Louise, and we would spend the night like that. The doctor finally gave us a medication that was experimental and that did marvels."[38] Pierre was also diagnosed with a behavioural disorder at an early age. An array of specialists examined the sensitive young boy, who seemed to leave intolerable disruption in his wake. None was able to offer useful advice or effective treatment. Again, L'Heureux-Dubé blamed herself. "I asked myself over and over what I did wrong. [I] felt so guilty. I wondered if it might have been different if I had stayed home, but others said no, it would have been the same or worse. And I think it would have killed me if I had stayed home, [with] no way to get away to another side of life."[39]

As the children grew older, they went off to camp in July and the family took its holidays in August, when Arthur could get away from Laval. At first, L'Heureux-Dubé rented a cottage on Lac Trois-Saumons just north of L'Islet, where her mother and sister Nicole had a small summer place.

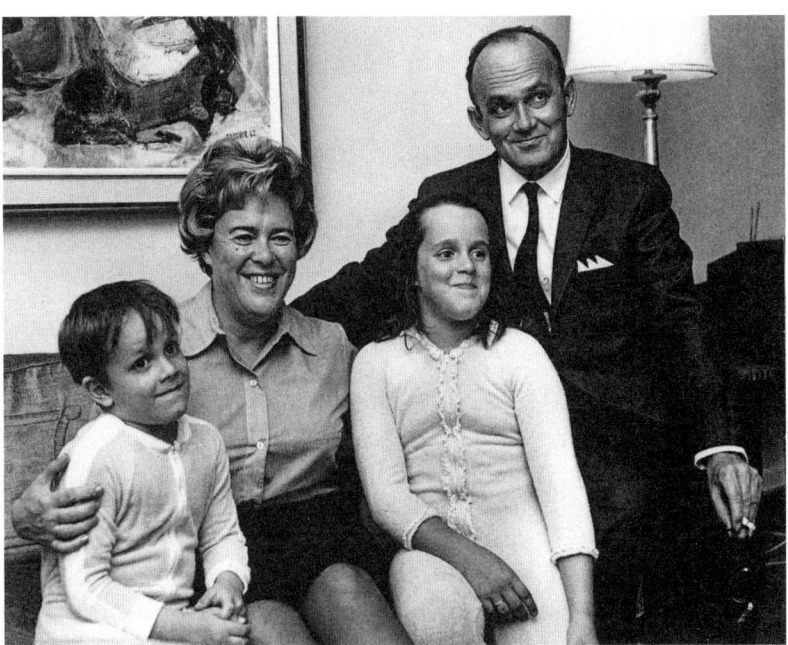

L'Heureux-Dubé family posing for a newspaper story about Claire, 1969.

If her work intervened, she left the children in the care of the nanny and went down to the city, returning on weekends. In the 1960s, as her law practice became more lucrative, the family purchased a fishing and hunting camp on a private lake in Portneuf, between Quebec City and Trois-Rivières. On Christmas holidays, they sometimes took skiing holidays or went south to Florida or the Caribbean.

Despite the pressures of work and childcare, the couple maintained an active social life. Arthur had his brothers and friends over to watch sports, listen to music, and drink beer. The two of them invited guests for cocktails and dinner, primarily friends of Arthur's, since he preferred the discussions of Laval professors to that of lawyers. Among their closest friends were Léon and Denyse Dion. Léon Dion was a professor of political science, widely credited as one of the greatest visionaries behind the Quiet Revolution.[40] Denyse, originally from France and a realtor, was one of the only other Laval wives who worked outside the home. Their son, Stéphane, who would later lead the federal Liberal party, often joined the Dubé children at their home for lunch.

Léon Dion and Denyse Dion, family friends of the L'Heureux-Dubés, at their Quebec City home, 1997.

Denyse Dion and L'Heureux-Dubé both braved criticisms from the neighbours that their careers interfered with the needs of their children. Denyse found herself drawn toward the young lawyer, and described her as "fresh water in the middle of the desert" and "the first authentic woman I met in Canada," adding that she "was not like the other women, who were just playing roles, repressed socialites. Claire was intelligent, gifted, and very direct. We both said what we thought."[41] One summer, Claire L'Heureux-Dubé and Denyse Dion broke all the rules of propriety and went off to Italy and Spain together for a holiday. L'Heureux-Dubé laughed at the memory: "At the time, Denyse said she couldn't go on a trip like this with anybody but me because in Canada, women were not traveling without their husbands. We were liberated women."[42]

The early 1960s were not easy times for L'Heureux-Dubé's family. Both parents were trying to establish themselves in professional careers. Their young children were experiencing physical and psychological health issues. The family had to endure the prying gaze of the neighbours and the press, who wanted to know how husbands coped when they lacked a stay-at-home wife, and how a working mother could possibly measure up. Claire L'Heureux-Dubé, who shouldered almost all of the home responsibilities herself, was sleepless but resolute. Arthur was sliding into depression and alcoholism. With the benefit of hindsight, their daughter, Louise, critiqued their decision to marry. "[My mother] did not have a knack for picking husbands. Regardless of the fact that she's not going to say that. Just no good was going to come out of this."[43]

15
Family Law
The Later Years of Practice

During Claire L'Heureux-Dubé's two decades in practice from 1952 to 1972, she witnessed significant structural change within the profession.[1] The Quebec City bar nearly doubled in size, although it continued to represent only about 15 percent of the province's lawyers.[2] Firm size also grew, with the largest firm boasting fourteen lawyers by 1972.[3] The bar remained overwhelmingly French Canadian.[4] There were only three Jewish lawyers; significantly, Sam Bard was no longer one of them.[5]

Transformation in the Bard Firm

In 1969, Sam Bard was named the first Jewish judge on the Superior Court in Quebec City. The judicial elevation surprised him because he had no political ties and had not sought the appointment.[6] The impetus came from Jewish lawyers in Montreal who were lobbying the government to overcome its historical reluctance to recognize meritorious Jewish candidates.[7] Their efforts aligned with those of Sydney Lazarovitz, who was networking within the Liberal party for a judicial appointment in Quebec City. In 1967, Lazarovitz had been named *bâtonnier* despite the considerable challenges he faced as the first Jew to hold the post.[8] To all observers, it seemed that if there were to be a Jewish judge, it would be Lazarovitz. Instead, when Minister of Justice John Turner made the appointment, he opted for Bard.[9]

Family Law 177

The appointment came as a shock not only to Sam Bard but also to his associates. L'Heureux-Dubé was returning from her summer holiday at the fishing camp when the news reached her. Although she was pleased for Sam, she was personally devastated. It was the only time she thought seriously about quitting practice. Her children were aged nine and five, household demands were huge, and the thought of trying to run the practice without her mentor nearly overwhelmed her. She also feared that Sam's Jewish clients would leave the firm after his departure. Worse, she was losing not only the firm's founder but a man she had come to love deeply. She collapsed in tears and wept for many days. After lengthy soul searching, she chose to continue. The turning point was her recognition of how many other members of the firm would suffer if it were to disintegrate.[10]

Bard's firm had seen several lawyers come and go over the two decades.[11] Three became permanent fixtures. Jacques Philippon, who started in 1959, developed a flourishing corporate practice with a full roster of his own clients.[12] Christine Tourigny, who arrived in 1970, developed a practice that was closely intertwined with L'Heureux-Dubé's. In later years, she would become widely recognized as one of the province's most influential

Bard Law Firm lawyers: *Left to right,* Sam S. Bard, Claire L'Heureux-Dubé, Christine Tourigny, Jacques Philippon.

feminists.[13] Roger Garneau, a brilliant litigator who joined in 1971, would become the firm's longest-serving member.[14] Gender-balanced in 1972 at 50 percent female and 50 percent male, the firm certainly stood out from the pack.[15] None of the other firms came close to these numbers, but the proportion of women practising across the city had increased tenfold, from the lonely two when Claire L'Heureux entered to twenty in her last full year of practice in 1972.[16] Province-wide that year, women accounted for 6.7 percent.[17]

A NEW FIELD OF PRACTICE:
THE BLOSSOMING OF MATRIMONIAL LAW

Although the vast majority of Quebec City law firms continued to operate general practices, specialization was in the air. Family law was one of the first fields to emerge as a distinct new field of practice.[18] Traditionally there had been no family law practice because divorce was virtually inaccessible in Quebec.[19] The *Civil Code,* which came into force in 1866, stated: "Marriage can only be dissolved by the natural death of one of the parties; while both live it is indissoluble."[20] When L'Heureux had first learned about family law from the dashing professor Jean Turgeon at Laval, separation was the only remedy for discordant couples. Even there, there was a double standard. A man could obtain *séparation de corps et de biens*† with proof of his wife's adultery. A woman had to prove that her husband was keeping "his concubine in their common habitation."[21]

Signs of change took the province by storm with the death of Maurice Duplessis on L'Heureux-Dubé's thirty-second birthday in September 1959. It marked the end of *La Grande Noirceur,* the Great Darkness. Within a year, the election of Jean Lesage's Liberals fast-tracked the province into *La Révolution Tranquille,* a "turning point" in which Quebec "took charge of [its] destiny."[22] Priests, nuns, and parishioners left the Church in droves, and a new elite of professionals and technocrats rose to power, "inspired by visions of economic progress, managerial competence, and a nationalism founded upon the power of the Quebec state."[23] In 1961, Marie-Claire Kirkland-Casgrain, the McGill law graduate admitted to the bar the same year as L'Heureux, was elected the first woman to sit in the Quebec legislative assembly.[24] In 1964, over the protests of lawyers and notaries, she

---

† separation as to bed and board

Family Law

Marie-Claire Kirkland-Casgrain, lawyer called to the bar the same year as L'Heureux-Dubé.

convinced the politicians to reverse the legal incapacity of married women under the *Civil Code*.[25] Divorce reform was next on the agenda. Réjane Laberge-Colas, who had written her bar exam alongside both Kirkland and L'Heureux, was elected president of the newly founded Fédération des femmes du Québec. She demanded divorce courts throughout the province.[26]

That would come under the leadership of federal Liberal minister of justice Pierre Elliott Trudeau, who declared that the state had no place in the bedrooms of the nation.[27] His 1968 *Divorce Act* extended access to divorce across the country, bringing Quebec spouses their first opportunity for judicial dissolution of marriage.[28] It provided that either spouse could terminate a marriage for adultery, cruelty, bigamy, homosexual act, lengthy imprisonment, and gross addiction to alcohol or drugs.[29] Divorce was also possible if the couple lived separately for three years.[30] The custody rules in Quebec, still covered under the *Civil Code,* retained the legal presumption that children should live with their father, although the court could order otherwise if it was to the children's "greater advantage."[31] In 1969, an amendment provided that custody decisions should also take account of "the conduct of the parties," their "condition, means, and other circumstances."[32]

When the floodgates opened, L'Heureux-Dubé was uniquely positioned to become Quebec City's pre-eminent family law practitioner. She was already known as one of the few lawyers who would take cases from the impoverished, desperate women who sought whatever legal relief could be had from impossible marriages before divorce came into the picture. When the bar decided to run seminars on the new *Divorce Act*, bâtonnier Lazarovitz was in charge of the programming. L'Heureux-Dubé pinpointed his intervention as determinative: "He phoned me to say, 'We'll have the bar meeting and you will make a speech on the Divorce Act.' I said, 'I don't know anything about divorce law.' He said, 'Learn it.'"[33]

And so she did. She researched the history of family law in England and France, and the transfer of these frameworks to English Canada and Quebec. She studied the constitutional issues raised by the new *Divorce Act* as well as its substantive and procedural provisions. She typed up a set of lecture notes and mounted the course at the bar school. "It put me on the map really, for the bar," she marvelled. "I was the expert from [that] minute on."[34] By 1970, she was lecturing on family law at Laval. With additional attention from press and television reporters hungry for information about the new divorce regime, her practice boomed. Her professional contemporaries acclaimed her the city's "matrimonial law specialist."[35]

To be fair, L'Heureux-Dubé's rise to prominence also occurred because there was not a lot of competition. Other lawyers were anxious to distance themselves from the opprobrium of marital disgrace. According to Roger Garneau, lawyers raced to avoid family law, "flicking their wrists" at the clients and their cases.[36] Malcolm Kronby, another early family law specialist who practised in Toronto, explained that the field had a "very bad reputation" everywhere. The focus on proving adultery triggered "fraud, perjury, corruption, and unethical lawyering."[37] Many counsel dismissed the field as "social work," not "real law." Julien Payne, one of Canada's foremost family law scholars, explained that family law was belittled as so much "milk and cookies."[38] Nicholas Bala, Canada's leading children's law expert, suggested that the root of the problem might have been anxiety over the tense emotional issues involved.[39] Family law soon became designated as stereotypically female work, given the high number of female clients and the relatively low fees that it was anticipated to generate. Payne acknowledged that in the 1960s and '70s, "family law was women's law," adding: "You will appreciate the correlation there in terms of status."[40]

Practising family law was not something L'Heureux-Dubé desired, nor something she gravitated toward in the way an outsider might lean toward an "outsider's" practice. It became the default option:

Family law never interested me in law school, and when I started, it was not [an area of practice, but] it came into full force as the only area in which women could practice [independently]. People had no confidence in women to handle money. Clients said, "I want to see a lawyer, not you." But with family law, they were ready to give women their heart if not their wallets. So I said okay – now I'll do it right. And then I got interested in it, and tried to make changes to the law, to make it into a respectable field of law, which it was not at the outset. I couldn't resist the challenge.[41]

Some claimed that divorce, coupled with the first access to the birth control pill, would vault Quebec women into full personhood.[42] L'Heureux-Dubé agreed that it was a "historic malfunction" that the Catholic Church had prohibited divorce in Quebec, and that greater access would prove beneficial:

[In my experience] divorce is for women. Six months afterward ... women admit they have never been so free [or] so happy. I'm totally unconventional when I say that. But Sam Bard used to say marriage is like a besieged tower. Everyone outside wants to get in, and everyone inside wants to get out.[43]

Nevertheless, she also had concerns about the law's capacity to resolve intimate human problems. She called for more training in family law at law schools and greater exposure of law students to psychiatry and psychology, and pointed to the importance of introducing expert social workers and psychologists into family law trials. She was critical of the adversarial system, where belligerent lawyers ushered terrified spouses into the witness box to reveal in open court the most private recesses of their love lives, their financial problems, and the most painful aspects of their marriages. *"[I]l paraît barbare,"*† she exclaimed.[44] Well ahead of her time she advocated mediation, even travelling with her teenage daughter, Louise, to attend an early conference on alternative dispute resolution in Toledo.[45] Although most lawyers were loath to take family cases, they were not above fretting that mediation would extinguish the practice. "I said 'it doesn't matter. [The adversarial process] is not good for women,'" recalled L'Heureux-Dubé.[46]

---

† "It seems barbaric"

The Growth of the Practice:
"Divorcing Half of Quebec City"

The first wave of clients reflected the pent-up demand. People who had been living apart for years flocked to obtain legal sanction. L'Heureux-Dubé jumped into the new practice with her typical enthusiasm. "I loved my clients," she said. The first to retain her was a man in his mid-seventies. He came into the office the day after the act was passed, and told her he had been living alone for twenty-five years and wanted a divorce. Staggered that a man of his age would want to go through a trial, she pressed him for a reason. He replied: "I don't want to die married."[47]

Indeed, the dam burst open on failed marriages. In 1960, there had been 85 requests for separation from bed and board in Quebec City. In 1968, within six months of the passage of the *Divorce Act*, there were 222 requests for divorce.[48] The process cost an average of $500, well within reach of a large cross-section of families.[49] In 1969, the provincial rate of divorce was 8.8 out of every 100 marriages. By 1972, this had doubled to 17.5.[50] The firm's caseload grew to encompass as many as ten clients a day, almost crushing L'Heureux-Dubé under the demand. She felt as though she were "divorcing half of Quebec City."[51] Justice Georges-René Fournier on the Superior Court, well known for his bad temperament, objected to the swelling numbers. "Why do you bring so many today?" he would complain to L'Heureux-Dubé in open court.[52]

The predominantly Catholic judges were brashly outspoken in their opposition to the new divorce law. L'Heureux-Dubé was dismayed when Chief Justice Frédéric Dorion stated publicly after the passage of the *Divorce Act* that he would never divorce anybody because it was against his religion. She added: "Cultures have long tentacles. It took the judges a long time."[53] But religion didn't stop the clients, primarily French-speaking Catholics, who thronged to see her. She described it as a felicitous balance: "My family law practice was mostly in French, my business law practice was mostly in English. [It was] a good division of labour."[54]

In the early years, her family clients were primarily women without means, but she turned no one away on financial grounds. "We would say, okay, you have no money? Pay when you can. Our firm never wrote a letter to collect money. [It was] the best way to practice law."[55] Within a few years, she began to receive retainers from wealthier clients: government ministers, lawyers, and judges, including one chief justice (not Dorion) who referred his daughter. A good number were the wives of physicians.

After several years, male clients began to come too, a change that piqued judges' curiosity. L'Heureux-Dubé was upset by what she took to be a deliberate effort to embarrass her when Justice Paul Miquelon joked, in front of her client: "How come you represent a man today? You always have women."[56]

L'Heureux-Dubé was surprised at the variety of emotions her clients displayed. "Some of them were crying. Some of them were not crying at all; they could kill the guy."[57] But there was often a certain pattern. "The women would come to my office and tell me their husbands had a mistress. I would ask, 'His secretary?' 'Yes,' they would say, so surprised that I had guessed. I heard it so often. The infidelity was almost always with the secretary."[58] Adultery usually provided the impetus to divorce, but cruelty was common as well. "Almost in every case, without fail, there was some beating or violence."[59] Mental cruelty and financial disagreements were pervasive.

L'Heureux-Dubé never assumed that an immediate divorce was the only option. Some of the clients were so emotionally fragile that she believed an adversarial court hearing would destroy them. She sent such women for psychiatric or psychological counselling, suggesting that they wait until they felt stronger before proceeding. Others explained that they were still in love with their husbands. For these, she advocated efforts to pursue reconciliation, even publishing an article on "The Right Not to Divorce" in 1969.[60] In some cases, she set up mediation sessions directly with the husbands. Some of the sessions resulted in reconciliation, others in financial arrangements that benefited her clients more than a judgment would have. It was an innovative technique, well ahead of most family law practices at the time.

Many of L'Heureux-Dubé's clients worried about how they would survive economically. She urged them to think realistically about whether a divorce was worth the financial consequences. "The courts assumed that since it was the husband who was working, it was all his money. We couldn't ask for much alimony, and women were not happy when I said, 'This is the maximum I can obtain.' Even when we achieved a reasonable result, it was with mixed feelings. I knew it was never enough."[61] After doing the calculations, some clients went back to their philandering husbands and stayed for the long term. Others did not. "We are not all Hillary Clinton," shrugged L'Heureux-Dubé.[62]

Where possible, she would urge her clients to establish themselves in the paid workforce before filing for divorce:

"You are an intelligent woman," I would say. "You could make your own livelihood. Get a job. Get established. You're losing time." ... When I saw that they could maybe survive by themselves, I said, "Why would you wait for the cheque of your husband every weekend, when you could work for pay?" If you worked, you didn't get very much alimony. It was contrary to their interests, but that was the reality. Even if they were awarded alimony, he wouldn't pay. So you had to explain the whole thing. "You will pick up the telephone to call him begging for the money. You will cry. If you could make a living, you'll get less alimony but at least you'll have something to eat." If they had no prospects at all, I would fight to the death for alimony for them.[63]

One client went back to a career in nursing. Later, when she returned to pursue the divorce, she thanked L'Heureux-Dubé profusely.

Claire L'Heureux-Dubé sought to make the law less intimidating for her clients. "The women were trembling. They were afraid to lose the children. They were afraid not to have money. You had to reassure them that you would do your very best to represent them, when you knew it wouldn't turn out well."[64] She would bring her clients to court before it opened, take them for coffee, and allow them to sit in the witness box, to become more comfortable with the room and the protocol. "Other lawyers weren't doing that," she explained, "but in family law I think [female lawyers] were more attuned to those problems. I wanted to make them at ease. It was so hard. They cried, and I very often was touched to tears. It was a very difficult practice."[65]

About 80 percent of the cases were uncontested, although even those clients had to go to trial to prove fault. Trials lasted an average of three to five days. L'Heureux-Dubé's longest took thirteen. She took care to ensure that her cases were winnable before she went to court with her clients, but no matter how good her case was, she faced challenges from the judges. "They didn't believe the women," she explained. "They thought they were exaggerating, that their stories were concocted. [We had to have] witnesses that he gave her a slap in the face."[66] She submitted photographs of bruises and called physicians to testify about injuries. When the judges said this was insufficient, she accused them of thinking that there was "never enough fault."[67] When the gender biases were palpable, she occasionally resorted to drama. One day, she got down on all fours insisting, "From what I understand, the woman must be on her knees with her husband walking on her, and you would still think it is not enough."[68]

Custody was another difficult battle. "The judges tended to give custody to the father, the patriarch ... under the *Civil Code*. The Anglophones had the 'tender years' doctrine,' [with a presumption that young children should be with their mothers]. We didn't [have that] in Quebec."[69] In L'Heureux-Dubé's view, it was better to replace *paternal* authority with *parental* authority, subject always to the best interest of the child.[70]

Alimony posed even greater challenges.[71] Husbands often tried to hide their assets, and L'Heureux-Dubé would be forced to cross-examine them and subpoena their financial records. "Some of them would lie through their teeth. In one case, what one husband said about his income was ridiculous. I had to order his American Express card records to show he was travelling in the south with his mistress."[72] But it was the judges who were the biggest barrier. "They wouldn't grant alimony – it was always asking too much."[73] L'Heureux-Dubé tried to explain to the judges that her weeping clients didn't have enough money to pay $1 a week for groceries, while their husbands were out drinking all night at the tavern. Convinced that the male judges had no idea of the cost of living, she challenged them: "*Monsieur le Juge*, do you know what it costs for milk?" "No," they would answer, "it's my wife who goes to the store." Courageously, she would reply that they should go themselves to "verify the cost."[74] She demanded that the judges take account of the income tax her clients had to pay even on their paltry alimony. Dismayed when they refused, she brought tax experts to court to testify how much tax would be paid. Quebec was no worse than the rest of the country in that respect. Lee Ferrier, one of the first family law specialists in Toronto, recalled that wives would get "twenty-five percent [of her husband's income, and] a few more throw-aways for the kids. Never more than a third. I mean it was awful, awful. I don't know how so many of them did it. They really got the short end. They either starved or family took them in. It was horrible."[75]

Some judges were incorrigible. Justice Gérard Corriveau was "a person with no manners, who would say anything that went through his head," recalled L'Heureux-Dubé. "He didn't know law at all. He was appointed by John Diefenbaker, who made the worst judicial appointments in Quebec. It was a clear case of patronage."[76] It was a view widely shared by others, with the *bâtonnier* and the bar strongly against the appointment. Yves Bernier, appointed to the Superior Court the same year as Corriveau, explained: "Corriveau was a very good person, but had no judgment as far as justice was concerned."[77] When Corriveau behaved particularly egregiously toward one of her female clients, L'Heureux-Dubé called for

Justice Gérard Corriveau, Quebec Superior Court.

a recess and approached the judge in his chambers. "Gérard – enough is enough," she told him. Waving her hand toward the hunting trophies – stuffed animal heads hung on the walls of the judge's office – she said, "Not all the animals are on the wall. I'll go to the appeal court and you will be ashamed."[78]

Appearing before Corriveau often provoked her. One case involved a "distinguished lady who was married to a prominent doctor."[79] Before L'Heureux-Dubé could even open the case, the judge launched into a long-winded address about the evils of divorce, emphasizing that when judges gave money to women, "they spend it with their lovers." She rose and told Corriveau that her female client was "absolutely shocked" at his outburst. But in practical terms, there was no way to challenge a judge for bias. It was perceived as contempt of court. "You would have risked your career to say that the judge is biased," explained L'Heureux-Dubé. She requested an adjournment, then sailed out of the court, banging the door, and went directly to the office of Chief Justice Frédéric Dorion. "I said, 'This man shouldn't be sitting. He should be in an asylum for crazy people. My client doesn't want anything to do with that judge. Please give me another judge.'"[80] The chief justice, who was familiar with Corriveau's foibles, acceded to her request.

Louise Galipeault, one of the other female lawyers practising in Quebec City, described L'Heureux-Dubé as "an excellent lawyer" to whom she referred a family member. "Claire would phone [her clients] at night [after court], to check that they were all right … not too much disturbed by the court day. [She was a] wonderful lawyer in all aspects."[81] Yves Bernier, in whose courtroom L'Heureux-Dubé appeared as an advocate, agreed. "She was well-prepared," and then he laughed, "and I think she spoke a lot."[82]

L'Heureux-Dubé's daughter, Louise, a young girl at the time, recalled that her mother became deeply involved with her family law clients. "She took the cases very personally. To the point where once she brought home [a] woman with four or five kids, [which] was truly scary to us. Here you are not in the perfect situation yourself, to say the least. These kids had no place to go … and they were truly frightened. She dealt with very high-profile cases of women that were beaten by their husbands. Her practice was pretty emotionally draining [but] she was very good at it. She had the right set of skills and was a fighter. Underneath, I think she was frightened herself."[83]

At times, clients could also be obstreperous. L'Heureux-Dubé recalled:

> A man would come in and say, "I don't want to pay the bitch a cent." I would never compromise. If I decided that was not a case I could win, with men particularly, I would say – "I can't win. You won't be happy with my services, perhaps you should look for somebody else." I would say, "This is what I can do for you. You earn so much, alimony would cost this much, [and] my fees would be this. If you don't like it, there are three hundred other lawyers, there's the door." I wasn't there to make money – but to be happy with myself when I finished a case.[84]

The worst case she ever had involved a male client referred by another firm. He had been represented by a lawyer who was named to the bench. Then his second lawyer was appointed to the bench before the trial began. In desperation, the firm referred him to L'Heureux-Dubé – one day before the divorce trial was to start. "I hated the case. But I took it as a service to another colleague. The client was awful, he was involved with bestiality, having sex with his dog, and I was so sorry [for his wife]. At one point they were arguing over the little black cat with the white tail, and I started to laugh so hard that I cried. It was one of those moments that [between] the tension and the story ... even the judge was laughing ... It was an awful thing."[85]

Her years in family law left L'Heureux-Dubé with a strong impression of the multiple challenges faced by women: "It took a lot of courage for women to go through [the process] at this time. They were not respected in court. They were not treated correctly – by the judiciary, by the lawyers, by their husbands."[86]

A Rising Public Profile: "We Need a Woman"

L'Heureux-Dubé's growing reputation resulted in a series of high-profile appointments. In 1967, the Quebec deputy minister of justice asked her to serve on the Conseil consultatif de l'administration de la justice, an advisory board with representatives from practice, academia, and government. The deputy minister's explanation, that they needed a woman, troubled L'Heureux-Dubé. She objected to being singled out on the basis of gender, and retorted that she was interested only if they wanted a competent woman. It took some time to smooth things out, but she eventually served on the council until 1973. She also served as vice president of the Canadian Consumers' Council between 1970 and 1973, and of the Vanier Institute of the Family from 1972 to 1973.

To her surprise, she was also named as Queen's Counsel in 1969. The honorary designation came through the intervention of Rémi Paul, the Quebec minister of justice, with whom she had been speaking at a conference in Ottawa.[87] The conversation turned to the QC designation that the government intended to bestow upon Pierre Trudeau, by then the prime minister of Canada. "I joked with him," recalled L'Heureux-Dubé. "You would give it to Trudeau, but you wouldn't give it to me because I'm a woman!" To her huge merriment, Paul turned to his secretary and said: "She will get a QC as well. Take it down."[88] L'Heureux-Dubé was named a QC the same day in September 1969 as Trudeau. It was a study in contrasts: complaining to the deputy minister about what she perceived as a gender-based female appointment to an advisory board, and needling the minister about the underrepresentation of women in the ranks of QCs.

Family Law

In 1969, Claude Gagnon, *bâtonnier* for the Barreau du Québec, urged L'Heureux-Dubé to run for election to its governing council.[89] Despite the pressures of her practice, she agreed to run out of respect for the *bâtonnier*. Elected in 1970, she was assigned to adjudicate disciplinary complaints against other lawyers. She expressed concern that the bar was too lenient with those who stole money from their clients. "They would suspend them for two months. I said we are not doing ourselves any favour with little taps on the wrist. It should be disbarment for life."[90]

She also recommended that a bar committee be struck to review misconduct allegations against Justice Gérard Corriveau. "Fifteen lawyers had spoken to the chief justice, to complain that they did not want to appear in front of him. I urged the committee that was set up to make a report to the newly formed Canadian Judicial Council [CJC], but nothing happened. The lawyers were so afraid their clients would be penalized. They wouldn't report half of the terrible things that went on in court, because they were afraid."[91] No report was made and no complaint launched with the CJC before her term expired. It was one of the reasons she chose not to run again.

Her most important outside work was with the ambitious project to overhaul the *Civil Code* led by Paul-André Crépeau.[92] It was a massive undertaking born out of the Quiet Revolution, designed to bring the *Civil*

Paul-André Crépeau, McGill law professor and president of the Civil Code Revision Office.

Code into a new century to reflect *la vie moderne*.⁹³ Crépeau's introduction to L'Heureux-Dubé had taken place in 1969, when he watched her appear before a legislative committee with Thérèse Casgrain to comment on a bill on matrimonial law. The bill was based on a report his Civil Code Revision Office had published several years earlier. The two lawyers were critical of the report, and Crépeau laughed as he recalled his reaction: "Claire put in a very intelligent and a very persuasive argument. I said to myself, 'My god, she's so bright! I have to have her with me, and not against me.'"⁹⁴

In 1969, he appointed L'Heureux-Dubé to the Committee on the Law on Persons and on the Family.⁹⁵ The appointment required weekly travel to Montreal. "I called it my *midi-minuit*," remembered L'Heureux-Dubé. "I left at noon, drove to Montreal for 3 p.m., met with the committee until 7 p.m., and then I drove back to Quebec City. Every week, in good weather and bad, storms, whatever, I went. I don't think I missed one."⁹⁶ Crépeau was only too conscious of the commuting risks. "Once a week she came up to Montreal from Quebec, often *entre nous* at 150 miles an hour. I was always in a panic by noon, fearing that Claire would not be with us for the meeting, but she always was."⁹⁷

Crépeau found her work exemplary. He described her as "open-minded," "friendly," "energetic," and "passionately committed to achieving results that were rigorous and intellectually meritorious."⁹⁸ By 1972, she was elevated to committee president when Justice Albert Mayrand departed.⁹⁹ Under her guidance, psychiatrists, sociologists, and social workers were consulted and research reports completed on Quebec law, comparative law, and the economic and social problems of divorce. The group committed itself to radical change. It advocated "the equality of husband and wife," with both spouses holding "identical rights and obligations in marriage."¹⁰⁰ The committee recommended the retention of the traditional separation from bed and board, for those whose religion or morality prevented them from seeking divorce. But it also endorsed full divorce when cohabitation had become "intolerable," or upon consent after one year's separation.¹⁰¹ Surprisingly, in retrospect, it also recommended a new rule, that marriage be declared "absolutely null" when contracted "by two persons of the same sex." The committee gave no explanation for this last proviso.¹⁰² Years later, L'Heureux-Dubé could not recall that this issue had ever been discussed, or that it had found its way into the report.

The content of the committee's two reports would ultimately find their way into the new *Civil Code* in 1991.¹⁰³ Years later, Crépeau marvelled at the committee's accomplishment:

When you think of it, it was extraordinary that the few of us had been given this opportunity, a tremendous responsibility to build a new *Civil Code*. The Quebec *Code* of the 19th century [was] paternalistic, absolutely *passé*. As far as the authority in the family, it was the authority of the husband and the father. "I'm the ruler and I can do as I will decide." We wanted a new *Code* that would reflect the modern values of the end of the twentieth century.[104]

Claire L'Heureux-Dubé and Roger Garneau at the latter's office.

L'Heureux-Dubé's reputation grew by leaps and bounds during these years. Louise Mailhot, who practised in Montreal at the time, had high praise: "She was the lead in family law in Quebec – she was the top."[105] "She was not liked by the sexist judges," recalled her partner Roger Garneau, but "she had influence and a certain radiance. *Elle diffuse la lumière.*† She was brilliant, quick, and she was loved. She gave to the family law its letters of *créance* – *les lettres de noblesse*. Respectability."‡, [106]

---

† "She was a source of light."
‡ "credentials, letters of nobility"

16
Practising as a Woman

When Claire L'Heureux graduated from Laval law school in 1951, the proportion of female lawyers in Quebec stood at 1.11 percent. Their presence more than doubled every ten years over subsequent decades. In her final year of practice, 1972, women represented 6.72 percent.[1] By the turn of the century, the last province to admit women to the bar would outstrip all the others to boast the largest proportion of female lawyers in North America, a remarkable 40 percent.[2] Observers tie the dizzying change of pace firmly to the social upheaval of the Quiet Revolution.[3] For L'Heureux-Dubé, whose last year in practice was in a profession that was 93.28 percent male, it must have felt like a belated surge: "The pyramid was all male when you went to court, from the clerk of the court to the lawyers to the judges."[4] It was her historical fate to be on the vertex of change, at the tip of the wedge that would propel women into law.

PRACTISING UNDER THE SPOTLIGHT:
"YOU HAD TO BE PERFECT IN EVERYTHING"

Women at the forefront faced enormous challenges. Male lawyers were reluctant to hire them. Clients were dubious: *"Ce n'est pas à la secrétaire que je veux parler mais à l'avocat."*[†,5] Without sponsorship from more powerful

---

† "I want to speak to the lawyer, not the secretary."

male lawyers, their careers languished and withered. There were daily reminders of the exception that they represented in a gender-divided world.

Even lunching with colleagues posed problems.[6] Women were barred from the rue Saint-Joseph tavern where L'Heureux-Dubé's colleagues gathered to eat in the early 1970s. Something of a coup occurred when they insisted she join them and offered to defend the case if a police officer should come. The tavern owner was stopped in his tracks the first time she arrived, but made an exception for the well-known lawyer. For L'Heureux-Dubé, the premises were integrated far earlier than the 1979 legal reform that opened taverns to women generally.[7] But both women and Jews were also unwelcome at the fancier private quarters in the Club de la Garnison de Québec, where the city's elite socialized and brokered deals. There, no exceptions were made. "A distinguished and select group steeped in tradition" was the motto.[8] The club insisted that women come through the back door and use a separate staircase. It took years before membership was opened to women or Jews.[9] "Sam Bard, Maurice Pollack, and I were part of the people they explicitly didn't want," explained L'Heureux-Dubé.[10] When the club finally admitted women, she refused to join on principle.

Nowhere was the aberrant status more evident than in court, where female lawyers were forced to tangle with hostile judges. Many judges had opposed the admission of women to the profession from the outset, worried that they would then aspire to become judicial "brethren." The first Canadian lawsuit over the right of women to practise law was a case in point. When Mabel French sought unsuccessfully to become the first female lawyer in New Brunswick in 1905, Chief Justice William H. Tuck had objected: "If this young lady is entitled to be admitted an attorney, she will in a year be entitled to be called to the bar, and, in a few years, will be eligible to be appointed to the bench." The concept of a female judge was to him a complete oxymoron, and he added: "If I dare to express my own views I would say that I have no sympathy with the opinion that women should in all branches of life come in competition with men. Better let them attend to their own legitimate business."[11] Judges who opposed the entry of women, who clung tenaciously to the all-male environment of the judiciary, were not disposed to behave kindly toward the first women who crossed their courtroom thresholds.

L'Heureux-Dubé recognized that the judges were harsher on her and other female lawyers. "The judges would look down on women, and try to take advantage of them. Some of the judges were particularly detestable, and made the young women cry.[12] *"J'ai vu de mes yeux de jeunes avocates pâlir, s'évanouir, trembler, pleurer même au moment de plaider en cour. Je me suis souvent demandé combien de vocations ont été perdues ou détournées simplement par intimidation.*"†, 13 She knew that, for many of the judges, deliberate disapproval always lurked below the surface: "The impression was that I should be home caring for my children. I know they were thinking that."14

Examples of egregious behaviour were not hard to find. One of the early female lawyers from Montreal described how she was treated when she arrived to plead a case in Quebec City. It was established custom that out-of-town counsel would first knock on the door of the judge's chambers to introduce themselves. When she did so in the company of her male colleague, the judge asked her to come in, "sit on his knee," and "give him a kiss." She continued: "I was very embarrassed. I refused to sit on his knee but did give him a peck on the cheek. I was really ashamed. It was like he was drawing attention to me sexually and also treating me like a little girl."15

L'Heureux-Dubé recalled that judges tended to be more familiar with female lawyers than with men. "They would say, *Oui, ma belle*‡ – perhaps meant nicely, but really it was an expression of familiarity or contempt in a way."16 Louise Mailhot, who became the first female articling student at Martineau Walker in Montreal in 1965, described similar treatment from both judges and male lawyers. "There was always a small comment about how you looked. They would call you *la belle* and *la jolie* [or] they always mentioned that I was a 'young colleague' – *ma jeune jolie* – to show I was inexperienced."17

Raymond Lessard, who was admitted to the bar in 1962 and practised with the Quebec City firm of Prévost, Gagné, Flynn, Chouinard et Jacques, agreed that discrimination was pervasive. He explained that male lawyers believed that women were unable to "focus."18 Women were dissuaded from courtroom "battles" because they were thought to be "too weak."19 "*C'est se faire dire que nous avons de l'intuition féminine et que nous sommes émotives plutôt que logiques et d'un esprit analytique,*"§ explained L'Heureux-Dubé.20 Male lawyers complained that female lawyers were "distracting" because they aroused sexual impulses in their male legal

---

† "I have seen with my own eyes young female lawyers turn pale, faint, tremble, and even cry when pleading in court. I have often wondered how many careers were lost or diverted simply by intimidation."
‡ "Yes, my beautiful [or, beautiful one/the pretty one/my young pretty colleague]."
§ "It is tantamount to being told that we have feminine intuition and that we are emotional rather than logical and of an analytical mind."

Louise Mailhot, Quebec lawyer, and later justice of the Quebec Superior Court and Quebec Court of Appeal.

adversaries.[21] Ironically, many of the men who saw gender discrimination saw it in reverse. Lessard remembered that male lawyers would meet to tell stories about female opponents. "They would say, 'The damn girl smiled to the judge and the judge smiled to her and I felt frustrated because she is good-looking and the judge doesn't listen to me anymore.'"[22]

A Canadian survey from the late 1960s elicited a string of negative stereotypes about female lawyers. Women were thought to be "incapable of being realistic or logical." They were accused of treating the practice of law as a "hobby." They were perceived as insufficiently dedicated or ambitious. "If they are single they have no family to feed and if they are married they have a husband who is the primary provider." Important business clients were "patronizing" to women, and could be "handled better by men."[23] Reacting to such attitudes, Toronto lawyer and federal cabinet minister Judy LaMarsh retorted in 1967: "We are like furniture to be looked over and overlooked."[24]

Women often felt that they were practising under a spotlight, that they had to be *"perfect in everything,"* emphasized Annette April, who was called to the Quebec bar in 1954. "They will forget errors coming from a man easier than for a woman."[25] Charlotte Whitton, elected the first female mayor of Ottawa in 1951, said it all in her oft-repeated quip: "Whatever

Raymond Lessard, Quebec City lawyer, Île d'Orléans, Quebec, 2010.

women do, they must do twice as well as men to be thought half as good."[26] For L'Heureux-Dubé, it seemed more like working *"trois fois plus pour n'être même pas reconnues égales."*[†, 27] The second half of Whitton's famous comment, "Luckily, it is not difficult," was filled with hubris. It is a remark that still makes people laugh. There is a touch of ruefulness in the humour, a poking at the cultural images of masculine dominance and bravado with a counter-image of female ambition and confidence.

Self-confidence at the level of Charlotte Whitton's was the *sine qua non* for the women who carved out the first successful law practices, yet traditional gender roles positively discouraged the cultivation of such attributes in women. A contemporary edition of *Roget's Thesaurus* listed "confidence," "self-reliance," "courage," "valour," "audacity," "fortitude," and "prowess" as synonyms of "manliness" and "manhood."[28] It equated "womanly" with "unmanly," "little bit of fluff," "softer," "weaker vessel," and "effeminate."[29] These were the early lessons from L'Heureux-Dubé's beloved Comtesse de Ségur series, which she had imbibed at her mother's knee in the solarium in Rimouski when the dishes were done and the sun was setting over the

---

† "three times as much and not even being acknowledged as equals"

St. Lawrence. *Les petites filles modèles* epitomized modesty, obedience, and charity. How did some women come to cherish instead *Les malheurs de Sophie*, the impish fictional waif who defied all prescriptions for docile femininity?

Resolute fortitude was the demeanour that L'Heureux-Dubé displayed as she grew in visibility and stature during her years in practice. She projected self-assurance, certainty, sure-footedness, and conviction. The young girl whom the nuns suspected lacked self-confidence had emerged from her convent education with a steadying belief in her own intelligence. She had survived the headwinds that buffeted the first women who went into law, landing on her feet in a supportive firm. She had overcome the resistance of clients, counsel, and judges who were deeply skeptical about women's entry into the legal profession.

Observers might have cited different explanations for her boldness. There was the female-centred focus of her family and convent education. There were her friends from childhood and convent days, with whom she kept in close contact, who surrounded her with a nurturing community of support. L'Heureux-Dubé herself would have pointed to the steel-willed backing of her mother, whose optimism and determination she strove to emulate. She might have added that she had been driven to forge a successful legal career in the face of her father's dogged objections. There was the unwavering admiration of Sam Bard and her law partners. And unlike many women, she had the reinforcement of a husband who stood solidly behind his wife's decision to maintain her own career. Arthur may not have been exactly the male equivalent of a devoted stay-at-home wife, to which many male lawyers attributed their success at the time, but he was one of the best on offer in the gendered environment of Quebec City.[30]

"LA TIGRESSE"

Self-confidence was essential but insufficient. It was a fine line that the first female lawyers walked. They were socialized to be female and perceived as such, but were trying to make their way in a masculine world. Confusion abounded when women and those who interacted with them attempted to superimpose the stereotypical characteristics of "femininity" on the traits of "aggression" and "dominance" that were thought to be the hallmarks of successful lawyers. Leaning too far toward the feminine side risked losing the respect of clients, lawyers, and judges. Being perceived as too masculine resulted in being branded as mean-spirited and abrasive.

Was there a balance that would prove workable? Would the female lawyer develop a distinct persona? Would her merger into the male profession make her into a "manly woman"? Would the masculinized image of male lawyers become softened at the edges as the profession absorbed women? At stake was nothing less than the very essence of traditional sex roles.

Some female lawyers consciously tried to deploy "charm" to avoid bruising male egos.[31] Suffrage advocate Thérèse Casgrain was famous for this. In his introduction to her autobiography, Frank R. Scott wrote:

> [S]he showed it is possible for a woman to play an active role in public life without losing any of her personal charm or giving up any of her duties as wife and mother. She was the most feminine of feminists, of whom a trade-unionist once said to me: "She makes every boy feel a man and every man feel a boy."[32]

Canadian female lawyers surveyed toward the end of L'Heureux-Dubé's years in practice raised a chorus of voices in agreement: "The woman lawyer who attempts to overcome her supposed sexual handicap by masculinising herself in appearance or manner," said one respondent, "is bound to defeat her purpose and suffer rebuffs." Instead, she should remain "feminine and charming without flaunting her sex"; this would cause "most men, to the extent that they remain conscious of her sex at all," to be "inclined to respond positively toward her."[33]

Roger Garneau observed that Claire L'Heureux-Dubé was always "*une femme charmante*. She charmed people. She charmed the judges. She was courteous, sincere, and frank."[34] Yet there were places where charm did little good. Justice Gérard Corriveau, brazenly displaying discriminatory attitudes in court, would never have been disarmed by charm. No doubt he would have been hard-pressed to choose the adjective "charming" in regard to L'Heureux-Dubé either. "Frank" might have been more in line with his experience.

And no abundance of charm could triumph, no matter what the circumstances, without a measure of tenacity. Toughness was an essential characteristic for the early female lawyers. In Raymond Lessard's eyes, L'Heureux-Dubé possessed this quality: "I would say she had a strong reputation. She wouldn't give it up."[35] Roger Garneau expanded: "She had to face old men, old judges, sometimes you might call them 'machos' – but she was respected because she was a fighter."[36] L'Heureux-Dubé's reaction to the discriminatory environment was to put on the strongest façade she could muster: "They learned not to try it with me. I was not a woman. I was the enemy. I encountered very few of these who tried to be flattering – I wasn't the type."³⁷ She had to banish all self-doubt and forge ahead. Within the bar, some lawyers tagged her with an unusual nickname: *La Tigresse*.† L'Heureux-Dubé was not nicknamed *Le Tigre*,‡ a nickname that might have symbolized courage, bravery, and heroism – in a man.³⁸ *La Tigresse* was a female tiger, a jungle image laden with a mixture of ferocity and sexualization. She did not object. She strove to maintain a delicate balance between femininity and the stereotypically masculine qualities of fearlessness and strength. She was inventing a new zone, somewhere between femininity and masculinity, with no role models to follow, no one from whom to take advice.

An Uneasy Relationship with Feminism:
"I Never Had the Idea That I Was on a Feminist Mission"

The first female lawyers were loath to wallow in complaints about discrimination. Surprisingly, many maintained that their sex was "neither a handicap nor an advantage."³⁹ One of the earliest surveys of female lawyers in Toronto, taken of the group that entered law school between 1916 and 1966, found that almost all who volunteered written comments endorsed the idea that "if a woman works hard and does a good job, she will be accepted."⁴⁰ Linda Silver Dranoff, a Toronto family lawyer who conducted the survey in the early 1970s, speculated that given the "deep-seated myths concerning women's intellect, motivation, and emotional stability," women might "*have* to deny their femaleness" in order to take themselves "seriously as lawyers."⁴¹ Others dubbed it the "ostrich syndrome."⁴²

Marguerite E. Ritchie, one of the early women in the federal department of justice, explained: "I have found that women are unwilling to admit discrimination, either because they are trying to conceal the fact from themselves or because they must play the role of 'Uncle Tom.'"⁴³ Dwelling upon discrimination could be overwhelming and self-defeating, and expressing objection was seldom career enhancing. Edra Sanders Ferguson, who practised law with her father and two brothers in St. Thomas, Ontario, in the 1930s and became Ontario's first Division Court judge in 1962, offered typical advice: "The best way to tackle prejudice is to ignore

---

† The Tigress
‡ The Tiger

it. The more women complain about sex prejudice, the more they draw attention to being women, rather than lawyers or doctors or what have you. Be confident. Be good at your job and you'll get there."[44] It was a stoicism shared by many, who coped with the challenges by trying to minimize them.[45]

L'Heureux-Dubé was firmly of this mindset. She asserted that "the profession was a gentleman's profession at the time, a small community, and we all belonged. I don't remember any case where a lawyer made disparaging comments, or made my life miserable."[46] To her mind, she was "not that kind of a feminist who said 'I'm a woman, you are discriminating.' I said to myself, 'They are not used to it, but eventually they will come to treat us as equals.'"[47] Asked whether being the only woman in so many venues had an effect on her, she replied: "I don't think it had any effect at all. I didn't realize it. I was doing what I wanted to do."[48] Confronted with the explicit rules denying women entrance to the Club de la Garnison, she explained:

> It was what was done. [There was] no public protest. I wasn't at that stage yet of my dissent. My colleagues who I dined with there never said, "Come with us, we'll break the rules." They could have. They didn't. The fact that you are alone, you have no support, means a lot. At the time, we were alone, the first ones. I suspect, if I had insisted on the front door, they would have manhandled me – carried me out. I was nobody, just a lawyer. I didn't try. The tavern was right in front of our place, so they breached the rules. The Club was an institution![49]

Throughout her convent education and law school years, L'Heureux-Dubé and her female classmates forged no philosophical or activist connections to feminism. They were travelling into uncharted territory as women, but they disavowed any identification with a wider movement. "We didn't see that we had a mission," L'Heureux-Dubé said. "We had enough on our plate just to find the money for our studies and to learn. I was not really conscious of discrimination against women at that time. Although women didn't get scholarships, we accepted it as a fact of life. It was nothing that would spur us to move to the barricades."[50]

To be sure, the post-suffrage years were not vibrant ones for the women's movement in Quebec or in the rest of Canada. Ten years after it was published in 1949, Simone de Beauvoir's classic treatise *Le deuxième sexe* was still not to be found in Montreal bookshops by order of the archbishop, Cardinal Paul-Émile Léger. That fall, an interview with de Beauvoir on Radio-Canada was partially censored due to pressure from Cardinal Léger.[51] When L'Heureux-Dubé launched her career in 1952, she was well ahead of the rebirth of organized feminism:

> I never thought of the fact that other women didn't have opportunities. When I was asked to help, I did, but I didn't have women's issues in mind. I treated my secretaries well. I had women clients, but I never had the idea that I was on a feminist mission. It was not in my parameter of views. It is very disappointing to some, I know, but it's true. The feminist movement was not advanced at the time, and I was not one who would have started it first. I had my career, my children. I was occupied twenty-four hours a day.[52]

L'Heureux-Dubé grew up in an era when there was almost no vocabulary to explain what women confronted. Conditions had not gelled to produce a vibrant contemporary women's movement that could document and analyze patterns of discrimination. L'Heureux-Dubé recalled that Thérèse Casgrain used the gender-neutral language of "justice" and "fairness" when she demanded votes for women and called for revision of

Thérèse Casgrain, founder of La Voix des femmes and advocate for female suffrage in Quebec.

La Voix des femmes. *Left to right*, [unidentified], Thérèse Casgrain, [unidentified], Simone Monet-Chartrand, [unidentified]. Man in front is the Right Honourable Paul Martin, Sr., minister of external affairs.

the Quebec *Civil Code*.⁵³ The word "feminism" was not *courant*.† Even "equality," she said, was a "notion which had not yet been developed."⁵⁴

But the world around L'Heureux-Dubé was about to change dramatically. The power of de Beauvoir's ideas had become irrepressible. Her book, which began circulating throughout Quebec in the 1960s, inspired a new generation of women.⁵⁵ Betty Friedan's blockbuster 1963 book *The Feminine Mystique,* which critiqued traditional sex roles and demanded expanded horizons for wives and mothers, was translated into French, attracted television coverage, and became a bestseller in Quebec.⁵⁶ Jeanne Sauvé, the charismatic speaker who had captivated L'Heureux-Dubé at the Jeunesse Étudiante Catholique conference in Montreal in 1945 and would go on to become Canada's first female governor-general, was quoted as saying: *"Je me demande si les Canadiennes françaises sont si heureuses dans leur foyer qu'on le suppose."*‡, ⁵⁷

---

† in common usage
‡ "I wonder if French Canadian women are as happy in their homes as they are thought to be."

La Fédération des femmes du Québec, first board of directors, 1966. *Top row, left to right*, Colette Beauchamp, Pauline Larochelle, Yvette Rousseau, Simone Chartrand, Fernande Cantero, Rita Cadieux; *middle row, left to right*, Réjane Laberge-Colas (president), Marie Gingras, Nicole Forget, Lise Trudeau, Raymonde Roy; *bottom row, left to right*, Cécile Labelle, Luce Dumoulin. *Absent from photo:* Monique Bégin (first vice president), Odette Dick, and Germaine Goudreault.

The rapid erosion of traditional gender roles has been described as central to the transformation of Quebec in the 1960s.[58] In 1961, Thérèse Casgrain founded the influential La Voix des femmes (Voice of Women), setting off a surge of activism in the province.[59] L'Heureux-Dubé did not join. A spiralling number of women's organizations banded together to form the Fédération des femmes du Québec in 1966.[60] Two female lawyers were among the sixteen signatories to the FFQ constitution: Réjane Laberge-Colas and Alice Desjardins.[61] The former would become the first woman appointed to the Quebec Superior Court.[62] The latter taught at the University of Montreal, the first female law professor in the country.[63] Quebec women rejoiced that the province that had been the last to allow women to vote, and to admit women into law, was now leading the country.[64] Once again, Claire L'Heureux-Dubé did not join up. The one explicitly female organization she did join, a province-wide group for female lawyers named Association des avocates, was short-lived, and her involvement was limited.[65]

The feminist movement continued to gain velocity. At the end of the decade, Quebec women joined others from across Canada to testify at the hearings of the Royal Commission on the Status of Women, where Monique Bégin, one of the FFQ founders, served as the commission secretary.[66] In 1970, the commission published its *Rapport Bird,* as it was called in French after its chair, Florence Bird. Although there was some uneasiness over the extent to which the report captured *le caractère québécois,* its demands for gender equality resonated throughout Quebec. The question was how to preserve the distinctiveness of Québécois culture while abandoning the dogma of *"les reines du foyer"* and *"la revanche des berceaux."*[†, 67] During the 1960s and '70s, Quebecers discarded Catholicism as a measure of identity, and the fight was on to shed the traditional image of Quebec women as docile, housebound mothers of large families.[68]

Rebellious younger feminists put such images behind them as they drew upon influences from France, English Canada, and the United States to fashion their own dynamic movement.[69] Labelling the Bird Report "conservative," they campaigned for free abortion on demand – *l'avortement libre et gratuit.* University students distributed the *McGill Birth Control Handbook,* a woman-focused how-to manual that achieved international acclaim. In 1972, the first women's studies course was launched at the Université du Québec à Montréal. Quebec feminists demonstrated against sexual violence, woman battering, capitalism, and colonialism. They demanded feminization of the French language and the arts, lesbian rights, unionization, and free daycare.[70] After the separatist Parti Québécois won the provincial election in 1976, feminists insisted upon equal time. The slogan of the Front de libération des femmes du Québec (FLFQ) would encapsulate it perfectly: *"Pas de libération des femmes sans Québec libre, pas de Québec libre sans libération des femmes."*[‡, 71]

It made Claire L'Heureux-Dubé distinctly uneasy. One event in particular left her decisively of the view that "feminism" was not for her. It involved a demonstration at the tavern on rue Saint-Joseph, the one that barred women but had made an exception for her when she lunched there with her colleagues. "One day a bunch of women invaded that tavern," she recalled, "crying out loud that they had a right to sit in a tavern just as men did." For a woman whose husband was losing his struggle with

---

† Quebec specificity; "queens of the household"; "revenge of the cradle"
‡ "No liberation of women without the liberation of Quebec. No liberation of Quebec without the liberation of women."

alcoholism, this would have rankled at some level, but her reaction was also entwined with the plight of her clients. She saw the feminist activism as nothing short of ridiculous:

> They called themselves feminists in a place where men were drinking their pay while their wives were crying in our offices unable to pay their debts. To me, they were a bunch of crazy women, while we were fighting for justice where justice counted, in courts and before the legislature. The word feminist for me from thereon was associated with those crazy women and I never wanted to be part of it.[72]

She had worked too hard to be taken seriously to risk being tarred with the radical actions of "crazy women."[73] Her sentiments were well captured by a 1972 Quebec newspaper article that focused on L'Heureux-Dubé's rise to prominence in an era of change: *"Féministe, elle ne l'est pas du tout, n'ayant jamais souffert de discrimination. « Quand les femmes auront conquis le pouvoir économique, ces deux mots – féminisme et discrimination – disparaîtront du langage », affirme-t-elle."*[†,74]

Shirley Tucker Parks, a federal government lawyer who was admitted to the Saskatchewan bar in 1953 and was to become a close friend of L'Heureux-Dubé's some years later, explained her similar sentiments. "I never thought of taking the label 'feminist' initially," she said. "You had to tread on your toes. You had to be a good lawyer, but you also had to be very careful how you presented yourself, if you were going to have acceptance in what you were trying to do. Certainly, there was no question of presenting yourself as a feminist. We were part of a cohort that preferred to think of ourselves as lawyers, not feminist lawyers."[75]

L'Heureux-Dubé repeatedly denied having experienced discrimination personally, but years of family practice had immersed her within a crucible of gender disparity. The unfairness she confronted in the courtroom built upon the sexism she had already experienced in her own life: her father's efforts to derail her legal career, the denial of scholarships, the dismissive treatment of female law students, the sexual harassment she suffered in her clerical position, the skepticism of lawyers, clients, and judges. She may have been uneasy with the word "feminism," but she had made an

---

† "A feminist she definitely isn't, having never suffered from discrimination. 'When women will have conquered economic power, these two words – feminism and discrimination – will disappear from the language,' she says."

Shirley Tucker Parks, lawyer and long-time friend of Claire L'Heureux-Dubé, Ottawa, 2009.

enormous contribution to the dismantling of sexism within the Quebec *Civil Code*. Julien Payne, one of Canada's most famous family law experts, called her "an egalitarian" whose "belief in equality came from the heart." She practised family law, he emphasized, and "she represented a lot of women, so dimes to doughnuts she learned about equality the hard way."[76] Now the struggles would move to the judiciary. What would the judges make of the changing world that was springing up around their courtrooms?

Quebec Superior Court

17
New Career Directions
"No" to Electoral Politics, "Yes" to the Bench, 1972–73

Claire L'Heureux-Dubé should have had an inkling that something was stirring when the phone call came in from Jean-Paul Lefebvre.[1] Lefebvre was a forty-six-year-old Quebec Liberal party operative, a confidante of Jean Marchand, who was co-chairing the party's 1972 federal election campaign.[2] Lefebvre asked to come to L'Heureux-Dubé's home to talk with her. To her surprise, he showed up with Prime Minister Pierre Elliot Trudeau.

THE PATH NOT TAKEN: LIBERAL POLITICS

The fifteenth prime minister of Canada had swept to power in 1968 riding the wave of "Trudeaumania" that washed over the country, and he was preparing to campaign for a second term in the fall of 1972.[3] Over half a century had passed since the federal suffrage was extended to Quebec women, yet none had ever been elected to Parliament, and some thought that change was long overdue.[4] Although much of the campaign would continue to be overtly sexist, Trudeau wanted some female candidates who could actually be elected.[5] There were rumours that Marc Lalonde, his principal secretary, who would later become minister responsible for the status of women, was compiling a list of eight women from Quebec, each one a potential candidate.[6] "I recommended that women run," confirmed Lalonde, but the desire for women was "widespread, stretching all the way to Trudeau himself."[7]

Les trois colombes at 24 Sussex Drive: *left to right,* Jean Marchand, Prime Minister Pierre Trudeau, Gérard Pelletier.

Why did they call on Claire L'Heureux-Dubé? As one of Quebec City's few high-profile female lawyers, she would undoubtedly have been an attractive prospect. And while she had no previous political involvement, there were some important links with the Liberals. The party's chief power broker in Quebec, Jean Marchand, was a friend of her brother-in-law Yves Dubé, who served as dean of social sciences at Laval University from 1968 to 1976. L'Heureux-Dubé first met Marchand when she, Marchand, and Yves Dubé had found themselves on a plane bound for Ottawa. The three spontaneously decided to get together that night, and it proved to be a most enjoyable evening. L'Heureux-Dubé remembered dancing with Marchand, who had a considerable reputation as flirtatious with women. Clearly, her charm was on full display. The dynamic cabinet minister impressed her. She perceived him as having entered politics "with his heart, to change things."[8]

Marchand first gained prominence during the 1949 Asbestos strike, where he stood out as an impassioned orator and brilliant labour organizer who "travelled the highways and back roads of Quebec," sleeping in workers' bedrooms, speaking in church basements, and singing ballads in cafés as he pressed for workers' equality. In 1965, he resigned as head of the Confederation of National Trade Unions (CNTU) to run for the Liberals. The triumvirate of Marchand, Trudeau, and Gérard Pelletier, dubbed the "three wise men" in English and *les trois colombes*† in French, burst onto the electoral scene that year. Marchand was appointed to cabinet immediately, as senior Quebec minister. He was to become one of Trudeau's closest colleagues and a lifelong friend.[9]

There were other linkages. Arthur Dubé knew Trudeau personally. The two had socialized years earlier, part of a small French Canadian cohort in Ottawa when Arthur had worked for the Department of Mines.[10] Although Arthur had never joined the Liberal party, both he and Yves were great admirers of Trudeau and his political philosophy. So it was that Arthur welcomed the prime minister as an old friend the evening that Trudeau and Lefebvre came calling.

In the family's living room, Trudeau quickly came to the point. He asked L'Heureux-Dubé to run as a Liberal in her home riding of Louis-Hébert, emphasizing that they wanted a woman. There are several versions of the ensuing conversation, all of them funny. L'Heureux-Dubé recalled that she delivered a flat rejection. "I said no, I'm not interested at all to go into politics. You're too late. My children are born. And you're too early, because they are not brought up." Then she added: "I accept on one condition. That I be defeated!"[11] Other recollections were of a longer exchange, with Trudeau protesting that she would not be defeated, that they "could put a dog there and get it elected," to which L'Heureux-Dubé retorted, "So, run the dog."[12]

Despite the humour, there was some probing on L'Heureux-Dubé's part. She wondered aloud whether women were wanted as mere window-dressing, and predicted that they would be relegated to the backbenches. She remonstrated that no one listened to women, and that female MPs would be no exception. When Trudeau insisted that he would appoint her to his cabinet, she registered total disbelief. "I'm not stupid. That's ridiculous. I said no."[13]

Years later, L'Heureux-Dubé admitted that she might also have been afraid. She had no first-hand experience of politics, and very little she could draw upon indirectly from family and colleagues. No one from her law firm had ever run for office. None of the women from her cohort at

---

† the three doves

Laval had tried her hand at politics. She had no money to fund a campaign. The challenges of scaling the walls of Laval and venturing into practice as one of only a few women in the capital had not daunted her. But her self-confidence faltered at the prospect of politics. She did not ask Trudeau for time to reflect on the offer. She never second-guessed the decision. She didn't look twice at the fork in the road. Her refusal made the headlines in the local newspaper: *"La famille avant la politique chez Madame Claire L'Heureux-Dubé."*† The laudatory article, which described her as *"humaine, dynamique, optimiste,"* and *"une travailleuse acharnée,"*‡ quoted her as saying: *"Mon schème de valeurs ne me permettait pas d'y penser. Ma priorité va à ma famille."*§, 14

Instead, she urged Trudeau and Lefebvre to consider Albanie Morin, a client of hers who lived in the riding. Recently widowed with grown children, Morin had retained L'Heureux-Dubé to handle her husband's estate. She was a teacher and translator, a rising municipal politician with the Council of Sillery who had just enrolled in law school. Her husband and sons had been Liberal party stalwarts. L'Heureux-Dubé recommended her without reservation. Although neither man committed himself that night, they pursued the lead. In the 30 October 1972 election, Albanie Morin sailed to victory in the Louis-Hébert riding and entered Parliament as one of the three first Québécoise MPs, along with Monique Bégin and Jeanne Sauvé.[15] She was re-elected in 1974 and served until her untimely death in 1976.[16]

"She Would Have Made a Great Politician"

Many have characterized Claire L'Heureux-Dubé as someone who could work a room like a natural politician.[17] Quick on her feet, humorous, well organized, and a glutton for long hours of work, she had many of the key attributes for electoral success. What if she had taken the bait and entered federal politics in the winnable riding of Louis-Hébert? Backed by the Quebec Liberal machine, chances are she would have won the seat that fall.[18] Entering Parliament as one of five women out of 264 MPs, with the prime minister intent on reserving a cabinet post for a woman, she might well have taken that prize.[19]

---

† "Family comes before politics at Madame Claire L'Heureux-Dubé's home"
‡ "human, dynamic, optimistic"; "a relentless worker"
§ "My set of values forbade me to consider it. My priority is my family."

The three Québécoise MPs elected in 1972: *clockwise from top left,* Albanie Paré Morin; Jeanne Sauvé, later Canada's first female governor-general; and Monique Bégin, a leading Quebec feminist.

Was it a lost opportunity?[20] Knowledgeable observers predicted that L'Heureux-Dubé could have been spectacularly successful as a politician.[21] Others suggested that the tumultuous political landscape ahead would have jeopardized her prospects. The oil embargo, the controversy over bilingualism, the introduction of unpopular wage and price controls, the divisive National Energy Program, the rise to power of René Lévesque's Parti Québécois in 1976 – all of these provoked bitter turmoil within the government.[22] Some wondered whether she would have resigned from cabinet on one provocation or another.[23] L'Heureux-Dubé herself had no regrets. "I would never have liked being a politician," she said. "I am a dissident, not a party person."[24] Of course, the opposite might also have occurred. Politics might have tempered her tendency to stand independently, a quality that was only reinforced within the judiciary.

The Judicial Path

It was the judicial door that opened next. This time the call came from Albanie Morin, the new Liberal MP for L'Heureux-Dubé's riding. Morin told her there was a judicial spot opening up and it was time to put a woman on the bench. Was she interested? Initially, L'Heureux-Dubé said no. "The judge post paid about $38,000," she explained. "I was making more than that for the first time in my life. It was too early for me. I told her to give me five years."[25] Morin phoned back weeks later to advise that someone more closely connected to the Liberal party was on the verge of getting the judgeship. As it turned out, the rumour mill was wrong.[26]

At the beginning of February 1973, another call came through, but L'Heureux-Dubé was out at a bar committee meeting. Over the next few days, repeated messages were left asking her to call "Mr. Lang." "I told my secretary, I don't know any Mr. Lang," she remembered. When she finally returned the call, she discovered it was Justice Minister Otto Lang. According to her recollection, he told her, "We've been trying to reach you for three days. You're harder to reach than the prime minister. We have signed the Order-in-Council naming you to the Quebec Superior Court."[27] With the stroke of a pen, on 8 February 1973, she became the first woman on the Superior Court in the district of Quebec, the second in the province, and the third in the country.[28]

This time she did not refuse. The cachet of the judicial designation, perennially a symbol of elevation in the eyes of the profession and particularly so for a woman, must have factored into her decision. "How could I say no?" she exclaimed.²⁹ She agreed to take the appointment, but remained adamant that she had never sought judicial office:

> I never asked to go to the Superior Court. In fact I didn't want to go. As a woman, it was not the same thing as a man who wants to go up and up. As a woman, we knew we had no chance. I don't dream about impossible things. In my time, it was not in the cards, not in the stars. [The judges] were all men in black robes. I didn't fit. I was just in the wilderness. There were no steps taken, talking to people, nothing. I was happy. The main thing, I think, is that I owed nothing to nobody. Of course you always owe to somebody ... you don't get there by yourself. But I never *asked* for a favour.³⁰

It is undisputed that L'Heureux-Dubé never asked for judicial appointment, unlike many others who lobbied either sporadically or incessantly. Yet the story she presented went beyond this. L'Heureux-Dubé would later maintain that she never agreed to let her name go forward, that the first she knew she was even being considered came when Lang phoned to tell her that the Order-in-Council had been signed.³¹ It underscored her message that she never asked, took no steps, and talked to no one. The problem is that those at the centre of the judicial appointments process flatly rejected any such notion. According to Otto Lang and Marc Lalonde, Orders-in-Council never went to cabinet without a positive commitment from the nominee ahead of time.³²

The discrepancy may be attributable to faulty memory.³³ Yet L'Heureux-Dubé's insistence that the judicial appointment was orchestrated entirely without her knowledge seems designed to buttress her depiction of herself as a woman "just in the wilderness," a complete outsider to the corridors of power. She bristled during a 1973 interview with a Quebec journalist who suggested that all judges came from "the establishment," retorting impatiently, *"Ce n'est pas vrai. Tout ce que j'ai, je l'ai gagné à la sueur de mon front."*†, ³⁴ By 1973, this was something of an overstatement. She had achieved success through the "sweat of her own brow," but in some ways she had become part of the establishment too. She was no longer the lower-middle-class girl from Rimouski, the customs inspector's daughter. She had negotiated the shoals of law school and bested male classmates from elite legal dynasties. She was a capable practising lawyer. She had

---

† "That's not true. Everything I have, I won by the sweat of my brow."

1014 Mont-Saint-Denis, L'Heureux-Dubé's home from 1969 to 1987.

been elected by her peers to sit on the bar council. She had a QC. Her success in law had enabled her to purchase her dream house four years earlier, at 1014 rue du Mont-Saint-Denis, one of the most exclusive streets in Sillery. It was no mansion on the Grande Allée handed down through generations of elite lawyers and judges, but it was a gracious home where she and Arthur planted flowering cherry and crabapple trees and rows of roses and tulips up the stone-edged tiered front path.[35]

Quebec was too small and too tight a community to give full credence to L'Heureux-Dubé's claim of lacking connections. She was the most senior female lawyer in the city and the wife of a Laval professor. Her mentor had been appointed a judge. Her husband knew the prime minister. Her brother-in-law knew Jean Marchand. And she knew Albanie Morin, whose political career she had herself set into motion. There is no question that she was an outsider by gender, that all of the judges were "men in black robes," but, as with many people new to power, she had yet to fully recognize that she was not a bit player any longer.

The journalist for *Action Québec* who interviewed L'Heureux-Dubé at her home painted a picture of a confident, well-spoken woman, "freshly coiffed" and wearing green eyeshadow, who spoke of the honour that surrounded judicial elevation and the integrity of the legal system. While they chatted, little Pierre, described as *"un diablotin aux cheveux cendrés,"*† ran in and out of the room, finding excuses to tap the piano keys, blow a few notes on the flute, and announce loudly that he "hated to go to the shopping centre with his mother." L'Heureux-Dubé took the interruptions in stride, stressing that she had never accepted that professional success should come at the expense of family life.[36] It was the sort of message that Sandra Day O'Connor, sworn in as the first woman on the US Supreme Court in 1981, would also emphasize. When she spoke, O'Connor liked to remind her avid audiences that she had come "with her bra and her wedding ring."[37] Speaking to the journalist that day, L'Heureux-Dubé was equally dismissive of her connections with the women's movement:

> *Elle n'a jamais senti le besoin de joindre les rangs des « Women's lib » qui se proposent de faire l'émancipation de la femme. « Pour moi, la discrimination n'a jamais été un problème. J'admets qu'elle existe et que de tels mouvements peuvent réveiller la population mais j'ai l'impression que personne ne croit vraiment à ces mouvements », dit-elle.*‡, 38

It was an interview designed to allay any fears that she might be stepping outside the feminine role, poised to foment radical change from the bench. She self-consciously portrayed herself as non-elite, someone who had worked hard to get where she was, and someone who would not shake up the court. It belied her reputation as *La Tigresse*.

Peeking behind the Scenes

What had occurred behind the scenes to orchestrate this precedent-setting appointment? A curtain of mystery veils most judicial appointments, but at least some details of this one have become clearer with time. One woman

---

† "a sandy-haired little devil"
‡ "She has never felt the need to join the ranks of 'Women's Lib' who propose to emancipate women. 'For me, discrimination has never been a problem. I admit that it exists and that such movements can awaken the population, but I am under the impression that no one really believes in these movements,' she said."

and four men seem to have been prime contributors: Albanie Morin, Otto Lang, Paul-André Crépeau, Gordon Henderson, and Jean Marchand.

There was no application process and there were no paper records to confirm who first suggested L'Heureux-Dubé, but all signs point to Albanie Morin. She was a strong advocate for female judges, her political career had been jump-started by L'Heureux-Dubé, she thought highly of her former lawyer, and she was the conduit for the confidential conversations that preceded the appointment.[39] Morin's daughter, who would go on to study law herself, emphasized that her mother admired Claire L'Heureux-Dubé, "consulted her when she was a practising lawyer in Quebec," and "probably studied law herself and influenced me in that direction, inspired by Claire L'Heureux-Dubé's example."[40]

The person to whom Morin would have pitched the idea was Otto Lang, the Liberal minister of justice from 1972 to 1975. Lang agreed to be interviewed about the appointment many years later, to the extent that he could do so without violating codes of confidentiality. "We were looking for people of quality," he explained, "and obviously there were some people who had good opinions about her."[41] Due to an increase in the size of the judiciary, Lang made more appointments during his term than in any comparable period in Canadian history. Women often make gains during periods of expansion, and the sheer number of new slots available in the courts certainly opened the way for more adventurous choices.[42]

Lang was also supportive of appointing women, which puzzled some of those who knew him personally. Shirley Tucker Parks, a classmate of Lang's at the University of Saskatchewan, expressed surprise that he would appoint the first woman to the Quebec district of the Superior Court.[43] Monique Bégin, who would later become a cabinet colleague of his, also would not have predicted that he would become a path-breaker for female judges, but added that he was "very intelligent," "extremely competent," and a "fair man."[44] Ed Ratushny, Lang's former executive assistant who was appointed his special adviser on judicial affairs shortly after L'Heureux-Dubé's appointment, remarked that "Otto Lang was always critiqued as being against women's issues." In his view, this was not "an accurate perception."[45]

Lang was willing to clarify his objectives. He was indeed looking for female candidates: "I came from a law school class at the University of Saskatchewan that had more women than usual. In 1953, when I graduated, there were five women out of twenty-seven students. One of those was Shirley Tucker Parks, [who] was such a champion of women lawyers. [And] I had three sisters and a mother who was a force."[46] John Turner,

Otto Lang, minister of justice at the time of L'Heureux-Dubé's first judicial appointment.

Lang's predecessor as justice minister, had started the ball rolling by appointing two women to superior courts, and Lang would appoint three more before his term ended.[47] The *Globe and Mail* quoted Lang as saying: "If I'm looking at an equal man and woman for an appointment, I'll appoint the woman."[48]

Lang's attitude can be contrasted with the views of US president Richard Nixon, whose 1971 tapes from the White House displayed his antipathy toward female judges. Tossing about the idea of nominating a woman to the Supreme Court, he complained: "I'm not for it. I don't think women should ever be allowed to vote even. I'm not for women, frankly, in any job. The reason ... is mainly because they are erratic. And emotional. Men are erratic and emotional too, but the point is a woman is more likely to be."[49] His grudging nomination to the Supreme Court of Mildred L. Lillie, then on the Court of Appeal for the Second Appellate District of California, was based on expedience: "[B]elieve me, women's lib is here, [and] it is a growing thing ... It isn't a man's world anymore, unfortunately. So I lean to a woman only because, frankly, I think at this time ... we got to pick up every half a percentage point we can."[50] The appointment was never completed. It would take another decade for Sandra Day O'Connor to achieve distinction as the first woman on the US Supreme Court in 1981.[51]

For his part, Otto Lang was more interested in appointments based on merit than on political affiliation. Had he been less interested in judges without party connections, L'Heureux-Dubé's long-standing political neutrality might have reduced her chances. When Lang taught law at the University of Saskatchewan, students in his constitutional law course asked him what it took to get "good appointments" rather than "just political appointees." He replied: "A minister of justice with guts."[52] In 1974, the *Montreal Gazette* listed the qualities Lang searched for in a potential judge:

> In recent months, [Justice Minister Otto Lang] has made a serious attempt to broaden his horizons in selecting the best possible man – not simply the best Liberal man – for the job ... When Otto Lang goes looking for a potential judge, as he often must these days, he is taking pains to consult respected individuals in bar associations, law societies, and in legal aid circles where younger lawyers are more prevalent. The minister of justice is looking at men who have spent a great deal of time in court as well as those who have seen little service there, because he feels members of the latter group sometimes exhibit skill at tackling the real issues in a case ... The human qualities Mr. Lang says he likes in a judge are "things like sympathy, generosity and charity" as well as integrity, ability to listen and an "impeccable personal life."[53]

What did it mean for the minister to "consult"? Historically, justice ministers had selected nominees based entirely on personal knowledge supplemented by whatever ad hoc advice might come from cabinet colleagues, MPs, lawyers, and judges.[54] Justice Minister Pierre Trudeau had initiated change in 1967. He submitted lists of names to a national committee on the judiciary set up by the Canadian Bar Association. The committee consulted on a confidential basis, and then pronounced individuals to be "well qualified," "qualified," or "not qualified." The minister was not required to accept the recommendation, but it generally carried the day.[55] Although the office of the deputy minister of justice also reviewed potential candidates, these opinions were given relatively less weight.[56] At the time of L'Heureux-Dubé's appointment, Lang combined his own ad hoc consultations with those of the CBA committee.[57]

The most influential individual Lang consulted turned out to be Paul-André Crépeau, the head of the project to revise the Quebec *Civil Code*, with whom L'Heureux-Dubé worked so closely in Montreal. Years back, when Crépeau was a McGill law professor and Lang was dean of law at the University of Saskatchewan, the two had become friends while serving on the executive of the Canadian Association for Law Teachers. Lang phoned Crépeau personally to ask about L'Heureux-Dubé, and Crépeau assured him that her work on family law reform had been stellar, and that she would make a great judge. Crépeau may also have hoped that as a sitting judge, L'Heureux-Dubé would have more time to devote to the *Civil Code* revision project than she had as a busy lawyer.[58]

Gordon Henderson entered the picture as chair of the CBA committee. Henderson was a prominent litigation and intellectual property lawyer in Ottawa, an individual for whom "everybody had high regard," according to Lang.[59] It is unclear whom Henderson actually consulted, or what the committee's recommendation was, but years later, Lang offered his opinion that the CBA national committee was preferable to local committees, which would be tried later. "There are so many reasons why [local committees] want their own candidates," he stressed. "Hatreds, jealousies, envies emerged. They would tell you one candidate was 'hopeless,' but it was not true. It was just that they wanted their own preferred candidates. They were very influenced by the 'old boy's club.' I think [Claire] would have been blocked by a local committee back then. [That was] less likely with a national committee."[60] Gordon Henderson, it appears, gave a green light.

To the extent that national consultation solicited more detailed and reliable information about strengths and weaknesses of candidates, it was a plus. The potential problem with consultation, even inside national committees, was the risk that tightly knit legal circles might lean toward replicating themselves. The homosocial predisposition to recognize merit within one's own group over others poses a significant threat to diversification within the justice system. A cautionary tale from south of the border demonstrated full well the perils of consultation. It was the American Bar Association Standing Committee on the Federal Judiciary that torpedoed Nixon's reluctant nomination of Mildred Lillie to the US Supreme Court in 1971. It ranked her as "unqualified" by a vote of eleven to one, while stating that she was "probably as good as any woman that could be considered for the Court."[61]

Musing later on what must have been an endorsement from the CBA committee, L'Heureux-Dubé expressed surprise that the bar supported a female candidate at the time. "We were only a few. They had so many of their own in the boys' club," she explained.[62] She was not the only one who was surprised. Monique Perron, who entered practice in Quebec City shortly after L'Heureux-Dubé, believed the men "did not want to see us elevated."[63] The *Montreal Gazette* reporter who wrote the article quoting Otto Lang's comments about judges had used exclusively male terminology: the goal was to find the "best possible man" for the position.[64] L'Heureux-Dubé's appointment as the first woman was "a surprise ... to me, to everyone," noted her law partner, Jacques Philippon.[65] Even her sister Nicole L'Heureux echoed the sentiment: "Were we surprised when Claire was appointed? She deserved it at the time. She was well known. She participated in the reform of the *Civil Code*. But yes, we were surprised!"[66]

The fourth man who had a direct hand in L'Heureux-Dubé's elevation was Jean Marchand. While she might have anticipated support from her charismatic former dance partner, his role was more mixed. It began when Lang brought L'Heureux-Dubé's name forward to cabinet to secure a formal Order-in-Council.[67] Files were never automatically accepted, but Lang's sometimes faced more challenges than others.[68] The *Windsor Star* noted that his colleagues often attacked him for "failing to show enough partisanship in judicial hiring" and for insisting that "ability comes first."[69] The *Globe and Mail* clarified: "It's doubtful whether any Minister of Justice could ever insulate himself completely from the pressures of his party and his Cabinet colleagues. Appointments are discussed in Cabinet, often heatedly, before they are made." It quoted Lang as retorting: "In the process we may have hair all over the place. It could be anybody's hair."[70]

The practice was for the minister of justice to put forward two to three names for every Order-in-Council.[71] Typically, he had one preferred candidate. "In most provinces," Lang recalled, "if I took a name and said this would be a superb appointment, [the] politics would be neutral. I would say, you've got old friends, but they don't compare. Usually they went along. In Quebec, it was more difficult, but we could work out compromises."[72] Jean Marchand held veto power over every Quebec judicial candidate by virtue of his role as head of the Quebec caucus. Marc Lalonde, Ron Basford, and Donald Macdonald often contributed to the debates, and Prime Minister Trudeau took a special interest in judicial appointments, particularly for Quebec.[73] All of them were at the table.

The group initially rejected L'Heureux-Dubé's candidacy, although this turned out to be only temporary. Lang recalled that it was Marchand who expressed resistance to her candidacy in the early stages.[74] Marchand was not known for sympathy toward feminism.[75] For a man who had spent his life in the male-dominated trade union movement, it was not "something that leaped to the top of his mind," according to Marc Lalonde.[76]

But Lalonde did not think that Marchand stood in the way of L'Heureux-Dubé's candidacy simply because she was female. It may have been that Marchand was irked that she had refused his party's request to run in the recent election. Or it may have been something completely different. Lang said that he was never sure whether it was Marchand himself who cast the veto or someone else from the Quebec caucus. He also did not know whether the veto was specifically directed at L'Heureux-Dubé or it was a matter of preferring another candidate instead.[77]

Whatever Marchand's motivation, he was open to reconsideration. Lang brought the nomination forward again, Marchand agreed to withdraw the Quebec caucus veto, and for reasons that Lang "could not recall," the Order-in-Council was signed.[78]

Women's Lib: A Significant Factor or Not?

Richard Nixon had complained that "women's lib" was a political force that had to be reckoned with in selecting candidates for the bench. Three years later, the *Globe and Mail* proclaimed that where judicial appointments were concerned, "Women's Lib has had virtually no impact."[79] Who was right?

Despite the *Globe and Mail*'s breezy dismissal, a more careful assessment suggests that the Quiet Revolution in Quebec and the second-wave women's movement throughout Canada had coalesced to produce a formidable demand for more women in positions of power. Crusty social attitudes were increasingly challenged as being out of sync with the dramatic gender changes taking place in education and employment, and grievances were proliferating.[80] In 1966, the dynamic feminist leader Laura Sabia called on Prime Minister Lester Pearson to set up a Royal Commission on the Status of Women. At the same time, she critiqued the absence of female judges, insisting that the question be "aired, discussed, and rectified."[81] The Royal Commission's 1970 report recommended reforms to the law, the economy, the family, education, the tax system, childcare, immigration, citizenship, the criminal justice system, women's prisons, and the role of women in public life.[82] A male *Toronto Star* columnist characterized it as a full-scale "call to revolution."[83] Marc Lalonde, who became a strong proponent of women's rights within the Liberal government, emphasized that recognition of the need for change went right to the top: "Trudeau was really supportive, and we wanted to proceed with the recommendations."[84]

Women were determined not to let the momentum falter. The Royal Commission's executive secretary, Monique Bégin, hired consultants to teach women how to lobby for implementation of the recommendations. It was a campaign that fell on particularly fertile ground in Quebec.[85] The Fédération des femmes du Québec (FFQ) published a forty-six-page guide to the report and distributed thousands of copies to eager discussion groups across the province.[86] Claire Lalonde, Marc Lalonde's wife, had been at the founding meetings of the FFQ, and described Quebec feminism as "exciting" and "serious," a movement of which she was proud to be a part.[87] Other prominent FFQ leaders were also married to powerful Liberal men. Rita Racette-Cadieux, the second president of the FFQ, was the wife of Fernand Cadieux, former president of the Jeunesse Étudiante Catholique and a man close to both Trudeau and Michael Pitfield (clerk of the Privy Council). Fernande Juneau was the wife of Pierre Juneau, co-founder with Trudeau of the dissident *Cité Libre,* first president of the Canadian Radio-television and Telecommunications Commission, and later president of the Canadian Broadcasting Corporation. It was a formidable network of women who brought pressure to bear on their powerful husbands to respond to feminist demands. Those who watched the process from within gave them credit for much of the changing environment.[88]

Governments across the country were setting up advisory councils on the status of women, including the exceptionally effective, well-funded Conseil du statut de la femme in Quebec.[89] Independent status-of-women committees furnished cauldrons of energy for young professional women eager to develop political skills.[90] By 1972, the National Action Committee on the Status of Women surfaced – a pan-Canadian feminist caucus composed of service groups, advocacy organizations, business clubs, arts and cultural groups, labour unions, religious institutions, and ethno-racial groups, whose political orientation ran the gamut from conservative to radical feminist.[91] In 1970, the Front de libération des femmes du Québec carried out an explosive Mother's Day demonstration in Montreal's Lafontaine Park, denouncing the celebration and demanding the right to abortion with picket signs that read: *"Reine un jour, esclave 364 jours."*[†, 92]

All of this certainly had an impact upon L'Heureux-Dubé's appointment. Gender had been the driving force behind Albanie Morin's overture to L'Heureux-Dubé. The Business and Professional Women's Clubs in Quebec wrote letters to a host of Quebec MPs, including Marchand,

---

† "Queen for a day, slave for 364 days"

Abortion rights protest.

Morin, Bégin, and Sauvé, lobbying for the appointment of a woman, particularly Claire L'Heureux-Dubé, whom they described as *"tout particulièrement qualifiée."*[†, 93] "It may have been like Sam Bard," L'Heureux-Dubé suggested, "when they decided to appoint a Jew. In my case, they may have decided to appoint a woman. That was exactly what Albanie told me: 'We feel it's time we put a woman on the bench.'"[94]

Was this some form of "affirmative action," a deliberate program to promote a previously disadvantaged group, simply functioning without the name? That was not the opinion of Shirley Tucker Parks, who was struggling at the time to forge a legal career in a male-dominant federal civil service. She stressed: "I would have to think Claire was the best choice for the job. [I] don't think Otto would have made the appointment if she wasn't the best choice on the list."[95] The comment, although quite likely accurate, misses the point. Claire L'Heureux-Dubé was the best choice for

---

† "especially qualified"

Justice Réjane Laberge-Colas, first woman appointed to the Quebec Superior Court and founder of the FFQ.

the job, but she would never have been appointed except for the government's conscious recognition that it needed a woman on the roster.

L'Heureux-Dubé was not someone who would ever claim membership in "women's lib." She was not like Réjane Laberge-Colas, the first woman appointed to the Superior Court in Montreal three years earlier, who had been the founding president of the FFQ.[96] She was not like Alice Desjardins, the country's first female law professor, who had signed the FFQ's inaugural constitution.[97] She was unattached to the burgeoning new feminist organizations. But when the politicians went looking, she was in the right place at the right time. Simply by virtue of being the most senior woman in private practice in Quebec, she was the obvious woman for the job.

Justice Alice Desjardins, first female law professor in Canada and first woman appointed to the Federal Court of Appeal.

Claire L'Heureux-Dubé, along with Réjane Laberge-Colas, Alice Desjardins, Albanie Morin, Monique Bégin, and Jeanne Sauvé, were all being propelled by the momentum of something much larger than their individual talents or ambitions. L'Heureux-Dubé's judicial appointment in 1973 was based on merit, but she was also situated at the forefront of feminist demands for revolution. Her opportunity emerged because the women's movement insisted on change. Whatever the *Globe and Mail* might think, women's lib *was* responsible. The irony was that Claire L'Heureux-Dubé rose to become a flag bearer for a movement to which she had never belonged.

18
First Months on the Bench, February to October 1973

A Frosty Welcome: "Like a Dog in a China Shop"

Claire L'Heureux-Dubé's status as an outsider flashed back into high relief when she took her place on the court.¹ There her rising public persona held little sway, because gender stood out above all else. That her reception would not be a warm one was evident from the outset. Even before the appointment was publicly announced, she happened to cross paths with the young daughter of another judge. Little knowing to whom she was speaking, the friendly girl chatted with L'Heureux-Dubé about what she had heard about the new judge: "Apparently they named a woman, apparently they can't *stand* her, she knows *nothing.*" L'Heureux-Dubé recalled laughing and replying, "[That's] nice to know."²

Her family, by contrast, was delighted, and turned out in force for the swearing-in ceremony on Friday, 9 March 1973. Her sisters Nicole and Louise were both there. Her mother, Marguerite, whose disability prevented her from attending, was euphoric about the appointment. Despite their strained relationship, her father, Paul, also appeared pleased. Arthur and the children sat in the front row. Arthur proudly reminded the children that their mother's elevation to the bench was clear confirmation of how smart she was.

At swearing-in ceremonies, it was traditional for the presiding chief justice to offer flattering remarks about an incoming judge. Instead, Chief Justice Frédéric Dorion gave only the briefest of welcomes to his court's

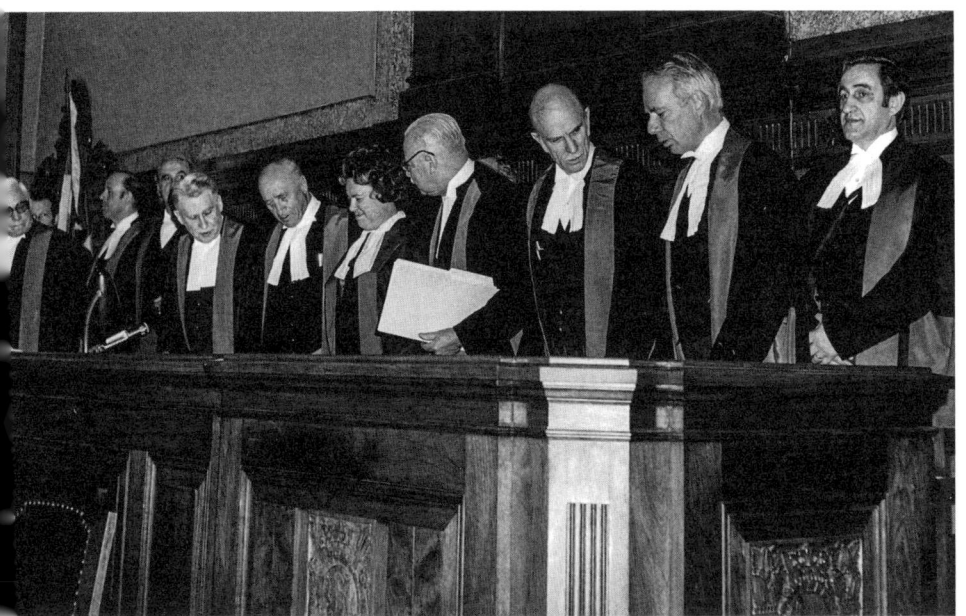

Superior Court judges at Claire L'Heureux-Dubé's Superior Court swearing-in ceremony, 9 March 1973.

newest member. He followed this studied diffidence with a lengthy tirade against *la déchristianisation de la société*,[†] union leaders, striking CEGEP (pre-university college) students, and the reprobates of society who demanded rights without responsibilities and laid their imbecility, viciousness, and crimes at the foot of society at large.[3] "He was so mad I was appointed," said L'Heureux-Dubé. "I was received like a dog in a china shop."[4]

Why was he so upset? "First, I was a woman," emphasized L'Heureux-Dubé. "Second, I was doing divorce and he was a fourth-degree *Chevalier de Colomb du Québec!*"[5] What was more, she had a passing familiarity with Dorion's own family challenges. When the marriage of Dorion's grandson unravelled, it was she who had acted as the divorce lawyer for the wife, a young woman who just coincidentally happened to be the daughter of one of the other Superior Court judges, Eugène Marquis.

Seventy-five-year-old Frédéric Dorion, who would retire six months after L'Heureux-Dubé's appointment, was a short stocky man, dour in demeanour and comportment, who represented another of Quebec's

---

† the de-Christianization of society

At the reception following the swearing-in ceremony. *Left to right,* Pierre Dubé *(back of head only),* Louise Dubé *(with roses),* Arthur Dubé, Claire L'Heureux-Dubé, René Letarte *(back only).*

illustrious legal dynasties.⁶ In the words of McGill professor Pierre-Gabriel Jobin, the chief justice was a man of "severe standards."⁷ In addition to his public remonstrations against divorce, Frédéric Dorion was given to railing against the legalization of abortion, which he equated with murder.⁸ He was also rumoured to harbour anti-Semitic sentiments and to sympathize with Nazi collaborators.⁹ His initial reaction to L'Heureux-Dubé may have related to her gender, her divorce law practice, and her long-time professional connection with Sam Bard.

It was an intimidating milieu, one woman moving into a courthouse with twenty male judges.¹⁰ Years later, she would describe the blanket of skepticism that greeted her: *"J'étais regardée par mes pairs comme une espèce d'animal spécial. Je sentais qu'ils croyaient que je ne serais jamais capable de faire le travail."*†, ¹¹ The first day she arrived at her chambers, Justice Jean-Robert Beaudoin, whose office was next door, came by to see her. "You are

---

† "I was looked on by my peers as some kind of special animal. It was my impression that they believed I would never be able to do the job."

First Months on the Bench

Justice Frédéric Dorion, ca. 1965.

happy today," he warned. "You'll be a slave for the rest of your days."[12] He was referring to what many of his brethren thought of their task: poorly paid drudgery, endless cases, all nose-to-the-grindstone. "There were no smiling judges on that bench," recalled L'Heureux-Dubé. "No joke types, just down to business."[13]

She may have hoped that Sam Bard, whose appointment to the Superior Court had occurred almost four years earlier, could smooth her path a little. Whatever promise this may have held turned out to be elusive. Bard could offer little hands-on help because he had transferred to the Montreal Superior Court a few months later, and the two no longer remained in close contact.[14] As seems to be typical of workplaces where homogeneity has been the tradition, very few of the other judges noticed that the first outsiders had a tough slog. Even Yves Bernier, who was not himself hostile to the idea of women on the bench and would later befriend L'Heureux-Dubé, thought that there were no challenges facing the first female judges. "It was very smooth," he stated. "I don't think anybody treated them differently."[15] It took another outsider to notice the difference. Melvin Rothman, who had been appointed to the Superior Court in Montreal in 1971, was one of few Jewish judges. He observed: "Women were not treated very well. I'm sure it was difficult as the lone woman in Quebec City. You would have thought that the other members of the court would have been more thoughtful and more progressive and more accepting. That wasn't always the case."[16]

THE CHALLENGE OF SETTLING IN

L'Heureux-Dubé's appointment was to replace Gérard Lacroix, the former Laval criminal law professor who was retiring after twenty years on the bench.[17] He was the larger-than-life figure who had excused her and Judith Gamache from his lectures on sexual assault. When L'Heureux-Dubé was ushered into Lacroix's chambers, which she had inherited along with the job, she was startled to find the room dominated by a crucifix. When she asked Lacroix about it, he explained that he used to kneel before it in his black tricorne hat, to offer prayers before leaving for court to condemn a prisoner to death. Lacroix's most notorious capital case had involved the murder trial of Wilbert Coffin, accused of killing three Americans who were hunting in the Gaspésie. Lacroix sentenced Coffin to death, and he was executed in 1956.[18] Canada's last hanging took place in Toronto's Don Jail in 1962, but the country did not finally abolish the death penalty until 1976.[19] Lacroix's dangling crucifix was an unsettling and sober reminder of the weight of office.

Otherwise, L'Heureux-Dubé found her new chambers more than adequate. The stone courthouse with its carved coats of arms, clock tower, and copper roof was a magnificent building, and it housed judges' offices that were spacious, high-ceilinged, and well lit with tall rectangular windows. The central uptown location in Vieux Québec offered access to restaurants, shops, and even a coiffeur. There was no cafeteria at the court, and many of the judges drove home for lunch. Since the courthouse was only a five-minute drive from her home, L'Heureux-Dubé also frequently returned to lunch with her children. The downside was that it made the social etiquette of the court even more austere. "There was no chit-chat, no socializing with the judges. [It was] not that kind of atmosphere," she recalled. "There were no dinners, no parties, no socializing at all as far as I was concerned."[20] It precluded any opportunity to diminish her sense of being an outsider.

One of the initial dilemmas was what to call the new female judge.[21] The lawyers and court personnel always addressed male judges as *Monsieur le juge*. The French word was not neutral, like the English "judge," but took a masculine form with the article *"le."* L'Heureux-Dubé objected to being addressed as *Monsieur le juge,* which was the designation most frequently blurted out by those appearing before her. "I said, 'You can do anything to me, but don't change my sex,'" she recalled. Instead, she opted for *Madame le juge.* "It took a long time before they got used to calling me *Madame le juge.* I was called *Monsieur le juge* for years, and I just joked about it."[22]

Some years later, Quebec feminists would insist upon referring to women as *Madame la juge* in a deliberate attempt to disrupt traditional male-centric language. The hope was that fully feminizing the word would promote the visibility of female judges and help educate the public that women could aspire to be professionals equal to men.[23] Although L'Heureux-Dubé had drawn the line at *Monsieur le juge,* she was averse to going any further. By the time the feminine article became *courant*,[†] she professed to be "too old to change." "I was *un avocat. Madame la bâtonnière* sounds awful to my ears. I can't change my grammar."[24] Here was another point at which she took issue with feminist strategy. "For me," she stressed, "it's superficial. This is not what feminism is all about."[25] It was a stance that did not soften with time. At her retirement from the Supreme Court of Canada, she was still insisting that the female lawyer who represented the Quebec bar be referred to as *le bâtonnier.*[26]

She had less difficulty adjusting to the long black toga with the red band that served as judicial garb in the Superior Court. L'Heureux-Dubé would later discover that the red band, which was not used by Court of Appeal judges, was meant to impress the trial witnesses with the importance of the court. "In the Court of Appeal," she explained, "there are no witnesses, just lawyers, so you don't need to impress anybody."[27] At the neck, male judges sported traditional white tabs, which L'Heureux-Dubé adopted as well. Some of the later female judges would substitute lace tabs, but L'Heureux-Dubé did not consider that until years later.[28] "I didn't wear lace at the throat. We were too few. We wouldn't have dared to wear anything other than what the men were wearing."[29]

As she was first getting her bearings, she discovered that her early case assignments would also pose a challenge. One of the first cases on her docket involved a water purification company that needed to haul heavy equipment down to the St. Lawrence River in order to construct water collectors and pumping stations.[30] The problem was that the machinery

---

[†] in common usage

Claire L'Heureux-Dubé at her Superior Court swearing-in, with judicial robes, sash, and white tabs and roses.

had to traverse Crown land, and the port authority refused access across its property. The water purification company was seeking an interlocutory injunction against the port authority. The law relating to interlocutory injunctions was technically complex, and L'Heureux-Dubé had little experience in the field. Her assignment to such a difficult case so early in her tenure caused her to wonder whether the chief justice was testing her.

Some of the other judges confirmed her suspicions, suggesting that Dorion was up to a "dirty trick." Male judges may also have been tested when they first began to sit, but for Quebec City's first female judge, it became a challenge of gender competence as well as judicial competence.

Counsel on the case also expressed surprise over the assignment. Jacques Marquis, the lawyer for the plaintiff, stopped by L'Heureux-Dubé's chambers to say, "It's not fair to give you a case like this. I'll go to the chief justice and ask that another judge be appointed."[31] While it was undoubtedly meant kindly, it further underscored the dubiousness that confronted the region's first female judge. Although she was troubled by the case assignment, she was more troubled by the offer to help her step down. Her pride overcame her anxieties, and L'Heureux-Dubé responded, "I'm going to preside over this and judge it. Forget it."[32] Things deteriorated when she entered the courtroom on the first day and found nine men seated in the front row, all members of the water purification company's board of directors. "When they saw a woman, they panicked," she recalled. "Women don't know anything. She's known for family law. [It's] terrible. I could see it in their faces. That's why Jacques Marquis had come to see me. I wasn't welcome. I could see that."[33]

She sat through the arguments, made full notes, and then put in long hours in the law library researching jurisprudence. There were no research assistants or law clerks attached to the court, so the full weight of responsibility rested on her shoulders. She decided to grant the injunction, stating in a twenty-three-page judgment that the plaintiff would suffer serious prejudice if it were not permitted to work after the investment of considerable sums and the hiring of entrepreneurs, while the defendant had demonstrated no serious prejudice and could be indemnified later if necessary. It was a decisive opinion on a hotly contested matter, something that would become a hallmark of her career as a judge. And she was not intimidated by having to rule on areas of law where she had not practised before: "No, law is law. It's just a matter of understanding the facts, a matter of judgment over the law." In fact, she boasted, "I liked the diversity."[34]

The switch from lawyer to judge was not a smooth one, but L'Heureux-Dubé was fiercely determined not to fail. She could see what an uneasy fit she made on an all-male court, and she chose to roll with the challenges and the uncertainties, making it up as she went along.

19
Immigration Commission of Inquiry, October 1973 to January 1976

The call came in August 1973, when Claire L'Heureux-Dubé was relaxing on the beach, enjoying the first holiday she had been able to take since her appointment to the Quebec Superior Court.[1] She and her family had rented a cottage in Old Orchard Beach, a resort town in Maine where many Quebec families spent their summers. There were no telephones and the call had to be relayed from a dispatcher twenty minutes away, who came searching for the lady judge. "You have a phone call from the minister," was the message, prompting her to panic over whether she had done something wrong.

She had not. It was Jean Marchand, relaying a request from the federal minister of manpower and immigration, Robert Andras, that she take a leave from the bench to chair a commission of inquiry relating to the Department of Manpower and Immigration in Montreal. The government divulged little to the public apart from announcing that there would be a "formal investigation into certain allegations of wrongdoing involving immigration matters in the Montreal area."[2] To L'Heureux-Dubé, Marchand privately confided that sexual scandal was suspected. It would take only a few months, he insisted, and the government needed her to undertake the task. She wondered whether Marchand, former minister of manpower and immigration and now minister of transport, might have singled her out for the job, but he laughingly denied any involvement.

L'Heureux-Dubé was worried that she knew nothing about immigration and that the work would require her to leave her family alone in Quebec City. It was the second factor that she stressed when she pleaded her case before Chief Justice Dorion. In one of his last official acts before retiring, Dorion briskly advised her that she was "in the service of [her] country" and could not refuse.[3] The appointment was finalized on 13 August 1973, the day that Dorion stepped down from his administrative judicial position.[4]

L'Heureux-Dubé suspected that she had been dispatched to Montreal because the judges wanted to get rid of her. As she learned more about the terms of the inquiry – the allegations that male immigration officers had slept with female applicants – she also asked herself whether the government was worried about sending the male judges, "because the women were beautiful and they were worried about another scandal."[5] In fact, L'Heureux-Dubé may have been picked because she was one of the most bilingual of the Quebec judges, and the inquiry would need to function in both languages. What she also did not know was that her fellow judges envied her because they viewed a commission of inquiry as a welcome departure from the daily grind of judging. She did not find out until years later that she could have refused the assignment.

First there was a flurry of arrangements for the care of her family. Arthur would remain in their home, but given his limited parental role, the couple agreed that it would be best to board the children. Young Pierre was becoming more and more difficult; "impossible" was the word L'Heureux-Dubé used.[6] So Louise, thirteen, and Pierre, nine, were moved to new schools in Quebec City where they could board during the week.[7] L'Heureux-Dubé drove to Montreal every Monday morning, supervised the inquiry from Monday to Friday, and picked up the children on Friday evenings. Family life was relegated to weekends. Despite Marchand's assurances, the inquiry would keep her away for two full years.[8]

PREPARING FOR AN INQUIRY

Initially, the unfamiliar prospect of chairing a commission of inquiry overwhelmed and reduced her to tears in the office. There were no instructions to guide commissions on the scope of the mandate, immunity, procedures, or expenses.[9] It was her colleague Yves Bernier, who had previously chaired another public inquiry, who came to her rescue. He gave her detailed advice, listened to her ideas about how to set up the research and the hearings, and offered confirmation that she was on the right track.[10] Ultimately, it was the Department of Manpower and Immigration that selected the files for review, arranged for physical facilities, dealt with

Justice Yves Bernier.

budgetary matters, and provided information and documentation. In retrospect, it was a tight relationship between the inquiry and the entity being inquired into that ought to have been avoided.

Joseph R. Nuss, then a partner at a Montreal litigation firm who had experience with commissions of inquiry, was hired as senior counsel.[11] Nuss found working with L'Heureux-Dubé exhilarating: "Her capacity for sustained work is absolutely phenomenal. This generated a reciprocal loyalty. You wanted to do things for Claire – wanted to get it done, and get it done right."[12] The task was daunting. The team examined 509 files that the department had earmarked as "potentially suspicious." It conducted 514 interviews with department officials, the immigrants named in the files, and representatives of concerned groups. It took evidence from

Immigration Commission of Inquiry

Joseph Nuss, senior counsel to the immigration inquiry, and Claire L'Heureux-Dubé dancing at Louise Dubé's wedding.

392 witnesses at formal public hearings. There were ninety-seven volumes of transcripts and 607 exhibits.[13] "All in all," explained Nuss, "as this type of commission goes, it was done very quickly. That's one of [Claire L'Heureux-Dubé's] great qualities, being very efficient, expeditious."[14]

The Inquiry Findings

The inquiry stemmed from complaints that Montreal federal immigration officers were admitting applicants despite false or missing documentation, that officers were accepting bribes, that external intermediaries were charging exorbitant fees for perfunctory representation, and that officers were soliciting sex from women seeking to settle in Canada. The problems first came to light when RCMP investigators working on another case made a surprise seizure of a "little black book" belonging to a Montreal immigration officer. Its contents included a long list of Caribbean female applicants, and further investigation commenced. Soon afterward, the department dismissed two immigration officers. A third opted for early retirement under a swirling cloud of rumours.[15]

The misdeeds were rooted in Canada's immigration history, the result of a set of policies designed to construct a "white" population of European origin. From the nefarious head tax imposed on Chinese immigrants, to the "continuous journey" regulations that excluded those from Asia who could not arrive on non-stop voyages, to the "inappropriate climate" assessments applied to immigrants of African origin, the historical landscape was littered with racist and discriminatory proscriptions.[16]

In 1967, a Liberal government intent upon reform announced that it would open the borders to more diverse newcomers. An earlier rule requiring immigrants to apply for permanent landed status before they arrived at the border was eliminated. One could now apply after entering as a visitor.[17] Equally important, individuals denied the right to remain could appeal to a newly created Immigration Appeal Board.[18] The ensuing flood of applications and appeals nearly overwhelmed an immigration department lacking the personnel, training, and resources to handle the claims. To deal with the huge backlog, special inquiry officers were authorized to grant permanent landed status. They were instructed to "use their discretion generously" under an environment of "amnesty" and "relaxed norms."[19]

The 1967 legal revisions set in motion a dramatic shift, from an immigrant cohort that was 76 percent European in 1966 to one that had dropped to 39 percent European by 1972. In 1974, a government Green Paper advised that Asian nations (led by India) and Caribbean countries (Jamaica and Trinidad) had replaced countries such as Germany and France "on the list of the first ten source countries."[20] The unprecedented racial diversity of the new applicants appears to have caused some discomfort to the predominantly white officials in the department.[21] It was no accident that of the "suspicious" files earmarked for examination, 60 percent involved immigrants (primarily male) from India, and 33 percent (almost entirely female) from the Caribbean.[22]

L'Heureux-Dubé began the commission's report by expressing compassion for the immigrants whose files the commission had reviewed. She depicted them as "poor and uneducated people who had sought desperately to settle in Canada as a way of escaping deprivation and ensuring the future of their families." In her words, they had fallen "into the hands of those ready, for money, to exploit them." In sum, "the human dimension of the inquiry was at times profoundly moving" and the scene of a "poignant human drama."[23]

Almost immediately, however, the focus of the inquiry shifted to the wrongdoing of the immigrants, who were characterized as using "deplorable" stratagems to jump the queue. "Phony" tourists paid the equivalent of several years' income in their country of origin to fly to Canada and then claimed to be so impressed with the country that they applied for landed status within days after arrival. The inquiry found evidence of false documentation regarding educational and employment skills. If applications were rejected, the immigrants had an automatic right of appeal that could take two years to process, during which time they could stay in the country and work.[24]

The commission found that immigrants from India had also pretended to be businessmen, a privileged category for entry. Very few had entrepreneurial experience, and none truly intended to set up businesses in Canada. They registered names of imaginary enterprises at the Montreal courthouse, claimed financial means from funds that revolved through the bank accounts of a sequence of immigrants, rented business premises that were never used, ordered goods then quickly cancelled, and occasionally even set up small businesses that were closed down once the proprietor was assessed as a businessman.[25]

The commission then turned its attention to unscrupulous outside intermediaries, many in Haiti and India, who facilitated these queue-jumping practices. They operated as travel agents, tour organizers, realtors, and recruitment agents for Canadian employers. Some posed as industrialists seeking workers for Canadian factories that turned out to be empty plants, full of rusty and useless equipment. They offered flight arrangements, temporary lodging, passports, border documentation, and the promise of good jobs. Some provided advice that actually assisted their clients to obtain landed status, but most charged sums that vastly exceeded the value of services rendered. Promised jobs could turn out to be illusory. Lodgings could be nothing more than unfurnished, empty factories. Clients could be forced to pay for flights several times over, with further fees demanded after arrival. One immigrant turned over his life savings, $40,000, to an intermediary in India.[26]

Stephen M. Byer, a Montreal lawyer who practised under a business named "Immigration Visa Services of Canada," was a homegrown intermediary. Byer was responsible for 268 of the irregular files, 84 from the

Caribbean and 162 from India. Charging over $1,000 per client, he "borrowed" letterhead from local businesses and provided immigrants with letters purporting to offer employment that he fraudulently signed with the names of company presidents. He furnished phony leases, backdated documents, falsified affidavits, counselled clients to give false statements to immigration officers, and told at least one immigrant to "put fifty dollars on the table" when he met with the special inquiry officer. Byer also purchased a list of applicants from one Montreal immigration officer and then aggressively solicited business from the named individuals.[27] It was a damning indictment, but because the commission's mandate was restricted to the department and its officers, the Montreal lawyer was left to the disposition of the criminal justice system and professional disciplinary processes.[28]

In contrast with the litany of misdeeds ascribed to immigrants and intermediaries, the commission seemed much gentler with the department itself. Although it identified 224 files of immigrants who were not bona fide visitors despite their claim at the port of entry, it stressed that beleaguered officers under time pressure had made "inevitable mistakes" and that there was "not a shred of evidence" that this was a result of "any wrongdoing in the department."[29] The commission unearthed twenty-seven files of phony businessmen, then attributed the errors to a "dearth of directions or guidelines," "lack of proper investigative facilities," and "officers' lack of training regarding business and legal matters."[30]

The commission was more critical of the sexual misdeeds. Lawrence Doiron, the immigration officer with the "little black book," was a man in his early forties, separated from his wife, who had been working with the department since 1967. Clearly a troubled employee, Doiron had a lengthy record of absenteeism and suffered from acute alcoholism. When the department found that he had been compiling names and phone numbers of female applicants and phoning them repeatedly to solicit sex, it dismissed him. By the time he testified at the inquiry, he was unemployed, destitute, and ready to make a clean breast of everything.[31] As L'Heureux-Dubé recalled years later, he seemed to be "very honest, very forthcoming. In the end, I thought he had nothing to lose."[32]

Doiron testified to having had sex with eighteen female applicants, sixteen of whom gave evidence to corroborate his story. He added that he had made advances over the telephone to nine more, of whom four came to his apartment, but that no sexual relations had occurred with these women.[33] Some of the women who had sex with Doiron explained their motivation as simply "liking" the officer. Others were less willing.

One testified that she "didn't want to, and I was crying. He put his arm around my neck and told me not to cry, that I shouldn't be afraid, and that if I wouldn't do it, I wouldn't get my papers."[34] The commission concluded that Doiron's dismissal was justified.

George-Étienne Desrochers, an officer in his mid-fifties, married with children, had joined the department in 1961. He admitted to sexual relations with four women who had applied for landed status. He had invited two others to meet him in the basement of the immigration office and "caressed" them there. One of the women testified that he told her "if I agree to go to bed with him, he would see that I have my papers." She became pregnant, and when she told Desrochers, he suggested an abortion. Because she was unable to obtain one, she gave birth and then put the child up for adoption. Since Desrochers had already taken early retirement from the department, the commission concluded he was beyond further disciplinary sanction.[35]

Victorin Bellemare, in his mid-forties, married with six children, was vice president of the union, and had been working with the department since 1960. Despite his denials and evasions, the commission found that he had had sex with at least one applicant and visited another at her home, where he touched and kissed her.[36] In spite of similar denials, officer Gaston Therrien was found to have offered to help a female applicant pay the rent if she would lease a room where he could visit her. He subsequently visited her at her apartment but made no sexual advances.[37] The commission recommended that both be disciplined.[38]

René Primeau struck up an apparently consensual cohabitation arrangement with a female applicant he had met at the department. The couple began to live together before the woman had received her landed immigrant status, and although the inquiry concluded that Primeau had not interfered with the handling of the file, it noted that he too deserved some disciplinary sanction.[39] Brian Purdon, a thirty-two-year-old supervisor in the department who had sold the list of applicants to lawyer Stephen Byer, commenced a sexual relationship with a woman he had met when she applied for landed immigrant status. He did not attempt to conceal the relationship from his departmental staff, and the two attended social events together. Although the commission determined that this was a "romantic relationship" that had lasted about a year, it labelled Purdon's acts as improper, and "particularly unfortunate" because, as supervisor, he might "well have jeopardized his ability to enforce his subordinates' adherence to the appropriate guidelines." It determined that this misconduct on its own merited a reprimand, but that combined with his misconduct in selling the list of applicants to Byer, his dismissal from the department was fully justified.[40]

The Commission's Conclusions: Queue-Jumping Immigrants

The focus on queue-jumping immigrants led inevitably to recommendations to crack down on miscreants seeking to settle in Canada: heavier penalties, detection and enforcement mechanisms, increased resources for officers, more explicit criteria for admission, mandatory visas from countries with significant illegal migration, modifications to social insurance cards to certify whether the holder was entitled to work in Canada, and a requirement that all employers screen job applicants more closely to ensure that they were legitimately entitled to work.[41] The evidence regarding unscrupulous intermediaries prompted the commission to suggest accreditation processes for immigration counsellors within Canada, and cooperation with foreign governments to expose fraudsters outside the country.[42]

There was scant sympathy regarding the economic, social, and political pressures that drove immigrants to use improper means to try to secure permanent settlement in Canada, a country which was itself overwhelmingly populated by immigrants. The only recommendation apparently offering support for immigrants was to set up legal aid clinics at the Toronto and Montreal airports, but the full intent of this became clearer when the commission noted that officers might feel "more at ease in denying entry" if legal representation were available.[43]

Asked decades later why her commission had come down so harshly on the immigrants, L'Heureux-Dubé replied: "I'm a law and order person. I'm not talking about refugees, [which is] quite different. But we can't open up to the whole world, and say to everyone, 'Come, come, come.' My vision is that we should have a fair system where people are integrated according to the possibilities Canada has. [Otherwise] you abolish all rules, and that is a free-for-all – who gets here first – and then we have chaos in the community."[44]

It was a response that accorded well with the sentiment of many Canadians, who worried that queue jumpers unfairly secured spots that properly belonged to more qualified immigrants. But it also presumed that the system processed applicants efficiently and fairly, according to transparent, uniform rules. All evidence pointed to the contrary, both through the long sweep of history and at the time of the inquiry.[45] As immigration supervisor Brian Purdon testified, "the place was a mess." He added: "I was wondering what the hell we were doing there. I wasn't the only one. Most of the officers were wondering what the hell they were doing there."[46]

By 1972, the legal regulations began to tighten again. Visitors were no longer permitted to apply for permanent residence from within Canada, nor could they appeal to the Immigration Appeal Board. In 1973, rights of appeal for others denied entry or refused at assessment were also severely restricted.[47] The path to permanent residence would become more challenging, a development that L'Heureux-Dubé's commission endorsed.

More Conclusions: A "Handful" of Gender-Neutral Officers Pursuing "Private Ambitions"

The commission found that nineteen female applicants had had sexual relations with Montreal immigration officers while their cases were pending. Thirteen others had been approached and invited but had avoided the sex. Six officers were involved.[48] The commission characterized this as "a handful of employees" who had had "intimate relations with women having business with the Department."[49] It was a rare lapse into gender-specific analysis, in a report that was otherwise resolutely gender-neutral. The sexual targets were *all female*, although nothing further was made of this. The summation failed to designate the gender of the "handful of employees," as though this were so obvious as not to warrant emphasis. But the genders of both applicants and officers was surely central to these events. Earlier in the report, figures indicated that approximately 94 percent of the Montreal officers were men.[50] The campaign to open up government positions equally to men and women was still in its infancy, and the possibility that an overwhelmingly male workplace might have had something to do with encouraging a culture of sexual entitlement on the part of men was not addressed.

Next, the commission pointed out that there were no official departmental directives regarding intimate or sexual relationships. It suggested that the department might have thought it "so obvious as not to require emphasis."[51] In fact, the line of permissible behaviour was not clearly understood within the department. It was not obvious to the supervisor who struck up a "romantic relationship" with a woman seeking landed status and brought her to social functions. It was not obvious to the six officers whose activities had landed them before the inquiry. The rules regarding sex on the job were unarticulated, as they were in most Canadian workplaces at the time.

The decade of the 1970s was about to usher in a new era of controversy over sexual norms. "Sexual harassment," a term describing coercive sexual behaviour toward vulnerable individuals by male employers or authority figures, came into circulation shortly after the inquiry issued its report. The phrase was coined by feminist activists in April 1975 in Ithaca, New York. *Ms.* magazine made it an explosive cover issue in 1977, and the first books on the topic would be published in the United States and Canada in 1978 and 1979. Within a decade, employers would begin promulgating rules and procedures governing coercive sexual relations on the job.[52] As with much of L'Heureux-Dubé's life, she was ahead of society, thrown into an inquiry where sexual harassment had unleashed a scandal before the concept itself had come into focus.

The commission made the right call in finding that the officers' behaviour was off limits. The report stated that it was "simply wrong" for an employee to have "an intimate or sexual relationship with a woman currently having business dealings with the Department."[53] However, it then went on to characterize the sexual overtures as "private" matters. In a conclusion that seems inherently contradictory, the report claimed that the officers had "seized opportunities *presented by their employment* to pursue *private* and in most cases questionable ambitions."[54] The sexual activities were not "private" but deeply connected to the positions of power that the officers held by reason of their employment at the immigration department. The female immigrants were vulnerable to the overtures of immigration officers in ways they would not have been to overtures from private citizens, because they were seeking settlement in Canada. The employment nexus was put into high relief with the finding that some of the sexual acts had occurred in the basement of the immigration office.

At points, the commission seemed curiously indifferent to the testimony it had heard. "There is no evidence that refusal of Doiron's advances by a woman immigrant affected his processing of her file," it noted. "Nor is there any evidence that Doiron made threats or gave promises of favourable treatment."[55] This flew in the face of the commission's own quotations from Doiron, where he admitted to telling a tearful immigrant that he would "arrange everything," and that a refusal of sex meant no papers would be issued.

The wider coercion and exploitation also appear to be submerged in the final report. Missing is any serious discussion about the position of the women immigrants, the exploitation they suffered when their applications became the trigger for sexual solicitation, and the harms they suffered from non-consensual, coercive sexual abuse. Instead, the report spoke of the department's having been brought "into disrepute," and of the officers who had become "personally vulnerable to blackmail."[56] The commission displayed a sensitivity to the plight of the officers that it did not extend to the female immigrants. The former were described as plagued by their conflicts of interest, while the latter were characterized as the recipients of undeserved advancement: "[B]ecause of the relationship [the officers] developed with some women, they might have felt obliged, either because of feelings of sympathy or from fear of being denounced, to deal favourably with their cases."[57]

With respect to the officer who had struck up an apparently consensual cohabitation arrangement with a woman whose file was pending, the power differential disappeared from the report while the commission focused instead on unmerited benefits accruing to the immigrant. "The woman moved in with him before she became a landed immigrant. Some might have thought, or think, that the woman hoped to benefit, and did benefit, by cultivating this relationship. Primeau might have become subject to pressure of a serious kind had the subject subsequently been refused landed immigrant status. He might well have been prompted to take positive and improper action to protect a woman he apparently loved." In the end, the report was left congratulating the officer: "In a way, he is to be complimented for his restraint in this respect, for the temptation to interfere must have been very real."[58]

Missing Pieces:
A Climate of Sexual and Racial Harassment

From the outset, L'Heureux-Dubé had been concerned not to allow the inquiry to become more explosive than necessary. "The Commission will not allow itself to be used as a forum for irresponsible allegations, or a platform for reckless sensationalism," she insisted.[59] Her chief counsel, Joseph Nuss, was even more forthright: "[There was] some delicacy in this, as there [is] in most commissions of inquiry of this nature, where there are allegations of wrongdoing. The reputations of a lot of people are at stake, including a lot of innocent people. In the Department of Immigration in Montreal, you have a great number of employees. Now, how many of them were involved in wrongdoing? You don't know, but the suspicion is cast on the whole group. You want to make sure that to the extent possible, innocent persons will not suffer damage to reputation and dignity."[60] The fears expressed by L'Heureux-Dubé and Nuss stemmed from anxiety to protect the reputations of men from false complaints, a perspective that had deep roots in Canadian law and society.[61] No concern was expressed about women who were too frightened or ashamed to speak about sexual abuse, or the pervasive silence that enabled guilty men to escape responsibility.

Many witnesses had testified that officers other than the six were involved in sexual relationships with applicants. Doiron had made it out to be an entrenched workplace norm, testifying that "everybody does it." He had named names for the commission. But L'Heureux-Dubé was more persuaded by a supervisor, who she recalled had testified with tears in his eyes that his officers were the "salt of the earth."[62] Years later, she explained:

> I believed him. My father was an immigration officer. I don't think everybody did it. I named the ones we found guilty. I couldn't say ... that it was a systemic problem. In a commission of inquiry, you have to think of the evidence you have. I was not a feminist. My main goal was to be fair with the evidence I had.[63]

It was an approach that was supported by the entire inquiry staff, hammered out after long discussions. Where any officer denied sexual involvement, the commission accepted the allegations as unproven unless there was "first hand evidence of impropriety." "Otherwise," stressed the report, "in the interests of fairness, the matter is best closed and forgotten."[64] Undoubtedly, without further probative evidence, this was the only path the commission could take. But the reluctance of women to report sexual assaults or divulge extramarital sexual experiences was common knowledge in the early 1970s. The added complexities posed when the victims were vulnerable, poor female immigrants seeking new lives in Canada from the very men who were propositioning them must also have been clear. The report made frequent mention of immigrants who refused to testify, who had eluded detection, or who had returned to their countries of origin. It is more likely than not that what the commission unearthed was a small fraction of the actual wrongdoing.

It would have been wiser to indicate that the allegations outstripped the evidence, but that there were a plethora of reasons why such evidence was elusive. There is no question that when evidence led only so far, the commission could do no more than make findings accordingly. But exoneration of the innocent should have been far from the main concern. It was more important, surely, to make every effort to eradicate the systemic attitudes or practices that might facilitate future misconduct. Instead of expressing caution and concern, the report found "the overwhelming majority of officers" to be "innocent of any wrongdoing."[65]

It was akin to depicting the few officers found to have had sexual relations with the female immigrants as "bad apples," isolated actors misbehaving against the backdrop of a department free from blemish. "By and large," concluded the commission, "the employees of the Department did their work adequately and honestly." The "misconduct" was "limited to a few employees," and was "fortunately not widespread."[66] Despite Doiron's testimony of a sexual free-for-all, of an office where the departmental supervisor was openly dating a woman he first met when she arrived at the office to seek landed immigrant status, the commission found the department to have had "no knowledge" of the misconduct prior to the RCMP investigation. It stated that it "could only have discovered these improper activities if it spied upon or used other unacceptable means to inquire into and observe the private lives of its employees."[67]

It would be unfair to fault L'Heureux-Dubé and her staff for their lack of understanding of the concept of sexual harassment. They were dealing with an inquiry prior to the explosion of public debate in the mid to late 1970s. However, L'Heureux-Dubé was no stranger to the dynamics of sexual coercion on the job. She had left a secretarial position during law school because of the blatant physical advances of a more powerful boss, behaviour that went unchecked even after she reported it to a manager. Like many other women at the time, she made no link between her own difficult experience and the sexual coercion directed at female immigrants who testified at the inquiry.

The findings were also free from racial analysis. From the outset, L'Heureux-Dubé had ordered that members of the press must not disclose the names, race, or nationality of any witnesses.[68] Ostensibly meant to protect the privacy of the individuals, this also stripped the discussion of racial analysis. Although she held private meetings with leaders of various ethnic communities from which the bulk of the immigrants came, when it came time to draft the report, L'Heureux-Dubé noted that "none of my report is based on these discussions."[69] It was not as though Quebec was a stranger to the dangerous dynamics of racial discrimination. Four years before the commission began its work, allegations of racism at Montreal's Sir George Williams University had led to public manifestations of anti-black hatred, riots, and arrests.[70]

L'Heureux-Dubé's commission heard testimony from several officers that the staff "joked among themselves about black immigrants and made remarks in bad taste," causing her to state that this was something the department should be vigilant to prevent. One immigration officer testified that department officers displayed "discriminatory attitudes," but she preferred the evidence of others who claimed there was a "total absence of discrimination in the handling of files." After concluding that she had found "no evidence of discriminatory attitudes or practices," she absolved the department of racism: "I am satisfied that there is no trace of discrimination in the policy of the Department, and that valuable efforts have been made by the Department to ensure the objective treatment of applicants."[71]

As with the "bad apple" approach to the sexual misconduct, this seems to outstrip the evidence as well as to constitute an unnecessary exoneration. The racial dimensions of the sexual abuse must have been evident to everyone at the inquiry. With few exceptions, all the women targeted for sexual overtures had been black Caribbean immigrants. It would be farfetched to assume that race had nothing to do with sexual solicitations made by officers in an all-white department, working in an office where jokes of unspecified "bad taste" were made about blacks. Asked to reflect on this further, with the benefit of hindsight, L'Heureux-Dubé admitted it was something that entirely escaped her notice. "I never thought about this issue," she said.[72]

The task of chairing the commission of inquiry turned out to be a difficult, challenging interlude at a very early stage in Claire L'Heureux-Dubé's judicial career. In many respects, she acquitted herself admirably, running a tight ship to produce a report in short order and within budget, with recommendations that were viewed as sensible at the time even if they may not have probed as deeply into the structural inequities of Canadian society as hindsight might have warranted.

It also positioned her as a woman to watch in the future. McGill law professor Pierre-Gabriel Jobin saw the inquiry as pivotal to L'Heureux-Dubé's future judicial elevation. "I think her first step in going up the scale was the Commission on Immigration. I think there was ambition there. Did I skip describing her as an ambitious woman? She has ambitions. [It] might have been part of the reasons why she accepted. She is a little bit like a star."[73]

20
Quebec Superior Court, 1976–79

A Woman Chief Justice

The biggest surprise that greeted Claire L'Heureux-Dubé upon her return to the bench in January 1976 was the new (associate) chief justice.[1] Gabrielle Vallée was named to the top post in August 1976.[2] It was a meteoric rise. Vallée was the nineteenth woman to graduate from law at Laval (L'Heureux-Dubé was ninth), and one of the few to enter private practice in Quebec City, four years after L'Heureux-Dubé. Her appointment as a judge, the second and only woman named during L'Heureux-Dubé's absence, came two months after L'Heureux-Dubé was seconded to the immigration inquiry. It took Vallée less than three years to attain the highest position on her court, the first woman in Canada to be thus honoured.[3]

A novice female judge catapulted to the top of the judiciary in Quebec City? How did this come to pass? It seems to have been more evidence of the Trudeau Liberal government's commitment to appoint women, despite the skepticism of the bar.[4] André Desmeules, who had graduated from Laval law several years after L'Heureux-Dubé and was appointed to the Superior Court the same day as Vallée, expressed the sentiment of many when he admitted he had not anticipated Vallée's initial judicial appointment. He was equally surprised at her elevation.[5] It seemed to some of the lawyers that women's path had suddenly become golden. Quebec lawyer Raymond Lessard captured their views: "[T]he government wanted women. If a woman wanted to be nominated, she could just walk into that path. She was offered the spot."[6]

Justice André Desmeules, Quebec Superior Court, 10 May 2010.

In one sense, it was true, and partly accounted as well for L'Heureux-Dubé's rise. But it was also not true. The government was beginning to make amends for decades of overlooking competent women. Women who would have made excellent lawyers, excellent judges, and excellent chief justices had been denied entry. With the emergence of the politically powerful feminist movement, the search was on for (a few) women to appoint. And there were just a few out there. They stood out in the sea of masculinity and got the offers. But were they *un*meritorious? What had it taken to break through those challenging barriers, to ascend to those precarious few spots in a male world? It may have seemed to some observers that promotions for the first women came easily, but this ignores the toil and fortitude it had taken to rise to an eligible position in the first place.

Besides the fact that her gender was now in vogue, Gabrielle Vallée was a natural choice. The first Laval female law graduate to enter practice with some of her male classmates, she was also highly popular with her peers, who had elected her the first female *bâtonnière* in Quebec in 1973.[7] Louis LeBel, who would later sit with L'Heureux-Dubé at the Supreme Court of Canada, described Vallée as a "very competent lawyer" who became a "very good manager" as the Quebec City chief justice.[8] She was reputed to be a brilliant administrator.⁹ She was also widely known for her political acumen. Her family background, with a father who had served as a deputy minister in the Quebec government, offered impeccable connections.¹⁰

And yet it was an appointment that brought little joy to L'Heureux-Dubé. The relationship between the two women was prickly at best. "She never liked me, and I never liked her," said L'Heureux-Dubé, adding: "Gaby was mean and overbearing."¹¹ L'Heureux-Dubé criticized the new chief justice for failing to pull her weight because she rarely sat on cases and spent her whole time in administration. She objected to the gossip that Vallée encouraged. She complained that people would come to the chief justice's office just to have coffee and swap stories about lawyers and judges, adding: "I couldn't relate to that. I never went."¹² She accused Vallée of playing favourites with those who curried favour, of behaving unfairly toward others, and of making "life miserable" for her in particular.¹³

It was an open secret that the two women rubbed each other the wrong way. Some wondered whether L'Heureux-Dubé might have been irked at being passed over for chief justice, given that she had preceded Vallée to the bench. She was quick to dispute that notion. "It's not that I was disappointed," she insisted, "but I didn't think she was a good appointment. [There were] so many others that probably would have fit the bill much better."¹⁴

Some of the negativity directed against Vallée seemed to be a product of her lack of femininity. L'Heureux-Dubé had described Gaby Vallée as "one of the boys" during her years of practice, and now she criticized her "masculine style" on the bench.¹⁵ It was a common reaction to the strikingly tall Vallée. L'Heureux-Dubé's Laval classmate Martial Asselin remarked that Vallée was "very manly," "very tough," and "a tall woman who never married."¹⁶ André Desmeules added: "Gaby was *'un garçon manqué'*† – like a man – not so feminine as Claire. She never married. I think she would have liked to, but she was so tall, so strong ... maybe she frightened men."¹⁷ Louis LeBel described Vallée as "quite a character," "aggressive," and "a bit abrasive at times."¹⁸ Raymond Lessard complained that Vallée was a woman who "felt that she had to be too much like tough males to get what she wanted," and a person who "got mad easily."¹⁹

The first women negotiating the path of an all-male profession encountered pitfalls at every turn. Presenting an overly masculine demeanour

---

† "a tomboy"

Justice Gabrielle Vallée.

Quebec Superior Court judges, 1976. *Front row, left to right,* Gérard Corriveau, Jean-Robert Beaudoin, Eugène Marquis, Paul Miquelon, André Trottier; *back row, left to right,* Claire L'Heureux-Dubé, Jean Moissan, Paul-Étienne Bernier, André Gervais, Georges Pelletier, Gabrielle Vallée, Maurice Jacques, Georges-René Fournier, Jean-Jacques Bédard, Gabriel Roberge, Louis Doiron.

seems to have been as risky as having an overly feminine one. Vallée's height was surely irrelevant, yet in a highly gendered world where women were always supposed to be shorter than their male counterparts, it clearly mattered. Her marital status was also beside the point, yet it was something people mentioned regularly and that occasioned intrusive speculation. It was something the shorter, married L'Heureux-Dubé must have known smacked of sexism. She did not draw attention to these attributes herself, yet she joined in the general objections to Vallée's "masculine" style. Vallée's death from cancer in 1984 ended her unprecedented rise through the judicial ranks, and also deprives us of any opportunity to explore her perspectives on her position within the legal profession and her relationship with L'Heureux-Dubé.[20]

The more "feminine" L'Heureux-Dubé may have had difficulty dealing with the new chief justice, but she had begun to make allies on the bench. Yves Bernier, who had been so helpful during the immigration inquiry, continued to mentor her. Several of her Laval classmates joined her on the court: André Trottier in 1974, Ovide Laflamme in 1976, and Jean Bienvenue in 1977. Jacques Philippon from her former law firm was appointed in 1977 as well.[21] She made new connections with colleagues in other courts at judicial conferences and educational seminars. She participated enthusiastically in the summer English courses that the Commissioner for Federal Judicial Affairs provided for Francophone judges. She played host when Anglophone judges were offered an opportunity to take French courses in Quebec City. The relationships she forged with judges from across the country at the Château Frontenac dinners and at receptions in her home created long-lasting bonds.[22] She volunteered for key roles in national legal organizations – director of the Canadian Judges Conference, president of the International Commission of Jurists – and regularly attended Canadian Bar Association annual meetings. All in all, it led to a warming of the climate that pervaded the judicial workplace. Even former chief justice Frédéric Dorion, now retired, managed to speak more highly of L'Heureux-Dubé as time passed.[23]

Judging on Circuit

Because she had grown up in Rimouski, L'Heureux-Dubé was assigned to the Bas-Saint-Laurent area, primarily in Rimouski and Rivière-du-Loup. She sat less frequently in Baie-Comeau, Sept-Îles, and Îles-de-la-Madeleine, and very rarely in Chicoutimi, Beauce, and Trois-Rivières. It was an entirely

Francophone area, and her cases on circuit – as in Quebec City – were almost exclusively heard in French. She loved to drive, even on the narrow, winding roads that traversed most of the area at the time. She would get up at 6 a.m. and drive three hours to Rivière-du-Loup, starting court at 9 a.m. For Rimouski, which took an extra hour, she would delay the opening of court until 10 a.m. Baie-Comeau and Sept-Îles were too far to drive, so she took the plane and stayed the week. Occasionally, the weather would ground the planes and she would have to spend the weekend too.

Some voiced concern that women judges might seek special accommodation to reduce their travelling because of family responsibilities. According to André Desmeules, it was an idea that caused many of the male judges to insist that if the women wanted to become judges, they must fulfill the same duties as the men. He, however, believed that "whether we like it or not ... women are different from men."[24] L'Heureux-Dubé was adamant that she expected no special treatment: "I would never have accepted to be treated differently."[25] In fact, it seems that Gaby Vallée took care to ensure that her only female colleague was travelling her full share on circuit, if not more so.

L'Heureux-Dubé dealt with the time away by hiring a live-in housekeeper. The young woman who filled the position, Monique Barabé, had worked previously for one of her divorce clients, whose family could no longer afford her services. "She was an extraordinary person," recalled L'Heureux-Dubé. "She was an educator, kindly but firm, and a good cook. The children were very comfortable with her, and we became very attached. And of course my husband was there in the house too, not exactly a stranger to the children."[26]

L'Heureux-Dubé found the most onerous part of a judge's work to be writing the decisions, but her self-discipline prevented any backlog from building. Judges were asked to render judgments within six months, but L'Heureux-Dubé pushed herself to write immediately, most often the evening after the trial ended. If it was a case that required legal research, she left it for later but drafted the factual findings immediately, even if it meant working long into the night. She drew upon her training in the classical French humanities, developing a structural format she described as the "facts, law, and solution," which she "tried to write clearly."[27]

She prided herself on being organized, on scheduling efficiently, on never wasting time, and on always being punctual. "I was never late for court," she stressed. "I was never late in writing a judgment."[28] On balance, she also found her responsibilities as a judge to be easier to manage than her work in the law firm. "In law practice, the hours were not so predictable," she explained. "At the courts, it was nine to five [and then I wrote decisions] until eleven. [And] the best thing about being a judge was you didn't have to bill your clients."[29] There was also lots of time off in December, and a generous full month in the summer.

CHARACTERISTICS OF A GOOD TRIAL JUDGE

What makes a good trial judge? Reflecting on this question today, a cross-section of trial judges and distinguished counsel unveiled a long list of personal characteristics: patience, empathy, compassion, intelligence, life experience, fairness, the capacity to listen, respect for others, humility, wisdom, the ability to assess a cross-section of people, openness to human frailty, decisiveness, a demeanour of openness and impartiality, an ability to intervene when necessary, and the common sense to be silent otherwise.[30] L'Heureux-Dubé listed "educated common sense," an "open mind," and "empathy" as the three qualities she felt were most critical.[31]

The equation, already a difficult one, was further complicated by gender. In our culture, then and now, personalities and behaviours are filtered through the lens of gender. In each new town, L'Heureux-Dubé was confronted with lawyers, judges, and court staff for whom her gender was startling. *"Être pionnière c'est, somme toute, devoir se prouver à chaque occasion plutôt que d'être acceptée à la face même de ses réalisations."*[†, 32] Stereotypical assumptions about women's lack of capabilities dogged her. "They had to be educated that a woman was just like another judge," she explained.[33] Some observers believed L'Heureux-Dubé was severe with the lawyers who appeared before her. It reflected the stereotypical gendered assessment that firm men were properly "assertive" while firm women were unfairly "aggressive." It may also have had some basis in fact.

L'Heureux-Dubé's daughter, Louise, remembered being in the courthouse elevator one day and overhearing two lawyers criticize her mother's treatment of counsel. "They didn't know who I was [but] they didn't like her," she recalled.[34] In 1979, *Le Soleil* reporter J.-Claude Rivard wrote, *"Elle a la réputation d'être exigeante à l'égard des avocats lorsqu'ils plaident devant*

---

† "Being a pioneer is, in the end, having to prove oneself at every opportunity rather than being accepted on the face of one's previous achievements."

elle."[†] L'Heureux-Dubé's quick retort was: *"C'est parce que je suis exigeante envers moi-même."*[‡, 35] The young girl from the convent who had quizzed classmates and nuns alike, posing questions and then more questions until she was satisfied, was of the same mind as the judge on the bench. It was something she was aware of, and she was quick to defend herself:

> We had a party one day at Roger Garneau's [my former partner] and one lawyer [told me], "Lawyers don't like you." I said, "I can't stand bad lawyers." "You didn't do your job," I would say. "I know the file better than you. You go out and study it and when you're ready, I will come back to you." I was rough. I was not tender. I've never been tender on the bench. I was strict because the litigants had a right to be represented correctly, and I couldn't accept that a lawyer couldn't do his job. But good lawyers loved me.[36]

It was a view of long standing. Near the end of her tenure at the Supreme Court of Canada, she quipped: *"Les bons m'aiment, les pourris me détestent, et c'est parfait pour moi."*[§, 37]

Other lawyers spoke highly of L'Heureux-Dubé as a judge. Jacques LeMay, who practised with the Quebec firm of Prévost, Gagné, Flynn, described her as "very well prepared," and someone who was "attentive ... to the evidence and whatever comments the lawyers made." In his opinion, she was both "charming" and "a very pleasant woman" on the bench.[38] Roger Chouinard, who was appointed to the Superior Court a few weeks before L'Heureux-Dubé, stressed that she was "lively" as a judge, but "well accepted" and "serious." "She was a good judge [with] a good reputation," he concluded.[39]

Louise Mailhot, who followed L'Heureux-Dubé to the Superior Court in Montreal in 1980, was equally positive. "She listened to lawyers, especially the young ones, and she would be helpful actually," she recalled. "She spoke her mind. And if it was in the direction she wanted to go, she would give the lawyers more opportunity to plead. In family law, especially, she had a very clear direction."[40] Melvin Rothman, who was sitting on the Superior Court in Montreal, recalled that she was a judge who "didn't hold back":

> She would ask questions without any hesitation if she felt there was something that wasn't clear, or she wanted to know, or if it sounded silly what

---

† "She has a reputation for being demanding of lawyers when they plead before her."
‡ "It is because I am demanding toward myself."
§ "The good ones like me, the rotten hate me, and it's all fine with me."

the witness was saying. She would ask questions and keep at it. She is extremely lively. She doesn't hide her concerns or euphemize. Did some of the lawyers find that difficult? Maybe some did. Trial lawyers much prefer a judge who sits there and listens at least until the very end, and then asks questions. They don't like interruptions and arguments with them. It's generally not considered a good idea to interrupt excessively because it does sometimes throw the witness off the track of what he wants to say. In Claire's case, I never found her interventions wildly excessive or mean or prejudiced.[41]

Life experience, the capacity to listen, and the ability to assess fairly were other touchstones. L'Heureux-Dubé was firmly of the view that she possessed all of these qualities. "I'm a decision-maker," she exclaimed. "I didn't find it difficult. I was fascinated by all those stories. I listened. With your experience of life, looking at all those stories, you understand. You give people the benefit of the doubt regarding their perceptions of the facts, although sometimes it is not a question of perception but outright lying. I didn't have a problem assessing credibility. [I'm] very intuitive, good at people. I have that natural aptitude to see through people."[42] It may have seemed overly confident, yet such characteristics were also essential to success. Self-doubt, second-guessing, and reluctance to draw clear conclusions can immobilize a trial judge.

On balance, L'Heureux-Dubé seems to have possessed a good number of the personality traits described as important for trial judges. Certainly intelligence, decisiveness, life experience, and compassion were evident, although patience may have been occasionally in short supply.

THE DOCKET OF CASES:
A CROSS-SECTION OF DISPUTES AND *"L'AFFAIRE DES TROIS CHAÎNES"*

Quebec Superior Court judges did not specialize at the time, and L'Heureux-Dubé was assigned a varied docket of cases. She assessed damages for motor vehicle collisions, ruled on personal injury suits, dealt with insurance indemnity suits, settled estate matters, and decided bankruptcy and debtor/creditor disputes. She ruled on the intricacies of the registration of civil judgments, assessed employment claims, dealt with zoning and property disputes, issued interlocutory injunctions against striking union members, and heard a variety of contract disputes. She considered marital separations, dealt with divorcing spouses, settled alimony obligations, and ruled on child custody.[43]

Because she had never practised criminal law, L'Heureux-Dubé restricted herself to civil cases by what she called a process of "natural selection."[44] "I didn't know anything about criminal law," she explained. "I was afraid of it. Probably the defence lawyers who criticized me [later in my career] would laugh to hear me say that."[45] That did not stop reporters from quizzing the new judge about her views. Peppered with questions about criminal law when she addressed the Press Club of Rimouski, she pronounced herself against any reintroduction of the death penalty and in favour of the rehabilitation of criminals. The reporters loved it, describing her as *"l'une des personnalités marquantes non seulement du monde juridique du Québec mais également dans le « clan » des réformistes de la société québécoise."*[†, 46]

Her years on the trial court reveal a judge firmly in control of her courtroom who was proficient in resolving disputes. Cases often arrived as a tangled mess of contradictory evidence, with litigants who were confused, angry, frightened, demanding, sometimes recalcitrant, and often bitter. She sorted through conflicting stories, separating contested from uncontested facts. She sifted through police reports from the scenes of automobile crashes, scrutinized expert analyses of medical injuries and psycho-social reports of marital discord, evaluated parenting skills, quantified temporary and permanent physical incapacities along with related psychological depressions, assessed loss of life expectancy, compared incomes against living expenses and debts, and calculated alimony amounts due. She gave each case careful, studied attention, and issued decisions that were tightly structured, thoughtfully reasoned, and clear.[47] In her increasingly capable hands, the decisions emerged as a tribute to the rationality of the judicial art. Someone had to sort out the contradictions, and she did so with finesse. Her decisions, almost all in French, were well organized, beautifully written, and cogently explained. Reading them, what emerges is a portrait of a talented judge who was skilled in managing judicial proceedings, analyzing facts, and interpreting the law.

The best known of L'Heureux-Dubé's trial decisions was *"L'Affaire des trois chaînes."*[48] The 1979 case involved the Quebec government's claim to the shoreline of non-navigable lakes and rivers. The government asserted that it held a long-standing right over strips of land 198 feet wide, the length of three surveyors' chains, around the tiny lakes and rivers where Quebec residents had traditionally built their vacation chalets. The government argued that it could expropriate the 198 feet without compensation

---

† "one of the notable personalities not only of Quebec's legal milieu but also in the 'clan' of Quebec society reformers"

whenever it wished. Edouard Healey, a forty-year-old Francophone electrician from Rimouski, had built a cottage on the edge of a lake in Fleuriault Township. His property was in the county of Matapédia on the southern tip of the Gaspé peninsula, an area flush with salmon and noted for its bucolic hills. When the province served Healey with an eviction notice, he refused to move. It was a test case that had the potential to affect thousands of cottage owners throughout Quebec.

The basis for the government's claim to *les trois chaînes* strips had originated historically to preserve fishing rights for the Crown when the lands were first put on the market.[49] A 1919 legislative amendment further stipulated that the Crown had "full ownership" of the strips.[50] Healey did not object to the Crown's reserve of fishing rights, but he disputed its claim to ownership. His property, like most of the cottage properties in Quebec, had been purchased from the Crown before 1919. The case turned on whether or not the amending statute was retroactive.

L'Heureux-Dubé refused to evict Healey. She decided that the government had failed to prove the retroactivity of the 1919 statute, and dismissed the case with costs.[51] Her decision contained seventy-nine pages of thorough legal analysis, and was so well crafted that it brought her to the attention of lawyers at the Department of Justice in Ottawa and was a key factor in her growing reputation as a leading trial judge.[52] But it was not to hold. The Quebec Court of Appeal unanimously reversed her judgment, concluding that the three-chain reserve "for fishing purposes" had preserved the Crown's right of ownership from the outset, and that the 1919 act was retroactive.[53] The Supreme Court of Canada did the same in a unanimous decision written by L'Heureux-Dubé's old Laval classmate, Julien Chouinard.[54]

Neither appellate decision tempered L'Heureux-Dubé's views. She thought the appellate courts wrong when their decisions were delivered, and time did not change her assessment. Decades after, she was still adamant about the correctness of her ruling:

> The guy's building was within the 198 feet from the lake. They said, "Get out – no compensation – you're on our property." I said, "This is not their property. It's only a right of use for fishing." If it had been their property, why would they sell it? Everybody who had a cottage on the lake was expropriated automatically by that law. That was to me, outside the good common sense. If the 1919 statute had been retroactive, it would dispossess without compensation all the owners of those lands. I could only imagine that if this was the case, it would have been said clearly. I went with the people rather

than the government on the theory that if there was a doubt about the intent of the government, the decision should favour the dispossessed people.⁵⁵

Public sentiment was with L'Heureux-Dubé. The Quebec government was besieged with demands to repeal the 1919 statute.⁵⁶ Before the year was out, it acted to abolish the reserve.⁵⁷

SIGNS OF INNOVATION

One of the most interesting decisions L'Heureux-Dubé issued from the trial bench involved a paternity case. This was her first opportunity to consider matters directly touching upon female sexuality. In *L. v. M.*, the plaintiff claimed that the defendant was the father of her two-year-old son, and that she had become pregnant while she and the defendant were living together. Their nine-month cohabitation was "public and notorious." Friends and both sets of parents were aware that the pair was sleeping together. The plaintiff testified that she had had sex with no one other than the defendant while they lived together. The defendant denied paternity, testifying that he never had sex with the plaintiff during the period of conception, that she had had sex with others during this time, and that she was a woman *"de moeurs plutôt légères."*†

L'Heureux-Dubé found the plaintiff's evidence more persuasive than the reticence and memory gaps of the defendant. She held that there was no proof that the young woman had had sex with others during the relevant time. Although the facts were not conclusive, they rendered the defendant's paternity probable, which was all that was required. As for the fact that the plaintiff had had another child from a previous liaison and lived for several years with yet another man, L'Heureux-Dubé dismissed this as insufficient to prevent a finding of paternity. She noted that courts retained some anxiety about making findings of paternity, and equated this with parallel problems in the area of rape law: *"Le courant jurisprudentiel moderne dénote un certain laisser-aller dans l'administration de la preuve en cette matière, ce qui, selon lui, pourrait donner ouverture à des abus sérieux. C'est le même type d'argument qui a prévalu dans certains milieux lorsqu'il s'est agi d'amender la législation relative au viol."*‡ Courts in general might be

---
† "with a rather loose lifestyle"
‡ "In modern jurisprudence there is a certain *laissez-faire* in the law of evidence, which could open the way to significant abuses. It is the same type of argument that has prevailed in some circles when it came to amending the legislation on rape."

afflicted with anxiety but Claire L'Heureux-Dubé was not. She pronounced the defendant the birth father.[58]

As a lawyer, L'Heureux-Dubé had crusaded for women's greater entitlement to alimony. Now as a judge, she was responsible for making the decisions. She was reluctant to be pigeonholed as a family law judge, but since she was seen as an expert in the rapidly expanding field and, unlike most other judges, was not loath to preside over family disputes, she was inundated.[59] Some of her decisions showed her prepared to grant substantial alimony to ex-wives. One alcoholic ex-husband with a long history of violence against his wife and children had threatened to dissipate his estate and leave his wife with nothing. Throughout their twenty-three-year marriage, the wife had worked side by side with her husband to build a successful business with assets totalling half a million. L'Heureux-Dubé ordered the ex-husband to pay a lump sum of $100,000 to support his wife and two children, along with over $1,000 a month in alimony.[60]

In other decisions, she strove to ensure that alimony more accurately reflected the actual costs of separated spouses. When she learned that a husband earned $634 a month while his wife, who had custody of two teenage children, had been forced onto social assistance, she raised the alimony from $40 to $60 a week.[61] She sided with an impoverished divorced wife who was living with her five children on family allowance. When the ex-husband sought to have his alimony reduced because he had been laid off from his job, L'Heureux-Dubé noted that he had made frivolous purchases and was boasting that he no longer wished to work only to pay alimony. She rejected his request.[62]

She was sympathetic to women whose husbands tried to take advantage of them financially, even where both spouses worked for pay. During marriage, one wife had turned over her full salary to her husband, who managed all the family finances. He had returned $10 a week to her for her personal expenses. L'Heureux-Dubé gave short shrift to a document the husband filed with the court stating that for a payment of $500, his wife had renounced all present and future claims to alimony. Looking at the expenses and means of the parties, L'Heureux-Dubé ordered the husband to pay $100 per month.[63] She was particularly dismissive of men who claimed that they could not pay alimony because they had expenses for new female companions.[64] She rejected one ex-husband's request, pointing out that he had been having an extramarital affair and financially supporting his lover and their two illegitimate children for nine years. She accused him of starving his first family to support the second, and increased his alimony.[65]

L'Heureux-Dubé was particularly innovative in child custody decisions. She was one of the first judges to ask the children of divorcing parents to come to her chambers. There, in the presence of counsel and a stenographer but without the parents, she examined the children privately regarding their wishes. "I was the only judge that received the children in my chambers," she recalled. "Some judges said, 'Never do that.' I said, 'Do you think they are animals or what?'"[66] Children's preferences governed her decision when she overturned an earlier ruling by Frédéric Dorion granting custody to a father in a divorce based on the wife's adultery. The father's international travels kept him away from home for long stretches, while the mother could offer more hands-on attention and affection. L'Heureux-Dubé sided with the children when they advised her that they preferred to live with their mother.[67]

Many of the decisions exhibited sensitivity to the child custody rights of mothers. She set aside an earlier paternal custody order and awarded custody of four children to a mother who had remarried and was getting her life back together after being hospitalized for depression.[68] She refused an abusive ex-husband's demand that she overturn the maternal custody order for a six-year-old boy, noting that his brutality toward his wife was no incentive to entrust his son to his care.[69] She awarded custody of a four-year-old girl to her mother, adding that although it might not be a rule of law, it was a rule of good sense that a young child benefited from contact with the mother.[70] She awarded interim custody to a female accountant, even though her profession entailed long hours and she had had a short-term liaison with another man. L'Heureux-Dubé did not cast the traditional aspersions upon a mother who pursued a career and personal social interests, or even an extramarital affair. She emphasized that this woman was an excellent mother, who never neglected the children and hired responsible caregivers to look after them when she was away.[71]

On the Other Hand ...

Despite her many years in practice championing women's family law rights, L'Heureux-Dubé also issued quite a few decisions in favour of divorcing husbands. Some of her decisions on alimony reflected the traditional patriarchal approach that was characteristic of the era. She accepted the presumption that if a divorced wife had moved in with another man, her new male partner should take over her financial support.[72] She declared that marriage did not guarantee a pension for life.[73] The husband should have the right to remake his life *"sans cette épée de Damoclès"*† hanging over him.⁷⁴ She granted a husband's request to cancel his alimony obligations even though his income had almost doubled since the separation and his wife was living on social assistance, because the wife had lived with several male companions after the split. L'Heureux-Dubé described the woman's refusal to accept cash from her live-in companions as her own largesse, which ought not to bind her former spouse: *"Si la requérante veut lui faire des libéralités, elle ne doit pas le faire au détriment de l'intimé."*‡,⁷⁵

Some of the alimony rulings that went against female claimants seem to have reflected her optimism that women could and should stand financially on their own two feet. She ordered a wife who earned approximately the same as her husband to contribute equally to the cost of supporting their child.⁷⁶ She denied alimony to a separated wife who was in the paid labour force, despite the fact that her husband earned more than double her salary, and emphasized that separation ought not to focus on revenue equalization.⁷⁷ She cancelled an earlier alimony order for a working widow who had married and then divorced a retired priest, despite the fact that the former priest's income had almost doubled since the divorce. The widow was in the paid workforce and financial ties should be cut cleanly, she stated: *"Il est reconnu que le mariage n'est pas une assurance tous risques à perpétuité, et que la pension alimentaire ne doit pas servir à pénaliser l'une des parties. Il n'y a pas de doute qu'en l'espèce, chacune des parties doit aujourd'hui être en mesure d'assumer son propre coût de vie."*§,⁷⁸ Marriage was not an insurance policy for life. Divorcing spouses should assume their own costs of living.

She was also open to paternal custody. She awarded provisional custody of four children to a truck-driver father despite his admission that he drank, that he used gross language and vulgarity in front of the children, and that his wife was an excellent mother. The cause of the marital breakup was the wife's serious affair, and after the children advised L'Heureux-Dubé in chambers that they wished to live with their father, she awarded him custody.⁷⁹ In another case, she refused to overturn an earlier award for paternal custody that had been based on a psycho-social expert report.⁸⁰

---

† "without this sword of Damocles"
‡ "If the applicant wishes to give him gifts, she must not do so to the detriment of the respondent."
§ "It is recognized that marriage is not a perpetual all-risk life insurance, and that alimony should not be used to penalize one of the parties. There is no doubt that in this case each party must now assume responsibility for his or her own cost of living."

She also refused to extend visiting access to a mother after hearing from the children in her chambers that their mother quarrelled with their father, once even brandishing a knife. In fact, L'Heureux-Dubé reduced her access.[81]

What conclusions can be drawn from L'Heureux-Dubé's years at the Quebec Superior Court? Her paternity decision demonstrated a more balanced assessment of credibility than was prevalent at the time, when the law tended to disbelieve the testimony of sexually adventurous women. Some of her rulings on maternal custody illustrated a growing regard for women's equality, and a corresponding disregard for the sexual double standard. She delved more deeply into family disputes than some lawyers or parties expected, consulting in chambers with children, scrutinizing expert reports from psychologists and social workers, and closely inspecting the dollar amounts that should be awarded in alimony claims.

On the other hand, the decisions by no means depicted an iconoclastic jurist, radically reformulating judicial precedents and jettisoning traditional legal analysis. She spoke publicly about the disparate roles of the courts and legislators: the former to apply the law, the latter to make it. As she explained to the *Rimouski Progrès-Echo*, judges were not to follow their individual consciences but to apply the law as scrupulously as possible.[82] She did not view alimony as a tool for income equalization. She was not averse to paternal custody, or to relieving some men of the burden of alimony payments.

She may have made some rulings that her male brethren on the bench would not have made, but this was not the record of a wild-eyed reformer, out to change the shape of the law. It was the dossier of an intelligent, industrious, productive judge, whose decisions were balanced, solid, and generally in conformity with established standards – with just a shimmer of non-conformity.

21
Family Tragedy
Arthur's Death, 11 July 1978

As if the judicial work schedule were not challenging enough, the stresses in Claire L'Heureux-Dubé's personal life were intensifying. During the 1970s, while she struggled to keep up with circuit rounds for the Superior Court and the demands of the Montreal immigration inquiry, each member of her family seemed to be spiralling out of control.[1]

Arthur's mental health problems were intensifying at an alarming rate. His depression hung over the household like a blanket of gloom. He often expressed regret that he had had children, muttering: "Why put more miserable people on this earth?"[2] There was a history of mental illness and alcohol abuse in Arthur's family. "And he drank way too much," recalled L'Heureux-Dubé. "He drank to forget his unhappiness. It was the only time he was jovial, happy, having fun."[3]

Family and friends remember joining L'Heureux-Dubé and her husband at restaurants where Arthur seemed seriously out of control. Her sister Louise described a group dinner at the Montreal landmark restaurant Ruby Foo's where Arthur was "almost in a manic mood," loudly ordering bottle after expensive bottle of fine wine. She and her husband, Joe, marvelled over what the bill must have been.[4] Long-time friend and Rimouski neighbour Jean Drapeau recalled Arthur during an evening at the Oak Room in the old Sheraton Hotel in Montreal. "My lord, he was hot," exclaimed Drapeau. The couple had words in front of everyone: "When [Claire] was not glad, she told him," he explained.[5]

Photo taken for family Christmas card, December 1977.

The cure Arthur sought for his depression – alcohol – was worse than the disease. Some of the warning signs had been present for years. In 1956, Arthur had been charged with drunk driving and lost his driver's licence for one year.[6] Early in his Laval career, he began dropping into local taverns after his classes were over, and although his faculty colleagues would leave after several drinks, Arthur could not stop. Nothing changed after marriage and the arrival of children. He would forget to come home for dinner, and after she cleaned up, L'Heureux-Dubé would take a taxi to the pubs – La Grande Hermine on avenue Cartier, Hotel Saint-Louis-Joliet near the Château Frontenac – to try to coax him to come home. On nights when he refused, she drove the car home "so that he would not be tempted to drive home and kill someone."[7] Arthur would sometimes stay out all night, and the lady who ran the tavern would keep him.

As Arthur's alcoholism worsened, he was seldom sober. A sense of duty toward his job kept him from drinking in the morning, which enabled him to deliver his lectures at the university. By 11 a.m., however, he would start drinking continuously for the rest of the day. L'Heureux-Dubé tried to get him to compromise, begging him not to start drinking before 7 p.m. His reply was, "You're asking too much."[8] Her efforts to get him to go to Alcoholics Anonymous failed. "I'm not sure he realized [alcohol] was the problem," she explained, "[and] he thought he was above that."[9] L'Heureux-Dubé recalled that Arthur was going through about $100 worth of beer every month. "A guy would come with a truck and throw the cases out. We had to have a basement bar, almost a store at home, to keep the beer."[10]

Arthur often invited friends home in the evening to drink and watch sports. His brothers Georges-Henri and Yves would sometimes join him on a Friday evening, and they remember Arthur as "happy and funny" in the early years, serving chicken wings and beer. They too were worried about his drinking, but attributed it to the heavy-drinking heritage of the Scottish and Irish side of their mother's family.[11] Increasingly, though, Arthur failed to emerge from the basement for dinner with the family. "If he had been there for dinner with the children, it would have been okay," L'Heureux-Dubé countered.[12]

Their daughter, Louise, remembered that her father "would go on binges for two to three days, cavorting. Even when he was home, he would hole up in the basement with his buddies. Other than making fancy, complicated [French Canadian] meals that nobody makes any more ... I never saw him make or do anything. My father never taught my brother to play baseball, and he was a big sports fan. He was so much in his own head, in his own struggles, he couldn't do anything."[13] He began to demean himself in front of others. L'Heureux-Dubé's sister Louise remembered Arthur saying to her, "Everything you see here, Claire did it all. She's so efficient, it's all thanks to her. She does it all by herself. I have nothing to do with this. I'm not important. I'm not contributing." She added: "[He] was a little bit drunk. I think he had a low opinion of himself. I think maybe he was a little overwhelmed by her way to function, to make money."[14]

Although L'Heureux-Dubé had been a strong proponent of marital counselling for many of her clients, and for many of the litigants who appeared before her in court, she did not suggest it to Arthur.[15] "It was not for us. We felt we knew what we needed to deal with the problem. It would have been the last thing to think of. My husband would have said, 'Are you crazy?'" She added wryly, "It was good for others but not for us. That's very often the case."[16]

Claire and Arthur grew further apart, their joint philosophy being "live and let live."[17] "He left me totally free, never asked where I was, what I did. Total freedom on both sides," she recalled. "If he slept away from home for a couple of days ... I don't care about those things. I'm not a jealous person at all. Sexual fidelity – I don't believe in it – it doesn't exist. My husband could sleep with whoever he wanted. What I cared about was the intellectual relationship, being together. I still loved the brilliant man, this wonderful brain. He was too brilliant for this world."[18] Then she conceded, "You lose a bit of your respect for someone who is drunk, and who doesn't know what he does. What you call love becomes a little more problematic. I still loved him and I still loved the man who was sober. [But it] became hard to have a family life."[19]

L'Heureux-Dubé never let Arthur's descent into alcoholism and depression derail her career. She retained her independence, compartmentalizing her life in such a way that she could continue to meet all the expectations of her busy career. She could not shake the thought that a divorce might have sent Arthur deeper into depression. "I had intuition ... [I] knew that that would destroy him," she explained. "When I mentioned that we could live apart, that he could come [to visit] any time so long as he wasn't drunk, that he was a good father [and] could have the children, no problem ... that, I think, was the start of his going ... deeper and deeper into the hole. I didn't want to be responsible for that."[20] Years later, she agonized over whether she had been wrong, and whether a separation might have lessened Arthur's drinking, might have made him become more responsible as a person and a father. Louise believed that her parents should have divorced. Reflecting on the situation years later, she marvelled at her mother's ability to continue: "I don't know how she survived. She had a lot to deal with."[21]

Pierre and Louise

Pierre's earlier behavioural difficulties also intensified. Specialists would later offer varying diagnoses from schizophrenia to bipolar disorders, but whatever the source of the problem, he was an extremely disruptive child. He played with matches in completely unsafe circumstances. He was expelled from every school he attended. From the age of twelve, he began to run afoul of the law, stealing and experimenting with drugs. L'Heureux-Dubé would be called back from her judicial circuit time after time because of Pierre's scrapes. The police came to their home to check on the wayward boy, a frightening development and a particularly acute embarrassment for a Superior Court judge.

Louise described her brother as "trouble from the first day," "very rebellious very early on." "He would talk to us in ways that were horrible,

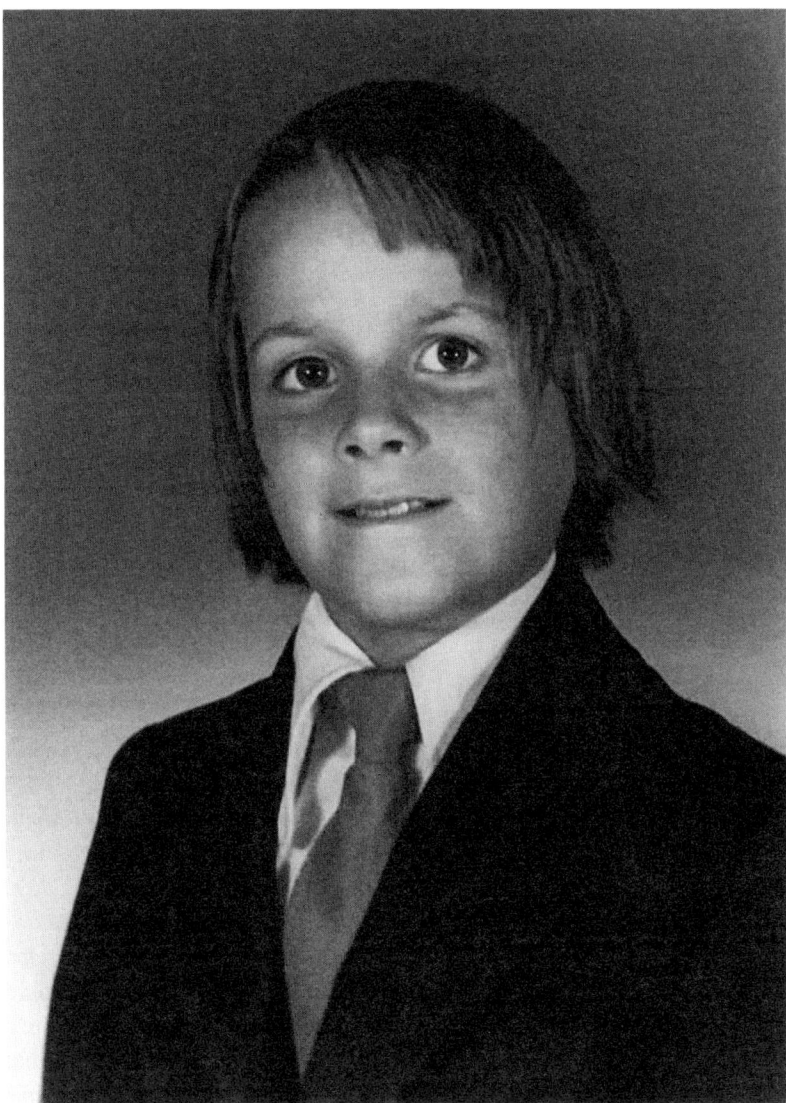

Son Pierre's school picture.

frightening. He needed a lot more help," she explained, "[and] he never got that. It was a disaster. It just got worse and worse and worse. It was a nightmare."[22]

L'Heureux-Dubé's sister Louise remembered Pierre when he was very little as "so bright, so smart." He used to amaze his cousins with his ability to solve the Rubik's Cube puzzle in minutes. But she noted that he "butted heads" with Arthur, each of them obstinate, inflexible, and strong-willed. She also worried that the nannies had spoiled Pierre, giving in to him when what he needed was a more disciplined framework. Louise worried too about her sister, wondering how L'Heureux-Dubé could possibly cope with Pierre as he became "more and more of a problem." She noted that it must have been her sister's "sense of optimism," her "hope that it would improve," that allowed her to keep going when "anybody else would have been brought down."[23]

In fact, L'Heureux-Dubé was distraught, terrified over what the future might hold for her son: "Pierre was very sensitive and brilliant. He was not a reader, but he could have been an engineer, because like his father he was good in math. It was heartbreaking, and I was so frightened."[24] She and Arthur took Pierre to see a psychologist, where the discussions were searingly unproductive. Pierre exploded with anger against Arthur during the sessions, accusing his father of being "always drunk, and if he wasn't, he walked like he was."[25] The specialist's response: Pierre would end up as a juvenile delinquent.

Daughter Louise seemed to be coping better, but she felt her mother's absences keenly. "My mother was in the first generation of working women," she explained, and there were "negative associations about that." Her schoolmates were all from "traditional" homes with working fathers and stay-at-home mothers. "I didn't know of any other classmates whose mothers worked," she continued. "There was a sense that working mothers would generate kids that were somehow deficient. I did feel this was imposed on me. I certainly bore the brunt of it."[26]

The feeling of being different, even deviant, marked the children whose mothers were the first to challenge the regimented postwar gender roles imposed on middle-class families. Betty Friedan's *The Feminine Mystique* would tackle this head-on, insisting that intelligent, educated women were leading stultified lives chained to sudsy dishpans in the suburbs. Her 1963 book opened the floodgates for the next generation of working women, but L'Heureux-Dubé, as usual, was ahead of the times, and her path-breaking career pulled her children into the frontlines of change as well, with predictable fallout.

Louise would later reflect negatively upon those years, faulting her mother for her time-consuming career. "Honestly, as a mother, she was tough. She didn't spend much time thinking about what we needed. Sometimes she would, but most of the time she was busy and concerned. [S]he had ... like ... the weight of the world on her shoulders. [And she]

Family Tragedy

Daughter Louise horseback riding, 1978.

was uni-dimensionally focused on law."²⁷ It was a sentiment that would have been recognizable to the children of Claire Kirkland-Casgrain, who had been called to the Quebec bar the same year as L'Heureux-Dubé. "If I wanted to have lunch with her, I needed to make an appointment," recalled her daughter, Lynne Casgrain.²⁸

Louise was equally critical of her father, whose physical presence in the home did little to dispel her sense of parental absence. "If he had been a different person, he could have helped more, been more attentive to the kids, [and] it might have worked," she mused. "[But] when his friends would call, they had to go out drinking, and if the kids were home he went anyway. At a certain point, it's very hard to tolerate on a day-to-day situation. There is no self-discipline, no ability to function for a family."²⁹ Louise never felt free to invite friends to her home, because she knew her father would be drinking. She recalled that although her mother attended all her school concerts, Arthur missed every one because he was drunk.

While other classmates went on family outings on weekends, Louise recalled that her parents never did. "There was no sense of family. That was the thing that was the hardest. There were four individuals and we divided up the house."[30]

Louise's survival strategy was to try to distance herself from the family. Her aunt Louise described her niece as "trying to steer away from it," to "detach herself from Pierrot's problems."[31] Despite her shyness, Louise felt safe at her all-girls' school, where she developed a close relationship with a best friend. She often took refuge at the home of her aunt Nicole and her grandmother. She took up horseback riding, a time-consuming sport that captured her interest, and by the time she reached CEGEP, she was spending nearly every afternoon at the stables. Intellectually gifted, Louise managed to keep her grades high throughout these years, and, influenced by her mother, she set her sights on law school.[32]

De Facto Separation and Arthur's Further Descent

Even as things continued to unravel, L'Heureux-Dubé refused to contemplate divorce. Instead, the couple observed a de facto separation. Arthur moved down to the basement, where he could drink uninterrupted. In some ways, it was the opposite of the Victorian gothic novel, where the estranged wife was hidden in the attic. L'Heureux-Dubé focused her energies upon her career, and maintained her social life with friends and colleagues. Her former law partner, Roger Garneau, recalled many receptions at L'Heureux-Dubé's home for lawyers and judges from across the country, including one where he met Justice Antonio Lamer.[33]

L'Heureux-Dubé entertained dinner guests without Arthur. Melvin Rothman, a Superior Court colleague from Montreal, remembered a dinner party where Arthur "dropped in and stayed for a drink" and talked to the guests for about five or ten minutes, adding tactfully: "Claire couldn't have had an easy life with respect to her husband."[34] Fellow Laval law graduate Monique Perron described similar incidents: "Sometimes Claire would invite five or six women for a very good dinner. Arthur would arrive, and she would say, 'Say hello to my friends,' and he didn't move. Her husband was very nice but drunk. [It was] very sad. She loved him. The next time she invited us, just the same. She could pass over things."[35]

Things became impossible during Arthur's sabbatical leave from Laval during the 1977–78 academic year. His moods were increasingly bitter, accusatory, and angry. L'Heureux-Dubé's sister Louise recalled: "[Although] Arthur was always nice to me, always ... you kind of had to avoid him when he was drinking. [I] don't think he was violent, [but] he was sourly and you didn't want to be around him."[36] Fewer and fewer of his friends dropped by, and even his brothers became loath to spend time with him. Georges-Henri Dubé watched his troubled sibling with alarm and despair, sensing that Arthur was "battling his own personality."[37] Yves Dubé, whose move to Ottawa kept him from seeing his brother for two years, spoke with great emotion of Arthur's wasted condition when he visited: "It was a great shock. Such a brilliant man. What people go through."[38] As Arthur's final months of sabbatical flew by, thoughts of trying to return to teaching seemed to overwhelm him. His relations with his wife and children became more volatile. At a family wedding, Arthur told some of his relatives that this would be the last time they would see him. Nobody knew what to make of his comments.[39]

On 11 July 1978, L'Heureux-Dubé's judicial session in Rivière-du-Loup came to a tragic halt when she received a message that Arthur had killed himself.[40] He had drunk himself into a stupor in the basement, emptying a whole bottle of cognac. Then, in an act of ultimate despair, he had shot his head off with a hunting rifle. The children were upstairs but did not hear the shot because the gardener was mowing the lawn. It was eighteen-year-old Louise who found him; she went looking for her father in the basement and saw blood spattered everywhere, her father's body mutilated beyond imagining. She screamed to Pierre not to come down, but the fourteen-year-old followed her and he too witnessed his father's destruction.[41]

Shocked and desolate with grief, L'Heureux-Dubé drove furiously for home. "It's so emotional, the sense of outrage, of injustice," she explained years later.[42] She was angry that Arthur had committed suicide in the home. "I can't understand that. Why did [he] do it in the house? Did he want to give us unnecessary pain? We had a cabin. He could have done it there. Or at the university. Then the children would have been spared the horror of seeing him. Imagine, his daughter had to see him with his head blown off. And I think he was partly responsible for the ruin of our son's life. Why did he do that?"[43] It was some time before she could come to grips with the anger. "Later, I was able to understand that he wasn't in his right mind. He was not responsible for what he was doing."[44]

L'Heureux-Dubé's family was grief-stricken at the news. Her sister Louise described the suicide as a shocking "tragedy."[45] Several of Arthur's Laval colleagues, especially Léon Dion, the husband of L'Heureux-Dubé's very close friend Denyse, helped arrange the funeral service, which went off "as well as could be expected."[46] The stress was acute. Like others, childhood friend Michèle Cloutier Mainguy arrived at the funeral with no advance warning of the cause of death. "The friend who told us ... simply said, 'Arthur is dead.' We arrived and I said, 'Was he sick?' Claire said, 'It's a suicide.' She's always been so open. I was a bit surprised."[47]

Years later, L'Heureux-Dubé reflected on her openness, which was a bold challenge to the stigmatization that keeps suicide hidden and largely misunderstood.

> Why do people hide suicide? [I guess that] it's the perception that it is a sin. I cannot see any other reason for societal condemnation of suicide. Since I'm not religious, [I] don't have those barriers. I had no reason to think you shouldn't talk about suicide. Maybe there are some people [who] would feel responsible. I never did that. That's his own demon. To me, there's nothing so bad about an individual making [such] a decision. Sometimes, there are signs that you need help. In his case, he didn't want any help. We didn't expect it, didn't see it coming, but it wasn't surprising when you look back.[48]

Her refusal to conceal the cause of Arthur's death was a courageous decision. It spoke to her forthright insistence upon the truth. Such openness about suicide was not commonplace, and many suffered behind veils of silence. L'Heureux-Dubé's disclosure helped usher in greater transparency, although it would eventually lead to greater public scrutiny than she could have imagined at the time. Suicide was also an issue L'Heureux-Dubé would later deal with on the Supreme Court of Canada, where she signed an opinion that would have struck down the criminal prohibition on assisted suicide as unconstitutional.[49] Although it was only a minority judgment and one she did not pen herself, it must have brought back intense memories of a tragic time in her own life. And it spoke to her renewed affirmation of the right to choose when to die.

Word of Arthur's death soon spread, and the horrific details became the source of gossip: the blood-spattered basement ceiling, the consternation of young Louise and Pierre discovering the body, his wife's frantic drive back from Rivière-du-Loup. Yet L'Heureux-Dubé steeled herself to get through it. Her sister Louise noted: "From what I heard from my mother and Nicole, Claire handled it well. She had good friends and good people to support her, but most of the strength came from within, from herself."[50]

The pain intensified when she reported to work only to discover that Chief Justice Gabrielle Vallée had taken it upon herself to send a death notice to the other judges without asking her, announcing that Arthur had "died in his sleep." L'Heureux-Dubé was appalled at the lie, and had the excruciating task of correcting the misinformation. She did not request bereavement leave. Adding aggravation to pain was the fact that Vallée had scheduled her to sit on circuit in far-flung Sept-Îles almost immediately after the funeral. Her colleagues offered to take her place so that she could be with the children, but she refused on principle. "I said no, I will go and tough her out."[51]

The family decided not to sell the house, but L'Heureux-Dubé could not bring herself to go down to the basement for years. She cleared out Arthur's Laval office, where she discovered more evidence of dysfunction. The office was disorganized, awash with papers covering every inch of space. Bugs were everywhere. The family photos that she and the children had given Arthur for his office had been thrown away. There was nothing to identify the person who had inhabited the premises. Determined to honour the brilliant man she had loved so much, she created a scholarship in her husband's name, and Arthur's colleagues and students came together to commemorate him, giving speeches in his honour.

Arthur's relatives rallied around L'Heureux-Dubé, offering support. There were agonized family conversations as to what had provoked Arthur's suicide, with no one able to say with any certainty what had caused it or what might have prevented it. L'Heureux-Dubé was deeply grateful that she was able to maintain close relationships with Arthur's brothers and sisters-in-law long after his passing, witness to their general agreement that she was not to blame.[52] Perhaps their daughter Louise summed it up best: "He struggled his entire life with depression and alcohol. I don't think he had a plan [or] knew what he wanted. He was just trying to survive. He ultimately failed at that. That part is just really sad."[53]

L'Heureux-Dubé maintained that no one should lose sight of the positive memories. "I think he was happier the twenty-two years he lived with me than he would have been otherwise," was her final comment.[54] She threw herself into her work, which she found to be both a distraction and an enormous comfort. "My husband took his own life, [but] I never looked back. [F]rom an early age, I had to take on responsibilities. My mother was sick ... then my sister died. I have the temperament of a survivor."[55] She compartmentalized her life, fine-tuning a mechanism that had always enabled her to turn things on and off. "[It helped me] to be busy intellectually. I think it was the greatest strength of my life, to be able to close off one aspect, and turn to my work. There was no point dwelling upon the suicide. And of course, I had my children after my husband died ... I had two children depending on me."[56]

Louise took refuge in flight. She began studying law at McGill University that fall, and graduated with honours three years later. She worked over the summers with the Heenan Blaikie law firm in Montreal, and practised tax law there until 1985. She returned home after concluding that law practice was not for her, but found the memories of her father's death overwhelming. Her mother urged her to do something different. With her financial support, Louise moved to Europe, where she studied German for a year and travelled for another year, before returning to complete an MBA degree at Yale University, where she met and married her first husband.[57]

Pierre's life would unfold in different directions, piling considerably more tragedy onto an already grief-stricken family.

Quebec Court of Appeal

22
Appointment to the Quebec Court of Appeal, 1979

The fall of 1979 was a momentous one for Claire L'Heureux-Dubé.[1] A vacancy opened up on the Quebec Court of Appeal when her former Laval classmate Julien Chouinard moved up to the Supreme Court of Canada.[2] On 16 October 1979, at the age of fifty-three, she was tapped to take his place, the first woman ever to join so rarefied a judicial circle in Quebec, and the second in Canada.[3]

A new cast of players came to power in Ottawa in June 1979, when Joe Clark defeated Pierre Trudeau and led the Progressive Conservatives to their first minority government in sixteen years.[4] Prime Minister Clark selected Jacques Flynn as his minister of justice, bringing him into the cabinet from the Senate because so few Conservative Quebec MPs had been elected. Flynn had practised law in Quebec City as the head of the prominent firm of Flynn, Rivard, Jacques, Cimon, Lessard et LeMay.[5] It was likely no accident that Flynn chose one of his former partners, Julien Chouinard, for the Supreme Court.[6] As a senior member of the Quebec bar, he would also certainly have known of L'Heureux-Dubé's reputation as a lawyer and judge.

There was another new player on the scene as well. Martial Asselin had served as a Conservative MP through the 1960s, had been appointed to the Senate in 1972, and was also brought into Joe Clark's cabinet in 1979 as minister of state for the Canadian International Development Agency. His position as one of the senior Quebec ministers gave him considerable influence over appointments. Although L'Heureux-Dubé knew neither Clark nor Flynn personally, she was well acquainted with Asselin, who

Jacques Flynn, minister of justice at the time of L'Heureux-Dubé's appointment to the Quebec Court of Appeal in 1979.

had been a classmate of hers and Chouinard's. Indeed, Asselin remembered fondly how much Claire L'Heureux had helped him catch up on his studies at Laval when his work as a student politician consumed the lion's share of his time. "I saw, even as a student, that she would be a very good lawyer," he recalled. "She was so bright. Claire was beautiful and she was joking very often. We were friendly."[7]

Plans were set in motion during a discussion on a plane en route to a Commonwealth conference in Zambia. Clark, his wife, feminist lawyer Maureen McTeer, Minister of Foreign Affairs Flora MacDonald, and Martial Asselin were all present. Their memories vary, but at some point during the long flight the conversation turned to the vacancy at the Quebec Court of Appeal.[8] Although McTeer does not remember the details, she was in favour of appointing a woman.[9] Clark was supportive, since he was "interested in ensuring there was a greater representation of women" in senior positions generally.[10] And Asselin piped up that he knew Claire L'Heureux-Dubé.[11]

All of them were well aware of the power of the feminist movement in Quebec, as well as the potential backlash that appointing a woman could provoke. McTeer elaborated:

> The women's movement [was] much more integrated into the fabric of Quebec life than was the case in English-Canada. [It was] a community-based, province-wide solidarity movement of which equality and fairness were integral. Joe hoped to appoint more women, but there was also a lot of resistance and flak. Martial Asselin was a very big supporter of women. He and Flynn were actively looking for appointments to the Senate at that time. It would have mattered that Flynn and Asselin pushed Claire. The resistors could be told, 'Look at these men, hardly revolutionaries – [they] think she is good.' It was, after all, only a token. The women who went first had to be better than the men – or at least as good. [Claire] was the right woman at the right place at the right time. It wasn't until later in her career that she became seen as a feminist. It would have been a barrier if she had been.[12]

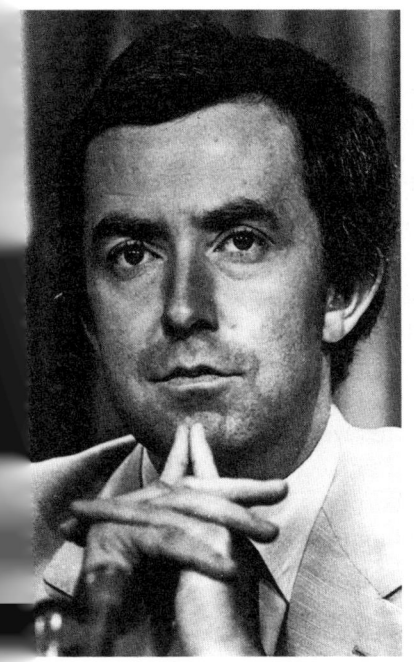

me Minister Joe Clark, who appointed aire L'Heureux-Dubé to the Quebec urt of Appeal in 1979.

Maureen McTeer, wife of Prime Minister Clark, who supported the appointment.

L'Heureux-Dubé was privy to none of this at the time, when appointment to the Court of Appeal required neither an application nor any particular process. Indeed, as appellate judge Yves Bernier explained, although "most of the Superior Court judges wanted the promotion," it was "looked down upon if you manoeuvred to get it." His recollection was that the chief justice and the *bâtonnier* would recommend someone to the minister of justice, there would be a quiet consultation, and then they would "just tell you that you had been appointed."[13] It is not clear to what extent there was a consultation with the bar, but it appears that Flynn did call the chief justice of the Court of Appeal, Édouard Rinfret, who consulted with Gabrielle Vallée from the Quebec Superior Court. Neither appeared to have rejected the candidacy out of hand. It was a much more streamlined process than initial appointments to the Superior Court. By the time judges became nominees for elevation to the appellate court, they had usually amassed a track record of decisions, a body of work that spoke for itself.

A plan was struck to assign L'Heureux-Dubé to the appeal court for a week of probation. Superior Court judges were occasionally appointed as ad hoc fill-ins or to alleviate backlog, but this appointment seems to have been sufficiently unusual that it was heralded in the press. An article titled *"À la Cour d'appel"* appeared in *Le Soleil* beside L'Heureux-Dubé's photo, indicating that as of the first week of October, she would sit as *"un juge suppléant,"*† the first Québécoise to ascend to the appellate bench.[14]

Although the timing, ten days after Chouinard's departure, should have made L'Heureux-Dubé twig, she maintained that she thought this was simply a regular one-week ad hoc appointment. When Gaby Vallée asked, she agreed to the assignment because she was curious about what went on at the Court of Appeal. Panels of three judges sat on appeal cases, and she was paired with Laurent-E. Bélanger and François Lajoie.[15] The trio heard nineteen matters during the five days, the hearings went well, and the panel made decisions without dissents. Bélanger wrote eight decisions, Lajoie four, and L'Heureux-Dubé two; the rest were delivered *sur le banc*‡ as a group.[16]

L'Heureux-Dubé wrote on the most important case: *Julien c. La Reine*, the appeal of a conviction on two counts of murder. Two bodies had been discovered in a rooming house after a deadly fire, and the accused was convicted on the testimony of Laurette Pelletier, who confessed that she saw him deliberately set the fire in a closet. The accused claimed that the

---

† "a temporary judge"
‡ from the bench

trial judge had erred in not permitting a psychiatrist to testify that Pelletier suffered from hysteria and a tendency to exaggerate. The trial judge had held that the psychiatric evidence was not presented as a legitimate attack on credibility but for the improper purpose of attacking the witness's competence in front of the jury. On appeal, L'Heureux-Dubé overruled him. The line between competence and credibility was very thin, she noted. Even though the judge had found the witness competent, the jury was entitled to hear about the two years of psychiatric treatment she had received and the diagnosis of hysteria. The defence arguments were buttressed by two letters Pelletier had written to the accused's legal aid lawyer after the trial, saying that she had perjured herself on the stand. L'Heureux-Dubé concluded that the psychiatric evidence and the subsequent renunciation were sufficient to overturn the convictions, and ordered a new trial.

It was a thorough twenty-six-page decision, reviewing all the relevant case law, that attracted the unanimous support of her colleagues. One of her earliest decisions to appear in the published law reports, it gave no hint of any "law-and-order" proclivity to come.[17] The two male judges reported that L'Heureux-Dubé was up-to-date on her law and able to handle the job. Only then did she discover that her two colleagues had been tasked with reporting on her aptitude for the job. "We gave you a thumbs-up," was how one of them put it.[18]

Within a week, Flynn phoned L'Heureux-Dubé to ask whether she would accept an appointment to the Court of Appeal.[19] She accepted without hesitation. "I [had become] impatient on the bench," she recalled, "because people were lying. I couldn't stand it. I don't think I would have lasted long on the Superior Court before being nasty."[20] Reflecting on this some years later, she added that negative attitudes were not uncommon among trial judges, who got fed up with the vicissitudes of witnesses. It was one of the unfortunate side effects of judging trials. The other plus side of her elevation was that appeals were heard only in Quebec City and Montreal. Travelling to Montreal was a cinch compared to her far-flung trial circuits. It was a much-needed respite for a woman who was now a single parent, trying to meet the needs of her nineteen-year-old daughter and fifteen-year-old son. L'Heureux-Dubé again emphasized that, to her, one of the most important aspects of her elevation was that she had not asked for it. "I never asked a favour," she emphasized. "I never asked anything from anybody. I didn't ask to go to the Court of Appeal, so I owed nobody anything. When you have strings attached, you are not free."[21] She prized her sense of autonomy and independence, traits that would emerge repeatedly in the coming decades.

André Desmeules, her colleague on the Superior Court, suggested that there may also have been another motivation: "I think she was glad to go there, especially since Gaby had been appointed chief justice."²² Gaby Vallée seems to have been passed right over when the call went out for a female appellate judge. L'Heureux-Dubé suspected that she may not have wished to leave her chief justice position, and added: "And of course, Martial Asselin had not been *her* classmate."²³ The previous antipathy between the two did not prevent Vallée from inviting L'Heureux-Dubé to lunch to celebrate the elevation, or L'Heureux-Dubé from sending an elegant letter thanking the chief justice for her generosity and *"le grand respect que tu as toujours démontré de mes délibérés."*†, ²⁴

Swearing-In: A Warmer Welcome

The swearing-in took place on 2 November 1979. This time, the official reception was much more welcoming. Chief Justice Rinfret delivered a flowery tribute, stating: *"Nous avons dérobé à la Cour supérieure une perle qui ornera désormais notre diadème."*‡, ²⁵ With a handwritten note on his official stationery, he forwarded to L'Heureux-Dubé copies of the many newspaper clippings that chronicled the event.²⁶ Seventy-four-year old Rinfret was a former Liberal politician who had been appointed directly to the Court of Appeal in 1952 and elevated to the position of chief justice in 1977. His graciousness toward L'Heureux-Dubé contrasted sharply with the earlier behaviour of Frédéric Dorion. The times were changing, and the warm greeting also reflected L'Heureux-Dubé's success in gaining acceptance from her fellow judges. A woman known for her charming personal notes, she sent Rinfret an eloquent thank-you letter a few days later.²⁷

L'Heureux-Dubé's speech that day was equally generous. She noted that 1979 marked the fiftieth anniversary of the Privy Council's Persons Case, *Edwards v. A.G. of Canada,* in which women had been legally recognized as "persons," creating a foundation of *"amitié et respect mutuel."*§ She expressed appreciation to Thérèse Casgrain, who had guided the hand of the premier who authorized women to practise law in Quebec in 1941, and expressed regret that Casgrain was not present on this historic occasion.

---

† "the great respect you have always shown for my deliberations"
‡ "We have stolen from the Superior Court a pearl that will now adorn our diadem."
§ "friendship and mutual respect"

Appointment to the Quebec Court of Appeal

Claire L'Heureux-Dubé with Chief Justice Édouard Rinfret at her Quebec Court of Appeal swearing-in, 2 November 1979.

She thanked by name many family members, friends, colleagues, and others whose kindnesses had been important. She spoke of the ideal of justice, which she hoped to hold close *"avec la grâce de Dieu et votre amitié."*[†, 28] Looking back over the photos of the swearing-in decades later, she recollected not only the sense of celebration but also the overwhelming fatigue. "I was so tired that day," she confessed.[29]

---

† "with the grace of God and your friendship"

L'Heureux-Dubé's family, former law partners, and close friends attended the ceremony, and then gathered for an informal reception at Denyse and Léon Dion's home. Joseph Nuss, counsel for the immigration commission of inquiry, who was there with his wife, recalled meeting Paul L'Heureux, Claire's father, for the first time. "Everything was very pleasant," he remembered, "including her father."[30] Official photographs were taken. The teenage children expressed pride in their mother. L'Heureux-Dubé spoke of the debt she owed her sister Nicole for taking such constant care of their ailing mother. She choked up with emotion over her husband, who was not there to share in this second swearing-in, his death a year earlier a poignant memory for all present. Her most vivid recollection of the event was complete exhaustion.

The press focused on the notoriety of the first female appellate appointment. L'Heureux-Dubé remained uneasy about this. She disavowed any *"mission spéciale"*[†] and claimed that all she wanted was to be *"un bon juge,"*[‡] but relented sufficiently to admit: *"C'est quand même bon pour les cercles féminins."*[§, 31] In case there remained any lingering doubt, J.-Claude Rivard, a reporter with *Le Soleil*, reminded all readers that *"on ne lui connaît pas une réputation de féministe."*[||, 32] And, as she said to Claude Roussin, who interviewed her for the Laval student newspaper: *"J'ai toujours prétendu et affirmé que la femme n'avait pas de rôle spécial à jouer dans le Barreau, dans la pratique et sur le banc. Un juriste, c'est un juriste; un juge, c'est un juge; un avocat, c'est un avocat, qu'il soit femme ou homme."*[#, 33] Despite her earlier references to the Persons Case and Thérèse Casgrain, her perspective had not shifted.[34] But was she nominated because she was a woman, queried the reporter? L'Heureux-Dubé refused to answer directly, replying that she did not agree with appointing women simply because of their gender: *"Je crois que c'est très mauvais pour les femmes d'ailleurs de nommer une femme parce qu'elle est femme; je crois que l'on doit nommer une personne, femme ou homme, parce qu'elle est compétente et c'est tout."*[††, 35]

---

† "special mission"
‡ "a good judge"
§ "It's still a good thing for women's circles."
|| "She is not known to be a feminist."
"I have always claimed and affirmed that being of feminine gender had no special role to play in the bar, in practice and on the bench. A jurist is a jurist; a judge is a judge; a lawyer is a lawyer, whether a woman or a man."
†† "I think it is very bad for women to appoint a woman because of her gender; I believe that we must appoint any person, woman or man, strictly on the basis of competence."

Appointment to the Quebec Court of Appeal

Quebec female judges and distinguished legal personalities, dinner of the Barreau du Québec. *Front row, seated, left to right,* Jeanne d'Arc Lemay-Warren, Réjane Laberge-Colas, [unidentified], Claire L'Heureux-Dubé, Claire Kirkland-Casgrain, Lyse Lemieux, Luce Patenaude; *second row, left to right,* [unidentified], Michèle Falardeau-Ramsay, [unidentified], [unidentified], [unidentified], Sylviane Borenstein, [unidentified], [unidentified], Alice Desjardins; *third row, left to right,* [unidentified], Hélène Dumont, Micheline Corbeil-Laramée, Claire Barrette-Joncas, [unidentified], Huguette St-Louis; *fourth row, left to right,* Michèle Rivet, Danièle Tremblay-Lamer, [unidentified], [unidentified], Juanita Westmoreland-Traoré.

The "woman factor" was disavowed repeatedly by women of L'Heureux-Dubé's generation as they struggled to assert their normalcy within all-male halls of power. It would take another generation to assert differently. Barbara Babcock, an American lawyer and law professor who entered law school twelve years after L'Heureux-Dubé and forged many "firsts" in her own career in Washington, DC, and on the faculty at Stanford law school, put it this way: "[When asked] 'How does it feel to get your job because you are a woman?' I developed a stock answer: 'It feels a lot better than *not getting it* because I am a woman.'"[36]

And of course, gender *was* one of the most salient features of the appointment. The court she was leaving had been slowly picking up additional female judges. On the Superior Court, after Réjane Laberge-Colas (1969) and L'Heureux-Dubé (1973), had come Gabrielle Vallée (1973), Claire Barette-Joncas (1975), Jeanne d'Arc Lemay-Warren (1976), and Lyse Lemieux (1978).[37] Across Canada, the same pattern was emerging. Louise Mailhot, whose appointment to the Superior Court would follow in 1980, noted that between 1943 and 1980, there were just thirty-three nominations of women to Canadian superior courts. However, there would be twenty-six nominations between 1980 and 1985, and fifty between 1985 and 1990. By the year 2000, female appointments would make up almost one-third.[38] From a tiny rivulet to a swelling stream, change was in process. But for Claire L'Heureux-Dubé, the pent-up pressure that would propel more women into the judiciary must have seemed ephemeral. She was alone and ahead of it all.

23
Appellate Judging, 1979–87

Despite the effusive welcome from Chief Justice Rinfret, Claire L'Heureux-Dubé's first days at the Court of Appeal were reminiscent of her bumpy beginning at the Superior Court.[1] Twenty-four cases were listed on the week's docket. The judges sat in panels of three, and the custom was to assign each judge to prepare one-third of the files in advance. Each would then brief the others thirty minutes before the hearings began. L'Heureux-Dubé recalled that she was nervous and had sacrificed sleep poring over her files to ensure that she was properly prepared.[2] One of her first cases involved a difficult contract dispute between a manufacturer of doors and window frames and a widow who rented the building and machinery for the enterprise.[3] "I had really studied that file, [but] there were all kinds of facts that were complicated. I was confused about dates. So when that case came up, I started asking questions," she recalled.[4]

Chairing her panel was George W.R. Owen, who was miffed at having to sit with a woman and felt no need to hide it. Sixty-seven years old, he had been appointed directly to the Court of Appeal from his Montreal law practice in 1955, and held one of the positions earmarked for Anglophone judges. L'Heureux-Dubé described him as a "big bulldog of a man" who "hated the idea of women on the bench."[5] In court that day, as L'Heureux-Dubé began to ask questions of the lawyers, he made a great show of looking at his watch. He had a luncheon appointment for 12:30 p.m., and it was 12:25. "Madam Justice L'Heureux-Dubé withdraws the question," he intoned. Then he poked L'Heureux-Dubé in the side and

293

growled, "Let's go out." The panel adjourned to the conference room, where he exploded: "I'm not going to endure you asking questions like this." L'Heureux-Dubé remembered "almost crying" and being "completely taken aback." When they resumed after lunch, she "didn't ask one question. So we finished. That was it."[6] Owen's heavy-handed intervention caused her to ask herself, "Why did I come here? If that was going to be my lot, I was much better alone in the Superior Court."[7]

RELATIONS WITH COLLEAGUES

L'Heureux-Dubé's rocky start was not atypical of what other women would find when they took postings as the first female appellate judges. Bertha Wilson, who in 1976 became the first woman to sit on the Ontario Court of Appeal, found many of her new colleagues less than receptive. When Ontario Chief Justice George Alexander Gale called a special meeting to warn his colleagues that the new judge would be female, a chorus of voices raised objections, including one senior judge who complained: "No woman can do my job."[8] Catherine Fraser, one of the early women appointed to the Alberta Court of Appeal in 1991, described her first years as a "burden."[9] Louise Mailhot, who in 1987 became the first woman to join the Montreal branch of the Quebec Court of Appeal, found the pervasive masculine culture very wearing. "At the daily coffee meetings ... they would only speak about hockey, golf, and baseball – exclusively. It could last hours." At official dinners, she remembered "this awful smell of the cigars and then the jokes that started ... with the Newfies and then the women. I felt overwhelmed."[10] It was sometimes deliberate, sometimes thoughtless, and each woman endured it in isolation. There were obvious parallels as well with the chilly reception directed toward Bora Laskin, the first Jewish judge appointed to the Ontario Court of Appeal in 1965.[11]

The other judge whom L'Heureux-Dubé recalled as continually difficult was Amédée Monet. She described Monet as "a great intellect" with "an original way of thinking," but "not easy."[12] Their relationship went back many years, when she had worked with the Civil Code Revision Office and interviewed him on family law reform. When she sent Monet a summary of his comments for his review, he replied that it was "not exactly what I said." L'Heureux-Dubé offered to correct the document if he would tell her where the discrepancies were, but he never responded. It was to be a pattern. He was "always questioning whatever you said," explained L'Heureux-Dubé.[13] He had a serious drinking problem as well. She would wind up clashing with Owen and Monet frequently when the three were assigned to sit together on appeal panels.

Over time, L'Heureux-Dubé encountered judges who were more supportive, and she slowly found her footing. Jean Turgeon, who had been one of her favourite law professors at Laval, took her under his wing. Called to the bar in 1933, Turgeon had practised law in Quebec City, taught part-time for twenty-five years at Laval, and been appointed directly to the Court of Appeal in 1969.[14] The most senior of the appellate judges in Quebec City, he served as the unofficial chief justice in the capital city. "[He was] like a father-figure. He protected me on the Court of Appeal," said L'Heureux-Dubé. Turgeon sensed that his new colleague's self-confidence had taken a bruising and he sought to intervene. "I remember one day he said, 'Come to my office,' after a hearing. He said, 'Why don't you believe in yourself? You're the one who is right,'" recalled L'Heureux-Dubé. Turgeon knew she had not had much experience in criminal law, and on that score, he was not above trying to influence her decisions. "He had the impression that women were very soft on crime," L'Heureux-Dubé explained. "When we went on the bench for a sentence hearing, he would say: 'Remember, they deserve it. Don't take it away from them.' He would always tell me that before we went into the court."[15]

Yves Bernier continued to dazzle L'Heureux-Dubé, as he had when they were both on the Superior Court: "He was a great judge, the brightest of my colleagues on the Court of Appeal. He listened. He had an open mind. He was not prejudging anything."[16] She deeply admired Albert Mayrand, whose encyclopedic knowledge of law, inspired writing style, and subtle humour gave her great pleasure.[17] She remembered the other Anglophone judge from Montreal, George Montgomery, as a "gentleman with a super mind."[18] John A. Nolan, a New Brunswick–born Irishman elevated from the Superior Court to the Court of Appeal in 1979, had a sense of humour that delighted her.[19] Melvin Rothman became a good friend whom she revered for his "wisdom" and "knowledge," someone "whose dissents were usually confirmed by the Supreme Court."[20] "Mel was one of the best judges on the Court of Appeal during my time," she said.[21] Two others she remembered with fondness were Laurent-E. Bélanger and François Lajoie, the judges who had given her the "test run" before her appointment.

Her male colleagues committed regular faux pas that might have unsettled many women, but L'Heureux-Dubé was determined not to let minor distractions bother her. One day, Fred Kaufman, a colleague she liked and admired, lightheartedly gave her a quick slap on the buttocks.[22]

Judges of the Quebec Court of Appeal. *Seated, left to right,* George H. Montgomery (1957–87), Marcel Crête (1972–88), Chief Justice Édouard-G.Rinfret (1952–80), George Robert Whittey Owen (1955–87), Jean Turgeon (1969–85); *standing, left to right,* Rodolphe Paré (1976–90), Laurent-E. Bélanger (1973–83), John A. Nolan (1979–86), Claire L'Heureux-Dubé (1979–87), Antonio Lamer (1978–80), Amédée Monet (1977–91), Fred Kaufman (1973–91), Yves Bernier (1973–91), François Lajoie (1970–84), André Dubé (1973–93), Albert Mayrand (1974–85).

Such an act would have been inappropriate at any time, but as luck would have it, this occurred just after an explosive incident in the 1984 federal election campaign, when Liberal leader John Turner had been caught on television giving a "pat on the bum" to Iona Campagnolo, a former MP who was the party president. The ensuing furor threatened to derail Turner's campaign, with protesters denouncing him as unfit to lead a new government.[23] Some of L'Heureux-Dubé's colleagues who noticed Kaufman's misstep cried out, "Fred, you'll be sued!" Anxious to defuse the situation, L'Heureux-Dubé just laughed and said, "Oh it's so nice. Oh Fred ... I miss it." This contrasted with Campagnolo's reaction, which was to turn the tables and give Turner a return pat, but there was a similarity in the way both women sought to recover from an embarrassing incident. Years later, L'Heureux-Dubé added: "The way I would take things would be more jokingly, trying not to make a drama about everything. I was the only one. I was not going to alienate everybody there."[24] For the only woman on the Court of Appeal during her nine-year tenure, it may have been the only realistic option. And it was a strategy that worked, that gained her a reputation as *"une femme attachante."*[†, 25]

THE ART OF NEGOTIATION ON APPELLATE PANELS

Appellate judging opened new vistas for L'Heureux-Dubé. She gave up the twin attributes of the trial judge, autonomy and isolation, for immersion in negotiation by triad. The Quebec Court of Appeal was composed of five judges from Quebec and eleven from Montreal. Each week, fresh trios were assigned to sit together. After hearing the lawyers' submissions, which were generally of a very high calibre, the judges adjourned to discuss the dispute. If all three could agree, the judge who had prepared the case would write the unanimous decision. Sometimes one of the three would write a concurring opinion; occasionally, all three did so. And there was always the prospect of a dissent if anyone disagreed. There was little hint of the reputation L'Heureux-Dubé would acquire on the Supreme Court of Canada as "the Great Dissenter." On the Quebec Court of Appeal, she dissented no more frequently than her colleagues. The essence of the job was learning to work with the other judges, to debate, to persuade, to compromise.[26]

L'Heureux-Dubé's Quebec Court of Appeal colleague Roger Chouinard emphasized that one of the most important characteristics of a successful appellate judge was to be able to "act as a group," adding that "if you are a lone wolf on appeal, it's hard." In this capacity, he felt that despite her status as the only woman, L'Heureux-Dubé learned to excel: "We have to be a mixer to a certain extent, to exchange our ideas in a correct way, to be able to accept the other opinions of others, [and] to convince others that ours are quite good. I think she had all [those] qualities."[27] Yves Bernier was slightly more cautious in his assessment. He saw L'Heureux-Dubé as "quite independent in her opinion," a stand-alone judge. "When we disagreed with her, she didn't like it. Then it was for us to show we were right

---

† "an endearing woman"

and she was wrong. [But] she was very open-minded, and when she saw that we were right, she would change her opinion altogether, [although] that was very rare."[28]

A Growing National and International Reputation

L'Heureux-Dubé's sociability as a host raised her profile and strengthened her connections with her colleagues. When judges from Montreal were sitting in Quebec City, she would invite them to visit at her home. One of her Montreal colleagues, Melvin Rothman, remarked on how many of the judges came to like her personally, appreciating how she "loved discussion, dinners with other people, [and that] she was just fun to be with."[29] McGill law professor Pierre-Gabriel Jobin, who worked with her on various comparative law organizations, added: "She was always making jokes, being kind with everybody. [She might have] vigorous arguments with judges on the issues, but she went along well with them."[30]

She was asked to speak at the Laval law school, and both her alma mater and the University of Montreal awarded her honorary doctorates. Her reputation spread well beyond Quebec. Before judicial education became established protocol, small groups of judges had begun meeting for informal discussions on law, and L'Heureux-Dubé was at the centre of it all. Educational conferences hosting up to sixty judges sprang up each summer at venues such as Jasper and St. Andrews by-the-Sea. She became a faculty instructor in family law, perhaps because she had done so much lecturing on the topic from her days as a practitioner. She travelled from Prince Edward Island to Vancouver, delivering summaries of the current state of the law based on detailed written materials that she hand-prepared in advance. While she laughed that "family law was not a big draw," and that some of the judges assigned to her sessions were "not happy," she also prided herself on being able to distribute papers that "covered everything in family law on every issue from coast to coast."[31] Supreme Court of Canada Justice Jean Beetz, who attended one of the conferences, congratulated her on producing "the best paper he'd seen."[32] She also made firm friendships with judges across Canada, some of whom later travelled to Quebec City to visit with her on holidays.

One or two American and English judges were often invited to speak on comparative law at the conferences, and L'Heureux-Dubé was thrilled at the opportunity to meet eminent international jurists. She developed a network of relationships with the chief justices of the Supreme Courts of

Washington State, Rhode Island, and California, and with US Supreme Court justice Ruth Bader Ginsberg, Lord Lane of the UK, and many others. The new connections led to invitations to speak at judicial education seminars outside the country. Along with Julien Payne, she established the Canadian branch of the International Society of Family Law, and that took her to conferences all over the world.[33]

It was at a judicial education conference that Rosalie Abella, later appointed to the Supreme Court of Canada, first met L'Heureux-Dubé. "I heard her before I saw her," laughed Abella. "I was sitting having breakfast and there was a table of male judges from Quebec. I just heard one female voice and I looked up, and there was a woman going up and down the row – it was a long table, six guys on each side – just going around to each person, hugging, kissing, and laughing with each of them. She was irresistible. It wasn't something you normally saw at a judicial conference."[34] L'Heureux-Dubé was making her mark, an increasingly well-known appellate judge who was becoming accepted by her colleagues as an equal while retaining as individualistic a personality as ever.

Court of Appeal Decisions

During her nine years on the court, L'Heureux-Dubé heard 1,311 appeal cases and 105 additional criminal sentence appeals, of which 150 were published in the official court reporter series.[35] In this era, there were no law clerks to provide assistance, and the range of legal matters was daunting: criminal, civil, municipal, labour, family, constitutional, administrative, social welfare, bankruptcy, insurance, and sales, among others.

L'Heureux-Dubé's Court of Appeal years spanned some of the most tumultuous political times in Quebec history. Her term began a few years after the 1976 election of René Lévesque's separatist Parti Québécois government. It continued through the turmoil of the first sovereignty referendum in 1980.[36] Not surprisingly, the volatility brought a number of controversial cases into her court. She gave a green light to the inquisitorial powers of the Keable Inquiry set up by Premier René Lévesque to examine the "dirty tricks" the police had perpetrated upon separatist groups.[37] But she stayed proceedings against an RCMP inspector charged with stealing computer records of PQ members, after an enraged Lévesque rose in the National Assembly to lambast a police witness in "colourful and abusive language."[38] She heard a defamation suit in the wake of Canada's decision to repatriate its constitution without the consent of Quebec, in which she supported four Quebec MPs who sought to stop the Saint-Jean-Baptiste Society from distributing material denouncing them for voting in favour of both repatriation and the *Canadian Charter of Rights and Freedoms*.[39] Following the bloodbath that Denis Lortie unleashed in the Quebec National Assembly when he killed three government employees and wounded thirteen others in an unsuccessful attempt to assassinate Lévesque, the media sued for access to the on-site video that had captured the carnage. Dissenting from her colleagues who supported the Assembly president's efforts to block the release, she would have ordered it produced for public access.[40] The cases tied her to the hotbed of political fervour, but her decisions offered no clue to her own predilections, whether sovereigntist or federalist.

The *Canadian Charter of Rights and Freedoms* was adopted in 1982, giving her a front-row seat in the first years of its interpretation, but there was little foreshadowing of the role she would play with respect to *Charter* or human rights law on the Supreme Court of Canada. L'Heureux-Dubé dismissed the few cases she heard. She rejected a *Charter* challenge against the law requiring compulsory seatbelts, ruling that freedom from seatbelt usage did not constitute a fundamental right.[41] She denied the disability challenge of a blind person who complained that his municipal council prohibited the tape-recording of debates.[42] She dismissed the human rights complaint of a woman who claimed she had been denied a rental apartment because she was divorced.[43]

Anti-Semitism appears to have been involved in another case she considered, an appeal launched by the director of the organizing committee for the 1976 Summer Olympics. The *Montreal Gazette* had described the plaintiff, a Jewish city councillor, as "a representative of the Jewish mafia in Montreal." He sued for defamation, and the jury awarded him $135,000. In the majority ruling, L'Heureux-Dubé's colleagues George Owen and Amédée Monet slashed the jury award to one-tenth, down to $13,500. In her dissent, L'Heureux-Dubé noted that the libel had impugned a man with a previously spotless reputation, and upheld the $135,000 award. Although two Jewish judges were then sitting on the Court of Appeal, neither had been appointed to hear the case. None of the three judges who did hear it, L'Heureux-Dubé included, made any reference to the obvious anti-Semitic overtones of the publication, or to Quebec's long-standing history of discrimination against its Jewish citizens.[44] Although the "Jewish mafia" reference mixed up its ethnic slurs, adopting a stereotype typically applied to Italians, it also played upon the long-standing derogatory characteristics incorrectly attributed to Jews: criminality and greed. The glossing over of the Jewish focus that was so central to the defamation was of a piece with the pattern of silence and denial that pervaded so much anti-Semitism in Quebec.

There was little in this record to reflect the equality rights champion that L'Heureux-Dubé would become.

Claire L'Heureux-Dubé's years as a Quebec appeal judge coincided with an active period for the feminist movement. Women streamed out of the home and into paid jobs, and by 1981 over half of Canadian women were in the workforce, despite the significant gender segregation and pay disparities that remained.[45] By 1987, women had reached parity in full-time university undergraduate populations.[46] There were sustained feminist demands for maternity leave and a fairer distribution of resources and workload within the family.[47] Divorce rates reached their highest ascendancy yet, 362 per 100,000 Canadians, in 1987.[48]

L'Heureux-Dubé's family law rulings demonstrated some sensitivity to these changes. Her appellate decisions built upon themes that had emerged during her trial court days, and evidenced a maturing of opinion. Alimony was one obvious area. While on the Superior Court, she had occasionally ordered lump sum awards, but her appellate decisions showed a growing preference for this approach. The family law lawyer who had lamented that her female clients were reduced to phoning their ex-husbands every Friday night, begging for the overdue weekly stipend, knew the value of a capitalized settlement. Now on the bench, L'Heureux-Dubé saw lump sums as a vast improvement over periodic alimony payments that forced the estranged parties to engage with each other for years. Where the parties had the means, it provided a clean break, *"la façon idéale"*† to effectuate a divorce.[49] Her colleagues were less enamoured of lump sums. George Owen insisted that they should be awarded only "in exceptional circumstances," and Amédée Monet was even more averse to them.[50] L'Heureux-Dubé complained that Owen and Monet were legally incorrect in designating lump sums as exceptional: "It's exceptional because people don't have the money, but nothing in the law prevents us awarding it."[51] Undeterred by their resistance, she approved more lump sums in later cases, reiterating that there was nothing "exceptional" about the award.[52]

In a clear break from her Superior Court rulings, L'Heureux-Dubé also began to reconsider her disavowal of the "equalization principle" for divorcing litigants. She had taken notice of a 1982 legal article written by

---

† "the ideal way"

Rosalie Abella, documenting how husbands improved their educational and career prospects during marriage while stay-at-home mothers diminished theirs.[53] L'Heureux-Dubé critiqued family lawyers for failing to produce detailed financial evidence, in contrast to commercial lawyers in contracts or insurance cases.[54] She disavowed the historical preference for paternal custody, noting that the "wellbeing of the children" was now the operative principle.[55]

Over Amédée Monet's dissent, she ordered an international diplomat to pay significant alimony to his ex-wife, who had shouldered all the domestic responsibilities of raising the couple's five children.[56] It was she who dissented when George Owen and Monet refused an ex-wife's claim to share in real estate property that her husband had bought in his own name during the marriage. Even if the ex-wife could not prove a common intention, L'Heureux-Dubé's strongly worded dissent insisted that the doctrine of unjust enrichment entitled her to half the property. L'Heureux-Dubé was a woman who had registered every matrimonial home she purchased in her own name, and she added on the record that she found it difficult to understand why such properties were put in the husband's name only. These problems were surfacing more and more as the mass of women entered the paid labour market. Judges needed to recognize *"une société ou aventure commune."*[†, 57] She dissented when her male colleagues refused to split the value of the family home between a divorcing husband and wife, repudiating their view that the domestic services and sums furnished by the wife to "make-do at the end of the month" did not warrant a significant share of the matrimonial home.[58]

But there were other cases in which her sympathies were drawn toward ex-husbands. She agreed with Monet and Jean Turgeon to reduce an ex-husband's alimony payments when he became unemployed.[59] She expressed concern over the plight of another ex-husband on social assistance who faced arrears of over $24,000 in alimony. Despite the poverty of his ex-wife, who was also on social assistance, she sided with Monet in cancelling his alimony retroactively.[60]

One of the biggest changes from her Superior Court years was the large number of criminal matters L'Heureux-Dubé heard in the Court of Appeal. The field may have been novel for her, yet her perspectives aligned snugly with those of her colleagues, and her three-person panels issued unanimous rulings on most criminal cases. Both Crown and defence won their share of the criminal appeals, with the early years showing more victories

---

† "a common society or venture"

for the Crown and later years more for the defence. In the few cases where she dissented from her colleagues, her opinions were evenly balanced between the Crown and the defence.[61] Little in her Court of Appeal criminal jurisprudence gave any hint of the reputation she would later develop on the Supreme Court as a "law-and-order" judge who vigorously protected victims' rights in sexual assault.

In fact, there were few cases involving sexual assault, and here L'Heureux-Dubé's rulings were mixed. Some seemed supportive of victim's rights. She upheld the kidnapping and sexual assault conviction of a thirty-year-old man who had tricked his neighbour, a developmentally disabled eighteen-year-old girl, into thinking that her mother wanted her to cooperate. L'Heureux-Dubé's panel found that the accused's false and fraudulent misrepresentations had vitiated the young woman's consent.[62] She held that prior sexual history had no relevance to a charge of sexual intercourse with a female person under fourteen.[63] She increased one rape sentence from eight to twelve years,[64] and refused to reduce the three-year sentence of a man convicted of incest with his daughter.[65]

But she dissented in a gross indecency case involving child witnesses, where the majority committed the accused for trial despite a lack of corroboration at the preliminary inquiry. In a lengthy and detailed opinion, L'Heureux-Dubé quoted law review articles from defence lawyers Morris Fish and Joseph Arvay regarding the presumption of innocence and corroboration. The goal of a preliminary inquiry was to ensure that the accused was not subject to the time, cost, and embarrassment of trial without sufficient evidence to warrant it. In her view, two unsworn, uncorroborated child witnesses could not meet that test.[66] And she joined her colleagues in another case to reduce the sentence of a man who had taken his underage niece to a hotel overnight, assigning him probation and 120 hours of community service instead of jail time.[67]

She signed on to a unanimous decision upholding a six-year sentence for attempted murder and use and possession of an illegal firearm in a case where a twenty-year-old accused man contracted with an eighteen-year-old to shoot his former girlfriend and her sister. One of the women was seriously injured, and was hospitalized and forced to undergo a tracheotomy. In a troubling observation, which L'Heureux-Dubé must have approved, the panel noted that the sentence should be upheld *"même si ce crime visait son ancienne concubine."*† It was a phrase that intimated that domestic situations somehow rendered violence less heinous.[68]

---

† "even if this crime was aimed at his former live-in mistress"

She reduced convictions from first- to second-degree murder where she felt that "planned and deliberate" premeditation had not been proven.[69] She upheld a reduced verdict of second-degree murder where the accused assassinated his former mistress and her five-year-old child on the ground that it was a "drama of passion."[70] She upheld a lesser verdict of involuntary homicide against a young soldier living on the Valcartier base who had fought with his inebriated seventeen-year-old girlfriend after they had sex and she insulted him. L'Heureux-Dubé ruled that the killing had been caused by sudden provocation.[71]

She quashed the conviction of an Indigenous man from the Kahwanake reserve for causing bodily harm with intent to wound, on the basis that he was acting in self-defence and all citizens had the right to protect themselves.[72] She acquitted a woman of impeding an agent of the peace in execution of his duties, because the constable had no power to arrest without warrant and Canadian citizens had no obligation to identify themselves to an officer unless required to do so by law.[73] She reduced a sentence of sixteen months to nine months for a woman who had defrauded the government of $200, finding her to be emotionally fragile and unable to support her child on her minimal earnings in a restaurant. Although she believed incarceration was necessary for deterrence, L'Heureux-Dubé also believed that the accused would deteriorate in prison, and that the shorter sentence was preferable.[74]

Despite the prevailing ethic of negotiation and harmony, disagreements between the judges occasionally became heated. Louis LeBel described one case shortly after he joined the Court of Appeal in which L'Heureux-Dubé, the senior judge on the panel, was at loggerheads with Maurice Jacques. It was a drug-trafficking conviction where the trial judge had imposed a $250 fine and probation, stating that drug crimes were less serious than thefts and break-and-enter cases. The Crown asked for eighteen months, arguing that the trial judge had failed to take account of the gravity of the infraction. L'Heureux-Dubé agreed with the light sentence, while Jacques wanted to increase it. "We reserved the matter," recalled LeBel, "[and] the two of them would barge into my chambers in turn to lecture me about sentencing law, about that case, [and] how the other was wrong. Eventually I went with Claire."[75] LeBel, who wrote the majority decision giving priority to rehabilitation, emphasized that the accused was employed, taking courses in Montreal, and living in a stable relationship with a young woman who was expecting a child. Jacques dissented, emphasizing that drug crimes were "real crimes," not "simply statutory infractions," and would have imposed nine months. LeBel's final comment, offered years after L'Heureux-Dubé had retired from the Supreme Court, was that she had "surprised" him with her strong views, since he believed she was "not usually" given to light sentences.[76] It may have reflected what he came to perceive about her on the nation's highest court, but was not an accurate assessment of her Court of Appeal years.

Overview

By and large, L'Heureux-Dubé's jurisprudence on the Court of Appeal can be characterized as "formalist" – regarding the law as a given and the judge's task as simply to apply recognized legal doctrines to the facts at hand. American jurist Richard Posner's description of "formalism" fit her decisions to a T: summarizing the decision of the court below and the arguments made by the parties to the appeal, reciting in detail the facts to which the law was to be applied, specifying and explaining the applicable legal rules, making copious references to authoritative texts, applying the rules extracted from these authorities to the arguments made by the parties, and striving for completeness by considering qualifications and side issues where relevant.[77]

A hallmark of her decisions was the logical and orderly format in which she presented her views. Tidily organizing her material under headings, she would provide a chronology of the history of the case, the facts, the legal precedents that applied, and succinct conclusions. Her former counsel at the immigration inquiry, Joseph Nuss, confirmed that she had a "fine reputation" for "writing very clear, sound reasons for judgment."[78] University of Ottawa law professor Marlène Cano agreed: *"[E]lle porte une attention particulière aux règles de droit et surtout aux pouvoirs d'intervention de la Cour d'appel ... Elle se soucie de l'objectivité judiciaire."*[†, 79] Although all the Quebec appellate judges were bilingual, they generally wrote decisions in their maternal language, with English-speaking judges such as George Owen, Fred Kaufman, William Tyndale, Melvin Rothman, and George Montgomery tending to write in English and the others in French. L'Heureux-Dubé wrote overwhelmingly in French, a language in which her writing talents, honed many years earlier under the scrupulous attention of the nuns, shone.[80]

---

† "She pays particular attention to the rules of law and, above all, to the powers of intervention of the Court of Appeal ... She cares about judicial objectivity."

Melvin Rothman concluded that all of her Court of Appeal colleagues "respected her, [and] thought she was a serious legal mind and a conscientious person," "honest," "professional," and "hard-working."[81] McGill law professor Pierre-Gabriel Jobin believed that she was "loved" on the Court of Appeal.[82] Her later colleague on the Supreme Court of Canada, Michel Bastarache, affirmed that she came "very well considered by judges in Quebec."[83] There were notable exceptions, of course. The pattern of disagreement with George Owen and Amédée Monet, which provoked some of her most vigorous dissents, may have presaged the rocky relationship she would come to have with her Supreme Court colleague Antonio Lamer. As for Lamer himself, the two were never assigned to sit on the same panel in the five months that their terms overlapped on the Court of Appeal.

During her Quebec Court of Appeal years, L'Heureux-Dubé seems to have mastered the art of negotiation required for successful appellate judges. Eventually the environment even came to feel collegial to her. Reflecting on what these years contributed to L'Heureux-Dubé's long-term judicial career, Alberta Chief Justice Catherine Fraser noted: "I think what that must have given her [was] a strength that she knew she could do the job and do it well. [She had] very strong analytical skills, [and] an ability to zero in on legal issues and human issues, wrap the two together, and come up with a rigorous judgment. She had rock-solid support from her colleagues on the Court of Appeal. Her time on the Quebec Court of Appeal gave her a strength that was long-lasting."[84]

By the end of her tenure at the Court of Appeal, L'Heureux-Dubé had come to think of most of her Quebec colleagues as family. She was willing to praise her fellow judges for their maturity, humanity, and intellectual capacities. In retrospect, she would describe her years there as the "happiest time of my life as a judge."[85] Despite the occasional glimpse of reform-mindedness in family law cases, and the occasional dust-ups with a few of her colleagues, she had overcome much of the outsider stigma that attended her arrival. She was also leaving behind a corpus of decisions that bore little hint of the mark she would make in the future.

24
More Family Traumas

Her Court of Appeal years witnessed increasing personal challenges for Claire L'Heureux-Dubé.[1] Trying to coordinate court sittings while supervising children and running a home would have presented complications for anyone, even someone as driven and well-organized as she. Although she was relieved of the full trial circuit, her travel schedule was still extensive. The court sat in Montreal and Quebec City, with judges from each city assigned to sit in both centres.[2] In recognition of the ingrown nature of the Quebec City bar, judges from Quebec were assigned more often to sit in Montreal, where they had fewer ties with the lawyers who appeared before them.[3] During her nine years on the Quebec Court of Appeal, L'Heureux-Dubé sat for 35.5 weeks in Quebec City and 60.5 weeks in Montreal.[4]

Fortunately, daughter Louise was at university in Montreal, a providential situation that enabled her mother to keep tabs on her during the Montreal sittings. Louise had left home one month after her father's suicide to enrol in law at McGill University, after which she practised at an elite Montreal law firm.[5] Initially, she rented an apartment with friends while her mother stayed at the Château Champlain, but later the two shared a rental apartment in Westmount.

It was a completely different situation for Pierre, who was just fifteen when his mother was elevated to the Court of Appeal. Although there were some periods when Pierre seemed happy, the boy who had presented so many difficulties as a child had not tempered over time. Arthur Dubé had once confessed to his brother that he thought Pierre hated him so

Vacation respite in Florida: Philippe Michaud (family friend from Rimouski), Claire L'Heureux-Dubé, and Pierre.

much that he wanted to go to prison just to punish his father.[6] Pierre's aunt Louise speculated that this was the source of the problem, that Pierre and Arthur were "two strong-headed, stubborn people that butted heads [with] violent arguments between them."[7] Some wondered whether the torturous father-son relationship even provoked Arthur to commit suicide. The tragic death of his father, for which he may have blamed himself, exacerbated Pierre's anger. "Pierre became impossible after Arthur's suicide," was how L'Heureux-Dubé put it.[8]

Pierre's Increasing Dysfunction

Pierre remained in the family home in Quebec City, causing L'Heureux-Dubé increasing worry about her protracted time away in Montreal. Evidence of his dysfunction mounted from every direction. Family law expert Julien Payne remembered phoning L'Heureux-Dubé at home one evening, when Pierre answered. "I'm not bilingual," Payne recalled, "but he gave me hell on the phone in French."[9] Pierre badgered his mother with telephone calls when she was away, often phoning at 1 a.m.[10] He called his sister and kept her on the phone for hours, claiming that green aliens were coming out of tables.[11] He stole and sold much of the movable property in the

Claire L'Heureux-Dubé and daughter, Louise, on holiday in Sweden.

house, including jewellery and the TV.[12] He lost so much time from school that he fell to the bottom of the class. He had trouble reading at age sixteen.[13] His mother's efforts to enrol him in a course on car mechanics failed.[14]

L'Heureux-Dubé's mother, Marguerite, and sister Nicole could offer little help, because of Marguerite's increasing incapacitation from multiple sclerosis. So L'Heureux-Dubé's sister Louise volunteered to come up from Illinois to look after Pierre shortly after Arthur's death, enabling L'Heureux-Dubé and her daughter to travel to Scandinavia to attend one of the international conferences. Difficulties immediately arose. When his Aunt Louise called him to get up for school in the morning, Pierre refused. "I would wake him, shake him, [and] had to say it a million times – you're late for school." When she finally got him up and drove him to school, Pierre went in the front door and out the back door. At the end of the day, the school called home to inquire where Pierre had been. "I didn't know he wasn't there," explained Louise. "Little did I know he just walked in and out."[15]

Thinking that perhaps she could cajole Pierre with home-cooked meals, Louise prepared special dinners: fresh salmon, home-made baked goods, apple pie. His flat refusal to eat reduced her to tears. "And if I didn't go buy the croissants that morning, he wouldn't eat them." She woke up one day to discover that Pierre had sprayed Coke all over the kitchen walls and strewn banana peels around. The police arrived to advise her that someone had shot a light out during the night, and demanded to know Pierre's whereabouts. A petrified Louise questioned her nephew, who denied everything. Later, she discovered that Pierre had a habit of sneaking out the basement window, prowling around all night long. Paul L'Heureux even paid a visit, hoping to help Louise with Pierre. But it took almost no time for Pierre and Paul to explode at each other, after an incident at a shopping mall when Pierre threw ink over the older man. "Pierre didn't understand why [his grandfather] reacted so violently. Oh, my gosh, he was mad. Pierre had no sense at all of what he was doing," explained Louise. Eventually Louise sought refuge with her own mother and Nicole, where she broke down uncontrollably. "They just said, 'Forget it.' They knew the problems already. Pierre was like a nightmare."[16]

Pierre was caught breaking and entering for the first time at the age of sixteen, and was sent to Juvenile Court.[17] Then he was arrested for stealing a video player, after the police stopped him as he was carrying the machine on his bike during the middle of the night. With his mother away, he called his Aunt Nicole to come and bail him out at the police station. Nicole and her mother felt they were living on pins and needles, terrified of what would come next.[18] Pierre bought a motorcycle and disturbed the entire neighbourhood with its noise.[19] He was arrested for speeding. He had a spate of motor vehicle accidents. He would go on binges, destroying property, smashing glass, breaking things.[20] When his sister was home from university, she asked him to back his car out of the driveway so she could move hers. He smashed her windshield.[21] He took drugs.[22] He stole and robbed.[23] The police were regularly at the L'Heureux-Dubé home to search for drugs and stolen property, sometimes phoning L'Heureux-Dubé at the courthouse to ask permission to search. "So many times we got [Pierre] out of jail," remembered his sister.[24]

Initially, L'Heureux-Dubé tried to fix things, to pass over what was happening, hoping that the situation would improve. "She was so optimistic," explained her sister Louise. "Pierrot would get better. She was going to get control of that. Pierrot would straighten out."[25] But after Pierre was consigned to a juvenile detention centre in Montreal and escaped, his mother had a change of attitude.[26] His aunt Louise, again visiting from Illinois, recalled what happened when Pierre showed up at home:

> Claire and I took him back in the car. He didn't want to go. Apparently the detention centre was just horrible. Claire had put pressure on them to take him back, and they had agreed. Claire was determined that he was going to go back. This time, she didn't give in. She told him he had to go back,

otherwise it was going to be much harsher. He didn't want to go. This was the most horrible car trip I've ever taken. Leaving him there was just heartbreaking, just awful.[27]

This was not the only escape from juvenile detention. Pierre ran away repeatedly.

L'Heureux-Dubé was cautious about whom she confided in, and her colleagues emphasized that she never sought sympathy and never slackened her pace of work.[28] Occasionally, when she was tied up in a hearing when the police called, her capable secretary, Yolande Lemelin, would fill in to respond to Pierre's debacles. "She was an extraordinary person," recalled L'Heureux-Dubé, "who saved me from many of those heartbreaking times."[29] She turned to her former law partner, Roger Garneau, who had practised as a Crown attorney before joining the Bard law firm, and asked him to take on Pierre's legal representation on one of the early drug charges.[30] Garneau took Pierre to the Hôtel-Dieu to see a psychiatrist, who convinced Pierre that he needed to be hospitalized. L'Heureux-Dubé was hopeful when she spoke to the psychiatrist, who told her that Pierre was "a wonderful boy" and that it was "the sickness" that made him behave so badly.[31] But no one seemed able to offer a cure. Garneau obtained an acquittal due the protracted delay in prosecution, but never acted for Pierre again: "Not because I refused, but because Claire did not ask."[32] It was characteristic of her not to burden friends and colleagues. L'Heureux-Dubé was particularly protective of her sister Nicole and aging mother: "You didn't want to put more problems on their shoulders, because they had their own."[33]

And, as always with explosive family problems, there were others who offered their own advice. Gisèle Blondeau-Labrie, one of L'Heureux-Dubé's long-time friends from her convent days, believed that Pierre was "very dependent on his mother," that he was "really a delinquent," and that "nothing made him happy."[34] Close childhood friend Jean Drapeau thought that after Arthur's death, L'Heureux-Dubé tried to do "everything for [Pierre] ... even maybe too much *maternalisme* with the boy."[35] Her Rimouski friend Philippe Michaud blamed lack of parental supervision: "The father not being there, and the mother was working, [Pierre] was probably alone too much when he was young."[36] Roger Garneau added: "She has been a good mother [but] Claire was very busy, everybody [was] around her, she was respected, honoured. Maybe he wanted her attention. But oh la la, he got it, in a bad way."[37] Her close female friend Denyse Dion, who had secured a job re-educating juvenile delinquent children, joked that now she was dealing with her friend Claire, whose "family was delinquent!"[38] All of this must have increased the pressure on L'Heureux-Dubé, who was already highly sensitive to her own responsibility. "[I] asked myself over and over what I did wrong. [I] felt so guilty. I wondered if things might have been different."[39]

Traumatized children almost always produce guilt in mothers. Our society's gendered expectations result in fingers pointed at female parents, who are expected to solve problems that are often irresolvable. Women are faulted for paying too little attention because they are preoccupied with their careers, or for smothering their children with disastrous results, or for failing to compensate for the absence of fathers, or for personality deficiencies, or for failing to provide proper emotional support, or for errors in judgment, or for being too lenient or too harsh. Mothers who are already suffering the pain of watching their troubled children's lives then reproach themselves, intensifying the heartache. Reflecting upon her experience for this biography, L'Heureux-Dubé found reliving the memories of Pierre's downward spiral almost too hurtful to bear. And her response was deeper guilt: "I feel guilty that I was not a good enough parent," she said with great sadness. Does the record support this? What is evident, to the contrary, is a mother who used every available opportunity to assist a son who was tragically spinning out of control.

If there was one ray of hope throughout these years, it was a facility known as Boscoville, an adolescent re-education centre in a suburb of Montreal. Founded in the 1940s, Boscoville was an internationally recognized residential facility that had disavowed the traditional disciplinary focus on physical restraint, hard labour, and religious observance. Premised on a philosophy of treatment known as "psychoéducation," the centre's methods elevated contact with nature, community, humanism, and "re-educative work."[40] Its directors identified the roots of delinquency in an adolescent's inner psyche and professed to care less about the criminal record of the resident than repairing his psychological damage. The treatment program entailed an intense cycle of activities to reinforce social skills, punctuated by "stages" through which each resident was to move, with educational training designed to enable the young person to regain confidence in his intellectual capacity. One of Boscoville's leading proponents, Noël Mailloux, vowed, *"Il n'y a pas de jeunes incorrigibles,"*† and in keeping with this philosophy, there were no fences or prison bars.[41] The

---

† "No youth is incorrigible."

facility initially boasted a success rate of 80 percent, giving it a pre-eminence in the field that would last well into the 1970s.[42]

L'Heureux-Dubé recalled Boscoville as "very famous, with a long waiting list."[43] She advocated that her son be placed there when he appeared again in Juvenile Court for the use of illegal drugs in the early 1980s. Boscoville staff claimed that terms of up to two years of secure custody were necessary to effect long-term inner transformation.[44] L'Heureux-Dubé recalled that Pierre was given an indeterminate term, and that she went to see him every week. She was impressed with her son's progress. She thought Boscoville was "an extraordinary place," where Pierre was doing "marvellously well." "He went through the three-month assessment, and moved to the next stage of sports and a job. With good behaviour, they graduated to productive jobs."[45] Pierre himself was less convinced, and he continued to run away, as he had from previous institutions. L'Heureux-Dubé arrived home one day, opened a closet door, and saw her son's feet. "I almost dropped dead," she recalled. "I could only see his toes. I thought he had hung himself." She had to call the staff at Boscoville to report Pierre's escape: "It was not easy for me to do that, but it was my duty. I had to convince him to go back. I had noticed such an improvement."[46]

Any hope that Boscoville would prove the making of Pierre was dashed when her son took advantage of the newly enacted Quebec *Youth Protection Act* to request a hearing in Juvenile Court.[47] "Unfortunately," stated L'Heureux-Dubé, "the law changed, and children had the right to go before the judge and ask to be let out. That's what he did. He said he wanted to go, and the judge agreed. My only hope was destroyed. The judge said, 'Fine, you don't want to be there, we will take you out of the institution.' Then he met up with others implicated in drugs and crime. That was the end of him."[48]

It is impossible to know whether L'Heureux-Dubé's assessment of this was accurate. Certainly, she knew her son and was in a good position to appraise his performance. And her views were seconded by the staff counsellors at Boscoville, who were giving Pierre good reports. But adolescent detention centres were notoriously difficult places despite their best intentions, and Pierre's efforts to secure his release suggest that he was not in accord with his mother's views. Whether Boscoville would have been able to add Pierre to its list of successes had he remained longer is also unclear. What is clear is that upon his exit from Boscoville, he toppled still further out of control.

Did L'Heureux-Dubé's experience with Pierre set in motion a shift in her thinking about criminal law? It is difficult to imagine that such personal anguish had no impact. In earlier press interviews, she had expressed a preference for criminal rehabilitation. Did she emerge from the Boscoville intervention with a growing appreciation for lengthy incarceration in detention centres? Asked this long after she had retired from the courts, she replied, "I can examine this more, but I [don't think it] came to my mind at all. I was never thinking of it. I don't think it had any influence on my decisions. I don't judge on anything else than the file."[49] It seems a somewhat simplistic response. Some think that the finest judges would be those whose minds are pristine, untouched by circumstances and beliefs. To imagine such a judge would be to construct a being who had negotiated life without developing any ideas, without being touched by pleasure or pain. Others have suggested that the best courts are peopled with individuals of wide-ranging backgrounds, who bring their diverse expertise to bear on the disputes before them while still demonstrating the ability to listen with open minds to the facts and submissions of the parties.

L'Heureux-Dubé's years at the Court of Appeal offered little to indicate that she would later develop a reputation as a tough-on-crime judge. The cases she adjudicated remained fairly evenly balanced between the defence and the Crown. But there was at least one case that hit uncomfortably close to home. In 1986, L'Heureux-Dubé was appointed to a three-person panel to hear *Adam v. R.* The panel had to decide whether a seventeen-year-old juvenile delinquent should be sheltered in Juvenile Court or tried for first-degree murder in adult court. Adam had imbibed a great quantity of alcohol and drugs before attending a school dance, and then had been seen kissing his girlfriend, Gisèle Legros, near midnight in front of the school. The next morning, the authorities discovered the girl's strangled and sexually assaulted body. Adam confessed that the two had argued, he had punched his girlfriend, and then vomited and blacked out. The question was whether he should be treated for rehabilitation, as the Juvenile Court had recommended, at the Philippe-Pinel Institute (an adolescent unit within an institution for the criminally insane) or transferred for trial to the Superior Court, where a verdict of murder would result in penitentiary time.[50]

Amédée Monet and Melvin Rothman opted for an adult trial. Writing briefly and bluntly, they concluded that juvenile rehabilitation resources were not unlimited, and Adam's wrongdoing was not attributable to society but to himself. L'Heureux-Dubé concurred in the result, but wrote at much greater length than her colleagues, chronicling Adam's woeful life history: a boy of superior intelligence with a poor self-image, acrimonious parents who separated early on, a mother with *"une vie de débauche,"*† an introduction to drinking and drugs in grade five, placement in group homes from the age of thirteen, documented incidents of sexual victimization by two adults, a long string of thefts and violence, and lockup in a secured facility in 1981. The reports filed by the social workers, psychologists, and criminologists were divided. Some recommended that Adam be placed in Boscoville, which accepted youths guilty of murder, for a minimum of three years. Others recommended adult facilities. L'Heureux-Dubé was obviously torn, and had agonized over whether to order that Adam face the prospect of the penitentiary. She noted that the teenage boy's rehabilitation must certainly be "possible," but everything would depend on his own decision to turn his life around. One could wish for a "miracle," but given that many of the experts doubted that juvenile resources would do the trick, she concluded that Adam should be subjected to lengthy institutionalization to teach him self-control. It was a harsh disciplinary approach to a seventeen-year-old boy.[51]

Reflecting on the case years later, she noted that it would have been important to reach a unanimous decision in such a difficult case, and added that Melvin Rothman was someone she particularly respected for his judgment in criminal cases. Both of these reasons would help to explain her opinion. That she chose to write in such detail also indicated her sensitivity to the issues, and her need to justify her conclusion. Despite her reluctance to acknowledge it, it would have been surprising if she had not brought to bear her personal and familial experience and anguish as she weighed the arguments of both sides.[52] The extent to which a growing acceptance of disciplinary incarceration would begin to drive her jurisprudence would become far clearer in the ensuing decades.

Yet Another Blow: Marguerite's Death

Marguerite L'Heureux, who was still living in the Quebec City family home with her daughter Nicole, was facing increasing health challenges. The degenerative multiple sclerosis had caused full paralysis, moving up from her feet to her arms and shoulders, curling her fingers into immobility. Marguerite described feeling like she was encased "in a steel corset" and "dependent on everybody."[53] The disease had no impact on her cognitive abilities, and she remained as intellectually engaged as ever. Even in

---

† "a life of debauchery"

her final years, she continued to study ancient and modern languages, poetry, and mythology. Her effervescent disposition never diminished. Everyone who knew her remarked on her continued optimism.

It was Nicole who provided the essential round-the-clock care, despite her teaching and research responsibilities as a faculty member at Laval law school.[54] Demonstrating some of the same organizational skills for which her sister Claire was renowned, Nicole delivered her lectures and published impressive legal treatises on banking and consumer law while serving as a full-time caregiver.[55] If she had to be away any longer than two hours, the only stretch her mother could manage alone, Nicole would rely upon the generosity of retired nuns who would volunteer to sit with Marguerite.

In 1982, Marguerite's ill health required hospitalization. Worried that her elderly mother would not recover, L'Heureux-Dubé contacted her father, and Paul L'Heureux returned from Montreal to see his wife. L'Heureux-Dubé described with visible emotion a wrenching scene in the hospital room that she witnessed between her estranged parents:

> She took his hand ... "I love you. I always loved you," and he cried. She was seventy-nine years old. He was living with another woman for more than twenty years, and they still loved each other. [I] don't know how to explain it ... it's very hard to know why I'm so moved by this ... total love but not being able to live together. Father took the easy way out but he never left her.[56]

The poignant moment passed, Marguerite rallied, and she managed to hang on for another year. She died at the age of eighty on 16 December 1983, and Paul married Francine Teasdale one year after.

The funeral was held in Quebec City, where the overwhelming memory of all who attended was of searingly cold wintry weather. People arrived at the funeral parlor for the service bundled up in fur coats, boots, scarves, and hats, but nothing could keep the frigid temperatures at bay. "It was just awful, it was so cold," remembered L'Heureux-Dubé's sister Louise. For Marguerite's surviving daughters, their overwhelming sadness made the funeral "a blur."[57] For Claire L'Heureux-Dubé, it was a wrenching loss, the permanent departure of the person who had been the single greatest influence on her life.[58]

Supreme Court of Canada

25
Appointment to the Supreme Court of Canada, 1987

Events unfolded first on the ski slopes outside Quebec City, where Claire L'Heureux-Dubé's former classmate, Supreme Court of Canada Justice Julien Chouinard, took a downhill tumble just after Christmas 1986. Since expert skiers do not often fall, his family insisted he undergo medical tests. Six weeks later, the fifty-eight-year-old judge was dead from a brain tumour. L'Heureux-Dubé was one of the many Quebecers who mourned the premature passing of the brilliant jurist and long-time public servant. Although the two had held quite different philosophies of life and law from their early days as rivals for the Laval medals, she was shocked and saddened at the loss of a principled and conscientious man, deeply knowledgeable in law, cut short in the prime of life.[1]

Rumours soon began circulating about prospective appointees for Chouinard's vacant seat. All the names floated were from Quebec, since three of the nine Supreme Court positions were constitutionally reserved for Quebec civil law appointees.[2] Louis LeBel, Paul-Arthur Gendreau, Claude Bisson, Marc Beauregard, and Maurice Jacques of the Court of Appeal, along with Alan Gold and Jules Deschênes of the Superior Court, James Hugessen of the Federal Court of Appeal, and Georges Pouliot of the Montreal bar were reputed to be under consideration. Lucien Bouchard, then Canada's ambassador to France, was also mentioned.[3] But the name most frequently touted was Montreal lawyer Yves Fortier, an Oxford-trained Rhodes Scholar and former president of the Canadian Bar Association.[4] Fortier was a close friend of Prime Minister Brian Mulroney, and the two had practised law together at Ogilvy Renault before Mulroney led the

Progressive Conservative party to victory in 1984.[5] The rumours were accurate: Prime Minister Mulroney offered Fortier the slot on the top court. Fortier turned him down.[6]

Speculation raged on. Whose name would come out on top next? Bertha Wilson had made history as the first woman on the Supreme Court of Canada in 1982, and the Canadian Press reported that feminists had "mounted a strong lobby" for another woman. Apparently spokeswomen for women's organizations had expressed serious disappointment when Mulroney appointed Gérard La Forest to the Supreme Court in 1985.[7] The insistence upon female representation on the bench, a perspective that would later evolve substantially beyond debate, was then still a controversial, hot-button issue. The top court had always been a geographically representative body, three spots reserved for Quebec, three for Ontario, two for the West, and one for the East, with religion and language points of consideration as well. But many court-watchers lost sight of that when they insisted that the "merit" principle should govern above all else, and disputed feminist demands to add gender to the list of necessary components for an inclusive national court. It also bears noting that the feminist demands focused exclusively upon gender. The equally important campaign for racial and Indigenous inclusivity in the judiciary had yet to reach the level of preliminary public notice.[8]

Brian Mulroney, who agreed to be interviewed about this appointment years later, explained that he had strong views about gender. "When it came time to fill [the] vacancy in Quebec, I told [my principal secretary] Bernard Roy and the justice minister [Ramon Hnatyshyn] that I wanted to do this with a woman, very likely from the Quebec City area." Gender had not been his first impulse when he considered Fortier. Why the preference for a woman now? "I felt that women were inadequately represented in all the courts," he said. "I think that the record will show that I appointed more women to cabinet and to the bench than any prime minister in history. I thought it was an important thing to do."[9]

This time, there was virtually no consultation process. Mulroney stressed that Supreme Court appointments were the prime minister's prerogative: "In my time, all Supreme Court appointments [were] chosen and made directly by the prime minister."[10] There were no constitutional impediments to such prime ministerial autonomy, although the provinces had long advocated for a greater role in the nomination and selection process.[11] After the enactment of the *Charter of Rights and Freedoms*, there was also a chorus of demands for more public involvement in recommending and vetting candidates.[12] But in 1987, Mulroney would brook no intrusion

Appointment to the Supreme Court of Canada

Prime Minister Brian Mulroney, who appointed L'Heureux-Dubé to the Supreme Court of Canada in 1987.

into his office's control of the process, and stressed that these appointments were "one way that the prime minister shapes the future of the country."[13] In fact, as he would later divulge to the press, he was "proud" that the candidate he recommended to the cabinet was his "personal choice."[14] It is an open question whether wider consultation with the bench and bar would have derailed his selection of a woman. In many quarters, there was still staunch resistance to the presence of women. Sometimes, decision-making processes of the few led more quickly to significant change.

Of the female candidates under scrutiny, according to the press, Claire L'Heureux-Dubé was the leading contender. Her name had circulated in

1980, when Antonio Lamer was appointed, and she was considered stronger than the other two mentioned: Louise Mailhot of the Superior Court and Micheline Audette-Filion of the Montreal bar.[15] Because both Mulroney and Bernard Roy had studied law at Laval and practised in Quebec, they knew of L'Heureux-Dubé's reputation as a practitioner and a judge.[16] They instructed Paul Tellier, clerk of the Privy Council, to have the Department of Justice put together a dossier on her and other possible candidates.[17] It was no surprise to the prime minister that when Bernard Roy brought the shortlist back to his office, Claire L'Heureux-Dubé was on top.[18]

Partisan politics had no place in the decision, stressed Mulroney: "I did not ever allow politics to enter the consideration in terms of Supreme Court of Canada appointments. We don't have the American tradition, where people maintain their political views and allegiances on the bench to advance political causes. I have no idea whether [Claire] was Conservative, NDP, or Liberal. I didn't ask."[19] In fact, he used L'Heureux-Dubé's appointment as a shield against criticism that he was making too many partisan appointments to administrative boards. L'Heureux-Dubé had no "association of any kind with the Conservative Party," he emphasized.[20] It was a point picked up in the press: reporters later emphasized that the appointment had "no hint of patronage."[21]

The only further consultation was with the chief justice. "Believing in no surprises, I always talked to Brian [Dickson] before I made an appointment," explained Mulroney. "[I] had him over to 24 Sussex for coffee, [and] said, 'Look ... I'm down to a choice here for the Supreme Court ... we have [a few] candidates and I think I am going to go with [L'Heureux-Dubé]. What is your view?'"[22] The answer must have been positive, because the next day Mulroney met with Roy and Tellier in his parliamentary office. "[I] remember making the decision. I looked at the list [and] said, 'I'm going to appoint Claire.' She was known as a person of great integrity and fearlessness. She didn't give a damn about what anybody else thought. I knew her background, record, [and] skills. [She] had the independence to be a superb member of the highest court."[23]

The Late-Night Telephone Call

On 14 April 1987, Mulroney placed a late-night telephone call to L'Heureux-Dubé and offered her the Supreme Court position. He recalled that she sounded both surprised and hesitant. She explained that she loved her job at the Court of Appeal and that she did not want to leave Quebec City for Ottawa. Mulroney responded that he and his wife, Mila, had learned to love Ottawa and he was sure she would too. He emphasized that by going to the Supreme Court, she would have an "opportunity to shape the future of this country unlike few others," and to "enter the history books of Canada big-time." With his signature self-confidence, he insisted, "I'm going to appoint you and you are going to accept." He gave her until eight the next morning to decide.[24]

A distraught L'Heureux-Dubé asked for more time to consider, and the prime minister retorted: "The appointment will be made at 8 a.m." Explaining his rationale for the time constraint years later, he said: "If you are the prime minister of Canada and you are going to offer somebody an appointment to the Supreme Court and she is going to need three weeks to decide, you've called the wrong person. Decisiveness is one of the important elements in a magistrate."[25] He was also bent on making the announcement on the fifth anniversary of the enactment of the *Charter,* three days away, a point that would later be celebrated in the media.[26]

It was a huge decision, and L'Heureux-Dubé badly needed someone to talk to about such a seismic shift in her life. She called Pierre Côté, the associate chief justice of the Superior Court, very late that evening and asked him to meet her at a twenty-four-hour local café, the Saint-Germain on rue Sheppard. The two met over sandwiches and beer, examining the situation from every angle until well into the morning. Côté was a natural choice for a sounding board. Called to the bar in 1948, he had started his law practice with Sam Bard and then left to become a partner with Lapointe, Roberge, Fortier, Côté, ultimately practising as a senior partner with his cousin Yves Pratte's law firm until his appointment to the Superior Court in 1969 and his elevation to the post of associate chief justice in 1984.[27] He and L'Heureux-Dubé had become firm friends on the court, often lunching in their offices, going for walks together, and consulting about cases.

At the café that night, L'Heureux-Dubé voiced her fear that she was unqualified. She characterized the Supreme Court judges as "great people" and fretted that she was "not of that calibre."[28] In particular, she worried that she had little experience with constitutional law and had adjudicated very few *Charter* cases. "The *Charter,* for me, was a monster," she remembered. "When you don't know, you are afraid."[29] It was a resurfacing of the lack of self-confidence that had affected her early convent years, and she was fortunate that Côté was there to respond. Although Pierre Côté

The Honourable Pierre Côté, Associate Chief Justice of the Quebec Superior Court, a former colleague of L'Heureux-Dubé's who advised her on the Supreme Court appointment.

neither urged her to accept or reject the offer, he scoffed at her doubts, reassuring her that there was no problem with her ability. "The big thing," he countered, "was to leave Quebec."[30]

Both of them were well aware that two of the Quebec Supreme Court judges who had preceded Chouinard, Yves Pratte and Louis-Philippe de Grandpré, had served less than two years and four years, respectively, before quitting to return to Quebec.[31] Moving to a predominantly Anglophone court located in Ontario, with all the linguistic and cultural isolation it would entail, was a daunting prospect. Because there was no requirement that Supreme Court judges be bilingual, there were always some judges who were unable or unwilling to speak French. By custom, the working language for group deliberations often defaulted to English. Many of the previous Quebec appointees had also found the Supreme Court "monastic" and Ottawa "stultifying."[32] As L'Heureux-Dubé noted, "when [Quebec] judges talk about the Supreme Court of Canada, they just roll their eyes. It's not the same world. French values are totally different from the English. French Canadians have a sense of community that the others don't have."[33] Even Mulroney recalled that he well understood L'Heureux-Dubé's hesitation about the dislocation: "[Claire] had a terrific lifestyle [in Quebec City]. So you pay a price in terms of comfort – it's not what you're used to."[34]

L'Heureux-Dubé left the café still uncertain what to tell the prime minister in a few hours. Eschewing any thought of sleep, at 6:30 she phoned a Supreme Court of Canada judge she considered a friend, William McIntyre. Born in Saskatchewan and elevated to the high court from the British Columbia Court of Appeal in 1973, McIntyre was someone with whom she had long collaborated in judicial education circles. His efforts to become fluent in French through judicial immersion courses in Quebec also endeared him to her.[35] When she asked for his advice, his blunt reply was that "rumours were flying" that she was "trouble" and that she would "not be welcomed" at the Supreme Court.[36] This would shortly become public knowledge when *Maclean's* revealed that her appointment "was initially opposed by some Supreme Court judges."[37]

L'Heureux-Dubé remembered her conversation with McIntyre as "the turning point." "[I] never backed down from a challenge," she explained. "[I] decided right then to accept the appointment."[38] It was the response of the risk-taking young girl who rebelled against her father's harsh discipline, the rebellious student who resisted the strict regulations at the convent, the courageous lawyer who railed against judges who discriminated against her family law clients. She made the affirmative phone call to Bernard Roy that morning. He advised the prime minister and the Order-in-Council was approved without delay. Mulroney made two other female judicial appointments that same day. Louise Mailhot was elevated from the Superior Court to take L'Heureux-Dubé's place as the only woman on the Quebec Court of Appeal.[39] Christine Tourigny, L'Heureux-Dubé's former law partner, was named to the Superior Court.[40] Mulroney was elated to inform L'Heureux-Dubé that she was one of a triumvirate of women appointed that day. Her former judicial adversary, George W.R. Owen, was less impressed. Sitting with Réjane Laberge-Colas in the judicial dining room in Montreal, he snorted: "They have appointed three women. Next time, dogs." An angry Laberge-Colas reportedly stood up and walked out.[41]

Reaction to the Appointment

The news shook up the Quebec bar.[42] Louis LeBel recalled: "Was the Quebec bar surprised? Possibly. Because it was a woman? Probably."[43] McGill law professor Pierre-Gabriel Jobin characterized the appointment as "controversial."[44] L'Heureux-Dubé's former Laval classmate Roch Bolduc explained: "I would have predicted she would have been a very good judge at the Superior Court, maybe the appeal court. But the Supreme Court of Canada? No. In those years, we couldn't imagine that."[45] Even Martial Asselin, who took personal pride in his role in her ascension on the bench and was quick to add that he had spoken highly of L'Heureux-Dubé to both Joe Clark and Brian Mulroney, admitted that he "did not predict she would sit at [the] Supreme Court of Canada."[46] An unidentified Montreal lawyer was quoted in *Maclean's* accusing L'Heureux-Dubé of being "strong on facts but short on law."[47]

Louise Mailhot recalled that some of the "negative comments" might have related to L'Heureux-Dubé's reputation as an expert in family law. Expressing her frustration, Mailhot added: "Claire was so intelligent, she could grasp any problem, but men were seen as the experts in commercial law, and women the 'soft' [areas]."[48] The family law tag was one that rankled with L'Heureux-Dubé. In an interview with the Canadian Bar Association's *National* magazine, she described family law as a specialty that emphasized "more compassion, more human feeling," but then she insisted: "I don't like to be categorized. Women have a role in every part of the law."[49] "*Comme juge et comme praticienne, j'ai touché à tout.*"[†, 50]

Other Quebec observers were less surprised at the appointment.[51] Her judicial colleague Roger Chouinard stressed that L'Heureux-Dubé was "well-placed" for the elevation. "She has the qualities, she has the friends, she had the set-up, she was well-known, well-appreciated."[52] Professor Jobin singled out other characteristics to account for the elevation: "She's an ambitious woman, a woman of networking. She had a natural sense of being at the right place at the right time, [to] be noticed by decision-makers."[53] His sense of L'Heureux-Dubé's socializing and conscious

---

† "As a judge and practitioner, I have touched on everything."

positioning for power contrasted with her own self-presentation as a woman who never sought judicial office, who never strategized for elevation. It offered an entirely new perspective on her rise through the ranks.

Judith Gamache-Côté, her Laval classmate and long-time friend, was valiantly supportive, emphasizing that she heard from other lawyers that L'Heureux-Dubé was promoted because she was "extremely competent." The comment prompted L'Heureux-Dubé to quip that it was "better than hearing you slept your way to the top."[54] Yves Fortier wrote her that she would be a "breath of fresh air" on the court.[55] And her former mentor, Sam Bard, sent a card addressed to "Claire the Supreme," adding that he had always known that she would "eventually end up on the Supreme Court."[56]

The Swearing-In

At the ceremony on 4 May 1987, the family was represented by L'Heureux-Dubé's two sisters, Louise and Nicole, her children, Louise and Pierre, and her father, Paul. The grandiose proceeding reminded her family of a "coronation," and they coined a new title – *"la cour suprême"* – as a nickname for Claire.[57] Did Paul L'Heureux finally concede that he had been wrong to try to keep his daughter from a career in law? L'Heureux-Dubé's sister Louise recalled that her father "looked proud but I don't think he said he was wrong. At the beginning, when she first got on the court, I think he resented it. Something like ... she had outshone him. At the end, when she made the Supreme Court of Canada, maybe he completely turned around. Maybe, although that's not his style. But he came."[58] L'Heureux-Dubé remembered one reporter asking her father if she had been "difficult to raise." "Not so much," retorted her father, "but she always had the last word."[59] The tumultuous father/daughter relationship had not mellowed.

Just before the ceremony was to begin, L'Heureux-Dubé retired to her office to don the traditional garb: a heavy scarlet robe trimmed with white mink fur, capped with an "archaic tri-corned hat."[60] Marie-Claire Belleau, who would serve as L'Heureux-Dubé's first law clerk, recalled that moment as the first sign of how much the new judge would alter the court's severe atmosphere. "I can see the sunshine coming into the corridor through those magnificent windows, and she's trying to put on her 'Santa Claus' gown and she's screaming with laughter," explained Belleau. The ruckus was so shocking that one of the judges came to Bertha

Wilson's office to ask what was going on. Wilson replied, "That's laughter!" Belleau explained that laughter was something no one ever heard in the austere Supreme Court hallways. And she added: "[Justice L'Heureux-Dubé] laughs with an open throat – it's just contagious."[61] The formal ceremony was somewhat more restrained. Chief Justice Dickson read the lengthy oath of office without a hint of facial expression.[62]

A bevy of reporters did their best to offer some context for a public eager for background on the new judge. The press seemed uncertain about L'Heureux-Dubé's ideological leanings. The *Globe and Mail* quoted one Montreal lawyer who claimed that she could not be "categorized," and a criminal lawyer who advised that she was "not predictable," while the *Montreal Gazette* described her as a "small-l liberal," someone "known for candor on the bench and for strong sympathy for social justice issues."[63] The *Toronto Star* described her as "headstrong, sometimes temperamental, but always candid."[64] Pointing up the cultural divide between Quebec and the rest of the country, the *Montreal Gazette* noted that the appointment had elicited "widespread and favourable reaction," while the *Toronto Star* complained that "apart from a few knowledgeable persons in legal and academic circles, her name is unfamiliar to the masses of Canadians who will be affected by her legal decisions."[65] The *Globe and Mail* characterized her as "a public dynamo who enthuses other people," with the "downside" being that "some think that is undecorous." In closing, the *Globe* added that the appointment was "not without detractors."[66]

The matter of gender also received an airing. The *Toronto Star* noted that there had been substantial pressure to appoint a woman, with L'Heureux-Dubé the obvious senior female candidate, and that she might not have been "according to the experts, the most qualified jurist in the province." For good measure, the paper noted that court observers had "said the same of [Bertha] Wilson, when she was elevated."[67] These were sentiments rarely voiced about male appointees, nor were they often expressed to question the merits of judges appointed due to geography. Appointees with obvious political ties might be more susceptible to attack, but even they rarely had their substantive qualifications openly doubted. The baseline for the concept of "merit" was never articulated, never publicly debated, never applied across the board. Yet when gender equity was introduced as a new variable, observers insisted that the all-important merit standard had been improperly overridden. Feminists characterized it as a surreptitious way of insisting that female candidates could never measure up.

Claire L'Heureux-Dubé's former law colleagues, Roger Garneau, Jacques Philippon, and Sam Bard, at the swearing-in ceremony, 4 May 1987.

In an interview with Kirk Makin of the *Globe and Mail*, L'Heureux-Dubé conceded that "it was not competence alone" that inspired the prime minister to telephone her with the offer.[68] But as she had with her earlier judicial appointments, she steadfastly characterized her own philosophy as "gender-blind."[69] And Makin described her as "unmoved by those who attribute her elevation partly to her sex." She retorted, "I was the right person in the right place at the right time. So what? All appointments are like that. It doesn't bother me whatsoever."[70] She did, however, emphasize that she believed in gender equality: "I always perceive myself as an equal. Like many women probably, I thought my competence would take me where I wanted to go."[71]

Rosalie Abella, then chair of the Ontario Labour Relations Board, made a perceptive comment to the *Ottawa Citizen:* "She doesn't lack any of the judicial qualities. Her insight, her analytical prowess, all of those things are there in spades. Over and above that, she defines herself according to her own standards and doesn't in any way worry about perception. If she feels like being effusive, she is effusive. If she feels like being creative and moving in new directions, she does it. She is all of the things that judges are supposed to be, plus she's Claire L'Heureux-Dubé."[72]

26
Early Days on the Supreme Court of Canada

THE SUPREME COURT "WELCOME": AN OUTSIDER AGAIN

Any glow from her swearing-in had faded before Claire L'Heureux-Dubé managed to hang pictures in her new wood-panelled office. A feeling of estrangement affects many new Supreme Court appointees. They are uprooted from their communities at an age when it is difficult to forge new friendships. Then they are transplanted into a job where their every action is publicly scrutinized through the unforgiving lens of judicial propriety. L'Heureux-Dubé described it as "living like a hermit in Ottawa," similar to a "monk's existence." She felt "cut off" from her friends and her life, suspended in "rarefied air."[1]

Once again, she found that her gender posed an added challenge. It is always difficult to diagnose why one is treated as an outsider and held at arm's length, and certainly some of the male Supreme Court judges must also have felt estranged from their colleagues at times. But in addition to the interpersonal factors that can impede comfortable relations, the first women faced a gendered layer of resistance as well. Bertha Wilson, who arrived in 1982, was met with a level of apprehension that she attributed to her sex.[2] The first woman appointed to the Supreme Court out of a cohort of fifty-eight judges appointed over 107 years, she felt forced "to prove herself" to a group of men who were skeptical about whether she had won the position "on her merits."[3] Bora Laskin, the chief justice at the time, exhibited nervousness during Wilson's swearing-in. Despite his own familiarity with outsider status and anti-Jewish discrimination during his early

Early Days on the Supreme Court of Canada 331

Justice Bertha Wilson, first woman appointed to the Supreme Court of Canada in 1982.

years on the bench, he displayed overt disappointment about a woman entering the ranks.[4] When Wilson entered the room for her first judicial conference with her male brethren, Antonio Lamer pointedly remained seated when the others rose to stand as she came through the door.[5] Wilson found herself routinely left out of the informal decision-making discussions that the male judges engaged in, which deeply disturbed her and impeded her ability to influence the court.[6]

Five years later, L'Heureux-Dubé found the chilliness still pervasive.[7] It was evident from her colleagues' first reaction to her candidacy. Gérard La Forest recalled that when Chief Justice Dickson advised the judges that

L'Heureux-Dubé was at the top of the prime minister's shortlist, their expressions of concern were such that Bertha Wilson went to his office and asked point-blank: "What's wrong with the woman?"[8] La Forest, who did not share his male colleagues' anxieties, attempted to reassure Wilson that there was "nothing wrong with the woman." But it was only too clear that the negative views voiced by some members of the bar and the press were shared by some of the male Supreme Court judges. The law clerks working at the court were appalled by the misogynistic reactions. They overheard comments that ran the gamut from speculation that L'Heureux-Dubé would never amount to much because she was a woman, to prurient gossip about her sexual reputation.[9] One law clerk was astonished when Antonio Lamer complained in front of her that he "did not want to work with a menopausal woman."[10] Underscoring it all was a clear reluctance to accept a second female judge.

Wilson took the cautionary step of dropping by L'Heureux-Dubé's office to warn her that even though she had been elevated to the nation's top court, "she would have to start to prove herself all over again."[11] It must have felt a bit like Sisyphus, fighting the same battle over and over, rolling the rock up the hill yet one more time. Then, as if to validate the warning, L'Heureux-Dubé discovered that one of her male colleagues, Willard (Bud) Estey, refused to speak with her. "He wouldn't talk to me for three months," she recalled. "After that, he sent me a note saying: 'You've passed your probation.'"[12] It was as though suspicion were a magnet that attached itself to female judges, subjecting them to "the sting of exclusion."[13] "We felt isolated. We were not part of the gang," was how L'Heureux-Dubé put it.[14]

It was a stark contrast with what L'Heureux-Dubé felt she had left behind. Every morning, the Quebec Court of Appeal judges had coffee together, a social gathering that she sorely missed at the Supreme Court. As her first law clerk, Marie-Claire Belleau, explained, "She missed the collegiality [and] the exchanges ... the capacity to sit down in the office and chat about a case. She spoke about it all the time."[15] L'Heureux-Dubé had spent years painstakingly overcoming the dubiousness that greeted her earlier judicial appointments, using every social grace she had to gain acceptance on the Quebec courts. Now it felt like starting all over again.

Gender is always intersectional, and L'Heureux-Dubé's outsider status was exacerbated by her identity as a Francophone from Quebec. She described it as "two solitudes," with the English-speaking judges from the rest of Canada having virtually "no knowledge of what we do [or] what we write in Quebec." She added, "In Quebec, I was part of life. The

Early Days on the Supreme Court of Canada 333

Claire L'Heureux-Dubé and Marie-Claire Belleau, her first Supreme Court law clerk.

Court of Appeal was much more social, much more French. *C'est la joie de vivre.*"[16] And she pointed to the experiences of two predecessors, de Grandpré and Pratte, who had both resigned, emphasizing that she was "not the only casualty."[17] Belleau, her Quebec Francophone law clerk who observed first-hand L'Heureux-Dubé's isolation at the Supreme Court, explained, "It's an Anglophone culture. One of the things about that is that the language is tiring, but it's mostly that you don't have the same cultural references. You always feel stupid. They haven't read the same things you've read, nor have you read what they've read."[18]

McGill law professor Pierre-Gabriel Jobin echoed this: "[Claire L'Heureux-Dubé] is from Rimouski, remember that. She evolved a great deal in Quebec City, but in those days, even as it is today, Quebec City is homogeneous, a French-speaking population with a bourgeoisie, [and] she was part of the bourgeoisie. Going up to the Supreme Court of Canada [was] a different ball game."[19] Teresa Scassa, the law clerk who succeeded Belleau, offered an illustration. "Culturally, in Ontario, people don't touch each other much. Whereas in Quebec, even somebody you were meeting for the first time, at a friend's house, a party, whatever, you would kiss on both cheeks. In Ontario, if you'd go to give someone a kiss on both cheeks, they'd take a step back because you don't touch other people. [There's] probably a gender dimension to it as well. [If you] get kissed by a woman, that means something different too. [I] can certainly understand that with judges of an older generation, predominantly from English-speaking provinces, there's always this disjunction. Justice L'Heureux-Dubé didn't dial it down."[20]

Montreal-born *Globe and Mail* reporter Kirk Makin, who did an in-depth interview with L'Heureux-Dubé shortly after her appointment, agreed: "A lot of Anglo-Canadians, probably even more so when you get into echelons like the top judiciary, are pretty conservative in their social interactions [and] very careful with their words. It's not every judge who runs up and hugs people, or comes out with some really funny line. There's a risk to doing that. Maybe less a risk in her own province than when she gets up there with the big boys from across the country in the Supreme Court."[21] Peter Sankoff, another of L'Heureux-Dubé's law clerks, added, "I'm sure her Francophone status mattered." He remembered that the other Anglophone clerks nicknamed her "Happy-Doobie," their translation of her French name: "She's a woman, and she's loud. [She] can take over the room. It can be hard to get words in and she speaks a lot. A lot of guys aren't going to take too well to that."[22]

Were things even minimally easier because there were now two women? Was there some solidarity in the isolation? Certainly Bertha Wilson was both welcoming and sympathetic to her new female colleague. And L'Heureux-Dubé was a great admirer of Wilson's intellect and principled reasoning.[23] But the two were badly mismatched in personality. Wilson was a "stoic Scot" who primarily "stuck to the work."[24] Their colleague Charles Gonthier explained that Wilson "didn't mince her opinions, but in terms of manner, Claire and Bertha were [at] almost opposite ends of the spectrum, Bertha much more reserved and Claire very much of the Latin temperament."[25] L'Heureux-Dubé's first clerk recalled Wilson as "happy" to have L'Heureux-Dubé on the court, but "very removed," and "reserved ... in a way that just kept a distance." Marie-Claire Belleau also sensed this had to do with the distinction between the Anglophone and Francophone backgrounds. "When you're French, you put the volume up, and when you speak to English people, you have to put the volume down. [Justice Bertha Wilson] was a very low-volume person. Justice L'Heureux-Dubé was very high."[26]

There was a palpable sense that L'Heureux-Dubé was different from the other judges who preceded her. Although her gender was central to this, it went beyond that. The sense of nervousness that attended her arrival also had to do with her flamboyant, passionate, overwhelming personality, which seemed all the more startling against the traditional backdrop of the inscrutable, staid judicial image. In many ways, she stood out in high relief.[27]

Of Cold Marble Hallways, Colleagues, and "Gopher Holes"

The Supreme Court building, situated on a high bluff overlooking the Ottawa River, is constructed of severe granite and set back from the street by a massive lawn and towering stone steps. Its cold, marble-columned lobby seems designed to intimidate. The nine judges' offices are lined up sequentially off a "silent marble corridor" that runs around three sides of the building, inspiring one judge to refer to his colleagues as "disappearing into their gopher holes."[28] In order of seniority, the bench that L'Heureux-Dubé joined consisted of Chief Justice Brian Dickson, Jean Beetz, Willard (Bud) Estey, William McIntyre, Antonio Lamer, Bertha Wilson, Gerald Le Dain, and Gérard La Forest. A sitting judge once compared joining the Supreme Court to being matched up with eight spouses, none of them of your choosing.[29] Who were the eight colleagues who greeted L'Heureux-Dubé, and how did they respond individually to their newest colleague?

Brian Dickson had been appointed to the court in 1973 and named chief justice in 1984. From the Prairies, he had practised corporate-commercial law in Winnipeg.[30] His biographers described him as the "leading figure" in the post-*Charter* transformation of the Supreme Court from a "cautious, narrow, and legalistic" body to an institution "at the centre of political life in Canada."[31] He had ushered in a sweeping new judicial style focused on "broad questions of policy," yet he was also a man of self-discipline and military precision, sometimes described as "old-fashioned and privileged."[32] L'Heureux-Dubé's recollection of their first conversation was that Dickson sounded like "the regiment master," giving an order to soldiers under his command.[33] She must have wondered about the parallels with her own father's harsh military persona. Dickson was "not very welcoming," she recalled.[34] It was a relationship that would change with time, as L'Heureux-Dubé's work ethic impressed the chief justice and his demeanour slowly began to warm.[35]

Although he was quoted in the press describing L'Heureux-Dubé as an appointee of "merit," Dickson may have chafed at the sense that she was also selected because of the pressure for more women on the court.[36] He was publicly critical of affirmative action in judicial appointment: "I don't think it is any compliment to the particular group that we will have a minimum of, say, three women on [the court] ... If they aren't the best persons to be sitting as judges of the court, then I think you cheapen the court, and I don't know where you would end up. If you once start recognizing an entitlement to a position on the court simply because of a particular sex or race or religion or what have you, then it becomes, I think, something very unmanageable and messy. If it is a woman who is truly outstanding in competition with any man, I think that is wonderful."[37] L'Heureux-Dubé, also a staunch opponent of affirmative action, would not have disagreed.[38] But it was not a principle either of them applied to the designation of seats based on geography, which seemed to have passed muster for generations without cheapening the court.

Jean Beetz, the next most senior of the judges, was a former Rhodes Scholar and dean of law from the University of Montreal who had served as legal adviser to Prime Minister Trudeau. An expert on constitutional federalism, Beetz was renowned as "erudite" and "profoundly cultured," a man whose French was "so vivid and exquisite that interpreters sometimes despaired of conveying its richness."[39] He also agonized over difficult judgments, and was "chronically slow" to reach decisions.[40] Beetz was a long-time supporter of women and had lobbied for the appointment of the first full-time female law professor at the University of Montreal.[41]

One might have predicted that Beetz would have offered warm overtures to his new female colleague from Quebec, but the distinct personalities of the two judges made that difficult. Beetz was a "retiring person who liked his privacy and wanted to maintain it."[42] He was "delicate," "timid," and "reserved."[43] He was far too polite to be inhospitable to L'Heureux-Dubé, but he was "a bit unsettled by her presence, by the space she would occupy."[44] Marie-Claire Belleau explained, "He's the kind of man she would approach, and he would step back. She's a bit too big in her ... extrovert personality."[45] The differences were exacerbated by Julien Chouinard's death. Beetz was in deep mourning over the loss of his beloved colleague, whom he had known since childhood and with whom he had had lunch every day at the court. "He was neither welcoming nor unwelcoming, just unbelievably sad and lost," according to Belleau.[46] Their shared tenure on the court was also brief. Struck down by a heart attack and then hit by cancer, Beetz retired in November 1988.[47]

One of the most abrasive of her new colleagues was Willard (Bud) Estey, the son of a former Supreme Court judge who had practised as a corporate litigator, served as chief justice of Ontario, and been appointed to the top court in 1977.[48] Although Estey was "very popular with the bar," his charm was scarcely visible at the Supreme Court by the time L'Heureux-Dubé arrived. His "volatile personality" had always made him a bit of a "loose cannon," but by the mid-1980s he was becoming "increasingly disaffected" over the court's new direction under the *Charter*.[49] Estey sometimes took out his frustrations on his law clerks and his colleagues, using his intelligence and caustic wit to devastate people with a bluntness that could become destructive. It would be an understatement to say that his welcome to L'Heureux-Dubé was non-existent.[50] Although their relations warmed after the "probation period," the overlap between the two was brief, since Estey was away presiding over a federal inquiry into the collapse of two banks in western Canada, and then on sick leave due to a blood clot that damaged his ophthalmic nerve. He announced his retirement in April 1988 and then attracted a storm of controversy with a volley of indiscreet comments to the press about past and ongoing political and judicial matters.[51]

William McIntyre, the judge L'Heureux-Dubé had phoned before accepting Mulroney's offer, had been appointed in 1979. He had practised law in Victoria before becoming a trial and appeal court judge in British Columbia. Despite his long-term friendship with L'Heureux-Dubé, the two were not destined to see eye to eye on jurisprudential matters, since McIntyre was a "deeply conservative advocate of judicial restraint," who was "sceptical of the *Charter* as an instrument of social change" and had been described by Dickson as "anchor[ing] the right wing of the court."[52] Nevertheless, McIntyre was one of the most effusive of L'Heureux-Dubé's new colleagues. He had "genuinely rejoiced" in Bertha Wilson's appointment, and Wilson considered him her "closest friend on the court."[53] His reception of L'Heureux-Dubé was similar. "He was very welcoming ... kind and nice to her in every way," recalled Belleau. "He was the most joyous and fun person. One Friday night, he came around to teach us how to make real martinis."[54] Whatever community he offered was brief, however. McIntyre retired in December 1988 at the age of seventy.[55]

The judge who was destined to be L'Heureux-Dubé's long-term nemesis was Antonio Lamer. Lamer grew up in Montreal's tough east end, where, as he was fond of saying, "everyone on his block except himself and another boy (who became a dentist) went to the penitentiary."[56] Lamer had practised law in Montreal, founded the Defence Attorneys' Association of Quebec, and taught criminal law at the University of Montreal. One of his law students, Louise Arbour, who would later join him on the Supreme Court of Canada, had dazzling memories of him as "far ahead of his time in terms of his outlook on abuse of power by the state."[57] Deeply affected by the abuses his clients suffered at the hands of the police, Lamer achieved legendary status even as a young criminal defence counsel, with lawyers lining up to watch his dynamic advocacy in court.[58]

Named to the Quebec Superior Court four years before L'Heureux-Dubé, Lamer was seconded to the Law Reform Commission of Canada in 1971, where he was serving as chair when he was elevated to the Quebec Court of Appeal in 1978. Prime Minister Trudeau appointed him to the Supreme Court in 1980.[59] Although his background in criminal law set him apart from most of his predecessors, the court's criminal caseload was steadily increasing, a pattern that would further escalate after the enactment of the *Charter*.[60] At his swearing-in, the Quebec deputy minister of justice had described Lamer as having *"un esprit audacieux à l'action percutante."*[†, 61]

Lamer had been one of the members of the court most vocally opposed to L'Heureux-Dubé's appointment. He "made my reputation a little less pleasant," was how she described it. "I knew from law clerks at the time that Lamer had mentioned if I were appointed, he would resign. He apparently said to the other judges, it would be over his dead body. He really tried to poison them against me. You can imagine the climate in which I came. I don't know why. We never sat together before. I had had him [as a guest] to my home when he was on the Quebec Court of Appeal. We often tried to invite our travelling colleagues to dinner."[62]

Since Antonio Lamer's death in 2007 made it impossible to ask him about his relationship with L'Heureux-Dubé for this biography, I asked his widow, Danièle Tremblay-Lamer, if she knew the background history to the antipathy. She agreed to speak on behalf of her deceased husband, but only because he was no longer able to contribute his own perspective. And she could only speculate. "I don't know if [it was] one event. Maybe he had somebody else in mind [for the vacancy]. When you want an expert in such and such, and then you get family law judges, you [might say] 'Oh my god, I'm stuck with Claire.' It happened with other colleagues that were appointed where he was not happy. She wasn't the only one."[63]

Lamer and L'Heureux-Dubé would disagree on many criminal justice and gender equality issues in the coming years, but it was more than simply an ideological fissure. Tremblay-Lamer explained it as based on personality: "It may be because of their different temper. She would have got on his

---

† "an audacious mind prone to powerful action"

Justice Antonio Lamer, appointed to the Supreme Court of Canada in 1980.

nerves, and he may have said something. He had a temper when he was frustrated, and he could be rude with colleagues, which my husband did not like. With flamboyant people, it can happen."[64] In some ways, it was the opposite of the personality divisions that separated L'Heureux-Dubé and Beetz. Here were two judges who were simply too much alike. Tremblay-Lamer explained that both were "vivacious," "flamboyant," "social," "Francophone," and "Latin." "It may have been one of the reasons their personalities collided," she suggested.[65] The same could be said about their driving habits. Each drove like a "bat out of hell" on their regular treks home from Ottawa to Montreal and Quebec City, respectively.[66] As Belleau put it, "Justice L'Heureux-Dubé and Justice Lamer both took too much space."[67] And those tensions were exacerbated by sexism. People characterized Lamer as an outgoing man, displaying jovial bonhomie. He didn't have to "dial it down" to fit in. L'Heureux-Dubé, with similar vivacious characteristics, was perceived as transgressive because of her gender.[68]

Four years older than L'Heureux-Dubé, Bertha Wernham Wilson had been born in Scotland, studied law at Dalhousie University, and practised at Osler's in Toronto, with a focus on research, for over fifteen years. In 1975, she became the first woman appointed to the Ontario Court of Appeal, and in 1982, the first woman appointed to the Supreme Court.[69] Known as a hard-working, principled, and compassionate jurist who shouldered more than her share of decision drafting, Wilson developed a reputation as a woman of iron will, whose jurisprudence helped lay the foundation for the interpretation of the new *Charter*.[70] Undoubtedly the two female judges found themselves strengthened in numbers, but their disparate temperaments made them anything but soulmates at the court.

Gerald Le Dain had served as a judge of the Federal Court of Appeal after a career as corporate counsel and as a law professor at McGill and Osgoode Hall Law School. He had chaired the impressive Le Dain Inquiry into the Non-Medical Use of Drugs, the first Canadian body to recommend, in 1973, the decriminalization of marijuana possession.[71] During his tenure at the Supreme Court, he buckled under his perfectionist work ethic. Tortured with indecision over the drafting of opinions, he required repeated hospitalization.[72] Le Dain's family had some experience with mental health challenges and he had lost his eldest daughter in a tragic car accident prior to his appointment to the Supreme Court.[73] Had Le Dain been healthier when L'Heureux-Dubé arrived, their similar family difficulties might have created a bond and the two might have become close colleagues. As it was, she saw little of Le Dain; he suffered a major depressive illness in the summer of 1988 and resigned in November.[74]

L'Heureux-Dubé's eighth colleague, Gérard La Forest, was a bilingual New Brunswicker and a Rhodes Scholar. He had practised in Grand Falls, taught law at the University of New Brunswick, served as law dean at the University of Alberta, and sat on the New Brunswick Court of Appeal. A former civil servant, he was deeply knowledgeable about the process of constitutional change, but tended to "defer to governments" and to take "a restrained approach under the *Charter* to matters of social policy."[75] L'Heureux-Dubé had previously met La Forest at the international Francophone legal conference in Tunisia that she attended in the early 1970s, where they "got along quite well."[76] Being able to converse easily in French

Early Days on the Supreme Court of Canada 341

Supreme Court of Canada judges as a group, 1987. *Top row, left to right,* Gérard La Forest, Bertha Wilson, Gerald Le Dain, Claire L'Heureux-Dubé; *front row, left to right,* William McIntyre, Jean Beetz, Brian Dickson, Willard (Bud) Estey, Antonio Lamer.

increased L'Heureux-Dubé's comfort level with La Forest.[77] Like McIntyre, La Forest distinguished himself by his sociable reception of the first two women on the high court.[78]

Overall, with several notable exceptions, the bench that greeted L'Heureux-Dubé upon her arrival at the Supreme Court of Canada was austere, constrained, retiring, in some respects suspicious, and to some degree downright hostile. The turnover resulting from several retirements would change the complexion of the bench a little in coming years, but the prevailing culture would not undergo dramatic transformation. The mannerisms with which L'Heureux-Dubé had eventually managed to charm the majority of the Quebec Court of Appeal would hold little sway in this venue.

A Context of Backlog, Feverish Work Pace, and Irrepressible *Joie de Vivre*

L'Heureux-Dubé's first "judicial conference" caused her to stumble in a way that she was loath to repeat. When the lawyers finished their oral arguments, the nine justices were in the habit of retiring immediately to the conference room, "an intimate but ornate library," to exchange their preliminary views.[79] Under Chief Justice Bora Laskin, the tradition had been established that each judge had an opportunity to speak, with the most recently appointed going first and the others following in reverse order of seniority. As explained by Laskin, the process, borrowed from Jewish traditions, was designed to reduce any danger that if the senior judges spoke first, they might unduly influence or intimidate their junior colleagues. Once there was a sense of what each judge thought, the chief justice would solicit a decision writer for the majority (possibly unanimous) side. Judges volunteered for this, and although it was the chief justice's call, he tended to give the most senior volunteer priority over junior colleagues. The draft decision would be circulated, and the judges would provide comments by written memo distributed to all. The draft might go through several rounds of amendment, and occasionally the shifting opinions would mean that the draft majority decision would morph into a dissent, and another judge would take over the writing of the majority opinion. Finally, individual judges would decide whether to sign on or to draft their own concurring or dissenting opinions.[80]

L'Heureux-Dubé knew nothing of her obligation to speak first when she filed into the conference room the first time.[81] She found herself seated at the round judicial table, directly across from Chief Justice Dickson. He began by saying: "Claire, what do you think?" Startled, she retorted: "What, I won't first have the benefit of your great minds?" Dickson replied curtly: "Claire, you'll get used to our ways."[82] It upset L'Heureux-Dubé all the more that she had no ready-made presentation. "She wasn't prepared," recalled Marie-Claire Belleau. After that, L'Heureux-Dubé always ensured that her clerks prepared written bench memos outlining the issues well before oral arguments were made.[83]

The Supreme Court was facing a substantial backlog when L'Heureux-Dubé arrived. Judgments had fallen from an average of 100 per year down to 54 in 1984, 75 in 1985, and 77 in 1986. In 1986, 65 appeals were on reserve, awaiting judgment. In 1987, there were 29 cases still awaiting judgment more than twelve months after argument, the highest number in over a decade.[84] For L'Heureux-Dubé's first five years on the bench, there was not a single year when at least one judge was not absent from the court through special commissions, illness, or death.[85] Settling in to assist with the catch-up, she soon became notorious for burning the midnight oil in her "gopher hole."[86] Putting her legendary work ethic into overdrive, she would get up at 6 a.m., swim, eat breakfast, and then work at the court from 8:00 a.m. to 2:00 a.m. As she had confessed to the press on her appointment, she still needed "very little sleep – just four hours a night."[87] In the early years, before the court created its own lunchroom, she ate lunch at her desk and dinner at Le Circle Universitaire, a private dining venue created by University of Ottawa alumni to promote French culture.

L'Heureux-Dubé was fortunate in her choice of staff. Soon after her arrival, she hired as her secretary Lisette Gammon, with whom she had grown up in Rimouski. Gammon was working in John Turner's office at the time, but L'Heureux-Dubé convinced her to transfer to the Supreme Court, where her intelligence and efficiency soon made her a stalwart of the busy judicial chambers. She had initially planned to retire after one year but ended up staying eight. She spoke positively about the job: "I loved it. It was just like working with a close friend, or almost a sister." She described L'Heureux-Dubé as an "active and outgoing person" who was "very generous." "We got along very, very well," she said.[88] L'Heureux-Dubé was equally effusive: "Lisette had my full confidence. I admired, respected, and loved her. And it was such a comfort to have her there when I felt so lonely, and I was so disturbed by the way that they treated me."[89]

L'Heureux-Dubé chose as her court attendant André Legault, a former military man and car salesman who had impressed her in the interview when he explained that he desired the position because *"[il] veut passer à l'histoire."*[†,90] In the twelve years he worked for her, the two became trusted confidants and close friends. Legault said, "I was awed by the title of working for a Supreme Court judge until I got to know Mme. L'Heureux-Dubé. The title kind of diminished compared to her character. She is much more than just a Supreme Court judge." She was, he emphasized, "the type of person who didn't differentiate" based on someone's wealth or status. His insight into L'Heureux-Dubé's character gave him an unusual vantage point: "With all her intelligence [and] her knowledge of the law, she always remained a little girl – very innocent and easily hurt – although people never knew that. She always put on this stern façade."[91] It was a side of L'Heureux-Dubé that few others ever saw.

---

† "he wants to go down in history"

When she started on the court, the judges were not provided with written briefs from the lawyers until the day before oral arguments. Despite Bertha Wilson's warning to L'Heureux-Dubé that the judges were "set in their ways" and that change was well-nigh impossible, she forged ahead with the suggestion that the written materials be circulated earlier. "I came to the court [conference] after a case and said, 'I have a point to make. Is it the time to do it?' Chief Justice [Dickson] replied, 'Go on.' I continued, 'We receive our files the day before we sit, and we sit thirty-three weeks. We hear lawyers for four days on the same case, as long as they want to talk. What should I do with *my lovers?*'" The startled judges laughed in unison, the written materials were produced earlier, and L'Heureux-Dubé described it as her "first adventure in change." Wilson came by later to admit that she had loved "the 's' at the end of Claire's lovers."[92]

Although L'Heureux-Dubé readily acknowledged that she was pulling her colleagues' legs a bit, it was also true that the woman who had always been known for her many romantic encounters continued her life in the same vein. She had a number of "loving friendships" and a number of long-term relationships. She even had a number of offers of marriage, all of which she turned down. "If I had found the perfect person, maybe," she admitted. "But I don't think so even then." There were many reasons to eschew another marriage.

> I was married once, and the lessons from my marriage did not compel re-marriage. I was too busy to live a normal married life and care for someone as much as one should. Children don't like the mother to be remarried, so that was one concern. And I think that relationships that remain at arm's length [have] a better chance of success at a certain age. I felt free [to be] alone with my profession [and] my travels and my family. I loved the freedom ... of being able to do what I want to do, and not being hampered by duties. When you have such an interesting and full life, you would be very demanding of a person who would want to marry you. You don't need it. Very often brilliant women marry guys that are not at their level at all – why? Loving friendship is much better than love. It's less tyrannical. If it is real love, it is tyrannical in many ways; I feel more comfortable in loving friendships. There were very close friends I could count on for company ... occasional lovers ... and lots of loving friendships.[93]

Homesick for Quebec, L'Heureux-Dubé tried to get back on weekends whenever she could. The lead foot for which she was famous would turn the drive home into a four-hour speeding expedition. Once there, she often stayed with her close friend Denyse Dion. In fact, one of her refrains in Ottawa was, "All I want to do is take the car and go home and share a pizza with Denyse Dion."[94] In summertime, she would arrive, take a quick swim in Denyse's backyard pool, and then fall sound asleep in the basement room. The four-hour nights were taking their toll. "I was so tired," she recalled, "I would sleep twnety-four hours just trying to recover."[95]

Others also offered L'Heureux-Dubé venues for respite. Her newfound friend, Ottawa lawyer Shirley Tucker Parks, suggested that L'Heureux-Dubé stay in her Clearwater, Florida, condo in the spring of 1988, when the court had a week's respite from sitting. After giving a speech in New Orleans, L'Heureux-Dubé stopped off for ten days. She was so enamoured of the Florida spot that she put in an offer to buy a condo of her own.[96] It was to become one of her treasured possessions. Although she rarely managed to get more than one or two months there per year, she relished the weather, the chance to invite friends and family, and the opportunity to relax. She was delighted when her daughter Louise used it for her honeymoon in October 1988.[97]

Such interludes were few and far between due to the perilous judicial workload of the era. "The pressure of the court makes people crazy," explained L'Heureux-Dubé:

> Particularly at that time, [when] they were dealing with a new thing, the *Charter* ... They didn't know how to go about it. When I arrived, it was doom and gloom. Everybody there was depressed [and] wanted to get out of there. I should have said no to going to the Supreme Court. I was unhappy. I would have been so happy at the Court of Appeal. I would have retired as a supernumerary judge at sixty-five. I would have enjoyed life. Instead, I got myself into the worst fifteen years of my life. I cried like a baby the first six months. I said it publicly – it's a prison, and it's a cemetery. The problem was I loved the challenge of the cases and the jurisprudence. The work was incredible, and I enjoyed every minute of that, but I didn't like any of the rest.[98]

Despite the stresses and strains, there was something irrepressible in Claire L'Heureux-Dubé that refused to be flattened. Her flirtatious sociability might not charm her Supreme Court colleagues, but she was not going to change her stripes one bit. Marie-Claire Belleau tried to convey what she observed of her mentor in those early months:

She was miserable at the time, but she had a *joie de vivre*. One evening, it was winter, [and she was coming down] those big corridors [on the] second floor of the Supreme Court. Justice L'Heureux-Dubé had one of these flowing skirts, and she was making it float in the air. "Marie-Claire, do you know what I'm doing tonight? I have a date and I'm going skating on the [Rideau] Canal." And it just made me feel that ... life started at sixty. I was twenty-five and she was almost sixty. And I saw her coming into my life, and I thought, "Life starts at sixty." She was lively [and] full of energy. She's a role model for me, at the personal level and at the professional level. I was smitten.[99]

27
Continuing Isolation on the Supreme Court

Eleven new judges joined the Supreme Court of Canada during Claire L'Heureux-Dubé's fifteen-year term, and although she forged some new collegial relationships, the chilliness that marred her arrival never fully abated.[1] The decade of the 1990s, under Chief Justice Antonio Lamer's leadership, witnessed an extraordinary level of disagreement on the Supreme Court bench.[2] It was, some said, like "flood waters bashing against each other" in a "court trying to negotiate [unresolved] tensions" across the larger community.[3] In the view of others, the hostility between Lamer and L'Heureux-Dubé lay at the core of the disharmony.

The Growing Tension with Tony Lamer

L'Heureux-Dubé often referred wistfully to the collegiality she had experienced on the Quebec Court of Appeal. She would claim that it stemmed from shared French Canadian cultural values, but this sense of community heritage never seemed to encompass Montrealer Antonio Lamer. The friction may have had to do in part with her dismissive attitude toward criminal law, the field that Lamer held so dear.[4] "I found criminal law simple," she was apt to say. "No nuances. It had one rule only: fairness to the accused." In fact, she added, you could "learn it by osmosis."[5] For his part, Lamer thought that L'Heureux-Dubé had "an aversion to criminal law."[6] His widow, Danièle Tremblay-Lamer, who agreed to be interviewed after his death, remembered acrimonious exchanges between the two:

Official Supreme Court photo, 1999. *Top row, left to right,* Ian Binnie, Jack Major, Michel Bastarache, Louise Arbour; *front row, left to right,* Beverley McLachlin, Claire L'Heureux-Dubé, Antonio Lamer, Charles Gonthier, Frank Iacobucci.

"[L'Heureux-Dubé] would just say, 'he's guilty, he's guilty,' which would annoy [the other judges] because they wanted to have a serious discussion. My husband [was] passionate about criminal law. Claire would drive him crazy when she wouldn't give it any attention."[7]

Former University of Ottawa law professor and Ontario judge David Paciocco saw the hostility as an inevitable outgrowth of disparate views on criminal law. He offered an example of the conversational sparring between the two judges:

> As [Justice Lamer] once said, "At the end of the trial, the only person who's going to be leaving in handcuffs is the accused." It may be apocryphal but I have this memory of someone telling me that Justice L'Heureux-Dubé

once said, "The difficulty with Tony is that he can't stand to have somebody leave the court in handcuffs." What they are doing matters. The Supreme Court matters. If they see someone getting in the way of what they want to accomplish, they see that person as a professional enemy.[8]

Former Lamer law clerk Jocelyn Downie speculated that the differences resulted from "profound disagreements about sexual assault." Lamer's beliefs about sexual assault, she noted, were those of the "typical defence criminal lawyer," and he would occasionally say things that were completely at odds with what L'Heureux-Dubé understood about sexual violence. "That level of disagreement," suggested Downie, "could affect everything."[9] Another law clerk, who did not want to be quoted for attribution, added that during a conversation about sexual assault with several law clerks, Lamer seemed to suggest that most complaints were fabricated: "[He said that] he didn't think he knew any woman who had been raped and he thought he would know if they had."[10]

The discord over criminal law was fundamental, but there were equally serious differences over issues of gender inequality. Lamer was "not a feminist," according to his former law clerk Catherine Dauvergne, and his tenure on the court "did not include leadership in responding to the challenge of legal feminism."[11] L'Heureux-Dubé too refused to identify as a feminist, but others often affixed the label to her, and at least one observer who knew them both attributed much of Lamer's aversion toward L'Heureux-Dubé to "anti-feminist discrimination."[12] Some of their disagreement also had roots in Lamer's days at the Law Reform Commission, when family law had come under review. On this topic, L'Heureux-Dubé and Lamer found themselves philosophically at "different ends of the spectrum."[13]

Lamer's driving philosophy was to restrain the state from overreaching in criminal law, a perspective honed as a criminal defence lawyer in Quebec during the Duplessis years. It was an era about which Quebec Chief Justice J.J. Michel Robert had quipped, "We'll say, to be elegant, that 'police conduct' toward the accused 'lacked monitoring.'"[14] L'Heureux-Dubé had also lived through the Duplessis years, but since she did not practise criminal law, she never saw the police abuses first hand. The abuses she was steeped in concerned women impoverished by divorce. By contrast, Lamer was personally embroiled in marital breakdown while on the Supreme Court, divorcing a long-time spouse.[15]

The larger-than-life personalities of the two judges may also have contributed to the tensions. Charles Gonthier, who joined the court in 1989, believed the dissension had to do with L'Heureux-Dubé's personality. "[She was] the type of person who relates to other people either very enthusiastically [and] warmly, or else she has really no common sort of feeling towards them. Her failings are more the extreme of her qualities, so to speak ... because she was [not] a person of natural moderation. In other words ... as much as she likes people, she may dislike people as well. And feel very strongly about it. And she's never had any qualms about expressing herself."[16] Gonthier added, "She had no sympathy at all with Justice Lamer. [Ideological differences] were part of it, but I think it went perhaps deeper than that. I think there was a lack of trust on her part."[17] Michel Bastarache, who joined the court in 1997, also pointed to L'Heureux-Dubé's personality: "One thing for sure, when [Claire] opposed him, she always had just the wrong words. It was almost always insulting. So that's why it went off the rails all the time."[18] The antagonistic approach was part of a pattern – similar to the run-ins she had had with some of the obstreperous Quebec trial judges when she practised family law, and with rancorous judges such as George Owen and Amédée Monet on the Court of Appeal. It was a resurfacing of *La Tigresse*, ready to pounce in the face of opposition. It was also something she fully recognized in herself. "Many people hate conflict but I love it," was how she described her own personality.[19]

Others traced the problem to Lamer's personality. Saskatchewan Chief Justice Edward Bayda said: "Tony was a very bullish person. You don't deal with Claire that way."[20] Supreme Court commentator Philip Slayton also described Lamer as "something of a bully," a tendency "exacerbated by his fondness for alcohol," and emphasized that other judges "chafed" under his regime as chief justice as well. According to Slayton: "[Lamer had] told more than one colleague at post-hearing conferences to 'shut up.' One judge wouldn't speak to [him] for several years, and two others are supposed to have left the court early because of their antipathy toward him."[21]

Gérard La Forest was quick to agree that the problems were not only between L'Heureux-Dubé and Lamer. "It wasn't confined to her," he stressed. "It wasn't just Claire who had difficulty with him. Brian Dickson was a superb chief justice, and anybody who followed him would have a hard act to follow. Things weren't as happy [under Lamer]." Asked what it was about Lamer's personality that created problems, La Forest said: "Without wanting to get into too much ... Lamer was vain. He's an example of a fellow who goes up one step too many."[22] Michel Bastarache felt that Lamer was "unfair with a lot of people. Nobody really disliked him, but they disliked what he did. He had his favourites [within the group of judges]. He was very much disliked by the staff because ... he treated people very badly. He was very harsh on people working regularly in the court. They were afraid of him."[23]

Even Lamer's more supportive judicial colleagues were willing to acknowledge his failings. Louise Arbour, who joined the court in 1999, said: "[Lamer] was the occupier of this grand office. He really had a sense of the office. [It was] one of his flaws."[24] Jack Major, appointed in 1992, said: "Tony enjoyed being high profile. But as he had a little bit of vanity, that kept growing as he stayed in office. The trappings of the office, after a while, consume them."[25] Others pointed out that L'Heureux-Dubé also had her share of run-ins with John Sopinka, Major, and others.[26] Yet rarely did the difficulties reach the conflagration point that they did where Lamer was concerned.

Constance Glube, Nova Scotia's first female Supreme Court judge and the first female chief justice of a superior court in Canada, wondered whether part of the disaffection might have reflected L'Heureux-Dubé's discomfort with Lamer's position as chief justice. "I always thought she would have made an interesting chief, if she had been appointed, and that she might have wanted it. Did she want it? Did she feel badly that she was passed over?"[27] When Prime Minister Brian Mulroney chose a chief justice to replace Brian Dickson, tradition would have indicated that he select the most senior of the French Canadian justices. In 1990, that would have been Lamer, who had joined the court in 1980, years before L'Heureux-Dubé's 1987 appointment and Gonthier's in 1989. Tradition was not always followed, however, as Bora Laskin's and Brian Dickson's appointments had illustrated. At the time of L'Heureux-Dubé's appointment, when everyone was speculating about who might take the posting at the Supreme Court, some ventured that the new female appointee might also become the next chief justice.[28] It had not happened.

L'Heureux-Dubé was quick to disavow any suggestion that Lamer's elevation to chief justice had exacerbated an already difficult relationship. Dickson had a strong influence on the selection of his successor, she stressed, and he was a proponent of returning to tradition, which meant the senior Quebec judge. Lamer was first in line.[29] Dickson's only concern about Lamer was his marital status, she added. "He went to Lamer and said, 'Clean up your act. Get married.' Lamer divorced [his first wife] right away, and married Danièle. He was named."[30] What was more, L'Heureux-Dubé was adamant that she had no desire to become chief justice. "Me? I was already in over my head. I didn't think I had the capacity, the authority, or the brain. I was very new at the court at the time. I was lost in a certain way. There was never any thought in my mind that I would fit the bill in any way possible. No way."[31]

Globe and Mail reporter Kirk Makin, who conducted in-depth interviews with both Lamer and L'Heureux-Dubé over their years on the court, had observations of his own:

> They both sort of became perceived as caped crusaders of opposing forces. He was the lion of the defence bar. She became the hero of Crowns [and] victims. [They were] both reformers in a different way. It's part of her charm and part of what infuriated certain people, [that] she was just so out there about what she thought. I came to view her as this fascinating, forthright, sometimes comical figure, who just has a congenital need to say what's on her mind. [Then] picture Lamer, the way he was, sitting back. He was in a way her equal in terms of his lack of innate caution. They both were outliers in terms of [being] outspoken, uncaring, let it all hang out ...
>
> People are so used to ... the judiciary cloaking everything in nuanced, subtle signals, little word phrases. They don't come right out and say it. And she would just sit there and come right out and say it. Much like Lamer. They both are in a category of their own when it comes to candour, devil-may-care, flaunting of their viewpoint.[32]

The Effect of the Hostilities on the Wider Court and Beyond

Over time, the acrimony became widely known within the court. Jack Major explained that Lamer and L'Heureux-Dubé "were at odds most of the time," and described it as "real animosity between the two of them."[33] Michel Bastarache called it a "continuing feud," adding: "It wasn't a very positive atmosphere in the court because of that."[34] L'Heureux-Dubé's law clerk Peter Sankoff said that "things could get a little snippy at times, to put it mildly. She and Lamer exchanged some unpleasant emails, the judicial equivalent of Armageddon."[35]

The sparks that flew often upset others. L'Heureux-Dubé remembered one shouting match where "Tony and I had harsh words, and Beverley [McLachlin] covered her eyes. She hates conflict."[36] One meltdown between L'Heureux-Dubé and Lamer grew so intense that the law clerks could overhear the shouting in the hallway. They described Lamer yelling at L'Heureux-Dubé, "No one wants you here. Why don't you just leave?

Justice Michel Bastarache, colleague of L'Heureux-Dubé on the Supreme Court of Canada, post-retirement, Ottawa, 2009.

You're nothing to the court. Why don't you resign?" She yelled back, "I'm going to be here after you are. Do what you like."[37] Even Mulroney knew of the hostilities. "She and Tony Lamer had some exchanges of views that I'm told were interesting," he said diplomatically.[38]

The feuding sometimes expressed itself humorously, although usually in jokes with an edge. One interchange arose out of an overture from Prime Minister Jean Chretien's office to L'Heureux-Dubé about potentially naming her lieutenant-governor of Quebec. She indicated that she was not interested in what she viewed as a figurehead position, but used the discussion to tease Lamer.[39] "We had a court dinner or something, and I said to Tony, in front of the others, 'I would like you to know before everybody knows that I was asked to be the lieutenant-governor of Quebec.' He looked at me with a smile up to his ears. [He] saw me gone already. I waited for a little moment. 'But Tony, I hate to disappoint you, but I refused.' Oh my gosh, his face went down. Everyone was laughing."[40]

A former law clerk, who preferred not to be named, remembered seeing the judges gathering for a meeting when L'Heureux-Dubé brought Lamer a cup of tea. Lamer's response, overheard by many, was, "Thank you, what did you put in it?" Ian Binnie, who joined the court in 1998, recalled another incident: "We were going to Lake Carling for the court retreat. The brochure for the hotel showed a giant bubble bath, [with] this rather attractive woman in the bubbles. [We were in the conference room] and somebody said, 'I can imagine Claire disporting in this bubble bath.' Tony muttered something to her – they sat next to each other in the conference [room]. She burst out laughing, and said, 'What Tony said was, 'Yes, face down.'"[41] A man famous for his own wry sense of humour, Binnie added: "On one level, you could say that is horrendous, but on another, the whole thing had got to a kind of bantering level. They knew they were expected to make remarks about each other, and did."[42]

L'Heureux-Dubé made things significantly more difficult by making no secret of the hostilities, speaking of it to friends, judges, lawyers, and law students. Binnie recalled sitting beside her at a dinner after a mooting event at the University of Western Ontario, while he was still a Toronto litigator and several years before he joined the court. He described the awkward interaction that ensued: "She launched into a denunciation of Tony Lamer. Why she should be sharing this with me seemed unusual."[43] Queen's law professor Don Stuart observed the same thing when L'Heureux-Dubé came to speak at the law school in Kingston. He recalled that she would say: "The whole problem is Tony." Stuart was taken aback that she was so critical in public.[44] Speaking with *Globe and Mail* reporter Kirk Makin several years after his retirement, Lamer professed to be stymied over L'Heureux-Dubé's public disparagement of him, saying, "I don't understand. Ask her. I never criticized her in public and never will." Then he added: "She said so much about me that at some point in time, her credibility suffered. I couldn't be that bad."[45]

Danièle Tremblay-Lamer said that L'Heureux-Dubé's critical comments were often relayed back to her husband. "People would mention to me, 'It's terrible what she's saying.'"[46] When she urged her husband to fight back, he refused, adding that he wouldn't stoop to "playing the same game." She thought her husband's silence was rooted in compassion. "[Claire] lost her husband. She had a very frustrating life. It may explain aspects of her personality."[47] Others noticed more of a pushback from Lamer. Louise Arbour added: "I don't know why it was so personal, so visible inside the court. Claire is not particularly discreet. [Tony was] perhaps more restrained, [but] the more public she became, the less he was restrained."[48] Professor Stuart witnessed both giving as much as they got: "Justice Lamer and Justice L'Heureux-Dubé were like oil and vinegar. Both were equally critical, [making] very clear cracks at each other [in

Claire L'Heureux-Dubé and Antonio Lamer on the bench.

public]. I'm a gossiping criminal law prof and it always surprised me nevertheless. They had no sense of privacy at all [and] no respect for the Supreme Court. [They should not have] put this into the public realm."[49]

L'Heureux-Dubé's Deepening Isolation on the Court

The discord with Lamer may have laid the foundation for L'Heureux-Dubé's discomfort on the court, but other Supreme Court judges felt the lack of community as well. The *Globe and Mail* described the court in the decade of the 1990s in harsh terms: "factionalized, overworked and demoralized."[50] Some of it was inevitably attributable to the institution itself. Frank Iacobucci, appointed in 1991, emphasized the distinction between the courts of appeal and the Supreme Court of Canada: "The opportunities for collegiality are greater in courts of appeal. There you sit in threes [and] you change the sittings. [With the Supreme Court,] it is nine people from all different parts of the country [and] different backgrounds, all of which contributes to its strengths. But because of that diversity, you don't have the kind of feeling [that you do] on the courts of appeal ... You're together all of the time, and you don't get relief. What surprised me was there wasn't this ethos of strong collegiality."[51]

Michel Bastarache was in complete agreement, adding that "when you're on the Court of Appeal, you're a bench of three, but you've got twenty friends out there in the corridor. You can go and sit down with them when you don't feel you're getting anywhere with the smaller group. They give you more perspective. When you are always with the same group, it's frustrating. It hampers open and free discussion. You're limited to these eight people. And it's not really eight because there's always been two or three who don't talk [and] won't share anything." It was, he concluded, "very circumscribed" and "difficult."[52] L'Heureux-Dubé's law clerk Cynthia Westaway believed that the structure created unavoidable "work stress," adding: "They went at each other [because] they needed an outlet. They were so pent up."[53]

L'Heureux-Dubé also contributed her share to the chilliness that some of her colleagues felt. Although she had been deeply offended by the reception she received upon her arrival, she did not hesitate to pass along her own thoughts to judges who came later. Iacobucci remembered her meeting him with the greeting: "Frank, I think you're terrific, but I wish you were a woman." As her law clerk David Wright observed, "she's not good at understanding how things she says are hurtful."[54] Given her adamant disavowal of affirmative action for judicial appointments, it was also a surprising comment. And as Iacobucci admitted, it "rankled a bit." He added that L'Heureux-Dubé's irrepressible personality did much to lessen the sting: "I think that the woman that I hugged the most, after my wife and my daughter, was Claire. And yet I could be disagreeing with her fundamentally on a legal question. That wouldn't matter in terms of the kind of person she was."[55] Observers suggested that L'Heureux-Dubé and Iacobucci temperamentally ought to have been closer, but that "they didn't trust each other on jurisprudence."[56]

The gender of an appointee was not L'Heureux-Dubé's only bone of contention. She also spoke critically to Louise Arbour when she was appointed in 1999. Arbour recalled: "In personal terms, she is very hard not to like, but she could not hide her disappointment when I was appointed. [She] made it very clear I was not her first choice. She was very happy when I left, that it made room for others."[57] Even after Lamer retired in 2000 and the next chief justice, Beverley McLachlin, made great efforts to foster a new atmosphere of cooperation, L'Heureux-Dubé remained at odds with those whom she felt had sided with Lamer. Arbour observed: "Our disagreements on criminal law issues [were] eminently predictable. I was pro-accused, she thought, and that was the end of it. She's very difficult to debate with. She was a handful. I figured out pretty quickly that there were tensions between Claire and Tony ... between Claire and the court, frankly."[58]

L'Heureux-Dubé's colleagues had differing recollections of her behaviour during the judicial conferences following the hearings. Michel Bastarache described her as "very undisciplined." Instead of following the custom of speaking in seniority, junior to senior, without interruption, he recalled that she "interrupted all the time. She didn't follow the rules. So if one or the other was saying something she didn't approve of, she would right away say she didn't approve, or ask a question. Tony would, every time, stop her and say, 'No, you know this is not the rule. Let the person have his say. You'll have your turn later.' Then she'd get into an argument with him right away."[59] Bastarache gave an illustration of the type of pointed exchanges that took place:

> I remember many times, especially on section 15 [*Charter*] cases, we'd go around the table, and [Lamer] spoke last. When he started saying something, he hadn't said ten words, she'd interrupt and say, "You don't believe in equality anyway, you never did." Where do you go from there? She did that often ... He would always fire back, so then they'd get into a real nasty discussion, and then everybody else just wanted to get out. There was no point in trying to get a real debate going.[60]

Frank Iacobucci admitted that, given her "energy," her "drive," and her "passion," L'Heureux-Dubé might have interrupted out of turn from time to time. "She would argue with you more than most ... but I don't recall it as being a negative thing."[61] Binnie was of a similar view. "She would interject with observations, [but] I certainly don't think she ever tried to monopolize the discussion. She had a habit ... she would make an intervention and then she would laugh ... [but I] don't remember dismissive comments, personally."[62]

L'Heureux-Dubé's notoriously long working hours also contributed to the insularity. She startled the RCMP security by ordering pizza to the courthouse at midnight.[63] She worked weekends. She thought nothing of phoning her clerks at 2 a.m. if she had a question about one of their memos. Then she moved a cot into her office and took to sleeping there overnight when she worked late. Someone objected that the cot "had to go," that it broadcast the wrong message that a judge was being "worked to the bone."[64] Others thought that the court had become her life, with some marvelling that her family tragedies had not caused her "to slide right off the rails completely" and some speculating that she might have retreated into her work to escape the memories of the devastation.⁶⁵ Her law clerks staunchly defended her work ethic, attributing it to her deep engagement in the work and her insistence upon producing the best decisions possible.⁶⁶

But quite a few of her colleagues felt there was grandstanding involved. Louise Arbour explained: "A lot of people ridiculed her self-described workaholic lifestyle. 'I sleep on my couch in my office' did not go [over] well. A lot of people [would] say, 'This is a job that virtually everybody else manages to do in reasonable hours. You must be slow if you can't manage.' What she portrayed as ... extreme devotion to work was perceived by others as 'What's your problem?'" While Arbour also agreed that L'Heureux-Dubé was "very curious" and "engaged," she added that her colleague's self-portrayal distanced her from the others in the court. The implication was that the other judges "did not work enough," or "did not care enough." "It was part of the 'me and them' image," Arbour added.⁶⁷ Jack Major emphasized that the hours she put in were not always on cases: "I said to her on a couple of occasions [that] I could spend as much time as you do here, Claire, if I read the *New York Times* on the computer."⁶⁸ Ian Binnie added that during her last years on the court, "by the time I got there, Claire devoted a lot of time to ... speeches, lectures ... and she was on this network of judges who give their thoughts to one another. She spent a lot of time, but much of it was networking the network."⁶⁹

Jack Major mentioned that he could not think of anybody who "disliked Claire on a personal basis." But equally, he could not think of "anybody that worked with her. She was sort of an island to herself in some respects." Major's last words on the subject captured it well: "Just frequently Claire was in her own zone, you might say."⁷⁰

28
Fifteen Years of Jurisprudence, 1987–2002
"The Great Dissenter"

"In her own zone" was how Jack Major described his colleague Claire L'Heureux-Dubé at the Supreme Court of Canada. It may have been apt for the last two-thirds of her tenure. It was not accurate for the first.[1] It is true that she came into the court marked as an outsider – by gender, French Quebec heritage, reputation as a specialist in family law, and flamboyant personality. But during her first five years, her jurisprudence was solidly in line with that of her colleagues. It was not until the 1990s that she began to gain a reputation as a leader on equality issues and a law-and-order judge on the criminal side. It was also then that she acquired the title of "the Great Dissenter."

During her fifteen years on the court, L'Heureux-Dubé participated in 1,219 decisions.[2] Her jurisprudence has inspired a stream of academic analysis, books, and law journal articles.[3] Instead of attempting to replicate that, this biography will focus on her reputation, the surprising change over time, and her proclivity for issuing dissents. Her contribution to Quebec civil law will not be probed here. Her erudite command of Roman and French law in *Houle v. Canadian National Bank* (1990), where she re-evaluated the proper recourse for abuse of contractual rights, and her expansion of compensation entitlements in *Augustus v. Gosset* (1996) and *Quebec (Public Curator) v. Syndicat national des employés de l'hôpital St-Ferdinand* (1996) are more properly left to the experts in civil law.[4] Instead, this biography will devote separate chapters to profiling six other important cases – *Seaboyer* (1991), *Moge* (1992), *Mossop* (1993), *Symes* (1993), the *Quebec*

Re-creation of cartoon of L'Heureux-Dubé, drawn by an unidentified law clerk.

Reference (1998), and *Baker* (1999) – before revisiting *Ewanchuk*, the cause célèbre that brought her to the centre of public attention.[5]

Most observers have characterized L'Heureux-Dubé as "progressive" in social justice matters and "conservative" in criminal law during her Supreme Court years.[6] In the field of social justice, she was perceived as an innovator who was eager to embrace novel claims, a human rights icon, and a judge who grounded equality law in social context evidence. She championed women's rights, gave unprecedented recognition to gays and lesbians, and supported victims of sexual assault.[7] In criminal law, she gained a reputation for being tough on criminals, willing to uphold convictions in the face of police misdeeds, and reluctant to accept defences based on technicalities.[8] One defence lawyer bluntly called her a judge "who never met a Crown attorney she didn't like."[9]

Many have found the two halves of this reputation inherently contradictory. Supreme Court colleague Louise Arbour expressed surprise that

Fifteen Years of Jurisprudence   361

L'Heureux-Dubé failed to demonstrate "empathy" toward or "understanding" of criminal defendants.[10] Law professor Rosemary Cairns Way pointed out that for an egalitarian judge, it was a gap that was "particularly troubling" in the context of an "anti-egalitarian" and "highly punitive" sentencing regime.[11] Former law clerk Teresa Scassa recalled asking L'Heureux-Dubé directly about the contradiction. She replied: "Well, I don't see it as inconsistent at all. I'm for the little guy. And in the criminal law context, the little guy is the victim."[12] In many ways, L'Heureux-Dubé provided an illustration of why it was almost impossible to slot judges into neatly defined categories.

A PROGRESSIVE EQUALITY LAW JUDGE

In fact, L'Heureux-Dubé's reputation as a progressive social justice jurist is one that accords with her last decade on the Supreme Court, but not the first third of her tenure. Equality-based constitutional claims came on stream in 1985, when section 15 of the *Canadian Charter of Rights and Freedoms* first came into effect. Initially, few cases came forward, and L'Heureux-Dubé mostly signed on to the opinions of others. She signed La Forest's majority decision in *Robichaud* in 1987, holding employers liable for the sexual harassment of their workers.[13] She signed Lamer's unanimous 1988 judgment in *Canadian Newspapers Company* to uphold the ban on publication of names of complainants of sexual assault.[14] She signed Gérard La Forest's unanimous 1988 family law decision in *Leblanc v. Leblanc*, awarding a wife the lion's share of property she had amassed during twenty-six years of marriage to an alcoholic husband.[15] In 1989, she signed Bertha Wilson's majority analysis of substantive equality in *Andrews,* John Sopinka's unanimous decision denying Joe Borowski standing to argue for the criminality of abortion, and the court's unanimous decision denying Jean-Guy Tremblay an injunction to stop the abortion of a fetus he had inseminated.[16] She signed Wilson's 1989 dissent in *Vorvis* asserting that an employer should pay punitive damages for the mental suffering of a fired employee, Brian Dickson's unanimous rulings that sexual harassment and discrimination based on pregnancy constituted sexual discrimination in *Janzen* and *Brooks* in 1989, and Dickson's majority decision upholding the criminal prohibition on hate propaganda in *Keegstra* in 1990.[17]

She wrote a few progressive early decisions herself. Her concurring opinion in *Gagnon* in 1988 refused to deny an injured worker employment insurance benefits because he had been temporarily unavailable for work.[18] Her dissent in *Prassad* in 1989 claimed that administrative fair process should be extended to an immigrant facing deportation.[19] Her dissent in 1989 in *Syndicat des employés de production du Québec et de l'Acadie* dealt with a claim for equal pay for work of equal value, and held that the human rights commission must entertain input from female CBC employees regarding the methodology to use to conduct the evaluation.[20]

But she also signed on to Sopinka's 1989 unanimous decision that compulsory retirement for firefighters over the age of sixty did not constitute age discrimination.[21] She signed on to Peter Cory's unanimous decision in 1992 denying the Canadian Council of Churches the right to challenge immigration legislation that made it more difficult to obtain refugee status.[22] She supported Sopinka's unanimous ruling in 1992 that reduced the rights of appeal for permanent resident non-citizens facing deportation after conviction for serious offences.[23]

A 1989 political science study described William McIntyre and Claire L'Heureux-Dubé as the Supreme Court judges "most inclined to favour judicial self-restraint."[24] In 1990, L'Heureux-Dubé herself published a law review article complaining that the courts were not "the best forum in which to settle political issues." She equated "attempts to promote political agendas through the courts" as "analogous to attempts to cure a headache with brain surgery."[25] It was reminiscent of a comment she had made to a Montreal reporter in 1987, stressing that judges must apply the *Charter* "*avec circonspection.*"[†] "*Nous ne sommes pas élus,*" she added, "*ce n'est pas à nous de faire la législation.*"[‡, 26]

It was not until 1991, with her path-breaking dissent in *Seaboyer,* that the jurisprudence for which she would become famous surfaced. It presaged a lineup of future equality decisions, including hallmarks such as *Moge, Mossop, Symes, Baker,* and *Ewanchuk.*[27] In 2001, a year before her retirement, she claimed in a *Queen's Law Journal* article that by her fourteenth year on the court, "the label that I now wear as a badge of honour is one that names me as a vigorous proponent of equality."[28] Although her later decisions drew the ire of many who favoured a conservative judicial approach, they also won her fulsome praise from equality advocates.[29]

---

† "with caution"
‡ "We are not elected"; "it is not up to us to pass legislation."

Reputation as a Law-and-Order Judge

Her criminal law reputation was something L'Heureux-Dubé chafed against. "The analysis is very superficial," she complained. "I never had a philosophy that I am for the Crown. I always wanted the thing to be right in the middle – not to bend for or against a side. [Supreme Court of Canada cases] are always grey, never black or white. If it were black or white, the issues would have been settled a long time before. We have to look at the grey cases and decide which way to go for the good of the country."[30]

Classifications of judicial decisions are bound to be complex, since the outcome of cases can hinge on many things that have little to do with any particular judge: the facts, the legal precedents, the quality of the arguments, the socio-political-economic context of the time, and the interactions between the judges on the panel, among other things. However, criminal cases composed the majority of the court's caseload, and quantitative analysis can point to some broader patterns. An assessment of her first five years and her final five years on the court demonstrated that L'Heureux-Dubé ruled for the Crown 76 percent of the time.[31] In this, she seemed in alignment with her other colleagues on the bench who, despite the stark divisions between judges in this era, also ruled for the Crown 65 percent of the time.[32] If there was a law-and-order inclination, it was shared by the other judges.

But L'Heureux-Dubé's criminal law decisions also varied markedly over time. During her first two full years on the court, she held for the Crown at exactly the same rate as the majority of the court: 74 percent in the first year and 78 percent in the second.[33] Then things began to change, with L'Heureux-Dubé ruling for the Crown more frequently than the majority every year thereafter, with the greatest disparity occurring in her last five years. In her thirteenth year, she ruled for the Crown 89 percent of the time, while the court ruled for the Crown 70 percent. In her fourteenth year, the numbers were 77 percent and 64 percent, and in her fifteenth year, 67 percent and 39 percent, respectively.

More useful still is to tally the number of times that L'Heureux-Dubé sided with Lamer, one of the judges reputed for taking the defence perspective. Here the results are surprising. Initially, there was little evidence of the divide that would open up between the two. In her first full year on the court, she agreed with Lamer on criminal cases 96 percent of the time. In her second to fifth years, she agreed with him 83, 75, 62, and 55

Claire L'Heureux-Dubé, Beverley McLachlin, and Antonio Lamer in happier times.

percent of the time, respectively. The numbers were still declining into her last five years on the court. In her eleventh year, she sided with Lamer 48 percent of the time, in her twelfth year 39 percent. It was almost a straight-line trajectory downward, from a surprising 96 percent accord with Lamer at the outset to a low of 39 percent in 1999, the year of Lamer's retirement.[34]

The most obvious conclusion is that the critics were wrong to define L'Heureux-Dubé as consistently pro-prosecution. This is an inaccurate characterization of the first third of her term, although a fair description by the end. The data call into question the notion that judges are predictable, and that more transparent, publicly accountable appointment procedures will allow a better assessment of judicial nominees. One cannot predict from a judge's past record what the future might hold.

By the 1990s, the signs of L'Heureux-Dubé's diminishing concern for the situation of the accused (or, put another way, growing recognition of the needs of vulnerable victims and the community) were evident. In 1990, in *Martineau,* she dissented from Lamer's groundbreaking decision that no one should be convicted of murder without subjective foresight of death.[35] She was the lone dissenter in *Swain* in 1991, where the automatic indeterminate detention of individuals found "not guilty by reason of insanity" was challenged under the *Charter*. Her colleagues all agreed to strike this down as unnecessarily harsh and discriminatory toward those with mental illnesses. L'Heureux-Dubé pronounced the mandatory deprivation of liberty for the criminally insane fully lawful.[36] In 1992, *Généreux* reviewed a *Charter* challenge against military tribunals that tried military personnel separately from the civilian criminal justice system. Lamer's majority judgment found the system flawed, ruling that a military court did not constitute an "independent and impartial tribunal." Once again alone in dissent, L'Heureux-Dubé took the position that the separate system was constitutional. It was essential, she said, to have "rigorous obedience to a rigid hierarchy." The military was "its own society" with "traditions, rules, and taboos which are not within the normal ken of outsiders."[37] In 2002, she took a position in *Sauvé* denying federal prison inmates the right to vote.[38] It was her later decisions – in quantity and quality – that merited the reputation she came to hold.

Shifting Approach over Time: "I Changed"

There had been little in L'Heureux-Dubé's record in the lower courts to predict her flowering as an activist social justice judge or her reputation as being tough on crime. Even after her elevation to the Supreme Court of Canada, it took years for both of these trends to surface.[39] Isolation and longevity may explain some of this. Initially at the nation's top court, she was striving to prove herself within an environment in which she was a stark outsider. She went with the flow. As she became more settled at the apex of the judicial pyramid, she gained confidence in her own experience and exercised greater independence. Did this reflect some alteration in judicial philosophy? Or was it the real core that she revealed in her last decade, aspects muted until she found her footing? Can we identify factors that may have contributed to this jurisprudential change? The question is best explored separately on the social justice issues and the criminal law front.

One factor that may account for the shifting social justice perspectives was the role of her law clerks. Introduced to the Supreme Court in 1968, the number of law clerks assigned to each judge had risen from one to two in the wake of the *Charter* in 1982, and to three in 1989.[40] During her fifteen years there, L'Heureux-Dubé worked with forty-three law clerks.[41]

Hired from the ranks of the top law students across the nation, the clerks recommended which appeals to accept, wrote "bench memos" summarizing the cases prior to oral argument, did extensive legal research, and often drafted and edited the decisions under instruction from their judges.[42] Some of the judges kept their clerks at "a considerable distance," taking "little or no interest in any opinions" they might offer.[43] L'Heureux-Dubé did not.

She was known for her free-wheeling discussions with clerks, even "late at night over a pizza" or at the weekend cottage.[44] "For me," she added, "it's been the greatest thing to have law clerks to be able to discuss with ... to explore ideas. They were the only ones we were talking to."[45] Markedly different from the more formal, reserved style of the other judges, L'Heureux-Dubé would invite her clerks into her chambers to celebrate their birthdays, their calls to the bar, and other occasions with champagne.[46] She may have felt isolated from her peers, but she was surrounded by a group of young, high-achieving, enthusiastic, newly minted law graduates with whom she interacted daily. Her law clerks worked around the clock, collecting "huge stacks of material" that she instructed them to compile. The voluminous materials stretched well beyond traditional cases and law texts to encompass philosophical, social, and economic literature, which she read at work, while travelling, and even on holidays.[47] Buttressed by teams of law clerks, top-flight researchers all, she found her horizons widening. Her own recognition of the context and consequences of decisions broadened significantly.

L'Heureux-Dubé's work ethic was invaluable to the task. Her court attendant André Legault explained that the heavy workload made it almost impossible to plan vacations and days off. "She didn't like laziness and she didn't like fools." He recalled that for many of the law clerks, the initial breaking-in period was a shock. The woman who brooked no slippage in standards from the lawyers who appeared before her was equally rigorous with her clerks. "The first memo the law clerks would write," recalled Legault, would be returned "full of red marks" and "scratches." As the one who had to return those to the clerks, he added ruefully, "I've seen more tears ..."[48]

Although L'Heureux-Dubé hired both male and female clerks, some noticed disparate treatment. Former law clerk Cynthia Westaway explained: "To be honest, there was an impression that she would be harder on women."[49] It was a sentiment echoed by other female clerks as well.[50] Westaway believed it was because L'Heureux-Dubé wanted "so much" for women that she "put them through the wringer more" than male clerks, who would "not need that extra toughness."[51] Whether they were male or female, Legault's assessment was that most of the clerks adjusted when they realized how hard L'Heureux-Dubé herself worked. "I'd say a good 90 percent loved her," he said.[52]

Former law clerk Laurie Sargent thought that the new social justice dimensions in L'Heureux-Dubé's judgments "surely had a lot to do with her clerks." Sargent contrasted the academic backgrounds of the law clerks with the doctrinal black letter legal education the judges had received years earlier: "It's a generational thing, being exposed to people who were now educated in law schools with feminist courses, critical legal studies courses, law and society courses."[53] Did L'Heureux-Dubé set about consciously to hire clerks with progressive social justice leanings? Jocelyn Downie, one of Lamer's former law clerks, commented that L'Heureux-Dubé had a reputation, more than the other judges, of hiring feminist clerks with human rights orientations.[54] L'Heureux-Dubé's own opinion was that she looked first for people who "knew how to write," and second for people who were "on the same wavelength as me. People who were interested in human rights issues, women's discrimination, people who understood the issues I was interested in. I had enough of quarrelling with my colleagues. I didn't want to quarrel with the clerks."[55] Writing skills aside, her sense of being an outsider, isolated on the court, appears to have led her to choose clerks likely to be more attuned to "the little guy," the community she was coming to define as in need of greater judicial support. This was the circle within which her most significant analysis and debate now occurred.

Did L'Heureux-Dubé think her clerks changed her mind on the cases? She thought that the law clerks did make a difference, especially in terms of the research they compiled. "When you write alone, you can't be as thorough. They would bring these things to me and say, 'Do you think we could incorporate that?' I would say yes or no." But "as far as changing my mind," she added, "I don't recall one incident."[56] Mind changing is one thing, introduction of new influences another. The clerks themselves often marvelled at how open to discussion L'Heureux-Dubé was with them. Clearly, given the differences in age and hierarchical position between judge and law clerk, these discussions could not be depicted as debates among equals. However, former law clerk Peter Sankoff sensed that L'Heureux-Dubé welcomed the views of her clerks. "We could call her at any time. She wanted to know anything we thought. She would always say, 'If you don't agree, come to me.' I got her to listen to my points. I'm not going to say I swayed her, but we talked a point through. I had her ear ... she would listen. [Some of the other] judges didn't want to have that conversation."[57]

Jocelyn Downie, who clerked for Lamer, agreed that L'Heureux-Dubé was open to discussing cases with her clerks in a way that was not common with many of the other judges, "who knew what they wanted their clerks to do, and that was that – you took instructions."[58] Teresa Scassa was equally surprised by L'Heureux-Dubé's receptivity to discussion: "What she did with it in the end was her own decision. But you could go to her and say, 'I'm really troubled by this.' She would listen and talk. [It was] remarkable."[59] And former law clerk Michelle Flaherty recalled a number of times when L'Heureux-Dubé initially took a position that she later completely departed from: "Her ideology sometimes sent her in particular directions,

L'Heureux-Dubé with law clerks Adam Dodek, Laurie Sargent, and Michelle Flaherty.

Fifteen Years of Jurisprudence

L'Heureux-Dubé with law clerk Teresa Scassa.

L'Heureux-Dubé with law clerks David Wright, Eric Marcoux, and Cynthia Westaway.

but not to the point of being close minded about other views."⁶⁰ L'Heureux-Dubé's openness to discussion with her law clerks contrasted with what some of her judicial colleagues felt was a lack of openness to discussion with them, and a particular rigidity of views.⁶¹

The new influences that the young law clerks brought to L'Heureux-Dubé's chambers did not fall into a vacuum. L'Heureux-Dubé had a personal history replete with incidents of discrimination. Her efforts to pursue a legal career had met with resistance from her father and Laval administrators, who did not believe that women could be lawyers. She had been denied a Laval scholarship on spurious grounds and ruled ineligible for a Rhodes Scholarship because of her gender. She had been sexually harassed as a secretary. Her job prospects as a legal practitioner were severely circumscribed by gender discrimination. She had observed multifaceted discrimination against female lawyers. She had seen her family law clients mistreated because of their gender. She had found herself treated differently as a female judge. It was first-hand life experience that potentially enhanced her ability to recognize discrimination and to comprehend the damage that inequality inflicted upon its victims. For decades L'Heureux-Dubé had resisted any suggestion that she had suffered from disparate treatment or that there was such a thing as a distinct female perspective. Now, as one of the nation's top judges, she was reading literature that articulated minority views, she was debating with law clerks who were eager to expand judicial horizons, and she was presented with more opportunities to issue decisions that attempted to dismantle discrimination. She embraced the challenge with enthusiasm.

The transformation in L'Heureux-Dubé's criminal law decisions presents a different set of questions. The first observation is that her law-and-order reputation became so dominant that almost no one seemed to recognize that she had ever produced a more pro-defence set of rulings. In fact, the quantifiable shift was news to her judicial colleagues, many of whom expressed astonishment over the numbers.⁶² L'Heureux-Dubé herself admitted that she was startled to see the statistical change in criminal law outcomes over time, and even more so by the symmetry between Lamer's and her decisions during the early years.⁶³ The reputation had overwhelmed the earlier record to the point of the latter's obliteration.

Did the troubled relationship between L'Heureux-Dubé and Lamer contribute to the change? Asked what might account for the discernible change, she burst out laughing and said: "Tony got bolder!"⁶⁴ She was quick to add, "I don't think I changed," but conceded that the conflicts between her and Lamer may have driven some of their criminal law rulings: "I figured out at one point that Lamer was [leaning toward] the defence beyond what was acceptable, so I dissented."[65]

Other observers agreed. Saskatchewan Chief Justice Edward Bayda thought that the conflict with Lamer "may have spurred [L'Heureux-Dubé] on to be more independent."[66] David Wright, another former law clerk, believed that "they were instrumental in forming each other's jurisprudence."[67] Rosalie Abella, at the time an Ontario Court of Appeal judge, offered a contextual explanation. She suggested that L'Heureux-Dubé's record could be understood only "if one remembers the climate in which her most important judgments" were produced:

> Judicially, she found herself for a full decade on a court in which the jurisprudential trajectory was criminal law. This concentration, perhaps an inevitable second chapter to the human rights–oriented *Charter* story launched by Chief Justice Dickson, exponentially expanded the rights of the accused and held the state to stricter account. It was not a comfortable philosophical environment for a judge whose sympathies lay openly with victims and the protection of the public ... [A]ll [her decisions] reflect her indomitable resistance to what she saw as a judicial flow of indifference to the rights of the victims of crimes.[68]

That "judicial flow" and that "resistance" became personified by two Supreme Court judges, unleashing a duet of opposites that echoed well into their retirement. Ten years after she left the court, L'Heureux-Dubé remained unrelentingly critical of Lamer's criminal decisions: "He was only for the criminal. He was a defence lawyer all his life, so he was a defence lawyer on the bench. He acted as if he were the Law Commission, not a judge. He didn't care what the law was. He just changed it to what he wanted it to be."[69] The concerns she expressed about Lamer's criminal law decisions must have been reciprocated by *his* dismay over *her* growing proclivity to dismiss the interests of the accused. When he gave an interview to *Globe and Mail* journalist Kirk Makin in 2002, Lamer summed it up: "Philosophically, we disagreed fundamentally about 90 per cent of everything."[70]

Did L'Heureux-Dubé's shift in social justice philosophy also help to explain the shift in criminal law rulings? Certainly, in the field of sexual assault, the two overlap. Greater protections for women and children who experience sexual and physical violence frequently result in reduced protections for men accused of these crimes. L'Heureux-Dubé's expanded focus on victims of abuse necessarily meant less openness to many defence arguments.

Were there other factors to account for the shift? They were unlikely to have included the influence of her law clerks, who were frequently anxious over L'Heureux-Dubé's prosecutorial leanings but failed to convince her in this field. Did her traumatic familial experience with the criminal activities of her son, Pierre, factor into her hardening law-and-order rulings? Did his involvement with illicit drugs convince her that criminalization was an important component of eradicating drug abuse? Did her experience with Pierre's stay at the Boscoville juvenile facility influence her thinking about the need for long stretches of incarceration? In her view, the short answer was no, that this was something separate, without influence on her jurisprudence.[71] The emphatic denial is not surprising, given the importance placed on judges' deciding cases strictly on the objective facts and law. Whether any of us is capable of shutting out searing personal events from our frameworks of analysis is less certain.

When asked for her wider reflections about the jurisprudential shifts, L'Heureux-Dubé was initially hesitant to consider such questions. That did not surprise her daughter, Louise Dubé, who described her mother as someone who preferred to attribute her judgments to "common sense." "I think the reality is more complex," explained Louise, "and I think she herself wants to discredit that complexity."[72] Over a decade after her retirement, in interviews for this biography, L'Heureux-Dubé recognized that she *had* changed her approach while on the bench. In a remarkably open assessment, she mused about that change:

> It's normal, we change with the dimension of the work. On the Superior Court, it's motor vehicle accidents, nothing of that kind of vision that you have to develop when you deal with the *Charter*, with ideas. At the Court of Appeal, there is a little more, but [we sat as] three colleagues on the bench, we were all close friends, [there was] more exchange between us. I compromised. I didn't actually compromise on principle. I was principled back then too, but [I] did not worry about changes that were not really important. I was more obedient to my three colleagues on the bench.
>
> [There is] no doubt the Supreme Court is making the law. You have to decide for the future. It's more of a question of principles and vision on the Supreme Court. You have to have a vision if you are making the law. [I] didn't have that before. When I went there, I didn't know who I was really. And I didn't want to know especially, except that I had to. At the Supreme

Court, we have to define ourselves much more – who we are, where we are, which we don't know before necessarily. I changed. It takes time to get there. You don't know quite what direction until you get there. I defined myself better [and] found out who I was. It's in the nature of the Supreme Court cases. They force you to find out who you are. I became more of myself.[73]

Her comments suggest that her evolving jurisprudence may have reflected the changing nature of the cases before her, the altered dynamics between judicial colleagues, and the need to articulate a stronger self-definition. Her comments fail to resolve the question of whether the new "principles and vision" were fresh perspectives for her, or simply a better-defined version of long-standing views, more of what she had always believed in her heart. Was it a coming to grips with a fresh new vision? Was it a matter of finding out who she really had been? Perhaps the best answer is that it was a combination of both.

"The Great Dissenter"

L'Heureux-Dubé's many dissents during her years on the Supreme Court ultimately brought her the title of "the Great Dissenter."[74] She was the second judge in the history of the court to be so labelled, after Bora Laskin, the first judge of Jewish heritage on the top court.[75] It was a designation that initially surprised L'Heureux-Dubé. "I didn't go there to do dissents," she emphasized.[76] "You don't dissent for the pleasure of dissenting. It's much harder to write a dissent and to try to destroy the other side than it is to say 'Yes' and do nothing. It takes a bit of courage."[77] She traced some of that courage to her family: "My mother was like that. My father was like that. And my grandfather and my grandmother. So I think it's in the genes not to be afraid."[78] It echoed her life history as a woman who had challenged the rules within her family, at the convent, in her selection of career, and as a practising lawyer. And it fit with her self-description as a person who loved conflict.

The first time she reflected in depth on the genre of dissents was in 1999, at a meeting of the International Association of Comparative Law, where she discovered that there was no tradition of dissenting judgments in France. The rationale? The French believed in the "stability of law."[79] L'Heureux-Dubé found this shocking: "It's totally ridiculous because society is not stable, so [the] law should move. Dissents are the law of the future."[80] A French law professor asked her to compose an article on dissents, and she began to work with her law clerk Laurie Sargent to produce an article that critiqued the concept of judicial unanimity, arguing that the goal should not be stability but justice. Sargent's enthusiasm would have added greatly, since she recalled studying L'Heureux-Dubé's dissents at McGill: "As a law student, I remember thinking how important it was to hear her voice coming through in dissent [in] the *Seaboyer* case and others. Finally there was a voice in jurisprudence that spoke to me."[81]

It was a philosophy often attributed to the American legal realist Karl Llewellyn, who conceived of the law as "constantly in flux as judges created and discarded law to meet social needs."[82] It was also another sign that L'Heureux-Dubé's philosophy had changed from her earlier formalist decisions grounded in judicial restraint, and that she had become more of a "realist" judge, described by American judge Richard A. Posner as someone who "realizes and is prepared within reason to act on the realization that, at any moment a significant portion of legal doctrines, procedures, usages and so forth, are obsolete and should be reformed or jettisoned."[83]

Marie-Claire Belleau and Rebecca Johnson, both former law clerks of L'Heureux-Dubé, calculated that she dissented in 39 percent of her written judgments, while penning separate concurring opinions in another 35 percent of her written reasons.[84] When the non-unanimous decisions of all twenty-six Supreme Court judges who sat between 1982 and 2008 are compared, her average rate of dissent of 63.3 percent was higher than that of any of her contemporaries, fully justifying her reputation as *"la grande dissidente."*[85] In their qualitative examination of L'Heureux-Dubé's dissents, Belleau and Johnson noted that although law was traditionally perceived to "sublimate the role of emotion in decision-making," her dissenting opinions "were deeply invested with passion and emotion," which in turn seemed to inspire "an interesting mixture of public adulation and fury."[86] They added that that there was "no pretence here of a supposed unemotional, neutral, and detached position." Indeed, because dissents were "located in the world, not of the real but of the possible," a judge could rely more heavily on the "tools of passion and desire," posing "challenges to deeper understandings of concepts like justice, objectivity and common sense."[87] Although dissenting opinions lacked the force of law, they were designed with different audiences in mind: judicial colleagues, the parties, future litigants, academics and law students, other courts, legislatures, and the public at large.[88]

Writing in the *Osgoode Hall Law Journal* two years before her retirement, L'Heureux-Dubé described dissents as "innovative yet, paradoxically, potentially stabilizing forces in the law, particularly when these opinions are oriented toward the future and invite dialogue with those who are unsatisfied with, or feel excluded by, the majority decision."[89] It was a perspective shared by American legal historian Melvin I. Urofsky, who described dissents as a powerful agent of dialogue that was "part of a larger conversation that goes on in a democracy."[90] In an interview with Laval law professor Louise Langevin five years after her retirement, L'Heureux-Dubé suggested that dissenting judges, often individuals "born before our time," could become "the voice of the future."[91] Occasionally, this brought little comfort to the litigators who appeared in front of her. Ottawa lawyer David Scott, QC, quipped: "Our motto was, 'If Justice L'Heureux-Dubé agrees with you, you're sinking.' She [once] asked me a question about the argument I was making, and then rephrased it perfectly, in a way that made it clear she both understood and supported the position we were taking. I felt my spirits sag."[92]

L'Heureux-Dubé's penchant for dissenting did not endear her to her colleagues, who often struggled to collaborate on reasons. Once a judge signalled an intention to issue a dissent, everything was put on hold. John Sopinka, who joined the court in 1988, explained to the *Ottawa Citizen*: "When somebody has announced they will be writing a dissent, it's courtesy that nobody concurs with the majority judgment until they've read the dissent ... to give the dissenter a chance to persuade the court that they're right."[93] Judicial colleague Michel Bastarache was of the view that L'Heureux-Dubé "always prided herself on being a dissenter," although he believed that there were real stresses associated with doing so. In his view, L'Heureux-Dubé was so often in dissent because "she never tried to convince [the others.] She tried to confront all the time. She was always in a confrontation, especially with Tony [Lamer], but almost as much with people like Jack Major."[94] Her former law clerk Pascale Fournier thought it might have reflected the challenges L'Heureux-Dubé had faced: "She had to fight hard to be where she was. It was my way or the highway. She was not willing to compromise. She had strong core values. I used to wonder why she wouldn't just change the tone of her decisions a little bit, and then she might have had the majority. But she was not willing to go there."[95] Louise Arbour was critical of L'Heureux-Dubé's dissents. "[Some thought that] Claire was just getting her name out there. She made very clear that when she saw a gender angle in something, she owned the issue. [I]f you believe that you need to construct your jurisprudence, then it's better you say something about everything. The quotable quote. You feel it's critical that the world understand you have a slightly different angle. It's all about you.'"[96]

L'Heureux-Dubé's former law clerk Andrew Lenz disagreed: "I think people believe that she kind of took pleasure in being an outlier and a contrarian. I don't think that's true. I think she was more cooperative with her colleagues than people give her credit for, and I think when she dissented it was because she felt she had to. I think she has strong views, for sure. But it wasn't like she was doing this for sport."[97] Alberta Chief Justice Catherine Fraser felt similarly: "I think she's a person of immense courage. I think if she were the only one that thought what she was doing was right, she would still pursue that and not be crushed by the burdens that put on her as a person. She's very strong, and not only intellectually but physically, morally, [and] psychologically." It was, Fraser added, "one of the reasons" that enabled her to become so "powerful."[98]

Selected Cases

29
Sexual Assault
Seaboyer, 1991

R. v. Seaboyer was the first blockbuster case to herald Claire L'Heureux-Dubé's emergence as a courageous dissenter, an equality advocate, and a judge who was prepared to short-circuit criminal defence arguments. *Seaboyer* was a signature decision, a milestone ruling that brought her into public view as no previous decision had done.[1] It was a sea change from her earlier, more cautious judicial pronouncements and a sign that she was going to stand, distinct, from her colleagues on the court. According to Toronto journalist Sean Fine, the "passionate eighty-six page" opinion made her "an instant hero to women."[2]

Like *Ewanchuk,* which followed eight years later, *Seaboyer* focused on sexual assault. At the heart of the case lay the treatment of women who testified about acts of sexual coercion. At issue was whether lawyers representing the accused men were entitled to inquire into women's sexual history. It was a touchy subject. For centuries, defence lawyers had had wide latitude to cross-examine complainants about their sexual pasts.[3] Questions could be asked about both reputation and conduct.[4] The criminal law had a long history of distinguishing between "pure" and "promiscuous" women, and many of the sex crimes defined in the *Criminal Code* had originally restricted protection to women of "previously chaste character."[5] In 1877, in its first ruling on the matter, the Supreme Court had proclaimed that evidence of extramarital sexual relations was "manifestly calculated to affect the character, and as a consequence, the credibility" of a woman who complained of rape.[6]

These rules became a major bone of contention for the feminist movement of the 1970s and 1980s. Feminists claimed that the wide-ranging cross-examinations constituted discrimination against sexually unconventional women and enshrined the "sexual double standard" in law. They emphasized that men accused of sexual assault were not subjected to scrutiny of their sexual histories.[7] They argued that the rules resulted in disproportionately low conviction rates in sexual assault cases. Statistics Canada recorded a 44.4 percent conviction rate for rape, compared with 85.5 percent for indictable offences generally.[8] Feminists took the position that a woman's prior sexual history was never relevant to the question of whether she had been sexually assaulted in the present.[9] They insisted that questions often asked by defence counsel – such as "do you live common law with a man?" "are you on the pill?" and "are you a prostitute?" – were designed to sully reputations rather than get to the truth. Feminists insisted that all women deserved protection from sexual assault.[10] Their arguments prompted federal legislators to pass "rape-shield" laws in 1982.[11]

The newly enacted section 277 of the *Criminal Code* stated that "evidence of sexual reputation, whether general or specific," was not admissible for the purpose of "challenging or supporting the credibility of the complainant."[12] But the revised law did not place all prior sexual history off limits. Defence lawyers were still entitled to introduce evidence about the complainant's prior sexual history *with the accused*. Evidence that the complainant had made prior false allegations of sexual assault was also admissible. Section 276 expressly permitted "rebuttal" evidence (to refute prosecution arguments regarding the complainant's "sexual activity or absence thereof"),[13] "identity" evidence (to establish "the identity of the person who had sexual contact with the complainant on the occasion" charged),[14] and "same occasion" evidence (evidence of other "sexual activity that took place on the same occasion," where that evidence related to the accused's belief that the complainant consented).[15]

The complex wording of the new sections reflected hard-fought battles between feminist law reformers and defence lawyers. What resulted was a tangled parliamentary compromise that pleased virtually no one. Defence lawyers objected that the new provisions deprived accused men of the right to a full and fair defence under sections 7 and 11(d) of the *Charter*.[16] Some Crown prosecutors added their objections as well; "sparing" the complainant "spoiled" the trial, argued one.[17] In contrast, feminists complained that the rape-shield provisions failed to encompass the wider prohibition needed to eradicate sexist rules of evidence.[18] As University of Ottawa law professor Elizabeth Sheehy put it, sexual history evidence "devastates women as witnesses." It causes them to become "flustered" or "embarrassed," or "to cry." It "unhinged" them. It was "used to make false insinuations." The better law, argued Sheehy, would have proclaimed sexual history "absolutely irrelevant."[19]

Seaboyer was the first case to bring the new rape-shield laws before the Supreme Court. Because the constitutional challenges began at the preliminary inquiry stage, little was known about the facts that gave rise to the prosecution. Seaboyer was charged with sexually assaulting a woman he had met in a Toronto tavern. His lawyer sought to question the complainant about her "past sexual life" and her "sexual conduct after the event."[20] The judge presiding at the preliminary inquiry stopped this line of questioning, citing the new rape-shield sections.[21] Seaboyer appealed the ruling through the Ontario Court of Appeal up to the Supreme Court of Canada.[22]

LEAF's Feminist Advocacy

The challenge to the rape-shield law caught the attention of a new legal advocacy organization, the Women's Legal Education and Action Fund. LEAF, as it was called, was the brainchild of a group of lawyers who had lobbied to secure women's rights during the negotiations over the *Charter*. Founded in 1985, the year that the section 15 equality provision of the *Charter* came into effect, the non-profit organization was designed to advocate a "more woman-centred view of the world" in Canadian law.[23] It was run by a new generation of self-identified "feminist lawyers" who were forging previously uncharted careers based upon the philosophy of gender equality.[24]

LEAF defined its mission as an "intervener" in sex equality cases. Bertha Wilson, one of the Supreme Court judges who offered the warmest welcome to interveners generally, described this as moving beyond "the narrow facts of the case" to "paint a broader picture" for the court. She would later credit LEAF with making "an impressive contribution to the decisions in many of the leading *Charter* cases," adding that it "represented a real effort on the part of a very diligent and dedicated group of counsel to discharge the role of intervener at its highest and most challenging level."[25] Sherene Razack, a sociologist at the University of Toronto, characterized the LEAF volunteers as a group marked by a surfeit of energy, motivated by shared goals, confident, full of hope, and undeterred by the enormity of the task at hand.[26] Not all commentators were as positive. Karen Selick, a conservative legal columnist, protested that "listening to a bunch of radical feminists beat their drums over and over again" would undoubtedly have an "impact on the decisions reached by the court."[27]

Was *Seaboyer* an ideal case for LEAF? Its early leaders hoped to "occupy the field" with *Charter* equality cases, helping to shape which issues were argued, in what ways, and in what order. Yet as early as 1988, one of its founders, Beth Symes, observed, "We have not occupied the field. Men have. We have been involved in damage control ... men have been popping up all over Canada in various courts challenging things that we as women fought to get, such as maternity benefits, such as rape-shield provisions."[28] She bemoaned the resources required to intervene in such cases.[29] Regardless of their sentiments, the LEAF lawyers did not hesitate when the rape-shield laws were challenged. *Seaboyer* would become one of the organization's early flagship cases.

Toronto labour lawyer Elizabeth Shilton, who spearheaded LEAF's intervention in *Seaboyer*, recalled the lead-up to the Supreme Court appearance.[30] The intervention at the Ontario Court of Appeal had gone badly. LEAF was just finding its feet. Feminists were uneasy about how to intervene to support a substandard rape-shield law that they felt did not go nearly far enough. Should they go in to try to shore up a bad law with traditional arguments that were calculated to find favour in the courts, or should they forge a purer argument based on fuller feminist analysis that was more likely to lose? Because there were very few female lawyers with appellate litigation experience, and virtually none expert in criminal law, the decision had been taken to hire a highly respected male criminal defence lawyer, Mark Sandler.

Sandler, who was a strong proponent of rape-shield protections, recalled that he was "delighted to act pro bono for LEAF."[31] It was a unique brief, the first time he had ever taken instructions from a committee that insisted upon hours of conference-call discussions. He recollected debates over philosophy and strategy that took place between "very knowledgeable," "very bright," "very committed women," leaving it crystal-clear that there were "no right answers." In the end, Sandler's seasoned criminal law advice prevailed: to recognize that it was "unlikely" that the legislation "would be upheld without any qualification," and to try to "save the most important parts."[32] The result was a disaster. A split Ontario Court of Appeal decision made the situation worse. The minority opinion struck down the entire rape-shield law as unconstitutional because it deprived the accused of a fair trial. The majority refused to strike down the provisions, but held that trial judges should be able to widen the kinds of sexual

Elizabeth Shilton, Toronto labour lawyer who spearheaded LEAF's intervention in the *Seaboyer* case at the Supreme Court of Canada.

history evidence that could be admitted, on a case-by-case basis.[33] For LEAF activists, it was a decision that made a bad law worse.

Shilton characterized the feminist response to the Ontario Court of Appeal debacle as vehement and unequivocal. LEAF was forced to restructure itself into a body that consulted with front-line women's organizations that would have an equal voice in framing the arguments. This was the last time a male lawyer would be selected based on reputation and criminal law expertise. The expertise that LEAF sought thereafter was in feminist theory. If the ranks of experienced feminist litigators were thin, then LEAF would consider itself an incubator for young talent. By the time the case reached the Supreme Court, LEAF was representing a host of organizations working on violence against women.[34] The coalition committee drew upon a dynamic group of young feminist Canadian law professors: Christine Boyle, Brettel Dawson, Renate Mohr, and Elizabeth Sheehy. The all-female litigation team they settled upon included Elizabeth Shilton, Helena Orton (LEAF's litigation director), Anne Derrick (a feminist Halifax lawyer with some criminal practice behind her), and Catharine MacKinnon (an American feminist law professor then visiting at Osgoode Hall Law School).

It was still an early stage for interveners at the Supreme Court, and no one was quite clear what the rules of engagement would be. Shilton recalled that there was a debate over whether an intervener was restricted to making its claim based on legal authorities, or whether it could file social context evidence, similar to what was described as a Brandeis brief in the United States.[35] The *Seaboyer* team chose to aim high. It compiled material on the historical and current realities of sexual assault, the ways in which rape functioned as a mechanism of male dominance, and the failures of the legal system to protect women's constitutional right to security.[36] LEAF also made the path-breaking argument that the section 15 guarantee of equality should be used to dismantle the discriminatory social practice of sexual assault.[37] From a sex equality perspective, it argued, evidence about a victim's sexual history was "simply never relevant."[38] It was an argument calculated to capture attention. It was L'Heureux-Dubé who accepted the challenge.

L'Heureux-Dubé's Dissent

That this dissent would not be a routine opinion was clear from the outset. Claire Klassen, the law clerk who assisted in the research and drafting in *Seaboyer*, observed that the case seemed to hold a special level of intensity for L'Heureux-Dubé: "Seaboyer was *so* close to Justice L'Heureux-Dubé. It was her first opportunity to demonstrate how the *Charter* jurisprudence had started to shift. So much of it was novel. There was a huge learning curve, with materials that were not standard judicial fare. There were new voices informing the court. Those voices really resonated with her."[39] Klassen remembered drafting, redrafting, and redrafting again. "It was some of the hardest work I've ever done," she added, explaining that the voluminous material they read on the pervasiveness and severity of sexual assault proved to be both unsettling and emotionally compelling.[40]

L'Heureux-Dubé's dissent situated the dispute squarely within a sociolegal framework. The problem as she saw it was rooted in gender inequality:

> Sexual assault is not like any other crime. In the vast majority of cases the target is a woman and the perpetrator is a man ... Unlike other crimes of a violent nature, it is for the most part unreported ... The prosecution and conviction rates for sexual assault are among the lowest for all violent crimes. Perhaps more than any other crime, the fear and constant reality of sexual

assault affect how women conduct their lives and how they define their relationship with the larger society. Sexual assault is not like any other crime.[41]

L'Heureux-Dubé drew extensively from material in LEAF's factum, the written document setting out its position before the court. She used the studies LEAF cited to provide statistics about the real-world experience of coercive sexuality – that one Canadian woman in five would be sexually assaulted during her lifetime.[42] For courts that had relied exclusively on statutes and case law in the past, it was unusual to make reference to secondary contextual sources, a novel judicial direction that would soon begin to gather wider momentum.[43] One year earlier, in one of her most famous presentations, Bertha Wilson had expressed the opinion that female judges would make a difference to the development of law, and that they might be more attuned to examining contextual factors than traditional male judges would be.[44] As L'Heureux-Dubé laid bare the widespread "myths" and "stereotypes" that underpinned popular understandings about women's character and sexuality, she did so with language not regularly seen in judicial opinions.

Adopting the phrase "Madonna-Whore Complex," she noted that women were "categorized into one-dimensional types" that slotted them into two groups: "They are maternal or they are sexy. They are good or they are bad." Then she added that "anything not 100 percent proper and respectable" was used to discredit the complainant, to imply that she had "consented to sex."[45] Quoting from judicial opinions and criminal law texts of "surprisingly recent vintage," she itemized concrete illustrations of pervasive "rape myths" that presented "formidable obstacles for complainants in their dealings with the very system charged with discovering the truth."[46] She reviewed research that demonstrated that juries were "reluctant to convict" when "any testimony about prior sexual history" was introduced – regardless of whether such information was ever verified.[47]

She took issue with the "unique evidentiary rules" fashioned under common law that treated sexual assault victims "with suspicion and distrust."[48] Premised on the belief that "extramarital sexual activity was abnormal for women," the judiciary had expressed its "contempt for the unchaste female accuser" by shifting the inquiry away from the conduct of the offender to that of the "moral worth" of the complainant.[49] Women who had had "consensual sex outside of marriage" were thought to have "a dual propensity: to consent to sexual relations at large and to lie."[50] L'Heureux-Dubé's own background provided her with a particular sensitivity to the sexual autonomy claims of women who were reputed to be flirtatious, who welcomed personal adventure. She knew from experience that the rigid line drawing was unfair, and that presumptions about women's predisposition to lie were incorrect. It was no accident that the woman who insisted on sexual autonomy in law was also reputed to be a non-conformist in her romantic life.

L'Heureux-Dubé's decision traced the history of earlier unsuccessful efforts to rid the *Criminal Code* of unfair evidentiary rules. A 1976 legislative revision, designed to shelter women from intrusive questioning about their sexual history, had boomeranged when the judges interpreted the change to provide "*less* protection to the complainant." As L'Heureux-Dubé recounted this "curious result," she added that it was "lamentable" that after Parliament sought to improve the law, a complainant "should walk away with less than she already had."[51] When this necessitated "the intervention of Parliament on a second occasion," defence counsel had mounted the very *Charter* challenge at issue in *Seaboyer.*[52] L'Heureux-Dubé also referenced the persistent and repeated efforts Parliament had made to try to eradicate the "corroboration rule," the traditional requirement that judges warn juries that it was not safe to convict on sexual assault in the absence of corroboration.[53] She sounded a note of caution about leaving rules of evidence to the discretion of judges, whose "experience, common sense and logic" might well be "informed by stereotype and myth."[54] The "demonstrated inability of the judiciary to change its discriminatory ways," and "overwhelming social science research that says that things have not changed," had convinced Parliament that the "discretion of judges" was "antithetical" to its goals.[55]

Citing both sections 15 and 28 of the *Charter*, L'Heureux-Dubé reasoned that the constitutional inquiry should not be confined to the "narrow interests of the accused," because complainants and the community at large had "a legitimate interest in ensuring that trials [were] conducted in a fashion that does not subordinate the fact-finding process to myth and stereotype."[56] She concluded that section 277 of the *Criminal Code*, which barred using prior sexual history as a tool for determining credibility, was constitutional. It was, she noted, an "uncontentious" position that was endorsed by the whole court.[57] In dissent, she also upheld the constitutionality of section 276 of the *Criminal Code*, which she concluded had sufficient exceptions carved into it to cover anything that could possibly prove relevant. If anything, the exceptions had been cast "overly broadly."[58]

The format of L'Heureux-Dubé's dissent presented a significant departure from the typical Supreme Court rulings, and she could find only one colleague to sign on with her: Charles Doherty Gonthier. Gonthier had been born in Montreal, and practised law there until he received his first judicial appointment in 1974. Although their paths had crossed during their years on the Quebec courts, the friendship blossomed after 1989, when Gonthier joined the Supreme Court of Canada. During the years they shared on the top court, the two became regular lunch partners in the Supreme Court dining room and over coffee in the court cafeteria.[59] They were an odd couple in some ways. L'Heureux-Dubé – fiery, impassioned, and impetuous – stood in stark contrast with Gonthier, a man noted for his patience, diplomacy, gentleness, and intellectual finesse.[60] Yet L'Heureux-Dubé was a huge admirer of Gonthier's "honesty" and "brilliance," and she characterized him as the "intellectual leader of the court."[61] Gonthier explained that he admired L'Heureux-Dubé's "quick wit," "intelligence," "enthusiasm," and "boundless energy."[62]

Adam Dodek, who clerked for L'Heureux-Dubé some years after the *Seaboyer* case, marvelled at the relationship between the two judges: "Their personalities were so different – yin and yang. Justice L'Heureux-Dubé might talk and talk and talk, and Justice Gonthier would say something at the end, and she would jump on it and say – 'Exactly! What Justice Gonthier just said!'"[63] Dodek described it as "a friendship of tremendous mutual respect, support, and admiration."[64] Although many others found the friendship puzzling, it seems to have created a jurisprudential bond that occasionally brought Gonthier into the orbit of L'Heureux-Dubé's most innovative decisions. *Seaboyer* was one such instance; *Ewanchuk* would be another.[65]

Beverley McLachlin:
"The Courts Must Seek a Middle Way"

Although the growing tensions between Chief Justice Lamer and L'Heureux-Dubé might have suggested that he would author the majority opinion, to the dismay of many female observers, Beverley McLachlin, the only other woman on the nine-person bench, wrote the majority decision striking down much of the rape-shield law.[66] The third woman appointed to the Supreme Court, McLachlin had arrived in 1989, but with the retirement of Bertha Wilson in 1991, there were just two women left.[67] A native of Pincher Creek, Alberta, the eldest child of Pentecostal parents who worked a ranch and a sawmill, McLachlin had practised law in Alberta and British Columbia before she joined the Faculty of Law at the University of British Columbia.[68] She moved through the judicial hierarchy at a meteoric pace,

Beverley McLachlin shortly after her appointment to the Supreme Court of Canada, with Brian Dickson and Claire L'Heureux-Dubé.

"faster than most litigants," as some were fond of saying.[69] In 2000, she would become the country's first female chief justice of Canada.[70]

McLachlin's authorship of an attack on the rape-shield law astonished women across Canada. It seemed to many a significant betrayal that one of the two remaining women on the Supreme Court of Canada would lead the charge against the hard-fought (and partial) legislative reform. Elizabeth Sheehy, who had sat in the Ottawa courtroom when *Seaboyer* was argued, recalled her dismay at watching McLachlin take over the questioning of counsel while her male colleagues sat back in silence. "It was very clear where she stood," added Sheehy. "[It was] a very interesting optic – the woman judge who clearly goes on the attack to demonstrate the weaknesses in the arguments."[71]

The reporters who covered the oral arguments at the hearing were equally surprised. The *Globe and Mail* captured the unfolding drama:

> Questions from the two female justices of the court indicated they may be on opposite sides. On the second day of hearings ... Madam Justice Beverley McLachlin asked a revealing question. When [Jeff Casey of the Ontario

Attorney General's office] advanced a hypothetical case to buttress his argument that a woman's sexual history was irrelevant even if she were a prostitute, Judge McLachlin said, "But isn't there going to be a question there, that the jury would not believe her [if she were a prostitute]? The difference to the accused is enormous. He could go to jail for life." During the presentation on Tuesday by the lawyer Marc Rosenberg, who represents one of the accused rapists, Judge L'Heureux-Dubé said any evidence of a woman's sex life before the offence is irrelevant. "Is it really relevant to know what she did with other persons? That's irrelevant in my view. What's the relevance of having sex with 25 other people?" she said.[72]

The courtroom jousting was prescient. McLachlin offered to write the majority opinion, and Lamer assigned it to her. She claimed in her decision that she was charting "a middle way" that offered "the maximum protection to the complainant compatible with the maintenance of the accused's fundamental right to a fair trial."[73] She upheld section 277, a ruling without controversy. Like L'Heureux-Dubé, McLachlin was troubled that the common law traditionally allowed the routine introduction of "evidence that the complainant had relations with the accused and others" to prove "that the complainant had consented" and "as undermining her credibility generally." She noted that the rules were based on "discredited" myths "that unchaste women were more likely to consent to intercourse, and in any event, were less worthy of belief." She explained, "The fact that a woman has had intercourse on other occasions does not in itself increase the logical probability that she consented to intercourse with the accused. Nor does it make her a liar."[74] She concluded, "There is no logical or practical link between a woman's sexual reputation and whether she is a truthful witness. It follows that the evidence excluded by s. 277 can serve no legitimate purpose in the trial."[75]

But when McLachlin turned to section 276, her analysis shifted. If L'Heureux-Dubé's decision was rooted in the recognition of gender inequality, McLachlin's operated from the presumption of gender equality.[76] It meant that unlike L'Heureux-Dubé, who took the *Charter* equality provisions as central to the analysis, McLachlin listed only the sections that dealt with the rights of the accused. She did not mention section 15 of the *Charter* when she struck down section 276 of the *Criminal Code* as an unconstitutional violation of the accused's rights of full answer and defence under the *Charter*.[77] She began by expressing approval for all of the exemptions already crafted into section 276. Then, unlike L'Heureux-Dubé, who had speculated that these exceptions might be overly broad, McLachlin went further to find that section 276 "overshoots the mark."[78] The problem she diagnosed was that by listing the exceptions, the legislation failed to recognize the "impossibility of predicting in advance what evidence may be relevant."[79] In the end, she left prior sexual history up to the trial judges, whom she hoped would demonstrate a "sensitive and responsible exercise of discretion."[80] These were, of course, the very trial judges that L'Heureux-Dubé had criticized in her dissent, whose preoccupation with women's prior sexual history had necessitated the law reform in the first place.[81]

L'Heureux-Dubé lamented that she could not convince her female colleague to side with her. "You always feel so sorry that you cannot get your colleagues to agree. [It left] a feeling of frustration. I thought Beverley was going backward ... and I don't understand why she wrote that. I couldn't understand why they would say it was unconstitutional. She wrote *Seaboyer* when she was very young on the court. She reacted like it was an ordinary case against a guy who wouldn't have the means to defend himself. She had not yet grasped these issues of sexual assault."[82] As for McLachlin, she told the *Ottawa Citizen*, "We knew what was at stake in that case and you make the choices. They're not always easy choices but you make the choice you think is right and after that it's over. You live with it."[83]

With the passage of time, L'Heureux-Dubé came to describe Beverley McLachlin as someone who grew in office: "She learned a lot [and] changed a lot. She moved very much."[84] Questioned again as to whether this description also characterized her, whether she had penned a frankly feminist decision in *Seaboyer* that might have been too radical for her even a few years earlier, she mused: "Did I change over time? Some of the women are tortured on the stand. The prior sexual history had absolutely no bearing on the guilt or innocence of someone. [The cases] force you to find out who you are. *Seaboyer* is an example."[85]

Asked by the *Ottawa Citizen* one year after *Seaboyer* whether she thought female judges made a difference, however, she held to her traditional line: "I'm sensitive, I'm listening and maybe I'm listening more than others because I'm a woman. But I don't see the world as men and women, I see the world as people and in that sense I'm not a feminist the way people define feminists – all for women. Women make a difference because of who they are, their experiences, but not necessarily a difference in the sense that they will be all for women. It doesn't mean that we always have a unanimous voice."[86] Reporter Stephen Bindman ended his profile with this concluding line: "Never was that clearer than in the Supreme Court's ruling on the rape shield law."[87]

The Aftermath: A Fierce and Effective Lobby

McLachlin's ruling unleashed a firestorm of protest.[88] The *Globe and Mail*'s Sean Fine reported that women's groups responded "with an almost visceral revulsion."[89] Philip Slayton said that prominent feminists accused her of "encouraging rape."[90] "Women's groups expressed outrage at yesterday's landmark ruling" was the lead story in the *Montreal Gazette*, which added that feminists feared an "open season" on women in the courtroom.[91] "I can't believe it," was the *cri de coeur* from a women's centre executive director quoted in the *Windsor Star*: "It totally negates the law. It's stating that rape is not an act of violence; it's an act of sexual activity."[92] "This is one of the most hotly contested issues in terms of basic values and conflict facing the women of this country," insisted University of Calgary law professor Sheilah Martin.[93]

Two hundred chanting protesters picketed in front of the Supreme Court.[94] Less than two weeks later, a dozen "rape-shield law protesters" splattered the front wall of the court with "human blood," asserting that the majority judgment would provoke sexual violence against women.[95]

Feminist demonstration at the Supreme Court after the *Seaboyer* ruling, 1991.

Protests were not restricted to feminist organizations. Ontario's attorney general and minister responsible for women's issues depicted the ruling as a "set-back for women."[96] A Gallup poll found that the majority of Canadians supported "the idea behind the rape-shield law that was struck down."[97]

LEAF litigator Elizabeth Shilton called the majority decision "devastating," although she admitted that she and her colleagues had had no realistic expectation that "the whole court was ready to sign on" to a feminist perspective on those "very difficult issues." As for McLachlin's leading the majority, Shilton added: "We didn't go into that naively thinking that women would side with us. But there was a lot of discussion about whether women judges make a difference. It was a good teaching tool about the complexities of gender in the judiciary."[98]

The most important thing for Shilton was L'Heureux-Dubé's dissent. "[Her] dissent made it clear that we had got our message across. We had done what we had gone up there to do. We certainly were very encouraged to continue what we were doing by that kind of dialogue between feminist litigators and feminist judges. We felt we had given her what she needed to write the decision that she wrote. She gave us back what we needed from her."[99] Elizabeth Sheehy described the elation of reading L'Heureux-Dubé's dissent:

> I thought it was a thing of beauty. She put law in context. She put sexual assault in context. [It was] a masterpiece of research and integration of social science knowledge into thinking through the criminal law. I thought it was also beautifully written. A dissent matters. It is like a record, an imprint on the world. At least somebody stood up for us. Justice Bertha Wilson had given us *Morgentaler* and *Lavallee,* big cases for women. But this was the first big social context decision, and it went well beyond [the earlier rulings]. It made me hopeful to think that a judge of the Supreme Court of Canada could understand and articulate so beautifully a feminist sense of the realities of sexual assault and the law's role in it. When you think about how women might write law differently, her judgment was a great example of what a difference feminists might make on the court, in how they read, interpret, and write the law.[100]

She added that feminists hoped that L'Heureux-Dubé's dissent would "rise like a phoenix from the fire."[101]

The LEAF lawyers might have been even more heartened had they known that retired Supreme Court justice Bertha Wilson had penned a

Sexual Assault 393

Elizabeth Sheehy, University of Ottawa professor of law, receives honorary doctorate, Law Society of Upper Canada.

handwritten personal note to her former colleague: "Dear Claire: Re Seaboyer – great judgement! I feel more relaxed about having left – hope you carry the day but not overly optimistic! Bertha."[102] The wide public support for her dissent must also have strengthened L'Heureux-Dubé's sense that she had done the right thing. As Alberta's first female chief justice, Catherine Fraser, observed: "She might have been on the minority side" but that didn't mean "that she would necessarily feel isolated." Fraser added: "She is someone who values the opinions of people whose judgments she trusts. If she was getting a lot of support outside of the court, that can mitigate any concerns that might arise otherwise. She had a lot of support across the country."[103]

The charges against Seaboyer never proceeded to trial. The complainant declined to continue with the case, and the Crown felt that the prosecution was barred by the lengthy delay between the assaults and the Supreme

Court ruling.¹⁰⁴ But the shock waves that rolled from the court to all corners of the country were based on far more than a rape trial run amuck. L'Heureux-Dubé's dissent was cited as the clarion call that mobilized "the strongest and most effective lobby effort by women's groups that Canada has ever witnessed."¹⁰⁵ Federal department of justice officials were taken aback by the level of "public outrage" and "public pressure" that mounted almost overnight, widespread impassioned demands that the government counteract the Supreme Court's majority decision.¹⁰⁶

The federal minister of justice, Kim Campbell, who described the *Seaboyer* judgment as "worrisome," initiated intensive consultations with women's groups.¹⁰⁷ Less than one year after *Seaboyer*, Campbell presented more legislative revisions: a clarification of the rules for admitting evidence of prior sexual history, a tough new definition of "consent," and restrictions on the defence of "mistake."¹⁰⁸ It was a strategy to "step outside *Seaboyer*'s framework," pursuing "substantive" rather than simply "evidentiary" amendments.¹⁰⁹ It was a brand-new law, subsequently upheld by the court, which would come to be known as the "No Means No Law."¹¹⁰ According to Mark Sandler, the new measures went far beyond the provisions under attack in *Seaboyer*, boldly challenging "stereotypical notions around sexual relations between men and women."¹¹¹ According to L'Heureux-Dubé, by the time the new situation was finally sorted out between the Supreme Court and Parliament, this served as one of the "clearest" illustrations of how her dissent could "become the law."¹¹²

The big question was what would happen to it in the hands of the judiciary. The explosive potential of the new "No means No" rules would become all too clear when *Ewanchuk* blew up eight years later.

30
Family Law and Spousal Support
Moge, 1992

Zofia was nineteen when she wed twenty-five-year-old Andrzej Moge in Poland in the mid-1950s.[1] In the grip of a communist government, the war-devastated country was facing economic depression and social unrest.[2] Andrzej was a welder and Zofia, who had dropped out of school after seventh grade, was a sales clerk. The young couple made plans to emigrate. By the time they arrived in Canada in 1960, the Moges had two children under the age of five. They settled in Winnipeg, where Andrzej secured continuing employment as a welder, and Zofia gave birth to their third child in 1966. Whatever dreams they had when they moved to Canada, it is likely that neither of them had the least notion that their marital struggles would become enmeshed in the law for almost two decades, capped off with a precedent-setting ruling from their adopted nation's top court.

Traditional versus Modern Marriages
and In Between

Many of the judges who examined the case grappled with whether to characterize the Moge marriage as "traditional" or "modern." Traditional marriage was understood to be a "life-long relationship," while a modern one was a union that lasted "only as long as the parties wish." A traditional husband was the breadwinner, providing his wife and children with financial

395

support until death. A traditional wife was the caregiver, responsible for raising the children, doing the laundry, housework, shopping, and cooking. Modern marriages embraced less rigid roles. Wives and husbands could both pursue careers in the outside labour force as economically self-sufficient actors.[3]

Most of the judges who deliberated on *Moge* characterized the marriage as traditional. One judge noted that he would have to "shut [his] eyes to social history" not to recognize that in mid-century Poland, as well as Canada, "marriage was intended as a life-long relationship."[4] Andrzej, with his welding job at Motor Coach Industries, was the primary wage earner. Zofia was the primary caregiver, who stayed home during the day to look after the children and the household. The one wrinkle was that Zofia also worked outside the home. Although she never learned to speak English well and never obtained further education or occupational training, she obtained a job as a maid at the historic Hotel Fort Garry. She cleaned rooms during the six-hour evening shift, between 5 and 11 p.m., five days a week. Most of the judges dismissed this as insufficient to fit the defining attribute of the modern marriage: economic independence for both spouses. They emphasized that Zofia looked after her home all day, and left it in the evening only to give a small supplemental boost to the family budget. And there was no crossover in return for Zofia's paid work. Andrzej did not undertake "additional responsibilities at home" to counterbalance Zofia's "efforts in the external work force."[5]

The analysis was largely inattentive to class. Whether "traditional" or "modern," many poor and immigrant families had always sent both spouses out to work to make ends meet.[6] What changed in the "modern" second half of the twentieth century was that more middle- and upper-class wives began to seek careers in the paid labour force for the first time, with or without children in the home.[7] In 1931, 20 percent of Canadian women were working for pay; by 1986, the number had more than doubled, to 55 percent. That same year, over half of women with children under the age of three were in the labour force.[8] The extent to which this new population of female workers was greeted with educational and employment opportunities equal to men was hotly contested. The extent to which "modern" husbands were willing to accept equal responsibility for the care of children and the home was also problematic. Zofia Moge's plight – working a minimum-wage job without education or training while shouldering all of the household and childcare needs – was by no means atypical.

The Unravelling of the Moge Marriage

The paper trail reveals little about the personal relations within the Moge family, or why the marriage fell apart in 1973. Gone was the era when getting a divorce required the parties to painstakingly display their grievances before the courts. Claire L'Heureux-Dubé had lived through an era when divorce was all but impossible, as her own parents' circumstances had illustrated. She had practised family law at a time when Quebec judges publicly denounced divorce, and presided over trial and appellate cases as marital dissolution slowly became more available. By the time she arrived at the Supreme Court, no-fault divorce was accessible to all.[9] A Manitoba court had granted Andrzej's petition for divorce in 1980, awarded Zofia custody of the children, and ordered Andrzej to pay $150 a month in spousal and child support.[10] Zofia managed to make ends meet by continuing to report for the evening shift at the Hotel Fort Garry, where she earned about $800 per month.[11] In what one judge described as nothing short of "miraculous," she not only also raised the three children "on her own" but "put them through university."[12]

Then disaster struck. In 1987, the Hotel Fort Garry closed and Zofia was out of a job. Her thirty-eight job applications elicited no job offers. Now dependent on unemployment insurance benefits, she returned to court to request an increase in support from her ex-husband. By this time, Andrzej and his new wife were on substantially sounder financial footing. He had purchased a home, he had a small income from investments, and his welding job was grossing almost four times the income his former family was living on.[13] The Manitoba court increased Andrzej's support payments to $400 a month.[14]

Several months later, Zofia landed intermittent part-time work as an office cleaner with the provincial government. Andrzej's discontent boiled over after he discovered that the Hotel Fort Garry had reopened but that Zofia had chosen not to return to the more remunerative night job because she preferred the morning shift of a government office cleaner.[15] Andrzej went back to court to request that his support obligations be terminated permanently.

In 1989, the Manitoba Court of Queen's Bench agreed with Andrzej. Half of the monthly support had been designated for the couple's youngest child, Edward, who was now a twenty-three-year-old university student. Due to Edward's age, the court cancelled his half outright, and no one appealed that part of the ruling. But the court also went on to cancel Zofia's half of the monthly support, stating that she had had more than enough time to become financially independent, and that "[s]he cannot expect that Mr. Moge will support her forever."[16] The Manitoba Court of Appeal overturned that ruling in a 2-1 decision, reinstating support of $150 per month to Zofia.[17] This is what propelled the *Moge* case to the Supreme Court.

WARRING SPOUSES: WARRING THEORIES

Two main doctrines of spousal support vied for acceptance in the late twentieth century. The differences are best appreciated at their polar extremes, where the theories can be described as the "pension for life" and the "clean break."

The pension for life was often described as the "traditional" model of spousal support. It was rooted in the idea that marriage should provide "economic security for women in a society where women's labour force participation was limited," and required husbands who abandoned the marriage without cause to pay for the rest of their lives.[18] Proponents argued that women's domestic roles deprived them of opportunities for financial self-sufficiency. Redressing economic disability through support payments recognized the value of their "contributions to the home and family."[19] Wives who had performed family responsibilities would be compensated for the costs of career diminishment, while husbands who had been freed up to work for pay would share the benefit of their extra career potential.[20]

The claim for long-term spousal support was often bolstered by concerns over the "feminization of poverty." Between 1971 and 1986, the number of Canadian women living below the poverty line grew by 110 percent, the number of men by 24 percent. The majority of poor women lived in single-parent family units, often as a result of skyrocketing divorce rates.[21] It spawned the well-worn dictum that middle-class women were "only one man away from welfare."[22] American sociologist Lenore Weitzman had startled many when she released her 1985 study showing that ex-wives suffered a 73 percent drop in income, while ex-husbands improved theirs by 42 percent.[23] In Canada, as well, divorce was often cited as one of the most important contributors to the feminization of poverty.[24] The lack of spousal support was one of the obvious culprits.[25]

In contrast, the clean-break philosophy emphasized "individual responsibility" and "finality" in relations between ex-spouses. Its proponents claimed that permanent spousal support was "insulting to women" because this reinforced oppressive gender stereotypes that infantilized and incapacitated women.[26] It was also "unjust to ex-husbands" to convert a host of physically and mentally competent women into "an army of alimony drones."[27] Using a commercial analogy, supporters of this theory noted that "one business partner does not support the other after a partnership dissolves."[28]

The clean-break theory also recognized the "impermanence," "fluidity," "autonomy," and "independence" of the members of the modern family unit.[29] It relieved people trying to dissolve their union from a "permanent debt relationship."[30] It rejected tying the economic status of the wife to the husband, balked at reaffirming a "patriarchal notion of the family," and refused to define an adequate standard of living for ex-wives as "the personal responsibility of individual men."[31] Instead, proponents argued it was preferable for each divorced spouse to secure his or her own economic needs, or for public agencies to step in to rescue the vulnerable.[32] They looked to the state rather than individual spouses to remedy the weaker position of women in the economy.[33] Furthermore, proponents of the clean-break theory emphasized that spousal support orders were unlikely to alleviate the feminization of poverty, because even if ordered, wealthier spouses rarely paid in practice.[34] In fact, the major contributors to the dissolved unit frequently started up new families, which drained their capacity to pay. "Even the most vigorous enforcement cannot extract money that is not there," was the cautionary refrain.[35] To the extent that clean-break theorists countenanced spousal support at all, they saw it as a short-term, rehabilitative, transitional measure.[36]

In an attempt to mediate, Parliament entered the fray. The 1985 *Divorce Act* set out four principles upon which spousal support should be based. Court orders should:

(a) recognize any economic advantages or disadvantages to the spouses arising from the marriage or its breakdown;

(b) apportion between the spouses any financial consequences arising from the care of any child of the marriage over and above the obligation apportioned between the spouses ...;

(c) relieve any economic hardship of the spouses arising from the breakdown of the marriage; and

(d) in so far as practicable, promote the economic self-sufficiency of each spouse within a reasonable period of time.[37]

The conflicts inherent in the four criteria were obvious from the start.

"Know Thy Judge"

In 1981, Rosalie Abella, then a Toronto provincial court family judge, had characterized the law on spousal support as a "patchwork of often conflicting theories and approaches" and "a Rubik's cube for which no one yet has written the Solution Book."[38] Seasoned family law practitioners often joked ruefully about the scattered rulings and the wide disparity in outcomes. Family law expert Julien Payne suggested abiding by "the golden rule of family law practice: 'Know Thy Judge.'" It was, he said, one of the only ports in the storm of unpredictability that felled inexperienced amateurs and experienced lawyers alike.[39] Many hoped for guidance from the top court, but due to the cost of appeals, family cases were few and far between at the Supreme Court of Canada. Prior to *Moge*, there had been four prominent exceptions: a dissent from Tony Lamer in 1983, and Bertha Wilson's majority decisions in a trilogy of cases in 1987.[40] Both judges had leaned toward the clean-break philosophy.

Lamer's dissent in *Messier v. Delage* claimed that the "evolution of society and of the status of women" required the re-examination of spousal support. "Women cannot on the one hand claim equal status without at the same time accepting responsibility for their own upkeep," he insisted.[41] Lamer cited a 1976 report of the Law Reform Commission of Canada, a body he had chaired at the time, for its recommendation that spousal support should not constitute a "guarantee of security for life for former dependent spouses."[42] It was up to the government, not ex-husbands, he argued, to resolve the larger social problem of the financial challenges facing ex-wives.[43] But Lamer's opinion was issued only in dissent. Julien Chouinard, writing for the majority, di+d not expressly side with the "pension for life" analysis, but he refused to cut off spousal support to an ex-wife in need.[44]

Three blockbuster decisions popularly known as "the trilogy," issued four years later, took Lamer's approach into majority territory. Bertha Wilson, then the only woman on the Supreme Court, decided in *Pelech v. Pelech, Richardson v. Richardson,* and *Caron v. Caron* that spousal support should be awarded only to cover short-term rehabilitation.[45] Commentators were sharply divided over what appeared to be a powerful new direction in family law.[46] Researchers who tracked the orders for spousal support reported that the numbers had begun to plummet and their duration was shortening.[47] The big question was whether this paved the way for a wholesale transformation in spousal support for the future.

Julien Payne's maxim "Know Thy Judge" came in for some scrutiny with the early clean-break Supreme Court decisions. Some might have thought Lamer's clean-break dissent was prescient for a man who would enter into a second marriage in 1987.[48] By contrast, Julien Chouinard, the author of the majority opinion that eschewed the clean break theory, was steeped in a traditional twenty-seven-year marriage when he issued the *Messier* decision.[49] Bertha Wilson's decision was more perplexing, and seemed to upend some presumptions about the gender of judges and judicial predilections for women's rights. Yet Wilson had forged a "modern" marriage with a minister, in which both followed their own professional careers, shared household responsibilities, and proudly acknowledged the egalitarian partnership they had created.[50] Her own experience may have underlain her optimistic assessment that women could stand on their own two feet, and should.[51]

Moge would offer L'Heureux-Dubé her first opportunity to weigh in on the complex question from the Supreme Court bench.[52] Few knew where she would settle. To the extent that upbringing and experience would govern, it was a mixed record. She had grown up in a traditional family, with a breadwinning father and homemaker mother. She had married in the mid-1950s like the Moges, but hers was a very "modern" union entered into by two professionals who both pursued their own careers. Like Zofia, L'Heureux-Dubé had shouldered the lion's share of responsibility for the children and the household, but never to the curtailment of her career. While she was in practice as a family lawyer, she had favoured the clean-break philosophy: urging female clients to become self-sufficient, worrying that spousal support orders were more often breached than paid, and favouring a lump-sum payment over monthly remittances. She told her clients that divorce was ultimately good for women, that they would eventually feel free. In an article she published while on the Court of Appeal in 1983, she rendered what sounded like something of a death knell for long-term spousal support:

> The newly acquired economic independence of each partner within marriage has brought about reform in divorce law that tends to do away with maintenance as a corollary measure to divorce ... Maintenance is on the way out,

except perhaps for the disabled housewife or as a transitory measure ... [T]here is some suggestion that ... spousal alimentary obligations should be the prime responsibility of the state, given the duration of marriage, the rate of remarriage, and the forming of new relationships outside marriage.[53]

Yet she was deeply aware of the financial cliffs over which so many divorced women toppled, unable to make ends meet with the paltry support orders handed down by male judges. Her earlier judicial decisions were mixed, some favouring the needs of dependent ex-wives, some favouring the wishes of ex-husbands to move on to new lives. She was the first judge on the Supreme Court of Canada to have specialized in family law practice. She was the first mother ever to sit at that level of court.[54] What would she do with *Moge*, a case that placed the competing visions so starkly before her?

Parasitical Divorcées
versus *Charter* Principles of Equality

"Supreme Court to decide if 19 years long enough for alimony payments" was the headline on the front page of the *Winnipeg Free Press* on 2 April 1992.[55] The prospect of Andrzej's loss was the worst nightmare possible for those who championed the clean break. They worried about parasitical divorcées who shunned the labour market to the chagrin of their struggling, hard-working ex-husbands.[56] The article quoted Andrzej Moge as saying he had given his wife "ample time to become self-sufficient" and that after nineteen years "he should not have to pay his wife Zofia a cent." It was not that she was "unable to support herself," but that she was "unwilling" to do so.[57] "She said she is going to make me broke up to my socks," he complained to the press.[58] Andrzej's counsel, Winnipeg family lawyer Douglas E. Johnston, expressed confidence that he would win this "watershed" case.[59] He pointed to the Supreme Court "trilogy" five years earlier, which espoused self-sufficiency, and disputed that marriage was the cause of Zofia's financial distress. He characterized the Moge relationship as a "modern marriage," and said if anyone had a responsibility to finance this ex-wife, it was the state.[60]

Zofia retained Winnipeg family lawyer Peter Bruckshaw, who had been called to the bar in 1989 and had practised for just two years. Bruckshaw explained that his work was almost entirely funded through legal aid at the time.[61] He recalled his client as a "quiet," "soft-spoken"

Peter Bruckshaw, Zofia Moge's lawyer in the Supreme Court case on spousal support.

woman, who "just wanted to help her son through school" and needed spousal support to do so. Bruckshaw had never been to the Supreme Court before, and had "no expectations that Mrs. Moge would win." At the oral hearing, he could see that L'Heureux-Dubé intended to take a lead role in the case because of her "intensity" and the "incredibly sharp" questions she posed. He remembered being struck by the "sense of courtesy" and "intellectual curiosity" that suffused the courtroom, something he had not experienced before.[62]

As it had in *Seaboyer,* the Women's Legal Education and Action Fund (LEAF) appeared as an intervener. The organization was again represented by Helena Orton, its Toronto litigation director, who had practised family law with Ottawa's first feminist law firm, Aitken, Greenberg, before joining LEAF in 1987. Her co-counsel was Alison Diduck, a Winnipeg family lawyer and law professor at the University of Manitoba.[63] LEAF argued that the issue was not whether the Moge marriage was "traditional" or "modern," but whether the *Charter* principles of equality should infuse spousal support law. LEAF's written factum contained a wealth of socio-economic data, including references to eighteen different studies describing

LEAF lawyer Alison Diduck, who appeared as an intervener in the *Moge* case.

women's unequal position within the contemporary family and the labour market, and their impoverished situation after divorce.[64] LEAF's goal was to challenge stereotypes and establish "the public importance of so-called private decisions," along with the centrality of social context.[65]

A Majority Decision from "the Great Dissenter"

The chief justice determined the size and composition of the panels, typically assigning nine judges in very important cases, seven in normal cases, and five in routine matters.[66] The numbers could morph still further when judges absented themselves due to illness or other activities, or when individual judges chose to recuse themselves from sitting. The panel that heard *Moge* numbered six, reduced from the original seven-judge bench, because Chief Justice Lamer recused himself. Judges were not required to give reasons for stepping aside, but there was speculation that Lamer might have felt that his recent divorce posed a conflict of interest. It had not stopped him from sitting on the *Pelech* trilogy and signing on to Wilson's majority clean-break decision a few years earlier, but he seemed disinclined to rule on spousal support again.[67]

Moge catapulted the court's "Great Dissenter" to the position of lead author. This time, L'Heureux-Dubé carried with her the majority of the six-person panel. She thought that it was "very significant" that Lamer was not on the panel. Stressing that his predilections for the clean break were well known, she wagered, "He wouldn't have changed his mind. If he had sat on the case, there would have been a division."[68] Wilson had retired, which eliminated the question of whether she would have advocated the *Pelech* perspective. The remaining panel included La Forest, Gonthier, Cory, and Iacobucci, all of whom signed L'Heureux-Dubé's *Moge* opinion, and McLachlin, who was the sole judge who did not. She wrote a brief concurring opinion.[69]

That L'Heureux-Dubé would write the majority decision became apparent right after the oral submissions at the case conference. None of the other judges volunteered and she expressed a strong interest in drafting. The handwritten notes she made at the time signified her excitement: "This is to be a major undertaking. Style will be important. Research must be thorough. Context is important. Speak of the feminization of poverty."[70] By this time, she had come to the conclusion that forcing self-sufficiency upon ex-spouses regardless of their circumstances was an error. It was a damaging legal trend and she wished to "destroy it forever," with a decision that "should be like *Seaboyer.*"[71] *Seaboyer* had heralded a marked departure for L'Heureux-Dubé, a newly articulated focus on the gender-based vulnerabilities of women to sexual assault. Now it was the financial devastation that so many women experienced upon divorce that would drive her analysis, overcoming any earlier hesitations she may have had about the usefulness of long-term alimony.

Her ruling clarified first that the *Pelech* trilogy did not tie the court's hands; she distinguished the earlier cases on factual grounds.[72] She quoted from *Messier v. Delage,* but here she referred to the majority opinion, not to Lamer's clean-break dissent. She quoted from Abella's widely cited 1981 paper on spousal support: "It is hard to be an independent equal when one is not equally able to become independent."[73] She dispensed with the distinction between "traditional" and "modern" marriages, because this required courts to make assessments based on "stereotypes."[74] The purpose of spousal support, she wrote, was to "relieve economic hardship" resulting from marriage or its breakdown, to alleviate the "effect of the marriage in either impairing or improving each party's economic prospects."[75] Those who advocated the "deemed self-sufficiency model" as the "pre-eminent objective" in the *Divorce Act* were incorrect. No single objective was paramount.⁷⁶ The "sink or swim" stance had contributed to the "feminization of poverty," and spousal support could help to alleviate that.⁷⁷

She conceded that marriage did not "automatically entitle a spouse to support," especially where the relationship had been equitable. She offered a "utopian" depiction of an egalitarian marriage where the clean break could operate with fairness: "[B]oth spouses maximize their earning potential by working outside the home, pursuing economic and educational opportunities in a similar manner, dividing up the domestic labour identically, and either making no economic sacrifices for the other or, more likely, making them equally."⁷⁸ In contrast, long-term support would be the preferable option in the more numerous cases where one spouse suffered economic disadvantages while the other reaped economic benefits. As she had recognized in *Seaboyer* with respect to sexual assault, inequality inside marriages was also deeply gendered:

> Women have tended to suffer economic disadvantages and hardships from marriage or its breakdown because of the traditional division of labour within that institution ... These sacrifices often impair the ability of the partner who makes them (usually the wife) to maximize her earning potential because she may tend to forego educational and career advancement opportunities. These same sacrifices may also enhance the earning potential of the other spouse (usually the husband) who, because his wife is tending to such matters, is free to pursue economic goals ... The curtailment of outside employment obviously has a significant impact on future earning capacity ... Often difficulties are exacerbated by the enduring responsibility for children of the marriage. The spouse who has made economic sacrifices in the marriage also generally becomes the custodial parent ...⁷⁹

It was an analysis based on "substantive" rather than "formal" equality, terms she would employ in a later spousal support decision.⁸⁰

Zofia Moge had sustained "substantial economic disadvantage" from her marriage and its breakdown. Her continuing responsibility for the children after the separation in 1973 had further reduced her ability to earn an income. She had failed to become economically self-sufficient "notwithstanding her conscientious efforts."⁸¹ The $150-a-month support awarded by the Manitoba Court of Appeal would never extricate her from financial insecurity, but family law could play "a limited role in alleviating the economic consequences of marriage breakdown."[82] In the final result, L'Heureux-Dubé refused to terminate Andrzej Moge's spousal support.

SOCIAL CONTEXT AND JUDICIAL NOTICE

As with *Seaboyer,* one of the controversial aspects of *Moge* was the material L'Heureux-Dubé relied upon to explain her decision. Judges customarily cited law reports, legal texts, and occasionally law review articles.[83] *Moge* expanded upon this dramatically. In addition to dozens of traditional sources, L'Heureux-Dubé listed sixteen sociological and economic studies, many of them familiar to her from her earlier work in family law reform while others were drawn from LEAF's factum.[84] L'Heureux-Dubé's judicial colleagues pointed out that she "more than any of the others" seemed to rely upon non-legal texts.[85] In many ways, it was reminiscent of her pathbreaking embrace of psycho-social expertise when she was trying family law cases in the Quebec Superior Court. But it was also a substantial departure from her "formalist" jurisprudence on the Quebec Court of Appeal.[86]

In applying the *Divorce Act,* L'Heureux-Dubé emphasized that it was an accepted rule of statutory interpretation that "Parliament must be taken as being aware of the social and historical context."[87] Data on the labour market, women and poverty, and the financial and social impacts of divorce provided the "social context" within which judges issued support orders. Under the doctrine of "judicial notice," these studies allowed her to import the "general economic impact of divorce on women" into the decision-making process.[88] It would be "perverse" to assume that Parliament's intention in enacting the act was to "financially penalize women," she wrote, and yet it was clear that the self-sufficiency model had "disenfranchised many women in the court room."[89] Her conclusion: "[T]he support model of self-sufficiency which Mr. Moge urges the Court to apply cannot be supported as a matter of statutory interpretation."[90]

Because it was expensive to retain experts to testify about the economic repercussions of a couple's marital roles, L'Heureux-Dubé urged more judges to take judicial notice of socio-economic reports.[91] Experts on the doctrine of judicial notice agreed that judges could incorporate into their decisions "not only facts of common notoriety but also indisputable matter contained in available sources of recognized accuracy."[92] Both Bertha Wilson and Brian Dickson had advocated a liberalized view of judicial notice, particularly in the era of the *Charter,* insisting that social science was superior to judicial "guesswork."[93] In the United States, the citation of social science research via the "Brandeis brief" was standard form.[94]

However, critics expressed concern that the concept was overused, and that one should not allow data to enter the courtroom untested by cross-examination.[95] What if judges based their rulings on invalid social science reports, or misinterpreted valid social science evidence? Some suggested it would be fairer for judges to advise counsel of these sources in advance, giving them a "reasonable opportunity to present information in rebuttal."[96] University of Ottawa law professor David Paciocco labelled L'Heureux-Dubé's use of extrinsic sources "unorthodox," although he noted that "the use of interdisciplinary materials – social science, philosophy, psychology – all of those things really came to life in her judgments. She was masterful at widening the nature of legal debate."[97]

Julien Payne agreed that L'Heureux-Dubé was "well known for engaging in analysis that involve[d] references to materials that were non-legal," adding that there was "some debate on whether you can do that, but Claire didn't have any hesitation." He added that others might use such evidence in coming to their decisions, but "wouldn't necessarily have acknowledged that." It was one of the reasons L'Heureux-Dubé experienced "resistance," he asserted, with critics claiming that her decisions were "driven by feminist policy making."[98] Queen's law professor Nicholas Bala agreed that the use of judicial notice for social context "opened [her] up to criticism."[99] The concern was that social context evidence, so important to the legislative and policy-making function, was out of place in the courtroom.

Two years after she released her *Moge* decision, L'Heureux-Dubé published an article in the *Ottawa Law Review* in which she defended the use of socio-economic sources as essential contextual background for sound judicial decision making. Judges applied rules through "a prism of personal experience," she stated, that sometimes provided "a perfectly adequate analytical framework" but occasionally did "not accord with reality." Judicial notice could play "a necessary role in re-aligning that prism with reality."[100] In family law, many assumptions were "based on male norms and values." This made it particularly important "to acknowledge and keep abreast of broad societal trends" so that decisions would "contemplate the human picture." She noted that the Supreme Court had slowly expanded the ambit of extrinsic evidence to include royal commission reports, law reform commission reports, legislative history, and some socio-economic data. The important thing, she stressed, was that the data be "acknowledged by the judge."[101] If judges openly cited social science reports rather than

Family Law and Spousal Support 409

hid behind untested hunches, their rulings could be challenged, and lawyers and other courts could revise case law to reflect better social science data. Ruth Sullivan, an expert on statutory interpretation, noted that L'Heureux-Dubé's comments exemplified her "judicial integrity," and demonstrated how social science data could be used "to challenge faulty or inadequate assumptions about women and their role in society."[102]

The Aftermath

On 17 December 1992, the *Moge* ruling made *The National,* the Canadian Broadcasting Corporation's flagship television news program, in a segment titled "Alimony Agony." A youngish-looking news anchor, Peter Mansbridge, called it "the ties that bind," while an even younger-looking news correspondent, Pamela Wallin, added: "The marriage breakup is making many Canadian women poor." Zofia Moge, wearing a pink sweater, black slacks, and blue slippers, was interviewed in her tiny Winnipeg apartment, seated on a sofa beside a doily-covered coffee table. "I am very happy I win," she told CBC reporter Saša Petricic, "because so many years I am so suffering ... by myself, with three children ... If I find a good job, I am never asking he should be paying me."[103]

Predictably, Andrzej Moge was less upbeat. He told newspaper reporters that he was "stunned," adding, "Everyone at work is laughing. They can't believe I'm paying so long."[104] Andrzej continued, "I am broke completely. If I would be in Poland, [Zofia] wouldn't get a penny from me."[105] Andrzej's lawyer added ominously that the support order "could continue until the day he dies!"[106] But the ruling was "cheered" by the couple's three children. The youngest, Ed Moge, told the press, "We know what our mom went through to raise us ... it was absolutely incredible all the sacrifices she had to make."[107]

Counsel for LEAF, Alison Diduck said that she "loved the outcome" and was "surprised" at how much of LEAF's argument "found its way into the decision."[108] Zofia's lawyer, Peter Bruckshaw, described himself as "surprised and delighted" by the decision, regretting that he had not sought an increase in spousal support instead of just defending against Andrzej's claim. He described *Moge* as "a decision discussed internationally," and much "more significant than I understood at the time."[109]

Globe and Mail reporter Sean Fine was fascinated by the ruling. The son of a single mother (his father had died when he was young), he characterized the decision as "a very human endeavour" and "wanted to find out more about the human being ... who wrote the judgment." He arranged an interview with L'Heureux-Dubé, and recalled years later the impression she left upon him:

> As everyone has no doubt described, she's so full of life [and] very warm. There's such an energy in her. She wrote with power. She could write in a very vivid way. When I asked her where her judgments [came] from, she pointed at her gut, and said, "It comes from here." She wasn't afraid to write strongly, to stake out strong positions on all sorts of issues – to be where her gut told her to be. And so, in that case, she was an original. [Canadian political scientist] Peter Russell used to tell me that judges were from the "mushy middle." She certainly wasn't. [There was] nothing mushy about her.[110]

Between 1987 and 1992, courts in all provinces had been moving toward the clean-break model from the *Pelech* trilogy. In what some observers described as "a revolution" in approach, *Moge* turned this around.[111] Toronto family law expert Linda Silver Dranoff, who tracked the impact of the ruling, documented thousands of published decisions that cited and applied L'Heureux-Dubé's *Moge* decision, resulting in spousal support in higher amounts for longer periods of time.[112] Not everyone was a fan of the new direction. Western University's law professor Jay McLeod denounced long-term spousal support as akin to "Chinese water-torture." He critiqued L'Heureux-Dubé's decision for its "political agenda" and for attempting to use spousal support "to redress systemic gender-based discrimination in society."[113]

Julien Payne counted *Moge* as one of the "most important judgments in family law" from the Supreme Court of Canada "in one hundred years," and "the most significant judgment" in L'Heureux-Dubé's career "regardless of field."[114] He added, "You're either pro-women or pro-men, [on] one or the other side of the plank. There are two philosophies. 'There's a good woman behind every man.' Or 'He earned it, it's his.' *Moge* was a sea change, a revolutionary change, [and] 'a Homemaker's Charter' ... that put money in women's pockets."[115] Laval law professor Louise Langevin lauded L'Heureux-Dubé's insertion of social context as forging the way for others, a ruling that *"a éventuellement trouvé une place dans les pratiques, les habitudes, et les jugements de ses collègues."*[†, 116]

---

† "in time found a place in the practices, habits, and decisions of her colleagues"

L'Heureux-Dubé wrote other important family law judgments at the Supreme Court, strengthening divorced women's mobility rights[117] and insisting that legal aid must be offered to women who resisted state efforts to take custody of their children.[118] In dissent, she also asserted that the *Charter* required that unmarried cohabiting persons of the opposite sex should have access to spousal support upon relationship breakdown,[119] and critiqued her colleagues for reducing spousal support drawn from an ex-husband's pension, an asset that had been previously equalized.[120] But none of these decisions eclipsed her pride in *Moge*. "I put all my heart and all my knowledge in *Moge*. It came from my experience with clients in family law, during my time on the Superior Court, and the Court of Appeal. It was so natural for me. [It was] the field I knew. I think if I hadn't written *Moge* it would never have been written. It's my heart."[121]

31
Human Rights for Same-Sex Couples
Mossop, 1993

Brian Mossop, whose case offered Claire L'Heureux-Dubé and her Supreme Court colleagues their first window into same-sex relationships, was a well-travelled, intellectually curious, politically engaged translator. Born in London, England, he immigrated to Toronto with his family at the age of four. Educated at East York Collegiate, Neuchâtel Junior College, the Université d'Aix-Marseille, the University of California, Los Angeles, Ohio State University, and the University of Toronto, he was drawn to languages. He studied French, German, Latin, Russian, and Ojibwa, and then began a doctorate in linguistics at the University of Toronto. In 1974, he began working as a translator with the federal government in Toronto.[1]

The government was frantically recruiting translators in the aftermath of the 1969 *Official Languages Act,* and Mossop passed the certification examination as a qualified translator. At the Department of the Secretary of State for almost twenty years and then with the Department of Public Works and Government Services until his retirement in 2014, he translated papers on meteorology, forestry, ecology, transport, penitentiaries, immigration, and refugees. He found the theoretical aspects of his work captivating, and also lectured on translation part-time at York University.[2]

Nineteen seventy-four was also the year when twenty-eight-year-old Mossop self-identified as "gay" and first crossed paths with Ken Popert, who would become his life partner. Twenty-seven-year-old Popert had just returned to Toronto, the city of his birth, after five years of graduate studies in anthropology and linguistics at Cornell University. Although

Human Rights for Same-Sex Couples 413

Ken Popert and Brian Mossop, whose claim became the first LGBT case heard at the Supreme Court of Canada, photo taken in Toronto, 1974.

Mossop's political activism had been devoted to the Communist Party of Canada up to that point, Popert was involved with the Gay Alliance Toward Equality and *The Body Politic* publishing collective.[3] The two men met at a gay rights march in Allen Gardens. It was a momentous time in Mossop's life: "Everything happened that summer. I started working in the Translation Bureau, I met Ken, and I came out [as gay], all in the space of eight weeks."[4] In 1976, Mossop and Popert jointly purchased a house in Riverdale and moved in together.[5]

Mossop soon became involved in gay activist work too. He joined the Committee to Defend John Damien, the Toronto jockey who was fired for being gay. He helped found the Right to Privacy Committee after the police raided gay bathhouses in the city. He was one of those arrested when the police raided the bathhouses again in 1981, and he helped organize the subsequent protest that led to "the biggest gay rights demonstration" yet seen in Canada.[6]

Bereavement Leave: A "Test Case" with Not Much "Prospect for Success"

On 3 June 1985, Mossop attended the funeral of Popert's father. One of the benefits of Mossop's unionized job was bereavement leave, and he applied for one day's paid leave after the funeral. He stated in the application that the deceased was "the father of my lover (male) of ten years, with whom I reside."[7] If he had been in a heterosexual relationship, this would have qualified for up to four days of paid leave. The collective agreement offered bereavement leave to employees after the death of members of their "immediate family." An extended list of people qualified, including common-law spouses, in-laws, wards, and any relative permanently residing in the household.[8] The union's efforts to include same-sex couples had failed when the government said no at the bargaining table.[9] The union decided to support Mossop's claim.[10]

Mossop's request was a "test case" that he did not expect to win, and sure enough, the government promptly denied the application. He grieved the denial, pointing out that under the collective agreement, a "common-law spouse" relationship was defined to exist "when, for a continuous period of at least one year, an employee has lived with a person of the opposite sex, publicly represented that person to be his/her spouse, and lives and intends to continue to live with that person as if that person were his/her spouse." The only difference in Mossop's situation was that he and Popert were not of opposite sexes.[11] The grievance was rejected.

That summer, Mossop launched a complaint with the Canadian Human Rights Commission (CHRC), claiming that the government had violated his rights as a gay man.[12] Once again, he did not think there was much prospect of success, but he went ahead since it "didn't involve an awful lot of work."[13] The CHRC's mission was to represent the public interest in human rights, not to represent individual complainants, and it took over the management of Mossop's case and hired the lawyers. Human rights complainants had the right to retain their own counsel at their own expense, but few did so. Mossop apparently had no idea that, as a separate party, he had the right to make independent representations with or without the assistance of a lawyer.[14] The consequences of this would become clear later.

There was vigorous debate over the role of law within the early gay liberation movement. Popert described *The Body Politic* collective as "state-averse," a group that would not have approved of the attempt to seek legal redress.[15] Mossop explained, "There were some who thought it was important to change the law. Others said no ... that the important thing was getting our ideas out into society through things like 'kiss-ins' and so on.'" According to Mossop, the naysayers felt that it was "more important to be in everyone's face – 'Here we are, we're not anything like you thought we were.'"[16] But Mossop viewed his case as a compromise, a potential launching pad to get gay issues into wider discussion:

> A lot of time was spent in the gay movement in the mid-1970s just trying to figure [ourselves] out ... What were we, and how did we fit in, and what should we say? What kind of positive discourse should we invent ...to think of an alternative way of talking about ourselves?[17]

Mossop believed that greater equality for gays and lesbians would follow once more people discovered that they knew someone who was gay and homosexuality was "no longer an abstraction." Perhaps this case would embolden those who were not yet public. "I think the main message was 'Come out of the closet now,'" he said.[18] The other focus was to alter the framework of discriminatory preconceptions. "When Ken and I met, the whole idea that gay men might have lasting relationships with each other was the opposite of the discourse that existed in society about homosexuality. [There was] no encouragement from society. As a result, we had to make our own arrangements. We devised a little ceremony for the anniversary of the day we met. We went down to the Eaton Centre and bought [two gold chains with entwined circles on them] and each year at the anniversary we exchange them. But in the early gay movement, the whole idea of gay marriage was repellent. We created our own relationship; we didn't want or need the blessing of the state."[19]

Popert emphasized that marriage "had a history of being a repressive institution" that could not "accommodate two equal adults." He characterized it as "an institution for one and a half people," and stressed that neither he nor his partner wanted "a parallel drawn" with the "husband and wife relationship." He added: "You can read gay marriage in a lot of different ways, one as a rejection of sexual liberation." He explained that it was "important to know" that this human rights complaint was conceptualized as a "broader approach," designed to head off the marriage debate by focusing on the "family relationship." The hope was that the case might promote a "platform for social and cultural change."[20]

The Canadian Human Rights Tribunal: The Meaning of "Family Status"

Beth Atcheson, a Toronto lawyer and also one of the founders of the Women's Legal Education and Action Fund (LEAF), was the tribunal adjudicator appointed to preside over a two-day human rights hearing in 1987. Mossop testified at the hearing about why he was waging such an extensive battle for something so small as one day of bereavement leave:

> [T]his is just another case of me being treated differently because I am gay. And every gay person, including me, has a long history of constantly being treated differently and in particular being treated as if our feelings or relationships don't count somehow. Getting a day of leave means something because it's a sort of official thing, it means that you're recognized as a unit in society.[21]

The *Canadian Human Rights Act* outlawed discriminatory treatment in employment "on a prohibited ground."[22] The problem was that the act did not prohibit discrimination on the basis of sexual orientation. When it was enacted in 1977, legislators had ranked gay and lesbian rights well below race, national or ethnic origin, colour, religion, age, physical handicap, and sex, all of which were incorporated into the act. The CHRC had repeatedly requested the government to add sexual orientation, without success.[23] In 1982, Justice Minister Mark MacGuigan had refused because of insufficient "social consensus."[24]

And so Mossop's complaint was filed under the category of "family status." The phrase was not defined in the act and the crux of the case was whether two gay men fit. The government had already conceded that unmarried heterosexual couples qualified if they had cohabited continuously for a year, publicly represented themselves as spouses, and intended to continue the relationship. In a measure of how differently gay men were seen, the CHRC led evidence of all of these things, but far more. Not only did Mossop and Popert live together, not only did they openly declare their same-sex status to family and friends, but they resided in a house that they co-owned and financed jointly. The two men shared a bank account, domestic tasks, and holidays. They were the beneficiaries of each other's will.[25]

Even further, one of the CHRC lawyers advised the tribunal that Mossop and Popert had a "monogamous" sexual relationship.[26] Reminiscing years later, Mossop said that the lawyers had never asked him if this was the case, and in fact it was inaccurate. "I found it so amusing, that whoever was representing me got up and … announced that we had a monogamous sexual relationship. We certainly did not. [He was] kind of reading in from what we thought of as heterosexual standards … into our relationship, even though I'd never actually told him anything about our sexual relationship."[27]

The evidence before the tribunal might have been more nuanced if anyone connected with the hearing had been an out gay or lesbian. None was. In fact, no experts on gay and lesbian issues were even called to testify. Instead, the CHRC called a scholar who specialized in gender and class, Margrit Eichler, a sociologist from the Ontario Institute for Studies in Education who researched family policy. This was her first time in the witness box as an expert. "I remember being excited to be asked," she explained, "and wondering 'Why me?'"[28] Eichler testified that there was no "standard definition" or "consensus" on the "fluid" concept of "family."[29] She criticized traditionally narrow definitions. While there was no "standard list of factors" to consider, she suggested that the Mossop-Popert relationship should qualify. The couple had lived in a joint residence for some time, with the expectation of continuance. They had an emotional and sexual relationship, an economic union, and shared housework.[30]

The federal government argued against a "sociological approach" to the term, suggesting instead that the "plain meaning of 'family status'" implied "certain traditional values and one common denominator … children." The government's lawyer added: "There is no need to argue that there will be no children in the type of relationship between Mr. Mossop and his lover."[31] Once again, the hearing was hampered by the lack of gay and lesbian expertise. Organizations of gay fathers existed at the time.[32]

Mossop testified that as a translator by profession, he knew that the usage of words shifted over time. "There's no single meaning of the word 'family' in the English language. It isn't just that the sociological facts differ about different types of living relationships but the word 'family' has different meanings." He thought the federal government should be taken to task for not having considered whether *heterosexual* common-law couples would meet its definition of "family." He explained, "There probably was an assumption that heterosexual couples are considered to be families," and added that this sort of "common wisdom" amounted to a "bias in favour of heterosexual people."[33]

Atcheson agreed that the "possibilities inherent in the term 'family'" were "many and complex." Rejecting the government's analysis, she concluded in her decision that it was problematic to rely upon "traditional values" or "common wisdom" because these might reflect "bias or prejudice against homosexuals in Canada."[34] The term "must be tested in today's world, against an understanding of how people are living and how language reflects that reality." Given that the act was "intended to address group stereotypes," Atcheson held that "homosexual couples" could constitute a "family."[35] She found Brian Mossop entitled to bereavement leave, and awarded additional compensation for damage to his "feelings and self-respect."[36] It was not to last. The federal government appealed to the Federal Court of Appeal, which ruled that the denial of bereavement leave to gay and lesbian couples did not violate the *Canadian Human Rights Act*.[37]

SURPRISES AT THE SUPREME COURT OF CANADA

The parties regrouped in Ottawa to argue an appeal before the Supreme Court in June 1992. It was the chief justice who decided how many and which judges should sit on any particular case, and in *Mossop*, Lamer assigned seven: himself, La Forest, L'Heureux-Dubé, Sopinka, Cory, McLachlin, and Iacobucci.[38] Both Brian Mossop and Ken Popert were in the courtroom for the oral submissions. René Duval, a Quebec litigator with experience in human rights law, acted for the CHRC. Barbara McIsaac, with the Department of Justice, represented the federal government. Gwen Brodsky, a Vancouver-based *Charter* expert who had been LEAF's first litigation director, was counsel for five intervener groups backing Mossop: Equality for Gays and Lesbians Everywhere (EGALE), the National Action Committee on the Status of Women, the National Association of Women and the Law, the Canadian Disability Rights Council, and the Canadian Rights and Liberties Federation.[39] Ian Binnie, then a senior partner with a large Bay Street law firm, represented groups opposed to gay and lesbian rights: the Evangelical Fellowship of Canada, the Pentecostal Assemblies of Canada, the Salvation Army, Focus on the Family, and REAL Women.[40] Binnie's clients had already made their views known outside the courtroom.

Human Rights for Same-Sex Couples

Supreme Court of Canada courtroom.

REAL Women complained that extending family benefits to more people would put "undue economic pressure on the government and the taxpayer," while the Salvation Army suggested that homosexual rights would provoke "a slide toward legalized pedophilia and bestiality."[41]

Although the judges preoccupied themselves with the legal "standard of review," the parties were far more interested in whether same-sex couples could form families, the issue that will be considered here.[42] Brian Mossop was asked at the outset of the hearing whether he wished to make any submissions himself, and he declined. "I regretted that as soon as it started," he explained. He regretted it because to his mind, the central issue of gay rights was never fully addressed. During the break, he approached one of the lawyers to see whether it was still possible for him to speak. The lawyer checked with the court. The answer came back that it was now too late.[43]

Two months later, before the Supreme Court judges had come to any agreement over the decision they should render in *Mossop*, the Ontario Court of Appeal issued a groundbreaking decision in *Haig*, a case of a man who had lost his job with the Canadian Armed Forces because he was gay. Haig had argued that it was a violation of his *Charter* rights that the *Canadian Human Rights Act* failed to provide protection against discrimination on the basis of "sexual orientation." The Ontario Court of Appeal agreed, held that the statute was constitutionally deficient, applied the equality provision of section 15 of the *Charter*, and "read in" the ground of "sexual orientation" to the act.[44] It was a bold move, ushering in broad human rights protection for gays and lesbians in one fell swoop.

Chief Justice Lamer apparently wondered whether the judges should hold off on circulating reasons in *Mossop* until it was clear whether the *Haig* case would also be coming up to the Supreme Court. Then Justice Minister Kim Campbell announced that the federal government would not appeal, that it would accept the *Haig* ruling and apply it across Canada.[45] In a surprising move, Lamer had the court registrar write to the lawyers who had appeared in the Mossop case, inviting them to make "supplementary submissions" regarding the relevance of *Haig*.[46] It was a call to place the *Charter* rights of gays and lesbians squarely into the mix.

Almost before the ink was dry, Barbara McIsaac and Ian Binnie both wrote back that it would be improper to expand the Mossop case this way. "The record as it now exists is not adequate," replied McIsaac.[47] "It would be inappropriate to alter fundamentally the nature of the Mossop case at this late stage," wrote Binnie, especially since "both the Canadian Human Rights Commission and Mr. Mossop expressly disavowed any reliance in this case on the *Charter*."[48] Adding more surprise to the situation, the CHRC indicated that it was of the same opinion. Instead of welcoming the chance to argue that *Haig* should be used to read in sexual orientation, providing not only a remedy for Brian Mossop but also much wider protection for gays and lesbians across the board, the CHRC agreed that the court should not reconvene.[49]

There were good reasons why the CHRC should have been first in line to argue the inclusion of sexual orientation within human rights statutes. Gordon Fairweather, chief commissioner of the CHRC, had told a Parliamentary committee in 1982 that he had hoped sexual orientation would be included when the legislation was first enacted in 1977. As for the concern that there might be inadequate social consensus for this, he replied bluntly, "We have found otherwise, frankly."[50] Why didn't the CHRC welcome the chance to reconvene and make the argument? William Pentney, general counsel to the CHRC, later explained that he had no idea whether the CHRC could attack its own enabling statute, a concern that would prove prescient several years later.[51] He also had no idea where the court might go if the *Charter* were argued. Might the court "topple the whole edifice" and declare the entire anti-discrimination provision unconstitutional? Or, if the court were to give the government time to re-enact the legislation, would the government produce an acceptable revised version? Equally problematic, might the court simply tell the parties that the issues were so complex that they should go back to the drawing board and begin the long, slow human rights process with a fresh complaint? Ultimately, Pentney recalled, the CHRC decided it too did not want a rehearing.[52]

Even EGALE chose not to argue that the *Charter* should import sexual orientation into the act. As their lawyer, Gwen Brodsky, put it, their only claim for section 15 was that it should be used as an interpretive backdrop to aid the court in finding that "family status" included gays and lesbians. Brodsky agreed with the other lawyers that it was too late to open up the case to a full-blown *Charter* challenge. And she added, "I frankly had no idea where Lamer was headed when he invited those additional submissions. It didn't make sense to me. Procedurally, it didn't seem plausible. The evidentiary record was limited to the decision of a tribunal where no *Charter* argument had been made."[53]

As for Brian Mossop, he had no inkling that he personally had the right to request that the case be reopened for new argument, as the chief justice had suggested. If he had received any correspondence from the chief justice on the matter, he did not recall it. "I didn't know I had the right" to reargue this, he emphasized. "I didn't know I had the right to have a lawyer. I thought it was up to the commission."[54] He was not surprised that the *Charter* had not been argued from the outset, adding: "On the day I went in [to the CHRC], at the very start, in June 1985, [section 15 of] the *Charter* had only been in effect for a few weeks. I don't think the concept of a *Charter* challenge existed. I doubt that was anyone's first thought."[55] Asked whether he *would* have wished to reconvene the hearing for supplementary submissions, even if this were at his own expense, he replied without hesitation, "Yes." He and his partner, Ken Popert, had fundraised for other gay legal campaigns in the past, and would have done so this time.[56] Years later, Ken Popert mused that the judicial system "missed a huge opportunity to nip the whole anguished gay marriage thing in the bud" by folding gays and lesbians into family status instead.[57] It was indeed a lost opportunity.

Lamer's Majority Decision: Gays Do Not Qualify as Family

The seven Supreme Court judges went back to drafting. On the question that mattered most to Brian Mossop, the court was almost evenly divided. Writing for four judges (Lamer, La Forest, Sopinka, Iacobucci), Lamer held that a gay relationship could not qualify under "family status." A minority composed of L'Heureux-Dubé, McLachlin, and Cory disagreed.

Lamer's decision sidestepped the contested definition of "family." Instead, he based his decision on the failure of Parliament to add "sexual orientation" into the *Canadian Human Rights Act* in the first place:

> When Mr. Mossop was denied bereavement leave in June 1985, the *CHRA* did not prohibit discrimination on the basis of sexual orientation. In my opinion, this fact is a highly relevant part of the context in which the phrase "family status" in the Act must be interpreted ... In the case at bar, Mr. Mossop's sexual orientation is so closely connected with the grounds which led to the refusal of the benefit that this denial could not be condemned as discrimination on the basis of "family status" without indirectly introducing into the *CHRA* the prohibition which Parliament specifically decided not to include.[58]

Lamer added that he would have preferred the parties to address the constitutionality of the legislation directly. "Relying on the reasons of the Ontario Court of Appeal in *Haig*, the appellant could then have challenged the constitutionality of s. 3 of the *CHRA* on the basis of the absence of sexual orientation from the list of prohibited grounds of discrimination. This would have enabled this Court to address the fundamental questions argued in the Ontario Court of Appeal in *Haig*. It would then have been possible to give a much more complete and lasting solution to the present problem."[59] Absent a *Charter* challenge, Lamer concluded that he had to dismiss Mossop's claim, "whatever may be my personal views in that regard."[60]

The CHRC was upset with the critique of its failure to argue the *Charter*. Commissioner Michelle Falardeau-Ramsay told the press that the CHRC was still recovering from a "rebuke" it had received from the Federal Court of Appeal for "trying to change the grounds of its complaint" in an earlier case. It was a "Catch-22 situation," she complained.[61] Gwen Brodsky agreed. "[It was] a bit of salt in the wound for me to draw from the majority judgment that perhaps we'd been remiss in not arguing a full-blown *Charter* challenge." Referring to Lamer's decision as a "dead-tree interpretive approach" that exemplified "traditional socially conservative legal reasoning," she added: "My thought was that even if a full-blown *Charter* challenge had been brought, the majority would not likely have ruled in our favour."[62] William Pentney, CHRC's counsel, reflected years later that it was not until he saw the decision that he sensed that the court had actually wanted the commission to present "a wholly new legal foundation" for the case. "There was a fair bit of court jurisprudence that suggested it was not really open to that," he noted, but "it sure would have been nicer to have wrapped it all up at the *Mossop* stage."[63]

Would a full-blown *Charter* challenge have secured equality for gays and lesbians in *Mossop?* Years later, L'Heureux-Dubé was uncertain. "It's complicated," she said. "I suspect there were too many hurdles."[64] Yet the evidence is less equivocal. Looking at it with hindsight, the panel of seven might just have done it then and there. The clues lay in the next gay and lesbian case that reached the Supreme Court, *Egan* in 1995, where the *Charter* was argued before the full nine-person panel of judges.[65] In *Egan*, five judges – Lamer, La Forest, Gonthier, Major, and Sopinka – ruled against same-sex couples, while a minority of four, L'Heureux-Dubé, Cory, Iacobucci, and McLachlin, held that governmental old-age pension benefits must not be restricted to heterosexual couples. But two judges who ruled *against* gays and lesbians in *Egan*, Gonthier and Major, were absent from the *Mossop* panel. If the judges from the *Mossop* panel of seven had ruled the same way on the *Charter* issues that they did later in *Egan*, there would have been a majority for Brian Mossop.[66] And it would have saved a lot of time and money for lesbian/gay/bisexual/transsexual (LGBT) litigants down the road.[67]

L'Heureux-Dubé's Dissent: An "Enriched Vision" of Family

L'Heureux-Dubé's dissent in *Mossop*, supported on this issue by both McLachlin and Cory, constituted an important judicial recognition of gay and lesbian families. It took her new line of jurisprudence from *Seaboyer*, expanded upon in *Moge*, to a higher level still, extending the mantle of human rights protection to gay and lesbian communities. Noting that the "social cost of discrimination" was "insupportably high," L'Heureux-Dubé endorsed the "living-tree doctrine" to indicate that the grounds of discrimination should be examined "in the context of contemporary values, and not in a vacuum."[68] She made reference to traditional sources such as cases, dictionaries, legislative debates, and law review articles. But once again she also cited census and demographic data, texts on family theory and policy, and books and articles about gay rights, gay couples, and gay parents.[69] Using references that would be particularly persuasive with feminist and anti-racist audiences, she quoted Adrienne Rich to stress that traditional families did not always produce ideal results, Audre Lorde to emphasize that differences should not be used to delegitimize some families, and Patricia Williams to demonstrate the complexity of overlapping categories of discrimination.[70]

Unlike Lamer, L'Heureux-Dubé dealt in detail with the concept of "family." Many Canadians did not "live within traditional families," she noted, and it was "possible to be pro-family without rejecting less traditional family forms." The debate about family presented society "with a false choice." All families should be enabled to "function as they can, free from discrimination." She rejected the narrow focus on procreation as promoting "an impoverished rather than an enriched vision." It ignored the fact that not all heterosexual couples had children, diminished the stature of adopted children, and erased the fact that many gays and lesbians were "involved in raising and nurturing children."[71]

Whereas Lamer had made reference to legislative debates to demonstrate that Parliament deliberately chose not to include "sexual orientation" in the *Canadian Human Rights Act*, L'Heureux-Dubé made reference to then justice minister Mark MacGuigan's comment in the House of Commons that the amendments included no definition for the phrase "family status" because the government relied upon the CHRC, tribunals, and the courts to interpret such terms.[72] Whereas Lamer had concluded that Mossop was discriminated against based on sexual orientation, not on family status, L'Heureux-Dubé wrote that this argument was "based on an underlying assumption that the grounds of 'family status' and 'sexual orientation' are mutually exclusive." In reality, categories of discrimination often overlapped, and ignoring the complexity of the interaction "misconceive[d] the reality of discrimination."[73] On the eve of her retirement, when asked by the press which judgment she was most proud of, it was *Mossop* that topped L'Heureux-Dubé's list.[74]

The Origins of This Dissent

Mossop was a precursor of the nationwide LGBT movement that would eventually see the law function as one of its most effective tools for dramatic social change. Other blockbuster cases would follow: *Egan*, where five of nine judges held that gay couples could be excluded from governmental old-age pension benefits;[75] *Vriend* in 1998, where the court unanimously found Alberta's human rights statute to be unconstitutional because it failed to include "sexual orientation";[76] *M. v. H.* in 1999, where the court held eight to one that a lesbian couple should not be excluded from the rules governing common-law relationships under the *Ontario Family Law Act*;[77] and *Reference re Same-Sex Marriage* in 2004, where the court unanimously upheld the constitutionality of legislation that would make same-sex marriages legal in Canada.[78] In every case that raised gay and lesbian rights during L'Heureux-Dubé's term on the court, she voted in favour of the LGBT litigants.[79] Shirley Tucker Parks, an Ottawa lawyer who became one of L'Heureux-Dubé's closest friends in the capital city, recalled that her friend was delighted to learn that some had christened her "the Queen of the Gays."[80]

L'Heureux-Dubé's early dissent in *Mossop* set the stage for what would ultimately emerge as a widespread campaign to use the law and the courts to accomplish cultural transformation. Her dissent constituted the most explicit and positive endorsement of gay and lesbian rights yet delivered from the nation's top court. It would become a flashpoint in the emerging debate over "judicial activism," the hotly contested struggle over the division of roles between the legislature and the courts.[81] How had she come to adopt this path-breaking analysis? As her friends would admit, L'Heureux-Dubé was personally somewhat uncomfortable with overt public displays of gay sexuality.[82] Yet she was always proud of her legal decisions on gay rights.[83] Tucker Parks explained that L'Heureux-Dubé took great satisfaction in supporting groups that had "not been treated fairly in the past."[84] In *Seaboyer*, she had responded to the vulnerabilities of women who had been sexually assaulted. In *Moge*, she sought to reduce the financial devastation of divorced women. Now, she moved further to extend rights to same-sex communities. University of Victoria law professor Rebecca Johnson, the law clerk who worked most closely with L'Heureux-Dubé on *Mossop*, tried to explain what it was like observing her decision-making process:

> It's amazing to see someone who was formed in the furnaces of so many different fires ... to see how she negotiated those tensions herself. Justice L'Heureux-Dubé carries in her this mode of judgment that is pretty strong. It's not that she can't revise her opinions, or is insufficiently nuanced, but there is an interior gut monitor that pushes her in a certain direction.[85]

Later, reflecting on her own life experience, L'Heureux-Dubé mentioned in particular one couple she knew from Rimouski, describing them as "wonderful people" who "shared the same artistic sense" and were "living together in a beautiful arrangement." "For me," she added, "homosexuals were not bad people."⁸⁶ It was a concrete reminder of Brian Mossop's belief that gay rights would achieve success based on the number of people who realized that they knew individuals who were gays and lesbians.

The sweeping format of L'Heureux-Dubé's dissent in *Mossop* brought forth a rare compliment from her colleague Beverley McLachlin, who noted in her brief separate remarks that L'Heureux-Dubé had "ably reviewed" Mossop's family status.⁸⁷ Some of the praise was due to Rebecca Johnson, who worked for many months on the background research for *Mossop*. As was not unusual at the Supreme Court at the time, she also helped to draft portions of L'Heureux-Dubé's dissent.⁸⁸ L'Heureux-Dubé frankly admitted that it was Johnson who brought to her the references to Adrienne Rich, Audre Lorde, and Patricia Williams, adding, "I am not a scholar. That's all Rebecca. That's what we asked [our clerks] to do – find the literature, find the law, find the jurisprudence." But she stressed that the final decision was hers: "I edited everything, word for word. I never let anything out [of which] I was not sure 100 percent."⁸⁹ Johnson concurred:

> Clerks are "pens" available to the judges. But those are her judgments ... I got back the old-style cut-and-paste. She had taken scissors and cut my text, [adding] handwritten parts in between. I learned about the craft of writing under her supervision. [W]hen it was things she didn't agree with, she would move [it], take it out, put it into her own words ... trying to find words to explain what she has decided.⁹⁰

It was an observation shared by other law clerks, who emphasized that L'Heureux-Dubé was tirelessly diligent in her research and in writing judgments, that she read all of the relevant materials voraciously, parsed every line of draft decisions, and took an active role in the preparation of speeches and articles.⁹¹

Ultimately, Johnson felt that under L'Heureux-Dubé's painstaking control, *Mossop* was a triumph:

> [It was] amazing to work with someone who holds such strong views, and see what they make possible ... in their willingness to speak [with] passion ... with commitment to justice – it's a gift. [It was] an amazing experience to be around her – but terrifying – like being close to a volcano – something of beauty and worrying that I would get singed a bit. At best, what it managed to do ... was allow people to see the possibility of their families reflected there even if the law wouldn't yet open the door to make it possible. It spoke

Human Rights for Same-Sex Couples 427

Rebecca Johnson, former law clerk to L'Heureux-Dubé.

to the aspirations and hopes and possibilities and fears and not just to the legal language of what the legislature had intended ... [and] who should be deferred to.[92]

Although he had never expected to win, Brian Mossop explained that he was "very pleased that it was just one vote difference." Equally important, he noted, "two of the people on my side were women."[93] But the highlight, the goal from the outset, was the media coverage that followed. Brian Mossop and Ken Popert called a Toronto Queen's Park press conference at which Mossop was quoted as saying: "This was our first attempt at this," and "eventually" he added, "Canadian lesbian and gay couples will be recognized as families."[94]

32
Tax Law and Sex Discrimination
Symes, 1993

Beth Symes decided to challenge Revenue Canada the year that the *Canadian Charter of Rights and Freedoms* came into force. Raised in Sioux Lookout, Fort Frances, and Winnipeg, she graduated from Queen's law school in 1976, was called to the Ontario bar in 1978, and opened a private law practice in Toronto directly after.[1] One of few women to open her own firm in that era, she partnered with two other young women in 1980. Their feminist law firm, Symes, Kiteley & McIntyre, did litigation, family, and labour law.[2] In the early years, money was tight. Without charge, Symes represented many clients with time-consuming cases no one else would take, including women suffering from sexual harassment, for whom legal remedies were particularly elusive. She often paid her office staff more than she took home from her law practice. Things had just begun to stabilize when her first daughter was born in 1981; a second arrived in 1985.[3]

Widely recognized even early in her career as one of Canada's most significant social justice lawyers, Symes worked with Toronto Rape Relief, eventually became president of the Canadian Institute for the Administration of Justice, and served on the task group to restructure the United Church of Canada. She volunteered with the Canadian Abortion Rights Action League. She was one of the women to conceive of the Women's Legal Education and Action Fund (LEAF) in 1982, designing its operations, fundraising for its creation in 1985, and nurturing it through its first decades of existence.[4] Her firm litigated *pro bono* cases that dealt with discrimination based on gender, race, class, and disability. She brought a constitutional

Tax Law and Sex Discrimination

Beth Symes, Toronto lawyer who challenged Revenue Canada over childcare expense deductions.

challenge to the Ontario government's rollback of social assistance payments to poor people. She represented clients who sought to stop landlords from refusing to rent to low-income tenants. She worked with Aboriginal women who were challenging sex discrimination under the *Indian Act*. She represented clients with mental disabilities and addictions.[5]

Although she would become a lifelong advocate for funded maternity leaves for women, she never took much time out herself.[6] "As a lawyer in private practice in a small firm, it just wasn't an option," she explained.[7] She took two weeks of maternity leave with the first child, and three months with the second. Two weeks after her first delivery, she was back defending hospital workers who had been fired for engaging in an illegal strike. She rented an extra room next to the arbitration hearing. "The arbitrator took breaks while I breastfed my daughter," she recalled. "I do not recommend this; I am not a role model for women lawyers." But the situation got her to thinking. "It was clear that I could deduct the cost of the room rental as a business expense. Why could I not deduct the cost of the nanny who cared for my daughter during the hearing?"[8]

Because both she and her spouse, Michael Symes, worked full-time, she employed a childcare worker, Shirley Simpson, to look after the girls. Symes paid Simpson above the prevailing market rates, increased her salary every year, paid her Canada Pension Plan and Unemployment Insurance premiums, and issued the proper T4 papers. In 1982, Symes spent over 80 percent of her income on childcare. Given the hours she devoted to her practice, she was earning less than minimum wage.[9]

Taking *Charter* Litigation to a Whole New Threshold

Back at her law office, as she wrote out paycheques for her office staff, paid her rent and utilities, paid the premium for her lawyer's insurance, and sent off her law society dues, she wondered some more. Why were all of these expenses, essential to the running of a legal practice, deductible from her earnings, but the childcare costs were not? To a feminist, it seemed odd. To a feminist lawyer, it seemed worth pursuing. She raised it with Mary Eberts, another co-founder of LEAF, who was then working as a litigator at a large Bay Street firm. They decided Symes would take the role of client, and that Eberts and her colleague Wendy Matheson would act as counsel.

All of them recognized that the only real solution for working parents was to create a publicly funded daycare program, as had opened up in Quebec, to provide childcare just as in public schools. But for years feminists had watched governments of all political stripes promise to create childcare programs in their election platforms, only to see them slip off the agenda after the politicians obtained power. So they decided to try litigation. The original plan was to find three women to bring a challenge collectively: Symes as the self-employed person, a second woman who was a salaried employee, and a third who was a student with income from a stipend or fellowship. They wanted to cover a wide spectrum of women with childcare needs. After further research and reflection, the strategy narrowed. As Symes recalled, "[i]t became clear that it would be better to just ... focus on business expenses in the first stage, rather than try to bring a full section 15 equality challenge to the entire tax act. If we were successful for the first step, it would put enormous pressure on the government to make fundamental changes."[10]

Tackling Revenue Canada meant wading into the tax world with a radically new argument, and taking *Charter* litigation to a whole new threshold. Mary Eberts described it as a plan "born in that time of possibility and expectation," when there was an aura of "excitement" about section 15.[11] Reflecting back, Symes laughed: "There is even an old adage: if you want to start a revolution, pay close attention to the *Income Tax Act*."[12] As *Globe and Mail* reporter Sean Fine wrote, "Such a case would have been unthinkable just a few years ago. Today, it exemplifies the strategies that women's advocates are developing in the second decade of the 1982 Canadian Charter of Rights and Freedoms. During the first 10 years, women won a series of major legal victories that set the groundwork for future equality challenges. Now, fresh from recent triumphs in divorce law and the rights of sexual abuse victims, feminists see a chance to win from the Supreme Court unprecedented social, political, and economic changes that will affect the everyday lives of women."[13]

The First Feminist Tax Case

Symes advised Revenue Canada that beginning in 1982 she would be deducting her full childcare expenses from her business income. Her goals were to draw public attention to "the personal and financial cost of childcare" and to "force the government to respond." She wanted to change the rules for women whose shift work and employment travel made licensed daycare unhelpful – women she represented in her practice, such as hospital employees who worked day, evening, and night shifts, seven days a week, and flight attendants who could be away from home for more than forty-eight hours a week.[14] She hoped to "regularize" the work of childcare providers who were forced by the tax laws to work as "part of an underground economy." Their absence from the tax system subjected them to "exploitation, such as physical and sexual abuse," she argued, and to working without health or unemployment insurance or pensions.[15] The Charter Committee on Poverty Issues, an intervener represented by Toronto human rights lawyer Raj Anand, agreed with Symes. Anand hoped that this case might open up the *Charter* to address new issues like poverty.[16] Intercede, an advocacy organization for domestic workers, also supported the lawsuit.

Symes put aside all the money she saved in taxes, ready to repay what she would owe to Revenue Canada if the claim were disallowed. She was completely open about the tax deduction she was taking. When she gave speeches to women lawyers and other groups about gender equality, she disclosed what she was doing and why. A number of other self-employed women, in law, medicine, other professions, and businesses, followed her lead and began to deduct the full cost of their childcare. Some started to speculate about whether other discriminatory income tax provisions could also be challenged.[17]

In 1985, Revenue Canada's assessors advised Symes that they were going to disallow the deductions for the entire four years. The rationale? Childcare costs were "not outlays or expenses incurred for the purpose of gaining or producing income from business." They were "personal or living expenses," which were not deductible under the *Income Tax Act*.[18] Symes objected and filed an appeal. She claimed that Revenue Canada was not treating her like a "serious business person with a serious expense incurred for a legitimate purpose."[19]

The Canadian Bar Association agreed. For the first time in its seventy-two-year history, the CBA decided to intervene in a court case. Paule Gauthier had been elected its first female president, and she urged the CBA to become involved. The CBA had 8,000 female lawyers among its 37,000 members, and surveys of the membership showed that female lawyers bore "almost double the responsibility for childcare as men."[20] CBA staff lawyer Melina Buckley took the position that "if existing business culture had not been based on a gendered division of labour, childcare expenses would always have been seen as business expenses."[21] Buckley recalled that *Symes* was her "first case" as a newly called lawyer, and that her twelve-year-old daughter sat in the courtroom to observe. "My younger children were six and four," she laughed. "I should have brought them too, and let them run around [the courtroom], just to underline the point."[22]

It took seven years. Revenue Canada dismissed the objection, and the matter went before the Federal Court Trial Division, the Federal Court of Appeal, and the Supreme Court of Canada. Symes won at the trial level, and lost everywhere else.[23] A full bench of the Supreme Court of Canada heard the final arguments on 2 March 1992. It was acknowledged to be the first high court tax case ever to be based "on a feminist analysis," and it was the first time that the Supreme Court allowed television cameras into its courtroom.[24] The seven male judges issued their ruling against Symes on 16 December 1993. L'Heureux-Dubé and McLachlin, the only two women then on the bench, dissented in her favour.[25]

Frank Iacobucci wrote for the men.[26] The son of Italian immigrants, he prided himself on having embarked upon a career in law when the barriers facing non-WASP and female entrants were slowly being dismantled.[27] From his impoverished youth in east-end Vancouver, he had acquired law degrees from the University of British Columbia and Cambridge, and practised corporate law in New York City. He had become a professor of law, dean of law, and vice president of the University of Toronto. In 1985, he had been appointed federal deputy minister of justice, and in 1988 chief justice of the Federal Court of Canada.[28] He was married to a woman with law degrees from Harvard and Cambridge, and they had three children.[29] He, like all six of the other male judges, each of whom was also married with children, had never been solely responsible for the care of his children.[30]

Iacobucci's 1991 appointment to replace Bertha Wilson had attracted some controversy. The press noted that unlike Prime Minister Brian Mulroney's earlier top court appointments, this had not met with universal acclaim and that Iacobucci had been "stung by the criticism."[31] Some critics complained that Iacobucci was "too close to Mulroney," having been his "key adviser" during the drafting of the Meech Lake constitutional accord.[32] The other critics were feminists who lamented that Wilson's replacement was not female, thus reducing the number of women on the Supreme

Justice Frank Iacobucci.

Court from three to two. By contrast, the Canadian Ethnocultural Council noted that Iacobucci's appointment had "increase[d] the ethnic minority representation by 100%."[33] Although Iacobucci was new to the court, he was also an acknowledged expert in tax and corporate law, which made him the obvious judge to write the decision.[34]

In his majority judgment, Iacobucci noted that it was judges who had originally defined childcare expenses as "personal expenses" and that the "increased participation of women in the Canadian workforce" indicated that it might be time for courts to review this.[35] There had been a "change in the social foundation," he conceded, and childcare expenses were "difficult to classify."[36] So far so good: this was not a categorical rejection of Symes's claim. But his decision took a U-turn when he referred to the provisions in the *Income Tax Act* that allowed *a portion of childcare expenses* to be deducted from income, business or otherwise.[37] He recognized that the provisions had set an unrealistically low cap. Less than a third of Symes's actual costs would be deductible under the existing rules.[38] Yet he concluded that when Parliament passed these sections, it intended them to be a "complete code" with respect to childcare expenses.[39] There was no "ambiguity" in the statutory language, so no need to consult "the values of the *Charter*."[40] As for the direct *Charter* challenge, he concluded that there was no violation of the equality provisions, despite the fact that women disproportionately bore the burden of childcare, because there was no evidence to show that women disproportionately *paid* childcare expenses.[41]

L'Heureux-Dubé's Dissent:
A "Male Standard" Based on the "Needs of Businessmen"

L'Heureux-Dubé believed, in contrast, that the case posed "fundamental and complex questions about the visions of equality and inclusivity that mould our legal constructs."[42] Relying upon the expert evidence of sociologist Patricia Armstrong, who had testified about the significant influx of women of childbearing age into the workplace in the late 1970s and early 1980s, L'Heureux-Dubé articulated a path-breaking feminist analysis that had been absent from previous tax cases.[43] She insisted that courts should not ignore "the contextual truth" when they examined what constituted "commercial needs" and "business expenses," concepts that were neither objective nor neutral but "wrought with male perspective and subjectivity."[44] The "male standard" had been used to frame "the backdrop of assumptions," with the assessment of legitimate expenses "constructed on the basis of the needs of businessmen."[45]

She observed that over the past decades the courts had adopted increasingly liberal interpretations of deductible business expenses.[46] The judges had allowed club dues and initiation fees, conference expenses, home office expenses, certain charitable donations, and the cost of luxury cars used for business. Also deductible was a portion of business entertainment and meal expenses, for example taking clients to nightclubs, parties, sporting events, lodges, and even yachts. Fines and penalties could also be considered business expenses. Even the cost of daycare centres was deductible in workplaces where an employer chose to set them up.[47] The costs incurred by businesswomen with children were "no less real, no less worthy of consideration and no less incurred in order to gain or produce income from business" than the costs of "lavish entertainment and the wining and dining of clients and customers," noted L'Heureux-Dubé.[48]

The fact that the *Income Tax Act* expressly allowed a small portion of childcare expenses to be deducted from income did not disentitle businesswomen from deducting the full cost. In L'Heureux-Dubé's view, both deductions could coexist.[49] Even if one believed that the act was ambiguous in this respect, the "prism of the values enshrined in the *Charter*" revealed that the Iacobucci decision impacted women differently than men. Because childcare responsibilities presented a "significant obstacle for women in the social and economic domain," the matter became "an equality issue." It was essential to interpret the *Income Tax Act* in a way that would accommodate "equality and the changing realities of our society."[50] Denying businesswomen the right to deduct childcare as a business expense amounted to a violation of the section 15 equality provision of the *Charter*.[51]

She also responded directly to the concerns Iacobucci had expressed over who actually paid for childcare. Referring to sociological evidence filed by Symes, L'Heureux-Dubé wrote: "[G]enerally women, rather than men, fulfil the role of sole or primary caregiver to children and, as such, it is they alone who incur and pay for such expenses. Men, until very recently, have rarely been primary caregivers, nor single parents and, as a result, they have not incurred direct childcare expenses."[52] Mary Eberts, who agreed with L'Heureux-Dubé on this point, would later add: "The scheme of the childcare deduction in the *Income Tax Act* required that the deduction be taken by the parent who had the lower income. Statistically, that was usually the woman. So, with all those women claiming the deduction, would it not have been appropriate for the court to have concluded [for the purposes of the case] that they had paid the expenses? ... Otherwise a whole lot of families would have been involved in lying to the government about who actually paid the costs for which the woman was claiming the deduction."[53]

In the concluding sections of her decision, L'Heureux-Dubé took issue with some of the criticisms levelled at Symes's action. The Federal Court of Appeal had characterized the challenge as "overshooting," adding: "At bottom, the approach put forward by the respondent risks trivializing the *Charter*."[54] Federal Court of Appeal Justice Décary had stated that he was "not prepared to concede that professional women make up a disadvantaged group."[55] L'Heureux-Dubé agreed that income tax deductions were not the "best way for governments to provide assistance with regard to the high cost of childcare," but stressed that Symes had raised a much narrower question: "The fact that Ms. Symes may be a member of a more privileged economic class does not by itself invalidate her claim under s. 15 of the *Charter*. She is not to be held responsible for all possible discriminations in the income tax system, nor for the fact that other women may suffer disadvantages in the marketplace arising from childcare."[56]

JUDGING AS WOMEN

Despite their disagreement over issues of gender in *Seaboyer*, Claire L'Heureux-Dubé and Beverley McLachlin's views coincided in *Symes*. McLachlin wrote a short separate dissenting opinion where she stated: "I agree with Justice L'Heureux-Dubé's interpretation ... of the *Income Tax Act* ... and s. 15 of the *Canadian Charter of Rights and Freedoms*, and with her conclusion that the appellant's childcare expenses are deductible as business expenses."[57] The two women would side together again in 1995, standing apart from all their male colleagues in the related case of *Thibaudeau*. There, also in dissent, they supported a mother who challenged the tax regime governing child support.[58] It was enough to rekindle the discussion Bertha Wilson had ignited with the speech she gave in 1990, the year of her retirement, titled "Will Women Judges Really Make a Difference?"[59]

Two years after that speech and one year prior to the *Symes* decision, reporter Stephen Bindman had asked McLachlin if she supported Bertha Wilson's comments that women judges would "make a difference." McLachlin had agreed: "I would hope that everyone on the court is looking out for women's interests and my observation is that they are. But there may be situations where we can bring a perspective that might not otherwise be brought forward."[60] Certainly the *Symes* decision suggested as much.

Earlier profiles of McLachlin and L'Heureux-Dubé published in the *Ottawa Citizen* had depicted McLachlin as a woman judge who viewed the law "in more traditional terms," someone who was more likely than L'Heureux-Dubé to "rally her male colleagues around her legal viewpoints."[61] Their shared dissent in *Symes* led some to wonder whether it was emblematic of changing perspectives on the part of McLachlin. L'Heureux-Dubé certainly thought so. In their early years together on the court, L'Heureux-Dubé believed that she and McLachlin had often been on the "same wavelength" on gender issues, but that McLachlin had been reluctant to take risks.[62] By the time of the *Symes* case, L'Heureux-Dubé was of the opinion that McLachlin's appreciation of gender discrimination had broadened.[63] That *Symes* dealt with childcare may also have tipped the balance. As a professional who was also a mother, McLachlin had personal experience with childcare needs.[64]

A 1998 study determined that the first three women appointed to the Supreme Court – Wilson, L'Heureux-Dubé, and McLachlin – were "more than twice as likely" as their male colleagues to support equality claims under the *Charter*.[65] L'Heureux-Dubé observed in an article she published in 2000 that the women who had sat on the Supreme Court of Canada since 1982 had "written or supported dissenting opinions more often than average, particularly in interpreting constitutional equality rights."[66] The "heightened propensity to dissent" among the female appointees to the Supreme Court was documented by scholars as well, although they stressed that the women did not always dissent "as a unified block" and were as likely to disagree with each other as with their male colleagues.[67] Their findings reflected the disparate results in *Symes* and *Seaboyer*.

The Uproar That Followed

The *Symes* case was an illuminating illustration of the complexities of feminist analysis and activism. L'Heureux-Dubé was a female judge who disavowed the label "feminist," who had written what many perceived as a frankly feminist dissent. Equally surprising was the division of opinion that the *Symes* case inspired among Canadian feminists. Feminists all agreed on many first principles: that women's equality depended upon high-quality, accessible, affordable childcare, and that Canada fell far short of this goal. Where they divided was over which strategies held the broadest scope for achieving the goal.[68]

Canada's largest feminist organization, the National Action Committee on the Status of Women, announced that it preferred Iacobucci's majority decision, which it described as "a victory for social equality, not a blow to women."[69] The Canadian Day Care Advocacy Association objected that the approach Symes had taken was "beneficial to middle-and-upper-class women at the expense of others."[70] Although the Canadian Advisory Council on the Status of Women refused to take a position on the case, it suggested that the childcare issue should be dealt with legislatively instead.[71] Even though Symes and Eberts had launched the lawsuit personally, and not under the auspices of LEAF, the organization was accused of being "elitist" because two of its founders were at the helm of the case.[72]

Some academics also criticized Symes's *Charter* challenge. Dalhousie law professor Faye Woodman took issue with a deduction that garnered a greater tax savings to those with higher incomes. Had Symes won, she argued, "the richer the taxpayer, the more her childcare expenses will be subsidized by other Canadian taxpayers."[73] University of Toronto law professor Audrey Macklin agreed:

> [A] tax deduction is an inappropriate response to the child care crisis ... *Symes* is not a case where a successful sex equality claim by a relatively privileged woman will have a "trickle down" effect on the women who are most in need of affordable, accessible childcare. I consider this to be the decisive factor tilting the balance in favour of depicting Symes' cause as one which champions class privilege as opposed to sex equality ... [H]er narrow and self-interested approach can only fragment and weaken the movement by and on behalf of all women, rich and poor, toward a comprehensive and accessible national day care program ... [T]hose interested in promoting equality for women ought to exercise caution when choosing their battles.[74]

Mary Eberts lamented that "people basically didn't get the notion of two-stage or incremental reform. Nor did the critics appreciate ... that many women with businesses of their own were far from wealthy elite women."[75] Some of the critics eventually softened their views, as they reflected that no other tax case had disallowed a business deduction on the basis that persons who were employees would not also get the deduction.[76] Claire Young, an early critic, later concluded that it had been unfair to criticize Symes for "inequities in the system," and that the "piling on of feminists" had been "unfortunate."[77] She believed it would have been fairer to view the challenge as the first of many cases seeking greater tax equity and as an impetus to future improvement. L'Heureux-Dubé's decision had taken the act "head-on," drawing attention to "horizontal equity." It was not a case of "businesswomen versus employees," but "businesswomen versus businessmen," bringing a "contextual approach to provisions that need that."[78] Indeed, Young noted that L'Heureux-Dubé's "analytical framework" added greatly to the possible success of future *Charter* challenges to inequitable gender discrimination and the increasing use of the tax system to deliver subsidies for social programs.[79]

University of Ottawa law professor Ellen Zweibel also admitted that she had been too critical of the case at first. "I made the mistake of thinking [Symes] was a socially and economically advantaged plaintiff," she explained. That Symes was a woman lawyer made it "easy" to "take potshots."[80] In retrospect, her views had changed. L'Heureux-Dubé's decision "unmasked the bias" in Iacobucci's decision: "Women's business realities are different. That's how the Act should have been interpreted. It was really a fabulous case, with huge implications. Every time I read *Symes* I see how much better things might have been in interpreting the *Income Tax Act* if that decision had gone the other way."[81] Claire Young speculated that if Symes had been successful, the government would have had to revise the Act, to rectify the perceived unfairness of giving the deduction to businesswomen only. "I think there would have had to be benefits for all," she mused.[82] It should not have been viewed as a "zero-sum game" for public resources.[83]

Although disappointed with the outcome, Mary Eberts was gracious about the loss. If litigants were going to lose on a sex equality case, this was the best gender split to receive. Eberts told the press she took heart from the L'Heureux-Dubé and McLachlin dissents: "I think a lot of women are going to be interested in the gender split on the court, and certainly from our point of view, the reasons of the minority on the court were gratifying. It showed that they did get our arguments."[84] Years later, she added: "[The dissent was] imbued with an understanding of women's lives. The judgment of Madam Justice L'Heureux-Dubé is still a *locus classicus* for how the *Charter* (section 15) should influence the development of the law."[85] Melina Buckley agreed: "I thought [the dissenting judgment] was brilliant. [L'Heureux-Dubé] was doing more than just dissenting, but hoping to put another step in equality rights jurisprudence – integrating the evidence [and] the record that was before her in a way that brought [together] the whole picture. As a lawyer in public interest cases, you know you're not always going to win, but you want to know you've been heard.

I definitely had that sense."[86] Buckley suggested that the loss also reflected the very high stakes: "[The majority judges] feared they would be opening up the whole *Income Tax Act* to challenge."[87]

THE FINANCIAL REPERCUSSIONS AND REFLECTIONS ON TEST CASE LITIGATION

Beth Symes had deliberately chosen not to request funding or assistance from LEAF, since she and Mary Eberts felt their personal ties to the organization made that inappropriate. A small group of female lawyers set up a committee to raise funds privately, and Eberts's Bay Street law firm agreed to bill at reduced rates.[88] The financial crunch came at the end of the road. Although Symes had sequestered all of the monies she deducted in the early 1980s, by the early 1990s, the interest penalties charged by Revenue Canada had reached 15 percent, escalating the monies owing to the government beyond the safeguarded funds.[89] Then, as Symes noted, "[n]ot only did I lose, but the Court also took the extraordinary step of ordering me to pay the government's legal costs at the Supreme Court of Canada and in the courts below."[90] After many observers protested the injustice of a punitive costs award in an equality test case, Justice Minister Allan Rock chose not to collect. This was cause for great relief, but there were still their own legal bills to pay, and every year, for the next five years, Eberts and Symes were both audited by Revenue Canada.[91]

How did Symes feel as the target of all this attention? She never forgot the biting comment the federal government lawyer made during the litigation: "Mrs. Symes, you chose to have children; personally, I chose to have cats."[92] She found the demeaning phrases Federal Court of Appeal judge Décary had used "crushing." She found it difficult to be characterized as a "rich, white, and privileged woman" when she was earning far less than any of the judges who heard her case and most of her academic critics. Noting that some of the judges had said other women should have brought the challenge, she retorted: "Whoever did they mean? Sole support mothers? Farmer women? Women who worked part-time? If I was having difficulty providing childcare, those with even less resources than I had were in a worse position. But that was not even questioned, nor was the issue of whether such women would be able to carry the costs and consequences of a court challenge of test case litigation."[93] She added:

Would I do it again? No. The personal cost of invasion of privacy was too high. I far prefer to be counsel. The experience has made me very aware of the stress and costs my clients face in such test case litigation, as well as women's enduring vulnerability to public censure when they seek to challenge legal and professional norms.[94]

The irony would not have been lost on L'Heureux-Dubé. One of Canada's most famous test-case litigation lawyers, a founder of LEAF whose clients provided the essential claimants for equality litigation, would not venture this way again.

33
More Deaths, 1987–94

The childcare responsibilities at the centre of public debate in *Symes* continued to affect Claire L'Heureux-Dubé personally, even though her children were no longer young. Louise was already launched on her own career, but twenty-three-year-old Pierre was still living in the family home in Quebec City. Consequently, their mother's move to Ottawa was disruptive. L'Heureux-Dubé was loath to interrupt her son's studies at the private Catholic college that he was then attending, and so delayed putting her home up for sale. She moved to Ottawa in May 1987 when she began hearing cases, and took an apartment in Cartier Place for the months before the summer recess. Come September and resumption of the gruelling Supreme Court schedule, she asked Denyse Dion to put the Quebec City house up for sale. It sold before the winter was out, and she tried to take care of Pierre's needs by renting him a nice apartment near the college.[1]

That fall she also purchased a modest townhouse at 174 Dufferin in the New Edinburgh neighbourhood of Ottawa. It was a community composed mainly of Anglophone residents, many of them civil servants, clustered around the spacious grounds of the governor-general's Rideau Hall residence. It had three bedrooms, "one for me and one for each of [the] children," as she put it. It also had a self-contained basement that she would later generously offer to friends who needed temporary lodging in Ottawa. Judicial colleague Douglas Campbell from British Columbia and the new head of the National Judicial Institute, George Thomson, both made temporary homes in the basement. "I gave them a lease with a *pied à terre*.

When you need it, you come. I charged nothing. That's friendship really."² It raised some eyebrows among people who were unaware that the arrangements were simply on a friendship basis. L'Heureux-Dubé explained: "One day, Chief Justice Tony Lamer came to see me. 'People are talking. You have men in your basement.' I said, 'You know, Tony, tell them I take them young and handsome.' That was the end of it. He stopped talking." Still angry years later, she added: "Isn't that incredible? Especially given his situation. I was furious."³

The Death of Paul L'Heureux

L'Heureux-Dubé's difficult relationship with her father came to an end in 1989. The parent who had opposed her entry into law and failed to attend her Laval law graduation had grudgingly come to accept his daughter's career success. L'Heureux-Dubé too had thawed. "I was so angry with my father when he left my mother. Then, I couldn't understand. I didn't realize that he had needs my mother could not satisfy." It was only later, she said, that she had become "more forgiving," "more understanding."⁴ Her growing generosity inspired her to host the reception at the Château Champlain for Paul L'Heureux and Francine Teasdale's wedding after her mother's death.⁵ However, her resentment toward Francine continued to simmer just below the surface. It was a recipe for more conflict when Paul's health began to deteriorate after he was diagnosed with cancer.

L'Heureux-Dubé had always been upset that her father had adopted Francine's children and grandchildren from a former marriage after abandoning his own family. Tensions boiled over when Paul decided to move from Montreal up to the Laurentians to be closer to Francine's children. Then, after he put a down payment on a house up north, Francine inexplicably refused to move. L'Heureux-Dubé believed that this drove her father into total despair. He had cancer, he was on a great deal of medication, and "he just apparently put down his medication and said 'I won't take any more. Take me to the hospital. I am going to die.'"⁶

All three of Paul's surviving daughters – Claire, Louise, and Nicole – travelled to be at his bedside. L'Heureux-Dubé remembered that he "had trouble breathing and needed a ventilator." She added: "He was in a terrible hospital. Louise, as a nurse, [had to] help him use it. If we hadn't been there around the clock, it would have been impossible."⁷ Whether by now estranged from her husband or simply overwhelmed by the L'Heureux sisters, Francine refused to visit. Paul died there in hospital, in what

L'Heureux-Dubé characterized as "a sort of suicide."⁸ "Then when he died, [Francine] insisted he be buried there, so he couldn't be buried next to our mother in the family plot. [A]ll she seemed interested in was the money in the estate. I was so disgusted, I refused to speak with her."⁹

The funeral was a low-key affair, held at the funeral home where Paul was cremated, in the suburb of Montreal where he lived. L'Heureux-Dubé's sister Louise remembered it as attended by "mostly family, with just a few people he had known from the customs." The three daughters were there, as well as Paul's sister and brother-in-law, Paul's half-brother Gaston, Francine and her children, and the Brillant daughters (long-time family friends from Rimouski), who were then living in Montreal. Pierre stunned the family when he told them he was hiding out in a Montreal apartment from "the Mafia-type people who wanted to break his legs."¹⁰ His aunt Louise remembered: "I was shocked. I didn't know what he had done, and he didn't tell us."¹¹

There were no speeches at the subdued gathering, "just people mingling around and saying hello to some of the people who came." The urn with Paul L'Heureux's ashes was interred as Francine Teasdale wished. Louise described it sadly as "an out of the way place," adding, "I wouldn't know where to find it."¹²

The Death of Pierre

During L'Heureux-Dubé's Supreme Court years, Pierre's mental health challenges intensified.¹³ He took refuge in alcohol and all sorts of drugs, legal and illegal, in a futile effort to cope with his mental illness.¹⁴ His substance abuse resulted in repeated hospitalizations, and although the medications prescribed by his doctors seemed to help, the minute he felt better, he stopped taking them, and the schizophrenia manifested itself again.¹⁵ His sister, Louise, described it as a "terrible" situation that got "worse." In her view, Pierre "was not really saveable after a while. He was a sad, sad, sad case. Your worst nightmare for your kids."¹⁶ His aunt Louise thought that Pierre's problems added enormously to the strain of his mother's years in Ottawa. "He was demanding so much attention, so much of her free time. Maybe another person ... it would have killed them. But she was so optimistic. Just like my mother. Pierrot would get better. She was going to get control of that. Pierrot would straighten out."¹⁷

Pierre came to Ottawa occasionally, usually when he was "really in bad shape." He would stay for a few weeks or a month and his mother would

Pierre Dubé, L'Heureux-Dubé's son, Quebec City.

try to "put him back on his feet," to "dialogue with him about his life."[18] He would convince her that he really wanted to turn his life around. At times, he did seem to recuperate, and there were short respites. One Christmas, L'Heureux-Dubé took him and Louise to Lake Tahoe to ski, and they spent a happy time together. Another year, L'Heureux-Dubé and Pierre were invited to have Christmas dinner at Beverley McLachlin's and the evening went off well.[19] While in Ottawa, Pierre met some of his mother's law clerks when he would come to the courthouse. François Lacasse developed a rapport with Pierre because both of them rode motorcycles. "[Pierre] had, at the time, probably the fastest production bike, top of the line, and he had modified it a bit. He was very proud of that motorcycle," recalled François.[20]

When Pierre crashed his motorcycle and was hospitalized at Montfort Hospital for a fracture in the spring of 1988, it was François who collected the damaged bike and had it repaired. He visited Pierre's hospital room, relaying reports back to L'Heureux-Dubé, who was then out of town, via long-distance telephone in an era before cellphones.[21] Pierre insisted on more pain relief, which the hospital staff, knowing of his drug addictions, refused. Pierre discharged himself on his own.[22] That same year, he crashed the sports car he was driving.[23] Marie-Claire Belleau witnessed the mounting toll this took: "Her son was always on drugs. [She] knew he was dangerous to himself and others. He didn't take his medication. She could do nothing. She felt she could not get him security or secure others from him."[24] And throughout it all, Belleau said, "I think she was an unbelievably loving mother."[25]

L'Heureux-Dubé never lost hope that her son would turn the corner. She rented a Montreal apartment for him in Westmount, but he could not cope.[26] She wondered whether Pierre would do better living in Rimouski. She drove back to the city of her youth, and prevailed upon the *recteur* of the Université de Québec à Rimouski to allow Pierre to enrol. She rented a furnished apartment and fully decorated it for him. The plan failed; he refused to attend classes.[27] With the assistance of Philippe Michaud, her childhood friend who had become a business leader in Rimouski, she found him a job with Quebec Telephone. He was fired when he didn't show up for work in the mornings.[28] For a while, Pierre lived with a young woman and her young child in an apartment in Quebec City. To his family, "they seemed to be in a relationship that was normal," but "things fell apart again."[29] L'Heureux-Dubé installed him in a new apartment and bought him furniture, but he destroyed everything. "She wanted so much to help him," recalled former law partner Roger Garneau. "How can a woman be such a good judge, such a brilliant woman, [and] be so weak with her delinquent child? How can she still hope that he will change? Nobody could. We were sad for her. We had pity for her."[30]

When Pierre ran afoul of the law and was called up before the Quebec courts, L'Heureux-Dubé would drive back for the remands, for the trials. "She was there the whole time. She was always supporting him," recalled former law clerk Andrew Lenz.[31] Pierre would show up at his mother's home in Ottawa drunk and on drugs, and trash her place, smashing glass, destroying everything within reach.[32] L'Heureux-Dubé's sister Nicole described Pierre's incessant demands for money. "He knew he could ask for money always, and she would give it. Claire would give him $130 to pay his rent and then he would return and say, 'I lost it, [it] fell out of my pocket,' and she would give him $130 again. She was generous, maybe too generous."[33] Louise Dubé remembered her brother extorting larger sums from his mother: "She gave him $25,000 one time, and $10,000 ... it was awful."[34] Nicole L'Heureux recalled Pierre's threats. "She was a Supreme Court judge. He was going, 'If you don't give me this, I'm going to say all these bad things to the journalists about you.' [He] threatened her all the time with all kinds of stuff."[35] Her judicial colleagues witnessed some of

Pierre's outbursts first-hand when he became disruptive inside the courthouse.³⁶ Her former law partners, family, and friends worried that Pierre would become more violent – possibly even kill his mother.³⁷

Things escalated in the fall of 1991, when Pierre showed up at his mother's Ottawa townhouse high on drugs and desperate for more. The details of what happened next are not entirely clear, but L'Heureux-Dubé's recollection is that Pierre drew a gun and began firing at the TV.³⁸ She told him to stop. She was so frightened that she fainted. "I was under a lot of pressure," she explained. "I was afraid he would do something – not to me, he never did anything to me personally or hurt me or anything – but possibly to someone, I don't know ..."³⁹ She said that Pierre called 9-1-1. The police arrived and saw the gun. "I was so under strain I don't remember if they asked me something or what, but they said, 'I think we better take him with us.' I didn't resist. I think I was at the end of the line. [He was] always destroying things. I had always succeeded in calming him, reasoning with him. That time, I guess it was too much."⁴⁰ Afterward, she telephoned her sister and wept.⁴¹

In 1992, as a result of this incident, Pierre was charged with "possession of a weapon for purposes dangerous to the public."⁴² L'Heureux-Dubé appeared in court to argue for her son's release on bail.⁴³ She was required to meet with André Marin, the Crown attorney in charge of the case, since she was the key Crown witness at the preliminary inquiry. She was not sanguine about his prospects for an acquittal. "I said to Pierre, 'What kind of defence can you make?' There was none. What else could they do? He had a weapon. It was true," she explained. "Marin handled [the case] with openness. He showed me his files. [I] thought it was extremely fair. I gave testimony. I said I didn't know he had a gun, or that it was in the house. I was afraid he would do damage. That's the truth."⁴⁴

On 26 October 1992, Pierre pleaded guilty before Ontario Superior Court judge David McWilliam, to the reduced charge of "mischief." It was helpful that L'Heureux-Dubé took the position that she knew her son was suffering a severe bout of depression and that she had never felt her life was in danger. Pierre's defence counsel filed a doctor's report explaining that Pierre was making "good progress," was "determined to turn his life around," and "realize[d] that alcohol aggravates his problem."⁴⁵ Pierre received a suspended sentence with three years' probation, and was ordered to "seek treatment for mental problems."⁴⁶ L'Heureux-Dubé thought the sentence was fair: "It was his first offence as an adult, possession of a gun for a purpose dangerous to the public peace. I don't think Pierre had anything given to him that he shouldn't have. It was a normal sentence."⁴⁷

Reporters caught wind of the case, and although some newspapers chose not to run the story because it was too personal, several accounts did appear.[48] "Mr. Dubé was charged after he allegedly loaded and unloaded a shotgun at Madam Justice L'Heureux-Dubé's home," was how *Lawyers Weekly* put it. Then "Madam Justice L'Heureux-Dubé 'fainted,' and police were called to the scene after the son dialed 911." The paper added that Pierre Dubé "had been receiving treatment at the Royal Ottawa Hospital [the psychiatric hospital in Ottawa] at the time of his arrest."[49] That L'Heureux-Dubé attended "every day of his court proceedings" was also recorded.[50] It would have been hard enough to bear in private. To have it exposed to the intrusive public glare must have made it more horrific.

Within a year, Pierre was arrested again, during an armed robbery when he threatened the manager of a small shop with a knife.[51] It was the beginning of the end. He developed an infection in prison, and was removed to a locked rehabilitation facility in Trois-Rivières in the early winter of 1994.[52] It took some time for the corrections personnel to diagnose how serious the illness was, but Pierre was eventually transferred to the hospital and the news reached his mother in February 1994. The court was sitting, but L'Heureux-Dubé was excused after she insisted that she could read the transcript from the hospital and put any questions she had to the lawyers in writing.[53] She drove to Trois-Rivières with a mountain of files, taking care to communicate closely with her law clerks back at the court, issuing instructions on draft memos and decisions by phone.[54] When she arrived, she was startled to learn that Pierre had pneumonia, and the doctors thought he might also have contracted Legionnaires' disease.[55] She checked into a hotel and spent every day at the hospital for about two weeks. Then Pierre appeared to rally, and it looked as if he would recuperate. L'Heureux-Dubé prepared to return to Ottawa. Pierre was well enough to warn his mother to be careful on the drive back because the roads were slippery. "He was very tender," recalled his relieved mother.[56]

No sooner had she returned to court than she was called out of the hearing with the tragic news that Pierre was dying. The latest diagnosis was flesh-eating disease. There was no cure.[57] In Trois-Rivières, she was devastated to see how sick her son was, how much pain he was suffering. He was only thirty years old but his body was breaking down completely. She sat at his bedside for what turned out to be the last week of his life.[58] When Pierre's kidney and lungs began to fail, she begged the doctors to take her kidney and one of her lungs for a transplant.[59] Her sisters were shocked, and relieved that none of the doctors took L'Heureux-Dubé's offer seriously.[60]

Waiting in the corridor, knowing her son was going to die, L'Heureux-Dubé wrote a heart-rending poem to him that would be read at his funeral.[61] Pierre died on 7 March 1994.[62] In the end, there was no definitive determination of what caused his death.[63]

THE AFTERMATH AND THE FUNERAL

The family waited until the fall to hold the funeral so that L'Heureux-Dubé's daughter, Louise, who then resided in California, could be with them.[64] Yolande Lemelin, L'Heureux-Dubé's former secretary at the Quebec Court of Appeal, generously helped organize the service. She arranged for the invitations, the music, and the singer.[65] L'Heureux-Dubé took nine days off to attend her son's funeral in Quebec City.[66] Her lifelong friend Jean Drapeau, the priest from Rimouski, officiated at the eulogy, and another Rimouski friend played the organ. The church was filled with her friends and family. All her Supreme Court colleagues were there, which overwhelmed her. The eulogy was short. Someone commented: "It's a short life."[67] Jean Drapeau remembered the day vividly. "For Claire ... I remember always. St. Dominique Church was beautiful. Claire had a wonderful display of white flowers all over."[68]

In expressing their condolences, some of those attending were quite blunt. Denyse Dion said, "Maybe it's the best thing for him. He's better dead, and she doesn't know how lucky she is."[69] Louise, L'Heureux-Dubé's daughter, agreed. "I was relieved when he died," she confided, "but Mom was not."[70] L'Heureux-Dubé's sister Louise was inclined to agree with Denyse and her niece. "It was something of a relief. He threatened her. There's nothing he didn't do. Pierre's problem was like a nightmare, just a bad dream. Claire forgets how bad it was toward the end. She forgot a lot."[71] The sentiment was shared by L'Heureux-Dubé's sister Nicole, who was overheard to add, "Good riddance."[72] Nicole insisted, "In French we would say *une épine* – a thorn in her back all the time. Or in her heart, because she loved that boy and did everything she could to try to help him. But there was nothing she could do. I would not have been able to cope the way she did."[73]

L'Heureux-Dubé's former law partner, Roger Garneau, hoped that Pierre's death would be something of a "release" for his mother: "For us, we were happy to find out that he died, and Claire lived. Because the opposite was possible. He was dangerous. But it has not been [a release] for Claire. It disturbed her enormously."[74] Louise agreed that her sister was inconsolable. "After all he had done, she had such optimism that she really felt it was horrible that he had died. She wished she could have done more for him. She felt she didn't do enough."⁷⁵ L'Heureux-Dubé's former law clerk Marie-Claire Belleau, who became one of her closest confidantes through this period, had flown in from Harvard, where she was pursuing graduate studies. "I heard over and over again, 'You must be relieved.' [It was a] most cruel thing to say. [She would have done] anything to save him. She wanted to change the story. It's a sad story ... of immense love. It was the end of the possibility of making it better. [T]he death of her child was like the end of the world."⁷⁶

Those gathered at the church were surprised by the arrival of a large group of long-haired bikers who approached the casket to deposit a floral tribute shaped to resemble a motorcycle. L'Heureux-Dubé's family and friends were disapproving of Pierre's biker acquaintances, whom they blamed for some of his troubles. L'Heureux-Dubé, however, stepped forward, received the floral arrangement, and graciously thanked them all.⁷⁷ The only thing that astonished the observers more was that she also stepped forward to take communion, something she had refused to do for decades.⁷⁸

After Pierre's death, L'Heureux-Dubé and her daughter found some solace in each other's company. Louise, who felt the need to be closer geographically, divorced her husband and moved back east from California. Mother and daughter tried to alleviate their grief by travel, and went to India together for a holiday. Louise recalled that her mother was not coping well. "At some point, we stopped to have lunch, [and] she [came] unglued. Then somehow she finds the strength to move on. [S]he had a life that would have been difficult for anyone – a life much harder than most people's lives."⁷⁹

Her long-time friends observed that it would take four years before L'Heureux-Dubé slowly began to recover from an all-encompassing grief. Simone Tardif described it as like "a big lead drape over her," as she struggled to make sense of the loss of her son. "I told her a hundred times, 'You have no guilt.' I don't know of anybody who has done so much for her son as you have. Claire should have let go. She always said, 'It's not easy.'"⁸⁰ Her court attendant, André Legault, remembered driving her to functions as she would be sobbing in the back seat of the car. "She would ask me to go around the block, and then she'd say, 'Let's get on with it. I'm okay now.' I think she got her strength from her mother. Claire was always talking about how positive her mother was. When things got tough, she'd swallow and say in French, 'Turn the page.'"⁸¹ L'Heureux-Dubé's sister Louise agreed:

Claire L'Heureux-Dubé and daughter, Louise, on holiday at the Taj Mahal in India.

"[Claire] had this really important job. Once she got into work, she must have wiped it all out. Just like my mother ... must be some kind of a gene there. She developed a mechanism for turning things on and off."[82]

L'Heureux-Dubé's colleagues at the Supreme Court were shocked by Pierre's death, another tragedy in a family already afflicted by so much loss. Her son's death brought her closer to some of her fellow judges, and often not those one would have anticipated. It wasn't Bertha Wilson who comforted her, as L'Heureux-Dubé admitted: "Bertha supported me every time I needed support, but I couldn't talk to her about my own things when my son died." Surprisingly, it was John Sopinka who filled this role on the court. "It was Sopinka I could talk to," she noted, "whom I couldn't stand intellectually on his judgments, but he was a person I really liked. He came and he cried with me."[83]

The other judges recalled how careful L'Heureux-Dubé was not to let her grief show in public. "We didn't hear about it except in a marginal way," Charles Gonthier remembered, even though he may have been the judicial colleague closest to L'Heureux-Dubé during this period. "Her personal life never prevented her from making her full contribution to the courts," he emphasized.[84] Gérard La Forest added, "She certainly kept on working away – enough that many of us didn't even know about what happened."[85] Jack Major was of the same view: "I think she was the most resilient person that I've met. That was the one characteristic of her that everybody admires. She had very tragic events in her life. It affected her, but she never seemed to be down. That's the one thing Claire never did was seek sympathy."[86] It was a sentiment with which L'Heureux-Dubé herself agreed: "I think I'm a survivor basically. I was busy intellectually. I think that was the greatest strength in my life, to be able to have an intellectual life. And my sense of duty is very strong. Both of my parents had an incredible sense of duty. Energy and optimism means happiness in a certain way."[87]

Many years later, Frank Iacobucci summed up his admiration for L'Heureux-Dubé's capacity to move forward:

> My affection for her is immensely influenced by the obstacles she overcame in her life. When you have your father leaving your mother, when her mother contracts a degenerative disease ... when you have your husband taking his life ... then a son who had issues ... The three most important men in her life are surrounded by tragedy, and she's in the middle. To get out of bed in the morning for most people after that would be something of a triumph. To stay with her practice, to become a judge, to be on the Supreme Court of Canada ... that's a triumph that I don't think anybody on the court before or after could equal. That's my assessment of her as a human being ... The courage, integrity, and resilience she had ... I think that's connected to whatever legacy unfolds.[88]

For all her resilience and ability to compartmentalize, an experience so personally devastating undeniably makes a substantial impact. Some observers raised more questions about whether Pierre's life might help to explain L'Heureux-Dubé's outlook on criminal law. The explosive 9-1-1 call in 1991, Pierre's criminal prosecution for threatening his mother in 1992, and his death in 1994 were all contemporaneous in timing with the statistical shift in pro-prosecution rulings.

Some observers continued to articulate the view that L'Heureux-Dubé held steadfast, that her own brushes with the criminal justice system did not dictate her changed judicial rulings. Law clerk François Lacasse, who later became a Crown prosecutor, conceded that Pierre had "an influence,"

More Deaths 453

Family gravesite, Quebec City, where son Pierre was interred alongside L'Heureux-Dubé's sister, mother, and husband. L'Heureux-Dubé's young grandson Simon stands in front of the headstone.

but believed that L'Heureux-Dubé's perspectives were much more complex. He noted that during the years she sat on the Supreme Court, the criminal law jurisprudence was undergoing dramatic transformation, with the *Charter* leaving many traditional doctrines unrecognizable. It wasn't so much that her philosophy evolved, but that the point of reference shifted from under her. If you "move the target," where you stand "in relation to that target" shifts, he emphasized.[89]

Marie-Claire Belleau was prepared to make the linkage far more definite. She believed that L'Heureux-Dubé's understanding of criminal law was "really rooted in her experience with her son." "A huge part of her understanding of the world," she added, "comes from that."[90]

34
The Quebec Secession Reference
"The Most Important Case," 1998

It was 20 August 1998. The grand hall of the Supreme Court building had been transformed into a television studio.[1] People were milling around, media stars were preparing to take to the air "live," and more than one hundred observers were anxiously counting the minutes to Chief Justice Antonio Lamer's formal pronouncement on the Quebec Secession Reference.[2] Court staff had spared no effort to ensure that the decision would not leak out in advance.[3] An entire nation waited transfixed to learn what the nine judges would say about whether the Quebec government, led by the separatist Parti Québécois (PQ) under Lucien Bouchard, could secede unilaterally from Canada. Some predicted that the case might ignite a "firestorm" in Quebec that could send "support for sovereignty soaring."[4] Commentators described it as one of the "most important cases in the Supreme Court's history."[5] Amid the high tension and drama, it seemed as though the "fate of the country hung in the balance."[6] Claire L'Heureux-Dubé, one of three Quebec judges on the nine-member panel, felt particularly responsible for the sensitive historic ruling.[7]

How did the case reach the doors of the Supreme Court?

Referenda, Patriation, References, and Accords

Four years after he first led the PQ to power, Premier René Lévesque called a referendum on sovereignty in 1980. His government asked the people of Quebec to vote "yes" on "sovereignty-association," a platform

Quebec Premier René Lévesque.

that encompassed political and legislative independence from Canada along with continued economic association.[8] The "no" side garnered 59.56 percent, and the "yes" side 40.44 percent. Lévesque's concession speech ended with a promise: *"À la prochaine fois."*[†, 9]

The uneasy relations between Quebec and the rest of Canada were tested further during the battles to "patriate" the constitution, to bring a new amending formula from Britain to Canada. Unable to obtain support from the provinces for a patriation package, Prime Minister Pierre Trudeau proposed to go it alone. A reference to the Supreme Court of Canada on

---

† "Until next time"

the legalities of constitutional amendment brought a split decision, which boiled down to the consensus that a unilateral federal request to Britain was legal in that no law was being violated, but unconstitutional because the government was breaching a rule of constitutional practice.[10] A return to the bargaining table brought all the provinces except Quebec into the fold. The subsequent enactment of the *Constitution Act, 1982* without the approval of Quebec further inflamed the Québécois.[11] The Meech Lake and Charlottetown Accords in 1987 and 1992, designed to obtain Quebec's consent for a revised constitutional framework, both failed dismally.[12]

Against this background, a new PQ premier, Jacques Parizeau, called a second referendum in 1995. It resulted in an even closer cliffhanger: 50.58 percent of the voters of Quebec voted "no" to sovereignty while 49.42 percent voted "yes."[13] Shaken to the core by the slim federalist victory, Prime Minister Jean Chrétien broke down behind the closed doors of his cabinet room and admitted that he had "almost lost the country" to the sovereigntists.[14] Canadian pundits stewed over a cascading series of options. Plan A would sidestep secession by accommodating Quebec's "legitimate desire for change." Plan B would "clarify the process of secession" while still striving to retain Quebec. Plan C following secession, also described as "looking into the abyss," would require the rest of Canada to decide whether the shrunken surviving territory should continue as a united country or dismember still further.[15]

Quebec City lawyer Guy Bertrand set Plan B in motion by seeking a declaration from the Quebec Superior Court that the province could not secede unilaterally. Refusing to sit by while the issue got bogged down in the lower courts, Chrétien elevated the action directly to the top court through a "reference" – a hypothetical question posed to the Supreme Court for its opinion on an important question of law or fact.[16] Three questions were put: (1) whether Quebec could secede unilaterally under Canadian constitutional law; (2) whether Quebec could secede unilaterally under international law; and (3) in the event of a conflict between domestic and international law, which one would take precedence.[17]

From the outset, the reference pleased no one. Federalists objected that it was useless to ask the court a question to which there was an obvious answer: everyone already knew, they insisted, that unilateral secession was unlawful. Further, asking the court how secession *should* occur strengthened the possibility that secession *would* occur.[18] Western University political scientist Robert Young noted that the legal ruling might detrimentally constrain the ability of both sides to manoeuvre in the uncertain negotiating terrain that would follow any "yes" vote.[19] Quebec separatists objected

Quebec Premier Jacques Parizeau.

to the legalization of a political issue, and claimed that federal judges could never control the democratic decisions of *"le peuple québécois."* They complained that delegating the decision to the court would "put Quebecers into a straightjacket tailored in English Canada." They disparaged the Supreme Court as "the leaning tower of Pisa," a biased institution that "always tilts the same way."[20] *Le Devoir* published an editorial cartoon depicting nine judges all leaning to one side with the caption "Official photograph of the Supreme Court justices."[21] Many expressed concern that the case rendered the court's entire legitimacy precarious.[22]

The situation was exacerbated when the Quebec government refused to participate in the reference, vowing to defy any decision that would thwart the democratic right of the people of Quebec to define their own destiny.[23] Gilles Duceppe, leader of the federal Bloc Québécois, threatened

Le Devoir editorial cartoon: "Official photograph of the Supreme Court justices."

to appeal any adverse ruling from the Supreme Court to the United Nations.[24] Undeterred, the Supreme Court used its *amicus curiae* power to appoint independent counsel to represent the interests of Quebec. How did the court select such a lawyer? L'Heureux-Dubé recalled that the three Quebec judges caucused to see whether they could think of a separatist lawyer from Quebec who might agree to take the brief. They came up with a list of names, but Chief Justice Lamer's efforts to secure a participant took some doing. Some of those called said they had conflicts because they had contracts with the government, some said they feared being blacklisted if they agreed, and others simply refused.[25] Finally, separatist lawyer André Joli-Coeur, a fifty-five-year-old administrative law specialist, agreed.[26] L'Heureux-Dubé described Joli-Coeur, as an "excellent lawyer," one with "guts" who "takes chances."[27] A long list of interveners also joined the lineup, including the governments of Saskatchewan, Manitoba, Yukon, and the Northwest Territories, four different Aboriginal groups, one women's organization, and one minority rights group. The facta and documentation filed by the parties were voluminous.[28]

Underscoring the acrimony, on the first day of oral submissions, a thousand demonstrators rallied on the steps of the courthouse, waving *fleur-de-lys* flags and chanting: "Democracy: for Quebecers to decide."[29] A small plane flown above the building by a separatist bush pilot trailed a banner that read *"le Québec aux Québécois."*[†,30] "Turmoil and uncertainty" were predicted in the run-up to the decision, the dollar plunged to a then-record low of 65.21 US cents, and the Canadian bond market took a dive.[31] It placed the court "in a tough corner," according to the *Globe and Mail*, "deciding whether the Constitution contains the tools of its own destruction," and forced to adjudicate "the nation's most explosive issue."[32]

The Hearing: "Bombastic Lawyers" and "Sphinx-Like Judges"

The contentious hearing lasted four full days. Yves Fortier, the lawyer who had refused Brian Mulroney's offer of appointment to the Supreme Court in 1987, acted for the federal government. He argued that the Constitution contained no formula for secession. Quebec should be told it could only secede through the complicated process of constitutional amendment under "the rule of law," necessitating support from the other partners within the Canadian federation. As everyone knew, given the foiled attempts to secure consensus among the provinces, this would never fly. Fortier also argued that international law offered no right to unilateral secession. Even if there were, in the event of a conflict between Canadian and international law, he insisted that it was well settled that domestic law prevailed.[33]

Cree Grand Chief Matthew Coon Come claimed that if Quebec was severable from Canada, then Quebec itself was severable, and so the Cree could secede too.[34] On behalf of the Chiefs of Ontario, Michael Sherry argued that "if there is a line up for the right of self-determination, in our view the First Nations are at the head of the line."[35] Representing the Ad Hoc Committee of Canadian Women on the Constitution, Anne Bayefsky insisted that unilateral secession was "illegal" and would mean "the end of Canada."[36] *Amicus curiae* André Joli-Coeur took a different tack, arguing that the Supreme Court should refuse to answer the questions entirely.

---

† "Quebec belongs to Quebecers."

The matter was too political, and the questions too hypothetical and theoretical to warrant a legal response.[37] John Whyte, the deputy attorney general of Saskatchewan, was the only lawyer to suggest compromise, characterizing Canada as a consensual, multilateral culture, where regard was always given to opposing interests.

Departing from their customary practice, the judges decided not to barrage the lawyers with questions during the oral submissions. Instead, Chief Justice Lamer collected written queries from each of the judges and read them out himself after the lawyers had wrapped up their arguments. It was a strategy initially recommended by L'Heureux-Dubé and Gonthier, who were worried that reporters would try to guess which way individual judges were leaning based on the questions they posed to the parties. The fear was that rampant speculation by the media would fuel tensions and provoke roller-coaster dips and swings in the financial markets. At Gonthier's suggestion, L'Heureux-Dubé took Jack Major to lunch to broach the idea. Major concurred and was able to obtain a consensus for the unusual process.[38] The unintended offshoot was that reporters depicted the inscrutable judges as "stone-faced" for the whole proceeding, and the lawyers were flummoxed, unable to hone their oral arguments midstream based on judicial probing.[39]

The Decision-Making Process:
Media Scrutiny and "Committee Consideration"

The public scrutiny of the court took on gargantuan proportions. The *Globe and Mail* ran photographs of each of the nine judges, with a brief summary of their persona attached. Lamer was described as having "roots that are three-quarters francophone and one-quarter Irish." L'Heureux-Dubé was described as the court's "most frequent dissenter," a judge who "tends to write from gut positions." Gonthier was described as "brilliant," but someone who maintained "a Sphinx-like silence at judgment-writing time." Cory was "an old-time liberal" who believed that "law should advance the cause of human dignity." McLachlin was "a classic liberal with a heart." Iacobucci was "a former deputy Attorney-General for the federal government" who was "often a swing vote." Major was "a plain-spoken conservative impatient with legal mumbo-jumbo." Bastarache was "a New Brunswick francophone who worked for the Yes committee on the 1992 Charlottetown Accord." Binnie, a Toronto lawyer and the most recent appointee to the high court, was described as having "represented the federal government in last year's controversial Nazi deportation cases at the Supreme Court."[40]

The *Globe and Mail* noted that the case would pose a "special challenge" to the judges of French Canadian origin, Lamer, L'Heureux-Dubé, and Gonthier. "Would they dare to favour their origins and render a decision that was not in the interest of the government that had appointed them?"[41] J.J. Camp, a former president of the Canadian Bar Association, noted that "the optics of, say, a 6–3 vote with the three Quebec judges being offside would be very bad."[42] Sean Fine, a *Globe* reporter who specialized in legal issues, focused specifically on Lamer and L'Heureux-Dubé in an article titled "Case puts spotlight on Dubé, Lamer." Stressing the diverse family backgrounds of both, Fine mentioned Lamer's Francophone father and English-speaking Irish mother, while highlighting L'Heureux-Dubé's Rimouski convent upbringing and a military father who "spent the Second World War overseas." Both represented, he wagered, "symbols of a national court."[43]

The key concern on Fine's mind, however, was the tension between the two judges. Noting that both had "pushed for more daring paths" for the court, Fine depicted Lamer as defying public opinion and the Justice Department in the field of criminal law "by spearheading a broadening of rights for accused people." As for L'Heureux-Dubé, Lamer's "most ardent foe," Fine claimed that "on family law and equality issues, she has staked out deeply felt positions for women and gays." He characterized the two as a "kind of odd couple," describing one as "the Chief Justice" and the other as "the chief maverick."[44] Would the court be able to "speak with one voice" in this case, given the long-standing antipathy between its two longest-serving members?[45]

All told, there were four Francophones, three Québécois, two Westerners, one New Brunswicker, and three Ontarians. Two had worked for the federal government. Apart from Bastarache, none was directly linked with the federalist side on the issue of secession, but separatists viewed all of them with suspicion because of their appointments by the prime ministers of Canada. Premier Bouchard described them as "nine persons whose federalist faith is not in doubt."[46] Montreal journalist and political scientist Josée Legault, a stalwart of the PQ, accused the entire bench of being "political mercenaries working to reinforce the Canadian state."[47]

Long afterward, L'Heureux-Dubé was prepared to concede that there were some real divisions between the Quebec judges and the others. "The

Quebec Premier Lucien Bouchard.

three French Canadians, Charles Gonthier, Tony Lamer, and I, were probably more concerned than the others about Quebec, and the others were probably more concerned about the Anglophone side of Canada."[48] But she agreed with the other judges that achieving a unanimous decision was terribly important, and stressed that the "case was more important than the judges."[49] As for the prediction that she and Lamer, traditional adversaries, might butt heads, in retrospect she laughed heartily. "We dissented in criminal law cases, but not usually in others."[50] Lamer's widow, Danièle

Tremblay-Lamer, was less effusive. She described the Quebec Secession case, which her husband felt to be one of the most important in his life, as an isolated example of a case "where they worked together," and "the only good example at the end" of their years on the bench together.[51] Ultimately, the two adversaries agreed, and along with the other seven judges they delivered a unanimous decision signed by "the Court" – a technique designed to assure the public that the ruling came from the nine judges collectively, without singling out any particular judge or judges as authors.[52]

Jack Major was the only one who spoke to the press about the dynamics on the court. He told the *Globe and Mail* that it had not been easy to obtain a unanimous judgment. "There were times when people had different points of view that hadn't been reconciled," he admitted. "It wasn't the kind of case that once it's argued everybody knows the answer." He explained that they had to "keep going around the table and around the table" to come to a consensus. "Some judges, if they had had their way, might have provided more detail on aboriginal issues or on border problems," he added.[53] Observers were eager to determine who had actually written the decision, and speculation centred on Gonthier.[54] While L'Heureux-Dubé was reluctant to breach judicial confidentiality, she revealed that Iacobucci had taken the leadership in developing the process that should be followed, that "Charles Gonthier was the soul of it," and that every judge participated in the drafting.[55] As for her own contribution, she recalled that apart from helping to formulate strategy, her role was to offer comments during the drafting.[56]

L'Heureux-Dubé on Separatism: "Deeply French, Proudly Canadian"

In his *Globe and Mail* feature, Sean Fine had characterized L'Heureux-Dubé as "deeply French."[57] Quoting her former law partner Roger Garneau, Fine described her as steeped in the "French spirit" through both education and culture.[58] She had paid an indisputable price for her Quebec heritage, sidelined by her ethnic roots on a majority Anglophone court where English was the primary working language. L'Heureux-Dubé was someone who cared deeply about her native language. She had laboured to master the intricacies of *la langue française* at the convent. In the lower courts, she had written her decisions almost exclusively in French, and had been highly regarded for her linguistic erudition. She had joined an organization to promote the use of French, L'Association pour le soutien et l'usage de la langue française, after her elevation to the Supreme Court.[59]

On the Supreme Court, the predominant practice was for the judges to write first in English, with French translations provided by professional staff translators.[60] It reflected the fact that most of the oral debates, deliberations, and sources were English, and that some of the Anglophone judges could not function in French. It also reflected the generosity of the Francophone judges, who sacrificed their greater proficiency in French to accept English as the working language, where the very stock-in-trade of the enterprise was words. For a bilingual country, it left much to be desired.

As L'Heureux-Dubé began to draft primarily in her second language,[61] some of her law clerks lamented that she wrote so infrequently in French. Francophone law clerk Michelle Flaherty explained, "She is an exquisite writer in French. She is like a poet. I found it very intimidating to write in French for her. I was so conscious of the calibre of her French writing."[62] L'Heureux-Dubé's daughter, Louise, agreed that her mother's written French was "exceptional," adding that there was a musical cadence to the writing, which she attributed to her mother's love of opera. It was as if a "musical gene" enlivened the French prose, along with a "gift" for linguistic precision.[63] Although everyone extolled L'Heureux-Dubé's proficient bilingualism, it was a significant loss to Canadian law that so many of her decisions were not written first in French.[64]

In theory, this should have been resolved through proper translation. Under the *Official Languages Act, 1988,* it was mandatory for every decision handed down by a federally established court to be published in both English and French.[65] As law clerk Teresa Scassa put it, in Canada language was "more than a symbol," and linguistic equality was a principle "upon which the political and social linguistic compromise" of the federal union had been based.[66] The problem with allowing one language to predominate on the court was that it was the French-translation decisions that became less precise, lacking in nuance, fluidity, and sophistication, and subject to multiple errors of interpretation.[67] Anxiety over this caused L'Heureux-Dubé to labour intensely over the translations. Her law clerk François Lacasse explained, "It was very important to her to make sure that the least was lost in translation as possible, hence her direct involvement. Before her, [I'm] not sure other judges were as concerned. When you have judges who can't read, write, or speak French, the translation of their judgments is quite literally beyond them. She would consider and reconsider and rewrite."[68]

By L'Heureux-Dubé's second year on the bench, she had begun the practice of writing judgments in both official languages. Instead of allowing the judgment in English to be the original version and the French to be listed as the *"version française,"* she adopted the practice of writing a second official judgment in French.[69] It was apparently the first time a judge had done this, unique in the annals of the court, but went largely "unnoticed," according to Scassa and Lacasse.[70] In contrast, L'Heureux-Dubé's notoriously exacting standards for translation did attract attention. Lacasse described it as "definitely challenging for someone who cares so much about language and grammar to be working in two languages," and a bit of "a nightmare for everyone."[71] It may also have underscored her passionate view that all judicial appointees should be fluently bilingual from the start. "It's a bilingual country," she emphasized. "People now should recognize that if they want to be in government service, they have to be bilingual."[72]

Sean Fine had depicted L'Heureux-Dubé as "deeply French," but he also described her as "proudly Canadian."[73] Her position on Quebec separatism was not much of a mystery. Her former law partner Roger Garneau stressed that she was "first a Canadian" and "an internationalist," who "doesn't like bonds."[74] It was a sentiment seconded by Saskatchewan Chief Justice Edward Bayda, a native of Alvena, Saskatchewan, and an admirer of L'Heureux-Dubé's: "She was a citizen of Quebec, a citizen of Canada, [and] a citizen of the world. [I] don't know that there was any hierarchy to them. All of those things were on kind of equal shares."[75] Although she had not been a Quebec resident during either the 1992 referendum on the Charlottetown Accord or the 1995 Quebec referendum, L'Heureux-Dubé openly stated, "Of course, if I had had the ability to vote, I would have voted 'no' without a scintilla of a doubt."[76] Her court attendant, André Legault, was incisive, "The political revolution in Quebec never interested Claire. She would say, 'I am who I am. I grew up the way I grew up. I'm going to make the best of myself. Don't dwell on what the English did to us. Just go and try to live your life. Stop the bitterness.'"[77] It was a philosophy that resulted in many rulings with a centralist perspective. According to Quebec law professor Andrée Lajoie, L'Heureux-Dubé was *"moins ouverte à la minorité québécoise, à laquelle elle n'est favorable que dans moins du tiers des pourvois,"*† ruling for Quebec in only four out of thirteen cases she heard during her tenure on the top court.[78]

---

† "less open to the Quebec minority, which she favours in less than a third of appeals"

Reflecting on her preference for a wider, international focus years later, L'Heureux-Dubé explained, "My father was an immigration officer. We lived always knowing about other countries. [I] don't want to be cut off from the world. The first thing I did was join the International Society of Family Law, the International Association of Comparative Law. I don't want Quebec to be just a little part of ourselves."[79] In contrast, she distanced herself from the separatist movement:

> The *Révolution Tranquille* was a great time, after Duplessis died. We felt that it would change ... the educational system, the religious influence on the politics, [and] the social science development of Quebec. My husband and I, and all the people around us, our friends, [and] our social community, were all of the same ideology. We didn't realize the slogan *"Maîtres chez nous"*† would lead to ... Lévesque forming his own party. I kind of liked Lévesque. He was honest. He did great things for French Canadians. He gave us pride in being French Canadian. We never had that before.
> But I didn't like his movement. I did not think the movement would go very far, given the type of people who adhered to it. It did not. I don't think Lévesque wanted separation really. It was a bargaining tool. He was a responsible person, and I am not sure if he had lived he would have continued on as a separate country. I think he would have negotiated something with the federal government to run Quebec according to our values and not according to the values of Canada, which may be different in many ways. I wasn't opposed to that. There was no doubt that the English didn't respect the French Canadians. They did it in all their colonies. They didn't give a chance to the French Canadians to develop their own skills. Lévesque said, "Wait – we are a great people." We took over all the businesses of the English in Quebec. But when Lévesque started with this separatism, that was too far for my husband and me. I never was a separatist and will never become one.[80]

In summary, L'Heureux-Dubé stressed that she was "a Quebec nationalist":

> Have you been to Montreal? It's a different world from Ontario. I lived in Ottawa for fifteen years and when I came back to Quebec [City] it was happiness incorporated. To live in my language, live in my values ... The core values of Quebec are important to me. I feel more comfortable in

---

† "Masters in our own house"

Quebec with our more socialist society, a more sharing society than in the rest of Canada. We pay more taxes. We have daycare. Although I am not a religious person, we were brought up in the community sharing of the Catholic Church. I love Canada, and we have succeeded in living together, but there are problems that we are trying to settle, so that Ottawa lets us live more like we want to live, which is different from the Anglophone world. I am all for more power to Quebec to realize our common goals, but I wouldn't go so far to think that it's necessary to separate.[81]

THE DECISION: VICTORY FOR BOTH SIDES

The court's unanimous decision surprised nearly everyone by rejecting the arguments raised by both sides. The sovereigntists lost their argument that secession was a unilateral political act. Quebec could not dictate the terms of secession, and could not rely on the right to self-determination to claim independence. The federalists lost their argument that a "yes" vote in any future referendum would place no reciprocal obligations upon the rest of Canada.

The court imposed a legal duty upon the federal government and the provinces to negotiate following a clear majority vote on a clear question. Observers noted that this ruled out any federal strategy of a nationwide anti-secession referendum.[82] The court stressed that there was no guarantee that negotiations would not end in an impasse. Issues such as the clarity of Quebec's future referendum question, the size of the requisite majority, and the good faith of the negotiations would be up to political actors, not the courts, to judge. The decision emphasized that the protection of minority and Aboriginal rights was a fundamental constitutional principle that would have to be taken into account in negotiating a divorce. The court identified four underlying constitutional principles as the basis for its position: federalism, democracy, constitutionalism and the rule of law, and respect for minorities. It fashioned a compromise decision that dealt less with the questions asked than with what the future process should be. L'Heureux-Dubé's verdict on the outcome was, "It was an excellent decision. We were honestly all on the same wavelength. We made so many efforts in such a short time. Everybody worked at it. After much drafting [and] redrafting, we all signed without any problem."[83]

Equally remarkable was the reaction of both sovereigntist and federalist forces. After some initial surprise, both sides claimed victory.[84] Prime Minister Chrétien applauded the court, saying it had "well-served all

Canadians by bringing clarity" and burying the principal myths that the partisans of separation had created.⁸⁵ In direct contradiction, Premier Parizeau characterized the decision as "a veritable boomerang on the federal government. The ruling validates our whole plan of 1995."⁸⁶ Guy Bertrand, the Quebec lawyer who had set the case in motion, declared it both a personal and federalist triumph: *"C'est une petite victoire personnelle ... c'est la fin du couteau sur la gorge pour tous les défenseurs de toutes les institutions canadiennes."*†, ⁸⁷ Speaking for the provincial premiers, Saskatchewan's Roy Romanow called the decision "probably as good a ruling as they could get."⁸⁸ Aboriginal Grand Chief Matthew Coon Come emphasized that *"la Cour a dit que les droits des autochtones dans une négociation sur la sécession devraient être considérés."*‡, ⁸⁹ The rest of the country also seemed content. Commentators were "almost universally laudatory."⁹⁰ The loonie moved up from its record low and the financial markets regained calm.⁹¹ Even the White House applauded the result.⁹²

Although there was no shortage of subsequent academic critique on the soundness of the ruling, Osgoode Hall law professor Patrick Monahan summed up the perspective most widely held:

> The existence of a "consensus" involving Jean Chretien and Lucien Bouchard on anything to do with Canadian federalism is no mean accomplishment. Surely the fact that these two habitual combatants both endorse the Supreme Court's opinion must count for something. And one cannot help but notice the fact that the political rhetoric in Quebec on the sovereignty issue appears to have muted considerably in the year since the Court's opinion was released. Moreover, the fact that Premier Bouchard has bestowed praise on a federal political institution has served to rehabilitate the reputation of the Court within Quebec, which is not only a positive development for Canadian federalism but also for the principle of the rule of law itself.⁹³

Toronto political scientist Peter Russell congratulated the court for having left most of the difficult negotiations "to the politicians and the political process," calling it "very wise."⁹⁴ Legal scholar Nathalie Des Rosiers applauded the balanced "tone" of the decision, the "sympathetic" approach to Quebec's "sensitivities," the "process-based solution," and the focus on

---

† "It is a small personal victory ... it is the end of the knife against the throat for all defenders of every Canadian institution."

‡ "The Court held that the rights of Indigenous peoples in negotiations on secession should be taken into account."

the need for reconciliation with minorities – both within and outside of Quebec. Her final conclusion: "The Supreme Court was the real winner in the battle."⁹⁵ And L'Heureux-Dubé's last word: "Without question it was the most important case I heard during my stay at the court. It's quite an achievement to make both parties happy. We wanted to do [something] good for the country – whether it's separation or not. I was happy."⁹⁶

35
Fairness in Immigration Law
Baker, 1999

The woman at the heart of the *Baker* case, Mavis Baker, was born in Jamaica in 1955.[1] In 1981, as a twenty-six-year-old African-Caribbean single mother who could not support her four children, she left her home and family in hopes of achieving economic independence in Canada.[2] Canada's history of racial preference for European immigrants was well known in the Caribbean, and Baker did not apply for permanent residence but entered the country as a temporary visitor.[3] She remained in Canada illegally, supporting herself as a household worker in the underground economy for eleven years.[4] During this time, she gave birth to four children: a boy in 1985, twins in 1989, and a boy in 1992, all of them Canadian citizens by birth.[5]

The father of two of them abandoned Baker, and then, after the birth of her last son, she was diagnosed with postpartum psychosis and paranoid schizophrenia. She lost her job, applied for welfare, and was hospitalized at Toronto's Queen Street Mental Health Centre. The twins were sent to live with their father and stepmother, while the other two children were placed in foster care.[6] After a year, medication improved Baker's health to the point where she could live independently, and the Children's Aid Society (CAS) returned her children from foster care. Although the twins remained with their father, the two family units became well integrated, with the twins' father offering psychological support to all of Baker's children. She was intent upon improving her education and securing employment.[7]

Her immigration status had never been regularized, however. Baker's application to stay in Canada was denied in 1987, and she received an order for deportation in 1992. In 1993, she applied for admission as a landed immigrant on "humanitarian and compassionate" grounds. Baker's physician advised that deportation would derail her health recovery, and that she needed to stay in Canada to continue treatment.[8] Her application noted that after more than a decade in Canada, she was far more Canadian than Jamaican. There was "nothing for her in Jamaica": no family ties, no community, no health care, no job.[9] The unemployment rate for adult women there had reached 65 percent. Twenty-five percent of the population lived below the international poverty line of US$1 a day.[10]

The CAS supported her application, emphasizing that Baker was the sole caregiver for two of her Canadian-born children, and that the other two depended on her for emotional support. A psychologist concluded that her deportation would detrimentally affect the emotional and cognitive development of all four children.[11] It was no answer to uproot the children to Jamaica, because it was a completely foreign land to them where they would be relegated to grinding poverty. The disruption to their schooling alone would have lifelong consequences. Since Baker had no one with whom to leave the children in Canada, if she were deported without the children, it would force them into institutional care. Whichever way the choice was made – to take the children or to leave them – the deportation of one parent would wrench the children from ongoing connection with the other parent.

In 1994, Baker's written application was summarily denied without a hearing. The perspective of immigration officer George Lorenz, who recommended deportation, was exposed when his rough notes surfaced later during the legal proceedings. He was angry that the immigration system was in disarray, and complained about the size of Baker's family:

This case is a catastrophy [sic]. It is also an indictment of our "system" that the client came as a visitor in Aug. '81, was not ordered deported until Dec. '92 and in APRIL '94 IS STILL HERE! The PC is a paranoid schizophrenic and on welfare. She has no qualifications other than as a domestic. She has FOUR CHILDREN IN JAMAICA AND ANOTHER FOUR BORN HERE. She will, of course, be a tremendous strain on our social welfare systems for (probably) the rest of her life. There are no H&C [humanitarian and compassionate] factors other than her FOUR CANADIAN-BORN CHILDREN. Do we let her stay because of that? I am of the opinion that Canada can no longer afford this type of generosity.[12]

Officer Lorenz had previously voiced similar sentiments about immigrants imposing a "constant drain on our system," comments that had been described as "inopportune and inappropriate" by previous courts.[13] Earlier courts had also overruled him for failing to consider the interests of children when rejecting a humanitarian and compassionate application.[14]

Some observers believed that immigration officers had begun to crack down on poverty-stricken single mothers because they were easy targets for meeting deportation quotas.[15] They criticized Officer Lorenz for relying upon popular stereotypes of immigrant workers as parasites upon Canadian largesse, for raising the spectre of the "Black welfare queen," and for exhibiting no awareness of Canada's reliance on human and economic resources from poorer nations.[16] They pointed out that contrary to myths that immigrants were a drain on the Canadian economy, they filled jobs Canadian-born citizens would not take, worked longer and harder, and helped offset declining population levels.[17] They objected to Officer Lorenz's view of domestic labour as unskilled, noting that those who cared for children, the sick, and the elderly applied physical and emotional labour, patience, and stamina.[18] They complained that Officer Lorenz had failed to recognize that as an undocumented worker, Baker would have had no access to public assistance for retirement, disability, or maternity, and that his rough notes betrayed discriminatory assessments of people diagnosed as "paranoid schizophrenic" as a permanent burden upon society. They argued that his deportation recommendation was really premised on the fact that Baker was sick and did not use birth control.[19]

But these arguments were all to come later. Initially, Officer Lorenz's supervisor simply incorporated the recommendation, without further reasons, into a deportation order. The Federal Court Trial Division and the Federal Court of Appeal refused to intervene.[20] Baker's children hired a lawyer and sought to be added as parties or as interveners in the case. The courts denied their request and awarded costs against the children. In the spring of 1996, immigration officials arrested Baker and the two children living with her. All three were detained several days at the immigration jail, despite there being no authority to arrest the children, who were Canadian citizens.

Baker's situation began to change when she obtained a legal aid certificate to hire Roger Rowe, a Montreal-born African Canadian lawyer with a poverty-law practice in Toronto. A founding member and president of the Canadian Association of Black Lawyers as well as a member of the Mayor's Committee on Race Relations, Rowe was offended by Officer Lorenz's resort to stereotypes, which he felt belittled all black people.[21] He

Fairness in Immigration Law

Roger Rowe, the Toronto lawyer who represented Mavis Baker.

believed that Baker had struggled to become a model citizen. Trying to protect her children, she had worked continuously until felled by temporary postpartum psychosis. He was drawn to his client, whom he described as "an excellent mother," and a woman who went to church "two to three times a week," who "inspired" him with her "gentle manner." He was convinced that if Mavis Baker were deported, she would perish on the street. His objective was to help her stay in Canada, for the sake of her children, her health, and her life.[22]

A MAJORITY DECISION:
ADMINISTRATIVE FAIRNESS AND THE BEST INTERESTS OF THE CHILD

At the Supreme Court of Canada, the case culminated in a 5–2 split, with Claire L'Heureux-Dubé penning a majority decision signed by Gonthier, McLachlin, Bastarache, and Binnie. Iacobucci and Cory concurred, but added a partial dissent on the effect of international law.[23] L'Heureux-Dubé found that Baker was within her rights to request admission upon "humanitarian and compassionate grounds" under section 114(2) of the *Immigration Act*.[24] Immigration experts noted that such claims were often made by individuals already in Canada, many of them "illegal de facto residents," often racialized women who came to Canada to take up positions as "domestic workers outside legal channels," established themselves over many years, and then sought to "regularize their status." The option to claim "humanitarian and compassionate grounds" recognized that people who had "severed ties with their home country" and "demonstrated an ability to be self-sufficient in Canada over a significant period of time" should not be subject to an "indefinite penalty for gaining illegal admission to the country."[25] Originally an exceptional power exercised by the minister of citizenship and immigration, the option had evolved over time to become a "front-line, high-volume" process in the hands of administrative personnel. Some believed it had become "too broad, too unstructured, and too difficult to supervise."[26] The question was what sort of judicial oversight should be put in place to constrain this.

In L'Heureux-Dubé's view, "procedural fairness" was a variable concept that should be adjusted to reflect the context of the particular statute and the rights involved.[27] She recognized on the one hand that immigration officers needed the flexibility to exercise considerable discretion, but noted on the other that Baker's immigration status was of extreme importance to her and her family. L'Heureux-Dubé overruled lower court rulings that had held that the duty of fairness in such matters was "minimal." She cautioned that claimants "whose important interests are affected by the decision in a fundamental way" must have a "meaningful opportunity to present the various types of evidence relevant to their case and have it fully and fairly considered."[28] She concluded that discretionary decisions "must be exercised in accordance with the boundaries imposed in the statute, the principles of the rule of law, the principles of administrative law, the fundamental values of Canadian society, and the principles of the *Charter*."[29]

L'Heureux-Dubé was also willing to move beyond the traditional common law position that reasons were not generally required for administrative decisions. She held that there was a duty here to provide a "written explanation" or "some form of reasons." There was no set format required, but since nothing else had been offered, she took Officer Lorenz's notes to be the reasons for this deportation order. At this point, the government's case toppled because Lorenz's notes failed the test for "reasonable apprehension of bias."[30] In compelling prose that extolled the benefits of immigration and took issue with discriminatory stereotypes, L'Heureux-Dubé wrote:

Canada is a nation made up largely of people whose families migrated here in recent centuries. Our history is one that shows the importance of immigration, and our society shows the benefits of having a diversity of people whose origins are in a multitude of places around the world. Because they necessarily relate to people of diverse backgrounds, from different cultures, races, and continents, immigration decisions demand sensitivity and understanding by those making them. They require a recognition of diversity, an understanding of others, and an openness to difference ...

[Officer Lorenz's] notes, and the manner in which they are written, do not disclose the existence of an open mind or a weighing of the particular circumstances of the case free from stereotypes. Most unfortunate is the fact that they seem to make a link between Ms. Baker's mental illness, her training as a domestic worker, the fact that she has several children, and the conclusion that she would therefore be a strain on our social welfare system for the rest of her life. In addition, the conclusion drawn was contrary to the psychiatrist's letter, which stated that, with treatment, Ms. Baker could remain well and return to being a productive member of society. Whether they were intended in this manner or not, these statements give the impression that Officer Lorenz may have been drawing conclusions based not on the evidence before him, but on the fact that Ms. Baker was a single mother with several children, and had been diagnosed with a psychiatric illness ... [H]is own frustration with the "system" interfered with his duty to consider impartially whether the appellant's admission should be facilitated owing to humanitarian or compassionate considerations.[31]

L'Heureux-Dubé stressed that the officer's decision was also unreasonable because it failed to recognize that "children's rights and attention to their interests" were "central" values in Canadian society.[32] In what heralded a bold new step, she buttressed this conclusion with international law. Canada had played a leading role in drafting the *Convention on the Rights of the Child*, a document signed by close to two hundred countries and ratified by Canada in 1991.[33] The convention provided that "in all actions concerning children, whether undertaken by public or private social welfare institutions, courts of law, administrative authorities or legislative bodies, the best interests of the child shall be a primary consideration."[34] Immigration lawyers had been arguing for years that Canada was posturing as a champion of the rights of children on the international scene while denying Canadian-born children the standing to dispute the deportation of their non-Canadian parents.[35] In 1995, the international Committee on the Rights of the Child charged with overseeing the convention specifically critiqued Canada's deportation practices: "The Committee regrets that the principles of non-discrimination, of the best interests of the child, and of the respect for the views of the child have not always been given adequate weight by the administrative bodies dealing with the situation of refugees and of immigrant children."[36]

L'Heureux-Dubé acknowledged that international conventions were "not part of Canadian law until they have been implemented by statute," and that the Convention on the Rights of the Child had not been "implemented by Parliament." Nevertheless, she was prepared to use it. Following international precedents from courts in India and New Zealand, she decided that "the values reflected in international human rights law may help inform the contextual approach to statutory interpretation and judicial review."[37] One year earlier, she had delivered a speech at an American judicial conference in which she stated that "growing international links and influences" were "changing judicial decisions, particularly at the level of top appellate courts throughout the world." She spoke positively about the "common understanding of the language of human rights that comes from a shared study and knowledge of international treaties and decisions."[38]

Cynthia Westaway, who clerked for L'Heureux-Dubé the year of the *Baker* decision, felt that L'Heureux-Dubé was "becoming a citizen of the world," "travelling in India," "doing international judicial education," taking "a broader vision," and "talking about globalization, the fact that you cannot operate in a Canadian vacuum [but] have to recognize international laws, international norms."[39] Michelle Flaherty, who worked as a law clerk the following year, emphasized how wide-ranging L'Heureux-Dubé's world-view had become by that stage of her career. "She was a woman of the world, who had all these international connections. She [had been] president of the International Commission of Jurists ... The Chief Justice of Zimbabwe would phone her for advice."[40] L'Heureux-Dubé explained that judges often discussed "common problems at international judicial conferences, by e-mail, and over the telephone," adding that the friendships that developed had enabled her to discuss "decisions of our court and theirs, and about issues that cross national boundaries." It was "bound to improve and refine the process of judicial globalization," she asserted.[41] She also attributed some of her knowledge about international law to her law clerks. "The law clerks educated me in many ways of things I was not aware. Because when I was in law school, international conventions were not discussed. They put us up to date on many of those international conventions."[42]

L'Heureux-Dubé characterized Officer Lorenz's reasons as failing to be "alive, attentive, or sensitive" to the interests of Baker's children. Indeed, he had taken the interests of the family, meant to work to the advantage of an applicant, and used it against Mavis Baker. Overall, he had "failed to give sufficient weight or consideration to the hardship that a return to Jamaica might cause Ms. Baker, given the fact that she had been in Canada for 12 years, was ill and might not be able to obtain treatment in Jamaica, and would necessarily be separated from at least some of her children."[43] Because the immigration officer had violated the principles of procedural fairness owing to a "reasonable apprehension of bias," and because the exercise of the "humanitarian and compassionate" discretion had been "unreasonable," L'Heureux-Dubé set aside the deportation order, and returned the matter to the government "for redetermination by a different officer."[44]

Iacobucci and Cory agreed that the case should be sent back for reconsideration, but they objected to referring to the "underlying values of an unimplemented international treaty in the course of the contextual approach to statutory interpretation and administrative law," because this might "adversely affect the balance maintained by our Parliamentary tradition, or inadvertently grant the executive the power to bind citizens without the necessity of involving the legislative branch." In short, to give domestic effect to an unratified treaty went against the separation of powers.[45] Apart from this partial dissent on the international treaty, they concurred with the majority decision.

David Wright, another law clerk in L'Heureux-Dubé's chambers that year, believed that getting a majority decision on a case as important as *Baker* mattered deeply to L'Heureux-Dubé. "Administrative law means a lot to her. Equality means a lot to her. International issues mean a lot to her. The rights of children. [In some ways] *Baker* brought all of those together." He also speculated that the composition of the seven-judge panel had been determinative. "Chief Justice Lamer and Justice Major were not sitting. [It] might have been very different had other judges been on the panel."[46]

RACELESSNESS, A CONTINUING THEME

Many observers thought that Mavis Baker's race had been a major factor driving the initial deportation order.[47] Immigration lawyers pointed to the wider background of deportations, a large proportion of which involved black families.[48] One observer compared Lorenz's objections to Mavis Baker to the themes of "sexual availability," "illegitimacy," and "excessive fertility" that had been crudely attached to Caribbean women in Canada for decades.[49] As University of Toronto law professor Audrey Macklin put it, "The coding jumps off the page: Jamaican woman, crazy, fecund, domestic worker, welfare queen. You name the stereotype: sleazy, not working, mentally ill, lots of babies."[50] Queen's law professor Sharryn Aiken agreed that the officer had used stereotypes of the "single mother," "paranoid schizophrenic," and "four children," adding that race was "implicit."[51]

Although Officer Lorenz never referred to "race" in his notes, race was the reason that Roger Rowe had been so offended. Rowe described the notes as laced with an "obvious racial animus of hostility," adding:, "I was struck by the arrogance ... the way we were all belittled. Lorenz was speaking about all black people, not just Ms. Baker ... all the stereotypes. As a black Canadian-born lawyer of West Indian heritage, I found the officer's comments offensive. It was his arrogant, insulting tone that gave me the incentive and wherewithal to pursue the appeal."[52] Rowe was equally upset that the Supreme Court had denied the African Canadian Legal Clinic, the Jamaican Canadian Association, and the Congress of Black Women the standing to intervene in *Baker*. He added that it had been a "slap in the face" to deny intervener status to a coalition that "wanted to raise [the] race issue."[53]

When the time for oral submissions arrived, Rowe found himself the only black lawyer in the courtroom. He felt he should have tackled the

Queen's University law professor Sharryn Aiken.

underlying racism, emphasizing that he "always wanted to do well by my community [and the] last thing I wanted for them to think was that I was oblivious to the issue of race." But as he explained to a group of law students years afterward, he lost his nerve:

> [Last winter I was invited to give a lecture on *Baker*] and for the first time, I had black female law students in the audience, and of course one of the issues they were concerned about was why I didn't raise the issue of race at the time. I apologized to those ladies. It bothered me that as the lone black lawyer in the pile, I was the one who wasn't raising the issue. And I'm the civil rights, human rights person who does all the advocacy work on behalf of the black community. It seems hypocritical, and I apologized to those ladies. [But when I stood up] looking at the complexion of the court ... they are totally out of touch with my reality, the reality of most black people, certainly the reality of Ms. Baker.
>
> Most judges are very uncomfortable talking about race. So in terms of how we framed the case, we had to think, "Do we want to make this about race?" – which we all know it's really about – or "Do we want the best chance of getting the largest number of judges on side?" [I knew] that this court wasn't going to look at race. We had to find another hook. I laid everything out as to why we framed it the way we did, and those women [law students] said, "Stop, you don't owe us any apology. We get it."[54]

What does it say about a country where racialized lawyers are afraid to raise legitimate arguments directly related to racism, for fear of backlash and negative repercussions against their clients? What does it say about a country with a Supreme Court bench that is all-white? The female litigators representing the Women's Legal Education and Action Fund (LEAF) had spoken movingly about what it meant to have women on the bench who might more fully understand the gender arguments they made – even in dissent. Roger Rowe had no such hope. The feminist movement that propelled the first women to the Supreme Court had not twinned its gender campaign with demands for racialized judges, and the anti-racism movement had not made independent headway on judicial appointments. There would be some talk about appointing an Ojibway judge, Murray Sinclair, in 2006, when a western spot came open on the top court, but there was an election, Liberal minister of justice Irwin Cotler was replaced by Conservative Vic Toews, and white judge Marshall Rothstein was appointed instead.[55]

In *Baker,* the all-white court sidestepped the issue of race, pinning blame on a "rogue immigration officer," race unspecified, who was unable to conduct himself properly and objectively.[56] It was a traditional Canadian legal stance, a failure to recognize or identify racism unless there had been overt name-calling. Incidents of implicit, semi-hidden racism are far more frequent, but they usually fly under the radar of legal authorities. Critics have pointed to the "dearth of judgments which have incorporated a 'race-sensitive' lens."[57] Audrey Macklin explained, "The way [our courts] deal with racism typically is, it's in the ether, but don't try to plant it on any individual. [We may have an] unfortunate history and practices, but don't try to pin it on any particular individual. We can see racism 'out there' but [it is] too scary to place it. Judges are really defensive about it. The idea of personalizing it is risky, because it can be personalized to them."[58] Sharryn Aiken added, "Had Justice L'Heureux-Dubé chosen to do so, she could have been more pointed [about the implicit racism] and it would have been helpful."[59]

Macklin emphasized that L'Heureux-Dubé had not shied away from objecting to stereotypes about mental illness, gender, and the receipt of social assistance. On the first two, she had first-hand life experience of her own with the unfairness of stereotypes. When it came to race, however, there was a gap. Macklin was critical: "Canada's multicultural history ... is invoked in a celebratory way. Why are we such a diverse multicultural country? Apparently because of our immigration practices. But here she confronts someone inside that system that she is celebrating. She does not comment on [the] anomaly. Either the system is not as romanticized as she thinks, or ... [someone at] the very heart of this multicultural immigration-loving society is behaving in ways that are not about those values. Here you present this feel-good Canadian image [by saying] that's not who we are, this guy is a random anomaly."[60]

Years later, L'Heureux-Dubé defended the absence of race analysis. "The decision by the officer was not based on race. It was based on her status as a person of little virtue that Canada didn't need. I never thought it was a case about an officer who hated blacks. I never thought it because it was not in the record. He detested people who are poor, who tried to exploit the system in his mind. [Race] may have been in his mind, but we couldn't go beyond his decision and say he was biased on race. How could we tackle this?"[61] As for the silence of Baker's counsel, she added:

> We can understand the frustration of a litigant in circumstances like this. I can understand his feelings knowing it as a black, and for him that was

it, because there is so much prejudice in society. I'm conscious of the fact that blacks and Aboriginals and other people ... maybe Islamic or whatever ... feel frustrated because they feel they are badly treated. I can understand that race is important. Maybe we should have been alerted. [The] fact that a lawyer doesn't raise what he thinks is the issue may say a lot about the way we treat race, but he had perfectly the right to do it. It's not necessarily bias from the court. It's [recognizing] that society is this way, and if they do something to raise this issue, that would create more problems than it settles for them. The answer of the bench would have been: [this] case is not about race.

While steadfast in her defence of the court, she then ruefully admitted that it was "not much of an answer."[62]

In some ways, it was the same story, and the same pattern that had unfolded when L'Heureux-Dubé chaired the 1976 Immigration Commission of Inquiry into the scandals linking white Montreal immigration officers with the exploitation of black Haitian women, and the commission had stripped its report of any analysis of racism.[63] It was also of a piece with L'Heureux-Dubé's 1983 Quebec Court of Appeal decision on the defamation of a Montreal Jewish politician, where the obvious anti-Semitic overtones had been glossed over, unreferenced and unconnected to the longstanding history of anti-Semitic discourse and practice in Quebec and Canada.[64]

L'Heureux-Dubé had been raised in an environment where people buried discussion about anti-Semitism and race discrimination, such as at the family dinner table when her parents chose not to talk about the forces of discrimination that made life so difficult for Jews in Quebec, even after she began working at one of the only Jewish law firms in town. One might argue that such silence was preferable to overt endorsement of discrimination, and certainly it was. But silence did not equate to an absence of prejudice. Failure to discuss discrimination encouraged the pretence, already widespread in Canada, that the society was tolerant and inclusive, needing nothing more than the correction of a few unrepresentative bad actors. In the mid-1970s and early 1980s, white people may have understood less about the dangers of burying race issues through omission, but by the turn of the century, demographic changes and widening sociocultural awareness of racism made this increasingly indefensible.

Is there any evidence that L'Heureux-Dubé's understanding of race had grown over time? Two years prior to *Baker*, she had heard the *R.D.S.* case, where Canada's first African Canadian female judge had been accused of bias against whites. The complaint of bias was based on critical comments the judge had made regarding the tendency of some police officers to "overreact" when dealing with non-white youths.[65] The majority of the Supreme Court bench rejected the bias complaint, but L'Heureux-Dubé and McLachlin jointly wrote the decision that was most supportive of the racialized female judge. They noted: "As a member of the community, it was open to [the judge] to take into account the well-known presence of racism in that community and to evaluate the evidence as to what occurred against that background. That [she] recognized that police officers sometimes overreact when dealing with non-white groups simply recognizes that in making her determination in this case, she was alive to the well-known racial dynamics that may exist in interactions between police officers and visible minorities."[66] This was a considerable stride forward in the judicial lexicon of race discrimination, a perspective directly opposed by Lamer, Sopinka, and Major, whose dissenting judgment insisted that the trial judge had improperly used racial "stereotypes" to assess evidence, and that "the appeal should not be decided on questions of racism."[67]

R.D.S. demonstrated that in certain cases, L'Heureux-Dubé could issue rulings that tackled racism explicitly. Yet *Baker* revealed that she, along with her Supreme Court colleagues, continued to hold a rudimentary understanding of the operation of racism. In *Baker,* she reprimanded an officer for stereotypical attitudes based on mental illness, gender, and poverty, but not race. L'Heureux-Dubé was correct to note that these issues had not been raised explicitly. Mental health advocates were upset at the level of antipathy directed at a woman who suffered from mental illness. Children's rights activists took up the cause of Baker's children. The Supreme Court was ready to put its judicial oversight stamp on the administrative process. And the unprofessional nature of the rough notes from what seemed like an out-of-control officer appalled everyone. But the one factor that had motivated Baker's lawyer above all else, what he and many from his community saw as egregious racism, was erased from the legal record.

Divided Response

Baker attracted substantial media attention, most of it negative.[68] The *National Post* dubbed it the "passport babies" case and the *Toronto Sun* called it "immigration-by-progeny: children conceived and born in the Great White North."[69] The *Globe* editors added, "[T]his country cannot go down a road in which illegal immigrants think if they have a child here, that child translates into a free passage for themselves into Canada ... This country must not permit the immigration process to become the legal equivalent of a shotgun wedding. When Ms. Baker's immigration appeal is heard again, the adjudicators should appreciate the sadness of her story but deport her nonetheless."[70] Margaret Wente opened her *Globe and Mail* column with a racially specific indictment: "On the face of it, Mavis Baker makes a pretty good poster person for tougher immigration laws. She's black, Jamaican, poor, uneducated, and prolific."[71]

The lawyers were significantly more supportive. Toronto lawyer Barbara Jackman, who had represented the Canadian Council of Churches as an intervener, lauded L'Heureux-Dubé's decision for "bringing human rights into the immigration process."[72] McGill law professor René Provost believed that the focus on international obligations marked *"un tournant dans la manière dont le tribunal utilise le droit international."*[†, 73] University of Toronto law professor Lorne Sossin extolled *Baker* as "arguably the farthest-reaching administrative law decision from the Supreme Court of Canada in a generation on the relationship between judicial review and administrative discretion."[74] Law professors David Dyzenhaus and Evan Fox-Decent characterized it as belonging to the "pantheon of great Canadian administrative law judgments."[75] According to Dyzenhaus, it established "for the first time in the common law world a general duty for administrative decision-makers to give reasons for their decisions."[76]

Audrey Macklin added, "On balance, it was a good decision [because of] the requirement of reasons. Here is somebody who [would seem to have] the least of claims to anything. She is here illegally ... a woman who is racialized, she's got a mental illness ... [and] she is asking for discretionary benefits. Our ideal immigrant is someone who hits the ground running and makes a ton of money, not her. She had very little to stand on. To say she is still entitled to be treated fairly, that she has the right to participate even if only in writing, that she is entitled to a decision-maker who is not biased against her ... that's really important. It created a kind of accountability that had not been there before."[77] Even the government seemed ultimately supportive, since it amended its legislation to stipulate that immigration officials must take into account "the best interests of a child directly affected" and "public policy considerations."[78]

---

† "a turning point in the way in which the court uses international law"

University of Toronto law professor Audrey Macklin.

Sharryn Aiken and Sheena Scott, who had acted as interveners on the issue of children's rights, heralded L'Heureux-Dubé's decision as "a step forward in taking children's rights seriously in the immigration context." But they also noted that the immigration bureaucracy was "resisting reform."[79] University of British Columbia law professor Catherine Dauvergne expressed similar concerns, suggesting that *Baker* had had "little influence in the actual outcomes of applications based on humanitarian and compassionate grounds."[80] It was a sentiment with which Roger Rowe agreed: "*Baker* created expectations that have not been fulfilled due to active resistance by immigration authorities and some lower courts, all of which has significantly limited its scope and effect."[81] Ironically, Lorne Sossin noted that the repercussions might have been the opposite of the court's objective. The immigration officers had apparently responded to the legal requirement to provide reasons "by having recourse to boiler-plate rationales, intended to immunize decisions from judicial scrutiny," and disclosing "far less about the reasoning process than was the case prior."[82]

Fairness in Immigration Law 485

Mavis Baker and two sons, ages six and thirteen, Toronto, 1998.

As for Mavis Baker, with Roger Rowe's continuing assistance, she obtained landed status as a permanent resident on 21 December 2001. "I am very proud," she told the press, adding optimistically that she hoped that "other people" would also benefit from the court ruling. The *National Post* reported that "unable to suppress her emotions, she hugged her lawyer, Roger Rowe."[83] Now in her sixties, Mavis Baker continues to live in Toronto with her children and grandchildren.

36
Epilogue on *Ewanchuk*

The firestorm that greeted Claire L'Heureux-Dubé's concurring opinion in *Ewanchuk* and Alberta judge John Wesley "Buzz" McClung's letter of response in the *National Post* continued to blaze long after its ignition in 1999. L'Heureux-Dubé was tagged as a radical feminist judge. McClung gained notoriety for his unprecedented critique. The Alberta judge went back on the record to claim that he had known nothing of Arthur Dubé's suicide when he accused L'Heureux-Dubé of causing male suicides in Quebec. McClung told the *National Post* that he was "just trying to give my friend Claire a prod because of her consistent anti-male response on these matters."[1] In a follow-up *National Post* interview, he could not resist adding that the *Ewanchuk* complainant was "not lost on her way home from the nunnery."[2]

Then he issued a public apology:

> For 40 years I have served the Courts of Alberta at 4 different levels and to the best of my ability. But last week I made an overwhelming error. When I read the Supplementary Reasons for Judgment of Madam Justice L'Heureux-Dubé in the Ewanchuk case, I allowed myself to be provoked into writing to the National Post. It was published on February 26th. The letter has been widely quoted and condemned.
>
> I wish to acknowledge that there was no justification for my doing so. I regret my reaction and appreciate that no circumstances could justify the media as the avenue for the expression of my disappointment. My letter

made reference to current suicide statistics in the Province of Quebec and was only included as a facetious chide to the Judge. I thought it would be so understood. What compounded my indiscretion was the fact, unknown to me, that Justice L'Heureux-Dubé had undergone a suicide bereavement in her own family. I immediately conveyed my explanation and apology to her later the same day. I sincerely regret what happened and have so advised her. It was a cruel coincidence to which she ought not to have been subjected. But it was a coincidence for which I am answerable.

On Saturday, February 27th, the National Post attributed to me further remarks about the Ewanchuk case. Any remarks were not designed to call into question the authority or finality of the Supreme Court of Canada resolution of the case, nor were they designed to impugn the complainant involved in the Ewanchuk assault. The discussion I had with Mr. Ohler, the reporter, was held as background to the issues in the case. I thought it was an off the record discussion as were discussions the previous day. Obviously Mr. Ohler did not. That in hindsight was also my mistake.

To be clear, I recognize the overriding authority of the Supreme Court of Canada and any suggestion to the contrary is incorrect. The Canadian system of justice could not function in the absence of a hierarchy of Courts. I deeply regret that what has happened has ignited a debate which could place the administration of justice in an unfortunate light. If so, that was unintentional as I have the highest regard for the justice system in which I serve.[3]

Globe and Mail columnist Margaret Bateman characterized it as a half-hearted apology, adding that it "included equivocations that give us glimpses of a man who blames others for provoking him, uses language recklessly and then claims his remarks were off the record, and tries to dissociate himself from what he must ultimately own – the meaning of his words, and their consequences."[4]

L'Heureux-Dubé chose not to reply to McClung publicly. The *Globe* described her as having "retreated into shocked silence as the attacks continued."[5] Years later, she admitted that the highly charged public debate caught her off-guard, for never in her "wildest dreams" had she imagined that her concurring decision would inspire such a backlash. "I didn't know McClung," she said, and had "nothing against him personally. I was not attacking McClung, but saying that the law cannot rely on myths and stereotypes."[6] Speaking with Laval law professor Louise Langevin in 2007, she added: *"Je me suis demandée pourquoi moi j'ai été catégorisée? La réponse qu'on m'a donné, « she is louder and clearer ». J'ai écrit selon mon tempérament, qui est clair, direct, pas ambigu et qui envoie le message de m'identifier beaucoup à l'égalité et aux droits des femmes.*"†,7

Outwardly L'Heureux-Dubé insisted that the public criticism only made her more confident in her views. There was no trace of the Laval student who chose not to challenge the male-only scholarships, the law graduate too shy to ask for a position in a Francophone law firm, the young judge who had allowed her Quebec Court of Appeal colleague to cut off her questions so rudely. "Criticism never deterred me," she insisted. "My temperament is a rebel."[8] When her law clerk Mimi Liu wondered whether the attacks might cause the judge to write decisions differently, L'Heureux-Dubé insisted, "I would write them all the same way."[9] Indeed, there was no evident change in tone or substance in the decisions she wrote during her remaining three years on the bench. It was a resurgence of her former reputation as *La Tigresse,* standing her ground, determined not to back away from an adversarial fight.

Inwardly, her feelings may have been more complex. It is a rare person who is not deeply affected when thrown into the middle of a contentious public conflagration. Even those who present themselves as impervious rarely escape unscathed. L'Heureux-Dubé's daughter, Louise, suggested that her mother was a "fighter," but that she was also a "very complicated person." Louise added:

> You get this story about women [who] need to be defended, this fighting spirit. My mother was afraid both for women and against criminal defendants. Underneath, I think she was frightened herself, unprotected against these men who took advantage ... *La Tigresse?* You can see it that way [but] I don't see it that way at all. If you poke her back, the bubble will deflate. She's very aggressive, [but I'm] not sure she can take as much as she dishes out. There are many layers there. She's a very anxious person. She paid quite a price. Then somehow she finds the strength to move on.[10]

Supreme Court judge Michel Bastarache saw something similar. "Claire looks self-assured, but she is not. Even in all her dissents, she puts a very brave face on it, but she was very insecure. I knew it. I saw her. When she was on the court, she kept saying, 'I don't feel any great pressure. It's a job.

---

† "I wondered why I was categorized? The answer I was given is, 'she is louder and clearer.' I wrote according to my temperament, which is clear, straightforward, unambiguous and sends out a message that identifies me very much with equality and the rights of women."

I just say what I think. I'm not afraid of speaking out.' In fact, it wasn't really true."[11]

Some of L'Heureux-Dubé's young law clerks also witnessed the personal toll close-up. David Wright recalled that the public discussion of Arthur's suicide quickly turned to erroneous rumours that her son, Pierre, had committed suicide as well. It was like piercing an unhealed wound. Wright added, "Sometimes, the words [and] the quotes can't capture ... the hurt of how she was treated."[12] Andrew Lenz agreed: "She feels things very deeply. When that whole McClung thing happened, that was very unfair. She didn't deserve that."[13] L'Heureux-Dubé's close friend Ottawa lawyer Suzanne Labbé was also aware of the pain. "I don't buy that she wasn't hurt. It must have been devastating. She did come out of it. Maybe looking back, she thinks it made her stronger."[14]

It was several years before L'Heureux-Dubé herself spoke publicly about the toll the *Ewanchuk* attack took. Surprisingly, she opened up with the press, the medium that had been such an agent of bombardment earlier. In an interview with Cristin Schmitz of *Lawyers Weekly* just weeks before her retirement from the Supreme Court of Canada in 2002, she admitted that she had been "distressed" over McClung's actions and explained that she thought she was "just doing [the] job" when she wrote the *Ewanchuk* opinion.[15] "I was accused of being a bully, among other things," she stated. "I feel that I was wrongly attacked ... and the message was, 'Shut up!'"[16]

An interview she gave to the *Globe and Mail* went still further. "I was flabbergasted that you could be attacked so personally," she admitted. "I don't mind criticism of my judgments – that is part of the territory – but personal attacks? As far as I'm concerned, it's not acceptable."[17] She went on to explain: "I can tell you it hurt – because of the personal attacks on my family, my husband. The implication was that I was responsible ... You know, you miss these people that you love. The attacks brought back all these memories. It was a very difficult period. Judges are just human beings, and we have feelings and reactions. I sometimes think people don't realize that we are not mechanical; we are not robots."[18]

The accusations McClung had flung would have been hurtful to anyone blamed for causing male suicide. There was a special edge given his aim specifically at L'Heureux-Dubé. She had never tried to hide the details of Arthur's self-inflicted death in an era when most people tried to conceal the ravages of family suicide. She had experienced deep grief over her husband's death, but she knew it stemmed from long-standing depression and mental illness. She took consolation from the fact that Arthur's siblings never blamed her or the marital relationship, indeed the opposite. Those who knew them said Arthur had been happier with her than he would have been without.[19] To have the tragedy dredged up years later by people who knew nothing about Arthur the person, his illness, or their relationship, and then to be privy to whispers and rumours circulated by others even less knowledgeable, must have been agonizing.

On the eve of her retirement, L'Heureux-Dubé was prepared to say that sexism was at the root of the imbroglio, a form of discrimination that she fought to remedy in law but rarely admitted as confounding her personal life. "Strong women judges who dare speak out for equal rights are lightning rods for unfair criticism," she told the *Lawyers Weekly*. "For example, if a man had written my concurring opinion in *Ewanchuk*, I would bet my right hand that the incident that followed would never have happened."[20] Political scientist Carl Baar agreed that no judge would have "made these comments or used this kind of language about a male colleague on the Supreme Court of Canada."[21] Rick Salutin, a *Globe and Mail* columnist, made the same point about Edward Greenspan: "I still wonder if Greenspan would have hit the same tone had the opinion been written by the guy. Bullying has its rules, just like a courtroom."[22] The male-dominated court had unanimously overturned McClung. Charles Gonthier had signed L'Heureux-Dubé's concurring decision. Yet it was only L'Heureux-Dubé who was excoriated. The anti-feminist, conservative organization REAL Women of Canada made the gendering explicit when its spokesperson, Gwen Landolt, was asked about Charles Gonthier. "REAL Women has no quarrel with him," she told the press.[23]

Dissension within the Supreme Court

Within the court, the reaction to the post-*Ewanchuk* free-for-all was tense. The law clerks were stunned, with some likening it to peering out at a train crash, none of them able to tear their eyes from the wreckage.[24] Within the judges' circle, dissension reigned. Although all of the judges had found McClung's outburst distasteful, some of L'Heureux-Dubé's colleagues believed that her concurring opinion had also gone "too far in dumping on the Alberta court," and that "the thing had got completely out of hand in both directions."[25] Several thought the best approach was for L'Heureux-Dubé to make a public statement accepting McClung's apology.

Frank Iacobucci spoke with L'Heureux-Dubé directly.[26] In his view, her best response was to take "the high road."[27] He thought that she should write a letter to McClung acknowledging the Alberta judge's apology. Iacobucci believed that she should tell McClung that she was pleased he had recognized "the error of [his] ways" and that she accepted his apology. He also thought it would be helpful to add something to the effect that she assumed that, as two judges, they would continue to work toward the administration of justice to the best of their abilities. He recommended that she release her letter publicly.[28] Although L'Heureux-Dubé initially seemed willing to consider this suggestion, she ultimately rejected his advice. Jack Major and Ian Binnie wondered whether she had consulted with friends outside the court, and then decided not to publicly accept McClung's apology.[29]

In fact, L'Heureux-Dubé was deeply upset by what she felt was a lack of support from her fellow justices. Law clerk David Wright observed that she was completely "isolated" on the court.[30] Her daughter, Louise, agreed: "I think she felt she was left alone and hung out to dry."[31] L'Heureux-Dubé would have preferred that Chief Justice Lamer issue a public defence of his court, specifically rebuking those who were proclaiming that "extreme feminist groups" had "overtaken the court." But Lamer remained silent.[32] The law clerks speculated behind the scenes about his motivation. Some, who knew only too well that Lamer found L'Heureux-Dubé "unbearable," wondered whether he might have shared some of McClung's critique. Others thought he may have held his peace because he did not wish to give McClung's diatribe the dignity of a response.[33]

Globe and Mail reporter Kirk Makin was not surprised that Lamer did not speak out. "I don't think that there was a really established protocol that the chief invariably comes to the defence of the beleaguered member of the court," he said. Then he added, "You could argue that Lamer could or should have come out and tried to still the roiling waters for the benefit of the court. He just let it happen."[34] In an article published at the time, Makin wrote, "To be sure, there is no love lost between the chief justice and Judge L'Heureux-Dubé. Yet, some legal observers believe that other members of the Supreme Court bench would have been happier had Chief Justice Lamer been in a position to defend Judge L'Heureux-Dubé against the recent attacks on her."[35]

Speaking some years later, retired judicial colleague Melvin Rothman, one of the few Quebec judges to have acknowledged the chilly climate that had marked L'Heureux-Dubé's early years on the Quebec bench, described himself as "shocked" by her treatment in the aftermath of the *Ewanchuk* case. Rothman believed that the chief justice's antipathy toward L'Heureux-Dubé was the real reason why Lamer did not step in to object publicly. "I don't think Brian Dickson would have permitted for ten seconds what Tony permitted," he insisted. "[Lamer] couldn't get along with Claire. Anything said against her, to tear her down, he would have accepted."[36]

L'Heureux-Dubé stepped up the pressure when she circulated a memo to her colleagues, praising Israeli Supreme Court President Aharon Barak for publicly rising to the defence of *his* court. This, she wrote, was what another chief justice had done when his court was subjected to unfair criticism.[37] Lamer took great exception. In a reply memo addressed to all the Supreme Court judges, he claimed that it would be inappropriate for him as chair of the Canadian Judicial Council to make comments on a case that had sparked complaints to that council. Lamer's memo continued:

> [M]y decision was to wait until the complaints have been disposed of and then, with your advice, decide whether to respond to these attacks and in what manner. I spoke to our colleague Mme Justice L'Heureux-Dubé, yesterday and told her how unfair I thought she was being indirectly accusing me of not coming to the defence of this Court. She told me others on this Court shared her views. I invite those persons to come forward and explain to me why and how I should respond now to the persons who have made such allegations without (you know what the Press can do with this) being perceived as interfering with the disposition of the two complaints.[38]

It was a defensible position.[39] As it turned out, Lamer seems to have felt that he was too close to the issue even to adjudicate the *Ewanchuk* complaints at the Canadian Judicial Council. He stepped aside, leaving other judges to conduct the review. He never did break his public silence.

Parallel Complaints to the Canadian Judicial Council

At the Canadian Judicial Council, REAL Women called for L'Heureux-Dubé's removal from the bench.[40] The essence of the complaint was that feminism was incompatible with judging. REAL Women alleged that L'Heureux-Dubé had failed to "impartially apply the law and decide cases in accordance with their legal merit," "consistently promoted her own feminist bias in her judgments," and "proceeded to quote feminist authors, including American feminist, Catharine MacKinnon."[41] Not only did she quote feminists but, according to the *National Post*, "her friends include a roster of feminists, both academic and on the bench."[42]

Epilogue on Ewanchuk   493

It fell to British Columbia Chief Justice Allan McEachern, who replaced Chief Justice Lamer as acting chair on the Canadian Judicial Council, to review the complaint. After examining the allegations, he concluded that there were no grounds to refer the case to a panel of CJC judges for further review, and dismissed the complaint. He found REAL Women's allegations meritless, ruling that that there was no evidence of any lack of impartiality or objectivity. He reminded REAL Women that all of the Supreme Court judges had agreed with the result.[43]

Twenty-four groups and individuals had lodged a parallel complaint against McClung.[44] Their complaint drew some fire from Edmonton lawyers, who sought standing to appear as well, claiming to act for lawyers across Canada who were concerned that "all the evidence comes out – not just sociological gibble."[45] It was a frontal assault on the social context approach that L'Heureux-Dubé had taken in her recent judgments. A Calgary women's group also wrote to the CJC charging that L'Heureux-Dubé had "disgraced the court by her longstanding and blatant partisanship with feminists" and by her "ungracious refusal" to accept McClung's apology.[46]

The McClung complaint was not dismissed at first instance. A CJC panel, composed of three chief justices from Nova Scotia, Quebec, and Ontario, found that McClung's initial judicial decision crossed "the boundary of appropriate judicial expression" and that his criticism of the complainant was "simply unacceptable for a judge." They characterized his letter to the *National Post* as "inappropriate," "impetuous," and "a significant indiscretion." They found the rationales he offered for his letter "not credible." As a whole, they concluded, McClung's conduct reflected "negatively on the judiciary." The CJC "rebuked" McClung but did not recommend his removal from the bench.[47]

It was, on balance, a vindication for the author of the concurring *Ewanchuk* decision. The acting chair of the CJC dismissed the complaint against L'Heureux-Dubé at first instance, without even sending it to a review panel. The review panel appointed by the CJC to hear the complaint against McClung found his behaviour "unacceptable." Some wondered whether the penalty of a "rebuke" was sufficient. But given that McClung had apologized to L'Heureux-Dubé, it would have been surprising to find any panel of judges recommending that he step down from the bench. Through it all, L'Heureux-Dubé must have found the CJC proceedings excruciating, required as she was to defend herself against the REAL Women organization and to endure yet more castigation from Alberta lawyers who intervened, and frustrated that the proceedings kept the controversy going. Law clerk Cynthia Westaway described it as "a very hard year for her."[48]

Shortly after the Canadian Judicial Council rulings, L'Heureux-Dubé delivered what the press dubbed a "hard-hitting address" to the Canadian Bar Association's annual meeting, where she objected to what she described as "bench bashing." She conceded that judges should not be "immune from criticism," and that there was no expectation that judicial decisions should be "popular" or "uncontroversial." But she asserted that attacks upon judicial institutions and individual judges were becoming "more and more frequent" and that the vocabulary bore fewer and fewer "signs of civility." She emphasized that the *Charter* had been democratically chosen by Canadian citizens, and that it was the duty of judges to ensure compliance with those rights.[49] The press marked it as the "first time a Supreme Court judge has so directly confronted the agenda of the top court's most vociferous and powerful critics."[50]

The Debate Expands

Far beyond the confines of judicial corridors and professional bar conventions, L'Heureux-Dubé's *Ewanchuk* decision took on a life of its own, initiating a "national debate about sex and the law."[51] Callers "jammed talk show lines" to weigh in on the broader implications for the relations between men and women.[52] Journalists observed that issues left "festering for years erupted in the public domain."[53] It reflected a society increasingly saturated with sex, where basic understandings about what constituted "consent" still remained largely unclear. The competing visions spelled out by McClung and L'Heureux-Dubé brought Canadians face to face with the necessity of hammering out how sex ought to be negotiated. Notions of free, voluntary, informed consent clashed with cultural norms surrounding techniques of seduction. The slogan "No means No" wrestled with "No really means Try Harder." There were disagreements over whether a woman's dress and reputation could be presumed to signal consent. The debates over "implied consent" constituted the equivalent of a Molotov cocktail thrown into the mix.

Joanne Wright, a political scientist at the University of New Brunswick who surveyed the public discourse that attended the *Ewanchuk* decision, concluded that the case and the backlash became "a focal point for society's fears and concerns about feminism in general." She observed that

Ewanchuk served as the terrain to debate "competing cultural-sexual scripts regarding appropriate sexual behaviour."[54] Wright suggested that the concept of implied consent had historically been misused by the courts, allowing judges to disregard women's non-consent by reason of their actions or dress.[55] She took issue with the characterization of men as "aggressive animals whose sexuality cannot be controlled," and stated that all the law required was that "men be sure that consent is present. If they are unsure, then it is their responsibility to *make sure*. Ideally, men should *want* to be sure." Indeed, she concluded, there "ought to be a more meaningful, more emancipatory, conception of consent for women."[56]

A new generation of female law students took inspiration from what they understood to be a strong new legal underpinning for women's sexual autonomy. They read L'Heureux-Dubé's decision as bolstering the proposition that women were free to accept or reject sexual interactions at any point, and that men had to pay greater attention to whether their prospective partner was genuinely willing. They signed up with LEAF chapters to supervise "No means No" workshops in local high schools. They found Canadian young people deeply confused about the concept of consent, and they chose the *Ewanchuk* case as the centrepiece for presentations to clarify matters.[57]

Those who preferred McClung's version argued that L'Heureux-Dubé's views were "removed from reality."[58] An Alberta reporter tried to showcase the illogic of the *Ewanchuk* consent rules with the following illustrations:

> If a friend nagged you into loaning him your car, we would call it acquaintance carjacking. If someone talked you into going on an unwanted trip by making you feel guilty about refusing, that would be kidnapping. If a relative from out of town wanted to stay at your place and did not take repeated hints that this wasn't such a good time, that would be no different from thugs forcing their way in at gunpoint.[59]

The argument was that the *Ewanchuk* rules simply would not work in the daily world. It was a sentiment shared by Toronto defence lawyer Alan Gold, one of the critics quoted in the media when the decision first came out. Interviewed years later, Gold took issue with L'Heureux-Dubé's elimination of implied consent. *Ewanchuk* went further than "No means No," he complained, to inscribe the "proposition that anything other than a crystal clear express 'Yes' means 'No.'" He added:

The sex act is not a real estate transaction. As the hormonal tide rises, the participants are beset by all kinds of desires, signals, ambiguity, internal debates ... *Ewanchuk* represented a radical feminist idea of how sex between males and females should take place. In the *Ewanchuk* world, there's no such thing as buyers' remorse in the sexual context. In the real world, that's a very real phenomenon. The model of sexual encounter adopted in *Ewanchuk* was simply not compatible with most people's perceptions and experience of the sexual encounter.[60]

Asked why L'Heureux-Dubé had become such a specific target, Alan Gold linked it to her high profile, her outspoken ways, the extent of her impact on criminal law, and her "law and order" agenda.[61]

In an interview over a decade after the Supreme Court ruling, Edward Greenspan, the Toronto defence lawyer who had published the angriest critique of *Ewanchuk,* stood his ground.[62] He explained that as early as the mid-1980s, he had become alarmed over "this whole new movement that was floating about in terms of sexual assault," attempting to import "victimology" into criminal law:

Toronto criminal lawyer Alan Gold.

I predicted *Ewanchuk*. I may not have predicted precisely what was said. But I predicted it because I was talking about pornography, sexual assault, how feminist pressure was influencing substantive as well as procedural law ... I deplored attempts to use the judicial council as an agency of the women's movement through the filing of complaints against judges who made passing remarks that didn't accord with their world view.

I also predicted ... that in 10 years from now ... they [would] have completed ... a judicial embracing of the feminist perspective. [Y]ou saw this coming a mile away ... in terms of treating sexual assault cases differently than all other cases.[63]

Greenspan disagreed with the new statutory rules regarding the definition of "consent" that had been enacted on the heels of the *Seaboyer* decision. He believed that men who did not understand that a woman had not consented ought not to be convicted because they did not have the *mens rea*, a guilty mind. He believed that women and children had a propensity to make false complaints. "In this day and age, I don't need *Ewanchuk* to tell me where I will draw the line in what I will say is a defence. My job is to raise a reasonable doubt."[64]

He conceded that McClung had done "a very stupid thing" in publishing that letter, but argued that L'Heureux-Dubé's "incendiary language" had left McClung "angry as hell."[65] He objected to the language L'Heureux-Dubé had used: "'Eradicate this thought,' 'It should never be thought again or said again.' What? You might hear that kind of language in show trials. To scold him in the very strong manner she did. To the point he should be removed from the bench! ... Her language made that inevitable." He continued: "[She] psychoanalyze[d] this judge and beat him up to the point where ... you know what the climate is, and the climate is to report [him]."[66] In Greenspan's view, feminists were out to unseat judges they did not agree with, and that was what drove McClung to write his protest letter. It was because McClung feared he was about to lose his job as a judge. The worst result would be a bench ultimately composed of feminists appointed to replace the disgraced McClungs.[67]

The polarizing debate about sex, consent, and the role of the criminal law was not resolved in the wake of *Ewanchuk*. But it served as a historically significant marker, offering multiple snapshots of what Canadians were prepared to articulate about intimate sexual relations. *Ewanchuk* had provided an inspiring call to arms and a lightning rod for pent-up anger. It came to stand in for years of simmering hostility. L'Heureux-Dubé's decision had undercurrents that went far beyond the actual judgment. It

Toronto criminal lawyer Edward Greenspan in his law office, 2013.

brought the defence bar's notion of fairness in criminal law crashing down upon the feminist notion of gender equality. Perhaps things had never been so raw, so explicit.

University of Ottawa law professor David Paciocco saw L'Heureux-Dubé as a judge who was "not prepared to accept the orthodox approach":

> The precedents were all liberty-regarding, concerned about wrongful convictions, due process. They purported to be faceless and genderless. To her credit, L'Heureux-Dubé recognized that they weren't. I think that when she approached these decisions, she did it from a group rights perspective, which is something that hadn't been done in the criminal law. It doesn't sit well with the classic conception of the criminal trial. But she saw another dimension to a fair trial. Why [was she] such a lightning rod? It was scary. Change was frightening. Especially [for] people who were invested in the doctrine. You come to believe in it, the way you see the world. Somebody comes along and wants to change it, it's scary. Whatever you may think of her particular decisions, you can't deny the impact that she had because of where she was and what she believed and her readiness to stick to it.[68]

Rosalie Abella, a judge who had been specifically targeted by the *National Post* as a "feminist friend" of L'Heureux-Dubé's, reflected that L'Heureux-Dubé got "swept up in something she would not have wanted" with *Ewanchuk*.[69] "It gave a lot of people an opportunity, a platform for saying things they wanted to say for a long time. It was the door that opened to feelings people had. She was the vehicle. She was the representative. It wasn't just about Claire. It was a class action."[70]

The Limelight Expands

The post-*Ewanchuk* limelight added heft to the reputation that was growing around L'Heureux-Dubé during her last decade on the court. She was deluged with invitations to speak. When she spoke at law schools, she spent time before the speech with the organizing committee and time afterward with the students. Law clerk Cynthia Westaway observed that "she built her reputation one event at a time. People felt they knew her."[71] Another law clerk, Teresa Scassa, emphasized L'Heureux-Dubé's populist appeal: "She was so open and so willing to engage with anyone. [She had] this very earthy sense of justice. Justice belonged to everybody. She walks into a class of law students, and is ... not remote, not formal and stuffy. She wins them over. A part of her just didn't see that divide between Supreme Court justices and everybody else."[72]

L'Heureux-Dubé's tiny stature belied her palpable physical presence in person. Law clerk Michelle Flaherty recalled being struck during her hiring interview with L'Heureux-Dubé, at how a woman whose build was so short "filled the room."[73] David Wright explained, "You've got to capture her personality. She is larger than life. She lights up a room."[74] Queen's law professor Don Stuart exclaimed, "Claire showed up and it was like the queen had arrived."[75] McGill law professor Pierre-Gabriel Jobin said, "She loves and seeks the company of others. She likes to have their attention. She's close to having the personality of a star, a diva maybe."[76] At one women's law conference, L'Heureux-Dubé arrived on stage and "the young women in the auditorium were on their feet. They were screaming ... like what I would have imagined at the Beatles' reception," recalled Halifax lawyer Darlene Jamieson. At the close, the crowd swarmed the judge to request her autograph.[77] At a 1999 evening in Quebec City to celebrate *Hommage à nos Pionnières,* L'Heureux-Dubé again stole the show.[78]

At a legal conference he attended with L'Heureux-Dubé at the University of Western Ontario, Ian Binnie marvelled at the after-dinner theatrics, when a male law student sang in her honour. "The lyrics went, 'I don't care what they say, I'm in love with L'Heureux-Dubé.' It was very witty, [and] a huge hit, [and it] ended to wide applause. Claire got up, dashed over to the student, and gave him a huge hug. He was twice as tall as she was. And [she] said, 'You've made my day, but you won't make my nights.' It brought down the house. Sensational."[79] Jack Major agreed: "It can't be questioned that during her period on the Supreme Court, she was probably the most recognized judge, and probably had the biggest single following. Criminal lawyers might have liked what Lamer said in different cases, but I think if you were rounding them up, you'd get a bigger crowd for Claire."[80] Rosalie Abella observed that it was through *Ewanchuk* that L'Heureux-Dubé became a "public persona." It was the twinning of the "vilification" she had suffered with her "singularly steadfast commitment to the rights of women, children, and minorities" that earned her a "place in history."[81]

The repercussions of the *Ewanchuk* case soon became evident to L'Heureux-Dubé herself. "It enlarged my horizon in so many ways. It mobilized people. It was my first connection with many ... all over the world."[82] Arline Pacht, a founder of the International Association of Women Judges (IAWJ), specifically cited *Ewanchuk* at a conference honouring L'Heureux-Dubé's retirement, when she described her as a "pacesetter" whose rejection of stereotypes had been an "all too singular voice."[83] The IAWJ would list *Ewanchuk* as one of L'Heureux-Dubé's most impressive accomplishments when it bestowed on her its Human Rights Award in 2012.[84] Although some observers predicted that generations of law students would be reading the *Ewanchuk* decision for years to come, few knew that the case would travel the globe. Irizel Collazo, a Puerto Rican lawyer, studied it in an international human rights class at the London School of Economics, where she recalled it as "one of the highlights" of her graduate education and L'Heureux-Dubé's decision as "particularly memorable."[85] Speaking to the *Globe and Mail* at her retirement, L'Heureux-Dubé mused, "That decision has been used all over the world in judicial education programs. It's incredible that something so small and ordinary and inconsequential brought such fury and had such influence."[86]

Epilogue for the Main Actors

One of the more memorable gifts that L'Heureux-Dubé received during her last decade on the court was a framed photo of Nellie McClung, Buzz

Epilogue on Ewanchuk

Nellie McClung, Canadian suffragist, and her famous quotation.

McClung's renowned suffragist grandmother. The photo was inscribed with Nellie McClung's famous quotation: "Never retract. Never explain. Never apologize. Just get the thing done and let them howl." L'Heureux-Dubé hung it in her Supreme Court chambers, where it provoked many visitors to smile over the irony. She loved the quote. And she recited it with great flourish at her retirement dinner.[87]

Although the relationship between L'Heureux-Dubé and McClung was never publicly smoothed over, behind the scenes civility reigned. When L'Heureux-Dubé learned that he had fallen ill, she sent him an encouraging note. He wrote back to convey his thanks. "For me," recalled L'Heureux-Dubé, "that was the closing of the book."[88] Apparently, it was less than full closure for McClung. According to Alberta legal lore, he remained haunted by the *Ewanchuk* events until his death in 2004.

Steve Ewanchuk was sent back to face the trial judge who had originally acquitted him. Now mandated by the Supreme Court to sentence Ewanchuk for sexual assault, the trial judge ordered a one-year jail term. It satisfied no one. Both the Crown and the defence appealed. The Alberta Court of Appeal increased the sentence to two years less a day, and the Supreme Court refused leave to appeal.[89]

After his release from prison, Ewanchuk's run-ins with the law continued. He was convicted in 2005 of sexually assaulting an eight-year-old girl.[90] The Crown sought to have him jailed indefinitely as a dangerous offender due to his lengthy prison record: three years for raping two 16-year-old girls in 1969, ten years for raping an 18-year-old nursing student while on parole in 1972, fifteen months for sexually assaulting a 14-year-old girl in 1989, three months for breaching a release condition forbidding him to employ girls under 18, and then, of course, two years less a day in the "No means No" case that brought him international infamy.[91] In 2007, the court rejected the Crown's "dangerous offender" application, and sentenced Ewanchuk to eleven years with mandatory supervision for ten years after parole.[92]

A Wider Stage

37
Judicial Education and International Influence

In the aftermath of the *Ewanchuk* case, a phenomenon that was already under way accelerated – the propulsion of Claire L'Heureux-Dubé onto the international stage. Alberta Chief Justice Catherine Fraser observed that few Canadians recognized what a significant "international presence" L'Heureux-Dubé developed. "We've had many great judges in Canada," she stated, "but I don't think we've ever had a judge from this country who has had an international influence like Claire." Her "very clear vision of equality," added Fraser, had made an "immense difference to lives of people not only in Canada but around the world."[1] Judicial education was the vehicle that made this possible.

THE CONTROVERSY OVER JUDICIAL EDUCATION:
"OPENING" JUDICIAL MINDS OR "ATTITUDINAL INDOCTRINATION"?

Historically, common law courts had had little use for judicial education.[2] Citing the twin principles of judicial independence and lifelong tenure, most judges appeared to be affronted by any suggestion that they required constant upgrading. The Canadian Judicial Council took the first step toward change when it introduced a voluntary seminar for judges in 1972.[3] In the early years, however, judicial education remained a haphazard patchwork of skills training and black letter law updates, run by volunteer judges.[4] These were the kinds of programs in which L'Heureux-Dubé had

Justice Catherine Fraser, chief justice of Alberta.

participated while still a Quebec appellate judge, when she lectured across the country about new developments in family law.

Chief Justice Brian Dickson effected larger changes when he oversaw the creation of the National Judicial Institute (NJI) in 1988, to develop nationally coordinated and more broadly conceived courses for judges.[5] The impetus was the *Canadian Charter of Rights and Freedoms,* which had turned the "spotlight of public opinion" onto the courts, intensifying demands for public accountability and sparking increasingly vitriolic critiques of judges.[6] Members of the public were lodging protests with the Canadian Judicial Council, the statutory body charged with investigating complaints about judges, at unprecedented rates, up almost tenfold from 1981 to the 1990s.[7] Many of the complaints were based upon perceived gender bias or insensitive comments about sexual assault, of the sort that Alberta judge Buzz McClung had made in the *Ewanchuk* case.[8] In 1989, a royal commission into the wrongful conviction of an Indigenous man, Donald Marshall Jr., recommended judicial training about "legal issues facing visible minorities."[9] In 1993, a task force on gender equality in the legal profession chaired by Bertha Wilson recommended mandatory courses for all judges on both gender and racial bias.[10] In 1994, the Canadian Judicial Council finally approved the development of new programs on gender and race.[11]

Two of the key advocates for "social context judicial education," as these programs came to be called, were Catherine Fraser and Claire L'Heureux-Dubé. Fraser fought for the new programming from within the Canadian Judicial Council. L'Heureux-Dubé was the "cheerleader in the background," a judge who had created a zone of legitimacy for social context analysis at the nation's highest court.[12]

Not surprisingly, the introduction of such judicial programs stirred up a storm of controversy, with opponents characterizing them as a cover for attitudinal indoctrination by representatives of an interest group.[13] Chief Justice Antonio Lamer, who had taken over the chair of the NJI from Dickson, articulated these concerns:

> I recognize that many Canadian judges are less than wholly supportive of social context education, primarily because they fear that it amounts to an attempt at indoctrination to a particular way of thinking about social context issues. To these colleagues, let me say that I have always believed very firmly, and continue to believe, that educational programs for judges must not and cannot be used as a vehicle for indoctrination of any kind.[14]

Lamer resisted calls to make such courses mandatory, or to allow anyone except judges to design and deliver the training, insisting that anything other "would threaten judicial independence in a fundamental way."[15]

Osgoode Hall law professor Allan Hutchinson disagreed. Contrary to suggestions that independent judges would "fall captive to the agenda of certain pressure groups," he argued that such programs would "open judicial minds, not close them."[16] Hutchinson added that judges had "already and always" fallen captive to the agenda of certain pressure groups: "[I]t is the rarely acknowledged and often unappreciated fact that the judiciary shares a social outlook and political affinity with the established interests of the status quo."[17] As NJI coordinators and Ottawa law professors Rosemary Cairns Way and Brettel Dawson put it: "Social context education was not about the *status quo:* rather it was about improving justice in those courtrooms."[18] The NJI began an in-depth study of social context judicial education in 1994.[19] Due to the skepticism of the bench, it was not until 1998 that the first intensive programs were ready to go.[20]

L'Heureux-Dubé, who was taking the lead in addressing social context at the Supreme Court, should have been "Exhibit A" for such training. But it was a sign of the tentativeness with which the judiciary approached the new direction that speaker/facilitators were deliberately culled to avoid adding fuel to the fire. L'Heureux-Dubé, known for her "courage" and "contrariness," was rarely invited. Whenever she was suggested as a potential speaker, there was always an objection that she was "too controversial," "too much of a firecracker."[21] An observer who attended one of the only events when L'Heureux-Dubé spoke at a social context program for Canadian judges, at a dinner in 2004, was shocked at the audience reaction to her speech. "There is a controversial divisiveness about Claire," the observer explained, "and there was a visceral reaction throughout the room. Had she gone too far? The room was split on whether or not they agreed with her."[22] And this was from a group of judges "willing to be identified" as registrants at the avant-garde social context workshops. It left L'Heureux-Dubé with few opportunities to take a hands-on role in social context Canadian judicial education. The irony was that the prophet without honour in her own country achieved acclaim as a superstar abroad.

The South Asia Pacific Project

It started with Naina Kapur, a feminist lawyer almost halfway around the world. Born in Uganda, Kapur was raised in Canada, took her legal education at King's College in the United Kingdom, and then moved to India to practise law. In 1992, she set up a public interest organization in New Delhi called Sakshi – meaning "Witness" – to focus on gender equality, sexual assault, violence against women, test case litigation, and law reform. She soon came to realize that without major changes within the judiciary, little could be achieved. "I had so much experience with biased judges," she observed. The "problem wasn't the law, but the attitude behind the law."[23]

Kapur presented the chief justice of India, Aziz Mushabber Ahmadi, with detailed case research on the overtly discriminatory attitudes of male judges. Ahmadi, whom Kapur described as a chief justice who was "open to new ideas," pledged his support for judicial training.[24] The two decided that it might be helpful to expand the initiative to include neighbouring countries in the Asia Pacific region and beyond. They invited Michael Kirby, a judge of the High Court of Australia, and Albie Sachs, a judge of the Constitutional Court of South Africa, to participate. Kapur and Ahmadi were also curious about the new experiments with social context education

Claire L'Heureux-Dubé and Chief Justice Aziz Mushabber Ahmadi of India.

in Canada. Ahmadi advised Kapur to speak with Claire L'Heureux-Dubé, whom he knew from her work with the International Commission of Jurists.[25] Kapur phoned L'Heureux-Dubé, they had a long conversation about violence against women in India, and L'Heureux-Dubé offered enthusiastic support for Kapur's desire to develop judicial training in the Asia Pacific. Remembering the discussion years later, L'Heureux-Dubé said, "[Naina] understands equality more than anybody I've seen. She is one of the people in my life who has impressed me the most."[26]

The other Canadian whom Kapur contacted was British Columbia judge Doug Campbell. Campbell had been offering training to lower court judges from the western provinces and northern territories on gender, race, and Indigenous issues independently of the NJI since 1988.[27] Known as one of the most adventurous of the early proponents of judicial education, he was also viewed as something of a maverick because his programming was premised on a clear acknowledgment that systemic discrimination was embedded in the justice system.[28] Kapur came away deeply impressed with Campbell's expertise, and she invited both Campbell and L'Heureux-Dubé to India to help develop the inaugural program.[29] The Canadian International Development Agency agreed to cover the travel expenses of

Naina Kapur, public interest and feminist lawyer in India, who worked with L'Heureux-Dubé on judicial education.

both Canadian judges.[30] A successful two-day meeting in December 1997 brought together twenty-six judges and twelve feminist NGO representatives from five Asia Pacific countries: India, Sri Lanka, Bangladesh, Nepal, and Pakistan. It resulted in a ringing endorsement for multination judicial education on equality issues.[31]

L'Heureux-Dubé described the 1997 meeting:

> [They had] invited all the chief justices [along] with an NGO from all of the countries. We knew that if we got the chief justices, we would get the others. My mission [was] to seduce the chief justices. I made a speech about equality. The chief justices were not really getting it the first day. They said, "All our judges are very fair. There is equality in our country." But the NGOs would say, "What about this case and that case?" That was the purpose, to put them in front of the chief justices. Ahmadi spoke about the importance of educating judges about equality. [I] interrupt[ed] him. I said, "I take your point. Education is key. But it takes three hundred years and we want justice now. You are the ones who are rendering justice." We related a number of decisions in Canada – *Seaboyer, Ewanchuk*. By the end, they were opening like flowers. They all agreed that we should go and do sessions with judges.[32]

Judicial Education and International Influence

L'Heureux-Dubé with Pakistani judges involved in a judicial education program.

And so began a ten-year operation of experiential workshops linking up judges and NGOs in the Asia Pacific region.[33] Drawing upon Doug Campbell's western Canadian programs, the sessions used small-group, role-playing formats to help build bridges. The participants visited courts, women's shelters, sexual assault centres, juvenile detention homes, and prisons.[34] The prisons could be particularly earth shattering. L'Heureux-Dubé offered one illustration:

> [Some women were in prison] because they were supposed to be adulterous. [In fact,] they had been sexually violated. The courts said, "He's a good guy, he couldn't have raped you." [They acquitted.] So then the women were put in jail as adulterers. We said, "These women are there because of you. You did this." And they were there with the children of the rape. These guys are the sons of a judge, a lawyer, very high up. They don't know what goes on down there. The judges cried. I cried. It doesn't mean it impressed all of them. [But] it was a wonderful program.[35]

There were "some rough spots," according to Campbell, when judges expressed strong vocal resistance, but there were many breakthrough moments.

"Gender issues are loaded with societal attitudes," observed Campbell. "Many judges would say 'I never understood any of this until I came to this meeting.'" It was, he concluded, "really powerful."[36]

Other Canadians, including Catherine Fraser and Kathleen Mahoney, joined teams of lawyers and judges from the countries involved, but it was Claire L'Heureux-Dubé who took centre stage. In her keynote lectures on equality, she broke away from years of denial back home, and spoke openly about her own experiences of discrimination in the workplace and as a judge. Moved by her honesty and the force of her personality, other judges would begin to acknowledge to what extent their own family backgrounds, upbringing, and experiences had shaped their beliefs and values. Kapur described L'Heureux-Dubé's unique contribution:

> It would get personalized. They would have to talk about it. All these judicial leaders saying things that most judges never talk about. [Claire L'Heureux-Dubé] would speak of what happened in Canada ... the judgments ... that she usually sat in dissent. She would say, "This is how it translated for me personally." She would put it within the equality paradigm. She was our "vision" person. She was the rolling pin, hitting someone on the head when they said the wrong thing. When they said something offensive, she would call them on it. But the thing is, they would love her. [S]he had the ability to evoke respect just by telling the truth. The motivation with which you do something determines the outcome. The root for Claire was passion, friendship, [and] reaching out. If I ever needed anything, she would say "yes." She showed me the interconnectivity of the world.[37]

Catherine Fraser emphasized that L'Heureux-Dubé "understood power." "She knew if you were going to make changes, you could spend a lot of time and a lot of years working all the way up through the system. Or alternatively you could go right to the top. She would say, 'We'll just go and get the chief justice on side and that will be it, and then we will work from there.' How did she do that? She is so persuasive as an individual and has such a dominating, magnetic personality. [She] found a way to connect with them emotionally on a personal level. She swirls into the meeting with the chief justice and she's grabbing them by the arm. Very few people could resist Claire."[38] Canadian Chief Justice Tony Lamer would certainly have disputed that. It underscored in bold relief the disparity between her isolation within the Supreme Court of Canada and her reception on the international scene.

Indeed, few of the Asia Pacific judges seem to have shared Lamer's hostility. Fraser described the energy L'Heureux-Dubé brought to the room: "I just remember how powerful she was, and how she commanded the room. How she swept in, like you are watching a force of nature."[39] Doug Campbell agreed that L'Heureux-Dubé lived up to her "larger than life" reputation. "She was the anchor. [She was] this wonderful, humorous person," with the perfect "skill set." He described her as "incredibly engaging," "bright," and "convincing to say the least."[40] He also valued her sense of timing. There would be "serious moments," he recalled, and then she "would lighten it up" with a burst of humour.[41]

Prabha Sridevan, a judge of the Madras High Court who participated in the training program in Delhi and went on to train other Indian judges herself, cited L'Heureux-Dubé as her "inspiration."[42] Shiranee Tilakawardane, a judge of the Supreme Court in Sri Lanka, described L'Heureux-Dubé's mentoring as life changing. "The more I talked with Claire," she said, "the more I could understand the things we had to face as judges. The difficult role we had to play with our own colleagues and the rest of the public. And the passion we both shared for the concept of true social justice." She explained how L'Heureux-Dubé showed the participants how to use international conventions to bring "gender justice to a higher level," specifically in "the Asian context." She depicted her as a Supreme Court *femme fatale*: "She would breeze in ... an extremely desirable, almost sexy, thoroughly informal person, whom even the chief justices could not resist. She almost beguiled men into understanding gender justice."[43]

Jessica Neuwirth, president of Equality Now, an international NGO dedicated to advancing human rights for women, recalled meeting judges in Nepal who had worked with L'Heureux-Dubé: "They "thought so highly of her. I was in this little, tiny home in Kathmandu, and she had been there. [T]hey were tough guys, but she had had such an impact on them. They definitely weren't feminist, and they weren't necessarily open to it, but they were open to Claire. She has such a sense of confidence. She really knows her power."[44] Baroness Helena Kennedy, a barrister and member of the British House of Lords, observed that L'Heureux-Dubé was able to "charm old patriarchal judges into rethinking their attitudes."[45] NJI academic director Brettel Dawson added, "If you've got a judge who's a star, who's charming and dances ... a Canadian judge from a pinnacle court who has a reputation *this* big, who comes and talks judge-to-judge with you, who has the courage or chutzpah or status to press you, to challenge you, to impress you, then I can see how minds would be changed."[46]

It was a glowing picture of what many understood to be L'Heureux-Dubé's unstoppable force. It may also have been something of an overstatement. Undoubtedly there were international judges who found her unconvincing, even off-putting, whose lives and judicial practices were not transformed by the judicial education workshops. Yet there were dramatic moments and evidence of substantial impact. And the success of the Asia Pacific program built upon itself, leading to further international expansion.

L'Heureux-Dubé, Campbell, and Fraser teamed up with Reem Bahdi, Canada's only Palestinian Canadian law professor, who was on the faculty at the University of Windsor, for a seven-year project in Palestine. Bahdi recalled L'Heureux-Dubé's riveting keynote speeches. She spoke "about the Universal Declaration of Human Rights, and how as judges they all had a responsibility as part of a global community to uphold certain values."[47] L'Heureux-Dubé spoke about how judges should handle issues of domestic violence and equality, and how to introduce international norms into domestic laws.[48] Her presence "carried a lot of weight," added Bahdi: "It seemed like she knew every single chief justice around the world."[49] One memorable session took the participants to a Palestinian prison, where the judges met children they had sentenced. "Senior judges started to cry," recalled Bahdi, "because [the] conditions of detention were not what they expected. The judges for the first time talked to the children they had sentenced. And the judges' attitudes changed. [T]hey were willing to go out and examine how their decisions were impacting people."[50] The Palestinian project ended prematurely with the expiry of funding in 2012,[51] but other connections were forged with Australia, New Zealand, Serbia, Croatia, Taiwan, Zimbabwe, and South Africa.[52]

Linkages with Female Judges across the World

Despite L'Heureux-Dubé's reluctance to identify as a "woman judge," she was not averse to working in associations limited to female judges. She confessed that she was not sure she "would have thought of it" by herself, but Bertha Wilson took the first step in 1987 when she wrote to all the female judges in Canada suggesting that they create a new association. L'Heureux-Dubé recalled that the majority replied "no."[53] Wilson was prepared to abandon the plan, but L'Heureux-Dubé was intrigued enough to suggest they give it another try. L'Heureux-Dubé contacted Arline Pacht, an American judge who had founded the International Association of

L'Heureux-Dubé with Baroness Brenda Hale, president of the International Association of Women Judges, London, 2012.

Women Judges (IAWJ).[54] Pacht accepted their invitation to come to Ottawa, where the idea was hatched to set up a Canadian chapter of the international organization. The international concept had more appeal, and the Canadian chapter bloomed. Membership grew from a small group to a large contingent that travelled to IAWJ biennial conferences around the world.

The Canadian women, who came to represent the second-largest delegation after the American judges, participated in IAWJ meetings that drew more than four thousand members from a hundred nations. They debated topics that included violence against women, international child abduction, incarcerated women, human trafficking, forced marriage, judicial independence, gender bias in the courts, and an international exchange of jurisprudence.[55] It was an attempt to bridge the isolation that so many female judges felt. Pacht described L'Heureux-Dubé as the "star attraction" of the Canadian branch, a "whirlwind" who had an "enormous influence."[56] Everywhere she travelled, she urged female judges to join the IAWJ.[57] Baroness Brenda Hale, the first woman on the Supreme Court of the United Kingdom (and now the first female president of the UK Supreme

Court), presented L'Heureux-Dubé with its Human Rights Award, the IAWJ's highest honour, at the close of the London conference in 2012.[58]

International Ties Expand

L'Heureux-Dubé relished her international contacts as much as they appreciated her. Catherine Fraser marvelled that "Claire was online" sharing ideas with judges globally "24 hours a day," and dubbed her addiction to email as "love at first byte."[59] L'Heureux-Dubé law clerk Mimi Liu described her "relentless" schedule: "If she's not sitting, or if she's not writing, she's travelling and speaking."[60] L'Heureux-Dubé volunteered months of her time to international organizations. She served as the vice president of the International Society of Family Law.[61] She served as president of the Canadian section of the International Commission of Jurists (ICJ). She became the first Canadian to hold the post of president of the larger international ICJ, a high-powered organization devoted to promoting the independence of the judiciary and the rule of law.[62] She served as president of the Quebec Society of Comparative Law and as president of the world congress that the International Association of Comparative Law held in Montreal.[63] Paul-André Crépeau, president of the Civil Code Revision Office, described the Montreal congress as a huge undertaking, in preparation for over three years and executed brilliantly by L'Heureux-Dubé: "It was extraordinary – the chair, the competence, and the way she hosted more than 450 delegates and 50 accompanying persons. She was just really at her best."[64]

By the time of her retirement, L'Heureux-Dubé had delivered over 240 speeches in locations as far away as Cape Town, Harare, Bangalore, London, Paris, Geneva, Fiji, Cameroon, Jerusalem, Honolulu, Suva, Alabama, Strasbourg, the Czech Republic, Slovakia, Hawaii, Guam, Auckland, Florence, Caracas, Wyoming, Durban, Sydney, Delhi, Moscow, Kathmandu, Tulsa, Brussels, Croatia, Moldova, Zimbabwe, Copenhagen, Vienna, Lahore, Morocco, and Buenos Aires.[65] Law clerk Adam Dodek believed that her international work may have made L'Heureux-Dubé feel "vindicated." Even if her own colleagues had not yet "seen the light," jurists and judges outside the country did. "She was very proud when aspects of her judgments [on equality] were adopted by other courts," he recalled.[66] And there were many examples in which to take pride.

Teresa Doherty, one of the first female judges in Papua New Guinea and Sierra Leone, explained that she looked to Canada when it came time to consider how international treaties and conventions could be used to interpret domestic law. "Canada was leading the path," she emphasized, and "Claire Dubé was in the forefront."[67] Anthony Gubbay, chief justice of Zimbabwe's Supreme Court, often referred to Canadian cases on constitutional human rights issues, and to L'Heureux-Dubé's decisions in particular. Her decisions "appealed" to him as "human" and "sensible," and he described *Ewanchuk* as particularly noteworthy and "impressive." "She was known the world over," he added, and "highly respected."[68] Gillian Lucky, a judge of the High Court in Trinidad and Tobago, wrote L'Heureux-Dubé that her "rulings and decisions" had had "a profound impact" on her and her colleagues.[69] Michael Kirby, a judge of the High Court of Australia, referred to L'Heureux-Dubé's decisions in his own rulings and emphasized that he had "great admiration" for L'Heureux-Dubé. He described her as "forward-looking, compassionate, energetic [and] imaginative."[70] Albie Sachs, judge of the Constitutional Court of South Africa, described L'Heureux-Dubé as "the prototype" of a judge for the twenty-first century, noting that her analysis of equality had "inspired" his court's constitutional interpretation as well.[71]

Cross-Cultural Challenges

As the Montreal immigration inquiry and the *Baker* case had demonstrated, L'Heureux-Dubé was not immune to the long-standing Canadian discomfort over the analysis of racism. She shared the traditional Canadian reluctance to discuss discrimination based on ethnicity and culture.[72] And the cross-cultural aspects of white Canadian judges delivering programs to Asia Pacific, Palestinian, and other racially diverse judges must have carried challenges. As Supreme Court colleague Louise Arbour put it, "The world is crawling with people who have good ideas, good intentions, but the interface is impossible because you know nothing about the environment with which you have to interact."[73] Did L'Heureux-Dubé's lack of expertise on discrimination based on race hamper the international judicial education?[74]

Naina Kapur believed not. Her observation was that race and ethnic differences never proved to be a fault line in India. "I get a lot of foreigners who come," she explained, "and I am sometimes skeptical. Claire became one of us. No one was ever beneath her. Her sense was that there are no boundaries. We are all one."[75] Much of L'Heureux-Dubé's effectiveness in these cross-cultural settings appears to have come from her refusal to stand

L'Heureux-Dubé in a "bug suit" at gender equality workshop in Nunavik.

on ceremony, to eschew the personal privileges that attended the office of a Supreme Court judge. Unlike some of the other judges, she never asked for first-class travel or better hotel rooms, and all of her time-consuming far-flung international work was done without remuneration.[76] She was completely comfortable blending into any local setting, as her colleague Doug Campbell indicated when he described their Indian travel together by coach, stuffed into a jam-packed train compartment, perched for hours on a tiny bench.[77] The idea is conveyed well in a photograph taken closer to home, of L'Heureux-Dubé in a "bug suit" on a rock in northern Nunavik, when she participated in a gender equality workshop and slept in a tent. It may have been part of being an "outsider" for so many years. She had developed a certain comfort within her own skin that served her well when she was transplanted to unfamiliar international settings.

As stories circulated about her disarming manner, international participants came away convinced that L'Heureux-Dubé had no ulterior motive, that she was driven by a sincere desire to share her vision of equality.[78] Kapur explained that it was the "informality, that instant 'let's be friends,'" that made the programs so successful.[79] Doug Campbell added,

"She could talk to anybody at any echelon in the judiciary, in politics, in government, on the street. She has a social manner about her that makes her accessible without any airs. She didn't come ... with any barriers whatever."[80] It also made a difference that L'Heureux-Dubé, a woman who prized her facility with languages, went out of her way to ensure that portions of her remarks were always translated into the language of the participants.[81] This is not to suggest that she somehow surmounted her lack of racial expertise. But it is undeniable that L'Heureux-Dubé's down-to-earth personality and her ability to communicate effectively with all kinds of people eased the way in her international work.

There is no question that some of L'Heureux-Dubé's greatest career successes were rooted in international judicial education. Her international work brought her "friendships that circled the world."[82] Not only did she travel the globe, but her ideas also took root internationally. It must have constituted an exhilarating sense of reward for the daughter of a customs and immigration officer who had gazed out so longingly across the waters of the St. Lawrence from the solarium in her childhood home.

As they observed her international networking, people described L'Heureux-Dubé as charming, charismatic, and gifted in "diplomacy."[83] She was praised for her skill in "relationship-building."[84] She was extolled for her ability to communicate effectively about issues of gender equality with male as well as female judges. None of these characteristics epitomized her Supreme Court years back home in Canada. In the international setting, she expended all of her energy to establish strong personal bonds with chief justices, recognizing them as essential to the project of gender sensitization, powerful pivots in any project for change. It seems completely opposite to her behaviour with Tony Lamer. On her own court, she had abandoned all hope early on of convincing Lamer and many of her male colleagues about her equality perspectives.

In her international keynote addresses and informal participatory sessions, L'Heureux-Dubé also opened up about the many ways in which her own life had been impacted by sex discrimination. In her efforts to inspire the international judges to re-examine their own prejudices, she took the step of naming her own experiences for what they were: sex discrimination. In these venues, she was prepared to do more than she had in Canada, and call it by name.

In her international work, she was not the same person as she was back in Ottawa. Her work in international judicial education constituted something separate and distinct.

38
Retirement
A Much-Heralded Exit

Speculation about Claire L'Heureux-Dubé's possible retirement began long before she left. During her early unhappy years on the court, she had often been heard vowing to quit the moment she reached the age of sixty-five.[1] She did not. Rumours hit the press in 1995 that she and Chief Justice Antonio Lamer were jockeying to outlast each other, with reports that L'Heureux-Dubé had "decided to remain as a thorn in Lamer's side."[2] Although Lamer would be the first to retire, he later told *Globe and Mail* reporter Kirk Makin, "I could have stuck it out until she was gone ... If that's her purpose in life, I'm flattered. I'm not going to start managing my life according to her fantasies."[3]

CHIEF JUSTICE LAMER'S RETIREMENT FROM THE COURT, 1999: THE FIRST OF THE TWO TO GO

Lamer's last year on the court was marred by gossip about his failing capacity: alcoholism, injudicious remarks from the bench, and growing apathy toward the responsibilities of office. It was sufficient to raise concern among his RCMP security detail and with officials at the Department of Justice.[4] L'Heureux-Dubé was one of the first to notice, since as the next in seniority she often had to step in for the chief. Their colleagues at the court also became alarmed.[5]

L'Heureux-Dubé thought that it was a combination of health problems, medications, and alcohol that caused Lamer's erratic behaviour. "It was known that he was drinking. I was sitting beside him and you could smell it. And his behaviour on the court – reading papers and so on. We would say, okay, drunk one day but next you're on top of it. But that was not what was happening. [It's] not that we were a temperance league, but it was affecting our work, how the court was perceived. When you are drunk you say all kinds of things that may reflect on the court."⁶ Supreme Court colleague Jack Major confirmed that Lamer "would obviously show signs of having a bottle of wine at lunch," and that the alcohol was taking its toll.⁷

Others noted that the heart medication and tranquillizers that Lamer was taking for an orthostatic tremor in his leg magnified the effects of the alcohol.⁸ *Lawyers Weekly* reported that he had become "forgetful" and "somewhat argumentative with both court staff and fellow judges," adding: "On occasion he expressed strong views about a case, only to turn around the next day to express equally strong opposite views – without always remembering his previous stance."⁹

Lamer's colleagues decided to confront him.¹⁰ "We felt we had no other option. You don't do that with great pleasure. It was the whole court. It was unanimous. A court cannot continue on with that kind of dagger over the head," L'Heureux-Dubé said.¹¹ She was not one of the three judges chosen to carry the message. It was Jack Major, Peter Cory, and Charles Gonthier who met with Lamer.¹² L'Heureux-Dubé recalled that her colleagues gave Lamer six months in the spring of 1999:

> They said, "You may be able to settle the problem in six months, but you must improve." At the end of August, he had not settled the problem, so they went back. They didn't say anything. He said, "I suppose I have to resign." And he did, at the convention of the Canadian Bar Association in August. I was there when he resigned. He was trembling. It was very hard for him to do that. I appreciate the fact that he did. You can give him credit for that.¹³

L'Heureux-Dubé added that it was "not the first time that judges had to resign after having medical problems." It was, she emphasized, "demanding to be a judge."¹⁴

Lamer's retirement allowed a temporary sense of decorum to settle over the feuding duo. At the ceremonial "swearing-out" event, L'Heureux-Dubé spoke on behalf of the court, and her words were generous: "Chief Justice, *vous avez bien mérité de la Patrie*,† the country is proud of you."¹⁵

---

† "you have been been a great credit to the Nation"

Eight years later, when Antonio Lamer died in 2007, onlookers also noted that L'Heureux-Dubé was prominent and visible, both at the memorial ceremony held at the Supreme Court and at the religious service in Montreal.

L'Heureux-Dubé's Departure from the Court, 2002: A "Cascade of Clairefests"

L'Heureux-Dubé delayed her retirement until almost the last moment. Just two months before she reached the age of compulsory judicial retirement at seventy-five, she stepped down on 1 July 2002.[16] Her daughter, Louise Dubé, observed that her mother "hated" that she had to retire, adding, "I think she felt she had things she hadn't finished."[17] But the unrelenting pace was punishing. As reluctant as her mother was, Louise believed that the weight of judicial responsibilities as well as the growing international dimensions of her work were becoming a "burden" that was simply too onerous.[18]

Louise Dubé, L'Heureux-Dubé's daughter.

Canadian Lawyer cartoon of Claire L'Heureux-Dubé with sword of justice in *retraite*.

The reporters who covered her leave-taking trained their focus on the controversial divisiveness that L'Heureux-Dubé had inspired. Writing for *Canadian Lawyer* and the *Ottawa Citizen,* Janice Tibbetts described her as the court's "most colourful character," and added, "Some say she has been Canada's single biggest contributor to the advancement of equality rights for minorities. Others contend she is a lightweight whose judgments are loaded with political statements rather than sound legal reasoning."[19] L'Heureux-Dubé's old nemesis, the *National Post,* summed up her career as follows: "The second woman to sit on the top court, she leaves behind an intellectual legacy admirers say heralds the future of Western legal philosophy and critics depict as a threat to the very foundations of Anglo-Canadian legal tradition."[20] The *Post* also quoted Edward Greenspan, who took direct aim at the *Seaboyer* case, insisting that L'Heureux-Dubé's decision had imperilled "the fundamental concepts of the rights of the accused which had been at the heart of the criminal justice system."[21] The CBC called L'Heureux-Dubé "one of Canada's greatest female legal pioneers."[22] *Lawyers Weekly* reporter Cristin Schmitz characterized her as the court's "most outspoken and tenacious champion for equal rights,"[23] and the *Globe and Mail*'s Sean Fine characterized her as "in a category of her own," a judge who "transcended the court."[24]

Despite the continuing debates over her legacy, her retirement elicited an unprecedented outpouring of adulation from those who had admired her career. Colleague Ian Binnie speculated that the hype surrounding L'Heureux-Dubé's retirement was "fuelled by the McClung controversy."[25] Indeed, many who had rallied to L'Heureux-Dubé's support in the wake of the *Ewanchuk* debacle took this as an opportunity to pay proper homage to what she had come to represent for them: a clear voice for female and lesbian/gay/bisexual/transsexual (LGBT) equality. The sheer number of celebrations left many flabbergasted. Beverley McLachlin, who had replaced Antonio Lamer as chief justice on 7 January 2000, dubbed the ensuing events a "cascade of Clairefests."[26] L'Heureux-Dubé's former law partner Jacques Philippon, exclaimed, *"Nous vivons l'année Claire L'Heureux-Dubé."*[†, 27] No one had seen anything to equal such festivities for a retiring Supreme Court judge. She had become a full-fledged feminist icon, a pop-culture celebrity, and a rock-star anomaly within the staid halls of the nation's top court.

The University of Ottawa held a conference in September 2002 to "capture and assess the contribution that this one woman had made to furthering a feminist analysis of the law in Canada."[28] The University of Ottawa also celebrated *"une soirée hommage,"*[‡] where the Claire L'Heureux-Dubé Fund for Social Justice was established.[29] The National Association of Women and the Law celebrated International Women's Day with a "Hats Off to Claire L'Heureux-Dubé" reception, where three hundred well-wishers came together in Ottawa to say "thank you."[30] Two former law clerks organized an international conference at the Château Frontenac in Quebec City that attracted a multitude of speakers and dignitaries who came to pay tribute, including Otto Lang, the minister of justice who had first appointed her.[31] The International Commission of Jurists put out a special booklet in her honour.[32]

An uproarious crowd of six hundred marked the retirement with a gala dinner in Toronto's Hilton hotel ballroom, hailing L'Heureux-Dubé as "a hero to equality workers everywhere."[33] The sold-out dinner co-hosted by the Ontario Bar Association and the Law Society of Upper Canada surprised some who had never thought of Toronto as L'Heureux-Dubé's "home base."[34] The raucous event included a presentation from the American Bar Association bestowing the Margaret Brent Award upon L'Heureux-Dubé,

---

† "We are having the year of Claire L'Heureux-Dubé."
‡ "a tribute evening"

and describing her as "one of Canada's national treasures." The High Court of Australia sent a video extolling her "magnificent work" on behalf of the LGBT community.[35] To remind the partygoers that there were still two sides to the assessment, a handful of demonstrators camped outside the Toronto hotel to protest L'Heureux-Dubé's decisions.[36]

Mirroring L'Heureux-Dubé's trademark sense of humour, Rosalie Abella, then a member of the Ontario Court of Appeal but later to be elevated to the Supreme Court, entertained an appreciative audience at the Ottawa soirée with irreverent sarcasm. Reading from a "fictitious" Supreme Court of Canada decision, she described the appellants as "the Charter of Wrongs, Inc." a "special interest group" whose publications included "the best-selling *Feminist Judges: None Is Too Many*." Abella purported to recount L'Heureux-Dubé's "frequent and enthusiastic interjections" during oral argument, while rejecting any suggestion that this conveyed the impression that she "might have made up her mind before hearing the appeal." Tongue-in-cheek, she added:

> Nothing could be further from the truth. When Justice L'Heureux-Dubé says "Ridiculous!" or "Can You Believe It?" or "Come *On!*" from the Bench, she is merely engaging in the judicial repartee that is necessarily part of oral argument. The very fact that she has agreed with the rest of the court in this case demonstrates her capacity to surprise.[37]

Before a different delighted Toronto crowd, Abella could not resist revisiting the *Ewanchuk* events, when she joked that L'Heureux-Dubé's retirement had been the subject of a "class action of women" who sought to set aside the requirement that she be forced to leave the court at age seventy-five. Purporting to read from the decision of the Alberta Court of Appeal, Abella claimed that "Justice McClung refused to set aside the mandatory provision and agreed instead with the trial judge who found that Justice L'Heureux-Dubé had consented, notwithstanding expert evidence from the *National Post* that she was the victim of battered judges' syndrome."[38]

Beverley McLachlin gave an equally humorous speech at the Toronto dinner. She recounted the conversation that the two female judges had had when McLachlin was first appointed. "I was contemplating these huge red robes with ermine with some consternation," McLachlin explained. L'Heureux-Dubé replied, "Well, you know they are very hot, but let me tell you my secret. I don't wear anything under them." To peals of laughter, McLachlin continued, "[Claire] said, 'Yes, Bev, *naked.*' So on June tenth, when you witness the swearing out ceremony and we are all in our red robes, I invite you to let your imaginations run wild."³⁹

McLachlin also shared the story of L'Heureux-Dubé's infamous overnight jail stint south of the border, caught with a speedometer clocked at "something in excess of a hundred miles per hour." It was in the late 1980s, and L'Heureux-Dubé had been arrested in North Carolina for speeding. The spectre of a sitting Supreme Court judge cooling her heels in a southern jail, "along with the other miscreants of the evening," as McLachlin described it, provoked further hilarity among the after-dinner crowd. For many of those assembled, L'Heureux-Dubé's driving habits were already legendary. She never braked until the last minute. Her foot-to-the-pedal, damn-the-torpedoes, full-speed-ahead proclivities were coupled with dramatic hand flourishes that punctuated her conversations. While her hands danced through the air, the neglected steering wheel would veer crazily to the left and right, causing mayhem with the surrounding traffic.⁴⁰ Yet she loved to drive, would buy a new-model car every three or four years, and would often travel non-stop from Ottawa to Quebec City, Quebec to Boston, or Quebec to Florida, sometimes fifteen hours at a stretch.⁴¹

Asked to tell the full story years later, L'Heureux-Dubé explained: "I pleaded guilty, got a $20 fine, $100 in costs, and was forbidden to drive in North Carolina."⁴² At a judicial conference years later, she met up with a North Carolina judge who invited her to speak to the judges in his state. She retorted, "I would love to, but I can't. I can't drive there." The southern judge professed shock, and after she laughingly related the details of her past indiscretion and arrest, he offered to research the case. Soon after, she received a letter saying that if she paid $100, she could obtain a pardon. "I never answered," L'Heureux-Dubé explained. She still drives to Florida. How does she get there? "Through North Carolina. I hope they have destroyed my file anyway," she said with a grin.⁴³

The official swearing-out at the Supreme Court on 10 June 2002 was preceded the evening before by a formal dinner with speeches. Small tables had been set up in the court dining room to accommodate all of the judges and their spouses, L'Heureux-Dubé's daughter, her sisters, and their spouses. The next morning, invited guests poured into the packed courtroom for prepared speeches from the chief justice, the federal and Quebec attorneys general, the president of the Canadian Bar Association, the *bâtonnière* of Quebec, as well as the honouree. In waning health, Lamer returned from retirement to sit on the front bench, despite his recent heart attack. In her speech, L'Heureux-Dubé made a special point of mentioning that she was "touched by his presence," in what people close to her observed

Beverley McLachlin with arm around L'Heureux-Dubé at retirement ceremony, 10 June 2002.

as a clearly genuine remark.[44] Lamer sat stolid and quiet, expressionless throughout the lengthy speeches.[45] L'Heureux-Dubé also made reference to "people near and dear to me who are not with us today," including "especially my mother, my husband and my son, who are in my thoughts on this moving occasion."[46] Sam Bard, who had passed away that January, was another significant absence.[47]

One of the most surprising moments came when Chief Justice McLachlin addressed the thorny issue of "feminism" in her official speech – offering her own reflections upon a label often applied to the outgoing judge. According to the *Oxford English Dictionary*, McLachlin explained, "a 'feminist' is a person who advocates for the rights of women, based upon the theory of equality of the sexes." Then she added, "According to this definition, Justice L'Heureux-Dubé is a feminist, as am I, as, I suspect, are most people in this room, indeed most Canadians. I say this because equality is more than a 'theory' in this country – it is constitutionally required. Of course, one can have different ideas about what this equality means, but there should be no dispute about the merits of the idea of sexual equality."[48]

McLachlin would exhibit even greater boldness in the foreword she wrote to a legal text published in 2004 to honour L'Heureux-Dubé's contributions: "Justice Claire L'Heureux-Dubé is invariably described as a 'feminist,'" she noted. "And although the label has not always been intended as a compliment, it is one she bears with pride."[49] Characterizing L'Heureux-Dubé as a "meteor speeding through our heaven," she added, "Claire has personally advised me that ... she's going to mellow out and take some time off. Somehow, I doubt it."[50]

In her reply, L'Heureux-Dubé sidestepped any self-identification with feminism, yet spoke with evident pride about the feminist strains she had discerned in the judgments of those who had preceded her. Referring to family and employment law decisions of the former chief justice Brian Dickson, she stated, "He was a true feminist ..."[51] who believed, as I do, in the 'revolutionary' notion that women are people entitled to the same respect, consideration and justice as every member of society."[52] She then added that "[i]f the court has been 'hijacked by feminists,' it started a long time ago," and made reference to other well-known decisions of Bora Laskin, Bertha Wilson, and Peter Cory.[53] But there would be no radical departure from her decades of resisting feminist labels, even in retirement.

L'Heureux-Dubé with grandson Simon on her lap at retirement ceremony. Frank Iacobucci looks on.

Speaking with the press, she added, "To be branded a 'feminist' I think is old stuff."[54]

In the final moments of the ceremony, L'Heureux-Dubé's four-year-old grandson, Simon, broke out from the audience, dashed toward his grandmother, and scrambled up on the elevated judges' bench.[55] The reporters noted that the young boy had been quietly singing "through most of the speeches."[56] Their coverage of the swearing-out featured a photo of L'Heureux-Dubé seated on her high-backed leather judicial chair with her grandson perched on her lap.[57]

And it did not stop even after the canapés and champagne glasses were removed from the reception that followed. In 2005, another fête at the Supreme Court honoured L'Heureux-Dubé three years after her retirement, when her former colleagues presented her with more than a dozen leather-bound volumes of the judgments in which she had participated.[58] Still another celebration at the Supreme Court in September 2012 marked the tenth anniversary of her departure from the bench.[59]

Activities Post Retirement

There was little discernible slowing of pace. L'Heureux-Dubé moved back to her beloved Quebec City and settled into a condo overlooking the Plains of Abraham.[60] She took a position as judge-in-residence at Laval University, where an annual prize was created in her name to recognize women whose careers exemplified the values of equality.[61] She was showered with more honours from Quebec, Canadian, and international organizations.[62] She returned on a part-time basis to her former Quebec City law firm in an advisory role as counsel.[63] Most of her activities were *pro bono*. She served as ombudsman of the City of Quebec and chair of the legal aid organization La Maison de justice. She became a board member of Avocats sans frontières, Lawyers Rights Watch, and the Equal Rights Trust. She spent hours on internet chats with judges across the world. Although she refused the lion's share of invitations, she continued to travel the world delivering speeches and facilitating judicial education: to Guyana, Palestine, Israel, Cameroon, Ireland, Paris, London, Strasbourg, and Geneva.[64]

She was involved in a Quebec commission on the salary of provincial judges and presided over an independent advisory committee to set the compensation for members of the Quebec National Assembly.[65] She vetted files on the torture of Afghan military detainees to assess whether federal

Reunion of former law clerks at the Supreme Court.

L'Heureux-Dubé over lunch at her Florida condo.

L'Heureux-Dubé's grandsons Simon and Daniel at her Quebec City condo.

government claims to cabinet secrecy were justified.[66] She participated in annual reunions with her former law clerks.[67] She continued to read all the Supreme Court decisions, writing often to her former colleagues to express her support or disagreement, comments that occasionally entered the public realm.[68] Ian Binnie once made a point of complaining that she had written to *Le Devoir* to attack one of his judgments. "I said, 'No, I didn't write *them,* they came to *me,*'" recalled L'Heureux-Dubé. "And your decision is still wrong."[69]

Despite all this activity, she expanded her personal and leisure activities. She nurtured relationships with long-time friends and colleagues. She indulged her lifelong passion for opera. She walked and swam daily. She read the *New York Times* and watched Jim Lehrer on PBS. She spent time with her grandchildren.[70] Her daughter, Louise, remarked that she was "surprised" at how much her mother seemed to love being a grandmother, and how wonderful she was with her grandchildren, who adored her in turn.[71]

More Controversies

Religion remained something of a powder keg for L'Heureux-Dubé, who much preferred secularism in the public setting. She spoke out in protest when the Supreme Court upheld the right of Jewish condo owners to install *sukkahs* (temporary huts constructed for a religious festival) on Montreal balconies in 2004. She spoke out again when the court upheld the right of Sikhs to carry kirpans in school in 2006. The court *"s'était trompée,*† she claimed. It had *"fait fausse route"*‡ in stretching the concept of "reasonable accommodations" too far.⁷² She critiqued the decision of a Montreal YMCA to frost over the windows of one of its exercise rooms at the request of a neighbouring synagogue.⁷³ She scrutinized the Bouchard-Taylor Commission in 2007–08, when it conducted consultations to determine what "reasonable accommodation based on religious beliefs" meant in the context of a modern Quebec. At the height of the debate, she told the press that she did not believe "that a fundamental right can be reasonable if it's not compatible with the notion of [sexual] equality."⁷⁴ When the Bouchard-Taylor Commission recommended that the government legislate to formalize secularism, she was elated.⁷⁵

In a lengthy Radio-Canada interview in May 2013, L'Heureux-Dubé argued that some rights were "more fundamental" than others, and that equality should trump religion.⁷⁶ In her view, "minorities" should "adapt to common values such as sexual equality."⁷⁷ A *Toronto Star* reporter described her as having "held nothing back in the May interview" in which she suggested that "complete face covering" for Muslim women was a sign of "oppression." L'Heureux-Dubé had advocated explicit rules based on secularism to "ensure that immigrants become like us."⁷⁸

Her anti-religious views had roots stretching back to the late 1940s, when she had renounced the Catholic Church long before the Quiet Revolution emptied Quebec churches. Her position stemmed from her personal history of living through *La Grande Noirceur*,§ a time when the grip of Catholicism had impeded life choices, particularly for women. In the twenty-first century, secularism had a distinct resonance in Quebec, as L'Heureux-Dubé explained:

> My public position on the neutrality of the state is precisely a fight against what was imposed on women during my life by the Catholic religion: submission of women to their husbands, denying abortion and divorce, and I can go on and on and on. [D]iscrimination against women, gays, etc. was what I fought during my practice at the bar and on the bench. Discrimination against women by religion, whatever religion, is to me unacceptable and as such must be denounced.⁷⁹

---

† "had made a mistake"
‡ "was on the wrong path"
§ The Great Darkness

She stressed that she was not a "hater of Islam" but that she was giving voice to the views of many who were concerned that their efforts to achieve sex equality must not be eroded by patriarchal religions.[80]

Yet her objection to Muslim women's religious garment failed to take account of the wider context. Quebec and Canada shared a history marred by racial and ethnic discrimination.[81] The anti-Muslim sentiment that surfaced in the aftermath of the 11 September 2001 destruction of the Twin Towers was merely the most recent manifestation of long-standing prejudices. The Rimouski of L'Heureux-Dubé's childhood had been entirely homogeneous, a community in which, as her sister Louise recalled, "foreigners" were "not to be trusted."[82] She had lived through decades of immersion within a racially and ethnically unequal society. Her judicial tenure had not broken with that experience, as the Montreal immigration inquiry and the *Baker* case had shown. She, like many others, did not appear to recognize the potential for damage when rules prohibiting religious dress were promulgated within a society exhibiting pervasive discrimination against Muslims. Widespread prejudice against Muslims in the post–9-11 world would cast a dangerous overlay upon advocacy for gender equality and secularism, and foster stark divisions.

That L'Heureux-Dubé took the position she did on Muslim women's dress was not surprising. Back in Rimouski, she had rebelled against the bishop's insistence that Catholic girls must wear long sleeves and eschew shorts. Her views reflected her gender equality ideals and her secular preferences. And she was by no means the only Quebecer, Canadian, or judge to fail to recognize the serious consequences of racial and ethnic discrimination. Most of us who occupy privileged positions fail to appreciate the full harms of racial and ethnic inequalities. But L'Heureux-Dubé was also someone who was in the habit of stating her views openly and powerfully, articulating her ideas in public in ways that made her vulnerable to being singled out. Once more, Claire L'Heureux-Dubé was about to become a public symbol for one side of an explosive controversy.

In the fall of 2013, the minority Parti Québécois government introduced a proposed Quebec Charter of Values.[83] The bill would have barred 600,000 workers in the public service from wearing religious garb while performing their duties.[84] The prohibition was slated to cover "objects such as headgear, clothing, jewellery, or other adornments which by their conspicuous nature overtly indicate a religious affiliation." Members of the public were also required to have their faces "uncovered" when receiving government services.[85] Journalists reported that this meant that Muslims, Sikhs, and

Jews who worked in the public sector would be forbidden to wear religious headwear such as hijabs, turbans, and kippahs, and Christians would be barred from wearing "bigger-than-average crucifixes."[86] People speculated that it would be mostly scarf-wearing Muslim women who would "lose good jobs as nurses, teachers, and daycare workers."[87]

The Quebec Bar Association came out against the proposed Charter.[88] Charles Taylor, co-chair of the commission that had initially recommended the legislation, objected that the new Charter had gone too far.[89] The Quebec Human Rights Commission issued a position paper calling the proposed legislation "a clear violation" of the *Canadian Charter of Rights and Freedoms,* Quebec's own *Charter of Rights,* and international law. The commission predicted that the new law would "hit a wall in the courts."[90] Its president, Jacques Frémont, added that there had been troubling anti-Muslim confrontations on buses, malls, and the streets. Citizens were accosting hijab-wearing women, telling them that they should go home. There were also reports of anti-Islam vandalism, including hateful graffiti scrawled on Quebec mosques, Muslim businesses, and cultural centres.[91]

The debate unleashed a wave of popular consternation in Quebec, and thousands marched in the streets. Some demonstrators urged support for the Charter of Values. Other marchers were opposed.[92] The press reported that the proposed Charter had "roiled Quebec," pitting "rural communities against urban, and religious minorities against some (though not all) women's rights advocates."[93] Some feminist organizations, such as the Conseil du statut de la femme, backed the proposed Charter. Others, such as the Fédération des femmes du Québec, were divided into factions, with one group supporting and the other in opposition.[94] National newspapers began to cover the controversy, and the rest of the country took up the debate, adding more fuel to the fire.[95]

Julie Latour, a pro-Charter feminist lawyer, expressed surprise over the criticism spreading across the country. She argued that laicism would ensure that "women's fundamental right to equality" was not "jeopardized by the application of religious or cultural precepts, whether pertaining to family law, education, labour law or the right to bodily integrity."[96] Latour noted that until the 1960s, Quebec had been pejoratively known as a "priest-driven province," and she found it "ironic to see that Quebec is now being decried by the rest of Canada for trying to further its laicization process."[97]

McGill women's history professor Andrée Lévesque disagreed. She reminded Quebecers that they were poorly positioned to impose a dress code: *"jusqu'à il y a cinquante ans, des hommes en robes longues et des soeurs à capines, le visage souvent encadré de mica qui empêchait une bonne vision périphérique, sillonnaient nos rues."*† What was more, *"la laïcité n'a jamais garanti l'égalité des sexes,"*‡ she pointed out.[98] Lévesque referenced France to prove her point, a country where sexism continued to reign despite its recent banning of the burqa.[99]

Although L'Heureux-Dubé was characterized as "a rare voice in the legal community to speak in favour of the PQ's proposal," she was also joined by others.[100] The pro-Charter petition that she signed in September 2013 was co-signed by thirteen lawyers, law professors, and retired judges under the name "Rassemblement pour la laïcité."§, [101] As had happened in the *Ewanchuk* public debate, however, criticism of the petition was overwhelmingly directed against L'Heureux-Dubé.

Indeed, she became something of an icon for the conflagration. *Toronto Star* columnist Haroon Siddiqui accused her of "extreme anti-Muslim bigotry." Taking issue with her assertion that there were "more hijabis and niqabis in Quebec than in Muslim countries such as Pakistan and Morocco," Siddiqui said, "She is either hallucinating or she travels in a cocoon." He added, "A woman's right to freedom of religion protects her right to wear the hijab. Her right to gender equality also protects her right to wear it. That's the Canadian way."[102] *Montreal Gazette* columnist Don Macpherson retorted that hearing a retired justice of the Supreme Court "sound like a talk-radio demagogue" made him "glad" that L'Heureux-Dubé was "no longer a judge."[103] *Globe and Mail* legal reporter Sean Fine explained that he was "quite distressed" by L'Heureux-Dubé's position. "She lent a credibility to that whole movement. It shocked me. Coming from a Supreme Court judge, who was associated with speaking up for minorities, she could give it a legitimacy [that it] did not deserve."[104]

A recent law graduate from the University of Ottawa who had represented the students one year earlier in presenting a gift to L'Heureux-Dubé on the tenth anniversary of her retirement wrote to the *Toronto Star*. Amna Qureshi described herself as "a hijab-wearing Muslim woman" who had been born and raised in "rural Alberta with parents who emigrated from Pakistan." She explained how inspired she had been when she and L'Heureux-Dubé had discussed their "shared passion for the law, equality, and justice" and their similar "experiences of living in small towns." She

---

† "Up until fifty years ago, men in long robes and nuns wearing capes, their faces often framed by sheets of mica which prevented good peripheral vision, walked our streets."
‡ "secularism never guaranteed gender equality"
§ "Coalition for Secularism"

Amna Qureshi presenting L'Heureux-Dubé with a gift on the anniversary of her departure from the bench.

described how standing beside L'Heureux-Dubé at the podium had been "a pivotal moment" in her life. When she learned that the retired judge had spoken out in support of the proposed Charter, Qureshi pronounced herself "disappointed" and "confused":

> I know a number of exceedingly intelligent, integrated, social, proudly Canadian women who wear the niqab as a personal choice. And I have advocated for women's right to wear the hijab or niqab on soccer pitches, in prisons, in the courtroom and elsewhere – all the while using you [Justice L'Heureux-Dubé] and your Supreme Court opinions as inspiration and support ... The oppression I have fought against is not from the religion I choose to follow or the garments I choose to wear, but from those who say women who dress provocatively are asking to be raped, who use a woman's demeanour to assess her credibility, and who dictate what women should or should not wear.[105]

L'Heureux-Dubé's public support of the proposed Charter also upset quite a few of her former law clerks, some of whom contacted her to try to talk her out of taking such a position.[106]

L'Heureux-Dubé and Quebec lawyer Julie Latour testifying on the proposed Quebec Charter of Values.

In February 2014, L'Heureux-Dubé appeared before the Quebec legislative committee reviewing the proposed Charter. She represented the organization known as Juristes pour la laïcité et la neutralité religieuse de l'État.[†, 107] Julie Latour joined her, presenting a brief for the Intellectuels pour la laïcité.[‡, 108]

L'Heureux-Dubé's group began by cautioning that the government should ascertain that there was a *"consensus social"*[§] before banning *"signes religieux"*[||] for public servants.[109] Their brief then offered arguments in favour of the bill. L'Heureux-Dubé asserted that although freedom of religion was a fundamental right, "the right to wear religious garb" such as a headscarf, a kirpan, or a crucifix was not.[110] She distinguished freedom of religious belief – a private matter – from *displays* of religious affiliation – a public matter that like freedom of expression could be overridden for legitimate competing reasons. She compared religious garb with political

---
† Jurists for Secularism and Religious Neutrality of the State
‡ Intellectuals for Secularism
§ "social consensus"
|| "religious signs"

expression, noting that there were long-standing restrictions upon political expression by public servants that could be extended to their wearing of religious symbols.¹¹¹ She emphasized the distinctive Quebec context, reflecting the historical choice to move from a religious state to a secular society. She took the position that the neutrality of the state was essential in a pluralistic society.¹¹² She submitted that the women of Quebec had undertaken *"une marche ardue vers l'égalité"*† and that they should not be blown off course by *"le vent des diktats de la religion."*‡, ¹¹³

The press depicted her as "the most prominent jurist to argue for the constitutionality of the ban."¹¹⁴ Indeed, her former position on the Supreme Court caused many to question her intervention. Daniel Jutras, the McGill dean of law, called it "unacceptable" to put "the weight of a retired Supreme Court justice behind [the ban]."¹¹⁵ L'Heureux-Dubé phoned him and insisted that a law dean had no right to criticize her, that she had a right to freedom of speech.¹¹⁶ Louise Arbour then felt it necessary to express her opposition to balance the scales, one retired Supreme Court justice to another. "I have no religious affiliations," Arbour pointed out. "I believe in a secular state."¹¹⁷ But she saw the proposed Charter as infused with "a very paternalistic attitude. 'We will fight their battles for them.' 'We know what's good for them.' It's the 'them' that bothers me."¹¹⁸

Arbour published an opinion column predicting that the Supreme Court would strike down the Quebec Charter as unconstitutional in violation of freedom of religion. She took issue with L'Heureux-Dubé's characterization of religion as a "private" matter distinct from public display. She argued that "freedom of religion will mean nothing if it is completely relegated to the private sphere." She conceded that in light of the history of religion in Quebec, where women were relegated to a "status of inferiority and submission," it was understandable to be "suspicious," and to be "unwilling to let our hard fought gains erode." But the proposed Charter would principally target "Muslim women who wear a headscarf," she pointed out. And it was "particularly offensive to advance our fight on the backs of those who are now among the most marginalized and whose access to the workplace is the best guarantee of both their autonomy and their integration." She criticized those who evoked nostalgic "images of a homogeneous Catho-secular society." She urged instead that "social cohesion comes from a generous and welcoming spirit that induces others to integrate."¹¹⁹

---

† "an arduous march toward equality"
‡ "the winds of religious dictates"

L'Heureux-Dubé told the press that it was "normal" for Supreme Court judges to disagree, and pointed out that "as a woman and judge from Quebec," she had often been "in a dissenting position." She maintained that the proposed Charter was constitutional. Alternatively, should it be found to contravene the *Canadian Charter of Rights and Freedoms,* she suggested that the Quebec government was in a "perfectly legitimate" position to use the "notwithstanding" override clause.[120]

Before the controversial Quebec Charter of Values was ever enacted, the PQ government lost power in an election that was contested in large part over the Charter itself.[121] The incoming Quebec Liberal government introduced its own bill in June 2015.[122] Less intrusive in scope, it would still have prohibited face coverings for all individuals giving or receiving public services. The legislative consultations dragged on, provoking more controversy.[123] In June 2016, someone dropped a pig's head at the door of the Quebec City mosque during the middle of the religious holiday of Ramadan. The attached card said *"bon appétit."*[124] On 29 January 2017, twenty-seven-year-old Alexandre Bissonnette, a Quebec university student known for his bitter anti-immigrant views, opened fire inside the same mosque. Six Muslim men were murdered as they knelt at worship, and nineteen others injured, in one of the worst religious massacres in Canadian history.[125]

Conclusion

Claire L'Heureux-Dubé's life and career unfolded amid a society engulfed in change. A nation with a distinct cultural history, Quebec saw its political, economic, and social framework shaped and reshaped through the Duplessis years of *La Grande Noirceur*, the Quiet Revolution, and the separatism of the Parti Québécois. The second-wave women's movement lobbed demands for gender equality onto centre stage, women poured into the paid workforce in unprecedented numbers, and female lawyers and judges fought to ascend to their rightful place. Lesbian and gay communities pressed claims for same-sex equality. The challenges posed by racial and ethnic discrimination were less visible but continued to fester. The legal profession grew exponentially. Law offices transitioned from small to large firms, from general practice to diverse specialties. The *Canadian Charter of Rights and Freedoms* resculpted the landscape, expanding popular notions of rights and investing judges with entirely new roles and responsibilities. Globalization broadened Canada's horizons and nurtured exhilarating visions of the country's place in the world.

Claire L'Heureux-Dubé travelled through this twisting terrain, at times typifying the norm, at others veering onto a singular path. She took her youthful bearings from the tranquil French Canadian town of Rimouski on the banks of the Lower St. Lawrence. She received a cloistered religious education from nuns in Catholic convents who were dedicated to moulding dutiful young women. Then, slightly ahead of the second-wave feminist movement that was beginning to gather steam, she chose to pursue post-secondary education. Living out her mother's dreams, she set off for law school. Although initially dubious that there would be any space for her within the practice of law, she found shelter and mentoring in the Jewish law firm of Sam Schwarz Bard. Isolated by gender, she bolstered her anomalous position within private practice through the accoutrements of conventional femininity. It was a strategy of legitimation, forging a parallel identity as a proper married woman, mother of two children, and an impeccable hostess presiding over a gracious home.

The advent of divorce transformed her practice, sequestering her within the new specialty of family law. This further underscored her aberrational status: a woman litigating divorce cases before an all-male judiciary bent on resisting modern ways. It evoked the exotic image of *La Tigresse,* a feral female combatant encroaching upon a masculine profession. Her professional success eventually brought her recognition as Quebec City's most illustrious female lawyer. Yet the struggle to maintain a functional work/life balance exacted an inhuman toll. When things eventually went awry, the voyeuristic public interest in L'Heureux-Dubé's personal life added to the burdens. It was a problem accentuated by gender. Male lawyers and judges were rarely evaluated for their skill in combining professional success with marital and family responsibilities.

L'Heureux-Dubé's judicial years brought new questions to the fore. How did she achieve her exceptional elevation to the bench? She described herself as completely surprised by the appointments, insisting that she had not strategized to achieve this, that, in fact, she had not even remotely imagined the prospect. Yet some observers saw her as a candidate with formidable networking skills, a talented and driven woman who positioned herself squarely in the forefront of opportunity. Still others saw an external and mounting tide of feminists demanding the diversification of an all-male judiciary, with L'Heureux-Dubé as the most viable female candidate of her time. Whatever the reasons, there is no doubt that her appointments to the bench were greeted with skepticism that was frankly gendered, and her relations with male colleagues were often frayed. Occasionally, her skills as *une femme charmante* overcame the resistance. When these did not, the rebellious streak she had honed at her father's knee and strengthened in her convent years re-emerged with a vengeance.

The promotion to the Supreme Court of Canada marked her as an outsider on multiple fronts: first as a woman, second as a Francophone Québécoise, and third as someone perceived to be a specialist in family law. The outsider status was something that she never overcame. But as her tenure lengthened, the "Great Dissenter" found her footing. She took pride in becoming a renegade, a risk taker who could chart the way for the law of the future. Her last decade on the court found her issuing a series of remarkable decisions in favour of those seeking remedies for discrimination on the basis of sex and sexual identity. Her innovative jurisprudence was buttressed by advocacy from *Charter* proponents such as the Women's Legal Education and Action Fund, and assisted by a generation of law clerks whose modern legal education pressed far beyond the formalistic doctrinal training she had imbibed at law school. Her decisions captured the attention of reform-minded activists and judges across the world, giving her still broader platforms from which to examine inequality. In what appears to have been a significant shift from her earlier years on the bench, L'Heureux-Dubé also explicitly began to articulate the linkages between the sex discrimination she had experienced – at home, at school, in practice, and on the bench – and the need for greater equality in law.

In contrast, her life experience had given her little first-hand connection with untoward police practices, and an all-too-vivid appreciation of what mental illness and substance abuse could do to wayward family members in need of restraint. During her most important years on the Supreme Court, her sympathy for women, children, gays, and lesbians, whom she depicted as "victims" or "the little guys," rarely extended to those accused of crime. Despite what she must have observed of anti-Semitism during her childhood and her years of practice with Sam Bard, and despite the racial, ethnic, and religious issues embedded in the Montreal immigration inquiry, *Baker*, and the divisive debates over the Quebec Charter of Values, the fuller dimensions of discrimination also seem to have eluded her. Where rights came into conflict, she opted for sexual equality as the main priority. Hers was a notion of gender that was "essentialized," lacking significant intersection with race, ethnicity, and religion, among other variables.

During her years on the Supreme Court, L'Heureux-Dubé came to embody the quintessential symbol of "feminism" in the minds of her detractors and supporters alike. Buzz McClung lambasted her "feminist bias."[1] The *National Post* described her *Ewanchuk* decision as a "feminist indictment of an entire sex."[2] Toronto defence lawyer Edward Greenspan accused her of delivering a "sermon of feminist theology."[3] Legal academics characterized her as a "self-proclaimed feminist" whose decisions relied on an "explicitly feminist analysis."[4] One analyst responded to the difficulties political scientists were having in pigeonholing L'Heureux-Dubé's judicial philosophy by noting that the decisions that could not easily be grouped under headings of "conservative" or "liberal" were best explained as "a consistent 'feminist' position."[5]

These depictions were all problematic. The Supreme Court judge who came to stand in as the figurehead for feminism consistently shrugged off any personal or professional linkages to the women's movement. She had launched her career well before second-wave feminism surged to the fore, and in the ensuing decades she chose to keep her distance. "I never belonged to a movement of feminists," L'Heureux-Dubé recalled. "I had plenty on my plate to work and have children. It was enough."[6] She also explained her long-standing disinclination to self-identify as stemming from her early disapproval of the campaign to tear down barriers to women's access to Quebec taverns.[7] And she added, "It's absolutely true I didn't want to be called a feminist because the perception was 'anti-men.' I am not anti-men at all."[8]

It is not surprising that a woman widely understood as a *femme fatale* might make such a claim. But it demonstrated a lack of expertise about the women's movement. While some feminists might describe themselves as anti-male, and still more might be perceived to be anti-male, feminism in the largest sense was not anti-male. Nor was it epitomized by a single campaign to degender Quebec taverns. Feminism was a multifaceted philosophy with a broad array of objectives and strategies.

The disjunction between L'Heureux-Dubé's disavowal of feminism and her public stature as a feminist icon could create awkward moments. In 2013, she attended a conference of female judges in Montreal where the evening program included a discussion with author Micheline Dumont, a Quebec historian who reviewed the contributions of the Quebec women's movement from the late nineteenth century to the present.[9] L'Heureux-Dubé stood up during the question period and took issue with Dumont's presentation. Insisting that feminism was "unnecessary," she added, "I am not a feminist. I am a humanist."[10] Once again, the explicit distinction evidenced very little knowledge about the efforts of many to define feminism as a movement dedicated to the eradication of discrimination in all aspects. By the late twentieth century, however imperfectly, feminism had moved well beyond gender to examine race, ethnicity, religion, disability, and class.

Dumont recalled being "absolutely stunned" at L'Heureux-Dubé's intervention, and described it as "paradoxical" that a judge who had been such a leading figure on gender equality issues would speak so dismissively about feminism. She countered L'Heureux-Dubé's assertion that feminism was "unnecessary" by insisting that the Quebec historical evidence was overwhelming. Feminism, she argued, had been essential to women's progress. A fervent debate followed before an astonished audience, with neither woman giving quarter.[11]

Dumont was correct. Without the organized feminist movement in Quebec, the law schools and the legal profession would not have opened their doors to women in L'Heureux-Dubé's era. It was feminist advocacy that provided the push necessary to position L'Heureux-Dubé for judicial appointment. Feminist organizations advanced the equality arguments that resonated with her and the feminist law clerks she hired at the Supreme Court. Feminist NGOs laid the groundwork for her success in international judicial education. L'Heureux-Dubé had been on the cusp of transformational changes in the status of women, ahead of the movement that so assisted her career. Like many other professional women of her generation, engaged full-time in the trailblazing effort to succeed in an entirely masculine milieu, she did not claim feminism on the way up.[12] The more difficult question was why she continued to take such a dismissive position even after retirement from the top court.[13]

For many feminists looking back over L'Heureux-Dubé's legacy, the distance she sought to maintain from the feminist movement was puzzling. It was not as though she disavowed the analysis or principles of feminism, although she preferred to use the language of "justice," "fairness," and "equality."[14] It was not as though she eschewed women's community, since she played a central role in female judicial organizations, and she nurtured long-standing female friendships in Quebec, the rest of Canada, and internationally. It was not as though she failed to recognize that sex discrimination posed personal challenges for her life and career, something she had begun to disclose publicly in her later years on the bench and in international settings. It was not as though she lacked for courage, even though it was obvious that identification as a feminist was dangerous for female judges.[15]

And, of course, it was not as though her resistance to self-identifying ever shielded her from anti-feminist attack. Those who opposed the *Charter*, who derided "activist" and "feminist" judges, subjected her to exceptional levels of venom that stung deeply and personally. One of her staunch critics, Toronto defence lawyer Alan Gold, professed astonishment when he was advised that L'Heureux-Dubé objected to being called a feminist. "That's bizarre," he retorted. "She's right out of the playbook."[16]

L'Heureux-Dubé's daughter, Louise, explained her mother's reluctance to identify as a feminist by emphasizing that she was "very individualistic" and "not the kind of person to join groups."[17] It fit with her insistence that she had never asked anything from anybody. It fit with her career path. An individualized perspective may have been inevitable for a woman whose life personified so many firsts. A lone woman moving through an unrelievedly male environment would have had little alternative but to develop an unhesitating reliance on herself alone. Alan Gold may unknowingly have put his finger on it when he added, "Well, she reached the same place on her own."[18]

In spite of L'Heureux-Dubé's intense individualism, she became a heroine to many communities that defined themselves by reference to movements for social reform. Younger female lawyers from the generation that came after her, many of whom embraced feminism as both a self-identity and a movement, lavished her with praise. LGBT communities elevated her to iconic status. She became revered by lawyers and judges who sought to eradicate sexism in international settings. Recognition that L'Heureux-Dubé had become an anti-feminist target brought her widespread acknowledgment and sympathy from feminists across Canada and internationally. For many years she shouldered criticism that belonged to the larger movement. That itself constituted an enormous contribution to the wider struggle for equality, and deserves historical recognition quite apart from the position she took or did not take with respect to feminism.

L'Heureux-Dubé's twenty-nine years on the bench served to deepen her individualist streak. She forged a particularly independent path on the bench. Her sense of nonconformity was exacerbated by the conflict-filled environment she inherited and helped to intensify on the top court. She delivered strong dissenting judgments that articulated a vision well beyond what most Canadians had come to imagine was possible from a judge. It may have been this individualist hyperconfidence that gave her the will and the capacity to write unprecedented decisions that expressed egalitarian perspectives in ways that had never been previously enunciated by the nation's Supreme Court. Perhaps it was this that enabled her to strike the chord that she did with vulnerable communities, who looked to her as their champion on the court, the first judge who truly heard their innovative claims. She took their written and oral submissions and fashioned decisions that spoke directly to them, that gave them fresh hope in the possibilities of law to refashion Canadian society.

It was a life and career that her mother, Marguerite, a woman unfairly constricted by her times and her disability, would have found immensely gratifying. Claire L'Heureux-Dubé's decisions may have generated enormous controversy, but few could deny that the energetic, risk-taking woman she epitomized – in all her contrariness and contradictions – represented a critical force on the Supreme Court at a critical time. A truly singular woman and an extraordinary judge, her influence was demonstrably and undeniably transformative.

Notes

ACKNOWLEDGMENTS

1 The interviewees were selected because of their knowledge regarding Claire L'Heureux-Dubé's personal and professional life: family members, individuals who went to school with her, individuals who worked with her in her law practice and on the bench, individuals who sat on the same courts, litigants and lawyers who appeared before her, journalists and commentators who observed her years on the bench, and individuals who could attest to her international activities. Claire L'Heureux-Dubé referred me to some, interviewees referred me to other interviewees, and some I identified through my own research into the sources.
2 The records held at Library and Archives Canada, MG 31, E110, vols. 1–490, contain decisions, notes, and correspondence from the judicial years, along with some personal correspondence and press clippings. Claire L'Heureux-Dubé requested that the records be closed for twenty-five years, but can also give individual authorization for conditional access.

INTRODUCTION

1 Interview with Louise Dubé, Boston, 22 May 2012.

CHAPTER 1: *EWANCHUK*

1 Hester Lessard, "Farce or Tragedy? Judicial Backlash and Justice McClung" (1999) 10:3 Const Forum Const 65; Joanne Wright, "Consent and Sexual Violence in Canadian Public Discourse: Reflections on *Ewanchuk*" (2001) 16:2 CJLS 173; Rebecca Johnson, "The Persuasive Cartographer: Sexual Assault and Legal Discourse in *R. v. Ewanchuk*" in Gayle M. MacDonald, ed., *Social Context and Social Location in the Sociology of Law* (Peterborough: Broadview Press, 2002) 247; Sheila McIntyre, "Personalizing the Political and Politicizing the Personal: Understanding Justice McClung and His Defenders" in Elizabeth Sheehy, ed., *Adding Feminism to Law: The Contributions of Justice Claire L'Heureux-Dubé* (Toronto:

Irwin Law, 2004) at 318; Constance Backhouse, "The Chilly Climate for Women Judges: Reflections on the *Ewanchuk* Decision" (2003) 15:1 CJWL 167.
2 *R. v. Ewanchuk*, [1999] 1 SCR 330 at 339–43, 368–69, overruling *R. v. Ewanchuk*, [1998] 6 WWR 8 (Alta CA), dismissing an appeal from an acquittal by Justice John C. Moore.
3 Ibid. at 339–43, 368–69; *R. v. Ewanchuk*, [1998] 6 WWR 8 (Alta CA) at 23–49; *R. v. Ewanchuk* (2002), 164 CCC (3d) 193 (Alta CA) at 21.
4 Ewanchuk had been convicted of sexual assault involving intercourse in 1989 and of rape three times in the 1960s and 1970s. *R. v. Ewanchuk* (2000), 276 AR 49 (Alta QB) at 55; *R. v. Ewanchuk* (2002), 164 CCC (3d) 193 (Alta CA).
5 Anne Marie Owens, "Attacker awaiting sentence," *National Post* (27 February 1999) A2.
6 *R. v. Ewanchuk*, [1999] 1 SCR 330 at 343–44.
7 *R. v. Ewanchuk*, [1998] 6 WWR 8 (Alta CA). Justice John Wesley McClung wrote the majority decision. Justice Peter Foisey, agreeing with McClung on the result, wrote a short concurrence. Chief Justice Catherine Fraser dissented, declaring that Parliament had tried to reject the "discredited theory of 'implied consent'" with no fewer than "three legislative attempts" (30). She insisted that Canadian women were "not walking around this country in a state of constant consent to sexual activity unless and until they say 'No' or offer resistance to anyone who targets them for sexual activity" (35).
8 *R. v. Ewanchuk*, ibid. at 18–23. Shawn Ohler, "'Best, worst' of British legal tradition seen in Judge McClung's decisions," *National Post* (27 February 1999) A3; Jill Mahoney and Sean Fine, "Judge McClung's story, life and times," *Globe and Mail* (6 March 1999) A1 and A4; Jim Farrell, "Jurist defended as man with deep feelings," *Calgary Herald* (28 February 1999) A3.
9 Interview with Claire L'Heureux-Dubé, Ottawa, 30 June 2010.
10 Peter McCormick, "Who Writes? Gender and Judgment Assignment in the Supreme Court of Canada" (2014) 5:2 Osgoode Hall LJ, 595, notes that "if more than one justice volunteers [to write], the more senior justice prevails." L'Heureux-Dubé had been appointed to the Supreme Court in 1987. Judges Gonthier, Cory, and McLachlin were appointed in 1989, Iacobucci in 1991, Major in 1992, Bastarache in 1997, and Binnie in 1998. Supreme Court of Canada, *The Supreme Court of Canada* (Ottawa: Supreme Court of Canada, 2000) at 22–23.
11 According to L'Heureux-Dubé, the process of deferring to the more senior judge was a matter of custom rather than firm rule, and could shift over time and according to the wishes of the chief justice: "There was an unwritten rule that when two or more volunteer, it goes to the senior [judge]. That was something that was not spelled out. Bertha [Wilson] told me, so it may not have been fully understood or accepted by all. It was also broken on occasion." Then she added, "I wanted to write *Ewanchuk*. Tony gave it to Major. I complained and said, 'I am the senior judge.'" Interview with Claire L'Heureux-Dubé, Clearwater, FL, 10–14 May 2009.
12 Interviews with Claire L'Heureux-Dubé, Clearwater, FL, 10–14 May 2009; Ottawa, 10 March 2010. On the friendship between Lamer and McClung, see Kirk Makin, "Close ties cloud process of judges judging judges," *Globe and Mail* (8 March 1999) A4: "When in Alberta, the Chief Justice of Canada can sometimes be found shooting ducks out of the sky with his friend – Mr. Justice John McClung of the Alberta Court of Appeal." Makin also described Jack Major as "a close friend of Judge McClung." See also "Hardly Impartial," Editorial, *National Post* (10 March 1999) A19, describing Jack Major as "a crony of Judge McClung." The reference to duck hunting appears to have come from a judge's conference at which Alberta Justice Catherine Fraser was speaking, when she criticized the absence of Lamer and McClung, noting that they were off hunting. "The boys have been hunting this afternoon," she stated; "I don't understand what it means that hunters want to blast the heads of ducks off." Apparently half the audience laughed; half sat stony-faced. Interview with Don Stuart, Kingston, ON, 4 May 2015.

13 Interview with Jack Major, Calgary, 13 November 2013.
14 Interview with Ian Binnie, Ottawa, 6 April 2011. Frank Iacobucci, who could not remember how the drafting judge was selected, agreed that Major's Alberta background was probably pivotal. Interview with Frank Iacobucci, Toronto, 26 October 2011.
15 Interview with Michel Bastarache, Ottawa, 24 November 2009. When asked whether she thought Bastarache may have been correct, L'Heureux-Dubé replied that he was "totally wrong"; discussion with Claire L'Heureux-Dubé, Quebec City, 11 July 2016.
16 Interviews with Claire L'Heureux-Dubé, Ottawa, 10 March 2010; Clearwater, FL, 25–27 November 2014.
17 Personal notes of L'Heureux-Dubé, 31 January 1999.
18 *R. v. Ewanchuk*, [1999] 1 SCR 330 at 340–50. There was a background to the issue, since one year earlier the Supreme Court had reviewed McClung's decision in a gay rights case, *Vriend v. Alberta* (1996), 184 AR 351, [1996] AJ No. 643 (CA). In that hearing, the lawyers seeking reversal of McClung's decision asked the Supreme Court to explicitly censure the homophobic comments he had made from the Alberta Court of Appeal bench. Lamer had objected during oral argument that judges were entitled to "free speech." The Supreme Court decision had overruled McClung without specifically critiquing his acerbic language: [1998] 1 SCR 493, 156 DLR (4th) 385. Some have suggested that the failure to rein in McClung in *Vriend* was a mistake, encouraging him to continue in the same vein in *Ewanchuk*. The remnants of *Vriend* continued to reverberate as the Supreme Court decided in what manner it should reverse McClung here. Interview with Rebecca Johnson, Victoria, 22 August 2013.
19 Interview with Claire L'Heureux-Dubé, Clearwater, FL, 25–27 November 2014.
20 *R. v. Ewanchuk*, [1999] 1 SCR 330 at 379–80. Philip Slayton described her concurring opinion as "an antiseptic one-paragraph" judgment and speculated that it might have been "strategic," relating to her desire to obtain the appointment as chief justice when Lamer resigned. Philip Slayton, *Mighty Judgment: How the Supreme Court of Canada Runs Your Life* (Toronto: Penguin, 2011) at 152.
21 *R. v. Ewanchuk*, ibid. at 361–79.
22 Ibid. at 369–79.
23 Interview with Stephen Bindman, Ottawa, 22 June 2015.
24 On the unparalleled nature of McClung's attack, see Alanna Mitchell, Jill Mahoney, and Sean Fine, "Legal experts outraged by personal attack on Supreme Court judge," *Globe and Mail* (27 February 1999) A1.
25 Justice J.W. McClung, "Right of reply," *National Post* (26 February 1999) A19.
26 Jill Mahoney, "'Personal and hurtful' comments stun colleagues," *Globe and Mail* (1 March 1999) A3.
27 "Judge L'Heureux-Dubé's husband had committed suicide in 1978, a fact widely known in Canadian legal circles"; Shawn Ohler, "Judge reiterates belief that teen wasn't assaulted," *National Post* (27 February 1999) A1. Interview with Claire L'Heureux-Dubé, Ottawa, 10 March 2010.
28 Interview with Jack Major, Calgary, 13 November 2013.
29 The suggestion was that McClung's animosity was also directed at his colleague Catherine Fraser, who had issued a dissent in *Ewanchuk*, an opinion that he perceived as even more irksome coming from a woman who had been elevated over her male peers to the position of chief justice on his own bench. Makin, "Close ties," see note 12 above.
30 Interview with Kirk Makin, Toronto, 9 April 2015.
31 Ibid.
32 Interview with Sean Fine, Toronto, 8 April 2015.
33 John Wesley McClung, nicknamed "Buzz," obtained his BA in 1957 and law degree in 1959 from the University of Alberta. Named by *Weekend Magazine* in 1975 as one of the country's top criminal lawyers, he practised in Edmonton until his appointment to the bench in

1976, followed by the Court of Appeal in 1980. Ohler, "'Best, worst,'" see note 8 above; Mahoney and Fine, "Judge McClung's story life and times," see note 8 above; Farrell, "Jurist defended," see note 8 above; "Tribute to Justice John Wesley McClung" (Winter 2004–05) 13:2 Architypes (Legal Archives Society of Alberta Newsletter) 2; Louis Knafla and Richard Klumpenhouwer, *Lords of the Western Bench: A Biographical History of the Supreme and District Courts of Alberta, 1876–1990* (Calgary: Legal Archives Society of Alberta, 1997) at 115–16.
34 Comment from an Alberta female judge who wished not to be identified.
35 Interview with Janice Tibbetts, Ottawa, 11 May 2015.
36 Interview with Claire L'Heureux-Dubé, Ottawa, 10 March 2010.
37 Kirk Makin advised that the *Post* had "targeted the courts and the *Charter* as one of the four or five topics they were going to make their name and reputation on," adding, "I was the guy who got scooped on that." Interview with Kirk Makin, Toronto, 9 April 2015.
38 Interview with Janice Tibbetts, Ottawa, 11 May 2015.
39 Ibid.
40 Shawn Ohler, "Judge apologizes for 'cruel' attack on senior justice," *National Post* (2 March 1999) A1.
41 L'Heureux-Dubé explained that she later learned that some of McClung's colleagues had advised against publishing the letter; interview with Claire L'Heureux-Dubé, Ottawa, 10 March 2010.
42 Penney Kome, former columnist with the *Calgary Herald*, notes that the *National Post* also hired anti-feminist reporters and columnists. Penney Kome, "I Too Was a Women's Libber" in Marguerite Andersen, ed., *Feminist Journeys/Voies féministes* (Ottawa: Feminist History Society, 2010) at 202.
43 Interview with Janice Tibbetts, Ottawa, 11 May 2015. Florian Sauvageau, David Schneiderman, and David Taras, *The Last Word: Media Coverage of the Supreme Court of Canada* (Vancouver: UBC Press, 2006) at 16–17.
44 McIntyre, "Personalizing the Political," see note 1 above at 318.
45 Tonda MacCharles, "Defence lawyer criticizes 'radical feminist' ruling," *Toronto Star* (26 February 1999) A7.
46 Nahlah Ayed, "L'Heureux-Dubé attacked as support for McClung builds," *Calgary Herald* (4 March 1999) A12.
47 Robert Fife, "McClung reprimanded for critical remarks made at L'Heureux-Dubé," *National Post* (22 May 1999) A4. The *Ottawa Citizen* editorial, "Judging the Judges" (3 March 1999) A13, complained that American law professor Catharine MacKinnon's *Toward a Feminist Theory of the State* was "the very paragon of fringe, illiberal feminist legal theory."
48 Shawn Ohler, "Women's group turns tables on L'Heureux-Dubé," *National Post* (4 March 1999) A5.
49 The Canadian Judicial Council dismissed the complaint; Canadian Judicial Council, Council File 98-129, 31 March 1999. See more detailed discussion in Chapter 36, "Epilogue on *Ewanchuk*."
50 Rosie DiManno, "Don't diss if you can't take it too," *Toronto Star* (1 March 1999) B1.
51 "Assaulting the law," Editorial, *National Post* (1 March 1999) at A19.
52 Marjaleena Repo, "The *Ewanchuk* ruling is no reason to rejoice," *Globe and Mail* (4 March 1999) A15.
53 "Consent means consent," *Ottawa Citizen* (2 March 1999) at A14; "Judging the judges," see note 47 above.
54 Shawn Ohler, "Groundswell of support rises for embattled McClung," *National Post* (3 March 1999) A6.
55 Edward L. Greenspan, "Judges have no right to be bullies," *National Post* (2 March 1999) at A18.

56 Tonda MacCharles, "Judge 'sorry' for outburst," *Toronto Star* (2 March 1999) A7.
57 McIntyre, "Personalizing the Political," see note 1 above at 313–46; Lessard, "Farce or Tragedy?" see note 1 above.
58 Jules Richer, "La juge L'Heureux-Dubé refuse de répliquer au juge McClung," *La Presse* (9 March 1999) B4.
59 Interview with Ann Robinson, Ottawa, 17 September 2008.
60 Nathalie Des Rosiers, "Être le miroir de son époque: la primauté du droit, la critique égalitaire, et la contribution de Madame la juge L'Heureux-Dubé" in Sheehy, *Adding Feminism to Law*, see note 1 above at 122.
61 Shawn Ohler, "McClung's letter outrageous, legal experts say," *National Post* (27 February 1999) A2; Mitchell, Mahoney, and Fine, "Legal scholar sees letter as personal attack on judge," *Globe and Mail* (27 February 1999) A6.
62 Ohler, "Judge reiterates belief," see note 27 above.
63 Interview with Claire L'Heureux-Dubé, Ottawa, 10 March 2010.
64 Mitchell, Mahoney, and Fine, "Legal scholar sees letter as personal attack on judge," see note 61 above; Janice Tibbetts, "Judge gets into deeper hot water," *Calgary Herald* (28 February 1999) A3; Janice Tibbetts "Top judge sorry for 'cruel' error," *Calgary Herald* (2 March 1999) A3.
65 Barbara Billingsley and Bruce P. Elman, "The Supreme Court of Canada and the Alberta Court of Appeal: Do the Top Courts Have a Fundamental Philosophical Difference of Opinion on Public Law Issues?" (2001) 39:3 Alta L Rev 703.
66 Rick Salutin, "Feminism, humanism and the battle of the judges," *Globe and Mail* (4 March 1999) D1.
67 The CJC "rebuked" McClung but did not recommend his removal from the bench; Canadian Judicial Council, Council File 98-128, 19 May 1999. See more detailed discussion in Chapter 36, "Epilogue on *Ewanchuk*."
68 McIntyre, "Personalizing the Political," see note 1 above at 322.
69 Henry Hess, "Women's groups applaud no-means-no ruling," *Globe and Mail* (26 February 1999) A7.
70 "Explicit bias," Editorial, *Law Times* (8–14 March 1999) 6.
71 Alex Kozinski, "An unfair attack on a decent judgment," *National Post* (8 March 1999) A18.
72 Interview with Michel Bastarache, Ottawa, 24 November 2009.

Chapter 2: Lineage

1 The full birth name was Marie Marguerite Antoinette Claire L'Heureux. Caroline Tanguay, OSU, with Louise Dumais, "Une grande Québécoise: L'Honorable Claire L'Heureux-Dubé, Cour suprême 1987–2002" (undated, unpublished manuscript). Sister Caroline Tanguay was one of Claire L'Heureux's teachers at the Ursuline convent; Louise Dumais assisted Sister Tanguay in compiling the manuscript.
2 Due to discrepancies in the birth records, the year is based on his published age at death, in his obituary. Between 1840 and 1880, 325,000 Quebecers emigrated to the United States. John Dickinson and Brian Young, *A Short History of Quebec*, 3rd ed. (Montreal: McGill-Queen's University Press, 2003) at 115.
3 Napoléon's parents were Jean Baptiste Edwidge L'Heureux and Luce-Léotine Drolet. The L'Heureux line has been traced back to Simon Lereau, also known as L'Hérault dit L'Heureux. from Saint-Cosme-de-Vair, near Rouen, France, who immigrated to Quebec around 1652. René L'Heureux, "Simon L'Hérault: Ier ancêtre canadien des familles L'Hérault et L'Heureux" (1969) 20:1 Mémoires de la Société Généalogique Canadienne-Française at 99–120; Simonne L'Heureux-Blouin, *Sortir du rang* (Sainte-Foy: Éditions du Givre, 1993); Nicole L'Heureux Généalogie (unpublished; copy on file with the author).

Notes to pages 23–26

4 Interview with Claire L'Heureux-Dubé, Ottawa, 30 October 2007. On the Quebec opposition to the Boer War, led by Henri Bourassa, see Susan Mann Trofimenkoff, *The Dream of Nation: A Social and Intellectual History of Quebec* (Toronto: Gage, 1983) at 169–71.
5 Bruna owned property in Vieux Québec, 55 Sous-le-Fort. Her father was a butcher or a grocer whose small fortune was the basis for his children's wealth. The uncle who stepped in was Adélard Lavoie. Nicole L'Heureux Généalogie; interview with Louise L'Heureux-Giliberti, Chicago, 20–21 April 2009; interview with Nicole L'Heureux, Clearwater, FL, 11–12 May 2009. See also Claire L'Heureux-Dubé, "Une vie" (undated, unpublished, and incomplete memoir covering the years of her youth) at 6–20.
6 L'Heureux-Dubé, ibid. at 20; interview with Nicole L'Heureux, ibid. Although these sources indicate that the connection occurred during the Boer War, this must have been in error, since Power was born in 1888 and the Boer War ended in 1902. On Power's injury on the battlefield during the Great War, see Norman Ward, ed., *A Party Politician: The Memoirs of Chubby Power* (Toronto: Macmillan of Canada, 1966).
7 Interview with Claire L'Heureux-Dubé, Ottawa, 30 October 2007; L'Heureux-Dubé, ibid. at 7.
8 Interview with Claire L'Heureux-Dubé, ibid.
9 Ibid.
10 The details about Napoléon in this chapter are from interviews with Claire L'Heureux-Dubé, Ottawa, 30 October 2007 and 1 November 2007; interview with Nicole L'Heureux, Clearwater, FL, 11–12 May 2009; interview with Louise L'Heureux-Giliberti, Chicago, 21 April 2009; L'Heureux-Dubé, "Une vie," see note 5 above at 7, 17–20.
11 The vast majority of middle-class French Canadian Catholic Quebec males received their secondary education in the *collèges classiques*, part of an educational network controlled by diocesan authorities and religious orders. Prior to 1945, the curriculum eschewed science and was dominated by classical humanism in the name of preserving French culture. Michael Gauvreau, *The Catholic Origins of Quebec's Quiet Revolution, 1931–1970* (Montreal: McGill-Queen's University Press, 2005) at 73–74.
12 Family stories vary regarding Napoléon's influence. Possibly Napoléon arranged for Paul to falsify his age, since he may have been too young to register. Possibly Napoléon facilitated the intercession of Chubby Power or some other Liberal patron.
13 Louise explained: "I think my father may have kept up some communication, but my mother didn't know about it, or she didn't want to know. She didn't want [my grandfather] to come over to the house, didn't want to see him. She was not a compromising person, and once she had made up her mind ... she was stubborn." Interview with Louise L'Heureux-Giliberti, Chicago, 21 April 2009.
14 L'Heureux-Dubé, "Une vie," see note 5 above at 18–19; interview with Nicole L'Heureux, Clearwater, FL, 11–12 May 2009.
15 Gaston L'Heureux, thirty-five years younger than his half-brother Paul, would later become a Quebec artist. L'Heureux-Dubé, ibid. at 18; Nicole L'Heureux Généalogie.
16 Obituary, Québec *Le Soleil* (14 June 1955) 27; Nicole L'Heureux Généalogie; L'Heureux-Dubé, ibid. at 6.
17 Marie Joséphine Antoinette (Fortin) Dion (1862–1940). The early family history is traced to Jean Guyon, born in 1592 in France, who departed for New France in 1634. Nicole L'Heureux Généalogie; L'Heureux-Dubé, ibid. at 22–24; Tanguay, "Une grande Québécoise," see note 1 above. The details about Antoinette that follow in this chapter are from interviews with Claire L'Heureux-Dubé, Ottawa, 30 October and 1 November 2007; interview with Nicole L'Heureux, Clearwater, FL, 11–12 May 2009; interview with Louise L'Heureux-Giliberti, Chicago, 21 April 2009.
18 Alexander Sedgwick, *Jansenism in Seventeenth-Century France* (Charlottesville: University Press of Virginia, 1977) at 194, 203–5. On the critique of Jansenism emerging from young

intellectuals in Quebec in the 1940s and 1950s, see Gauvreau, *Catholic Origins*, see note 11 above.
19 Interview with Claire L'Heureux-Dubé, Ottawa, 30 October 2007.
20 Antoinette's father, Louis-Gaspard Fortin (1820–63), was the son of Charles Fortin, a mayor and surveyor (1796–1853), and Anastasie Langelier. Antoinette's mother, Virginie Agathe Martin (1837–1902), was the daughter of Edouard Martin, a merchant, and Catherine Lepage. The couple's three children were Elzire, Marie, and Antoinette. After Louis-Gaspard's death, Virginie married Dr. François-Xavier Napoléon Dion, with whom she had five more children. Nicole L'Heureux Généalogie.
21 Louis-Victor Dion (1859–1910) was the son of William Dion and Zoé Hammond. His first marriage was to Vitaline Sirois. He married Marie Joséphine Antoinette Fortin in 1890. Their four children were Marie Marthe (1893–1958), Évelyne (1894–1973), Marguerite (1903–83), and Martin (1904–15). Nicole L'Heureux Généalogie; L'Heureux-Dubé, "Une vie," see note 5 above at 21.
22 L'Heureux-Dubé, ibid. at 21-23; Tanguay, "Une grande Québécoise," see note 1 above.
23 Interview with Claire L'Heureux-Dubé, Ottawa, 30 October 2007.
24 Details about Marguerite that follow in this chapter are from interviews with Claire L'Heureux-Dubé, Quebec City, Ottawa, Rimouski, and Clearwater, FL, on 17 September, 30 October, 1 November, and 2 December 2007; 29–30 April, 1–2 May, and 23–25 July 2008; 5 and 7 March, 27–28 April, and 10–14 May 2009; interview with Nicole L'Heureux, Clearwater, FL, 11–12 May 2009; interview with Louise L'Heureux-Giliberti, Chicago, 20 April 2009; L'Heureux-Dubé, "Une vie," see note 5 above at 27–28; Tanguay, "Une grande Québécoise," see note 1 above.
25 Schooling did not become compulsory in Quebec until 1943, and there was no network of public secondary schools before 1954. Catholic girls who could afford to do so studied privately in convents. By 1917, there were at least thirty-two religious teaching communities running 586 boarding schools for girls, but among girls aged sixteen, only a fifth studied in convents in 1911. This proportion increased to a quarter in 1921, and to a third for the two decades following. Anglophone girls had access to public high schools up to grade eleven, after which they could attend university. Clio Collective, *Québec Women: A History*, trans. Roger Gannon and Rosalind Gill (Toronto: Women's Press, 1987) at 223, 241–47; Micheline Dumont and Nadia Fahmy-Eid, *Les couventines: l'éducation des filles au Québec dans les congrégations religieuses enseignantes 1840–1960* (Montréal: Boréal Express).
26 Interview with Nicole L'Heureux, Clearwater, FL, 11–12 May 2009.
27 Tanguay, "Une grande Québécoise," see note 1 above.
28 Interview with Louise L'Heureux-Giliberti, Chicago, 20 April 2009; interview with Nicole L'Heureux, Clearwater, FL, 11–12 May 2009.
29 L'Heureux-Dubé, "Une vie," see note 5 above at 27–28.
30 Unless otherwise indicated, details about Paul that follow in this chapter are from interviews with Claire L'Heureux-Dubé, Quebec City, Ottawa, Rimouski, and Clearwater, FL, on 17 September, 30 October, 1 November, and 2 December 2007; 29–30 April, 1–2 May, and 23–25 July 2008; 5 and 7 March, 27–28 April, and 10–14 May 2009; interview with Nicole L'Heureux, Clearwater, FL, 11–12 May 2009; interview with Louise L'Heureux-Giliberti, Chicago, 20–21 April 2009; L'Heureux-Dubé, "Une vie," ibid. at 28–30; and Tanguay, "Une grande Québécoise," see note 1 above.
31 Interview with Dr. Marcèle Dorion, Quebec City, 30 April 2008; interview with Philippe Casgrain, Montreal, 23 August 2008; interview with Philippe Michaud, Rimouski, 24 July 2008.
32 L'Heureux-Dubé, "Une vie," see note 5 above at 28–30.
33 Interview with Claire L'Heureux-Dubé, Ottawa, 30 October 2007.
34 Ibid.

35 Interviews with Claire L'Heureux-Dubé, Ottawa, 30 October and 1 November 2007; interview with Louise L'Heureux-Giliberti, Chicago, 20 April 2009.
36 Jean R. Brillant, "Le Lt-Colonel Paul-H. L'Heureux, Un homme attachant," *En Garde* 1:2 (October 1983) at 22.
37 Interview with Claire L'Heureux-Dubé, Clearwater, FL, 10–14 May 2009; interview with Louise L'Heureux-Giliberti, Chicago, 20 April 2009; interview with Nicole L'Heureux, Clearwater, FL, 11–12 May 2009.
38 Interview with Michèle Cloutier Mainguy, Quebec City, 2 May 2008.
39 L'Heureux-Dubé, "Une vie," see note 5 above at 29–30.

Chapter 3: Early Years

1 Christian Blais et al., *Québec: quatre siècles d'une capitale* (Québec: Assemblée nationale du Québec, 2008) at 3.
2 Ibid. at 142, 147, 360; Jacques Lacoursière and Pierre Caron, *Québec et sa région* (Montréal: Éditions de l'homme, 2008) at 276–77.
3 Dominion Bureau of Statistics, Canada, *Seventh Census of Canada, 1931*, vol. 2, *Population by Areas* (Ottawa: J.O. Patenaude, 1933) at 250.
4 Andrée Lévesque, *Making and Breaking the Rules: Women in Quebec 1919–1939* (Toronto: McClelland and Stewart, 1994) at 18; Blais et al., *Québec*, see note 1 above at 420–24; John Dickinson and Brian Young, *A Short History of Quebec*, 3rd ed. (Montreal: McGill-Queen's University Press, 2003) at 198–210; Clio Collective, *Quebec Women: A History*, trans. Roger Gannon and Rosalind Gill (Toronto: Women's Press, 1987) at 185.
5 Blais et al., ibid. at 420; Dickinson and Young, ibid. at 292–93; Lacoursière and Caron, *Québec et sa région*, see note 2 above at 50–53; Gaston Deschênes, *Le parlement de Québec: histoire, anecdotes et légendes* (Sainte-Foy: Éditions Multimondes, 2005) at 94; Susan Mann Trofimenkoff, *The Dream of Nation: A Social and Intellectual History of Quebec* (Toronto: Gage, 1983) at 187, 218–19, 239, 243–45.
6 Lévesque, *Making and Breaking the Rules,* see note 4 above at 18–19, 29, 35, 136.
7 Dickinson and Young, *A Short History of Quebec*, see note 4 above at 239, 271; Clio Collective, *Quebec Women,* see note 4 above at 252; Trofimenkoff, *The Dream of Nation*, see note 5 above at 187, 218–19, 239, 243–45.
8 Unless otherwise indicated, the details that follow are drawn from interviews with Claire L'Heureux-Dubé, Quebec City, Ottawa, Rimouski, and Clearwater, FL, 17 September, 30 October, 1 November, and 2 December 2007; 29–30 April, 1–2 May, and 23–25 July 2008; 5 and 7 March, 27–28 April, and 10–14 May 2009.
9 Claire L'Heureux-Dubé, "Une vie" (undated, incomplete, and unpublished autobiographical manuscript) at 23.
10 Interview with Louise L'Heureux-Giliberti, Chicago, 20 April 2009.
11 L'Heureux-Dubé, "Une vie," see note 9 above at 28.
12 Dickinson and Young, *A Short History of Quebec*, see note 4 above at 66. According to Claire, her mother "said she breastfed us each for two years in order to avoid pregnancy ... that was the pill in those days."
13 They rented at 842 avenue Cartier, then numbered as 28½, from 1927 to 1929. There was one year at 5 Aberdeen with Napoléon L'Heureux, and then at 44½ Dorchester in 1930 and 91¾ rue des Franciscains in 1931. By 1932, the family was at 7 avenue Désy, later numbered as 695. *Marcotte Québec et Lévis adresses, Enr. (Directory), 1927–28* (Québec: Arthur Marcotte, 1927) at 144–46; *Directory 1929–30* at 121, 787; *Directory 1930–31* at 828, 869–70; *Directory 1932–33* at 170; *Directory 1933–34* at 149–50.
14 L'Heureux-Dubé, "Une vie," see note 9 above at 26–27; interview with Louise L'Heureux-Giliberti, Chicago, 20 April 2009.

15 *Marcotte Québec et Lévis adresses, Enr. (Directory), 1932–33, 1933–34, 1934–35* (Québec: Arthur Marcotte, 1932, 1933, 1934); L'Heureux-Dubé, ibid. at 25.
16 Interview with Nicole L'Heureux, Clearwater, FL, 11–12 May 2009.
17 Interview with Claire L'Heureux-Dubé, Clearwater, FL, 10–14 May 2009.
18 Ibid.
19 L'Heureux-Dubé, "Une vie," see note 9 above at 16, 30–31.
20 Institution Saint-Joseph dirigée par Les Sœurs de Saint-Joseph de Saint-Vallier, *Bulletins mensuels,* October 1933, November 1934, January 1935.
21 Interview with Claire L'Heureux-Dubé, Ottawa, 1 November 2007.
22 Interview with Claire L'Heureux-Dubé, Clearwater, FL, 10–14 May 2009.
23 Interview with Claire L'Heureux-Dubé, Ottawa, 30 October 2007.
24 Caroline Tanguay, OSU, with Louise Dumais, "Une grande Québécoise: L'Honorable Claire L'Heureux-Dubé, Cour suprême 1987–2002" (undated, unpublished manuscript).
25 Interview with Claire L'Heureux-Dubé, Ottawa, 30 October 2007.
26 Marie-Ange Caron et al., *Mosaique rimouskoise: une histoire de Rimouski* (Rimouski: Comité des fêtes du cent cinquantième anniversaire de la paroisse Saint-Germain de Rimouski, 1979) at 471–92.
27 Interview with Claire L'Heureux-Dubé, Ottawa, 30 October 2007.
28 Tanguay, "Une grande Québécoise," see note 24 above; interview with Philippe Michaud, Rimouski, 24 July 2008; Jeannot Bourdages et al., *Rimouski depuis ses origines* (Rimouski: Société d'histoire du Bas-Saint-Laurent, Société de généalogie et d'archives de Rimouski, 2006) at 136.
29 Interview with Claire L'Heureux-Dubé, Rimouski, 23–25 July 2008.
30 Ibid.
31 Real Bernier, *Rimouski, métropole du Bas-Saint-Laurent* (Thesis, École des Hautes Études Commerciales de Montréal, 1941) at 9–11; interview with Claire L'Heureux-Dubé, Ottawa, 30 October 2007.
32 Interview with Claire L'Heureux-Dubé, Quebec City, 27–29 April 2009.
33 L'Heureux-Dubé, "Une vie," see note 9 above at 36–37.
34 Bourdages et al., *Rimouski depuis ses origines,* see note 28 above at 27, 91. Translations from Mi'kmaq to French suggest diverse meanings: *terre de l'orignal, rivière du chien, demeure du chien* (land of the moose, dog river, home of the dog).
35 The population was 1,804 in 1901, 5,589 in 1931, and 7,000 in 1940. Pierre Bruneau, "Rimouski: ville moyenne et capitale régionale" (1996) 49:2 Revue d'histoire du Bas-Saint-Laurent at 88–89; Bourdages et al., *Rimouski depuis ses origines,* see note 28 above at 121, 129–30, 157–73; Bernier, *Rimouski,* see note 31 above at 23–24, 68–69; Caron et al., *Mosaique rimouskoise,* see note 26 above at 461.
36 Interview with Claire L'Heureux-Dubé, Ottawa, 30 October 2007. The 1851 census showed a population of 3,653. Of the 48 *étrangers,* 43 were Irish, 2 English, 1 Greek, 1 from Jersey, and 1 from Newfoundland. Between 1931 and 1961, the city welcomed only 100 immigrants from foreign countries, principally Europe. Bourdages et al., ibid. at 113–17, 232.
37 Some newcomers were also assimilated. Sixty immigrant Irish children orphaned by typhoid were adopted into Rimouski families in the 1840s, quickly picked up the French language, and were immersed in the French Canadian culture. Bourdages et al., ibid. at 116–17, 150, 184. Bernier, *Rimouski,* see note 31 above at 29–30, estimates that in 1941 there were just twenty-five Anglo-Saxon Protestant families that had not yet "assimilated." Interview with Jean-Marie Joly, Ottawa, 21 March 2009; interview with Lisette Gammon, Ottawa, 16 November 2007.
38 Interview with Louise L'Heureux-Giliberti, Chicago, 21 April 2009.
39 Ibid.
40 *Le Progrès du Golfe* (15 November 1929) 4.

41 Caron et al., *Mosaique rimouskoise,* see note 26 above at 355–62; Bourdages, *Rimouski depuis ses origines,* see note 28 above at 223; interview with Jean-Marie Joly, Ottawa, 21 March 2009.
42 Bernier, *Rimouski,* see note 31 above at 42, 46–47; Caron et al., ibid. at 429, 667–76; Yves Tremblay, *Du notable et de l'homme d'affaires: l'élite économique de Rimouski, 1890–1960* (Rimouski: Corporation Rimouski, 1996) at 31; Bourdages et al., ibid. at 149, 178–79; Bruneau, "Rimouski," see note 35 above at 88.
43 Unless otherwise indicated, sources for the description of the house are interviews with Claire L'Heureux-Dubé and Nicole L'Heureux, Clearwater, FL, 11–12 May 2009; interview with Louise L'Heureux-Giliberti, Chicago, 20 April 2009; interview with Jean Drapeau, Rimouski, 24 July 2008; interview with Michèle Cloutier Mainguy, Quebec City, 2 May 2008; interview with Philippe Casgrain, Montreal, 23 August 2008; L'Heureux-Dubé, "Une vie," see note 9 above at 32–37. The L'Heureux household account ledger shows a purchase price of $3,750, a down payment of $100, and mortgage payments of $100 generally paid four times a year. Interview with Philippe Michaud, Rimouski, 24 July 2008; Tanguay, "Une grande Québécoise," see note 24 above.
44 Interview with Claire L'Heureux-Dubé, Ottawa, 2 December 2007. Household ledgers show amounts of $1 to $5 paid every few months to the Sisters of Charity convent, as wages for the maids.
45 Rue Saint-Germain was one of three principal roads, named *le chemin du Roi* in 1853 and changed to Saint-Germain during one of the first sessions of the municipal council in 1869. It was among the first streets to have wooden sidewalks. Bourdages et al., *Rimouski depuis ses origines,* see note 28 above at 136.
46 The homes of the richest families – Casgrains, Carons, and Dubés (no relation to Claire's husband's family) – were slightly further west on another stretch of Saint-Germain, near the bridge that crossed the Rimouski River. Jules Brillant, another wealthy Rimouski resident, lived further away in a more isolated part of the city. Interview with Jean-Marie Joly, Ottawa, 21 March 2009.
47 Tanguay, "Une grande Québécoise," see note 24 above; L'Heureux-Dubé, "Une vie," see note 9 above at 37; Serge Bernier, *Canadian Military Heritage,* vol. 3, *1872–2000* (Montreal: Art Global, 2000) at 71–72.
48 Interview with Louise L'Heureux-Giliberti, Chicago, 20 April 2009.
49 Ibid.
50 Interview with Claire L'Heureux-Dubé, Ottawa, 7 October 2007.
51 Interview with Claire L'Heureux-Dubé, Ottawa, 30 October 2007.
52 Ibid.
53 Interview with Nicole L'Heureux, Clearwater, FL, 11–12 May 2009.
54 L'Heureux-Dubé, "Une vie," see note 9 above at 23; interview with Nicole L'Heureux, ibid.; Nicole L'Heureux Généalogie.
55 Interview with Louise L'Heureux-Giliberti, Chicago, 20 April 2009.
56 L'Heureux-Dubé, "Une vie," see note 9 above at 35.
57 Interview with Louise L'Heureux-Giliberti, Chicago, 20 April 2009; interview with Nicole L'Heureux, Clearwater, FL, 11–12 May 2009.
58 Interview with Nicole L'Heureux, ibid.
59 Interview with Jean Drapeau, Rimouski, 24 July 2008.
60 Interview with Louise L'Heureux-Giliberti, Chicago, 20 April 2009.
61 Ibid.
62 L'Heureux-Dubé, "Une vie," see note 9 above at 36; Tanguay, "Une grande Québécoise," see note 24 above.
63 Interview with Michèle Cloutier Mainguy, Quebec City, 2 May 2008.
64 Interview with Louise L'Heureux-Giliberti, Chicago, 20 April 2009.

65 Comtesse de Ségur, *Les petites filles modèles* (Paris: Hachette, republished 1991).
66 Comtesse de Ségur, *Les malheurs de Sophie* (Paris: Librairie Hachette, 1911).
67 Interview with Claire L'Heureux-Dubé, Ottawa, 30 October 2007.

CHAPTER 4: GROWING UP IN RIMOUSKI

1 Unless otherwise indicated, all information is drawn from interviews with Claire L'Heureux-Dubé in Quebec City, Ottawa, Rimouski, and Clearwater, FL, on 17 September, 30 October, 1 November, and 2 December 2007; 29–30 April, 1–2 May, and 23–25 July 2008; 5 and 7 March, 27–28 April, and 10–14 May 2009.
2 Interview with Michèle Cloutier Mainguy, Quebec City, 2 May 2008.
3 Interview with Nicole L'Heureux, Clearwater, FL, 11–12 May 2009; interview with Claire L'Heureux-Dubé, Ottawa, 30 October 2007.
4 Interviews with Claire L'Heureux-Dubé, see note 1 above; interview with Michèle Cloutier Mainguy, Quebec City, 2 May 2008; interview with Louise L'Heureux-Giliberti, Chicago, 20 April 2009.
5 Interview with Louise L'Heureux-Giliberti, ibid.
6 Claire L'Heureux-Dubé, "Une vie" (undated, incomplete, and unpublished autobiographical manuscript) at 36–37.
7 Interview with Michèle Cloutier Mainguy, Quebec City, 2 May 2008.
8 Caroline Tanguay, OSU, with Louise Dumais, "Une grande Québécoise: L'Honorable Claire L'Heureux-Dubé, Cour suprême 1987–2002" (undated, unpublished manuscript).
9 Interview with Louise L'Heureux-Giliberti, Chicago, 20 April 2009.
10 Interview with Michèle Cloutier Mainguy, Quebec City, 2 May 2008.
11 Interview with Jean-Marie Joly, Ottawa, 21 March 2009.
12 Interview with Louise L'Heureux-Giliberti, Chicago, 21 April 2009.
13 Interview with Louise L'Heureux-Giliberti, Chicago, 20 April 2009.
14 The club had a membership restricted to lawyers, engineers, and businessmen, with three exceptions: the court stenographer, the telegrapher, and the customs agent. Yves Tremblay, *Du notable et de l'homme d'affaires: l'élite économique de Rimouski, 1890–1960* (Rimouski: Corporation Rimouski, 1996) at 46–47.
15 Serge Bernier et al., *Military History of Quebec City, 1608–2008* (Montreal: Art Global, 2007), notes at 236: "English was the language of organization, administration, and training in Battery B in Québec City."
16 Interview with Louise L'Heureux-Giliberti, Chicago, 20 April 2009.
17 Interviews with Claire L'Heureux-Dubé, see note 1 above; interview with Nicole L'Heureux, Clearwater, FL, 11–12 May 2009; interview with Louise L'Heureux-Giliberti, ibid.; Tremblay, *Du notable et de l'homme d'affaires,* see note 14 above at 35, 52, 121.
18 Interview with Claire L'Heureux-Dubé, 30 October 2007.
19 Interview with André Legault, Ottawa, 10 December 2007.
20 L'Heureux-Dubé, "Une vie," see note 6 above at 38.
21 Interview with Nicole L'Heureux, Clearwater, FL, 11–12 May 2009.
22 The household account ledger (1935–47) shows numerous payments to physicians, and the $198.70 payment to the Sanatorium Prévost.
23 Interview with Claire L'Heureux-Dubé, Ottawa, 1 November 2007.
24 Interview with Louise L'Heureux-Giliberti, Chicago, 20 April 2009. Originally founded by the Dames de la Congrégation, the orphanage was taken over by the Sisters of Charity, who had arrived in Rimouski in 1871 to tend victims of typhoid. After several destructive fires, a new building constructed in 1909 served as both an orphanage and a hospice for women. S. Vachon, ed., *Centenaire de Rimouski – album-souvenir 1829–1929* (Rimouski: n.p., n.d.) at 44.

25 Interview with Jean-Marie Joly, Ottawa, 21 March 2009.
26 Interview with Claire L'Heureux-Dubé, Ottawa, 1 November 2007.
27 Correspondence from Louise L'Heureux-Giliberti, 18 December 2007.
28 L'Heureux-Dubé, "Une vie," see note 6 above at 38.
29 Ibid. at 38.
30 Ibid.
31 Interview with Louise L'Heureux-Giliberti, Chicago, 20 April 2009.
32 Interview with Nicole L'Heureux, Clearwater, FL, 11–12 May 2009.
33 Interview with Claire L'Heureux-Dubé, 30 October 2007.
34 Ibid.
35 Letter from Marguerite to Claire, from the Sanatorium Prévost in Montreal, 6 March 1936.
36 Interviews with Claire L'Heureux-Dubé, Ottawa, 5 March 2009; Clearwater, FL, 10–14 May 2009.
37 Interview with Michèle Cloutier Mainguy, Quebec City, 2 May 2008.
38 Interview with Claire L'Heureux-Dubé, Ottawa, 5 March 2009.
39 Tanguay, "Une grande Québécoise," see note 8 above.

CHAPTER 5: LIFE AS A *PENSIONNAIRE* WITH THE URSULINES

1 Caroline Tanguay, OSU, with Louise Dumais, "Une grande Québécoise: L'Honorable Claire L'Heureux-Dubé, Cour suprême 1987–2002" (undated, unpublished manuscript). Unless otherwise indicated, all other information is drawn from interviews with Claire L'Heureux-Dubé in Quebec City, Ottawa, Rimouski, and Clearwater, FL, on 17 September, 30 October, 1 November, and 2 December 2007; 29–30 April, 1–2 May, and 23–25 July 2008; 5 and 7 March, 27–28 April, and 10–14 May 2009; interview with Lisette Gammon, Ottawa, 16 November 2007; interview with Louise L'Heureux-Giliberti, Chicago, 20 April 2009; interview with Michèle Cloutier Mainguy, Quebec City, 2 May 2008; interview with Thérèse Dionne Lecomte, Rimouski, 24 July 2008.
2 Tanguay, ibid.: "*un besoin d'un certain encadrement*" ("a need for some framing").
3 Constructed in 1906 and substantially expanded in 1917, the convent hired labourers desperate for work during the Depression to add a fireproof wing in 1934. It was sold to the Université du Québec à Rimouski in 1968. Ibid.; Les Ursulines, *À Rimouski, il était un monastère* (Rimouski: Ursulines de Rimouski, 1995) at 32, 99–100, 125–26, 135, 142–43, 150, 481; Jeannot Bourdages et al., *Rimouski depuis ses origines* (Rimouski: Société d'histoire du Bas-Saint-Laurent, Société de généalogie et d'archives de Rimouski, 2006) at 194; S. Vachon, ed., *Centenaire de Rimouski – album-souvenir, 1829–1929* (Rimouski: n.p., n.d.) at 46.
4 Nicole Thivierge, "Les femmes dans l'histoire de Rimouski: la face cachée du développement" (1996) 49:2 Revue d'histoire du Bas-Saint-Laurent 97 at 99.
5 Tanguay, "Une grande Québécoise," see note 1 above.
6 Micheline Dumont and Nadia Fahmy-Eid, *Les couventines: l'éducation des filles au Québec dans les congrégations religieuses enseignantes, 1840–1960* (Montréal: Boréal Express, 1986) at 54.
7 Tanguay, "Une grande Québécoise," see note 1 above; Dumont and Fahmy-Eid, ibid. at 61.
8 The teaching curriculum in the province of Quebec depended on the religion of the students. The Anglo-Protestant pupils completed primary courses (or elementary school) and secondary courses (or high school), and then had direct access to university. Within the French Catholic system, education had traditionally consisted of a *cours primaire-élémentaire* (four years), *modèle* (two years), and *académique* (two years). In 1923, the four-year elementary program was expanded to six years, the two-year *modèle* was renamed *cours primaire-complémentaire,* and the final component was increased to three years and renamed *cours primaire-supérieur.* If successful in completing this program, the student received a Diploma

of Matriculation (Versification). Claire entered the Ursuline convent with four years of elementary schooling already completed (two in public school in Quebec City, and two in public school in Rimouski). She obtained her diploma of matriculation in 1943. Dumont and Fahmy-Eid, ibid. at 37–38; Les Ursulines, *À Rimouski*, see note 3 above at 36, 41, 165–67.

9 Tanguay, "Une grande Québécoise," see note 1 above: *"Guimpes et coiffes amidonnées, d'un blanc éblouissant sur les robes noires, voiles noirs ou blancs, pas feutrés, chuchotements, cliquetis des grains du grand rosaire que les religieuses portent à la ceinture";* Les Ursulines, ibid. at 131–32.
10 Les Ursulines, ibid. at 116–17.
11 Dumont and Fahmy-Eid, *Les couventines,* see note 6 above at 203–4.
12 Interview with Claire L'Heureux-Dubé, Ottawa, 2 December 2007.
13 Dumont and Fahmy-Eid, *Les couventines,* see note 6 above at 17.
14 Les Ursulines, *À Rimouski,* see note 3 above at 38. Despite this, there was occasionally a whiff of scandal. Claire recalled that the girls from one family, who came from just outside Rimouski, were rumoured to be victims of paternal incest. Interview with Claire L'Heureux-Dubé, Ottawa, 5 March 2009.
15 Dumont and Fahmy-Eid, *Les couventines,* see note 6 above at 212–13.
16 Ibid. at 58–59, 222.
17 L'Heureux household expense ledgers showed mortgage payments for the family home as $100 paid four times a year.
18 Tanguay, "Une grande Québécoise," see note 1 above.
19 Interview with Nicole L'Heureux, Clearwater, FL, 11–12 May 2009; interview with Claire L'Heureux-Dubé, Quebec City, 29–30 April 2008.
20 Tanguay, "Une grande Québécoise," see note 1 above; Les Ursulines, *À Rimouski,* see note 3 above at 130; Dumont and Fahmy-Eid, *Les couventines,* see note 6 above at 15–16, 284.
21 Dumont and Fahmy-Eid, ibid. at 15, 284.
22 Interview with Claire L'Heureux-Dubé, Ottawa, 30 October 2007.
23 Les Ursulines, *À Rimouski,* see note 3 above at 32–34, 55–58, 78–79, 180, 195; interview with Claire L'Heureux-Dubé, Rimouski, 23–25 July 2008.
24 Interview with Lisette Gammon, Ottawa, 16 November 2007.
25 Dumont and Fahmy-Eid, *Les couventines,* see note 6 above at 61–62, 285.
26 Ibid. at 17.
27 Interview with Claire L'Heureux-Dubé, Rimouski, 23–25 July 2008.
28 Tanguay was a graduate of the convent who entered as a postulant in 1928; Les Ursulines, *À Rimouski,* see note 3 above at 121–22.
29 Tanguay, "Une grande Québécoise," see note 1 above.
30 Ibid.
31 "Mlle Claire L'Heureux" Certificat, 17 June 1938.
32 In her second year, Claire was first in a class of twenty-five students; her highest grades were in religious instruction, religious history, mathematics, English, geography, and *leçons de choses* (show and tell). In December 1940, she was second in a class of fourteen students. Monastère des Ursulines de L'Immaculée Conception de Rimouski, *Bulletin Mensuel,* Mademoiselle Claire L'Heureux, Cours élem, univ., 2e année, 22 December 1938; Collège des Ursulines de Rimouski, *Bulletin Mensuel,* Mademoiselle Claire L'Heureux, *Syntaxe latine,* 26 December 1940.
33 Interview with Louise L'Heureux-Giliberti, Chicago, 21 April 2009.
34 Interview with Louise L'Heureux-Giliberti, Chicago, 20 April 2009.
35 Interview with Yves Dubé, Ottawa, 18 September 2008.
36 Interview with Jean Drapeau, Rimouski, 24 July 2008.
37 Tanguay, "Une grande Québécoise," see note 1 above.

38　Interview with Claire L'Heureux-Dubé, Ottawa, 30 October 2007.
39　Interview with Louise L'Heureux-Giliberti, Chicago, 20 April 2009.
40　Interview with Yves Dubé, Ottawa, 18 September 2008.
41　Interview with Lisette Gammon, Ottawa, 16 November 2007.
42　Interview with Louise L'Heureux-Giliberti, Chicago, 20 April 2009.
43　Interview with Louise Dubé, Boston, 22 May 2012.
44　Interview with Claire L'Heureux-Dubé, Ottawa, 30 October 2007.
45　Interview with André Legault, Ottawa, 10 December 2007.
46　Serge Bernier et al., *Military History of Quebec City, 1608–2008* (Montreal: Art Global, 2007) at 264.
47　Jean R. Brillant, "Le Lt-Colonel Paul-H. L'Heureux, Un homme attachant," *En Garde* 1:2 (October 1983) at 22–23.
48　Les Ursulines, *À Rimouski*, see note 3 above at 173; interview with Jean-Marie Joly, Ottawa, 21 March 2009.
49　Marie-Ange Caron et al., *Mosaique rimouskoise: une histoire de Rimouski* (Rimouski: Comité des fêtes du cent cinquantième anniversaires de la paroisse Saint-Germain de Rimouski, 1979) at 377–80.
50　Tanguay, "Une grande Québécoise," see note 1 above; Brillant, "Le Lt-Colonel Paul-H. L'Heureux," see note 47 above at 23.
51　Brillant, ibid. at 22–23.
52　Interview with Claire L'Heureux-Dubé, Rimouski, 23–25 July 2008; email correspondence from Claire L'Heureux-Dubé, 21 August 2009; text from "Le lieutenant-colonel Paul H. L'Heureux," plaque presented to Claire L'Heureux-Dubé on the occasion of the "dîner régimentaire annuel des officiers du régiment Les Fusiliers du St-Laurent, Rimouski, 30 mars 1996."
53　Tanguay, "Une grande Québécoise," see note 1 above; Caron et al., *Mosaique rimouskoise*, see note 49 above at 382; Bourdages et al., *Rimouski depuis ses origines*, see note 3 above at 226; Les Ursulines, *À Rimouski*, see note 3 above at 193; interview with Thérèse Dionne Lecomte, Rimouski, 24 July 2009; interview with Jean-Marie Joly, Ottawa, 21 March 2009; interview with Jean Drapeau, Rimouski, 24 July 2008.
54　Interview with Claire L'Heureux-Dubé, Ottawa, 30 October 2007.
55　Interview with Claire L'Heureux-Dubé, Clearwater, FL, 10–14 May 2009.
56　By 1938, eleven classical women's colleges had been set up across the province, although the programs were far from uniform and few students were enrolled. It was not until 1951 that the female classical colleges adopted the same program of studies as the male seminaries. Les Ursulines, *À Rimouski*, see note 3 above at 121, 142, 170, 182–85; Caron et al., *Mosaique rimouskoise*, see note 49 above at 211; Clio Collective, *Quebec Women: A History*, trans. Roger Gannon and Rosalind Gill (Toronto: Women's Press, 1987) at 244–47; Dumont and Fahmy-Eid, *Les couventines*, see note 6 above at 106, 110.
57　The household account book kept by Claire's parents recorded payments to Bellevue of $18.19 in October 1941, $43.70 (for Claire and Louise) in November 1941, $45.47 in December 1941, $40.50 in January 1942, $63.56 in February 1942, $60.00 in March 1942, $68.20 in April 1942, $60.50 in May 1942, and $68.48 in June 1942. The sums often included additional payments of $4 for "extra milk."
58　Les Ursulines, *À Rimouski*, see note 3 above at 185–86.
59　Dumont and Fahmy-Eid, *Les couventines*, see note 6 above at 108–9.
60　Les Ursulines, *À Rimouski*, see note 3 above at 193, lists seven in Claire's year, because one of the eight left early.
61　Interview with Claire L'Heureux-Dubé, Ottawa, 30 October 2007.
62　Ibid.
63　Ibid.

64 Paul Émile Farley et Gustave Lamarche, *Histoire du Canada, Cours supérieur* (Montréal: Clercs de St-Viateur, 1935) at 299. The authors discussed the Indigenous peoples under the title "*Peuplades sauvages en Amérique*," noting at 8, "*Les Peaux-Rouges ... n'étaient que faiblement civilisés et les Esquimaux vivaient dans la barbarie complète*" ("Red-skins ... were barely civilized and Eskimos lived in complete barbarity"). The English version of the Durham Report described the French as having the "unreasoning tenacity of an uneducated and unprogressive people."
65 Interview with Claire L'Heureux-Dubé, Ottawa, 5 March 2009.
66 Tanguay, "Une grande Québécoise," see note 1 above.
67 Ibid.
68 Les Ursulines, *À Rimouski*, see note 3 above at 195.
69 Interview with Charles Gonthier, Ottawa, 14 September 2008.
70 Louise Dubé, Claire's daughter, commented: "I know she did phenomenally well at school and was exceptionally talented. Was she really a leader then, or were there other girls who had as much leadership? Was she charismatic then, or does that come as a result of the success you have in life? Do people ascribe it to you because you are successful? I don't know if she always had this charisma. My suspicion is yes, that this was inbred. At least that's the way they tell it now." Interview with Louise Dubé, Boston, 22 May 2012.

CHAPTER 6: COLLÈGE NOTRE-DAME-DE-BELLEVUE

1 Unless otherwise indicated, all information is drawn from interviews with Claire L'Heureux-Dubé in Quebec City, Ottawa, Rimouski, and Clearwater, FL, on 17 September, 30 October, 1 November, and 2 December 2007; 29–30 April, 1–2 May, and 23–25 July 2008; 5 and 7 March, 27–28 April, and 10–14 May 2009. The description of the Collège Notre-Dame-de-Bellevue is also derived from interviews with Gisèle Blondeau-Labrie, Quebec City, 1 May 2008; Jeanne D'Arc LeMay-Warren, Pointe-au-Pic, QC, 8 August 2009; Judith Gamache-Côté, Quebec City, 1 May 2008; Marcèle Dorion, Quebec City, 30 April 2008; Monique Perron, Quebec City, 2 May 2008; Nicole L'Heureux, Clearwater, FL, 11–12 May 2009; and Louise L'Heureux-Giliberti, Chicago, 20 April 2009.
2 Jean R. Brillant, "Le Lt-Colonel Paul-H. L'Heureux, Un homme attachant," *En Garde* 1:2 (October 1983) at 23.
3 Interview with Claire L'Heureux-Dubé, Ottawa, 30 October 2007.
4 The household account book kept by Claire's mother recorded payments to Bellevue of $65.00 in September 1943, $89.46 in October 1943, $73.50 in November 1943, $72.31 and $100.00 in December 1943, $75.36 in February 1944, $71.00 in March 1944, $56.75 in May 1944, $65.25 in June 1944, $40.00 in September 1944, $53.37 in October 1944, $59.00 in November 1944, $61.95 in December 1944, $58.00 in January 1945, $60.36 in February 1945, $58.00 in March 1945, $47.00 in April 1945, $45.00 in May 1945, $46.22 in June 1945, $83.74 in December 1945, $86.60 in February 1946, $77.00 in March 1946, and $73.97 in June 1946.
5 As quoted in Caroline Tanguay, OSU, with Louise Dumais, "Une grande Québécoise: L'Honorable Claire L'Heureux-Dubé, Cour suprême 1987–2002" (undated, unpublished manuscript).
6 Interview with Marcèle Dorion, Quebec City, 30 April 2008.
7 Cited in Josée Lebrun, *Les cours lettres-sciences 1916–1960* (Mémoire de maîtrise en histoire, Université de Sherbrooke, 1985) at 63–64, as quoted in Micheline Dumont and Nadia Fahmy-Eid, *Les couventines: l'éducation des filles au Québec dans les congrégations religieuses enseignantes, 1840–1960* (Montréal: Boréal Express, 1986) at 23.
8 Interview with Jeanne D'Arc LeMay-Warren, Pointe-au-Pic, QC, 8 August 2009.
9 Dumont and Fahmy-Eid, *Les couventines*, see note 7 above at 143.

10 In 1924, there was one college with 36 students. In 1934, there were five colleges with 100 students. By 1944, there were twelve colleges with 295 students. Ibid. at 198–211, 223–24.
11 Interview with Jeanne D'Arc LeMay-Warren, Pointe-au-Pic, QC, 8 August 2009.
12 Ibid.
13 Dumont and Fahmy-Eid, *Les couventines,* see note 7 above at 287, 290.
14 Interview with Gisèle Blondeau-Labrie, Quebec City, 1 May 2008; interview with Jeanne D'Arc LeMay-Warren, Pointe-au-Pic, QC, 8 August 2009; interview with Louise L'Heureux-Giliberti, Chicago, 20 April 2009.
15 Interview with Louise L'Heureux-Giliberti, ibid.
16 Claire L'Heureux-Dubé, "Une vie" (undated, incomplete, and unpublished autobiographical manuscript) at 20.
17 Interview with Louise L'Heureux-Giliberti, Chicago, 20 April 2009.
18 Named Gabrielle Massicotte at birth, she was from Trois-Rivières. Massicotte eventually became the director general of the Congregation of Notre Dame. Interview with Claire L'Heureux-Dubé, Quebec City, 29–30 April 2008; interview with Jeanne D'Arc LeMay-Warren, Pointe-au-Pic, QC, 8 August 2009.
19 Interview with Gisèle Blondeau-Labrie, Quebec City, 1 May 2008. When the two women renewed their friendship a decade later, Gisèle discovered that Claire had kept all of her letters.
20 Interview with Jeanne D'Arc LeMay-Warren, Pointe-au-Pic, QC, 8 August 2009.
21 Interview with Gisèle Blondeau-Labrie, Quebec City, 1 May 2008.
22 Interview with Marcèle Dorion, Quebec City, 30 April 2008.
23 Lili (Éliane) Depeyre, Marcèle Dorion, and Thérèse Martel became doctors.
24 Marthe Godbout was the daughter of Quebec premier Adélard Godbout, the leader of the Liberal party who bowed to the feminist lobby led by Thérèse Casgrain and passed a women's provincial suffrage bill in 1940. See Thérèse F. Casgrain, *A Woman in a Man's World* (Toronto: McClelland and Stewart, 1972) at 94. Marthe moved back to her father's farm after he lost the election to Duplessis, and later worked at a penitentiary in Cowansville.
25 Gisèle Blouin studied agriculture at Laval, where she met and married a linguistics professor, Denis Gendron.
26 Cécile Dubé married after receiving her *baccalauréat,* and moved to the United States with her husband, Pascal Lévesque, a metallurgical engineer.
27 Frère S.-G. Donatien-Marie, *Évolution des structures de la J.E.C. canadienne de 1935 à 1961* (PhD thesis, Faculty of Education, University of Ottawa, 1962) at 11, 30, 38, 47–49, 61, 88, 113, 116.
28 Interview with Claire L'Heureux-Dubé, Ottawa, 5 March 2009.
29 Donatien-Marie, *Évolution des structures de la J.E.C. canadienne,* see note 27 above at 71–74, 267–69. The organization had two parallel branches, one masculine and one feminine, which came together for the 1945 national congress. Jeanne Mathilde Benoit Sauvé, who rose to prominence as an organizer within the JEC, later became the first woman from Quebec to serve as a federal cabinet minister, and was the first female governor-general. Shirley Wood, *Her Excellency Jeanne Sauvé* (Toronto: Macmillan, 1986). Gérard Pelletier, who served as the JEC national president from 1940 to 1944, was one of the founders of *Cité Libre* with Pierre Elliot Trudeau. He worked as a journalist and served in the Trudeau cabinet. Other presidents included Pierre Juneau, Guy Rocher, and Fernand Cadieux. Influential individuals involved also included Maurice Pinard, Claude St-Laurent, Guy Côté, Rock Demers, Marc and Claire Lalonde, Jean-Guy and Berthe Bellemare, Maurice Leroux, Camille Laurin, Yvon Gauthier, Maurice Sauvé, Gilles and Paule Ste-Marie, Simonne and Michel Chartrand, Guy Cormier, Renée and Jean-Paul Geoffroy, and Réal Michaud. Michael D. Behiels, *Prelude to Québec's Quiet Revolution* (Montreal: McGill-Queen's University Press, 1985); interview with Monique Bégin, Ottawa, 4 September 2011.

30 Interview with Claire L'Heureux-Dubé, Ottawa, 5 March 2009.
31 Interview with Jean Drapeau, Rimouski, 24 July 2008.
32 Interview with Gisèle Blondeau, Quebec City, 1 May 2008.
33 Interview with Louise L'Heureux-Giliberti, Chicago, 20 April 2009.
34 Interview with Claire L'Heureux-Dubé, Ottawa, 1 November 2007.
35 Ibid.
36 Georges-Alexandre Courchesne was born in 1880 in Saint-Thomas-de-Pierreville. Ordained a priest in 1904, he became a bishop of the diocese of Rimouski in 1928. He was named the first archbishop when the archdiocese of Rimouski was created in 1946. He died in 1950. André Chapeau et al., *Les évêques catholiques du Canada/Canadian R.C. Bishops 1658–1979* (Ottawa: Centre de recherche en histoire religieuse du Canada, Université Saint Paul, 1980) at 67; interview with Jean-Marie Joly, Ottawa, 21 March 2009; interview with Philippe Casgrain, Montreal, 23 August 2008; interview with Yves Dubé, Ottawa, 18 September 2008.
37 Interview with Philippe Casgrain, ibid.
38 Interview with Jean-Marie Joly, Ottawa, 21 March 2009.
39 Interview with Nicole L'Heureux, Clearwater, FL, 11–12 May 2009.
40 Interview with Claire L'Heureux-Dubé, Ottawa, 5 March 2009.
41 Ibid.
42 Ibid.
43 Interviews with Claire L'Heureux-Dubé, Ottawa, 1 November 2007; Quebec City, 27–28 April 2009.
44 Interview with Michèle Cloutier Mainguy, Quebec City, 2 May 2008.
45 Marie-Ange Caron et al., *Mosaique rimouskoise: une histoire de Rimouski* (Rimouski: Comité des fêtes du cent cinquantième anniversaires de la paroisse Saint-Germain de Rimouski, 1979) at 720–36; interview with Thérèse Dionne Lecomte, Rimouski, 24 July 2008.
46 Interview with Nicole L'Heureux, Clearwater, FL, 11–12 May 2009.
47 Interview with Lisette Gammon, Ottawa, 16 November 2007; interview with Michèle Cloutier Mainguy, Quebec City, 2 May 2008; interview with Thérèse Dionne Lecomte, ibid.; interview with Jean Drapeau, Rimouski, 24 July 2008.
48 Interview with Claire L'Heureux-Dubé, Ottawa, 5 March 2009.
49 Ibid.
50 The age restriction had been legislated in the wake of a Montreal cinema fire that killed a number of children. Interview with Jean-Marie Joly, Ottawa, 21 March 2009.
51 Interview with Philippe Casgrain, Montreal, 23 August 2008.
52 Interview with Michèle Cloutier Mainguy, Quebec City, 2 May 2008.
53 Interview with Thérèse Dionne Lecomte, Rimouski, 24 July 2008.
54 Interview with Jean Drapeau, Rimouski, 24 July 2008.
55 Interview with Philippe Michaud, Rimouski, 24 July 2008.
56 Interview with Monique Perron, Quebec City, 2 May 2008.
57 André Boissinot eventually became the pharmacist at Hôpital du Saint-Sacrement.
58 Interview with Jean Drapeau, Rimouski, 24 July 2008.
59 Brillant, "Le Lt-Colonel Paul-H. L'Heureux," see note 2 above at 23.
60 He also sent a book, *The Faerie Queene* by Edmund Spenser, which she could not read. Interview with Louise L'Heureux-Giliberti, Chicago, 20 April 2009; email correspondence from Louise L'Heureux-Giliberti, 22 August 2009.
61 Louise L'Heureux-Giliberti learned years later that her father had become involved with the wife of an English officer. Decades later, after her own husband died, this woman apparently travelled to Canada, hoping to marry Paul L'Heureux. Louise explained that she got short shrift: "He put her back on the ship." Interview with Louise L'Heureux-Giliberti, Chicago, 20 April 2009.

62 Brillant, "Le Lt-Colonel Paul-H. L'Heureux," see note 2 above at 23.
63 Interview with Louise L'Heureux-Giliberti, Chicago, 20 April 2009.
64 Interview with Nicole L'Heureux, Clearwater, FL, 11–12 May 2009.
65 Interview with Louise L'Heureux-Giliberti, Chicago, 20 April 2009.
66 Interview with Marcèle Dorion, Quebec City, 30 April 2008.
67 Interview with Jean Drapeau, Rimouski, 24 July 2008.
68 Interview with Louise L'Heureux-Giliberti, Chicago, 20 April 2009; email correspondence from Louise L'Heureux-Giliberti, 17 November 2007.
69 Interview with Claire L'Heureux-Dubé, Ottawa, 30 October 2007.
70 Interview with Louise L'Heureux-Giliberti, Chicago, 21 April 2009.
71 Tanguay, "Une grande Québécoise," see note 5 above.

CHAPTER 7: THE DECISION TO GO TO LAW SCHOOL

1 Constance Backhouse, *Petticoats and Prejudice: Women and Law in 19th-Century Canada* (Toronto: Women's Press, 1991) at chs. 10–11; Constance Backhouse, "To Open the Way for Others of My Sex: Clara Brett Martin's Career as Canada's First Woman Lawyer" (1985) 1 CJWL 1; "Woman's rights," *Canadian Illustrated News* (Montreal) (21 November 1874) at 323–24; "Female students-at-law," Toronto *Daily Mail* (6 April 1892); "Women as lawyers," Toronto *Daily Mail* (7 April 1892); Untitled (June 1896) 32 Can LJ 784.
2 Backhouse, *Petticoats and Prejudice*, ibid., ch. 11; Cameron Harvey, "Women in Law in Canada" (1970) 4 Man LJ 9 at 17–18; Cecilia Morgan, "An Embarrassingly and Severely Masculine Atmosphere: Women, Gender and the Legal Profession at Osgoode Hall, 1920s–1960s" (1996) 11:2 CJLS 19 at 21; Mary Jane Mossman, *The First Women Lawyers: A Comparative Study of Gender, Law and the Legal Professions* (Oxford: Hart Publishing, 2006) at 76, 87; Mary Kinnear, "That There Woman Lawyer: Women Lawyers in Manitoba 1915–1970" (1992) 5 CJWL 411.
3 *An Act Respecting the Bar*, SQ 1941, c. 56, s. 1.
4 Margaret Gillett, *We Walked Very Warily: A History of Women at McGill* (Montreal: Eden Press, 1981) at 303–14.
5 Born into a family of Lithuanian Jewish immigrants in Lancaster, Ontario, in 1871, and raised in Montreal, Jacobs graduated from McGill Law in 1893, took his master's in law at Laval in 1894, and began practice in Montreal in 1894. Bernard Figler, QC, *Sam Jacobs: Member of Parliament* (Gardenvale, QC: Harpell's Press Co-operative, 1970); Constance Backhouse, "Anti-Semitism and the Law in Québec City: The Plamondon Case, 1910–15" in Daniel W. Hamilton and Alfred L. Brophy, eds., *Transformations in American Legal History – Law, Ideology, and Methods; Essays in Honor of Morton J. Horwitz* (Cambridge, MA: Harvard Law School, 2010) at 303–25.
6 *Langstaff v. Bar of the Province of Québec* (1915), 47 CS 131 at 139–40, 145. Born of Scottish parents in Prescott, Ontario, in 1887, Langstaff had married at age sixteen, but separated from her husband and moved with her eight-year-old daughter to Montreal in 1906. There she found work as a secretary in Jacobs's law office. Gillett, *We Walked Very Warily*, see note 4 above at 303–14; Gilles Gallichan, *Les québécoises et le barreau: l'histoire d'une difficile conquête 1914–1941* (Sillery, QC: Septentrion, 1999) at 25–36; Fiona M. Kay, "Crossroads to Innovation and Diversity: The Careers of Women Lawyers in Quebec" (2002) 47 McGill LJ 699 at 706–8; Ian C. Pilarczyk, *A Noble Roster: One Hundred and Fifty Years of Law at McGill* (Montreal: McGill University Faculty of Law, 1999) at 58–59.
7 Montréal *Le Pays* (25 July 1914) 2: "*Un juge vient de dénoncer le danger des grâces féminines sur ceux qui pour être sur le banc des dieux ne sont pas moins de chair et d'os et sujets aux faiblesses des autres hommes. Les magistrats ne sont pas en pierre, paraît-il, et malgré l'apparence granitique de leur front rigide où toutes les lames des humaines émotions viennent se briser, ils*

ne sont pas insensibles aux chaudes effluves que versent deux prunelles lumineuses et à l'emprise d'un timbre de voix velouté, sorti de la gorge satinée comme une pêche, telle la chanson des heures, d'un gong harmonieux. Ils pourraient perdre la boule et prononcer la sentence que mimerait la séduisante avocate." ("A judge has just denounced the danger of feminine graces to those who, despite sitting on the bench of the gods, are no less flesh and bones and subject to the weaknesses of other men. Magistrates are not made of stone, it seems, and in spite of the granite appearance of their rigid brows, where all waves of human emotions come to break, they are not insensitive to the warm outpouring of two luminous eyes, or the influence of velvet tones, issuing from a peach-like satin throat, like the song of the hours from a harmonious gong. They could lose their bearings and pronounce the sentence mimicked by the seductive lawyer.")

8 Montréal *Le Pays* (20 February 1915) 2: "*Tel, qui ne craindrait pas de souiller une fillette de son ignoble convoitise, criera comme un paon à l'idée qu'une femme pourrait plaider une cause scabreuse, un régal pour les hommes mais une avocate, disent-ils, n'a pas grâce d'état pour l'entendre sans danger! ... Les causes grivoises, ce sont les avocats qui les font telles, avec leurs questions enlacées ainsi que les mailles d'un filet d'oiseleur, leurs insinuations malsaines, leurs sous-entendus perfides, leurs quidproquos libidineux*" ("He who would not hesitate to soil a young girl with his ignoble covetousness will cry like a peacock at the idea that a woman could plead a scabrous cause, a feast for men, whereas a woman lawyer, they say, has no grace of state to hear it safely! ... The scabrous cases are made such by the male lawyers with their questions entwined like the meshes of a fowler's net, their unhealthy insinuations, perfidious undertones, and libidinous double entendres"). Justice Saint-Pierre noted: "Let us for a moment picture to ourselves a woman appearing as defending or prosecuting counsel in a case of rapt [rape] and putting to the complainant the questions which must of all necessity be asked in order to make proof of the acts which are of the essence of the crime or which are equally necessary to meet and repeal the charge. No woman possessing the least sense of decency could possibly do so without throwing a blur upon her dignity and without bringing into utter contempt the honor and respect due to her sex." *Langstaff v. Bar of the Province of Québec*, see note 6 above at 139–40. For the next twenty-five years, Quebec women continued to obtain law degrees. More than twenty graduated between 1914 and 1941, the year of first admission to the bar. Some sought calls in neighbouring provinces, and then transferred back to work in Quebec law firms under the radar of the Barreau. Others found alternate careers in journalism and international women's organizations. Pilarczyk, *A Noble Roster*, see note 6 above at 60–65; Jean Hétu, *Les diplômés de la Faculté de droit de l'Université de Montréal depuis 125 ans* (Montréal: Éditions Thémis, 2003) at 3, 49, 51, 55, 63, 68, 69, 72–73, and "Corrections et ajouts" at 9.

9 King's Bench judges Horace Archambeault, Norman William Trenholme, Louis-Philippe Pelletier, and Henry George Carroll ruled against Langstaff, holding that under Quebec law, women had historically been excluded from the practice of law, and the court should not introduce a change that was "*si considérable et si extraordinaire*" without sanction from the legislature. Joseph Lavergne, in dissent, took the position that there was no express legislative exclusion, and that women should be admitted to all the liberal professions, as they had been in the United States, France, Scandinavia, and the rest of Canada. *Langstaff v. Barreau du Québec* (1916), 25 BR 11. The court ordered Langstaff to pay the Barreau over $500 in costs. Sam Jacobs's request that the bar forgo the collection of these costs because the case was in the public interest was rejected. Despite the setback, Langstaff continued to work in Jacobs's Montreal firm, in her words, doing "a little secretarial work, a little bookkeeping, and a little law." She took on the role of "alter ego" to Sam Jacobs, successfully managing the firm during his frequent absences on legal and political matters. She also published the *French-English, English-French Law Dictionary* (Montréal: Wilson et Lafleur, 1937). Langstaff did not seek admission after 1941 because she had not obtained

an undergraduate degree, which was by then a prerequisite. As noted in Harvey, "Women in Law in Canada," see note 2 above at 20, many prominent members of the Quebec bar did not, at the time, possess such a degree themselves. Langstaff died in 1975. J. Michel Doyon, *Les avocats et le barreau, une histoire* (Québec: Barreau du Québec, 2009) at 111–13, 122; Gillett, *We Walked Very Warily*, see note 4 above at 306; Mossman, *First Women Lawyers*, see note 2 above at 86, 104–5, 110. In 2006, Montreal *bâtonnier* Me Julie Latour presented Langstaff with a posthumous honorary admission to the bar. "Admission d'Annie MacDonald Langstaff au barreau," *Faculté de Droit* (McGill Faculty of Law) (Spring-Summer 2007) at 18; Julie Latour, "Remise de la médaille à feu Annie MacDonald Langstaff par le bâtonnier de Montréal, Me Julie Latour à l'occasion de la journée du barreau, le 7 septembre 2006" (unpublished speech).

10 "Le féminisme au barreau," Québec *L'Action Catholique* (28 November 1916) 1.

11 "Mme Langstaff est un Catholique Romaine," Montréal *Le Pays* (17 January 1917) 4; Gallichan, *Les québécoises et le barreau*, see note 6 above at 37–57.

12 "Les femmes n'entreront pas au barreau," Québec *Le Soleil* (14 December 1916) 1.

13 Six bills were defeated in 1920, 1927, 1928, 1929, 1930, and 1931. "No vote taken on admitting women to bar," *Montreal Gazette* (19 February 1930) 1, 5; Gallichan, *Les québécoises et le barreau*, see note 6 above at 61–97. Harvey, "Women in Law in Canada," see note 2 above at 19, notes that the League for Women's Rights, under the dynamic leadership of Thérèse Casgrain, lobbied for the change.

14 Père Léon, "Femme avocat," Québec *Bulletin paroissial de Limoilou* (April 1925), cited in Gallichan, *Les québécoises et le barreau*, ibid. at 69.

15 Gérard Lacourcière, "La femme doit-elle être admise au barreau," Université de Laval *Le Béret* 2:14 (8 February 1929) 6.

16 Joseph Noonan, "La femme avocate," Université de Montréal *Le Quartier Latin* 12:18 (2 February 1930) 5.

17 SQ 1941, c. 56; Gallichan, *Les québécoises et le barreau*, see note 6 above at 99–113. The Order of Notaries held out until 1956, and it was not until 1958 that Louise Dumoulin, the twenty-four-year-old daughter of Exchequer Court Judge Jacques Dumoulin, was sworn in as the first female notary in the Quebec Superior Court. "Quebec's first woman notary," *Montreal Gazette* (13 June 1958) 10.

18 Gallichan, *Les québécoises et le barreau*, see note 6 above at 101–2, 115–16. Monk (McGill BCL 1923) had been admitted to the Nova Scotia bar in 1934, became a Queen's Counsel in 1955, and practised in Montreal until 1979. Suzanne Raymond (later Suzanne Raymond-Filion) graduated from the University of Montreal in 1939. She worked for the Wartime Prices and Trade Board during the war, and then retired to raise her children. In the 1960s, she returned to university to study theology. Hétu, *Les diplômés*, see note 8 above at 63; Louise Mailhot, *Les premières! L'histoire de l'accès des femmes à la pratique du droit et à la magistrature* (Cowansville, QC: Éditions Yvon Blais, 2013) at 45–46. Marcelle Hémond was the first woman to plead before Le tribunal correctionnel in Montreal in 1943. She married lawyer Roger Lacoste in 1944, and raised her children while practising with the firm of Lacoste et Lacoste. She served as secretary and then president of the council of the Hôpital Sainte-Justine from 1966 to 1980 (ibid. at 49). Constance Garner Short (McGill BCL 1936) practised at the elite Montreal firm of Campbell, Meredith and became the first woman to plead before the Quebec Court of Appeal in 1947; Declan Brendan Hamill, "The Campbell, Meredith Firm of Montreal: A Case-Study of the Role of Canadian Business Lawyers, 1895–1913" in Carol Wilton, ed., *Inside the Law: Canadian Law Firms in Historical Perspective* (Toronto: University of Toronto Press, 1996) at 129.

19 Gillett, *We Walked Very Warily*, see note 4 above at 311–12.

20 Alison Prentice et al., *Canadian Women: A History* (Toronto: Harcourt Brace Jovanovich, 1988) at 303–11; Clio Collective, *Quebec Women: A History*, trans. Roger Gannon and Rosalind Gill (Toronto: Women's Press, 1987) at 293.

21 Quoted in Hélène Dumont, ed., *Femmes et droit: 50 ans de vie commune ... et tout un avenir* (Montréal: Éditions Thémis, 1991) at 313.
22 Interview with Thérèse Dionne Lecomte, Rimouski, 24 July 2008.
23 Interview with Michèle Cloutier Mainguy, Quebec City, 2 May 2008. Micheline Dumont and Nadia Fahmy-Eid, *Les couventines: l'éducation des filles au Québec dans les congrégations religieuses enseignantes 1840–1960* (Montréal: Boréal Express), note at 198–211, 223–24 that women were largely restricted to jobs as secretaries, nurses, librarians, social workers, or music teachers, or entrance to religious orders.
24 Elizabeth C. Monk, Suzanne Raymond-Filion, Marcelle Hémond, Constance Garner Short, Françoise Lefebvre Houde, M. Pauline-D. Cazelais, Ruth L. Hill, Marie-Paule Laurin, Mignonne Legault, Suzanne Barrière, Jeanne D'Arc Lemay. Gallichan, *Les québécoises et le barreau*, see note 6 above at 116, lists names up to July 1946.
25 The 1941 census recorded 129 women lawyers out of a total of 7,920 members of the profession; Canada Department of Labour, *Occupational Trends in Canada 1931–1961* (Ottawa: 1963) at 40 and 45. Statistics Canada reported higher numbers for female law students: 4.4 percent on Canadian-wide data for the year 1945: *Survey of Higher Education and Universities: Enrolment and Degrees*, cited in D.A.A. Stager with H.W. Arthurs, *Lawyers in Canada* (Toronto: University of Toronto Press, 1990), table 4.3 at 96–97. The Ontario numbers, more accurately tracked than other provinces so far, show that 3.7 percent of those called to the bar in 1945 were female: Constance Backhouse, "A Revolution in Numbers: Ontario Feminist Lawyers in the Formative Years, 1970s to 1990s" in Constance Backhouse and W. Wesley Pue, eds., *The Promise and Perils of Law: Lawyers in Canadian History* (Toronto: Irwin Law, 2009) 265 at 274, citing data prepared by Susan Lewthwaite, Research Coordinator, Corporate Records and Archives, Law Society of Upper Canada.
26 Interview with Marcèle Dorion, Quebec City, 2 May 2008.
27 Unless otherwise indicated, all information about Claire L'Heureux-Dubé's decision is drawn from interviews with her in Quebec City, Ottawa, Rimouski, and Clearwater, FL, on 30 October, 1 November, and 2 December 2007; 29–30 April 2008; 5 March, 10–14 May, and 21 September 2009; and 10 March 2010.
28 Jeanne D'Arc Lemay was born in 1922 in Saint-Agapit, QC, to Arthur Lemay, a grain merchant, and Corinne Beaudoin. She began her studies at Bellevue in 1933, and graduated with a BA in 1941. She credited her interest in law to her fascination with the political rallies she attended with her father, where so many lawyers gave superb public orations before excited crowds. She began legal studies at Laval along with her older sister, Thérèse. Thérèse and Édith, a third sister, graduated after Jeanne. Although Jeanne D'Arc Lemay is usually credited as Laval's first female graduate in law, one of her classmates, Magdeleine Therrien-Ferron from Nicolet, graduated one year earlier, in 1945. Because her marks were insufficient for an LL.L., Therrien-Ferron received only an LL.B., did not get called to the bar, and did not practise, which may be why her designation as "the first" has been overlooked: Sylvio Normand, *Le droit comme discipline universitaire: une histoire de la Faculté de droit de l'Université Laval* (Québec: Presses de l'Université Laval, 2005) at 248; correspondence from Sylvio Normand, 21 July 2010. Unspecified rumours of scandal also appear to have attached themselves to her; it is unclear whether they were due to her relations with male suitors or to her left-wing politics. Interview with Jeanne D'Arc Lemay-Warren, Pointe-au-Pic, QC, 8 August 2009.

Jeanne D'Arc Lemay inspired many women with her path-breaking choice. She was appointed directrice du service des écoles de protection de la jeunesse au ministère de bien-être social in 1948, a position that government rules forced her to leave when she married in 1953. After a number of years at home, she took up practice in Montreal. She was named judge of the Juvenile Court in 1970, and judge of the Superior Court in 1976. Interview with Jeanne D'Arc Lemay-Warren, ibid. Another path-breaker, Alice Desjardins, recalled being inspired to go into law after seeing a *La Presse* photograph of lawyer Maître

Jeanne D'Arc Lemay, in a large hat. "She just looked wonderful. I said I want to be like her. I think we influenced each other without really knowing each other." She later met Jeanne D'Arc and related this story, and Jeanne D'Arc said, "It must have been the hat." Desjardins added: "We both laughed. Especially because I never wear hats." In 1987, Desjardins became the first woman appointed to the Federal Court of Appeal. Interview with Alice Desjardins, Ottawa, 2 July 2009.

29 Dumont and Fahmy-Eid, *Les couventines,* see note 23 above at 273, point out that despite the official message that marriage and motherhood were the chief ends of educated women, celibate nuns were the ones who shaped and delivered the curriculum. Their very presence offered role models of professional women whose education had been put to use in earning a living.

30 Interview with Claire L'Heureux-Dubé, Ottawa, 30 October 2007.

31 Interview with Claire L'Heureux-Dubé, Ottawa, 2 December 2007. By contrast, others who chose law in this era credited growing up as the *only* girl in a family of boys. Mary Anne Richey, one of the early women lawyers and judges in Arizona, who entered law school at the University of Arizona the same year as Claire began at Laval in 1948, credited her "rough and tumble" childhood with two brothers with convincing her that she could succeed in a "man's world." Barbara Ann Atwood, *A Courtroom of Her Own: The Life and Work of Judge Mary Anne Richey* (Durham, NC: Carolina Academic Press, 1998) at 76.

32 Interview with Claire L'Heureux-Dubé, Ottawa, 30 October 2007.

33 Ibid.

34 Constance Backhouse, "A Revolution in Numbers: Feminist Lawyers in Canada" (unpublished manuscript).

35 Interview with Claire L'Heureux-Dubé, Ottawa, 30 October 2007.

36 Interview with Charles Gonthier, Ottawa, 14 September 2008.

37 Interview with Louise L'Heureux-Giliberti, Chicago, 20 April 2009.

38 Interview with Nicole L'Heureux, Clearwater, FL, 11 May 2009.

39 Interview with Marcèle Dorion, Quebec City, 30 April 2008. Paul L'Heureux "was not for her going through law"; interview with Gisèle Blondeau-Labrie, Quebec City, 1 May 2008.

40 Louise, who hated science and disliked the nursing program, completed her training and took up a placement at a hospital in New Rochelle, New York, which her father arranged so that she could improve her English. There she met and married Dr. Joseph J. Giliberti, an Italian-American oncologist. Her husband practised medicine in Korea during the war, in Ware, Massachusetts, and finally in Rockford, Illinois, where Louise stayed home to raise their four children, Gina, Anne, John, and Michele. Louise subsequently completed a BA degree in sociology, a master's degree in the history of art from Rockford College, and a curatorship from the School of the Art Institute of Chicago. She worked as a curator in museums in Rockford and Chicago, and as a docent at the Art Institute of Chicago. Interview with Louise L'Heureux-Giliberti, Chicago, 20–21 April 2009; email correspondence between Louise and Claire, 17 November 2007.

41 Interview with Claire L'Heureux-Dubé, Ottawa, 30 October 2007.

42 Lemay-Warren also emphasized that although her father gave his consent to his daughters' decisions to enter law, it was her mother who provided the funds for the tuition. Interview with Jeanne D'Arc Lemay-Warren, Pointe-au-Pic, QC, 8 August 2009.

43 The first Latina judge on the US Supreme Court, Sonia Sotomayor, also cited a desire to challenge naysayers as one of the primary influences in her decision to study law. Sonia Sotomayor, *My Beloved World* (New York: Alfred A. Knopf, 2013).

44 Interview with Claire L'Heureux-Dubé, Ottawa, 30 October 2007.

45 Claire recalled that Judith Gamache, her classmate at Laval Law, "was the same – we never thought we could earn a living."

46 Pilarczyk, *A Noble Roster,* see note 6 above at 65.

47 Morgan, "An Embarrassingly and Severely Masculine Atmosphere," see note 2 above at 27.
48 Kinnear, "That There Woman Lawyer," see note 2 above at 415, 423.
49 Anna R. Hayes, *Without Precedent: The Life of Susie Marshall Sharp* (Chapel Hill: University of North Carolina Press, 2008) at 421.
50 Working in the post office building, Claire's father was one of the first to see posters advertising new positions, and he used his business and government connections to secure the two jobs.
51 Interview with Thérèse Dionne Lecomte, Rimouski, 24 July 2008.
52 A niece of Jules Brillant, Rimouski's most successful businessman, filled Claire's position. The niece had served with the marine forces, and thus was more desirable to the veterans' office.
53 Jeannot Bourdages et al., *Rimouski depuis ses origines* (Rimouski: Société d'histoire du Bas-Saint-Laurent, Société de généalogie et d'archives de Rimouski, 2006) at 268–70; Jean R. Brillant, "Le Lt-Colonel Paul-H. L'Heureux, Un homme attachant" *En Garde* 1:2 (October 1983) at 23.
54 Interview with Nicole L'Heureux, Clearwater, FL, 11–12 May 2009.
55 Interview with Claire L'Heureux-Dubé, Ottawa, 1 November 2007. Years later, André Legault, a court attendant at the Supreme Court of Canada, recounted: "Madam Justice L'Heureux-Dubé used to tell me the story of working as a secretary ... and she would say, 'I'm smarter than he is, and I'm gonna prove it' – that's the way she was." Interview with André Legault, Ottawa, 10 December 2007.
56 From his first posting as the manager of the Banque d'Hochelaga, Brillant founded the Compagnie de pouvoir du Bas-Saint-Laurent, became vice-president of the Banque provinciale du Canada, purchased the *Progrès du Golfe* newspaper and CJBR radio, ran the telephone company, and served as president of the chamber of commerce from 1926 to 1947. Bourdages et al., *Rimouski depuis ses origines,* see note 53 above at 218, 264; Yves Tremblay, *Du notable et de l'homme d'affaires: l'élite économique de Rimouski, 1890–1960* (Rimouski: Corporation Rimouski, 1996) at 52, 94–95; Marie-Ange Caron et al., *Mosaïque rimouskoise: une histoire de Rimouski* (Rimouski: Comité des fêtes du cent cinquantième anniversaires de la paroisse Saint-Germain de Rimouski, 1979) at 446–58.
57 Interview with Nicole L'Heureux, Clearwater, FL, 11–12 May 2009. Brillant also lent Claire $250 to pay for her first year of fees to the bar. She reminisced: "He loaned it to me, and then he insisted I pay it back! A multi-millionaire!" Interview with Claire L'Heureux-Dubé, Clearwater, FL, 10–14 May 2009.

CHAPTER 8: LAVAL LAW SCHOOL STUDENT BODY

1 Unless otherwise indicated, all information about the Laval law school is drawn from interviews with Claire L'Heureux-Dubé in Quebec City, Ottawa, Rimouski, and Clearwater, FL, on 30 October, 1 November, and 2 December 2007; 29–30 April 2008; 5 March, 10–14 May, and 21 September 2009; and 10 March 2010.
2 Interview with Claire L'Heureux-Dubé, Ottawa, 2 December 2007.
3 Ibid.
4 Sylvio Normand, *Le droit comme discipline universitaire: une histoire de la Faculté de droit de l'Université Laval* (Québec: Presses de l'Université Laval, 2005) at 130.
5 Interview with Claire L'Heureux-Dubé, Ottawa, 1 November 2007. Such experiences were not unusual. Dalhousie law dean Horace Read told Bertha Wilson in the mid-1950s that she should "just go home and take up crocheting" instead of law, and dissuaded her from accepting a scholarship to do graduate legal studies at Harvard because there would "never be women academics teaching in law schools." Ellen Anderson, *Judging Bertha Wilson:*

Law as Large as Life (Toronto: University of Toronto Press, 2001) at 38. A female student had a similar experience in the early 1960s with another dean of law in western Canada, G.P.R. Tallin: "He called me in for a little chat and explained that although he knew that I was quite clever enough to do all these things it really wasn't suitable. I was baffled. He said, very embarrassed, 'Well, some times of the month you just might not be up to it.'" Mary Kinnear, "That There Woman Lawyer: Women Lawyers in Manitoba 1915–1970" (1992) 5 CJWL 411 at 425.

6 Interview with Claire L'Heureux-Dubé, Ottawa, 2 December 2007.
7 The school of social sciences, opened by Père Georges-Henri Lévesque in 1938, emphasized a scientific rather than religious approach. It consequently developed a suspect reputation during the Duplessis era. Johanne Daigle, "Innover dans l'action: l'implication des femmes dans l'assistance sociale à Québec, 1850–1960" (Paper presented at the Canadian Committee on Women's History conference, Vancouver, 14 August 2010).
8 Interview with Claire L'Heureux-Dubé, Ottawa, 2 December 2007.
9 Letter from Guy Hudon, CR, Faculté de droit, to Claire L'Heureux, 21 June 1948.
10 Interview with William Tetley, Montreal, 23 April 2010. The same held true at the University of Montreal law school, where scholarships depended on family connections to the Duplessis regime; interview with Roger Chouinard, Quebec City, 11 May 2010.
11 Interview with Claire L'Heureux-Dubé, Ottawa, 1 November 2007.
12 Normand, *Le droit comme discipline universitaire,* see note 4 above at 147, observes that between 1947 and 1963, male Laval law graduates *"sont issus de familles appartenant aux classes favorisées."*
13 Interview with Annette April, Montreal, 4 June 2010. April recalled that in response to the snobbishness of the Quebec elite, students from outside the capital would occasionally socialize separately.
14 Interview with William Tetley, Montreal, 23 April 2010.
15 Interview with André Desgagné, Quebec City, 10 May 2010; interview with Roger Chouinard, Quebec City, 11 May 2010; interview with Calin Morin-Melihercsik, Quebec City, 11 May 2010.
16 Interview with Robert Auclair-Hallé, Quebec City, 7 August 2009; interview with Annette April, Montreal, 4 June 2010; interview with William Tetley, Montreal, 23 April 2010.
17 Interview with Robert Auclair-Hallé, ibid. Normand, *Le droit comme discipline universitaire,* see note 4 above at 144–46, remarks that the number of students in first-year law remained stable from 1946 to 1957, with a low of fifty-one and a high of sixty-eight.
18 Philippe Casgrain was born in Rimouski in 1927. His parents were Lydie Prince and lawyer Perreault Casgrain, who would serve as a Quebec cabinet minister from 1942 to 1944 and president of the Canadian Bar Association in 1966–67. Called to the bar in 1952, Philippe was one of the first Francophones to obtain a position, and then become a partner, with an English firm in Montreal: Magee, O'Donnell and Byers. He then became a founding partner of the bilingual firm Byers Casgrain, which merged with Fraser Milner Casgrain in 2000. *Bâtonnier* in Montreal in 1980–81, a member of the American College of Trial Lawyers, and a recipient of the Merit of the Bar in 2001–02, Casgrain was reputed to be a "real lion in court," an "ebullient personality," "dramatically dressed and impeccably groomed," with the "charisma and cool intellect of a matinee idol." He could quote Balzac with ease during legal argument, and always carried a handkerchief in his pocket "in case a woman needed to dry her tears." Kathryn Leger, "Saying goodbye to Philippe Casgrain," *Montreal Gazette* (5 March 2010) B2; Alan Hustak, "Quebec lawyer Philippe Casgrain had a natural charm," *Globe and Mail* (21 March 2010); interview with Robert Auclair-Hallé, Quebec City, 7 August 2009.
19 Born in 1928 in Quebec City, Jean Bienvenue practised law with Premier Jean Lesage and Jean Turgeon, and worked as a Crown prosecutor. Elected in Matane in 1966, he served

in Premier Robert Bourassa's cabinet until his defeat in 1976 and appointment to the Superior Court in 1977. Ignace-J. Deslauriers, *La Cour supérieure du Québec et ses juges: 1849–1er janvier 1980* (Québec: Bibliothèque nationale du Québec, 1980) at 70–71. During a murder trial in Trois-Rivières in 1995, Bienvenue incited public outcry when he stated, during the sentencing of the female accused: "It has always been said, and correctly so, that when women – whom I have always considered the noblest beings in creation and the noblest of the two sexes of the human race – it is said that when women ascend the scale of virtues, they reach higher than men, and I have always believed this. But it is also said, and this too I believe, that when they decide to degrade themselves, they sink to depths to which even the vilest man could not sink. Alas, you are indeed in the image of these women so famous in history. The Delilahs, the Salomes, Charlotte Tardif, Mata Hari, and how many others who have been a sad part of our history and have debased the profile of women. You are one of them, and you are the clearest living example of them that I have seen. At the Auschwitz-Birkenau concentration camp in Poland, which I once visited horror-stricken, even the Nazis did not eliminate millions of Jews in a painful or bloody manner. They died in the gas chambers, without suffering." A vocally unrepentant Bienvenue was the focus of a panel of inquiry for the Canadian Judicial Council, in which four of the five members recommended his removal from the bench. The majority of the CJC, twenty-one chief justices, agreed with the recommendation, while seven chief justices expressed disapproval of the conduct but did not support removal. Upon learning of this, Bienvenue resigned in 1996, before the minister of justice could take steps to bring the matter before Parliament. Report to the Canadian Judicial Council by the Inquiry Committee Appointed under Subsection 63(1) of the *Judges Act* to Conduct a Public Inquiry into the Conduct of Mr. Justice Jean Bienvenue of the Superior Court of Quebec in *R. v. T. Théberge* (1996); Ed Ratushny, "Speaking as Judges: How Far Can They Go?" (2000) 11 NJCL 293 at 345–60.

20 Julien Chouinard was born in 1929 in Quebec City to Joseph Julien Chouinard and Berthe Cloutier. He received his BA from Laval in 1948 and his LL.L. in 1951. A Rhodes scholar and athlete, he studied at Oxford before he began law practice in 1953 with Prévost, Gagné, Flynn, Chouinard et Jacques. He taught corporate law at Laval law school, and served as commanding officer of the Sixth Field Regiment, RCA, with the rank of lieutenant-colonel. In 1965 he became provincial deputy minister of justice, ran unsuccessfully as a Conservative in the federal election of 1968, and returned to the provincial government, where he served as secretary-general of the executive council from 1968 until his appointment to the Quebec Court of Appeal in 1974. He was appointed to the Supreme Court of Canada in 1979. James G. Snell and Frederick Vaughan, *The Supreme Court of Canada: History of the Institution* (Toronto: Osgoode Society for Canadian Legal History, 1985) at 235, 417; Donn Downey, "Julien Chouinard: Supreme Court judge was top civil servant for Quebec premier," *Globe and Mail* (9 February 1987).

21 Martial Asselin was born in La Malbaie in 1924 to Ferdinand Asselin, manager of the Bell/Charlevoix Telephone Company, and Eugénie Tremblay. He received his LL.L. from Laval in 1951, and was called to the bar the same year. He served as mayor of La Malbaie from 1957 to 1963 and Conservative MP for Charlevoix from 1958 to 1963, and was re-elected in 1965 and 1968. Appointed to the Senate in 1972, he became its deputy speaker in 1984 and served as lieutenant-governor of Quebec from 1990 to 1996. "Martial Asselin," in *Canadian Who's Who* (Toronto: University of Toronto Press, 2005); interview with Martial Asselin, Quebec City, 7 August 2008.

22 Roch Bolduc was born to Antoinette St-Pierre and Edgar Bolduc in Saint-Raphaël-de-Bellechasse in 1928. His father, who ran the general store, died in 1939, and his mother struggled to continue the business and raise nine children. Bolduc received his BA from Laval in 1948 and his LL.L. in 1951, and then studied public administration at the University of Chicago in 1952–53. Over the next thirty-three years, he served as a member of the Public

Service Commission, deputy minister, and associate secretary to the Treasury Board of Canada Secretariat. He was one of the leaders of the Quiet Revolution, introducing to the civil service competitive exams, recruitment, and promotion, a code of ethics, and arbitration for dismissal. He taught public administration at the University of Montreal, Laval, Concordia, and the Université du Québec à Montréal. He was appointed to the Senate in 1988. Interview with Roch Bolduc, Quebec City, 7 August 2009.

23 Born to Anna-Marie Ducharme and Major Arthur J. Lapointe (a Liberal MP from 1935 to 1945), Gabriel Lapointe completed the master of public administration program at Harvard, and became one of the first full-time Crown attorneys in Montreal in 1961. In 1966 he switched to criminal defence. He served as Montreal *bâtonnier* from 1986 to 1987. In 1999, he received the Mérite du Barreau de Montréal. The carnival queen kidnapping was one of a rash of such pranks across North America. Lapointe and three co-conspirators rented a black limousine, picked up the young woman, who was waiting for her escort (Martial Asselin), and delayed her arrival at the ceremony by several hours. Her father, the mayor, and the chief of police wanted to press charges, and the Laval authorities wanted to expel the students. Martial Asselin, president of the student association, successfully advocated against the prosecution. Interview with William Tetley, Montreal, 23 April 2010; interview with Annette April, Montreal, 4 June 2010; interview with Martial Asselin, Quebec City, 7 August 2008; Lise I. Beaudoin, "Me Gabriel Lapointe s'éteint à l'âge du 70 ans," *Le Journal* (Barreau du Québec) 31:16 (1 October 1999).

24 Interview with Roch Bolduc, Quebec City, 7 August 2009.

25 Born into a farming family in 1926 in Sacré-Cœur-de-Marie, Quebec, Robert Auclair-Hallé was raised by a great-uncle who was a miner in Thetford Mines. He studied social sciences at Laval before entering law, and worked with Jean Marchand during the Asbestos strike in 1949. He practised union labour law in Chicoutimi, then worked as assistant to the deputy minister of labour in Quebec. He served as a judge of the labour court from 1979 to 1996. Interview with Robert Auclair-Hallé, Quebec City, 7 August 2009; John Dickinson and Brian Young, *A Short History of Quebec*, 3rd ed. (Montreal: McGill-Queen's University Press, 2003) at 287–89.

26 Pierre Marseille, from Quebec City, practised corporate and commercial law there with the firm of St. Laurent, Gagné and Pratte, which was reconfigured to become the Létourneau firm. Interview with Roch Bolduc, Quebec City, 7 August 2009; interview with Robert Auclair-Hallé, Quebec City, 7 August 2009.

27 William Tetley, born in 1927, took his bachelor's degree and first-year law from McGill, then transferred in second year to study law at Laval. He recalled his immersion in the French Canadian culture with its *bonhomie* and *joie de vivre* to be a welcome change from his English Montreal upbringing. He was called to the bar in 1952 and practised for eighteen years in Montreal with Martineau, Walker, Allison, Beaulieu, Tetley and Phelan. He was elected a Liberal member of the National Assembly of Quebec in 1968, and served as a cabinet minister until 1976, when he became a law professor at McGill. An award-winning author, his scholarly expertise encompassed maritime law and Quebec politics. Interview with William Tetley, Montreal, 23 April 2010.

28 Jacques Alleyn's father was a notary, and there were other lawyers in the family. He joined his uncles' law firm upon graduation, and moved to head the legal department at CBC in 1962. Interview with Jacques Alleyn, Ottawa, 9 September 2009.

29 André Desgagné, whose family came from Saguenay-Lac-Saint-Jean, where his father was a land surveyor, studied philosophy at Laval prior to entering law. In 1959, he received a *diplôme d'études supérieures en droit public* in Paris, with a thesis on Quebec family law, and recalled that Claire, who was in Paris with her husband when André was defending his thesis, attended the public defence and then celebrated his success over dinner with him and Arthur Dubé. Desgagné began to teach at Laval Law in September 1959, where

he became an important force for change and a role model for new faculty. Normand, *Le droit comme discipline universitaire,* see note 4 above at 143, 167–70; interview with André Desgagné, Quebec City, 10 May 2010.

30 Besides Julien Chouinard and Claire L'Heureux-Dubé, who served on the Supreme Court of Canada, Jean Bienvenue, Paul Gervais, Ovide Laflamme, Georges Savoie, and André Trottier were appointed to the Superior Court. Gilles Carle and André Lévesque were appointed to the Provincial Court, and Robert Auclair-Hallé to the provincial labour court.

31 *Annuaire général de l'Université Laval pour l'année académique 1951–52* (Québec: Université Laval, 1951) at 261 shows two women, Claire and Judith, among fifty-one graduates. In the fall of 1948, no women enrolled in a class of fifty-five at the University of Montreal; email from Monique Laforest, Faculté de droit, Université de Montréal, 17 January 2008. There were three women in a class of forty at McGill law school; email from Mary House, University Archives, McGill University, 28 January 2008. One was Marie-Claire Kirkland; interview with Marie-Claire Kirkland Strover, Montreal, 23 August 2008.

32 Judith studied with the Sœurs de la Présentation à Saint-Hyacinthe near Montreal, and passed through a number of schools before she moved to the Ursuline convent in Rimouski shortly after Claire left. She continued her studies at Jésus-Marie Collège in Quebec City. Despite her impoverishment, she travelled at will on her father's railway passes. A claims agent with the Canadian National Railway, his travel privileges extended to his family even after his death. Judith helped fund her law studies by registering in social sciences courses, for which she obtained a bursary. The law faculty academic director, Guy Hudon, forbade law students to cross-register, but when Judith pointed out that without the bursary she would be forced to leave, he advised her to "be discreet about it." Interview with Judith Gamache-Côté, Quebec City, 1 May 2008.

33 Gilles Gallichan, *Les québécoises et le barreau: l'histoire d'une difficile conquête 1914–1941* (Sillery, QC: Septentrion, 1999) at 116; *Annuaires généraux de l'Université Laval pour l'année académique 1943–44, 1944–45, 1945–46, 1946–47, 1947–48, 1948–49* (Québec: Université Laval, 1943–48); interview with Nicole L'Heureux, Clearwater, FL, 11 May 2009; interview with Monique Perron, Quebec City, 2 May 2008.

34 Six female students at Osgoode Hall Law School formed the Osgoode Women's Legal Society between 1943 and 1946. They dined together monthly, picketed the law school over the exclusion of women from juror roles at the mock trial, and protested the rule that the student president must be male. Constance Backhouse, "Gretta Wong Grant: Canada's First Chinese-Canadian Female Lawyer" (1996) 15 Windsor YB Access Just 3 at 30–31.

35 Interview with André Desgagné, Quebec City, 10 May 2010.

36 Interview with Jacques Alleyn, Ottawa, 9 September 2009.

37 Constance Backhouse, *Petticoats and Prejudice: Women and Law in 19th-Century Canada* (Toronto: Women's Press, 1991) ch. 10.

38 Cecilia Morgan, "An Embarrassingly and Severely Masculine Atmosphere: Women, Gender and the Legal Profession at Osgoode Hall, 1920s–1960s" (1996) 11:2 CJLS 19 at 51; Cameron Harvey, "Women in Law in Canada" (1970) 4 Man LJ 9 at 13; Kinnear, "That There Woman Lawyer," see note 5 above at 414, 426; Ian C. Pilarczyk, *A Noble Roster: One Hundred and Fifty Years of Law at McGill* (Montreal: McGill University Faculty of Law, 1999) at 65–66; interview with Suzanne Labbé, Ottawa, 12 August 2009.

39 Jeanne D'Arc Lemay, "Le droit moderne et la femme," *Le Carabin* 2:4 (14 November 1942) 8, as quoted in Mélanie Brunet "Le droit n'ajoutera rien au charme d'une jeune fille," in Élise Detellier and Éric Mauras, eds., *Société et exclusion* (Montréal: Université de Montréal, Département d'histoire, 2004) at 143.

40 Interview with Claire L'Heureux-Dubé, Ottawa, 10 March 2010.

41 Interview with Calin Morin-Melihercsik, Quebec City, 11 May 2010. She recalled that the male student who rescued her was Jean Bienvenue.

42 Interview with Jacques Alleyn, Ottawa, 9 September 2009; interview with Georges-Henri Dubé, Rimouski, 24 July 2008; interview with André Desgagné, Quebec City, 10 May 2010; interview with Stuart Wright, Quebec City, 10 May 2010; interview with André Desmeules, Quebec City, 10 May 2010.
43 Interview with Robert Auclair-Hallé, Quebec City, 7 August 2009.
44 Interview with Roch Bolduc, Quebec City, 7 August 2009.
45 Ibid.
46 Ibid.

CHAPTER 9: LAVAL LAW SCHOOL FACULTY AND CURRICULUM

1 Unless otherwise indicated, all information is drawn from interviews with Claire L'Heureux-Dubé in Quebec City, Ottawa, Rimouski, and Clearwater, FL, on 30 October, 1 November, and 2 December 2007; 29–30 April 2008; 5 March, 10–14 May, and 21 September 2009; and 10 March 2010.
2 Interview with Robert Auclair-Hallé, Quebec City, 7 August 2009.
3 Ibid.; interview with Stuart Wright, Quebec City, 10 May 2010; interview with Calin Morin-Melihercsik, Quebec City, 11 May 2010.
4 Interview with André Desgagné, Quebec City, 10 May 2010.
5 Interview with Robert Auclair-Hallé, Quebec City, 7 August 2009.
6 Ibid.
7 Sylvio Normand, *Le droit comme discipline universitaire: une histoire de la Faculté de droit de l'Université Laval* (Québec: Presses de l'Université Laval, 2005) at 13–15, 88–94, 115–23, 131. In 1854, Queen Victoria chartered four faculties at the first Catholic Francophone university in North America: theology, arts, law, and medicine; Laval University, *L'Université Laval depuis ses origines...* (undated, unreferenced pamphlet). In 1925, the Quebec bar gave students a choice between a three-year articled clerkship or a three-year university law degree. After 1947, the three-year university law degree became compulsory. J.E.C. Brierley, "Quebec Legal Education since 1945: Cultural Paradoxes and Traditional Ambiguities" (1986–87) 10 Dal LJ 5 at 7–8, 34; Yves Pratte (Dean of Law, Laval University), "The Faculty of Law at Laval University" (1965–66) 16 UTLJ 175 at 175–76; Walter S. Johnson, "Legal Education in Quebec" (1905) 4 Can L Rev 491 at 491–99.
8 Normand, *Le droit comme discipline universitaire,* ibid. at 132–38; interview with Pierre-Gabriel Jobin, Montreal, 23 April 2010.
9 Normand, ibid. at 152, notes that in the curriculum of 1945, the teaching of civil law constituted 35.5 percent of the program; if the course on civil procedure was added, that figure became 47.5 percent.
10 Less emphasis was placed on the other courses: criminal law, municipal law, constitutional law, commercial and maritime law, industrial legislation, parish law, administrative law, corporate law, and tax and accounting. Ibid. at 153; Brierley, "Quebec Legal Education since 1945," see note 7 above at 19.
11 Normand, ibid. at 156, notes that faculty cited Pierre-Basile Mignault, *Le droit civil canadien basé sur les 'Répétitions écrites sur le code civil' de Frédéric Mourlon avec une revue de la jurisprudence de nos tribunaux* (Montréal: Théoret, Wilson et Lafleur, 1916) and brief commentaries in articles.
12 Interview with William Tetley, Montreal, 23 April 2010.
13 Normand, *Le droit comme discipline universitaire,* see note 7 at 156; Brierley, "Quebec Legal Education since 1945," see note 7 above at 22.
14 Interview with Monique Perron, Quebec City, 2 May 2008, referring to Maurice Gagné, son of the Honourable Jules-Arthur Gagné, who had taught at Laval from 1922 to 1952. Perron, who studied law from 1955 to 1958, added that the students already had all the

notes, since these had been handed down from previous generations of students, and that without the compulsory attendance that was taken daily, the classroom would have been empty.
15 Trudeau said that his law professors "nauseate[d]" him and so he just studied "as much as is barely necessary." John English, *The Life of Pierre Elliott Trudeau*, vol. 1, *Citizen of the World, 1919–1968* (Toronto: Knopf Canada, 2006) at 133.
16 Scott, who began law school in 1955, added: "We were by and large an undistinguished lot, and it was well understood that not much was expected of us ... On all sides it was expected that we would be the drones of the profession." Ian Scott with Neil McCormick, *To Make a Difference: A Memoir* (Toronto: Stoddart, 2001) at 25.
17 Laura Kalman, *Legal Realism at Yale, 1927–1960* (Chapel Hill: University of North Carolina Press, 1986); Morton Horwitz, *The Transformation of American Law, 1870–1960: The Crisis of Legal Orthodoxy* (New York: Oxford University Press, 1992).
18 Normand, *Le droit comme discipline universitaire*, see note 7 above at 156; Brierley, "Quebec Legal Education since 1945," see note 7 above at 22.
19 Interview with Robert Auclair-Hallé, Quebec City, 7 August 2009; interview with Martial Asselin, Quebec City, 7 August 2008; interview with Jacques Philippon, Quebec City, 28 April 2009; interview with Stuart Wright, Quebec City, 10 May 2010. A survey of the profession commissioned by the Quebec bar in 1966–67 found that 42 percent of the law students reported that they had worked during the school year, with a higher proportion among the younger cohorts; Cadres Professionnels Inc., *Les avocats du Québec: étude socio-économique* (Montréal: n.p., 1968) at 18.
20 André Desmeules, who began practice in Quebec City in 1956, explained that many corporate clients were English-speaking, that insurance reports had to be written in English, and that lawyers had to "speak English every day." Interview with André Desmeules, Quebec City, 10 May 2010. Raymond Lessard, who was called in 1962 and practised with the firm of Prévost, Gagné, Flynn, Chouinard et Jacques, estimated that his business law practice was approximately 90 percent in English, adding that "it was typical of the country at the time." Interview with Raymond Lessard, Île d'Orléans, 11 May 2010.
21 In 1946, Guy Hudon and Laurent Lesage were both hired as career professors. Hudon continued to practise before the courts and to work as legal counsel to the government and on legislative drafting. He served as the first full-time dean from 1956 to 1962. Normand, *Le droit comme discipline universitaire,* see note 7 above at 141–43, 253; William Tetley, QC, "Louis-Philippe Pigeon," online: McGill University <http://www.mcgill.ca/maritimelaw/tetley/pigeon>.
22 This description is drawn from interviews with Martial Asselin, Quebec City, 7 August 2008; Roch Bolduc, Quebec City, 7 August 2009; Robert Auclair-Hallé, Quebec City, 7 August 2009; Pierre-Gabriel Jobin, Montreal, 23 April 2010; and Raymond Lessard, Île d'Orléans, 11 May 2010.
23 Student agitation and the advent of the Quiet Revolution in the 1960s would finally force the faculty to modernize. Brierley, "Quebec Legal Education since 1945," see note 7 above at 36–37.
24 Marie-Louis Beaulieu was born in 1896 in Saint-Georges de Beauce to Alcide Beaulieu, lumber merchant, and Agnès Morency. He graduated from law at Laval in 1923, and was called to the bar the same year. He practised with Charles-Napoléon Dorion, Paul Fontaine, and René Chalout, obtained his doctorate in law in 1938, and began his academic career in the faculty of social sciences in 1939, where he defended the newly established school against attacks by Duplessis and the leaders at the faculty of law. Responding to a denunciation from Judge Ferdinand Roy, the dean of the law faculty, Beaulieu urged future lawyers and notaries to study social sciences. He transferred to part-time teaching in law in 1940, and to full-time teaching in 1952. Jean-Charles Bonenfant, "Me. Marie-Louis Beaulieu,

1896–1971" (1971) 9 (4th series) Proceedings of the Royal Society of Canada 37; Sylvio Normand, "Le Professeur Marie-Louis Beaulieu, 1896–1971," (1993) 2:3 Laval droit 7; Normand, *Le droit comme discipline universitaire,* see note 7 above at 104, 141–43, 156, 160–69; interview with Robert Auclair-Hallé, Quebec City, 7 August 2009; interview with André Desgagné, Quebec City, 10 May 2010.
25 Interview with Claire L'Heureux-Dubé, Ottawa, 1 November 2007.
26 Interview with Roch Bolduc, Quebec City, 7 August 2009; interview with Robert Auclair-Hallé, Quebec City, 7 August 2009.
27 Born in Saint-Georges d'Henryville, Quebec, in 1905 to Arthur Pigeon, a notary and lawyer, and Maria Demers, Louis-Philippe Pigeon graduated from Laval Law in 1928, and practised law with St-Laurent, Gagné, Devlin et Taschereau. In 1940, he became law clerk of the Quebec legislature before joining the firm of Germain, Lapointe, Thibaudeau et Roberge. He also worked as legal adviser to Premiers Godbout and Lesage, drafting legislation to reform women's rights, education, and labour. Peter McCormack, *Supreme at Last: The Evolution of the Supreme Court of Canada* (Toronto: Lorimer, 2000) at 60; Normand, *Le droit comme discipline universitaire,* see note 7 above at 96; Louis-Philippe Pigeon, "The Necessity of Law Reform" (1947) 25 Can Bar Rev 955; Tetley, "Louis-Philippe Pigeon," see note 21 above.
28 Tetley, ibid.
29 Tetley added that Lévesque insisted that law was no loss, that he was attracted only to journalism. "Listen, I'm not interested in passing those exams, because I'll never practice. All I want to do in life is to write, nothing else." Ibid.
30 Interview with Roch Bolduc, Quebec City, 7 August 2009; interview with Jacques Alleyn, Ottawa, 9 September 2009; interview with Robert Auclair-Hallé, Quebec City, 7 August 2009; interview with Jacques Philippon, Quebec City, 28 April 2009; interview with Stuart Wright, Quebec City, 10 May 2010.
31 Interview with Claire L'Heureux-Dubé, Ottawa, 1 November 2007.
32 Born in Montréal in 1911 to Louis-Philippe Turgeon and Esther Rolland, Jean Turgeon was called to the bar in 1933. He sojourned for a year in Toronto with the law firm of Blake, Lash, Anglin and Cassels, and then returned to Quebec to practise. He sat on the Court of Appeal from 1969 to 1985. "Jean Turgeon" in *Galerie des bâtonniers et bâtonnieres de 1960–1969,* online: Barreau de Québec <http://www.barreau.qc.ca/quebec>.
33 Interview with Claire L'Heureux-Dubé, Ottawa, 1 November 2007.
34 Jean-Charles Bonenfant was born in Saint-Jean-de-l'Île-d'Orléans in 1912, and obtained his bachelor and master of law degrees from Laval. Admitted to the bar in 1935, he worked as a journalist and then secretary to Premier Duplessis, leaving that post in 1939 to become the librarian at the Legislative Assembly of Quebec. In 1969, he became a full-time professor at Laval. Ernest Caparros, "Jean-Charles Bonenfant (1912–1977)" (1979) 20 C de D 7; Édith Deleury, ed., *Hommage à Jean-Charles Bonenfant* (Montréal: Les Cahiers de Droit, 1979) at 13–23.
35 Interview with Claire L'Heureux-Dubé, Ottawa, 2 December 2007.
36 At Osgoode in the mid-1930s, Margaret Campbell led six other women in her class in a walkout when a professor mentioned a joke that could not be told in their presence. At the University of Manitoba, Annette Elliott, who studied in the late 1970s, recalled that a few professors would ask her "to run an errand if a salacious joke was to be told." Mary Kinnear, "That There Woman Lawyer: Women Lawyers in Manitoba 1915–1970" (1992) 5 CJWL 411 at 426. Barbara Ann Atwood, *A Courtroom of Her Own: The Life and Work of Judge Mary Anne Richey* (Durham, NC: Carolina Academic Press, 1998) notes at 83 that Mary Anne Richey (who started law school in Arizona the same year as Claire at Laval) expressly declined to leave the room. Her professor then subjected her to a barrage of questions, including how much penetration was required for the commission of the crime of rape. "The slightest penetration," replied Richey, without faltering.

37 Interview with Judith Gamache Côté, Quebec City, 1 May 2008. Born in Quebec in 1898, to Cyrille Lacroix (a merchant) and Kate Neiland, Gérard Lacroix was admitted to the bar in 1923 and practised law with Elysée Thériault, Valmore Bienvenue, and Paul Lebel. He was appointed a Crown attorney in 1934. He taught law at Laval for twenty-seven years, and after his appointment to the Superior Court in 1951, he presided over a number of murder trials. His students described him as "funny" and "charming." "Gérard Lacroix" in *Galerie des bâtonniers et bâtonnières de 1950–1959*, online: Barreau de Québec <https://www.barreau.qc.ca/quebec>; Normand, *Le droit comme discipline universitaire*, see note 7 above at 137; interview with Roch Bolduc, Quebec City, 7 August 2009; interview with Robert Auclair-Hallé, Quebec City, 7 August 2009.

38 Interview with Monique Perron, Quebec City, 2 May 2008. Pierre-Gabriel Jobin recalled that in 1963, when he was in first-year law at Laval, Professor Lacroix announced with great embarrassment that this was the first year that sexual offences were to be taught in class to everyone together. For at least a few years previously, Lacroix had lectured separately to the male students and then taken the female students to a French restaurant on the Place de l'Hôtel de Ville, where he lectured to them in a private dining room over lunch. Interview with Pierre-Gabriel Jobin, Montreal, 23 April 2010.

39 Interview with Claire L'Heureux-Dubé, Quebec City, 25 July 2008.

40 Interview with Claire L'Heureux-Dubé, Ottawa, 1 November 2007. Margaret Campbell and a female classmate recalled that they were the targets of sexual advances from one "lecherous old goat" on the Osgoode Hall faculty in the mid-1930s. Kinnear, "That There Woman Lawyer," see note 36 above at 31; transcript of the Osgoode Society interview with Margaret Campbell by Christine Kates, May 1990, at 10.

41 Tetley, "Louis-Philippe Pigeon," see note 21 above; interview with Martial Asselin, Quebec City, 7 August 2008; interview with Robert Auclair-Hallé, Quebec City, 7 August 2009.

42 Interview with Claire L'Heureux-Dubé, Ottawa, 1 November 2007.

43 Gerald Hallowell, ed., *The Oxford Companion to Canadian History* (Don Mills, ON: Oxford University Press, 2004) at 50, 131, 146, 188, 195, 215, 272, 329, 418, 471, 522; John Dickinson and Brian Young, *A Short History of Quebec* (Montreal: McGill-Queen's University Press, 2003) at 290–99.

44 Interview with Martial Asselin, Quebec City, 7 August 2008; interview with Robert Auclair-Hallé, Quebec City, 7 August 2009.

45 The case did not become a reported judicial decision.

46 Interview with Claire L'Heureux-Dubé, Ottawa, 5 March 2009. *Picard v. Warren*, QR [1951] KB 554; [1952] 2 SCR 433; email correspondence from Claire L'Heureux-Dubé, 1 July 2010.

47 Interview with Claire L'Heureux-Dubé, Ottawa, 5 March 2009. Although Claire did not remember the name of the accused, it may have been the 1948 trial of twenty-three-year-old Ovila Vallières, convicted in Quebec City of killing a man with a piece of wood. The date of execution was fixed for 25 February 1949, but an Order-in-Council was never issued to carry it out. Library and Archives Canada, "Persons Sentenced to Death in Canada, 1867–1976: An Inventory of Case Files in the Fonds of the Department of Justice," RG 13, vol. 1673 (1, 2), file CC655, 1948–49.

48 Interview with Calin Morin-Melihercsik, Quebec City, 11 May 2010.

49 Interview with Judith Gamache Côté, Quebec City, 1 May 2008.

50 Interview with Claire L'Heureux-Dubé, Ottawa, 1 November 2007.

51 Interview with André Desgagné, Quebec City, 10 May 2010.

52 Interview with Roch Bolduc, Quebec City, 7 August 2009.

53 Ibid.

54 Louis Baudoin, "Examens de droit civil dans les universités de la province de Québec" (1947) 7 La Revue du Barreau de la Province de Québec 477 at 489–90.

55 Interview with Robert Auclair-Hallé, Quebec City, 7 August 2009.

56 Interview with Roch Bolduc, Quebec City, 7 August 2009; interview with Martial Asselin, Quebec City, 7 August 2008; interview with Jacques Alleyn, Ottawa, 9 September 2009.
57 Interview with Martial Asselin, ibid.
58 Ibid.; interview with Jacques Alleyn, Ottawa, 9 September 2009; interview with Roch Bolduc, Quebec City, 7 August 2009; interview with Robert Auclair-Hallé, Quebec City, 7 August 2009.
59 Claire's Laval transcript shows:

1ᵉ année, pour l'examen final 1948–49 (1st year, for the 1948–49 final examination). Total grades: 153.05 out of 185.

Droit romain (Roman Law) 25.5/30; Droit municipal (Municipal Law) 23.4/30; Droit paroissial (Parish Law) 7.5/10; Droit administrative (Administrative Law) 9.0/10; Droit criminel (Criminal Law) 14.2/15; Histoire et Introduction (History and Introduction) 13.5/20; Comptabilité (Accounting) 8.75/10; Droit civil (Civil Law) 51.2/60.

2ᵉ année, 1949–50. Droit civil (Civil Law) 54/60; Procédure civile théorique (Theoretical Civil Procedure) 36.5/40; Droit constitutionnel (Constitutional Law) 12.4/20; Législation fiscale (Tax Legislation) 8.5/10; Droit des corporations (Corporate Law) 7.9/10; Droit criminel (Criminal Law) 14/15.

3ᵉ année, 1950–51. Droit civil (Civil Law) 105.3/120; Procédure civile théorique (Theoretical Civil Procedure) 03.5/110; Droit administratif (Administrative Law) 6.5/10; Droit municipal et scolaire (Municipal and School Law) 14.5/20; Droit paroissial (Parish Law) 8.5/10; Droit criminel (Criminal Law) 48.4/60; Droit constitutionnel (Constitutional Law) 14.2/20; Législation fiscale (Tax Legislation) 14.9/20; Droit des corporations (Corporate Law) 19.1/30; Droit commercial et maritime (Commercial and Maritime Law) 79/100; Droit aérien (Aviation Law) 20/20; Législation ouvrière (Labour Legislation) 35/40; Droit international (International Law) 14/20.

Licence en droit *cum laude* Degree in Law *cum laude*).

Ignace-J. Deslauriers, *La Cour supérieure du Québec et ses juges: 1849–1ᵉʳ janvier 1980* (Quebec: Bibliothèque nationale du Québec, 1980), noted at 144 that upon graduation *cum laude*, Claire received the "*Prix spéciaux droit civil et droit ouvrier en 1951.*"

60 Interview with Claire L'Heureux-Dubé, Ottawa, 1 November 2007.
61 The university law faculties operated this additional program until 1968, when the Quebec bar assumed responsibility for the fourth-year practical component: an obligatory period of articling *(stage)*, a series of practical courses run by the bar in Quebec City, Montreal, Ottawa, and later in Sherbrooke, and a set of professional examinations. J.E.C. Brierley, "Historical Aspects of Law Teaching in Quebec" in Roy J. Matas and Deborah J. McCawley, eds., *Legal Education in Canada: Reports and Background Papers of a National Conference on Legal Education Held in Winnipeg, Manitoba* (Montreal: Federation of Law Societies of Canada, 1987) at 148; Brierley, "Quebec Legal Education since 1945," see note 7 above at 29–30, 36.
62 Normand, *Le droit comme discipline universitaire,* see note 7 above at 106; interview with Jacques Alleyn, Ottawa, 9 September 2009.
63 Interview with Roch Bolduc, Quebec City, 7 August 2009. André Desgagné added that Chouinard's connections to powerful elites aided his success in the Rhodes Scholarship competition; interview with André Desgagné, Quebec City, 10 May 2010.
64 Interview with Roch Bolduc, ibid.; interview with Roger Chouinard, Quebec City, 11 May 2010.
65 Interview with Jacques Alleyn, Ottawa, 9 September 2009.

66 Interview with Claire L'Heureux-Dubé, Ottawa, 1 November 2007.
67 The twenty-six were as follows: in January 1942, Elizabeth C. Monk and Suzanne Raymond-Filion; in July 1942, Marcelle Hémond and Constance Garner Short; in June 1944, Françoise Lefebvre Houde; in July 1945, M. Pauline-D. Cazelais, Ruth L. Hill, Marie-Paule Laurin, and Mignonne Legault; in July 1946, Suzanne Barrière and Jeanne D'Arc Lemay; in July 1947, Lilian Balangero, Thérèse Cromp, Lucille Gauthier, and Françoise Perron; in July 1948, Nancy Rosina Gigot and Joan Catherine Gilchrist; in July 1949, Hélène Gélinas; in January 1950, Frieda Simon; in July 1950, Camille Messara, Marguerite Choquette, and Thérèse Lemay-Lavoie; in January 1951, Louise Boucher, Léda Tremblay, Gertrude Wasserman, and Ginette Fournier. Gilles Gallichan, *Les québécoises et le barreau: l'histoire d'une difficile conquête 1914–1941* (Sillery, QC: Septentrion, 1999) at 116.
68 Born in 1927 to Charles-Aimé Kirkland (a Montreal physician and Liberal MP) and Rose Demers, Marie-Claire Kirkland graduated with a BA and BCL from McGill. She practised law in Montreal for nine years and married Claire's classmate Philippe Casgrain. The marriage produced three children and ended in divorce seventeen years later. After her second marriage, to lawyer Wyndham Strover, she took the name Kirkland-Strover. Elected to the Legislative Assembly of Quebec in 1961, she was the chief advocate of the legal reforms in 1964 guaranteeing the right of married women to administer their own property, and in 1970 delineating the pecuniary relationship between husband and wife. In 1973, she became the first female judge of the Provincial Court, now the Court of Québec. Interview with Marie-Claire Kirkland-Strover, Montreal, 23 August 2008; "Marie-Claire Kirkland" in *Canadian Who's Who* (Toronto: University of Toronto Press, 2005).
69 Réjane Laberge-Colas was born in Montreal in 1923 to Xiste Laberge (a dentist) and Isabelle Lefebvre. She worked for five years as in-house counsel for Aluminium Secretariat Ltd., then moved to practise law with Geoffrion et Prud'homme in 1957. Married to Émile Colas, a fellow lawyer, she had three children. In 1967, she became the founding president of the Fédération des femmes du Québec. In 1969, she was named to the Quebec Superior Court by federal justice minister John Turner. Obituary, *Globe and Mail* (24 August 2009) S11; Deslauriers, *La Cour supérieure*, see note 59 above at 77; Paul Jones and Donna Clark, *Who's Who of Canadian Women* (Toronto: Who's Who Publications, 1998) at 196; "Réjane Laberge-Colas" in *Biographies canadiennes-françaises, 1920–1970* (Montréal: Éditions biographiques canadiennes-françaises, 1970) at 368.

CHAPTER 10: LIFE OUTSIDE OF LAW SCHOOL

1 Unless otherwise indicated, all information is from interviews with Claire L'Heureux-Dubé in Quebec City, Ottawa, Rimouski, and Clearwater, FL, on 30 October, 1 November, and 2 December 2007; 29–30 April 2008; 5 March, 10–14 May, and 21 September 2009; and 10 March 2010.
2 The original price was $3,750 in 1935. Claire recalled that her father sold the house for $13,000, but her sister Nicole remembered that the price was lowered to $10,000 because the home was sold to a family friend, Dr. Simard. Interview with Nicole L'Heureux, Clearwater, FL, 11–12 May 2009.
3 Yves Michaud, "L'extension du territoire urbanisé de Rimouski (de 1860 à nos jours)" (1996) 49:2 Revue d'histoire du Bas-Saint-Laurent 36 at 39–40; Jeannot Bourdages et al., *Rimouski depuis ses origines* (Rimouski: Société d'histoire du Bas-Saint-Laurent; Société de généalogie et d'archives de Rimouski, 2006) at 227. The house was never rebuilt, and the location is now the site of a boulevard that runs along the river, a service station, and a Tim Hortons coffee outlet.
4 The new dwelling, which cost $13,000, had a living room, dining room, kitchen, three bedrooms (one on the main floor and two on the second floor), and an unfinished basement.

5 Interview with Claire L'Heureux-Dubé, Ottawa, 1 November 2007.
6 Ibid.
7 Ibid.
8 Examples from Laval included Thérèse Lemay-Lavoie, who had to delay her studies after marriage to a doctor, and Magdeleine Therrien-Ferron, who finished her degree but never practised after her marriage to a doctor. Others whose marriage and family interfered with a legal career included Calin Morin, Hélène Cannon, and Andrée Morin.
9 Interview with Annette April, Montreal, 4 June 2010.
10 Interview with Nicole L'Heureux, Clearwater, FL, 11–12 May 2009.
11 Interview with Annette April, Montreal, 4 June 2010.
12 Interview with Claire L'Heureux-Dubé, Ottawa, 1 November 2007.
13 Interview with Claire L'Heureux-Dubé, Quebec City, 27–28 April 2009.
14 Interview with Claire L'Heureux-Dubé, Ottawa, 1 November 2007; interview with Yves Dubé, Ottawa, 18 September 2008.
15 Interview with Yves Dubé, ibid.; interview with Georges-Henri Dubé, Rimouski, 24 July 2008.
16 Interview with Yves Dubé, ibid.
17 Ibid.; interview with Georges-Henri Dubé, Rimouski, 24 July 2008; interview with Jean Drapeau, Rimouski, 24 July 2008; interview with Jean-Marie Joly, Ottawa, 21 March 2009; interview with Roch Bolduc, Quebec City, 7 August 2009. Carnegie Institute of Technology became Carnegie Mellon University in 1967.
18 Interview with Claire L'Heureux-Dubé, Quebec City, 27–28 April 2009.
19 Interview with Georges-Henri Dubé, Rimouski, 24 July 2008; interview with Nicole L'Heureux, Clearwater, FL, 11–12 May 2009.
20 Interview with Louise L'Heureux-Giliberti, Chicago, 21 April 2009.
21 Ibid.
22 Lucie had found the regimen at Notre-Dame-de-Bellevue exhausting, since her illness made it difficult for her to get up for six o'clock Mass and to master the curriculum. The nuns did not realize that Lucie's incapacity related to her health, and were angry with their young pupil. Seeking the shelter of her earlier educational home, Lucie returned to the Ursuline monastery in Rimouski for her last years of schooling.
23 Interview with Claire L'Heureux-Dubé, Ottawa, 2 December 2007.
24 Interview with Louise L'Heureux-Giliberti, Chicago, 21 April 2009.
25 Interview with Nicole L'Heureux, Clearwater, FL, 11–12 May 2009.
26 Lucie's report cards from the Collège des Ursulines and Notre-Dame-de-Bellevue, retained by the family, show her consistently at the bottom of her class between 1939 and 1949.
27 Interview with Louise L'Heureux-Giliberti, Chicago, 21 April 2009.
28 Ibid.
29 Ibid.
30 Interview with Claire L'Heureux-Dubé, Ottawa, 30 October 2007.
31 Interview with Claire L'Heureux-Dubé, Quebec City, 27–28 April 2009.
32 Interview with Claire L'Heureux-Dubé, Ottawa, 30 October 2007.
33 Ibid.
34 Interview with Nicole L'Heureux, Clearwater, FL, 11–12 May 2009.
35 From 1964 onward, Nicole L'Heureux was listed as practising from her home, 1690 Parc Chesnaye, in the *Canadian Law List, 1964–1973* (Toronto: Canada Law Book). Nicole's recollection is that she was appointed at Laval in 1969, the same year as Édith Deleury, who had worked as a teaching assistant at Laval since 1967 while finishing her doctorate. The two of them became the second and third women appointed to teach in a Quebec law faculty, following the appointment of Alice Desjardins at the University of Montreal in 1961. Ann Robinson followed, hired as *directrice des études* at Laval's law school in

December 1969. The *Canadian Law List, 1970* (published in the spring of 1970) showed Édith Bonnet as a *professeur adjoint*. By 1971, Nicole L'Heureux, Édith Bonnet, and Gisèle Harper were listed together. Interview with Nicole L'Heureux, Clearwater, FL, 11–12 May 2009; Interview with Ann Robinson, Ottawa, 17 September 2008.

CHAPTER 11: ENTRY

1 *L'Événement Journal* (undated clipping). Unless otherwise indicated, all information is from interviews with Claire L'Heureux-Dubé in Quebec City, Ottawa, Rimouski, and Clearwater, FL, on 30 October, 1 November, and 2 December 2007; 29–30 April 2008; 5 March, 10–14 May, and 21 September 2009; 10 March and 30 June 2010.
2 The numbers were calculated from the entries in the *Canadian Law List, 1952* (Toronto: Cartwright and Sons, n.d.), at 679–83. Claire L'Heureux did not appear until 1953. Gender data from 1950–51 compiled by the Barreau du Québec showed women across the province as 1.11 percent of the practicing bar, twenty-one individuals in total: untitled, undated list showing members, women, and men from 1942 to 1999. The other female was Ginette Fournier, who had opened her own law office one year earlier (ibid. at 682).
3 André Desgagné, a classmate of L'Heureux from the Saguenay-Lac-Saint-Jean, emphasized the difficulty of setting up in practice in Quebec City: "Society was not wide open like today. And if you didn't know anyone in the profession, your chances were not very great. We began from zero, to set up a new law firm. The first objective was to pay the rent. It took three long years before we had some revenue." Interview with André Desgagné, Quebec City, 10 May 2010. Roger Chouinard, from Chicoutimi, described Quebec City at the time: "It's a closed milieu – a town of the family compact. They called it the *Grande Allée*, referring to the name of the street, and the people who lived in that class. It's a fable to a certain extent. But there was a certain protection between a certain number of families." Interview with Roger Chouinard, Quebec City, 11 May 2010. Roch Bolduc explained that classmates who came from small towns often returned home, their only option to practice as notaries in the hinterland. Interview with Roch Bolduc, Quebec City, 7 August 2009.
4 Interview with Calin Morin-Melihercsik, Quebec City, 11 May 2010.
5 Ibid.; interview with Annette April, Montreal, 4 June 2010.
6 Cameron Harvey, "Women in Law in Canada" (1970–71) 4 Man LJ 9 at 11, noted that based on responses of 267 Canadian female lawyers, it was "much more difficult for women lawyers as opposed to men to obtain a *first* job or position of employment."
7 Interview with William Tetley, Montreal, 23 April 2010.
8 Interview with Raymond Lessard, Île d'Orléans, QC, 11 May 2010.
9 Interview with Louis LeBel, Ottawa, 8 July 2010.
10 Letter dated 17 June 1952.
11 Laval professor Marie-Louis Beaulieu, who taught her labour law, had told her about the ILO. Although no written records of the rejection survive, L'Heureux noted: "I was disappointed. I don't remember exactly whether I had big hopes, but it was a try. Already then, I was a person of the world. Canada was too small. The province was too small. I wanted to go away somewhere. If they had hired me, I'm sure my life would have been quite different."
12 Interview with Jeanne D'Arc Lemay-Warren, Pointe-au-Pic, Quebec, 8 August 2009. Judith Gamache, L'Heureux's only female classmate, admitted that she was "too shy" to seek a job with a firm. Interview with Judith Gamache-Côté, Quebec City, 1 May 2008.
13 Interview with Calin Morin-Melihercsik, Quebec City, 11 May 2010.
14 Sam Jacobs hired Annie Langstaff, Quebec's first female law graduate. Jewish lawyer E.F. Singer was the only Toronto lawyer to offer an articling position to Ethelbert Lionel Cross,

one of Canada's early black lawyers, who was called to the bar in 1924: Constance Backhouse, *Colour-Coded: A Legal History of Racism in Canada, 1900–1950* (Toronto: University of Toronto Press, 1999) chs. 4 and 5. In 1953, Toronto Jewish lawyer Samuel Gotfried hired Lincoln Alexander, who later became Ontario's first black lieutenant-governor: Samuel Gotfried, Osgoode Society for Legal History interview, Toronto, 1990. In 1960, Toronto Jewish lawyer David Lewis hired black lawyer Julius Isaac, who later became chief justice of the Federal Court of Canada: Philip Girard, *Bora Laskin: Bringing Law to Life* (Toronto: University of Toronto Press, 2005) at 265.

15 Interview with Calin Morin-Melihercsik, Quebec City, 11 May 2010. The comments were echoed by a Rimouski childhood friend: "[She] went to a Jew's office, and he sent her to court to plead. The French Canadian lawyers didn't give her a chance. It was that Jew one who did [the] most for her." Interview with Thérèse Dionne Lecomte, Rimouski, 24 July 2008.

16 Interview with Claire L'Heureux-Dubé, Clearwater, FL, 10–14 May 2009.

17 For details, see Constance Backhouse, "'We Don't Hire a Woman Here': Claire L'Heureux-Dubé and the Career Prospects for Early Female Law Graduates from Laval University" (2014) 39:2 Queen's LJ 355. The first twenty women, in order of registration, were: Jeanne D'Arc Lemay (1942), Thérèse Lemay (1942), Magdeleine Therrien (1942), Lucille Gauthier (1944), Ghislaine Gagné (1945), Pauline Shink (1945), Marguerite Choquette (1947), Ginette Fournier (1947), Claire L'Heureux (1948), Judith Gamache (1948), Jacqueline Beaupré (1949), Édith Lemay (1949), Calin Morin (1949), Lucile Thibault (1949), Annette April (1950), Hélène Cannon (1950), Andrée Morin (1950), Madeleine Rousseau (1950), Gabrielle Vallée (1950), and Louise Galipeault (1951). Gilles Gallichan, *Les québécoises et le barreau: l'histoire d'une difficile conquête 1914–1941* (Sillery, QC: Septentrion, 1999) at 116; *Annuaires généraux de l'Université Laval pour l'année académique 1943–44, 1944–45, 1945–46, 1946–47, 1947–48, 1948–49, 1949–50, 1950–51* (Québec: Université Laval, 1943–50).

18 Micheline Dumont, *Le féminisme québécois raconté à Camille* (Montréal: Éditions du remue-ménage, 2008); Clio Collective, *Quebec Women: A History*, trans. Roger Gannon and Rosalind Gill (Toronto: Women's Press, 1987); Mona-Josée Gagnon, *Les femmes vues par le Québec des hommes: 30 ans d'histoire des idéologies 1940–1970* (Montréal: Éditions du jour, 1974).

19 Three more of the twenty went into private practice years later: Jeanne D'Arc Lemay-Warren, Jacqueline Beaupré, and Annette April. Lucille Gauthier may have practised in western Canada as well. For details, see Backhouse, "'We Don't Hire a Woman Here,'" see note 17 above.

20 Ginette Fournier was admitted to the bar in January 1951 and opened her office in late 1951 or early 1952. The *Canadian Law List, 1952*, see note 2 above, showed her practising in her own firm at 136 Blvd. Langelier, Quebec, from 1952 to 1955. The dates are confirmed by the *Tableau de l'ordre des avocats de la province de Québec, 1952–53; 1953–54; 1955–56* (Montréal: Barreau du Québec, 1952–55). Her brother, François Fournier, practised in the same building with Lavergne, Leahy et Fournier. The 1956 listing showed that she moved to 126 St.-Pierre St. The next year, she disappeared from the *Canadian Law List, 1957* (Toronto: Cartwright and Sons, n.d.). L'Heureux recalled her as "quiet, modest, and not aggressive," as someone who was very nice but may not have had what it took to succeed in practice. Calin Morin recalled her as "very short," "very intelligent," and "very funny." Her contemporaries recall that she went back to study social work at Laval, and worked in that field thereafter. The *Tableau de l'ordre des avocats de la province de Québec, 1970–71* (Montréal: Barreau du Québec, 1970) noted that she was with the Service de réadaptation sociale, Inc. Interview with Calin Morin-Melihercsik, Quebec City, 11 May 2010; *Annuaire général de l'Université Laval pour l'année académique 1948–49, 1949–50, 1950–51* (Québec: Université Laval, 1948–50); Gallichan, *Les québécoises et le barreau*, see note 17 above at 116; interview with Claire L'Heureux-Dubé, Ottawa, 30 June 2010.

21 For details, see Backhouse "'We Don't Hire a Woman Here,'" see note 17 above.

22 Ibid.
23 Interview with Claire L'Heureux-Dubé, Ottawa, 21 September 2009. The firm opened in 1955 at 72 Côte de la Montagne with three partners, Romeo Depeyre, Gaston Michaud, and Henry Beaudry, all of whom had been admitted to the bar in 1954. Although Vallée was also admitted to the bar that year, she did not join until 1956. Vallée was the first female lawyer elected *bâtonnière* in Quebec in 1973. She was appointed to the Quebec Superior Court in 1973, and became its associate chief justice in 1976, the first female associate chief justice of a federal superior court. She died in 1984. Ignace-J. Deslauriers, *La Cour supérieure du Québec et ses juges: 1849–1er janvier 1980* (Québec: Bibliothèque nationale du Québec, 1980) at 62; *Hommage à nos pionnières* (Québec: n.p., 1999); *Canadian Law List, 1956–1973* (Toronto: Cartwright and Sons and Canada Law Book, n.d.).
24 For details, see Backhouse, "'We Don't Hire a Woman Here,'" see note 17 above.
25 Interview with Claire L'Heureux-Dubé, Quebec City, 27–28 April 2009.
26 Ibid.
27 Interview with Sydney Robins, former treasurer of the Law Society of Upper Canada, Toronto, 29 June 2010. The conference, which led to the launching of the National Association of Women and the Law, was organized by two professors at the University of Windsor, Christine Davies and Gabriella Lang.

Chapter 12: Sam Bard

1 Unless otherwise indicated, information in this chapter is drawn from interviews with Claire L'Heureux-Dubé in Quebec City, Ottawa, Rimouski, and Clearwater, FL, on 30 October, 1 November, and 2 December 2007; 29–30 April 2008; 5 March, 10–14 May, and 21 September 2009; 10 March and 30 June 2010. The *Canadian Law List, 1952* (Toronto: Cartwright and Sons, n.d.) listed two Jewish lawyers in the city: Sydney Lazarovitz and Sam Schwarz Bard.
2 L'Heureux had been earning $75 a month as a secretary. Interview with Claire L'Heureux-Dubé, Ottawa, 1 November 2007. The salary increased over the years and was always paid according to Bard's quaint custom of inviting each member of the firm into his office at the end of the week to hand over a little brown envelope with the cash, adding, "I'm satisfied with your work." Interview with Roger Garneau, Quebec, 28 April 2009.
3 Interview with Claire L'Heureux-Dubé, Quebec City, 27–28 April 2009.
4 Interview with Jacques Philippon, Quebec City, 28 April 2009. Annette April, one of the Laval cohort of twenty who worked as in-house corporate counsel, estimated that she earned 30–35 percent less than male lawyers at Bell Canada; interview with Annette April, Montreal, 4 June 2010. But male earnings also varied greatly. Roger Chouinard, who was admitted to the bar in 1954, opened his own firm with another male lawyer in Chicoutimi one year later. He admitted that he "would have done better to work as a labourer at the Price Company," but he recalled that those who set out on their own in Montreal "worked for nothing, just to hold the place and the possibility of meeting clients." Interview with Roger Chouinard, Quebec City, 11 May 2010. Laval classmate Jacques Alleyn, who joined the firm of his uncle, Richard R. Alleyn, KC, earned $240 a month to start. Interview with Jacques Alleyn, Ottawa, 9 September 2009. Louis St. Laurent, at the opposite end of the legal hierarchy, earned $50,000 a year in 1941. Dale C. Thomson, *Louis St. Laurent: Canadian* (Toronto: Macmillan of Canada, 1967) at 14.
5 Comment from Sam Bard in "Women in Law: A Video by Perry Bard" (1994).
6 Rose Ortenberg (1884–1961) immigrated from Suceava, Austria (now Romania) with her father, David (Stupak) Ortenberg. Some sources give Suceava as Rose's birthplace, others Russia. "L'hon. Juge Samuel Schwarz Bard" in Ignace-J. Deslauriers, *La Cour supérieure du Québec et ses juges: 1849–1er janvier 1980* (Québec: Bibliothèque nationale du Québec,

1980) at 66; "Our Family Roots – the Goldstein & Krolik Roots," online: RootsWeb <http://wc.rootsweb.ancestry.com>; Arthur D. Hart, *The Jew in Canada* (Toronto: Jewish Publications, 1926; repr. Toronto: Now and Then Books, 2010) at 185; Exposition Shalom Quebec <http://www.shalomquebec.org>.

7 Alan Davies, ed., *Antisemitism in Canada: History and Interpretation* (Waterloo, ON: Wilfrid Laurier University Press, 1992); Pierre Anctil and Gary Caldwell, *Juifs et réalités juives au Québec* (Québec: Institut québécois de recherche sur la culture, 1984); Morton Weinfeld, "The Jews of Quebec: Perceived Antisemitism, Segregation, and Emigration" (1980) 22:1 Jewish Journal of Sociology 5; Harold Troper, *The Defining Decade: Identity, Politics, and the Canadian Jewish Community in the 1960s* (Toronto: University of Toronto Press, 2010) at 9–10.

8 Jacob experienced close brushes with bankruptcy, and Rose underwent lengthy institutionalization. Interview with Claire L'Heureux-Dubé, Quebec City, 25 July 2008.

9 Bard's uncle Benjamin Ortenberg, whose business had been financially devastated by the call for a boycott of Jewish stores, was one of the plaintiffs. The other was Louis Lazarovitz, whose son, Sydney, was also beaten by the mob. Sydney Lazarovitz would later open a law practice, but the absence of Jewish lawyers at the time meant that Montreal lawyers Sam Jacobs and Louis Fitch argued the case. Defeated in first instance, the claim succeeded on appeal in 1914. Constance Backhouse, "Anti-Semitism and the Law in Quebec City: The Plamondon Case, 1910–1915" in Daniel W. Hamilton and Alfred L. Brophy, eds., *Transformations in American Legal History – Law, Ideology, and Methods; Essays in Honor of Morton J. Horwitz* (Cambridge, MA: Harvard Law School, 2010) at 303–25; Sylvio Normand, "L'affaire *Plamondon*: un cas d'antisémitisme à Québec au début du XXIème siècle" (2007) 48 C de D 477.

10 Interview with Joel Bard, Boston, 8 July 2010.

11 In an educational system divided between Roman Catholic and Protestant schools, *An Act to Amend the Law Concerning Education, with Respect to Persons Professing the Jewish Religion*, SQ 1903, c. 16, provided that Jews were to be treated the same as Protestants with respect to school taxes and attendance. Weinfeld, "The Jews of Quebec," see note 7 above at 6–7, noted that Jewish parents gravitated to the Protestant system, which had less religious teaching. English was favoured as the language of entrepreneurial opportunity and as facilitating linkages to relatives and friends who had moved to the United States and other parts of Canada. See David Fraser, *"Honorary Protestants": The Jewish School Question in Montreal, 1867–1997* (Toronto: University of Toronto Press, 2015).

12 Louis Rosenberg, *Canada's Jews: A Social and Economic Study of Jews in Canada in the 1930s* (orig. pub. 1939; repub. Montreal: McGill-Queen's University Press, 1993) at 175–92; Mario Nigro and Clare Mauro, "The Jewish Immigrant Experience and the Practice of Law in Montreal, 1830 to 1990" (1998–99) 44 McGill LJ 999 at 1009.

13 Interview with Joel Bard, Boston, 8 July 2010.

14 His choice of Laval instead of McGill for law may have reflected the lower cost of living at home in Quebec City. It may also have reflected growing anti-Semitism at McGill. Nigro and Mauro, "The Jewish Immigrant Experience," see note 12 above at 1012–14, note that "devices, open or camouflaged" limited the number of Jewish law students at McGill. There were never formal quotas for Jewish law students, and there was a noteworthy openness in the 1920s when the proportion of Jewish law students reached 39–44 percent. But after this was identified as the Jewish Problem in the 1930s, the numbers dropped to 5 percent in 1935–36, and rose to only 15 percent in 1939. By contrast, there were so few Jewish law students at Laval that they may have been viewed as novelties. Gerald Tulchinsky, *Canada's Jews: A People's Journey* (Toronto: University of Toronto Press, 2008) at 318; Pierre Anctil, "Interlude of Hostility: Judeo-Christian Relations in Quebec in the Interwar Period, 1919–39" in Davies, *Antisemitism in Canada*, see note 7 above at 140–45.

15 The level of discrimination in other professions that required obtaining a job as an employee, such as architecture, accountancy, and engineering, made these occupations off-limits to Jews. Self-employment opportunities in law, medicine, dentistry, and pharmacy made these occupations more attractive. According to the 1931 census, Jewish lawyers and notaries in Canada represented 4.35 percent of the occupational group, but only 1.51 percent of the population. Rosenberg, *Canada's Jews,* see note 12 above at 3–4, 193; Nigro and Mauro, "The Jewish Immigrant Experience," see note 12 above at 1009.

16 *Canadian Law List, 1938* (Toronto: Cartwright and Sons, n.d.); Deslauriers, *La Cour supérieure de Québec et ses juges,* see note 6 above at 66; "Bard, Samuel Schwarz" in Dr. Eli Gottesman, ed., *Who's Who in Canadian Jewry* (Montreal: Jewish Institute of Higher Research, 1965) at 55.

17 Nigro and Mauro, "The Jewish Immigrant Experience," see note 12 above at 1017–22, 1042. Anctil, "Interlude of Hostility," see note 14 above at 153, described the mid-1930s as "the most difficult period of economic hardship in the interwar period" and "the peak moment of anti-Jewish sentiment in twentieth-century Quebec." See also Philip Girard, *Bora Laskin: Bringing Law to Life* (Toronto: University of Toronto Press, 2005); Martin L. Friedland, *My Life in Crime and Other Academic Adventures* (Toronto: University of Toronto Press, 2007) at 42, 80–81; Harry Arthurs, "The Toronto Legal Profession: An Exploratory Survey" (1971) 21 UTLJ 498.

18 Aaron Ezekiel Hart is recognized as the first Jewish lawyer to practise law in Quebec City in the early nineteenth century. Hart, *The Jew in Canada,* see note 6 above at 374. A search of the *Canadian Law List* from 1900 to 1931 did not reveal any Quebec City lawyers with names that were not English or French. It is not always possible to determine ethnicity by last name, but the absence of names suggesting minority ethnicity is significant. In 1932, Lazarovitz became the first of his generation to open a Quebec City law office. Between 1933 and 1937, there was no listing for Lazarovitz. He reappeared with the firm of "Lazarovitz & Chaloult" in the *Canadian Law List, 1938* (Toronto: Cartwright and Sons, n.d.). *Canadian Law List, 1932–52* (Toronto: Cartwright and Sons, n.d.); *Canadian Jewish Review* (1 December 1961) 54.

19 Sam Schwarz Bard was admitted to the bar in 1936, and opened his practice in 1938. *Canadian Law List, 1932–39,* ibid.

20 He changed his professional name to Sam S. Bard in the *Canadian Law List, 1948* (Toronto: Cartwright and Sons, n.d.). His listing in the files of the Barreau, *Tableau de l'ordre des avocats de la province de Québec, 1965–66* (Montréal: Barreau du Québec, 1965) did not shift to "Bard, Sam S." until 1965. Sam's son, Joel, recalled that his father consciously dropped the "Schwarz" in part because people so often misspelled it, and in part out of a desire to Canadianize or "de-ethnicize" it. Interview with Joel Bard, Boston, 8 July 2010. Nigro and Mauro, "The Jewish Immigrant Experience," see note 12 above at 107, noted that anti-Semitism forced some Jewish lawyers to mask visible signs of Jewish identity.

21 Brauna, the daughter of Henry Lax and Lottie Goodman, graduated with a bachelor of household science degree. She would become the president of the Cercle des femmes canadiennes à Québec, a member of the Conseil d'administration des dames du Québec, and a member of the Comité d'honneur de l'orchestre symphonique de Québec. The couple had a daughter, Perry, a graduate of McGill, the University of Wisconsin, and the San Francisco Art Institute, who became an artist, and a son, Joel, a graduate of Yale University and Boston University, who practised law in Boston. "L'hon. juge Samuel Schwarz Bard" in Deslauriers, *La Cour supérieure de Québec,* see note 6 above at 66; interview with Joel Bard, ibid.; interview with Perry Bard, Montreal, 23 August 2010.

22 Clara Goodman graduated from McGill law school in 1921, before women could be admitted to the Quebec bar. She worked briefly with the Taschereau law firm in Quebec City; in what capacity is unclear. When her mother was diagnosed with tuberculosis, she left

law to become a full-time caregiver. Interview with Perry Bard, ibid.; interview with Brauna Hendler, Montreal, 23 July 2010.

23 Interview with Joel Bard, Boston, 8 July 2010; "Bard, Samuel Schwarz" in Gottesman, *Who's Who in Canadian Jewry,* see note 16 above at 55.

24 *Canadian Law List, 1938–42* (Toronto: Cartwright and Sons, n.d.); "L'hon. Juge Samuel Schwarz Bard" in Deslauriers, *La Cour supérieure de Québec,* see note 6 above at 66; interview with Joel Bard, ibid. Information about Bard's position as military judge advocate came from Claire L'Heureux-Dubé, since his children had no recollection of this.

25 Maurice Pollack, president of the committee charged with the construction, whose daughter was to be married in the synagogue the next day, spoke publicly to calm the fears: "*Il ne fallait pas non plus perdre confiance face aux Canadiens français, qui étaient des gens foncièrement honnêtes, qui travaillaient avec application, craignaient le châtiment de Dieu et savaient faire preuve d'ouverture envers autrui.*" Brauna Hendler remembered that the apprehension was so great in the Jewish community that all the homes of those who had governing positions with the synagogue, including hers, had security guards posted at the driveways. She credited the arson with helping to turn the situation around, prompting more responsible people to speak out against anti-Semitism. Interview with Brauna Hendler, Montreal, 26 July 2010. Israel Medresh, "L'assaut contre la synagogue de Québec" in *Le Montréal juif entre les deux guerres,* tr. Pierre Anctil (Sillery, QC: Septentrion, 2001) at 153–55; Guy Wagner-Richard, "Le cimetière juif de Québec: Beth Israel Ohev Sholom" (Sillery, QC: Septentrion, 2000) at xxiv; Charles C. Pollack, "Recollections of My Father" (undated, unpublished text); Pierre Anctil, "Bâtir une synagogue à la haute-ville" in Pierre Anctil and Simon Jacobs, eds., *Les juifs de Québec: quatre cents ans d'histoire* (Québec: Presses de l'Université du Québec, 2015) at 139–62. On the municipal by-laws and expropriation efforts that greeted earlier attempts to construct a new synagogue, see Tulchinsky, *Canada's Jews,* see note 14 above at 316–18.

26 David Rome, *Early Anti-Semitism: The Voice of the Media,* pt. 1 (Montreal: National Archives, Canadian Jewish Congress, 1984); David Rome, *Clouds in the Thirties: On Anti-Semitism in Canada, 1929–1939* (Montreal: Canadian Jewish Congress, 1977–81); Lita-Rose Betcherman, *The Swastika and the Maple-Leaf: Fascist Movements in Canada in the Early Thirties* (Toronto: Fitzhenry and Whiteside, 1975); Esther Delisle, *The Traitor and the Jew: Anti-Semitism and the Delirium of Extremist Right-Wing Nationalism in French Canada from 1929–1939* (Montreal: Robert Davies Publishing, 1993); Irving Abella and Harold Troper, *None Is Too Many* (Toronto: Lester and Orpen Dennys, 1982); Gary Caldwell, "L'antisémitisme au Québec" in Anctil and Caldwell, *Juifs et réalités juives au Québec,* see note 7 above at 293–325; Ruth Klein and Frank Dimant, eds., *From Immigration to Integration: The Canadian Jewish Experience – A Millennium Edition* (Toronto: B'nai B'rith Canada, 2001); Pierre Berton, "No Jews Need Apply," *Maclean's* (1 November 1948) 7, 55–57.

27 The play was written in the spring of 1938, during Abbé Groulx's boycott campaign against Jews. The script was intended to "bring out the difference between dishonest and profiteering Jews and honest but too naïve French Canadians." Max Nemni and Monique Nemni, *Young Trudeau: Son of Quebec, Father of Canada* (Toronto: McClelland and Stewart, 2006) at 58.

28 Marilyn Bernard, "Vivre, s'intégrer et interagir en étant minoritaires à plusieurs égards: le cas des femmes juives à Québec des années 1940 à aujourd'hui" (MA thesis, Université Laval, 2008) at 137, 164. George Stein, owner of a metal-processing business, was quoted as saying: "Here in Quebec City, we've never really had much anti-Semitism. I am in contact with French-speaking people all the time. Some people hardly know what a Jew is. They don't realize it's a religion. They think it's a race." Undated, unidentified clipping in collection of the Maurice Pollack Foundation, Montreal.

29 Interview with Perry Bard, Montreal, 23 August 2010.
30 Interview with Joel Bard, Boston, 8 July 2010; interview with Brauna Hendler, Montreal, 26 July 2010; Nigro and Mauro, "The Jewish Immigrant Experience," see note 12 above at 1014; Bernard, "Vivre, s'intégrer et interagir," see note 28 above at 142.
31 Interview with Joel Bard, ibid.
32 Interview with Perry Bard, Montreal, 23 August 2010. In an interview years later in a feature for the *New York Times* on Jews who had left Quebec City, long after Sam Bard had moved from Quebec to Montreal, he was quoted as saying: "I wouldn't want you to think we were driven out. No pogroms, nothing like that. My wife and children learned to speak French, and we made good friends among the French Canadians. We decided to leave because there were better opportunities for us in Montreal, that's all." Clyde H. Farnsworth, "Jews dwindle in the capital of Quebec," *New York Times* (16 August 1995).
33 Jack Jedwab, "The Politics of Dialogue: Rapprochement Efforts between Jews and French Canadians: 1939–1960" in Ira Robinson and Melvin Butovsky, eds., *Renewing Our Days: Montreal Jews in the Twentieth Century* (Montreal: Véhicule Press, 1995) at 42–74.
34 The address was initially 59 St. Joseph St., renumbered as 771 in 1956. *Canadian Law List, 1948–61* (Toronto: Cartwright and Sons, and Canada Law Book, n.d.).
35 Interview with Jacques Alleyn, Ottawa, 9 September 2009; interview with Donald Carr, Toronto, 10 September 2009; interview with André Desgagné, Quebec City, 10 May 2010; interview with Jacques Lemay, Quebec City, 5 May 2010; interview with Melvin Rothman, Montreal, 12 August 2008; interview with Monique Perron, Quebec City, 2 May 2008; interview with Raymond Lessard, Île d'Orléans, QC, 11 May 2010; interview with Brauna Hendler, Montreal, 26 July 2010; interview with Jacques Philippon, Quebec City, 28 April 2009; interview with Roger Garneau, Quebec City, 28 April 2009; interview with Nicole L'Heureux, Clearwater, FL, 11–12 May 2009; interview with Roger Chouinard, Quebec City, 11 May 2010; interview with Louise Dubé, Boston, 22 May 2012.
36 Interview with Perry Bard, Montreal, 23 August 2010.
37 Joel Bard recalled his father counselling a niece to consider carefully the pressures of being a mother and being a lawyer at the same time. "I said, 'Dad, what are you talking about? You worked with Claire Dubé all these years.' He said yes, but she felt a lot of pressure." Interview with Joel Bard, Boston, 8 July 2010.
38 Ibid.; interview with Perry Bard, Montreal, 23 August 2010; interview with Roger Garneau, Quebec City, 28 April 2009; interview with Jacques Philippon, Quebec City, 28 April 2009.
39 Fred Kaufman, *Searching for Justice: An Autobiography* (Toronto: University of Toronto Press, 2005) at 92; Michael Brown, *Jew or Juif? Jews, French Canadians, and Anglo-Canadians, 1759–1914* (Philadelphia: Jewish Publication Society, 1986).
40 In 1951, census data for Quebec City showed a population that was 94.7 percent Francophone, 4.9 percent Anglophone, and 0.21 percent Jewish. Canada, *Ninth Census of Canada, 1951* (Ottawa: Ministry of Trade and Commerce, 1953), tables 42, 57 at 42–48, 57–58. Brown, ibid., noted that the Jews tended to identify with Anglo-Canada. Yet Rosenberg, *Canada's Jews*, see note 12 above at 260, noted that in the city of Quebec, 89.76 percent of the Jewish population was able to speak French in 1931. Jedwab, "The Politics of Dialogue," see note 33 above at 42–74; Morton Weinfeld, "The Jews of Quebec: An Overview" in Robert J. Brym, William Shaffir, and Morton Weinfeld, eds., *The Jews in Canada* (Toronto: Oxford University Press, 1993) at 171–92.
41 Interview with Joel Bard, Boston, 8 July 2010.
42 Ibid. Roger Garneau sponsored Sam Bard to become one of the first Jewish members of the Cercle Universitaire de Québec. The two clubs later merged to become the Cercle de la Garnison de Québec. Interview with Roger Garneau, Quebec, 28 April 2009.
43 Interview with Pierre-Gabriel Jobin, Montreal, 23 April 2010; interview with Nicole L'Heureux, Clearwater, FL, 11–12 May 2009; "L'hon. Juge Samuel Schwarz Bard" in

Deslauriers, *La Cour supérieure de Québec,* see note 6 above at 66. In a book review he published in 1957 about a new text on corporate finance in Canada, Bard described himself as an associate professor of commercial law. Book Review of *Corporation Finance in Canada* (1957) 35 Can Bar Rev 982.

44 Interview with Steven B. Katkin, Montreal, 20 August 2010.
45 *Canadian Law List, 1963* (Toronto: Canada Law Book, n.d.), showing a QC received in 1961.
46 The Honourable Ian Binnie, "In Praise of Oral Advocacy" (2003) 21:4 Advocates' Soc J 3.
47 Veronica H. Ashenhurst, "Mentoring the Lawyer, Past and Present: Some Reflections" (2010–11) 42:1 Ottawa L Rev 125.
48 Fiona M. Kay, John Hagan, and Patricia Parker, "Principals in Practice: The Importance of Mentorship in the Early Stages of Career Development" (2009) 31:1 Law & Pol'y 69; Fiona M. Kay and Jean E. Wallace, "Is More Truly Merrier? Mentoring and the Practice of Law" (2010) 47:1 Canadian Review of Sociology 1; Fiona M. Kay and Jean E. Wallace, "Mentoring as Social Capital: Gender, Mentors, and Career Rewards in Law Practice" (2009) 79:4 Sociological Inquiry 418.
49 Interview with Claire L'Heureux-Dubé, Ottawa, 1 November 2007.
50 Interview with Claire L'Heureux-Dubé, Quebec City, 25 July 2008.
51 Interview with Claire L'Heureux-Dubé, Ottawa, 2 December 2007; and Quebec City, 25 July 2008.
52 Kelly Pullen, "The Problem with Women," *Toronto Life* (May 2010) 42–48.
53 Interview with Philippe Casgrain, Montreal, 23 August 2008.
54 Interview with William Tetley, Montreal, 23 April 2010.
55 Interview with Roch Bolduc, Quebec City, 7 August 2009.
56 Interview with Claire L'Heureux-Dubé, Ottawa, 5 March 2009.
57 "She never brought that home. It was nothing we talked about, not a point of contention." Interview with Louise L'Heureux-Giliberti, Chicago, 21 April 2009.
58 Claire L'Heureux-Dubé's daughter, Louise, whose second husband was Jewish, added: "My mother had always incredible respect for the Jewish religion because of Sam Bard. [She thought] the Jewish religion was a better family religion, [and that it had] a better educational system for kids." Interview with Louise Dubé, Boston, 22 May 2012.

Chapter 13: Business Law Practice

1 The *Canadian Law List, 1952* (Toronto: Cartwright and Sons, n.d.) listed 239 lawyers in the city. The Barreau du Québec, using different data, reported 278 lawyers in Quebec City, and 1,899 in the province, for a ratio of 14.6 percent. *Tableau de l'ordre des avocats de la province de Québec, 1952–53* (Montréal: Barreau du Québec, 1952).
2 The firm of St. Laurent, Taschereau, Letourneau, Johnston, Noel et Pratte at 65 rue Sainte-Anne was composed of the Right Honourable L.S. St. Laurent KC, LL.D., PC, André Taschereau KC, LL.D., Roger Letourneau KC, Renault St. Laurent KC, Jean Paul St. Laurent, C. Douglas Johnston, KC, Camil Noel KC, Yves Pratte, and Louis Pratte. The St. Laurent firm also handled constitutional law, bankruptcy and insolvency, and securities law. Dale C. Thomson, *Louis St. Laurent: Canadian* (Toronto: Macmillan of Canada, 1967) at 10, 61, 67, 76; *Canadian Law List, 1952,* ibid.
3 The office at 80 rue Saint-Peter was composed of the Honourable J.O. Gagnon KC, V.A. de Billy KC, Jacques de Billy KC, Gilles de Billy KC, André Gagnon, and Claude Gagnon. *Canadian Law List, 1952,* ibid.
4 Interview with André Desmeules, Quebec City, 10 May 2010; interview with Nicole L'Heureux, Clearwater, FL, 11–12 May 2009.
5 *Canadian Law List, 1952,* see note 1 above, showed the firm with two lawyers, Sam S. Bard and Pierre Côté. Côté left to practise with the Pratte firm in 1953. *Canadian Law List, 1953*

(Toronto: Cartwright and Sons, n.d.) showed the firm as Bard, Dussault & L'Heureux, with Georges Dussault as a new member along with Claire L'Heureux. Dussault, who had been admitted to the bar in 1949, left in 1957 for the attorney general's office. Quebec City firms were small. Apart from the nine-person St. Laurent firm, there was one six-lawyer firm, six four-lawyer firms, sixteen three-lawyer firms, and twenty-five two-lawyer firms. Seventeen lawyers practised with the provincial attorney general's department. Eighty-five lawyers operated sole practices. *Canadian Law List, 1952,* ibid.

6 *Canadian Law List, 1953* (Toronto: Cartwright and Sons, n.d.). The Bard firm had no partnership structure, so there was never a question of elevation to partnership.
7 "Me Claire L'Heureux, B.A. LL.L.," Québec *Le Soleil* (29 September 1952) 1.
8 Letter from André Michaud to Mlle Claire L'Heureux, 1 October 1952.
9 "Charmant précédent à la cour du Recorder," *L'Événement Journal* (30 September 1952) 9.
10 Unless otherwise indicated, information is from interviews with Claire L'Heureux-Dubé in Quebec City, Ottawa, Rimouski, and Clearwater, FL, on 30 October, 1 November, and 2 December 2007; 29–30 April 2008; 5 March, 10–14 May, and 21 September 2009; 10 March and 30 June 2010.
11 Interview with Roger Garneau, Quebec City, 28 April 2009.
12 Lazarovitz's parents were Louis Lazarovitz and Fanny Serchuk. He clerked with Chaveau Rivard. He married Marja Herscovitz in 1941 and they had two children: Julie Ann and Lynn Lazarovitz. *Canadian Jewish Review* (1 December 1961), Maritimes section, 54; "La famille Lazarovitz" and "Sydney Lazarovitz" in Exposition Shalom Québec, online: <http://www.shalomquebec.org>; "Lazarovitch, Sydney" in Dr. Eli Gottesman, ed., *Who's Who in Canadian Jewry* (Montreal: Jewish Institute of Higher Research, 1965) at 38. Sydney's older sister, Sadie Lazarovitz (1906–99) was one of the first women to graduate in law from McGill in 1928, before women were permitted to enter the Quebec bar. She received her call to the bar in Nova Scotia in 1929, married Ottawa lawyer Abraham Lieff, and worked in his Ottawa law firm until the late 1940s. Her husband was appointed Carleton County magistrate in 1937, and became the first Jewish judge of the Ontario Supreme Court in 1963. Sadie was active in the Liberal Party, serving as secretary of the National Federation of Liberal Women. "Sadie Lazarovitz" in Exposition Shalom Québec, ibid.
13 Interview with Claire L'Heureux-Dubé, Quebec City, 27–28 April 2009. André Desgagné stated that Lazarovitz had "a reputation as a fast operator," whereas Bard had "a better reputation." Interview with André Desgagné, Quebec City, 10 May 2010. Raymond Lessard described Bard as "a gentleman," and Lazarovitz as "a gentlecrook." Interview with Raymond Lessard, Île d'Orléans, QC, 11 May 2010. Roger Garneau stated that when you needed "a nice lawyer," you went to Bard; when you had a "dirty job," you went to Lazarovitz. Interview with Roger Garneau, Quebec City, 28 April 2009. Roger Chouinard agreed: "I think Lazarovitz was a far better lawyer than Bard, but I don't know as a man." Interview with Roger Chouinard, Quebec City, 11 May 2010. Louis LeBel added: "Sam Bard was always known as a lawyer that you could entirely trust. His word was worth any writing. Sydney had a reputation of being a little less reliable. You had to take some precautions, I was told, although I had dealings with him [and] I had absolutely no complaints, no reservations." Interview with Louis LeBel, Ottawa, 8 July 2010.
14 Pierre-Gabriel Jobin stated: "But you must be aware about anti-Semitism. Bard was viewed as a nice Jew (but as a Jew). Lazarovitz was ... more [of] a wheeler-dealer." Interview with Pierre-Gabriel Jobin, Montreal, 23 April 2010. "Lazarovitch, Sydney" in Gottesman, *Who's Who in Canadian Jewry,* see note 12 above at 38, noted that Lazarovitz was the past president of the Beth Israel Congregation and B'nai Brith, a member of the national executive of the Zionist Organization of Canada, and a member of the Canadian Jewish Congress, Montefiore Club, Canadian Friends of Hebrew University, and Canadian Israeli Navy League. Brauna Hendler recalled that Lazarovitz was "very community-conscious – you could always go to him for a favour ... when you needed help without pay. Sam was involved

with the Jewish community, but as a citizen, not so much as a doer." Interview with Brauna Hendler, Montreal, 23 July 2010.
15 Hendler recalled that "Sydney didn't lose any clients to Sam, and Sam didn't take any clients away from Sydney. Both were successful." Interview with Brauna Hendler, Montreal, 23 July 2010.
16 Interview with Claire L'Heureux-Dubé, Quebec City, 27–28 April 2009.
17 The Bard firm took out an advertisement in the *Canadian Law List, 1960* (Toronto: Canada Law Book Company, n.d.) stating: "References Bank of Montreal, St. Roch Branch, Quebec City; The Toronto-Dominion Bank, St. James and McGill Streets, Montreal." The Montreal banks must have been connected with some of the referral work the firm received from Montreal lawyers.
18 Interview with Joel Bard, Boston, 8 July 2010; interview with Brauna Hendler, Montreal, 23 July 2010; Pierre Anctil, "Maurice Pollack: homme d'affaires et philanthrope" in Pierre Anctil and Simon Jacobs, eds., *Les juifs de Québec: quatre cents ans d'histoire* (Québec: Presses de l'Université du Québec, 2015) at 119–37.
19 Rivka immigrated to Canada from Russia in 1906. "La famille Pollack" in Exposition Shalom Québec, see note 12 above; "Maurice Pollack Foundation" in *The Canadian Encyclopedia* (Toronto: Historica-Dominion, 2010), online: <http://www.thecanadianencyclopedia.com>; interview with Joel Bard, ibid.; interview with Brauna Hendler, ibid.; interview with Lana Harper, Montreal, 20 August 2010; transcript of Isabelle Wolfe's interview with Charles C. Pollack (Groupe Vélocité, September 2008).
20 Transcript of Isabelle Wolfe's interview with Charles C. Pollack, ibid.; Charles C. Pollack, "Recollections of My Father" (undated, unpublished text).
21 Sylvia Raff, "Speech to the Montreal Jewish Historical Society" (29 October 1987); Anctil, "Maurice Pollack," see note 18 above at 119–37.
22 Transcript of Isabelle Wolfe's interview with Charles C. Pollack, see note 19 above; Pollack, "Recollections of My Father," see note 20 above.
23 Interview with Claire L'Heureux-Dubé, Quebec City, 25 July 2008.
24 Interview with Claire L'Heureux-Dubé, Quebec City, 27–28 April 2009. On the opposition to unions on the part of wealthy Jewish philanthropists, see Gerald Tulchinsky, *Canada's Jews: A People's Journey* (Toronto: University of Toronto Press, 2008) at 145–52.
25 Pollack was quoted as saying: "If it doesn't hurt, it's not charity." Interview with Lana Harper, Montreal, 20 August 2010; transcript of Isabelle Wolfe's interview with Charles C. Pollack, see note 19 above; interview with Brauna Hendler, Montreal, 23 July 2010.
26 Pollack made large gifts to the Quebec City Synagogue, University of Laval, McGill University, Yeshiva University in New York, the Quebec Symphony Orchestra, the Montreal Symphony Orchestra, the YMHA, various hospitals, and the Bar-Ilan University in Israel. "Pollack, Maurice" in Gottesman, *Who's Who in Canadian Jewry*, see note 12 above at 504; "La famille Pollack" in Exposition Shalom Québec, see note 12 above; "Quebec leader receives award," *Canadian Jewish Chronicle* (26 February 1965) 10; Pollack, "Recollections of My Father," see note 20 above; Anctil, "Maurice Pollack," see note 18 above at 119–37.
27 William Kaplan, *State and Salvation: The Jehovah's Witnesses and Their Fight for Civil Rights* (Toronto: University of Toronto Press, 1989); William Kaplan, *Canadian Maverick: The Life and Times of Ivan C. Rand* (Toronto: University of Toronto Press, 2009) ch. 4.
28 Kaplan, *State and Salvation,* ibid. at 118. Sandra Martin, "Obituary, Glen How," *Globe and Mail* (21 January 2009) S8, gives the date of his admission to the bar as 1943.
29 Kaplan, *Canadian Maverick,* see note 27 above at 130. Montreal Jewish lawyers Albert L. Stein and Samuel Stein, and McGill constitutional law professor F.R. (Frank) Scott, were others who helped litigate in the province of Quebec. See also Laurel Sefton MacDowell, *Renegade Lawyer: The Life of J.L. Cohen* (Toronto: University of Toronto Press, 2001) at 156.
30 Interview with Perry Bard, Montreal, 23 August 2010.

31 Interview with Joel Bard, Boston, 8 July 2010.
32 Interview with Steven B. Katkin, Montreal, 20 August 2010. Katkin recalled that such statements were made publicly at a bar convention in Quebec City in the 1970s, when Sam Bard was belatedly heralded as one of the more principled lawyers of his era for providing legal services to the Jehovah's Witnesses.
33 Interview with Claire L'Heureux-Dubé, Quebec City, 27–28 April 2009.
34 Ibid.
35 Ibid.
36 *Saumur v. Quebec (City)*, [1953] 2 SCR 299. The Duplessis government responded with a new law that provided that door-to-door distribution of pamphlets that contained abusive or insulting attacks against religious beliefs did not constitute the free exercise of religion. Saumur again went to court to challenge it. Sam Bard was counsel of record along with Glen How. The Supreme Court dismissed their client's claim on the technical ground that Saumur's fear that he might be charged did not give him sufficient interest or standing to challenge the law: *Saumur v. Le Procureur Général de la Province de Québec*, [1964] SCR 252. Sam Bard took on many other Jehovah's Witnesses cases that never reached appellate courts or got reported. Kaplan, *Canadian Maverick*, see note 27 at 128–35; Martin "Obituary, Glen How," see note 28 above; Donald Fyson, "Roncarelli v. Duplessis" in Gerald Hallowell, ed., *Canadian History* (Don Mills, ON: Oxford University Press, 2004) at 548–49.
37 Interview with Jacques Philippon, Quebec City, 28 April 2009. Philippon joined the firm in 1959.
38 Interview with Claire L'Heureux-Dubé, Quebec City, 27–28 April 2009.
39 Ibid.
40 Ibid.
41 Interviews with Claire L'Heureux-Dubé, Quebec City, 25 July 2008 and 27–28 April 2009.
42 Judith Gamache obtained her first job as *greffier* with the Cour du Bien-être social through the direct intervention of Premier Maurice Duplessis, who took great pride in his personal control of all government positions. In 1954, she married Charles Côté, an engineer who built roads, and the couple moved to Îles de la Madeleine, where her daughter was born. She continued her career there as *protonotaire* and justice of the peace from 1956 to 1962. She returned to Quebec City and re-entered practice from 1966 to 1971 as the director of legal aid. Interview with Judith Gamache-Côté, Quebec, 1 May 2008.
43 "La diffusion de tribunaux familiaux dans la province serviraient la famille," Québec *Le Soleil* (5 October 1966) 35; "Conférence de Me Claire L'Heureux sur les faillites dans le district" and "Danger de s'illusionner sur le montant du chiffre d'affaires, Conférence de Me Claire L'Heureux" (undated, unreferenced clippings).
44 "Pour les femmes comme pour les hommes – un devoir pour tous: prendre position face aux problèmes actuels," in Québec *Le Soleil* (1 December 1967) 24.
45 The organization had been founded in 1947. Micheline Dumont, *Le féminisme québécois raconté à Camille* (Montréal: Éditions du remue-ménage, 2008) at 94.
46 Correspondence in files of the Canadian Federation of Business and Professional Women's Clubs, President Elsie Gregory MacGill, 10 October 1962, 15 May 1963, 26 April 1964. I am indebted to Crystal Sissons for locating these records.
47 Interview with Claire L'Heureux-Dubé, Ottawa, 10 March 2010.
48 Interview with Claire L'Heureux-Dubé, Clearwater, FL, 10–14 May 2009.
49 Interview with Claire L'Heureux-Dubé, Quebec City, 27–28 April 2009.
50 Interview with Perry Bard, Montreal, 23 August 2010.
51 Interview with Jacques Philippon, Quebec City, 28 April 2009.
52 Interview with Melvin Rothman, Montreal, 12 August 2008.
53 Interview with Claire L'Heureux-Dubé, Quebec City, 27–28 April 2009.

54 Monique Perron, who graduated in 1958 from Laval law school and interned briefly with the Bard firm, was not impressed with the practice: "It was dull, dull, dull ... bland. In this office the practice was very quiet, dull in my opinion. I thought, I won't spend my life going to the court bringing some documents to start a case to collect money." Interview with Monique Perron, Quebec City, 2 May 2008.
55 Interview with Claire L'Heureux-Dubé, Clearwater, FL, 10–14 May 2009.
56 Ibid.
57 L'Heureux recalled that "the Jews all spoke French, but only street-quality French – not a great French, but they could speak it. Most of the business was in English." Ibid.
58 "English-speaking North America for too long has permitted itself to believe that its language is the natural one of commerce and the legal profession has been symptomatically intransigent in so far as transnational linguistic considerations are concerned. The legal profession will no longer have the privilege of being solipsistic in its outlook. Opportunities following the possible signing of the Canada-US-Mexico Free Trade Agreement, for example, will go to those firms who are able to function effectively in English, French and Spanish and it does no good to sit on the shore of the ocean like some King Canute commanding the tide not to come in." Claire L'Heureux-Dubé, "The Legal Profession in Transition" (1992–93) 13 N Ill UL Rev 95.
59 Interview with Claire L'Heureux-Dubé, Clearwater, FL, 10–14 May 2009.
60 Ira Robinson, "No Litvaks Need Apply: Judaism in Quebec City" in Anctil and Jacobs, *Les juifs de Québec,* see note 18 above at 33–34; Pierre Anctil, "La grande migration est-européenne au début du XXe siècle" in Anctil and Jacobs, *Les juifs de Québec* at 81–110; Ira Robinson, "Finding a Rabbi for Quebec City" in Anctil and Jacobs, *Les juifs de Québec* 181 at 193.
61 Across the province, lawyers reported working 39 percent in English, 57 percent in French, and 4 percent in other languages. In Quebec City, the proportion of French was higher, with French-speaking lawyers working 21 percent of the time in English and 75 percent of the time in French. Cadres professionelles Inc. en collaboration avec Bélanger, Chabot, Angers et associés Inc., *Les avocats du Québec: étude socio-économique* (Montréal: Cadres Professionnels Inc., 1968) at 37–38. Before he became prime minister, Louis St. Laurent, raised in a bilingual milieu, conducted his practice primarily in English: Thomson, *Louis St. Laurent,* see note 2 above at 58–60.
62 Canada, Royal Commission on Bilingualism and Biculturalism, *Preliminary Report of the Royal Commission on Bilingualism and Biculturalism* (Ottawa: The Commission, 1965). Data from a 1966 survey of the province found that lawyers who did 90 percent of their work in English averaged $24,000 annually before taxes, while those who did only 10 percent of their work in English earned $16,400. English-speaking lawyers reported net income of $18,260, Jewish lawyers $16,020, and French-speaking lawyers $14,750, with the average income 18.5 percent lower than Ontario lawyers. Cadres professionnels, ibid. at 80–96; David R. Gilbert, "The Lawyers of Quebec" (June 1969) 3:2 Law Soc'y Gaz at 118–19.
63 Interview with Nicole L'Heureux, Clearwater, FL, 11–12 May 2009.
64 Interview with Steven B. Katkin, Montreal, 20 August 2010.
65 Interview with Perry Bard, Montreal, 23 August 2010.
66 Interview with Melvin Rothman, Montreal, 12 August 2008.
67 Interview with Roger Garneau, Quebec City, 28 April 2009.
68 A survey conducted by the Barreau du Québec in 1966 reported that lawyers worked on average 41.3 hours a week at the beginning of their careers (49 percent of the respondents had been called before 1950), and 45.5 hours in 1966. The 49.2-hour figure was given as the highest worked in 1966. Jews reported working approximately 5 hours more per week. Cadres professionnels, *Les avocats du Québec,* see note 61 above at 38–39, 129.

69 Interview with Joel Bard, Boston, 8 July 2010.
70 Interview with Steven B. Katkin, Montreal, 20 August 2010.
71 Interview with Melvin Rothman, Montreal, 12 August 2008.
72 Interview with Raymond Lessard, Île d'Orléans, QC, 11 May 2010.
73 Interview with Louis LeBel, Ottawa, 8 July 2010.

Chapter 14: Marriage and Children

1 Unless otherwise indicated, information is from interviews with Claire L'Heureux-Dubé in Quebec City, Ottawa, Rimouski, and Clearwater, FL, on 30 October, 1 November, and 2 December 2007; 29–30 April 2008; 5 March, 10–14 May, and 21 September 2009; 10 March and 30 June 2010; and 4–5 July 2013.
2 Interview with Claire L'Heureux-Dubé, Ottawa, 10 March 2010.
3 Interview with Claire L'Heureux-Dubé, Clearwater, FL, 10–14 May 2009.
4 At age fifty-two, Paul L'Heureux replaced the retiring Receveur des douanes et de l'accise, M. Savard. The senior post required him to supervise 800–1,000 employees. The promotion was announced in "Nommé receveur," an undated newspaper clipping in Claire L'Heureux-Dubé's files.
5 Interview with Claire L'Heureux-Dubé, Clearwater, FL, 10–14 May 2009.
6 This may have been more common among path-breaking career women than historical perceptions suggest. Judith McKenzie, *Pauline Jewett* (Montreal: McGill-Queen's University Press, 1999), noted at 143 that Jewett defied the dominant sexual mores in the 1950s and 1960s, exhibiting the same rebelliousness she demonstrated in her philosophical and intellectual thinking.
7 Interview with Yves Dubé, Ottawa, Ottawa, 18 September 2008.
8 Interview with Claire L'Heureux-Dubé, Clearwater, FL, 10–14 May 2009.
9 Informal discussions during "Challenges of Writing Biographies of Feminist Legal Icons" (American Society for Legal History workshop, Atlanta, 9–10 November 2011).
10 Interview with Louise Dubé, Boston, 22 May 2012.
11 Interview with Yves Dubé, Ottawa, Ottawa, 18 September 2008.
12 Jean Pineau, "Les régimes matrimoniaux" *Cours de Thémis* (Montréal: Faculté de Droit, 1972), noted at 13 that 75 percent of people in Quebec, particularly in rural and working-class populations, married without marriage contracts. L'Heureux-Dubé explained that contracts were *de rigueur* in professional circles, and that her own parents had also used one when they married. On the parental views of the marriage: interview with Georges-Henri Dubé, Rimouski, 24 July 2008; interview with Yves Dubé, Ottawa, 18 September 2008.
13 Comments from Claire L'Heureux-Dubé, during interview with Georges-Henri Dubé, Rimouski, 24 July 2008.
14 Teasdale had also been married with three children, and worked with the federal unemployment insurance office. Claire L'Heureux-Dubé described her father as very much in love with Francine, and stated that he adopted her children and grandchildren as his own, to the detriment of his relations with his own family. Marguerite was bitter about the new woman, and would contemptuously ask her husband: "How is the spare?" His daughters felt similarly, and disparaged their father's new love interest, a woman they felt was "of another class," whose apparent beauty and dancing ability far outstripped her intellectual capacities. "She may have been good for dancing and sex, but that's all," insisted L'Heureux-Dubé. "She was not my particular type of person." Interviews with Claire L'Heureux-Dubé, Ottawa, 30 October 2007; 27–28 April 2009; comments from Claire L'Heureux-Dubé during interview with Marcèle Dorion, Quebec City, 30 April 2008.
15 He would play dominoes with his invalid wife, put up the winter storm windows, and often bring gifts – a dishwasher, bottles of perfume, and other luxury presents.

16 Interview with Claire L'Heureux-Dubé, Ottawa, 30 October 2007.
17 Interview with Claire L'Heureux-Dubé, Quebec City, 29–30 April 2008.
18 Cécile Brosseau, "Claire L'Heureux-Dube, la femme des défis," *La Presse* (12 February 1975).
19 Claire L'Heureux-Dubé, Notes for speech at swearing-in ceremony, 9 March 1973.
20 John Dickinson and Brian Young, *A Short History of Quebec*, 3rd ed. (Montreal and Kingston: McGill-Queen's University Press, 2003), reported at 307 that only 30 percent of Quebec women used contraception before 1960. The collapse of Church influence and introduction of the birth control pill were not felt until the second half of the 1960s, when the provincial fertility index fell from 3.4 children per woman in 1960 to 2.0 in 1970. Quebec's birth rate, once one of the highest in the Western world, had dropped to one of the lowest by the 1980s.
21 Within the first of week of marriage, L'Heureux-Dubé opened a letter from Household Finance addressed to her husband, to discover that Arthur owed $3,000, the same amount as his annual salary. Yves Dubé, Arthur's brother, explained: "He never took money seriously." Interview with Yves Dubé, Ottawa, Ottawa, 18 September 2008.
22 Interview with Claire L'Heureux-Dubé, Quebec City, 4–5 July 2013.
23 The full birth name was Marie Jennifer Louise Dubé; date of birth 13 May 1960.
24 The full birth name was Joseph Arthur Pierre Dubé; date of birth 29 January 1964.
25 Interview with Claire L'Heureux-Dubé, Quebec City, 4–5 July 2013.
26 Interview with Nicole L'Heureux, Clearwater, FL, 11–12 May 2009; interview with Yves Dubé, Ottawa, 17 September 2008.
27 Mary Kinnear, "That There Woman Lawyer: Women Lawyers in Manitoba 1915–1970" (1992) 5 CJWL 418 noted: "It was usual for the woman to retire from professional work on marriage, and it was a commonplace that women put their families first when family responsibilities conflicted with work demands." She added at 432: "Women lawyers who worked before 1970 identified the fact that women were the primary care-givers in a family as a major reason for both their low numbers and their relative lack of success in the profession."
28 Interview with Claire L'Heureux-Dubé, Ottawa, 10 March 2010.
29 Even the most committed advocates of women's equality in the workforce in this era were of the view that women should shoulder domestic responsibilities. Margaret Hyndman, an influential Toronto lawyer and the head of the Business and Professional Women's Club's committee on equal pay for equal work, declared that although married women had the right to work outside the home, unpaid domestic labour remained their responsibility. Hyndman noted: "When a man applies for a job, his employer does not ask whether he is properly taking care of his home and family. Neither should he consider this angle when he is employing a woman. For a married woman to work successfully, however, she should have the understanding of her husband. If she is falling down on the job of caring for her home in taking the job, it is up to him to check her. If on the other hand her work is suffering because of home ties her employer can check her." "Equality for Women Would Obviate Club Says B and P President," unidentified clipping, 1948 Scrapbook, vol. 31, CFBPWC, Library and Archives Canada, cited in Ruth A. Frager and Carmela Patrias, "Human Rights Activists and the Question of Sex Discrimination in Postwar Ontario" (December 2012) 93/4 Canadian Historical Review 583 at 583.
30 In 1941, 8 percent of working women were married; in 1951, the rate was over 17 percent. Clio Collective, *Quebec Women: A History*, trans. Roger Gannon and Rosalind Gill (Toronto: Women's Press, 1987) at 294.
31 Brosseau, "Claire L'Heureux-Dubé, la femme des défis," see note 18 above.
32 Undated, unreferenced newspaper clipping in scrapbook held by Paul L'Heureux.
33 Interview with Claire L'Heureux-Dubé, Ottawa, 10 March 2010.

34 Pamela Burton, *From Moree to Mabo: The Mary Gaudron Story* (Crawley, Western Australia: UWA Publishing, 2010) at 350.
35 Interview with Gisèle Blondeau-Labrie, Quebec City, 1 May 2008.
36 Interview with Jean Drapeau, Rimouski, 24 July 2008.
37 Interview with Simone Tardif, Montreal, 4 August 2008.
38 Interview with Claire L'Heureux-Dubé, Clearwater, FL, 10–14 May 2009.
39 Ibid.
40 Jocelyn Létourneau, "Quieter Revolutions," *The Walrus* (October 2010) 52.
41 Interview with Denyse Dion, Quebec City, 1 May 2008.
42 Comments from Claire L'Heureux-Dubé during interview with Denyse Dion, Quebec City, 1 May 2008.
43 Interview with Louise Dubé, Boston, 22 May 2012.

CHAPTER 15: FAMILY LAW

1 Unless otherwise indicated, information is from interviews with Claire L'Heureux-Dubé in Quebec City, Ottawa, Rimouski, and Clearwater, FL, on 30 October, 1 November, and 2 December 2007; 29–30 April 2008; 5 March, 10–14 May, and 21 September 2009; 10 March, 30 June, and 13 September 2010.
2 There were 239 lawyers in 1952, 326 in 1962, and 445 in 1972. *Canadian Law List, 1952, 1962, 1972* (Toronto: Cartwright and Sons and Canada Law Book, n.d.). The percentage is more difficult to assess since sources differ on provincial numbers. In 1962, the ratio appeared to be about 13 percent of the province's lawyers; in 1972, 15.4 percent of the provincial total. *Canadian Law List, 1962*, ibid., showed 326 lawyers in Quebec City. Bélanger, Chabot, Angers et associés Inc., *Les avocats du Québec: étude socio-économique* (Montréal: Cadres Professionnels Inc., 1968) at 103, showed 2,510 lawyers in the province, for a ratio of 13 percent. The *Tableau de l'ordre des avocats de la province de Québec, 1962–63* (Montréal: Barreau du Québec, 1962) showed 2,604 in the province, for a ratio of 12.5 percent. *Canadian Law List, 1972*, ibid., listed 445 lawyers in Quebec City. The city numbers were not consistent with the *Tableau de l'ordre des avocats de la province de Québec, 1972–73* (Montréal: Barreau du Québec, 1972), which showed 590 in Quebec City and 3,823 in the province, for a ratio of 15.4 percent.
3 In 1962, the city's two largest firms still had only nine lawyers apiece. Both were reconfigurations from the St. Laurent firm. Roger Letourneau, Charles Stein, C. Douglas Johnston, Jean Leahy, Pierre Marseille, E. Anthony Price, Jacques Delisle, Pierre LaRue, and Pierre Verge practised in one. Yves Pratte, Pierre Côté, Louis Pratte, Charles Tremblay, André Miville-Dechene, Jean Beauvais, Monique Perron, Jean Demers, and Céline Turcotte practised in the other. The former prime minister had returned to practise in the four-person firm of St. Laurent & St. Laurent with Renault St. Laurent, Ivan Mignault, and André Desmeules. *Canadian Law List, 1962*, ibid.
    By 1972, there were fourteen firms with more than five lawyers. There were three nine-person law firms, one ten-person firm, one eleven-person firm, one thirteen-person firm, and one fourteen-person firm. The largest was composed of Roger Letourneau, Charles Stein, C. Douglas Johnston, Isidore C. Pollack, Claude Pratte, Pierre Marseille, Jacques Delisle, Pierre LaRue, Jean Belleau, Jean Marier, Jacques Gingras, Pierre Cimon, Jean DuBlois, and Pierre Pelletier. The number of lawyers with the government had grown from 17 to 31, and the number of sole practitioners from 85 to 148. *Canadian Law List, 1972*, ibid.
4 There were a small number of Anglophone lawyers of English and Irish heritage. Only two other names in the *Canadian Law List, 1972*, ibid., suggest diverse heritage. Lubin Lilkoff,

admitted to the bar in 1958, was a Francophone from Bulgaria; he worked briefly for the Bard firm. Vincent Kooiman, admitted to the bar in 1960, appears to have been the only other. Interview with Louis LeBel, Ottawa, 8 July 2010.
5 In 1972, the three were Sydney Lazarovitz, Isidore C. Pollack, and Gerald Roiter. Roiter was Lazarovitz's son-in-law, admitted to the bar in 1969, who began his practice with Lazarovitz's firm that year. Isidore (Zeke) C. Pollack was admitted to the bar in 1938, and opened his legal practice with Angers, Caisse and Pollack in Montreal. He served with the military from 1939 to 1946, and joined the Department of External Affairs in 1947. In 1951, he moved back to Quebec City to become president of M. Pollack Ltd. In 1961, he opened a law office as a sole practitioner at 725 St. Joseph St. E. He joined the firm of Letourneau, Stein, Marseille, Delisle et LaRue from 1969 to 1977, where he focused more on managing the family business than upon practice. *Canadian Law List, 1961–72*, ibid.; interview with Lana Harper, Montreal, 20 August 2010; interview with Brauna Hendler, Montreal, 23 July 2010; Charles C. Pollack, "Recollections of My Father" (undated, unpublished text).
6 Interview with Joel Bard, Boston, 8 July 2010.
7 The Montreal Lord Reading Law Society was formed in 1948, after the Quebec bar decided to hold its annual convention in Mont-Tremblant Lodge, a facility that refused admission to Jews. The society was named after Rufus Daniel Isaacs, a Jewish statesman in Britain, who became the Lord Chief Justice of England and took the title of Lord Reading. The campaign resulted in the appointment of Harry Batshaw, the first Jew named to the Superior Court in Montreal, in 1950. "These Fifty Years: The Lord Reading Law Society 1948–1998" (unpublished history compiled by the society on its fiftieth anniversary, 1998); Mario Nigro and Clare Mauro, "The Jewish Immigrant Experience and the Practice of Law in Montreal, 1830–1990" (1999) 44 McGill LJ 999 at 1016.
8 Lazarovitz was elected *délégué du barreau du Québec* from 1961 to 1963, and again in 1966–67. He was elevated to *bâtonnier* in 1966–67. *Canadian Law List, 1961–67*, see note 2 above; Nigro and Mauro, ibid. Louis LeBel recalled: "The only time I saw different treatment for Jewish lawyers was at the time Sydney decided to run for *bâtonnier*. Then it started. That was one point where there was clearly anti-Semitism on the part of a number of Quebec City lawyers. At the time, I think some senior lawyers were very opposed to his candidacy, and Sydney Lazarovitz essentially won with the votes of young lawyers, the young bar, and probably the smaller firms." Interview with Louis LeBel, Ottawa, 8 July 2010; interview with Raymond Lessard, Île d'Orléans, QC, 11 May 2010; interview with Pierre-Gabriel Jobin, Montreal, 23 April 2010.
9 Whether the decision was due to the disparate reputations of Lazarovitz and Bard, whether due to Lazarovitz's alleged difficulties with past taxes, or whether due to Bard's greater acculturation outside of the Jewish community, is unclear. Interview with Steven B. Katkin, Montreal, 20 August 2010.
10 L'Heureux-Dubé and Jacques Philippon bought the business from Bard, taking on all of his files, and later reimbursing him with a portion of the fees for each of his files they completed.
11 Georges Dussault joined in 1953, and left in 1957 for the attorney general's office. Maurice Lahoud worked from 1957 to 1959, after which he was no longer listed as a lawyer. Denys Aubé worked from 1957 to 1961, when he set up a practice with Marcel Turgeon. Lubin L. Lilkoff started in 1959 but left the next year. *Canadian Law List, 1953–72*, see note 2 above.
12 Born in 1932 in Quebec City, Jacques Philippon was a second-generation lawyer. He graduated from Laval law school in 1958, was admitted to the bar that year, and took one year of graduate studies at the London School of Economics. The death of his lawyer father, Horace, brought him home, and Nicole L'Heureux, who had been his classmate, referred

him to the Bard firm. "There might be some who could see some problem for me to go with a Jewish firm," recalled Philippon, "but I didn't. I was working for Sam Bard, but I was also doing my own practice. I had the same arrangements as Claire from the beginning. It was one of the reasons I joined. I had my own clients, because of my father's reputation and my own relationships. I was glad also that part of the practice was in English." He was appointed to the Quebec Superior Court in 1977. Interview with Jacques Philippon, Quebec City, 28 April 2009; *Canadian Law List, 1959–72*, ibid.

13 Born in 1943 in Quebec City, Christine Tourigny graduated in law from Laval in 1966, and was admitted to the bar in 1969. Her lawyer father had served in the Duplessis cabinet, and her brother was a lawyer. Christine Tourigny practiced family law with the firm from 1970 to 1979. She served as the province's first secretary general of the Secrétariat à la condition féminine from 1979 to 1982. From 1982 to 1985, she worked as the deputy minister of the litigation branch of the Quebec Ministry of Justice. She was appointed to the Quebec Superior Court in 1985 and the Quebec Court of Appeal in 1987. In recognition of her contribution to family law and equality issues in Quebec, Tourigny became the first recipient of the Prix d'excellence du Comité sur les femmes dans la profession du Barreau du Québec in 1998. After her death in 1998, the prize was named the Mérite Christine-Tourigny. *Canadian Law List, 1970,* ibid.; "Tourigny, Christine" in Marie Paule Desjardins, *Dictionnaire biographique des femmes célèbres et remarquables de notre histoire* (Montréal: Guérin, 2007) at 472; Kim G. Kofmel, ed., *Who's Who of Canadian Women,* 5th ed. (Toronto: Trans-Canada Press, 1988) at 470.

14 Roger Garneau was born in Arthabaska, Quebec, in 1936. Both his father and grandfather had been notaries. He obtained his LL.L. from Laval in 1960, was admitted to the bar in 1961, and studied for one year at the London School of Economics. He began practice in 1962 with Drouin, Drouin, Bernier et Drouin at the rate of $70 per week. He left in 1966 for a full-time post as a Crown attorney, but was soon lured by Pierre Côté to move to Yves Pratte's firm (see note 3 above), where he did civil litigation, damages, contracts, and insurance law. When Côté was appointed a judge and Pratte left to run Air Canada, the firm dissolved. L'Heureux-Dubé invited Garneau to join her firm and he accepted. He did some commercial practice but soon gravitated to family law, and took over L'Heureux-Dubé's files when she was appointed to the bench. *Canadian Law List, 1971,* ibid.; interview with Roger Garneau, Quebec City, 28 April 2009.

15 The four-member firm was composed of L'Heureux-Dubé, Philippon, Garneau, and Tourigny.

16 In 1952, the *Canadian Law List, 1952,* see note 2 above, listed only one female lawyer (Ginette Fournier) in Quebec City since Claire L'Heureux-Dubé had yet to be registered. This represented 0.4 percent of the 239 lawyers listed. In 1972, the 20 women represented 4.49 percent of the 445 lawyers in Quebec City. Names can be problematic as an identifier of gender, but based on the *Canadian Law List, 1972,* ibid., the female lawyers in practice in 1972 (listed in order of year of admission) were Claire L'Heureux-Dubé, 1952; Gabrielle Vallée, 1954; Louise Galipeault and Claire J. Jacques, 1955; Nicole L'Heureux and Lise R. Lavallée, 1958; Monique Perron, 1959; Anne Cuddihy-Dubé, 1964; Andrée Genest, 1965; Marie J. Cantin and Gisèle Côté-Harper, 1966; Paule Gauthier and Jackie C. Beausoleil, 1967; Alice Mercier, 1968; Christine Tourigny, Delpha Bélanger, and Ann Robinson-Chouinard, 1969; Lise Morency, 1970; and Charlotte Rogerge and Nicole Bélanger, 1971.

17 There are varying numbers regarding the proportion of female lawyers in the province. Tables inserted into the *Tableau de l'ordre des avocats,* see note 2 above, showed 6.7 percent. Maude Rochette, *Les femmes dans la profession juridique au Québec: de l'access à l'intégration, un passage couteux* (Québec: Les Cahiers de recherche du GREMF, 1990) at 60, using Statistics Canada data for 1971, showed 5.1 percent for Quebec (225 women out of 4,400), with a ratio of 4.7 percent across Canada (775 women out of 16,305).

18 Lee Ferrier, one of the first lawyers in Toronto to specialize in family law, recalled that before the mid-1960s, "There was nobody in the country – in Canada – [this is] not an exaggeration – who was doing family law exclusively." Interview with Lee Ferrier, Toronto, 8 August 2012. Other new growth areas included labour and municipal law. Interview with Louis LeBel, Ottawa, 8 July 2010; Yves Ouellette, "La profession d'avocat: perspective d'avenir" in J. Bouchard, ed., *Le Barreau du Québec à 125 ans – son passé, son avenir* (Barreau du Québec, 1974).

19 Quebec was not among the provinces that had previously used de facto jurisdiction to provide litigants with divorce decrees on limited grounds. Quebec couples willing to travel to Ottawa could bring ad hoc petitions on a case-by-case basis, seeking a parliamentary divorce from the Senate of Canada, but few did so. L'Heureux-Dubé was involved with only two clients who obtained the federal remedy; she retained Ottawa lawyers to represent them. Constance Backhouse, "Pure Patriarchy: Nineteenth-Century Marriage" (1986) 31:2 McGill LJ 265; Constance Backhouse, *Petticoats and Prejudice: Women and Law in Nineteenth-Century Canada* (Toronto: Women's Press, 1991) at 167–99, 204.

20 Statutes of Lower Canada 1865, c. 41, art. 185. The *Code* represented a more patriarchal version of gender equality than had prevailed earlier in Quebec, under the Custom of Paris and the material realities of a pre-industrial economy. Jan Noel, *Along a River: The First French-Canadian Women* (Toronto: University of Toronto Press, 2013).

21 *Civil Code*, ibid., art. 187–88. Germain Brière, *Cours de droit civil: la famille* (Ottawa: Université d'Ottawa, 1958–59), noted at 169: "*la femme ne pouvait demander la séparation de corps pour cause d'adultère du mari, que s'il tenait sa concubine dans la maison commune.*" The gender disparity was challenged by the Montreal Local Council of Women and the Alliance canadienne pour le vote des femmes au Québec when the Dorion Commission examined women's civil rights in 1930. The commission dismissed the critique: "Everyone knows that in fact, the wound to the heart of the wife is not usually as severe as the wound to the husband who has been deceived by his wife ... [in] a woman's heart, forgiveness is naturally easier." The concubine provision was finally removed by *An Act to amend the Civil Code*, SQ 1954–55, c. 48, s. 1, which amended article 188 to read: "A wife may demand the separation on the ground of her husband's adultery." Clio Collective, *Quebec Women: A History*, trans. Roger Gannon and Rosalind Gill (Toronto: Women's Press, 1987) at 255–61; Jennifer Stoddart, "Quebec's Legal Elite Looks at Women's Rights: The Dorion Commission 1929–1931" in David H. Flaherty, ed., *Essays in the History of Canadian Law* (Toronto: Osgoode Society for Canadian Legal History, 1981) at 323.

22 Jocelyn Létourneau, "Quieter Revolutions," *The Walrus* (October 2010) 50.

23 Clio Collective, *Quebec Women,* see note 21 above at 274; Michael Gauvreau, *The Catholic Origins of Quebec's Quiet Revolution, 1931–1970* (Montreal: McGill-Queen's University Press, 2005) at 247.

24 She opened a private practice in Montreal, where she married another lawyer, Rimouski-born Philippe Casgrain, whose flamboyance had so impressed his classmates when he studied at Laval with Claire L'Heureux. It was Kirkland-Casgrain's status as a married woman that caused difficulties when she tried to rent a Quebec City apartment after her election. "My signature had no legal value," she exclaimed decades later. "My husband had to take the train from Montreal to sign. I found it so unfair that a young woman lawyer, of the age of majority, elected by majority of her constituents, with three children, couldn't sign a lease." Interview with Marie-Claire Kirkland-Strover, Montreal, 23 August 2008; "Marie-Claire Kirkland" in *Canadian Who's Who* (Toronto: University of Toronto Press, 2005). In the *Globe and Mail* on 31 March 1962, Kirkland-Casgrain commented on the risks facing the female politician: "If I remain silent, I am useless. If I talk too much, it is a woman's fault. If I dwell on woman's rights, I am narrow. If I neglect them, women will ask why they elected me. If I tackle large problems of finance and make a

mistake, it is because I am a woman. And you can imagine what would be said if I tried to use charm?"

25 *An Act respecting the legal capacity of married women*, SQ 1964, c. 66. A woman no longer needed her husband's signature to transact business. She could sign contracts and her husband no longer had exclusive authority to choose the conjugal domicile. She was authorized to engage in a calling distinct from that of her husband, launch a lawsuit, or act as the executor of a will. Article 174 of the *Civil Code* was amended to read: "The wife participates with the husband in ensuring the moral and material control of the family, in providing for its maintenance, in bringing up the children and preparing their establishment in life." This signified an end to the absolute control of the husband and total obedience on the part of the wife, and an increase in the wife's control over property, but it did not equalize the spouses in every respect: Germain Brière, Albert Mayrand, Roger Comtois, and Guy M. Desaulniers, *Lois nouvelles* (Montréal: Presses de l'Université de Montréal, 1965); Clio Collective, *Quebec Women*, see note 21 above at 321–24; Micheline Dumont, *Le féminisme québécois raconté à Camille* (Montréal: Editions du remue-ménage, 2008) at 107. Kirkland-Casgrain was also instrumental in the enactment of *An Act respecting matrimonial regimes*, SQ 1969, c. 77, expanding the rights of married women and replacing community property with a partnership of acquests – *la société d'acquêts*. In 1973, she established the Conseil du statut de la femme, which became a sponsor of research, funding, and information, and was later transformed into a ministry with responsibility for enforcing laws against discrimination. Emilia B. Allaire, *Têtes de femmes; essais biographiques* (Québec: Éditions de l'équinoxe, 1964); Claire Kirkland-Casgrain, "A Woman in Politics, My Own Story," *Chatelaine* (September 1976) 47; Diane Lamoureux, *Fragments et collages: essai sur le féminisme québécois des années 70* (Montréal: Éditions du remue-ménage, 1986) at 72–74; Yoland Cohen, "From Feminine to Feminism in Quebec" in Françoise Thébaud, ed., *A History of Women in the West* (Cambridge, MA: Harvard University Press, 1994) at 563.

26 Karin Moser, "La lutte des femmes du Québec," Montréal *L'Évangeline* (29 June 1967); Clio Collective, *Quebec Women*, see note 21 above at 337.

27 John English, *The Life of Pierre Elliott Trudeau*, vol. 1, *Citizen of the World, 1919–1968* (Toronto: Knopf Canada, 2006) at 447.

28 *Divorce Act*, S.C. 1968, c. 24.

29 Ibid., s. 3 listed grounds as follows: (a) has committed adultery; (b) has been guilty of sodomy, bestiality, or rape, or has engaged in a homosexual act; (c) has gone through a form of marriage with another person; (d) has treated the petitioner with physical or mental cruelty of such a kind as to render intolerable the continued cohabitation of the spouses. S. 4 added: (a) imprisonment for three years in the previous five-year period, or imprisonment for two years for an offence for which the spouse was sentenced to death or ten years or more; (b) three years of gross addiction to alcohol or narcotics with no reasonable expectation of rehabilitation; (c) desertion for three years with no knowledge of the spouse's whereabouts; (d) non-consummation.

30 Ibid., s. 4(e) required that spouses live separate and apart for a period of not less than three years. However, five years was required if the spouse who deserted the marriage was the party seeking the divorce. S. 9 barred judges from issuing a divorce if it appeared that the parties had "connived" or "colluded" to prove fault, or if the marital offence had been "condoned." The admissions and consent of the parties were expressly declared insufficient evidence of proof.

31 Brière, *Cours de droit civil*, see note 21 above, described the situation during marriage at 151: "*Les pères et mères ne sont toutefois pas placés sur un pied d'égalité, puisque l'exercice de l'autorité est confié au père seul, durant le mariage (art. 243). Cette disposition s'explique par le principe selon lequel le père est le chef de la famille et aussi par le fait que l'autorité n'est vraiment efficace que si elle est une; d'ailleurs la mère est soumise à la puissance maritale.*"

Upon separation, Brière noted at 152, 178: "*en principe, la garde des enfants appartient au mari durant cette période (cela est conforme à l'art. 243); mais le tribunal ou le juge peut l'attribuer à la femme ou même à un tiers, si tel est l'avantage des enfants. (art. 200)*"; "*la séparation de corps laisse subsister la puissance paternelle; cependant, le droit de garde, qui en est le principal attribut, appartient à l'époux qui a obtenu la séparation à moins que le tribunal n'en décide autrement pour le plus grand avantage des enfants.*" On the criteria for awarding custody, Brière wrote at 178: "*La femme peut donc présenter une requête en vue d'obtenir la garde des enfants. Pour l'accueillir ou la rejeter, les tribunaux prendront en considération l'intérêt des enfants; entreront en ligne de compte l'âge et la religion des enfants, la capacité des parents de prendre soin de leurs enfants, les facilités d'instruction et d'éducation, l'indignité des parents.*" *Civil Code,* Statutes of Lower Canada, 1865, c. 41, arts. 200, 214; Backhouse, *Petticoats and Prejudice,* see note 19 above at 204.
32 *An Act to amend the Civil Code,* SQ 1969, c. 74, s. 14, amending article 212.
33 Interview with Claire L'Heureux-Dubé, Ottawa, 30 June 2010.
34 Ibid.
35 Interview with Jacques LeMay, Quebec City, 5 May 2010.
36 Interview with Roger Garneau, Quebec City, 28 April 2009. Jacques LeMay added: "Very few lawyers in Quebec practised family law. I maybe had a few matrimonial cases, but it was not a field of practice I enjoyed." Roger Chouinard agreed: "As a lawyer, I tried to avoid family law. It was a sentimental business." Interview with Jacques LeMay, Quebec City, 5 May 2010; interview with Roger Chouinard, Quebec City, 11 May 2010.
37 Interview with Malcolm C. Kronby, Toronto, 30 September 2010. Called to the Ontario bar in 1959, he practised family law exclusively after 1965, and became the author of *Canadian Family Law,* 10th ed. (Mississauga: John Wiley and Sons, 2010).
38 Julien Payne obtained his law degree at London University, moved to Canada in 1960, and taught law at the University of Saskatchewan, University of Western Ontario, University of Alberta, and University of Ottawa. He was one of the architects of the 1968 *Divorce Act.* Interview with Julien Payne, Ottawa, 7 July 2009.
39 Nicholas Bala taught at Queen's law school and received the Law Society Medal from the Law Society of Upper Canada in 2009. Interview with Nicholas C. Bala, Kingston, 12 August 2009.
40 Interview with Julien Payne, Ottawa, 7 July 2009.
41 Interview with Claire L'Heureux-Dubé, Quebec City, 27–28 April 2009.
42 Johanne Daigle, "Le siècle dans la tourmente du féminisme" (2000) 3:2 Globe: Revue Internationale d'Études Québécoises 65 at 81–82.
43 Interview with Claire L'Heureux-Dubé, Quebec City, 27–28 April 2009.
44 Claire L'Heureux-Dubé, "Le droit de ne pas divorcer" (1969) 10 C de D 121 at 132–34.
45 Interview with Louise Dubé, Boston, 22 May 2012; Louise Mailhot, *Les premières! L'histoire de l'accès des femmes à la pratique du droit et à la magistrature* (Cowansville, QC: Éditions Yvon Blais, 2013) at 115.
46 Interview with Claire L'Heureux-Dubé, Quebec City, 27–28 April 2009.
47 Interview with Claire L'Heureux-Dubé, Clearwater, FL, 10–14 May 2009.
48 L'Heureux-Dubé, "Le droit de ne pas divorcer," see note 44 above at 127.
49 Prior to 1968, parliamentary divorces (which few Quebec couples sought) had cost in the range of $1,000 to $5,000, with some lawyers demanding fees of up to $3,000 even for uncontested divorces. Interview with Lee Ferrier, Toronto, 8 August 2023; Zoe Bieler, "The great divorce rush continues in Quebec," *Montreal Star* (20 January 1973).
50 Statistics Canada, Institut de la statistique du Québec, "Nombre de divorces et indice synthétique de divortialité, Québec, 1969–2005" in *Le bilan démographique du Québec: Édition 2009* (Québec: Institut de la statistique du Québec, 2008) at 80. Different numbers were listed in Laurent Roy, *Le divorce au Québec; évolution récente* (n.p.: Gouvernement du Québec, Division des études démographiques, Registre de la population) at 10, showing

8.7 divorces per 100 marriages in 1969, 13.9 in 1970, 14.5 in 1971, 17.6 in 1972, and 22.0 in 1973. Marriage rates began to fall dramatically as well. The percentage of women married in Quebec was 92.8 percent in 1972 but 67.5 percent in 1979. Suzanne Messier, *Chiffres en mains* (Québec: Éditeur officiel, 1982) cited in Lamoureux, *Fragments et collages,* see note 25 above at 74.
51 Interview with Claire L'Heureux-Dubé, Ottawa, 10 March 2010.
52 Interview with Claire L'Heureux-Dubé, Clearwater, FL, 10–14 May 2009.
53 Interview with Claire L'Heureux-Dubé, Quebec City, 27–28 April 2009.
54 Interview with Claire L'Heureux-Dubé, Ottawa, 30 June 2010.
55 Interview with Claire L'Heureux-Dubé, Quebec City, 27–28 April 2009.
56 Ibid. She described Paul Miquelon as "not particularly pleasant," but someone who "rendered good decisions, especially in criminal law."
57 Interview with Claire L'Heureux-Dubé, Clearwater, FL, 10–14 May 2009.
58 Ibid.
59 Ibid.
60 L'Heureux-Dubé, "Le droit de ne pas divorcer," see note 44 above at 139.
61 Interview with Claire L'Heureux-Dubé, Clearwater, FL, 10–14 May 2009.
62 Ibid.
63 Interview with Claire L'Heureux-Dubé, Clearwater, FL, 25–27 November 2014.
64 Interview with Claire L'Heureux-Dubé, Clearwater, FL, 10–14 May 2009.
65 Ibid.
66 Interview with Claire L'Heureux-Dubé, Quebec City, 27–28 April 2009.
67 Ibid.
68 Ibid.
69 Ibid.
70 Madam Justice Claire L'Heureux-Dubé, "Deciding Child Custody: New Developments in Quebec" in Ian F.G. Baxter and Mary A. Eberts, eds., *The Child and the Courts* (Toronto: Carswell, 1978) at 125.
71 Quebec marriage was based on the legal concept of "community of property." All the property that the two spouses obtained after marriage became their "joint" property, although the husband alone had the right to administer and dispose of it. Couples could opt out by signing special marriage contracts permitting a wife to retain control over her own property. Bettina Bradbury et al., "Property and Marriage" (1993) 26:51 Histoire sociale/Social History 9; Backhouse, "Pure Patriarchy," see note 19 above; Backhouse, *Petticoats and Prejudice,* see note 19 above at 167–99.
72 Interview with Claire L'Heureux-Dubé, Clearwater, FL, 10–14 May 2009.
73 Interview with Claire L'Heureux-Dubé, Quebec City, 27–28 April 2009.
74 Ibid.
75 Interview with Lee Ferrier, Toronto, 8 August 2012.
76 Claire L'Heureux-Dubé's comments during interview with Yves Bernier, Quebec City, 30 April 2008. Corriveau was appointed to the Quebec Superior Court on 30 March 1961. He had run unsuccessfully for the Progressive Conservative party in the federal election of 1949 in the riding of Dorchester. Ignace-J. Deslauriers, *La Cour supérieure du Québec et ses juges: 1849–1er janvier 1980* (Québec: Bibliotheque nationale du Québec, 1980).
77 Interview with Yves Bernier, ibid.
78 Claire L'Heureux-Dubé's comments during interview with Yves Bernier, ibid.; Mimi Liu, "A 'Prophet with Honour': An Examination of the Equality Jurisprudence of Madam Justice Claire L'Heureux-Dubé of the Supreme Court of Canada" (2000) 25:2 Queen's LJ 417 at 419; interview with Roger Garneau, Quebec City, 28 April 2009.
79 Interview with Claire L'Heureux-Dubé, Quebec City, 27–28 April 2009.
80 Ibid.
81 Interview with Louise Galipeault-Moisan, Le Portage, QC, 30 July 2010.

82　Interview with Yves Bernier, Quebec City, 30 April 2008. He was appointed to the Superior Court in 1961.
83　Interview with Louise Dubé, Boston, 22 May 2012.
84　Interview with Claire L'Heureux-Dubé, Quebec City, 27–28 April 2009.
85　Ibid.
86　Ibid.
87　Rémi Paul served as the minister of justice with the Union Nationale party from 23 July 1969 to 12 May 1970.
88　Interview with Claire L'Heureux-Dubé, Quebec City, 27–28 April 2009.
89　Claude Gagnon was elected *bâtonnier* for Quebec City and for the province at large in 1969. *Canadian Law List, 1969–71*, see note 3 above. He would later serve as president of Le Cercle Universitaire and be instrumental in the dismantling of its discriminatory admission rules.
90　Interview with Claire L'Heureux-Dubé, Ottawa, 30 June 2010; *Canadian Law List, 1970–71*, ibid.
91　Interview with Claire L'Heureux-Dubé, Quebec City, 27–28 April 2009. The Canadian Judicial Council, composed of chief justices and associate chief justices of Canada's superior courts, was established in 1971 to adjudicate complaints about judicial misconduct. Ed Ratushny, "Speaking as Judges: How Far Can They Go?" (2000) 11 NJCL 345.
92　Paul-André Crépeau was appointed president of the Civil Code Revision Office in 1965, asked to serve by Deputy Minister of Justice Julien Chouinard, whom he knew from their days as Rhodes Scholars at Oxford. Interview with Paul-André Crépeau, Montreal, 1 October 2010.
93　Paul-André Crépeau, *La réforme du droit civil canadien: une certain conception de la recodification, 1965–1977* (Montréal: Éditions Thémis, 2003) at 3–6. Born in Gravelbourg, Saskatchewan, in 1926, Crépeau received a BA from the University of Ottawa in 1946, a Licence in Philosophy from the University of Ottawa in 1947, a law degree from the University of Montreal in 1950, a Bachelor of Civil Law degree as a Rhodes Scholar at Oxford in 1952, and a doctorate from the Université de Paris in 1955. He joined the law faculty at the University of Montreal from 1955 to 1959, and taught at the McGill Faculty of Law from 1959 to 1994. Interview with Paul-André Crépeau, ibid.; André Poupart, "Crépeau, Paul-André" in *The Canadian Encyclopedia* (n.p.: Historica-Dominion, 2010); "Professor Paul-André Crépeau," online: McGill University <http://www.mcgill.ca/wainwright/chair/crepeau>.
94　Interview with Paul-André Crépeau, ibid. The reforms that Casgrain and L'Heureux-Dubé opposed were enacted as *An Act respecting matrimonial regimes*, SQ 1969, c. 77. The community of property regime was replaced by a partnership of acquests in the absence of other provisions chosen by the spouses. Spouses were authorized to modify their choice of matrimonial regime during the marriage. The need to obtain authorization to accept a succession, a gift, or the function of testamentary executor was removed. Jeanne Dansereau, "Le bill 10: une affaire de participation," *La Presse* (5 June 1969).
95　Correspondence from Paul-André Crépeau, 15 December 2010.
96　Interview with Claire L'Heureux-Dubé, Quebec City, 27–28 April 2009.
97　Interview with Paul-André Crépeau, Montreal, 1 October 2010.
98　Ibid.
99　Correspondence from Paul-André Crépeau, 15 December 2010.
100　Civil Code Revision Office, *Report on the Family, Part I* (Montreal: Québec Official Publisher, 1974) at 12, 16, 141, 148.
101　Ibid. at 24, 225–32. Where both parties did not consent, divorce was to be granted after three years of separation, regardless of whether or not the party seeking divorce was the deserter.

102 Ibid. at 103.
103 *Report on the Family, Part I* was published by the Civil Code Revision Office in Montreal on 31 May 1974. *Part II* was published on 10 October 1975. The other members of the committee included Jean-Guy Cardinal (professor and notary), Denyse Fortin (notary), Ethel Groffier-Atala (professor), Denyse Guay-Archambault (lawyer), Albert Mayrand (judge of the Court of Appeal), and Roland Milette (notary). The recommendations built upon previous legislation that had begun to modernize the *Civil Code:* SQ 1964, c. 66, declaring the legal capacity of married women; SQ 1969, c. 74, on the solemnization of civil marriage; SQ 1969, c. 77, reforming matrimonial regimes; SQ 1970, c. 62, granting rights to children born out of wedlock and their parents; and SQ 1971, c. 85, lowering the age of majority and making provision for the legitimacy of children born outside of marriage. The Civil Code Revision Office presented the *Draft Civil Code* and explanatory *Commentaries* to the National Assembly in 1978. The framework became the new *Civil Code of Québec,* SQ 1991, c. 64, which came into force on 1 January 1994. "Professor Paul-André Crépeau," see note 93 above.
104 Interview with Paul-André Crépeau, Montreal, 1 October 2010.
105 Born in Montreal in 1940, Louise Mailhot studied law at the University of Montreal and McGill, and was admitted to the bar in 1966. She practised employment and public law in Montreal, was appointed to the Superior Court of Quebec in 1980, and became the first woman appointed to the Court of Appeal of Quebec in Montreal in 1987. Interview with Louise Mailhot, Gananoque, ON, 20 May 2009.
106 Interview with Roger Garneau, Quebec City, 28 April 2009.

CHAPTER 16: PRACTISING AS A WOMAN

1 Barreau du Québec data from 1950–51 showed women across the province composing 1.11 percent of the practising bar, 21 individuals in total. Data for 1960–61 showed 69 female lawyers, or 2.93 percent. Data for 1970–71 showed 193 female lawyers, or 5.6 percent. Data for 1972–73 showed 292 female lawyers, or 6.72 percent. Untitled, undated list showing members, women, and men from 1942 to 1999.
2 The 1999 percentages were: Quebec, 40.0; Prince Edward Island, 35.2; Yukon, 34.6; Ontario, 30.2; Nova Scotia, 28.2; Northwest Territories and Nunavut, 28.1; British Columbia, 27.6; Newfoundland, 26.8; Alberta, 26.4; New Brunswick, 26.1; Saskatchewan, 24.7; and Manitoba, 24.0. Fiona M. Kay and Joan Brockman, "Crossroads to Innovation and Diversity: The Careers of Women Lawyers in Quebec" (2007) 47 McGill LJ 699 at 701–9.
3 The Quiet Revolution created the conditions for a strengthening women's movement, the explosion of public educational opportunities for women, the secularization of female Quebec religious orders, the hope that law could be a useful tool in the struggle to achieve gender equality, the regulatory expansion of the state, which increased the need for lawyers, and the exodus of men who would have become lawyers in past decades into new opportunities for Francophones in business and commerce. Mélanie Brunet, "Simply Catching Up? The 'Feminization' of Law Schools in Quebec since the 1960s" (Presentation delivered at the Osgoode Society for Canadian Legal History's Thirtieth Anniversary Symposium, Osgoode Hall, 30 October 2009); Kay and Brockman, ibid. at 709.
4 Comment from "Women in Law: A Video by Perry Bard" (1994). Unless otherwise indicated, information is drawn from interviews with Claire L'Heureux-Dubé in Quebec City, Ottawa, Rimouski, and Clearwater, FL, on 30 October, 1 November, and 2 December 2007; 29–30 April, 1–2 May, and 23–25 July 2008; 5 March, 27–28 April, 10–14 May, and 21 September 2009; 10 March, 30 June, and 13 September 2010; and 4–5 July 2013.
5 Claire L'Heureux-Dubé, quoted in Cécile Brosseau, "Claire L'Heureux-Dubé, la femme des défis," *La Presse* (12 February 1975) D3.

6 Mabel Van Camp, one of the first women to be appointed to the Ontario Supreme Court, recalled that women had difficulty being accepted "socially – on the golf course, going out to lunch – [it's] easier to take another man along." Linda Silver Dranoff, "Women as Lawyers in Toronto" (1972) 10 Osgoode Hall LJ 177 at 182.

7 Interview with Roger Garneau, Quebec City, 28 April 2009. Licensed taverns served beer by the glass and had a monopoly on draft beer. They provided "a place for male socialization" in urban working-class neighbourhoods. Small groups of Quebec feminists, members of the Front de libération des femmes, first demonstrated against the gender bar in taverns in the years 1970–72, but legislation to admit women was not enacted until 1979. Diane Lamoureux, *Fragments et collages: essai sur le féminisme québécois des années 70* (Montréal: Éditions du remue-ménage, 1986) at 127; Micheline Dumont, *Le féminisme québécois raconté à Camille* (Montréal: Éditions du remue-ménage, 2008) at 128; John Dickinson and Brian Young, *A Short History of Quebec*, 3rd ed. (Montreal: McGill-Queen's University Press, 1983) at 232.

8 Promotional pamphlet for the Club de la Garnison de Québec.

9 For a wider analysis of the anti-Semitic policies of Canadian private clubs, see Harold Troper, *The Defining Decade: Identity, Politics, and the Canadian Jewish Community in the 1960s* (Toronto: University of Toronto Press, 2010) at 248–62.

10 Interview with Claire L'Heureux-Dubé, Ottawa, 30 June 2010.

11 *In re Mabel P. French* (1905), 37 NBR 359 (Ct of King's Bench). French was admitted to the bar a year later (21 April 1906), after the New Brunswick legislature passed a special act allowing it; SNB 1906, c. 5.

12 Interview with Claire L'Heureux-Dubé, Quebec City, 27–28 April 2009.

13 Claire L'Heureux-Dubé, "Femmes et droit: le regard d'une pionnière, une vision du passé et de l'avenir" in Hélène Dumont, ed., *Femmes et droit: 50 ans de vie commune ... et tout un avenir* (Montréal: Éditions Thémis, 1991) at 315.

14 Interview with Claire L'Heureux-Dubé, Quebec City, 27–28 April 2009.

15 The interviewee who related this anecdote asked not to have it attributed to her by name. Shirley Tucker Parks, admitted to the Saskatchewan bar in 1953, had similar experiences with a Saskatchewan judge, who "wouldn't issue a writ to me unless I held his hand first. He was considered a ladies' man. I took a lot of ribbing." Interview with Shirley Tucker Parks, Ottawa, 19 November 2009.

16 Interview with Claire L'Heureux-Dubé, Quebec City, 27–28 April 2009.

17 Interview with Louise Mailhot, Gananoque, ON, 20 May 2009.

18 Interview with Raymond Lessard, Île d'Orléans, QC, 11 May 2010. Lessard's firm hired two women in 1971: Lise Morency (admitted to the bar in 1970) and Claire J. Jacques (admitted to the bar in 1955, and wife of one of the partners). *Canadian Law List, 1963–71* (Toronto: Cartwright and Sons, and Canada Law Book, n.d.).

19 Toronto lawyer Maureen Sabia, then practising with the government, stated: "Women are very often encouraged to draft wills or work on real estate ... you're told you can't go into court and battle it out because you're too weak." *Toronto Star* (29 October 1971).

20 L'Heureux-Dubé, "Femmes et droit," see note 13 above at 314.

21 Jennifer K. Bankier, "Women and the Law School: Problems and Potential" (1974) 22:5 Chitty's LJ 171 at 174: "One interviewer [of a female articling student in Ontario] said that he found the concept of women as litigation lawyers very difficult to accept because if he finds a woman on the other side of the court he wants to make love to her instead of arguing with her, and he finds it distracting."

22 Interview with Raymond Lessard, Île d'Orléans, QC, 11 May 2010.

23 The comments are from a survey that sent 640 questionnaires to female lawyers across Canada. There was a return rate of 43 percent, or 267. There were 117 respondents who were called in the 1960s, 72 in the 1950s, 41 in the 1940s, and 36 earlier. One did not indicate call date. Cameron Harvey, "Women in Law in Canada" (1970–71) 4 Man LJ 9 at 12.

24 *Globe and Mail* (19 April 1967). Judy LaMarsh graduated from law at Osgoode Hall in 1950, practised with her father's law firm in Niagara Falls, was elected as a Liberal to Parliament in 1960, and served as the second woman appointed to the federal cabinet from 1963 to 1968. Judy LaMarsh, *Memoirs of a Bird in a Gilded Cage* (Toronto: McClelland and Stewart, 1969).
25 Interview with Annette April, Montreal, 4 June 2010.
26 Patricia T. Rooke and R.L. Schnell, *No Bleeding Heart: Charlotte Whitton, a Feminist on the Right* (Vancouver: UBC Press, 1987) at 2.
27 L'Heureux-Dubé, "Femmes et droit," see note 13 above at 314.
28 Peter Mark Roget, *Thesaurus of English Words and Phrases* (Toronto: Longmans, Green, 1947) at 328, 440.
29 Roget, ibid. at 120, 702.
30 John J. Robinette, considered the leading Canadian barrister of his time, itemized the two things needed to be a successful lawyer: "a pair of strong legs and an understanding wife." Jack Batten, *Robinette: The Dean of Canadian Lawyers* (Toronto: Macmillan of Canada, 1984) at 150.
31 Anna R. Hayes, *Without Precedent: The Life of Susie Marshall Sharpe* (Chapel Hill: University of North Carolina Press, 2008), described various efforts taken by Sharpe, the first woman in the United States to be elected chief justice of a state supreme court in 1974, to accomplish this end.
32 Thérèse F. Casgrain, *A Woman in a Man's World* (Toronto: McClelland and Stewart, 1972) at 10.
33 Harvey, "Women in Law in Canada," see note 23 above at 14.
34 Interview with Roger Garneau, Quebec City, 28 April 2009.
35 Interview with Raymond Lessard, Île d'Orléans, QC, 11 May 2010.
36 Interview with Roger Garneau, Quebec City, 28 April 2009.
37 Interview with Claire L'Heureux-Dubé, Quebec City, 27–28 April 2009.
38 Roget, *Thesaurus,* see note 28 above, lists "tiger" as synonymous with these at 328.
39 *Globe and Mail* (20 October 1944), quoting British Columbia lawyer Mrs. S.M.G. Duff and Toronto lawyer Vera Parsons, who added that women should be treated as "just another black-robed advocate" who asked "no quarter from legal adversaries."
40 Dranoff, "Women as Lawyers in Toronto," see note 6 above at 179.
41 Ibid. at 189.
42 Lynn Smith, Marylee Stephenson, and Gina Quijano, "The Legal Profession and Women: Finding Articles in British Columbia" (1973) 8 UBC L Rev 146.
43 Quoting Ritchie's letter accompanying the return of her survey responses, in Harvey, "Women in Law in Canada," see note 23 above at 13.
44 The comment, made in 1966, was quoted ibid. at 22.
45 Harvey, ibid. at 14, noted that there was "a significant number of women who very definitely indicated that not only had they never experienced any discrimination, but that they had always been treated respectfully simply as lawyers and that they could not be happier in their chosen profession."
46 Interview with Claire L'Heureux-Dubé, Quebec City, 27–28 April 2009.
47 Ibid.
48 Interview with Claire L'Heureux-Dubé, Clearwater, FL, 10–14 May 2009.
49 Interview with Claire L'Heureux-Dubé, Quebec City, 27–28 April 2009.
50 Interview with Claire L'Heureux-Dubé, Clearwater, FL, 10–14 May 2009.
51 Andrée Lévesque, "Grâce à Simone de Beauvoir" in Marguerite Andersen, ed., *Feminist Journeys/Voies féministes* (Ottawa: Feminist History Society, 2010) 219 at 219.
52 Interview with Claire L'Heureux-Dubé, Clearwater, FL, 10–14 May 2009.
53 Correspondence from L'Heureux-Dubé, 25 October 2015.
54 Ibid.

55 Francophone women voice extensive tributes to de Beauvoir in Andersen, *Feminist Journeys/ Voies féministes*, see note 51 above.
56 Dumont, *Le féminisme québécois raconté à Camille*, see note 7 above at 106–7. Other influential feminist texts included Kate Millett's *Sexual Politics* (published in 1969, translated into French in 1971), Shulamith Firestone's *The Dialectic of Sex* (published in 1970, translated into French in 1972), and Germaine Greer's *The Female Eunuch* (published in 1970, translated into French in 1971). Clio Collective, *Quebec Women: A History*, trans, Roger Gannon and Rosalind Gill (Toronto: Women's Press, 1987) at 358.
57 Dumont, ibid. at 101.
58 Michael Gauvreau, *The Catholic Origins of Quebec's Quiet Revolution, 1931–1970* (Montreal: McGill-Queen's University Press, 2005) at 233. Michèle Jean, *Québécoises du 20ᵉ siècle* (Montréal: Éditions Quinze, 1977) at 34, identifies three new strains of feminism that emerged in the province from the 1960s through the 1980s: radical feminism, socialist feminism, and Québécois feminism.
59 Thérèse Forget Casgrain was born to an upper-class family in Montreal in 1896, married lawyer and MP Pierre-François Casgrain in 1916, and led the campaign for provincial suffrage for decades. She stood unsuccessfully for provincial election as an independent Liberal, as a member of the Co-operative Commonwealth Federation, and later for the New Democratic party. She was appointed to the Senate in 1970. Other leaders within the Voix des femmes included Mariana Jodoin, Ghislaine Laurendeau, Simonne Monet-Chartrand, Léa Roback, Solange Chaput-Rolland. Casgrain, *A Woman in a Man's World*, see note 32 above at 157; Dumont, *Le féminisme québécois raconté à Camille*, see note 7 above at 101.
60 Mona-Josée Gagnon, *Les femmes vues par le Québec des hommes: 30 ans d'histoire des idéologies 1940–1970* (Montréal: Éditions du jour, 1974) at 106.
61 Clio Collective, *Quebec Women*, see note 56 above at 337.
62 Réjane Laberge-Colas was appointed to the Superior Court of Quebec in Montreal in February 1969. Jean, *Québécoises du 20ᵉ siècle*, see note 58 above at 42; Paul Jones and Donna Clark, *Who's Who of Canadian Women* (Toronto: Who's Who Publications, 1998) at 196; "Réjane Laberge-Colas" in *Biographies canadiennes-françaises, 1920–1970* (Montréal: Éditions biographiques canadiennes-françaises, 1970) at 368.
63 Alice Desjardins graduated in law from the University of Montreal in 1957, and was called to the bar in 1958. She became the first female tenure-stream Canadian law professor when she was appointed to the University of Montreal in 1961. She obtained an LL.M. from Harvard in 1967 and worked at the Constitutional Review Section of the Privy Council Office from 1969 to 1974, when she moved to the Department of Justice. She was elevated to the Quebec Superior Court in 1981, and became the first woman appointed to the Federal Court of Appeal in 1987. Interview with Alice Desjardins, Ottawa, 2 July 2009.
64 Dumont, *Femmes et droit*, see note 13 above at 31–32. She also noted that Yvette Dussault-Mailoux had become the first woman named to Magistrate's Court in 1964, that Claire Barrette-Joncas would become the first to preside over a jury trial on assizes in 1975, and that Gabrielle Vallée would become the province's first female (associate) chief justice on 12 August 1976.
65 Although she was elected its vice president, she does not recall extensive or lengthy involvement. "Me Claire L'Heureux, vice-présidente de l'Association des avocates" (undated, unlabelled clipping).
66 Lamoureux, *Fragments et collages*, see note 7 above at 55–56; Dumont, *Le féminisme québécois raconté à Camille*, see note 7 above at 115.
67 Gagnon, *Les femmes vues par le Québec des hommes*, see note 60 above at 82, 143.
68 Diane Lamoureux, *L'amère patrie: féminisme et nationalisme dans le Québec contemporain* (Montréal: Éditions du remue-ménage, 2001) at 105, 115.

69 Francine Descarries, "Le projet féministe à l'aube du 21ᵉ siècle: un projet de libération et de solidarité qui fait toujours sens" (1998) 30 Cahiers de recherche sociologique 179 at 179–210; Francine Descarries, "Le mouvement des femmes Québécois: état des lieux" (undated, unpublished manuscript). At 1, Descarries described the Quebec feminist movement at the end of the 1960s as "*un moment sans précédent de discours, de revendications et de pratiques féministes*" ("an unprecedented moment of feminist discourses, demands, and practices").
70 Clio Collective, *Quebec Women*, see note 56 above at 346, 357–66; Dumont, *Le féminisme québécois raconté à Camille*, see note 7 above at 121–31, 137–53. Dumont noted at 162: "*À la fin des années 1970, presque toutes les québécoises ont été touchées d'une manière ou d'une autre par les féministes ou par le mouvement des femmes*" ("By the end of the 1970s, almost all women in Quebec were affected in one way or another by feminists or by the women's movement").
71 Lamoureux, *L'amère patrie*, see note 68 above at 132, 138–48. The FLFQ was officially created in November 1969. Michèle Jean, *Québécoises du 20ᵉ siècle*, see note 58 above at 42–43.
72 Correspondence from Claire L'Heureux-Dubé, 25 October 2015.
73 Similar thinking dogged Gloria Steinem, an internationally famous feminist from the United States, who was told when she started to write about the women's movement for New York magazines: "You've worked so hard to be taken seriously. Don't get involved with these crazy women." She dismissed the caution and became an international leader of the women's movement. Philip Galanes, "The fights of their lives," *New York Times* (15 November 2015) 17.
74 Lily Tasso, "La famille avant la politique chez Madame Claire L'Heureux-Dubé" (clipping dated 5 October 1972, in scrapbook held by Paul L'Heureux).
75 Interview with Shirley Tucker Parks, Ottawa, 19 November 2009.
76 Interview with Julien Payne, Ottawa, 7 July 2009.

Chapter 17: New Career Directions

1 Unless otherwise indicated, information is from interviews with Claire L'Heureux-Dubé in Quebec City, Ottawa, Rimouski, and Clearwater, FL, on 30 October, 1 November, and 2 December 2007; 29–30 April 2008; 5 March, 10–14 May, and 21 September 2009, 10 March, 30 June, and 13 September 2010; and 30 August 2012.
2 Federal cabinet ministers Robert Andras and Jean Marchand co-chaired the 1972 federal election campaign. Joseph-Yvon-Jean-Paul Lefebvre, born 1926, had risen through the ranks of the Jeunesse Étudiante Catholique, inspired by his interest in adult education, to work with Jean Marchand at the Confédération des syndicats nationaux and then to serve as the Liberal member of the Quebec legislature for the riding of Ahuntsic from 1966 to 1970. He was close to Gérard Pelletier, Fernand Cadieux, Marc Lalonde, and Pierre Elliott Trudeau, and worked in the federal public service after the 1972 election. Lefebvre later served as secretary general of the Liberal party, Section Quebec. Interview with Marc Lalonde, L'Île-Perrot, QC, 16 August 2012; interview with Monique Bégin, Ottawa, 4 September 2011; Monique Bégin's email correspondence of 5 September 2011; Pierre G. Normandin, *The Canadian Parliamentary Guide 1970* (Ottawa: Gale Canada, 1970) at 758–59; John English, *The Life of Pierre Elliott Trudeau*, vol. 2, *Just Watch Me, 1968–2000* (Toronto: Knopf Canada, 2009) at 175.
3 John English, *The Life of Pierre Elliott Trudeau*, vol. 1, *Citizen of the World, 1919–1968* (Toronto: Knopf Canada, 2006).
4 Micheline Dumont, *Le féminisme québécois raconté à Camille* (Montréal: Éditions du remue-ménage, 2008) at 165.

5 The Liberal platform, "The Land Is Strong," offered evidence of economic growth and then stated: "Behind these statistics is a man with a good job and a steady wage; a man and a woman starting a new family in a new house; another man with a good job because Canadian products sell so well abroad; still another man with a good job because Canadian enterprise has the confidence in itself and in the country to re-invest to create the new jobs our young people want." English, *Just Watch Me,* see note 2 above at 178; interview with Monique Bégin, Ottawa, 4 September 2011.
6 Monique Bégin recalled that although she never saw the reputed list, she was told she was number eight, and that other names included Rita Cadieux and Monique Coupal. Many refused to run. The campaign organizers on the English Canadian side apparently told Trudeau that "there were no women capable." As a result, the only Liberal women elected in 1972 were from Quebec. Interview with Monique Bégin, ibid.
7 Interview with Marc Lalonde, L'Île-Perrot, QC, 16 August 2012.
8 Interview with Claire L'Heureux-Dubé, Quebec City, 30 August 2012.
9 English, *Citizen of the World,* see note 3 above.
10 In the 1940s, a small group of French Canadians living in Ottawa (among them Arthur Dubé and Gérard Morin, correspondent of *Le Soleil*) would dine at Le Canton, a Chinese restaurant favoured by Pierre Trudeau.
11 Interview with Claire L'Heureux-Dubé, Quebec City, 27–28 April 2009.
12 Interview with Claire L'Heureux-Dubé, Quebec City, 30 August 2012. L'Heureux-Dubé's memory retained several versions of the conversation. André Legault recalled hearing from her a still different version: "Trudeau approached her and said, 'You'd be a good minister in my cabinet.' She said 'I know nothing about being elected ... whether people would vote for me.' He said, 'Don't worry – I've got a place for you to run, even a dog could get elected there.' She said, 'So you think I'm a dog!' And he said, 'No, that's not what I meant.' They were laughing about it." Interview with André Legault, Ottawa, 10 December 2007.
13 Interview with Claire L'Heureux-Dubé, Quebec City, 27–28 April 2009.
14 Lily Tasso, "La famille avant la politique chez Madame Claire L'Heureux-Dubé" (clipping dated 5 October 1972, in scrapbook held by Paul L'Heureux).
15 Dumont, *Le féminisme québécois raconté à Camille,* see note 4 above at 165; Michèle Jean, *Québécoises du 20ᵉ siècle* (Montréal: Éditions Quinze, 1977) at 43.
16 Albanie (Paré) Morin was born on 30 April 1921 in St. Elizabeth, Manitoba. Her husband, George Morin, ran an automobile sales and repair business. She began her career as a secretary. After she married, she completed her university education, with degrees in history, education, and translation. She served as the assistant deputy chair of the House of Commons Committee of the Whole from 1974 to 1976. She had completed all of her law courses but had not yet been called to the bar when she died on 30 September 1976. Interview with Albanie Morin (daughter of Albanie Paré Morin), Montreal, 1 August 2008; Wayne D. Madden, *Canadian Women M.P.s and M.L.A.s* (Fort McMurray, AB: A Little Bit of Hope [Madden], 1998) at 12; Jean Bannerman, *Leading Ladies Canada* (Belleville, ON: Mika Publishing, 1977) at 263–64.
17 "If she's in a room, she'd know everybody in the room by the time the evening's over." Interview with Julien Payne, Ottawa, 7 July 2009.
18 When the Liberals recruited Monique Bégin to run in 1972, they offered her a "safe" Montreal seat, pledged to run no fewer than three Québécoises, and provided financial support for the campaign. L'Heureux-Dubé's entrance into politics would likely have been similarly assisted. Interview with Monique Bégin, Ottawa, 4 September 2011.
19 Ibid.; interview with Marc Lalonde, L'Île-Perrot, QC, 16 August 2012. In addition to the three Quebec Liberal women, the two other female MPs were Grace MacInnis (New Democratic party, Vancouver–Kingsway) and Flora MacDonald (Progressive Conservative, Kingston and the Islands). Grace MacInnis was the daughter of J.S. Woodsworth, the

founder of the Co-operative Commonwealth Federation predecessor party to the NDP, and had held the seat since 1965. As for all of the others, this was their first term as MP. Sunny P. Lewis, *Grace: The Life of Grace MacInnis* (Madeira Park, BC: Harbour Publishing, 1993); Ann Farrell, *Grace MacInnis: The Story of Her Love and Integrity* (Markham, ON: Fitzhenry and Whiteside, 1994); Madden, *Canadian Women M.P.s and M.L.A.s,* see note 16 above at 12.

20 See Constance Backhouse, "What If? Career Paths Not Taken: Claire L'Heureux-Dubé and Politics" (2014) 29 CJLS 273.

21 Interview with Monique Bégin, Ottawa, 4 September 2011; interview with Marc Lalonde, L'Île-Perrot, QC, 16 August 2012; interview with Stéphane Dion, Lake Couchiching, ON, 6 August 2011; interview with Allan Rock, Ottawa, 6 September 2012.

22 English, *The Life of Pierre Elliott Trudeau,* 2 vols., see notes 2 and 3 above; Stephen Clarkson and Christina McCall, *Trudeau and Our Times,* 2 vols. (Toronto: McClelland and Stewart, 1990–94).

23 Interview with Monique Bégin, Ottawa, 4 September 2011.

24 Interview with Claire L'Heureux-Dubé, Quebec City, 4–5 July 2013.

25 Interviews with Claire L'Heureux-Dubé, Ottawa, 21 September 2009; Quebec City, 30 August 2012. The salary of $38,000 is set out in the subsequent letter from the deputy minister of justice confirming the judicial appointment on 13 February 1973.

26 The alternate candidate, André Desmeules, who had been active in the youth wing of the Liberal party, was apparently on the shortlist for the position that L'Heureux-Dubé received, but did not obtain an appointment until 18 October 1973, some months after she did.

27 Interview with Claire L'Heureux-Dubé, Ottawa, 21 September 2009.

28 She replaced Gérard Lacroix, her former Laval professor, who retired on 17 January 1973. Ignace-J. Deslauriers, *La Cour supérieure du Québec et ses juges: 1849–1er janvier 1980* (Québec: Bibliothèque nationale du Québec, 1980) at 33, 144. Réjane Laberge-Colas had been appointed by Justice Minister John Turner and Prime Minister Trudeau to the Superior Court of Quebec in Montreal on 20 February 1969. She had graduated from the Faculty of Law at the University of Montreal (LL.L. *cum laude*), and ranked first at the bar exams in 1952. She was married to Émile Colas, a Montreal lawyer, and the couple was part of a tight network of successful Liberal professionals. Her first five years in practice were as in-house counsel with Aluminium Secretariat. She had just joined the law office of Geoffrion et Prud'homme in 1969 when she was appointed to the court. Interview with Monique Bégin, Ottawa, 5 September 2012; Jean, *Québécoises du 20e siècle,* see note 15 above at 42; Alison Prentice et al., *Canadian Women: A History* (Harcourt Brace Jovanovich, 1988) at 346; Lucie-Anne Fabien, "Décès de l'honorable Réjane Laberge-Colas – 1923–2009," *Canada Newswire* (10 August 2009); Deslauriers, ibid. at 45. The second woman was Mabel Margaret Van Camp, who was appointed by Justice Minister Turner and Prime Minister Trudeau to the Supreme Court of Ontario in 1971. Born in Blackstock, north of Toronto, in 1920, Van Camp graduated from Osgoode Hall Law School and was called to the bar in 1947. She practised in Toronto with Beaudoin, Pepper and Van Camp until her appointment. Mabel Van Camp Obituary, William Illsey Atkinson, "I am the damn judge," *Globe and Mail* (9 August 2012) R5.

There had been prior appointments to lower levels of court. Helen Kinnear was appointed to the county court of the County of Haldimand, Ontario, in 1943, the first to be appointed to such a high judicial post in the British Commonwealth. She was the first woman in the Commonwealth to receive a KC (1934), the first woman to appear before the Supreme Court of Ontario, and the first to appear before the Supreme Court of Canada. Others who were not lawyers by training were appointed earlier: Emily Murphy, Canada's first female police magistrate, was appointed in Edmonton in 1916; Alice Jamieson was appointed a police magistrate in Calgary in 1916; and Helen Gregory MacGill was appointed to the Juvenile Court of Vancouver in 1917. Edra Sanders Ferguson was appointed

Ontario's first Division Court judge, as well as judge of the Juvenile and Family Court in 1962. See Cameron Harvey, "Women in Law in Canada" (1971) 4 Man LJ 9 at 20–22.
29 Interview with Claire L'Heureux-Dubé, Quebec City, 27–28 April 2009.
30 Interviews with Claire L'Heureux-Dubé, Ottawa, 5 March 2009; Ottawa, 21 September 2009; Quebec City, 30 August 2012.
31 L'Heureux-Dubé maintained this consistently during her interviews, as well as in a public presentation, "Conversation with the Hon. Justice Claire L'Heureux-Dubé" at the University of Ottawa Faculty of Law, 25 September 2012, despite contradictory recollections from the former Liberal cabinet ministers concerning protocol operating at the time.
32 Interview with Otto Lang, Winnipeg, 4 September 2009; interview with Marc Lalonde, L'Île-Perrot, QC, 16 August 2012. They stressed that the advocacy required at cabinet meetings was such that it would have been folly to put forward a file where the candidate had not previously agreed to the appointment. It would have meant expending political capital for no end, plus experiencing political embarrassment with a resulting loss in status.
33 On the "elusive quality of recollection," see Gregory Cowles, "The liars' club: Is there such a thing as a reliable memoir?" *New York Times Book Review* (25 October 2015) 20. Two alternate explanations are both less likely. One suggestion is that the process may have been initiated independently by Albanie Morin, who prevailed upon L'Heureux-Dubé after their first discussion to send in a résumé, even if only because it might be useful for other purposes. After L'Heureux-Dubé did so, this may have allowed Morin to take the candidacy forward, keeping the judicial appointment a live issue. Another possibility relates to Paul-André Crépeau, who had been badgering L'Heureux-Dubé to accept a full-time position with the Civil Code Revision Office, which she had declined, saying the pay was unsustainable. She had apparently joked that if she became a judge, maybe she could negotiate a secondment to Crépeau's office. Crépeau may have taken this to signify L'Heureux-Dubé's desire for a judicial appointment, and confirmed this with Lang, who later consulted him regarding the appointment. Neither of these versions overrides Lang's and Lalonde's assertions that no Order-in-Council would go forward without the candidate's prior agreement.
34 Nicole Beaulieu, "Première femme nommée juge à la Cour supérieure de Québec," *Action Québec* (10 March 1973).
35 She recalled selling her old house for $27,000 and bargaining down the asking price for the Mont-Saint-Denis house from $85,000 to $55,000. She paid off the mortgage in five years. "I was responsible for the tulips, my husband had the roses," L'Heureux-Dubé recalled. "We won a prize for those gardens."
36 Beaulieu, "Première femme," see note 34 above.
37 Linda Hirshman, *Sisters in Law: How Sandra Day O'Connor and Ruth Bader Ginsburg Went to the Supreme Court and Changed the World* (New York: HarperCollins, 2015), introduction.
38 Beaulieu, "Première femme," see note 34 above.
39 Morin had also taken steps to seek a reference from L'Heureux-Dubé's former Laval classmate Gilles Carle, who was a family friend of hers. He recommended L'Heureux-Dubé highly. Marc Lalonde has been suggested as the other possible initiator, but he denied any involvement. Interview with Marc Lalonde, L'Île-Perrot, QC, 16 August 2012.
40 Interview with Albanie Morin (daughter of Albanie Paré Morin), Montreal, 1 August 2008.
41 Interview with Otto Lang, Winnipeg, 4 September 2009.
42 Otto Lang's 161 new appointments constituted a 45 percent increase over John Turner's 111 new appointments, and Turner's record itself constituted a significant increase over that of his predecessor. The growth in number of positions resulted from improved retirement options and an increase in the number of judges. Within a two-week period early in 1973, Lang appointed Jean Beetz and Fred Kaufman to the Quebec Court of Appeal, and Willard Estey, Charles Dubin, and G. Arthur Martin to the Ontario Court of Appeal; later that spring, he appointed Brian Dickson to the Supreme Court of Canada. Bora Laskin was

also elevated within the Supreme Court of Canada, becoming the country's first Jewish chief justice. It was Otto Lang who made the decision to depart from tradition by elevating Laskin over the more senior Justice Ronald Martland. Trudeau was initially preoccupied with impending fatherhood and expected precedent to be followed, but when Lang suggested the Laskin elevation, he supported the idea with enthusiasm. Ed Ratushny, "Judicial Appointments: The Lang Legacy" (1977–78) 1 Advocates' Q 2 at 4–7, 16; Philip Girard, *Bora Laskin: Bringing Law to Life* (Toronto: University of Toronto Press, 2005); Government of Canada, *Guide to Canadian Ministries since Confederation July 1, 1867 to February 1, 1982* (Ottawa: Government of Canada, 1982) at 157.
43 Interview with Shirley Tucker Parks, Ottawa, 19 November 2009.
44 Interview with Monique Bégin, Ottawa, 19 July and 5 September 2012.
45 Interview with Ed Ratushny, Ottawa, 15 August 2009; Ratushny, "Judicial Appointments," see note 42 above at 7.
46 Interview with Otto Lang, Winnipeg, 4 September 2009.
47 The second, Gabrielle Vallée, was also appointed to the Quebec Superior Court in 1973. Ratushny noted that there were few women who had the "ten years standing at the bar required by the *Judges Act*," but that the problem was exacerbated because "a higher percentage of women lawyers have declined to let their names stand for judicial appointment for personal reasons." He added: "[I]t is probably fair to say that Mr. Lang's greatest disappointment in relation to judicial appointments was his limited success in being able to appoint more women to the bench." Ratushny, "Judicial Appointments," see note 42 above at 14–15.
48 Geoffrey Stevens, "What makes a good judge?" *Globe and Mail* (8 March 1974): "There are special problems, Mr. Lang says, in recruiting women judges. Women account for only 3 per cent of the practising lawyers in Canada. Many of them are in fairly narrow specialties such as institutional work (with trust companies and the like) and family law; relatively few do litigation work. Although women are entering law schools in ever-increasing numbers, the ten year rule means that it will be some time before there is a large pool to draft from."
49 National Archives and Records Administration transcript, cited in John Dean, *The Rehnquist Choice* (New York: Simon and Schuster, 2001) at 104, 113, 155.
50 Ibid. at 113.
51 Sandra Day O'Connor, *Out of Order* (New York: Random House, 2014).
52 Interview with Otto Lang, Winnipeg, 4 September 2009.
53 Don Sellar, "Here comes the judge – but whose choice?" *Montreal Gazette* (2 April 1974).
54 Ratushny, "Judicial Appointments," see note 42 above at 6.
55 The CBA committee was composed of two members each from Ontario and Quebec, and one each from all the other provinces except Prince Edward Island and Newfoundland. The chair requested each member to make discreet telephone inquiries about the candidate. Once the responses were received, the chair formulated a final assessment and submitted it to the minister. If the minister disagreed with a negative assessment by the committee, he might request reasons and/or reassessment. The ratio of names submitted to appointments made was approximately four to one. Ibid. at 6–11. Geoffrey Stevens noted that although the opinions were not binding on the government, "as far as can be determined only once since 1967 has an individual been appointed who was deemed to be not qualified; that was to a county court in Ontario." Geoffrey Stevens, "Judicial appointments," *Globe and Mail* (7 March 1974) 6.
56 A reference on file from Deputy Minister of Justice Donald S. Maxwell, stating that L'Heureux-Dubé would be a very good candidate, came too late in the process to be influential. "It just shows how out of the loop he was," reflected Lang, noting that judicial appointments constituted "a separate operation from the deputy minister and the bureaucracy." Interview with Otto Lang, Winnipeg, 4 September 2009.

57 Shortly after her appointment, the consultation process intensified. Otto Lang felt "overwhelmed by the number of judicial vacancies and underwhelmed by his lack of information on which to make these decisions," according to Ed Ratushny. Ratushny was charged with taking proactive measures to conduct broader consultations with the bench, bar, and legal academia to gather "as much relevant information as possible about every name recommended," even before deciding to refer someone to the CBA committee. Email from Ed Ratushny, 16 August 2009; Ratushny "Judicial Appointments," see note 42 above at 6–11.
58 It was L'Heureux-Dubé's suspicion that Crépeau may have hoped that once she was a judge, she could be seconded to assist him. In fact there would be no release time from the court, and she continued her *Civil Code* work on a voluntary basis on top of her judicial responsibilities. Interview with Paul-André Crépeau, Montreal, 1 October 2010.
59 Interview with Otto Lang, Winnipeg, 4 September 2009.
60 Ibid.
61 Dean, *The Rehnquist Choice,* see note 49 above at 235.
62 Interview with Claire L'Heureux-Dubé, Ottawa, 21 September 2009.
63 Interview with Monique Perron, Quebec City, 2 May 2008.
64 Sellar, "Here comes the judge," see note 53 above.
65 Interview with Jacques Philippon, Quebec City, 28 April 2009.
66 Interview with Nicole L'Heureux, Clearwater, FL, 11–12 May 2009.
67 Interview with Otto Lang, Winnipeg, 4 September 2009; Ratushny "Judicial Appointments," see note 42 above at 4.
68 Ratushny, ibid. at 6–11.
69 Brian Kappler, "You scratch my back," *Windsor Star* (24 August 1974).
70 Stevens, "Judicial appointments," see note 55 above at 6.
71 Interview with Otto Lang, Winnipeg, 4 September 2009.
72 Lang noted that Manitoba was even "harder" than Quebec in this process. Ibid.
73 Ratushny, "Judicial Appointments," see note 42 above at 12; interview with Otto Lang, ibid.
74 Interview with Otto Lang, ibid.
75 Interview with Monique Bégin, Ottawa, 19 July 2012.
76 Interview with Marc Lalonde, L'Île-Perrot, QC, 16 August 2012. Lalonde added, with a smile, "Madeleine Parent was not a member of the CNTU," referring to the Confederation of National Trade Unions/Confédération des syndicats nationaux.
77 Otto Lang's recollection was that the Marchand veto might also have been lodged at an earlier stage of consideration, when a Montreal judgeship was under consideration and someone had raised L'Heureux-Dubé's name as a candidate. The position was filled by Albert Malouf on 24 May 1972. L'Heureux-Dubé maintained that she had no inkling that she was being considered for an earlier Montreal judicial position. Interview with Otto Lang, Winnipeg, 4 September 2009.
78 Ibid.
79 Stevens, "What makes a good judge?" see note 48 above.
80 Gail Cuthbert Brandt et al., *Canadian Women: A History,* 3rd ed. (Toronto: Nelson, 2011) at 527.
81 Letter of Laura Sabia, 18 April 1966, quoted in Cerise Morris, "No More Than Simple Justice: The Royal Commission on the Status of Women and Social Change in Canada" (MA thesis, McGill University Department of Sociology, January 1982) at 114.
82 Morris, ibid.
83 Anthony Westell, "Report is more explosive than any terrorists' time bomb," *Toronto Star* (8 December 1970).
84 Interview with Marc Lalonde, L'Île-Perrot, QC, 16 August 2012. Lalonde cited his wife, Claire, as a guiding force in his feminist education, along with books he read by Simone de Beauvoir, Benoîte Groult, Germaine Greer, and Margaret Mead. Monique Bégin attested

to Lalonde's support, noting that he believed in feminism and knew it was politically important. Interview with Monique Bégin, Ottawa, 19 July 2012.
85 Interview with Monique Bégin, ibid.
86 Dumont, *Le féminisme québécois raconté à Camille,* see note 4 above at 133.
87 Comments of Claire Lalonde during interview with Marc Lalonde, L'Île-Perrot, QC, 16 August 2012.
88 Interview with Monique Bégin, Ottawa, 4 September 2011 and 5 September 2012.
89 The Conseil du statut de la femme published a groundbreaking document in 1978 titled *Pour les Québécoises: égalité et indépendance.* Cuthbert Brandt et al., *Canadian Women,* see note 80 above at 531–32.
90 Ibid. at 532.
91 Jill Vickers, Pauline Rankin, and Christine Appelle, *Politics as if Women Mattered: A Political Analysis of the National Action Committee on the Status of Women* (Toronto: University of Toronto Press, 1993).
92 Dumont, *Le féminisme québécois raconté à Camille,* see note 4 above at 126–27.
93 Letters from Georgette Leblanc, Présidente, Les Clubs de Femmes de Carrières libérales et commerciales de la province de Québec, to MPs Jean Marchand, Jeanne Sauvé, Albanie Morin, Monique Bégin, Gérard Duquet, Ovide Laflamme, and Raynald Guay, 5 February 1973.
94 Interviews with Claire L'Heureux-Dubé, Ottawa, 21 September 2009; Quebec City, 30 August 2012.
95 Tucker Parks had moved to Ottawa from Saskatoon after graduating from the University of Saskatchewan, on her father's suggestion that it might be easier for a woman to find a job in the public service than in private practice back home. She spent twenty-two years with Central Mortgage and Housing, "until it became obvious that no matter how hard I worked, I would never get to be general counsel," at which point she moved to the Department of Justice until her retirement. Interview with Shirley Tucker Parks, Ottawa, 19 November 2009.
96 "Réjane Laberge-Colas (1923–2009) – Décès d'une pionnière de la magistrature," *Le Devoir* (11 August 2009).
97 Alice Desjardins was appointed to the Faculty of Law at the University of Montreal in 1961. Interview with Alice Desjardins, Ottawa, 2 July 2009.

CHAPTER 18: FIRST MONTHS ON THE BENCH

1 Unless otherwise indicated, information is from interviews with Claire L'Heureux-Dubé in Quebec City, Ottawa, Rimouski, and Clearwater, FL, on 30 October, 1 November, and 2 December 2007; 29–30 April 2008; 5 March, 10–14 May, and 21 September 2009; 10 March, 30 June, and 13 September 2010; 30 August 2012; and 4–5 July 2013. See also Claire L'Heureux-Dubé, "Outsiders on the Bench: The Continuing Struggle for Equality" (2001) 16 Wis Women's LJ 15.
2 Interview with Claire L'Heureux-Dubé, Ottawa, 13 September 2010.
3 Allocution de L'Honorable Frédéric Dorion, Juge en Chef de la Cour Supérieure, à la Prestation de Serment de Me Claire L'Heureux-Dubé Comme Juge de la Cour Supérieure, le 9 Mars 1973, à Québec (copy of speech held in private papers of Claire L'Heureux-Dubé).
4 Interview with Claire L'Heureux-Dubé, Ottawa, 21 September 2009.
5 Interview with Claire L'Heureux-Dubé, Ottawa, 13 September 2010. Les Chevaliers de Colomb du Québec (Knights of Columbus) was a lay Catholic order dedicated to the celebration of religion, the family, and fraternity, founded in the United States in 1882 and named in honour of Christopher Columbus, affirming the "discovery of America as a Catholic event." Christopher J. Kauffman, *Faith and Fraternalism: The History of the Knights of Columbus, 1882–1982* (New York: Harper and Row, 1982) at 1, 16.

6 Born in Saint-Joseph-de-Lévis, Quebec, in 1898, Frédéric Dorion graduated from the Collège de Charlesbourg and the Séminaire de Québec, studied law at Laval, was called to the bar in 1920, and had practised law with his two brothers, Noël and Charles Napoléon. All three brothers served as federal MPs, Noël also in the cabinet as secretary of state, and both Charles Napoléon and Frédéric were elected *bâtonniers.* Frédéric Dorion was appointed to the Superior Court in 1957, and became associate chief justice in 1961 and chief justice in 1963. He had become supernumerary on 2 February 1973, although he retained his post as chief justice until he was replaced by Jules Deschênes on 14 August 1973. He retired on 23 August 1973. Frédéric was also author of the 1965 Dorion Report on bribery and corruption within the federal government. Ignace-J. Deslauriers, *La Cour supérieure du Québec et ses juges: 1849–1er janvier 1980* (Québec: Bibliothèque nationale du Québec, 1980) at 11, 50, 129; "(Frédéric) Dorion" in B.M. Greene, ed., *Who's Who in Canada 1962–63* (Toronto: International Press, 1962–63) at 1275; "L'honorable Noël Dorion" in *Biographies canadiennes françaises, 1920–1970* (Montréal: Éditions biographiques canadiennes-françaises, 1970) at 233; Charles Napoléon Dorion" in J.A. Fortin, *Biographies canadiennes françaises, 1965* (Montréal: Éditions biographiques canadiennes françaises, 1965) at 478. The additional description is from interviews with Claire L'Heureux-Dubé.
7 Interview with Pierre-Gabriel Jobin, Montreal, 23 April 2010.
8 "Le juge Frédéric Dorion s'élève contre l'avortement," *L'Action Québec* (2 August 1973).
9 In 1949, while an MP, Dorion acted as counsel for Count Jacques Charles Noel Duge de Bernonville, a police official from Vichy France who had served as an aide to Gestapo chief Klaus Barbie. France was seeking his extradition for collaboration with the Nazis. Dorion defended his client not only in court but also in the House of Commons, where he opposed the extradition: "I am sure that if it had been Communist Jews who had come here instead of French Catholics, we would not have heard a word about them." Lorne Slotnick, "Barbie aide was the darling of Quebec's conservatives," *Globe and Mail* (11 February 1983).
10 In February 1973, the Quebec Superior Court at the District of Quebec was composed of the following judges, in order of seniority: Eugène Marquis, Antoine Lacourcière, Paul Lesage, Chief Justice Frédéric Dorion, Paul Miquelon, Jean-Robert Beaudoin, Yves Bernier, Gérard Corriveau, Georges Pelletier, Édouard Laliberté, Georges-René Fournier, Albert Mayrand, André Dubé, Jean-Jacques Bédard, Pierre Côté, Jacques Dufour, Vincent Masson, Sam Schwarz Bard, Ivan Mignault, Toussaint McNicoll. The latter was not the most junior but rather the most recent to the courthouse since he had transferred from Chicoutimi in 1971. Deslauriers, *La Cour supérieure du Québec et ses juges,* see note 6 above at 10–56.
11 Nicolas Tremblay, "Parfum de sagesse," in *Femmes: 100 Québécoises au sommet d'action* (Laval, QC: Entreprendre Magazine, 1999) at 43. Her sentiments would be shared by Constance Glube, the first woman appointed to the Supreme Court of Nova Scotia in 1976, three years later. "Walking into the common room for judges that first day was not easy," she recalled. "It was not easy being a woman who was one of the early ones." Interview with Constance Glube, Halifax, 28 October 2014.
12 Interview with Claire L'Heureux-Dubé, Ottawa, 13 September 2010. Jean-Robert Beaudoin was born in Thetford Mines in 1911 and graduated from the Séminaire de Québec in 1931 and Laval law school in 1934. Admitted to the bar in 1934, he was appointed to the Superior Court in 1960, and would become supernumerary in 1976. Deslauriers, *La Cour supérieure du Québec et ses juges,* see note 6 above at 66; Kathryn O'Handley, ed., *Canadian Parliamentary Guide, 1995* (Ottawa: Gale Canada, 1995) at 928.
13 Interview with Claire L'Heureux-Dubé, Ottawa, 13 September 2010.
14 Bard was appointed in 1969 and transferred to the District of Montreal on 1 June 1973. Deslauriers, *La Cour supérieure du Québec et ses juges,* see note 6 above at 27.
15 Interview with Yves Bernier, Quebec City, 30 April 2008. He was elevated from the Superior Court to the Court of Appeal in 1973. Deslauriers, ibid.

16 Interview with Melvin Rothman, Montreal, 12 August 2008. Deslauriers, ibid. at 45.
17 Deslauriers, ibid. at 50.
18 Coffin, a forty-year-old mining prospector, was tried, convicted, and sentenced to hang in August 1954. Appeals to the Court of Appeal and the Supreme Court were unsuccessful. *R. v. Coffin*, [1956] SCR 191. There was no recommendation for mercy, and the hanging took place in Montreal on 10 February 1956. Library and Archives Canada, "Persons Sentenced to Death in Canada, 1867–1976: An Inventory of Case Files in the Fonds of the Department of Justice," RG 13, vol. 1729–32, file CC786, 1954–64. Controversy attended the case, with concerns that circumstantial evidence was used to obtain an unjust conviction.
19 Ronald Turgsin and Arthur Lumas were the last two hanged in 1962. James H. Marsh, ed., *The Canadian Encyclopedia, Year 2000 Edition* (Toronto: McClelland and Stewart, 1999) at 398. *Criminal Law Amendment Act (No. 2)* SC 1974-85-76, c. 105 at ss. 25–28.
20 Interview with Claire L'Heureux-Dubé, Quebec City, 30 August 2012.
21 Mabel Van Camp, appointed to the Ontario Supreme Court in 1971, experienced similar problems. Since she was unmarried, some suggested she be called "Miss Justice." This struck others as too reminiscent of "injustice" and the clerks and lawyers settled on "Madam Justice" instead. Mabel Van Camp Obituary, William Illsey Atkinson, "I am the damn judge," *Globe and Mail* (9 August 2012) R5.
22 Interview with Claire L'Heureux-Dubé, Quebec City, 30 August 2012. In 1993, during oral argument for the case of *Symes v. Canada* at the Supreme Court of Canada, she had to remind federal government lawyer John Power, who had addressed his submissions to "My Lords" that if he wished the two female justices then on the top court to listen, he should use "My Lords, My Ladies." Rebecca Johnson, *Taxing Choices: The Intersection of Class, Gender, Parenthood, and the Law* (Vancouver: UBC Press, 2002) at 88.
23 Nicole Brossard, *La letter aérienne* (Montréal: Éditions du Remue-ménage, 1985).
24 Interview with Claire L'Heureux-Dubé, Quebec City, 30 August 2012.
25 Ibid.
26 DVD of Retirement Ceremony, 2002.
27 Interview with Claire L'Heureux-Dubé, Ottawa, 13 September 2010.
28 Ibid. She wore lace tabs at her 2002 retirement ceremony from the Supreme Court of Canada; DVD of Retirement Ceremony.
29 Louise Mailhot recalled that she was the first to wear lace tabs after her appointment to the Quebec Superior Court in 1980: "I bought a blouse in a Scottish shop with all the big Scottish lace, and I tacked it to some of my official blouses. I started that. Then we had meetings across Canada, and the other judges and lawyers started to imitate us. They would say where do you buy them, and I would bring the lady judges to this one store, and now this is across Canada." Interview with Louise Mailhot, Gananoque, ON, 20 May 2009.
30 *Bureau d'assainissement des eaux du Québec métropolitain v. Le conseil des ports nationaux*, 22 mai 1973, La Cour supérieure, District de Québec, No 14-237, Bibliothèques et Archives nationales du Québec.
31 Interview with Claire L'Heureux-Dubé, Quebec City, 30 August 2012.
32 Ibid.
33 Ibid.
34 Ibid.

Chapter 19: Immigration Commission of Inquiry

1 Unless otherwise indicated, information is from interviews with Claire L'Heureux-Dubé in Quebec City, Ottawa, Rimouski, and Clearwater, FL, on 30 October, 1 November, and 2 December 2007; 29–30 April 2008; 5 March, 10–14 May, and 21 September 2009; 10 March, 30 June, and 13 September 2010; and 30 August 2012.

2 Arthur Blakely, "Immigration probe on in Montreal," *Montreal Gazette* (14 August 1973); "Immigration: un juge enquêtera à Montréal," *La Presse* (14 August 1973). Marchand was probably the one who made the contact because of his personal knowledge of L'Heureux-Dubé. Robert Andras served as minister of manpower and immigration in the Trudeau cabinet between 27 November 1972 and 13 September 1976. Government of Canada, *Guide to Canadian Ministries since Confederation July 1, 1867 to February 1, 1982* (Ottawa: Government of Canada, 1982) at 159.
3 Interview with Claire L'Heureux-Dubé, Quebec City, 30 August 2012.
4 Ignace-J. Deslauriers, *La Cour supérieure du Québec et ses juges: 1849–1er janvier 1980* (Québec: Bibliothèque nationale du Québec, 1980) at 11, 50, 129, 144.
5 Interview with Claire L'Heureux-Dubé, Quebec City, 30 August 2012.
6 Interview with Claire L'Heureux-Dubé, Clearwater, FL, 10–14 May 2009.
7 Louise attended Saint-Joseph de Saint-Vallier and the Collège Notre-Dame-de-Bellevue, and Pierre was at Saint-Jean-Berchmans.
8 L'Heureux-Dubé's leave began 13 August 1973. The formal appointment occurred on 30 October 1973. Hearings took place from 23 April 1974 to 19 August 1975. The final report was filed on 19 January 1976, and she returned to the Superior Court that month. Privy Council Order 1973-3454; Deslauriers, *La Cour supérieure du Québec et ses juges*, see note 4 above at 144; *Report of the Commission of Inquiry Relating to the Department of Manpower and Immigration in Montreal* (Ottawa: Information Canada, January 1976) [hereafter *Report*].
9 Interview with Claire L'Heureux-Dubé, Quebec City, 30 August 2012.
10 Interview with Yves Bernier, Quebec City, 30 April 2008. In 1962, he had been seconded to chair a royal commission on pilotage, an inquiry that was intended to take six months but lasted nine years.
11 Born in 1934 in Montreal to Jewish parents, Hungarian-born Eugene Nuss and Piroska Schwartz, Joseph Nuss was married to Marissa Orenstein, whose family had been neighbours and close friends of Bora Laskin's family in Thunder Bay. Called to the bar in 1959, he practised with Ahearn, Nuss, and Drymer, sat on a Quebec bar committee to study the *Public Inquiries Act,* and appeared before the Commission of Inquiry on the Disruption of Shipping on the Great Lakes. Yves Fortier, who would later chair the Montreal law firm of Ogilvy Renault, was the lawyer L'Heureux-Dubé first approached for the position. Since he was already occupied with another inquiry on sugar, Fortier recommended Nuss, who had been a McGill law classmate. Nuss was later appointed to the Quebec Court of Appeal. Interview with Joseph R. Nuss, Montreal, 14 August 2008. Roger D. Pothier was the other counsel who served the inquiry.
12 Interview with Joseph R. Nuss, ibid.
13 These files constituted approximately 1 percent of the files processed in Montreal between 1970 and 1972. *Report,* see note 8 above at 12, 17.
14 Interview with Joseph R. Nuss, Montreal, 14 August 2008.
15 *Report,* see note 8 above at 4, 27.
16 Freda Hawkins, *Canada and Immigration: Public Policy and Public Concern,* 2nd ed. (Montreal: McGill-Queen's University Press, 1988); Constance Backhouse, *Colour-Coded: A Legal History of Racism in Canada 1900–1950* (Toronto: University of Toronto Press, 1999); R. Bruce Shepard, *Deemed Unsuitable* (Toronto: Umbrella Press, 1997); Sean Mills, "A Place in the Sun: Haiti, Haitians, and the Remaking of Quebec" (unpublished manuscript).
17 *Report,* see note 8 above at 19, 227–28; *Immigration Act,* RSC 1952, c. 325; 1967 Regulations, P.C. 1967-1616 of 16 August 1967, later RSC 1970, c. I-2.
18 *Report,* ibid.; *Immigration Act,* ibid.; *Immigration Appeal Board Act,* RSC 1970, c. I-3.
19 *Report,* ibid. at 19–21, 136, 229–30; Project 80, introduced 23 June 1972; Project 97, "Operation Make My Country Your Country," established under Bill C-197, which came into force 15 August 1973.

20 *Report of the Canadian Immigration and Population Study: Green Paper on Immigration,* vol. 1 (Ottawa: Manpower and Immigration, Information Canada, 1974) at 32.
21 The evidence of this included testimony of racist commentary in the workplace, and the racialized dimensions of the sexual overtures made by officers to immigrants.
22 *Report,* see note 8 above at 24. The other countries included Greece (4), Portugal (3), Hungary (2), Colombia (2), Uganda (2), and one each from Kenya, Zambia, Pakistan, Philippines, Yugoslavia, Italy, South Africa, United States, Scotland, Israel, Ecuador, and Uruguay.
23 Ibid. at 18.
24 Ibid. at 22–23.
25 Ibid. at 23–24, 52–53.
26 Ibid. at 24, 38–42, 72–77.
27 Ibid. at 44–48, 83–95.
28 Ibid. at 4, 94–96, 145. At the time of the inquiry hearings, Byer was awaiting criminal trial.
29 Ibid. at 36–37.
30 Ibid. at 59, 62, 66–68.
31 Ibid. at 112–14.
32 Interview with Claire L'Heureux-Dubé, Quebec City, 30 August 2012.
33 *Report,* see note 8 above at 112–14.
34 Ibid. at 115.
35 Ibid. at 120–22.
36 Ibid. at 122–27.
37 Ibid. at 129–31.
38 Ibid. at 127, 131.
39 Ibid. at 131–33.
40 Ibid. at 127–29, 135–38.
41 Ibid. at 37–38, 155–58.
42 Ibid. at 157; "Some immigration officials preyed on alien women, report shows," *Toronto Star* (27 January 1976) A8.
43 *Report,* ibid. at 38, 157.
44 Interview with Claire L'Heureux-Dubé, Quebec City, 30 August 2012.
45 Lisa Rose Mar, *Brokering Belonging: Chinese in Canada's Age of Exclusion, 1885–1945* (Toronto: University of Toronto Press, 2010), noted that the immigration system was corrupt, with a network of kickbacks that reached the highest levels of the Liberal party and resulted in a quarter of the Chinese population being undocumented workers in the 1930s.
46 *Report,* see note 8 above at 136.
47 Ibid. at 19, 155, 229.
48 Ibid. at 111–12.
49 Ibid. at 22.
50 Ibid. at 130. Of the thirty-three officers who testified, only two were women.
51 Ibid. at 108.
52 Constance Backhouse, "Sexual Harassment: A Feminist Phrase That Transformed the Workplace" (2012) 24:2 CJWL 275; Carrie N. Baker, *The Women's Movement against Sexual Harassment* (Cambridge: Cambridge University Press, 2008) at 27–31, 35, 207. The first books were Lin Farley, *Sexual Shakedown: The Sexual Harassment of Women on the Job* (New York: McGraw Hill, 1978); Constance Backhouse and Leah Cohen, *The Secret Oppression: Sexual Harassment of Working Women* (Toronto: Macmillan, 1978); Catharine A. MacKinnon, *Sexual Harassment of Working Women* (New Haven, CT: Yale University Press, 1979).
53 *Report,* see note 8 above at 108, 122.
54 Ibid. at 135 [emphasis added].
55 Ibid. at 116.

56 Ibid. at 138.
57 Ibid. at 134–35, 138.
58 Ibid. at 132–33.
59 Ibid. at 8.
60 Interview with Joseph R. Nuss, Montreal, 14 August 2008.
61 Constance Backhouse, *Carnal Crimes: Sexual Assault Law in Canada, 1900–1975* (Toronto: Irwin Law, 2008).
62 Interview with Claire L'Heureux-Dubé, Quebec City, 30 August 2012.
63 Ibid.
64 *Report,* see note 8 above at 133–34.
65 Ibid. at 134.
66 Ibid. at 22, 155.
67 Ibid. at 134–35.
68 Ibid. at 10.
69 Ibid. at 12.
70 *"Ninth Floor,"* a National Film Board documentary released in 2015, documented the 1969 complaints by racialized students of discriminatory evaluations by a professor, a sit-in protest that began without violence, allegations of misdoing by undercover police, "Black Power" protests, unruly crowds of whites chanting messages of hate, and riots involving police, the public, and the students, along with significant criminal justice consequences.
71 *Report,* see note 8 above at 100–1.
72 Interview with Claire L'Heureux-Dubé, Quebec City, 30 August 2012.
73 Interview with Pierre-Gabriel Jobin, Montreal, 23 April 2010.

Chapter 20: Quebec Superior Court

1 Unless otherwise indicated, information is from interviews with Claire L'Heureux-Dubé in Quebec City, Ottawa, Rimouski, and Clearwater, FL, on 30 October, 1 November, and 2 December 2007; 29–30 April 2008; 5 March, 10–14 May, and 21 September 2009; 10 March, 30 June, and 13 September 2010; and 30 August 2012.
2 Ignace-J. Deslauriers, *La Cour supérieure du Québec et ses juges: 1849–1er janvier 1980* (Québec: Bibliothèque nationale du Québec, 1980) at 61. Eugène Marquis, who had succeeded Frédéric Dorion as chief justice, retired in July 1976. The chief justice position had reverted to Montreal, to Jules Deschênes, but the Quebec City bar always referred to the top judge in their court as the "chief justice," even though the formal title was associate chief justice.
3 The Quebec district of the Quebec Superior Court would add only one other woman during L'Heureux-Dubé's tenure there: Lyse Lemieux, appointed in 1978 (transferred to Montreal in 1980). The Montreal district of the Quebec Superior Court would boast three women during the same period: Réjane Laberge-Colas, appointed in 1969; Claire Barette-Joncas, appointed in 1975; and Jeanne d'Arc Lemay-Warren, appointed in 1976. Ibid. at 10–56. Vallée was also the first woman to become a member of the Canadian Judicial Council. Louise Mailhot, *Les premières! L'histoire de l'accès des femmes à la pratique du droit et à la magistrature* (Cowansville, QC: Éditions Yvon Blais, 2013) at 122.
4 Minister of Justice Ron Basford, who had succeeded Otto Lang in 1975, made the appointment.
5 Interview with André Desmeules, Quebec City, 10 May 2010.
6 Interview with Raymond Lessard, Île d'Orleans, 11 May 2010.
7 Mailhot, *Les premières!* see note 3 above at 122.
8 Interview with Louis LeBel, Ottawa, 8 July 2010.

9   Interview with Calin Morin, Quebec City, 11 May 2010. Calin Morin had come to know Vallée when they were both studying law at Laval, and also described her as a "very open person," whom she liked a lot.
10 Ibid.
11 Interview with Claire L'Heureux-Dubé, Ottawa, 21 September 2009; Quebec City, 30 August 2012.
12 Interview with Claire L'Heureux-Dubé, Quebec City, 30 August 2012.
13 Interview with Claire L'Heureux-Dubé, Ottawa, 30 June 2010.
14 Interview with Claire L'Heureux-Dubé, Quebec City, 30 August 2012.
15 Interview with Claire L'Heureux-Dubé, Ottawa, 21 September 2009; Quebec City, 30 August 2012.
16 Interview with Martial Asselin, Quebec City, 7 August 2008.
17 Interview with André Desmeules, Quebec City, 10 May 2010.
18 Interview with Louis LeBel, Ottawa, 8 July 2010.
19 Interview with Raymond Lessard, Île d'Orléans, 11 May 2010.
20 She died on 2 June 1984. Mailhot, *Les premières!* see note 3 above at 204.
21 Deslauriers, *La Cour supérieure du Québec et ses juges,* see note 2 above at 10–56.
22 Library and Archives Canada, Correspondence with Edythe I. MacDonald, Department of Justice, MG 31, E110, box 4.
23 L'Heureux-Dubé observed that the chief justice relaxed his critical views somewhat as her term wore on.
24 Interview with André Desmeules, Quebec City, 10 May 2010.
25 Interview with Claire L'Heureux-Dubé, Quebec City, 30 August 2012.
26 Ibid.
27 Ibid.
28 Interview with Claire L'Heureux-Dubé, Clearwater, FL, 10–14 May 2009.
29 Interview with Claire L'Heureux-Dubé, Quebec City, 30 August 2012.
30 Interviews with Harvey Strosberg, Edward Greenspan, Mark Sandler, Malcolm Mercer, Robert Wadden, Mary Lou Benotto, Harriet Sachs, Thea Herman, and Nancy L. Backhouse, Toronto, 8 and 26 May 2013; 24 and 26 June 2013.
31 Interview with Claire L'Heureux-Dubé, Quebec City, 4–5 July 2013.
32 Claire L'Heureux-Dubé, "Femmes et droit: le regard d'une pionnière, une vision du passé et de l'avenir" in Hélène Dumont, ed., *Femmes et droit: 50 ans de vie commune ... et tout un avenir* (Montréal: Éditions Thémis, 1991) at 314.
33 Interview with Claire L'Heureux-Dubé, Quebec City, 30 August 2012.
34 Interview with Louise Dubé, Boston, 22 May 2012.
35 J.-Claude Rivard, "Pour Claire L'Heureux-Dubé être juge, c'est exercer le plus beau métier du monde," Québec *Le Soleil* (20 October 1979) A-7.
36 Interview with Claire L'Heureux-Dubé, Quebec City, 30 August 2012.
37 Manon Cornellier, "Dissidente suprême," *L'Actualité* (1 October 1999) at 72.
38 Interview with Jacques LeMay, Quebec City, 5 May 2010. LeMay was a graduate from Laval who was called to the bar in 1963. He practised automobile, insurance, and product liability litigation.
39 Interview with Roger Chouinard, Quebec City, 11 May 2010.
40 Interview with Louise Mailhot, Gananoque, ON, 20 May 2009.
41 Interview with Melvin Rothman, Montreal, 12 August 2008.
42 Interview with Claire L'Heureux-Dubé, Quebec City, 30 August 2012.
43 The 457 unreported trial decisions that survive from the years 1976–79 are held at the Bibliothèques et Archives nationales du Québec (BAnQ).
44 Interview with Claire L'Heureux-Dubé, Quebec City, 30 August 2012. She heard only two criminal cases before her elevation to the Court of Appeal. *La Reine v. Dubé,* unreported,

Cour supérieure, District de Rimouski, No. C.S.Q. 100-36-017-75, 23 February 1976, BAnQ, was an appeal from a ruling of the Court of Sessions of the Peace acquitting the accused of obtaining a driver's licence while under suspension. In the trial *de novo,* she noted that the licence had been suspended after the accused caused an automobile accident while driving without insurance. He applied for a new driver's licence under a false name, but his ruse was unveiled when he was involved in yet another accident. She found him guilty and fined him $500. In *R. v. Genest,* unreported, Cour supérieure, District de Québec, No. 200-05-004293-762, 10 February 1977, BAnQ, the Crown argued that she should overrule a lower court's acquittal of a man charged under the *Juvenile Delinquents Act* with using pornography to induce two boys into sexual immorality. The lower court judge had found the acts unpremeditated and the Crown overzealous, taking judicial notice that pornography was available on newsstands and in cinemas across Quebec, with "*les oeuvres du Marquis de Sade*" available "*partout.*" She dismissed the appeal, noting that the act permitted only limited rights of review based on the public interest or the good administration of justice.

45 Interview with Claire L'Heureux-Dubé, Quebec City, 30 August 2012.
46 "Le juge Claire L'Heureux-Dubé au club de presse," *Rimouski Progrès-Echo* (17 March 1976) C23, announcing the event of 18 March 1976; N.P. (initials only), "Claire L'Heureux-Dubé: une vision humaine de la justice," *Rimouski Progrès-Echo* (24 March 1976) A-15.
47 See, for example, *Lessard v. Location Québec Auto Inc.,* unreported, Cour supérieure, District de Québec, No. 10-434, 26 May 1977, BAnQ; *Beland v. Bertrand,* unreported, Cour supérieure, District de Québec, No. 200-05-004005-752, 12 May 1977, BAnQ; *Voyer v. Bouillon,* unreported, Cour supérieure, District de Rimouski, No. 100-05-000163-74, 12 October 1976, BAnQ; *Dumont v. Gendron,* unreported, Cour supérieure, District de Rimouski, No. 100-05-000133-74, 4 May 1977, BAnQ; *Michaud v. Pelletier,* unreported, Cour supérieure, District de Kamouraska, No. 250-05-000031-75, 26 April 1978, BAnQ.
48 *Le Procureur général de la Province de Québec v. Edouard Healey,* Cour supérieure, District of Rimouski, No. 100-05-000600-722, 29 January 1979; reported as [1979] CS 286.
49 *An Act to amend and consolidate the laws relating to fisheries,* SQ 1888, c. 17, s. 1, provided that any sales or grants of Crown land would henceforth be "subject to a reserve, for fishing purposes, of three chains in depth of the lands bordering on non-navigable rivers and lakes in the province."
50 The statute was amended in 1919 by *An Act to amend the Quebec fish and game laws,* SQ 1919, c. 31, s. 1, replacing the words "for fishing purposes" with the words "in full ownership by the Crown."
51 She also ruled that Healey's lake did not come within the scope of the legislation at all. The lake was of "*très petites dimensions,*" there was no archival record of any navigation, and an engineer had testified that it was "*ni navigable ni flottable.*"
52 Edythe MacDonald, then a senior counsel with the federal Department of Justice, made reference to this decision in writing to the minister of justice on 18 July 1979, to comment on the importance of appointing a woman to the Supreme Court of Canada.
53 [1983] CA 573.
54 [1987] 1 SCR 158.
55 Interview with Claire L'Heureux-Dubé, Ottawa, 10 March 2010.
56 Email correspondence from Dominique Langis, counsel for Healey, 11 January 2013.
57 *Loi sur les terres du domaine de l'état,* LQ 1987, T-8.1. The change of government also facilitated the repeal. The Liberal government of Robert Bourassa had replaced the Parti Québécois government of René Lévesque in 1985.
58 *L. v. M.,* unreported, Cour supérieure, District de Kamouraska, No. 250-05-000389-77, 5 April 1979, BAnQ.
59 It was the same situation over in Montreal, where Réjane Laberge-Colas, the first female judge to sit on the Superior Court there, was also shouldering a majority of family law

cases. Mailhot, *Les premières!* see note 3 above at 97. Some judges expressed particular concerns about the complexities of assessing family law cases. Interview with Alice Desjardins, Ottawa, 2 July 2009; interview with Lee Ferrier, Toronto, 8 August 2012.

60 *M. v. C.*, unreported, Cour supérieure, District de Québec, No. 200-12-013200-754, 23 June 1976, BAnQ.
61 *St-H. v. H.*, unreported, Cour supérieure, District de Québec, No. 10-874, 12 April 1973, BAnQ.
62 *L. v. G.*, unreported, Cour supérieure, District de Kamouraska, No. 250-12-000115-75, 7 February 1979, BAnQ.
63 *D. v. B.*, unreported, Cour supérieure, District de Québec, No. 7219-D, 6 July 1973, BAnQ.
64 In one case, the husband had revenues surpassing $1,800 per month, but claimed he could not pay more than $300 for his wife and two children. Ordering him to double his payment to $600 a month, L'Heureux-Dubé asked rhetorically how, if he could not make ends meet for himself and his new companion with revenues of $1,800, he thought his wife could manage for herself and their two children. *L. v. L.*, unreported, Cour supérieure, District de Rimouski, No. 100-05-000570-75, 8 December 1977, BAnQ.
65 His middle-aged ex-wife had never worked outside the home, while the new female partner had. L'Heureux-Dubé concluded that if ex-wives were increasingly being asked to cover their own living costs, concubines should not be exempt. *St-P. v. P.*, unreported, Cour supérieure, District de Québec, No. 200-12-014661-764, 23 July 1976, BAnQ. She also rejected another husband's request to halt his alimony payments because he was living with and supporting a companion who had three children. His wife and three children had been forced onto social assistance. It was, L'Heureux-Dubé noted, a case where the state was assuming the cost of the legitimate family while the husband assumed the cost of his concubine and her children. *B. v. B.*, unreported, Cour supérieure, District de Québec, No. 200-12-015293-765, 3 May 1977, BAnQ.
66 Interview with Claire L'Heureux-Dubé, Quebec City, 30 August 2012.
67 *P. v. G.*, unreported, Cour supérieure, District de Québec, No.578-D, 11 July 1973, BAnQ.
68 The father had lost the children to foster homes, and she found that his life was even less stable than the mother's. She disregarded the social worker's recommendation in favour of paternal custody, noting that all four children had told her in chambers that they wished to live with their mother. She also admitted that she had probed well beneath the surface of this case, adding, "*Peut-on blâmer le juge d'être parfois plus curieux que les procureurs et les parties ne le désireraient?*" *P. v. L.*, unreported, Cour supérieure, District de Québec, No. 200-12-012398-757, 11 May 1976, BAnQ.
69 *B. v A.*, unreported, Cour supérieure, District de Québec, No. 200-12-014219-761, 9 March 1977, BAnQ.
70 The father planned to ask his parents to look after the child while he was out at work, whereas the mother was intending to stay at home. L'Heureux-Dubé noted that it would be exceptional for a court to grant custody to a father who intended to leave a child with his parents. *R. v. D.*, unreported, Cour supérieure, District de Québec, No. 200-12-016873-771, 9 September 1977, BAnQ.
71 *M. v. St-L.*, unreported, Cour supérieure, District de Hauterive (Baie-Comeau), No. 655-12-000615-79, 26 July 1979, BAnQ.
72 *C.v. F.*, unreported, Cour supérieure, District de Rimouski, No. 100-12-000027-74, 20 September 1978, BAnQ.
73 She supported an ex-husband who sought to vacate an earlier court order to pay alimony to his former wife. The financial circumstances of the parties had not changed, but the former wife was now living with a boyfriend with whom she shared rent and food. Quoting from an article by Me Derek Guthrie in the *Revue du Barreau*, she stated that living with another man was a valid defence to a wife's claim for support, because there was a presumption of fact that she would receive support from the new partner. *R. v. B.*, unreported,

Cour supérieure, District de Québec, No. 3020-D, 18 April 1973, BAnQ, quoting (1965) 25 Revue du barreau 525 at 538.
74 She denied a wife's claim for alimony from an adulterous husband, noting that the right to alimony was not automatic, that the couple had lived together only six months, that the wife was in the workforce, and that she had already found a new male partner. *A. v. B.*, unreported, Cour supérieure, District de Québec, No. 200-12-015730-776, 9 March 1977, BAnQ.
75 *P. v. A.*, unreported, Cour supérieure, District de Québec, No. 200-05-002065-74, 1 April 1977, BAnQ.
76 She denied the request for $50 per week from the ex-husband, and substituted an order for $20, "*en proportion de leurs moyens respectifs, compote tenu de leurs obligations.*" *M. v. M.*, unreported, Cour supérieure, District de Québec, No. 200-12-013850-764, 2 March 1976, BAnQ.
77 The couple had married in middle age after each was widowed, the marriage had lasted only four years, and she found that neither party's conduct had been above reproach. *D'A. v. M.*, unreported, Cour supérieure, District de Rimouski, No. 100-05-00004-74, 17 June 1976, BAnQ.
78 The marriage had been brief. *L. v. R.*, unreported, Cour supérieure, District de Québec, No. 8226-D, 8 July 1977, BAnQ.
79 *L. v. L.*, unreported, Cour supérieure, District de Québec, No. 6568-D, 19 April 1973, BAnQ.
80 The mother lived in Quebec City while the children lived with their father in Chicoutimi. L'Heureux-Dubé recognized that this placed additional burdens and travel costs upon the mother, but her advice was that the mother should consider moving to Chicoutimi and looking for work there. *J.-B. v. B.*, unreported, Cour supérieure, District de Québec, No. 200-05-000448-741, 16 November 1976, BAnQ.
81 *P. v. P.*, unreported, Cour supérieure, District de Québec, No. 200-6752-D, 2 March 1976, BAnQ.
82 N.P., "Claire L'Heureux-Dubé," see note 46 above.

Chapter 21: Family Tragedy

1 Unless otherwise indicated, information is from interviews with Claire L'Heureux-Dubé in Quebec City, Ottawa, Rimouski, and Clearwater, FL, on 30 October, 1 November, and 2 December 2007; 29–30 April 2008; 5 March, 10–14 May, and 21 September 2009; 10 March, 30 June, and 13 September 2010; 30 August 2012; and 4–5 July 2013.
2 Interview with Claire L'Heureux-Dubé, Quebec City, 27–28 April 2009.
3 Interview with Claire L'Heureux-Dubé, Rimouski, 23–25 July 2008.
4 Interview with Louise L'Heureux-Giliberti, Chicago, 21 April 2009.
5 Interview with Jean Drapeau, Rimouski, 24 July 2008.
6 Arthur pleaded guilty in magistrate's court to illegally driving an automobile while his faculties were impaired by alcohol on 27 August 1956, and was fined $50 or one month, with a licence suspension of one year. He appealed the conviction, although the outcome was not listed in the archival record. Library and Archives Canada, MG 31, E110, 70.7.
7 Interviews with Claire L'Heureux-Dubé, Quebec City, 27–28 April 2009; 4–5 July 2013.
8 Interview with Claire L'Heureux-Dubé, Quebec City, 4–5 July 2013.
9 Ibid.
10 Comments by Claire L'Heureux-Dubé during interview with Georges-Henri Dubé, Rimouski, 24 July 2008.
11 Interview with Yves Dubé, Ottawa, 18 September 2008; interview with Georges-Henri Dubé, ibid.
12 Interview with Claire L'Heureux-Dubé, Quebec City, 27–28 April 2009.

13 Interview with Louise Dubé, Boston, 22 May 2012.
14 Interview with Louise L'Heureux-Giliberti, Chicago, 21 April 2009.
15 L'Heureux-Dubé advocated using the Service de thérapie conjugale, a new marital counselling office that had asked the judges to refer appropriate cases. "We were at the front of this new process," she recalled.
16 Interview with Claire L'Heureux-Dubé, Quebec City, 4–5 July 2013.
17 Interview with Claire L'Heureux-Dubé, Clearwater, FL, 10–14 May 2009.
18 Interview with Claire L'Heureux-Dubé, Quebec City, 27–28 April 2009.
19 Ibid.
20 Interview with Claire L'Heureux-Dubé, Quebec City, 4–5 July 2013.
21 Interview with Louise Dubé, Boston, 22 May 2012.
22 Ibid.
23 Interview with Louise L'Heureux-Giliberti, Chicago, 21 April 2009.
24 Interviews with Claire L'Heureux-Dubé, Clearwater, FL, 10–14 May 2009 and 25–27 November 2014.
25 Interview with Claire L'Heureux-Dubé, Clearwater, FL, 10–14 May 2009.
26 Interview with Louise Dubé, Boston, 22 May 2012.
27 Ibid.
28 Claire Kirkland-Casgrain Obituary, Lisa Fitterman, "Quebec's first female legislator," *Globe and Mail* (2 April 2016) S12.
29 Interview with Louise Dubé, Boston, 22 May 2012.
30 Ibid.
31 Interview with Louise L'Heureux-Giliberti, Chicago, 21 April 2009.
32 Interview with Louise Dubé, Boston, 22 May 2012.
33 Interview with Roger Garneau, Quebec City, 28 April 2009.
34 Interview with Melvin Rothman, Montreal, 12 August 2008.
35 Interview with Monique Perron, Quebec City, 2 May 2008.
36 Interview with Louise L'Heureux-Giliberti, Chicago, 21 April 2009.
37 Interview with Georges-Henri Dubé, Rimouski, 24 July 2008.
38 Interview with Yves Dubé, Ottawa, 18 September 2008.
39 Interview with Gisèle Blondeau-Labrie, Quebec City, 1 May 2008; interview with Georges-Henri Dubé, Rimouski, 24 July 2008.
40 Accounts vary as to where she was when the news came through – Rivière-du-Loup or Rimouski.
41 Interview with Gisèle Blondeau-Labrie, Quebec City, 1 May 2008.
42 Interview with Claire L'Heureux-Dubé, Ottawa, 5 March 2009.
43 Interview with Claire L'Heureux-Dubé, Rimouski, 23–25 July 2008.
44 Ibid.
45 Interview with Louise L'Heureux-Giliberti, Chicago, 21 April 2009.
46 Ibid.
47 Interview with Michèle Cloutier Mainguy, Quebec City, 2 May 2008.
48 Interview with Claire L'Heureux-Dubé, Clearwater, FL, 25–27 November 2014.
49 *Rodriguez v. British Columbia (Attorney General)*, [1993] 3 SCR 519 was a case where a terminally ill patient sought physician-assisted suicide. The court upheld the criminal prohibition 5 to 4. L'Heureux-Dubé signed Beverley McLachlin's dissenting opinion. The criminal provision would be overruled unanimously in *Carter v. Canada (Attorney General)*, [2015] 1 SCR 331, over a decade after L'Heureux-Dubé retired.
50 Interview with Louise L'Heureux-Giliberti, Chicago, 21 April 2009.
51 Interview with Claire L'Heureux-Dubé, Ottawa, 30 June 2010.
52 Interview with Georges-Henri Dubé, Rimouski, 24 July 2008.
53 Interview with Louise Dubé, Boston, 22 May 2012.

54 Comments by Claire L'Heureux-Dubé during interview with Georges-Henri Dubé, Rimouski, 24 July 2008.
55 Interview with Claire L'Heureux-Dubé, Ottawa, 5 March 2009.
56 Ibid.
57 Interview with Louise Dubé, Boston, 22 May 2012.

CHAPTER 22: APPOINTMENT TO THE QUEBEC COURT OF APPEAL

1 Unless otherwise indicated, information is from interviews with Claire L'Heureux-Dubé in Quebec City, Ottawa, Rimouski, and Clearwater, FL, on 30 October, 1 November, and 2 December 2007; 29–30 April 2008; 5 March, 10–14 May, and 21 September 2009; 10 March, 30 June, and 13 September 2010; 30 August 2012; and 4–5 July 2013.
2 He was appointed to the Supreme Court of Canada on 24 September 1979. James G. Snell and Frederick Vaughan, *The Supreme Court of Canada: History of the Institution* (Toronto: Osgoode Society for Canadian Legal History, 1985) at 235, 417.
3 On the date of appointment, see Minute of a Meeting of the Privy Council, 16 October 1969, Ottawa. Ignace-J. Deslauriers, *La Cour supérieure du Québec et ses juges: 1849–1er janvier 1980* (Québec: Bibliothèque nationale du Québec, 1980) at 144; "Juge à la Cour d'appel," Québec *Le Soleil* (18 October 1979) A14. Bertha Wilson had preceded her on the Ontario Court of Appeal in 1975: Ellen Anderson, *Judging Bertha Wilson: Law as Large as Life* (Toronto: University of Toronto Press, 2001) at 84.
4 Jim Lotz, *Prime Ministers of Canada* (Winnipeg: Bison Books, 1987). Joe Clark was prime minister from 4 June 1979 to 3 March 1980.
5 *Canadian Law List 1952–70* (Toronto: Cartwright and Sons, n.d.) listed him with Prévost, Gagné et Flynn; in 1964, with Prévost, Gagné, Flynn, Chouinard et Jacques; in 1968, with Prévost, Flynn, Rivard, Jacques, Cimon, Lessard et LeMay; and in 1970, with Flynn, Rivard, Jacques, Cimon, Lessard et LeMay. Appointed a senator in 1962, Flynn held the post of minister of justice from 4 June 1979 to 2 March 1980.
6 Julien Chouinard began law practice in 1953 with Prévost, Gagné, Flynn, Chouinard et Jacques. He entered the provincial public service in 1965 as deputy minister of justice. After he failed in his federal political bid for office as a Conservative in 1968, he returned to the provincial government as secretary-general of the executive council, and then served as a judge of the Quebec Court of Appeal from 1974 to 1979. Donn Downey, "Julien Chouinard: Supreme Court judge was top civil servant for Quebec premier," *Globe and Mail* (9 February 1987).
7 Martial Asselin served as president of the Laval University Student Council from 1949 to 1950, and as the Conservative MP for Charlevoix from 1958 to 1963. He was re-elected in 1965 and 1968. Appointed to the Senate in 1972, he served as deputy speaker in 1984 and lieutenant-governor of Quebec from 1990 to 1996. "Martial Asselin" in *Canadian Who's Who* (Toronto: University of Toronto Press, 2005); interview with Martial Asselin, Quebec City, 7 August 2008.
8 Interview with Martial Asselin, ibid. L'Heureux-Dubé later heard Asselin recount a version of this story over dinner with judges at the Supreme Court of Canada, confirming that he had lobbied the prime minister to appoint her. The news came as a great surprise to her. Interview with Claire L'Heureux-Dubé, Quebec City, 30 August 2012.
9 McTeer recalled the flight but not the specifics: "I'd like to be able to say, 'Oh yes, it was discussed on the plane,' but we're talking so many years ago. [We were] looking for ... an opportunity to show that there were women who had done a tremendous number of things. I know I had encouraged Joe quite a bit. It was pathetic how few women there were." Interview with Maureen McTeer, Ottawa, 7 June 2013.
10 Clark does not recall the exact circumstances of the appointment, but noted that when he took over as prime minister, he had been surprised to discover that all but one deputy

minister was male, and he was determined to see more women elevated to key posts. Interview with Joe Clark, Ottawa, 7 March 2014.
11 Interview with Martial Asselin, Quebec City, 7 August 2008; interview with Claire L'Heureux-Dubé, Quebec City, 29–30 April 2009.
12 Interview with Maureen McTeer, Ottawa, 7 June 2013.
13 Interview with Yves Bernier, Quebec City, 30 April 2008. On the growth of the court from four judges in 1849 to seventeen, see Deslauriers, *La Cour supérieure du Québec et ses juges*, see note 3 above at 52.
14 Québec *Le Soleil* (3 October 1979) A16.
15 Bélanger (age sixty-eight) had been sitting on the appellate court since 1973 and Lajoie (age fifty-seven) since 1970. Deslauriers, *La Cour d'appel du Québec et ses juges*, see note 3 above at 15–17.
16 There were also two concurring opinions issued, one from Lajoie and the other from L'Heureux-Dubé. Library and Archives Canada (LAC), Jugements Rendus, Claire L'Heureux-Dubé, JCA (*ad hoc*), nos. 1–19, MG 31, E-110, box 70.
17 *Raymond Julien v. R.*, [1980] CA 89; LAC, Jugements Rendus, Claire L'Heureux-Dubé, JCA (*ad hoc*), no. 1, MG 31, E-110, box 70.
18 Interview with Claire L'Heureux-Dubé, Quebec City, 4–5 July 2013.
19 André Cedilot, "Première femme juge à la Cour d'appel," *La Presse* (3 November 1979) C3, gave the nomination date as 16 October.
20 Interview with Claire L'Heureux-Dubé, Quebec City, 4–5 July 2013.
21 Interviews with Claire L'Heureux-Dubé, Ottawa, 5 March 2009; Quebec City, 30 August 2012.
22 Interview with André Desmeules, Quebec City, 10 May 2010.
23 Interview with Claire L'Heureux-Dubé, Quebec City, 30 August 2012.
24 Correspondence from L'Heureux-Dubé to Vallée, 24 October 1979 (letter held in private papers of Claire L'Heureux-Dubé).
25 Cedilot, "Première femme juge à la Cour d'appel," see note 19 above.
26 Ibid.; Claude de Cotret, "Une première: un juge féminin à la Cour d'appel," Montréal *Le Journal* (3 November 1979; "First woman appointed to appeal court," *Montreal Gazette* (3 November 1979).
27 Correspondence from L'Heureux-Dubé to Édouard Rinfret, 20 November 1979 (letter held in private papers of Claire L'Heureux-Dubé). Édouard Rinfret was born in 1905 in Saint-Jérôme, called to the bar in 1928, and elected an MP for the Quebec riding of Outremont in 1945. Re-elected in 1949, he served as postmaster-general until 1952. Édouard Rinfret, Parliament of Canada biography, online: <https://lop.parl.gc.ca/Parlinfo/Files/Parliamentarian.aspx?Item=b745e5cf-e635-463f-9b17-d993fa12b459&Language=E& Section=ALL>.
28 Speaking notes from Claire L'Heureux-Dubé.
29 Interview with Claire L'Heureux-Dubé, Quebec City, 30 August 2012.
30 Interview with Joseph Nuss, Montreal, 14 August 2008.
31 Cedilot, "Première femme juge à la Cour d'appel," see note 19 above.
32 J.-Claude Rivard, "Pour Claire L'Heureux-Dubé être juge, c'est exercer le plus beau métier du monde," Québec *Le Soleil* (20 October 1979) A7.
33 Claude Roussin, "Hommage à Claire L'Heureux-Dubé," *Aristide* 6:3 (November 1979) 4.
34 Even after her retirement, although she recognized that her judicial appointments were influenced by "pressure from society ... feminists who became powerful enough to influence the nomination process," she continued to insist: "I'm very averse to quotas. I'm not a woman for women for women. I say that they should be considered on the same footing as men." Interview with Claire L'Heureux-Dubé, Clearwater, FL, 25–27 November 2014.
35 Roussin, "Hommage à Claire L'Heureux-Dubé," see note 33 above.
36 Barbara Babcock, *Fish Raincoats: A Woman Lawyer's Life* (New Orleans: Quid Pro Quo Books, 2016) at i.

37 Deslauriers, *La Cour supérieure du Québec et ses juges,* see note 3 above at 10–56.
38 Louise Mailhot, *Les premières! L'histoire de l'accès des femmes à la pratique du droit et à la magistrature* (Cowansville, QC: Éditions Yvon Blais, 2013) at 75. From 1943 to 1980, there were 29 new nominations and 4 promotions. From 1980 to 1985, there were 21 new nominations and 5 promotions. From 1985 to 1990, there were 35 new nominations and 15 promotions. The combined total was 76 nominations in ten years, compared with 33 in the first thirty-seven years.

Chapter 23: Appellate Judging

1 Unless otherwise indicated, information is from interviews with Claire L'Heureux-Dubé in Quebec City, Ottawa, Rimouski, and Clearwater, FL, on 30 October, 1 November, and 2 December 2007; 29–30 April 2008; 5 March, 10–14 May, and 21 September 2009; 10 March, 30 June, and 13 September 2010; 30 August 2012; and 4–5 July 2013.
2 Yves Bernier noted that when he first arrived at the Court of Appeal in 1973, the "belief at the time [was] that you should not be tainted by previous knowledge of the case before the lawyers came before you and explained what the situation was. I thought this was terrible. We couldn't put good questions when we had no knowledge of the case. I asked them to send me the file with the dossier with all the evidence, the transcript, and pleadings from both sides. I made a little résumé and sent it to my colleagues. That's the way it began. Then it became a policy – a big change." Bernier's view was that L'Heureux-Dubé was one of the most diligent of his colleagues in preparing before the hearings. "We had meetings before sitting and reviewed the cases we had during the day. [Claire] remembered all the important things of every case. She could glance through a book very fast and remember what was important. She has a very good memory. And she worked from 5 a.m. [and] slept very little." Interview with Yves Bernier, Quebec City, 30 April 2008.
3 *Roger Lavigne c. Dame Joseph Loubier Nadeau,* unreported, Quebec Court of Appeal, Claire L'Heureux-Dubé, JCA, Jugement 37, issued 28 January 1980, Library and Archives Canada (LAC), MG 31, E-110, box 70.
4 Interview with Claire L'Heureux-Dubé, Quebec City, 4–5 July 2013.
5 Interviews with Claire L'Heureux-Dubé, Ottawa, 13 September 2010; Quebec City, 4–5 July 2013. Born in Malta in 1912, George Owen was the son of Frank W. Owen, a businessman, and Annie Birchall. He graduated from McGill with a BA, MA, and BCL, and studied at the École libre des sciences politiques in Paris. Admitted to the bar in 1937, he practised with Meredith, Holden, Heward and Holden. Ignace-J. Deslauriers, *La Cour d'appel du Québec et ses juges: 1849 à 1980* (Québec: Comité général des juges de la Cour supérieure de la province de Québec, 1980) at 17.
6 Interviews with Claire L'Heureux-Dubé, Ottawa, 13 September 2010; Quebec City, 4–5 July 2013. The story later circulated among other judges. Interview with Melvin Rothman, Montreal, 12 August 2008.
7 Interview with Claire L'Heureux-Dubé, Quebec City, 4–5 July 2013.
8 Ellen Anderson, *Judging Bertha Wilson: Law as Large as Life* (Toronto: University of Toronto Press, 2001) at 85–88.
9 Catherine A. Fraser was appointed to the Court of Queen's Bench in Alberta in 1989 and the Alberta Court of Appeal in 1991. She became chief justice of Alberta in 1992. Louise Mailhot, *Les premières! L'histoire de l'accès des femmes à la pratique du droit et à la magistrature* (Montréal: Éditions Yvon Blais, 2013) at 127; interview with Catherine Fraser, Edmonton, 12 November 2013.
10 Interview with Louise Mailhot, Gananoque, ON, 20 May 2009. The last sentence in the quotation comes from Donalee Moulton, "Mailhot honoured for a singular career," *Lawyers Weekly* (18 October 2013) 23.

11 Philip Girard, *Bora Laskin: Bringing Law to Life* (Toronto: University of Toronto, 2005) at 322–24, 338–41.
12 Interview with Claire L'Heureux-Dubé, Quebec City, 4–5 July 2013.
13 Ibid.
14 Deslauriers, *La Cour d'appel du Québec et ses juges*, see note 5 above at 29.
15 Interview with Claire L'Heureux-Dubé, Clearwater, FL, 10–14 May 2009.
16 Interviews with Claire L'Heureux-Dubé, Quebec City, 25 July 2008 and 30 August 2012. Bernier was elevated to the Court of Appeal in 1973. Deslauriers, *La Cour d'appel du Québec et ses juges,* see note 5 above at 20.
17 Albert Mayrand was elevated to the Court of Appeal in 1974. Ibid. at 17. On his *"parcimonie de mots qui démontre la sobriété et la sagesse du juriste,"* see Me. Simon Venne, "Hommage à Albert Mayrand," *8ᵉ Conférence Albert-Mayrand* (Montréal: Éditions Thémis, 2004) at 4.
18 Interview with Claire L'Heureux-Dubé, Quebec City, 4–5 July 2013. A graduate of Bishop's University and McGill, George Montgomery was admitted to the bar in 1936 and named to the Court of Appeal in 1957. Deslauriers, ibid. at 26.
19 Born in McAdam, New Brunswick, in 1911, John Nolan studied at the Catholic High School in Montreal and graduated from McGill law school in 1937. He practised in Montreal with O'Brien, Stewart and Hall, and was appointed to the Superior Court in 1969. Deslauriers, *La Cour d'appel du Québec et ses juges,* see note 5 above at 27.
20 Melvin Rothman was born in Montreal in 1930, studied at McGill, and was called to the bar in 1954. He practised with the Montreal firm of Phillips and Vineberg before his appointment to the Superior Court in 1971 and to the Court of Appeal in 1983. Interview with Melvin Rothman, Montreal, 12 August 2008.
21 Interview with Claire L'Heureux-Dubé, Quebec City, 4–5 July 2013.
22 Ibid. Fred Kaufman was born in Vienna in 1924. He began his studies in England but later obtained degrees from the University of Sherbrooke, the University of Montreal, and McGill. Prior to being called to the bar in 1955, Kaufman worked as a journalist in Sherbrooke and Montreal. He later practised with Cohen, Leithman and Kaufman, a firm that later became Kaufman, Yarosky and Fish. He was named to the Court of Appeal in 1973. Deslauriers, *La Cour d'appel du Québec et ses juges,* see note 5 above at 24.
23 John Ibbitson, "John of the 79 days," *Globe and Mail* (25 November 2011).
24 Interview with Claire L'Heureux-Dubé, Quebec City, 4–5 July 2013.
25 Interview with Marie-Claude Belleau, Ottawa, 11 December 2013.
26 Alice Desjardins, the first woman appointed to the Federal Court of Appeal in 1987, stated: "On an appeal court, you have to learn to work with your colleagues. You prepare for a case, and you hear it, and then the chips fall somewhere. And through the discussion you either say 'it makes sense,' or you say 'this is where we part company.' It's entirely different [from the Superior Court]. You're not as lonely because you're very much alone as a trial judge. But it's more difficult if you disagree. You've got to fight more." Interview with Alice Desjardins, Ottawa, 2 July 2009.
27 Interview with Roger Chouinard, Quebec City, 11 May 2010.
28 Interview with Yves Bernier, Quebec City, 30 April 2008.
29 Interview with Melvin Rothman, Montreal, 12 August 2008.
30 Interview with Pierre-Gabriel Jobin, Montreal, 23 April 2010.
31 Interview with Claire L'Heureux-Dubé, Quebec City, 4–5 July 2013.
32 Ibid.
33 Ibid. She served as vice president of the international organization, and recalled attending biennial meetings in Berlin, Uppsala, San Francisco, Paris, Louisiana, Belgium, and Vienna. She helped co-convene the conference in Montreal on violence in the family.
34 Interview with Rosalie Abella, Ottawa, 9 November 2007.

35 Audiences de la Cour d'appel du Québec, Madame le juge L'Heureux-Dubé faisant partie du Banc. Library and Archives Canada holds a complete run of the 1,311 decisions in which L'Heureux-Dubé participated, along with additional files of Appeals on Sentence, and Judge Sitting Alone: LAC, MG 31, E-110, boxes 70–76. The reported decisions are in the annual volumes from 1979 to 1987 of the *Recueils de jurisprudence du Québec, Cour d'appel*. The numbers above do not include the decisions issued from the week she sat as an ad hoc appellate judge prior to her appointment.

36 Graham Fraser, *René Lévesque and the Parti Québécois in Power* (Montreal: McGill-Queen's University Press, 2001); René Lévesque, *Memoirs* (Toronto: McClelland and Stewart, 1986).

37 The issue was whether a police officer must identify his confidential sources on the witness stand. In her lengthy majority opinion, L'Heureux-Dubé held that the commission had been set up by a democratic government to examine the conduct of the provincial police, and that the officer must testify. Jean Turgeon agreed but Amédée Monet dissented, holding that the officer should be sheltered from having to divulge his sources. *Émile Bisaillon v. Jean-F. Keable et Le Procureur Général de la Province de Québec*, [1980] CA 316; *Henri-Paul Vignola v. Jean-F. Keable*, [1980] CA 531. On appeal, the Supreme Court of Canada upheld the inquiry's investigative powers with respect to municipal and provincial police activities, but found the federal RCMP to be outside the scope of a provincial inquiry. *Attorney General of Quebec and Jean Keable v. Attorney General of Canada*, [1983] 1 SCR 218.

38 A police defence witness testified that the PQ had retained prostitutes to obtain information on federal public employees. The trial judge ordered a stay of proceedings under ss. 7 and 11 of the *Canadian Charter of Rights and Freedoms*, holding that the premier's highly publicized outburst made it impossible to empanel an impartial jury. L'Heureux-Dubé's majority decision stated: "*[L]e pouvoir judiciaire se trouve ici paralysé de par la nature même des actes posés par le chef du pouvoir exécutif, lui-même chargé de veiller à sa bonne administration, il s'agit là d'un cas unique, sans précédent dans les annales judiciaires … [Je] n'ai aucune hésitation à privilégier la présomption d'innocence dont tout accusé doit bénéficier dans notre système judiciaire, présomption qui me paraît ici mise en péril.*" *R. v. Claude Vermette*, [1984] CA 466 at 469–70. The Supreme Court of Canada overturned her decision, ruling that the charges should be examined afresh at a new trial. Only one of the judges at the Supreme Court supported the majority opinion that L'Heureux-Dubé had co-signed: Justice Antonio Lamer. *R. v. Vermette*, [1988] 1 SCR 985.

39 The MPs objected to the accusations that they had collaborated in the betrayal of Quebec and the disappearance of the Quebec people, and charged that the text was defamatory and a call to violence. Marcel Crête and L'Heureux-Dubé issued an interlocutory injunction to halt the distribution of the material they labelled defamatory. She found the posters to be "*une atteinte abusive à la réputation des appelants et un exercice abusif du droit à la liberté d'opinion et d'expression.*" Albert Mayrand dissented, noting that public discussion on divergent political ideas often made use of colourful and vigorous vocabulary. It was the price of free expression. *Jean-Guy Dubois v. La Société St-Jean-Baptiste de Montréal*, [1983] CA 247; Fraser, *René Lévesque*, see note 36 above; Lévesque, *Memoirs*, see note 36 above.

40 The trial judge had placed a videotape of the carnage, created by government surveillance cameras, under embargo for the duration of the trial. After the verdict but before the appeal was complete, the press sought access to the tape. L'Heureux-Dubé's colleagues, Gérald McCarthy and François Chevalier, noted that the president of the National Assembly opposed the release of the videotape, and rejected the media request. L'Heureux-Dubé's dissent noted that the order preventing media dissemination had been made to safeguard the accused's rights to a fair trial, but did not stand indefinitely: "*La publicité des débats judiciaires est à la base de notre société démocratique … Que les dossiers de Cour sont publics*

est un corollaire de la publicité des débats." Freedom of expression would not violate the accused's rights to a fair trial in this case. *Denis Lortie v. R.,* [1985] CA 451 at 457–58.

41 The ruling also added that even if the plaintiff had discharged his burden of proof, the law was a reasonable limit in a free and democratic society. *Jacques A. Léger v. Ville de Montreal,* #1104, LAC, MG 31, E-110, box 75, heard in Montreal, 13 May 1986, with Marc Beauregard and Gérald McCarthy.

42 The challenge was brought under the Quebec *Charter of Human Rights and Freedoms* by a blind individual of a political party different from the mayor's, on the basis of handicap and political conviction. *Réjean Morel v. La Corporation de Saint-Sylvestre,* #1304, LAC, MG 31, E-110, box 76, heard in Quebec City, 14 April 1987, with Marc Beauregard and Louis LeBel.

43 When the landlord learned that the complainant was the divorced mother of two young children, she inquired who would take care of the children when they came home from school. Dissatisfied by the prospective tenant's response, the landlord advised her that others had rented the apartment. Later inquiries determined that the landlord had not rented the apartment and was entertaining other inquiries from potential renters. The trial judge had dismissed the claim, finding that the landlord was not motivated by discrimination but had an honest concern to ensure that renters had peaceful possession. Jean Turgeon wrote the unanimous decision, signed by L'Heureux-Dubé and Yves Bernier, affirming the trial judge's decision, noting that this landlord had previously rented to some divorced women and that the discrimination had not been proven. *La Commission des Droits de la Personne du Québec v. Oliva L'Homme,* #205, LAC, MG 31, E-110, box 71, heard in Montreal, 18 November 1980.

44 *The Montreal Gazette Ltd. v. Gerald M. Snyder,* [1983] CA 604. L'Heureux-Dubé's dissent was upheld when the case was appealed to the Supreme Court of Canada, with dissenting opinions from Antonio Lamer and William McIntyre that would have placed a cap on non-pecuniary damages for defamation. *Snyder v. Montreal Gazette Ltd.,* [1988] 1 SCR 494.

45 Gail Cuthbert Brandt et al., *Canadian Women: A History,* 3rd ed. (Toronto: Nelson, 2011) at 437–58.

46 Ibid. at 501.

47 Ibid. at 437–58.

48 Ibid. at 485.

49 *Droit de la Famille – 182,* [1985] CA 92.

50 *D.M. v. K.D.,* #326, LAC, MG 31, E-110, box 72, heard in Montreal, 23 November 1981.

51 Interview with Claire L'Heureux-Dubé, Clearwater, FL, 25–27 November 2014. In this case, the ex-husband had a farm worth $200,000 and an annual income of about $25,000. The middle-aged ex-wife was unemployed, and L'Heureux-Dubé wanted to approve a lump sum of $15,000. Her ruling affirmed the trial judge's original award of $175 alimony per week as well as a lump sum of $15,000. L'Heureux-Dubé emphasized that, in contrast to her colleagues on the bench, she did not believe that the allocation of "*une somme globale*" was exceptional or rare. Owen, who reluctantly signed on to L'Heureux-Dubé's decision, was clearly troubled by the lump sum, but decided that the husband had the means to pay and that it did not "shock" his sense of justice sufficiently to warrant interfering with the trial judge's decision. Monet, who dissented, would have cancelled the lump sum entirely (ibid.).

52 In *Droit de la Famille – 182,* see note 49 above, Marcel Nichols concurred with L'Heureux-Dubé's decision to award a lump sum of $5,000 where the ex-husband had a good salary and retirement pension, as well as ownership of the expensive family home, an automobile, and company shares, while the middle-aged ex-wife had been absent from the workforce for thirty-one years, was of fragile health, and had significant debts and no assets. Amédée Monet dissented, holding that a party who claimed a lump sum had a certain burden of proof, which the ex-wife had failed to discharge.

In *M.E.S. v. C.F.Co.,* #1112, LAC, MG 31, E-110, box 75, heard in Montreal, 15 May 1986, and reported as *Droit de la Famille – 287,* [1986] RJQ 1650 (CA), Marc Beauregard wrote the unanimous opinion, with which L'Heureux-Dubé and Gérald McCarthy concurred, ordering an ex-husband to pay a lump sum of $20,000 to his former wife.

In *Dame L.L. v. R.D.,* #1076, LAC, MG 31, E-110, box 75, heard in Montreal, 19 March 1986, L'Heureux-Dubé, Fred Kaufman, and William Tyndale all agreed to the doubling of the lump sum, from the $10,000 ordered by the trial judge to $20,000, for a wife who was forced to leave the conjugal home at the age of forty-seven, after twenty-one years of marriage and three children.

In *P.D. v. F.D.,* #1155, LAC, MG 31, E-110, box 75, heard in Montreal, 16 September 1986, with Marcel Nichols and Claude Vallerand, L'Heureux-Dubé upheld a lump sum order of $10,000 against an ex-husband doctor with annual revenues of $77,761 and clear capacity to pay.

In *R.B. v. Dame S.G.C.,* #1154, LAC, MG 31, E-110, box 75, heard in Montreal, 17 September 1986, with Marcel Nichols and Claude Vallerand, L'Heureux-Dubé approved a lump sum of $25,000, which the trial judge had ordered to be paid to the ex-wife after the conjugal home was sold. When the ex-wife remarried before the house was sold, her ex-husband sought cancellation of the order. L'Heureux-Dubé refused, noting that the lump sum was not a pure *"libéralité"* but was for the upkeep of the ex-wife and in exchange for her promise not to apply for future alimony. *"La paiement de la somme globale s'impose donc plus qu'auparavant puisque l'intimée s'est portée co-propriétaire de la maison où elle loge ses enfants."*

53 Rosalie S. Abella, "Economic Adjustment on Marriage Breakdown: Support" in *Family Law and Social Policy Workshop Series* (Toronto: Faculty of Law, University of Toronto, 1982).

54 *Droit de la Famille – 182,* see note 49 above.

55 Dissenting from her male colleagues, Marcel Nichols and Gérald McCarthy, she noted that the father based his claim on the primordial nature of parental authority, but *"s'il fut un temps dans notre droit où la puissance paternelle et à sa suite l'autorité paternelle et le lien biologique dominaient toute autre considération dans l'attribution de la garde d'un enfant, ces temps sont révolus." G.C. v. T.V.-F.,* #1140, LAC, MG 31, E-110, box 75, heard in Montreal, 11 June 1986, reported as *Droit de la Famille – 320,* [1987] RJQ 9 (CA). The Supreme Court of Canada agreed with her. *T.V.-F. v. D.F.,* [1987] 2 SCR 244, per Beetz, J.

56 The couple had travelled the world during the twenty-three-year marriage as part of the diplomat husband's eighteen international postings, living in luxury with cars, chauffeurs, and gardeners. The wife had handled all the domestic tasks while raising five children. After the divorce, the ex-husband remarried, secured a diplomatic posting in Scotland, paid for his new wife's son to study at the Sorbonne, and vacationed in Egypt, Tunisia, and Greece. The ex-wife was sleeping on a sofa in a small rental apartment, had no car, took no holidays, sold her jewels, and was accepting charity from a generous aunt. L'Heureux-Dubé awarded $24,000 per year. Claude Vallerand concurred, Amédée Monet dissented. *Droit de la Famille – 193,* [1985] CA 252.

57 The couple both worked as full-time professors and deposited almost all their revenue to a joint bank account. They both agreed to purchase the properties and all payments were drawn from their joint bank account. The majority decision, written by Owen and signed by Monet, concluded that the wife had not proven that there was an *"entente tacite"* ("tacit agreement") between the parties or that she had contributed one-half of the purchase price. *G.S. v. M.C.,* [1982] CA 361.

58 The property was an old schoolhouse that the husband bought for $1,500 and renovated into a family home that had increased in value to $29,000. The wife had been primarily engaged in the home, raising four children, but contributed $2,000 of her employment

income to repairing the house. Upon divorce, the issue was how to divide the value of the home. The two male judges, Marc Beauregard and Rodolphe Paré, found that the domestic services and sums furnished by the wife to "make-do at the end of the month" did not serve to enrich the "*patrimoine*" of the husband because they were neither exceptional nor causal. L'Heureux-Dubé, in dissent, would have attributed $12,500 to recognize the wife's contribution: "*[P]ar son travail et par sa contribution financière au cours du mariage, l'intimée a fait un apport direct à l'enrichissement du patrimoine de l'appelant.*" Droit de la Famille – *271*, [1986] RJQ 689 (CA).

59 *C.L. v. Dame J.F.*, #101, LAC, MG 31, E-110, box 71, heard in Montreal, 18 March 1980.

60 William Tyndale dissented, characterizing the man's defiance of the original alimony judgment as close to contempt of court. *A.C. v. M.S.*, #1213, LAC, MG 31, E-110, box 75, heard in Montreal, 10 December 1986, reported as *Droit de la Famille – 356*, [1987] RJQ 764 (CA).

61 These conclusions are drawn from a review of every reported decision between 1979 and 1987, and every unreported archival decision in 1979, 1980, 1986, and 1987, along with every unreported appeal on sentence from 1979 to 1987. She participated in 17 reported criminal decisions and 61 unreported archival criminal decisions, as well as 105 additional appeals on sentences. See note 35 above.

62 *Gaetan Frechette v. R.*, #1130, LAC, MG 31, E-110, box 75, heard in Montreal, 9 June 1986. This was a unanimous panel with Gérald McCarthy and Marcel Nichols.

63 *Jean-Marc Langlois v. R.*, #1224, LAC, MG 31, E-110, box 75, heard in Montreal, 12 January 1987, with Marc Beauregard and Gérald McCarthy.

64 *R. v. Louis-Marie Collin*, #S-50, LAC, MG 31, E-110, box 76, heard 9 September 1982, with François Lajoie and Maurice Jacques. The rape had been committed with a gun, in the presence of the young child of the victim, and there was psychiatric evidence that the accused posed a danger to society.

65 *David Pootogee v. R.*, #S-77, LAC, MG 31, E-110, box 76, heard 11 July 1984. The crime involved aggravating threats, and the daughter gave birth to a child as a result of the sexual relations.

66 The lower court had quashed the committal for trial because the only evidence implicating the accused was the unsworn testimony of two boys. L'Heureux-Dubé's colleagues, George Owen and John Nolan, overruled that decision. They overlooked the lack of corroboration at the preliminary inquiry because both boys would have turned fourteen by the time of trial. *Le Procureur Général de la Province de Québec v. Fernand Poirier*, [1981] CA 227.

67 The accused, who was the uncle of the victim, was convicted of taking a child younger than fourteen years of age out of the care of her parents and committing a criminal act. Acquitted on a separate charge of attempted rape, he pleaded intoxication and argued that the victim suffered no violence. The lower court sentenced him to one year. Given that the accused was a gainfully employed contractor, the panel decided that community service was preferable to prison. *Leoli Laflamme v. R.*, #1053, LAC, MG 31, E-110, box 75, heard in Quebec, 11 February 1986. The unanimous decision was written by George Montgomery and signed by L'Heureux-Dubé and Gérald McCarthy.

68 *Pasqualino Ragozzino v. R.*, #1151, LAC, MG 31, E-110, box 75, heard in Montreal, 15 September 1986, with Marcel Nichols and Claude Vallerand.

69 *Jacques Vaudry v. R.*, #57, LAC, MG 31, E-110, box 71, heard in Montreal, 22 January 1980, with Chief Justice Marcel Crête and Yves Bernier. The death ensued from a late-night altercation in the parking lot of a bar, where the accused argued with the victim over cars blocking the exit. The victim was attempting to leave when the accused returned to his automobile, at the suggestion of his companion, to look for a knife, and then attacked. L'Heureux-Dubé's unanimous ruling emphasized that everything unrolled quickly and in

the context of an argument already heated up by alcohol. Substituting murder in the second degree, she sentenced the accused to fourteen years before eligibility for parole.

In *Normand Fortin v. R.*, #234, LAC, MG 31, E-110, box 72, heard in Quebec, 30 March 1981, two masked men held up a grocery store, where one fired his gun in the air and then toward the owner of the store, who died one hour later. Because the first bullet had been fired in the air, L'Heureux-Dubé found that there was not necessarily an intention to kill, and that the jury had not given the accused the benefit of the doubt on premeditation. She quashed the conviction of first-degree murder and substituted second-degree murder, but did not alter the sentence. Her unanimous ruling was signed by François Lajoie and Marc Beauregard.

70 *Marc-Michel Collin v. R.*, #1158, LAC, MG 31, E-110, box 75, heard in Montreal, 16 September 1986, with Claude Vallerand and Marcel Nichols. The jury had rejected the accused's claim of mental insanity caused by epilepsy, and the appeal court did not disturb this finding.
71 *Le Procureur Général du Québec v. Michel Martel*, #1051, LAC, MG 31, E-110, box 75, heard in Quebec City, 10 February 1986, with George Montgomery and Gérald McCarthy. The accused's request to reduce the sentence was rejected, despite his youthful age of twenty-one, because he had previous convictions for assault and assault causing bodily harm.
72 *William Meloche v. R.*, [1980] CA 117. Yves Bernier and L'Heureux-Dubé wrote separate concurring opinions. Chief Justice Marcel Crête, dissenting, would have upheld the conviction.
73 A Métro subway employee who believed that the woman had committed a municipal infraction was attempting to arrest her. *R. v. Sylvie Gagné*, #1210, LAC, MG 31, E-110, box 75, heard in Montreal, 9 December 1986. Amédée Monet and Walter Tyndale signed on to the unanimous decision.
74 *Aline Boily Chastenay v. R.*, #S-100, LAC, MG 31, E-110, box 76, heard 5 March 1986. The unanimous opinion was written by Marc Beauregard, and signed by L'Heureux-Dubé and Melvin Rothman.
75 Interview with Louis LeBel, Ottawa, 8 July 2010.
76 Ibid.
77 Richard A. Posner "Judicial Opinions and Appellate Advocacy in Federal Courts – One Judge's Views" (2013) 51 Duq L Rev 3 at 7.
78 Interview with Joseph Nuss, Montreal, 14 August 2008.
79 Marlène Cano, "Claire L'Heureux-Dubé et le droit de la famille: juge innovateur/innovatrice" (1991) 98:1 Queen's Quarterly 131 at 153, 155.
80 For examples of rare English-language decisions, see *G.G.F. v. J.E.W.*, #1072, LAC, MG 31, E-110, box 75, heard in Montreal, 17 March 1986, with an all-English panel of Fred Kaufman and William Tyndale, and *Trans-Quebec Helicopters Ltd. v. Heirs of the Estate of the Late David Lee*, #125, LAC, MG 31, E-110, box 71, heard in Montreal, 21 April 1980, and reported as [1980] CA 596.
81 Interview with Melvin Rothman, Montreal, 12 August 2008.
82 Interview with Pierre-Gabriel Jobin, Montreal, 23 April 2010.
83 Interview with Michel Bastarache, Ottawa, 24 November 2009.
84 Interview with Catherine Fraser, Edmonton, 12 November 2013.
85 Interviews with Claire L'Heureux-Dubé, Quebec City, 30 August 2012 and 4–5 July 2013.

Chapter 24: More Family Traumas

1 Unless otherwise indicated, information is drawn from interviews with Claire L'Heureux-Dubé in Quebec City, Ottawa, Rimouski, and Clearwater, FL, on 30 October, 1 November, 2 December 2007; 29–30 April 2008; 5 March, 10–14 May, and 21 September 2009; 10 March, 30 June, and 13 September 2010; 30 August 2012; and 4–5 July 2013.

2 Cases from the following districts were heard in Montreal: Beauharnois, Bedford, Drummond, Hull, Iberville, Joliette, Labelle, Montreal, Pontiac, Richelieu, St-François, St-Hyacinthe, Terrebonne. Quebec heard all of the other districts. Library and Archives Canada (LAC), "La cour d'appel du Québec," MG 31, E-110, box 4.
3 Yves Bernier explained: "In Quebec, [we] knew everybody intimately most of the time, [and it was] difficult to say that you were not influenced. I preferred [to sit in Montreal] where I was not too familiar with the lawyers." Interview with Yves Bernier, Quebec City, 30 April 2008.
4 Audiences de la Cour d'Appel du Québec, Madame le juge L'Heureux-Dubé faisant partie du Banc. LAC, MG 31, E-110.
5 Interview with Louise Dubé, Boston, 22 May 2012.
6 Interview with Georges-Henri Dubé, Rimouski, 24 July 2008.
7 Interview with Louise L'Heureux-Giliberti, Chicago, 21 April 2009.
8 Interview with Claire L'Heureux-Dubé, Clearwater, FL, 10–14 May 2009. Dealing with intractable children was something L'Heureux-Dubé shared with some of the other women who were early appointees to their nation's highest courts. Mary Gaudron, Australia's first female judge on the High Court, was once quoted as saying: "As one who has been the mother of a teenager for 24 years straight, and is still not out of the woods in that regard, I find it very difficult to make an argument in favour of motherhood." Pamela Burton, *From Moree to Mabo: The Mary Gaudron Story* (Crawley, Western Australia: UWA Publishing, 2010) at 370.
9 Interview with Julien Payne, Ottawa, 7 July 2009.
10 Interview with Nicole L'Heureux, Clearwater, FL, 11–12 May 2009.
11 Interview with Louise Dubé, Boston, 22 May 2012.
12 Interview with Louise L'Heureux-Giliberti, Chicago, 21 April 2009; interview with Simone Tardif, Montreal, 4 August 2008.
13 Interview with Nicole L'Heureux, Clearwater, FL, 11–12 May 2009.
14 Ibid.
15 Interview with Louise L'Heureux-Giliberti, Chicago, 21 April 2009.
16 Ibid.
17 Interview with Louise Dubé, Boston, 22 May 2012.
18 Interview with Louise L'Heureux-Giliberti, Chicago, 21 April 2009.
19 Interview with Nicole L'Heureux, Clearwater, FL, 11–12 May 2009.
20 Interview with Roger Garneau, Quebec City, 28 April 2009.
21 Interview with Simone Tardif, Montreal, 4 August 2008.
22 Interview with Jean Drapeau, Rimouski, 24 July 2008.
23 Interview with Claire L'Heureux-Dubé, Clearwater, FL, 10–14 May 2009.
24 Interview with Louise Dubé, Boston, 22 May 2012.
25 Interview with Louise L'Heureux-Giliberti, Chicago, 21 April 2009.
26 Interview with Louise Dubé, Boston, 22 May 2012.
27 Interview with Louise L'Heureux-Giliberti, Chicago, 21 April 2009.
28 Interview with Frank Iacobucci, Toronto, 26 October 2011; interview with Jack Major, Calgary, 13 November 2013; interview with Charles Gonthier, Ottawa, 14 September 2008.
29 Interview with Claire L'Heureux-Dubé, Quebec City, 4–5 July 2013. Lemelin's husband, Charles, was a social science professor and a friend of Arthur's. L'Heureux-Dubé had suggested that Lemelin come to work at Sam Bard's law firm, where she had been employed until she followed Bard to the bench. She transferred to L'Heureux-Dubé's chambers when Bard moved to Montreal.
30 Interview with Louise L'Heureux-Giliberti, Chicago, 21 April 2009.
31 Interview with Claire L'Heureux-Dubé, Clearwater, FL, 25–27 November 2014.
32 Interview with Roger Garneau, Quebec City, 28 April 2009.

33   Interview with Claire L'Heureux-Dubé, Clearwater, FL, 25–27 November 2014.
34   Interview with Gisèle Blondeau-Labrie, Quebec City, 1 May 2008.
35   Interview with Jean Drapeau, Rimouski, 24 July 2008.
36   Interview with Philippe Michaud, Rimouski, 24 July 2008.
37   Interview with Roger Garneau, Quebec City, 28 April 2009.
38   Interview with Denyse Dion, Quebec City, 1 May 2008.
39   Interview with Claire L'Heureux-Dubé, Clearwater, FL, 10–14 May 2009.
40   Louise Bienvenue, "The Complete Re-education of Delinquents in Boscoville (1940–1971): A Pivotal Moment in the History of Social Intervention in Quebec" (2009) 50:3 Recherches sociographiques 507.
41   Dominican priest Father Noël Mailloux served as the first director of the Institute of Psychology at the University of Montreal. Ibid.
42   The facility closed in 1997. For reference to critiques of Boscoville in the 1980s, see ibid.; Marc Leblanc, "De l'efficacité d'internats québécois" (1985) 14:2 Revue canadien de psycho-éducation 113; Marc Leblanc, *Boscoville: la rééducation évaluée* (Montréal: Éditions Hurtubise, 1983).
43   Interview with Claire L'Heureux-Dubé, Clearwater, FL, 10–14 May 2009.
44   Bienvenue, see note 40 above. In the 1980s, all records of the residents at Boscoville were destroyed, in a deliberate attempt to ensure that the juvenile past could never catch up with a resident's life, and so it is not possible to locate Pierre's individual diagnoses and treatments.
45   Interview with Claire L'Heureux-Dubé, Clearwater, FL, 10–14 May 2009.
46   Ibid.
47   *Youth Protection Act,* LRQ, c.P. 34.1, had been enacted in 1979 in response to critiques that the *Juvenile Delinquents Act,* RSC, c. 160, had insufficient protection for due process. Section 95 of the Quebec statute permitted a child under the age of eighteen to apply to the tribunal for review of a decision entrusting him or her to an institution operating a rehabilitation centre.
48   Interview with Claire L'Heureux-Dubé, Clearwater, FL, 10–14 May 2009.
49   Interview with Claire L'Heureux-Dubé, Clearwater, FL, 25–27 November 2014.
50   *Adam v. R.,* #1043, LAC, MG 31, E-110, box 75, heard in Montreal, 22 January 1986.
51   Ibid.
52   The choice of a disciplinary approach also reflected advice she had given to Nova Scotia's first female Supreme Court judge, Constance Glube, in the late 1970s, when Glube sought her counsel at a judicial education conference about her own young son, who was involved with drugs, break-ins, and theft. Glube remembered that in a deeply meaningful, heart-to-heart conversation they had about their shared family problems, L'Heureux-Dubé advised "tough love." It was a sentiment with which Glube agreed, noting that her family had tried everything else – psychiatrists, psychologists – and nothing was working. "Claire was extremely helpful to me, because she understood. When I unburdened myself ... she was kind to me." Interview with Constance Glube, Halifax, 28 October 2014.
53   Interview with Claire L'Heureux-Dubé, Ottawa, 30 October 2007.
54   At L'Heureux-Dubé's urging, Paul L'Heureux transferred the ownership of the Quebec City house to Nicole, in recognition of the long years during which she nursed her invalid mother.
55   The University of Laval website indicated that Nicole L'Heureux commenced her career as a teaching assistant at the Faculty of Law in 1968 and became a full professor in 1977. She taught courses in commercial law, banking and financial institutions, law of finance and international payments, and consumer law. Her publications included Nicole L'Heureux, *Droit de la consommation* (Montréal: Sorej, 1981), and Nicole L'Heureux, *Droit bancaire,* 4th ed. (Montréal: Éditions Yvon Blais, 2004), treatises published in multiple editions in multiple languages. Her accomplishments were remarkable, given her many

decades of providing constant nursing care for her mother. After her mother's death, Nicole developed her career internationally, delivering judicial education, accepting academic visiting appointments to European universities, and participating in conferences. In 1983, at the age of seventy, she married Ray Kuntz, an American she met while holidaying in Florida, and they made their home in Florida. Interview with Nicole L'Heureux, Clearwater, FL, 11–12 May 2009.
56 Interview with Claire L'Heureux, Ottawa, 30 October 2007.
57 Interview with Louise L'Heureux-Giliberti, Chicago, 21 April 2009.
58 Interview with Claire L'Heureux-Dubé, Ottawa, 17 September 2007. Others who made the same remark included Roger Garneau (interview, Quebec City, 28 April 2009); Charles Gonthier (interview, Ottawa, 14 September 2008); André Legault (interview, Ottawa, 10 December 2007).

CHAPTER 25: APPOINTMENT TO THE SUPREME COURT OF CANADA

1 Chouinard's death occurred 6 February 1987. Donn Downey, "Julien Chouinard: Supreme Court judge was top civil servant for Quebec Premier," *Globe and Mail* (9 February 1987) A14; interview with Marie-Claire Belleau, Quebec City, 30 April 2008.
2 The *Supreme Court Act, 1985*, RSC 1985, c. S-26, s. 6, required that three of the judges be trained in Quebec civil law.
3 David Vienneau, "Appointment likely as Supreme Court loses another justice," *Toronto Star* (15 April 1987) A10; David Vienneau, "Appointment to High Court critical," *Toronto Star* (29 March 1987) B5; Canadian Press, "Who'll fill Chouinard's seat on top court?" *Montreal Gazette* (9 February 1987) A5; Kirk Makin, "New judge called likely chief justice," *Globe and Mail* (10 February 1987) A15.
4 Born in Quebec City in 1935, Yves Fortier obtained a BA from the University of Montreal in 1955, a Bachelor of Civil Law from McGill in 1958, and a Bachelor of Letters from Oxford University in 1960. He was called to the bar and joined Ogilvy Renault in 1961, and was elected president of the Canadian Bar Association in 1982. He represented Canada in a maritime boundary dispute with the United States in 1984. Drew Hasselback, "Yves Fortier to leave Norton Rose," *Financial Post* (24 October 2011); Spyros Bourboulis, "The Diplomat," Canadian Bar Association *National* (January-February 2014) 12.
5 Gordon Donaldson, *The Prime Ministers of Canada* (Toronto: Doubleday Canada, 1997).
6 Anthony Wilson-Smith, "A New Face on the Bench," *Maclean's* (27 April 1987) 11; Bourboulis "The Diplomat," see note 4 above at 13: "At the mention that he once turned down a seat on the Supreme Court, [Fortier will] tell you that he would have preferred that that story had never gotten out. 'It's now public knowledge, but I didn't like it to be discussed,' he says." On the rumours that Fortier was asked, and turned down the position, see also interview with Louis LeBel, Ottawa, 8 July 2010. LeBel, frequently named as a contender, was appointed in 2000. The rejection did Fortier's career no long-term damage. In 1988, Mulroney appointed him ambassador to the United Nations, and he went on to serve as Canada's representative on the UN Security Council, as a corporate board chair, and as an international arbitrator.
7 Canadian Press, "Who'll fill Chouinard's seat on top court?" see note 3 above; Ellen Anderson, *Judging Bertha Wilson: Law as Large as Life* (Toronto: University of Toronto Press, 2001).
8 The *Report of the Royal Commission on Aboriginal Peoples,* which advocated the appointment of an Aboriginal judge to the top court, was not filed until 1996. Canada, *The Report of the Royal Commission on Aboriginal Peoples*, vol. 6 (Ottawa: Supply and Services Canada, 1996) at 129. See also James C. Hopkins and Albert C. Peeling, "Aboriginal Judicial Appointments to the Supreme Court of Canada" (Paper prepared for the Indigenous Bar Association, April 2006); Richard Devlin, A. Wayne McKay, and Natasha Kim, "Reducing

the Democratic Deficit: Representation, Diversity, and the Canadian Judiciary, or 'Towards a Triple P Judiciary'" (2000) 38 Alta L Rev 734. Prime Minister Mulroney would subsequently demonstrate a desire for greater ethnic diversity, with appointments of the first Ukrainian Canadian (John Sopinka, 1988) and the first Italian Canadian (Frank Iacobucci, 1991).

9 Interview with Brian Mulroney, Montreal, 22 August 2013.
10 Ibid.
11 The *Constitution Act, 1867 (U.K.)*, 30 & 31 Vict., c. 3, and *Constitution Act, 1982 (U.K.)*, 1982, c. 11, made no reference to the process of nomination and selection of Supreme Court judges. On the demands for more provincial influence, see Claire L'Heureux-Dubé, "Nomination of Supreme Court Judges: Some Issues for Canada" (1991) 20 Man LJ 600. The Victoria constitutional conference in 1971 elicited an agreement that appointments to the Supreme Court would be subject to provincial consultation, but after the wider constitutional proposals failed, no changes were made. Efforts at constitutional reform that culminated in the Meech Lake Agreement (1987) and Charlottetown Accord (1992) also contained provisions to give the provinces a greater role in the selection of Supreme Court justices; none were enacted. James G. Snell and Frederick Vaughan, *The Supreme Court of Canada: History of the Institution* (Toronto: Osgoode Society for Canadian Legal History, 1985) at 276.
12 Proposals included nominations from a body representing governments, the legal community, and non-lawyers; L'Heureux-Dubé, ibid. In Claire L'Heureux-Dubé, "La Nomination des Juges: Une Perspective" (1994) 25:2 Rev Gen 295, she reported on the arguments for and against, without concluding which process would be preferable. Peter Russell explained the rationale for more public involvement as a need for a more "democratic" method of appointment to a court that would adjudicate disputes about the powers of government and the rights of citizens. P.H. Russell, "Meech Lake and the Supreme Court" in K.E. Swinton and C.J. Rogerson, eds., *Competing Constitutional Visions: The Meech Lake Accord* (Toronto: Carswell, 1988) at 97 and 104–5. Two years after her retirement from the court, L'Heureux-Dubé appeared before a Commons justice committee that was studying possible reform to the judicial appointment process. She cautioned against subjecting nominees to public confirmation hearings as was done in the United States, but recommended that the government appoint a committee of experts, including the Supreme Court chief justice and a couple of MPs, who could privately screen contenders. Noting that the current process kept candidates as well as the public "out of the loop during the selection process," she added: "In my case, I would have liked somebody to interview me." Janice Tibbetts, "Public must see how justices are picked: ex-judge," *Ottawa Citizen* (5 April 200) A3. At her retirement, she stressed the usefulness of a "non-partisan, broad-based" screening committee with representation from the provinces, the public, academics, and lawyers; Cristin Schmitz, "Top court 'can always be improved,'" *Ottawa Citizen* (5 May 2002) A4.
13 Interview with Brian Mulroney, Montreal, 22 August 2013. Before his term as prime minister ended in 1993, Mulroney would appoint nine Supreme Court judges: Gérard La Forest, Claire L'Heureux-Dubé, John Sopinka, Charles Gonthier, Peter Cory, Beverley McLachlin, William Stevenson, Frank Iacobucci, and Jack Major.
14 Maurice Jannard, "Claire L'Heureux-Dubé à la Cour suprême," *Montréal La Presse* (16 April 1987). Jannard also reported that Marc Lortie, press secretary to the Quebec premier, advised that there had been "*discussions approfondies*" between Quebec and Ottawa prior to the appointment, a pattern he indicated was ongoing: "*M. Lortie a affirmé que pour chaque nomination à la Cour suprême Ottawa consulte largement le Québec.*"
15 Vienneau, "Appointment to High Court critical," see note 3 above; David Vienneau, "PM ponders crucial appointment of justice to top court," *Toronto Star* (23 February 1987) A8. Audette-Filion was rumoured to have turned down an earlier offer of appointment to the Quebec Court of Appeal.

16 Roy and Mulroney both graduated from Laval with LL.L. degrees in 1964, and then practised law at Ogilvy Renault in Montreal. Konrad Yakabuski, "Bernard Roy was Brian Mulroney's right-hand man," *Globe and Mail* (15 April 2013).
17 Frank Iacobucci was the deputy minister of justice at the time, and recalled that Paul Tellier instructed them to put together dossiers on two candidates: L'Heureux-Dubé and another individual whom he did not name. He recalled that the recommendation on L'Heureux-Dubé was positive. Interview with Frank Iacobucci, Toronto, 26 October 2011.
18 Interview with Brian Mulroney, Montreal, 22 August 2013.
19 Ibid.
20 Richard Cleroux, "Tory appointments spark Commons row," *Globe and Mail* (24 November 1987) A11.
21 Ken McQueen, "Second woman named to Supreme Court," *Ottawa Citizen* (16 April 1987) A1; "Quebec woman to SCOC," *Halifax Chronicle-Herald* (16 April 1987) 4, noted that L'Heureux-Dubé had "no political background."
22 Interview with Brian Mulroney, Montreal, 22 August 2013.
23 Ibid.
24 Ibid.
25 Ibid.
26 Jeff Sallot, "Second woman appointed to top court," *Globe and Mail* (16 April 1987) A1.
27 *Canadian Law List, 1952* (Toronto: Cartwright and Sons, n.d.) listed Côté with Bard in the Bard Côté law firm, although this early position was not listed in his biographical entry in Ignace-J. Deslauriers, *La Cour supérieure du Québec et ses juges: 1849–1er janvier 1980* (Québec: Bibliothèque nationale du Québec, 1980) at 78.
28 Interview with Claire L'Heureux-Dubé, Quebec City, 30 August 2012.
29 Ibid.
30 Ibid.
31 Pratte, who had also been dean of the Laval law school from 1962 to 1965, served as special legal counsel to Quebec premiers Jean Lesage and Daniel Johnson, and chair of Air Canada from 1968 to 1975. Appointed to the Supreme Court in the fall of 1977, he resigned in the spring of 1979. De Grandpré was a career litigator and former president of the bars of Montreal and Quebec; he was appointed to the Supreme Court on 1 January 1974 and resigned in 1977. Philip Girard described their reasons for quitting as similar: "after their high-flying careers and busy social lives in Montreal, the Supreme Court seemed a dull back-water, and [Chief Justice Bora] Laskin's blunt management style a provocation." Philip Girard, *Bora Laskin: Bringing Law to Life* (Toronto: University of Toronto Press, 2005) at 416, 441.
32 Ibid. at 373.
33 Interview with Claire L'Heureux-Dubé, Quebec City, 27–28 April 2009.
34 Interview with Brian Mulroney, Montreal, 22 August 2013.
35 W.H. McConnell, *William R. McIntyre: Paladin of the Common Law* (Montreal: McGill-Queen's University Press, 2000).
36 Interview with Claire L'Heureux-Dubé, Quebec City, 29–30 April 2008.
37 Anthony Wilson-Smith, "A New Face on the Bench," *Maclean's* (27 April 1987) 11.
38 Interview with Claire L'Heureux-Dubé, Quebec City, 29–30 April 2008.
39 Louise Mailhot, *Les premières! L'histoire de l'accès des femmes à la pratique du droit et à la magistrature* (Cowansville, QC: Éditions Yvon Blais, 2013) at 205.
40 The official date of the appointment was 15 April 1987. Ibid. at 199.
41 Interview with Claire L'Heureux-Dubé, Ottawa, 13 September 2010.
42 Jacques LeMay, who had practised law with Julien Chouinard and Jacques Flynn, confessed that many of the lawyers were "surprised it was a woman appointed to the Supreme Court." Interview with Jacques LeMay, Quebec City, 5 May 2010. Interview with Jeanne D'Arc Lemay-Warren, Pointe-au-Pic, QC, 8 August 2009: "I knew she would ... go far, but then,

I didn't think of the Supreme Court of Canada." Interview with Robert Auclair, Quebec City, 7 August 2008: "We could not foresee that she would be appointed to the Supreme Court of Canada."
43 Interview with Louis LeBel, Ottawa, 8 July 2010.
44 Interview with Pierre-Gabriel Jobin, Montreal, 23 April 2010.
45 Interview with Roch Bolduc, Quebec City, 7 August 2009.
46 Interview with Martial Asselin, Quebec City, 7 August 2008.
47 Wilson-Smith, "A New Face on the Bench," see note 37 above.
48 Interview with Louise Mailhot, Gananoque, ON, 20 May 2009. The emerging family law bar, accustomed to such aspersions, was pleased with the appointment. Toronto family lawyer Malcolm Kronby emphasized that she was the first on the court with any expertise in family law: "We were very pleased to see somebody from her background appointed." Interview with Malcolm C. Kronby, Toronto, 30 September 2010. Queen's law professor Nicholas Bala added that she was the "first mother on the Supreme Court of Canada" – an important attribute in diversifying the court. Interview with Nicholas C. Bala, Kingston, 12 August 2009.
49 "Courting on High: '*Pourvu qu'elle ne change pas*,'" Canadian Bar Association *National* 14 (5 May 1987) 4.
50 Michel A. Auger, "Les femmes ont une part égale à jouer dans les grandes institutions de la société," *Le Devoir* (18 April 1987).
51 Interview with Yves Bernier, Quebec City, 30 April 2008: "I was not surprised she was chosen. She was well known because she is an extrovert. She makes friends with everybody. Women had to be appointed to the Supreme Court of Canada, which was another factor in favour of her." Interview with André Desmeules, Quebec City, 10 May 2010: "She's so full of talent [and] has so much energy. I was not surprised." Jacques Alleyn confessed that he had "no idea" who might have nominated his "outspoken" classmate, but that he was "pleasantly surprised" because it was "high time that they found women candidates for these appointments." Interview with Jacques Alleyn, Ottawa, 9 September 2009.
52 Interview with Roger Chouinard, Quebec City, 11 May 2010.
53 Interview with Pierre-Gabriel Jobin, Montreal, 23 April 2010.
54 Comments from Claire L'Heureux-Dubé during interview with Judith Gamache-Côté, Quebec City, 1 May 2008.
55 Comments from Claire L'Heureux-Dubé during interview with Denyse Dion, Quebec City, 1 May 2008.
56 Interview with Claire L'Heureux-Dubé, Clearwater, FL, 10–14 May 2009.
57 Comments from L'Heureux-Dubé's brother-in-law Joe Giliberti during interview with Louise L'Heureux-Giliberti, Chicago, 21 April 2009.
58 Interview with Louise L'Heureux-Giliberti, Chicago, 21 April 2009.
59 Comments from Claire L'Heureux-Dubé during interview with Marcèle Dorion, Quebec City, 30 April 2008.
60 Florian Sauvageau, David Schneiderman, and David Taras, *The Last Word: Media Coverage of the Supreme Court of Canada* (Vancouver: UBC Press, 2006) at 20.
61 Interview with Marie-Claire Belleau, Quebec City, 30 April 2008.
62 Dickson's demeanour at the swearing-in is captured in the *Hon. Claire L'Heureux-Dubé Swearing-In Ceremony* DVD, held by the Registrar of the Supreme Court of Canada.
63 Kirk Makin, "Long hours, teamwork a habit for new Supreme Court judge," *Globe and Mail* (23 April 1987) A1; Canadian Press, "Who'll fill Chouinard's seat on top court?" see note 3 above; "Someone of Merit," Editorial, *Montreal Gazette* (20 April 1987) B2.
64 David Vienneau, "Second woman appointed to Supreme Court," *Toronto Star* (16 April 1987) A1.
65 "Someone of Merit," see note 63 above; "Picking a Judge," Editorial, *Toronto Star* (18 April 1987) B2.

66 Makin, "Long hours, teamwork a habit," see note 63 above.
67 Vienneau, "Appointment to high court critical," see note 3 above.
68 Makin, "Long hours, teamwork a habit," see note 63 above.
69 Peggy Curran, "Second woman named to Canada's top court," *Montreal Gazette* (16 April 1987) A1.
70 Makin, "Long hours, teamwork a habit," see note 63 above.
71 Ibid.
72 Stephen Bindman, "Hard work, compassion propel judge to success," *Ottawa Citizen* (24 April 1987) A9.

Chapter 26: Early Days on the Supreme Court of Canada

1 Interview with Claire L'Heureux-Dubé, Clearwater, FL, 10–14 May 2009; Stephen Bindman, "Judging in a man's world," *Ottawa Citizen* (13 April 1992) at A3.
2 Frank Iacobucci, named as Wilson's successor in 1991, noted that she had confided in him that the court was "not the friendliest of environments," and that there were "some who were cool to her." Iacobucci explained: "I think [Bertha Wilson] went on a court where she knew she was not the rest of the court's choice. Some members of the court may have wanted others. As you can expect from Ontario, there's a big pool of men to draw from." Interview with Frank Iacobucci, Toronto, 26 October 2011.
3 Ellen Anderson, *Judging Bertha Wilson: Law as Large as Life* (Toronto: University of Toronto Press, 2001) at 127, 154.
4 On Laskin's challenges as the first Jewish judge, see Philip Girard, *Bora Laskin: Bringing Law to Life* (Toronto: University of Toronto Press, 2005) at 322–24, 338–41. Some of his displeasure at Wilson's appointment can be traced to his lobbying for the appointment of Charles Dubin instead. Ibid. at 439.
5 Anderson, *Judging Bertha Wilson,* see note 3 above at 150. Anderson noted at 414 that Lamer explained this many years later, at the unveiling of Wilson's portrait in 1999, as intending to signal that it was inappropriate to show "traditional gallantry" by standing to honour Wilson as a woman.
6 Ibid. at 128, 150, 153–34, and 164.
7 Frank Iacobucci stated: "I have a sense that when Claire went on the court, there would be hangovers from that," referring to Wilson's experience that some of the men were cool to her. "I think Claire met that kind of feeling. Bertha told me that when Claire came on, there were still elements of that." Interview with Frank Iacobucci, Toronto, 26 October 2011.
8 Interview with Gérard La Forest, Ottawa, 30 June 2014.
9 Comments shared by law clerks serving at the time who wished not to be identified by name.
10 The former law clerk, who asked to remain anonymous, added that as a young female clerk, she felt that she ought not to express her shock or bewilderment in front of the judge: "I could not understand the link between menopause and the work of a judge. [But] I could not react. Today, I wish that I could have reacted to tell him how upsetting an attack on the dignity of this woman it was."
11 Interview with Claire L'Heureux-Dubé, Quebec City, 29–30 April 2008; Kirk Makin and Graeme Smith, "Gatecrashing the old boys' club," *Globe and Mail* (2 May 2002) A8; Cristin Schmitz, "Lists Former Colleagues with 'Beautiful Minds,'" *Lawyers Weekly* (17 May 2002) at 23.
12 Makin and Smith, ibid. The judge was not named in the article but was revealed in interviews with Claire L'Heureux-Dubé, Clearwater, FL, 10–14 May 2009.
13 "Top court 'can always be improved,'" *Ottawa Citizen* (5 May 2002) A4.
14 Cristin Schmitz, "Our One-on-One with Justice Claire L'Heureux-Dubé," *Lawyers Weekly* (17 May 2002) at 18, 23.

15 Interview with Marie-Claire Belleau, Quebec City, 30 April 2008.
16 Interview with Claire L'Heureux-Dubé, Clearwater, FL, 10–14 May 2009; Stephen Bindman, "Judging in a man's world," see note 1 above.
17 Interview with Claire L'Heureux-Dubé, Clearwater, FL, 10–14 May 2009.
18 Interview with Marie-Claire Belleau, Quebec City, 30 April 2008.
19 Interview with Pierre-Gabriel Jobin, Montreal, 23 April 2010.
20 Interview with Teresa Scassa, Ottawa, 16 May 2014.
21 Interview with Kirk Makin, Toronto, 9 April 2015.
22 Interview with Peter Sankoff, Ottawa, 27 June 2014.
23 Louise Langevin, "Hon. L'Heureux-Dubé, Claire: entrevue réalisée avec l'Hon. L'Heureux-Dubé," 26 March 2007 at l'Université Laval, Québec (copy on file with the author).
24 Interview with Frank Iacobucci, Toronto, 26 October 2011.
25 Interview with Charles Gonthier, Ottawa, 14 September 2008.
26 Interview with Marie-Claire Belleau, Ottawa, 11 December 2013.
27 Interview with Rosemary Cairns Way, Ottawa, 29 April 2014. Cairns Way was a law clerk to Gerald Le Dain from 1987 to 1988.
28 Anderson, *Judging Bertha Wilson,* see note 3 above at 162, quoting Justice Estey.
29 This is an unattributed comment made by a sitting judge.
30 Robert J. Sharpe and Kent Roach, *Brian Dickson: A Judge's Journey* (Toronto: University of Toronto Press, 2003) chs. 1–6; DeLloyd J. Guth, ed., *Brian Dickson at the Supreme Court of Canada 1973–1990* (Winnipeg: University of Manitoba, 1998) at 3.
31 Sharpe and Roach, ibid. at 5.
32 Ibid. at 158; Guth, *Brian Dickson at the Supreme Court of Canada,* see note 30 above at xviii; Philip Slayton, *Mighty Judgment: How the Supreme Court of Canada Runs Your Life* (Toronto: Penguin, 2011) at 274.
33 The conversation was reported in Sharpe and Roach, *Brian Dickson,* see note 30 above at 62.
34 Interview with Claire L'Heureux-Dubé, Ottawa, 30 June 2014.
35 From the position of retirement, she added: "[Chief Justice Dickson] had stature. He was a man of duty. He was kind and he was severe. He had authority. He was very fair. He had common sense and he was humble. When we were in conference, he was always very thoughtful in his explanations." Interview with Claire L'Heureux-Dubé, Clearwater, FL, 25–27 November 2014. The genuine affection she developed for Dickson was discernible to his two biographers, who noted that she "wept when Dickson broke the news of his retirement." Sharpe and Roach, *Brian Dickson,* see note 30 above at 465.
36 "Someone of Merit," Editorial, *Montreal Gazette* (20 April 1987) B2.
37 In the same article where he discredited affirmative action for the court, he supported it in justifying his decision in *Action Travail des Femmes v. C.N.R.* regarding other employment venues: "I think, increasingly, Canadian society is recognizing that the disadvantaged, the Native people, women, various cultural groups, and racial groups, linguistic groups deserve a better break than they have been getting. So on a sort of broad basis I think I would be inclined to favour it." The Hon. Mr. Justice Robert J. Sharpe, "Brian Dickson: Portrait of a Judge" (1998) 17:3 Advocates' Soc J 3.
38 Notes from interview with Madam Justice L'Heureux-Dubé upon her retirement, *Crown Prosecutors' Review,* unreferenced copy: "I am totally opposed to quotas. There are sufficiently talented and competent women lawyers in this country that they can compete on merit alone." See also her comment, "*nommer une femme pour nommer une femme n'est pas mon genre*": Langevin, "Hon. L'Heureux-Dubé, Claire," see note 23 above.
39 Sharpe and Roach, *Brian Dickson,* see note 30 above at 143–44; Sharpe, "Brian Dickson: Portrait of a Judge," see note 37 above; James G. Snell and Frederick Vaughan, *The Supreme Court of Canada: History of the Institution* (Toronto: Osgoode Society for Canadian Legal History, 1985) at 225–26; Girard, *Bora Laskin,* see note 4 above at 415–16.

40 Sharpe and Roach, ibid. at 19, 144; Girard, ibid. at 432.
41 Interview with Alice Desjardins, Ottawa, 2 July 2009. Desjardins became the first tenure-stream female law professor in Canada, hired at the University of Montreal in 1961. Beetz was a faculty member at the time, and recruited Desjardins, stating that "women had been keeping the primary school and secondary school in Quebec for generations, and it was time that they had women at the university." Beetz went on to become the dean from 1968 to 1970.
42 Sharpe, "Brian Dickson: Portrait of a Judge," see note 37 above.
43 Interview with Marie-Claire Belleau, Ottawa, 11 December 2013.
44 Ibid.
45 Ibid.
46 Ibid.
47 Anderson, *Judging Bertha Wilson,* see note 3 above at 416.
48 Sharpe and Roach, *Brian Dickson,* see note 30 at 186; Girard, *Bora Laskin,* see note 4 above at 440.
49 Sharpe and Roach, ibid. at 286; Girard, ibid. at 440–41.
50 Schmitz, "Our One-on-One with Justice Claire L'Heureux-Dubé," see note 14 above at 18, 23.
51 Estey's controversial press comments, which attracted a complaint to the Canadian Judicial Council and resulted in his withdrawal from participation in twenty-five cases on which he had sat but for which judgment had been reserved, included disparagement of the *Charter,* critique of the *Morgentaler* decision, support for free trade, a parliamentary presentation questioning the constitutionality of the Nisga'a Treaty, and opposition to the proposed Meech Lake Accord: Sharpe and Roach, *Brian Dickson,* see note 30 at 375, 427–30; Anderson, *Judging Bertha Wilson,* see note 3 at 376; David Vienneau, "Appointment likely as Supreme Court loses another justice," *Toronto Star* (15 April 1987) A10. Upon her retirement, L'Heureux-Dubé admitted that although Estey was "not comfortable with having a woman coming to the court," the two became "very, very, very good friends," and that she had "enjoyed his wit." Schmitz, "Our One-on-One with Justice Claire L'Heureux-Dubé," see note 14 above at 18, 23.
52 W.H. McConnell, *William R. McIntyre: Paladin of the Common Law* (Montreal: McGill-Queen's University Press, 2000); Sharpe and Roach, *Brian Dickson,* see note 30 above at 186–87, 362; Rae Corelli, "Here Come the Judges," *Maclean's* (11 January 1988) at 36; Anderson, *Judging Bertha Wilson,* see note 3 above at 152, quoting David Vienneau, "'Conservative' judge quits Supreme Court," *Toronto Star* (11 February 1989) A1.
53 Anderson, ibid. at 152–54; McConnell, ibid. at 76.
54 Interview with Marie-Claire Belleau, Ottawa, 11 December 2013.
55 Sharpe and Roach, *Brian Dickson,* see note 30 above at 18.
56 McConnell, *William R. McIntyre,* see note 52 above at 82; Hon. J.J. Michel Robert, "Antonio Lamer: The Man, His Life and Times" in Adam Dodek and Daniel Jutras, eds., *The Sacred Fire: The Legacy of Antonio Lamer (Chief Justice of Canada)* (Markham, ON: LexisNexis, 2009) at 3–4.
57 Interview with Louise Arbour, Saint-Faustin Lac-Carré, QC, 24 July 2014.
58 Interview with Danièle Tremblay-Lamer, Ottawa, 12 March 2015.
59 Ignace-L. Deslauriers, *La Cour supérieure du Québec et ses juges: 1849–1ᵉʳ janvier 1980* (Québec: Bibliothèque nationale du Québec, 1980) at 145.
60 Peter McCormick, *Supreme at Last: The Evolution of the Supreme Court of Canada* (Toronto: Lorimer, 2000) at 85, 111, noting at 108 and 131 that the largest part of the caseload, 37.1 percent, involved criminal appeals during the years of Dickson's chief justiceship, rising to 43.6 percent under Lamer's chief justiceship.
61 As quoted by Anne Roland, "Le juge en chef Lamer et l'administration de la Cour suprême du Canada: une vision en action" in Dodek and Jutras, *The Sacred Fire,* note 56 above at 15.

62 Interviews with Claire L'Heureux-Dubé, Ottawa, 30 June 2010, 30 June 2014; interview with Claire L'Heureux-Dubé, Quebec City, 27–29 April 2009.
63 Interview with Danièle Tremblay-Lamer, Ottawa, 12 March 2015.
64 Ibid.
65 Ibid.
66 On L'Heureux-Dubé's driving, I can attest personally to the speed. On Lamer's, see comments of Teresa Scassa, who was given a lift back to Montreal with Lamer after her law clerk interviews in 1987. Scassa noted that driving beyond the speed limit amused Lamer, who told her that the police were often on his tail, lights flashing, until they "ran his plates," realized that the licence belonged to a Supreme Court justice, and abandoned the chase. Interview with Teresa Scassa, Ottawa, 16 May 2014. One might contrast this with Supreme Court Justice Louise Arbour, who recounted an anecdote of driving furiously down a street, late in picking up her daughter from childcare, only to be stopped by an officer for speeding. He checked her licence and came back apologizing that he had stopped her at all. She said: "Officer, write that ticket!" Interview with Don Stuart, Kingston, 4 May 2015.
67 Interview with Marie-Claire Belleau, Ottawa, 11 December 2013.
68 Interview with Teresa Scassa, Ottawa, 16 May 2014.
69 Anderson, *Judging Bertha Wilson*, see note 3 above, chs. 1–5.
70 Ibid. at 149–279; Kim Brooks, ed., *Justice Bertha Wilson: One Woman's Difference* (Vancouver: UBC Press, 2009); Jamie Cameron, ed., *Reflections on the Legacy of Justice Bertha Wilson* (Markham, ON: LexisNexis, 2008).
71 Sharpe and Roach, *Brian Dickson*, see note 30 above at 296.
72 Ibid. at 18, 374, 430–32; McConnell, *William R. McIntyre*, see note 52 above at 86–87: Harry W. Arthurs, "In Memoriam: A Locomotive of a Man" (2007) 45 Osgoode Hall LJ 655 at 662.
73 Bruce B. Ryder, "To Make a Difference" (2007) 45 Osgoode Hall LJ 655 at 659, noted the tragic death of the daughter.
74 Sharpe and Roach, *Brian Dickson*, see note 30 at 18, 374, 430–32; McConnell, *William R. McIntyre*, see note 52 at 86–87.
75 Sharpe and Roach, ibid. at 18, 297, 473; McConnell, ibid. at 87.
76 Interview with Gérard La Forest, Ottawa, 30 June 2014.
77 Interview with Marie-Claire Belleau, Ottawa, 11 December 2013.
78 Ibid.; Anderson, *Judging Bertha Wilson*, see note 3 above at 153; McConnell, *William R. McIntyre*, see note 52 above at 76.
79 Florian Sauvageau, David Schneiderman, and David Taras, *The Last Word: Media Coverage of the Supreme Court of Canada* (Vancouver: UBC Press, 2006) at 20.
80 Anderson, *Judging Bertha Wilson*, see note 3 above at 152; interview with Gérard La Forest, Ottawa, 30 June 2014; Bertha Wilson, "Decision-Making in the Supreme Court" (1986) 36 UTLJ 227.
81 The appointment date of 15 April 1987 was followed by L'Heureux-Dubé's first hearing on 4 May 1987.
82 Interview with Claire L'Heureux-Dubé, Ottawa, 30 June 2014.
83 Interview with Marie-Claire Belleau, Ottawa, 11 December 2013.
84 Guth, *Brian Dickson at the Supreme Court of Canada*, see note 30 above at 297, 307–8.
85 Anderson, *Judging Bertha Wilson*, see note 3 above at 416.
86 Justice Gérard La Forest noted that L'Heureux-Dubé developed a reputation as working "more than anybody else." Interview with Justice Gérard La Forest, Ottawa, 30 June 2014.
87 Kirk Makin, "Long hours, teamwork a habit for new Supreme Court judge," *Globe and Mail* (23 April 1987) A1.
88 Interview with Lisette Gammon, Ottawa, 16 November 2007.
89 Interview with Claire L'Heureux-Dubé, Ottawa, 30 June 2014.
90 Ibid.

91 Interview with André Legault, Ottawa, 10 December 2007.
92 Interview with Claire L'Heureux-Dubé, Ottawa, 30 June 2014.
93 Interview with Claire L'Heureux-Dubé, Clearwater, FL, 25–27 November 2014.
94 Interview with Claire L'Heureux-Dubé, Ottawa, 30 June 2010.
95 Comments from Claire L'Heureux-Dubé during interview with Denyse Dion, Quebec City, 1 May 2008.
96 Interview with Claire L'Heureux-Dubé, Clearwater, FL, 10–14 May 2009.
97 Ibid.
98 Interviews with Claire L'Heureux-Dubé, Clearwater, FL, 10–14 May 2009; Ottawa, 30 June 2010.
99 Interview with Marie-Claire Belleau, Ottawa, 11 December 2013.

CHAPTER 27: CONTINUING ISOLATION ON THE SUPREME COURT

1 Peter McCormick, *Supreme at Last: The Evolution of the Supreme Court of Canada* (Toronto: Lorimer, 2000) at 121–24, listed John Sopinka (1988), Charles Doherty Gonthier (1989), Peter deCartaret Cory (1989), Beverley McLachlin (1989), William Alexander Stevenson (1990), Frank Iacobucci (1991), John C. Major (1992), Michel Bastarache (1997), Ian Corneil Binnie (1998), Louise Arbour (1999), and Louis LeBel (2000).
2 Emmett Macfarlane, *Governing from the Bench: The Supreme Court of Canada and the Judicial Role* (Vancouver: UBC Press, 2013), noted at 123 that the Laskin court saw unanimity rates of over 80 percent, the Dickson court 64.7 percent, Lamer's court 58.4 percent, and the first decade of McLachlin's court 62.8 percent.
3 Interview with Rebecca Johnson, Victoria, 22 August 2013.
4 Criminal law was the subject of the largest number of decisions written by Lamer, and "a passion that began long before he came to the Supreme Court." Catherine Dauvergne, "Chief Justice Lamer's Leadership in Feminist Times" in Adam Dodek and Daniel Jutras, eds., *The Sacred Fire: The Legacy of Antonio Lamer (Chief Justice of Canada)* (Markham, ON: Lexis-Nexis, 2009) at 369.
5 Interview with Claire L'Heureux-Dubé, 25 July 2008.
6 Interview with Danièle Tremblay-Lamer, Ottawa, 12 March 2015.
7 Ibid.
8 Interview with David Paciocco, Ottawa, 11 June 2015.
9 Interview with Jocelyn Downie, Halifax, 24 October 2014.
10 Interview with former Lamer law clerk who asked not to be quoted as the source for this comment.
11 Dauvergne, "Chief Justice Lamer's Leadership in Feminist Times," see note 4 above at 353, 377. Dauvergne qualified this statement by adding that Lamer did not meet feminist argument "with protracted resistance."
   Lamer did not take it lightly when accusations of sexism were directed at the judiciary. Sparks flew when a Canadian Bar Association task force on gender equality reported that almost half of the 132 women judges who replied to its survey had "personally experienced discrimination" from male chief justices or colleagues. *Touchstones for Change: Equality, Diversity and Accountability, a Report on Gender Equality in the Legal Profession* (Ottawa: Canadian Bar Association, August 1993) at 192. Chief Justice Lamer demanded that Bertha Wilson, who had chaired the study, reveal the names of the women who had complained. When Wilson, who had conducted the survey under the promise of full confidentiality, refused to do so, he became enraged. Ellen Anderson, *Judging Bertha Wilson: Law as Large as Life* (Toronto: University of Toronto Press, 2001) at 349–50.
   After retirement, Lamer also took issue with Wilson's complaint that she and L'Heureux-Dubé had been shut out of judicial discussions on the court. He accused Wilson of refusing to engage in the "horse-trading that unites judges and results in strong common opinions,"

branding her "stubborn as a mule." Kirk Makin, "Lobbying hurt court, book says," *Globe and Mail* (11 March 2002) A9. "There was no little clique," Lamer told the *Lawyers Weekly*, "no little gang. Like-minded people tend to congregate ... I guess some of us just figured, 'well, there's no point in going and trying to convince Bertha that it's going to be this, and not that,' because she is not going to change her mind ... and maybe she felt isolated about that, but we never isolated her." Cristin Schmitz, "Former Chief Justice Lamer Reflects on His Brightest, Darkest Moments as Canada's Top Jurist," *Lawyers Weekly* (29 March 2002) 1 at 1, 7. University of Toronto law professor Jim Phillips, a former law clerk to Wilson, wrote back that Lamer had failed "to take into consideration that, had she been invited to participate in more of the informal discussions among the judges forming majority opinions without the benefit of her input, she might have been able to change their minds." Letter to the Editor, *Lawyers Weekly* (18 April 2002) 5.
12 Interview with Melvin Rothman, Montreal, 12 August 2008. Rothman knew both from his years as a Quebec judge.
13 Interview with Julien Payne, Ottawa, 7 July 2009; Robert J. Sharpe and Kent Roach, *Brian Dickson: A Judge's Journey* (Toronto: University of Toronto Press, 2003) at 187.
14 Hon. J.J. Michel Robert, "Antonio Lamer: The Man, His Life and Times" in Dodek and Jutras, *The Sacred Fire,* see note 4 above at 4–5.
15 On the divorce and his remarriage to Danièle Tremblay, see "Chronology" in Dodek and Jutras, ibid. at 483–84.
16 Interview with Charles Gonthier, Ottawa, 14 September 2008.
17 Ibid.
18 Interview with Michel Bastarache, Ottawa, 24 November 2009.
19 Interview with Claire L'Heureux-Dubé, Quebec City, 29–30 April 2008.
20 Interview with Edward Bayda, Regina, 23 October 2009.
21 Philip Slayton, *Mighty Judgment: How the Supreme Court of Canada Runs Your Life* (Toronto: Penguin, 2011) at 215–16. Jack Major later disputed that Lamer had ever told a colleague to "shut up": Cristin Schmitz, "Supreme Court's Judges Confronted Top Judge in 1999," *Lawyers Weekly* (29 April 2011). L'Heureux-Dubé observed that unhappiness over Lamer's elevation to chief justice was one reason Bertha Wilson retired early. "This was not the only reason. She wasn't well, [but] he came in in 1990, and she left in 1990. She said, 'I prefer to leave now. I know what's going to happen.'" Interview with Claire L'Heureux-Dubé, 25–27 November 2014.
22 Interview with Gérard La Forest, Ottawa, 30 June 2014.
23 Interview with Michel Bastarache, Ottawa, 24 November 2009.
24 Interview with Louise Arbour, Saint-Faustin Lac-Carré, QC, 24 July 2014.
25 Interview with Jack Major, Calgary, 13 November 2013.
26 For comments indicating that L'Heureux-Dubé's disagreements with Sopinka, Major, Iacobucci, and others were very pointed, see interview with Jack Major, Calgary, 13 November 2013; interview with Michel Bastarache, Ottawa, 24 November 2009; interview with Louise Arbour, Saint-Faustin Lac-Carré, QC, 24 July 2014.
27 Interview with Constance Glube, Halifax, 28 October 2014. On her career, see Allison Lawlor, "Constance Glube: Canada's first female chief justice," Obituary, *Globe and Mail* (3 March 2016) S6.
28 See, for example, Michel Vastel, "Mme L'Heureux-Dubé est nommée à la Cour suprême," *Le Devoir* (16 April 1987), who noted that L'Heureux-Dubé could in theory succeed Chief Justice Dickson, and suggested that other alternatives might include Francophone Ontario judge Le Dain and Francophone New Brunswick judge La Forest. Vastel then added that the alternating appointments probably would take more notice of Quebec judges over Anglo-Canadian judges, rather than French-speaking or English-speaking capabilities.

29 Interview with Claire L'Heureux-Dubé, Clearwater, FL, 25–27 November 2014.
30 Ibid.
31 Ibid.
32 Interview with Kirk Makin, Toronto, 9 April 2015.
33 Interview with Jack Major, Calgary, 13 November 2013.
34 Interview with Michel Bastarache, Ottawa, 24 November 2009.
35 Interview with Peter Sankoff, Ottawa, 27 June 2014. The child sexual abuse case of *R. v. F.F.B.*, [1993] 1 SCR 697, offered a vehicle for two former L'Heureux-Dubé law clerks to explore some of the hostility that suffused the court during this era; Marie-Claire Belleau and Rebecca Johnson, "Faces of Judicial Anger: Answering the Call" in M. Jézéquel and N. Kasirer, eds., *Les sept péchés capitaux et le droit* (Montréal: Éditions Thémis, 2007) 13. The enmity was not unprecedented at the court. A century earlier, in 1880, Justice Samuel Henry Strong, himself known for having disorganized work habits and taking unwarranted leaves, had launched into a virulent attack against his fellow judge William Alexander Henry, calling Henry's decisions "long, windy, incoherent, masses of verbiage, interspersed with ungrammatical expressions, slang and the veriest legal platitudes inappropriately applied." The comments were made in a letter to the prime minister, which also called for Henry's removal from the court; James G. Snell and Frederick Vaughan, *The Supreme Court of Canada: History of the Institution* (Toronto: Osgoode Society for Canadian Legal History, 1985) at 37–39.
36 Interview with Claire L'Heureux-Dubé, London, UK, 3 May 2012.
37 This anecdote is a composite description of several exchanges, offered by several law clerks who asked not to be identified.
38 Interview with Brian Mulroney, Montreal, 22 August 2013.
39 Interview with Claire L'Heureux-Dubé, Quebec City, 30 August 2012. In 1996, Jean Chretien's chief of staff took L'Heureux-Dubé to lunch and indicated that the prime minister was considering appointing her to the vice-regal post in Quebec. She recalled: "I joked, if I accepted you would roll over in your tomb. I will be very vocal. I will rewrite the speeches of the Péquistes. It is not to your advantage and certainly not to mine." In the summer of 1996, the famous Québécois actor from the *La famille Plouffe* series, Jean-Louis Roux, was appointed to the post instead. Caroline St-Pierre, "Jean-Louis Roux, actor and co-founder of TNF, dies at 90," *Montreal Gazette* (29 November 2013).
40 Interview with Claire L'Heureux-Dubé, Quebec City, 30 August 2012.
41 Interview with Ian Binnie, Ottawa, 6 April 2011.
42 Ibid.
43 Ibid.
44 Interview with Don Stuart, Kingston, ON, 4 May 2015.
45 Transcript of interview between Kirk Makin and Antonio Lamer, 2002. I am indebted to Kirk Makin for sharing this extract with me.
46 Interview with Danièle Tremblay-Lamer, Ottawa, 12 March 2015.
47 Ibid.
48 Interview with Louise Arbour, Saint-Faustin Lac-Carré, QC, 24 July 2014.
49 Interview with Don Stuart, Kingston, ON, 4 May 2015.
50 Kirk Makin and Renata D'Aliesio, "Chronicle of a lion in winter," *Globe and Mail* (7 May 2011) A4.
51 Interview with Frank Iacobucci, Toronto, 26 October 2011.
52 Interview with Michel Bastarache, Ottawa, 24 November 2009.
53 Interview with Cynthia Westaway, Ottawa, 17 October 2014.
54 Interview with David Wright, Toronto, 4 May 2014. He added: "At the same time, she is one of the most loving, loyal, supportive [people]."

55 Interview with Frank Iacobucci, Toronto, 26 October 2011.
56 Interview with David Wright, Toronto, 4 May 2014. Wright speculated that if Iacobucci had been on the court when L'Heureux-Dubé arrived, "he might have eased [her] path."
57 Interview with Louise Arbour, Saint-Faustin Lac-Carré, QC, 24 July 2014.
58 Ibid.
59 Interview with Michel Bastarache, Ottawa, 24 November 2009.
60 Ibid.
61 Interview with Frank Iacobucci, Toronto, 26 October 2011. Iacobucci also recalled that L'Heureux-Dubé once circulated a draft dissenting judgment describing his opinion as "unconscionable." He remembered being "very upset," and going to speak with her to say, "You cannot say that. It means no conscience." He said, "She seemed surprised when I told her. She took the word out."
62 Interview with Ian Binnie, Ottawa, 6 April 2011.
63 Sean Fine, "The Most Important Woman in Canada," *Saturday Night* (December 1995) 46.
64 Interview with Edward Bayda, Regina, 23 October 2009, recounting what he had heard about objections to the cot.
65 Ibid.
66 Interview with Andrew Lenz and François Lacasse, Ottawa, 5 August 2014; interview with Teresa Scassa, Ottawa, 16 May 2014. Judicial colleague Charles Gonthier, who lunched with her most days after the court set up a judges' dining room in the building, was another one who admired the work ethic: "There are so many things I suppose that revealed her qualities, her ways. She certainly worked longer hours. She was a very hard worker, and very thorough, and her decisions were very well researched, carefully drafted." Interview with Charles Gonthier, Ottawa, 14 September 2008.
67 Interview with Louise Arbour, Saint-Faustin Lac-Carré, QC, 24 July 2014.
68 Interview with Jack Major, Calgary, 13 November 2013.
69 Interview with Ian Binnie, Ottawa, 6 April 2011.
70 Interview with Jack Major, Calgary, 13 November 2013.

CHAPTER 28: FIFTEEN YEARS OF JURISPRUDENCE

1 Major joined the court in 1992, when the change to L'Heureux-Dubé's jurisprudence had begun to appear. However, he expressed great surprise that this was a change from early years, something that he said neither he nor his colleagues knew. Interview with Jack Major, Calgary, 13 November 2013.
2 The full list of Supreme Court cases heard by L'Heureux-Dubé can be drawn from the Canadian Legal Information Institute, online: <http://www.canlii.org>. See <http://scc-csc.lexum.com/scc-csc/en/d/s/index.do>.
3 Elizabeth Sheehy, ed., *Adding Feminism to Law: The Contributions of Justice Claire L'Heureux-Dubé* (Toronto: Irwin Law, 2004); Marie-Claire Belleau and François Lacasse, eds., *Claire L'Heureux-Dubé à la Cour suprême du Canada 1987–2002* (Montréal: Wilson et Lafleur, 2004). The full volume of *Canadian Journal of Women and the Law* (2003) 15:1, contained Daphne Gilbert, "Unequaled: Justice Claire L'Heureux-Dubé's Vision of Equality and Section 15 of the *Charter*" at 1–27; Andrée Lajoie, Cécile Bergada, and Katherine Gauthier, "Claire L'Heureux-Dubé, la Cour suprême et les minorités" at 28–52; Rosemary Cairns Way, "Culpability and the Equality Value: The Legacy of the *Martineau* Dissent" at 53–72; Michelle Boivin, "Les principes féministes en action: l'oeuvre judiciaire de l'honorable juge Claire L'Heureux-Dubé ou 'voir juste, voir claire/e'" at 73–101; Joan Brockman, "Aspirations and Appointments to the Judiciary" at 138–66; Constance Backhouse, "The Chilly Climate for Women Judges: Reflections on the Backlash from the *Ewanchuk* Case" at 167–93.

4 *Houle v. Canadian National Bank*, [1990] 3 SCR 122, opened the door under art. 1024 of the *Code civil* to greater judicial recourse for the abuse of contractual rights, without an obligation to prove malice or bad faith. Her ruling was described by one civil law commentator as providing "*nouvelles solutions à de vieux problèmes*": Boivin, ibid. at 100. *Augustus v. Gosset*, [1996] 3 SCR 268, overruled a long-standing Supreme Court precedent in order to provide compensation under arts. 1053 and 1056 of the *Code civil* for grief and distress (*solatium doloris*) to the mother of a son who had been wrongfully shot by police. It was praised for recognizing the "importance of emotions and interpersonal relations in women's lives": Louise Langevin, "L'œuvre de Claire L'Heureux-Dubé: une lecture féministe de l'arrêt *Augustus c. Gosset*" (2003) 15:1 CJWL 122 at 122–37. *Quebec (Public Curator) v. Syndicat national des employés de l'hôpital St-Ferdinand*, [1996] 3 SCR 211, awarded compensation to patients with mental disabilities who experienced deprivation of care during an illegal hospital strike, on the basis that this interfered with their right to security, inviolability, and dignity under the *Quebec Charter of Human Rights and Freedoms*. L'Heureux-Dubé's dissent in *Béliveau St-Jacques v. Fédération des employées et employés de services publics inc.*, [1996] 2 SCR 345, took issue with the decision of the majority to deny to a victim of sexual harassment any recourse to exemplary damages under the *Quebec Charter of Human Rights and Freedoms* because it also constituted a "workplace injury" compensable under the *Loi sur les accidents du travail et les maladies professionnelles*. See also Louise Langevin, "Le harcèlement sexuel au travail: l'impact de la décision *Béliveau Saint-Jacques*" (1997) 9 RFD 17; DeLloyd Guth, "Text and Consequence Serve the Rule of Law's Method" in Belleau and Lacasse, ibid. at 743–49.

5 *R. v. Seaboyer*, [1991] 2 SCR 577; *Moge v. Moge*, [1992] 3 SCR 813; *Canada (Attorney General) v. Mossop*, [1993] 1 SCR 554; *Symes v. Canada*, [1993] 4 SCR 695; *Reference re Secession of Quebec*, [1998] 2 SCR 217; *Baker v. Canada (Minister of Citizenship and Immigration)*, [1999] 2 SCR 817; *R. v. Ewanchuk*, [1999] 1 SCR 330.

6 Donald R. Songer, Susan W. Johnson, C.L. Ostberg, and Matthew E. Wetstein, *Law, Ideology, and Collegiality: Judicial Behaviour in the Supreme Court of Canada* (Montreal: McGill-Queen's University Press, 2012); C.L. Ostberg and Matthew E. Wetstein, *Attitudinal Decision Making in the Supreme Court of Canada* (Vancouver: UBC Press, 2007); Emmett Macfarlane, *Governing from the Bench: The Supreme Court of Canada and the Judicial Role* (Vancouver: UBC Press, 2013) at 60.

7 Sheehy, *Adding Feminism to Law*, see note 3 above; Belleau and Lacasse, *Claire L'Heureux-Dubé*, see note 3 above; *Canadian Journal of Women and the Law* (2003) 15:1, see note 3 above; interview with Nathalie Des Rosiers, Ottawa, 19 September 2008; interview with Anne Derrick, Halifax, 20 February 2009.

8 Interview with Don Stuart, Kingston, 4 May 2015; interview with Teresa Scassa, Ottawa, 16 May 2014; interview with David Wright, Toronto, 7 May 2014; interview with Peter Sankoff, Ottawa, 27 June 2014; interview with Pascale Fournier, Montreal, 7 July 2015; interview with Janice Tibbetts, Ottawa, 11 May 2015.

9 <http://www.wednesday-night.com/L-Heureux-Dube.asp. The criminal defence lawyer was not named.

10 Interview with Louise Arbour, Saint-Faustin Lac-Carré, QC, 24 July 2014.

11 Rosemary Cairns Way, "Culpability and the Equality Value: The Legacy of the *Martineau* Dissent" (2003) 15:1 CJWL 53 at 71.

12 Interview with Teresa Scassa, Ottawa, 16 May 2014.

13 *Robichaud v. Canada (Treasury Board)*, [1987] 2 SCR 84.

14 *Canadian Newspapers Co. v. Canada (Attorney General)*, [1988] 2 SCR 122.

15 *Leblanc v. Leblanc*, [1988] 1 SCR 217.

16 *Andrews v. Law Society of British Columbia*, [1989] 1 SCR 143; *Borowski v. Canada (Attorney General)*, [1989] 1 SCR 342; *Tremblay v. Daigle*, [1989] 2 SCR 530.

17 *Vorvis v. Insurance Corporation of British Columbia*, [1989] 1 SCR 1085; *Janzen v. Platy Enterprises Ltd.*, [1989] 1 SCR 1252; *Brooks v. Canada Safeway Ltd.*, [1989] 1 SCR 1219; *R. v. Keegstra*, [1990] 3 SCR 697. She arrived at the court too late to be included on the panel that heard *R. v. Morgentaler*, [1988] 1 SCR 30, in which Sopinka, writing for a unanimous seven-person bench, struck down the criminal prohibition on procuring abortion as a violation of the *Charter*. The case was argued in 1986, the year before her appointment.
18 *Canada (Canada Employment and Immigration Commission) v. Gagnon*, [1988] 2 SCR 29; see also *Jove v. Canada (Unemployment Insurance)*, [1988] 2 SCR 53.
19 *Prassad v. Canada (Minister of Employment and Immigration)*, [1989] 1 SCR 560.
20 *Syndicat des employés de production du Québec et de l'Acadie v. Canada (Canadian Human Rights Commission)*, [1989] 2 SCR 879.
21 *Saskatchewan (Human Rights Commission) v. Saskatoon (City)*, [1989] 2 SCR 1297; *Saskatchewan (Human Rights Commission) v. Moose Jaw (City)*, [1989] 2 SCR 1317.
22 *Canadian Council of Churches v. Canada (Minister of Employment and Immigration)*, [1992] 1 SCR 236.
23 *Canada (Minister of Employment and Immigration) v. Chiarelli*, [1992] 1 SCR 711.
24 F.L. Morton, Peter H. Russell, and Troy Riddell, "The *Canadian Charter of Rights and Freedoms*: A Descriptive Analysis of the First Decade, 1982–1992" (1995) 5 NJCL 37.
25 Claire L'Heureux-Dubé, "The Length and Plurality of Supreme Court of Canada Decisions" (1990) 28 Alta L Rev 581 at 582.
26 Michel C. Auger, "Les femmes ont une part égale à jouer dans les grandes institutions de la société," *Le Devoir* (18 April 1987).
27 Other notable cases include *Norberg v. Wynrib*, [1991] 2 SCR 226, where she signed McLachlin's concurring opinion holding that a doctor had breached his fiduciary duty when he had sexual relations with a drug-addicted patient; *Dickason v. University of Alberta*, [1992] 2 SCR 1103, where her dissent found that a university policy of mandatory retirement at age sixty-five was a violation of human rights legislation; *R. v. Osolin*, [1993] 4 SCR 595, where she dissented in holding that defence counsel could not cross-examine a sexual assault complainant on private medical records; *R. v. Park*, [1995] 2 SCR 836, where she wrote a concurring opinion narrowly defining the "air of reality" required to raise the defence of mistaken belief in consent in sexual assault cases; *Gould v. Yukon Order of Pioneers*, [1996] 1 SCR 571, where her dissent would have upheld a human rights ruling that restricting organizational membership to men constituted sex discrimination.
28 Claire L'Heureux-Dubé, "What a Difference a Decade Makes: The Canadian Constitution and Family Law since 1991" (2001) 27 Queen's LJ 361 at 372.
29 Nathalie Des Rosiers described L'Heureux-Dubé's decisions as powerfully evocative of women's lived experience. Interview with Nathalie Des Rosiers, Ottawa, 19 September 2008. Halifax litigator Anne Derrick extolled her jurisprudence as resonating well beyond legal circles, giving heart to members of vulnerable communities who were surprised and heartened to find a judge who recognized the profound damage inflicted by discrimination. Interview with Anne Derrick, Halifax, 20 February 2009.
30 Interview with Claire L'Heureux-Dubé, Ottawa, 30 June 2014.
31 Since she did not start on the court until 15 April 1987, the first five years run from 15 April 1987 to the end of April 1988, and so on annually. She retired on 1 July 2002 but continued to deliver decisions from cases heard previously until the end of December 2002. Thus, the sample for the last five years was based on the calendar year from 1 January 1998 to the end of December 1998, and so on annually until the end of December 2002. L'Heureux-Dubé ruled for the Crown as follows: 1987–88, 74%; 1988–89, 78%; 1989–90, 72%; 1990–91, 68%; 1991–92, 78%; 1998, 88%; 1999, 69%; 2000, 89%; 2001, 77%; and 2002, 67%.
32 The Crown was successful in the court's majority opinion as follows: 1987–88, 74%; 1988–89, 78%; 1989–90, 66%; 1990–91, 55%; 1991–92, 66%; 1998, 76%; 1999, 59%; 2000, 70%; 2001,

64%; and 2002, 39%. Several theories have been advanced to explain this. Some suggested that the Crown chose to appeal only when it thought it had a strong case: interview with Claire L'Heureux-Dubé, Ottawa, 30 June 2014. Others explained the lopsided proportion of success in criminal but not in civil cases by suggesting that since many convicted individuals might be represented by legal aid lawyers, they might have less reluctance to launch appeals, and their lawyers might be less well prepared due to restricted funding: Richard A. Posner, "Judicial Opinions and Appellate Advocacy in Federal Courts – One Judge's Views" (2013) 51 Duq L Rev 3.

33 Many of these decisions were unanimous, but there were some cases where L'Heureux-Dubé voted for the Crown and the majority voted against, and some cases where the majority voted for the Crown and L'Heureux-Dubé voted against.

34 The only year to depart from this was 2000, directly after Lamer's retirement, when he delivered several held-over decisions from cases on which he had sat during his last year, 1999. Of the seven held-over decisions on which they both sat, she agreed with Lamer on four, siding with him 57 percent of the time. Lamer delivered no decisions in 2001 or 2002, so no comparisons could be made for L'Heureux-Dubé's last two years.

35 *R. v. Martineau*, [1990] 2 SCR 633. Lamer used ss. 11 and 7 of the *Charter* to extend to the crime of felony murder the common law presumption against convicting a person of a true crime without proof of intent or recklessness. L'Heureux-Dubé held that there was no *Charter* violation if the test of objective foreseeability was met.

36 *R. v. Swain*, [1991] 1 SCR 933. Lamer wrote the majority opinion, signed by Wilson, La Forest, Sopinka, Gonthier, and Cory.

37 *R. v. Généreaux*, [1992] 1 SCR 259. See also *R. v. Forster*, [1992] 1 SCR 339.

38 *R. v. Sauvé*, [2002] 3 SCR 519. This is often referred to as *Sauvé II*, because a previous case, *Sauvé v. Canada*, [1993] 2 SCR 438, had resulted in a unanimous nine-judge ruling that earlier legislation restricting the ability of all prisoners to vote was overbroad. Parliament had then enacted new legislation denying prisoners serving sentences of two years or longer the right to vote. In the subsequent challenge in 2002, Chief Justice McLachlin, writing for the majority, held that the denial of suffrage violated the *Charter*. L'Heureux-Dubé signed on to the dissenting opinion of Gonthier that the prisoners had not experienced a violation of their equality rights.

39 She was not the first judge to record such a pattern, for others had also changed in office. Chief Justice Brian Dickson's biographers described his transformation from a trial and appellate judge who wrote technical, doctrinal, precedent-controlled judgments to a leading exponent of progressive social-context and policy-based opinions in his later years on the Supreme Court. They attributed the alteration to the advent of the *Charter* as well as the flowering of new dimensions in Dickson's character – he had "grown as a judge and become more confident in the Court's ability to make law." Robert J. Sharp and Kent Roach, *Brian Dickson: A Judge's Journey* (Toronto: University of Toronto Press, 2003) at 24. Likewise, Bertha Wilson's biographer's account of her long career of research in a corporate-commercial, male-dominated Bay Street law firm and the bulk of her Court of Appeal decisions offered few hints of the fulsome equality rights jurisprudence she later produced on the Supreme Court. Ellen Anderson, *Judging Bertha Wilson: Law as Large as Life* (Toronto: University of Toronto Press, 2001). South African jurist Albie Sachs extolled both Dickson and Wilson for leading the Supreme Court of Canada toward a "modern" approach and a "broad, empathetic vision of a diverse society," when he explained that their judicial inspiration was "the main reason for emulating Canada's approach to constitutional rights" in his own country. Sean Fine, "Anti-apartheid hero makes a special plea to Canada," *Globe and Mail* (28 November 2015) A4.

40 Sharpe and Roach, ibid. at 207.

41 Janice Tibbetts, "Farewell Claire," *Canadian Lawyer* (September 2002) 39.

42 Based on interviews with sitting and former judges and law clerks, Emmett Macfarlane, *Governing from the Bench: The Supreme Court of Canada and the Judicial Role* (Vancouver: UBC Press, 2013), noted at 106 that law clerks' involvement typically ranged from researching and editing to producing full drafts of the reasons themselves. F.L. Morton and Rainer Knopff, *The Charter Revolution and the Court Party* (Peterborough, ON: Broadview, 2000) at 110.
43 Philip Slayton, *Mighty Judgment: How the Supreme Court of Canada Runs Your Life* (Toronto: Penguin, 2011) at 237.
44 Ibid. at 237.
45 Interview with Claire L'Heureux-Dubé, Clearwater, FL, 25–27 November 2014.
46 Interview with Teresa Scassa, Ottawa, 16 May 2014.
47 Ibid.
48 Interview with André Legault, Ottawa, 10 December 2007.
49 Interview with Cynthia Westaway, Ottawa, 17 October 2014.
50 See, for example, interview with Michelle Flaherty, Ottawa, 29 October 2014; interview with Pascale Fournier, Montreal, 7 July 2015. Several of the female applicants who interviewed for law clerking positions with L'Heureux-Dubé recalled her asking probing questions about whether they had young children, were due to give birth, or planned to become pregnant during their time at the court. L'Heureux-Dubé then told them that the work hours were not conducive to parenting. Years later, L'Heureux-Dubé had no recollection of such conversations; interview with Claire L'Heureux-Dubé, Clearwater, FL, 25–27 November 2014. But there were too many reports contradicting her memory to dismiss the stories as inaccurate. The information comes from a number of interviewees as well as people who heard of the incidents, which were widely discussed among law clerks and judges. Ian Binnie recalled hearing that L'Heureux-Dubé had dismissed one interviewee, telling her that it would be "impossible to have a single mother" as a law clerk. "Here was this great champion of women and women's rights, but when it came to a matter that touched her personal modus operandi there was a different response." Interview with Ian Binnie, Ottawa, 6 April 2011. In contrast, Lamer clerk Catherine Dauvergne recalled that she first met the chief justice when she was six months pregnant, and that she became pregnant with her second child while at the court. She noted that Lamer was "not at all concerned about my pregnancy," except to occasionally send up "morning snacks to the clerk offices for me." Dauvergne, "Chief Justice Lamer's Leadership in Feminist Times" in Adam Dodek and Daniel Jutras, eds., *The Sacred Fire: The Legacy of Antonio Lamer (Chief Justice of Canada)* (Markham, ON: Lexis-Nexis, 2009) at 353–54. Another former Lamer clerk, Jocelyn Downie, added that Lamer often hired feminist law clerks, noting that both she and Elizabeth Grace, whose feminism was "all over" their résumés, were chosen. "He wasn't particularly looking for feminists to hire," she added, "but he didn't hold it against us." Interviews with Jocelyn Downie, Halifax, 28 October 2014 and 18 July 2016.
51 Interview with Cynthia Westaway, Ottawa, 17 October 2014.
52 Interview with André Legault, Ottawa, 10 December 2007. As for the 10 percent, where individual clerks' work ethic or other skills created a mismatch, her former law clerks observed that she "didn't suffer that lightly [and] the relationship deteriorated." Interview with Peter Sankoff, Ottawa, 27 June 2014; interview with Teresa Scassa, Ottawa, 16 May 2014.
53 Interview with Laurie Sargent, Ottawa, 26 September 2014. She added that "Brian Dickson had the same trajectory, as did Bertha Wilson."
54 Interview with Jocelyn Downie, Halifax, 28 October 2014.
55 Interview with Claire L'Heureux-Dubé, Clearwater, FL, 25–27 November 2014.
56 Ibid.
57 Interview with Peter Sankoff, Ottawa, 27 June 2014.

58 Interview with Jocelyn Downie, Halifax, 24 October 2014.
59 Interview with Teresa Scassa, Ottawa, 16 May 2014.
60 Interview with Michelle Flaherty, Ottawa, 29 October 2014.
61 Jack Major observed that L'Heureux-Dubé was not "analytical." He added: "This sounds worse than it is, [but] I think Claire was result-driven. If she thought something was right, ancient precedents and flim-flam and the rest of it wouldn't interfere. To her, she felt that would be an injustice. [I]f what she perceived to be the right answer was deterred by precedent, she'd find a way to just breeze by that. She was clearly motivated, I think, by helping the underdog. And she and I were not kindred souls that way. We had different points of view on most things." Interview with Jack Major, Calgary, 13 November 2013. Michel Bastarache agreed, but only to a certain extent. "She'd know the solution, know where she wanted to go, and then she would have to send someone to bring her the legal reasoning in a form that would go into a good judgment. That was sort of the reverse of the way I worked. We had different approaches, but in the end, most often we agreed." Where he differed from some of his colleagues was on how to classify L'Heureux-Dubé's judicial style. "A lot of the judges thought [Claire] was very opinionated, [but] I didn't really find that. I just thought that she put a lot of energy into explaining her position, [and] was very forceful in making [the] argument. I don't think that's the same as being opinionated. I think she got a 'bad rap' for that." And he recalled that, more than some of their other colleagues, she was open to "reconsideration." "Some of the others would not [reconsider]," he emphasized. "They won't budge. She didn't have a sense of losing 'face.'" Bastarache added that if anyone deserved the label "ideological," it was Lamer, Major, and Iacobucci. "You couldn't discuss with them," he complained. Interview with Michel Bastarache, Ottawa, 24 November 2009.
62 Interview with Claire L'Heureux-Dubé, Ottawa, 30 June 2014; interview with Louis LeBel, Ottawa, 8 July 2010; interview with Jack Major, Calgary, 13 November 2013; interview with Louise Arbour, Saint-Faustin Lac-Carré, QC, 24 July 2014.
63 Interview with Claire L'Heureux-Dubé, Ottawa, 30 June 2014.
64 Ibid.
65 Ibid.
66 Interview with Edward Bayda, Regina, 23 October 2009.
67 Interview with David Wright, Toronto, 7 May 2014.
68 Rosalie Abella, "The Jurisprudence of Claire L'Heureux-Dubé" (Pamphlet of International Commission of Jurists [Canadian Section], *A Tribute* [2002]).
69 Interview with Claire L'Heureux-Dubé, Quebec City, 27–28 April 2009.
70 Transcript of interview between Kirk Makin and Antonio Lamer, 2002. I am indebted to Kirk Makin for providing me with extracts from this interview.
71 Interview with Claire L'Heureux-Dubé, Clearwater, FL, 25–27 November 2014.
72 Interview with Louise Dubé, Boston, 22 May 2012.
73 Interviews with Claire L'Heureux-Dubé, Ottawa, 30 June 2014; Clearwater, FL, 25–27 November 2014.
74 Marie-Claire Belleau and Rebecca Johnson, "Judging Gender: Difference and Dissent at the Supreme Court of Canada" (2008) 15:1–2 International Journal of the Legal Profession 57 at 60. During Chief Justice Lamer's leadership in the 1990s, the level of discord affected others on the court as well. Observers singled out "the gang of five," composed of Lamer, Sopinka, Cory, Iacobucci, and Major, as tending to vote *en bloc*. A smaller, more fragmented bloc of four, composed of L'Heureux-Dubé, La Forest, Gonthier, and McLachlin, was sometimes dubbed "the outsiders." The gang of five was perceived to be partial to the accused in criminal matters, and restrained on equality rights, whereas the four outsiders were understood to be generally less supportive of the accused and stronger on *Charter* equality rights. Peter McCormick, *Supreme at Last: The Evolution of the Supreme Court of*

Canada (Toronto: Lorimer, 2000) at 134–36; Peter McCormick, "Birds of a Feather: Alliances and Influences on the Lamer Court 1990–1997" (1998) 36 Osgoode Hall LJ 339. Others identified three blocs of judges: one wing dominated by Sopinka, Major, and Lamer, another by L'Heureux-Dubé, Gonthier, and La Forest, with the three remaining judges more of a conundrum: Iacobucci and Cory facing off against McLachlin. Donald R. Songer, Susan W. Johnson, C.L. Ostberg, and Matthew E. Wetstein, *Law, Ideology, and Collegiality: Judicial Behaviour in the Supreme Court of Canada* (Montreal: McGill-Queen's University Press, 2012) at 104. These authors noted at 171–72: "Justices Gonthier, La Forest, and L'Heureux-Dubé, who were found at the most liberal extreme of the economic ideological dimension, turned out to be the least liberal justices on the criminal factor. In contrast, Justices Major and Sopinka, who occupied the most conservative position on economic cases, turned out to be the most liberal justices on criminal decisions that scored strongly on the ideological factor."

75 Marie-Claire Belleau and Rebecca Johnson, "La dissidence judiciaire: réflexions préliminaires sur les émotions, la raison et les passions du droit" in Belleau and Lacasse, *Claire L'Heureux-Dubé*, see note 3 above at 712.

76 Interview with Claire L'Heureux-Dubé, Ottawa, 10 March 2010.

77 Cristin Schmitz, "Leaving after 15 Years on Bench, Justice L'Heureux-Dubé Says She's 'Extremely Serene,'" *Lawyers Weekly* 22:2 (10 May 2002).

78 Cristin Schmitz, "Our One-on-One with Justice Claire L'Heureux-Dubé," *Lawyers Weekly* 22:3 (17 May 2002) 18.

79 Interview with Claire L'Heureux-Dubé, Clearwater, FL, 25–27 November 2014.

80 Ibid.

81 Interviews with Claire L'Heureux-Dubé, London, UK, 3 May 2012; and Ottawa, 10 March 2010; interview with Laurie Sargent, Ottawa, 26 September 2014. The article was published as Claire L'Heureux-Dubé, "La pratique des opinions dissidentes au Canada – l'opinion dissidente: voix de l'avenir?" (2000) 8 C du Cons Const 85 (Dossier: Débat sur les opinions dissidentes).

82 Karl Llewellyn, "Some Realism about Realism: Responding to Dean Pound" (1931) 44 Harv L Rev 1222 at 1235.

83 Richard A. Posner, "Judicial Opinions and Appellate Advocacy in Federal Courts – One Judge's Views" (2013) 51 Duq L Rev 3 at 18.

84 Belleau and Johnson, "La dissidence judiciaire," see note 75 above at 700–1; Belleau and Johnson, "Judging Gender," see note 74 above at 61.

85 Marie-Claire Belleau, Anik Lamontagne, and Rebecca Johnson, "Les décisions de la juge McLachlin à la Cour suprême du Canada: une analyse statistique comparative" in David Wright and Adam Dodek, eds., *Public Law at the McLachlin Court: The First Decade* (Toronto: Irwin Law, 2011) at 47, 51.

86 Belleau and Johnson, "La dissidence judiciaire," see note 75 above at 700.

87 Ibid. at 718–19.

88 Marie-Claire Belleau and Rebecca Johnson, "I Beg to Differ: Interdisciplinary Questions about Law, Language and Dissent" in Logan Atkinson and Diana Majury, eds., *Law, Mystery and the Humanities: Collected Essays* (Toronto: University of Toronto Press, 2008) ch. 6.

89 Claire L'Heureux-Dubé, "The Dissenting Opinion: Voice of the Future?" (2000) 28:3 Osgoode Hall LJ 495 at 498, 504.

90 Melvin I. Urofsky, *Dissent and the Supreme Court: Its Role in the Court's History and the Nation's Constitutional Dialogue* (New York: Pantheon, 2015) at 36. Quoting Chief Justice Charles Evans Hughes at 12, Urofsky characterized dissents as "an appeal to the brooding spirit of the law, to the intelligence of a future day."

91 Louise Langevin, "Hon. L'Heureux-Dubé, Claire: entrevue réalisée avec l'Hon. L'Heureux-Dubé," 26 March 2007 at l'Université Laval, Québec (copy on file with the author).

92 Interview with David Scott, Toronto, 1 September 2010.
93 Stephen Bindman, "Decision-making in the inner sanctum: The judges: Canada's top court at work," *Ottawa Citizen* (12 April 1992) at A4.
94 Interview with Michel Bastarache, Ottawa, 24 November 2009.
95 Interview with Pascale Fournier, Montreal, 7 July 2015.
96 Interview with Louise Arbour, Saint-Faustin Lac-Carré, QC, 24 July 2014.
97 Interview with Andrew Lenz and François Lacasse, Ottawa, 5 August 2014.
98 Interview with Catherine Fraser, Edmonton, 12 November 2013.

Chapter 29: Sexual Assault

1 *R. v. Seaboyer*, [1991] 2 SCR 577 [hereafter *Seaboyer*].
2 Sean Fine, "The Most Important Woman in Canada," *Saturday Night* (December 1995) 46. The article profiled Beverley McLachlin, with the comments about L'Heureux-Dubé as comparative points.
3 *Seaboyer*, see note 1 above at 670.
4 Adelyn L. Bowland, "Sexual Assault Trials and the Protection of 'Bad Girls': The Battle between the Courts and Parliament" in Julian V. Roberts and Renate M. Mohr, eds., *Confronting Sexual Assault: A Decade of Legal and Social Change* (Toronto: University of Toronto Press, 1994) at 242.
5 Constance Backhouse, *Carnal Crimes: Sexual Assault Law in Canada, 1900–1975* (Toronto: Irwin Law, 2008).
6 *Laliberté v. The Queen* (1877), 1 SCR 117.
7 This is not to suggest that they should be, since evidence of prior sexual acts should be no more probative with respect to the accused than with respect to the complainant. Both are unreliable predictors. The issue is the imbalance. The sexual "double standard" was described by Michael D. Smith, "Language, Law and Social Power: *Seaboyer: Gayme v. R.* and a Critical Theory of Ideology" (1993) 51 UT Fac L Rev 118 at 152–53, as a "sex-specific ethics" or "a faith" – "an ethic without an epistemology – a particular system of attaching values to conduct without the slightest comprehension of how or why people believe that the system is true. It is a creed whose articles never really require articulation, because its believers rarely encounter anyone who does not already believe it, silently and by heart."
8 Audrey A. Wakling, *Corroboration in Canadian Law* (Toronto: Carswell, 1977) at 122, citing data for 1972. For data from earlier decades, see Backhouse, *Carnal Crimes*, see note 5 above at 265, 419–20.
9 National Association of Women and the Law, "A Brief on Bill C-49" (submitted to the Legislative Committee on Bill C-49 of the House of Commons, 20 May 1992) at 3.
10 Although there were feminists who raised the intersecting issues of class, race, and ethnicity in this debate, this did not dominate the analysis, and despite its importance, it was missing from the process of legislative reform and the judicial analysis. An essentialist version of gender – with respect to both the complainant and the accused – dominated the opinions of both majority and dissent.
11 *Criminal Code*, R.S.C. 1985, c. C-46 at ss. 276 and 277, formerly ss. 246.6 and 246.7. The first rape-shield laws had been enacted in 1974 in Iowa, Florida, Michigan, and California. By 1980, forty-six states and the federal government had enacted rape-shield statutes. "Comments" (1985) Wis L Rev 1219.
12 *Criminal Code*, ibid. at s. 277, formerly s. 246.7.
13 For example, if there was evidence of vaginal injury or bruises that the Crown argued resulted from the rape, the defence was permitted to introduce evidence that the woman had had sex with her boyfriend or someone else that would account for the injuries.

14 For example, if the woman contracted a sexually transmitted disease that she suspected came from the assailant, he would be able to introduce evidence that an identifiable third person with that disease could have transmitted it.
15 Often referred to as the "gang rape exception," it accepted that if the accused witnessed the woman being sexually assaulted by another man, he might assume that she would consent to sexual contact with him, without consulting her. As one scholar observed, it appeared to codify the defence of mistake and accepted a male-defined standard of consent. T. Brettel Dawson, "Sexual Assault Law and Past Sexual Conduct of the Primary Witness: The Construction of Relevance" (1987–88) 2 CJWL 310 at 319.
16 *Canadian Charter of Rights and Freedoms*, Part I of the *Constitution Act, 1982*, being Schedule B to the *Canada Act 1982* (U.K.), 1982, c. 11, s. 7: "Everyone has the right to life, liberty and security of the person and the right not to be deprived thereof except in accordance with the principles of fundamental justice." Section 11(d): "Any person charged with an offence has the right to be presumed innocent until proven guilty according to law in a fair and public hearing by an independent and impartial tribunal."
17 David H. Doherty, counsel in Toronto's Crown Law Office, critiqued the new law in an article advocating that the criminal justice system "should place the liberty of the individual at the top of the hierarchy of the values reflected in the system," even if this required that the witness "must endure a degree of embarrassment and perhaps psychological trauma." David H. Doherty, "'Sparing' the Complainant 'Spoils' the Trial" (1984) 40 CR (3d) 55 at 63, 66. For a critique of his analysis, see Dawson, "Sexual Assault Law and Past Sexual Conduct of the Primary Witness," see note 15 above at 315; Camille LeGrand, "Rape and Rape Laws: Sexism in Society and Law" (1973) 61 Cal L Rev 915. Doherty became a judge in 1988, and was elevated to the Ontario Court of Appeal in 1990.
18 Margaret Mitchell, a New Democratic party MP from Vancouver known for her concern about violence against women, was the only woman on the Justice and Legal Affairs Standing Committee when the reforms were debated. She argued on 4 April 1982 that there should be a blanket prohibition on all prior sexual history: "I believe the bill states that previous sexual history of a woman with a person other than the accused may be admissible in evidence under certain circumstances. Of course we would agree with ... the views of many women's organizations that there really should be no question permitted as to the sexual activity of the complainant." Ottawa, House of Commons, Minutes of Proceedings and Evidence, Issue No. 77, First Session of the Thirty-Second Parliament, 1980–81–82, at 39.
19 Interview with Elizabeth Sheehy, Ottawa, 1 April 2015.
20 *Seaboyer*, see note 1 above; *R. v. Gayme* (1987), 37 CCC (3d) 53 at paras. 19–20 [hereafter *Gayme*]. Smith, "Language, Law and Social Power," see note 7 above, noted at 144 that the singling out of these facts from a host of other potential descriptions suggests at the outset that rape mythology is at work. "[W]e are told only that 'the accused was charged with sexual assault of a woman with whom he had been drinking in a bar.' What does this statement, by itself, tell us and more important, what is it intended to tell us? Certainly there were other, less connotative ways to describe the relationship between the defendant and the primary witness. The latter might have been presented, for example, as 'a woman with whom the accused had no prior relationship' or 'a woman he had met by chance in a public place.' More important, there was no need to mention their association at all, since it had no bearing on the issues before the court."
21 The rulings at the preliminary inquiries were discussed in *Seaboyer*, see note 1 above; *R. v. Gayme*, [1985] O.J. No. 599 (Supreme Court of Ontario).
22 Seaboyer's case was heard together with another appeal by an eighteen-year old man named Gayme, who was defending himself against a charge of sexual assault upon a fifteen-year-old girl in the basement of a Toronto school. Gayme's lawyer sought to question the

complainant about whether she had been "very free with sexual favours," and had performed sexual acts with other students "sometimes at her own insistence." *Seaboyer,* see note 1 above; *Gayme,* see note 20 above at paras. 19–20. Smith, "Language, Law and Social Power," see note 7 above, also took issue with the selective facts in the majority judgment in *Gayme,* see note 20 above at 145–47: "What do the facts as cited tend to suggest, given commonly held assumptions about gender roles, male and female sexuality, and the nature of sexual assault? The primary witness in *Gayme* was rather young; young enough, perhaps, that she might be presumed by the more traditionally minded not to be sexually active. Such a presumption, however, is undermined by the reference to evidence of ... sexual activity. Thus the reader's subjective perception of the primary witness is potentially transformed, through subtle textual cues, from 'virginal child' to 'seductive temptress.' [Identification of] the sexually active 15-year-old primary witness [as] the sexual aggressor implicitly raises the all-too-familiar spectres of fabrication and the 'child seductress' myth."

23 Section 15(1) of the *Canadian Charter of Rights and Freedoms* provided that "[e]very individual is equal before and under the law and has the right to the equal protection and equal benefit of the law without discrimination and, in particular, without discrimination based on race, national or ethnic origin, colour, religion, sex, age or mental or physical disability." Women's Legal Education and Action Fund (LEAF), *Equality and the Charter: Ten Years of Feminist Advocacy before the Supreme Court of Canada* (Toronto: Emond Montgomery, 1996) at xi; Sherene Razack, *Canadian Feminism and the Law: The Women's Legal Education and Action Fund and the Pursuit of Equality* (Toronto: Second Story Press, 1991) at 12. LEAF's finances came from the Women's Program of the federal Department of the Secretary of State, the Court Challenges Program, and the Ontario Litigation Fund, along with private donations. See Christopher P. Manfredi, *Feminist Activism in the Supreme Court: Legal Mobilization and the Women's Legal Education and Action Fund* (Vancouver: UBC Press, 2004) at 13–14.

24 Constance Backhouse, "'A Revolution in Numbers': Ontario Feminist Lawyers from the 1970s to the 1990s" in Constance Backhouse and W. Wesley Pue, eds., *Essays in the History of the Canadian Legal Profession* (Toronto: Irwin Law, 2009) at 265–94.

25 Women's Legal Education and Action Fund, *Equality and the Charter,* see note 23 above at ix. From 1985 to 1999, the Supreme Court did not reject a single application for intervener status from LEAF. Manfredi, *Feminist Activism in the Supreme Court,* see note 23 above at 15.

26 Razack, *Canadian Feminism and the Law,* see note 23 above at 46–49.

27 Karen Selick, "Methinks the Lady Doth Protest Too Much," *Canadian Lawyer* 24:2 (February 2000) 62.

28 Razack, *Canadian Feminism and the Law,* see note 23 above at 61.

29 Ibid.

30 Interview with Elizabeth Shilton, Boston, 25 October 2014.

31 Interview with Mark Sandler, Toronto, 27 March 2015.

32 Ibid. Razack, *Canadian Feminism and the Law,* see note 23 above, noted at 55–56 that the LEAF brief failed to make any reference to section 15 equality issues, and conceded (with examples) that there might be instances where a woman's prior sexual history would be relevant. She described the approach as "conservative" and "ill-advised," and noted that a group of feminists working on the possibility of civil remedies for women harmed by pornography was highly critical of the brief.

33 *R. v. Seaboyer* (1987), 37 CCC (3d) 53 [hereafter *Seaboyer 1987*]. The majority ruling was written by Grange, with Martin and Thorson concurring; the dissent was written by Brooke, with Dubin concurring. The majority upheld the constitutionality of the rape-shield law, but recognized the right of any accused who could demonstrate a constraint on his particular rights to claim a "constitutional exemption."

34 The Barbara Schlifer Clinic, Metro Action Committee on Public Violence Against Women and Children, Metropolitan Toronto Special Committee on Child Abuse, Women's College Hospital Sexual Assault Care Centre, and the Canadian Association of Sexual Assault Centres. Women's Legal Education and Action Fund, *Equality and the Charter,* see note 23 above at 175.
35 Interview with Elizabeth Shilton, Boston, 25 October 2014.
36 *Seaboyer and Gayme v. The Queen* factum of LEAF, in Women's Legal Education and Action Fund, *Equality and the Charter,* see note 23 above at 173–90.
37 Women's Legal Education and Action Fund, *Equality and the Charter,* ibid. at 175–99.
38 Elizabeth J. Shilton and Anne S. Derrick, "Sex Equality and Sexual Assault: In the Aftermath of *Seaboyer*" (1991) 11 Windsor YB Access Just 107 at 118.
39 Interview with Claire Klassen, Edmonton, 27 July 2015.
40 Ibid. Reading all of the background social-context information in preparation for the drafting had a long-term effect on Klassen: "What I read to assist Justice L'Heureux-Dubé really stuck with me. When I left the court, for about fifteen years thereafter, I was a volunteer at our sexual assault centre, doing lectures on various areas of law."
41 *Seaboyer,* see note 1 above at 648–49.
42 Ibid. at 648–58. Her dissent contained twenty-six citations of material referred to in LEAF's factum.
43 John T. Saywell, *The Lawmakers: Judicial Power and the Shaping of Canadian Federalism* (Toronto: University of Toronto Press, 2002), noted at 243 that in 1957 there were 10 references to secondary literature in 60 decisions. From 1991 to 1996, there were 2,817 academic citations in 680 decisions.
44 Bertha Wilson, "Will Women Judges Really Make a Difference?" (1990) 28 Osgoode Hall LJ 507–22, a text of the speech made at Osgoode Hall Law School earlier that year.
45 *Seaboyer,* see note 1 above at 651–54, 659.
46 Ibid. at 660.
47 Ibid. at 664, citing Hubert S. Feild and Leigh B. Bienen, *Jurors and Rape* (Lexington, MA: Lexington Books, 1980); Eugene Borgida and Phyllis White, "Social Perception of Rape Victims: The Impact of Legal Reform" (1978) 2 Law and Human Behavior 339; Gary D. La Free, "Variables Affecting Guilty Pleas and Convictions in Rape Cases: Toward a Social Theory of Rape Processing" (1980) 58 Social Forces 833; Gary D. La Free, Barbara F. Reskin, and Christy A. Visher, "Jurors' Responses to Victims' Behavior and Legal Issues in Sexual Assault Trials" (1985) 32 Social Problems 389; Katherine Catton, "Evidence Regarding the Prior Sexual History of an Alleged Rape Victim – Its Effect on the Perceived Guilt of the Accused" (1975) 33 UT Fac L Rev 165.
48 *Seaboyer,* see note 1 above at 665.
49 Ibid. at 660, quoting Harriet R. Galvin, "Shielding Rape Victims in the State and Federal Courts: A Proposal for the Second Decade" (1986) 70 Minn L Rev 763 at 792–93.
50 *Seaboyer,* see note 1 above at 666.
51 Ibid. at 670–73, referring to *Criminal Law Amendment Act, 1975,* SC 1974–75–76, c. 93, s. 8 and *Forsythe v. The Queen,* [1980] 2 SCR 268, as critiqued by Wilson dissenting in *R. v. Konkin,* [1983] 1 SCR 388.
52 *Seaboyer,* see note 1 above at 706.
53 Ibid. at 673–76, noting failure of the 1976 legislation that repealed the s. 139 requirement to warn about corroboration, and the necessity in 1982 to enact *An Act to amend the Criminal Code in relation to sexual offences and other offences against the person and to amend certain other Acts in relation thereto or in consequence thereof,* SC 1980–81–82–83, c. 125, which instructed judges in s. 246.4 *not* to instruct the jury that it would be unsafe to convict without corroboration.

54 *Seaboyer*, see note 1 above at 679–80.
55 Ibid. at 707.
56 Ibid. at 695–99. Section 28 provided: "Notwithstanding anything in this Charter, the rights and freedoms referred to in it are guaranteed equally to male and female persons."
57 Ibid. at 683.
58 Ibid. at 683–85, 690.
59 Interview with Charles Gonthier, Ottawa, 14 September 2008.
60 This description comes from the eulogy delivered by L'Heureux-Dubé at his funeral, 20 July 2009.
61 Interview with Claire L'Heureux-Dubé, Ottawa, 30 June 2014.
62 Interview with Charles Gonthier, Ottawa, 14 September 2008.
63 Interview with Adam Dodek, Ottawa, 30 May 2014.
64 Ibid.
65 The two were not always in sync, as evident in Gonthier's majority decision on the taxation of child support, from which L'Heureux-Dubé and McLachlin dissented: *R. v. Thibaudeau*, [1995] 2 SCR 627. In *M v. H.*, [1999] 2 SCR 3, L'Heureux-Dubé signed on to the majority judgment ruling that provincial legislation excluding same-sex couples from the legal definition of marriage was in breach of the *Charter*, while Gonthier dissented.
66 Her opinion was signed by Lamer, La Forest, Sopinka, Cory, Stevenson, and Iacobucci.
67 Peter McCormick, *Supreme at Last: The Evolution of the Supreme Court of Canada* (Toronto: Lorimer, 2000) at 121–24.
68 Philip Slayton, "Judging Beverley," *Maclean's* (6 July 2009) at 48–52.
69 Robert J. Sharpe and Kent Roach, *Brian Dickson: A Judge's Journey* (Toronto: University of Toronto Press, 2003) at 301. Like L'Heureux-Dubé, she was propelled into the judiciary by a surge of interest in locating some women for the bench. She was appointed to the Vancouver County Court in 1981, appointed to the British Columbia Supreme Court months later, elevated to the Court of Appeal in 1985, appointed chief justice of the British Columbia Supreme Court that same year, and appointed to the Supreme Court of Canada in 1989. Slayton, ibid. at 48–52.
70 Philip Slayton, *Mighty Judgment: How the Supreme Court of Canada Runs Your Life* (Toronto: Penguin, 2012) at 156. Slayton added that "some believed that Justice Frank Iacobucci, considered the intellectual leader of the court, would have been a better choice, and that ... simple gender had triumphed." Slayton, "Judging Beverley," ibid. at 48–52. In fact, McLachlin was the most senior of the Anglophone judges on the court, whose turn it was by tradition, with two years more experience than Iacobucci.
71 Interview with Elizabeth Sheehy, Ottawa, 1 April 2015.
72 David Shoalts, "Judges seem divided on victim's history," *Globe and Mail* (1 April 1991).
73 *Seaboyer*, see note 1 above at 598. For a critique of McLachlin's decision, see Renate M. Mohr and Julian V. Roberts, "Sexual Assault in Canada: Recent Developments" in Roberts and Mohr, *Confronting Sexual Assault*, see note 4 above at 10.
74 *Seaboyer*, ibid. at 604. She left unexplored the third, less often articulated explanation for the impugned rule: that women with prior sexual histories were not worthy of protection in law. In other words, raped or not, they were not the sort of women for which men should be put in jail. She also did not make reference to other critiques that attacked the linking of chastity with credibility generally. Borgida and White, "Social Perception of Rape Victims," see note 47 above at 340: "If [a woman's sexual behavior is directly related to her credibility as a witness] then one might expect that prior sexual history testimony would also be admissible in any trial in which a woman served as a witness. Moral character, however, is not permitted to impeach the credibility of a witness in any other area of criminal law."

75 *Seaboyer*, ibid. at 612.
76 Diana Majury, "*Seaboyer* and *Gayme:* A Study in Equality" in Roberts and Mohr, *Confronting Sexual Assault,* see note 4 above at 269.
77 At 614, McLachlin explained that prior sexual acts might relate to a complainant's "bias or motive to fabricate" or "explain the physical conditions on which the Crown relies ... such as semen, pregnancy, injury or disease." At 615–16, she turned to "evidence as to pattern of conduct," and offered the following illustration: "A woman alleges that she was raped. The man she has accused of the act claims that she is a prostitute who agreed to sexual relations for a fee of twenty dollars, and afterwards, threatening to accuse him of rape, she demanded an additional one hundred dollars. The man refused to pay the additional amount. She had him arrested for rape." At 613, McLachlin tied her analysis to the defence of mistake, which allowed accused men to assert that they had an "honest belief" that the complainant had consented to the sex: "The basis of the accused's honest belief ... may be sexual acts performed by the complainant at some other time or place," she wrote. It was an analysis to which L'Heureux-Dubé would strongly object four years later, in *R. v. Park,* [1995] 2 SCR 836 at paras. 14–53.
78 *Seaboyer,* see note 1 above at 616.
79 Ibid. at 631–32.
80 Ibid. at 634.
81 McLachlin's decision was critiqued for creating the impression that sexist beliefs were "relics of the past" that had been "expunged from the legal system," which was in itself "a highly dubious proposition," and for disguising the fact that her analysis was "rife with, and in effect serves to legitimate, the myths she claims have been dispelled." Smith, "Language, Law and Social Power," see note 7 above at 151. Other critiques came from two of the LEAF litigators, who wrote: "The Court appears to find sexual history evidence as relevant as it ever was; now, however, it is relevant to such issues as motive to fabricate and 'similar fact' situations. But what are these issues, other than credibility and consent in very thin disguises? How far has our society really come in laying aside the sexual double standard? If judges cannot see through these disguises, can they really exercise discretion in a manner consistent with the principles of equality mandated by the *Canadian Charter of Rights and Freedoms?* ... The majority of the Court makes it clear that 'relevance' is to be the hallmark of admissibility. Women inevitably ask: 'relevance' to what? And according to whom? We understand that beliefs are derived from the experience of the person making the determination about relevance. The consequence is that those with power can define their experience as objective fact. Power, in our society, has historically been distributed along gender lines." Shilton and Derrick, "Sex Equality and Sexual Assault," see note 38 above at 118.
82 Interview with Claire L'Heureux-Dubé, Clearwater, FL, 25–27 November 2014.
83 Stephen Bindman, "Judging in a man's world," *Ottawa Citizen* (13 April 1992) at A3.
84 Interview with Claire L'Heureux-Dubé, Clearwater, FL, 25–27 November 2014.
85 Ibid.
86 Bindman, "Judging in a man's world," see note 83 above.
87 Ibid.
88 She was not the first woman to be lambasted for her position on the rape-shield law. Louise Arbour, who would be appointed to the Supreme Court in 1999, had appeared as counsel for the Canadian Civil Liberties Association when *Seaboyer* was argued earlier at the Ontario Court of Appeal. When Arbour submitted that the rape shield should be struck down as unconstitutional, the howls of protest from across the country caused the press to focus on the CCLA's "macho, male-focused" perspective" – which feminist organizations labelled "diametrically opposed" to the "rights and liberties" of women. Kelly Toughill, "Women take aim at civil liberties group," *Toronto Star* (30 August 1992) A1. The quote was from Christie Jefferson, executive director of LEAF. Over fifty members of the CCLA resigned

their memberships in protest over the position CCLA had taken: F.L. Morton and Rainer Knopff, *The Charter Revolution and the Court Party* (Peterborough, ON: Broadview, 2000) at 73. Arbour recalled years later that the "flak" that her advocacy attracted made it "the case from hell." Interview with Louise Arbour, Saint-Faustin Lac-Carré, QC, 24 July 2014. Arbour reflected: "I have not always taken the popular path and this was one of them. I'm still convinced that [our argument] acknowledged the tremendous defect and abuse of the previous evidentiary regime. Rules of absolute exclusion of evidence on their face have to be extremely well justified ... The way cases present themselves and the factual variety and complexity is such that I thought it was not prudent to articulate the case that way."

89 Sean Fine, "The Most Important Woman in Canada," *Saturday Night* (December 1995) 46. Mohr and Roberts, "Sexual Assault in Canada," see note 73 above, noted at 10 that women's groups almost unanimously characterized the decision as striking "a devastating blow to women's rights in Canada."

90 Slayton, *Mighty Judgment,* see note 70 above at 158–61, quoting Fine, ibid. Fine had quoted Patricia Marshall, who would later co-chair the Mulroney government's commission on violence against women as warning: "Rape is going to flourish." Fine had also quoted UBC law professor Christine Boyle as bemoaning the McLachlin decision: "What's the point of being in law? If law's not capable of responding to concerns about the way women are treated in sexual assault trials, is it the kind of arena in which women should be active?"

91 Stephen Bindman, Irwin Block, Catherine Buckie, "Rape victims' past can be used at trial," *Montreal Gazette* (23 August 1991) A1.

92 Grace Macaluso, "Rape shield decision called 'major setback,'" *Windsor Star* (23 August 1991) at A2.

93 David Vienneau, "The sexual history of rape victims," *Toronto Star* (22 March 1991) F1.

94 Alana Kainz, "Angry women rap high court," *Ottawa Citizen* (27 August 1991).

95 "Rape-shield law protesters splash 'blood' on court wall," *Montreal Gazette* (7 September 1991). Although one of the protesters, law student Pamela Cross, was quoted by name in the article, the police decided to lay no charges since they had not witnessed the splattering, and the article noted: "The protesters casually strolled away after police arrived."

96 Library and Archives Canada, Claire L'Heureux-Dubé Fonds, MG 31, E110, vol. 44, dossiers 13–16. Attorney General Howard Hampton and Minister Responsible for Women's Issues Anne Swarbrick were mentioned in undated, unreferenced press clipping as complaining to Prime Minister Kim Campbell about the urgency of finding an alternative to the law that had been struck down.

97 "Most back rape-shield law," *Montreal Gazette* (13 January 1992).

98 Interview with Elizabeth Shilton, Boston, 25 October 2014.

99 Ibid.

100 Interview with Elizabeth Sheehy, Ottawa, 1 April 2015. *R. v. Morgentaler,* [1988] 1 SCR 30, struck down as unconstitutional the criminal law prohibiting abortions except under stringent circumstances; *R. v. Lavallee,* [1990] 1 SCR 852, involved a feminist reinterpretation of the common law rules of self-defence.

101 Elizabeth Sheehy, "Legalising Justice for All Women: Canadian Women's Struggle for Democratic Rape Law Reforms" (1996) 6 Australian Feminist Law Journal 87 at 90. Several years earlier, Sheehy had predicted that if the laws restricting cross-examination on prior sexual history were struck down, voices would clamour for the government to use the "override clause" in the *Charter.* Section 33, dubbed the "override clause," had been added to the constitutional patriation package to assure suspicious legislators that if the courts ran off the rails in interpreting the new constitution, Parliament could re-enact the laws it wanted by proclaiming them under the protection of section 33. However, the Quebec government had been the first to use section 33 to protect its French-language preferences, giving the use of the override clause a bad odour among the larger Anglophone (anti-Francophone?) population in Canada. Political scientist Christopher Manfredi speculated

that had *Seaboyer* arrived first, the feminist Attorney General of Canada (and future prime minister) Kim Campbell would have enjoyed broad public support had she decided to use the override to defend vulnerable victims of rape and strike down a judicial opinion widely viewed as illegitimate. Christopher Manfredi *Judicial Power and the Paradox of Liberal Constitutionalism* (Norman: Oklahoma University Press, 1993) at 204–5, 210.

102 Note from retired Justice Bertha Wilson, held in Claire L'Heureux-Dubé's private personal papers.
103 Interview with Catherine Fraser, Edmonton, 12 November 2013.
104 The Gayme prosecution also died for the same reasons. Gary Oakes, "Crown withdraws charges in 'rape shield' cases," *Toronto Star* (20 February 1992) A2; Majury, "*Seaboyer* and *Gayme*," see note 76 above at 272.
105 Mohr and Roberts, "Sexual Assault in Canada," see note 73 above at 10; Bowland, "Sexual Assault Trials and the Protection of 'Bad Girls,'" see note 4 above at 257–61. Majury, "*Seaboyer* and *Gayme*," see note 76 above, described at 286 the dissenting opinion as "one of the strongest, most overtly inequality-based, contextualized judgments I have read."
106 Sheila McIntyre, "Redefining Reformism: The Consultations That Shaped Bill C-49" in Roberts and Mohr, *Confronting Sexual Assault*, see note 4 above at 295.
107 "Justice minister aims to save rape shield law," *Ottawa Citizen* (29 August 1991).
108 Bill C-49, which received Royal Assent on 23 June 1992, as described by Mohr and Roberts, "Sexual Assault in Canada," see note 73 above at 10–11; McIntyre, "Redefining Reformism," see note 106 above at 306–10.
109 McIntyre, "Redefining Reformism," ibid. at 296–97.
110 Ibid. at 302.
111 Interview with Mark Sandler, Toronto, 27 March 2015; *R. v. Darrach*, [2000] 2 SCR 443. Kent Roach, *The Supreme Court on Trial: Judicial Activism or Democratic Dialogue* (Toronto: Irwin Law, 2001), noted at 272–73 that this exemplified the "democratic dialogue" between the court and Parliament. Had the section 33 override been used, "Parliament would have won its shouting match with the Court, but after a five-year cooling-off period, it would have had to revisit the matter by deciding whether the expired override should be renewed." In what he described as a "more constructive and more permanent response," the new reforms dealt with the crime far more comprehensively.
112 Interview with Claire L'Heureux-Dubé, Clearwater, FL, 25–27 November 2014. The legislative revisions created a shift on the part of defence lawyers, who began to seek court-ordered disclosure of the complainant's counselling and other personal records in order to suggest "false memory," motive to fabricate, consent, or grounds for "mistake." Sheehy, "Legalising Justice for All Women," see note 101 above, described at 104 the records sought as therapeutic records, crisis counselling records, psychiatric records, hospital records, birth control records, abortion records, residential school records, juvenile records, child welfare records, immigration and family court records, and school records. Sheehy noted at 105 that disclosure of records required that women submit to public scrutiny the details of their lives and suffering if they were to be believed, and at 107 that many women would withdraw from prosecution, refusing to tolerate this loss of privacy.
In *R. v. O'Connor*, [1995] 4 SCR 411, Lamer, Sopinka, Cory, Iacobucci, and Major expressed a majority preference for defence counsel to have wide-ranging access to the medical, counselling, and school records of Aboriginal complainants alleging sexual abuse from the bishop who ran the Indian residential school they had attended as youngsters. In a dissenting judgment supported by La Forest and Gonthier, L'Heureux-Dubé would have prescribed much narrower access. She stated at 481: "[T]he assumption that private therapeutic or counselling records are relevant to full answer and defence is often highly questionable, in that these records may very well have a greater potential to derail than to advance the truth-seeking process." She also noted at 487–88 that disclosure would have a disproportionate effect on women, since sexual assault was a gendered crime, affecting

primarily women and children, many of whom sought counselling or therapy in the aftermath of the attacks. She added at 488: "This Court has recognized the pernicious role that past evidentiary rules in both the *Criminal Code* and the common law, now regarded as discriminatory, once played in our legal system. We must be careful not to permit such practices to reappear under the guise of extensive and unwarranted inquiries into the past histories and private lives of complainants of sexual assault." To the surprise of some, McLachlin also penned a short opinion concurring with L'Heureux-Dubé's dissent.

Feminist groups lobbied the government with a platform of "No records. No time. No reason." Sheehy, "Legalising Justice for All Women," ibid., noted at 111 that women lawyers within the Department of Justice drafted an amendment that was "a far sight better than the courts will ever give us, and that may protect some number of women." Parliament introduced amendments to the *Criminal Code* in 1997, a package that differed significantly from the parameters set out in *O'Connor*, and attempted to narrow access to records. The new legislation essentially adopted the higher threshold for disclosure proposed in L'Heureux-Dubé's dissent. Queen's law professor Don Stuart described her dissent on the need to protect the privacy of sexual assault victims as leaving a "huge legacy. Parliament actually enacted word for word what Justice L'Heureux-Dubé had in mind." Interview with Don Stuart, Kingston, 4 May 2015.

R. v. Mills, [1999] 3 SCR 668, dealt with a *Charter* challenge to the amendments. Upholding the new legislation, McLachlin and Iacobucci wrote a majority judgment that was signed by L'Heureux-Dubé, Gonthier, Major, Bastarache, and Binnie. Chief Justice Lamer dissented in part. The press reported that Parliament had used L'Heureux-Dubé's "ringing dissent" in *O'Connor* "as a blueprint for Bill C-46, which protects complainants' privacy and which was upheld in 1999 by an almost unanimous court in *R. v. Mills.*" Cristin Schmitz, "A Supreme Court Judge for All Seasons," *Lawyers Weekly* 22:3 (10 May 2002).

Chapter 30: Family Law and Spousal Support

1 Zofia was born in 1937 and Andrzej in 1931. Her birth name is not referenced in any of the documentation. Different sources gave the date of marriage as either 1955 or 1957. The midpoint, 1956, has been used here. John Douglas, "Supreme Court to decide if 19 years long enough for alimony payments," *Winnipeg Free Press* (2 April 1992) A1; George Nikides and Kevin Rollason, "Love ends, but alimony may not," *Winnipeg Free Press* (18 December 1992) A1. Unless otherwise indicated, all facts come from the three court decisions: *Moge v. Moge* (1989), 60 Man R (2d) 281 [hereafter *Moge 1989*]; *Moge v. Moge* (1990), 64 Man R (2d) 172 [hereafter *Moge 1990*]; *Moge v. Moge,* [1992] 3 SCR 813 [hereafter *Moge*].
2 "History of Poland (1945–1989)," *New World Encyclopedia,* online: <http://www.newworldencyclopedia.org/entry/History_of_Poland_(1945-1989)>.
3 *Moge 1990,* see note 1 above at 173; *Moge,* see note 1 above.
4 *Moge 1990,* ibid.
5 Ibid. at 173–74.
6 Alison Prentice et al., *Canadian Women: A History* (Toronto: Harcourt Brace Jovanovich, 1988) at 218–39.
7 Ibid. at 311–17.
8 Morley Gunderson, Leon Muszynski, and Jennifer Keck, *Women and Labour Market Poverty* (Ottawa: Canadian Advisory Council on the Status of Women, 1990) at 13–15. The reasons for this surge included growing demand for female employees in the gendered service sector, growth in part-time jobs, rising unemployment (of men), declining fertility, increases in women's educational attainments, increased access to childcare, and the growing financial needs of families for housing and consumer goods.
9 *Moge 1990,* see note 1 above; divorce was available upon proof of a one-year separation.

10 Justice Nitikman's unreported judgment granting the separation and $150 a month in support for Zofia and the three children was dated 22 November 1974; *Moge*, see note 1 above at 825. Reference to the divorce decision was made in *Moge 1990*, see note 1 above.
11 *Moge 1990*, ibid. at 174, noted that the husband's gross monthly income was in the vicinity of $1,300 while the wife's was $780 one year after the divorce.
12 Douglas, "Supreme Court to decide if 19 years long enough for alimony payments," see note 1 above, quoting Peter Cory's comment during oral argument at the Supreme Court of Canada.
13 *Moge 1990*, see note 1 above at 174, listed the husband's earnings as $1,925 gross per month, with the wife's unemployment benefits at $594 per month. The Unemployment Insurance data registered a lower level of $570 gross; *Moge 1989*, see note 1 above.
14 Mullally J.'s unreported judgment of 14 October 1987 was referred to in *Moge 1989*, ibid. The order was divided: $200 for the youngest son, who was attending university but still living at home, and $200 for Zofia.
15 Zofia was grossing about $800 a month in the government job; *Moge 1989*, ibid. Reference to the speculative hotel salary of $1,000 was found in *Moge*, see note 1 above at 827.
16 *Moge 1989*, ibid. at 282–83.
17 *Moge 1990*, see note 1 above. Archibald Kerr Twaddle and Joseph Francis O'Sullivan issued the majority decision; Bonnie M. Helper, the first woman to sit on the Manitoba Court of Appeal, wrote in dissent that sixteen years after the separation, "Mr. Moge's obligation was at an end."
18 Carol J. Rogerson, "The Causal Connection Test in Spousal Support Law" (1989) 8 Can J Fam L 95–132.
19 Patricia Proudfoot and Karen Jewell, "Restricting Application of the Causal Connection Test: *Story v. Story*" (1990) 9 Can J Fam L 143.
20 Rogerson, "The Causal Connection Test in Spousal Support Law," see note 18 above.
21 Gunderson et al., *Women and Labour Market Poverty*, see note 8 above at 7–35; Dana G. Stewart and Linda E. McFadyen, "Women and the Economic Consequences of Divorce in Manitoba: An Empirical Study" (1992) 21 Man LJ 80 at 81.
22 Margrit Eichler, "The Limits of Family Law Reform or, the Privatization of Female and Child Poverty" (1990–91) 7 Can Fam LQ 59 at 62.
23 Lenore J. Weitzman, *The Divorce Revolution: The Unexpected Social and Economic Consequences for Women and Children in America* (New York: Free Press, 1985). Margrit Eichler described the Weitzman study as having "an almost galvanizing effect on the legal, sociological and policy communities" in "The Limits of Family Law Reform," ibid.
24 Stewart and McFadyen, "Women and the Economic Consequences of Divorce in Manitoba," see note 21 above; Gunderson et al., *Women and Labour Market Poverty*, see note 8 above at 7–35.
25 Between 1986 and 1989, Manitoba courts awarded spousal support to only 11 percent of divorcing women, with a median monthly amount of $266. Stewart and McFadyen, ibid. at 81–82, 89. A 1981 Alberta study found that even when there were dependent children, only 18 percent of wives received spousal support, and a 1983 Ontario study found the average amount of spousal support was 20 percent of the husband's net income. Julien D. Payne, "Permanent Spousal Support in Divorce Proceedings. Why? How Much? How Long?" (1987) 6 Can J Fam L 384 at 385–86. Mary E. O'Connell, "Alimony after No-Fault: A Practice in Search of a Theory" (1988) 23 New Eng L Rev 437, noted at 438 that "alimony has a small but crucial role to play in remedying male and female economic disparity."
26 Proudfoot and Jewell, "Restricting Application of the Causal Connection Test," see note 19 above; Michael J. Trebilcock and Rosemin Keshvani, "The Role of Private Ordering in Family Law: A Law and Economics Perspective" (1991) 41 UTLJ 533 at 536.
27 *Doyle v. Doyle*, 5 Misc.2d 4, 158 NYS2d 99, 912 (1957), as quoted in O'Connell, "Alimony after No-Fault," see note 25 above at 490.

28 O'Connell, ibid. at 444.
29 Mary Ann Glendon, *The New Family and the New Property* (Toronto: Butterworths, 1981) at 11, 31.
30 Katharine K. Baker, "Contracting for Security: Paying Married Women What They've Earned" (1955) 55 U Chicago L Rev 1193 at 1197.
31 Eichler, "The Limits of Family Law Reform," see note 22 above at 62.
32 Glendon, *The New Family and the New Property*, see note 29 above at 47.
33 Eichler, "The Limits of Family Law Reform," see note 22 above.
34 Stewart and McFadyen, "Women and the Economic Consequences of Divorce in Manitoba," see note 21 above at 81–82, 89.
35 Glendon, *The New Family and the New Property*, see note 29 above at 82.
36 Rogerson, "The Causal Connection Test in Spousal Support Law," see note 18 above.
37 *Divorce Act*, RSC 1985, c. 3 (2d Supp.), s. 15(7).
38 Rosalie S. Abella, "Economic Adjustment on Marriage Breakdown: Support" (1981) 4 Fam L Rev 1 at 1, as cited in *Messier v. Delage*, [1983] 2 SCR 401 at 409 [hereafter *Messier*].
39 Payne, "Permanent Spousal Support in Divorce Proceedings," see note 25 above at 386–87.
40 *Messier*, see note 38 above; *Pelech v. Pelech*, [1987] 1 SCR 801 [hereafter *Pelech*]; *Richardson v. Richardson*, [1987] 1 SCR 857 [hereafter *Richardson*]; *Caron v. Caron*, [1987] 1 SCR 892 [hereafter *Caron*].
41 *Messier*, ibid. at 420–21, 427.
42 Law Reform Commission of Canada, *Family Law* (Ottawa: Information Canada, 1976) at 42–43.
43 *Messier*, see note 38 above at 426–27.
44 Ibid. Lamer's dissent was signed by Bertha Wilson and William McIntyre. The majority decision, written by Julien Chouinard and signed by Ritchie, Beetz, and Estey of a seven-judge panel, opted to continue the spousal support, noting that the ex-husband had the means to pay, and the ex-wife had been able to find only part-time work as a translator, for $5,000 a year.
45 *Pelech*, see note 40 above; *Richardson*, see note 40 above; *Caron*, see note 40 above. David G. Duff, "The Supreme Court and the New Family Law: Working through the *Pelech* Trilogy" (1988) 42:2 UT Fac L Rev 542 at 548. The facts showed that Mr. Pelech's net worth had increased from $128,000 at the time of separation to $1.8 million at the time of his wife's petition for relief, while she was unable to work and reduced to living on welfare. Wilson noted: "[T]o burden the [husband with continued care] ... for no other reason than they were once husband and wife seems to me to create a fiction of marital responsibility at the expense of individual responsibility. I believe that the courts must recognize the right of an individual to end a relationship as well as begin one and should not, when all other aspects of the relationship have long since ceased, treat the financial responsibility as continuing indefinitely into the future." *Pelech v. Pelech* (1987), 7 RFL (3d) 225 at 271 (SCC).
46 J.G. McLeod asserted that the rulings, originally based upon separation agreements and minutes of settlement, should be extended to all spousal support decisions; J.G. McLeod, "Annotation" (1987) 7 Reports of Family Law (3d) 225. Martha Bailey characterized it as deeply problematic, likely to produce greater poverty among women; Martha J. Bailey, "Pelech, Caron, and Richardson" (1989–90) 3 CJWL 615.
47 J.C. MacDonald, "Consultation with Family Law Lawyers on the Divorce Act, 1985" (Ottawa: Department of Justice, May 1989). Canada, Department of Justice, *Evaluation of the Divorce Act* (Ottawa: Department of Justice, 1989) at 73–80, 130, noted that spousal support awards occurred in about 6 percent of the cases surveyed, with a trend toward fixed-term awards.
48 "Chronology" in Adam Dodek and Daniel Jutras, eds., *The Sacred Fire: The Legacy of Antonio Lamer (Chief Justice of Canada)* (Markham, ON: Lexis-Nexis, 2009) at 483–84.

49 Chouinard married Jeannine Pettigrew in 1956. The couple had three children: Julien, Lucie, and Nicole, and was still married at the time of Chouinard's death in 1987. Donn Downey, "Julien Chouinard: Supreme Court judge was top civil servant for Quebec Premier," *Globe and Mail* (9 February 1987).

50 Ellen Anderson, *Judging Bertha Wilson: Law as Large as Life* (Toronto: University of Toronto Press, 2001) at 349–50.

51 Mary Jane Mossman explained Wilson's views as stemming from the belief that "societal, rather than familial, support was appropriate for dependency at marriage break-down," noting that Wilson preferred "the communal responsibility of the state." Mary Jane Mossman, "Bertha Wilson: 'Silences' in a Woman's Life Story" in Kim Brooks, ed., *Justice Bertha Wilson: One Woman's Difference* (Vancouver: UBC Press, 2009) 297 at 309. Colleen Sheppard, "Feminist Pragmatism in the Work of Justice Bertha Wilson" in Jamie Cameron, ed., *Reflections on the Legacy of Justice Bertha Wilson* (Markham, ON: LexisNexis, 2008) 83 at 90, described Wilson's judgment as "support for a more robust public responsibility for economic well-being and resistance to the logic of the privatization of economic responsibilities."

52 Very few family law matters came to the Supreme Court of Canada during L'Heureux-Dubé's tenure. There were only nine cases prior to *Moge*, and she wrote just one decision: the unanimous judgment restoring state guardianship for a child in *New Brunswick (Minister of Health and Community Services) v. C. (G.C.)*, [1988] 1 SCR 1073. La Forest wrote the unanimous judgment on marital property division in *Leblanc v. Leblanc*, [1988] 1 SCR 217. Sopinka delivered the unanimous reasons regarding the wardship of a child in need of protection in *B.(B.) v. Child and Family Services*, [1989] 1 SCR 291. Gonthier wrote the unanimous judgment regarding the division of property on a divorce in *Elsom v. Elsom*, [1989] 1 SCR 1367. Cory wrote for the majority (including L'Heureux-Dubé) and McLachlin wrote for the dissent regarding constructive trust and marital property division in *Rawluk v. Rawluk*, [1990] 1 SCR 70. Wilson wrote the unanimous decision regarding the splitting of pension assets upon divorce in *Clarke v. Clarke*, [1990] 2 SCR 795. Gonthier wrote the unanimous decision on the division of property after a divorce in *M.(M.E.) v. L.(P.)*, [1992] 1 SCR 183 and *T.(K.N.) v. P.(G.R.)*, [1992] 1 SCR 210. Cory wrote the unanimous decision on spousal support in *Strang v. Strang*, [1992] 2 SCR 112.

53 Claire L'Heureux-Dubé, "Family Law in Transition: An Overview" in Rosalie S. Abella and Claire L'Heureux-Dubé, eds., *Family Law: Dimensions of Justice* (Toronto: Butterworths, 1983) 301 at 303, 305–6.

54 Judicial colleague Louise Arbour took issue with this designation, concerned that it might unfairly diminish Bertha Wilson's contribution as a jurist because she was not a mother. She also laughed over the public unveiling of her own status as "the first unwed mother on a court of appeal" in a legal magazine article that appeared when she was appointed to the Ontario Court of Appeal. "I had never made a secret of the fact that I was unmarried and had three children," she noted, but "this was surprising news to some. I said to Charlie Dubin, 'It gives the wrong impression that unwed mothers have a crack at the good jobs.'" Interview with Louise Arbour, Saint-Faustin Lac-Carré, QC, 24 July 2014.

55 Douglas, "Supreme Court to decide if 19 years long enough for alimony payments," see note 1 above. The claim to spousal support had first been made in 1973, when the couple initially separated, and was first ordered upon the judicial separation in 1974.

56 Carol Smart, "Marriage, Divorce, and Women's Economic Dependency: A Discussion of the Politics of Private Maintenance" in Michael D.A. Freeman, *The State, the Law, and the Family: Critical Perspectives* (London: Tavistock, 1984) at 9–23.

57 Douglas, "Supreme Court to decide if 19 years long enough for alimony payments," see note 1 above.

58 George Nikides and Kevin Rollason, "Love ends, but alimony may not," *Winnipeg Free Press* (18 December 1992) A1.

59 Johnston had graduated from the University of Manitoba Faculty of Law in 1985, and was called to the bar of Manitoba in 1986. The reference to the case as a watershed is found on Johnston's web page, where he indicated he was involved in the *Moge* litigation; Myers Weinberg LLP website, online: <http://www.myersfirm.com/person/douglas-e-johnston>. Reference to his confidence comes from interview with Alison Diduck, Winnipeg, 28 July 2014.
60 As indicated in L'Heureux-Dubé's handwritten notes, prepared during oral argument, Library and Archives Canada (LAC), Claire L'Heureux-Dubé Fonds, MG 31, E110, vol. 50, dossier 16.
61 Interview with Peter Bruckshaw, Winnipeg, 23 July 2014; St. Mary's Law LLP website, online: <http://www.stmaryslaw.com/St._Marys_Law/Lawyers_Peter_Bruckshaw_St._Marys_Law.html>.
62 Interview with Peter Bruckshaw, ibid.
63 Interview with Alison Diduck, Winnipeg, 28 July 2014.
64 "*Moge v. Moge* Factum," in Women's Legal Education and Action Fund, *Equality and the Charter: Ten Years of Feminist Advocacy before the Supreme Court of Canada* (Toronto: Emond Montgomery, 1996) at 321–39; interview with Alison Diduck, ibid.
65 Interview with Alison Diduck, ibid.
66 This was a tradition that had developed under Chief Justice Dickson. Peter McCormick, *Supreme at Last: The Evolution of the Supreme Court of Canada* (Toronto: Lorimer, 2000) at 106–8, 129–31.
67 Lamer's participation in spousal support cases while undergoing a marital dissolution himself had generated earlier discomfort. Julien Chouinard had indicated that he felt it was improper, as noted by a former law clerk who wished not to be identified. Lamer was also missing from the six-person panel that heard another spousal support claim, *Strang v. Strang*, [1992] 2 SCR 112, on 1 April 1992, the same day as *Moge*. In *Strang,* Cory wrote for a unanimous panel, refusing to reduce the support that the Alberta Court of Appeal had ordered a chartered accountant to pay to his former wife of a twenty-nine-year marriage, a bookkeeper with a grade ten education. Unlike *Moge,* the decision did not canvas the detailed arguments concerning the philosophy of spousal support.
68 Interview with Claire L'Heureux-Dubé, Clearwater, FL, 25–27 November 2014.
69 *Moge,* see note 1 above at 877–83. William Stevenson, who was also assigned to sit on the case, retired before the decision was released on 17 December 1992, and took no part in the decision. McLachlin's concurrence, which Gonthier signed in addition to signing L'Heureux-Dubé's decision, expressed concern that experts should not be required in most cases, to save on cost and an overburdened justice system. L'Heureux-Dubé had strong views about McLachlin's pattern of writing separate short opinions, adding: "When she doesn't want to compromise herself on something I have said, she does three paragraph quotable-quotes, I call it. I had the feeling she shared my views but she was afraid to sign on to everything I say. But she was always more or less sincere." Interview with Claire L'Heureux-Dubé, ibid.
70 L'Heureux-Dubé's handwritten notes from case conference, LAC, Claire L'Heureux-Dubé Fonds, MG 31, E110, vol. 50, dossier 16.
71 Ibid.
72 *Moge,* see note 1 above at 835–39. She distinguished the trilogy as based on factual agreements the parties had hammered out earlier, noting that there was no such consensual agreement in *Moge*.
73 Abella, "Economic Adjustment on Marriage Breakdown," see note 38 above at 4.
74 *Moge,* see note 1 above at 845, 847.
75 Ibid. at 848–49.
76 Ibid. at 852–53.
77 Ibid. at 853.

78 Ibid. at 864–65.
79 Ibid. at 861–64.
80 *G.(L.) v. B.(G.)*, [1995] 3 SCR 370. In this spousal support case, L'Heureux-Dubé's concurring opinion, signed by La Forest and Gonthier, affirmed an order for spousal support, noting that the 1985 *Divorce Act* had moved away from the tendency to favour a "clean break." She examined the substantive rather than formal equality of the spouses in the marriage and at the time of the divorce, rejected the presumption of economic self-sufficiency, and utilized criteria that would take into account the advantages and disadvantages to spouses accruing from the marriage or its breakdown.
81 *Moge,* see note 1 above at 876–77.
82 Ibid. at 865. This view was reinforced by others, who emphasized that family law was "incapable of solving the problem of poverty of women and children" and should not be pursued "at the expense of societal reforms ... a comprehensive reform of the income security system ... employment equity programs and through parental benefit programs"; Eichler, "The Limits of Family Law Reform," see note 22 above. Others noted that the larger context of Zofia's economic vulnerability included government responsibility for the gendered provision of language and job training to male "heads of households," as well as employer responsibility for discriminatory wages paid in traditionally female jobs; Colleen Sheppard, "Uncomfortable Victories and Unanswered Questions: Lessons from *Moge*" (1995) 12 Can J Fam L 283.
83 McCormick, *Supreme at Last,* see note 66 above, noted at 142–43 that prior to the Laskin years, the court was reluctant even to cite law journal articles, but that academic authorities became common references in the Laskin, Dickson, and Lamer years, reinforcing a more "contextualist" style.
84 Examples included Gunderson et al., *Women and Labour Market Poverty,* see note 8 above; Weitzman, *The Divorce Revolution,* see note 23 above; Canada, Department of Justice, *Evaluation of the Divorce Act – Phase II: Monitoring and Evaluation* (Ottawa: Department of Justice, 1990); Statistics Canada, *Women in Canada: A Statistical Report,* 2nd ed. (Ottawa: Ministry of Supply and Services, 1990); National Council of Welfare, *Women and Poverty Revisited* (Ottawa: Ministry of Supply and Services, 1990); *Report of the Social Assistance Review Committee: Transitions* (Toronto: Ministry of Community and Social Services, 1988).
85 Interview with Jack Major, Calgary, 13 November 2013.
86 On the distinction between "formalism" and "legal realism," see Richard A. Posner, "Judicial Opinions and Appellate Advocacy in Federal Courts – One Judge's Views" (2013) 51 Duq L Rev 3 at 7.
87 *Moge,* see note 1 above at 857.
88 Ibid. at 873.
89 Ibid. at 857.
90 Ibid.
91 Ibid. at 874.
92 Edmund M. Morgan, "Judicial Notice" (1944) 57 Harv L Rev 269 at 272–74, 286, 290.
93 Bertha Wilson, "Decision-Making in the Supreme Court" (1986) 36 UTLJ 227 at 243–44; Robert J. Sharpe and Kent Roach, *Brian Dickson: A Judge's Journey* (Toronto: University of Toronto Press, 2003) at 310.
94 The famous "Brandeis brief" was first submitted in *Muller v. Oregon,* 208 US 412 (1908). "Legal realism" had surfaced in the United States in the 1930s, suggesting that society would be better off if judges were informed by empirical social science research than if they acted in ignorance of the consequences of their decisions. Although courts were initially suspicious of such data, by the end of the twentieth century American scholars agreed that it was difficult to find a Supreme Court constitutional decision implicating an empirical question in which at least one side "did not cite to social science research." Both "liberal"

and "conservative" judges embraced the practice. John Monahan and Laurens Walker, "Social Authority: Obtaining, Evaluating and Establishing Social Science in Law" (1986) 134:3 U Pa L Rev 477; John Monahan and Laurens Walker, "Empirical Questions without Empirical Answers" (1991) Wis L Rev 569; John Monahan and Laurens Walker, "Twenty-Five Years of *Social Science in Law*" (University of Virginia School of Law, Public Law and Legal Theory Research Paper Series No. 2010–09), February 2010, 4, 24–25.
95 Morgan, "Judicial Notice," see note 92 above at 293.
96 Ibid. at 294.
97 Interview with David Paciocco, Ottawa, 11 June 2015.
98 Interview with Julien Payne, Ottawa, 7 July 2009.
99 Interview with Nicholas Bala, Kingston, 12 August 2009.
100 Claire L'Heureux-Dubé, "Re-examining the Doctrine of Judicial Notice in the Family Law Context" (1994) 26 Ottawa L Rev 551 at 559.
101 Ibid.
102 Ruth Sullivan, "The Era of Concealed Underlying Premises Is Over: L'Heureux-Dubé J.'s Contribution to Statutory Interpretation" in Elizabeth Sheehy, ed., *Adding Feminism to Law: The Contributions of Justice Claire L'Heureux-Dubé* (Toronto: Irwin Law, 2004) 49 at 64.
103 CBC-TV Prime Time News, "Divorce – Alimony Agony" (17 December 1992), online: <http://www.cbc.ca/archives/categories/society/family/splitting-up-canadians-get-divorced/alimony-agony.html>.
104 Nikides and Rollason, "Love ends, but alimony may not," see note 1 above.
105 "Just Call Me Mr. Moge," *Lawyers Weekly* 13:30 (10 December 1993).
106 CBC-TV Prime Time News, "Divorce – Alimony Agony," see note 103 above.
107 Nikides and Rollason, "Love ends, but alimony may not," see note 1 above.
108 Interview with Alison Diduck, Winnipeg, 28 July 2014.
109 Interview with Peter Bruckshaw, Winnipeg, 23 July 2014.
110 Interview with Sean Fine, Toronto, 8 April 2015.
111 E. Llana Nakonechny, "Spousal Support Decisions at the Supreme Court of Canada: New Model or Moving Target?" (2003) 15 CJWL 102 at 103; National Council of Welfare, *Women and Poverty Revisited,* see note 84 above at 73–74.
112 Linda Silver Dranoff, "Fair" (unpublished manuscript submitted to the Feminist History Society, 2016) at 282.
113 James G. McLeod, "Case Comment *Moge v. Moge*" (1993) 43 RFL (3d) 455 at 455–64. McLeod did concede, however, that the result was correct, adding that it was "difficult to imagine how anyone (aside from, perhaps, a frustrated payer) could think that the support should have been terminated." Recalling McLeod's mesmerizing lectures, Julien Payne remembered him comparing marital property division to "being hit by a two-by-four." Interview with Julien Payne, Ottawa, 7 July 2009.
114 Interview with Julien Payne, ibid. Payne noted that the only other family law judgment that was comparable in significance was Laskin's dissent in *Murdoch v. Murdoch,* [1975] 1 SCR 423.
115 Interview with Julien Payne, ibid.
116 Louise Langevin, "Honorable Claire L'Heureux-Dubé: créatrice de la langue d'égalité," DRT-150492, Recherche dirigée Université Laval (17 April 2007) at 2.
117 *Gordon v. Goertz,* [1996] 2 SCR 27. The case involved a divorced mother from Saskatoon who had been awarded custody of her child; her ex-husband had been awarded generous access. The mother wished to move to Australia to pursue a professional education, and sought permission from the court to move the child with her. The Supreme Court found that the mother's move to Australia was in the best interests of the child, and varied the terms of the custody to allow her to move. L'Heureux-Dubé wrote a concurring opinion

emphasizing that the notion of custody encompassed the right to choose the child's place of residence. She went further than most of her colleagues in stating that the non-custodial parent also bore the onus of proving that the change of residence would be detrimental to the best interests of the child.

118 *New Brunswick (Minister of Health and Community Services) v. G. (J.)*, [1999] 3 SCR 46. A single mother sought legal aid representation to assist her to resist the state's application for protective custody of her children. When the province advised that its legal aid program did not cover custody, she claimed this was a breach of her section 7 *Charter* rights. The Supreme Court unanimously held that this was a violation of section 7, but L'Heureux-Dubé wrote a concurring opinion (signed by McLachlin) noting that it also violated the principle of gender equality under section 15 because women, and especially single mothers, were disproportionately affected by child protection proceedings.

119 *Nova Scotia (Attorney General) v. Walsh*, [2002] 4 SCR 325, in which she asserted that there was no significant distinction between property division and support.

120 *Boston v. Boston*, [2001] 2 SCR 413. LeBel wrote the dissent, which L'Heureux-Dubé signed, emphasizing the unfairness of depriving women, after a long-term marriage, of their entitlement to a standard of living congruent with that during the marriage. The majority reduced the ex-wife's spousal support by two-thirds because the support was drawn from pension income, an asset that had been previously equalized under the earlier division of assets.

121 Interviews with Claire L'Heureux-Dubé, Ottawa, 27–28 April 2009 and 30 June 2014; Clearwater, FL, 25–27 November 2014.

Chapter 31: Human Rights for Same-Sex Couples

1 Brian Robert Mossop, "Publications and Curriculum Vitae," online: <http://www.yorku.ca/brmossop>.
2 Mossop taught at Glendon College, York University, from 1980 until his retirement in 2014. Ibid.
3 Interview with Ken Popert, Toronto, 7 August 2014. When *The Body Politic* ceased publication in 1986, Popert continued to publish *Xtra!* under the auspices of the Pink Triangle Press.
4 Interview with Brian Mossop, Toronto, 31 July 2014.
5 Ibid.
6 Ibid.
7 *Mossop v. Canada (Secretary of State)* (1989), 10 CHRR D/6064 at 6065 [hereafter *Mossop 1989*].
8 Ibid. at 6066 listed "father, mother, brother, sister, spouse (including common-law spouse resident with the employee), child (including child of common-law spouse), ward of the employee, father-in-law, mother-in-law, and a relative who permanently resides in the employee's household or with whom the employee permanently resides."
9 Ibid. at 6067–68.
10 Interview with Brian Mossop, Toronto, 31 July 2014.
11 *Mossop 1989*, see note 7 above at 6066–67.
12 He might never have carried this further except that the Translation Bureau was located in the same building as the CHRC, and he knew one of the young lawyers who worked there, Maryka Omatsu. The two had an informal conversation about the situation one day, and she suggested that he file a complaint. Interview with Brian Mossop, Toronto, 31 July 2014.
13 Ibid.
14 Ibid.

15 Interview with Ken Popert, Toronto, 7 August 2014.
16 Interview with Brian Mossop, Toronto, 31 July 2014.
17 Ibid.
18 Ibid.
19 Ibid.
20 Interview with Ken Popert, Toronto, 7 August 2014.
21 *Mossop 1989,* see note 7 above at 6068, citing transcript, p. 16.
22 *Canadian Human Rights Act,* SC 1976–77, c. 33, s. 7(b).
23 The *Minutes of Proceedings of the Parliamentary Standing Committee on Justice and Legal Affairs* no. 115 (20 December 1982) noted at 19 that the CHRC had recommended the introduction of "sexual orientation" annually since 1979.
24 MacGuigan added that under section 15 of the *Charter,* it was "open to the courts, if they feel that we have misread the situation, to add that as a requirement." Ibid. at 19–20.
25 *Re Attorney-General of Canada and Mossop* (1991), 71 DLR (4th) 661 at 664 [hereafter *Mossop 1991*].
26 Interview with Brian Mossop, Toronto, 31 July 2014.
27 Ibid.
28 Interview with Margrit Eichler, Toronto, 11 August 2014.
29 *Mossop 1989,* see note 7 above at 6072–73.
30 Ibid. at 6072-3.
31 Ibid. at 6080. The lawyer was Robert Cousineau.
32 Interview with Brian Mossop, Toronto, 31 July 2014.
33 *Mossop 1989,* see note 7 above at 6081.
34 Ibid. at 6091–92.
35 Ibid. at 6094.
36 Ibid. at 6098; decision dated 13 April 1989.
37 *Mossop 1991,* see note 25 above at 673–75, 676. The Federal Court of Appeal struck down virtually every aspect of the tribunal's reasoning. It noted that the dispute really centred on discrimination on the basis of sexual orientation. As the legislative history of the act demonstrated, Parliament had declined to add sexual orientation to the lists of prohibited grounds. The court concluded that to adopt a "living tree" approach toward "discerning new grounds of discrimination" would "usurp the function of Parliament."
38 Peter McCormick, *Supreme at Last: The Evolution of the Supreme Court of Canada* (Toronto: Lorimer, 2000) at 106–8, 129–31.
39 Brodsky explained that the multi-issue coalition reflected the "depth and breadth" of the equality rights movement at the time, that the groups involved were "meeting pretty regularly, unlike now, on a national basis to discuss what we were doing – activism, litigation both." She added, "What distinguished us as interveners is we were up against a tendency among lawyers representing lesbian and gay clients to argue in the format of an idealized definition of family, accompanied by a *Better Homes & Gardens* checklist – financial dependence, bank accounts, wills, and so on. Lawyers representing lesbian and gay litigants were trying to show that lesbians and gays are actually straighter than straight. The coalition wanted to resist that. The endeavour was not to show how lesbians and gays fit into a rigid heterosexist formulation of family, but rather to bring an end to bias in the law." Interview with Gwen Brodsky, Vancouver, 16 October 2014.
40 *Canada (Attorney-General) v. Mossop,* [1993] 1 SCR 554 [hereafter *Mossop*].
41 Doug Harrington, "Court needs to bring family up to date," *Ottawa Citizen* (24 February 1993) A9.
42 The "standard of review" question was whether the court should show deference to the expertise of the hearing adjudicators, or supervise their decisions more strictly, demanding that all rulings be "correct." Barbara McIsaac recalled "being thrown off at the Supreme

Court of Canada because the court was more interested in the question of the standard of review than anything else." Interview with Barbara McIsaac, Ottawa, 2 August 2014. Brian Mossop recalled that he and other gay activists who were with him complained that the discussion was not "about our issues – whether it was discrimination based on sexual orientation." Interview with Brian Mossop, Toronto, 31 July 2014. La Forest wrote for six of the seven judges on the standard of review. He held that courts must require that human rights adjudicators be "correct" in their legal analysis – a more intrusive standard than applied to tribunals in fields such as labour relations and telecommunications. L'Heureux-Dubé, the only dissenter on this point, held that courts should defer to human rights tribunals, intervening only if their findings were patently unreasonable. She was of the view that Mossop's claim should be supported because Atcheson's original decision was both "well-written and well-thought out." *Mossop*, see note 40 above; interview with Claire L'Heureux-Dubé, Clearwater, FL, 25–27 November 2014.

43 Interview with Brian Mossop, ibid.
44 *Haig v. Canada* (1992), 94 DLR (4th) 1 (Ont CA). The court relied upon *Schachter v. Canada*, [1992] 2 SCR 679, issued one month earlier, for authority to add the missing ground to the legislation, rather than simply declare legislation "inoperative" or offer the government a "breathing period" to figure out how to correct the legislation.
45 Stephen Bindman, "Gay rights up to courts," *Ottawa Citizen* (2 November 1992).
46 Library and Archives Canada (LAC), Claire L'Heureux-Dubé Fonds, MG 31, E110, vol. 52, dossier 2–3, contains copies of the correspondence that Lamer sent to the litigants; *Mossop*, see note 40 above. L'Heureux-Dubé stated that Lamer would not have communicated with the parties about rearguing the case without consulting the other members of the panel, and that the panel must have agreed, since he went ahead and requested this. Interview with Claire L'Heureux-Dubé, Clearwater, FL, 25–27 November 2014.
47 LAC, Claire L'Heureux-Dubé Fonds, ibid., correspondence from Barbara McIsaac to the Registrar of the Supreme Court, 4 November 1992.
48 Ibid., correspondence from Ian Binnie to the Registrar of the Supreme Court, 6 November 1992.
49 *Mossop*, see note 40 above at 579, where Lamer stated: "The Court invited the parties to this appeal to submit new arguments ... The appellant chose not to take this approach, however, and insisted that this Court dispose of its action solely on the basis of the meaning of 'family status.'"
50 *Minutes of Proceedings of the Parliamentary Standing Committee on Justice and Legal Affairs* (21 December 1982) at 44–45.
51 Interview with William Pentney, Ottawa, 11 August 2014. In *Cooper v. Canada (Human Rights Commission)*, [1996] 3 SCR 854, La Forest's majority decision held that the commission did not have the jurisdiction to question the constitutional validity of its enabling statute.
52 Interview with William Pentney, ibid.
53 Factum of EGALE et al., 5 November 1992; interview with Gwen Brodsky, Vancouver, 16 October 2014.
54 Interview with Brian Mossop, Toronto, 31 July 2014. William Pentney, commenting on the failure to advise Mossop that he had the right to make separate arguments and be represented by a lawyer, recalled that "at that stage, having complainants represented separately was very much not the norm. The model was that the commission had carriage of the case. Very few independent complainants had their own counsel." Interview with William Pentney, Ottawa, 11 August 2014.
55 Interview with Brian Mossop, ibid.
56 Ibid.
57 Interview with Ken Popert, Toronto, 7 August 2014.

58 *Mossop,* see note 40 above at 580.
59 Ibid. at 579.
60 Ibid. at 581.
61 Sean Fine, "Gay man's argument rejected by top court," *Globe and Mail* (26 February 1992) A2. The case was that of Mary Pitawanakwat.
62 Interview with Gwen Brodsky, Vancouver, 16 October 2014.
63 Interview with William Pentney, Ottawa, 11 August 2014.
64 Interview with Claire L'Heureux-Dubé, Clearwater, FL, 25–27 November 2014. She added: "I never thought we could have gone further and settled the thing for the gays [in *Mossop*]. A new hearing, a new set of facts ... always the possibility that things don't turn out like you want. It's true [*Mossop*] didn't advance the case as it should [have]. But there ... would be other [occasions]."
65 *Egan v. Canada,* [1995] 2 SCR 513 [hereafter *Egan*].
66 Ibid. If the seven judges who sat on *Mossop* had ruled the same way on a full-blown *Charter* challenge in *Mossop*, Mossop would have won 4–3, with L'Heureux-Dubé, Cory, Iacobucci, and McLachlin siding with Mossop, and Lamer, La Forest, and Sopinka siding against him. Lamer's vote in *Egan* seemed odd, given that he had asked the parties to reargue the case with a *Charter* challenge and critiqued them for failing to do so. L'Heureux-Dubé did not find Lamer's negative vote surprising, and expressed the view that he was "too much of a male womanizer" to support "the gay type." Interview with Claire L'Heureux-Dubé, Clearwater, FL, 25–27 November 2014.
67 The tide would finally turn in *Vriend v. Alberta,* [1998] 1 SCR 493 [hereafter *Vriend*], when all nine judges sat again: eight found the denial of human rights protection for gays and lesbians to be unconstitutional; Sopinka took no part in the decision.
68 *Mossop,* see note 40 above at 615, 621.
69 Margrit Eichler, *Families in Canada Today: Recent Changes and Their Policy Consequences,* 2nd ed. (Toronto: Gage, 1988); Gregory M. Herek, "Myths about Sexual Orientation: A Lawyer's Guide to Social Science Research" (1991) 1 Law & Sexuality 133; Didi Herman, "Are We Family? Lesbian Rights and Women's Liberation" (1990) 28 Osgoode Hall LJ 789; Sylvia A. Law, "Homosexuality and the Social Meaning of Gender" (1988) Wis L Rev 187; Mary Mendola, *The Mendola Report: A New Look at Gay Couples* (New York: Crown, 1980); Bruce Ryder, "Equality Rights and Sexual Orientation: Confronting Heterosexual Family Privilege" (1990) 9 Can J Fam L 39; Meryn E. Stuart, "An Analysis of the Concept of Family" in Ann L. Whall and Jacqueline Fawcett, eds., *Family Theory Development in Nursing: State of the Science and Art* (Philadelphia: F.A. Davis, 1991) at 31.
70 Adrienne Rich, "Husband-Right and Father-Right" in *On Lies, Secrets, and Silence* (New York: Norton, 1979); Audre Lorde, "Age, Race, Class, and Sex: Women Redefining Difference" in *Sister Outsider* (Freedom, CA: Crossing Press, 1984) at 114; Patricia J. Williams, *The Alchemy of Race and Rights* (Cambridge, MA: Harvard University Press, 1991). Most of these sources had not been cited by any of the parties in their facta.
71 *Mossop,* see note 40 above at 627, 631, 634.
72 Ibid. at 620, citing *Minutes of Proceedings of the Parliamentary Standing Committee on Justice and Legal Affairs,* no. 115 (21 December 1982) at 73. See also *Minutes of Proceedings of the Parliamentary Standing Committee on Justice and Legal Affairs* no. 115 (20 December 1982) at 17.
73 *Mossop,* see note 40 above at 645.
74 Cristin Schmitz, "Our One-on-One with Justice Claire L'Heureux-Dubé," *Lawyers Weekly* 22:3 (17 May 2002).
75 *Egan,* see note 65 above. Although unanimous in the first stage of the section 15 analysis, the court split 4-1-4 on the question of whether section 1 permitted the exclusion of gay couples; L'Heureux-Dubé, in dissent, held that it was unlawful to exclude them.

76 *Vriend*, see note 67 above. Although the court was unanimous on the initial point, Major dissented on the remedy. The majority "read in" the missing protection for sexual orientation, whereas Major recommended striking down the legislation and leaving it to the provincial government to decide whether to re-enact with or without the use of the "notwithstanding" clause.
77 *M. v. H.*, [1999] 2 SCR 3. Gonthier dissented.
78 *Reference re Same-Sex Marriage*, [2004] 3 SCR 698.
79 Andrée Lajoie, Cécile Bergada, and Katherine Gauthier, "Claire L'Heureux-Dubé, la Cour suprême et les minorités" (2003) 15:1 CJWL 28 at 35.
80 Interview with Shirley Tucker Parks, Ottawa, 19 November 2009.
81 Critics castigated the judiciary for caving in to groups that were attempting to use the courts rather than Parliament to advance their causes. Address of Ted Morton to the Donner Canadian Foundation, 2000, as reported in Florian Sauvageau, David Schneiderman, and David Taras, *The Last Word: Media Coverage of the Supreme Court of Canada* (Vancouver: UBC Press, 2006) at 62–63. The editors of the *Ottawa Citizen* described it as neither a "triumph" nor a "defeat" for gays, but a message to Parliament: "In coming just one vote shy of giving Mossop his day, and in virtually inviting a new case, the Supreme Court justices have sent Parliament a warning: Act soon, or we'll do it for you." "Top Court Forces MPs to Act," Editorial, *Ottawa Citizen* (26 February 1993) A10. Barbara McIsaac indicated that a succession of federal ministers of justice had been supportive of adding "sexual orientation" into the human rights statute, but none of them had been able to get the revision enacted. "There wasn't enough political will to take on the issue. It was one of the classic situations where it's not politically expedient to move that quickly." She saw the outcome in *Mossop* as "a situation of the court giving signals, but giving the government an opportunity to do it. [The court] seemed to be conscious of the fact that this was thought to be a social policy decision, not a court-imposed decision." Interview with Barbara McIsaac, Ottawa, 2 August 2014. McGill law professor Stephen Toope said recognition of gay rights, like the issue of abortion, "makes legislators nervous." It was easier for them to say: "Let the courts do it. They bear the heat." Sean Fine, "Court sets seal on gay revolution," *Toronto Globe* (24 November 1992) A1, A6. Human rights expert Ken Norman, a law professor at the University of Saskatchewan, stated: "It is a revolution in progress ... What politicians won't do willingly, the courts may require. The gay community is a case study in how a stigmatized minority group can achieve dramatic political change without the support of vote-conscious politicians in the era of the *Canadian Charter of Human Rights and Freedoms*" (ibid.).
82 Interview with Shirley Tucker Parks, Ottawa, 19 November 2009; interview with Simone Tardif, Montreal, 4 August 2008; interview with David Wright, Toronto, 7 May 2014.
83 Interview with Shirley Tucker Parks, ibid.; interview with Simone Tardif, ibid.; interview with David Wright, ibid.
84 Interview with Shirley Tucker Parks, ibid.
85 Interview with Rebecca Johnson, Victoria, 22 August 2013.
86 Interview with Claire L'Heureux-Dubé, Quebec City, 27–29 April 2009.
87 *Mossop*, see note 40 above at 649: "The factors which give this relationship 'family status' are ably reviewed by Justice L'Heureux-Dubé and need not be repeated. I would dispose of the appeal as proposed by L'Heureux-Dubé J."
88 Interview with Claire L'Heureux-Dubé, Clearwater, FL, 25–27 November 2014. Although none of L'Heureux-Dubé's clerks would reveal whether they had actually written portions of decisions, she developed a reputation, as did a number of other Supreme Court judges, for relying upon her clerks to write. Richard A. Posner, "Judicial Opinions and Appellate Advocacy in Federal Courts – One Judge's Views" (2013) 51 Duq L Rev 3, noted at 24 that this practice had become the norm south of the border, where American judges routinely assigned their law clerks to write the draft decisions, and then expended their own efforts

on editing those drafts. Some of L'Heureux-Dubé's colleagues made greater use of clerks to do their writing than she did. Others still insisted on drafting from scratch. Her colleague Ian Binnie was quick to stress that he thought L'Heureux-Dubé "closely supervised" her clerks. "She is a very bright woman," he added. "She certainly didn't put herself in a position of saying things she didn't intend to say." Interview with Ian Binnie, Ottawa, 6 April 2011. It was not a generosity that L'Heureux-Dubé extended to Lamer, whom she accused of hiring law clerks and making them write his decisions. "Each one would write one part, 1, 2, 3, and he would not even read it before it was circulated to the other judges." Interview with Claire L'Heureux-Dubé, Quebec City, 27–28 April 2009.
89 Interview with Claire L'Heureux-Dubé, Clearwater, FL, 25–27 November 2014.
90 Interview with Rebecca Johnson, Victoria, 22 August 2013.
91 François Lacasse, who clerked during L'Heureux-Dubé's first year on the court, explained that "everything that came out of her chambers when I was there was her work product, not mine. It never happened that we would write, she would change a sentence and a comma, and sign off." Andrew Lenz, who clerked in 1991–92, described how L'Heureux-Dubé read voraciously all of the memos, articles, and cases that the clerks located, and then discussed them with her clerks. She would also go over the various draft decisions with her clerks, "line by line, in English, in French." Laurie Sargent, who clerked in the later years, 1999–2000, affirmed that the pattern did not change over time, and described the process of drafting L'Heureux-Dubé's speeches. "We did the background, [but she would] depart from the text and make it so much more interesting. Ultimately it was her own when it came to the presentation." Sargent emphasized that L'Heureux-Dubé "always read everything" the clerks produced, and was "very engaged" with the writing. The clerks "did a lot" on the drafting of decisions, "but there was not a word that she hadn't scrutinized carefully [or] rewritten. It was not in any way a clerk-driven process." Interview with François Lacasse, Ottawa, 5 August 2014; interview with Andrew Lenz, Ottawa, 5 August 2014; interview with Laurie Sargent, Ottawa, 26 September 2014.
92 Interview with Rebecca Johnson, Victoria, 22 August 2013.
93 Interview with Brian Mossop, Toronto, 31 July 2014.
94 David Vienneau, "Top court denies family benefits to gay couples," *Toronto Star* (26 February 1993) A1 at A14; Anita Elash and Peter Stockland, "Gays unfazed by court setback," *Toronto Sun* (26 February 1993) 3.

Chapter 32: Tax Law and Sex Discrimination

1 Interview with Beth Symes, Toronto, 17 July 2015; Beth Symes, "Henderson Lecture" (unpublished, undated manuscript).
2 The partners were Fran Kiteley and Elizabeth McIntyre.
3 Interview with Beth Symes, Toronto, 17 July 2015.
4 Along with Mary Eberts, Beth Atcheson, and Jennifer Stoddart, Symes co-authored the feasibility study in 1984, and they worked together on research, education, and litigation as the project evolved. LEAF announced its first two cases on 17 April 1985, the day the equality section of the *Charter* first came into effect, and Symes noted that it made for a "wonderful spectacle on the hill. We raised $20,000 that day in Ottawa and $25,000 in Toronto." Sherene Razack, *Canadian Feminism and the Law: The Women's Legal Education and Action Fund and the Pursuit of Equality* (Toronto: Second Story Press, 1991) at 34–41, 48, 61.
5 Interview with Beth Symes, Toronto, 17 July 2015; Symes, "Henderson Lecture," see note 1 above.
6 Long after she had stopped having children herself, Symes became one of the main proponents for the creation of a maternity leave policy for the Scott & Aylen law firm, with which she later practised. As a bencher between 2003 and 2015, she helped the Law Society

of Upper Canada design a funded maternity leave program for self-employed female lawyers.
7 Interview with Beth Symes, Toronto, 17 July 2015.
8 Symes, "Henderson Lecture," see note 1 above.
9 Ibid.
10 Interview with Beth Symes, Toronto, 17 July 2015.
11 Interview with Mary Eberts, Toronto, 30 July 2015.
12 Symes, "Henderson Lecture," see note 1 above.
13 Sean Fine, "Women to seize opportunities under the Charter," *Globe and Mail* (21 August 1992) A4.
14 Symes, "Henderson Lecture," see note 1 above.
15 Ibid.
16 *Symes v. Canada*, [1993] 4 SCR 695 [hereafter *Symes*].
17 Claire F.L. Young, "Impact of Feminist Analysis on Tax Law and Policy" in *1992 Institute of Continuing Legal Education* (Toronto: Canadian Bar Association, 31 January 1992) at 12.
18 *Symes v. Canada*, [1993] 4 SCR 695; [1993] SCJ No. 131 at 7 [hereafter *Symes 1993 SCJ*].
19 *Symes v. Canada (FCTD)*, [1989] FCJ No. 400 at 11 [hereafter *Symes 1989*].
20 Ellen Roseman, "Childcare goes to top court," *Globe and Mail* (27 February 1993) B21.
21 Ibid.
22 Interview with Melina Buckley, Vancouver, 24 July 2015. Buckley later rewrote the decision of *Symes v. Canada* on behalf of the Women's Court of Canada, a project dedicated to rewriting Supreme Court decisions from a feminist perspective. Melina Buckley, "*Symes v. Canada*" (2006) 18:1 CJWL 27.
23 *Symes 1989*, see note 19 above; *Symes v. Canada (FCA)*, [1991] FCJ No. 537 [hereafter *Symes 1991*]; *Symes*, see note 16 above.
24 Young, "Impact of Feminist Analysis on Tax Law and Policy," see note 17 above at 1–2; "Child Care Costs: Public Policy Trails Work Reality," Editorial, *Ottawa Citizen* (4 March 1992) A10. Two earlier tax challenges to the lack of deductibility of childcare as business expenses had occurred prior to the *Charter. No. 68 v. Minister of National Revenue* (1950), 52 DTC 236 (TAB) involved a married female optometrist. *Macquistan v. Minister of National Revenue* (1965), 65 DTC 236 (TAB) involved a married physician. Both lost.
25 *Symes*, see note 16 above.
26 The opinion was also signed by Lamer, La Forest, Sopinka, Gonthier, Cory, and Major.
27 Describing his decision to enter law, Iacobucci said, "It hit me as the first time that my name or my background could be thought of as some sort of burden or handicap. We don't have to go very far back in history to see how inaccessible the legal profession was to minority groups ... and women ... really an ugliness about the profession. In some ways, when I thought about those things, they were incentives for me to try a little more." Interview with Frank Iacobucci, Ottawa, 21 June 2000. Iacobucci had publicly acknowledged his debt to his parents during his judicial swearing-in to the Supreme Court in December 1990. "He spoke in Italian to offer 'a thousand thanks and a big hug' to his late mother ... and his ailing steel-worker father ... for their hard work." Stephen Bindman, "The judges: A personal look at the Supreme Court justices," *Ottawa Citizen* (11 April 1992) B2.
28 Bindman, ibid.
29 His wife, Nancy Elizabeth Eastham, had a BA from Mount Holyoke, an LL.B. from Harvard, and a Dip. Int. Law from Cambridge; Frank Iacobucci's printed curriculum vitae.
30 Rebecca Johnson, *Taxing Choices: The Intersection of Class, Gender, Parenthood, and the Law* (Vancouver: UBC Press, 2002) at xi.
31 Stephen Bindman, "Iacobucci: The making of a Supreme Court justice," *Ottawa Citizen* (25 January 1991) A13. On the universal support for the previous seven appointments, see David Vienneau, "New high court judge unfazed by criticism," *Toronto Star* (23 January

1991) at A21, who noted: "Iacobucci's friends say the controversy dampened what should have been one of the happiest days of his life. It's not something he wishes to talk about during an interview in his new office." Although L'Heureux-Dubé was also a previous Mulroney appointee, Vienneau apparently overlooked the critical comments on her ascension to the Supreme Court.

32 Stephen Bindman, "Judge credits immigrant parents' views," *Vancouver Sun* (24 January 1991) at E7.
33 Graham Fraser, "Federal judge named to Supreme Court: No obligation to pick woman, PM says," *Globe and Mail* (22 December 1990) at A10.
34 He was the co-editor of six editions of *Materials on Canadian Income Tax*. Ibid.; Iacobucci printed curriculum vitae.
35 *Symes 1993 SCJ*, see note 18 above at 19–20.
36 Ibid. at 20, 25.
37 *Income Tax Act*, RSC 1952, c. 148, as amended. Section 63 had introduced a deduction of $500 per child to a maximum of $2,000 per family in 1972, increasing to $1,000 (maximum $4,000) in 1976, and $2,000 (to a maximum of $8,000) in 1983. *Symes 1991*, see note 23 above at 5. As all commentators noted, these amounts did not reflect the actual cost of childcare. Claire F.L. Young, "Child Care – A Taxing Issue?" (1994) 39 McGill LJ 539.
38 Audrey Macklin, "*Symes v. M.N.R.:* Where Sex Meets Class" (1992) 5 CJWL 498 at 499.
39 *Symes 1993 SCJ*, see note 18 above at 26–29, 34. The federal government had failed to argue section 63 as a complete code at trial, conceding the point to Symes. As commentators noted, this suggested that "the government itself did not initially understand its own legislation as precluding other legitimate business expenses." Johnson, *Taxing Choices*, see note 30 above at 115.
40 *Symes 1993 SCJ*, see note 18 above at 30.
41 Ibid. at 35.
42 Ibid. at 41.
43 Young, "Impact of Feminist Analysis on Tax Law and Policy," see note 17 above, noted at 11 that the "rhetoric" seen in this case was "highly unusual."
44 *Symes 1993 SCJ*, see note 18 above at 48.
45 Ibid. at 51–52.
46 *Symes 1989*, see note 19 above at 4; Faye Woodman, "A Child Care Expenses Deduction, Tax Reform and the Charter: Some Modest Proposals" (1990) 8 Can J Fam L 371 at 375, 377.
47 *Symes 1993 SCJ*, see note 18 above at 51. Neil Brooks, "The Principles Underlying the Deduction of Business Expenses" in Brian G. Hansen, Vern Krishna, and James A. Rendall, eds., *Essays on Canadian Taxation* (Toronto: Richard De Boo, 1978) 249 at 260; Johnson, *Taxing Choices*, see note 30 above at 40. Although the legal principles underlying the judicial analysis had not been altered, some of these court decisions had later been reversed by legislative amendments, when the government tightened up the deductions businessmen were taking. Golf club and other private club initiation fees and dues, hunting cabins, private airplanes and yachts came off the list. Deductions for business meals and luxury cars were reduced. Interview with Kim Brooks, Halifax, 27 October 2014.
48 *Symes 1993 SCJ*, ibid. at 55. As Audrey Macklin noted: "The fact that these expenditures also have a 'personal' element was never treated as a complete bar. Thus, the courts have in the past permitted businessmen to deduct club fees because men like to conduct business with each other over golf. Chances are that few women would ever have been able to avail themselves of such a deduction, not only because golf is primarily played by men, but also because many clubs refused to admit women as members. Because some men believe expensive cars enhance their professional image, driving a Rolls Royce has been held to be an incident of a professional business." Macklin, "*Symes v. M.N.R.*," see note 38 above at 507.

49 *Symes 1993 SCJ*, ibid. at 61.
50 Ibid. at 62.
51 Claire L'Heureux-Dubé, "What a Difference a Decade Makes: The Canadian Constitution and the Family since 1991" (2001) 27 Queen's LJ 361 at 369, noted that the thrust of her dissent was not based directly on the *Charter* but on parsing the statute's language in light of *Charter* values.
52 *Symes 1993 SCJ*, see note 18 above at 49.
53 Interview with Mary Eberts, Toronto, 30 July 2015. Melina Buckley also disputed Iacobucci's reasoning when she subsequently rewrote the decision as a member of the fictional Women's Court of Canada: "Perhaps the most problematic aspects of this reasoning is Iacobucci J.'s finding that while it had been demonstrated that women disproportionately incur the social costs of childcare it had not been proven that they disproportionately pay childcare expenses ... Ms. Symes does not need to prove that women disproportionately pay for childcare in order for her claim to succeed. The clear evidence accepted at trial is that she paid for childcare in order to earn income through her professional business. Ms. Symes's situation reflects the norm in Canadian society that women are primarily responsible for childcare and that they pay for it economically." Buckley, "*Symes v. Canada*," see note 22 above at 59.
54 *Symes 1991*, see note 23 above at 12.
55 Ibid. at 14.
56 *Symes 1993 SCJ*, see note 18 above at 64.
57 Ibid. at 68.
58 *R. v. Thibaudeau*, [1995] 2 SCR 627 [hereafter *Thibaudeau*]. The mother failed in her challenge to the tax rules that allowed the payer of child support to deduct support payments from income, while the recipient had to include the payments in income for tax purposes. McLachlin and L'Heureux-Dubé were the only two dissenters. Despite the government's "win" in *Thibaudeau*, Parliament amended the *Income Tax Act* in 1997 to end the requirement that the custodial parent include child support as part of taxable income. Claire L'Heureux-Dubé, "It Takes a Vision: The Constitutionalization of Equality in Canada" (2002) 14 Yale JL & Feminism 363 at 372.
59 Bertha Wilson, "Will Women Judges Really Make a Difference?" (1990) 28 Osgoode Hall LJ 507–22, a text of the speech made at Osgoode Hall Law School earlier that year.
60 Stephen Bindman, "Judging in a man's world," *Ottawa Citizen* (13 April 1992) at A3.
61 Ibid.
62 Interview with Claire L'Heureux-Dubé, Clearwater Beach, FL, 25–27 November 2014.
63 Ibid. Two years earlier, the conservative group REAL Women had sought McLachlin's removal from the bench after a speech in which she said that criminal laws against abortion and prostitution were "based on outdated sexual stereotypes and lead to unfair and unequal treatment of women." The Canadian Judicial Council had dismissed the complaint, concluding that McLachlin's speech "contributed to a greater understanding and sensitivity as to how the criminal law has impacted upon the lives of women." Bindman, "Judging in a man's world," see note 60 above at A3.
64 Stephen Bindman, "Sitting in judgment," *Ottawa Citizen* (11 April 1992) B1.
65 Candace C. White, "Gender Difference in the Supreme Court of Canada" (MA thesis, Department of Political Science, University of Calgary, December 1998), noted at 55 that McLachlin supported 75 percent of the section 15 challenges, L'Heureux-Dubé 71 percent, and Wilson 50 percent, whereas the court mean was 35 percent. See also Peter McCormick, "Birds of a Feather: Alliances and Influences on the Lamer Court 1990–1997" (1998) 36 Osgoode Hall LJ 339.
66 Claire L'Heureux-Dubé, "The Dissenting Opinion: Voice of the Future?" (2000) 28:3 Osgoode Hall LJ 495 at 512.

67 F.L. Morton, P.H. Russell, and T. Riddell, "The Canadian Charter of Rights and Freedoms: A Descriptive Analysis of the First Decade, 1982–1992" (1994) 5 NJCL 1; Peter McCormick, *Supreme at Last: The Evolution of the Supreme Court of Canada* (Toronto: James Lorimer, 2000); Marie-Claire Belleau and Rebecca Johnson, "Judging Gender: Difference and Dissent at the Supreme Court of Canada" (2008) 15:1–2 International Journal of the Legal Profession 57 at 62. It was also a pattern that did not hold after L'Heureux-Dubé's retirement, when the two remaining female judges (now Chief Justice Beverley McLachlin and Louise Arbour) along with the women who followed them on the court no longer continued to dissent markedly from their male colleagues. Indeed, Belleau and Johnson noted at 63–67 that the higher proportion of female dissents may have been triggered by the "trailblazing" position rather than gender itself. Marie-Claire Belleau, Anik Lamontagne, and Rebecca Johnson, "Les décisions de la juge McLachlin à la Cour suprême du Canada: une analyse statistique comparative" in David Wright and Adam Dodek, eds., *Public Law at the McLachlin Court: The First Decade* (Toronto: Irwin Law, 2011) 39; Marie-Claire Belleau, Rebecca Johnson, and Annie Packwood, "L'honorable Louise Charron: une analyse quantitative comparée de sa jurisprudence" (University of Ottawa Faculty of Law Working Paper Series, October 2013).
68 Johnson, *Taxing Choices,* see note 30 above, summarized the range of feminist academic perspectives at 163–66.
69 "Women's group backs court ruling," *Globe and Mail* (18 December 1993) at A5.
70 Ibid.
71 "L'affaire Beth Symes et les services de garde," *Le Devoir* (23 March 1993) A6.
72 Razack, *Canadian Feminism and the Law,* see note 4 above at 58.
73 Woodman, "A Child Care Expenses Deduction, Tax Reform and the Charter," see note 46 above at 383.
74 Macklin, "*Symes v. M.N.R.,*" see note 38 above at 509–15.
75 Interview with Mary Eberts, Toronto, 30 July 2015.
76 The point was made by Beth Symes in "Henderson Lecture," see note 1 above.
77 Interview with Claire Young, Advocate Harbour, NS, 10 July 2015. For her earlier criticisms: Claire F.L. Young, "Impact of Feminist Analysis on Tax Law and Policy," see note 17 above at 13–14; Claire F.L. Young, "Child Care – A Taxing Issue?" see note 37 above; Claire F.L. Young, "Case Comment on *Symes v. The Queen*" (1991) British Tax Review 105; Claire F.L. Young, "Child Care and the *Charter:* Privileging the Privileged" (1994–95) 2:1 Rev Const Stud 20; Claire F.L. Young, "Taxing Times at the Supreme Court of Canada: The Contributions of Justice L'Heureux-Dubé to a Better Understanding of the Application of the Charter to the Income Tax System" in Elizabeth Sheehy, ed., *Adding Feminism to Law: The Contributions of Justice Claire L'Heureux-Dubé* (Toronto: Irwin, 2004) 229.
78 Interview with Claire Young, ibid.; Young, "Impact of Feminist Analysis on Tax Law and Policy," ibid. at 13–14; Young, "Child Care – A Taxing Issue?" ibid.
79 Young, "Taxing Times at the Supreme Court of Canada," see note 77 above at 241.
80 Interview with Ellen Zweibel, Ottawa, 18 July 2015.
81 Ibid. Rebecca Johnson, a former L'Heureux-Dubé law clerk, went on to write a book centred on the *Symes* case. In it she predicted that had Symes prevailed, it would have hastened a reclassification of childcare as "public and not private." Johnson, *Taxing Choices,* see note 30 above at 187. Johnson raised a series of interesting questions at xi: "Should the government be responsible for subsidizing childcare, or are childcare needs the private responsibilities of individual parents? Was it appropriate to blur the traditional distinction between the 'public' domain of work and the 'private' domain of home and children? Even if government were to subsidize childcare, should the subsidy take the form of limited tax deductions, or should it take the form of a national daycare system? What were the needs and responsibilities of mothers who work for pay? Was there any distinction to be drawn

between the childcare needs of wage earners and business-income earners? What about the women providing care for their own children in their own homes? Should their childcare work not be valued? Should the discussion of childcare focus on the needs of mothers or the needs of parents? Should gender neutrality be fostered by treating all parents equivalently, or were there differences between being a mother and being a father? If there was an unequal division of childcare labour within families, was this a legal or social problem? Should those struggling to advance the cause of equality in the domain of the family deploy the strategy of litigation or pursue other strategies of social/legislative reform?"

82 Interview with Claire Young, Advocate Harbour, NS, 10 July 2015.
83 Nancy Staudt, "Tax Talk" (2003) 51:5 Can Tax J 1931 at 1947.
84 Cristin Schmitz, "Lawyer Can't Claim Nanny as Business Expense," *Lawyers Weekly* (28 January 1994) at 4.
85 Interview with Mary Eberts, Toronto, 30 July 2015.
86 Interview with Melina Buckley, Vancouver, 24 July 2015.
87 Ibid.
88 Roseman, "Childcare goes to top court," see note 20 above.
89 On the interest rate in 1991, see David A. Steele, "The Deductibility of Childcare Expenses Re-examined: *Symes v. R.*" (1991) 7 Can Fam LQ 315 at 336.
90 Symes, "Henderson Lecture," see note 1 above.
91 Ibid.
92 Ibid.
93 Ibid. Melina Buckley had also raised the same point, suggesting that the case might have been more successful with an unmarried plaintiff, or a female entrepreneur who was making very little money, perhaps someone like a hairdresser making $20,000 a year. Interview with Melina Buckley, Vancouver, 24 July 2015.
94 Symes, "Henderson Lecture," see note 1 above.

Chapter 33: More Deaths

1   Interview with Claire L'Heureux-Dubé, Ottawa, 30 June 2014.
2   Ibid.
3   Ibid.
4   Interview with Claire L'Heureux-Dubé, Ottawa, 27–28 April 2009.
5   Claire L'Heureux-Dubé described her sentiments about paying for the reception: "My mother was dead. I said he had a new companion." Interview with Claire L'Heureux-Dubé, Quebec City, 12 July 2016.
6   Interview with Claire L'Heureux-Dubé, Ottawa, 27–28 April 2009.
7   Ibid.
8   Ibid.
9   Ibid.
10 Interview with Louise L'Heureux-Giliberti, Chicago, 21 April 2009.
11 Ibid.
12 Ibid.
13 Interview with Claire L'Heureux-Dubé, Rimouski, 23–25 July 2008; interview with Louise Dubé, Boston, 22 May 2012.
14 Interview with Marie-Claire Belleau, Quebec, 30 April 2008, and Ottawa, 11 December 2013.
15 Interview with Claire L'Heureux-Dubé, Clearwater, FL, 25–27 November 2014.
16 Interview with Louise Dubé, Boston, 22 May 2012.
17 Interview with Louise L'Heureux-Giliberti, Chicago, 21 April 2009.
18 Interview with Claire L'Heureux-Dubé, Clearwater, FL, 25–27 November 2014.

19 Ibid.
20 Interview with Andrew Lenz and François Lacasse, Ottawa, 5 August 2014.
21 Ibid.
22 Interview with Claire L'Heureux-Dubé, Clearwater, FL, 25–27 November 2014.
23 Interview with Andrew Lenz and François Lacasse, Ottawa, 5 August 2014.
24 Interviews with Marie-Claire Belleau, Quebec, 30 April 2008; Ottawa, 11 December 2013.
25 Ibid.
26 Interview with Nicole L'Heureux, Clearwater, FL, 11–12 May 2009.
27 Interview with Jean Drapeau, Rimouski, 24 July 2008; interview with Nicole L'Heureux, Clearwater, FL, 11–12 May 2009.
28 Interview with Philippe Michaud, Rimouski, 24 July 2008.
29 Interview with Louise L'Heureux-Giliberti, Chicago, 21 April 2009.
30 Interview with Roger Garneau, Quebec City, 28 April 2009.
31 Interview with Andrew Lenz and François Lacasse, Ottawa, 5 August 2014.
32 Interview with Roger Garneau, Quebec City, 28 April 2009.
33 Interview with Nicole L'Heureux, Clearwater, FL, 11–12 May 2009.
34 Interview with Louise Dubé, Boston, 22 May 2012.
35 Interview with Nicole L'Heureux, Clearwater, FL, 11–12 May 2009.
36 Several Supreme Court judges described these; none wished to be quoted.
37 Interview with Roger Garneau, Quebec City, 28 April 2009.
38 Various accounts deal with the incident: interview with Claire L'Heureux-Dubé, Clearwater, FL, 25–27 November 2014; Janice Tibbetts, "Supreme Court's great dissenter," *National Post* (27 February 1999) A3; "Particulars," *Lawyers Weekly* 11:31 (13 December 1991) 4; "Committal for Trial of Justice's Son is Gossip, Not News, Reader Feels," Editor's Note, Letters to Editor, *Lawyers Weekly* 11:35 (24 January 1992). Interview with Nicole L'Heureux, Clearwater, FL, 11–12 May 2009; interview with Yves Bernier, Quebec City, 30 April 2008; interview with Simone Tardif, Montreal, 4 August 2008; interview with Shirley Tucker Parks, Ottawa, 19 November 2009.
39 Interview with Claire L'Heureux-Dubé, Clearwater, FL, 25–27 November 2014. Others recall that Pierre made multiple threats to kill his mother, once at the point of a knife. Interview with Simone Tardif, ibid.; interview with Shirley Tucker Parks, ibid.
40 Interview with Claire L'Heureux-Dubé, ibid.
41 Interview with Nicole L'Heureux, Clearwater, FL, 11–12 May 2009.
42 Tibbetts, "Supreme Court's great dissenter," see note 38 above.
43 Janice Tibbetts, "Farewell Claire," *Canadian Lawyer* (September 2002) 39; interview with Claire L'Heureux-Dubé, Clearwater, FL, 25–27 November 2014.
44 Interview with Claire L'Heureux-Dubé, ibid.
45 "Justice: son on probation for threat to mother," *Ottawa Citizen* (27 October 1992) H6.
46 Ibid.
47 Interview with Claire L'Heureux-Dubé, Clearwater, FL, 25–27 November 2014.
48 Stephen Bindman, who was the national legal affairs correspondent for Southam News based in Ottawa, noted that there were discussions in his office over the appropriateness of the coverage. They ultimately decided it was not something the paper would normally be interested in, that they would be writing about it only because of who the victim was, and they decided not to. Interview with Stephen Bindman, Ottawa, 22 June 2015. *Lawyers Weekly* decided otherwise, and published the following in its column titled "Particulars," see note 38 above: "Pierre Dubé, son of Supreme Court of Canada Justice Claire L'Heureux-Dubé, was committed for trial on a charge of possession of a weapon for a purpose dangerous to the public peace following a preliminary hearing in Ottawa. His trial date will be set in January. Mr. Dubé was released on his own recognizance." *Lawyers Weekly* subsequently provided more details: "Committal for Trial of Justice's Son Is Gossip," see note 38 above.

Southam's later reported on the hearing to set a date for pretrial, "Pretrial date set for son of judge," *Ottawa Citizen* (12 January 1992) A8, and the sentencing, "Justice: son on probation for threat to mother," see note 45 above.

49 "Committal for Trial of Justice's Son Is Gossip," ibid. "Pretrial date set for son of judge," ibid., noted that the pretrial date was set for February 5.
50 This was recounted belatedly, upon L'Heureux-Dubé's retirement: Tibbetts, "Farewell Claire," see note 43 above.
51 Interview with Roger Garneau, Quebec City, 28 April 2009.
52 Ibid.
53 Interview with Claire L'Heureux-Dubé, Clearwater, FL, 25–27 November 2014.
54 Interview with Laurel Broten, Halifax, 25 July 2014.
55 Interview with Louise L'Heureux-Giliberti, Chicago, 21 April 2009.
56 Interview with Claire L'Heureux-Dubé, Clearwater, FL, 25–27 November 2014.
57 Ibid.
58 Interview with Gisèle Blondeau-Labrie, Quebec City, 1 May 2008.
59 Interviews with Marie-Claire Belleau, Quebec City, 30 April 2008; Ottawa, 11 December 2013.
60 Interview with Louise L'Heureux-Giliberti, Chicago, 21 April 2009.
61 Interview with Gisèle Blondeau-Labrie, Quebec City, 1 May 2008.
62 Interview with Claire L'Heureux-Dubé, Clearwater, FL, 25–27 November 2014.
63 Pierre's sister, Louise, added: "What happened to him was quite a mystery. I read the autopsy report, [and] it still doesn't make sense. You can't have renal failure for as long as he did without being treated. Clearly there was negligence there, and [my mother] could have sued. She chose not to." Interview with Louise Dubé, Boston, 22 May 2012.
64 Interview with Claire L'Heureux-Dubé, Clearwater, FL, 25–27 November 2014.
65 Interview with Claire L'Heureux-Dubé, Ottawa, 30 June 2014.
66 She left Ottawa on 10 September and returned on 19 September 1994.
67 Interview with Louise L'Heureux-Giliberti, Chicago, 21 April 2009; interview with Claire L'Heureux-Dubé, Clearwater, FL, 25–27 November 2014.
68 Interview with Jean Drapeau, Rimouski, 24 July 2008.
69 Interview with Louise Dubé, Boston, 22 May 2012; interview with Louise L'Heureux-Giliberti, Chicago, 21 April 2009.
70 Interview with Louise Dubé, Boston, 22 May 2012.
71 Interview with Louise L'Heureux-Giliberti, Chicago, 21 April 2009.
72 Interviews with Marie-Claire Belleau, Quebec City, 30 April 2008; Ottawa, 11 December 2013.
73 Interview with Nicole L'Heureux, Clearwater, FL, 11–12 May 2009.
74 Interview with Roger Garneau, Quebec City, 28 April 2009.
75 Interview with Louise L'Heureux-Giliberti, Chicago, 21 April 2009.
76 Interviews with Marie-Claire Belleau, Quebec City, 30 April 2008; Ottawa, 11 December 2013.
77 Interview with Jean Drapeau, Rimouski, 24 July 2008; interview with Louise L'Heureux-Giliberti, Chicago, 21 April 2009.
78 Interview with Louise L'Heureux-Giliberti, ibid.
79 Interview with Louise Dubé, Boston, 22 May 2012. Louise subsequently married again, to an American in Boston, with whom she had two boys, Simon Pierre Harris (1998) and Daniel Louis Dubé Harris (2002).
80 Interview with Simone Tardif, Montreal, 4 August 2008.
81 Interview with André Legault, Ottawa, 10 December 2007.
82 Interview with Louise L'Heureux-Giliberti, Chicago, 21 April 2009.
83 Interview with Claire L'Heureux-Dubé, Ottawa, 5 March 2009.

84 Interview with Charles Gonthier, Ottawa, 14 September 2008.
85 Interview with Gérard La Forest, Ottawa, 30 June 2014.
86 Interview with Jack Major, Calgary, 13 November 2013.
87 Interview with Claire L'Heureux-Dubé, Ottawa, 5 March 2009.
88 Interview with Frank Iacobucci, Toronto, 26 October 2011.
89 Interview with Andrew Lenz and François Lacasse, Ottawa, 5 August 2014.
90 Interviews with Marie-Claire Belleau, Quebec, 30 April 2008; Ottawa, 11 December 2013.

Chapter 34: The Quebec Secession Reference

1 Anne Roland, "Le juge en chef Lamer et l'administration de la Cour suprême du Canada: une vision en action" in Adam Dodek and Daniel Jutras, eds., *The Sacred Fire: The Legacy of Antonio Lamer* (Markham, ON: LexisNexis, 2009) at 24.
2 Interview with David Wright, Toronto, 7 May 2014; Florian Sauvageau, David Schneiderman, and David Taras, *Last Word: Media Coverage of the Supreme Court of Canada* (Vancouver: UBC Press, 2011) at 116.
3 "Chief Justice Lamer was very proud of the fact that there was not a trickle. Nobody knew what was going to come out." Interview with David Wright, Toronto, 7 May 2014.
4 Robert A. Young, "A Most Politic Judgement" (1998) 10:1 Const Forum Const 14.
5 Adam M. Dodek, "Chief Justice Lamer and Policy Design at the Supreme Court of Canada" in Dodek and Jutras, *The Sacred Fire,* see note 1 above at 93; Chantal Hébert, "La cause du siècle," *La Presse* (16 February 1998) A1.
6 Jamie Cameron, "To the Rescue: Antonio Lamer and the Section 2(b) Cases from Quebec" in Dodek and Jutras, *The Sacred Fire,* ibid. at 241–42.
7 *Reference re Secession of Quebec,* [1998] 2 SCR 217 [hereafter *Quebec Secession Reference*]. The nine judges who heard the case were Lamer, L'Heureux-Dubé, Gonthier, Cory, McLachlin, Iacobucci, Major, Bastarache, and Binnie.
8 Kristen Pue, "Reference re: Secession of Quebec, in Context" (17 August 2012), online: University of Alberta Centre for Constitutional Studies <http://ualawccsprod.srv.ualberta.ca/ccs/>.
9 Michel Lévesque and Martin Pelletier, *Les référendums au Québec: bibliographie* (Québec: Bibliothèque de l'Assemblée nationale du Québec, 2005) at 15.
10 *Re Resolution to Amend the Constitution (Patriation Reference),* [1981] 1 SCR 753.
11 Enacted as Schedule B to the *Canada Act 1982,* 1982, c. 11 (UK).
12 John Dickinson and Brian Young, *A Short History of Quebec,* 3rd ed. (Montreal: McGill-Queen's University Press, 2003) at 354–56.
13 Sauvageau et al., *Last Word,* see note 2 above at 93.
14 Ibid. at 94.
15 Alan C. Cairns, "The Quebec Secession Reference: The Constitutional Obligation to Negotiate" (1998) 10:1 Const Forum Const 26; Young, "A Most Politic Judgement," see note 4 above at 14. For exploration of Plans B and C, see Robert A. Young, *The Secession of Quebec and the Future of Canada* (Montreal: McGill-Queen's University Press, 1998).
16 *Supreme Court Act,* RSC 1985, c. S-26, s. 53.
17 *Quebec Secession Reference,* see note 7 above.
18 Young, "A Most Politic Judgement," see note 4 above at 15; Patrick Monahan, "The Public Policy Role of the Supreme Court of Canada in the Secession Reference" (1999–2000) 11 NJCL 65.
19 Young, *The Secession of Quebec,* see note 15 above at 362.
20 The "leaning tower of Pisa" reference was attributed to former premier Maurice Duplessis, but picked up by Quebec Deputy Premier Bernard Landry. Young "A Most Politic Judgement," see note 4 above at 14–15.

21 *Le Devoir* (17 February 1998) A6.
22 Young "A Most Politic Judgement," see note 4 above at 14–15.
23 Monahan, "The Public Policy Role," see note 18 above.
24 Graham Fraser, "Supreme Court tackles big questions on Quebec secession," *Globe and Mail* (16 February 1998) A4.
25 Interview with Claire L'Heureux-Dubé, Ottawa, 30 June 2014.
26 Evelyn J.C. Davidson, *Who's Who in Canadian Law.* 2nd ed. (Toronto: Trans-Canada Press, 1982).
27 Interview with Claire L'Heureux-Dubé, Ottawa, 30 June 2014.
28 Warren J. Newman, *The Quebec Secession Reference: The Rule of Law and the Position of the Attorney General of Canada* (Toronto: York University, 1999) at 32–35.
29 Sean Fine, "Judges' delicate task: address the nation's most explosive issue," *Globe and Mail* (20 August 1998) A1. Sauvageau et al., *Last Word,* see note 2 above at 106, estimated the crowd at only five hundred.
30 Rhéal Séguin, "Separatists flying high at top court," *Globe and Mail* (17 February 1998) A1.
31 Graham Fraser, "Ottawa girds for Quebec ruling," *Globe and Mail* (20 August 1998) A1.
32 Fine, "Judges' delicate task," see note 29 above.
33 Canada, Factum of the Attorney General of Canada (No. 25506) (1997) at paras. 85, 101, 112, 186.
34 Elizabeth Thompson, "We'll stay in Canada, Crees vow," *Montreal Gazette* (18 February 1998) A1.
35 Graham Fraser, "Crees 'call on Canada' to ensure their status protected," *Globe and Mail* (18 February 1998) A4.
36 Ibid. Although women's organizations were not of one uniform opinion about secession, Bayefsky's organization was the only one to appear as an intervener.
37 *Quebec Secession Reference,* see note 7 above (Factum of the Respondents).
38 Interview with Claire L'Heureux-Dubé, Ottawa, 30 June 2014.
39 Paul Wells, "Full speed ahead for Lamer," *Montreal Gazette* (17 February 1998) A8.
40 Photos and captions in *Globe and Mail* (20 August 1998) A4.
41 Sean Fine, "Canada, Quebec and the Supreme Court of Canada," Editorial, *Globe and Mail* (16 February 1998) A18.
42 Fine, "Judges' delicate task," see note 29 above.
43 Fine, "Case puts spotlight on Dubé, Lamer," *Globe and Mail* (16 February 1998) A1.
44 Ibid.
45 Ibid.
46 Transcript of "Preliminary Statement by Lucien Bouchard, Premier of Quebec, The Day Following the Opinion of the Supreme Court of Canada on the Reference by the Federal Government" (Office of the Premier of Quebec, 21 August 1998) at 190, online: Secrétariat aux affaires intergouvernementales canadiennes <http://www.saic.gouv.qc.ca>.
47 Josée Legault, "How to deny Quebec's right to self-determination," *Globe and Mail* (21 August 1998) A19, A23.
48 Interview with Claire L'Heureux-Dubé, Ottawa, 30 June 2014.
49 Ibid.
50 Ibid.
51 Interview with Danièle Tremblay-Lamer, Ottawa, 12 March 2015.
52 Peter McCormick, "'By the Court': The Untold Story of a Canadian Judicial Innovation" (2016) 53:3 Osgoode Hall LJ 1048.
53 Sean Fine, "Behind the scenes as history was made," *Globe and Mail* (21 August 1998) A1; Sean Fine, "Court sought to create a judgment that will stand the test of time," *Globe and Mail* (21 August 1998) A8.

54 Manitoba law professor DeLloyd J. Guth publicly speculated that the final decision bore "unmistakeable tracings of the Gonthier pen, his method and his mind." DeLloyd Guth, "Method and Matter in the Gonthier Legacy: Legal History and Judgment Writing, 1989–2003" in Michel Morin et al., eds., *Responsibility, Fraternity and Sustainability in Law* (Markham, ON: LexisNexis, 2012) at 47. Ian Binnie added, "Justice Gonthier was ideally suited to the challenge." Ian Binnie, "Justice Charles Gonthier and the Unwritten Principles of the Constitution" in Morin et al., *Responsibility, Fraternity and Sustainability in Law* at 442. Legal journalist Philip Slayton wrote, "Gonthier wrote the core of the judgment, and formulated the four principles." Philip Slayton, *Mighty Judgment: How the Supreme Court of Canada Runs Your Life* (Toronto: Penguin, 2011) at 85.
55 Interviews with Claire L'Heureux-Dubé, Ottawa, 30 June 2014, and Clearwater, FL, 25–27 November 2014.
56 Ibid.
57 Fine, "Case puts spotlight on Dubé, Lamer," see note 43 above.
58 Ibid.
59 Interview with Robert Auclair, Quebec City, 7 August 2008. Auclair had founded the organization to promote the use of French in the workplace and government in tandem with the Quiet Revolution, and to ensure that the highest quality of French was encouraged.
60 Teresa Scassa, "Language of Judgment and the Supreme Court of Canada" (1994) 43 UNBLJ 169 at 173–75. The Francophone judges from Quebec occasionally wrote in French and then had the decision translated into English, but these cases were "relatively few."
61 Interview with Peter Sankoff, Ottawa, 27 June 2014. The choice of language for the first draft of her decisions frequently followed the language of the parties, and sometimes the language of the law clerk working on the case. Sankoff recalled that occasionally, if there weren't French sources, she would also choose to draft in English for a more eloquent result.
62 Interview with Michelle Flaherty, Ottawa, 29 October 2014.
63 Interview with Louise Dubé, Boston, 22 May 2012.
64 Some marvelled at L'Heureux-Dubé's English decisions too. Janice Tibbetts, an Anglophone reporter who frequently covered the Supreme Court, thought she was "a beautiful writer," who said things in a "strong, clear, very passionate way." Tibbetts marvelled at her ability to write so well in her second language, and noted that it was a "gift to journalists." Interview with Janice Tibbetts, Ottawa, 11 May 2015.
65 Scassa, "Language of judgment and the Supreme Court of Canada," see note 60 above at 181. Scassa noted that the act said nothing about the authenticity of the two versions, or how conflicts between the two versions might be resolved.
66 Ibid.
67 Ibid. at 178, 181–82.
68 Interview with François Lacasse, Ottawa, 5 August 2014.
69 Ibid.
70 Scassa, "Language of judgment and the Supreme Court of Canada," see note 60 above at 176; interview with François Lacasse, ibid.
71 Interview with François Lacasse, ibid.
72 Interview with Claire L'Heureux-Dubé, Clearwater, FL, 25–27 November 2014. She added: "I would go further – all professionals should be bilingual in Canada and the universities should do what they should have done a long time ago, not to give a diploma until the candidate is bilingual. If they can learn engineering, law, medicine, they surely can learn a language."
73 Fine, "Case puts spotlight on Dubé, Lamer," see note 43 above.
74 Ibid.

75 Interview with Edward Bayda, Regina, 23 October 2009.
76 Email correspondence from Claire L'Heureux-Dubé, 7 July 2014.
77 Interview with André Legault, Ottawa, 10 December 2007.
78 Andrée Lajoie, Cécile Bergada, and Katherine Gauthier, "Claire L'Heureux-Dubé, la Cour suprême et les minorités" (2003) 15:1 CJWL 28 at 39–40.
79 Interview with Claire L'Heureux-Dubé, Ottawa, 30 June 2014.
80 Interview with Claire L'Heureux-Dubé, Clearwater, FL, 10–14 May 2009.
81 Interview with Claire L'Heureux-Dubé, Ottawa, 30 June 2014. The reference to the values of the Catholic Church was interesting, given her anti-religious perspectives. Also interesting was her failure to mention the social science tradition at Laval University, shaped by scholars such as Georges-Henri Lévesque, Fernand Dumont, Léon Dion, and Vincent Lemieux, whose research and teaching sought to "instill a collective sense of purpose for Quebeckers" that inspired the Quiet Revolution and broke with the Church's former isolationism and conservative tendencies. Antonia Maioni, "Vincent Lemieux: first came the Laval school," *Globe and Mail* (23 July 2014) A11.
82 Peter Oliver, "Canada's Two Solitudes: Constitutional and International Law in *Reference re Secession of Quebec*" (1999) 6 International Journal on Minority and Group Rights 65 at 88.
83 Interview with Claire L'Heureux-Dubé, Ottawa, 30 June 2014.
84 Joan Bryden, "Federalist, separatist camps can both claim victory," *Ottawa Citizen* (21 August 1998) A1; Jim Bronskill, "Ruling is prudent, legal scholars say," *Ottawa Citizen* (21 August 1998) C4.
85 Graham Fraser, "Political leaders react cautiously," *Globe and Mail* (21 August 1998) A7; Katia Gagnon, "Bouchard et Chrétien heureux du jugement," *La Presse* (22 August 1998) A1.
86 "Charest dismisses Bouchard's call for another referendum," *Ottawa Citizen* (22 August 1998) B2.
87 Jules Richer, "Une victoire personnelle pour l'avocat Guy Bertrand," *La Presse* (21 August 1998) B-4.
88 John Gray, "Premiers cautious but hopeful that nation can be made to work," *Globe and Mail* (21 August 1998) A6.
89 Gilles Toupin, "Pour les autochtones, une porte ouverte à l'autodétermination," *La Presse* (22 August 1998) B5; Chris Cobb, "Native groups pleased with court ruling," *Ottawa Citizen* (21 August 1998) C5.
90 Monahan, "The Public Policy Role," see note 18 above; Huguette Young, "Le jugement s'annonce plus nuancé que prévu," Ottawa *Le Droit* (20 August 1998) 20; Yves Boisvert, "Les experts réagissent de façon positive," *La Presse* (21 August 1998) B1; Isabelle Ducas, "Chacun y trouve son compte," Ottawa *Le Droit* (21 August 1998) 4. There were a few critics; see, for example, Ted Morton, "A ticket to separate," *Ottawa Citizen* (22 August 1998) B7.
91 Graham Fraser, "The Quebec ruling: Canada must negotiate after Yes vote," *Globe and Mail* (21 August 1998) A1.
92 "White House lauds ruling," *Globe and Mail* (27 August 1998) A6. Federalists and separatists continued to disagree on the interpretation, both eventually enacting legislation to reflect their understanding of the ruling. The federal *Clarity Act,* SC 2000, c. 26, stipulated that before the rest of Canada needed to negotiate, the House of Commons was entitled to decide whether the referendum question was "clear" and whether a "clear majority" had voted in favour of secession. The House of Commons was also to ensure that the views of various political actors in Canada and representatives of the Aboriginal peoples of Canada had been considered, and that "changes to the borders of the province," "minority rights," and the rights of "Aboriginal peoples" were on the negotiating table. Premier Lucien Bouchard's PQ government enacted legislation declaring that the Quebec people had the

"inalienable right to freely decide the political regime and legal status of Quebec" acting "through its own political institutions," and that in any subsequent referendum "50% of the valid votes cast plus one" would suffice. *An Act respecting the exercise of the fundamental rights and prerogatives of the Québec people and the Québec State,* RSQ 2000, c. E-20.2.
93 Monahan, "The Public Policy Role," see note 18 above. The reduced appetite for secession in Quebec continued; Lysiane Gagnon, "A dim future for sovereignty," *Globe and Mail* (26 March 2014) at A13, noted that "two-thirds of Quebeckers, including 20% of those who would vote Yes, do not want a referendum on sovereignty."
94 Bronskill, "Ruling is prudent, legal scholars say," see note 84 above.
95 Nathalie Des Rosiers, "Secession: From Quebec Veto to Quebec Secession: The Evolution of the Supreme Court of Canada on Quebec-Canada Disputes" (2000) 13 Can JL & Jur 171 at 171–83. At the time, Des Rosiers was a law professor at the University of Western Ontario. She would later become dean of law at the University of Ottawa.
96 Interview with Claire L'Heureux-Dubé, Ottawa, 30 June 2014.

Chapter 35: Fairness in Immigration Law

1 The facts are from *Baker v. Canada,* [1995] FCJ No. 1441 (Federal Court of Canada – Trial Division) [hereafter *Baker 1995*]; *Baker v. Canada,* [1996] FCJ No. 1570 (Federal Court of Appeal) [hereafter *Baker 1996*]; *Baker v. Canada,* [1999] 2 SCR 817 [hereafter *Baker*]; the facta submitted by the parties and interveners; interview with Roger Rowe, Toronto, 1 November 2014; Valerie Lawton, "Jamaican woman's deportation halted," *Toronto Star* (10 July 1999); and "Jane-Finch lawyer fights for his community" (Winter 2005) 9:1 Ont. Law. Gaz.
2 The economic instability of Jamaica has been attributed to colonialism, the legacy of slavery, trade inequity, foreign debt, and Cold War political destabilization. George Beckford and Michael Witter, *Small Garden, Bitter Weed: Struggle and Change in Jamaica,* 2nd ed. (London: Zed Press, 1982); Michael Manley, *The Politics of Change: A Jamaican Testament* (Washington, DC: Howard University Press, 1990) at 124.
3 Sharryn J. Aiken, "From Slavery to Expulsion: Racism, Canadian Immigration Law and the Unfulfilled Promise of Modern Constitutionalism" in Vijay Agnew, ed., *Interrogating Race and Racism* (Toronto: University of Toronto Press, 2007) at 63–84; Vijay Agnew, ed., *Racialized Migrant Women in Canada* (Toronto: University of Toronto Press, 2009) at 11–17; Peter S. Li, *Destination Canada: Immigration Debates and Issues* (Don Mills, ON: Oxford University Press, 2003); Sunera Thobani, "Closing Ranks: Racism and Sexism in Canada's Immigration Policy" (2000) 42:1 Race and Class 35; Ninette Kelley, "Non-Citizens and State Sovereignty under the Charter" in David Dyzenhaus, ed., *The Unity of Public Law* (Oxford: Hart, 2004) 253 at 256. Preference was given to northern Europeans until the late-nineteenth and early-twentieth centuries, when men from India, China, and Japan gained entry in limited numbers, but their wives and children were mostly kept out. Blacks and Jews were particularly unwelcome. Some changes occurred after the Second World War, when nationalist movements in Asia and Africa, the horrors of the Nazi regime, and the civil rights movement in the United States made it more difficult to maintain overtly racist policies. But it was not until 1962 that explicit racially discriminatory admissions provisions were eliminated and replaced by criteria that emphasized skills, education, and training. The *Immigration Act* of 1971 opened up immigration still further, but barriers to racialized women remained. Women have less access to money, education, and information, all significant under the selection criteria. Despite the chronic labour shortages of domestic workers in the Canadian economy, domestic service was not listed as an eligible occupation. Audrey Macklin, "Foreign Domestic Worker: Surrogate Housewife or Mail Order Servant? (1992) 37:3 McGill LJ 681, recounted at 734–35 the surge of protest from the African Canadian

community in 1977 regarding the "Case of the Seven Jamaican Women," against the "racist and sexist policy of the government toward domestic workers."
4 Women who were visible minority and foreign-born remained consistently the lowest earners in the Canadian labour market. Monica Boyd and Jessica Yiu, "Immigrant Women and Earnings Inequality in Canada" in Agnew, *Racialized Migrant Women in Canada*, see note 3 above at 208–32; C. James, C. Jansen, and D. Plaza, "Issues of Race in Employment: Experiences of Caribbean Women in Toronto" (Fall 1999) 19:3 Canadian Woman Studies 129.
5 *Baker*, see note 1 above at 825.
6 Ibid. at 825–26.
7 Ibid. at 826.
8 Ibid.
9 Ibid. at 827; interview with Roger Rowe, Toronto, 1 November 2014.
10 Joan French, "Hitting Where It Hurts Most: Jamaican Women's Livelihoods in Crisis" in Pamela Sparr, ed., *Mortgaging Women's Lives: Feminist Critiques of Structural Adjustment* (London: Zed Book, 1994) at 165; Hope Lewis, "Universal Mother: Transnational Migration and the Human Rights of Black Women in the Americas" (2001) 5 J Gender Race & Just 197 at 228.
11 *Baker*, see note 1 above at 826; *Baker 1995*, see note 1 at 6.
12 *Baker*, ibid. at 827–28.
13 *Tylo v. Canada (Minister of Citizenship and Immigration)* (1995), 90 FTR 157, 26 Imm LR (2d) 250, where despite the critique, the rejection of the request for permanent residence was upheld by the Federal Court Trial Division. In *Munir v. Canada (Minister of Citizenship and Immigration)* (1993), 66 FTR 64, 24 Imm LR (2d) 143, Officer Lorenz's recommendation was overturned because he had refused to decide the issue before him. In *Tejani v. Canada (Minister of Citizenship and Immigration)* (1994), FCJ No. 1416, counsel on both sides raised concerns about Officer Lorenz's comments concerning a request for humanitarian and compassionate review.
14 *Marques v. Canada (Minister of Citizenship and Immigration)* (1995), 116 FTR 241, 27 Imm LR (2d) 209. In *Bawuah v. Canada (Minister of Citizenship and Immigration)* (1995), CarswellNat 2249, the Federal Court Trial Division sent the case (a humanitarian and compassionate review that was predicated in part upon the existence of a Canadian-born child) back for reconsideration by another reviewing officer, mentioning that Officer Lorenz's notes were "not supported by material on the file" and that his recommendation was "scanty in view of the facts."
15 Interview with Roger Rowe, Toronto, 1 November 2014.
16 Ibid; interview with Audrey Macklin, Toronto, 7 January 2015; Sharryn Aiken and Sheena Scott, "Baker v. Canada (Minister of Citizenship and Immigration) and the Rights of Children" (2000) 15 J L & Soc Pol'y 211 at 221.
17 Thobani, "Closing Ranks," see note 3 above at 37, noted that the postwar economic boom in Canada was underwritten by the significant labour provided by Third World immigrants. Thobani noted at 45 that population levels in Canada would fall below replacement levels without continued immigration.
18 Lewis, "Universal Mother," see note 10 above at 230; Macklin, "Foreign Domestic Worker," see note 3 above.
19 Simone A. Browne, "Of 'Passport Babies' and 'Border Control': The Case of *Mavis Baker v. Minister of Citizenship and Immigration*" *Atlantis* 26:2 (Spring 2002) 97 at 98, 102, 106.
20 *Baker 1995*, see note 1 above; *Baker 1996*, see note 1 above.
21 Interview with Roger Rowe, Toronto, 1 November 2014. Rowe was also a recipient of the Law Society of Upper Canada's Lincoln Alexander Award, named after Canada's first African Canadian lieutenant-governor. He practised in the low-income, racialized neighbourhood of the Jane-Finch corridor.

22 Interview with Roger Rowe, ibid.; Virginia Galt, "'Excellent' mom faces new fight to stay here," *Globe and Mail* (10 July 1999) A3.
23 *Baker*, see note 1 above. This chapter will not focus upon another significant part of the judgment, which dealt with the standard of judicial review. L'Heureux-Dubé held that the minister had wide discretion when it came to deportation and humanitarian and compassionate grounds, which would incline a court to exercise deference. However, the importance of the interest affected by the decision warranted closer scrutiny. She chose "reasonableness *simpliciter*" as the appropriate judicial standard of review, rather than the more deferential "patent unreasonableness" standard or the least deferential "correctness" standard.
24 RSC 1985, c. I-2., s. 141(2). The section was first enacted in 1976; SC 1976, c. 52, s. 115(2): "The Governor in Council may by regulation exempt any person from any regulation made under subsection (1) or otherwise facilitate the admission of any person where the Governor in Council is satisfied that the person should be exempted from such regulation or his admission should be facilitated for reasons of public policy or due to the existence of compassionate or humanitarian considerations." Macklin, "Foreign Domestic Worker," see note 3 above at 737, noted that although the section "was originally intended to be an exceptional remedy for isolated cases," it became "the standard statutory route to permanent residence for thousands of foreign domestic workers in the absence of a regulation formally exempting domestic workers from the point system method of assessment." She added that the point system drew upon notions of male breadwinners and skills assessment that unfairly disadvantaged women, and domestic workers in particular.
25 Aiken, "From Slavery to Expulsion," see note 3 above at 98–99.
26 Lorne Sossin, "From Neutrality to Compassion: The Place of Civil Service and Legal Norms in the Exercise of Administrative Discretion" (2005) 55 UTLJ 427 at 434.
27 *Baker*, see note 1 above at 837. She noted that she was drawing upon her earlier analysis of the duty of fairness in *Knight v. Indian Head School Division No. 19,* [1990] 1 SCR 653.
28 *Baker*, ibid. at 843.
29 Ibid. at 855.
30 Ibid. at 842–49.
31 Ibid. at 850–51.
32 Ibid. at 858–60.
33 Factum of Respondents, *Baker*, ibid.
34 *Convention on the Rights of the Child,* Can TS 1992, art. 3, as cited in *Baker,* ibid. at 829.
35 Interview with Roger Rowe, Toronto, 1 November 2014.
36 Committee on the Rights of the Child, "Concluding Observations of the Committee on the Rights of the Child: Canada," adopted 9 June 1995, as cited in Daniela Bassan, "The Canadian *Charter* and Public International Law: Redefining the State's Power to Deport Aliens" (1996) 34:3 Osgoode Hall LJ 583 at 622; Aiken and Scott, "Baker v. Canada," see note 16 above at 213.
37 *Baker*, see note 1 above at 860–61.
38 Claire L'Heureux-Dubé, "The Importance of Dialogue: Globalization and the International Impact of the Rehnquist Court" (1998) 34 Tulsa LJ 15 at 16, 24.
39 Interview with Cynthia Westaway, Ottawa, 17 October 2014.
40 Interview with Michelle Flaherty, Ottawa, 29 October 2014. This was confirmed by interview with Anthony Gubbay, Vancouver, 9 July 2015.
41 L'Heureux-Dubé, "The Importance of Dialogue," see note 38 above at 26.
42 Interview with Claire L'Heureux-Dubé, Clearwater, FL, 25–27 November 2014.
43 *Baker,* see note 1 above at 861–63.
44 Ibid. at 864–65.
45 Ibid. at 865–66. Jutta Brunnée and Stephen J. Toope, "A Hesitant Embrace: *Baker* and the Application of International Law by Canadian Courts" in Dyzenhaus, *The Unity of Public*

Law, see note 3 above at 357, critiques this position, and also critiques L'Heureux-Dubé's majority reasoning for being too cautious.
46 Interview with David Wright, Toronto, 7 May 2014.
47 Aiken and Scott, "Baker v. Canada," see note 16 above at 219, 221, 236–37.
48 The African Canadian Legal Clinic's brief to the UN World Conference on Racism (2001) noted that racist anti-immigration sentiment had fuelled the mass expulsion of long-term African Canadian residents from Canada, pointing out that while African Canadians composed only 3 percent of the population of Ontario, approximately 60 percent of the people deported from Ontario since 1995 had been people of African descent. Aiken, "From Slavery to Expulsion," see note 3 above at 106; Roger Rowe, "*Baker* Revisited 2007" (January 2008) 38:3 Journal of Black Studies 338 at 339.
49 Browne, "Of 'Passport Babies' and 'Border Control,'" see note 19 above.
50 Interview with Audrey Macklin, Toronto, 7 January 2015.
51 Interview with Sharryn Aiken, Kingston, 8 January 2015.
52 Interview with Roger Rowe, Toronto, 1 November 2014; Rowe, "*Baker* Revisited," see note 48 above at 339–40.
53 Interview with Roger Rowe, ibid. Jack Major, for the court, refused to grant leave to the interveners who sought to address the problem of racial bias in immigration law, policy, and decision making: Order of Major J., 31 March 1998; Factum of coalition of proposed interveners.
54 Interview with Roger Rowe, ibid.
55 Interview with Claire L'Heureux-Dubé, Clearwater, FL, 25–27 November 2014.
56 Browne, "Of 'Passport Babies' and 'Border Control,'" see note 19 above.
57 Aiken, "From Slavery to Expulsion," see note 3 above at 73; Constance Backhouse, *Colour-Coded: A Legal History of Racism in Canada, 1900–1950* (Toronto: University of Toronto Press, 1999).
58 Interview with Audrey Macklin, Toronto, 7 January 2015.
59 Interview with Sharryn Aiken, Kingston, 8 January 2015.
60 Interview with Audrey Macklin, Toronto, 7 January 2015.
61 Interview with Claire L'Heureux-Dubé, Clearwater, FL, 25–27 November 2014.
62 Ibid.
63 *Report of the Commission of Inquiry Relating to the Department of Manpower and Immigration in Montreal* (Ottawa: Information Canada, January 1976).
64 *The Montreal Gazette Ltd. v. Gerald M. Snyder*, [1983] CA 604.
65 *R. v. S. (R.D.)*, [1997] 3 SCR 484. An African Canadian youth was riding his bicycle when he saw an African Canadian friend being arrested by a white police officer. He stopped to ask his friend if he should call his mother. The officer told the youth that he would be arrested if he spoke again. The youth continued to ask if he should call, the officer arrested him, and later the officer testified that the youth had pushed him and run into his legs with the bicycle. The youth denied this. They were the only two witnesses at the trial: the accused and the police officer. In her ruling in Youth Court, Corinne Sparks acquitted the African Canadian accused, saying, "I believe that probably the situation in this particular case is the case of a young police officer who overreacted. And I do accept the evidence of [R.D.S.] that he was told to shut up or he would be under arrest. This seems to be in keeping with the prevalent attitude of the day." The white Crown attorney launched an appeal based upon a "reasonable apprehension of bias" of the African Canadian trial judge. The majority of the Supreme Court held that the comments did not disclose bias, although their rulings disapproved, in varying levels, of the overtly racialized comments made by the trial judge.
66 Ibid. at 512.
67 Major authored the dissent, which was signed by Lamer and Sopinka. Ibid. at paras. 1–25.
68 Aiken and Scott, "Baker v. Canada," see note 16 above at 241.

69 *National Post* (30 October 1998) A1; *Toronto Sun* (22 February 1999) 15.
70 "Having Children Can't Be the Path to a Passport," Editorial, *Globe and Mail* (12 July 1999) A10.
71 Margaret Wente, "Margaret Wente on Canada's porous immigration system," *Globe and Mail* (13 July 1999) A20. Wente ultimately supported the outcome: "Ms. Baker has been living in Canada for 18 years now. We've spent hundreds of thousands of dollars trying to get rid of her. She has, with tremendous tenacity, resisted. After all this time, I figure, she's ours."
72 Valerie Lawton, "Jamaican woman's deportation halted," *Toronto Star* (10 July 1999) 1.
73 René Provost, "Le juge mondialisé: légitimité judiciaire et droit international au Canada" in Marie-Claire Belleau and François Lacasse, *Claire L'Heureux-Dubé à la Cour suprême du Canada 1987–2002* (Montréal: Wilson et Lafleur, 2004) at 571.
74 Sossin, "From Neutrality to Compassion," see note 26 above at 428.
75 David Dyzenhaus and Evan Fox-Decent, "Rethinking the Process/Substance Distinction: *Baker v. Canada*" (2001) 51 UTLJ 193 at 193–94.
76 Dyzenhaus, *The Unity of Public Law*, see note 3 above at 1.
77 Interview with Audrey Macklin, Toronto, 7 January 2015.
78 *Immigration and Refugee Protection Act,* SC 2001, c. 27, s. 25(1): "The Minister shall, upon request of a foreign national who is inadmissible or who does not meet the requirements of this Act, and may, on the Minister's own initiative, examine the circumstances concerning the foreign national and may grant the foreign national permanent resident status or an exemption from any applicable criteria or obligation of this Act if the Minister is of the opinion that it is justified by humanitarian and compassionate considerations relating to them, taking into account the best interests of a child directly affected, or by public policy considerations."
79 Aiken and Scott, "Baker v. Canada," see note 16 above at 240, 246, 253.
80 Catherine Dauvergne, "How the Charter has Failed Non-Citizens in Canada: Reviewing Thirty Years of Supreme Court of Canada Jurisprudence" (2013) 58:3 McGill LJ 663 at 687, citing an unpublished manuscript by Catherine Dauvergne, "Humanitarianism and Compassion in the Federal Court: An Empirical Review of 500 Judicial Review Decisions."
81 Rowe, "*Baker* Revisited," see note 48 above at 338.
82 Sossin, "From Neutrality to Compassion," see note 26 above at 445.
83 Interview with Roger Rowe, Toronto, 1 November 2014; Charlie Gillis, "Mother in battle over deportation legally a resident," *National Post* (22 December 2001) at A8.

Chapter 36: Epilogue on *Ewanchuk*

1 As quoted in Cristin Schmitz, "Dubé Speaks Out on Ewanchuk Controversy," *Lawyers Weekly* 22:2 (10 May 2002) 3.
2 Shawn Ohler, "Judge reiterates belief that teen wasn't assaulted," *National Post* (27 February 1999) A1. Cristin Schmitz, "Judicial Council Blasts McClung's 'Unacceptable' Comments," *Lawyers Weekly* 19:5 (4 June 1999) 2.
3 *Globe and Mail* (2 March 1999) A4. McClung misspelled "Ewanchuk" as "Ewenchuk" throughout, an error corrected by the *Globe and Mail* in its published version of the judge's text.
4 Margaret Bateman, "Spotlight on Judge McClung," *Globe and Mail* (4 March 1999) A15.
5 Kirk Makin and Graeme Smith, "Gatecrashing the old boys club," *Globe and Mail* (2 May 2002) A8.
6 Interview with Claire L'Heureux-Dubé, Ottawa, 10 March 2010.
7 Louise Langevin, "Hon. L'Heureux-Dubé, Claire: entrevue réalisée avec l'Hon. L'Heureux-Dubé," 26 March 2007 at l'Université Laval, Québec, at 26 (copy on file with the author).
8 This was not reported until the year of her retirement. Makin and Smith, "Gatecrashing the old boys club," see note 5 above.

9   Mimi Liu, "A 'Prophet with Honour': An Examination of the Equality Jurisprudence of Madam Justice Claire L'Heureux-Dubé of the Supreme Court of Canada" (2000) 25 Queen's LJ 417 at 473, referring to an interview on 19 February 1999.
10 Interview with Louise Dubé, Boston, 22 May 2012.
11 Interview with Michel Bastarache, Ottawa, 24 November 2009.
12 Interview with David Wright, Toronto, 7 May 2014.
13 Interview with Andrew Lenz and François Lacasse, Ottawa, 5 August 2014.
14 Interview with Suzanne Labbé, Ottawa, 12 August 2009.
15 Schmitz, "Dubé Speaks Out on *Ewanchuk* Controversy," see note 1 above.
16 Ibid.
17 Makin and Smith, "Gatecrashing the old boys club," see note 5 above.
18 Ibid.
19 Interview with Georges-Henri Dubé, Rimouski, 24 July 2008.
20 Schmitz, "Dubé Speaks Out on *Ewanchuk* Controversy," see note 1 above. Writing in "Making a Difference: The Pursuit of a Compassionate Justice" (1997) 31 UBC L Rev 1 at 7, L'Heureux-Dubé added, "Women judges and adjudicators are finding themselves the targets of unfairly harsh criticism and allegations of bias, particularly – but not exclusively – when they have relied on a new perspective or more inclusive principles." Law clerk David Wright wondered why it was that some of Lamer's comments on issues relating to race – that the Chinese were gamblers, for example – which he articulated in open court during oral arguments, escaped public notoriety almost entirely. Interview with David Wright, Toronto, 7 May 2014.
21 Tonda McCharles, "Public attack on judge sparks calls for censure," *Toronto Star* (27 February 1999) A27. See similar comments from Ontario bencher Carole Curtis in Cristin Schmitz, "Critics Call for Judge's Ouster," *Lawyers Weekly* (12 March 1999) 10, in which she said, "It seems that women judges are fair game in a way that men are not. A male Court of Appeal judge would never say those things about a male Supreme Court of Canada judge. He would never have written the letter. He would never have taken [a male judge's opinion] as a personal thing. He would never have made personal comments. He might have commented on the judgment [but] he would never have reduced it to a personal level."
22 Rick Salutin, "Feminism, humanism and the battle of the judges," *Globe and Mail* (4 March 1999) D1.
23 Shawn Ohler, "Women's group turns tables on L'Heureux-Dubé," *National Post* (4 March 1999).
24 The law clerks who offered this comment asked to remain unidentified.
25 The judges described McClung's behaviour as "unfortunate," "inappropriate," and "totally out of line," but they also believed that L'Heureux-Dubé's decision was "a little inflammatory" and "quite vehement." Interview with Jack Major, Calgary, 13 November 2013; interview with Michel Bastarache, Ottawa, 24 November 2009; interview with Ian Binnie, Ottawa, 6 April 2011.
26 Interview with Claire L'Heureux-Dubé, Ottawa, 10 March 2010.
27 Interview with Frank Iacobucci, Toronto, 26 October 2011.
28 Ibid.
29 Interview with Jack Major, Calgary, 13 November 2013; interview with Ian Binnie, Ottawa, 6 April 2011.
30 Interview with David Wright, Toronto, 7 May 2014.
31 Interview with Louise Dubé, Boston, 22 May 2012.
32 Robert Fife, "MPs split over censuring McClung," *National Post* (27 February 1999) A3, reported that neither the office of Justice L'Heureux-Dubé nor the office of Chief Justice Lamer had any comment to make.
33 The law clerks who offered these comments asked to remain unidentified.

34 Interview with Kirk Makin, Toronto, 9 April 2015.
35 Kirk Makin, "Close ties cloud process of judges judging judges," *Globe and Mail* (8 March 1999) A4.
36 Interview with Melvin Rothman, Montreal, 12 August 2008.
37 As described during the interview with Claire L'Heureux-Dubé, Ottawa, 10 March 2010.
38 Memorandum to Members of the Court from The Chief Justice re "Role of the Chief Justice," 17 March 1999, copy in personal papers of Claire L'Heureux-Dubé, shared with the author.
39 *Globe and Mail* reporter Kirk Makin agreed: "Since he is the chairman of the council that will ultimately decide the fate of both judges, Chief Justice Lamer has been prevented from publicly defending his own colleague." Makin, "Close ties cloud process of judges judging judges," see note 35 above.
40 Celeste McGovern, "No Such Word as 'Yes,'" *Alberta Report* 26:2 (15 March 1999) 29. The Canadian Judicial Council, created in 1971, referred complaints to the chair or vice chair of its Judicial Conduct Committee. If the complaint was considered serious enough to merit further consideration, it was referred to a panel of up to five committee members who could decide whether a public inquiry was needed. The federal minister of justice or attorney general of any province could also request an inquiry, in which case the appointment of an inquiry committee was mandatory. The CJC did not have the power to remove a judge from office, but could recommend such action to Parliament if the judge was considered incapacitated or disabled by age, by infirmity, by misconduct, by failure to execute the office, or by having been placed in a position incompatible with the execution of the office. Carla Yu, "The Judges Prepare for War," *Alberta Report* 26:15 (5 April 1999) 20; Geoffrey Scotton, "Lawyers Seek Standing at a McClung Hearing," *Lawyers Weekly* 18:44 (2 April 1999) 2.
41 Canadian Judicial Council, Council File 98-129, Letter from Jeannine Lebel, National President, to Mr. Justice Antonio Lamer, 31 March 1999; Christin Schmitz, "CJC dismisses bias complaint against Dubé," *Lawyers Weekly* 19:13 (13 August 1999) 3.
42 Janice Tibbetts, "Supreme Court's great dissenter," *National Post* (27 February 1999) A3.
43 Canadian Judicial Council, Council File 98-129, Correspondence from Jeannie Thomas, Canadian Judicial Council, to Jeannine Lebel, REAL Women of Canada, 31 March 1999.
44 The National Association of Women and the Law, the National Council of Women of Canada, the Feminist Legal Analysis Section of the Canadian Bar Association – Ontario, the Metropolitan Action Committee on Public Violence Against Women and Children, and federal NDP leader Alexa McDonough were among the complainants. "Judge apologizes for 'cruel' attack on senior justice," *National Post* (2 March 1999) A1. Canadian Judicial Council, Council File 98-129, 19 May 1999.
45 Scotton, "Lawyers Seek Standing at a McClung Hearing," see note 40 above.
46 Yu, "The Judges Prepare for War," see note 40 above.
47 The panel was composed of Nova Scotia Chief Justice Constance R. Glube, Quebec Chief Justice Pierre Michaud, and Ontario Chief Justice R. Roy McMurtry. The complaint also made allegations of homophobia based upon McClung's decision in *Vriend* v. *Alberta* (1996), 184 AR 351, [1996] AJ No. 643 (CA), rev'd [1998] 1 SCR 493, 156 DLR (4th) 385. The evidence the panel reviewed included the written public apology McClung had tendered to L'Heureux-Dubé and published in the *Globe and Mail* (2 March 1999) A3, along with McClung's separate letter to the CJC insisting that "L'Heureux-Dubé's criticism was unfair and uncarned and diverged from the Commonwealth tradition of impersonal appellate disagreement." Canadian Judicial Council, Council File 98-128, Correspondence from Hon. Chief Justice Constance R. Glube to the Hon. Justice John W. McClung, 19 May 1999; Schmitz, "Judicial Council Blasts McClung's 'Unacceptable' Comments," see note 2 above; Mark Bourrie, "McClung survives judicial council probe; McClung rebuked but not removed," *Law Times* (31 May – 6 June 1999) 1, 4. See also Ed Ratushny, "Speaking

as Judges: How Far Can They Go?" (2000) 11 NJCL 387; Sheila McIntyre, "Personalizing the Political and Politicizing the Personal: Understanding Justice McClung and His Defenders" in Elizabeth Sheehy, ed., *Adding Feminism to Law: The Contributions of Justice Claire L'Heureux-Dubé* (Toronto: Irwin Law, 2004) at 342; Canadian Judicial Council, *Ethical Principles for Judges* (Ottawa: Canadian Judicial Council, 1998) at 24; Richard J. Scott, "Accountability and Independence" (1996) UNBLJ 45 at 27–36.
48 Interview with Cynthia Westaway, Ottawa, 17 October 2014.
49 Cristin Schmitz, "'Activism' Critics Posing Threat to Judicial Independence: Dubé," *Lawyers Weekly* (3 September 1999) 1.
50 Ibid.
51 McGovern, "No Such Word as 'Yes,'" see note 40 above at 28–29.
52 Ibid.
53 Ibid.
54 Joanne Wright, "Consent and Sexual Violence in Canadian Public Discourse: Reflections on *Ewanchuk*" (2001) 16:2 CJLS 173 at 173–74.
55 Ibid. at 199.
56 Ibid. at 183, 201–2.
57 The workshops were led by female and male law students, and were aimed at male and female high school students. They focused on educating young people about their legal rights and responsibilities regarding sexual relations: the law of sexual assault, consent, and sexting. Correspondence from Mayoori Malankov, University of Ottawa law school, 18 April 2016, 6 May 2016; Discussions during the Feminist Legal Issues seminar, University of Ottawa, January 2016.
58 The comment was made by REAL Women's spokesperson, Gwen Landolt, as quoted in McGovern, "No Such Word as 'Yes,'" see note 40 above at 32.
59 Ibid. at 28–29. McGovern noted that she was quoting from Cathy Young's recently published book *Ceasefire! Why Women and Men Must Join Forces to Achieve True Equality* (New York: Free Press, 1999).
60 Interview with Alan D. Gold, Toronto, 5 August 2009.
61 Ibid.
62 Edward L. Greenspan, "Judge Kozinski, I beg to differ," *National Post* (11 March 1999) A18.
63 Interview with Edward Greenspan, Toronto, 1 August 2013.
64 Ibid.
65 Ibid.
66 Ibid.
67 Ibid.
68 Interview with David Paciocco, Ottawa, 11 June 2015.
69 Tibbetts, "Supreme Court's great dissenter," see note 42 above, noted: "Her friends include a roster of feminists, both academic and on the bench, including Rosalie Abella, an Ontario Court of Appeal judge who could be in line for a Supreme Court appointment."
70 Interview with Rosalie Abella, Ottawa, 9 November 2007.
71 Interview with Cynthia Westaway, Ottawa, 17 October 2014.
72 Interview with Teresa Scassa, Ottawa, 16 May 2014.
73 Interview with Michelle Flaherty, Ottawa, 29 October 2014.
74 Interview with David Wright, Toronto, 7 May 2014.
75 Interview with Don Stuart, Kingston, 4 May 2015.
76 Interview with Pierre-Gabriel Jobin, Montreal, 23 April 2010.
77 Interview with Darlene Jamieson, Halifax, 19 February 2009, describing a National Association of Women and the Law conference that she recalled as taking place in 1997.
78 Interview with Joseph Nuss, Montreal, 14 August 2008.
79 Interview with Ian Binnie, Ottawa, 6 April 2011.
80 Interview with Jack Major, Calgary, 13 November 2013.

81 Rosalie Abella, "The Jurisprudence of Claire L'Heureux-Dubé" (Pamphlet of International Commission of Jurists [Canadian Section], *A Tribute* [2002]).
82 Interview with Claire L'Heureux-Dubé, Ottawa, 10 March 2010.
83 Arline Pacht, "Gender Equality: Thoughts on Causes and Cures for Gendered Victimhood" in Marie-Claire Belleau and François Lacasse, *Claire L'Heureux-Dubé à la Cour suprême du Canada 1987–2002* (Montréal: Wilson et Lafleur, 2004) at 418–20.
84 "The Honourable Claire L'Heureux-Dubé – a living legend," *International Association of Women Judges News* (5 May 2012).
85 Interview with Irizel Collazo, San Juan, Puerto Rico, 29 August 2014.
86 Kirk Makin and Graeme Smith, "Gatecrashing the old boys club," *Globe and Mail* (2 May 2002) A8.
87 DVD of the Ontario Bar Association Retirement Dinner, Toronto, 6 May 2002.
88 Makin and Smith, "Gatecrashing the old boys club," see note 5 above.
89 Justice John C. Moore's one-year sentence was not reported. The Alberta Court of Appeal decision to increase the penalty (having credited him with house arrest from June 1994 until October 2000) was reported as *R. v. Ewanchuk*, [2002] AJ No. 516. The Supreme Court's refusal of leave to appeal was reported as *R. v. Ewanchuk*, [2002] SCCA No. 469.
90 The multiple sexual assaults occurred while Ewanchuk was in a "position of trust" with the young girl. "Child, 9, testifies in Ewanchuk sexual assault trial," *Edmonton Journal* (26 October 2005); "Tearful Ewanchuk denies molesting young girl," *Edmonton Journal* (2 November 2005); "Edmonton sexual predator with 35-year history of sex crimes loses latest appeal," *Canadian Press* (31 March 2010).
91 Chris Purdy, "Ewanchuk guilty of sex assault: dangerous offender status sought for molester of girl," *Edmonton Journal* (8 November 2005) B1; "Sex offender fighting prison, cancer," *Edmonton Journal* (23 October 2006), reporting the fifteen-month sentence as taking place in 1986; "No means No sex offender sentenced to prison," *CTV News* (22 February 2007); "Edmonton sexual predator with 35-year history of sex crimes loses latest appeal," ibid.
92 Florence Loyie, "Ewanchuk faces up to ten years," *Edmonton Journal* (27 January 2007) A3; "Top court denies sex predator's appeal," *Edmonton Journal* (1 April 2010) B3; "Edmonton sexual predator with 35-year history of sex crimes loses latest appeal," ibid; Tony Blais, "Sex predator loses appeal," *Toronto Sun* (13 October 2010); "'No means No' sex offender, Steve Ewanchuk, to remain behind bars," *Canadian Press* (31 March 2015). The sentence was actually 16.5 years, but it was reduced to 11 due to time served at the remand centre while in custody. "No statutory release for 'No means No' offender," *Hamilton Spectator* (16 May 2014); "Parole board detains 'No means No' sex offender until end of prison term," *Canadian Press* (17 May 2014).

CHAPTER 37: JUDICIAL EDUCATION AND INTERNATIONAL INFLUENCE

1 Interview with Catherine Fraser, Edmonton, 12 November 2013.
2 Livingston Armytage, *Educating Judges* (Geneva: Kluwer International, 1990); Rosemary Cairns Way, "Contradictory or Complementary? Reconciling Judicial Independence with Judicial Social Context Education" (unpublished manuscript) at 4.
3 Ibid. The Canadian Judicial Council was established by Parliament under the *Judges Act*, RSC 1985, c. J-1 in 1971.
4 Cairns Way, "Contradictory or Complementary?" see note 2 above at 4–5. Skills included case management, judgment writing, and computer use.
5 National Judicial Institute Letters Patent (Canada, Minister of Consumer and Corporate Affairs, 18 April 1988); Cairns Way, ibid. at 5–6.
6 Cairns Way, ibid. at 1–7; Rosemary Cairns Way and T. Brettel Dawson, "Taking a Stand on Equality: Bertha Wilson and the Evolution of Judicial Education in Canada" in Kim

Brooks, ed., *Justice Bertha Wilson: One Woman's Difference* (Vancouver: UBC Press, 2009) at 278–89.
7 Canadian Judicial Council, *Annual Report, 2001–02* (Ottawa: Canadian Judicial Council, 2002), online: Canadian Judicial Council <http://www.cjc-ccm.gc.ca>. The CJC was chaired by the chief justice of the Supreme Court of Canada, and was composed of the chief justices, associate chief justices, and some senior judges from provincial and federal superior courts of the provinces and territories. Complaints to the CJC increased from 22 in 1980–81, to 52 in 1985–86, 98 in 1990–91, and 200 in 1995–96.
8 Ibid.
9 Nova Scotia, *Royal Commission on the Donald Marshall, Jr., Prosecution*, vol. 8, *Digest of Findings and Recommendations* (Halifax: Royal Commission on the Donald Marshall, Jr., Prosecution, 1989) at 26.
10 Canadian Bar Association Task Force, *Touchstones for Change: Equality, Diversity and Accountability: The Report of the Canadian Bar Association Task Force on Gender Equality in the Legal Profession* (Ottawa: Canadian Bar Association, 1993) at 192.
11 The CJC decision was not released in a public document, but was cited in Cairns Way, "Contradictory or Complementary?" see note 2 above at 14.
12 Other leading advocates were University of British Columbia law dean Lynn Smith, Ontario Superior Court judge Katherine Swinton, and then deputy minister of justice Frank Iacobucci. Interview with Brettel Dawson, Ottawa, 16 July 2015; interview with Rosemary Cairns Way, Ottawa, 5 May 2015; interview with Catherine Fraser, Edmonton, 12 November 2013; Lynn Smith, *Statement of Needs and Objectives for Continuing Judicial Education on the Social Context of Judicial Decision-Making* (Ottawa: National Judicial Institute, 1996) at 1; Katherine Swinton, *Report to the National Judicial Institute on Social Context Education for Judges* (Ottawa: National Judicial Institute, 1996). Alberta Chief Justice Catherine Fraser was described by many as one of the most tenacious and effective advocates for social context education at the CJC. Reflecting years later on the respectability that social context education eventually came to hold, Fraser cited Frank Iacobucci's depiction of it as the "jewel in the crown of the NJI," adding, "It took a lot of people a lot of time to put those jewels in that crown ... knock 'em down, drag 'em out every time" (ibid.). Lynn Smith described the objectives of social context judicial education: "'Social context' refers to background factors which may inform judicial decision-making. Examples include the history, culture, economic and social circumstances of aboriginal peoples, the current situation of immigrant and visible minority populations in Canada, and the issue of systemic racism, the changing role of women, their economic and social circumstances and the implications flowing from a commitment to equality between the sexes, and the circumstances and needs of persons with disabilities and the consequences of the requirement that they be accommodated" (ibid.). Cairns Way characterized L'Heureux-Dubé as a vocal proponent of social context education, adding that it was clear that L'Heureux-Dubé believed that judicial education had to go beyond "black letter updates from other judges and appropriately screened professors without political views." However, she observed that L'Heureux-Dubé was "never front and centre" in the NJI work, but remained a "strong voice in the background."
13 Beverley McLachlin attempted to explain the push-back in 1995: "To understand one must evaluate it from the psychological perspective of the judge who is to be educated. Stripped of candy-coating, the proposition that a judge needs to be educated on equality amount[s] in the eyes of some to saying that the judge is deficient, perhaps even biased. That the bias may be subconscious and founded in his upbringing and life experience does little to soften the affront the judge may feel. Moreover, the judge, trained to skepticism, independence and a critical mind, may view those urging the proposition of bias as non-neutral representatives of an interest group – and conclude that it is his duty to assess their message

critically, rather than in a spirit of acceptance. We should not be surprised then that the judge may deny the need for such education, or alternatively, participate in it only superficially, on the basis that while someone else might need this, he or she is O.K." Beverley McLachlin, "Judicial Neutrality and Equality" (Paper delivered at Aspects of Equality: Rendering Justice Conference, Hull, QC, November 1995). From her position as chief justice, McLachlin endorsed social context education explicitly in 2004, when she stated, "Context, policy, and philosophy have always been part of judging. What the Charter has done is to bring this kind of thinking out of the closet ... Judges now openly acknowledge that before they make decisions that affect peoples' lives or government policy, they must have some understanding of the circumstances or context of the problem before us and the implications of deciding one way or another." As quoted in Cairns Way and Dawson, "Taking a Stand on Equality," see note 6 above at 289.

14 Antonio Lamer, "Social Context Education" (1997) 10 National Judicial Institute Bulletin 1 at 6.

15 Antonio Lamer, "The Rule of Law and Judicial Independence: Protecting Core Values in Times of Change" (1996) 45 UNBLJ 15 at 17.

16 He added, "Requiring public officials to attend seminars on violence against women or racism cannot be construed, as many judges seem to do, as a campaign of political correctness. At their best, criticism and education can combine to prod a reluctant judiciary to bring out for scrutiny their basic operating assumptions and to evaluate them in light of the demands of a society that professes to be democratic and egalitarian in its practices and aspirations." Allan C. Hutchinson, "Towards Judicial Accountability – Are the Excuses Getting Lamer?" (1996) 45 UNBLJ 97 at 98–100.

17 Ibid. at 98.

18 Cairns Way and Dawson, "Taking a Stand on Equality," see note 6 above at 289.

19 Ibid. at 286.

20 Cairns Way "Contradictory or Complementary?" see note 2 above at 17. Two of the key controversies were whether non-judges could design and deliver such programs to judges, and whether all judges ought to be required to attend. Proponents of social context education complained that confining workshops solely to judges would only compound the problem of a homogeneous judiciary that was struggling to understand issues of inequity in the first place. Bertha Wilson agreed, "I have never heard judges resist instruction in judgment-writing on the ground that it was delivered by those non-judges especially schooled in the area of the English language"; as quoted in Ellen Anderson, *Judging Bertha Wilson: Law as Large as Life* (Toronto: University of Toronto Press, 2001) at 347. Supporters also argued that seminars that were not mandatory risked preaching only to the converted. As the programs eventually developed, the judges did indeed retain firm control and all attendance remained voluntary, but there slowly emerged recognition of the need for some participation from community groups who could lend their expertise to the planning and delivery (Cairns Way, "Contradictory or Complementary?" at 22).

21 The individual who made this comment preferred to remain anonymous, but added that the negative sentiments slowly diminished after her retirement, as L'Heureux-Dubé came to take on more of an aura of a "senior stateswoman judge."

22 The observer who described this event wished to remain anonymous.

23 Interview with Naina Kapur, by phone from Ottawa, 20 April 2010.

24 Ibid.

25 Ibid.; interview with Claire L'Heureux-Dubé, Clearwater Beach, FL, 25–27 November 2014. L'Heureux-Dubé's curriculum vitae showed that she served as president of the International Commission of Jurists (Canadian Section) from 1981 to 1983, as vice president (International Board) from 1992 to 1998, and as president from 1998 to 2002.

26 Interview with Claire L'Heureux-Dubé, Clearwater Beach, FL, 25–27 November 2014.

27 The programming was organized through the Western Judicial Education Centre, a project of the four western provinces and two territories, directed by Campbell, then a provincial court judge, who was given half-time leave from judicial duties. The programming was delivered almost exclusively to provincial court judges. It focused on equality training and was designed and delivered by judges working with disadvantaged community representatives. Funding came from the federal, provincial, and territorial governments, law societies, law foundations, continuing legal education organizations, and judges' associations. It had drawn attention across Canada and internationally by the time Campbell was appointed to the Federal Court of Canada in 1995. Interview with Doug Campbell, Toronto, 21 April 2015.
28 Cairns Way and Dawson, "Taking a Stand on Equality," see note 6 above at 286.
29 Interview with Naina Kapur, by phone from Ottawa, 20 April 2010.
30 Ibid.; interview with Doug Campbell, Toronto, 21 April 2015; interview with Claire L'Heureux-Dubé, Clearwater Beach, FL, 25–27 November 2014.
31 Interview with Naina Kapur, by phone from Ottawa, 20 April 2010.
32 Interview with Claire L'Heureux-Dubé, Clearwater Beach, FL, 25–27 November 2014.
33 Interview with Naina Kapur, by phone from Ottawa, 20 April 2010; interview with Doug Campbell, Toronto, 21 April 2015; interview with Claire L'Heureux-Dubé, ibid. The funding, from the Ford and other foundations, flowed through Kapur's NGO Sakshi. The Canadian International Development Agency covered the travel expenses of the Canadian participants. The Canadian judges did the consultations as volunteers, using their non-sitting days for the meetings, which were usually held three times a year, with the largest gatherings in January, when all five countries attended.
34 Interview with Naina Kapur, ibid.; interview with Doug Campbell, ibid.; interview with Claire L'Heureux-Dubé, ibid. Brettel Dawson, academic director at the NJI, praised the resource kit – a "red box on sexual assault" – that was developed as part of this programming. "It asked judges to answer the question 'If your daughter was raped, would you report it?' and then unpacked the responses to determine why so many answered 'no.'" Interview with Brettel Dawson, Ottawa, 16 July 2015.
35 Interview with Claire L'Heureux-Dubé, ibid.
36 Interview with Doug Campbell, Toronto, 21 April 2015.
37 Interview with Naina Kapur, by phone from Ottawa, 20 April 2010.
38 Interview with Catherine Fraser, Edmonton, 12 November 2013.
39 Ibid.
40 Interview with Doug Campbell, Toronto, 21 April 2015.
41 Ibid.
42 As quoted in Aparna Karthikeyan, "Beyond the courtroom," *Bangalore Chennai Delhi Hyderabad Kochi Thiruvananthapuram* (31 January 2013) (copy on file with author).
43 Interview with Shiranee Tilakawardane, London, UK, 3 May 2012. In correspondence to L'Heureux-Dubé from Sri Lanka on 21 October 2007, Tilakawardane wrote: "In our part of the world, [we] see human contact at its worst. People like you give us back hope and belief in humanity."
44 Interview with Jessica Neuwirth, New York City, 16 October 2008.
45 Correspondence from Baroness Helena Kennedy, QC, 1 August 2015.
46 Interview with Brettel Dawson, Ottawa, 16 July 2015.
47 Interview with Reem Bahdi, London, ON, 2 May 2015.
48 Mimi Liu, "A 'Prophet with Honour': An Examination of the Equality Jurisprudence of Madam Justice Claire L'Heureux-Dubé of the Supreme Court of Canada" (2000) 25:2 Queen's LJ 417 at 437.
49 Interview with Reem Bahdi, London, ON, 2 May 2015.
50 Ibid.

51 Interview with Doug Campbell, Toronto, 21 April 2015; interview with Brettel Dawson, Ottawa, 16 July 2015.
52 Interview with Catherine Fraser, Edmonton, 12 November 2013; interview with Claire L'Heureux-Dubé, Clearwater Beach, FL, 25–27 November 2014.
53 Interview with Claire L'Heureux-Dubé, ibid.
54 Arline Pacht, "Gender Equality: Thoughts on Causes and Cures for Gendered Victimhood" in Marie-Claire Belleau and François Lacasse, eds., *Claire L'Heureux-Dubé à la Cour suprême du Canada 1987–2002* (Montréal: Wilson et Lafleur, 2004) at 411.
55 http://www.iawj.org; "International Association of Women Judges" pamphlet indicated the IAWJ was founded in 1991.
56 Interview with Arline Pacht, London, UK, 3 May 2012.
57 Interview with Claire L'Heureux-Dubé, Clearwater Beach, FL, 25–27 November 2014.
58 "The Honourable Claire L'Heureux-Dubé – a living legend" *IAWJ News* (5 May 2012).
59 Catherine Fraser, "The Unfinished Journey – the Pursuit of Equality and Law Reform: A Global View" (introductory remarks for Claire L'Heureux-Dubé, Toronto, 6 May 2002).
60 Liu, "A 'Prophet with Honour,'" see note 48 above at 421.
61 Interview with Claire L'Heureux-Dubé, Quebec City, 4–5 July 2013.
62 Ibid.; "A Tribute by the International Commission of Jurists (Canadian Section)" pamphlet in honour of L'Heureux-Dubé, 2002. Hugh Verrier, senior partner at the New York law firm of White and Case, recalled how L'Heureux-Dubé connected his firm with a human rights activist in Russia who was attempting to intercede on behalf of a man held in a Russian prison without charge for years. Due to the *pro bono* work of Verrier's firm, the prisoner was released and the wider context that permitted the incarceration came under examination. Verrier noted: "She was amazing at the opening of this, and just moved effortlessly to put people in touch with each other to insist that something be done." Interview with Hugh Verrier, New York City, 18 October 2008.
63 Interview with Claire L'Heureux-Dubé, Clearwater Beach, FL, 25–27 November 2014. The congress was held in 1990.
64 Interview with Paul-André Crépeau, Montreal, 1 October 2010.
65 Fraser, "The Unfinished Journey," see note 59 above; List of International Activities prepared by L'Heureux-Dubé, 2014 (held by author).
66 Interview with Adam Dodek, Ottawa, 30 May 2014.
67 Interview with Teresa Doherty, London, UK, 3 May 2012.
68 Interview with Anthony Gubbay, Vancouver, 9 July 2015.
69 Correspondence from Justice Gillian Lucky to L'Heureux-Dubé, 22 November 2016.
70 Correspondence from Michael Kirby, Sydney, 13 July 2015.
71 As noted in Manon Cornellier, "Dissidente supreme," *L'Actualité* (1 October 1999) 68, 71.
72 For a discussion of the Canadian tradition of professing "racelessness," see Constance Backhouse, *Colour-Coded: A Legal History of Racism in Canada, 1900–1950* (Toronto: University of Toronto Press, 1999).
73 Interview with Louise Arbour, Saint-Faustin Lac-Carré, QC, 24 July 2014.
74 Although the initial calls for social context judicial education had focused on race, Indigeneity, and gender, Catherine Fraser noted that the international programs she delivered with L'Heureux-Dubé were "largely on gender issues in various areas ... family law, criminal law, civil law." Interview with Catherine Fraser, Edmonton, 12 November 2013.
75 Interview with Naina Kapur, by phone from Ottawa, 20 April 2010.
76 Interview with Reem Bahdi, London, ON, 2 May 2015.
77 Doug Campbell described a side trip the two of them made to the Taj Mahal, with the return trip by coach, relegated to a small bench in a tightly packed train compartment for four and a half hours. "I had never been in a crowd like that in my life," he said. "There were hundreds and hundreds of people waiting for a train on a platform. Claire said, 'Okay

fine,' we made our way to the door, I saw benches with sleeping lofts above. She said, 'Sit down,' and we slipped in while everybody else loaded on behind." Interview with Doug Campbell, Toronto, 21 April 2015.

78 Kapur described nervous organizers who went to meet L'Heureux-Dubé at the airport in advance of one of the early meetings. They were horrified to discover the name card they brought was missing the accent in Dubé. They wondered if they had picked up the wrong person when L'Heureux-Dubé swept by exclaiming, "Call me Claire." Kapur also recalled an incident when L'Heureux-Dubé asked the taxi driver to take her to his home in a crowded neighbourhood in old Delhi, "She stayed in his house with his family and got to know them," Kapur recalled, adding, "Nobody does this!" Interview with Naina Kapur, by phone from Ottawa, 20 April 2010.
79 Ibid.
80 Interview with Doug Campbell, Toronto, 21 April 2015.
81 Interview with Catherine Fraser, Edmonton, 12 November 2013.
82 Ibid.
83 Interview with Reem Bahdi, London, ON, 2 May 2015.
84 Ibid.

Chapter 38: Retirement

1 Interview with Louise Mailhot, Gananoque, ON, 20 May 2009.
2 Sean Fine, "The Most Important Woman in Canada," *Saturday Night* (December 1995) 46.
3 Kirk Makin, "Judicial rivalry a legend unto itself," *Globe and Mail* (2 May 2002) A8; Transcript of interview between Kirk Makin and Antonio Lamer, 2002; I am indebted to Kirk Makin for sharing this with me.
4 Philip Slayton, *Mighty Judgment: How the Supreme Court of Canada Runs Your Life* (Toronto: Penguin, 2012) at 85.
5 L'Heureux-Dubé's recollection was that the RCMP officers brought their concerns to her as the senior puisne judge. She then advised her colleagues, but they were aware of the problem already. Interview with Claire L'Heureux-Dubé, Clearwater Beach, FL, 25–27 November 2014.
6 Ibid.
7 Cristin Schmitz, "Supreme Court's Judges Confronted Top Judge in 1999," *Lawyers Weekly* (29 April 2011).
8 Ibid.
9 Ibid.
10 The confrontation was chronicled in Slayton, *Mighty Judgment,* see note 4 above at 85.
11 Interview with Claire L'Heureux-Dubé, Clearwater, FL, 25–27 November 2014.
12 Kirk Makin and Renata D'Aliesio, "Chronicle of a lion in winter," *Globe and Mail* (7 May 2011) A4–A5, reported that Major, Cory, and Gonthier were chosen because they "had nothing to gain by speaking to the chief" because "not one of them was looking for his job."
13 Interview with Claire L'Heureux-Dubé, Clearwater, FL, 25–27 November 2014.
14 Ibid.
15 These were the words the newly appointed chief justice, Beverley McLachlin, later borrowed, with attribution, to complete her foreword in the volume of essays honouring Lamer. Right Hon. Beverley McLachlin, PC, "Foreword" in Adam Dodek and Daniel Jutras, eds., *The Sacred Fire: The Legacy of Antonio Lamer (Chief Justice of Canada)* (Markham, ON: LexisNexis, 2009) at vii.
16 She advised the federal minister of justice of her retirement on 1 May 2002: Kirk Makin, "Gatecrashing the old boys club," *Globe and Mail* (2 May 2001) A8.
17 Interview with Louise Dubé, Boston, 22 May 2012.

18 Ibid.
19 Janice Tibbetts, "'Great dissenter' to leave top court," *Ottawa Citizen* (5 September 2001) A5; Janice Tibbetts, "Farewell Claire," *Canadian Lawyer* (September 2002) 39.
20 Luiza Chwialkowska, "Retiring judge tough on crime but 'progressive,'" *National Post* (2 July 2002) A6.
21 Ibid.
22 "Supreme Court justice L'Heureux-Dubé retires," CBC (28 June 2002), online: <http://www.cbc.ca/canada/story/2002/06/28/dube020628.html>.
23 Cristin Schmitz, "Leaving after 15 Years on Bench, Justice L'Heureux-Dubé Says She's 'Extremely Serene,'" *Lawyers Weekly* 22:2 (10 May 2002).
24 Interview with Sean Fine, Toronto, 8 April 2015.
25 Interview with Ian Binnie, Ottawa, 6 April 2011.
26 "Remarks of the Right Honourable Beverley McLachlin, P.C. at the Retirement Ceremony of the Honourable Claire L'Heureux-Dubé," 10 June 2002.
27 Jacques Philippon, "Allocution prononcé par ..." in Marie-Claire Belleau and François Lacasse, *Claire L'Heureux-Dubé à la Cour suprême du Canada 1987–2002* (Montréal: Wilson et Lafleur, 2004) at 17.
28 "Introduction" in Elizabeth Sheehy, ed., *Adding Feminism to Law: The Contributions of Justice Claire L'Heureux-Dubé* (Ottawa: Irwin, 2004) at 6. The papers were published in Sheehy's volume as well as a special issue of the *Canadian Journal of Women and the Law* (2003, 15:1).
29 The event occurred on 25 September 2002. The $170,000 fund, consisting of donations from judges, law professors, lawyers, and other supporters, was used to promote equality activities between 2002 and 2010. Projects included a book publication subvention; a summer institute on feminism, media, and the law in Chaffey's Locks, ON, in 2004; a summer camp on Indigenous women's issues in Nunavik in 2005; a travel grant for students from Rimouski to participate in Carrefour international bas-laurentien pour l'engagement social in 2006; a summer writing institute for Indigenous women in Saskatchewan in 2007, a summer institute for pan-Canadian young feminists in Montreal in 2008, and a social justice summer fellowship in 2010. Final Report, The Claire L'Heureux-Dubé Fund for Social Justice, University of Ottawa Faculty of Common Law, July 2010.
30 Bonnie Diamond, "Hats Off to Claire L'Heureux-Dubé," *Jurisfemme* 21(2) (Summer 2002) at 16.
31 The clerks were François Lacasse and Marie-Claire Belleau, the conference was held in 2003, and many of the papers were published in Belleau and Lacasse, *Claire L'Heureux-Dubé à la Cour suprême du Canada*, see note 27 above. Interview with Otto Lang, Winnipeg, 4 September 2009.
32 *1987–2002: Un hommage rendu par la Commission internationale de juristes (Section canadienne)*.
33 Kevin Bourassa and Joe Varnell, "A Tribute to Madame Justice L'Heureux-Dubé," 6 May 2002, online: Equal Marriage for Same-Sex Couples <http://www.samesexmarriage.ca/advocacy/dube.htm>.
34 Interview with Louise Arbour, Saint-Faustin Lac-Carré, QC, 24 July 2014.
35 DVD of the Ontario Bar Association Retirement Dinner, Toronto, 6 May 2002. Comments sent via video from Justice Edwin Cameron of South Africa did not arrive in time for presentation.
36 On the crowd of revellers and small group of protesters, see Bourassa and Varnell, "A Tribute to Madame Justice L'Heureux-Dubé," see note 33 above.
37 Rosalie Silberman Abella, "Tribute to Justice Claire L'Heureux-Dubé, Faculty of Law, University of Ottawa, 25 September 2002." In her remarks at the Toronto dinner, Beverley McLachlin also roasted L'Heureux-Dubé for her transparent reactions during judicial conferences: "She would listen to one of her fellow judges expound views, according to

her facial expression, with mounting disbelief. If she agrees, she turns her hearing aid up – 'Wait a minute, I want to hear this.'" DVD of the Ontario Bar Association Retirement Dinner, Toronto, 6 May 2002.
38 DVD of the Ontario Bar Association Retirement Dinner, ibid.
39 "A Tribute to Madame Justice L'Heureux-Dubé," see note 33 above; DVD of the Ontario Bar Association Retirement Dinner, ibid.
40 The description is from personal observation. Several anecdotes also illustrate this well. Driving from Quebec to Ottawa in the fall of 2010, L'Heureux-Dubé "ran into a truck." She left the banged-up car in the driveway of the friend with whom she was staying, attaching a note to suggest that it should be checked to see if it could be "fixed" or, alternatively, that the repair person should order her a new car. "The other side was already bad," she added, "so we are settling both sides at the same time. It's a blessing in disguise. It will be back to me at the end of the week and it saves the parking!" Interview with Claire L'Heureux-Dubé, Ottawa, 13 September 2010. At the Toronto dinner, Beverley McLachlin described being driven by L'Heureux-Dubé to a luncheon that Chief Justice Dickson was giving on his farm. "We got lost three times," McLachlin said, "neither of us being very good on directions, but we still got there half an hour early." DVD of the Ontario Bar Association Retirement Dinner, ibid.
41 Interview with Claire L'Heureux-Dubé, Quebec City, 29–30 April 2008.
42 Interview with Claire L'Heureux-Dubé, Clearwater, FL, 25–27 November 2014.
43 Ibid. There are various versions of this story, some quite embellished: Interview with André Legault, Ottawa, 10 December 2007; interview with Jack Major, Calgary, 13 November 2013, where he noted, "She tells that story herself!"
44 The full statement was, "I also want to take the opportunity presented by this special occasion to thank former Chief Justice Lamer for his patience with my many dissents and to wish him well." "Remarks of the Honourable Claire L'Heureux-Dubé on the Ceremony to Mark Her Retirement" (10 June 2002). The remarks astonished her sister Louise, who was well aware of the antipathy between the two judges, but it was also her observation that the sentiment was heartfelt. Interview with Louise L'Heureux-Giliberti, Chicago, 21 April 2009. On Lamer's presence on the front bench, see Janice Tibbetts, "Supreme Court peers praise retiring 'great dissenter,'" *National Post* (11 June 2002) A9.
45 DVD of Retirement Ceremony.
46 "Remarks of the Honourable Claire L'Heureux-Dubé," see note 44 above.
47 Bard experienced a period of dementia after his retirement from the Montreal Superior Court; he died in January 2002. Interview with Perry Bard, Montreal, 23 August 2010.
48 "Remarks of the Right Honourable Beverley McLachlin," see note 26 above.
49 The Right Honourable Chief Justice Beverley McLachlin, PC, "Foreword" in Sheehy, *Adding Feminism to Law,* see note 28 above at 1.
50 "Remarks of the Right Honourable Beverley McLachlin," see note 26 above.
51 Here she referenced the Supreme Court decision on sexual harassment in *Janzen v. Platy Enterprises Ltd.,* where Dickson quoted Catharine MacKinnon.
52 "Remarks of the Honourable Claire L'Heureux-Dubé," see note 44 above.
53 Ibid., citing *Murdoch, Rathwell, Action Travail des Femmes, Brooks, Janzen, Sorochan, Pettkus v. Becker, Lavallee,* and *Peter v. Beblow.*
54 Schmitz, "Leaving after 15 Years on Bench," see note 23 above.
55 DVD of Retirement Ceremony.
56 Sue Bailey, "Supreme Court pays tribute to colourful, contentious judge," *Globe and Mail* (11 June 2002) A8.
57 "La juge Claire L'Heureux-Dubé tient son petit-fils Simon Harris dans ses bras durant l'hommage," *La Presse* (11 June 2002) A9.
58 Cristin Schmitz, "Claire L'Heureux-Dubé on Life after the Supreme Court," *Lawyers Weekly* 25:1 (6 May 2005).

59 Amna Qureshi, "Retired Supreme Court Justice wrong to endorse Quebec values charter," *Toronto Star* (28 September 2013).
60 Interview with Claire L'Heureux-Dubé, London, UK, 3 May 2012.
61 Claude Vaillancourt, "Trois premières récipiendaires du prix Claire-L'Heureux-Dubé," Québec *Le Soleil* (12 March 2004).
62 Companion of the Order of Canada, Grande officiére de l'Ordre national du Québec, Prix les assises – Touchstone – and Prix de l'alliée de la COIS (Canadian Bar Association), Prix Femme de Mérite (Fondation Y des femmes). She had already received honorary doctorates from Dalhousie, University of Montreal, Laval, University of Ottawa, Université du Québec à Rimouski, University of Toronto, Gonzaga University (WA), University of Windsor, York, and Concordia. Two additional ones were added after retirement: the Law Society of Upper Canada and the University of Victoria. Correspondence from L'Heureux-Dubé, 1 July 2010, and "List of Honours" file kept by L'Heureux-Dubé.
63 Claude Vaillancourt, "La juge L'Heureux-Dubé dans l'arène," Québec *Le Soleil* (28 August 2003) A13. The position of "counsel" was described as "typically awarded to senior lawyers who are not partners of a firm, but act as advisers to other lawyers, work on client matters, and help attract new business through their contacts." Janet McFarland, "Former OSC head to counsel Toronto law firm," *Globe and Mail* (5 April 2016).
64 Schmitz, "Claire L'Heureux-Dubé on Life after the Supreme Court," see note 58 above; interviews with Claire L'Heureux-Dubé, Ottawa, 30 June 2010, and Clearwater, FL, 25–27 November 2014; email correspondence from L'Heureux-Dubé, 13 April 2014 and 22 August 2010.
65 Rhéal Séguin, "Overworked Quebec politicians deserve salary increase, committee report says," *Globe and Mail* (30 November 2013) A15.
66 Hugo de Grandpré, "Les documents sur la torture de détenus afghans seront étudiés," *La Presse* (15 July 2010) A11; Colin Freeze and Daniel LeBlanc, "Vetting of Afghan-detainee files left unfinished, panel says," *Globe and Mail* (24 June 2011) A4; interview with Claire L'Heureux-Dubé, Ottawa, 30 June 2010.
67 Interviews with Claire L'Heureux-Dubé, ibid. and Clearwater, FL, 25–27 November 2014.
68 Interview with Claire L'Heureux-Dubé, ibid.
69 Interview with Claire L'Heureux-Dubé, London, UK, 3 May 2012; Schmitz, "Claire L'Heureux-Dubé on Life after the Supreme Court," see note 58 above.
70 Interviews with Claire L'Heureux-Dubé, Ottawa, 30 June 2010, and Clearwater, FL, 25–27 November 2014.
71 Interview with Louise Dubé, Boston, 22 May 2012.
72 Hélène Buzzetti, "La Cour suprême s'est trompée," *Le Devoir* (9 November 2007) A3.
73 Ingrid Peritz, "Ex-Supreme Court justice said to be a Quebec charter backer," *Globe and Mail* (23 September 2013).
74 Ibid.
75 Ibid; Julie Latour, "Equality, democracy and religion: revisiting the secularism charter," *The Common Room: CBA Women Lawyers' Forum Newsletter* (September 2014).
76 Allan Woods, "Ex-Supreme Court judge expected to back Quebec values charter," *Toronto Star* (23 September 2013).
77 Peritz "Ex-Supreme Court justice said to be a Quebec charter backer," see note 73 above.
78 Woods, "Ex-Supreme Court judge expected to back Quebec values charter," see note 76 above.
79 Correspondence from Claire L'Heureux-Dubé to Constance Backhouse, 5 August 2016.
80 Interview with Claire L'Heureux-Dubé, Quebec City, 14 July 2016.
81 Constance Backhouse, *Colour-Coded: A Legal History of Racism in Canada 1900–1950* (Toronto: University of Toronto Press, 1999); R. Bruce Shepard, *Deemed Unsuitable* (Toronto: Umbrella Press, 1997); "Anti-Semitism and the Law in Québec City: The Plamondon Case, 1910–15" in Daniel W. Hamilton and Alfred L. Brophy, eds.,

Transformations in American Legal History – Law, Ideology, and Methods; Essays in Honor of Morton J. Horwitz (Cambridge, MA: Harvard Law School, 2010) at 303–25; Alan Davies, ed., *Antisemitism in Canada: History and Interpretation* (Waterloo: Wilfrid Laurier University Press, 1992); Pierre Anctil and Gary Caldwell, *Juifs et réalités juives au Québec* (Québec: Institut québécois de recherche sur la culture, 1984); Morton Weinfeld, "The Jews of Quebec: Perceived Antisemitism, Segregation, and Emigration" (1980) 22:1 Jewish Journal of Sociology 5; Harold Troper, *The Defining Decade: Identity, Politics, and the Canadian Jewish Community in the 1960s* (Toronto: University of Toronto Press, 2010) at 9–10.
82 Interview with Louise L'Heureux-Giliberti, Chicago, 21 April 2009.
83 Bill 60, National Assembly of Quebec, "Charter affirming the values of State secularism and of religious neutrality and of equality between men and women, and providing a framework for accommodation requests" (2013) [hereafter Bill 60].
84 Don Macpherson, "The ex-judge and the veil," *Montreal Gazette* (24 September 2013), online: *Montreal Gazette* <http://blogs.montrealgazette.com/2013/09/24/the-ex-judge-and-the-veil/>; Canadian Press, "Ex-justices weigh in on Quebec charter," *National Post* (8 February 2014) A10; Fannie Olivier and Lia Levesque, "Denis Lebel, Harper's Top Quebec Minister, Not Upset about Values Charter," 24 September 2013, online: Huffington Post <http://www.huffingtonpost.ca/2013/09/24/quebec-values-charter-supreme-court-judge-n-3983466.html>; Les Perreaux, "Rights body, PQ butt heads," *Globe and Mail* (18 October 2013) A7.
85 Bill 60, see note 83 above.
86 Macpherson, "The ex-judge and the veil," see note 84 above; Canadian Press, "Ex-justices weigh in on Quebec charter," see note 84 above; Sue Montgomery, "PQ's minority candidates cheered charter," *Montreal Gazette* (8 April 2014) B5; Olivier and Levesque, "Denis Lebel, Harper's Top Quebec Minister," see note 84 above; Les Perreaux, "Identity politics fail to sway voters," *Globe and Mail* (5 April 2014) A3. Presumably if hijabs (scarves that covered women's hair) were prohibited, the proposed law would also have prohibited the cloaks that covered more: chadors (garments that drape down from the hair to a woman's feet), niqabs (cloaks covering face, mouth, and nose but not the eyes), and burqas (covering the entire face and bodies, leaving only a mesh screen to see out).
87 Perreaux, "Rights body, PQ butt heads," see note 84 above.
88 Sean Fine, "Ex-Supreme Court judge backs charter," *Globe and Mail* (14 February 2014) A4. L'Heureux-Dubé was critical of the Quebec Bar for taking such a position without a full consultation of its membership. Background correspondence from Claire L'Heureux-Dubé to *Le Devoir*, copy of email, 29 January 2014, in possession of Claire L'Heureux-Dubé.
89 Interview with Claire L'Heureux-Dubé, Clearwater, FL, 25–27 November 2014.
90 Perreaux, "Rights body, PQ butt heads," see note 84 above. L'Heureux-Dubé was critical of the commission, and suggested that its position did not take account of the more nuanced court rulings regarding fundamental liberties. Background correspondence from Claire L'Heureux-Dubé to *Le Devoir*, copy of email, 29 January 2014, in possession of Claire L'Heureux-Dubé.
91 His comments followed reports of incidents in August and September 2013, reported in *Le Soleil* and the *Huffington Post Quebec*; Graeme Hamilton, "PQ to public: Help us 'improve' charter," *National Post* (18 September 2013) A1; Ingrid Peritz, "Anti-Islam vandalism stokes concerns," *Globe and Mail* (22 February 2014) A6; Perreaux, "Identity politics fail to sway voters," see note 86 above.
92 Canadian Press, "Retired Supreme Court judge Claire L'Heureux-Dubé adds her support to Quebec values charter," *National Post* (24 September 2013), online: *National Post* <http://news.nationalpost.com/2013/09/24/parti-quebecois-religion-plan-gets-support-from-retired-supreme-court-judge/>; Hamilton, ibid.

93 Fine, "Ex-Supreme Court judge backs charter," see note 88 above.
94 Kevin Dougherty, "Maltais denies stacking council with supporters," *Montreal Gazette* (21 September 2013) A4.
95 Canadian Press "Retired Supreme Court judge Claire L'Heureux-Dubé adds her support to Quebec values charter," see note 92 above; Hamilton, "PQ to public," see note 91 above; Ayesha Chaudhry, "Don't politicize women's bodies," *Globe and Mail* (5 August 2014) A11; Emmett Macfarlane, "Secular charter case shows Supreme Court judges can be ideological – and wrong," *Globe and Mail* (1 October 2013); Haroon Siddiqui, "Quebec charter's authoritarian streak: Siddiqui," *Toronto Star* (28 September 2013); Fine, "Ex-Supreme Court judge backs charter," see note 88 above.
96 Latour, "Equality, democracy and religion," see note 75 above.
97 Ibid.
98 Andrée Lévesque, "Opposition à la Charte des valeurs québécoises proposée par le gouvernement du PQ" (September 2013) (copy on file with the author).
99 Ibid. On the banning of the burqa as well as the niqab in Belgium and Switzerland, see Chaudhry, "Don't politicize women's bodies," see note 95 above, who argued that "neither forced veiling nor deveiling actually serves the interests of women."
100 Peritz, "Ex-Supreme Court justice said to be a Quebec charter backer," see note 73 above.
101 Petition, "La Laïcité: un principe rassembleur une charte de la laïcité serait une avancée historique pour le Québec." The law professor signatories were Henri Brun, Maurice Arbour, Guy Tremblay, and Guillaume Rousseau. The lawyer signatories were Julie Latour, André Binette, François Côté, Denis Langlais, Éric Poirier, André Joli-Coeur, Marie-Laure Leclercq. The other retired judge was Huguette St-Louis, chief judge of the Court of Québec.
102 Siddiqui, "Quebec charter's authoritarian streak," see note 95 above.
103 Macpherson, "The ex-judge and the veil," see note 84 above.
104 Interview with Sean Fine, Toronto, 8 April 2015.
105 Amna Qureshi, "Retired Supreme Court justice wrong to endorse Quebec values charter," *Toronto Star* (28 September 2013).
106 Critics of L'Heureux-Dubé's position on the Quebec Charter included Michelle Flaherty, who admitted that there was "no way to talk about her position on the hijab that doesn't take away from the accomplishments that she's otherwise had." Peter Sankoff compared it to "taking a sledgehammer" to the complicated issue. Laurie Sargent explained L'Heureux-Dubé's position on the Quebec Charter as related in large part to "gender equality issues," but added, "Some of her mistakes are rooted in her deepest flaws." Interview with Michelle Flaherty, Ottawa, 29 October 2014; interview with Peter Sankoff, Ottawa, 27 June 2014; interview with Laurie Sargent, Ottawa, 26 September 2014.
107 Mémoire présenté à la Commission des institutions, Assemblée nationale du Québec, Projet de loi n. 60, par Les Juristes pour la laïcité et la neutralité religieuse de l'État, 18 décembre 2013 (copy on file with the author).
108 They were followed by other Charter proponents representing a public-sector union, an educational association, a historical society, student activist leaders, and former politicians. Hamilton, "PQ to public," see note 91 above. Chris Selley, "Pauline Marois' union dupes," National Post (13 September 2013) A10; Kevin Doughherty, "Maltais denies stacking council with supporters," Montreal Gazette (21 September 2013) A4; Hugo Prévost, "Les Janettes manifestent au centre-ville de Montréal," *Sherbrooke Tribune* (28 October 2013) 7; Graeme Hamilton, "Charter hearing invites circus," National Post (10 January 2014) A1; Graeme Hamilton, "Cue the Quebec charter experts," National Post (15 January 2014) A1; Paul Journet, "Un ex-chef du Bloc appuie la Charte," La Presse (17 January 2014).
109 Mémoire présenté à la Commission des institutions, see note 107 above at 1–2.
110 Fine, "Ex-Supreme Court judge backs charter," see note 88 above; Tu Thanh Ha, "Former judges split on Quebec charter," *Globe and Mail* (8 February 2014) A9; Speaking Notes of

Claire L'Heureux-Dubé, "Projet de loi sur la laïcité" (February 2014), copy on file with author.
111 Marco Bélair-Cirino, "Un grand pas vers l'égalité homme-femme," *Le Devoir* (1 February 2014); Speaking Notes of Claire L'Heureux-Dubé, ibid.
112 Mémoire présenté à la Commission des institutions, see note 107 above at 7–8.
113 Bélair-Cirino, "Un grand pas vers l'égalité homme-femme," see note 111 above; Speaking Notes of Claire L'Heureux-Dubé, see note 110 above.
114 Fine, "Ex-Supreme Court judge backs charter," see note 88 above.
115 Ibid.
116 Interview with Claire L'Heureux-Dubé, Clearwater, FL, 25–27 November 2014.
117 Interview with Louise Arbour, Saint-Faustin Lac-Carré, QC, 24 July 2014.
118 Ibid.
119 Louise Arbour, "Quebec risks losing its mind," *Globe and Mail* (12 February 2014) A13; Louise Arbour, "Le chant des sirènes," *La Presse* (7 February 2014).
120 Tu Thanh Ha, "Former Supreme Court justices offer conflicting views of Quebec's secular charter," *Globe and Mail* (7 February 2014).
121 Daniel Leblanc, "Liberals vow their charter will be based on 'consensus,'" *Globe and Mail* (9 April 2014) A7.
122 Bill 62, An Act to foster adherence to State religious neutrality and, in particular, to provide a framework for religious accommodation requests in certain bodies, was introduced to the Quebec National Assembly on 10 June 2016, by Minister of Justice Stéphanie Vallée. The bill was designed to bar public servants from wearing face-covering religious garb at work, and to prevent members of the public from covering their faces while receiving government services. The bill would permit accommodation under certain circumstances, but not to the detraction of security or identification. On 15 November 2016, the bill was passed in principle and sent to committee for clause-by-clause consideration. Parliamentary proceedings, online: <http://www.assnat.qc.ca/en/travaux-parlementaires/projets-loi/projet-loi-62-41-1.html>.
123 Ingrid Peritz, "Religious-headgear debate returns to Quebec with Bill 62," *Globe and Mail* (8 February 2017) A5; Nadia El-Mabrouk, "La laïcité, assise de la cohésion sociale," *La Presse* (18 February 2017); Janice Arnold, "Quebec's Bill 62 violates key rights," *Canadian Jewish News* (22 April 2017); Raquel Fletcher, "Quebec's Bill 62 aims to impose religiously neutral public services," *Global News* (18 October 2016), online: <http://globalnews.ca/news/3010994/quebecs-bill-62-aims-to-impose-religiously-neutral-public-service/>; Samer Mazjoub, "These two Quebec bills are apparently targeting Muslims," *Huffington Post* (22 April 2017), online: <http://www.huffingtonpost.ca/samer-majzoub/quebec-muslims-hate-crimes_b_7621612.html>. Claire L'Heureux-Dubé emphasized that the bill was "strongly criticized" by the opposition Parti Québécois and the third party, Coalition Avenir Québec, "for not going far enough." Email communication from Claire L'Heureux-Dubé, 25 December 2016. In contrast, Quebec philosopher Charles Taylor lamented the new bill, calling it the "anti-Charter" and stating that "it should be dead." CBC Radio, *Sunday Morning*, 22 January 2017.
124 Ian Austen and Craig S. Smith, "Quebec mosque shooting kills at least 6," *New York Times* (29 January 2017).
125 Nicolas Van Praet, André Picard, Rhéal Séguin, Sean Gordon, and Verity Stevenson, "Suspect in Quebec mosque attack charged with six counts of murder," *Globe and Mail* (30 January 2017); Konrad Yakabuski, "An attack Quebeckers must never forget," *Globe and Mail* (31 January 2017) A8; "The Quebec City mosque: What we know so far," *Globe and Mail* (10 February 2017), online: <http://www.theglobeandmail.com/news/national/quebec-city-mosque-shooting-what-we-know-so-far/article33826078/>.

Conclusion

1 Justice J.W. McClung, "Right of reply," *National Post* (26 February 1999) A19.
2 Janice Tibbetts, "Fathers' group to file complaint against high court," *National Post* (13 March 1999) A6; "Assaulting the law," *National Post* (1 March 1999).
3 Edward L. Greenspan, "Judges have no right to be bullies," *National Post* (2 March 1999) at A18; Edward L. Greenspan, "Judge Kozinski, I beg to differ," *National Post* (11 March 1999) A18.
4 Elizabeth Sheehy, "Introduction" in Elizabeth Sheehy, ed., *Adding Feminism to Law: The Contributions of Justice Claire L'Heureux-Dubé* (Toronto: Irwin Law, 2004) at 6; Sheila McIntyre, "Personalizing the Political and Politicizing the Personal: Understanding Justice McClung and His Defenders" in Sheehy, *Adding Feminism to Law* at 313; Shelley A.M. Gavigan, "Outside/In: Lesbian and Gay Issues as a Site of Struggle in the Judgments of Justice Claire L'Heureux-Dubé" in Sheehy, *Adding Feminism to Law* at 347.
5 Candace C. White, "Gender Difference in the Supreme Court of Canada" (MA thesis, Department of Political Science, University of Calgary, December 1998) at 56, 121.
6 Interview with Claire L'Heureux-Dubé, Clearwater, FL, 10–14 May 2009.
7 Correspondence from Claire L'Heureux-Dubé, 25 October 2015.
8 Interview with Claire L'Heureux-Dubé, Clearwater, FL, 25–27 November 2014.
9 Dumont was the author of *Le féminisme québécois raconté à Camille* (Montréal: Éditions du remue-ménage, 2008), trans. to English in Micheline Dumont, *Feminism à la Québécoise* (Ottawa: Feminist History Society, 2012).
10 Interview with Micheline Dumont, Sherbrooke, QC, 29 December 2015, as supplemented by women who were present at the event but preferred to keep their identity confidential.
11 Ibid. After the set-to, at least some members of the audience described themselves as deeply upset, wondering if L'Heureux-Dubé did not identify as a feminist judge, who could ever call themselves feminist? Dumont added, "After the outburst women [judges] from New Brunswick [and] Saskatchewan came to me [saying], 'We don't understand.' They were very upset at her position. Many people came to me and told me, 'Well, she shouldn't have said that.'" Dumont remembered thinking that L'Heureux-Dubé's decisions had been so important to women, "especially on *Seaboyer*. For me, it was always feminist. But she wouldn't admit that she is a feminist, or that feminism is necessary. I cannot explain it. Is it her age? I am eighty myself!" Dumont admitted that she had not been quick to identify herself as a feminist in the early years of the second wave: "I was busy with my family, I went to France." She thought initially that the women protesting abortion and taverns were "absolutely foolish." But over time, as she read more about feminism, "It was like we were sleeping, and suddenly ... 'oh I understand.'" In the end, Dumont pronounced herself dismayed and mystified by L'Heureux-Dubé's position.
12 Her predecessor Bertha Wilson had also resisted identifying with feminism. Constance Backhouse, "Justice Bertha Wilson and the Politics of Feminism" in Jamie Cameron, ed., *Reflections on the Legacy of Justice Bertha Wilson* (Markham, ON: LexisNexis, 2008) at 33–52.
13 Her close contemporary, federal government lawyer Shirley Tucker Parks, who had also not self-identified as a feminist during her career, took a different stance. Recalling that she too had been labelled a feminist despite the absence of any direct involvement in the organized movement, she said, "By the very fact that you did what you did, you soon began to be tagged as a feminist. And I didn't mind at all." Interview with Shirley Tucker Parks, Ottawa, 19 November 2009.
14 After her retirement, L'Heureux-Dubé was asked whether her definition of "justice" included "feminism." She replied, "Yes. I worked very hard for women and children, and that is

part of feminism. But does [my definition of justice] include other things? Yes." She added, "I am a feminist but a larger feminist, in the sense of justice for all, equality." "Thinking about feminism today, I realize that fighting for justice and fairness for women is feminism," she admitted, but she held to the view that "equality" was a better word. It was a "vocabulary question," as she defined it. Interview with Claire L'Heureux-Dubé, Clearwater, FL, 25–27 November 2014; correspondence from Claire L'Heureux-Dubé, 25 October 2015. Mimi Liu, "'A Prophet with Honour': An Examination of the Gender Equality Jurisprudence of Madam Justice Claire L'Heureux-Dubé of the Supreme Court of Canada" (2000) 25 Queen's LJ 419, quoted L'Heureux-Dubé as saying, "If the word 'feminist' means justice for everyone including women, I am a feminist." In 2009, L'Heureux-Dubé also stated, "You had to fight every step of the way. We had to battle every minute with the judges. I was sensitive to injustice. I really was acting like a feminist, although I didn't use the word." Interview with Claire L'Heureux-Dubé, Quebec City, 27–29 April 2009. Former law clerk Teresa Scassa recalled L'Heureux-Dubé as resistant to the label "feminist" throughout her time on the court. Interview with Teresa Scassa, Ottawa, 16 May 2014. According to former law clerk Laurie Sargent, self-identification as a feminist never occurred: "It didn't get fully internalized, that's for sure." She explained, "[Although] she definitely would not call herself a feminist, in my mind she absolutely was. The whole thing was infused by a feminist approach to law, to constitutional interpretation. But it is true; she was not very comfortable with the word." Interview with Laurie Sargent, Ottawa, 26 September 2014.

15 Justice Wendy Baker of the Supreme Court of British Columbia, a self-identified feminist, wrote in 1996 that she was "conscious that there are those who consider feminism to be an alarming form of judicial bias," and described a formal grievance made against her as a judge by a disgruntled male litigant, whose main complaint seems to have been that she was "known to have been a feminist." Baker maintained that feminism was not evidence of "judicial partiality nor a threat to judicial independence." Wendy Baker, "Women's Diversity: Legal Practice and Legal Education – A View from the Bench" (1996) 45 UNBLJ 199. Legal scholars Isabel Grant and Lynn Smith (the latter subsequently appointed a British Columbia judge) argued in 1991 that the "dangers in assuming that given positions are 'objective' or neutral ... [meant that] criteria such as 'objectivity' [were] not, in reality, very helpful." They added, "While impartiality and fairness must remain centrally important goals for the judiciary, it must also be recognized that every person sees issues from a perspective, and ... legal principles naturally tend to reflect the perspectives of those who developed them ... The point is that no one is 'objective' in the sense of being without a frame of reference, yet we sometimes fail to notice the frame of reference of those who have been in a position to define the very terms and concepts in which we think." Isabel Grant and Lynn Smith, "Gender Representation in the Canadian Judiciary" in *Appointing Judges: Philosophy, Politics and Practice: Papers Prepared for the Ontario Law Reform Commission* (Toronto, Ontario, 1991) at 79. Legal theorist Kenneth C. Davis added, "Almost any intelligent person will initially assert that he wants objectivity, but by that he means biases that coincide with his own." Kenneth C. Davis, *Administrative Law Treatise*, 2nd ed. (San Diego: K.C. Davis) at 377–78.

16 Interview with Alan Gold, Toronto, 5 August 2009.
17 Interview with Louise Dubé, Boston, 22 May 2012.
18 Interview with Alan Gold, Toronto, 5 August 2009.

Illustration Credits

Every effort has been made to identify, credit appropriately, and obtain publication rights from copyright holders of the material reproduced in this book. Notice of any errors or omissions in this regard will be gratefully received and correction made in subsequent editions.

10 / Steve Ewanchuk. *Edmonton Journal, 26 May 1999,* A1

12 / John (Jack) C. Major. *Supreme Court of Canada/Philippe Landreville*

15 / John Wesley "Buzz" McClung. *Edmonton Journal, 14 February 1996,* A1

17 / Edward Greenspan. *University of Western Ontario/Craig Glover*

28 / Marguerite Dion. *Claire L'Heureux-Dubé*

31 / Paul Henri L'Heureux, ca. 1924. *Claire L'Heureux-Dubé*

36 / Claire at age three with carriage, Quebec City. *Claire L'Heureux-Dubé*

37 / Louise and Claire on cannon, ca. 1935, Plains of Abraham. *Claire L'Heureux-Dubé*

38 / Louise and Claire with Paul L'Heureux at Anse au Foulon. *Claire L'Heureux-Dubé*

40 / Cathédrale Saint-Germain, Rimouski. *Constance Backhouse, 2008*

43 / Quai de Rimouski, 1913. *Université du Québec à Rimouski, Collection Lionel-Pineau/L.O. Vallée*

44 / Saint-Germain children's birthday party in park. *Michèle Cloutier Mainguy*

45 / 188 rue Saint-Germain, late 1940s. *Claire L'Heureux-Dubé*

49 / Doll with melted legs. *Les malheurs de Sophie* (Paris: Librairie Hachette, 1911) at 11

52 / Four L'Heureux sisters at Le Bic. *Claire L'Heureux-Dubé*

53 / Claire as a teenager with bicycle. *Claire L'Heureux-Dubé*

53 / Children at the beach at Rocher Blanc. *Claire L'Heureux-Dubé*
56 / Marguerite and Paul L'Heureux beside their home in Rimouski. *Claire L'Heureux-Dubé*
64 / Monastère des Ursulines, Rimouski. *Philippe Michaud*
65 / Community of Ursulines, 1931. *Les Ursulines de Rimouski*
67 / Dramatic production at the Monastère des Ursulines. *Claire L'Heureux-Dubé*
68 / Dormitory at the Monastère des Ursulines. *Les Ursulines de Rimouski*
72 / Lieutenant-Colonel Paul L'Heureux with military colleagues. *Claire L'Heureux-Dubé*
75 / Graduation at the Monastère des Ursulines, June 1943. *Les Ursulines de Rimouski*
77 / Claire in front of Hôtel Clarendon. *Claire L'Heureux-Dubé*
79 / Students from Collège Notre-Dame-de-Bellevue, 1941–42. *Claire L'Heureux-Dubé*
84 / Claire L'Heureux, age sixteen. *Claire L'Heureux-Dubé*
86 / Claire and André Boissinot on the beach at Rocher Blanc, ca. 1946. *Claire L'Heureux-Dubé*
87 / Quebec City restaurant. *Claire L'Heureux-Dubé*
87 / Formal ball at the Collège Notre-Dame-de-Bellevue, 1946. *Claire L'Heureux-Dubé*
90 / Collège Notre-Dame-de-Bellevue graduation, 1946. *Claire L'Heureux-Dubé*
95 / First four women called to Quebec bar. *Barreau du Québec, 1942; originally published in La Presse, 10 September 1942*
97 / Jeanne D'Arc Lemay-Warren. *Jeanne D'Arc Lemay-Warren*
99 / Four L'Heureux sisters in front of Rimouski home. *Claire L'Heureux-Dubé*
101 / Thérèse Dionne Lecomte. *Thérèse Dionne Lecomte*
105 / Jean Bienvenue. *Bibliothèque et Archives nationales du Québec, Fonds Gabriel Desmarais (Gaby), P795,S1,D3838*
107 / Laval Law graduating class, 1951. *Archives de l'Université Laval, U539/47/4*
108 / Women law students relaxing at Lac Sept-Îles. *Claire L'Heureux-Dubé*
110 / Roch Bolduc. *Roch Bolduc*
112 / Library of the Laval Faculty of Law, 1933. *Archives de l'Université Laval, U519/3310,1,1*
119 / Martial Asselin. *Constance Backhouse*
121 / Claire L'Heureux, call to the bar, 1952. *Claire L'Heureux-Dubé*
124 / Letter from Sam Schwarz Bard. *Collection of Claire L'Heureux-Dubé; photo courtesy of Constance Backhouse*
126 / Formal ball with Gabriel Gagnon. *Claire L'Heureux-Dubé*
128 / Arthur Dubé graduating from Carnegie Institute of Technology, Pittsburgh. *Claire L'Heureux-Dubé*
138 / Marguerite Choquette. *Barreau du Québec*

Illustration Credits

139 / Louise Galipeault, admission to Quebec bar, 1955. *Louise Galipeault*
142 / Sam S. Bard. *Joel and Perry Bard*
146 / Sam Bard skiing on the Plains of Abraham, 1930s. *Joel and Perry Bard*
152 / Sydney Lazarovitz. *Barreau du Québec*
154 / Maurice Pollack. *Lana Harper and the Pollack Foundation*
161 / Louis LeBel. *Constance Backhouse*
163 / Claire L'Heureux on deck of cruise ship. *Claire L'Heureux-Dubé*
164 / Claire L'Heureux at cocktail hour on cruise ship. *Louise Dubé*
166 / Claire L'Heureux and Arthur Dubé's wedding, 1957. *Claire L'Heureux-Dubé*
168 / Arthur and Claire. *Louise Dubé*
169 / Mother and children at Christmas, ca. 1964. *Claire L'Heureux-Dubé*
172 / Gisèle Blondeau. *Gisèle Blondeau*
173 / L'Heureux-Dubé family, 1969. *Claire L'Heureux-Dubé*
174 / Léon Dion and Denyse Dion. *Stéphane Dion*
177 / Bard Law Firm lawyers. *Claire L'Heureux-Dubé*
179 / Marie-Claire Kirkland-Casgrain. *Marie-Claire Kirkland-Casgrain*
186 / Gérard Corriveau. *Bibliothèque et Archives nationales du Québec, Fonds Gabriel Desmarais (Gaby), P795,S1,D4170_002*
189 / Paul-André Crépeau. *Paul-André Crépeau*
191 / Claire L'Heureux-Dubé and Roger Garneau. *Constance Backhouse*
196 / Louise Mailhot. *Denis Gendron; courtesy of Louise Mailhot*
197 / Raymond Lessard. *Constance Backhouse*
202 / Thérèse Casgrain. *Library and Archives Canada, Dupras & Colas/PA-127291*
203 / La Voix des femmes. *Alain Chartrand*
204 / La Fédération des femmes du Québec, first board of directors. *Bibliothèque et Archives nationales du Québec, P783,S2,SS9*
207 / Shirley Tucker Parks. *Constance Backhouse*
212 / Les trois colombes at 24 Sussex Drive. *Duncan Cameron/Library and Archives Canada, C-25003*
215 / Albanie Paré Morin. *Albanie Paré Morin's daughter, also named Albanie Morin*
215 / Jeanne Sauvé. *Barbara Woodley*
215 / Monique Bégin. *Monique Bégin*
218 / 1014 Mont-Saint-Denis. *Constance Backhouse*
221 / Otto Lang. *Otto Lang*
227 / Abortion rights protest. *Fédération du Québec pour le planning des naissances*
228 / Réjane Laberge-Colas. *Bibliothèque et Archives nationales du Québec, Fonds Gabriel Desmarais (Gaby), P795,S1,D15621_1*
229 / Alice Desjardins. *Yousuf Karsh/Library and Archives Canada, e010750296*
231 / Judges at Claire L'Heureux-Dubé's Superior Court swearing-in. *Claire L'Heureux-Dubé*
232 / At reception following swearing-in. *Claire L'Heureux-Dubé*

233 / Frédéric Dorion. *Harvey/Bibliothèque et Archives nationales du Québec, P428,S3,SS1,D44,P107*
236 / Claire L'Heureux-Dubé at Superior Court swearing-in. *Claire L'Heureux-Dubé*
240 / Yves Bernier. *Bibliothèque et Archives nationales du Québec, Fonds Gabriel Desmarais (Gaby), P795,S1,D3884*
241 / Joseph Nuss and Claire L'Heureux-Dubé dancing at Louise Dubé's wedding. *Joseph R. Nuss*
254 / André Desmeules. *Constance Backhouse*
256 / Gabrielle Vallée. *Bibliothèque et Archives nationales du Québec, Fonds Gabriel Desmarais (Gaby), P795,S1,D4050_001*
256 / Quebec Superior Court judges, 1976. *Claire L'Heureux-Dubé*
270 / Photo taken for family Christmas card, December 1977. *Claire L'Heureux-Dubé*
273 / Pierre's school picture. *Claire L'Heureux-Dubé*
275 / Louise horseback riding, 1978. *Claire L'Heureux-Dubé*
284 / Jacques Flynn. *Canadian Press/Fred Chartrand*
285 / Prime Minister Joe Clark. *Canadian Press/Fred Chartrand*
285 / Maureen McTeer, wife of Prime Minister Clark. *Maureen McTeer*
289 / Claire L'Heureux-Dubé with Chief Justice Édouard Rinfret at Quebec Court of Appeal swearing-in. *Claire L'Heureux-Dubé*
291 / Quebec female judges and distinguished legal personalities, dinner of the Barreau du Québec. *Claire L'Heureux-Dubé*
296 / Judges of the Quebec Court of Appeal. *Claire L'Heureux-Dubé*
308 / Vacation respite in Florida. *Claire L'Heureux-Dubé*
309 / Claire L'Heureux-Dubé and daughter, Louise, on holiday in Sweden. *Claire L'Heureux-Dubé*
321 / Prime Minister Brian Mulroney. *Yousuf Karsh*
324 / Pierre Côté. *Bibliothèque et Archives nationales du Québec, Fonds Gabriel Desmarais (Gaby), P795,S1,D4167*
329 / Claire L'Heureux-Dubé's former law partners at the swearing-in ceremony. *Claire L'Heureux-Dubé*
331 / Bertha Wilson. *Michael Bedford*
333 / Claire L'Heureux-Dubé and Marie-Claire Belleau. *Marie-Claire Belleau*
339 / Antonio Lamer. *Supreme Court of Canada/Paul Couvrette*
341 / Supreme Court of Canada judges as a group, 1987. *Supreme Court of Canada*
348 / Official Supreme Court photo, 1999. *Supreme Court of Canada/Larry Munn*
353 / Michel Bastarache. *Constance Backhouse*
355 / Claire L'Heureux-Dubé and Antonio Lamer on the bench. *Claire L'Heureux-Dubé*
360 / Cartoon of L'Heureux-Dubé. *Drawn by unknown law clerk; re-creation by Rachel Robertson*
364 / Claire L'Heureux-Dubé, Beverley McLachlin, and Antonio Lamer in happier times. *Claire L'Heureux-Dubé*

Illustration Credits

368 / L'Heureux-Dubé with law clerks Adam Dodek, Laurie Sargent, and Michelle Flaherty. *Adam Dodek*
369 / L'Heureux-Dubé with law clerk Teresa Scassa. *Claire L'Heureux-Dubé*
369 / L'Heureux-Dubé with law clerks David Wright, Eric Marcoux, and Cynthia Westaway. *David Wright*
383 / Elizabeth Shilton. *Elizabeth Shilton*
388 / Beverley McLachlin with Brian Dickson and Claire L'Heureux-Dubé. *Claire L'Heureux-Dubé*
391 / Feminist demonstration at the Supreme Court, 1991. *Ottawa Citizen/Paul Latour; reprinted with permission*
393 / Elizabeth Sheehy. *Elizabeth Sheehy*
403 / Peter Bruckshaw, Zofia Moge's lawyer. *Peter Bruckshaw*
404 / LEAF lawyer Alison Diduck. *Alison Diduck*
413 / Ken Popert and Brian Mossop. *Brian Mossop*
419 / Supreme Court of Canada courtroom. *Supreme Court of Canada/Philippe Landreville*
427 / Rebecca Johnson. *Rebecca Johnson*
429 / Beth Symes. *Beth Symes*
433 / Frank Iacobucci. *Frank Iacobucci*
445 / Pierre Dubé, Quebec City. *Claire L'Heureux-Dubé*
451 / Claire L'Heureux-Dubé and daughter, Louise, at Taj Mahal. *Claire L'Heureux-Dubé*
453 / Family gravesite, Quebec City. *Claire L'Heureux-Dubé*
455 / René Lévesque. *Yousuf Karsh*
457 / Jacques Parizeau. *Assemblée nationale du Québec*
458 / *Le Devoir* editorial cartoon. *Garnotte/McCord Museum, M2007.69.265*
462 / Lucien Bouchard. *Assemblée nationale du Québec*
473 / Roger Rowe. *Roger Rowe*
478 / Sharryn Aiken. *Sharryn Aiken*
484 / Audrey Macklin. *Audrey Macklin*
485 / Mavis Baker and two sons. *National Post/Hans Deryk*
496 / Alan Gold. *Alan Gold*
498 / Edward Greenspan. *Constance Backhouse*
501 / Nellie McClung and her famous quotation.
506 / Catherine Fraser. *Catherine Fraser*
509 / Claire L'Heureux-Dubé and Chief Justice Aziz Mushabber Ahmadi of India. *Claire L'Heureux-Dubé*
510 / Naina Kapur. *Naina Kapur*
511 / L'Heureux-Dubé with Pakistani judges. *Claire L'Heureux-Dubé*
515 / Baroness Brenda Hale and L'Heureux-Dubé. *Constance Backhouse*

518 / L'Heureux-Dubé in a "bug suit" at gender equality workshop in Nunavik. *Claire L'Heureux-Dubé Fund for Social Justice*
522 / Louise Dubé. *Louise Dubé*
523 / *Canadian Lawyer* cartoon of Claire L'Heureux-Dubé. *Pascal Elie, artist*
527 / Beverley McLachlin with L'Heureux-Dubé at retirement ceremony. *Montreal Gazette/Tom Hanson*
528 / L'Heureux-Dubé with grandson Simon at retirement ceremony. *Ottawa Citizen/Tom Hanson*
530 / Reunion of former clerks at the Supreme Court. *Claire L'Heureux-Dubé*
530 / L'Heureux-Dubé at her Florida condo. *Claire L'Heureux-Dubé*
531 / L'Heureux-Dubé's grandsons at her Quebec City condo. *Claire L'Heureux-Dubé*
536 / Amna Qureshi presenting L'Heureux-Dubé with a gift on the anniversary of her departure from the bench. *Véronique Larose*
537 / L'Heureux-Dubé and Julie Latour testifying on the proposed Quebec Charter of Values. *Globe and Mail/Clément Allard*

Index

Note: "Claire" is used when describing Justice L'Heureux-Dubé's youth and her student years. After her call to the bar in 1952, use of "L'Heureux" is made in recognition of her independent adulthood. After 1957, her married name, "L'Heureux-Dubé" is used. "(f)" after a page number indicates an illustration.

Abella, Justice Rosalie: about Justice L'Heureux-Dubé, 299, 329, 371, 499, 500, 525, 692n69; spousal support, 400, 405
abortion cases, 205, 226, 227(f), 361, 392, 659n100
L'Action Catholique, 94
Action Québec, 219
Ad Hoc Committee of Canadian Women on the Constitution, 459, 682n36
Adam v. R. murder case, 314–15, 634n50
administrative law, 474, 477, 483
L'Affaire des trois chaînes (land rights case), 262–64
Affaire Plamondon, 143
affirmative action, 227, 336, 356, 640nn37–38
African Canadian community. *See* black community
African Canadian Legal Clinic, 478, 688n48
age discrimination case, 362
Ahmadi, Chief Justice Aziz Mushabber, 508–9(f), 510
Aiken, Sharryn, 478(f), 480, 484
Aitken, Greenberg law firm, 403

Alberta Court of Appeal, 9, 14, 502, 665n67, 693n89
alimony. *See* spousal support
Alleyn, Jacques: about Alleyn, 106, 115, 120, 572n28, 583n4; about Claire, 108, 638n51
Alliance canadienne pour le vote des femmes au Québec, 598n21
American Bar Association, 223, 524–25
Anand, Raj, 431
Andras, Robert, 238, 607n2, 616n2
Anse au Foulon cove, 37–38(f)
anti-Semitism: club membership, 147, 194, 604n9; lawsuits, 143, 300–1, 481, 629n44; lawyers, 93, 148–49, 176, 596n8; name change, 585n20; synagogue arson, 144, 586n25; university law school, 584n14
appellate court. *See* specific provincial Court of Appeal
April, Annette, 196, 582n19, 583n4
Arbour, Justice Louise: about, 348(f), 642n66, 664n54, 677n67; about Justice Lamer, 337–38, 351, 354; about Justice L'Heureux-Dubé, 354, 356–57, 358, 360–61, 375, 517; Quebec Charter

713

of Values, 538–39; rape-shield law, 658n88
Arcand, Adrien, 144
Archambeault, Justice Horace, 565n9
Armstrong, Patricia, 434
Arosa Line, 162–64
Asbestos strike (1949), 111, 212
Asia Pacific region (judicial education), 508–14, 696n34
Asselin, Martial: about, 106, 119(f), 571n21, 572n23, 624n7; about Justice Vallée, 255; judicial appointment process, 283–85, 326, 624n8; law school, 118–19
Association des avocates, 204, 606n65
L'Association pour le soutien et l'usage de la langue française, 463–64, 683n59
Atcheson, Beth, 416, 418, 673n4
Aubé, Denys, 596n11
Auclair-Hallé, Robert: about, 106, 572n25, 573n30; law school, 109, 111, 115
Audette-Filion, Micheline, 322, 636n15
Augustus v. Gosset (1996) compensation case, 359, 647n4
Australia (High Court), 525
Avocats sans frontières, 529

Babcock, Barbara, 291
Bahdi, Reem, 514
Baker, Mavis, 470–71, 485(f)
Baker, Justice Wendy, 706n15
Baker v. Canada (1999) immigration law case, 470–85, 685n1, 688n53, 689n71
Bala, Nicholas, 180, 408, 600n39, 638n48
Barabé, Monique, 258
Barak, Israeli Supreme Court Chief Justice Aharon, 492
Bard, Joel (son of Samuel Bard), 144, 145, 160, 585n21, 587n37
Bard, Perry (daughter of Samuel Bard), 144, 145, 585n21
Bard (Schwarzbard), Samuel: about, 141, 142(f)–49, 583n1, 583n6, 584n8, 584n14, 585n20, 587n32, 587n43; appointments, 147, 176, 233, 588n45, 596n9, 614n14; death, 527, 700n47; law firm, 144, 145, 177(f), 323, 329(f), 585n19, 586n24, 587n34, 596n10, 637n27; relationship with Claire L'Heureux, 4, 124(f)–25, 137, 140, 141, 147–49, 156, 327; relationship with Sydney Lazarovitz, 151;
reputation, 151, 589nn13–14, 590n15; on working women, 145, 587n37
Bard Côté law firm, 323, 637n27
Bard law firm: bilingual firm, 151–57, 590n17; lawyers, 150, 177(f), 588n5, 589n6, 596nn10–11, 597n15; operating costs, 151; secretarial pool, 159–60; types of clients, 151–59, 590n17, 591n32, 591n36; workday routine, 160–61
Barreau du Québec (Bar of Quebec): bâtonnières, 235, 254; bâtonniers, 93, 105, 106, 176, 189, 596n8, 602n89, 614n6; Charter of Values, 533–34, 702n88; disciplinary complaints, 189; female judges, 291(f); female lawyers statistics, 193, 581n2, 603n1; law school curriculum, 119–20, 578n61; lawyer and law firm statistics, 588n1, 595n3; surveys, 160, 575n19, 592n68
Barrette-Joncas, Claire, 291(f), 292, 606n64
Barrière, Suzanne, 567n24
Basford, Justice Ron, 224, 618n4
Bastarache, Justice Michel: about, 348(f), 460, 548n10; about Justice Lamer, 350–51; about Justice L'Heureux-Dubé, 19, 306, 350, 357, 375, 488–89, 651n61; about Justices L'Heureux-Dubé and Lamer, 352; about Justices L'Heureux-Dubé and McClung, 690n25; decision-writing protocol, 11, 549n15; immigration law case, 473; judicial collegiality, 356; post-retirement, 353(f); sexual assault case, 660n112
bâtonniers/bâtonnières. See Barreau du Québec (Bar of Quebec)
Batshaw, Harry, 596n7
Bayda, Chief Justice Edward, 350, 371, 465, 646n64
Bayefsky, Anne, 459, 682n36
Beaudoin, Justice Jean-Robert, 232–33, 256(f), 614n12
Beaulieu, Marie-Louis, 103, 114, 120, 122, 575n24, 581n11
Beauregard, Marc, 629n52, 630n58, 631n63, 631n69, 632n74
Beetz, Justice Jean, 298, 335, 336, 341(f), 641n41, 663n44
Bégin, Monique, 205, 214–15(f), 220, 226, 227, 608n6, 608n18
Bélanger, Justice Laurent-E., 286, 295, 296(f), 625n15

Belleau, Marie-Claire: about Justice
  L'Heureux-Dubé, 327–28, 332–33, 334,
  336, 340, 342, 345–46, 374; about
  Justice McIntyre, 337; about Justices
  L'Heureux-Dubé and Lamer, 339–40;
  female judicial dissent, 374, 677n67;
  Francophone judicial collegiality, 332–
  33, 334; with Justice L'Heureux-Dubé,
  333(f); on Pierre Dubé's death, 446,
  450, 453; tribute conference, 524,
  699n31
Bellemare, Victorin, 245
bereavement leave, 414, 668n8
Bernier, Justice Yves: about, 185, 240(f),
  296(f), 602n82, 614n15, 616n10, 627n16;
  about Justice L'Heureux-Dubé, 187,
  239, 257, 295, 297–98, 638n51; court
  assignments and influence, 633n3;
  criminal cases, 631n69, 632n72; female
  judges, 233; hearings preparation, 626n2;
  judicial appointments process, 286
Bertrand, Gérard, 106
Bertrand, Guy, 456, 468
bias. *See* judicial bias
Bienvenue, Jean, 105(f), 257, 573n30,
  573n41
Bienvenue, Valmore, 105–6, 570n19
bilingualism: class status, 55, 557n15;
  courts, 305, 325, 464–65; law firms, 113,
  151–52, 159, 592nn57–58, 592nn61–62.
  See also language
Bill C-49 legislation, 394, 660n108,
  660nn111–12
Billingsley, Barbara, 18
Bindman, Stephen, 13, 390, 436, 679n48
Binnie, Justice Ian: about, 348(f), 460–61,
  548n10; about Justice L'Heureux-Dubé,
  357, 358, 499–500, 524, 530, 650n50,
  672n88; about Justice L'Heureux-Dubé
  and Justice Lamer, 354; about Justice
  L'Heureux-Dubé and Justice McClung,
  11, 491, 690n25; decision-writing protocol, 11; immigration law case, 473; law
  clerks, 650n50, 672n88; on mentorship,
  147; same-sex couples case, 418–19, 420;
  secession case, 683n54; sexual assault
  case, 660n112
Bird, Florence, 205
Bissonnette, Alexandre, 539
Black, Conrad, 15
black community: deportations and
  stereotypes, 478, 688n48; judicial bias

complaints, 481–82, 688n65; racialized
  lawyers, 478–80, 481
Bloc Québécois, 457–58
Blondeau, Gisèle, 80, 81, 90(f), 171–72(f),
  311, 562n19, 562n25
The Body Politic (gay rights publication),
  413, 415, 668n3
Boer War, 23, 552n4
Boissinot, André, 85–86(f), 87(f), 101,
  563n57
Bolduc, Roch: about, 106, 571n22; about
  Claire, 110, 148, 326; law school, 109–
  10(f), 111, 114, 118; on private law practices, 581n3; on Rhodes Scholarship, 120,
  578n63
Bonenfant, Jean-Charles, 115, 576n34
Bonnet, Édith, 580n35
"bonnets and crinolines" reference (sexual
  assault case), 8, 9, 14, 19
books (children), 48–49(f), 50, 69
Borowski v. Canada (Attorney General)
  (1989) abortion case, 361
Boscoville juvenile re-education centre,
  312–13, 315, 634n42, 634n44
Boston v. Boston (2001) spousal support
  case, 411, 668n120
Bouchard, Quebec Premier Lucien, 461,
  462(f), 468, 684n92
Bouchard-Taylor Commission, 532
Bourassa, Robert, 620n57
Boyle, Christine, 12, 383, 659n90
Brandeis brief, 384, 408, 666n94
Brillant, Agnès, 102
Brillant, Major Jean R., 71
Brillant, Jules A., 102, 124, 569n52,
  569nn56–57
Brillant family, 444
Britton, Louise Weibel, 100
Brodsky, Gwen, 418, 421, 422, 669n39
Brooks v. Canada Safeway Ltd. (1989)
  sexual discrimination case, 361
Bruckshaw, Peter, 402–3(f), 409
Buckley, Melina, 432, 439–40, 674n22,
  676n53, 678n93
Business and Professional Women's
  (BPW) Club, 157, 591nn45–46, 594n29
business expenses (income tax), 434–35,
  675nn47–48
Byer, Stephen M., 243–44, 245–46, 617n28

Cadieux, Ferdinand, 226, 607n2
Cadieux, Rita, 608n6

Cairns Way, Rosemary, 361, 507, 640*n*27, 694*n*12
Calgary Herald, 16
Camp, J.J., 461
Campagnolo, Iona, 296
Campbell, Douglas, 442, 509, 511, 512, 513, 518–19, 696*n*27, 697*n*77
Campbell, Prime Minister Kim, 394, 420
Campbell, Margaret, 576*n*36, 577*n*40
Canada: criminal law reform, 379, 380, 386, 394, 654*nn*17–18, 656*n*51, 656*n*53, 660*n*108, 660*nn*111–12; elections, 213–15; female judges associations, 515–16; female lawyers statistics, 93, 96, 193, 567*n*25, 603*n*2; immigration and population, 472, 686*n*17; immigration policy, 242, 470, 685*n*3; judicial appointments reform, 320, 636*n*12; judicial education, 505–8, 693*n*4; prisoners right to vote legislation, 649*n*38; repatriation and defamation appeal, 299–300, 628*n*39
Canada (Attorney-General) v. Mossop (1993) same-sex couples case, 67, 412–27, 657*n*65, 671*n*66, 671*n*75
Canada (Canada Employment and Immigration Commission) v. Gagnon (1988) case, 361–62
Canadian Advisory Council on the Status of Women, 438. *See also* Conseil du statut de la femme; National Action Committee on the Status of Women; Royal Commission on the Status of Women
Canadian Armed Forces (sexual orientation discrimination), 419–20
Canadian Association of Black Lawyers, 472
Canadian Bar Association: annual meetings, 257; gender equality task force, 643*n*11; interveners, 432; on judicial appointment, 326; on judicial decision, 18; judiciary committee, 222, 223, 611*n*55, 612*n*57; president, 105, 319, 570*n*18, 635*n*4
Canadian Bill of Rights, 155
Canadian Charter of Rights and Freedoms: criminal caseload, 338, 641*n*60, 649*n*35; equality challenges, 361, 381, 389–90, 403, 411, 430–35, 649*n*39, 655*n*23, 657*n*56, 658*n*81, 668*n*118, 676*n*51; judicial activism, 15; judicial candidates process, 320, 636*nn*11–12; judicial concerns, 337, 340, 345, 362, 494, 506, 641*n*51, 694*n*7; jurisprudence shift, 365, 371, 453, 649*n*39; media, 15, 550*n*37; notwithstanding clause, 538–39; opinions on, 323, 494, 533–34; override clause, 659*n*101; previous to, 122, 155; prisoner voting rights, 365, 649*n*38; repatriation and defamation appeal, 299–300, 628*nn*38–39, 629*nn*41–42; sexual assault case challenge, 380–81, 386, 654*n*16; sexual orientation discrimination challenge, 416, 419–21, 422–23, 669*n*24, 670*n*44; tax law discrimination challenge, 428–41
Canadian Civil Liberties Association (CCLA), 658*n*88
Canadian Cod Liver Oil Research Institute, 100, 102
Canadian Consumers' Council, 188
Canadian Council of Churches, 483
Canadian Council of Churches v. Canada (Minister of Employment and Immigration) (1992) case, 362
Canadian Day Care Advocacy Association, 438
Canadian Ethnocultural Council, 434
Canadian Human Rights Act, 416, 418, 419–20, 422, 424, 670*n*44, 672*n*81
Canadian Human Rights Commission (CHRC), 414–18, 420, 668*n*12, 669*n*23, 670*n*54
Canadian International Development Agency (CIDA), 508–9, 696*n*33
Canadian Judges Conference (Conférence canadienne des juges), 257
Canadian Judicial Council (CJC): bias complaints, 492–94, 506, 691*n*40, 691*n*47; disciplinary complaints, 106, 189, 570*n*19, 602*n*91, 641*n*51, 676*n*63, 694*n*7; female appointment, 618*n*3; judicial education, 505, 693*n*4; on sexual assault case, 16, 18, 550*n*47, 551*n*67
Canadian Lawyer (cartoon), 523(f)
Canadian Newspapers Co. v. Canada (Attorney General) (1988) sexual assault case, 361
Cannon, Hélène, 580*n*8
Cannon, Lucien, 94
Cano, Marlène, 305
capital punishment. *See* death penalty
Carle, Gilles, 109, 573*n*30, 610*n*39
Caron v. Caron (1987) spousal support case, 400–1

Carroll, Justice Henry George, 565n9
Casgrain, Lynne, 275
Casgrain, Perreault, 105, 570n18
Casgrain, Philippe, 81–82, 84–85, 105, 148, 570n18, 579n68, 598n24, 606n59
Casgrain, Thérèse Forget, 190, 199, 202(f)–3, 203(f), 288, 562n24, 566n13, 602n94, 606n59
Cathédrale Saint-Germain, 39–40(f)
Catholic church. *See* Roman Catholic church
Cercle de la Garnison de Québec, 147, 587n42
Charlottetown accord, 456
Charter Committee on Poverty Issue, 431
Charter of Rights of Freedoms. *See Canadian Charter of Rights and Freedoms*
child care expenses, 429–30, 431, 434, 439, 674n24, 675n37, 675n39, 677n81
child custody: children's preference, 266, 268, 621n68; maternal, 411, 621n68, 667n117; paternal, 185, 266, 267–68, 302, 621n70, 622n80, 630n55
child support, 267, 397, 436, 657n65, 676n58
children (imprisonment), 514
Children's Aid Society (CAS), 470, 471
children's books, 48–49(f), 50, 70, 197–98
children's rights, 475–76, 484
Choquette, Marguerite (Margot), 108, 138(f), 140
Chouinard, Justice Julien: about, 106, 571n20; about Justice Lamer, 665n67; appointment, 283, 624n2, 624n6; death, 319, 635n1; decisions, 263, 400, 401, 663n44; law school, 106, 118–19, 120, 578n63; marriage, 401, 664n49; scholarship, 120, 578n63
Chouinard, Roger, 260, 297, 326, 581n3, 583n4, 589n13, 600n36
Chrétien, Prime Minister Jean, 456, 467–68
chronology (life of Claire L'Heureux-Dubé), xv–xviii
church. *See* Roman Catholic Church
cinemas, 83–84, 563n50
Cité Libre, 226
Civil Code (Quebec): child custody, 185; law school, 112, 574n9; marriage and divorce, 178, 598nn20–21; reforms, 179, 189–91, 222–23, 599n25, 599n31, 600n32, 602n92, 602n101, 603n103, 612n58

Civil Code Revision Office, 189–91, 516, 603n103
Claire L'Heureux-Dubé Fund for Social Justice (Fonds pour la justice sociale Claire L'Heureux-Dubé), 524, 699n29
Clarity Act (2000), 684n92
Clark, Prime Minister Joe, 283–85(f), 624nn3–4, 624n10
class status, 34, 43, 54–57
Cloutier, Denis, 53(f)
Cloutier, Huguette, 44(f), 53(f)
Cloutier, Jacques, 53(f)
Cloutier, Louis, 53(f)
Cloutier, Pierre, 53(f)
Cloutier Mainguy, Michèle: about Claire, 44, 44(f), 48, 52, 53(f), 54, 59, 82–83, 85; on Arthur Dubé, 278; on women's career choices, 96
Club de la Garnison de Québec, 147, 194, 201, 587n42, 604n8
Club Rimouski, 55, 557n14
Coffin, Wilbert, 234, 615n18
Collazo, Irizel, 500
collective rights vs individual rights, 130
Collège Notre-Dame-de-Bellevue (Quebec City): curriculum, teachers, and rules, 73, 77–80; female students, 78, 79(f), 562nn24–26; formal ball, 87(f); graduation, 90(f); tuition, 76, 560n57, 561n4
Commissioner for Federal Judicial Affairs, 257
Committee on the Law on Persons and on the Family, 190
Committee on the Rights of the Child, 476, 687n36
common law and evidentiary rules, 385–86, 389, 474, 483, 649n35, 660n112
Comtesse de Ségur children's books series, 48–49(f), 50, 70, 197–98
Confederation of National Trade Unions (CNTU), 213, 612n76
conferences (female judges), 543, 705nn10–11
Congrégation de Notre-Dame, 66
Congress of Black Women, 478
Conseil consultatif de l'administration de la justice, 188
Conseil du statut de la femme, 226, 534, 599n25, 613n89. *See also* Canadian Advisory Council on the Status of Women; National Action Committee

on the Status of Women; Royal Commission on the Status of Women
Constitution Act, 1982, 456, 636*n*11, 681*n*11
constitutional principles, 467
constitutional reform, 320, 636*n*12
convent schools: classical courses, 73–75, 560*n*59; recruitment, 66, 559*n*14; student life, 65–67(f); tuition, 66, 559*n*17
Convention on the Rights of the Child, 475–76
Coon Come, Cree Grand Chief Matthew, 459, 468
Corriveau, Justice Gérard, 185–86(f), 189, 199, 256(f), 601*n*76
Cory, Justice Peter: about, 460; about Justice Lamer's capacity, 521, 698*n*12; appointment, 548*n*10; immigration law case, 362, 474, 477; judicial discord, 651*n*74; same-sex couples case, 418, 422, 423, 671*n*66; sexual assault case, 657*n*66, 660*n*112; spousal support case, 405, 662*n*12, 664*n*52; tax law case, 674*n*26
Côté, Pierre, 323–24(f), 588*n*5, 597*n*14, 637*n*27
Cotler, Irwin, 479
Courchesne, Archbishop Georges-Alexandre, 81–82, 563*n*36
Courts of Appeal (Canada) and judicial collegiality, 355, 356
Crépeau, Paul-André: about Justice L'Heureux-Dubé, 190–91, 516, 612*n*58; Civil Code Revision Office, 189(f)–91, 602*nn*92–93; judicial appointments process, 220, 222–23, 610*n*33, 612*n*58
Crête, Chief Justice Marcel, 296(f), 628*n*39, 631*n*69, 632*n*72
Criminal Code of Canada: evidentiary rules, 385–86, 389–90, 656*n*51, 656*n*53; law school, 112; reforms, 379, 380, 386, 394, 654*nn*17–18, 656*n*51, 656*n*53, 660*n*108, 660*nn*111–12

dangerous offenders, 502, 693*nn*91–92
Dauvergne, Catherine, 349, 484, 643*n*11, 650*n*50
Dawson, Brettel, 383, 507, 513, 696*n*34
de Beauvoir, Simone, 201–2, 203, 606*n*55
de Grandpré, Justice Louis-Philippe, 324, 333, 637*n*31
death penalty, 117, 234, 262, 577*n*47, 615*nn*18–19
Décary, Justice Robert, 436, 440

defamation lawsuits: anti-Semitism, 143, 300–1, 481, 629*n*44; repatriation, 299–300, 628*n*39
demonstrations: judicial decisions, 525; Quebec Charter of Values, 534; rape-shield law, 391(f), 659*n*89, 659*n*95; separatism, 459, 682*n*29
Department of Manpower and Immigration inquiry, 238–52
Depeyre, Lili (Éliane), 87(f), 89–90(f)
deportation, 471–72, 474–75, 477, 478, 686*nn*13–14, 688*n*48
Depression, 42
Derrick, Anne, 383, 648*n*29
Des Rosiers, Nathalie, 18, 468–69, 648*n*29, 685*n*95
Desgagné, André: about, 106, 572*n*29; about Claire, 108, 118; law practice, 581*n*3; law school, 111, 578*n*63; lawyer reputations, 589*n*13
Desjardins, Alice: about, 229(f), 291(f), 606*n*63; appellate justice, 567*n*28, 627*n*26; law professor, 204, 228, 580*n*35, 613*n*97, 641*n*41
Desmeules, André, 254(f); about Justice L'Heureux-Dubé, 288, 638*n*51; about Justice Vallée, 255; English-language discourse, 575*n*20; on female justices, 253, 258; judicial candidate, 609*n*26
Desrochers, George-Étienne, 245
Le Devoir (editorial cartoon), 457, 458(f)
Dickson, Chief Justice Brian: abortion rights case, 361; about, 335–36, 341(f); affirmative action, 335–36, 640*n*37; appointment process, 322, 331, 351, 644*n*28; feminist, 528, 700*n*51; judicial education, 506; judicial notice, 407–8; jurisprudence shift, 649*n*39; relationship with Justice L'Heureux-Dubé, 342, 344, 640*n*35; swearing-in ceremony, 328, 638*n*62
Diduck, Alison, 403–4(f), 409
Diefenbaker, Prime Minister John, 185, 601*n*76
Dion, Denyse, 174–75, 174(f), 290, 311–12, 345, 442, 449
Dion, Léon, 174–75, 174(f), 277–78, 290, 684*n*81
Dion, Louis-Victor (maternal grandfather of Claire), 26, 553*n*21
Dion, Marie-Marthe (maternal aunt of Claire), 37, 39, 57, 78, 102, 553*n*21

Dion, Stéphane, 174–75
Dion (Fortin), Antoinette (maternal grandmother of Claire), 26–27, 34, 46, 89, 552*n*17, 553*n*20
Dionne, Yves, 83
Dionne-Lecomte, Thérèse, 83, 85, 96, 100, 101(f)
discrimination of Jews. *See* anti-Semitism
divorce: child custody, 185, 266, 267–68, 667*n*117; church prohibition, 181; civil law reforms, 179, 190, 599*n*25, 599*nn*29–31, 600*n*32, 602*n*94, 602*n*101, 603*n*103; client types, 182–88; equalization principle, 267, 268, 301–2, 411; feminization of poverty, 398, 405, 406; gender inequality, 178, 301, 406, 411, 598*n*21, 666*n*80, 668*n*118; judicial bias, 182–87; justices, 400–2; legal aid, 411, 668*n*118; legal costs, 182, 600*n*49; mediation vs adversarial system, 181, 183; statistics, 182, 301, 600*n*50; "the trilogy," decisions, 400–1, 405, 410, 663*n*46, 665*n*72. *See also* family law; marriage; spousal support
Divorce Act (1968), 179, 180, 599*nn*29–30, 600*n*38
Divorce Act (1985), 399–400, 666*n*80
Dodek, Adam, 368(f), 387, 516
Doherty, Justice Teresa, 516–17
Doiron, Lawrence, 244–45, 248
domestic workers (immigration), 470, 471, 474, 685*n*3, 687*n*24
Dorion, Chief Justice Frédéric: about, 187, 231–32, 233(f), 614*n*6; case assignments, 237; child custody decision, 266; on divorce, 182; immigration inquiry, 239; Nazi collaboration case, 232, 614*n*9; relationship with Justice L'Heureux-Dubé, 230–31, 257, 619*n*23
Dorion, Marcèle, 80, 87(f), 89, 90(f), 96, 98–99
Downie, Jocelyn, 349, 367, 368, 650*n*50
Dranoff, Linda Silver, 200, 410
Drapeau, Jean: about Arthur Dubé, 269; about Claire, 44, 47, 69, 81, 85, 86, 172; about Claire's parents' marriage, 89; about Pierre Dubé, 311, 449
Drapeau, Marguerite, 44, 87(f)
Drouin, Thérèse, 87(f)
Dubé, Arthur (husband): about, 126–27; alcohol abuse and depression, 168, 269–72, 274, 275, 276–77; with Claire, 168(f); courtship, 125–26, 127–28; debt, 168, 594*n*21; family portrait, 173(f), 270(f); as father, 169; father-son relationship, 307–8; graduation, 128(f); holidays, 168(f), 173–74; impaired driving, 270, 622*n*6; marriage, 164–66(f), 271–72, 276, 593*n*12; political connections, 213, 608*n*10; sabbatical, 276–77; suicide, 13, 277–79, 486, 487, 489, 549*n*27, 623*n*40; supports Claire's career, 5, 167; at swearing-in, 230, 232(f)

Dubé, Cécile, 80, 87(f), 90(f), 562*n*26
Dubé, Georges-Henri (brother-in-law), 271, 277
Dubé, Louise (daughter): about brother, 272–74, 444, 446, 449, 680*n*63; as child, 168–69(f), 172–73, 594*n*23; family portrait, 173(f), 270(f); father-daughter relationship, 271, 275–76; father's suicide, 277, 279, 280; law school, 280, 307; marriages and divorce, 280, 345, 450, 680*n*79; mother as grandmother, 531; mother as justice, 372, 464; mother as lawyer, 187, 259; mother not as feminist, 544; mother-daughter relationship, 274–75, 309(f), 450–51(f); mother's character, 6, 187, 488, 561*n*70; mother's isolation on court, 491; mother's marriage, 165, 175, 272; mother's respect for Jews, 588*n*58; mother's retirement, 522(f); mother's written French, 372, 464; school, 239, 616*n*7; survival strategies and horseback riding, 275(f), 276, 280; at swearing-in, 230, 232(f), 327

Dubé, Pierre (son): as adult, 445(f); as child, 169(f), 173, 219, 594*n*24; death and funeral, 444–45(f), 446–53, 680*n*63; family portrait, 173(f), 270(f); father's suicide, 277; father-son relationship, 307–8; firearms possession, 447–48, 679*n*48, 680*nn*49–50; holiday with mother, 308(f); juvenile delinquency, 307–15, 634*n*44; mental illness, 173, 272–74, 308, 444, 446, 448, 680*n*49; motorcycle, 445; school, 239, 273(f), 442, 616*n*7; suicide rumour, 489; at swearing-in, 230, 232(f), 237; threatens mother, 446–47, 679*n*36, 679*n*39

Dubé, Yves (brother-in-law), 69, 127, 165, 212, 271, 277

Duceppe, Gilles, 457–58
Duff, S.M.G., 200
Dumont, Micheline, 543–44, 567*n*23, 705*nn*9–11
Duplessis, Quebec Premier Maurice: civil service, 116, 591*n*42; death, 178; election, 33–34; on freedom of religion, 154–55, 591*n*36; "leaning tower" reference, 681*n*20; police conduct, 349; post, 466; scholarships and political affiliations, 104, 570*n*10; on social sciences, 570*n*7, 575*n*24; tax status case, 157
Dupuis-Couillard, Jacques, 106
Durham Report (Lord Durham), 74, 561*n*64
Duval, René, 418
Dyzenhaus, David, 483

Eberts, Mary (lawyer), 430, 431, 435–36, 438, 439, 440, 673*n*4
L'École Saint-Germain, 59
education: classical courses, 28–29, 73–74, 78, 560*n*59, 562*n*10; curriculum, 64–66, 73, 558*n*8, 561*n*64; social sciences, 570*n*7; women, 28–29, 65–66, 77–78, 103, 553*n*25, 562*n*10
Edwards v. A.G. of Canada women's rights case, 288
EGALE (Equality for Gays and Lesbians Everywhere), 418, 421
Egan v. Canada (1995) same-sex couples case, 423, 424, 671*n*66, 671*n*75
Eichler, Margrit, 417
Elman, Bruce, 18
employment (women), 396, 661*n*8, 686*n*4
employment insurance case, 361–62
English language: judicial decision translations, 463–65, 683*nn*60–61, 683*nn*64–65, 683*n*72; working language of judges, 305, 325, 632*n*80; working language of lawyers, 159, 592*nn*57–58, 592*nn*61–62, 595*n*4. *See also* language
Equal Rights Trust, 529
Equality Now, 513
Estey, Justice Willard (Bud): about, 336–37, 341(f); conduct complaint, 337, 641*n*51; family law decisions, 663*n*44; on judges' offices, 335, 640*n*28; relationship with Justice L'Heureux-Dubé, 332, 336–37, 639*n*12, 641*n*51

Ewanchuk, Steve: on judicial dispute, 17; media interview, 10(f); prior convictions, 9, 548*n*4; sentence and dangerous offender, 502, 693*nn*89–92
Ewanchuk sexual assault case. *See R. v. Ewanchuk*

Fahmy-Eid, Nadia, 567*n*23
Fairweather, Gordon, 420
Falardeau-Ramsay, Michelle, 291(f), 422
family (definition), 417–18
family law: family status, 416–18; law reforms, 179, 190, 599*n*25, 599*nn*29–31, 600*n*32, 602*n*94, 602*n*101, 603*n*103; lawyers, 178–81, 598*n*18, 600*n*36; paternity case, 264–65; same-sex couples rights, 412–27. *See also* divorce
Farley, Paul Émile, 74, 561*n*64
Federal Court of Appeal: female lawyer appointment, 567*n*28; immigration case, 472; same-sex couples case, 418, 422, 669*n*37; tax law case, 432, 436, 440
Federal Court Trial Division, 432, 472, 686*nn*13–14
federal elections (female candidates), 211, 608*n*6, 608*nn*18–19
Fédération des femmes du Québec (FFQ), 179, 204, 204(f), 226, 228, 534, 579*n*69
female justices: appointments, 225–29, 253–57, 283, 292, 613*n*89, 618*nn*2–3, 624*n*3, 626*n*38, 640*nn*37–38; associations, 514–16; conferences, 543, 705*nn*10–11; decisions and gender differences, 390, 392, 432, 434, 436–37, 674*n*22, 675*n*43, 676*n*65, 677*n*67; formal dinner, 291(f); gender as challenge, 258, 293–94, 295–297, 330–32, 490, 614*n*11, 639*n*2, 639*n*5, 639*n*7, 639*n*10, 690*nn*20–21; judicial robes, 235, 615*nn*28–29; social context opinions, 385, 392; title, 234–35, 615*nn*21–22. *See also* justices; male justices
female lawyers: barriers, 103–4, 569*n*5; emotions, 156; feminist, 200–7, 381–84, 383(f); first women-at-law, 19, 137–40, 582*n*17, 582*n*19; gender discrimination, 135–36, 193–201, 581*n*3, 581*n*6, 604*nn*6–7, 604*n*11, 604*n*15, 604*n*19, 604*n*23, 605*nn*44–45; graduates, 19, 137–40, 582*n*17, 582*n*19; law students, 107–8(f),

109, 116–18, 573n31, 573n41, 576n36, 577n38; lawyer-mother status, 167–75, 258, 541; legal action and legislative reform, 93–96, 564nn6–9, 565nn8–9, 566n13, 566n17; lists, 579n67, 582n17, 597n16; marriage vs career, 125, 169–70, 580n8, 594n27, 673n6; maternity leave policy, 673n6; salary disparity, 141, 583n4; self-confidence, 197; statistics, 96, 178, 193, 567n25, 581n2, 597nn16–17, 603nn1–2; surveys, 196, 200, 604n23; tax law case, 428–41. *See also* lawyers; male lawyers

feminist movement: about, xiii; demonstrations, 205–6, 226, 227(f), 391(f), 604n7, 659n89, 659n95; development, 201, 202(f)–6, 606n55, 607nn69–70; female judicial appointments, 225–29, 613n89; female lawyers, 200–7, 381–84, 383(f); judicial bias, 492–93, 544, 691n47, 706n15; judicial decision analysis, 432, 434, 437–38, 674n22, 675n43, 677n68; judiciary, 349, 542–45, 550n47, 643n11; organizations, 381–84, 459, 492–93, 682n36, 691n44; principles, 437–38, 677n68; on sexual assault and sexual history, 380, 653nn9–10; tavern discrimination, 194, 201, 205–6, 604n7; types of, 606n58; writers, 201–2, 203, 606nn55–56

feminization of poverty, 398, 399, 405, 406, 666n82

Ferguson, Edra Sanders, 200–1, 605n44, 609n28

Ferrier, Lee, 185, 598n18

Fine, Sean: on *Charter* challenge, 431; on Justice L'Heureux-Dubé retirement, 523; on Justice McClung, 14; on Quebec Charter of Values, 535; on secession case, 461, 463; on sexual assault case, 379, 391, 653n2, 659n89; on spousal support case, 409–10

firefighters age discrimination case, 362

fishing rights, 263, 620nn49–51

Flahaut, Jean, 77–78

Flaherty, Michelle, 368(f), 464, 476, 499, 703n105

Flynn, Jacques, 283, 284(f), 285, 624n5

Flynn, Rivard et al. law firm, 283, 624n5

Fonds pour la justice sociale Claire L'Heureux-Dubé (Claire L'Heureux-Dubé Fund for Social Justice), 524, 699n29

formalism, 305, 374, 407

Fortier, Yves, 319–20, 327, 459, 616n11, 635n4, 635n6

Fournier, François, 137, 582n20

Fournier, Justice Georges-René, 182, 256(f)

Fournier, Ginette, 137–38, 581n2, 582n20

Fournier, Pascale, 375

Fox-Decent, Evan, 483

Francophone judges: judicial decisions language, 463–65, 683nn60–61, 683nn64–65, 683n72; secession case challenges, 461, 462(f)

Fraser, Alberta Chief Justice Catherine: about, 294, 506(f), 626n9; about Justice L'Heureux-Dubé, 306, 376, 393, 505, 512, 513, 516; on hunting, Justices Lamer and McClung, 548n12; judicial education, 507, 512, 694n12, 697n74; sexual assault case, 548n7, 549n29

Fraser Milner Casgrain law firm, 105, 570n18

freedom of religion, 155, 535, 537, 538

Frémont, Jacques, 534, 702n91

French, Mabel, 194, 604n11

French language: associations, 463–64, 683n59; judicial decisions translations, 463–65, 683nn60–61, 683nn64–65, 683n72. *See also* language

French law, 373–74

Friedan, Betty, 203, 274

Front de libération des femmes du Québec (FLFQ), 205, 226, 227(f), 604n7, 607n71

Fusiliers du Saint-Laurent Rimouski, 70–71, 560n52

Gagnon, Claude, 189, 602n89

Gagnon, Gabriel, 125, 126(f)

Gale, Chief Justice George Alexander, 294

Galipeault, Louise, 139(f)–40, 187

Gamache-Côté, Judith: about, 107(f), 108(f), 581n12, 591n42; about Justice L'Heureux-Dubé, 327; court clerk, 156–57; law school, 107, 108(f), 113, 568n45, 573nn31–32

Gammon, Lisette, 343

Garneau, Roger: about, 178, 597nn14–15; about Arthur Dubé, 276; about Justice

L'Heureux-Dubé, 192, 199–200, 463, 465; about Pierre Dubé, 311, 446, 449; on family law, 180; Jewish lawyers, 587n42, 589n13; with Justice L'Heureux-Dubé, 191(f), 329(f)
Gaudron, Mary, 171, 633n8
Gauthier, Lucille, 579n67, 582n17, 582n19
Gauthier, Paule, 432, 597n16
gay rights movement, 415–16, 418, 424, 669n39
gender bias, 19, 171, 182–87, 507, 653n10
gender diversity: judicial appointments, 292, 320, 328–29, 336, 626n38, 640n38; law firms, 178, 597nn16–17
gender equality: and feminism, 201–7, 542–45, 705n14; judicial education, 507, 513, 518, 694n12; salaries, 141, 362. *See also Canadian Charter of Rights and Freedoms*; human rights
gender identity (children's books), 48–49(f), 50
gender inequality: divorce, 178, 301, 406, 411, 598n21, 666n80, 668n118; earnings, 141, 583n4, 686n4; female justices, 330–32, 490, 519, 639n2, 639n5, 639n7, 639n10, 690n21; female lawyers, 103–4, 135–36, 194–201, 569n5, 581nn2–3, 581n6, 604n11, 604n15, 604n19, 604n23, 605nn44–45; legal aid, 411, 668n118; marriage, 406, 598n24, 599n25, 601n71; motherhood, 170, 594n29
Gingras, Dr. Gustave, 57, 557n22
Ginsberg, Justice Ruth Bader, 299
Globe and Mail newspaper: immigration law case, 483, 689n71; judicial collegiality, 334, 355; on Justice L'Heureux-Dubé, 328, 329, 523; on Justices L'Heureux-Dubé and Lamer, 352; on Justices L'Heureux-Dubé and McClung, 486–87, 489, 491, 689n3; Quebec Charter of Values case, 535; Quebec secession case, 459, 461, 463; sexual assault cases, 14–18, 388–89, 391
Glube, Justice Constance, 351, 614n11, 634n52, 691n47
Godbout, Quebec Premier Adélard, 95, 116, 562n24, 566n17, 576n27
Godbout, Marthe (daughter of Adélard Godbout), 87(f), 90(f), 562n24
Gold, Alan, 16, 495–96(f), 544, 545
Gonthier, Justice Charles Doherty: about, 348(f), 386–87, 460, 657n60; about

Justice Lamer, 521, 698n12; about Justice L'Heureux-Dubé, 74–75, 98, 349–50, 387, 646n66, 657n65; about Pierre Dubé, 451–52; appointment, 548n10; immigration law case, 473; as outsider, 651n74; prisoners' right to vote case, 649n38; same-sex couples case, 423; secession case, 460, 461, 462, 463, 683n54; sexual assault cases, 11, 14, 490, 660n112; spousal support case, 405, 664n52, 665n69, 666n80; tax law case, 674n26
Goodman, Clara, 144, 585n22
Gorlick, Barry (CBA), 18
The Great Darkness *(La Grande Noirceur)*, 178, 532
Greenshields, Chief Justice Robert-Alfred-Ernest, 95–96
Greenspan, Edward, 16–17(f), 19, 490, 496–97, 498(f), 523
Gubbay, Justice Anthony, 517

Haig v. Canada (1992) sexual orientation case, 419–20, 422, 670n44
Hale, Justice Baroness Brenda, 515(f)–16
Hampton, Howard, 392, 659n96
Healey, Edouard (*L'Affaire des trois chaînes* land rights case), 262–64, 620nn49–52, 620n57
Heenan Blaikie law firm, 280
Hémond, Marcelle, 95(f)–96, 566n18, 567n24
Henderson, Gordon, 220, 223
Hnatyshyn, Ramon, 320
homophobia, 117–18, 549n18, 691n47. *See also* gay rights movement
Hôtel Clarendon, 77(f)
Hotel Fort Garry, 396, 397
Hôtel Saint-Louis, 39
Houle v. Banque canadienne nationale (1990) contract case, 359, 647n4
How, W. Glen, 154–55, 590n28, 591n36
Hudon, Guy, 104, 111, 113–14, 116, 573n32, 575n21
human rights: activist imprisonment, 697n62; appeals cases, 629nn41–43; equality decisions, 365, 648n27; same-sex couples, 412–27, 671n75; sexual orientation, 424, 549n18, 671n67, 672n76, 691n47; women, 513. *See also Canadian Charter of Rights and Freedoms*; gender equality

Human Rights Award, 500, 515–16
Hutchinson, Allan, 507, 695n16
Hyndman, Margaret, 100, 170, 594n29

Iacobucci, Justice Frank: about, 348(f), 432–33(f), 460, 674n29, 675n34; appointment, 433–34, 548n10, 635n8, 674n31; on decision-writing protocol, 549n14; as ideological, 651n61, 651n74; immigration law case, 474, 477; judicial appointments tradition, 637n17, 639n2, 657n70; on judicial collegiality, 355, 356, 357, 639n2, 639n7, 646n61; judicial education, 694n12; on Justice L'Heureux-Dubé and Justice McClung's apology, 490–91; relationship with Justice L'Heureux-Dubé, 357, 452, 646n61; same-sex couples case, 418, 421–23, 671n66; secession case, 463; sexual assault cases, 657n66, 660n112; spousal support case, 405; swearing-in, 674n27; tax law case, 432–34, 676n53
immigration: admission rights, 471, 474; children's rights, 475–76, 484; and deportation, 362, 471; law reform, 242, 616n19; population level, 472, 686n17; to Quebec, 42, 555nn36–37; queue-jumping, 246–47, 617n45; status, 470–71, 474
Immigration Act (1971), 474, 685n3, 687n24
Immigration and Refugee Protection Act (2001), 483, 689n78
Immigration Appeal Board, 242, 247
immigration applicants: homeland statistics, 242, 617n22; intermediaries, 242–44; stereotypes, 242, 471–72, 474–75, 477, 478, 481, 617n21, 686nn13–14; testimony, 250
Immigration Commission of Inquiry (1973-76): findings, 241–49, 616n8, 617nn21–22, 617n28, 617n45; preparations, 239–41, 616n13; racial analysis, 251–52, 481; testimony, 250
immigration law: fairness case, 470–85, 685n1; racial bias, 478–79, 688n53
immigration officers: applicant stereotypes, 471–72, 474–75, 477, 478, 481, 617n21, 686nn13–14; directives, 247–48; sexual misconduct inquiry, 238–52
immigration policy: children's rights, 483; racial discrimination, 685n3

Immigration Visa Services of Canada, 243–44
implied consent, 9, 385, 494–97, 548n7, 692nn57–59
Income Tax Act: business expenses, 434–35, 675nn47–48; child care expenses, 432, 434, 435–36, 675n37, 675n39; child support amendment, 676n58
India (judicial education), 508–13
Indigenous peoples: decision-making and social context, 694n12; history curriculum, 74, 561n64; judicial diversity, 320, 635n8; judicial race relations, 506–7; rights and Quebec secession, 459, 467, 468, 684n92; sexual abuse complainants, 660n112
International Association of Comparative Law, 466, 516, 697n63
International Association of Women Judges (IAWJ), 500, 514–15, 697n55
International Commission of Jurists (Commission internationale de juristes), 257, 476, 509, 516, 524, 695n25
International Comparative Law Association, 373
international judicial education, 508–14, 695n25, 696n27, 696nn33–34
International Labour Organization (ILO), 136, 581n11
International Society of Family Law, 299, 466, 516, 627n33

Jackman, Barbara, 483
Jacob, Marthe, 53(f)
Jacob, Monique, 53(f)
Jacobs, Samuel William KC, 93–94, 143, 564n5, 565n9, 581n14, 584n9
Jacques, Justice Maurice, 256(f), 304, 631n64
Jamaica, 470, 478, 685n2
Jansenism movement, 26, 552n18
Janzen v. Platy Enterprises Ltd. (1989) sexual discrimination case, 361, 700n51
Jehovah's Witnesses, 154–55, 591n32
Jeunesse Étudiante Catholique (JEC), 81, 203, 226, 562n29, 607n2
Jewish judges, 176, 233, 294, 300, 589n12, 639n4
Jewish lawyers: anti-Semitism, 93, 143–44, 176, 585n15, 596nn7–8; bilingual, 159, 592n57; law firms, 144, 176, 585n18, 596n5; law school, 584n14; in Quebec

City, 141, 150–51, 583n1; recruitment, 137, 581n14, 582n15; reputation, 151, 589nn13–14, 590n15
Jews: anti-Semitism, 143–45, 584n9, 585n15, 585n17, 586n25, 586nn27–28, 587n32, 604n9; club memberships, 147, 194, 604n9; education, 143, 584n11; freedom of religion, 531–32; immigration, 143; name change, 144, 585n20; population (Quebec City), 147, 587n40
Jobin, Pierre-Gabriel: about Justice L'Heureux-Dubé, 252, 298, 306, 326–27, 499; on chief justice, 232; on female law students, 577n38; Francophone justices, 333; on Jewish lawyers' reputation, 589n14
Johnson, Rebecca, 374, 425–27(f), 677n67, 677n81
Johnston, Douglas E., 402, 665n59
Joli-Coeur, André, 458, 459–60
Joly, Jean-Marie, 82
judicial activism, 425, 672n81
judicial appointments: lobbying, 226, 227–28; patronage, 185, 322, 601n76; process, 219–25, 610nn31–32, 610n39, 610n42, 611nn55–56, 612n57; veto power, 224–25, 612n77; women, 219–25, 228, 609n28, 611nn47–48
judicial bias: cartoon, 457, 458(f); complaints, 492–94, 691n40, 691n44, 691n47; gender, 19, 171, 184–87, 507, 653n10, 690n21, 706n15; racial, 478–79, 481–82, 507, 688n53, 688n65; religion, 182
judicial education, 298–99, 505–19, 693n4, 694nn12–13, 695n16, 695n20, 697n74
Julien c. La Reine murder case, 286–87
Juneau, Fernande, 226
Juneau, Pierre, 226, 562n29
justices: characteristics, 259–61, 297, 323, 627n26; complaints toward, 106, 189, 492–94, 506, 570n19, 602n91, 676n63, 691n40, 691n47, 694n7; discretion, 386; English-language decisions, 305, 632n80; ethnic background, 432, 674n27; formalism, 305; Francophone, 325, 332–34, 461–62; legal realism, 113, 374, 666n94; salary, 216, 609n25; secondary sources, 385, 656n43. *See also* female justices; male justices
Jutras, Daniel, 538

juvenile delinquency, 313–15, 634n47, 634n50
Juvenile Delinquents Act (Quebec), 634n47
juvenile detention centres, 310–11, 312–13, 314

Kapur, Naina, 508–9, 510(f), 512, 517, 518, 698n78
Katkin, Steven (Samuel Bard's nephew), 147, 160, 161, 591n32
Kaufman, Justice Fred, 295–96(f), 305, 627n22, 629n52, 632n80
Keable inquiry, 299, 628n37
Kennedy, Baroness Helena, 513
Kirby, Justice Michael, 508, 517
Kirkland-Casgrain (Kirkland-Strover), Marie-Claire: about, 122, 579n68, 598n24; as judge, 291(f); as politician, 178–79(f), 599n25; as working mother and criticism, 275
Klassen, Claire, 384, 656n40
Kozinski, Justice Alex, 19
Kronby, Malcolm C., 180, 600n37, 638n48

La Forest, Justice Gérard: about, 335, 340–41(f); about Justice Lamer, 350; about Justice L'Heureux-Dubé, 341, 452, 642n86; appointment, 320; chief justice appointment process, 644n28; family law cases, 361, 670n51; on female judicial appointments, 331–32; judicial discord, 651n74; same-sex couples case, 418, 421–23, 671n66; sexual assault case, 657n66, 660n112; spousal support case, 405, 664n52, 666n80; standard of review, 669n42; tax law case, 674n26
Labbé, Suzanne, 489
Laberge-Colas, Réjane: about, 122, 204(f), 228(f), 291(f), 579n69, 606n62; family law cases, 620n59; female judicial appointments, 228(f), 292, 325–26, 609n28; treatment by male justices, 325–26; women's organization, 179, 204(f), 204
Lacasse, François, 445, 452–53, 464, 465, 524, 673n91, 699n31
Lachance, Anita, 44(f)
Lacourcière, Gérard, 94–95
Lacroix, Justice Gérard, 116, 234, 577nn37–38, 609n28, 615n18
Laflamme, Ovide, 257, 573n30

Lajoie, Andrée, 465
Lajoie, Justice François, 286, 295, 296(f), 625n16, 631n64, 631n69
Lalonde, Claire, 226, 612n84
Lalonde, Marc: feminism, 225, 612n84; judicial appointments process, 211, 224, 607n2, 610nn32–33, 610n39, 612n76
Lamarche, Gustave, 74, 561n64
LaMarsh, Judy, 196, 605n24
Lamer, Chief Justice Antonio: about, 296(f), 335, 337–38, 339(f), 341(f), 348(f), 460; animosity toward Justice L'Heureux-Dubé, 306, 338–40, 347–55(f), 357, 371, 443, 461, 462–63, 491–92, 497, 520, 526–27, 645n37, 690nn32–33, 700n44; bias complaint case, 482, 688n67; colleague relationships, 350–51, 644n21; criminal law, 347–49, 643n4; criminal law rulings vs Justice L'Heureux-Dubé, 363–64, 649nn34–35; death and funeral, 522; decision-writing protocol, 10–11, 548n10; defamation lawsuit, 629n44; defence of court, 491–92, 691n39; driving habits, 339, 642n66; failing capacity, 520–21, 698n5; on female judicial appointments, 331, 639n5; on free speech entitlement, 549n18; friendship with Justice McClung, 11, 548n12; on gender equality, 643n11, 644n12; judicial discord, 349, 643n11, 651n74; judicial education and social context, 507; on Justice McClung's apology, 491, 690nn32–33; with Justices L'Heureux-Dubé and McLachlin, 364(f); law clerks, 650n50, 672n88; marital status, 349, 351, 644n15; personality traits, 338–39, 349–51, 644n21; race discrimination, 690n20; retirement, 520–22; same-sex couples case, 418, 420–23, 670n46, 670n49, 671n66; secession case process, 454, 460, 461, 463, 681n3; sexual assault case, 10–11, 361, 548n10, 657n66, 660n112; spousal support case, 400, 663n44; spousal support case judicial panel recusal, 404–5, 665n67; on supplementary submissions, 420, 670n46, 670n49; swearing-out event, 521; tax law case, 674n26; treatment of females, 332, 639n10
land rights case, 262–64, 620nn49–52, 620n57
Landolt, Gwen, 16, 490, 495, 692n58

Lane, Justice Lord, 299
Lang, Otto: judicial appointments, 216–17, 220–21(f), 222, 224, 610nn32–33, 610n42, 611nn47–48, 611n56, 612n57, 612n77; tribute conference, 524
Langevin, Louise, 375, 410, 487–88
Langstaff, Annie MacDonald, 93–94, 564nn6–7, 565nn8–9, 581n14
Langstaff v. Bar of the Province of Québec (1915) women's rights case, 93–94, 564nn6–7, 565nn8–9
language: bilingualism, 113, 151–52, 159, 305, 325, 464–65, 592nn57–58, 592nn61–62; class status, 55, 557n15; English as working language, 159, 305, 325, 592nn57–58, 592nn61–62, 595n4, 632n80; French-language associations, 463–64, 683n59; judicial decisions translations, 463–65, 683nn60–61, 683nn64–65, 683n72
Lapointe, Gabriel, 106, 572n23
Lapointe, Roberge, Fortier, Côté law firm, 323
Larue, Abbé, 165
Laskin, Chief Justice Bora: chief justice appointment process, 351; dissenter, 373; judicial appointments, 610n42; judicial conferences tradition, 342; management style, 637n31; spousal support decision, 667n114; treatment of, 294
Latour, Julie, 534, 536–37(f)
Laval University, 73, 575n24, 684n81
Laval University, Faculty of Law: female faculty, 131, 580n35; female graduates, 19, 137–40, 582n17, 582n19; fourth year, 120–22; graduating class (1951), 107(f); law students, 102, 104–20; library, 112(f); male law students, 104, 570n12; professors and curriculum, 112, 113–18, 316, 574n7, 574nn9–11, 574n14, 575n21, 634n55
Lavoie, Aurore (second wife of Napoléon L'Heureux), 25
Lavoie, Bruna (grandmother of Claire), 24, 25, 552n5
Lavoie, Lucie, 44(f)
law clerks: about, 366, 650n42; about Justice L'Heureux-Dubé, 327–28, 332, 358, 367, 536, 650n50, 703n106; cartoon of justice, 360(f); Charter of Values reaction, 536, 703n106; on judicial animosity (Justices L'Heureux-Dubé

and Lamer), 349, 352–54, 643*n*10, 645*n*35, 645*n*37; on judicial collegiality, 332, 356; reunions, 530, 530(f); role, 365–70, 426–27(f), 650*n*42, 672*n*88, 673*n*91; on treatment of female justices, 332, 639*nn*9–10; tribute conference, 524, 699*n*31

law firms: bilingual practice, 113, 575*n*20; gender, 178, 597*nn*16–17; operating costs, 151; statistics, 176, 595*n*3

Law Reform Commission of Canada, 338, 349, 400

law schools, 112–20, 574*nn*9–11, 574*n*14, 575*n*15, 575*n*21, 575*nn*23–24, 578*n*61

Law Society of Upper Canada, 140, 524, 583*n*27, 673*n*6

law students: bar examinations, 120–22; employment during law school, 113, 575*n*19; fourth year, 119–20, 578*n*61; leisure time, 113; "No means No" workshops, 495, 692*n*57; oral examination, 118; from privilege, 104, 570*n*12; statistics, 104–10, 570*n*17; survey, 575*n*19. *See also* female lawyers; male law students

Law Times, 19

lawsuits, 143, 299–301, 481, 628*n*39, 629*n*44

lawyers: bilingual, 159, 592*nn*57–58, 592*nn*61–62; counsel adviser, 529, 701*n*63; family law, 178–81, 598*n*18, 600*n*36; language, 176, 595*n*4; race relations, 137, 478–80, 481, 581*n*14, 582*n*15; routines and working hours, 160, 592*n*68. *See also* female lawyers; male lawyers

Lawyers Rights Watch, 529

Lawyers Weekly, 448, 489, 490, 521, 523, 679*n*48, 680*nn*49–50

Lax, Brauna, 144, 585*n*21

Lazarovitz, Sydney: about, 151, 152(f), 583*n*1, 589*n*12, 589*n*14; anti-Semitism lawsuits, 584*n*9; *bâtonnier* appointment, 176, 596*n*8; divorce law seminars, 180; law firm, 144, 176, 585*n*18, 596*n*5; relationship with Sam Bard, 151; reputation, 151, 589*nn*13–14, 590*n*15

Le Dain, Justice Gerald, 335, 340, 341(f), 644*n*28

Le Dain Inquiry into the Non-Medical Use of Drugs, 340

LEAF (Women's Legal Education and Action Fund). *See* Women's Legal Education and Action Fund (LEAF)

LeBel, Justice Louis: about Chief Justice Vallée, 255; about Justice L'Heureux-Dubé, 161, 304–5; appointment, 635*n*6; in chambers, 161(f); on female justice appointment, 254; on Jewish lawyers, 589*n*13; spousal support case, 668*n*120; on treatment of women lawyers, 136

Leblanc v. Leblanc (1988) family law case, 361, 664*n*52

Lefebvre, Jean-Paul, 211, 214, 607*n*2

legal realism, 113, 374, 407, 666*n*94

Legault, André, 56–57, 343, 366, 450, 465, 569*n*55, 608*n*12, 650*n*52

Legault, Josée, 461

Léger, Cardinal Paul-Émile, 201–2

Legros, Gisèle, 314

Lemay, Édith, 117–18

LeMay, Jacques, 260, 600*n*36, 619*n*38, 637*n*42

Lemay-Lavoie, Thérèse, 138–39, 140, 580*n*8

Lemay-Warren, Jeanne D'Arc: about, 97(f), 291(f), 567*n*28; appointment, 97(f), 292; education, 78, 99, 568*n*42; law practice barriers, 103, 136, 582*n*19; on male law students, 109

Lemelin, Yolande, 311, 449, 633*n*29

Lemieux, Lyse, 291(f), 292

Lenz, Andrew, 376, 446, 489, 673*n*91

LePage, Dr. Victor, 129

Lesage, Quebec Premier Jean, 178, 576*n*27

Lessard, Raymond: about, 136, 195, 197(f); about Chief Justice Vallée, 255; about Jewish lawyers, 589*n*13; about Justice L'Heureux-Dubé, 161, 199; on female justice appointment, 253; on gender discrimination, 195; law practice, 575*n*20, 604*n*18; women and law practice barriers, 136

Letarte, René, 232(f)

Lévesque, Andrée, 534–35

Lévesque, Pascal, 87(f), 562*n*26

Lévesque, Quebec Premier René, 115, 299, 300, 454–55(f), 466, 576*n*29, 628*n*38

L'Heureux, Claire
— education, early: 63–90
age sixteen, 84(f); boyfriends and social activities, 82–86(f), 87(f); *Civil Code* as

graduation present, 90; classical studies and tuition, 73–90, 560n57, 561n4; convent education, 63–67(f), 68–70, 73–90, 558n8, 559n28, 559n32; convent school troublemaker, 69–70, 79; father, 88, 89, 563n60; female classmates, 79(f), 80, 562nn24–26; French grammar education, 73–74; in front of Hôtel Clarendon, 77(f); graduation, 89(f), 90(f); mother's influence, 76–77, 89; parents' marriage, 89; religious influence, 80–82; school formal ball, 87(f); wartime memories, 70–72, 560n52

— *education, legal: 93–131*
academic results and transcript, 118–19, 578n59; Arthur Dubé courtship, 125–26, 127–28; bar examination, 120; barriers to women, 103–4, 116, 569n5; called to the bar, 121(f), 122; classmates, 104–10, 119, 570n17, 573n31; collective rights vs individual rights, 130; criminal law education, 116, 117, 577n47; employment during law school, 113; father's influence, 98–99, 100, 568n39, 569n50; female law school friendships, 107–8(f), 109, 573n31; fourth year, 120; graduating class (1951), 107(f); law school decision, 93–102, 567n27, 568n31; legal vs secretarial career, 100, 568n45, 569n55; male law students, 104–6, 109–10; on Maurice Duplessis, 117; mother's influence, 102; National Assembly debates, 116–17; professors, 115; religious views, 130; romances, 101–2, 125–26(f), 127–28; secretarial work, 100, 102, 123–24, 569n52, 569n55; sexual harassment, 123–24; social life, 101–2, 123–31; social status, 104; student loan, 102, 569n57

— *family heritage and childhood: 23–50*
birth name, 551n1; childhood home (Rimouski), 43–45(f), 46, 48, 56(f), 99(f), 123, 556nn43–46, 559n17, 579nn2–3; childhood homes, 35, 554n13; class status, 54–57; convent school, 60; elementary education, 36, 59; family leisure, 37(f)–38(f), 54; father, 38(f), 46–47; maternal family history, 26–29, 552n17, 553nn20–21; money attitudes, 55–56; mother, 27, 29, 57–60, 558n35;

move to Rimouski, 39–50; orphanage, 58; paternal family history, 23–25, 551nn2–3, 552nn4–6, 552nn11–13, 552n15; sisters and friends, 35–36(f), 37–38(f), 44(f), 51–52(f), 53(f)–54, 99(f); troublemaker, 47, 50, 58

— *law practice: 135–67*
bilingualism, 159, 592nn57–58, 592nn61–62; business law, 150–61; clients, 155–57; on cruise, 162, 163(f), 164(f); first case, 156; Jewish law firm, 124(f)–25, 140, 148–49, 588n58; language of legal profession, 159, 592nn57–58, 592nn61–62; law firm job offer, 124(f)–25; marriage contract and wedding, 164–66(f), 593n12; mentorship, 124(f)–25, 140, 147–49; newspaper announcement, 150–51; parents' separation, 165–67, 593n14; salary, 141, 583n2; speeches, 157; women and law career, 140, 583n27; workday routine and working hours, 160–61. *See also* L'Heureux-Dubé, Justice Claire: law practice

L'Heureux, Gaston (half-brother of Paul Henri), 25, 78, 444, 552n15

L'Heureux, Louise (sister): about, 568n40; about Arthur Dubé, 269, 277, 278; about Claire, 37(f), 54, 69, 149, 230, 274, 278, 327, 450–51, 452, 588n57, 700n44; about Pierre Dubé, 274, 309–10, 444, 449–50; caregiver, 129–30; as child, 35, 44(f); education, 69–70, 73–74; father, 38(f), 46, 98, 99, 443, 444, 563n61, 568n40; mother, 34, 47–48, 88–89, 316; orphanage, 58; sisters, 51–52(f), 53(f), 54, 99(f)

L'Heureux, Lucie (sister): as child, 35, 44(f), 52(f), 53(f); education, illness, and death, 129–30, 580n22, 580n26; sisters, 52(f), 99(f)

L'Heureux, Marie (paternal aunt), 24

L'Heureux, Napoléon (paternal grandfather), 23–25, 35, 78, 81, 551nn2–3, 552n6, 552nn11–13, 552n15

L'Heureux, Nicole (sister): about Claire, 101, 125, 224, 230, 327; about Pierre Dubé, 446, 448, 449; on archbishop, 82; as child, 35, 44(f), 53(f), 57; father, 88, 98, 443; law career, 99, 108, 130–31, 160, 316, 580n35, 634n55; mother's care-

giver, 130–31, 315–16, 634n54; sisters, 51–52(f), 99(f)
L'Heureux, Paul Henri (father): about, 23, 24–25, 29–31(f), 32; about Claire, 4, 38(f), 88, 100, 230, 290, 327; affair, 563n61; bilingual, 55, 557n15; civil service career, 25, 30, 35, 39, 54, 55, 123, 162, 552n12, 557n14, 569n50, 593n4; class status, 55, 557n14; with daughters, 38(f); death and funeral, 443–44, 678n5; as disciplinarian, 46–47; family finances, 35, 100; grandson Pierre, 310; local politics, 100–1; marriage to Francine, 316, 443, 593n14, 678n5; marriage to Marguerite, 27, 34, 56(f), 58–59, 76, 88–89, 165–67, 593n15; military service, 30–31(f), 32, 70–72(f), 76, 88, 560n52; religious views, 81
L'Heureux (Dion), Marguerite (mother): about, 23, 27, 28(f), 29, 553n21, 553n25; about Arthur Dubé, 127–28, 165; about Claire and influence on, 4, 76–77, 89, 98, 102, 115, 230; birth of children and birth control, 35, 554n12; child-rearing, 36, 46, 48, 52, 59; class status and bilingualism, 55; death and funeral, 315–16; father-in-law, 25, 552n13; as good cook, 47–48; letter writing, 57, 59, 558n35; marriage and separation, 27, 34, 56(f), 58–59, 76–77, 88–89, 165–67, 316, 563n61, 593nn14–15; money attitudes, 27, 55–56; multiple sclerosis, 57–60, 129–31, 557n22; religious views, 36, 42, 81; siblings, 553n21
L'Heureux-Dubé, Justice Claire
— *Immigration Commission of Inquiry: 238–52*
appointment and family arrangements, 238–39, 616n8; findings, 241–49; preparations, 239–41, 616n13; recommendations, 246, 481; sexual and racial harassment, 249–52, 481
— *judicial education: 505–19*
awards, 500, 515(f)–16; with chief justice (India), 509(f); cross-cultural challenges and effectiveness, 517–19, 697n74, 697n77; female judges associations, 514, 515(f)–16; on gender equality, 513, 518(f)–19; international influence, 508, 509(f), 510, 511(f)–14, 516–19, 695n25; international meeting, 510; judicial education and social context, 507–8, 694n12; with Pakistani judges, 511(f); personality and reputation, 508, 512–13, 518–19, 695nn21–22, 696n43, 698n78; women's rights (wrongful convictions), 511
— *law practice: 167–207*
birth of children, 168–69; challenges as a woman, 136, 193–207, 581nn10–11; Civil Code reform, 190, 602n94, 602n101; divorce clients, 182–88; divorce law specialist, 180, 541; family law, 176–92; on feminism, 201–6; first home, 169; full-time lawyer, 137, 140, 582n15; gender disparity, 194–95, 201, 205–7, 541; holidays (Denyse Dion), 174–75; holidays (family), 168(f), 173–74; on judicial bias, 185–87; justice vs payment for service, 187; as "*La Tigresse*," 199–200, 541; law firm purchase, 177(f), 596n10; lawyer-mother status, 167–75, 541; male clients, 187–88; marriage and children, 162–75; mediation vs adversarial system, 181, 183; nickname, 200; as outsider, 180; on parental vs paternal authority, 185; Quebec bar council election, 189; Queen's Counsel (QC) designation, 188; reputation, 188–92, 541; with Roger Garneau, 191(f); self-confidence, 197–98; social life, 173–74; tavern demonstrations, 205–6; treatment of female lawyers, 194–95, 201; worst case, 187–88. *See also* L'Heureux, Claire: law practice
— *personal life and family tragedy: 269–80, 307–16, 442–53*
bilingual, 30, 55, 100, 125, 239, 464–65, 683n72; compartmentalization, 272, 279, 450–52; daughter, 241, 443, 451(f); dinner parties, 276; driving habits, 526, 700n40; family gravesite, 453(f); family holidays, 238, 445; family portrait, 173(f), 270(f); father, second marriage, 443; grandson, 453(f), 528(f); holidays, 238, 445, 451(f); husband, alcohol abuse, 270–71, 276; husband, suicide, 277–79, 623n40; hyphenated surname, 167; lawyer-mother status, 167–75; life and career summary, xv–xviii, 3–7, 540–45; on marital counselling, 271, 623n15; marriage, 167–75, 271–72, 276; mother, 316, 450–51, 635n58; personal

challenges, 307–16; residences, 442–43; son, 274, 308(f), 312, 446, 448–53, 680n66. *See also* Dubé, Arthur (husband); Dubé, Louise (daughter); Dubé, Pierre (son)

— *Quebec Court of Appeal: 281–316*
alimony, 301–2, 629n51, 629n52, 630nn55–58, 863n60; appointment, 283–92, 624n3; characteristics of appellate justice, 297–98, 627n26; compartmentalization, 311; court assignments and influence, 307, 633nn2–3; criminal law cases, 286–87, 302–5, 631n61, 631nn68–69, 632nn70–74; decisions overview, 299–306, 625n16, 628n35; divorce cases, 301–2, 629nn51–52, 630nn55–58, 631n60; educational conferences, 298–99, 309; equalization principle, 301–2; family law association, 299, 627n33; family law education, 505–6; on female judicial appointments, 290–91(f), 625n34; first case, 293–94, 626n6; formalism, 305; as the "Great Dissenter," 297; hearings preparation, 626n2; holiday with daughter, 309(f); honorary doctorates, 298; judicial relationships, 294–99, 304–5, 306, 350; jurisprudence shift, 313–14, 315, 372, 634n52; with justices, 296(f); as "law and order" justice, 287, 303; paternal custody, 302, 630n55; probation period, 286–87; reputation, 298–99, 627n33; secretary, 311; sexual assault cases, 303, 631nn62–67; son and jurisprudence shift, 313–14, 315, 634n52; son and juvenile detention centres, 310–11; swearing-in, 288, 289(f)–92; working hours and travel schedule, 307, 626n2, 633n2

— *Quebec Superior Court: 211–68*
alimony and revenue equalization, 267, 268, 622n77; alimony decisions, 265, 266–67, 268, 621nn64–65, 621n73, 622n74, 622n76; case assignments challenges, 235–37; characteristics as justice, 259–61; child custody decisions, 265, 266, 267–68, 621n68, 621n70, 622n80; children in chambers (child custody cases), 266, 267, 268; civil case dockets and decisions, 261–68, 619n43, 620n47, 620n51; criminal cases and decisions, 619n44; on death penalty, 262; dinner parties, 276; divorce cases and decisions, 231, 265–68, 621nn64–65; electoral candidate refusal, 213, 214–16, 608n12, 608nn17–18; family law cases and decisions, 264–68, 620n59, 621nn64–65; female judicial appointments, 227–29, 255, 257; female justices, challenges, 230–34, 258, 614n11; on feminism, 219, 235; home, 218(f), 610n35; judicial appointment process, 216–25, 610nn31–32; judicial circuit, 257–59; judicial judgments, 258; judicial relationships, 257, 287, 619n23; judicial robes, 235, 615n28; jurisprudence shift, 372; justices (1976), 256(f); lawyer-mother status, 258; on *le bâtonnier* title, 235; as non-elite, 217–19; as outsider, 230–31(f); paternity cases and decisions, 264–65; political connections, 211–12; relationship with Justice Vallée, 258, 288; swearing-in, 230–32(f), 231(f), 236(f); title, 234–35, 615n22; treatment by lawyers, 259–61; working hours, 258–59

— *retirement: 522–39, 698n16*
awards, 524–25, 529, 701n62; cartoon, 523(f); Charter of Values support and reaction, 533–39, 702n88, 702n90, 703n106, 704n123; Charter of Values testimony, 537, 537(f), 538; counsel adviser, 529, 701n63; decision reading, 529; Florida condo, 530(f); freedom of religion (private vs public display), 537, 538; grandmother, 528(f), 529, 531(f); international judicial education, 529; judge-in-residence, 529; judicial robes and swearing-out ceremony, 525–26; law clerk reunions, 529, 530(f); post-retirement activities, 529-31, 530(f), 531(f); religious views and gender equality, 531–33; retirement date, 522, 698n16; retirement reactions, 523(f)–29

— *Supreme Court of Canada: 319–502*
about, 341(f), 348(f), 541–42; about Justice Lamer's capacity, 520, 521, 698n5; about Justice McClung's personal attacks and apology, 489–92, 497, 502, 689n8, 690n25, 690n32; about Justice Wilson, 334; administrative law, 474–77; affirmative action, 336, 640n38; animosity with Justice Lamer, 338–39(f), 347–55(f), 349, 357,

370–71, 461, 462–63, 491–92, 497, 520, 522; appointment, 319–29(f), 335–41(f), 548n10, 637n21, 638n62, 640nn37–38, 642n81; assisted suicide case, 278, 623n49; awards, 500; on bilingual justices, 465, 683n72; cartoon, 360(f); on *Charter* cases jurisprudence, 323, 362, 494, 649n39; on a chief justice appointment, 351–52, 644n28; children's rights, 475–76; compartmentalization, 343; conferences, 373; court attendant, 343; on criminal law, 347–49; criminal law rulings vs Justice Lamer, 363–64, 649nn34–35; decision statistics, 363–64, 646n2, 648nn31–32, 649nn33–35, 649n38; decision-writing protocol, 10–11, 548nn10–11; decisions and gender differences, 437, 676n65; decisions in French, 463–65, 683nn60–61, 683nn64–65, 683n72; on discrimination, 370, 475–77, 481, 490, 542, 643n11, 690n20; on dissents, 374–75, 394, 646n61, 660n112; driving habits, 339, 526, 642n66, 700n40, 700n43; early days, 330–46; equality decisions, 362, 648n27, 649n38; on family status, 424; as female appointment, 322, 328–29(f), 335–41(f), 637n21; female law clerks treatment, 366–67, 650n50; on feminism and not identifying as, 349, 437, 486, 528, 542–45, 700n51, 705n11, 706n14; feminization of poverty, 405, 406; formalism vs realism, 374, 407; French-language decisions, 463–65, 683nn59–61, 683nn64–65, 683n72; gender as challenge, 330–32, 639n7; gender equality task force, 349, 643n11; gift (Nellie McClung photo), 500–1; "Great Dissenter" title, 3, 373–76, 651n74; immigration law case, 473–77, 687n45; on income tax and childcare, 436; international human rights law, 476; as internationalist, 465, 466; isolation on court, 332–33, 490–92, 690n25, 690n32; judicial activism, 425; on judicial appointments reform, 636n12; judicial approach and decision-making process, 425–26, 498–99, 651n61; on judicial bias complaints and "bench-bashing," 494; judicial conferences, 342, 357, 642n81, 646n61; judicial notice and social context, 407–9;

judicial relationships, 334, 335–41(f), 350–51, 491–92, 497, 520, 644n26; judicial robes, 327–28; jurisprudence shift, 360–73, 646n1, 649n39; on justice vs stability, 374; with Justices McLachlin and Lamer, 364(f); as "*La Tigresse*," 198–200, 488; as law and order judge, 360–61, 363–65, 370, 372, 496; law clerks, 327–28, 332–33(f), 334, 365–68(f), 369(f), 370, 375, 376, 384, 426–27(f), 477, 488, 489, 499, 650n50, 650n52, 672n88, 673n91; law conference reception, 499, 692n77; lawyer-mother status, 402, 664n54; on *le bâtonnier* title, 235; marriage and substantive vs formal equality, 406, 666n80; with McLachlin and Dickson, 388(f); nicknames, 334; as outsider, 330–35, 347–58, 646n56, 646n61, 651n74; personal life and friendships, 344–45; personality traits, 334–35, 336, 338–39, 345–46, 349–50, 356, 387, 499, 645n54, 657n65, 692n77; on procedural fairness, 474, 477, 687n27; Quebec justices and judicial collegiality, 325, 332–33, 347; Quebec lieutenant-governor candidate, 353, 645n39; as "Queen of the Gays," 425; race analysis, 480–82; realism, 374; religious views and church values, 467, 684n81; reputation and influence, 499–500, 545; retirement celebrations, 524, 526–29, 527(f), 528(f), 699n35, 699n37; same-sex couples case, 418, 422, 423–26, 671n64, 671n66, 671n75, 672n87; secession case, 461–63, 467, 469; secretary, 343; on separatism, 463, 465–67; sexual assault case, 10–13, 384–87, 389–90, 392–94, 425, 523, 549n15, 660n102, 660n105; sexual assault case reaction, 16–19, 550n47, 550n49; social justice, 361, 371–72; socio-economic sources, 407–9; song, 500; spousal support case, 401–2, 404–7, 410, 411, 425, 664n52, 665n60, 665n69, 665n72, 667n117, 668nn118–20; staff, 343; standard of judicial review, 474, 669n42, 687n23; swearing-in ceremony, 327–29(f), 638n62; swearing-out ceremony, 526–27(f), 528, 700n44, 700n51; tax law case, 434–37, 676n51; work ethic and working hours, 343, 345, 366,

642n86; written briefs and oral arguments process, 344
Liberal Party of Canada, 211–15, 607n2, 608n5, 608n18
Lillie, Mildred L., 221, 223
Liu, Mimi, 488, 516
Llewellyn, Karl, 374
Lorde, Audre, 423–24, 426
Lorenz, George, 471–72, 474–75, 477, 478, 686nn13–14
Lortie, Denis, 300, 628n40
Lucky, Justice Gillian, 517

M. Pollack Ltd., 124, 596n5
M v. H. (1999) family law case, 424, 657n65
Macdonald, Donald, 224
MacDonald, Flora, 284, 608n19
MacGuigan, Mark, 416, 424, 669n24
MacKinnon, Catharine, 12, 17, 383, 492, 550n47
Macklin, Audrey, 438, 478, 480, 483, 484(f), 675n48
Maclean's, 325
Macpherson, Don, 535
Madame le juge title, 234–35
"Madonna-Whore Complex," 385
Mahoney, Kathleen, 18, 512
Mailhot, Louise: about, 196(f), 603n105; about Justice L'Heureux-Dubé, 192, 260, 326, 638n48; about male judges and lawyers, 195, 294; appointment, 322, 325; judicial robes, 615n29
Mailloux, Noël, 312–13, 634n41
Major, Justice John (Jack): about, 348(f), 460; about Justice Lamer, 351, 352, 521, 644n21, 698n12; about Justice L'Heureux-Dubé, 351, 352, 358, 359, 452, 500, 644n26, 646n1, 651n61; about Justices L'Heureux-Dubé and McClung, 491, 690n25; appointment, 548n10; bias complaint case, 482, 688n67; friendship and hunting with Justice McClung, 11, 548n12; interveners, 688n53; judicial animosity, 352; judicial discord, 651n74; on male and female judges, 14; same-sex couples case, 423, 672n76; secession case, 463; sexual assault cases, 1, 549n14, 660n112; tax law case, 674n26
Makin, Kirk: about Justice L'Heureux-Dubé, 329, 334, 352, 520; about Justice McClung, 14, 491, 492, 691n39; judicial animosity, 352, 520; newspaper wars, 550n37
male justices: judicial opinion vs female justices, 385, 437, 676n65, 677n67; treatment of female justices, 230–34, 258, 293–97, 490, 643n11, 690nn20–21; treatment of female lawyers, 194–96, 604n15. *See also* female justices; justices
male law students, 108–9, 573n41
male lawyers, 195–96, 604n19, 604n21, 604n23, 605n30. *See also* female lawyers; lawyers
Manitoba Court of Appeal, 398, 406–7, 662n17, 666n82
Manitoba Court of Queen's Bench, 397–98
Mansbridge, Peter, 409
Marchand, Jean, 212(f)–13, 220, 224–25, 238, 607n2, 612n77, 616n2
Marcoux, Eric, 369(f)
Margaret Brent Award, 524–25
marijuana decriminalization, 340
Marin, André, 447
Marquis, Justice Eugène, 231, 256(f), 618n2
Marquis, Jacques, 237
marriage: gay rights perspective, 415–16; gender inequality, 406, 598n24, 599n25, 601n71; traditional vs modern, 395–96, 398–99; working women, 170–71, 594n30. *See also* divorce
Marseille, Pierre, 106, 118, 119, 572n26
Marshall, Donald J. inquiry, 506–7
Martel, Thérèse, 87(f), 90(f)
Martin, Clara Brett, 93, 108
Martin, Paul, 203(f)
Martin, Sheilah, 391
Martineau Walker law firm, 195
Masson, Paul, 83
Mastercraft uniform factory, 153
Matheson, Wendy, 430
matrimonial law. *See* family law
Mayor's Committee on Race Relations, 472
Mayrand, Justice Albert, 190, 295, 296(f), 627n17, 628n39
McCarthy, Gérald, 628n40, 629n52, 630n55, 631nn62–63, 631n67, 632n71
McClung, Justice John Wesley "Buzz": about, 14, 15(f), 549n33; friendship with Justices Lamer and Major, 11, 548n12;

homophobic comments, 549n18; judicial bias complaints, 493–94, 691n44, 691n47; personal attack on Justice L'Heureux-Dubé (letter and apology), 13–15, 487–88, 497, 502, 550n41, 689n3; sexual assault case, 9, 548n7; sexual assault case reaction, 16–19, 551n67; treatment of female justices, 14, 549n29, 550n34
McClung, Nellie, 14, 500, 501(f), 502
McEachern, Chief Justice Allan, 493
McGill Birth Control Handbook, 205
McGill University law school: anti-Semitism, 584n14; female students, 144, 280, 307, 573n31, 585n22, 589n12; professors, 189(f), 340, 602n93
McGovern, Celeste, 495, 692n59
McIntyre, Justice William: about, 335, 337, 341(f); about Justice L'Heureux-Dubé, 325, 337; decisions, 629n44, 663n44; judicial self-restraint, 362
McIntyre, Sheila, 18–19
McIsaac, Barbara, 418, 420, 669n42, 672n81
McLachlin, Justice Beverley: about, 348(f), 387–88(f), 437, 460, 657n69; about Justice Lamer, 698n15; about Justice L'Heureux-Dubé, 352, 426, 524, 525–26, 527(f)–28, 672n87, 699n37, 700n40; appointment, 548n10, 657n70; assisted suicide case, 623n49; decisions and gender differences, 436–37, 676n65, 677n67; equality rights, 648n27, 649n38; gender equality, 437, 527–28; immigration law case, 473; on judicial collegiality and discord, 352, 356, 651n74; judicial complaint, 676n63; judicial education and social context, 694n13; with Justice L'Heureux-Dubé, 527(f); with Justices L'Heureux-Dubé and Lamer, 364(f); same-sex couples case, 418, 422, 423, 671n66; sexual assault case, 11, 387–88, 549n20, 657n66, 657n74, 658n77, 658n81, 660n112; speeches, 525–26, 527–28, 676n63, 699n37; spousal support case, 405, 664n52, 665n69; tax law case, 436–37
McLeod, Jay, 410, 667n113
McTeer, Maureen, 284–85(f), 624n9
McWilliams, Justice David, 447
mediation vs adversarial system (family law), 181, 183

Meech Lake accord, 456
Mère Sainte-Thérèse de l'Enfant Jésus, 74
Messier v. Delage spousal support case, 400, 405
Michaud, Philippe, 85, 311, 446
military tribunal case, 365
Miquelon, Justice Paul, 183, 256(f), 601n56
Moge, Andrzej, 395–96, 397, 402, 409, 661n1
Moge, Ed (son of Andrzej and Zofia Moge), 409
Moge, Zofia, 395–96, 397, 402, 406, 409, 661n1, 662nn13–15, 666n82
Moge v. Moge (1989), 397–98, 662nn14–15
Moge v. Moge (1990), 397, 662nn10–11, 662n13, 662n17
Moge v. Moge (1992) spousal support case, 395–411, 665n69, 665n72, 666n82. See also spousal support
Mohr, Renate, 383
Monahan, Patrick, 468
Monastère des Ursulines de L'Immaculée Conception (Rimouski): about, 63–64(f), 65(f)–66, 68(f), 558n3; classical courses, 73–75, 560n56; student recruitment, 66, 559n14
Monet, Amédée, 296(f); about Justice L'Heureux-Dubé, 294–95, 306, 350; criminal cases, 314, 632n73; defamation case, 300–1, 629n44; police conduct inquiry, 628n37; spousal support case, 301, 302, 629nn51–52, 630nn56–57
Monet-Chartrand, Simone, 203(f), 204(f)
Monk, Elizabeth Carmichael, 95(f)–96, 566n18, 567n24
Montgomery, Justice George, 295, 296(f), 305, 627n18, 631n67, 632n71
Montreal Gazette, 300–1, 328, 535, 629n44
Montreal Local Council of Women, 94, 598n21
Morin, Albanie: electoral candidate, 214–15(f), 608n16; judicial appointment process, 216, 220, 226–27, 610n33, 610n39
Morin, Calin: about Ginette Fournier, 582n20; about Justice Vallée, 619n9; law school, 108(f), 109, 117–18, 573n41; marriage and career choice, 580n8; women and law practices, 136, 137, 582n15
Morton, Ted, 16

Mossop, Brian: about, 412–13(f), 414, 668n2; decision reaction, 427; human rights complaint as test case, 414–15, 668n12; on supplementary submissions, 419, 420, 421, 669n42, 670n54; testimony, 417–18
Mossop v. Canada (Secretary of State) (1989) same-sex couples case, 412–27, 657n65, 671nn66–67, 671n75, 672n81
motherhood guilt, 172, 312, 633n8
Mulroney, Prime Minister Brian: on judicial animosity, 353; judicial appointments, 319–21(f), 322–23, 325, 635n6, 635n8, 636nn13–14; law school, 322, 637n16
murder cases: death penalty, 117, 234, 262, 577n47, 615nn18–19; decisions, 286–87, 314–15, 364–65, 634n50, 649n35
Murdoch v. Murdoch (1975) family law case, 667n114
Muslims: mass murder shootings, 539; traditional dress bans, 532–39, 702n86, 702n91, 703n99, 704nn122–23

National Action Committee on the Status of Women, 226, 438. *See also* Canadian Advisory Council on the Status of Women; Conseil du statut de la femme; Royal Commission on the Status of Women
National Assembly shooting, 300, 628n40
National Association of Women and the Law (NAWL), 140, 499, 524, 583n27, 692n77
National Judicial Institute (NJI), 506, 509, 694n12
National Post, 13, 14–19, 482, 513, 550n37, 550n42
Nepal (judicial education), 510, 513
Neuwirth, Jessica (Equality Now), 513
New Brunswick v. G. (J.) (1999) child custody case, 411, 668n118
newspapers, 13–19, 388–89, 391, 482–83, 550n37, 550n42
Nixon, President Richard, 221, 223, 225
"No means No" reference (sexual assault case), 8, 9, 394, 494–97, 660n108, 660nn111–12
Nolan, Justice John A., 295, 296(f), 627n19, 631n66
Noonan, Joseph, 95
North Shore Paper company, 123

Notre-Dame-de-Bellevue. *See* Collège Notre-Dame-de-Bellevue (Quebec City)
Nova Scotia (Attorney General) v. Walsh (2002) spousal support case, 411, 668n119
nuns. *See* Ursuline nuns
Nuss, Joseph R., 240–41(f), 290, 305, 616n11

O'Connor, Justice Sandra Day, 100, 219, 221
Official Languages Act (1988), 464, 683n65
Ogilvy Renault law firm, 319, 616n11, 635n4, 637n16
Ontario Bar Association (retirement dinner), 524, 699n35, 699n37
Ontario Court of Appeal: rape-shield laws, 382–83, 655n32; sexual assault case, 658n88; sexual orientation discrimination, 419–20, 422, 670n44
Ontario Family Law Act, 425
Ontario Superior Court, 447
Orphelinat du Couvent des Soeurs de la Charité (orphanage), 58, 557n24
Ortenberg, Rose (Sam Bard's mother), 143, 583n6, 584n8
Orton, Helena, 383, 403
Osgoode Hall Law Journal, 374
Osgoode Hall Law School (Toronto): faculty, 113, 340; female students, 108, 573n34, 577n40
Osgoode Women's Legal Society, 108, 573n34
Ottawa Citizen, 16, 523, 679n48
Ottawa Law Review, 408
Ouellet, Andrée, 44(f), 53(f)
Ouellet, Jacques, 44(f)
Ouellet, Raymonde, 44(f), 53(f)
Owen, Justice George W.R.: about, 296(f), 626n5; decisions in English, 305; defamation lawsuit decision, 300–1, 629n44; family law decisions, 301, 302, 629n51, 630n57; on female judicial appointments, 293–94, 325–26; relationship with Justice L'Heureux-Dubé, 293–94, 306, 350, 626n6; sexual assault decision, 631n66

Pacht, Arline, 500, 514–15
Paciocco, David, 348–49, 408, 498
Pakistan (judicial education), 510, 511(f)

Palestine (judicial education and prison), 514
Paré, Justice Rodolphe, 296(f), 630n58
Parent, Alphonse-Marie, 103
Parizeau, Quebec Premier Jacques, 456, 457(f), 468
Parsons, Vera, 200
Parti Québécois (PQ), 299, 539, 628n38. *See also* Quebec Secession Reference (1998)
paternity case, 264–65
patronage appointments, 185, 322, 601n76
Paul, Rémi, 188, 602n87
Payne, Julien: about Pierre Dubé, 308; family law, 180, 299, 410, 600n38, 667n114; on judicial notice, 408; on Justice L'Heureux-Dubé, 207; "Know Thy Judge," 400, 401; law school, 667n113
Le Pays, 94, 564n7, 565n8
Pelech v. Pelech (1987) spousal support case, 400–1, 663n45
Pelletier, Gérard, 81, 212(f), 213, 607n2
Pelletier, Laurette, 286–87
pension benefits, 423, 424, 671n75
Pentney, William, 420–21, 422–23, 670n54
Perron, Monique, 85, 108, 158, 223–24, 276, 592n54
Persons Case (women as persons), 288
Pharmacie Boissinot, 85
Philippe-Pinel Institute (juvenile detention centre), 314
Philippon, Jacques, 177(f), 224, 257, 329(f), 524, 596n10, 596n12
Phillips, Jim, 643n11
Phillips and Vineberg law firm, 158, 627n20
Pigeon, Louis-Philippe, 114–15, 116, 576n27
police conduct inquiries, 299, 628n37
Pollack, Maurice: about, 124, 152–54(f), 590n19; church boycott, 153; philanthropy, 154(f), 590nn25–26; on synagogue arson, 586n25; union relations, 153, 590n24; wartime contract, 153
Popert, Ken, 412–13(f), 415–16, 668n3
Posner, Justice Richard A., 305, 374
Potvin, Abbé, 80
poverty (women), 398, 471, 662n25, 663n46
Power, Charles (Chubby) Gavan, 24, 552n6

Prassad v. Canada (Minister of Employment and Immigration) (1989) case, 362
Pratte, Yves, 323, 324, 333, 637n31
La Presse, 18
Prévost, Gagné et al. law firm, 195, 260, 571n20, 575n20, 624nn5–6
Price Brothers sawmill, 42, 55
Primeau, René, 245, 249
prisoners: human rights activist, 697n62; right to vote rulings, 365, 649n38
prisons, 511, 514
Provost, René, 483
Purdon, Brian, 245–46, 247

Quebec: abortion, 205; anti-Semitism, 143–45, 148–49, 584n9, 584n14, 585n15, 585n17, 585n20, 586n25, 586nn27–28, 587n32; birth control and birth rate, 594n20; *Charter* clauses, 538–39, 659n101; child care, 430; cinemas, 83–84, 563n50; civil law, 359, 647n4; class status, 54–57, 104, 570n13; cultural attitudes toward women, 34, 96, 97, 170, 205, 567n23, 568n29, 594n30; divorce law, 178, 598n19; divorce statistics, 182, 600n50; education, 28–29, 64–66, 73–75, 77–78, 552n11, 553n25, 558n8, 560n56, 561n64; elections, 539; emigration, 23, 551n2; English- vs French-language legal discourse, 159, 592nn57–58, 592nn61–62; feminist movement, 204–5, 225–29, 606nn58–59, 607nn69–70, 613n89; immigration, 42, 143, 555nn36–37; Jewish law firms, 141, 144, 150–51, 583n1, 585n18; Jewish population, 147, 587n40; Jews and education, 143, 584n11; land rights case and statutes, 262–64, 620nn49–52, 620n57; lawyers and law firm statistics, 150, 176, 588nn1–3, 595nn2–3; lieutenant-governor, 106, 353, 571n21, 645n39; marriage contracts, 165, 593n12; patriarchy, 34; secession participation, 457–58; Second World War, 70–72, 560n52; secularism and legislative bills, 533–39, 702n83, 702n86, 703n101, 703n108, 704nn122–23; sovereignty referendums, 454–55, 456, 468, 684n92, 685n93; women, education, 28–29, 77–78, 553n25; women, employment and marriage, 34, 96, 97, 170, 205, 567n23, 568n29, 594n30; women judges, 291(f);

Index 735

women lawyers, 93–96, 178, 193, 564*nn*6–7, 565*nn*8–9, 566*n*13, 566*n*17, 597*nn*16–17, 603*nn*1–2; women politicians, 213–15; women's suffrage legislation, 34, 562*n*24
Quebec Bar. *See* Barreau du Québec (Bar of Quebec)
Quebec Charter of Human Rights and Freedoms, 647*n*4
Quebec Charter of Values, 533–39, 702*n*83, 702*n*86, 703*n*101, 703*n*108
Quebec City: about, 33; Jewish lawyers, 141, 150–51, 583*n*1; Jewish population, 147, 587*n*40; lawyer statistics, 150, 176, 588*n*1, 595*nn*2–3
Quebec Court of Appeal: appointments, 286, 603*n*105, 625*n*13; collegiality, 332–33, 347; criminal cases, 302–5, 631*n*61, 631*nn*68–69, 632*nn*70–74; defamation case, 299–300, 628*n*39; family law cases, 301–2, 629*nn*51–52, 630*nn*55–58, 631*n*60; judicial robes, 235; judicial triad and appeals process, 297–98, 304–5, 627*n*26; justices, 286, 296(f), 625*n*13; land rights case, 263; sexual assault cases, 303, 631*nn*62–67
Quebec Human Rights Commission (QHRC), 534, 702*n*90
Quebec Legislative Assembly, 116–17
Quebec Provincial Court (Cour du Québec), 122, 579*n*68
Quebec (Public Curator) v. Syndicat national des employés de l'hôpital St-Ferdinand (1996) compensation entitlement case, 359, 647*n*4
Quebec Secession Reference (1998): *amicus curiae* court power, 458; constitutional principles, 467, 683*n*54; critics, 456–59; decision and reaction, 467–69, 683*n*54, 684*n*92; decision-making process and media scrutiny, 460–63; demonstrations, 459, 682*n*29; Francophone judges, 461–62; hearing submissions, 459–60; interveners, 458; judges, 454, 460–62, 681*n*7; media coverage, 454, 457, 459, 460; secession as political process, 468; secession options, 456
Quebec Society of Comparative Law, 516
Quebec Superior Court: appointments, 106, 176, 216–25, 573*n*30, 583*n*23, 596*n*7, 596*n*9, 596*n*12, 597*n*13, 602*n*82, 603*n*105, 606*n*62, 610*nn*31–32, 618*n*3; case assignments, 235–37, 261–62; chambers and courthouse atmosphere, 234; chief justice title, 618*n*2; child custody case, 266, 267–68, 621*n*68, 621*n*70, 622*n*80; civil cases, 261–64, 619*n*43, 620*nn*51–52; conduct inquiries, 570*n*19; criminal cases, 619*n*44; female justice title, 234–35; female justices appointments, 122, 292, 579*n*69, 618*n*3, 620*n*59, 626*n*38; female notary, 566*n*17; judicial circuits, 257–59; judicial robes, 235, 615*nn*28–29; justices, 256(f), 614*n*10; paternity case, 264–65; patronage appointment, 185, 601*n*76; secession options, 456; spousal support cases, 265, 266–67, 621*nn*64–65, 621*n*73, 622*n*74, 622*n*76; swearing-in ceremony and justices, 231(f)
Quebec Winter Club, 147
Queen's Counsel (QC), 147, 188
Quiet Revolution: French-language associations, 463–64, 683*n*59; legal education changes, 575*n*23; post-Duplessis, 466; Roman Catholic Church, 466, 684*n*81; visionaries, 174, 571*n*22; women's movement, 137, 193, 225–29, 603*n*3
Qureshi, Amna, 535–36(f)

R. v. Ewanchuk sexual assault cases, 8–19, 486–502, 548*n*2, 548*n*4, 548*n*7, 693*n*89, 693*nn*91–92. *See also* Ewanchuk, Steve
R. v. Généreux (1992) military tribunal case, 365
R. v. Keegstra hate propaganda case, 361
R. v. Lavallee (1990) abortion rights case, 392, 659*n*100
R. v. Martineau (1990) murder case, 364–65, 649*n*35
R. v. Morgentaler (1988) abortion rights case, 361, 392, 648*n*17, 659*n*100
R. v. Sauvé (2002) prisoners' right to vote case, 365, 649*n*38
R. v. Seaboyer sexual assault case, 362, 379–94, 405, 523, 648*n*27, 653*n*7, 653*n*13, 654*nn*14–15, 654*nn*20–22, 655*n*33, 658*n*81, 658*n*88, 659*nn*89–90, 660*n*105, 660*nn*111–12
R. v. Swain murder case, 365, 649*n*36
R. v. Thibaudeau (1995) tax and child support case, 436, 657*n*65, 676*n*58
race relations: analysis, 251–52, 618*n*70; black lawyers, 478–80, 481; judiciary, 478–82, 506–7

Racette-Cadieux, Rita, 226
racial bias, 478–79, 481–82, 507, 688*n*53, 688*n*65
rape-shield law: *Charter* override clause, 659*n*101; decision critique, 391–94, 658*n*88; legislative reform, 380–81, 382, 653*nn*9–11, 653*n*13, 654*nn*14–15, 654*nn*17–18, 655*n*32; protest, 391(f)
Ratushny, Ed, 220, 611*n*47, 612*n*57
Raymond-Filion, Suzanne, 95(f)–96, 566*n*18, 567*n*24
Razack, Sherene, 381
R.D.S. bias complaint case, 481–82, 688*n*67
REAL Women of Canada, 16, 418–19, 490, 492–93
realism, 113, 374, 407, 666*n*94
Reference re Same-Sex Marriage (2004) case, 425
Reference re Secession of Quebec (1998). *See* Quebec Secession Reference (1998)
referendums (Quebec sovereignty): polls, 468, 685*n*93; results, 454–55, 456
Régiment de Montmagny, 30–31(f)
religion. *See* Roman Catholic Church
religious mass murder shootings (Muslims), 539
Revenue Canada tax law case, 428–41
Révolution Tranquille. *See* Quiet Revolution
Rhodes Scholarship, 120, 578*n*63
Rich, Adrienne, 423, 426
Richardson v. Richardson (1987) spousal support case, 400–1
Rimouski: about, 39–43(f), 44–45, 555*nn*34–37; economic conditions and class status, 42, 43, 55, 556*nn*45–46, 557*n*14; fire, 123; orphanage, 58, 557*n*24
Rimouski Lecture Club, 101
Rimouski Press Club, 262
Rinfret, Justice Édouard, 286, 288–89(f), 296(f), 625*n*27
Ritchie, Marguerite E., 200, 605*n*43
Rivard, J.-Claude, 259, 290
Robert, Quebec Chief Justice J.J. Michel, 349
Robichaud v. Canada (Treasury Board) (1987) sexual harassment case, 361
Robins, Justice Sydney, 140, 583*n*27
Robinson, Ann, 18, 580*n*35
Rock, Allan, 440

Rodriguez v. British Columbia (Attorney General) (1993) assisted-suicide case, 278, 623*n*49
Roman Catholic Church: boycotts, 153; censorship, 201–2; convent schools, 65–67; divorce prohibition, 181; on Judaism, 42, 153; lay orders, 231, 613*n*5; treatment of women, 82, 532; values, 467, 684*n*81
Roman law, 112, 115
Romanow, Saskatchewan Premier Roy, 468
Rosenberg, Marc, 389
Rosenfeld, Florence Margulis, 100
Rothman, Justice Melvin: about, 615*n*16, 627*n*20; about Justice L'Heureux-Dubé, 161, 233–34, 260–61, 276, 295, 298, 306; about Justices L'Heureux-Dubé and Lamer, 491–92, 643*n*12; decisions, 314, 315, 632*n*74; English-language decisions, 305; law firm reputation, 158; on treatment of women, 233–34
Rothstein, Justice Marshall, 479
Roussin, Claude, 290
Rowe, Roger, 472–73(f), 478–79, 484–85, 686*n*21
Roy, Bernard, 320, 322, 325, 637*n*16
Royal Canadian Mounted Police (RCMP) computer theft case, 299, 628*n*38
Royal Commission on Bilingualism and Biculturalism, 159, 592*n*62
Royal Commission on the Status of Women, 205, 225–26. *See also* National Action Committee on the Status of Women
Russell, Peter, 18, 410, 468, 636*n*12

Sabia, Maureen, 225, 604*n*19
Sachs, Justice Albie, 508, 517, 649*n*39
Saint-Pierre, Justice Henri-Césaire, 94, 564*n*7, 565*n*8
Salutin, Rick, 18, 490
Salvation Army, 418, 419
same-sex couples human rights cases, 412–27, 657*n*65, 671*nn*66–67, 671*n*75, 672*n*81
Sanatorium Prévost, 57, 557*n*22
Sandler, Mark, 382, 394, 660*n*108
Sankoff, Peter, 334, 367–68, 683*n*61, 703*n*106
Sargent, Laurie, 367, 368(f), 650*n*53, 673*n*91, 703*n*106, 705*n*14

Saskatchewan (Human Rights Commission) v. Saskatoon (City) (1989); *Saskatchewan (Human Rights Commission) v. Moose Jaw (City)* age discrimination case, 362
Saumar, Laurier, 154–55, 591*n*32, 591*n*36
Saumur v. Quebec (City) (1953) freedom of religion case, 155, 591*n*36
Sauvé, Jeanne, 81, 203, 215(f), 227, 562*n*29
Sauvé v. Canada (1993) and *Sauvé II* prisoners' right to vote case, 365, 649*n*38
Scassa, Teresa: about Justice Lamer, 642*n*66; about Justice L'Heureux-Dubé, 361, 368, 499, 705*n*14; bilingual decisions, 464, 465, 683*n*65; Francophone vs Anglophone judicial differences, 333–34; with Justice L'Heureux-Dubé, 369(f)
Schmitz, Cristin, 489, 523
Schwarzbard, Jacob (Sam Bard's father), 143, 584*n*8
Schwarzbard, Samuel. *See* Bard (Schwarzbard), Samuel
Scott, David QC, 375
Scott, Frank R., 199, 590*n*29
Scott, Ian, 113, 575*n*16
Scott, Sheena, 484
Seaboyer sexual assault case. *See R. v. Seaboyer* sexual assault case
Second World War, 70–72
Selick, Karen, 381–82
separatism (demonstrations), 459, 682*n*29
sex discrimination. *See* gender inequality; judicial bias; tax law discrimination case
sex offenders, 502, 693*nn*89–92
sexual assault cases: about, 8–19, 379–94; "bonnets and crinolines" reference, 8, 9, 14, 19; complainants, 8–9, 13, 361; conviction rates, 380, 653*n*8; decision critiques, 16–19, 550*n*47, 550*n*49, 551*n*67; decisions, 10–13, 384–94, 548*n*11, 549*nn*14–15, 549*n*18, 549*n*20, 648*n*27, 655*n*33, 658*n*81, 658*n*88, 659*nn*89–90, 660*n*105, 660*n*112; female decisions, 16–19, 390, 392; implied consent, 9, 385, 494–97, 548*n*7, 692*nn*57–59; international judicial education, 511, 696*n*34; judicial discord, 349; law students treatment, 117–18, 577*n*45; legislation reforms, 385–86, 394, 656*n*51, 656*n*53, 660*n*108, 660*nn*111–12; media coverage, 13–19, 550*n*41; "No means No" reference, 8, 9, 394, 494–97, 660*n*108, 660*nn*111–12; sentences, 502, 693*nn*89–92; sexual history, 371–81, 385–86, 394, 653*n*7, 653*n*9, 653*n*13, 654*nn*14–15, 654*nn*20–22, 657*n*74, 658*n*77, 659*n*101, 660*n*112; statistics, 385; wrongful convictions, 511
sexual behaviour and implied consent (public discourse), 494–97, 692*n*57
sexual harassment, 116, 123–24, 248, 361, 576*n*36, 577*n*40
sexual history, 371–81, 385–86, 394, 653*n*7, 653*n*9, 653*n*13, 654*nn*14–15, 654*nn*20–22, 657*n*74, 658*n*77, 659*n*101, 660*n*112
sexual misconduct inquiry, 238–52
sexual mores, 163, 593*n*6
sexual orientation and human rights, 416–20, 422, 424, 669*n*23, 669*n*37, 670*n*44, 671*n*67, 672*n*76
Sheehy, Elizabeth, 12, 380–81, 383, 388, 392–93(f), 659*n*101
Sherry, Chief Michael, 459
Shilton, Elizabeth, 382, 383(f)
Short, Constance Garner, 95(f)–96, 566*n*18, 567*n*24
Siddiqui, Haroon, 535
Sikh traditions (freedom of religion), 531–32
Simpson, Shirley, 430
Sinclair, Justice Murray, 479
Sir George Williams University, 251, 618*n*70
Sister Sainte-Héléna/Mère Sainte-Héléna (Gabrielle Massicotte), 79–80, 89, 97, 562*n*18, 568*n*29
Slayton, Philip, 350, 391, 549*n*20, 683*n*54
Snyder, Gerald M., 300–1, 629*n*44
social context judicial education, 507–8, 694*nn*12–13, 695*n*16, 695*n*20, 697*n*74
social justice grants, 524, 699*n*29
social sciences, 114, 120, 570*n*7, 575*n*24
Société des enfants de Marie, 81
Les Soeurs des Saints-Noms de Jésus et de Marie, 66
Le Soleil, 94, 290
Sopinka, Justice John: abortion case, 361, 648*n*17; about Justice L'Heureux-Dubé, 351, 451, 644*n*26; appointment, 635*n*8; bias complaint case, 482, 688*n*67; on decisions and dissent, 375, 651*n*74; deportation case, 362; same-sex couples case, 418, 421–23, 671*n*66; sexual assault

cases, 657n66, 660n112; spousal support case, 664n52; tax law case, 674n26
Sossin, Lorne, 483, 484
spousal support: challenges, 183–84; decisions, 265, 266–67, 395–411, 621nn64–65, 621n73, 622n74, 622n76, 630nn56–58, 631n60, 663nn45–47, 665n69, 665n72, 668nn119–20; feminization of poverty, 398, 399, 405, 406, 666n82; increase request, 397, 662nn13–14; lump sum awards (clean break), 301, 398–99, 400, 401, 629nn51–52; payment orders, 265–68, 621nn64–65, 662nn10–12; and revenue equalization, 267, 268, 622n77; statistics, 398, 400–1, 662n25, 663n47. *See also* divorce
Sri Lanka (judicial education), 510, 513
Sridevan, Justice Prabha, 513
St. Joseph Street tavern, 194, 201, 205–6
St. Laurent, Prime Minister Louis, 106, 150, 583n4, 588n2, 592n61
Stuart, Don, 354–55, 499, 660n112
students. *See* law students
suicide (assisted), 278, 623n49
Sullivan, Joan, 140
Sullivan, Ruth, 409
Sun Trust, 102, 123–24
Superior Court. *See* Quebec Superior Court
Supreme Court of Canada: agreement rates, 33, 34, 35, 36, 347, 363–64, 643n2, 648n32, 649n38; *amicus curiae* power, 458; appointments, 106, 328–29, 548n10, 571nn20–22; appointments process, 319–21(f), 351, 635n2, 635n6, 635n8, 636nn11–14, 644n28, 657n70; assisted suicide case, 278, 623n49; backlog, 342–43; building, 335; cartoons, 360(f), 457, 458(f), 681n20; cases, 377–441, 454–502; chief justice, 351, 404, 418, 491–92, 644n28, 665n66, 691n39; consensus, 463; court language, 325, 463–65, 683nn60–61, 683nn64–65, 683n72; court retreat, 354; courtroom, 419(f); criminal caseload, 338, 641n60; decision-writing protocols, 10–11, 548nn10–11, 549nn14–15, 549n20; decisions and feminist analysis, 432, 674n22; decisions and gender differences, 437, 676n65, 677n67; ethnic diversity, 320, 432, 635n8, 674n27; female justices treatment, 349, 643n11; Francophone justices, 325, 332–34, 461–62; immigration law case, 470–85, 685n1; interveners, 381–84, 403–4, 431, 478–79, 655n25, 688n53; judicial activism, 425, 672n81; judicial bias complaints, 492–94, 691n40; judicial collegiality, 337, 340–41(f); judicial conferences, 342, 357, 643n11, 646n61; judicial discord, 335–41, 347–58, 490–92, 640n29, 645n35, 651n74; judicial nominees, 319; judicial notice and social context, 407–9, 666n83; judicial panels, 404, 418, 665n66; judicial robes, 327–28, 525–26; justices, 341(f), 348(f), 460–61, 643n1; law clerks, 365–68(f), 369(f), 370; lawyer briefs, 344; race-sensitivity gap, 478–82; same-sex couples case, 418–21, 657n65, 671nn66–67, 671n75, 672n81; secession reference case, 463, 467–69, 681n7, 683n54, 684n92; secondary sources, 385, 656n43; sexual assault case, 10–13, 384–94, 548n11, 549nn14–15, 549n18, 549n20, 648n27, 655n33, 658n81, 658n88, 659nn89–90, 660n105, 660n112; spousal support case, 265, 266–67, 395–411, 621nn64–65, 621n73, 622n74, 622n76, 630nn56–58, 631n60, 663nn45–47, 665n69, 665n72, 668nn119–20; standard of judicial review, 419, 474, 669n42, 687n23; swearing-in ceremonies, 328, 638n62; swearing-out event, 521–22
Swarbrick, Anne, 392, 659n96
Symes, Beth, 382, 428–29(f), 431–32, 440–41, 673n4
Symes, Michael, 430
Symes, Kiteley & McIntyre law firm, 428, 673n2
Syndicat des employés de production du Québec et de l'Acadie v. Canada (Canadian Human Rights Commission) (1989) employment case, 362

Tanguay, Sister Caroline, 68, 73, 551n1, 559n28
Tardif, Simone, 172, 450
Taschereau, Quebec Premier Louis-Alexandre, 33
taverns (women barred), 194, 201, 205–6, 604n7
tax law discrimination case, 428–41, 674n24, 674n26, 676n58, 678n93

Taylor, Charles, 531–32, 534, 704*n*123
Teasdale, Francine (second wife of Paul Henri L'Heureux), 166, 316, 443, 444, 593*n*14, 678*n*5
Tellier, Paul, 322, 637*n*17
Tetley, William, 106, 113, 114–15, 136, 148, 572*n*27
Therrien, Gaston, 245
Thomson, Justice George, 442
Tibbetts, Janice, 14, 15, 523, 683*n*64
La Tigresse, 198–200, 350, 488
Tilakawardane, Justice Shiranee, 513, 696*n*43
Toews, Vic, 479
Toronto Star, 16, 328, 535
Toronto Sun, 482
Tourigny, Christine, 177(f)–78, 325, 597*n*13, 637*n*40
Tousignant, Fabienne, 87(f)
Tremblay, Jean-Guy, 361
Tremblay v. Daigle (1989) abortion rights case, 361
Tremblay-Lamer, Danièle, 291(f), 338–39, 347–48, 351, 354, 463, 644*n*15
Trottier, Justice André, 256(f), 257, 573*n*30
Trudeau, Prime Minister Pierre Elliott: anti-Semitism, 144, 586*n*27; constitution repatriation, 455–56; family law, 179; female electoral candidates, 211–13, 608*n*12; judicial appointments, 211, 212(f), 222, 224, 253–54; law school, 113, 575*n*15; Queen's Counsel designation, 188; women's rights, 225
Tuck, Justice William H., 194, 604*n*11
Tucker Parks, Shirley, 206, 207(f), 220, 227, 345, 425, 604*n*15, 613*n*95, 705*n*13
Turgeon, Justice Jean, 115, 178, 295, 296(f), 302, 576*n*32, 596*n*11, 628*n*37, 629*n*43
Turner, John, 176, 220–21, 296, 610*n*42
Tyndale, Justice William, 305, 629*n*52, 631*n*60, 632*n*73, 632*n*80

University of Montreal law school: female law students, 573*n*31; female professors, 204, 228, 229(f), 606*n*63, 613*n*97; law students, 113, 575*n*15
University of Ottawa conference, 524
Urofsky, Melvin I., 375, 652*n*90
Ursuline nuns: convent teachers, 63–64(f), 65(f)–66, 67(f)–70, 74, 79–80, 97, 568*n*29; orphans treatment, 58, 68(f); on student potential, 74, 97, 568*n*29.

See also Collège Notre-Dame-de-Bellevue (Quebec City); Monastère des Ursulines de L'Immaculée Conception (Rimouski)

Vallée, Gabrielle (Gaby): chief justice appointment, 253–56(f), 257, 606*n*64, 611*n*47, 618*nn*2–4, 619*n*20; death notice (Pierre Dubé), 278–79; judicial appointments process, 286, 288, 292; law practice, 139, 140, 583*n*23; masculinity characteristics, 161, 255–57; relationship with Justice L'Heureux-Dubé, 255
Vallières, Ovila, 117, 577*n*47
Vanier Institute of the Family, 188
La Voix des femmes, 203(f), 606*n*59
Vorvis v. Insurance Corporation of British Columbia (1989) employment case, 361
Vriend v. Alberta (1996) sexual orientation case, 549*n*18, 691*n*47
Vriend v. Canada (1998) sexual orientation case, 424, 671*n*67, 672*n*76

Wallin, Pamela, 409
Wartime Prices and Trade Board, 100
water purification company, 235–37
Weitzman, Lenore, 398
Wente, Margaret, 483, 689*n*71
Westaway, Cynthia, 356, 366–67, 369(f), 476, 494, 499, 650*n*50
Western Judicial Education Centre, 696*n*27
Whitton, Charlotte, 196–97
Whyte, John, 460
Willats, Anna, 19
Williams, Patricia, 424, 426
Wilson, Justice Bertha: about, 334, 340, 341(f); about Justice Lamer, 644*n*21; about Justice L'Heureux-Dubé, 328, 332, 334, 344, 451; appointment, 320, 337, 624*n*3; decision-writing protocol, 548*n*11; decisions and gender differences, 385, 437, 676*n*65; employment case, 361; female judges association, 514; female judges speech, 436; gender as challenge, 294, 330–31(f), 332, 569*n*5, 639*n*2, 639*nn*4–5, 639*n*7; gender equality task force, 643*n*11; on interveners, 381; judicial education, 695*n*20; judicial notice, 407–8; jurisprudence change, 649*n*39; not feminist, 705*n*12; sexual assault case, 392–93, 660*n*102; spousal

support case, 400, 401, 663nn44–45, 664nn51–52
women: category stereotypes, 385; cultural attitudes toward, 96, 97, 205, 567n23, 568n29; education, 28–29, 65–66, 73–75, 77–78, 553n25, 560n56, 562n10; employment, 396, 661n8, 686n4; federal elections, 211, 608n6, 608nn18–19; legally as persons, 288; marriage (working mothers), 170–71, 594n30; motherhood guilt, 172, 312, 633n8; poverty, 398, 471, 662n25, 663n46; wrongful conviction, 511. *See also* female justices; female lawyers; gender equality; gender inequality
Women's Legal Education and Action Fund (LEAF): beginnings, 428, 673n4; feminist advocacy, 381–84, 392, 438, 655n23, 658n81; intervener factums, 403–4, 407, 479, 655n25, 656n42, 666n84
women's movement. *See* feminist movement
women's rights. *See* feminist movement
Woodman, Faye, 438
Wright, David: about Justice Lamer, 371, 690n20; about Justice L'Heureux-Dubé, 356, 371, 477, 489, 491, 499, 645n54, 646n56; with Justice L'Heureux-Dubé, 369(f)
Wright, Joanne, 494–95

Young, Claire, 438–39
Young, Robert, 456
Youth Protection Act (Quebec), 313, 634n47
YWCA and tax-exempt status, 157

Zimbabwe (chief justice), 476, 517
Zweibel, Ellen, 4

PUBLICATIONS OF THE OSGOODE SOCIETY FOR CANADIAN LEGAL HISTORY

2017

Constance Backhouse, *Claire L'Heureux-Dubé: A Life*

Dennis G. Molinaro, *An Exceptional Law: Section 98 and the Emergency State, 1919–1936*

2016

Lori Chambers, *A Legal History of Adoption in Ontario, 1921–2015*

Bradley Miller, *Borderline Crime: Fugitive Criminals and the Challenge of the Border, 1819–1914*

James Muir, *Law, Debt, and Merchant Power: The Civil Courts of Eighteenth-Century Halifax*

2015

Barry Wright, Eric Tucker, and Susan Binnie, eds., *Canadian State Trials. Volume IV: Security, Dissent and the Limits of Toleration in War and Peace, 1914–1939*

David Fraser, *"Honorary Protestants": The Jewish School Question in Montreal, 1867–1997*

C. Ian Kyer, *A Thirty Years' War: The Failed Public/Private Partnership That Spurred the Creation of the Toronto Transit Commission, 1891–1921*

Dale Gibson, *Law, Life, and Government at Red River: Settlement and Governance, 1812–1872, Volume 1*

2014

Christopher Moore, *The Court of Appeal for Ontario: Defining the Right of Appeal, 1792–2013*

Dominique Clément, *Equality Deferred: Sex Discrimination and British Columbia's Human Rights State, 1953–84*

Paul Craven, *Petty Justice: Low Law and the Sessions System in Charlotte County, New Brunswick, 1785–1867*

Thomas Telfer, *Ruin and Redemption: The Struggle for a Canadian Bankruptcy Law, 1867–1919*

2013

Roy McMurtry, *Memoirs & Reflections*

Charlotte Gray, *The Massey Murder: A Maid, Her Master and the Trial That Shocked a Nation*

C. Ian Kyer, *Lawyers, Families, and Businesses: The Shaping of a Bay Street Law Firm, Faskens 1863–1963*

G. Blaine Baker and Donald Fyson, eds., *Essays in the History of Canadian Law, Volume XI: Quebec and the Canadas*

2012

R. Blake Brown, *Arming and Disarming: A History of Gun Control in Canada*

Eric Tucker, James Muir, and Bruce Ziff, eds., *Property on Trial: Canadian Cases in Context*

Shelley A.M. Gavigan, *Hunger, Horses, and Government Men: Criminal Law on the Aboriginal Plains, 1870–1905*

Barrington Walker, ed., *The African-Canadian Legal Odyssey: Historical Essays*

2011

Robert J. Sharpe, *The Lazier Murder: Prince Edward County, 1884*

Philip Girard, *Lawyers and Legal Culture in British North America: Beamish Murdoch of Halifax*

John McLaren, *Dewigged, Bothered and Bewildered: British Colonial Judges on Trial*

Lesley Erickson, *Westward Bound: Sex, Violence, the Law, and the Making of a Settler Society*

2010

Judy Fudge and Eric Tucker, eds., *Work on Trial: Canadian Labour Law Struggles*

Christopher Moore, *The British Columbia Court of Appeal: The First Hundred Years*

Frederick Vaughan, *Viscount Haldane: The Wicked Step-father of the Canadian Constitution*

Barrington Walker, *Race on Trial: Black Defendants in Ontario's Criminal Courts, 1850–1950*

2009

William Kaplan, *Canadian Maverick: The Life and Times of Ivan C. Rand*

R. Blake Brown, *A Trying Question: The Jury in Nineteenth-Century Canada*

Barry Wright and Susan Binnie, eds., *Canadian State Trials. Volume III: Political Trials and Security Measures, 1840–1914*

Robert J. Sharpe, *The Last Day, the Last Hour: The Currie Libel Trial* (new edition)

2008

Constance Backhouse, *Carnal Crimes: Sexual Assault Law in Canada, 1900–1975*

Jim Phillips, R. Roy McMurtry, and John Saywell, eds., *Essays in the History of Canadian Law, Volume X: A Tribute to Peter N. Oliver*

Gregory Taylor, *The Law of the Land: Canada's Receptions of the Torrens System*

Hamar Foster, Benjamin Berger, and A.R. Buck, eds., *The Grand Experiment: Law and Legal Culture in British Settler Societies*

2007

Robert Sharpe and Patricia McMahon, *The Persons Case: The Origins and Legacy of the Fight for Legal Personhood*

Lori Chambers, *Misconceptions: Unmarried Motherhood and the Ontario Children of Unmarried Parents Act, 1921–1969*

Jonathan Swainger, ed., *The Alberta Supreme Court at 100: History and Authority*

Martin Friedland, *My Life in Crime and Other Academic Adventures*

2006

Donald Fyson, *Magistrates, Police and People: Everyday Criminal Justice in Quebec and Lower Canada, 1764–1837*

Dale Brawn, *The Court of Queen's Bench of Manitoba 1870–1950: A Biographical History*

R.C.B. Risk, *A History of Canadian Legal Thought: Collected Essays*, edited and introduced by G. Blaine Baker and Jim Phillips

2005

Philip Girard, *Bora Laskin: Bringing Law to Life*

Christopher English, ed., *Essays in the History of Canadian Law, Volume IX: Two Islands, Newfoundland and Prince Edward Island*

Fred Kaufman, *Searching for Justice: An Autobiography*

2004

John D. Honsberger, *Osgoode Hall: An Illustrated History*

Frederick Vaughan, *Aggressive in Pursuit: The Life of Justice Emmett Hall*

Constance Backhouse and Nancy L. Backhouse, *The Heiress versus the Establishment: Mrs. Campbell's Campaign for Legal Justice*

Philip Girard, Jim Phillips, and Barry Cahill, eds., *The Supreme Court of Nova Scotia, 1754–2004: From Imperial Bastion to Provincial Oracle*

2003

Robert Sharpe and Kent Roach, *Brian Dickson: A Judge's Journey*

George Finlayson, *John J. Robinette: Peerless Mentor*

Peter Oliver, *The Conventional Man: The Diaries of Ontario Chief Justice Robert A. Harrison, 1856–1878*

Jerry Bannister, *The Rule of the Admirals: Law, Custom and Naval Government in Newfoundland, 1699–1832*

2002

John T. Saywell, *The Law Makers: Judicial Power and the Shaping of Canadian Federalism*

David Murray, *Colonial Justice: Justice, Morality and Crime in the Niagara District, 1791–1849*

F. Murray Greenwood and Barry Wright, eds., *Canadian State Trials. Volume II: Rebellion and Invasion in the Canadas, 1837–38*

Patrick Brode, *Courted and Abandoned: Seduction in Canadian Law*

2001

Ellen Anderson, *Judging Bertha Wilson: Law as Large as Life*

Judy Fudge and Eric Tucker, *Labour before the Law: Collective Action in Canada, 1900–1948*

Laurel Sefton MacDowell, *Renegade Lawyer: The Life of J.L. Cohen*

2000

Barry Cahill, *"The Thousandth Man": A Biography of James McGregor Stewart*

A.B. McKillop, *The Spinster and the Prophet: Florence Deeks, H.G. Wells, and the Mystery of the Purloined Past*

Beverley Boissery and F. Murray Greenwood, *Uncertain Justice: Canadian Women and Capital Punishment*

Bruce Ziff, *Unforeseen Legacies: Reuben Wells Leonard and the Leonard Foundation Trust*

1999

Constance Backhouse, *Colour-Coded: A Legal History of Racism in Canada, 1900–1950*

G. Blaine Baker and Jim Phillips, eds., *Essays in the History of Canadian Law, Volume VIII: In Honour of R.C.B. Risk*

Richard W. Pound, *Chief Justice W.R. Jackett: By the Law of the Land*

David Vanek, *Fulfilment: Memoirs of a Criminal Court Judge*

1998

Sidney Harring, *White Man's Law: Native People in Nineteenth-Century Canadian Jurisprudence*

Peter Oliver, *"Terror to Evil-Doers": Prisons and Punishments in Nineteenth-Century Ontario*

1997

James W. St. G. Walker, *"Race," Rights and the Law in the Supreme Court of Canada: Historical Case Studies*

Lori Chambers, *Married Women and Property Law in Victorian Ontario*

Patrick Brode, *Casual Slaughters and Accidental Judgments: Canadian War Crimes and Prosecutions, 1944–1948*

Ian Bushnell, *The Federal Court of Canada: A History, 1875–1992*

1996

Carol Wilton, ed., *Essays in the History of Canadian Law, Volume VII: Inside the Law – Canadian Law Firms in Historical Perspective*

William Kaplan, *Bad Judgment: The Case of Mr. Justice Leo A. Landreville*

Murray Greenwood and Barry Wright, eds., *Canadian State Trials. Volume 1: Law, Politics and Security Measures, 1608–1837*

1995

David Williams, *Just Lawyers: Seven Portraits*

Hamar Foster and John McLaren, eds., *Essays in the History of Canadian Law, Volume VI: British Columbia and the Yukon*

W.H. Morrow, ed., *Northern Justice: The Memoirs of Mr. Justice William G. Morrow*

Beverley Boissery, *A Deep Sense of Wrong: The Treason, Trials and Transportation to New South Wales of Lower Canadian Rebels after the 1838 Rebellion*

1994

Patrick Boyer, *A Passion for Justice: The Legacy of James Chalmers McRuer*

Charles Pullen, *The Life and Times of Arthur Maloney: The Last of the Tribunes*

Jim Phillips, Tina Loo, and Susan Lewthwaite, eds., *Essays in the History of Canadian Law, Volume V: Crime and Criminal Justice*

Brian Young, *The Politics of Codification: The Lower Canadian Civil Code of 1866*

1993

Greg Marquis, *Policing Canada's Century: A History of the Canadian Association of Chiefs of Police*

Murray Greenwood, *Legacies of Fear: Law and Politics in Quebec in the Era of the French Revolution*

1992

Brendan O'Brien, *Speedy Justice: The Tragic Last Voyage of His Majesty's Vessel* Speedy

Robert Fraser, ed., *Provincial Justice: Upper Canadian Legal Portraits from the Dictionary of Canadian Biography*

1991

Constance Backhouse, *Petticoats and Prejudice: Women and Law in Nineteenth-Century Canada*

1990

Philip Girard and Jim Phillips, eds., *Essays in the History of Canadian Law, Volume III: Nova Scotia*

Carol Wilton, ed., *Essays in the History of Canadian Law, Volume IV: Beyond the Law – Lawyers and Business in Canada 1830–1930*

1989

Desmond Brown, *The Genesis of the Canadian Criminal Code of 1892*

Patrick Brode, *The Odyssey of John Anderson*

1988

Robert Sharpe, *The Last Day, the Last Hour: The Currie Libel Trial*

John D. Arnup, *Middleton: The Beloved Judge*

1987

C. Ian Kyer and Jerome Bickenbach, *The Fiercest Debate: Cecil A. Wright, the Benchers and Legal Education in Ontario, 1923–1957*

1986

Paul Romney, *Mr. Attorney: The Attorney General for Ontario in Court, Cabinet and Legislature, 1791–1899*

Martin Friedland, *The Case of Valentine Shortis: A True Story of Crime and Politics in Canada*

1985

James Snell and Frederick Vaughan, *The Supreme Court of Canada: History of the Institution*

1984

Patrick Brode, *Sir John Beverley Robinson: Bone and Sinew of the Compact*

David Williams, *Duff: A Life in the Law*

1983

David H. Flaherty, ed., *Essays in the History of Canadian Law, Volume II*

1982

Marion MacRae and Anthony Adamson, *Cornerstones of Order: Courthouses and Town Halls of Ontario, 1784–1914*

1981

David H. Flaherty, ed., *Essays in the History of Canadian Law, Volume I*